, TED "

LIKE THE ROMAN

Also by the author

Moral Desperado: A Life of Thomas Carlyle (1995)
Power and Place: The Political Consequences of King Edward VII (1998)

Forthcoming:
Nor Shall My Sword: The Reinvention of England
(to be published 1999)

LIKE THE ROMAN

The Life of Enoch Powell

Simon Heffer

Weidenfeld & Nicolson
LONDON

First published in Great Britain in 1998
by Weidenfeld & Nicolson

A CIP catalogue record for this book is available
from the British Library.

ISBN 0 297 84286 2

Typeset by Selwood Systems, Midsomer Norton
Set in Minion
Printed in Great Britain by
Butler & Tanner Ltd
Frome and London

Weidenfeld & Nicolson
The Orion Publishing Group Ltd
Orion House
5 Upper Saint Martin's Lane
London, WC2H 9EA

To Pam, who was there

Then, 'twas before my time, the Roman
At yonder heaving hill would stare:
The blood that warms an English yeoman,
The thoughts that hurt him, they were there.

A. E. Housman, *A Shropshire Lad*, No. XXXI

Tell us what it is that binds us together; show us the clue that leads through a thousand years: whisper to us the secret of this charmed life of England, that we in our time may know how to hold it fast.

J. Enoch Powell, speech to the Royal Society of St George,
22 April 1961

Man first puts himself in relation with Nature and her Powers, wonders and worships over those; not till a later epoch does he discern that all Power is Moral, that the grand point is the distinction for him of Good and Evil, of *Thou shalt* and *Thou shalt not*.

Thomas Carlyle, *On Heroes, Hero-Worship and the Heroic in History*

Too often today people are ready to tell us: 'This is not possible, that is not possible.' I say: whatever the true interest of our country calls for is always possible. We have nothing to fear but our own doubts.

J. Enoch Powell, speech to the Conservative party
conference, October 1968

Passionate people think little of what others are thinking: the condition they are in raises them above vanity.

Friedrich Nietzsche, *Daybreak: Thoughts on the Prejudices of Morality*

I am not engaged in breaking down but in breaking open; but in saying here is a stone, let us see what is behind the stone.

J. Enoch Powell, interview, April 1966

What in me is dark
Illumine, what is low raise and support;
That to the height of this great argument
I may assert eternal Providence,
And justify the ways of God to men.

John Milton, *Paradise Lost*, Book I

I just don't like America, or Americans. It is like saying you like sugar in your tea. *De gustibus non est disputandum.*

J. Enoch Powell, interview, 1986

CONTENTS

ILLUSTRATIONS

With some friends in Wolverhampton, 1973
A target for satire, 1968[2]
'Judas was paid! Judas was paid! I am making a sacrifice!' Saltaire, 1974[1]

Between pages 720 and 721
With Pamela at the count in South Down, 1974
The Brigadier on manoeuvres in Ulster, 1978
With Ted Curtis, c. 1976
Susan's wedding, 1977
Holding the baby at the Christening of his first grandchild, Simon Day, 1983
On the stump with Jim Molyneaux, 1987
With his agent, Jeffrey Donaldson, by the Mountains of Mourne, 1983
Dressed for wet rain with Andrew Freeth, 1984
The elder statesman and his wife, at Lord Duncan-Sandys's memorial service,
    1988
Four old stagers at the 80th birthday dinner, 1992
With his family before the 80th birthday dinner
At the 80th birthday dinner with Greville Howard
Bearing Patch, 1993
With Richard Ritchie, 1989
With his granddaughter Rachel Day, 1990
With his grandchildren James and Julia Lavin, 1996
Meeting Johnnie Heffer, 1996
The Last Post: Warwick, 1998
In the library[3]

Sources
Unless otherwise credited all photographs are reproduced by kind permission
    of Mrs Pamela Powell

[1] PA News
[2] *Private Eye*
[3] Carole Cutner

ACKNOWLEDGEMENTS

John Enoch Powell resolutely refused to write his own biography. Using one of his favourite metaphors, he stated that to do so would be like returning to his own vomit. Nonetheless, he accumulated a massive personal archive of letters, memoranda and other materials from his schooldays onwards. In late 1994 he wrote to me to say he had heard I would be interested in writing 'a – or even the – biography' of him. I went to his home in South Eaton Place to be shown the formidable array of private papers, stored in safes in his boiler room and in his attic. He told me he did not want an 'official' biography, largely because such a designation brings with it certain restrictions that can interfere with the truth. I agreed. The only condition under which I undertook this book was that my access to his most private papers would not occur until after his death, and therefore the book could not be published in his lifetime. This was a straightforward condition for a biographer, but a sad one for a friend. As it turned out, the work that had to be done even before the personal and private papers were reached was so extensive that it was scarcely finished by the time of his death over three years later. Although I could not read his private papers during his lifetime, he did give me complete co-operation in every other respect, not least extensive interviews in which my every question was fully and unambiguously answered. So my first debt is to my subject, for his confidence in choosing me to be the first and last biographer to have access both to his memory and to his private papers, and for the generosity with which he helped me. His death robbed me, like so many others, of a most valued and special friend, and his loss is irreparable. I hope I have upheld the principles of our friendship by approaching his life in the objective spirit he would have wanted.

An army of people helped me in one way or another. I am especially indebted to the Powell Estate and to its Literary Trustees for granting me permission to quote from the archive of J. Enoch Powell. Many people gave their time to speak to me about Powell, or went to trouble to answer letters of inquiry. I am especially grateful to Greville Howard for the invaluable assistance and constant support he gave me as chairman of Powell's Literary Trustees. His advice on many other matters has been essential to me and constitutes a conspicuous act of friendship. Similarly, I must thank Powell's other trustees – Richard Ritchie, Lord Biffen and Professor John Ramsden – for their help and advice. Mr Howard, Mr Ritchie and Lord Biffen all granted me extensive interviews about Powell, for which I am additionally grateful. Professor Ramsden made a detailed reading of the text and offered many helpful suggestions, for which I particularly thank him. Nicholas Budgen was responsible for suggesting to Powell that I might be his biographer, and he helped me greatly with recollections, support and encouragement throughout the writing of this book. Michael Strachan was indispensable to me, lending me letters, answering endless questions and giving me advice that drew not just on his ancient friendship with and knowledge of Powell, but on his own distinguished record as an author. He played a larger part in this book than he will ever know.

For sharing with me their memories of Powell I am grateful to Lord Molyneaux, Lady Thatcher, Lord Harris of High Cross, Lord Weatherill, Lord Alport, Lord Deedes of Aldington, Lord Carr of Hadley, Lord Fanshawe of Richmond, Lord Gilmour, Lord Griffiths of Fforestfach, Lord Braine of Wheatley, Lady Butler of Saffron Walden, the late Lady Maude, Sir Hardy Amies, the late Sir David Hunt, the late Sir Brian Warren, Sir George Godber, General Sir Charles Dunphie, Sir Donald Sinden, Denis Hills, Ian Beddows, Jeffrey Donaldson, Mrs Barbara Hawkins, Tony Benn, George Jones, Clement Jones, Mrs Bee Carthew (now Miss Muir), the late Roy Lewis, Canon Donald Gray, Matthew d'Ancona, Andrew Alexander, Peter Lilley, Alan Clark, Colonel Kenneth Post, Miss Hester Curtis, Martin Freeth, Frank Field, Canon Eric James, Jonathan Aitken, William Waldegrave, Gerry Malone, Bernard Harrison, the late Geoffrey Parkhouse, Mrs Michael Strachan, Charles Moore, A. J. Marsden, Mrs Marjorie Dyson, Bryan Rayner, Stephen Robinson, Bernard Jenkin, Frank Judge, Peter Clarke, David Clarke, James Ramsden, Professor J. M. Thoday, C. Howard Wheeldon, Mrs Fiona Shackleton and Philip Beddows.

Michael Cockerell generously allowed me to see transcripts of interviews conducted for his 1995 BBC documentary about Powell, *Odd Man Out*. I thank him for that and for numerous other incidences of help, advice and support. I have an enormous debt to David Ashton, who generously gave me his prodigious store of press cuttings, extending over twenty years, about Powell, and which saved me weeks of work in newspaper libraries. Other friends and colleagues helped find and provide me with various research materials, and for that I am grateful to Lord Patten, Sir Robin Day, Paul Foot, Francis Wheen, Mark Garnett, Miss Elizabeth Fleming, Miss Rebecca Hardy, Mrs Quentin Letts, Neil Hamilton, Mrs Julia Cooper, Mrs Alan Tritton, Mrs Barbara Finney, Hywel Williams, Mme Radoslaw Sikorski, Peter Hennessy, Richard Thorpe, Miss Sarah Baxter, Andrew Bailey, Ferdinand Mount, Dr Ann Ridler, Professor Robert B. Todd, Kerrod Burt, Tim Dickenson, Simon Pearce, Ian Hunter, Miss Jayne Mays, Miss Lisl Biggs-Davison and Miss Claire Gannaway.

The staff of the Public Record Office, Kew, provided me with great help in my researches there into the ministerial papers of the periods 1955–8 and 1960–3. For access to papers held in its archive at the Bodleian Library, Oxford, I am obliged to the Conservative party, and particularly to Alistair Cooke, who facilitated that access, and to Dr Martin Maw, who gave me tireless and unfailingly courteous assistance.

I have a special debt to Miss Fiona McPhillips, whose own significant expertise in the classics helped illuminate that part of Powell's life for me. Miss Sally Chatterton was a constant support to me in discharging many necessary and important tasks with great good humour, speed and initiative. Miss Emily Hohler generously conducted some time-consuming research on my behalf, and Miss Elizabeth Anderson facilitated it. Miss Candice Walker, Miss Jenny Jones and Miss Davina Broadly were all enslaved to the photocopier for longer than was humane. Mrs Monica Wilson helped me greatly in finding my way around the Powell archive. Miss Fiona Graham assisted with technical matters. My parents-in-law, Mr and Mrs Peter Clee, provided frequent hospitality on various research trips. So too did Mr and Mrs Richard Ehrman, Mr and Mrs Peter Luff and Dr and Mrs Niall Ferguson.

The editor of the *Daily Mail*, Paul Dacre, gave me much moral and practical encouragement over the years in which I wrote this book. I owe him a lot. I was greatly helped by Stuart Proffitt in planning how and in what form I should write it. Andrew Roberts heroically read my manuscript in close detail at a late stage and I am much in his debt. The support and enthusiasm of my publisher, Anthony Cheetham, my editor, Ion Trewin and his assistant Rachel Leyshon, have been indispensable to me. My agent, Miss Georgina Capel, has once again proved herself peerless. The manuscript was magnificently copy-edited by Peter James, who saved me from some grave errors.

Two debts supersede all others: first, to Mrs Pamela Powell, who has at every stage in this book's creation been on hand with help, information, support, encouragement, advice, extensive hospitality and, above all, patience and under-standing. Those who knew her husband knew also the epic part she played in his life and in his success. She has been scarcely less important to his biographer, and it is a great happiness to me that she has accepted the dedication of this book.

Finally, and above all, my wife Diana and my sons Fred and Johnnie have put up with far more than I had a right to expect them to in their unsought vocations as literary widow and orphans. Their forebearance and loyalty have been essential and deeply appreciated. It is good manners for an author to say he could not have written his book without the help of his wife. In my case, it happens to be true.

24 August 1998   Simon Heffer
                                                        Great Leighs

1

'MY EARLIEST DWELLING'

John Enoch Powell was a little blond boy. When his mother took him to the barber for his first haircut, on 10 November 1913 at the age of seventeen months old, she collected a bright yellow curl from the clippings and preserved it in a small envelope. All mothers treasure their children, but in John Enoch's case the regard was especially intense. His mother would be the making of him, and he would never forget it. That he kept the curl in its envelope all his life, for it to be found in his effects after his death in February 1998, was above all an act of devotion towards the woman who had first collected it, and who had indispensably shaped him.

In 1909 that woman, Ellen Mary Breese, had married Albert Enoch Powell, a Birmingham elementary school master. He was thirty-seven; she was twenty-three. They had met the previous year. She was the daughter of a policeman; he the son and grandson of scrap-metal dealers. Ellen, like her husband, was of non-conformist stock. John Breese, her grandfather, had been born in 1828 at Forton in Shropshire, just over the border from Staffordshire. He was apprenticed to a jobbing tailor named Scarratt around Newport, Shropshire. Having acquired enough skill to set up in business on his own, he toured grand houses and made liveries for footmen and coachmen. He married Mary Ann Betteley, and together they ran the Crown and Cushion, a public house in Newport High Street, though John continued his tailoring up until his death in 1916, at the age of eighty-eight. His great-grandson, John Enoch, remembered him in this extreme old age, climbing a mound in the summer of 1915 to look at the memorial to the Duke of Sutherland at Lilleshall. 'John Breese', he recalled, 'was a man strict in his standards and cautious in his judgments. "I find no fault in him" was the limit of his approbation when his grand-daughter presented her future husband and, later, her first and only child.'[1]

John and Mary's second son and third child, Henry William Breese, enlisted in the Liverpool police. He was discharged from the force on a pension at the age of twenty-two, after being injured in an affray at the docks. Shattered by this calamity, he became an alcoholic. He had married an Eliza Burns, had eight daughters and was deeply disapproved of by his parents, who never came to terms with their son's condition. They made what contribution they could by taking the eldest daughter, Ellen Mary, and bringing her up in Newport as their own child. She was intelligent and industrious, and won a scholarship to the local Ladies' College, Merevale. 'There was no keeping Nellie Breese back,' her son recalled. 'She painted, she acted, she revelled in languages.' She was told she could hold her own at Girton: but John Breese could not afford that.

Albert Powell, her husband, was the fourth-generation descendant of Welsh emigrants to the Black Country. His family had once moved from Radnorshire to the coalfields of South Wales to find work in the mines. When that dried up Albert's grandfather, Samuel, moved to Wednesbury in Staffordshire, four miles from Wolverhampton, to work in a colliery. His son Enoch, Albert's father, was born in 1846 in Smethwick, on the borders of Staffordshire and Warwickshire, and a few miles nearer Birmingham. According to his grandson and namesake, Enoch was 'a determined but somewhat cantankerous character'.[2] He was apprenticed to Chance Brothers, a firm of glass-makers, but by the 1870s was a scrap-metal dealer. He was a political radical and a Methodist – probably Calvinist – lay preacher. The years after the Franco-Prussian War were a boom time for the scrap trade. For a while Enoch and his wife, Felicia Holloway, lived in some style in a big house off Smethwick High Street, and had a trap pulled, it was said, by 'the finest trotting pony in the West Midlands'.[3] Albert Enoch, their only child, was born into this relative prosperity on 12 September 1872; but before his childhood was much advanced the boom was over, and 'many blast furnaces in the Black Country were blown out never to be re-lit'.

The family was ambitious, blessed with a strong native intelligence, and (in keeping with the temper of the times) much concerned with self-improvement. However, the fine education planned for Albert Powell could now not be afforded, so it was a relief to his father and mother when, at the age of sixteen in 1888, he found a position with the Birmingham School Board as a pupil teacher. His work entailed having to control classes of sixty children in elementary schools. When he proved he could do this he went for two years to a teacher-training college at Saltley. It was a Church of England establishment that required Albert Enoch, with his father's permission, to desert his Methodist roots in the interests of advancement. In 1892, his training completed, he returned to what would be a lifelong career as an elementary school teacher. Sixteen years later, in 1908, he looked out of a window at Dudley Road Schools and was attracted by the sight in the playground of a new supply teacher, who would become his bride.

Upon their marriage, Albert and Ellen Powell moved to a Victorian semi-detached house by a railway cutting in Flaxley Lane, Stechford, Birmingham. They chose Stechford because all the trains stopped there before travelling on to New Street station in the heart of the city. In this house John Enoch (named after his two grandfathers) was born on 16 June 1912, at ten minutes to ten in the evening during a violent thunderstorm. His parents knew him as Jack. There would be no more children. This, too, was central to the forming of Jack's character. Without brothers or sisters he was thrown on adult company, principally that of his parents, and especially that of his mother; and he would acquire their interests and disciplines, notably academic and self-improving – and he would acquire them precociously.

'My father', he recalled, 'was, as it were, a warm presence and another boy around the place. But my childhood is very much my mother.'[4] His mother saw Jack's education as her first duty. Such was her own thirst for learning that she had taught herself Greek (using the New Testament as her primer) while attending Merevale. She had a 'phenomenal' knowledge of the Bible.[5] She had distinguished herself in French and Latin and had longed to study Greek, but there had been no mistress at the college to teach her, which is why, being immensely determined, she taught herself. For her own son, Mrs Powell put the alphabet up on cards around the walls of the kitchen for him to learn; his earliest memory was of saying his elementary lessons to her as she stood cooking at the stove or washing at the sink. This form of education, reminiscent of John Stuart Mill's, was no pain to Jack. 'I'm not one of those who thinks of his childhood as an unhappy time. Home, entirely happy. If I could remake it and reconstruct it I wouldn't know what to do to have made it better.'[6]

He recalled of his mother that 'her constant injunction was what you start you must finish. Your motto ought to be "thorough".'[7] Her main ambition for him was not just that he should be brilliant; it was that he should be happy. When, later in his life, others looked quizzically at the sort of upbringing Powell had had, he would maintain that 'nothing was oppressive about my childhood, about that I am certain, but I don't think one can ever be certain how much is due to one's environment and how much one brought when one came here. My own belief is that the sort of person we are going to be, and the sort of things – different according to setting – we are going to do is settled by the time we are born.'[8] The most important thing was that 'there was an atmosphere of scholarship at home'. His parents were both highly self-disciplined people, with solid achievements to show for their self-discipline; it was a lesson they easily imparted to their son, and which he would take to an extreme. Jack may have acquired physical resemblances to his father, but seemed in character to take after his mother. One who knew both his parents commented that 'Powell's father was a very distinguished-looking man with a somewhat ruddy complexion set off by white hair and carefully trimmed white moustache, very upright ... He looked more like a soldier than a school master. Mrs Powell was slight and rather pale and did not smile as readily as her husband, who seemed always to be in cheerful good spirits.'[9]

Jack's mother had given up teaching on her marriage. The three of them lived, to begin with, on Mr Powell's wages of forty-eight shillings a week, an income comparable with that of the drivers of the steam-engines that clattered past their house. Mr Powell had one mildly remunerative sideline: he had, with two fellow teachers, written some arithmetic textbooks, and would receive small royalty cheques for them up to the 1950s. From the beginning, Jack was brought up in a climate of strict economic rigour. Nearly sixty years later he recalled: 'My mother ran the house on a scrupulous budget. My father turned over to her everything he earned. They decided together what to save and what to spend, and she administered it. She did this so well that we were never conscious of lacking for anything.'[30] So effective was the regime that, when Jack was six, the family could afford a house at 52 Woodlands Park in the smarter Birmingham suburb of King's Norton: they were also helped financially by the fact that Jack's father had become headmaster of the George Dixon Elementary School in Edgbaston.

As elementary schools went, the George Dixon was relatively genteel, set in a respectable area. Mr Powell was remembered fondly by his old pupils. He was interested in ornithology, and kept a great collection of stuffed birds in glass cases in his study. As a treat for the children, he would bring them out and pass them round the classroom, lecturing on the names and habitats of the birds. The school had a good reputation for drilling its pupils in the basic skills of literacy and numeracy, and Albert Powell himself would supervise each child's annual reading examination.

He was strict about manners, but enjoyed a joke with his pupils. One, Marjorie Dyson, recalled seventy years later the ceremony when it came to leaving the school. A week before the end of term 'he would say, in front of the whole school, "any pupil who is wanting their leaving certificate will, next week, seek me out. I shall be somewhere about the school. I don't want to hear anyone ask for a stiff cat, or a stiffy cat, but a cer-tif-i-cate." When at last we found him we would say with great precision: "Please sir, may I have my learning certificate?" He would reply: "Oh! So you want your stiff cat do you?" ' Mrs Dyson added, 'I have remembered him fondly all my life.'[11]

Nellie Powell had given up teaching only in the strict professional sense. Her son became her star pupil. By three he had mastered the alphabet, and was beginning to read simple books. At four he was ploughing through the *Harmsworth Encyclopaedia*, a progress interrupted temporarily while his eyes suffered as a side-effect of the measles. The encyclopaedia had been published in instalments some years earlier, and had been bound by Jack's great-grandfather, who in turn had passed it on to Nellie. 'It displayed to me', he remembered in old age, 'an illimitable vista over the ocean of knowledge, and many of its illustrated entries remain indelible memories.'[12] Along with Richard Jefferies's *Bevis*, it would become one of the two favourite books of Jack's childhood. It could be assumed that his mother had pushed him intellectually, but he denied this. 'I was not driven,' he told an interviewer in his eighty-first year. 'I have no sense of having been physically or mentally pushed, but the implication of the environment was that there was no point in education unless one was academically successful.'[13] The plain fact was that Jack needed no encouragement to learn: he had an innate urge to do so, which his mother identified and capitalised upon.

He soon showed such a capacity for absorbing knowledge, and his mother was so intense in her instruction of him, that by the age of three he was nicknamed 'the Professor'. His grandfather Enoch also had a collection of stuffed birds, and when the Powells went to visit the old man Jack would spend hours looking at them and asking his father – a more exact ornithologist than his grandfather – questions about them. When, long after old Enoch's death in August 1914 – he died predicting it would be a long war, and telling Jack to be a good boy to his mother – the boy had mastered the details of the habits and characteristics of the birds, he would solemnly impart the information to everyone else. 'I used to like to get visitors in front of these cases and lecture them – aged three – and one of them called me "the Professor". And I think from an early age I imagined I would be a professor.'[14]

Jack was vaguely conscious of the Great War: one of his earliest memories, when only just over two years old, was of the tumult that bank-holiday weekend in August 1914 when the conflict began. On his journeys with his mother around Birmingham in subsequent years he saw wounded soldiers at New Street station, and German prisoners of war at work in the streets and in the countryside around the city. There were occasional Zeppelin raids, during which the family sheltered in a cupboard under the stairs. On a train ride into New Street Jack remembered his parents pulling the blinds down so the Zeppelins would not see the lights. His childish pleasures of a non-academic sort were simple: he loved gardening, and especially digging. His parents would encourage him in this enterprise, using each hole he had dug to bury rubbish in.

By the age of six Jack had become an addictive reader, mainly of history books borrowed from the local library. It was at this time that he went with his parents to Caernarvon Castle. Entering one room he removed his cap. Asked by his father why, he replied it was because it was in that room the first Prince of Wales had been born. His instinctive regard for institutions and rank was already apparent; it was part of the Toryism he would later describe as 'congenital'.[15] His political outlook was not hereditary; his father was, after the split in that party in 1916, a Lloyd George Liberal. This action was more than just about politics: it was also indicative of Powell's innate romanticism, evident in a national, historical context then as it would be throughout the rest of his life. 'It shows how early this thread begins,' he said nearly eighty years later. 'It's the thread of a nation, the belief in a nation as the thing which explains and justifies everything.'[16]

II

On Sunday evenings Albert and Nellie would hear lectures by Jack on subjects he had learned from his week's reading of his library books. They would encourage him while he lectured standing on a chair, reading out notes he had made. 'My parents must have been terribly patient to put up with this,' he said in 1970. 'The other thing I can remember doing on Sunday evenings at home was that I used to conduct evensong and deliver a sermon. We had a great deal of fun at home.'[17] His father's responsibility in his son's extra-curricular education would instil in him a love of the English language, and a precision in its use: Borrow, Carlyle, Emerson, Thoreau and Mark Twain were the staples of his early diet. He told his son that 'to speak and write good English was the supreme achievement'.[18]

As Jack grew older, his pleasures remained solitary. He was not wilfully anti-social, but his preoccupation with activities of the mind created an intellectual isolation for him. Although in adolescence and early adulthood this would cause him some loneliness, he was not always aware of it, and would soon come to regard his intellectual independence as a great personal strength. Neither was his solitude confined to his books. Once old enough to venture afield on his own, he would go into Worcestershire and walk the lanes and fields with pre-war Ordnance Survey maps, developing a love for the landscape and for cartography that would last all his life. In the years before his marriage, especially, long and vigorous walks would be one of his most important recreations, and part of his nurturing process as a poet and a romantic.

His parents made the financial sacrifices necessary to give him a good education. There was no elementary school for him: a friend of his mother's, Miss Mabel Pane, ran a dame school in King's Norton, and Jack attended it until the age of eleven. His character seems to have been almost fully formed by his years with Miss Pane: 'She was a great teacher. She prepared for a secondary education large numbers who went on to distinction later at schools, at university and in life. But to all her pupils she gave more than a firm grounding in schoolwork and a love of books and learning. She set them standards of conduct, courtesy and sincerity which only a truly good person could have done.'[19] These were lessons, academic and personal, that were only reinforced by his schoolteacher parents when he went home. For all Miss Pane's intellectual rigour, his mother still found the time to drill Jack in additional subjects, constantly providing him with the academic head start he would need to succeed.

After Miss Pane's he went for three years to a secondary school in King's Norton before winning a scholarship to King Edward's School in Birmingham, which he entered in 1925 at the age of thirteen. He remembered his masters at his secondary school vividly; what struck him was how they had almost all been in the war, and the effect the war had had on them. He felt a shadow of sorts being cast over him and his generation, with the memory of the war saturating everyday life. He formed the general belief that, one day, the two armies would meet again and this time fight it out to a finish.

Having conceived the ambition that Jack should go to King Edward's, his mother intensively coached him for his scholarship examinations, concentrating on what she knew to be his two weakest subjects – mathematics and science. Such was her success that, when Jack won his scholarship, he was initially placed on the science side of the school. Under the distinguished Chief Master Robert Carey Gilson, it had an unusual ethos of high academic achievement matched with individual responsibility. It was, in the words of Powell's distinguished contemporary Roy Lewis, 'a very good and solid old-fashioned grammar-school'.[20] It was mainly a middle-class establishment, the grander sons of Birmingham being sent there, but also the brighter sons of tradesmen and the lower-middle class. The boys of the mid-1920s sat at old desks set out in rows, and saw scratched on them the names of boys from twenty years earlier, many of which appeared more formally on the school's war memorial. In an era when schools were largely ruled by the principle of *mens sana in corpore sano*, games were however not compulsory. They could not be, since the school playing fields were so far from the school itself. This suited Powell, who felt no affinity for ball games and would rather spend the time feeding his insatiable hunger for knowledge. It was 'a school for work. Boys who worked liked it. Boys who didn't work didn't like it.'[21]

After a term on the science side, the head of classics – perceiving Powell's ability at a subject he was studying only as a sideline – made a plea for him to be transferred to that side of the school. The transfer was agreed, and Powell went home for his Christmas holidays in 1925 to have some more intensive coaching. In just over two weeks his mother – to her delight – taught him Greek. By the time he went back to school she had brought him up to a level most of his schoolfellows would only attain after two years; when he brought out his translation of the fifth century BC Greek historian Herodotus twenty years later, he mentioned her important role in its production. Upon joining the classical form he told his classmates that within two terms he would be top; he was. 'He was really unlike any schoolboy one had known,' recalled one of his contemporaries, the Rev. Professor C. F. Evans. 'He was austere. One seldom, if ever, saw him standing up against a wall with his hands in his pockets just talking. He didn't play games ... he was either at his books or if not he was walking purposefully from A to B with a goal in mind with either his books under his arm or his clarinet, pale, head rather forward, shoulders slightly stooped. He was quite a phenomenon.'[22] The school had a strong tradition of both divinity and Hellenism: Powell was soon encouraged to read the Greek Testament 'with more than a cursory eye to the commentaries and the textual criticism; and in the process I discovered that the Gospel was "not true". The historical and internal evidence would not support the narrative.' The experience would have a profound effect on his religious belief, and on the rest of his life and work.

He acquired the nickname 'Scowelly Powelly' – 'I had a bad habit of frowning.'[23] Another contemporary, Denis Hills, felt that 'he could not smile', and had 'a crocodile face' of such ferocity that even the naughtiest boys were not prepared to tease him.[24] To his schoolfriends he seemed austere, failing to join in their games, or even to talk to them. Hills recalls seeing Powell each morning on the train into Birmingham. 'He was pointed out to me as a boy to stay clear of – "an unfriendly fellow, talks to no-one". Powell had a pale face, was never without his cap, carried an armful of books (Greek texts?) and kept to himself. His penetrating blue eyes, furrowed brow and set mouth discouraged familiarity, and he was reputed to be cleverer than any of the masters.'[25] Hills felt that Powell made 'a fetish' of his personality; he also regretted that this man who would, in later life, come to adore institutions 'did nothing for the school' – except, of course, win it huge academic distinction. In his fifth form he won all three school classics prizes, for Thucydides, for Herodotus and for Divinity, though two or three years younger than anyone else who had won them. He set himself the aim of becoming an authority on Thucydides and Herodotus, an aim he achieved in publishing works on both shortly before the war.

He also began, at this precocious age, his translation of all nine books of Herodotus, the earliest surviving prose work in European or Semitic literature, with the exception of certain books of the Bible. He completed a translation of the first section of the work during the 1926 Christmas holidays, when he was just fourteen. He arrived in the sixth form at the school two years before his contemporaries. One classics master whose life Powell made particularly difficult because he knew more than the teacher was called Mr Heath – C. H. Heath, a distinguished classicist who had taught at the school since 1900. It was in the sixth form, which could be noisy and rowdy, that Powell demonstrated his powers of concentration; schoolfellows remember his working intently despite noise and distractions going on around him.[26]

Always determined to be correctly dressed, Powell did not just adhere to the cap – which most boys longed not to wear – but kept on his mackintosh, buttoned up, almost regardless of the weather. His was an intimidating presence. 'We thought', said Roy Lewis, 'that the masters were afraid of him.'[27] Hills, speaking when he and Powell were both in their eighties, remembered him as having 'a stern look' identical to that which he carried for the rest of his life.[28] It was on the train journeys to school, however, that Powell showed he could, if pressed, be one of the boys. One of his schoolfellows' favourite games, into which he would occasionally be enlisted, was to see whether they could unscrew the luggage rack in the compartment of the train during the fourteen minutes' journey from King's Norton to New Street; and when they had unscrewed it, they would throw it out of the window, not minding whether it caused a derailment. Also, it was a point of honour for King Edward's boys to alight from the train at New Street while it was still moving, to avoid a long walk back to a footbridge. The Chief Master took strong exception to this, and the habit stopped, not because it was causing harm to any of the boys but because other passengers, not realising the train was still moving, were getting out behind the boys and having a shock. Powell's contributions to general horseplay were, though, rare. His contemporary Rowland Ryder, later a distinguished cricketer, remembered being flung against Powell in a railway-carriage while Powell was engrossed in a book. 'I was terrified and apologised profusely,' Ryder recalled. 'He grunted amiably and went on with his reading.'[29]

There were few diversions from scholarship in Powell's career at King Edward's. He realised he should maintain a decent level of physical fitness, and decided to take up gymnastics: not because it had any particular attraction for him, but because he reasoned it was one of the most efficient ways to take the necessary exercise. So good did he become that he won a medal for it. He was similarly calculating about the choice of the clarinet as his musical instrument, though he did have, and would develop further, an intense passion for music. 'I wanted to learn a musical instrument and I worked it out that if there was one instrument that was always in demand with bands and orchestras, it was the clarinet. So I chose it for that reason.'[30] He became proficient to the point where he was considering applying for the Royal Academy of Music, as a prelude to a career as a musician. However, at sixteen, his parents' influence led him to agree that he would try for a scholarship to Cambridge. There had to be sacrifices. Ambition had been bred into him at home: 'This was how one got on and up.'[31] He had excelled at music, but the opportunities offered by a degree at Cambridge were clearly greater. So 'I put my clarinet away for the last time – I've never looked at a sheet of music since; though music remained very important to me throughout ... my pre-war life, that was put behind me.' The notion of Cambridge had been planted in Powell's mind in 1927 by Mr Sheldon, the lower-sixth master. 'Powell,' Sheldon told him, 'you will not go up to Oxford, for two reasons: you cannot write an English essay and a combination of you and Balliol would be intolerable. You will instead go up to Cambridge and write one of your Latin proses, which will win you a major open scholarship at Trinity.'[32]

Although the courtesy and respect Powell faultlessly practised as an adult were already ingrained in him by the time he went to school, he could be provoked. He recalled an incident when, in the fifth form, a master had told him for no apparent reason, 'Don't be idle.' Powell retorted, 'Idle's the word, is it?' and then proceeded to deluge the master with one completed exercise after another until the man admitted defeat; he was more careful with what he said to Powell after that.[33] His effect on his contemporaries was equally startling. One of them, the Rev. Henry Jamieson, later to be Moderator of the Church of Scotland, could remember nothing about any of the fifteen other boys in his form, but could recall Powell vividly. In their form room 'there were two rows of tables and he was in the back, I was in the front – it was done by seniority, not ability. I remember there was always a feeling of this brilliant mind at the back of you. It was almost a relief when he sometimes got pulled up. I shall never forget when the Head did this once. Enoch had translated the Latin phrase *natura loci* as "the topography of the locality". The Headmaster gave him a wry look. "Pole" he boomed – that was how he pronounced Powell – "the nature of the locality would have been enough." Enoch had, even then, a precise way of speaking that didn't always go down well with the other boys.[34]

In the sixth form Powell began a love affair with German language and culture. 'There is a critical faculty,' he later explained, 'which is awoken by German scholarship, which has always been lacking in the English scholarship. The scientific approach to language and literature, and the structure of the German language is conducive to this.'[35] His first German reading book was the libretto of Wagner's *Flying Dutchman*; before long he had moved on to less exotic writings, soon embarking upon German philosophy. It was the start of the process that would turn him into an atheist, the final act of which would be his immersion in the writings of Nietzsche once he had finished his under-graduate life at Cambridge. As he marched towards atheism – for the moment without the steamrollering help of Nietzsche – he met with none of the resistance from his parents that, for example, Carlyle had when he, over a century earlier, had began to have 'doubts' that were confirmed by a reading of different German influences. His father had never taken religion particularly seriously, as was shown by the ease with which he 'converted' to Anglicanism to enter his teacher-training college. His mother had been raised by her grandparents as a low-church Anglican, but began to have 'doubts' in the early 1920s, when Jack was still a small boy. It was when Jack was nine, and it was thought his father had cancer of the throat, that Mrs Powell's doubts became too strong to contain. The diagnosis was wrong. Her husband survived; but her doubts could not be reversed. She did not let her own feelings affect Jack's religious education, as he was too young to understand such things; but, when her son began to assert his own independence on the matter during his late adolescence while reading his Greek Testament, she put no obstacle in his way.[36]

Powell complemented this philosophical submergence with a wider reading of contemporary history, particularly books about the Great War. By the time he left school in 1930, before the rise of Hitler, he was confirmed in his instinctive view that the war was not over, merely stayed, to be rejoined soon. He did not, then, feel the contradiction about his addiction to the culture of the nation that would, once more, be his country's enemy. The language opened doors for him intellectually; it was a love for the language itself that he found so irresistible. 'I remember,' he wrote in 1970, 'as sharply as Keats recalled first looking into Chapman's *Homer*, the moment – it must have been in 1927 – when I opened my first German book. Here was the language I had dreamt of but never knew existed: sharp, hard, strict but with words which were romance in themselves, words in which poetry and music vibrated together.'[37] German was Powell's fifth language, but not the last he would study at school; he had also, by the time he left, acquired a decent command of Italian.

III

The liberality of the regime at King Edward's allowed boys to wander out of school during their lunch hours. Powell would go home on the train for lunch with his mother; and, if time allowed before his next lesson, rather than have to make idle conversation with his schoolfellows, he would wander the ten minutes or so from the school to John Bright Street, which had several second-hand bookshops. There he would browse, especially in the 'penny boxes' the book-sellers placed outside their windows, where bargains were within the reach of the pocket of a schoolboy. Some of the books he collected in that way were on his shelves for the rest of his life: the vellum-bound seventeenth-century edition of Macrobius, or Smith's *Classical Dictionary*. His voracious reading outside the curriculum would help give him the head start that would both get him to Cambridge and set him apart from the other classicists there – 'I am sure that a disproportionate share of my classical knowledge when I left school', he wrote thirty years later, 'had come not out of the prescribed textbooks, but out of the second-hand bargains which I bought and studied "on the side".'[38]

Books assumed an enormous importance in his life. At thirteen he would sit by the fireplace in the family's dining room and read J. G. Frazer's *The Golden Bough*, a hard-headed study of comparative religions, in the one-volume abridgement; it so enraptured him that he graduated on to the three-volume edition. 'I cannot imagine', he wrote in 1962, 'how different my mental and religious life would have been if the impact of J. G. Frazer had come at another time or not at all.'[39] It was 'the most powerful intellectual experience of my boyhood'.[40] Frazer began the process of making Powell an atheist: Nietzsche merely provided the iron confirmation. In 1934 Powell would tell his best friend, Ted Curtis, that 'until I read *The Golden Bough* and St Paul's *Epistle to the Galatians* at 13 years of age, I was an Orthodox Churchman'.[41] At around the same time Powell first read *Sartor Resartus*, Carlyle's semi-autobiographical philosophical novel about the discovery of a form of post-Christian religion, and found it 'intoxicating'. Given that his mother seemed to have provided most of his intellectual stimulation up to this point, the adventure with *Sartor* represented an important departure. His father was the Carlylean, and had predicted to his son that he would find *Sartor* as great an experience as he had done at a similar age. More than that, it was his reading of *Sartor* that precipitated Powell more deeply into German culture, particularly into the brand of German religious thought Carlyle had imbibed from Goethe and which would, for Powell and for many later readers, make Carlyle the bridge to Nietzsche. Powell would find the temptation to read German, especially Goethe, hard to resist all his life. His empathy with Carlyle was made the more special by his discovery of the Sage as a man who revered the German language, and was as excited by it as Powell was himself.

Powell decided on scholarship as a career. He determined that, in the first instance, Thucydides would be the basis of that scholarship, and he would compile the definitive edition of his works. It was in turning up articles on him that he came across one written, to his horror, by a classicist called John U. Powell. There could not, Jack Powell decided, be two John Powells writing in this limited field. 'This is terrible,' he thought. 'My work will be confused with his.' He had always signed himself J. E. Powell; now he decided to sign his middle name in full, and became J. Enoch Powell. So he was for the rest of his life.[42]

As a senior boy, Powell cut a severe figure. Dr Lawrence Paling, a contemporary, remembered him as 'very pale, [with] rather staring eyes, always dressed in a dark grey suit – a chapel suit, you might call it. We didn't have to wear a uniform except a school cap or, by this stage, a prefect's cap.'[43] Although Hills remembered Powell as 'solitary, and too wrapped up in himself to contribute to the communal life of the school', he nonetheless matched his intellectual excellence by becoming a prefect.[44] For the last four years he was at school he was, as well as winning many prizes for Greek and Divinity, top of his form.

In 1929, having passed the Higher School Certificate with distinction in Latin, Greek and Ancient History, Powell won the school's Lee Divinity Prize for an essay on the New Testament: he went into the examination having memorised, in Greek, the whole of St Paul's *Epistle to the Galatians*. The textual mysteries of this part of the Bible would obsess him all his life; he would return to them sixty years later and make them the subject of his last book. The books he won as prizes stimulated years of intense study; Herodotus and Thucydides were both trophies. For now, the command he had of the texts as a schoolboy would set him up for his academic career. In December 1929 he went to Cambridge to sit the scholarship paper in classics for Trinity College, with which his school had a strong connection and from which most of its classics masters had come. He won the top award the College had to offer. Unbeknown to him, his parents had arranged to find the money to send him to Cambridge whether he won the scholarship or not – 'but I got all the scholarships there were, and I made a profit of some three hundred pounds on my three years as an undergraduate.'[45]

These examinations, taken when Powell was seventeen, were an early display of his intellectual arrogance. Sir Ronald Melville, who sat the exams at Trinity with him, recalled that 'the exams mostly lasted three hours. Powell left the room halfway through each of them. We did not know who he was and wondered why.'[46] Melville met Powell, whom he did not know at Cambridge, many years later, when Powell explained what he had done: in the mere one-and-a-half hours he had spent on Greek prose composition, he had given the examiners two versions of the same piece, one in the style of Thucydides and another in the style of Herodotus. Powell described more than sixty-five years after the event how he had tackled another of the papers, involving a translation of a passage from Bede. He began by translating it into Platonic Greek, but – and this was obviously an examination Powell did not leave halfway through – there was still time to try something else. 'In the remaining hour and a half I tore it up and translated it again into Herodotean Greek – Ionic Greek – (which I had never written before) and then, still having time to spare, I proceeded to annotate it. One of the notes was reported to my school by the director of studies at Cambridge: "I adopt, without undertaking to defend, the form recommended by Dindorf for Herodotus." I think that it was regarded as rather a portent.'[47]

2

THE SADNESS OF SPRING

Shortly after arriving at Trinity at the start of Michaelmas Term 1930, Powell was found by Henry Jamieson, his fellow Edwardian, sitting on packing cases in his room reading a Greek text. 'Come and have some tea,' Jamieson said. 'Thank you very much,' Powell replied, 'but I came here to work.'[1] Powell reflected late in his life that, at that stage, 'I knew nothing else to do but to work. . . . I had no social life as an undergraduate.'[2] Another schoolfellow, C. F. Evans, recalled a similarly frosty response to a social overture, when he found Powell on a cold day in November 1930 in a room 'quite bare except for the College furniture . . . there was no fire, there were no pictures, Powell was sitting in his overcoat with a rug across his knees and . . . surrounded by eighteenth-century folios'.[3] Evans tried another tack, walking to the mantelpiece and taking out a cigarette. 'Would you mind not smoking?' Powell asked him. 'And so I left.'

Lawrence Paling had become secretary of the Cambridge branch of the Old Edwardians, and had to collect Powell's half-crown subscription. 'He was always courteous, always paid up,' Paling recalled, 'but never came to any of our dinners or anything like that.'[4] In that first year, on a visit to Powell, Paling too found an extraordinary sight awaiting him. 'I remember finding him in his rooms in the dead of winter with no fire on to keep him warm. He was sitting in an overcoat, with a blanket over his knees and mittens on his hands. He told me that it wasn't a matter of economy, but that the coal fire made him sleepy and he could work longer without it.' To maintain fitness, Powell started walking daily to the railway station and back, which took him an hour. It was a utilitarian pursuit: the route from Trinity to Station Road is probably the least aesthetically pleasing in Cambridge – but then aesthetics were not the issue. The routine provided him with a talking-point when, as a fellow, he joined Trinity's High Table. He told the other dons that he knew, from personal experience, 'that the best roast beef to be had in Cambridge was to be had at the refreshment room at the Cambridge station'.[5] The image of the young Powell tucking in to a cheap dinner, on his own, in this drab Fenland canteen before his solitary journey back to Trinity and his books is almost tragic.

He became a virtual recluse, ever to be found in his rooms behind a 'sported oak': the outer door of the two to his room being firmly locked, signifying that he did not wish to be disturbed. Unless going to lectures or supervisions, he would stay at his books from 5.30 in the morning until 9.30 at night. 'This was not because I disliked my fellows, that's not the point at all,' he explained. 'It was that I didn't know there was anything else to do and since I wasn't thrown into a social environment in which I worked as I always had done and always have done since, and have swum and swum happily, I didn't get into the water. But it is true that the social life of a college was a social life completely unfamiliar to me. Even the sheer mechanics of it, of how to tie a bow-tie, were unknown to me and I had no environment which would, as it were, tell me how to tie the bow-tie.'[6] He saw fellow undergraduates who he felt were nearly as clever as he was, but who had been brought up to have much else in their lives besides: 'which is why my elder daughter was put down for Eton before she was born', he said over half a century later.[7] As an atheist he never went to chapel, so avoided the society which that might have entailed: he never, in fact, set foot in the College chapel until 1951.[8] Only once did he have doubts about what his regime was doing to him. In 1931 Cambridge felt the distant shock of an earthquake. He remembered waking up at five that morning, as the tremor hit the city, 'and seeing the attachment for the window swinging backwards and forwards and saying it's right, I evidently am overworking'.[9] As he put it, later on in life, to his wife: 'I knew I was a bit of a swot.'[10]

Later, he would regret his obsession with work, and the way in which it made him miss out on the normal pleasures of youth. 'I worked too hard in my first year or so: I worked too long. I didn't get the maximum benefit either out of the brain, or out of Cambridge, in those first one or two years.'[11] Though not yet a Nietzschean, Powell was instinctively in sympathy with the man who would, for nearly two decades, be his main intellectual influence. In an apophthegm 'on education' written in 1881, Nietzsche had observed, 'I have gradually seen the light as to the most universal deficiency in our kind of cultivation and education: no one learns, no one strives after, no one teaches – *the endurance of solitude*.'[12]

'I saw my life when I went up to Cambridge,' Powell recalled, 'and I saw it far too much, I realise in retrospect, as a simple condition of the prize-scholarship-winning knowledge-eating process of the working side of my school life.'[13] He found he could create an environment in which he could concentrate on classical texts without any distractions, to an extent that far exceeded that of the normal undergraduate; he was already at the level of a research fellow. Still not nineteen, he made his first contribution to a learned classical journal – in German, for the *Philologische Wochenschrift*, on the subject of a line in Herodotus. It was the start of a distinguished career of writing frequently for the classical press, in English, German and Italian, that would end only when the war came.[14] Yet he doubted now whether he wanted to be a professional scholar. In his first year at Cambridge he had discussed with the University appointments board the possibilities of entry into the diplomatic service. He wanted a career in which he could use his languages, and learn more of them. He also wished to live and work abroad. However, the idea was abandoned once he won his first tranche of academic distinctions in the summer of 1931, and realised that an academic career would, at least to start with, be irresistible. He would find that, within those confines, he would be able to travel and develop his polyglot interests. Perhaps the diplomatic service was better avoided; Trinity was, at the time, a breeding ground for some of the century's most notorious spies. 'I never had the good fortune to meet them,' Powell remarked.[15] In Nevile's Court at Trinity, once he became a fellow, Powell had rooms next to the historian Steven Runciman who, when he long after claimed to have known 'all the Cambridge traitors', left Powell feeling rather inadequate: 'I must confess', he wrote in 1991, 'to having never had the faintest idea at all of what was going on'; but then he was not one to mix, even in his own College.[16]

He had set a standard for reclusiveness early on, politely refusing the invitation from the Master and his wife to join other freshmen scholars at the traditional dinner soon after he arrived at Trinity. The Master's wife recalled that no one had ever refused before; and Powell's stated reason was 'pressure of work'.[17] To please his father, who felt it was something his undergraduate son must do, Powell took out life membership of the Cambridge Union. The main use of the Union to him was that he could eat dinner there on a Saturday and read the German newspapers. He never attended its debates, and played no part in politics while at the University. He was simply not interested, and did not have the time to be interested. The main thing for which Powell's happy but eccentric home life had not prepared him was socialising: and women in particular were, and for some time yet would remain, an unknown species.

'They didn't exist,' he said when asked sixty-five years later about any undergraduate encounters with them. Asked what he thought about women at that stage in his life, Powell answered: 'What a lyrical poet who doesn't know women thinks about them ... they're part of the vocabulary of poetry.'[18] He had an instinctive sense of the difference, and – despite the strong and contrary example of his mother – in some respects what he felt was the inferiority, of women, something reinforced by his reading of Nietzsche. It was not a view he would modernise later. 'I didn't think they would approach advanced learning in the same mood or manner as a man would ... because the analytical faculty is underdeveloped in women.'[19] It may also be, as some psychologists claim, that the effect of a strong parent on a child, particularly a mother on a son, can restrict the child's ability to interact with the opposite sex. However, Powell admitted he had no self-confidence at that time in relation to women, and was convinced he lacked allure for them: 'I'm not sure that many young men of the age of Cambridge undergraduates do have an attraction for the opposite sex.'[20]

He was determined to approach Cambridge, with all that University's additional attractions, no differently from King Edward's. 'When a young man comes to the university at seventeen or eighteen years of age,' he would tell his colleagues and students at Sydney eight years later, 'his character, both intellectual and moral, is no longer pliable. It is already all but fixed.'[21] It certainly seems to have been so in Powell's case. For all his glittering success as a schoolboy, and for all the belief that he was bound to repeat it at university, he was confronted by the 'drawling disgust' of A. S. F. Gow, his director of studies at Trinity, when he first told him what classical literature he had read. He recalled Gow saying to him, 'Well, I must say, for a scholar of this college this reading list is exceedingly thin.'[22] The problem, which Powell claimed to have all his life, was that he read 'painfully slowly', a legacy, he felt, of his interest in textual criticism, where such intensive study was essential.

He did not entirely fail to make friends. One fellow classicist drawn to him was Ted Curtis, a year older but a contemporary in the University, who was at Clare. Curtis was popular and had an outgoing personality, the complete opposite of Powell; he had been to St Olave's School in the City of London, so was like Powell a grammar school boy. His first glimpse of Powell was in the University scholarships examination at the beginning of the Lent Term, 1931 – their second term at Cambridge. Curtis, writing to his mother about his own difficulties with the examination, said that 'the papers today were rotten: one genius who just translated as though it were French went out at half-time to the consternation of everyone'.[23] The genius was Powell. Curtis formed a friendship with Gow, Powell's tutor, and this encouraged Powell to take the initiative in the relationship. He invited Curtis, in the summer of 1931, to come to London with him to hear a lecture by a French archaeologist. It was the first of many such excursions: Powell discovered that 'the same aspects of the world appeared to us interesting or ridiculous'.[24] Thus encouraged, Curtis broke through Powell's shell of isolation, took him around with him and helped him to become less of a recluse; he also brought him home in the vacation to meet his family in London.

It was early in 1931 that Powell first saw A. E. Housman, the Kennedy Professor of Latin, and a man with whom he had much in common. Housman had been a grammar school boy from the West Midlands who, with far less ease than Powell – his early academic career had been a disaster – had risen to the top of classical scholarship, with a fellowship at Trinity. To the wider world he was better known as a poet, especially as the author of *A Shropshire Lad*, a collection of lyrics largely about premature death published with astonishing success in 1896. Powell, too, was an aspiring poet, and his subject matter would to a great extent reflect Housman's.

Powell's first glimpse of Housman was on 'a freezing and foggy night ... I was up before the term started ... and was passing disconsolate through Nevile's Court, Trinity, on the way to my chilly attic in New Court. There was a sudden gleam of light as the Fellows' door into the cloister opened; and a taut figure strode rapidly to a nearby staircase and disappeared up the wooden stairs with a twitch of the gown.'[25] To Powell, the Professor was 'no more ... than a vague legend attached to a name'. The recollection was not principally one of Housman; it was one of inner suffering. 'Here', Powell recalled, 'was someone who for whole decades had survived the heart-chilling loneliness of Cambridge. Could I not manage to resist it with the same stony manfulness?' However, he also maintained that 'I have no sense of fear or anxiety when I find myself alone, either physically or intellectually'.[26] Powell further defined Housman's solitude as that of a man 'used to the loneliness of one who perceives what others cannot perceive', a loneliness to which Powell himself would become used.

As a second-year undergraduate later in 1931 Powell attended some of Housman's lectures. He found himself 'gripped by the spectacle of that rigorous intellect dissecting remorselessly the textual deformations of poetry which his sensitivity would not permit him to read without betraying his emotions'.[27] It was the 'ruthless and fearless logic with which he dissected the text', in this climate of 'suppressed emotion', that so entranced him.[28] Above all, Housman's intellectual courage, and his determination to stand by a point of view once arrived at, whatever the opposition, would be his greatest legacy to Powell. He had gone up to Cambridge never having heard of Housman or of *A Shropshire Lad*, and it had only been at the start of his second year that his director of studies had said to him, 'I think we might put you down for Housman's lectures and see how you react'.[29] After that, Powell had never missed a Housman lecture for the rest of his time as an undergraduate, 'thrilled' as he recalled 'by the profundity, precision and logic with which he dissected Latin poetry, by which he was so moved as to be sometimes unable without emotion to read it aloud in translation'. Housman made Powell aware that he, too, was a gifted textual critic. As a textual critic, Housman was superb, if recondite. Powell remembered that his lectures would always begin with a room full, and end up with just six: 'but they were the six who understood exactly what he had to say'.[30]

To an extent, Powell modelled himself on Housman. He applied himself with the same intellectual rigour, and read and, eventually, wrote poetry with the same intensity; and he disappeared into his own private world hardly able to communicate with anyone outside, as Housman did. As with Housman, it was the boiling up of private and intense emotions within the pressure-cooker of his temperament that helped form Powell as a poet. A contemporary classicist and a future comrade in the army, David Hunt, felt that Powell had imbibed many of Housman's personal mannerisms, not least his brusqueness of manner and his bluntness in his written criticism.[31] Powell had heard Housman lecture on Lucretius, Horace, Virgil and Catullus, and recalled that 'the exhilaration was produced by watching what seemed to be a mental machine of great power and precision applied to material at first sight unexpected; namely, to determining the meaning of a piece of poetry and the form and wording of it which originally left the poet's pen or arose in his mind'.[32] The effect on Powell was inevitable: 'under the radiation of this display of a great critical mind in action, one's own powers, such as they might be, developed – above all, the spirit of bold but temperate self-reliance without which no great criticism is possible'.

Slowly, he formed a distant relationship with Housman. It was hard, because like Powell Housman was uncommunicative, reserved and solitary. At the end of the second term in which he had attended his lectures, Powell ventured to send him a suggested amendment to Book, IX, line 214 of Virgil's *Aeneid*, replacing *solita aut* with *aut solitas*. He recalled that he felt this was 'greatly daring'. Term was ending, 'and I had some days to spend in expectation of the lightning'. Housman, writing from his favourite hotel in Paris, replied tersely: 'Dear Mr Powell. You analyse the difficulties of the passage correctly, and your emendation removes them. Yours sincerely, A. E. Housman'. Powell admitted that 'no praise in the next forty years was ever to be so intoxicating'.

When he came to write his own poetry within a few years – poetry that relied on Housman's metrical forms and subject matter, but which he claimed to have written with Wagner's music in his head – Powell, too, would invest it with the same emotional intensity that his mentor did.[33] It was not, though, until some time after he had encountered Housman that he first read *A Shropshire Lad*. Later on, he and Housman would meet regularly at High Table, but here things were difficult. Housman had let it be known he did not want to discuss either the classics or poetry, but preferred, if he had to make conversation, to talk about food and wine; Housman's entries in the Kitchen Book at Trinity were legendary. 'I have to confess', Powell recalled forty years later, 'that the correct use of red pepper was the only actual piece of learning I ever imbibed from him in personal intercourse.'[34]

As he had at school, Powell made a forbidding impression upon his contemporaries. One of them, Jasper Rootham, writing in the 1980s recalled him walking along Trinity Street to lectures: 'The face was parchment yellow, tight drawn, the hands were crossed behind the back, the gait stooping but deliberate. The hair was crew cut (a rarity then) and the dark blue Trinity gown was carried as though the wearer had been born in it.'[35] Powell became known as the man who never spoke: *Granta* dubbed him 'The Hermit of Trinity'. While still an undergraduate he would get up at 5.30 a.m. each day and spend an hour translating Herodotus into the English of the Authorised Version, using as his text the copy he had won as a prize at school, and continuing the long and lonely task started there. He would complete it shortly before taking his degree, with help from his mother in checking and revision; but it was just a first draft, and one Powell would later devote much time to rewriting.

His rewards for such dedication were, though, immediate. At the start of his second term, in January 1931, it was announced that he had won the University's Craven Scholarship, only the second time since its foundation in 1647 that it had been taken by a freshman. The following term he won the Trinity Greek

Prose Prize. During this period he was supervised occasionally by Walter Hamilton, a junior fellow of Trinity who would become Headmaster successively of Westminster and Rugby, and Master of Magdalene College Cambridge. 'I formed the opinion', Powell noted sixty years later, 'that my Latin and Greek were better than his; but I also gained a respect for him that lasted all our lives.'[36] Occasionally he broke the routine of incessant work. In the winter of 1931–2 he and Curtis, who shared a devotion to Wagner, made the journey to London, to try to get into the opera at Covent Garden. It being booked solid, they settled for the new Noël Coward production, *Cavalcade*, at Drury Lane. Seeing its revival in 1995, Powell recalled how keen the sense of national consciousness had been for him and his peers so soon after the Great War; it was a sense he was never to lose, and a symbol of the inevitable intrusion of national romanticism into his life, even at this intense academic stage.

In his long vacation in 1932 he made another important discovery, relatively near to his parental home, when he heard of a collection of third- and fourth-century A D papyri in the library of the Selly Oak College in Birmingham. The collection – which had never been published – had been donated by the classicist James Rendel Harris, whom Powell went to see; the old man was then in his eighties, and almost blind. 'It was', Powell later recalled, 'one of the important encounters of my life.'[37] Rendel Harris had made the collection while curator of the Rylands Library in Manchester. He had often travelled to Egypt with two spinsters to see papyri that were being unearthed during excavations for nitrate near the Nile delta. As it was illegal to export the documents, Rendel Harris had smuggled them out in the women's hat boxes.

Powell persuaded Rendel Harris to authorise him to take the papyri to the British Museum, where they were mounted for him, the Selly Oak trustees agreeing to provide funds for the purpose. That done, he set about examining, classifying and translating them. He found on them fragments of classical writings, but also notes and minutiae of everyday life, including recipes and money orders. He worked on the documents for three years, starting while still an undergraduate. When his book on them was published in 1936, it was his first great original contribution to classical scholarship.

II

Powell's hard work for his finals in May 1933 was suddenly threatened with futility. He had been sickening with tonsillitis since the Easter vacation, which he had partly spent on a walking tour of the Welsh marches with Curtis, their first such holiday. On his return to Cambridge the tonsillitis felled him and, because of his refusal to stop working, he weakened further and contracted pyelitis, an inflammation of the kidney, shortly before he was due to sit his examinations. He ran a terrible fever, and it was feared he would have to take an *aegrotat* – a degree deriving its name from the Latin for 'he is sick'. However, Canon Frederick Simpson, who lived on the same staircase in Trinity Great Court – though they had never spoken, since Simpson was as private as Powell – effected a rescue when he heard from their bedmaker that Powell was so ill. He had him admitted to the Evelyn Nursing Home, and had the Tripos papers, as the Cambridge degree courses are known, and an invigilator, sent in for him to take there. There were seven papers in all, and Powell had a temperature of 104 degrees when he sat the last one. Nonetheless, he achieved his first, to match the one taken in the first part of his Tripos. It had required some exertion on Simpson's part: 'Apparently,' Powell recalled, 'Simpson went straight to my tutor, Mr Dykes, insisted that arrangements be made for me to take the papers in hospital, and pushed the matter as far as a personal and acrimonious altercation with the chairman of the examiners, Professor F. M. Cornford.'[38] It was only by accident that Powell subsequently learned of the efforts made on his behalf.

Although Powell had made few friends, one or two of his seniors had found him sufficiently interesting to try to penetrate his private world. At the neighbouring college, St John's, the classics don Martin Charlesworth told one of his undergraduates at the time of Powell's brilliant graduation: 'That man Powell is extraordinary. He is the best Greek scholar since Porson. But he's very shy. I'm doing something about it.'[39] Charlesworth persisted, over the years that Powell remained in Cambridge, in including 'John Enoch', as he called him, in lunches, dinners and other academic–social events that he organised. Slowly, Powell came out of his shell. He did not, though, come to like Cambridge sufficiently to want to stay there, as Housman had done, immured in loneliness.

Upon his graduation, Powell won the Craven travelling scholarship. He used it to fund a series of visits to Italy, reading Greek manuscripts – mainly Thucydidean – in libraries. In 1933–4, after a walking tour of Cornwall with Curtis, he went to Venice, Florence and Parma, and was captivated by the Italian life and language. The following year he went to Venice again, Naples and Turin, a city he enjoyed more than any other. He returned to Florence, where he devoted more time than he should to finishing Tasso's *Gerusalemme Liberata* – he had the habit of always finishing a work he had started, however difficult or potentially unrewarding it might seem – and took in Rome and the Vatican, having returned home briefly between each of his research trips. He found his work physically difficult: the strain on the eyes was such that it was hard for him to read meaningfully for more than ten minutes at a time. There were barely any facilities for making photographic replicas of the manuscripts he read; hence the length of time his work took.

Italy had other benefits. He became fluent in the language, and had an education in aesthetics. He saw the realities of fascism, which further confirmed his view of the likelihood of war. He also met other travelling scholars, and made friendships outside his existing, somewhat confined, circle. While in Turin in March–April 1935 he wrote to his parents complaining that, despite his name-change, he was being further confused with J. U. Powell, his fellow classicist. J. U. Powell had been listed to give a speech at a papyrology congress that was, in fact, to be given by J. E. Powell. However, a few days later J. E. Powell wrote to his parents to tell them that J. U. Powell had died suddenly. 'If I may say so in such a matter, this will be a great convenience . . . the cause was pneumonia: but we know better! The shock of seeing himself booked to speak at Florence on *I papiri greci Rendel Harris* proved too much for the poor old gentleman.'[40]

The only record of Powell's having kept a diary in his life was during his stay in Turin in the spring of 1935 ('to write a diary every day', he observed in 1977, using one of his favourite metaphors, 'is like returning to one's own vomit').[41] It seems to have been kept largely for the entertainment of his parents, who were always keen to know what he was doing; and he was as keen to have them know. As might be expected of so introverted a man with such close ties to his parents and so few friends, his letters home are, at this stage in his life, intelligent and informative but occasionally Pooterish. He seems to have been a hyp-ochondriac, constantly alert to, and complaining of, bad throats and colds, and there are many touching assurances to his mother that he is taking precautions against catching a chill, and dressing properly. His diary is full of complaints about the noise he has to endure from other readers when he works in the library, and about it being either too hot or too cold, or too sunny or too dark. Having kept the diary for a few days in which there were many such assaults on his sensibilities, Powell tells his parents: 'I soon discovered the weakness of diary-keeping. After a bad day it obliges you to remind yourself of all the worst which has come to pass just before retiring, and this is undesirable. Consequently, the diary has languished this week. . . .'[42]

In between these two Italian tours a great spiritual crisis occurred in Powell's life. He was still sure there would be another war, but even the coming to power of Hitler in January 1933 did not, at the time, strike him as conclusive. He was more concerned about France's potential as a force for continental instability.[43] The events in Germany distressed him not merely for the threat they posed to his country, but because of his love for German culture. However, he was not yet shaken out of his regard for his spiritual homeland. Nonetheless, events there imposed upon him a sense of time running out; the belief that war was inevitable had been supplemented by, and then subjugated to, the belief that he would die in the resumed hostilities. He told his father, in 1934, 'I want to be in the army from the first day that Britain goes to war.' His father replied, 'Well, my son, if you had said the opposite to me you would still have had my support, but I am glad that that is the conclusion to which you have come.'[44]

His main intellectual recreation at this time – though his work on the Rendel Harris papyri was continuing – was Nietzsche: 'In my early twenties I read all

Nietzsche – not just the main works but the minor works as well, all of them, and every scrap of published correspondence. Nietzsche alone of men out of books has a share in the loyalty and affectionate gratitude which otherwise belongs only to living teachers.'[45] The effect of reading him, and imbibing his detestation of Christianity and its regard for the weak, compounded the effect of Frazer and the early Carlyle, and the influence of his mother's withdrawal from the church. His study of the New Testament in Greek also fuelled his doubts, because of the 'extreme unrealism' of what he read. Thus his initial easy atheism became committed, even militant; and the poetry he began to write contained more than its share of Nietzschean themes, principally the triumph of the strong over the weak, of light over darkness. Although some thought the moustache he had been cultivating since school was in imitation of Nietzsche, Powell said he grew it because his father had one.

He would note with irony that his reading of Nietzsche ran contemporaneously with the gradual explosion of Germany into war. For Powell, Nietzsche would eventually become more than just a philosopher, he would become a model for life: and not just intellectual life at that. There were as many similarities between the two men as there were distinct differences: not least, at this stage in Powell's life, that both were brilliant classical scholars, heavily influenced by their mothers – in Nietzsche's case inevitably, as his father had died while he was a small child. Powell's precocity at King Edward's matched Nietzche's at Pforta seventy years earlier. Although the years to 1949 would comprise the period of Nietzsche's greatest influence over Powell – they coincide with his period of militant atheism – much of the power of Nietzsche's thought, and above all the example of his intellectual courage and originality – were to live with Powell for ever. It was the certainty of Nietzsche that so attracted him, and the philosopher was never more certain than on the question of the death of God. 'What thinking person', he had asked, 'still needs the hypothesis of a God?'[46] For Powell, constructing his own self-contained existence without recourse to God became a fundamental intellectual and moral challenge. For the best part of twenty painful years he held to it.

He took Nietzsche undiluted, and not least of the attraction to him of the German's rationale was the argument that Christianity was a betrayal of the precepts of the ancient culture they both revered. The Greeks, Nietzsche had argued, had seen their gods not as masters above them, but as reflections of the most successful of their own caste; this had enhanced the Greeks' nobility. 'Christianity, on the other hand, crushed and shattered man completely, and submerged him as if in deep mire,' Nietzsche had written. 'Then, all at once, into his feeling of complete confusion, it allowed the light of divine compassion to shine, so that the surprised man, stunned by mercy, let out a cry of rapture, and thought for a moment that he carried all of heaven within him. All psychological inventions of Christianity work towards this sick excess of feeling, toward the deep corruption of head and heart necessary for it. Christianity wants to destroy, shatter, stun, intoxicate: there is only one thing it does not want: moderation, and for this reason, it is in the deepest meaning barbaric, Asiatic, ignoble, un-Greek.'[47]

During 1934 his last feelings of romance about Germany finally faded, when, on 1 July, he heard the news of the 'night of the long knives', the mass murder ordered by Hitler of hundreds of Brownshirts under the homosexual Ernst Röhm. The events of the preceding eighteen months had failed to puncture Powell's German dream: 'As with every spiritual homeland,' he recalled, 'it was not of this world.'[48] Yet once this news arrived Powell

> sat for hours in a state of shock, shock which you experience when, around you, you see the debris of a beautiful building in which you have lived for a long time ... so it had all been illusion, all fantasy, all a self-created myth. Music, philosophy, poetry, science and the language itself – everything was demolished, broken to bits on the cliffs of a monstrous reality. The spiritual homeland had not been a spiritual homeland after all, since nothing can be a homeland, let alone a spiritual homeland, where there is no justice, where justice does not reign ... overnight my spiritual homeland had disappeared and I was left only with my geographical homeland.

His imaginings of war became more urgent still. In the spring of 1935 he was living in a German house in Venice, where he met the eminent Jewish classicist Paul Maas, a professor from Königsberg. Before long Maas had confirmed, and amplified, all the doubts and fears Powell had about the Third Reich, and about the certainty of war. Moving on to Florence, to the Congresso Internazionale di Papirologia to present a paper on the Rendel Harris papyri, Powell had a 'furious' argument with an official of the British Council, who was a sympathiser of the British Union of Fascists and told Powell of the importance of their country following Mosley.[49] In Powell's papers is a handwritten note from this time, which he appears to have sent in a letter to his parents: 'Where infernal politics and foreign policies are concerned, it is an Englishman's duty, when on the continent of Europe, to keep his ears, his eyes and particularly his mind, open – and his mouth shut.'[50]

On 8 October 1934, Powell was elected a fellow of Trinity at the remarkably early age of twenty-two. He had secured this position with a dissertation entitled 'The Moral and Historical Principles of Thucydides, and their Influence in Later Antiquity' -proof he was more than simply a textual critic. *The Times* reported his election, listing the prizes he had won at Trinity: Craven Scholar, College Greek and Latin Prose Prizeman, Percy Pemberton Prizeman, Members' Latin Prizeman, Porson Prizeman, Sir William Browne Medallist, Craven Student, Research Scholar, Yeats Prizeman and Lees Knowles Exhibitioner, not forgetting his first class with distinction in both parts of the Tripos. The historian of

Cambridge between the wars, T. E. B. Howarth, describes Powell as 'something of a prodigy'; his academic achievements were stupendous.[51] Howarth also notes that, as with Housman, 'the drier the subject matter the more satisfaction he appeared to find in it'.[52]

It was not until the summer of 1935 that he settled down in Cambridge. Special leave of absence as a fellow was granted to him to study abroad, but that ended at Easter 1935. He took up residence again at Trinity, teaching and working on the texts of Thucydides and Herodotus. He supervised undergraduates at Jesus and Pembroke, and lectured in the University. His main activity was researching his lexicon to Herodotus, which he would complete in 1937 and publish the following year. Both A. S. F. Gow, in a conversation with whom Powell came up with the idea, and another Trinity fellow, Ernest Harrison, arranged to find money from a College fund to help Powell complete the project.

Slowly, Powell the lover of institutions began to appreciate the qualities of his University and his College. Although at first he had been unwilling to surrender to the pressures put on him by the Fellows of Trinity to join their number, if only for a few years, he began to see it would not be too bad for him. He eventually accepted under protest, his protests directed mainly at his father, who had applied great pressure upon him. Albert Powell's argument was, however, cogent: he told his son that, having been a fellow of Trinity, he could then be anything else he liked. Powell's father had retired in July 1932, and with his wife had moved from Birmingham to the Sussex coast; their devotion to their son, which had always been complete, took on a new intensity. With a view to staying for the shortest term possible, Powell agreed to accept the fellowship when the time came. 'But even then,' he recalled, 'it was always suffocating to me, always overpowering.'[53]

The 'suffocation' was something he always felt when entering the Great Gate at Trinity: 'I felt I was going out of the world into something enclosed, that all my instincts were to get out of what was enclosed into the world.'[54] His father had told him it would be contrary to the laws of biology for him not to want to be a teacher; and Powell, who as a child had wanted to be a professor, now felt that ambition mature. 'I do have, I think,' he told the writer Geoffrey Parkhouse in 1970, 'a means of making an instant approach and contact with an elder boy or a young man. Indeed, one of the reasons why I was determined not to spend my life at university was precisely because this was so strong that I felt that it either had to be me or them – that they'd eat me body and soul. It would be my students and not me. I could never endure the idea that I would spend my life in college.'[55] Despite the greater availability of luxury to him as a fellow, he made no compromises in his personal austerity. His sitting room was described by a friend as 'resembling in its Spartan simplicity the room of a first-year student at the Potsdam military academy'.[56]

As an undergraduate, Powell had written – but not published – a rather precious essay entitled 'On Cambridge, by a Cambridge undergraduate'. In it, he showed he had formed an early view of the difficulties of taking a fellowship: 'Several hundreds of the acutest and most original minds in England are cast together in a heap, housed in compartments like those of a beehive, one above and beside the other, tied to Cambridge for eleven months out of the twelve all the days of their life, virtually forbidden to marry by force of circumstances, given old men and undergraduates for companions – and then commanded to be happy.'[57] His later reluctance to join their number was hardly surprising.

Both as an undergraduate and as a fellow, he would spend much of his free time alone: even the walking holidays around England in the Easter and long vacations were not always made in Curtis's company, and he would sleep on railway stations or in barns. This was because of his natural asceticism, not out of poverty; Powell had won sufficient scholarships and awards to be as well off as most apparently better-born undergraduates, and, at about £400 a year, better off than many men with families to support. Writing to his parents from Cardiganshire in July 1935, during a long north–south walk along the border, Powell said that 'for the purpose of seeing and covering ground on foot, the lone traveller has a great advantage over the one that goes in company ... the reason chiefly is, that being free to follow his own inclination absolutely in the matter of speed, rests, time for food and drink, the individual moves quicker and more effortlessly'.[58] The sentiment could be used as a metaphor for other parts of his life. He was fascinated by landscape, but, by his own admission, 'blind' to buildings; he would never look inside an old church when he came across one.[59] That revelation would come later. When Curtis went with him on these walks they tended to the Welsh Marches, and the land along Offa's Dyke, and Powell would occupy himself reading Dante's *Inferno*, or competing with Curtis for which of them could make the better Latin translation of *The Times*'s first leader.

It was not until May 1935, when Powell came back into residence at Trinity, that he first actually spoke to Housman; he found himself sitting next to the Professor at High Table. They were not to have many such discussions. On a sunny spring morning the following year Powell was walking across Great Court when he noticed the College flag at half-mast. He went into the porter's lodge to inquire; the porter told him, with what struck Powell was an interesting false emphasis, 'Professor Housman's *died*, Sir.' There was a twist; 'in the service-sheet at his funeral,' Powell remembered, 'there was a misprint right in the middle of his own specially composed hymn'. It was a cause of amusement that night at dinner that, as one don put it, 'of all people, for this to have happened to Housman!'[60] He found High Table dominated by his once and future benefactor Canon Simpson, conducting 'conversations which extended at least three places to left and right of him and opposite'.[61] Simpson's main sparring partner was a Professor Hardy, who 'sustained a long-running cricket fantasy, in which

Simpson and he were captains respectively of the God Eleven and the No God Eleven'. Powell, judged by Hardy to be 'pure 100 per cent atheist', was deputed to be one of the main batsmen in Hardy's team. 'The competition', Powell recalled, 'was conducted only by losing runs through inadvertent acknowledgements of the position of the other side, as occurred when the Junior Bursar, de Bruyne, improved the heating in the College Chapel and had to be dropped in consequence from the No God Eleven altogether.'[62]

It was also at Trinity that, on the advice of a mathematician, Powell had his first encounter with the philosophical discipline that would dominate his political life, and afford him great, if nearly posthumous, distinction in it: economics. He had been told to read Malthus' *Essay on the Principle of Population*, and did so with 'excitement'.[63] Malthus said resources could never increase at a rate sufficient to feed the growth in the population; if 'prudence' were not applied to the use of these resources, 'misery' would result.

His Herodotean work had taken a great step forward in the spring of 1935. He received a telegram from his parents while in Florence to tell him that the Cambridge University Press had agreed to publish his lexicon. This was a conspicuous success for him, but he also demonstrated, in his reply to his parents, just how much he depended on their support in his lonely and earnest existence: 'So far as I can see, the older I grow and the more I succeed, the more I shall want help from my mother and father.'[64] The connections made with German scholars on his European travels resulted in his acquiring some of the research materials of two German Herodoteans, Ludwig Kalpers and Fritz Nawak, including thousands of word-slips they had used for compiling their own lexicon twenty-five years earlier. He paid 600 marks for the material from a Freiburg classics professor, W. Aly, concluding the deal in Florence.[65] This provided an enormous short-cut, and allowed him the time to develop a new system of his own to indicate variants of words between the standard texts and the versions of them he had found in Italian libraries; for the benefit of future scholars, Powell deposited the slips in the Wren Library at Trinity. A by-product of his work was that he was forced to improve his own poor handwriting, to avoid the likelihood of literal errors that would sabotage the credibility of his lexicon. His concentration on the work was intense: he told another Trinity fellow, T. C. Nicholas, that if all the text of Herodotus were to disappear he could reproduce it by heart.[66] The painstaking task reinforced his view, often expressed to friends in later life, that 90 per cent of any job was sheer drudgery.

He used the preface to his own lexicon to attack an earlier German attempt, by Johannes Schweighauser in 1824, as 'a pretence', since it had missed 1,200 words used by Herodotus.[67] The claim he made for his own work was that it combined 'the advantages of a lexicon with those of an index; it is an index in so far as it notes every occurrence of every word or name used by Herodotus, και [and] alone excepted; it is a lexicon in the sense that all words are translated and the references classified by meaning and construction'. It was well received. Noting it in the *Classical Review*, W. L. Lorimer of St Andrew's complimented Powell's 'amazing industry, much thought and care, and fine scholarship'.[68] The form of the work was, he added, 'well nigh perfect', and Lorimer hoped Powell would move on after his 'eagerly awaited translation of Herodotus and critical edition of Thucydides to produce a similar lexicon to Thucydides.' Even today, Powell's work still excites regard. Robin Lane Fox, of New College, Oxford, has said that although the lexicon is 'an entirely mechanical production with no intellectual power' it is 'nonetheless invaluable'; it showed, he felt, the strength of Powell's 'sharp, clear and nit-picking mind' as a classicist.[69]

In January 1936 Powell gave an address on 'The War and its Aftermath in their Influence on Thucydidean Studies' to the Classical Association of Westminster School. His alertness to the intentions of the regime in Germany, and to its nature, was being maintained not just by his contacts with German scholars, but by his assiduous reading of diplomatic and political events. He now applied a classical mirror to what was going on. He said that, since the advent of dictatorship in Italy, there had been a decline in study of the free Greek and Rome republics. Because of the search for anti-fascist sentiment, he said:

> It is obviously safer to begin by choosing a more congenial subject than a free Athens or a free Rome. In Germany the effect of National Socialism has been the opposite. Racial doctrines and political antipathy to the whole Roman Empire and its cognate ideas have had the result of discouraging study of the Italic peoples and of Rome, mistress of the world. On the other hand, a peculiar kinship has been detected between the ancient Greeks and modern Germans. Not only the Greek civilisation in general, but Thucydides in particular, has proved exceptionally congenial. The intensely political outlook of Thucydides may be made serviceable to a doctrine which asserts the absolute dominion of the State over every phase of individual existence; and, as the more striking figures of Caesar and Augustus had already been captured as prototypes by Mussolini, Hitler might well be made to look very like Pericles – or Pericles, rather, to look like Hitler.[70]

With hindsight, his fixation with the forthcoming war is clear: he also felt, through his reading of Nietzsche, that he had come to understand the German mind, which added to his conviction based on the historical evidence that there would be another war. Yet, for all the threat Germany posed, he remained addicted to German culture. 'The happiest and most glorious hours of my life with books', he later said, 'have been with German books.'[71] He went to see the commandant of the Cambridge University Officer Training Corps, to ask what he should do to ensure being able to enlist in the army on day one of the war. When he told the commandant he had no military training at all – he had not even been in the cadets at school – he was told there was little that could be done for him. He was assured, though, that he had been put on a list, whose scope he avoided by enlisting as a private soldier in 1939. Otherwise, he feared for his fate: 'I was lucky to escape Bletchley,' he observed, referring to the code-breaking centre that became the repository of the country's leading academics.[72] At another juncture, he asked a senior fellow at Trinity whether his fellowship could be suspended if he chose to go to Abyssinia to fight against the invading Italians.[73]

For all his growing dislike of Trinity, its resources did offer him certain unpredictable stimulations. He would frequently avail himself of his privilege as a fellow to go into the Wren Library at any time and read old manuscripts lodged there. On one such excursion he found the laws of the ancient Welsh king Hywel the Good. Powell had a smattering of Welsh, and such was his interest in his discovery that he taught himself sufficient medieval Welsh to start a translation. He wrote up his discovery in the *Journal of Celtic Studies*, which alerted another scholar with an interest in Hywel, Stephen Williams of Swansea University. The two men collaborated on an edition of Hywel's laws, eventually – after the vicissitudes of travel and war – published in 1942 as *Llyfr Blegywryd*.

III

At the end of 1936 – Powell could date it exactly, because it was the very day, 10 December, that Edward VIII abdicated – he arrived at the British School in Rome; it was the last stop on his tour of Italian libraries, and he was there for the month of the Christmas vacation. At lunch the next day he met a young artist, Andrew Freeth, of whom he would become a close friend, and for whom he would act as a muse, over the next fifty years. Powell remembered asking him, 'What is your name?' The man replied, 'My name is Freeth.' Powell asked him, 'What does it mean?' Freeth, with the common sense that would commend him to Powell, said, 'It doesn't mean anything. It's a name.'[74] (It did, in fact, mean a Scottish font.) Freeth almost immediately made his first drawing of Powell. In Italy on a travelling scholarship too – he had just won the Rome scholarship in engraving – Freeth was Powell's age, and also from Birmingham. He painted or drew Powell at almost every stage in his life, and in turn later became fascinated by Powell's political theorising. Powell was studying manuscripts of Thucydides in the Vatican library, and Freeth recalled later that Powell was praying that the Pope, who was ill, would not die: because if he did the library would close, and Powell would be unable to work; the Pope did not die, and Powell finished his task.[75]

One of Powell's problems was that he increasingly defined himself not as a scholar, but as a poet, and somewhat unrealistically longed for the freedom to write poetry in the manner of the romantics. Throughout his early twenties he had been writing verse, in Housman's manner, and by 1937 had enough publishable lyrics – fifty in all – to put out a collection of them. He received a sheaf of rejection slips from the main publishing houses, and realised he would be published only if he subsidised the operation himself. The money needed to publish his slim volume was lent him by Canon Simpson, to whom Powell had shown his poetry; when, in January 1940, he had raised enough from the sales of his second volume, *Casting Off*, to pay him back, Simpson used the money to plant cherry trees along the Coton footpath on the Backs in Cambridge.[76] Maurice Cowling, commenting on the poems in his study of Powell's thought, describes them as 'restrained and pessimistic, and written out of a high sense of human destiny'. This is the mark, once more, of Nietzsche as much as of Housman, though Cowling also talks of it as registering 'the resigned, masculine gloom of the Trinity ethos into which he had been inducted'.[77]

First Poems – which Powell had initially entitled *The Chaplet* – was the first of four books of verse Powell would publish: the second came in 1939, the last two jointly in 1951. Of the first three he wrote that they were 'dominated by the War – the War foreseen, the War imminent, the War actual'.[78] This was a Housmanic theme, and it is quickly apparent that the form as well as the subject matter owes much to Powell's teacher – though Powell claimed that 'Tennyson and Milton were the principal fountains from which I drank'.[79] He wrote most of the poems in Cambridge between the autumn of 1935 and late 1936. On to Housman's perceptions Powell grafted his own sensitivities, especially an obsession with what he would call in one of his most important speeches a quarter of a century later 'the sadness of spring'.[80] It is a pain described in *A Shropshire Lad*, most notably in the poem 'Loveliest of trees, the cherry now', which was read at Powell's funeral. In his introduction to the *Collected Poems*, Powell recalled that 'in old age it is no longer possible to credit the sheer, almost physical agony which is caused in youth by the passage of time, when the turning of spring into summer arouses pain as lively as the pain of toothache. The succession of the seasons is like a recurrent inescapable catastrophe, which sweeps away what is young and beautiful, and what is beautiful because it is young.'[81] It was also, as he wrote forty years later 'unfair that such an explosion of life, such a miracle of colour and joy, should take place and that we, the human spectators, are left unchanged and the course of our life still set irreversibly onwards to its end'.[82] While not imagining he was the first to feel such things, Powell knew that 'its poignancy was enhanced in the years before 1939 for those who, like myself, lived under the shadow of the conviction that the hostilities temporarily suspended in November 1918 would presently be renewed on a similar scale of brutality and intensity'.

He had felt driven to poetry because 'pain of this sort demands utterance, and when it cries out, it cries out anywhere and anyhow in poetry', though over half a century later he would admit it was 'not entirely inaccurate' to detect in his verse 'self-absorbed romanticism'.[83] In the first of the poems, Powell makes quite clear what had provoked him:

> But when the spring to hill and coomb
> Returned in warmth and rain,
> The torture of the trees in bloom
> Stung me to speech again.[84]

It is a theme expanded in the next poem:

> No eyes have I but for the sight
> Of early bloom that summer drought
> Untimely kills; I love the light
> That soonest flickers and is out.[85]

It is a useful metaphor, because of its close association with Powell's main preoccupation, death. In his 28th lyric he says that the blossoms of spring give:

> What all our wisdom would not buy;
> Their life for us they yearly live,
> And year by year for us they die.[86]

There is a risk that this tone can spill over into the unpleasantly self-pitying, which it appears to do in the next lyric:

> Oh, sweet it is, where grass is deep,
> And swifts are overhead,
> To lie and watch the clouds, and weep
> For friends already dead.[87]

It is the sort of tone that gave rise to so many parodies of Housman; it is one Powell handles better elsewhere, as he develops the notion that the coming around of spring is a sign of ageing, year on year, and a propulsion towards the grave:

> How many springs, before my sighing
> Is hushed, and healed my sore,
> And I in wintry dark am lying?
> How many summers more?[88]

The loss of his youth, the recognition of which is promoted by the return of spring, is particularly painful:

> And so your coming makes me glad,
> With youthful grace that holds the eye,
> And yet my heart within is sad
> For youth of mine gone by.[89]

If both the form and the tone are derivative, and often the metaphors less than fresh, with clear echoes of a variety of poets from Henry Vaughan to William Wordsworth, Powell still brings to his verse an intensity of feeling that fully conveys his psychological obsessions, most notably the agony of getting older:

> It is not only when I go
> On journeys, that I feel
> The steel wheels grind and pound below
> Along the rails of steel.
>
> Their voices, faint or louder,
> I hear them night and day;
> They pound my life to powder,
> They grind my years away.[90]

The poems seem to be a search for inner strength, but with death used as the best and most noble antidote to the loneliness that seeps out of so much of the poetry. There is also, in one of the poems that embodies these feelings, the clearest presentiment of a predominant theme not just of much of Powell's later poetry, but of much of his life after the war:

> Below the turf his straight limbs lie,
> A stone is at his head.
> O God of battles, why am I
> Alive when he is dead?[91]

Yet the most famous of all Powell's verse, the third poem in this first volume, reflects a Nietzschean ideal of youth, strength and vitality: the ideal, inevitably and frustratingly transient, that he felt the need to pursue:

> I hate the ugly, hate the old,
> I hate the lame and weak,
> But more than all I hate the dead
> That lie so still in their earthen bed
> And never dare to rise.
>
> I only love the strong and bold,
> The flashing eye, the reddening cheek,
> But more than all I love the fire
> In youthful limbs, that wakes desire
> And never satisfies.[92]

However, he makes his own 'desire' explicit in the 45th lyric:

> yet not for life
> Is my desire,

> But first to close the eyes of those
> Who brought me to the light,
> And then before my youth is o'er
> To die in fight.[93]

In the previous poem, he had written that:

> To-night on years I shall not see
> My thought more warmly runs:
> Clearer to-night is borne to me
> The murmur of the guns.[94]

Yet for all this – patently sincere – longing to make the final sacrifice, there remains, at the very close of the volume, an almost atavistic need for security and comfort, for a condition in which bravado and manliness can without shame be cast aside:

> Mother, with longing ever new
> And joy too great for telling
> I turn again to rest in you
> My earliest dwelling.[95]

Compared with poetic contemporaries, Powell is a reactionary; not-withstanding the debt to Housman, these are verses that would have sat better in the world immediately after August 1914, though their gloom – there is none of Rupert Brooke's 'swimmers into cleanness leaping' here – is a more modernistic component, almost ironically transmitted in such conventional verse forms. The limited nature, at this time, of Powell's social and emotional experiences inevitably constrained him as a poet; but what enabled him to make his first venture into verse as successful as it was was the fact that what he did feel – about war, death, solitude, the end of youth – he felt with an almost unbearable intensity. The *Times Literary Supplement* was complimentary, inevitably noting that the poems captured a little 'the tone and temper' of *A Shropshire Lad*.[96] The review added that Powell 'crystallises his feeling with a poignant economy seldom met with in a first book of poems'. Powell sent a copy to the poet laureate, John Masefield, who replied, 'I am reading these with a great deal of admiration for their concision and point.'[97] Hilaire Belloc, similarly favoured, wrote, 'I have read them with the greatest pleasure and interest. It is most kind of you to have thought of sending them to me and most flattering to me. I shall always retain them.'[98]

It is certainly true that, like many young men educated in an all-male atmosphere, Powell at the time he wrote this poetry formed a close intellectual and spiritual attachment to at least one other young man. Because of the intensity with which he had applied himself to his studies, Powell was emotionally immature; as a result he had his schoolboy crushes late in life, and it is easy for those who do not properly appreciate the peculiar forces at work in his background to come to the erroneous conclusion that he was homosexual, as at least one acquaintance of Powell's claimed shortly after his death.[99] Powell's muse was, in fact, A. W. J. 'Tommy' Thomas, an undergraduate reading classics at Pembroke whom Powell had supervised, and three years younger than him. Thomas's letters to 'Dear Powell' are largely reports of his own activities, with occasional discussions of classical themes; and the one letter in the Powell papers to Thomas from him is affectionate, but neither passionate nor remotely erotic. The two men were separated in 1937 when Thomas, who was in the colonial service, was posted to Malaya.

Powell made Thomas's effect on the poems explicit in a letter he sent him in November 1937. He referred to criticism Thomas had made of the poems during a walking holiday the two men had had earlier in the year at Anglesey, but added,

> The book has also another and a deeper connection with you, which it would be foolish for me to try to deny, when I remember that nearly all the poems in it were written between January 1936 and June 1937. I believe, as you know, that nothing can be poetry which is not universal, and there is certainly not a single line in First Poems which has any personal reference; but it is equally certain that the book would either have been very different or would not have been written at all, but for the accident of my supervising for Pembroke in the Lent Term last year.[100]

When questioned towards the end of his life about the apparent homoerotic tone of some of his poetic work, Powell replied, 'Does one not love young men, from being young?' He amplified this point by saying, 'One's love is for a whole generation that is doomed.'[101] The love was not sexual; it was the pain, as Housman put it, of 'The lads who will die in their glory / And never grow old'. Having had so austere an upbringing, Powell was bewitched by the *jeunesse d'orée*, and sought to celebrate it. He had an almost childish regard for the hero whose heroism was rooted in physical courage, a regard which caused him to manifest affection in the form of a schoolboy crush. He was also socially and emotionally limited to an extent that eliminated women from his life until they forced themselves into it after the war: when he would turn out to be not in the least homosexual. In Thomas he thought he had found someone who could share, in its full depth, his own intellect and sensitivity. To judge from Thomas's letters to Powell, it would be exaggerating to say that he appreciated or understood the earnestness of Powell's feeling for him, or of his commitment. Thomas had, though, burrowed deep into Powell's soul and, for reasons that will become apparent, would be rooted there for ever.

IV

Powell was determined to broaden his experience as far as he could before the war, as he expected, consumed him; and was still determined to get out of Cambridge, where, he said, he still felt 'oppressed and suffocated'.[102] At a College feast in the spring of 1937, the guest of honour, Lord Wright, a law lord, said that 'our Government is doing its best to prevent war'. Powell, on the fellows' table, shouted out, 'But we *want* war.'[103] That same year, driving to Boar's Hill with Gilbert Murray, who had just retired as the Regius Professor of Greek at Oxford, Powell said, 'There's no hope for us unless we go to war with Germany,' at which Murray looked him 'straight in the eyes' and said, 'I think so too.'[104] It was a battle which, like many others in his life to come, Powell had elevated to a high pitch of romanticism; but, when the time came, his approach to the conflict would become necessarily highly practical. The prospect of war, the uncertainty of when it would come, and the sense of imprisonment Powell felt at Cambridge made a cocktail that depressed him deeply. After a trip to Anglesey during the 1937 long vacation he went to see his parents and broke down in tears in front of them, 'because I felt I had no future and that every man's hand was against me'. He soon, though, pulled himself together.[105]

He planned to go to Moscow to read manuscripts there in the second part of 1937, and began to try to learn enough Russian to get by. However, another opportunity intervened. He had hoped to beat Nietzsche's record of becoming a professor at the age of twenty-four, when he had taken up the chair in classics at Basel, and in 1935–6 started applying for vacancies. He was not, unsurprisingly, immediately successful. 'Redbricks looked favourably on my applications,' he said later, 'until they discovered I was 23.'[106] However, when offered the chair in Greek in the University of Sydney in 1937 – 'sight unseen' as he later put it, since he had been interviewed by Sydney's Professor of Mathematics, who happened to be in Cambridge and had had the task deputed to him – he was still, at twenty-five, the youngest of his rank in the British Empire.[107] Sydney was the first university not to be frightened off by his youth. He would succeed an Oxford man, William John Woodhouse, who was about to retire – he in fact died in October 1937 – and who had been professor since 1901: Powell was only the fourth occupant of the chair. Greek was highly valued at Sydney; it had been one of the foundation subjects in the University's curriculum when it was established in 1852. However, Woodhouse had a growing difficulty – which Powell would inherit – that Greek was being less and less taught in Australian schools. A one-year preparatory course had therefore been established at the University in 1930 to help attract more undergraduates, but Woodhouse had also taken the message of Greek around the schools of New South Wales, and beyond.

Powell had amassed formidable references with which to impress Sydney when making his application for the chair. His Trinity colleague Ernest Harrison spoke of the 'astonishing merit' of Powell's dissertation on Thucydides, and praised his *Lexicon to Herodotus* and his work in papyrology.[108] Contrary to the impression Powell might give, Harrison added that 'nor is he a recluse: he takes his part well in the social life of the Fellows, and is observant of the world and its affairs'. Paul Maas wrote from Königsberg to say, 'I know few philologists who in such a high degree combine scientific with artistic gifts, and depth of learning with attractive personality. ... In Mr Powell I see the worthy pupil of his great master A. E. Housman.'[109] Powell's former director of studies at Trinity, F. H. Sandbach, wrote that 'If the University of Sydney were to appoint Mr Powell to the Chair of Greek, they would secure a man of great learning and one whose publications would bring them credit; they would also gain a strong, human and interesting character.'[110]

On his appointment being confirmed, Powell composed a limerick, which he sent to Curtis, and which also refers to Thomas:

> When they heard that he'd gone to Malaya
> They exclaimed: 'What a long way awaya!'
> But he won't be as far
> From where libraries are
> As the failure that's gone to Australia![111]

In a mood of elation – 'I tried to escape from Cambridge and eventually succeeded' – Powell took a seat on the first flying-boat to make the trip to Singapore, and reached Sydney sixteen days after leaving Poole harbour.[112] He was one of only two through passengers on the flight, completed by a Qantas de Havilland after Singapore, through the Dutch East Indies to Darwin and Sydney. 'It was an exacting routine,' he recalled, half a century later. 'Three or four times a day, the flying-boat landed on a sheet of water – lake or river or sea. Nightly the crew and passengers were transported to a neighbouring city for a few hours' rest before the ferociously early take-off the next morning.'[113] His mother had supervised his packing, for which Powell was grateful: heating on the flying-boat was primitive, with a cardigan necessary at low altitude and an overcoat above 10,000 feet – both items she had insisted upon. Among the stops was one at Rome, where he saw Andrew Freeth, and then Greece, a place which – for all its historic and intellectual power over Powell – 'does not amuse or interest me greatly', as he told his parents.[114] However, 'when this afternoon I found myself passing over the country which had stretched out its tentacles over two millennia, caught me in Birmingham and drawn me to Australia, I could not contemplate without some emotion the unfamiliar places to which names so familiar belong'.

Powell had never flown before, and the change to land-planes after Singapore was a shock. Each time he came into land, and saw earth rather than water beneath him, he thought the plane about to crash, and braced himself for imminent death. There had been another upset on the voyage: 'the news of Eden's resignation reached us at Karachi and came as a shock', he told his parents from Singapore, referring to the departure of the Foreign Secretary from the Government in protest at Neville Chamberlain's decision to recognise Italy's annexation of Abyssinia. 'We get deeper and deeper in the mire.'[115] Two days were lost to mechanical failure *en route*, expanding the fourteen-day journey to sixteen. Parts of the trip were, as Powell put it, 'primitive'. On Timor, the facilities comprised merely a hut. A table contained the hunks of bread and beer that were the only refreshment, consumed under a hanging acetylene lamp, and the tablecloth had to be taken outside and shaken every ten minutes to remove the thick layer of insect life that had settled upon it. It was, Powell said, 'a deeply formative experience'. The flying-boat flew at low levels, giving him 'an immense geography lesson in the extent and majesty of the British Empire'.[116] Of all the stops between Crete and Indonesia only one out of almost twenty was not either under British rule or British authority – 'Alexandria, the Lake of Galilee, Habbaniya, Basra, Abu Dhabi, Mekran, Karachi, Jaipur, Allahabad, Calcutta, Akyab, Rangoon, Penang, Singapore – one was witnessing the ubiquity of a power on which the sun had not yet set. I saw; I felt; I marvelled.' It was a potent fuel to pour on the fires of his incipient romanticism.

His was the first flight to land at Calcutta; he found India 'the most striking frontispiece of the Empire'. It awakened a longing that would never be satisfied, but which war would allow him the opportunity to try to appease five years later. He took with him on the journey *Ecce Homo*, Nietzsche's autobiography. Yet a break with his intellectual past was, in some measure, enforced by this great journey; 'his world', he later wrote of himself, 'was expanding with explosive speed'.[117] He found work *en route* 'nearly impossible', but told his parents from 2,000 feet over Queensland that 'I have been able to do more than 20 pages of the Herodotus book and to write about 50 lines of English verse on the flight thus far.'[118]

Writing in the 1960s, on his first trip to America, Powell recalled how it had felt to settle down in Sydney. He remembered 'the dull pang ... it was the heartache of the exile, the oppressive sense of being remote, so remote, from everything that ultimately mattered, from all that gave one birth'.[119] He did not intend to stay for long: circumstances, he felt sure, would not allow it. Powell told the University's vice-chancellor, to his astonishment, that he would be returning home to join the army immediately war was declared. 'He looked at me', Powell recalled, 'like some visitor from out of space.'[120] His feelings towards Germany were now of 'great hatred as well as fear ... a fear of my country being defeated'.[121] Yet, as well as promising to leave precipitately, Powell had also pledged to raise the status and quality of Greek studies within the University. First, though, he would have to take control of his new milieu. 'I sensed', he recalled, 'the spirit of the early colonial university, something equally unknown to Oxbridge, and to Redbrick, a defiant assertion of the culture of the old world in a harsh and, by nature, unfriendly environment. It was this tang of defiance, still perceptible in the air, which gave life inside and outside the university its peculiar exhilaration.'[122] There was one immediately gratifying experience for him; meeting his new colleagues, part of his reputation had preceded him – 'I find everybody here talking about *First Poems*. There will be hardly any need to carpet-bag the booksellers.'[123] Within a couple of months a student was giving a lecture to the University Literary Society entitled 'Professor Powell as a poet'. The Professor told his parents: 'scurrilous no doubt, but it means a few more sales'.[124]

Acclimatising was a shock. It was the hottest March for thirty years, and Powell's natural desire to explore on foot was prevented by the extreme heat and humidity. Sydney was infested with mosquitoes, and he had to sleep under a net. Having lived at the Australian Club for a week after his arrival, he told his parents of his routine: 'Rise, early morning tea and wash at 6.30; tram to University, arriving about 7.45, breakfast in Union 8.15; university work and teaching during morning; lunch in Union at "high table" 12.45; private work during afternoon; tea I am making arrangements to make over my own gas-ring; dinner in Union, 6.30; return by tram to town and trifle away time till bed at 10pm.'[125] He used his tram journey to maintain a daily intake of Schopenhauer, the effect of whom was to intensify still further the atheistic feelings and understanding of the will acquired from Nietzsche. He lectured for six hours a week, and took an additional four hours of tutorials. It left him much time for his own private projects, which suited him perfectly.

On Sundays he would go for day-long walks of about twenty miles in the bush, 'clambering in and out of precipitous ravines along tracks distinguishable only as a trickle of whiter sand from boulder to boulder through semi-tropical vegetation (plus giant ants and the occasional snake) which is in exactly the same condition as when Captain Cook arrived. . . . In such places you can go all day without seeing a human being; and this I appreciate perhaps most of all,' he told his parents. 'For, changing from a semi-monastic life to one in which I am talking to people in one way or another for five and a half days in the week with little intermission, I have, as you will appreciate, developed quite a ferocious thirst for silence and solitude when I can get it. On Saturday afternoons I go out into the quadrangle from my work (the University is quite deserted then) and stand sucking the silence up like water in a drought. Of my ever being lonely there is no question; I can never be lonely enough.'[126] Six weeks into his stay he wrote home that 'I am as happy as anyone can be who is absolutely on his own and separated from the only two people he cares about; and yet that degree of happiness is no contemptible one. For I was plainly built for a self-sufficient type of existence.'[127] Self-sufficiency could have its drawbacks: one Monday morning his Greek class went uninstructed because the Professor had been stranded, and had spent the night in a cave by the light of a gumstick fire. His students were, he found on his return, more 'surprised by the taste for exploration than by the getting lost'.[128] He spread his wings in other ways, too: the Australian Broadcasting Corporation gave him a regular half-hour programme with a brief to talk about 'antiquity in the news', beginning a part-time career as a broadcaster that was to last for most of the rest of his life.

Despite this impression that Powell led a solitary life, he soon made friends with his professorial colleagues, reporting to his parents that he was on 'good terms' with them. Unlike on his arrival at Trinity, he made time to attend a soirée for new teaching staff, and went to pay his respects to Mrs Woodhouse, his predecessor's widow. He dined regularly in the homes of colleagues. He did, however, like the Australian Club for being 'just the kind of unsociable, heavily upholstered atmosphere to which I am used'; but after the expiry of a short honorary membership arranged by the University he was looking for new lodgings, as the £26 5s entrance fee and £21 annual subscription were not, he felt, good value for one who would be in Australia for only eight months of the year, and who might be off to the war at any time. He was offered a room at Wesley College, where a colleague lived: 'but the snag was not only the High Table, at which it was hoped I would dine frequently, but the chapel', he told his parents. 'I was quite frank about my never under any circumstances being seen in that.'[129] He soon found another honorary membership compatible with atheism, at the University Club, and, not wanting the bother of moving again, decided to stay there for good.

The official history of Sydney University records that 'the arrival of Powell stirred the Greek department'.[130] Woodhouse's teaching had been lecture-based; Powell's approach was of classwork and one-on-one teaching. Writing to his parents in March 1938 about his students, he said that 'they have realised already that this term Greek is a subject where work and plenty of it has to be done ... nothing of the sort has ever been seen here before, but the powers that be are in favour'.[131] The department, though, was sufficiently small to be stirred easily. Until Powell's arrival the teaching staff had comprised only the Professor, though he would now be joined by a lecturer and a part-time lecturer. Between thirty and forty undergraduates attended the beginners' classes; only ten or a dozen enrolled as honours students. These small numbers allowed Powell the luxury of undertaking a great deal of one-on-one teaching, or what he later described as 'informal encounters between students and professor'.[132] He was depressed by the non-availability of most standard Greek texts in the Sydney bookshops, books readily found in the classics departments of most English schools. He persuaded the University authorities to start a papyrological collection as a memorial to Woodhouse, because such a collection would enable original research to be done.

Predictably, some students were bemused by their new teacher. 'Going was heavy at first,' Powell recalled. 'There was suspicion that the Englishman was leg-pulling, "trying it on" and perhaps, one never knew, intending not to play the game, come examination time.' His experimental approach, however, soon won over his students.

> One method we all enjoyed was to put up a Greek text which contained a corruption and then, picking on one student, not always of the brightest, take him on from one deduction to another, always asking questions but never answering them, until he produced the emendation which restored the sense and explained the error. The class waited for the ritual conclusion: 'Ladies and gentlemen, you will all, I am sure, wish me to congratulate Bloggs on a most brilliant discovery. I should invite him to publish it in a learned journal without delay but for the fact that he has been anticipated by Porson' (or whatever other famous scholar it might be).

He soon won a reputation as a devoted teacher, prepared to take pains with any student of whatever ability, provided the student showed a genuine interest and a will to arrive at the truth.

His intellectual intention, beyond sheer textual criticism, was that 'the detail of Greek scholarship was to be made a school for severe and disciplined reasoning'. He wanted Greek civilisation 'to be made a challenge to uncritical acceptance of modern conventions, moral and social. They were different, fearfully different, these Greeks, whose voices we could still hear and (at a pinch) understand. What had we in the vast, sprawling suburbs of Sydney with the gardens and the poinsettias and jacarandas, that would deserve their envy rather than their contempt?' It was all very well Powell seeking to challenge and expand the comprehension of his students, and shake them out of the closeted understanding life in the New World had imposed upon them; but it was going to a new country, and challenging his own view – hitherto exclusively developed in old civilisations – that had had the profound effect on him that was the necessary prelude to taking on his students in this way. A colleague told Powell that his students had 'detested' him for the first fornight, but 'now I have won them all over completely'.

Powell's sense of nation was already well developed, and was offended when, from the great distance of Sydney, he read of the moment when (as he put it half a century later) 'the House of Commons fawned upon a Prime Minister for capitulating to Hitler'.[133] It made him feel shame, which he was determined that, when the time came, he would do all he could to eradicate. His words to the vice-chancellor already looked less eccentric. 'I used to fancy that I heard a sound which nobody around me was hearing – the sound of German divisions marching on the other side of the earth.' It was a sentiment he captured in one of the poems in his second volume of verse, *Casting Off*, after he had attended Speech Day in a school in New South Wales:

> Row upon row they stood to sing,
> A thousand at a word,
> And loud arose 'God save the King'.
> But as I watched and heard,
> The upturned faces in the light
> Of early afternoon
> Reminded me of crosses white
> Beneath a silent moon.[134]

His letters to his parents contain constant references to the coming war: on 19 March 1938 he tells them, 'I am inclined to think that one of these fine days the UK will declare war and you will get a cable to say I am returning.'[135]

One of Powell's colleagues at Sydney, Professor A. P. Treweek, remembered him as out of the ordinary: aloof, as always, but so hopeless at communicating with women that he actively shunned them, and often dealing with colleagues with a complete absence of tact. 'He was quick to speak his mind, and to hell with the consequences,' Treweek said. 'We were never close friends, but our working relationship was good. Powell was never afraid of unpopularity and often rubbed people up the wrong way. He seemed to avoid women as much as possible. He was something of a misogynist. They seemed to unsettle him and make him nervous. If a female student wanted to discuss something with him, he would ask me to see her.'[136] Powell admitted, 'I did not encourage women students' because 'I felt they were unlikely to enjoy my method of handling the classics.'[137] He agreed this was a weakness of his, but maintained that women were unlikely to have 'the critical view which I endeavoured to instil. . . . they have a different biological purpose and that conditions a great deal and conditions the way they think as well as live and are.' In refusing to teach one of them because of her 'idleness, ignorance and stupidity' he had the support of other colleagues, who knew her shortcomings. One colleague told him that 'as her period with me was the last of the morning, she had been weekly expecting an invitation to lunch, and instead of that to her astonishment she got turned out altogether!'[138] Powell told his parents that 'that illustrates perfectly the whole impossibility of teaching women. The whole time they're not thinking about Greek, but about whether you're handsome or ugly, polite or discourteous, about whether in short there's any chance of a match – what can you do with material like that?' He added: 'It's true, I have always insisted that sexual attraction is an essential element in successful teaching, and so I still believe: but the trouble is that this in my case gives me command over my own sex, but none over the opposite.'

Treweek was formally appointed, in June 1938, an assistant professor, which released Powell to spend more time continuing Woodhouse's evangelism in schools. Treweek had a high regard for Powell as a scholar. 'He had an immense capacity for detail without being swamped by it. His *Lexicon to Herodotus* . . . is the most fantastically accurate work of this type that I have ever handled. When he came to Sydney he was very much under the influence of A. E. Housman . . . he also wrote savage but justified invectives in the style of Housman, on various matters of Greek scholarship; in fact his preface to Herodotus VIII was so fierce that the Cambridge Press refused to print anything of it beyond part of the first sentence.'[139] However, he and other colleagues found Powell's obsessive attention to work ludicrous. Treweek recalled that 'his scholarly achievements were very strong, but of narrow interest. He found faults in Greek texts where there were none. He couldn't read a page without finding mistakes – so much so that at times he was referred to as a textual pervert.'[140]

Two other qualities of Powell's struck his associates at Sydney: the rigidity of his atheism, and his commitment to his poetry. The latter was an essential outlet for the variety of boiling emotions – the apparent certainty of an early death, the estrangement from home and family, the loneliness bred by his failure to connect with the opposite sex or with many of his own, and his deep, romantic, cultural sensitivity – now surging within his psyche. For all he had achieved he was still only twenty-five, and remained, in his own view, an outsider. A decision he took during the summer of 1938 confirmed a further estrangement: he asked, when his Trinity fellowship expired that autumn, that the College should not give him another one. As a mark of his respect for the College, he gave £60 to endow a biennial poetry prize in his name when he left for Australia. When war broke out, he sent the College his books and research on Thucydides, in a carton thoughtfully marked 'RIP JEP'.

Powell's school visits, as related in his letters home, seem to have been a success. During term time he restricted his visits to New South Wales; in the shorter vacations he explored the rest of the continent. He went to every school in the Commonwealth of Australia where Greek was taught, and to Australia's five other universities. Within a year of his arrival at Sydney, he had made contact with all classics teachers in the other universities. He welcomed the chance to travel, and came to love Australia; he recalled Perth framed 'against the desert sunsets from the end platform of the overland train across the Nullarbor; Hobart in delicious orchard valleys, the trees ringed with heaps of apples; Brisbane's lights seen from the neighbouring hills, as splendid a vision as Hongkong or any other in the world; Melbourne in the long avenues of autumn trees; at Adelaide I remember my colleague FitzGerald's volumes of aboriginal vocabularies, compiled year after year on journeys into the interior.'[141] These meetings with his peers he found were 'heightened and given a kind of never-never quality by the strange un-European sense of distance and discovery'.

In schools, he would speak to classics teachers and to headmasters who might have been in favour of other language studies – German was particularly popular, and frequently forced Greek out of the curriculum. He would teach classes of boys, demonstrating his own excitement and trying to communicate it to them. Having undertaken his first such programme, at Sydney Grammar School in March 1938, he wrote home: 'From now on we go at it hammer and tongs, one school per week; and as the ultimate 'villains of the piece' are the educational authorities, who are hostile to Greek, we are getting introductions to them also and shall deal with them in rotation. In the end, something is bound to shift; and if the numbers for Greek are not doubled within four years, it will be surprising.'[142]

After Sydney Grammar, Powell chose North Sydney High School. He found twenty-two boys studying Greek, more than in any other single school in the state. He soon made contacts at a third school, Shore, where he was invited to dine with the Headmaster and his colleagues; and was asked by the Father Superior to Riverview College. Urged on by these successes, he tackled the authorities, as he wrote to his parents on 17 April 1938: 'I have ... bearded the Director of Education in his lair. I am further to make contact with the Chief Inspector of Secondary Schools. The Director (Thomas is his name) was disposed to favour my plans and is writing a circular letter about me to his myrmidons.'[143]

Even the official history of the University notes that Powell's relations with colleagues and students were 'formal'.[144] It also notes that he was on good terms with several professorial colleagues including, unsurprisingly, Eben Waterhouse, who held the chair in German. He also became friends with the University's Chancellor, Mr Justice Halse Rogers, telling his parents in March 1938 that 'I confided to him my schemes for private teaching and personal propaganda and obtained his enthusiastic support for both. He will be a very useful big gun for the siege trains in case of heavily fortified opposition anywhere.' Two other men in Sydney befriended him, and he remembered them fondly: Sammy Angus, an Ulsterman and a widower in his late fifties, Professor of Theology in the Presbyterian college, who had recently been a central figure in a heresy trial after sceptical remarks he had made in a book, and which had caused him to be deprived of his teaching post; and Richard Windeyer, a King's Counsel and celebrated criminal lawyer who had met Powell through his membership of the University Senate. Windeyer was described by Powell as 'the Marshall Hall of Australia', after the legendary British barrister. He kept a yacht in Sydney Harbour on which Powell was a frequent guest, giving the lie to his otherwise austere reputation.

Powell gave his inaugural lecture as Professor of Greek at a degree ceremony on 7 May 1938, in the presence of the Governor of New South Wales, Lord Wakehurst. He laced his remarks with an aggression typical of the way in which he was advancing the cause of his subject: 'I feel that it would be improper for me to fight on the defensive, or to take the line of justifying the existence of my own branch of university studies ... the only university in Australasia which maintains a chair of Greek must be sufficiently satisfied already of the value of Greek studies.'[145] What he wanted to do instead was analyse the motives of Greek scholarship, and in doing so he set out much of his own attitude to life. Speaking of the curiosity that drives men to acquire knowledge unnecessary for a satisfactory existence, he spoke of the devotion of much of that curiosity 'to the human past, to the attempt to reconstruct that vast jig-saw puzzle of which infinitely more pieces are lost than remain, or can ever be rediscovered'.[146] Above all, this was a cultural jigsaw puzzle that those of Western stock could understand: 'it belongs to us and we are of it'.

He told his audience he considered part of his mission in teaching Greek to be 'the cultivation of good taste':[147]

> Ours is an age when the engines for the diffusion of bad taste possess great force. With rare exceptions, the cinema, the newspaper and the wireless tend powerfully to promote vulgarity. By day and night in our cities the eye and the ear are continually assaulted by objects of bad taste. And the need of counteracting these influences is not at its least among a nation like the Australian, which has no tradition to fall back upon, and none of the sober and steadying influences of a 'past at its doors'. Now, Greek scholarship in all its activities demands the constant exercise of taste.

This taste was exceptionally important, he added, in the matter of textual criticism, for aesthetic judgments had to be made in helping to decide whether part of a text was corrupt, or accurate. Powell explained what he meant with reference to his own creative activity, remembering hearing Housman say at Cambridge about a corrupt epithet of Lucretius' that 'a modern poet, I suppose, might write such a phrase as that and fancy that it was good, but Lucretius could never have done so'. Powell said the remark stayed with him, 'and whenever I have achieved a daring adjective in a poem, "and fancy that it is good", my conscience asks me whether Lucretius and Housman would have thought the same or not'.[148]

In the rest of his lecture, Powell ranged widely: on how the study of Greek was superior to that of Latin, because Latin was but a derivative of the older language; on how translating English into Greek made one realise how shoddy one's English was, and therefore what a help Greek was in becoming a stylist, and in the art of using language precisely; how understanding the way in which Greek texts had been transmitted down the centuries required, too, the development of historical sense; and, above all, the importance in everyday life of 'independent judgment' and 'healthy scepticism'. This was an early indication of the qualities he would bring to bear in his political life; but, with more direct relevance to that, he said that, for example, 'year after year political parties secure a return to power by promising the electorate that they will do what any one of those electors, with a few minutes of clear and dispassionate reflection, could perceive to be either impossible or disadvantageous'.[149]

His next point clearly displayed his preoccupation with the coming catastrophe: how 'the world has recently been treated for nearly a decade to the unusual spectacle of a great empire deliberately taking every possible step to secure its own destruction, because its citizens were so obsessed by prejudice, or incapable of thinking for themselves, as never to perform the few logical steps necessary for proving that they would shortly be involved in a *guerre à outrance*, which could be neither averted nor escaped'.[150] It all proved the truth of something said by the comic poet Epicharmus – 'keep a clear head and don't believe what you are told' – even, Powell said, when you were told it by the Professor himself, 'unless independently it commends itself to your reason'. All this, with its apocalyptic undertone, was used to demonstrate the importance of not taking Greek texts at their face value, as well as indicating what the sceptical regard for Greek texts taught one about the modern world.

Powell did not allow his teaching responsibilities to interfere with his output of research. He had been contributing to the *Classical Quarterly* regularly while at Trinity, mostly textual notes on Herodotus, in the course of which he had greatly changed scholars' notions of what had come to be the accepted text. Once at Sydney he sent the *Quarterly* a disquisition on the Cretan manuscripts of Thucydides, in which – buried in a footnote – he mounted a scathing attack on the abilities of the last classicist to address the subject in those pages, a man called Lockwood. Powell said that the 'only rational basis' for a treatment of Aristophanes' manuscripts in general was 'analysis of content combined with dating'. The way in which Lockwood, the previous year, had addressed the manuscripts of Aristophanes in the British Museum 'would be futile, even if treated intelligently; for it assumes that 6 MSS out of 240 are likely to have individual importance or to be closely related among themselves from the simple circumstance of their being conveniently accessible together in the British Museum'. The Powell who had spent the previous years dredging the dark libraries of Western Europe in the restless search for the most obscure manuscripts continued: 'Mr Lockwood, however, has treated the subject unintelligently – namely, by counting the agreements and disagreements of one London MS with one or more of the other five.' His conclusion was typically uncompromising. 'If not competent to relate the London MSS to the tradition as a whole, Mr Lockwood should have contented himself with correcting slips and noting anticipated conjectures.'[151] Such attacks smelt of arrogance, but they were Powell's way of maintaining the sanctity of the true text, of not cheapening the subject by cutting corners, by exhorting other scholars to address texts with the same painstaking detail (however time-consuming) as he did.

In 1938 Powell returned to his translation of Herodotus, completed five years earlier. His greater maturity as a writer and stylist, and his minute acquaintance with the text acquired by compiling the *Lexicon* and the critical edition of Book VIII, led him to find great dissatisfaction with what he had written as a schoolboy and undergraduate. He embarked on a revision 'so drastic as to amount to almost complete re-writing'.[152] This was three-quarters complete when war broke out; and Powell put the manuscript away, expecting never to have to the opportunity of completing it.

From mid-1938 onwards Powell's gaze was directed at Europe, with imminent expectation of war. Reading of German troop-movements in the newspapers in May 1938, he wrote home of his belief that 'about another week … should see the United Kingdom at war'.[153] Whenever he went away from Sydney – as he did that month to Hobart, to carry the classics message to Tasmanian schools – he took with him his return air-ticket to England, his passport and an emergency stash of travellers' cheques, to be ready to go home at any time. He planned to go across the Pacific to America and thence to Britain as 'the safest route home'. After his first term in Sydney, at the end of May, he admitted to his parents that he was actually happy – 'the dangerous epithet' -and 'sorry that the course of events is going to take me so prematurely from the department I am building up'.[154] In a separate note enclosed with this letter, entitled 'Sober reflections (also not to be taken too seriously)' he said that 'I grow more and more ashamed of spending nine-tenths, and more, of my time and thought upon a hobby … hobby is the right description of my Greek scholarship; for neither shall I ever be a true scholar nor in my heart do I wish to be one.' A proper 'attachment to antiquity' was not, as it should have been, 'the dominating passion' of his life; and he claimed the labour he lavished on the *Lexicon to Herodotus* was expended with 'an inward sneer and an ever-present feeling of disgust', when he ought to have been regarding it as 'his life's work'. He said he was not interested in Greek antiquity, and that 'Greek literature is to me merely words on paper to be juggled with: nothing more.' He had specialised as a textual critic too early, and this had done him 'irremediable' harm. He saw his calling as that of the poet, but was afraid he would harm that too by his work as a professor when, instead, he should have been reading and writing poetry. As a concession to the poetic impulse he not only stopped walking on Sunday mornings and used the time, instead, to write poetry, but he substituted the complete works of D. H. Lawrence for those of Schopenhauer.

In August 1938, between the second and third terms of the academic year, he undertook to see Australia from end to end by train: a three-week trip to Melbourne, Geelong, Perth, then back to Sydney via Adelaide, meeting colleagues as he went. In Adelaide he saw the blossom coming out in orchards, the first he had seen in eighteen months, 'but blossom here doesn't seem the same, after what to me is no winter'.[155] He took his passport with him, as usual, though he thought Germany would now wait awhile before launching 'a short, sharp winter coup against Czechoslovakia'.[156] He was scheduled to return home in November anyway, during the Australian long vacation, but found himself less moved by anticipation of that than by his 'dread' of having to go back to Australia the following March. He told his parents he hoped and prayed the 'explosion' in Europe would happen while he was in England.[157] Meanwhile, he resolved to apply for every chair in Greek that came up at an English university.

Back in Sydney on 11 September, he wrote home somewhat dramatically that 'I do not really expect this letter to reach you before the outbreak of war' – his permanent pessimism had caused one of Sammy Angus's women friends to accuse Powell of being 'Mother's one little ray of sunshine'.[158] He said that the imminence of war was causing him 'continual and suffocating anxiety', which he was relieving by listening constantly to *Tristan und Isolde*. A week later he wrote fulminating after Chamberlain's first visit to Hitler at Berchtesgaden: 'I do here in the most solemn and bitter manner curse the Prime Minister of England for having cumulated all his other betrayals of the national interest and honour, by his last terrible exhibition of dishonour, weakness and gullibility. The depths of infamy to which our accurst "love of peace" can lower us are unfathomable.' He added, in a letter concluded with the exclamation 'GOD SAVE THE KING', that 'immediate war' was 'our only chance of salvation', and that his highest ambition was to meet his death in it – together, if necessary, with his poor parents.[159] He had arranged with Imperial Airways to have a seat on the first flying-boat out of Sydney after the declaration.

In the week leading up to Munich he could hardly concentrate on his work: he prepared himself to make for home at any moment; and then 'our traitor Prime Minister and our cowardly nation, which richly deserves the inevitable destruction to which it has devoted itself, have presented us with another year or two of life lived in fear, at the mercy of our slavemasters'.[160] Ironically, he took the message of Wagner's *Ring* as his motto: 'Sterben ist besser als in Furcht leben,' it is better to die than live in fear. The imprecation at the end of his letters has become 'GOD SAVE THE KING AND DAMN THE ACCURSED MINISTERS OF THE KING'; and he quotes at his parents the line he would utter again in his most famous speech, thirty years later: 'whom the Gods wish to destroy, they first make mad'.[161] Now, until the time for his scheduled return home for the Christmas holiday, he had to concentrate on his work. He had cut down his teaching since Treweek's appointment, but now complained that, because of the amount of committee work he had to do, he had become 'a kind of politician'.[162] He had at least worked out the secret of committees: that he who is prepared can usually get his own way because of the under-preparation of everyone else. It was a lesson to be of great use to him later on.

He began the haul back to England in the first week of November, reaching London on 14 November. Having three months in Europe he took the opportunity to travel. His first stop was Königsberg, to visit Paul Maas. Powell was

arrested and interrogated by the Gestapo for not having a visa; in his absence
in Australia, he had not heard that they had been introduced for travellers from
Britain. While there he spoke to members of the anti-Nazi movement, and also
to Jewish friends to whom he had been introduced by Maas; the awfulness of
what was happening was fully brought home to him. Travelling back through
Berlin he went to the British embassy, outside which he found a massive queue,
mainly of Jews, waiting to get visas. 'I humbly took my place in the queue, and
duly reached the front door of the embassy. At that moment, a door opened,
and a man ushered out some visitor. He caught sight of me and said: "Are you
British?" I said "Yes." He said "Come inside." I'll never forget the look on the
faces of those other people who were waiting.' Powell managed to secure Maas
a visa to come to Britain, of which Maas (who subsequently taught at Oxford)
availed himself days before the declaration of war. Maas and Powell corresponded with each other, in English and in Greek, until Maas's death.

Powell returned to his post at the end of February 1939. He went via Rome
again, and saw Freeth. He stayed briefly in Singapore with 'Tommy' Thomas,
who had been assigned to the Malayan civil service, and who was leaving for
China to learn Cantonese as Powell went on to Australia. Both men, according
to Powell, knew they would never see each other again; Thomas was killed when
the Japanese stormed the colony in February 1942. Powell remembered their
taking leave of each other as 'the most horrible parting of my life'. It would
haunt him for ever.

While at home Powell had been interviewed for the Professorship of Greek
and Classical Literature at Durham University, a post he was set to take up on 1
January 1940, at the end of the next Australian academic year. On returning to
Sydney he awaited confirmation and, when it arrived on 3 May 1939, announced
his intention to resign his chair as from 31 December. He found it painful to tell
friends such as Windeyer – a man he now regarded as 'my best friend this side
of the Equator' – that he would be leaving, and his decision caused great
disappointment to them and to the University, as he admitted to Ted Curtis in
a letter on 10 April.[163] However, there was nothing they could have done about
it.

In addition to his teaching, Powell was maintaining a high output of written
work, and not just in the English-language classical journals; he contributed to
German ones too. In early 1939 he completed a lengthy article for the *Journal of
Hellenic Studies* on the sources of Plutarch's *Alexander*, demonstrating a whole
new specialist area of research and textual criticism. It was another display of
Powell's academic certainty. 'The sources of Plutarch's *Alexander*', he wrote,
'have hitherto been a subject passed by without examination in detail, not
because examination was superfluous but because the task was considered
hopeless on account of its apparent complexity.' That was not how he saw it.
'Our enquiry has shown the fallacy of that appearance and the way in which the

biography, in combination with the two orations, has to be treated as a historical source; all passages under suspicion of deriving from the spurious letters of Alexander are to be rejected; the rest represents an imperfect and often careless epitome, which may be supplemented from Arrian, of an encyclopedic Alexandrine biography.'[164] It was a tone of conviction that would, later, distinguish his political pronouncements.

Also at that time he published the further fruits of his Herodotean scholarship of earlier in the decade: his *History of Herodotus*, an undergraduate textbook study of the methods of composition used by the historian in his work, was welcomed by an Oxford don, A. R. W. Harrison, in the *Classical Review*, as 'the first really systematic attempt to apply the study of cross references in Herodotus to the problem of the composition of his history'.[165] Powell divided up Herodotus' career as a writer into three periods, giving his reasons for doing so. Harrison commended his methods: 'The reasoning is subtle and compact and the conclusions are stated with admirable clarity.' He also noted though, that in some respects the work suffered from 'over-compression', and that Powell was occasionally guilty of exaggerating inconsistencies. He also took issue with Powell's contention that Herodotus could not have intended his work to be both recited in public and copied out for distribution in written form; and there was a suggestion that Powell, through his now customary discounting of the quality of the work done by his predecessors in the field, might have taken too narrow an approach. Harrison's conclusion was, however, that the book would inevitably form the basis of all future research into the matter. In his preface, Powell illuminated the deeply utilitarian approach that was his trademark: 'Those who wish to know that the historian was related to the epic poet Panyassis or enjoyed the personal friendship of Pericles must get their information elsewhere.'[166] There was also a further sign of intellectual arrogance: 'As I care more about the soundness than the novelty of my reasoning and conclusions, acknowledgement to predecessors is rare. I have, besides, profited much more often from their mistakes than their successes.' Disdainfully, he concluded that anyone trying to outline the compositional process 'finds himself face to face with the whole forces of prejudice and thoughtlessness'.

No sooner had Powell reached Australia than Hitler invaded Czechoslovakia, which only confirmed all Powell had thought of Chamberlain the previous autumn. 'Oh to be at war, to have a chance to kill and be killed!' he wrote to his parents on 19 March. 'I wish I were a German, and not an English cur.'[167] When Chamberlain gave guarantees to Poland, Powell simply expected him to renege upon them. He found it hard to re-engage with Australia, telling his parents that, mentally, he was still living in Europe. There were, also, other important considerations: his mother appears to have remonstrated with him during his visit home about the state of his clothes and his personal appearance. He reassured her: 'I am behaving myself like a good boy sartorially: have had my boots soundly repaired, keep my wardrobe organised, and in all respects obey instructions.' Three weeks later, writing to Curtis, he made the point again about mentally living in Europe, 'divided by a kind of gauze from all the people here who go about their own Australian affairs'.[168]

That summer Blackwell's published Powell's second volume of poetry, *Casting Off*. It was a matter of 'great satisfaction' to Powell that the firm would publish his work under their own imprimatur and not as a private edition, as in the case of *First Poems*; Powell still, though, had to guarantee the firm against financial loss on the deal.[169] The inspiration was his journey across the world to Australia, and his experience of Asia *en route*. Although the 'Australasian tapestry' was now the backdrop, nostalgia and longing for the familiar sights of England that had infused *First Poems* was here too; like John Cowper Powys describing the composition of *Wolf Solent*, these are thoughts 'written in a foreign country with the pen of a traveller and the ink-blood of his home'.[170] The themes familiar from *First Poems* are still there – melancholy, isolation, death and, pre-eminently, war. The opening lyric, from which the volume took its title, recreates Powell's departure on his flying-boat, and the sight of the friends and families left behind on the quayside, 'Where the streams of human woe / Burst their banks and overflow'.[171] In another poem, the sense of isolation to which Powell would rarely admit is starkly brought out:

> Now I alone sit by the fire,
> And one remains of three;
> For two have got their heart's desire
> And left their grief to me.[172]

Occasionally, his form is more experimental than before: for example, a poem on Tristan and Isolde (Powell's Germanicism is frequently reflected) changes metre two-thirds of the way through to describe Powell's arrival, with a friend, at Euston station. There is more poetry of the experience, and less of the imagination, the experiences either of travel, or of nostalgia. In a rare excursion into sonnet form, nostalgia for his walking holidays in the Marches provides Powell with one of his best poems:

> When I remember, now the summer's done,
> I think there never has been such a year,
> And never like of it will be, I fear,
> In aftertime. For since I first begun
> To know and feel, I never drank the sun
> With such a thirsty fervour, never yet
> Had such a wholesome appetite for sweat
> On toiling hill-roads, never found such fun
> Under the hedges, halting many a time

To plunder damsons, where the Severn comes
East out of Wales; and blackberries were prime
In flowery Hereford; but oh! The plums:
Why, folks at Ross were giving them away.
There never has been such a year, they say.[173]

Such work is evidence of a slight broadening of poetic influences upon him, out from Housman, towards Edward Thomas. His metaphors seem to have become more vivid since his first poems, too:

I thought that all at once my brain
Burst open; and, as in the dark
When rockets burst, a glittering rain
Was dashed and scattered all about
Of coloured stars, each star a spark,
Each spark a fragment of a dream
Long known and cherished.[174]

Sometimes, as in the poem 'Speech Day' (quoted earlier in this chapter), Powell records his experiences without embellishment, the better the convey the intensity of his own emotions. When speaking of war now he has become more like Brooke, regarding the impending challenge as a passionate encounter:

Their faces all, both man and boy,
With a lover's flush are fired;
They haste with swinging steps of joy
To meet their long-desired;

And every eye is glistening
With hope no more denied;
For now the marriage-morn will bring
The bridegroom to the bride.[175]

There are suggestions of sexual love, or at least of sexual attraction, in several of the poems – though there is no evidence that Powell had had any direct experience of women by this stage in his life or, despite the assertions to the contrary, of homoerotic activity. In a foreshadowing of the main themes of his last volume of poetry, *The Wedding Gift*, sexual notions are often mixed with religious ideas; in one poem, seeing 'A waxen Virgin Mary / With folded, waxen hands' is the prelude to 'when, by chance encountered, / You fix your eyes on mine, / I tremble, and remember / The Virgin of the shrine'.[176] Yet the predominant feeling that accompanies contemplation of the opposite sex is one of inability to manage the emotions provoked:

> Sooner or later I shall get my chance.
> And unsuspecting friends will find a way
> To give me something longer than a glance,
> Taken by stealth from day to lucky day;
> And while they introduce us, I shall stand
> Reserved and stiff and wondering what to say:
> But when she looks at me and takes my hand,
> I'll wish myself a hundred miles away.[177]

On another occasion, the sight of 'someone with dark, tumbled hair and supple shoulders' has the bizarre effect of starting him 'somehow wondering / Whether round Harlech castle-wall / The rooks at wind-play rise and fall, / And far below, the shimmering dune / Bakes in a sun-soaked afternoon'.[178] The sight of a woman's face elsewhere works:

> like a fever on my mind,
> Stirring within me, buried deep,
> These other seeds, so joined and such,
> That, having ages lain asleep,
> In long-forgotten loins, now spring
> To life and torment at your touch.[179]

This is precisely the sort of poetry that he was wont to dismiss as being 'a work of the imagination'. That was a remark he made in response to an inquiry about one of his less subtle erotic poems:

> I did not speak, but when I saw you turn
> And cross your right leg on your left, and fold
> Your hands around your knee, I felt a flow
> Of white-hot lava seething up the old
> Volcano shaft.[180]

It was written as an exercise,' he said in 1995, though he described it, with some irony, as 'a perfect love-poem'.[181] Inevitably, such outpourings from one apparently so buttoned up as Powell were bound to provoke curiosity, and they still do, which is why he ends the same volume with a tease, albeit one that has inevitably (and without, as usual, any evidence) been interpreted as a hint of homosexuality:

> I smile at the fuss
> When I hear them discuss
> My poems – *our* poems;
>
> And when anyone asks
> If he rightly unmasks
> My meaning – *our* meaning,

> I simply say, Yes;
> For I dare them to guess
> My secret – *our* secret.[182]

The *Times Literary Supplement*'s reviewer said that 'in Mr Powell's verse lyrical feeling, reflection, and an epigrammatic conciseness are pleasantly balanced'.[183] The reviewer's only reservation was that 'his more personal lyrics are apt to be too private and confidential to communicate their feeling to the outsider'. Yet he concluded: 'But the verse is always simple and sensitive.' The *Cambridge Review* said that 'Mr Powell's verse rings of A. E. Housman,' but added that Powell was differentiated from the master by feeling: 'Housman has an intensity which Powell lacks.'[184]

The stress Powell felt about the international position, and his trauma after wishing Thomas farewell on the way to certain death at Singapore, meant that he composed little poetry once he returned to Australia.[185] Thomas wrote to him from Amoy in Malaysia, where he was now posted, to say he expected to be in a Japanese prison camp within three to four months; and Powell, who shared this deeply pessimistic streak with his friend, saw no reason to doubt it. He was frustrated, though, that war was not more imminent: his contacts in Sydney journalism, who knew more than they published, and the Foreign Office people from Canberra whom he occasionally met, assured him privately that hostilities were not about to break out. By the end of June he was complaining to his parents about 'the slimy cowardice of the English' almost as if he were no longer one of them. 'It is the English, not their Government; for if they were not blind cowards, they would lynch Chamberlain and Halifax and all the other smarmy traitors.'[186] He regretted that the only impediment to his health was that his eyes were very tired, the result of years peering at faded manuscripts in ill-lit libraries. 'I am afraid I'll never be able to shoot. And what else do I care about but to kill and be killed?'

He was still afraid the conflagration would be so sudden and so total that he might never get home. He felt he had to confront the reality that he and his parents might never see each other again; and wrote on 9 July to reassure them that the strength of the bond between them, in his view, meant that never to meet again need not be tragic. The definition of himself as one prepared to die for his country was, he believed, shared explicitly by them. It was time to make a statement of higher beliefs, or, as he put it, 'I want first of all to make once and for all a statement of policy.' He continued:

> We, that is the three of us, look forward to my return to England and fear whatever might prevent it because we desire and hope for a more or less lengthy period of *regular* and *familiar* association before that day on which that association will become impossible to all eternity. This is what we still hope to 'win from the void and formless infinite', this, but nothing less. By which I mean that

one or two brief snatched meetings are valueless and perhaps worse than that. Our only prospect of joy in one another is realizable only with time. Βίος τέλεις, as Aristotle calls it.

He continued:

> And now you know the point that I am coming to. If war breaks out, it is perfectly indifferent to our happiness whether or not we succeed in seeing one another again, except for a fallacious sentiment which we must endeavour to educate out of ourselves. The fallacy is to confound such a reunion in such circumstances with that regular association which I have described. It is the same pitious [sic] fallacy which summons children to a deathbed, when life in the proper sense is already over. It is a confusion of thought that we must learn to laugh at and make merry over, as we laugh at the comedy of cemeteries.[187]

He had decided he would die in the war, and decided with such certainty that he would never come to terms with being wrong about it, least of all when he saw others meet the fate he had settled upon for himself. The letter ends: 'God Save the King. God help Thomas.'

In August 1939 Powell went to New Zealand to explore classical studies there. On the night before his departure he had been invited to dine with Sir Hubert Murray, brother of Gilbert, who was on his way back to Papua, New Guinea, where he was governor. Drawing on the full expertise of the foreign service, he assured Powell there would be no war.[188] Powell went first to Auckland, whence he wrote to his parents of his fears of 'another Munich' that would deprive him of the war he so badly wanted.[189] In Wellington he was invited to dine at the Wellington Club, and fell into conversation with some of the members about the difference between the official and market rates of exchange between Australian and New Zealand pounds. 'In the course of the meal,' Powell later recalled, 'I enquired of my affable neighbour where I could get some Australian pounds exchanged at a good rate. I only understood the sudden cessation of cordial relations with him when, on inquiring after the meal as to his identity, I was told, "That is the Governor of the Bank of New Zealand." '[190]

Such amusements were soon to belong to the past: as Powell sailed home the hour for which he had waited had come. Reaching Sydney on 4 September 1939 he found 'with a sort of fierce joy that Australia, alone of the Dominions, had not declared war but had simply announced that, as the King Emperor was at war with Germany, Australia was automatically at war too'.[191] On his last night in New Zealand, dining with some professors in Otago, he was told of their certainty that the Japanese would be coming for them; they had seemed far more alert to the threat and intensity of war than the Australians.

Immediately upon returning to Sydney Powell began to make arrangements for his part in the war. He was determined not to be trapped in Australia or ordered into any reserved occupation, so his first step was to go into hiding. At the dead of night on 4/5 September he went into his office to write and deliver his letter of resignation. He summoned Treweek to his office and told the somewhat stunned man what he would have to do to run the department. In a dramatic act typical of his sense of the romantic, he then left a note pinned to his door explaining to his students and colleagues what he had done. Contrary to legend, it was not in Greek. Powell spent 5 September walking the streets of Sydney, still striving to remain out of contact. The next day, having wired his parents to expect him, he was on an aeroplane home, with a Russian dictionary and grammar on the folding table in front of his seat: he was convinced that 'Russia would hold the key to our survival and victory,' as it had in 1812 and 1916.[192] He was no lover of the Soviet system, and recognised the familiar 'smell of dictatorship' emanating from Moscow. His view was, though, that if teaming up with Satan was a necessary requirement for beating Germany, so be it. Detesting Baldwin and Chamberlain for their approach to Hitler, he saw the much despised Ribbentrop–Molotov pact of non-aggression between the Germans and the Russians as a necessary act for Russia's self-defence and survival. He did not, then or later, regard Bolshevism with any fear because he did not see Russia as a militarily aggressive power towards Western Europe. Germany, on the other hand, wanted to 'crush nationhood'.

His last sight of Australia was during an evening stopover at Darwin, where he watched huge hermit crabs on the beach, saw a 'gaunt, deserted' canning factory on the horizon, and, in an omen of the life to come, the digger hat and bayonet of a sentry. He still fancied he could hear the boots of the German armies drilling through the earth and reaching him in Australia. 'The aircraft which took off a few minutes after was flying towards the war.'[193]

3

THE SEPARATING FLAME

Powell had, at last, found something that truly motivated him. He would recall that 'one of the happiest days of my life was the 20th of October 1939. It was then for the first time I put on the King's coat.'[1] His country had, at last, motivated itself as a nation; and he would have his chance to help wipe away the shame of appeasement. The national cohesion he was witnessing would leave its mark on him for the rest of his life. It was the summit of his *alter ego* as a romantic. Joining the fight was 'the most total self-description of which one is capable'. It was 'the most important thing I ever did, perhaps the only important thing I ever did'.[2]

He put on the King's coat as private 5110957 of the Royal Warwickshire Regiment, which he joined at Budbrooke Barracks, just outside Warwick. It had not been easy to enlist, despite his being only twenty-seven years old, fit and able. The War Office told him they did not want professors, particularly those with no Territorial Army background, at that time; it was still the phoney war, and a call-up was proceeding slowly. Basing himself with his parents at their retirement home at Seaford in Sussex, he started frequenting recruiting stations; but it was no use. Powell heard that men who had travelled from the colonies and dominions especially to enlist were allowed to do so. So he engaged in the subterfuge of going to Australia House and having them certificate him as an Australian, on the strength of his being Professor of Greek at Sydney – 'reckon you'll do' was how the Australian official put it.[3] He took the document with which they provided him to a recruiting office at Edgware, whence he emerged as a private soldier, nearly a month after returning home. He had wanted to join the Warwickshires because it was the only regiment with which he had a connection; his father's teacher-training college had a volunteer battalion of the regiment attached to it. He felt he must have been the only Englishman to join the British Army by getting in as an Australian. Three days after enlisting he received a cheerful letter from Thomas in Malaya, who told him: 'I am still here, and will remain so until captured by either the Russians or the Japanese.'[4]

He was a member of recruit squad 12, run by a Sergeant Lucas and a Corporal Donnelly. In that squad of thirty men he did three months of basic training. There were several Oxford undergraduates in the squad but also some youths from Birmingham, two of whom were just out of Wakefield gaol. Patrick Ryan, one of Powell's fellow recruits, recalled that 'the Brummie boys teased the undergrads a bit, but Powell spoke their language, and anyway he could freeze them out with a look'.[5] Ryan remembered that there was nothing superior in Powell's attitude. He was keen to learn all he could about soldiering as quickly as possible. 'His high intellect was obvious, but he was surprisingly down-to-earth. None of your head-in-the-air academic. It was as though he had been stripping a Bren gun all his life. He was always best at everything, even drill on the barrack square.' In theory, Powell the instinctive Tory loved institutions. However, he had not much liked those of which he had so far had experience. His school and university had been solely academic. Because of his academic superiority, he had always been apart from others in those institutions. The training of a private soldier was different; it was a great equaliser. Powell was happy not least because, for almost the first time in his life, he had something in common with his fellows; he welcomed 'the framework in which men understand each other, because they are subject to the same rules'.[6] For a time – until he showed that his intellectual skills could as easily be applied to military life – he was not unusual; he had subjugated his individuality, and his individual quality, for the national effort. He felt he 'belonged'. On his first day at the barracks he settled down, in great contentment, with a plate of potatoes, faggots and peas – 'good Black Country fare'.[7]

On his arrival, another recruit came up to him to ask him whether he could fight; Powell replied that he had come to learn precisely how to do just that. His comrade, Private Arthur 'Dixie' Lee, said he had meant fists, not guns. When Powell looked bemused Lee told him, 'Never mind, I'll look after you.' In time, Lee became Powell's batman. Even the hardened NCOs who ran his squad were soon intimidated by him. They would address him as 'Mister', even though he was not yet an officer cadet. 'So I was a strange figure,' he recalled, 'although I felt that I fitted in. I remember Corporal Donnelly running after me one day when we were going on parade shouting out: "Mr Powell, Mr Powell, the bolt of your rifle is up!" There was a sense that I was a man from a different world and yet there was neither hostility nor unnaturalness.'[8] He recalled that he took to being a private soldier 'like a duck to water. It's the nicest thing to be. It seemed to me such a congenial environment, but the whole institution of the army, the framework of discipline, the exactitude of rank, the precision of duty was something almost restful and attractive to me.'[9]

As soon as he had a uniform to put on, Andrew Freeth painted him in it. Powell told him: 'Andrew, this war will last ten years, and by the end of it I shall be a general.'[10] As well as fulfilling his romantic urge to fight for his country, joining the army gave him a freedom he had hardly experienced before. 'The outward trappings of conformity', he later said, 'are a helpful vehicle towards unique self-expression. . . . Provided that you conform, you can think anything.'[11] He was later to think the same about the House of Commons and the Anglican church, and to make the mistake of thinking such reasoning applied to the Conservative party. He took pride in his outward appearance, and paid particular attention to drill. He said he would remember all his days a compliment paid him by his platoon sergeant, when he heard him say to the company commander that Powell was the smartest soldier in the company. Powell made no secret of the fact that 'I wanted to end the war so to speak, or perhaps not so to speak, riding into Berlin on a white horse.'[12] Having been in intensely competitive institutions almost all his life, he was amazed to meet no resentment about his ambition: quite the opposite, as his fellow private soldiers were glad to have one among them who sought responsibility. The one deficiency in his soldierly attributes was his shooting, which he described as 'awful'. Spending extra time on the range trying to improve it, he was engaged in conversation by a senior officer. Powell told him, 'I shall end the war as a major-general.' He recalled. 'He didn't dispute it, but must have found it rather odd.'[13]

During November 1939 Powell used a leave to go to Cambridge. He visited Deighton Bell, one of the town's second-hand booksellers, and found a copy of Clausewitz's *On War* in the original German. He soon found he was 'unable to put it down. He lunched with Martin Charlesworth and met, for the first time, Jasper Rootham, who had observed him quizzically from afar when they had been undergraduates. The two men would become lifelong friends. Rootham – who had just ceased to be Neville Chamberlain's private secretary – recalled Powell engaging in a denunciation 'of the base treachery of Army lorries which, because he started thinking about something else while he was at the wheel, drove themselves into the most improbable places'.[14] Mastering the art of driving was something with which Powell would have recurring trouble during his otherwise glittering service career. He also clashed in his early weeks with the military authorities, because of his habit of taking long walks. He was twice arrested by the Military Police for wandering around the countryside: they told him soldiers did not go for walks.

It was highly unusual for a man in basic training to be promoted, but Powell was; and he invested his first leap in rank with huge significance. 'The promotion from private to lance-corporal was the largest gulf I have ever crossed in any part of my career,' he reflected later.[15] He also marked his first day as a lance-corporal by putting three men on a charge. 'I was quite right to do so, but I can't rightly say what the offence was.' In a later interview, his memory had improved: he had found them 'urinating in the barrack room'.[16] Despite the challenges of soldiering, Powell found other intellectual diversions. He continued to teach himself Russian, studying with his usual intensity, to allow him to read it fluently: he never spoke it. 'Literally I put my Greek away, and I took my Russian out. For, not mistakenly, I thought that Russia would be decisive in the war.' He had no interest in pursuing his classical studies: 'I sensed that I would be either be killed or do something else.'[17]

His basic training over, Powell was marked out as officer material. Wisely, he turned down an offer to have officer training with the Military Police. He went instead in the freezing January of 1940 to begin a four-month cadetship at Aldershot. Many of his platoon of thirty were candidates for the Intelligence Corps, and there mainly because they could speak two modern languages. Their task at Aldershot was to prove, before moving on to specific intelligence training, that they were capable of being infantry officers: which meant more square-bashing and stripping Bren guns. Occupying the bed next to him was a man who had begun, just before the war, to show promise as a couturier, but whose main value to the army was his fluency in French and German – Hardy Amies. The next bed was occupied by another classicist, who had known Powell by repute before the war, and who would make a name in diplomacy after it – David Hunt.

Hunt was an archaeologist, with a close interest in Greek history, and had been particularly impressed by Powell's *Lexicon to Herodotus* – though he thought that, in including every word in Herodotus, excluding only 'and' but including every use of the definite article, Powell had 'gone a bit far'.[18] In his memoirs of the war, Hunt recalls the impression Powell made at Aldershot. 'He was reserved, taciturn and generally believed in the platoon to be modelling himself on the Prussian Great General Staff.'[19] Later, Hunt added that 'the rest of the platoon used to think had he had quite a congenital sympathy with the ideas of Prussian militarism', a sympathy confirmed to Hunt by Powell's habit of speaking German in conversation.[20] Powell was still devoted to reading *Vom Kriege* each evening before lights out; because the light in the room was so bad, he turned his bed round so his head was under the electric bulb. Given that Clausewitz's was a long book, and the cadets were worked so hard that Hunt imagined Powell could not have had much more than ten minutes a day for reading, he doubted whether he managed to finish it during their course. Amies remembered Powell reading the Bible too, in Greek.[21]

He also remembered Powell being aloof, 'but not offensively so ... he was greatly respected by all the other men'. He would not join in the general row-diness, nor go on beer-drinking expeditions. He would, instead, keep himself to himself, confiding in Amies only that he had had the happiest time of his life in Australia; he would occasionally discuss the war and military strategy with Hunt, though he did let on to him that when the war was over, and if he survived, he would not be returning to academic life.

Powell developed an important extra-curricular interest during his cadetship: he served for a short time as editor of *Battledress*, 'The Cadet Magazine'. As well as writing the editorial, he printed two of his own poems – 'Over your Grave in Far Japan' and 'My hand is on the Lamp' – that would appear, with only the slightest revision, in his collection *Dancer's End*, published in 1951. The editorial shows Powell's cast of mind in the spring of 1940. He recalled how, on a stopover at Darwin on his way home the previous September, he had shocked his companions on the flying-boat by professing that the war would last ten years: a view he claimed, now, was quite usual. He explained his own pessimism, and described the 'metaphysical miscalculation' that prevented 'the people of the Empire from apprehending the nightmare vastness of the struggle that is beginning'.[22]

'In most ages and in most wars,' he wrote, 'there has been some ground of compromise, some basis of possible understanding, on which combatants might at length make peace when force of arms had declared for one side or the other, or shown that neither had it in their power to attain their end by that means.' This was manifestly not the case with the Great War, 'upon the second phase of which we entered in 1939'. He defined a new motive for warfare: 'these wars of unlimited objectives, as they may be called, are the wars of opposing meta-physics, or, if you like it better, ideologies'. Powell used his knowledge of German history and culture to debunk the notion that the war was against the Nazi party, not the German people as a whole. The party, he said, identified with some of the strongest traits of that people: 'anti-Semitism, the faith in the hero-leader, the application of Darwinian "survival of the fittest" to foreign politics, the love and admiration of force and power for their own sake, and, above all, the readiness to sacrifice the present and the material for the future and the abstract'. Nothing, he continued, could be less like the English cast of mind; if an anthology were made of references to England in the best German prose and poetry of the nineteenth century, he claimed, the 'dominant note' of the extracts would be 'contempt'. There was no possibility of compromise.

Powell defined the necessary British war aims as the 'destruction – not merely the defeat – of the German field armies, and a permanent crippling of German industry and commerce sufficient to reduce the Reich in a generation to an agricultural state of some twenty millions' as others were suggesting at the time. In a typically Powellish flourish, he seemed to conclude that this was unlikely unless a great change of national attitude were brought about: 'When I find this war, in the ninth month of its second phase, still referred to coyly as the "national emergency", when I find German music enjoying an undiminished popularity in England, and when I notice the coolness of the nation and the public towards that army of theirs which alone will have to achieve the almost impossible, then I cannot help but wonder.'

The routine at Aldershot was deliberately exhausting, starting with the cold shower that followed reveille at seven o'clock – in the coldest winter in living memory – to be followed by an early parade before breakfast. Much ground had to be covered as quickly as possible, and the cadets were in the hands of sergeant instructors. After lunch, most afternoons were occupied by a long march. Powell's comrades noted the undiluted enthusiasm with which he took to his tasks. There was a little time for recreation in the evening before lights out at ten o'clock, which gave Powell an opportunity to delve more deeply into Clausewitz. He was not especially impressed with the training. Only one officer had battle experience, from the Great War: the others, he sensed, knew no more about it than the men they were instructing.

The previous year, Powell had congratulated Ted Curtis on obtaining a commission in the territorials before the outbreak of hostilities.[23] He had been determined to catch up, and overtake, his friend, to whom he had not written since enlisting, his silence being maintained 'out of a kind of pique and false pride', as Powell later admitted.[24] On 12 May 1940 he wrote to Curtis, who was with the British Expeditionary Force in France, to report that 'after four months as a cadet and three as a private and lance-corporal, not to mention five weeks during which he declined my services altogether, His Britannic Majesty, upon whose enemies confusion, has yesterday been pleased to commission me in the General List as a second lieutenant, a rank which, while far from corresponding to my merit or ambitions, confers upon me the privilege, which I have long impatiently expected, of corresponding with you without dishonour'.[25] Powell was commissioned into the Intelligence Corps. In October 1941, as he left on his first overseas posting, he transferred at his own request back into the Royal Warwickshires. He was inordinately proud of that regiment; and though he never saw active service with it, being detached from it to serve on the General Staff, he maintained his loyalty to it throughout the war. He always wore its insignia, even having the buttons sewn on to his tunic when he was a brigadier in India.

After ten days' leave, spent in Seaford, Powell was sent to a field-security course at Sheerness on the Isle of Sheppey. It was a few days before Dunkirk. On arrival, he wrote to his parents that he had stopped by a village near Sittingbourne to see Thomas's parents – 'the combination which produced the miracle'.[26] While he had been glad to meet his friend's family, Powell reported that:

> the whole encounter, renewing my recollection of the last 5 years, made me feel enormously old, and more than that, shrivelled and dried up. The plain fact is that I have had my cake and eaten it. With the wrong sex and in unfavourable circumstances I have had and finished what is likely to be the one real love-affair of my life, together with its accompanying minor ones, like the satellites of a planet. Henceforward the only emotions of which I am capable seem to be hatred, ambition and selfishness, and I feel possessed and burnt up with them. If I survive the present hostilities, which I increasingly pray God I may not, there will be little humanity left in me at all, and certainly no poetry.

A fellow subaltern, A. J. Marsden, who in civilian life had been a German teacher, found himself attracted to Powell by the force of his concentration. Marsden asked him at the end of one day's instruction whether he would like to come for a walk. Powell was still not good at making friends: 'Nobody has ever asked me to go for a walk before,' he replied. 'Yes, I will come.'[27] They strode out quickly, keen to stretch their legs after a day indoors, and after nine miles and two hours of rapid walking Marsden felt the time might have come to return. He asked Powell whether he would like to turn back, and Powell said no. 'I was rather surprised,' Marsden recalled, 'as he looked rather fragile.' Powell told Marsden of his habit of long, hilly walks in the Black Country and Shropshire; and Marsden, who had been a cross-country runner, was happy to keep on. They walked for three more hours – it was nearly midnight by now – and Powell still wanted to continue. They were walking on the road, and carrying straight on, hoping that as they were on an island they would eventually come round in a circle. The weather was fine, and they carried on walking through the whole night. Powell was in his service dress; Marsden in battledress. They were back for breakfast at eight o'clock, having walked for thirteen hours non-stop. Marsden found it hard to stay awake the following day during their classes, but Powell seemed unaffected by the exertion. On other weekends Powell and Marsden went for walks, and Powell would pause now and again and write poetry.

When the time came to pass out from Sheppey the officers formed a single file to shake hands with their instructors as a farewell. The senior instructor said to Powell, 'Well, Mr Powell, do you think you have benefited from the course?' and Powell answered, 'Thank you. I feel that we might have been better employed guarding the coast during the evacuation from Dunkirk.' While on the course at Sheerness Powell met Malcolm Muggeridge, who was one of the sergeant instructors. Muggeridge recalled 'this strange-looking man who then had a rather remarkable moustache – it was almost a soupstrainer moustache – which added to the comedy. I asked him why afterwards, and with his usual honesty he replied that he grew it to convey an impression of Nietzsche.'[28]

The following month Powell went on two more general intelligence courses, at Swanage in Dorset. There he met Michael Strachan, a fellow second lieutenant who would become, with Andrew Freeth and Ted Curtis, one of the highly exclusive circle of Powell's closest friends. As with Freeth and Curtis, the friendship with Strachan came about almost involuntarily, or by force of circumstance; Powell never set out to make friends, however lonely he was, and this feature of him – with perhaps one exception concerning his first affair with a woman – remained constant for the rest of his life. Strachan was a rare brother officer who could share his intellectual interests. He was not yet twenty-one, and had interrupted his studies at Cambridge to join the army, being commissioned at the end of May 1940. Like Powell he was virtually bilingual in German, and both men were on the same two courses. The first, in a large hotel on the sea front, was about military intelligence and the German Army; the second was in a smaller hotel and dealt in more detail with the organisation of the German Army and with interrogation techniques. Hardy Amies was on this course too, and the others included former foreign correspondents, businessmen who had travelled in Germany before the war, and former undergraduates such as Strachan.

Strachan and Powell soon discovered their shared interest in languages and literature, and Strachan found he could learn a lot from Powell. For his part, Powell was intrigued by Strachan's very different background from his own, his having grown up on a large country estate. Powell was attracted too by Strachan's far less austere view of life. When not posted together Powell and Strachan maintained throughout the war a frequent and candid correspondence.

Powell was still not convinced the Government would have the gumption to do what was necessary in the event of invasion. He began to write memoranda about the conduct of the war, concerning at this stage the fall of France and the defence of Britain, which would become an outlet for him throughout the next five years.[29] He was fearful Britain might give in or be overwhelmed, and could not see how the sheer numbers could be amassed to overcome the numerical might of the German Army. He believed 'it is unlikely that America would in any circumstances be willing to send overseas a force of that magnitude'.[30] The participation of Russia on Britain's side was essential to victory, and there was no prospect of that in July 1940. He recalled that he and a brother officer had agreed that 'if the King Emperor made peace we would shoot ourselves with our service revolvers' as, in such a humiliating circumstance, 'an officer had no justification to go on living'.[31] Such a capitulation did not come. After his courses Powell was posted first as intelligence officer to an infantry brigade at a stately home near Bisley in Surrey, then to HQ Western Command at Chester; he spent part of the late summer and autumn of 1940 riding around the coasts of the Wirral and Lancashire on a motor-bike, looking for places the enemy might land. He had learned to ride the motor-bike while in Surrey. It had been a difficult initiation, with Powell riding the machine into a large yew hedge – so that only the back wheel was visible – just when he thought he had mastered it.

The recurring theme of Powell's war, other than his frequent and rapid promotions, would be his failure, despite repeated attempts, to see action. He had asked to be in a combatant unit. When commissioned into the General List, he asked to be allowed to go into armour. He tried to be transferred into the Royal Inniskilling Dragoon Guards, but failed, and instead was sent off to staff college. In early November 1940 he heard he was to be posted to the Intelligence Training Centre at Matlock in Derbyshire, as an instructor. After three weeks he was posted again, in the rank of captain, to Headquarters 9th Armoured Division at Guilsborough, Northamptonshire. Soon after his arrival the Blitz began. From his barracks, Powell had the salutary experience of seeing the sky illuminated over Coventry. He was once more busily writing poetry, and still reading constantly. His learning was the stuff of legend, and brother officers were always trying to catch him out. One at Aldershot succeeded in discovering that Powell had never read the great Portuguese poet Camões. When the two next met, a couple of years later in Cairo, Powell told him he had now read every word of Camões, a study he had embarked upon on arriving in Egypt, having taught himself Portuguese before leaving England.

His study of Russian soon came in useful. Russia was still neutral – and would be until June 1941 – and Powell found his aptitudes called upon while visiting some friends in the War Office in the winter of 1940–1. He liked, when he visited the building, to wander around wherever he wished, making a mockery of security; so he would take his tunic off and leave it in a friend's office, since being without it did not draw attention to his rank, and made it look as though he belonged in the building. He went into the Russian Section and was told by a Major Saul there was a crisis: they had lost their Russian translator, yet the Russian parachute manual had to be translated urgently so that it could be used for training in Manchester. Powell volunteered; Saul was sceptical, but tore the book down the spine, handed him the first chunk, and told him to take it away and see how he got on. Powell returned to Guilsborough and, between eleven and twelve at night when his other duties had finished, sat in his billet translating it. Having completed one part, he took back his translation to the War Office, to be handed another. 'Being a new subject,' he recalled, 'there weren't any dictionaries which contained the parachute technical terms. One had to work them out from the context. I hope I wasn't responsible for any casualties.'[32] At this time he wrote, unsolicited, a memorandum to the General Staff about how he felt the war could be won: by bringing in Russia on the side of the Allies. The word went round that Powell, notorious for being a Russian speaker, was clearly also a communist. Just over six months later, Russia did enter the war on the Allied side, a moment Powell described as 'like coming out of darkness into light'.[33]

While at Guilsborough Powell was corresponding with Strachan, who had been in prisoner-of-war camps interrogating German pilots captured during the Battle of Britain. Although Strachan had been on a commando raid in February 1941 he, like Powell, did not feel he was a 'proper soldier'. He wrote to his friend saying that the 9th Armoured Division 'was the sort of formation I would like to be part of'.[34] Powell asked his commanding officer, Major-General Brocas Burrows, to request that Strachan be posted to their outfit as divisional intelligence officer, with a strong encomium about his friend's capabilities. Late in the winter of 1941, Strachan and Powell were reunited, but not for long.

A few months after Strachan's arrival, Powell – who had greatly impressed Burrows, and had been earmarked for speedy promotion – was summoned to the Staff College at Camberley. His excellence as an intelligence officer meant he arrived for staff training at a much earlier stage in his career than would normally have been the case, another factor in keeping him from the front line. He spent the summer of 1941 there, a frustrating experience, though he shared a room with an escaped French officer, with whom he would endlessly and enjoyably talk about theories of military strategy. On 23 June, the day after the German invasion of the Soviet Union, Powell heard there was to be a mission to Russia. He immediately wrote to Burrows to ask whether he could go. Burrows made inquiries, but was told it had already departed. 'Anyway,' he told Powell kindly, 'I am sure that you will be wiser to finish your Staff College Course before launching forth on to Missions. . . . I trust that all goes well with you and that you are being a model pupil.'[35]

Writing to Strachan on 22 July, Powell showed the signs of intellectual isolation, rebuking his friend for not having replied to an earlier letter and urging him to try to join him on a weekend pass to Cambridge. He reported that 'amid increasing boredom I am contriving to keep myself fitfully amused and instructed by planning a campaign to capture Kirkenes and Petsamo and conquer Finland . . .'.[36] He also revealed he had made an appointment to see Burrows early in August because 'I want him to help me to get some green trousers'; in other words, to be posted to the Inniskilling Dragoons, where there was a better chance of going into battle. 'How exactly he will entertain this affront to his regt it is difficult to forecast,' Powell added, swearing Strachan to secrecy about his plan. Nevertheless, Powell would look back on his time at Camberley as by far the most valuable part of his training. He made his trip to Cambridge, without Strachan, who was detained at Guilsborough. 'I feel lonely here now,' Powell wrote to him on 17 August from Trinity, 'as though like Nietzsche in his post-1879 period, I were attempting a philosophical task to which my previous life had indeed been a preparation but which remained *rätselhaft* and *unverständlich* for that previous life.'[37] He frequently consulted Strachan about intelligence matters – though plainly there were limits to what could be discussed in a letter – but from his repose at Trinity asked him, 'Can you look round for some instances for me of German rectitude in observance of the rules of war?'

His latest importuning of Burrows did not result in his seeing active service. 'It transpired that the Inniskillings are better off for Officers than any other Regiment in the Army.'[38] Powell then asked the General to try the 15/19th Hussars, but Burrows had to report to him that that regiment could fill its vacancies purely from its reserve. Burrows assured Powell, who by now was deeply disenchanted, that 'there is nothing personal whatsoever in their decision'.[39] Before Burrows could try his luck on Powell's behalf with a cavalry regiment, Powell was posted, still in the rank of captain, to General Headquarters Middle East in Cairo. Burrows told him: 'I do not think you should be disappointed, because I am rapidly becoming persuaded that it is there that the fighting will occur and therefore that the principal interest and excitement will take place.'[40] However, Powell told Colonel T. Robbins, an instructor on his staff course, 'I am afraid I must admit this is a disappointment.'[41] Robbins replied that he shared Powell's surprise at the posting, but hoped it would be 'very brief'. He warned Powell,

'Wherever you go you will have to suffer fools gladly – flattery is the only antidote to flatulence when it is in the head.'[42]

II

Powell left for Cairo in early October 1941. Before embarking, he had been to Seaford to see his mother and father, for a poignant farewell, every detail of which his father vividly recalled in a letter to him two years later: 'If I lived for another 70 years, your farewell could never lose its intensity, nor its air of finality – temporary as I know it to be. I see you again vividly in my mind's eye standing on the door-step stroking your mother's cheek and bidding her: Be a good mother. I see you saluting us at the gate, making a right turn in the fashion of a private in the Warwicks, and then resolutely marching off up the road out of sight to whatever fate may hold in store.'[43] His mother told him that the image of their son marching off to war 'for a long time . . . kept recurring with deep emotion'.

The flight to Egypt was tortuous. First he flew to Shannon, in civilian clothes, and was asked by an Irish customs officer whether he was a Treasury civil servant, like the man who had been processed before him. Thinking this was part of the cover, Powell said he was, but on trying to discover from the other man which unit he really belonged to, was dumbfounded to learn he really was a Treasury civil servant. Thence he flew to Lisbon, and had the uncomfortable experience of dining next to a table of Germans in his hotel. After a difficult stopover in Malta – the flying-boat was almost knocked to pieces in rough seas taking off – he at last reached Cairo. Ted Curtis, like Powell now a captain, was staff officer in charge of transport there. Seeing his friend's name on the list of arriving personnel, he was waiting to meet his flying-boat at the landing-stage on the Nile; and Powell, writing home on 19 October, two days after his arrival, said that Curtis 'has looked after me ever since like a mother'.[44] Curtis's first achievement was to persuade the normally frugal Powell to accept a long-term billet at one of Cairo's plusher hotels, and Powell was delighted to have an intelligent and sympathetic companion to take with him on his weekly half-holiday, for the inspection of antiquities.

Powell's posting initiated another epic correspondence between him and his parents, which would last for the next four and a half years. He wrote to them at least weekly; they to him, with news of the home front, at least twice weekly. He was as candid with them as always: what he could tell them now was restricted only by the official censor. As when in Europe and Australia, his letters are the best indication of the progress of his soul and the intense closeness of his relationship with them. All his letters end 'God Save the King'. He regarded his posting as extremely temporary, and told his parents, soon after his arrival, that

on Christmas Day – being three months after the end of his course at Camberley – he would apply to rejoin his regiment and go into combat.[45]

Powell made a name for himself rapidly as an intelligence officer. He soon
came to the attention of his superiors, and within six weeks was sounded out
about becoming deputy head of a small inter-services unit known as MI (Plans).
It used intelligence gathered from all the forces to target and disrupt the enemy's
supply lines. Powell carried on this work throughout 1942 in the thick of the
campaign in North Africa. By mid-December he was doing the work of an
officer one rank above him, and his promotion to major seemed a matter of
time. 'The work I do', he told his parents in January 1942, 'is appreciated very
near the top and some of it goes right to the top.'[46]

Cairo was not disagreeable at that stage of the war, and Powell found another
friend already there besides Curtis. Andrew Freeth's fluency in Italian was put
to use at the Combined Services Detailed Interrogation Centre on the outskirts
of the city, where he interrogated Italian prisoners of war. He was keeping his
hand in by drawing portraits of captured Italian generals whom he had also had
to interrogate, 'and who complained bitterly when sugar was put into the
macaroni'.[47] Freeth's wife – he had married in late 1940, with Powell refusing to
attend the wedding because he disapproved of such liaisons in wartime – had
managed to find a job there too, so they were together. Powell also made contact
with a Professor Waddell, a prominent papyrologist in Cairo, who gave him
access to what Powell described as 'the most considerable reference library in
this continent'; so, if he had the time and inclination for private study, he now
had the facilities in which to pursue it.[48] Twice a week Powell would dine with
Curtis, and once with Freeth: living in a grand hotel, it amused him to be able
to entertain Mr and Mrs Freeth to dinner. He was at his desk, apart from a short
break for lunch, from 8.15 a.m. until 8.15 p.m. Despite this activity, he devoted
between half an hour and an hour to language studies before he went to sleep
each night – tackling in turn Spanish, Portuguese and Russian. Sundays were
still free, and he and Curtis would go the edge of Cairo and walk into the desert
to see the pyramids – or, as he told his parents in terms designed not to worry
the censor by giving his location away, 'certain conical objects'.[49] Soon, life would
get harder.

For over three months – from 25 January to 1 May 1942 – Powell stopped
writing to his parents. There is no explanation in his letter once the cor-
respondence is resumed, though Powell assures them that he has never stopped
thinking of them, and that he understands they might be angry at his silence.
The war in North Africa was intense at this stage – the key Libyan port of
Benghazi fell at the end of January, and Rommel continued to drive the 8th
Army back towards Cairo – and Powell may have been precluded from writing.
However, he had suffered great personal unhappiness, with the realisation that
Thomas would have been in the front line of the Japanese invasion of Singapore.

They had both known he would die, and their instincts were right. Thomas, a civilian in the colonial service, had joined the Chinese Volunteer Corps in Singapore and went to the front to await the Japanese invasion on 7 February 1942. The fighting in his sector that day was intense, and he was never seen again. During the spring of 1942, Powell learned that he was 'missing'.

Life for Powell, though, went on. At least when he wrote on 1 May it was with good news: he had just been promoted major, backdated to December 1941. Soon afterwards he voiced a rare political opinion: 'Wars, I think, make people conservative – English wars at least – because in the last analysis the people undertake to support them not for the present nor the future, but for the memory of a dream, the associations of infancy and childhood.'[50]

His skills as a textual critic could be put to some use. A signal was intercepted saying the Germans intended to send a division to Athens at the rate of 'a platoon a day'. Being particularly concerned with the amounts of men and *matériel* being brought through the Balkans to North Africa, he brooded on this unusual arrangement; 'and in the middle of the night, while visiting Eighth Army headquarters, I jumped out of the truck where I was sleeping shouting: "trains, trains!" ' He realised the noun *Zug* meant train as well as platoon; and, as the reinforcements would be arriving by the trainload and not by the platoon, it would make a great difference to the forces who might be opposing them. While at HQ, Powell ran into David Hunt again, whom he now outranked, a major to Hunt's captain. 'He was the quintessential staff officer,' Hunt recalled, 'but he needn't have rubbed it in so much.' He felt Powell was somewhat out of place: he turned up in blistering desert heat in full khaki drill, finding Hunt and his men in shorts and desert boots. The air of formality this imposed upon the operation was something of a shock to the men; Hunt noted that Powell was no readier to compromise about his way of doing things than when they had last met at Aldershot.

Powell was not shy to use his intellect and his intuition, even if it involved highlighting the shortcomings of his superiors. In the spring of 1942 aerial photographs of North African ports under German occupation were coming into the Cairo headquarters. They were used, with help from Ultra decoded messages, to identify which ships were where; but Powell began to wonder whether his commanding officer was identifying the ships correctly. 'So I began duplicating his work by having an extra copy made of the report of the reconnaissance, and identifying the ships myself; one worked with the Lloyd's Register. One day I went in, when I had completed the identification of the ships which were at Benghazi, and dropped it in his in-tray and left it. A bell rang; I went in and saluted. "Powell, you will do this work in future." That was the British Army at its greatest.'[51]

He admired Rommel as a magnificent military strategist, and certainly as one who provided him as a staff officer with a constant intellectual challenge. At the end of June 1942 Rommel was at El Alamein, and seemed unstoppable; sensitive documents were being burned in Cairo, and the British had a contingency plan to retreat into Palestine. However, Powell worked out that Rommel lacked the tanks he would need to make the last push on to Cairo and drive the British out. Also, to outflank the British the tanks Rommel did have would need to traverse salt marshes, in which Powell knew they would sink: he and a team of men had made a reconnaissance near El Alamein and tried the same manoeuvre with a relatively light lorry, which had had to be dug out.[52] Nonetheless, Powell began to contemplate his own mortality again, despite the previous month having been so optimistic about seeing the end of hostilities that he had asked his parents to consider what the best course of his life might be after that time. Now, he told them that 'I have had Thomas incessantly in mind in these last days. But his chances, poor chap! were infinitely bluer.'[53] By mid-July Powell was discussing the longer term with his parents again, revealing that he viewed a 'return to Durham or to any form of academic life with aversion'.[54] What he most wanted was to have the financial independence 'to think or write or neither as I pleased. I am not interested in a third "career".' However, he could not imagine how he would ever have that independence.

In August he met Nicholas Hammond, another classicist he had known in Cambridge before the war. With great certainty, Powell told him that 'Rommel was finished and the Germans would be out of Africa soon, and that he was going on to India where an important job had to be done.'[55] Nonetheless, in June he and Curtis had made a plan for such an eventuality: they each had an emergency stash of provisions in knapsacks that would last them while they made an escape to Palestine. From there the plan was to go to India, and eventually to China, which (backing on to Russia as it did) Powell felt would be the last redoubt against the Axis.[56] As Powell was starved of the chance to fight, he wrote to his parents that Thomas 'has become the personification of my conscience; as though my military omissions and commissions were seen and silently rebuked by him'.[57]

On 29 July 1942 Powell wrote to Strachan to say that 'my immediate superior today informed me that at an unknown distance of time he expected to be promoted, and that he had recommended me to succeed him. Although the whole of this is rendered hypothetical by a recent change higher up, he invited me to consider whom I should wish to have as G2 [his second-in-command]. I informed him that I should ask for you.'[58] Although Powell stressed this was still 'a remote and doubtful possibility', he urged Strachan to consider whether he would like to come if the option arose. He had a similar conversation with Curtis, who had just been promoted major.

At the end of August, Powell became head of the unit and was promoted lieutenant-colonel. He wrote to his parents that he now faced 'the most difficult of all the steps on the ladder – Lt Col to Brig [which was, in fact, two steps]. I give it one to two years.'[59] He apologised for writing so infrequently, but said he was doing the work of three people. He was also having no luck in persuading his superiors to let him have a second-in command: in mid-September he was told he could not have Strachan, who at twenty-three was deemed too young, but could have Curtis. However, just when Powell thought this settled, Curtis was barred from the post on security grounds, as he had become engaged to be married to the widow of an Italian, an enemy alien. He was sent to Palestine, and Powell had to carry on alone.

The three months before El Alamein, the crucial battle in October 1942 in which Montgomery's 8th Army defeated Rommel's Afrika Korps and turned the tide of the whole war against Germany, were a time of intense emotional strain. Never had he wanted so much to be in the front line. He came to know brother officers who were going into battle, and longed to be with them, feeling a sense of failure that he was not. Ever after, it was the sacrifice he saw them make at El Alamein – those who were, as he put it in a poem, destined to be on the other side of 'the separating flame' – that became the ultimate symbol of the mental torture he felt at being unable to fight. He was working to the limit of his endurance, as he repeatedly told his parents, and as the great battle approached had no time for recreation or reflection. He told his parents on 18 September of a new longing he had suddenly conceived: 'I have an overwhelming desire (not due, I am certain, to mere absence) to acquire that intimate knowledge of the British Isles and their inhabitants which to acquire requires more than the hasty glance which the person in employ can give.'[60] He was still, without any practical ideas of how to attain it, striving to secure financial independence.

El Alamein made him realise the limited future he had in North Africa. 'I must ask for your understanding and sympathy with a resolution which I have already begun to try to put into effect,' he wrote home on 11 November 1942. 'It appeared in my mind more suddenly, decidedly and utterly imperatively than any since I became a soldier. I have this day asked my chief to assist me in getting to the Far East.'[61] He said he was 'bidden, beckoned by the ghost of Thomas, living or dead'. His chief had promised, in the light of Powell's excellent work, to do what he could when the time came. Although Powell had not been in the front line during Rommel's defeat, his superiors were well aware that without his intelligence work, disrupting the German supply lines, it could not have been achieved.

He acquired a temporary second-in-command, enough to allow him a week's leave in November, which he spent in Haifa visiting Curtis. He had not wanted to leave Cairo, but his superiors ordered him to rest.[62] Things had quietened down, a lull that fed the intensity of his desire to get to India and Burma. Before leaving for Palestine he had been to Tobruk, now ruined, and which he had 'done some little towards reducing to its present appalling state'. Returning to Cairo, he had 'a feeling of anticlimax' when told he would be going nowhere for the foreseeable future.[63] There was not nearly the same pressure of work as before to occupy him; so, thanks to the high quality of Cairo's second-hand bookshops, he took to re-reading one of the favourite authors of his youth, Richard Jefferies, and indulged his longing for England by reading Cobbett's *Rural Rides*. He also read one of his father's favourite books, Gilbert White's *Selborne*, which he found 'formless and slovenly'.[64] He never read the newspapers or listened to the wireless because, as he told his mother and father, 'I know too much of the truth to be able to stand the published version.'[65]

While the rest of the army celebrated Christmas, Powell spent Christmas Day at work writing, for circulation among senior colleagues, an essay entitled '1943'. He told his parents it contained 'my strategic and political convictions as they have built themselves up during the last three years'.[66] He was deeply frustrated: 'I seem no nearer to Burma,' he added, 'but keep my ears and eyes open and shall not miss a chance.' As if to emphasise the point, his letters now end 'GOD SAVE THE KING (and Emperor of India)'. Powell had decided Britain would not now be conquered, and would in time win the war in Europe. Like Lord Lansdowne in 1917, he had concluded that it was 'perfectly obvious' the Central Powers could not win. Like Lansdowne, he wanted to make peace with them. 'Let them settle scores with their unsuccessful regimes, let them deal with the dictators that had brought them to that pass, but no need to carry on the chess game to the point of sweeping all the pieces off the board and smashing the board up as well into the bargain.'[67] Powell's immense respect for human life meant that, even in this most just of wars, he regarded the growing demand, particularly among the Americans, for the enemy to make an unconditional surrender as 'the most barbaric and inhuman concept ... you do not have to destroy your opponent; you merely have to prove to him that he cannot win.'[68] Not least for this reason, the Americans were a group towards whom Powell was nurturing a growing distrust.

In '1943' he made these points, and posed questions about what sort of victory there would be, and what would be done with it. 'Never, indeed, since Rome has there been a national will so strong, steady and persistent as Britain's,' he wrote.[69] He described the British Empire as the 'moral counterpart' of the country's 'unique strategic situation', though he knew that like all empires it would fall eventually. With defeat no longer a possibility, decisions about the future had to be taken; and 'the decision of 1943 will determine our history and our greatness for centuries'. He hoped Britain would pay more attention to history than she had after the Great War, when the humiliation of Germany had broken with the traditional conduct of foreign policy, and the Americans had led Britain to agree to the redrawing of the map of Europe. Powell felt the terms imposed on Germany after her forthcoming defeat could not possibly be so severe as in 1919. 'As soon as Germany is prepared to accept these terms, whatever they may be, the war, so far as Britain is concerned, is won.' The terms had to be the evacuation by Germany of all her occupied territories, although the events of 1940 had shown that 'Britain need not dread all Europe united against her.'

Powell discounted any presence by the British in Europe, but the lesson of 1941–2 was that Britain should control the hitherto French-dominated southern shore of the Mediterranean, and thus remain a force in North Africa. He was not concerned with French sensibilities: 'we have defeated France. Hardly has a European nation been more mercilessly crushed. Her country occupied, her navy sunk, her colonies conquered or seized, her self-respect so humiliated that it is doubtful if she can ever look the world in the face again.' With Germany within her pre-1938 boundaries and France out of North Africa, Powell felt there could not be a better result; and it would be a settlement Britain alone would make, without recourse to the wisdom and efforts of the Americans. As for the war in the East, there was only one aim: 'that Britain is determined to defend her own and not hold it on the sufferance of other nations'. In dealing with Japan, 'the prime motive, undoubtedly, is revenge', but there was the scarcely less important purpose of re-establishing the eastern Empire in a more defensible form. This would mean securing a base in what had been French Indo-China as 'an Eastern Malta' to keep open access to that Empire.

Powell was sceptical about America's role in this theatre. He felt material help had been given to Britain by America only once it was clear that Britain would not be overrun. Further, he felt America's war aims were not remotely coincidental with Britain's, not least the aim to destroy Japan's naval power – 'Britain cannot view with satisfaction the elimination of the world's third naval power; for the existence of Japan's navy always offers the means to counterbalance America in the Pacific while confronting her in the Atlantic.' The survival of Japan was vital if, as Powell was convinced, America was to be prevented from further world domination, and if Britain was to be able to win a war against America in the Atlantic. The whole thesis must have had a striking effect on Powell's senior colleagues.

When, in January 1943, he pointed out again to his superiors his relative underemployment, he was told to take over the duties of another lieutenant-colonel in intelligence. He found himself in command of thirty officers rather than just two, and with most of the intelligence reports in North Africa passing across his desk. 'For a week it has been frantic getting settled,' he told his parents, 'but calm and efficiency are now again in sight.'[70] Though it was not the change Powell had sought, the greater responsibilities enhanced his promotion prospects, and he remained convinced the war had many more years to run in which he could see action. He volunteered to revert to the rank of major if that would help get him moved. He was becoming more and more driven by forces he could not control.

'I have in these weeks', he wrote home on 7 February,

had a stronger sense than ever before of an inward voice directing my actions in places where logic and reason will not help. This is what Socrates called the δαίμων, and Goethe after him the 'dämon', of which 'I know that my redeemer liveth' is yet another expression. I well know this to be merely an involuntary personification of the internal circumstance which interacts with external circumstance. I am not fooled; but in times when this force is operative, one is stronger and better for the conviction which it inspires, that the path so dictated is the right path, though it were 'the path leading unto destruction'. Life and death themselves belong to a lower level of things than that in which this power operates.[71]

This might seem like the first stirrings of Powell's dormant religious sensibilities, and his emergence from atheism; but he gives another clue in the postscript to this letter. 'If you see Mrs Thomas, you will be sure to convey to her as best you are able that I share some minute part of her trouble.'

For all Powell's desire to move east, he contemplated for a moment staying his hand. He was warned that the post of deputy director of military intelligence, with the rank of full colonel, would shortly become vacant, and was his for the taking. 'I was prepared to defer my Eastward movement', he told his parents some months later, 'in order to gain rank, improve my record and widen my horizon.'[72] Then, in early February, he was asked whether he would transfer his whole operation to Algiers, to help finish off the war in North Africa speedily now Rommel had moved back west. It meant not widening his horizon and not being promoted, but the challenge and variety were enough of a compensation for him. It also gave him a bargaining counter to secure the posting to him of Strachan, and, once he had flown to Algiers, he set about that straight away.

In February 1943 a signal arrived for Strachan, by this time based at Scotch Corner in Yorkshire as liaison officer for the Inns of Court Regiment, to which he had been attached when 9th Armoured Division was disbanded, requesting he be posted to Allied Force Headquarters, Algiers, with the rank of major. Strachan and his senior officers were impressed that the signal was marked 'signed Eisenhower'; but it was merely a sign, as Strachan later found out, of how well Powell had learned to work the system. Powell had tried to warn Strachan that there was, at last, movement on the matter, but the mail was unreliable and his letter – in which he also urged Strachan to visit his parents in Sussex before coming out – did not arrive until after he was on his way to North Africa.

As had been the plan, Strachan took up Powell's old post as the unit's second-in-command on 2 April 1943. He was not entirely happy about the posting, as he, like Powell, was keen to do some fighting and had been conducting a campaign to those ends. However, any resentment was soon forgotten. On his arrival in Algiers, Strachan reported to Powell at the city's St George's Hotel, where he was required to sign a piece of paper that constituted a solemn oath of secrecy, and an undertaking that he could never in future undertake any military role where there was any possibility of his being taken prisoner. Powell, too, had had to sign this undertaking – made necessary by his access to Ultra material – though it would not stop him repeatedly soliciting for the chance to go into battle. Besides Strachan, Powell had on his team a squadron leader from the RAF, a Royal Navy Lieutenant and a US army captain, as well as an ATS officer secretary. Strachan found the life demanding but exciting and stimulating. 'It was then that I learned a lot from Enoch about the sheer technique of handling a lot of work. He delegated a small amount. Perhaps that was a fault. If what he did delegate was not up to his standards, there was a big fuss. The pressure was considerable. The service chiefs wanted a daily report for their 9am conferences to enable them to decide on targets. This, of course, meant us starting work at four in the morning to prepare this report. Then we would work on through the day until about 6pm.'[73] Some days, the work would go on even longer.

The intelligence gathering never stopped: throughout the day, as new information came in, it was collated and, if urgent, acted upon without waiting for the next day's meeting. Powell had developed a penchant for the card-index system – something that would feature in the organisation of his constituency campaigns when he became a politician – and updating this was a main responsibility of those in the unit. There were also regular visits from the Head of Deception Planning, the Head of Security, the local Head of the Secret Intelligence Service, and frequent requests for information from the Joint Intelligence Committee, Allied Forces. When the day was finally over, Powell and Strachan would go to an American army mess down the hill from the St George's Hotel, and would, most nights, eat American food. Strachan recalled that Powell ate heartily, but drank little, preferring to watch his second-in-command consume a bottle of the local wine.

In Algiers Powell came across the American mind, not just the American cuisine, for the first time, and found it bemusing. Early in 1943 when the Germans counter-attacked near Gafsa and captured fifty American tanks, he recalled that 'the British staff were almost as aghast as if the war had been lost; after fighting the Germans in the desert for two years, we knew what Rommel could do with a few captured tanks. The Americans couldn't understand. "Hell," they said, "there's plenty more where those came from." '[74] In professional intercourse with senior American officers, he confirmed for himself one of America's main war aims: to end the British Empire. He became America's sworn opponent. He had found the Americans, he later recalled, 'gauche and amateurish' in their approach to a war that he, for one, was fighting with unusual dedication and professionalism.[75]

In a letter home just before going to Algiers, on 16 February 1943, he revealed that:

> the thought struck me for the first time today that our duty to our country may not terminate with the peace – apart, I mean, from the duty of begetting children to bear arms for the King in the next generation. To be more explicit, I see growing on the horizon the greater peril than Germany or Japan ever were; and if the present hostilities do not actually merge into a war with our terrible enemy, America, it will remain for those of us who have the necessary knowledge and insight to do what we can where we can to help Britain be victorious again in her next crisis.

He added: 'Where, and how, if at all, I can play my part in this, I do not yet see: yet I feel somehow that there will be no return to the life of an individual ever again.'[76] His parents hinted to him in letters that his personality was changing, that he was becoming almost a stranger to them. He was pained by this, and wrote reassuringly that 'I don't think you could be more constantly in my mind, waking or sleeping. Last night, sleeping in an aircraft with 6 Americans, I dreamt of you and thought that Mother was in some trouble, whereupon I woke up and found I was crying freely.'[77] Not, of course, able to tell his parents of the location of his new posting, the address 'as from' at the top of his letter of 28 February alerted them that he was writing in code, and that counting every tenth letter they would find his destination: the letter began 'Wanted to warn you that lengthened gaps may now intersperse letters I write and thus...'

Whatever the spiritual effects of the war upon him, the political ones were becoming as pronounced. He apologised for inflicting his views, and their consequences, on his parents. 'You have never expressed any decided political opinions, and indeed I do not know if or how far you assent to the proposition that almost unlimited sacrifices of individual life and happiness are worth while to preserve the unique structure of power of which the keystone (the only conceivable and indispensable keystone) is the English Crown. I for my part find it the nearest thing in the world to an absolute (as opposed to a relative) value: it is like the outer circle that bound my universe, so that I cannot conceive anything beyond it.'[78] Though his parents were no fools, the sheer force of his personality and the scale of his achievements meant he came to dominate them as he became older. When he would seek to translate these philosophical views into direct political action, they would follow him.

Those not, like Strachan, bound to Powell by close ties of friendship, but who came across Powell the staff officer – such as Jasper Rootham, who was serving in Cairo as a captain on the staff when Powell was a major and had not then come to know him well – recalled the chilly, correct, charmless way in which he did business. Rootham, like Powell deputising for a more senior officer at an important meeting, recalled the 'odious correctitude' with which Powell operated; and noted that when, quite improperly for a junior officer, he had interrupted Powell and proceeded to browbeat him on the ground that the two of them went back a while, Powell looked at him 'with icy dislike'.[79] He was, as Strachan observed, swift to expose the 'brainlessness' of senior officers himself, which not only made him mildly unpopular and somewhat feared, but also left him with little ground to stand on when the same tactic was tried on him. An RAF officer working with him on photographic reconnaissance, J. M. Thoday, found him 'not the easiest person to get along with', and remembered that gossip had it that Powell worked long hours except on Christmas Eve, 'when he stayed up all night as a demonstration that war was a serious matter'.[80]

However, Powell's staff could not but respect him. Thoday remembered that he had everything at his fingertips. Needing the information in order to show the photographic interpreters how critical it was that they had missed a 220 foot ship that had unloaded in Tobruk, he immediately said it could carry enough ammunition for two days' full battle for Rommel's forces, or seven days' supply for Tobruk's anti-aircraft defences – a revealing figure of a kind not taken into account by those historians and others who purport to judge the efficacy of bombing.'

The success with which Powell had conducted his operation in Cairo led to his being gazetted a military MBE on 18 February 1943, 'for gallant and distinguished services in the Middle East'.[81] He told his parents, apologetically, that he had not been able to 'escape' it: 'I know this will be a sad blow to father, being worse than the OBE. However, you must have the fortitude to bear the disgrace.'[82] Powell's embarrassment seems to have been caused by the fact that the military MBE was a staff officer's award, and he was not happy with a reminder of that status. Sadly for him, his growing distinction hardened the view of his commanding officer, Major-General Kenneth Strong, that Powell had better stay on his command. Powell increased his efforts to make it clear he was intent on winding up MI (Plans) and securing a posting to India; Strachan remembers that it was then, and not just after he arrived on the sub-continent, that he had conceived the ambition to be viceroy.[83] The General enlisted the support of equally senior RAF and naval commanders in his battle with higher authority to retain Powell. Powell was livid, and threatened to go over Strong's head; there was talk of his being court-martialled for refusal to obey orders. Strachan acted as mediator between both sides in what became a battle of wills.

A more exacting conflict, whose outcome was far from certain, now gripped Powell. If he could participate in the war against Japan, he could help protect the cornerstone of the Empire against the imperialist designs of the Americans. He told Thoday he had applied for a posting to the Far East because 'the war in Europe is won now, and I want to see the flag back in Singapore'.[84] Powell had had a walk-on part in the Algiers conference of May 1943, where Churchill had met Allied commanders including Montgomery and Eisenhower. He watched Churchill fail to persuade the Americans that the Mediterranean should be the first priority for the Allies in obtaining dominance over the Nazis. Even though, by stalling, Churchill won the argument anyway, Roosevelt's resistance was simply further proof for him that the Americans were determined to undermine British power.

III

Strachan has left the most vivid contemporary snapshot of Powell's pre-political life in his *Blackwood's* magazine article of 1949, 'Teaching the Professor'. The events related took place in June 1943, when, with Rommel beaten, Powell and he were on their way back to Cairo formally to disband MI (Plans). Reckoning that driving a thirty-hundredweight truck across 3,000 miles of North Africa – for that, with the detours they would have to make in wartime, was the distance to be covered – was the best way to get themselves and the highly sensitive files of MI (Plans) back to base, Powell had taken the decision three weeks earlier that drive they would. Strachan could not believe he was serious. The main drawback was that no driver would be available, as it would effectively have meant posting a soldier from one theatre of operations to another. The two men would, therefore, have to drive themselves. This in turn led to the subsidiary drawback: Powell still could not drive. He did possess a certificate authorising him to drive any government vehicle, but this, according to Strachan, had been presented to him while at his officer Cadet Training Unit 'by an over-optimistic sergeant instructor before his first and only driving lesson'. His determination was not, though, to be countered.

Strachan begins by describing the events of their first morning on the road. They had parked their truck, christened Pinafore, in a disused railway cutting sixty miles east of Algiers. It was 6.30 a.m., and Powell was trying to cook sausages. The fire he had lit was being uncooperative, so he threw some petrol over it, causing the flames to flare up and singe his moustache. He cut his finger trying to cook the sausages and the water he was boiling fell over the flames and put the fire out. Strachan, who was more practical, offered to help. 'You keep away,' Powell snarled at him. 'If they want to be bloody-minded, I'll show them, by God I will.'[85] The breakfast was not a success, nothing in Powell's life having prepared him for the culinary challenges he was now facing. Strachan tactfully drank his disgusting tea and ate his undercooked sausages, while Powell, unused to failure, stomped around muttering, 'Bloody inefficient! Bloody inefficient!', too angry to eat.

Strachan gives a clear description of Powell at the age of thirty-one: 'Stockily built, with a pale face and brown hair *en brosse*. His eyes were greenish, very penetrating and rather sinister; they indicated something of their owner's intellectual brilliance and something of his force of character.' The plan for the trip – which Powell had estimated would take fourteen days – was that, *en route*, Strachan should teach him to drive properly. Strachan could not believe his friend's lack of ability was as serious as Powell suggested, though he was soon disabused of that. He also felt that 'it would be a distinctly agreeable experience ... for me to give instructions to the Professor for a change'. Strachan had never seen Powell's shortcomings exposed; he recalled how patient and courteous he had been with him, in the preceding months, when Strachan had made mistakes; he would have to act with similar compassion.

Powell's main problem with driving was the concept of steering. He had, eventually, learned how to master the motor-bike, and felt he could steer a truck in the same way, by swaying around in his seat. It did not occur to him to turn the steering-wheel. He had put himself in charge of navigation, and therefore chose a road not long into their journey that was marked 'Closed to WD [War Department] transport'. They soon learned why: it was narrow and began to wind upwards tortuously into the hills. 'Good practice for steering,' Powell noted, while Strachan, sweating profusely, sat next to him. His instructor was just complimenting himself on how quickly his pupil had mastered the art of steering when, suddenly, Powell lost control of the truck. It was only prevented from plunging down a precipice by running into a stone parapet. Minimal damage was done; the main casualty was a huge tin of tomatoes, which split open and garnished the rest of their food supply: for the rest of the journey 'we never picked anything up without looking to see which part of it had the tomato ketchup on'. The two men were soon on their way again. So as not to destroy Powell's confidence, Strachan let him drive a little further.

As with every new skill he had to master, Powell took it extremely seriously. The truck broke down, and Strachan diagnosed a petrol blockage. He went to try to fix it, while Powell sat in the cab. Suddenly, the fuel started to course through. 'She'll start now,' said Strachan when he returned to the cab. ' "I thought she would," replied the Professor. He had the instruction book on his knees: "You had only one petrol tank turned on; I presumed that one had run dry, so I turned on the other one." "Oh," I said.' Powell, deciding he had now learned to drive, insisted on splitting the driving-time exactly between himself and Strachan. As they passed into Tunisia through what had recently been battlefields he managed to avoid any further accidents, and his instructor felt able to relax. They soon settled into a routine. Stopping at seven-thirty each evening, as night fell, Strachan would make a fire and cook the supper while Powell turned the back of the van into a dining room. They would eat and talk and then, at ten, bed down in the back of the van under their mosquito nets.

In his account, Strachan paints a precise picture of Powell's eccentricity:

The Professor was habitually an early riser and I always awoke to find him offering me a mug of tea while still polishing away at what he called his 'collection of brass'. I, like other normal people, wore a shirt and shorts and nothing much else. The Professor, who spent most of the war in Egypt and Africa or places even hotter, invariably wore a shirt with collar and tie, long drill trousers and boots, a tailored drill jacket with brass buttons and regimental badges, and a Sam Browne. As he said, wearing his full uniform 'kept up his morale', and it certainly did not make him feel the heat any more than other people.

Despite their long friendship, Powell and Strachan ran out of conversation. This was, as Strachan pointed out, not just boring but dangerous, since it could help the driver to fall asleep; sometimes the silences were as long as three hours. The two men hit on a scheme. Powell would lecture Strachan on classical history when the latter was driving. When Powell was driving, Strachan would lecture him on something of which he had specialist knowledge. This presented two difficulties for the younger man. He knew Powell's range of expertise was 'mortifyingly wide' and therefore finding a matter in which he was better versed than the Professor was hard. Also, Powell's driving was still so lacking in brilliance that Strachan did not feel he could concentrate both on delivering a lecture and on watching the road. In the end, though, they hit on a subject that Powell knew nothing of and in which Strachan could instruct him with ease: horses and hunting.

As it turned out, each became inordinately interested in what the other had to tell him. As they drove through the site of Carthage, Powell gave a detailed description of the Punic Wars. When they stopped for the evening he would illustrate verse forms to Strachan and teach him the Greek alphabet. Strachan, in return, would draw pieces of harness and give Powell intricate descriptions of the parts of a horse that would have been impossible while Powell was driving. He repeated to Powell the tales of Surtees, and found Powell identifying particularly with the eccentric Squire Mytton. ' "By Jove!" he exclaimed one day when I had finished a more or less true account of an eventful day's hunting, "what I've been missing! – 'the image of war without its guilt and only twenty-five per cent of its danger!' I believe that fellow Jorrocks knew what he was talking about." Then quite solemnly he said, "I've made up my mind. I shall hunt." I never took him seriously, of course. The idea of the Professor hunting was diverting – but quite preposterous.'

Powell, to his amusement and Strachan's anger, crashed the truck outside Tunis; it was towed into the city where, thanks to Powell's pulling rank, a team of mechanics worked through the night to repair it. Strachan made up his mind to drive the rest of the way, but Powell talked him out of it on the ground that to do so would be a personal failure for Strachan as an instructor. Between Tunis and Cairo they inspected sites of German resistance, and the remaining destruction and debris. They continued on through Libya with Powell, by this stage, lecturing about Plato. Strachan was attacked by fleas. His scratching their bites deeply irritated Powell, who refused to talk unless he stopped. Strachan said he could not stop until the fleas ceased biting him, and hoped they would bite Powell as well, to bring home to him the full measure of the discomfort. As a result, some long pauses opened up in the lecture programme.

After seven days – half the scheduled trip – the two men had covered 1,200 miles, or somewhat less than half the journey. Powell's driving improved, but, just when Strachan thought it safe for him to relax, something frightful would happen to keep him again on the alert. In Tripoli, and again in Benghazi, Powell almost ran over Arabs. 'What particularly disturbed me', Strachan recalled, 'was that the Professor seemed to have no sense of guilt or of danger.' As a result, it was hard for him to make Powell drive more carefully. They passed on through Tobruk and by El Alamein; and on the final evening Powell asked Strachan whether he would pass him fit to drive. Strachan retailed to Powell some of the hair-raising things he had done, and asked him whether he thought that it would be commensurate with his reputation as an instructor to pass him. Powell was reluctant to take the point, so Strachan made a proposal. If, when they completed their journey the next day, Powell could drive safely right through the middle of Cairo to GHQ, Strachan would certify he could drive. 'The astounding thing', Strachan noted, 'was that he did it.' Powell looked back on the journey as 'one of the good things I have done in my life'. He told his mother and father that 'when we saw the pyramids appear, we sang Rule, Britannia, Land of Hope and Glory and God Save the King'.[86]

Soon after their safe arrival Powell scoured the second-hand bookshops and bought some Surtees, and other books on hunting. He took Strachan to tea at Gezireh, a luxurious country club for expatriates. He had an ulterior motive: he wanted Strachan to take him to the polo field, and explain the rudiments of that game to him. Strachan had other ideas: he wanted to sleep. Soon, they would go their separate ways and not meet until after the war. Powell had made a massive impact on his younger friend. Speaking in 1970, Strachan was unequivocal about his qualities: 'Powell is the most brilliant intellect I have known. He introduced me to a wealth of literature I had never come across.' As an officer, Powell 'would do even the most routine piece of work himself if there was no one else available to do it. He was a hard task master, but then it was interesting and exciting work and he never let up himself.' Another quarter-century on, Strachan noted that 'I learned an enormous amount from Powell: how to analyse a problem, even sometimes how to solve it – and just how much can be achieved by individual effort. He introduced me to whole new areas of literature from George Borrow to Dante. He also demonstrated how relatively easy it was in the army to get posted to where you wanted to be.'[87]

Throughout this time in North Africa, Powell was writing poetry. He mentioned this to Strachan, but did not let him see it. 'He told me that he often composes spontaneously. He said that he would have an idea for a poem in his head when he goes to bed, just an idea, then wake up in the night with the whole thing composed.'[88] Strachan saw a side of Powell few were permitted to see. 'When I was in the army,' Powell later recalled, 'a fellow officer described me as the most bloody-minded officer in the Middle East.'[89] The bloody-mindedness was not simple stubbornness, nor a desire to create difficulties: it was a straight-forward belief that he was right, and that he was determined to prove, both by logic and by empiricism, that he had found the best solution to any problem.

Once in Cairo, Powell resumed his desperate campaign for a posting to the Far East. 'I wanted', he wrote forty years later, 'to get into the war against Japan as soon as the crisis of the war with Germany was past, with a view, as I used to put it, to "getting into Singapore before the Americans".'[90] He was also con-cerned to find something suitable for Strachan, whom he had had brought out all the way from England for what turned out to be less than two months' work. Eventually, he used his clout to secure him a place at the Staff College at Haifa, with an attachment to an armoured regiment to fill in the time before the course started. Strachan ended his war in North Italy as a lieutenant-colonel; but, before he and Powell parted in Cairo, they made a bet: Powell would pay for Strachan to have a day's hunting if he became a brigadier before Strachan became a lieutenant-colonel; or vice versa.

Before leaving Algiers Powell had turned down a promotion to colonel that would have trapped him in North Africa indefinitely. He fully expected still to have to drop down to major if he was to go east without a posting to a specific job carrying with it the responsibilities of a lieutenant-colonel.[91] He was also unwilling to accept a definite posting of this sort, in case it tied him to a non-combatant job. The 'red hat' of the colonel was offered again, and refused again, when he reached Cairo. Both Curtis and Strachan told him he had been foolish to reject the promotion, and for a time Powell was plagued by rare self-doubt. In the end, he convinced himself that his consistency, of wishing to stick to his resolve to go to India and Burma, was right, and no amount of rank could have compensated for it.[92] His fear, made explicit to his parents, was that America and not the forces of the Crown would reconquer the British colonies, and that would be the end of the Empire 'not later than the lifetime of my children, should I have any'. He added that 'these convictions of mine take on a certain lively reality and pathetic force from my relationship with Thomas, the cir-cumstances of whose probable death render him symbolic in my mind'. The trouble was that Powell still found himself 'utterly in doubt of my objects and standards, without firm ground anywhere. In this darkness instinct tells me that a rigid self-consistency and adherence to resolutions once taken is the only hope of stability.'

He languished in the blistering heat of the Egyptian summer throughout July, reading Surtees and writing poetry; he sent fourteen new poems to his parents in early August, inviting their critical appreciation. While he waited for the confirmation of Strachan's place at Haifa, he felt he could not deal with his own advancement. Strachan's future was settled at the end of July: now Powell moved on to the offensive on his own account. His commanding officer, at last, honoured the earlier pledge to do what he could for Powell, and the India command were ordered to give him a first-grade appointment, so that he could keep his rank of lieutenant-colonel.[93]

On 7 August he heard he had secured a posting to India, persuading the Director of Military Intelligence (India), General Cawthorn, to take him on his staff in Delhi to organise joint service intelligence. He headed for the sub-continent a fortnight later, after a brief trip to Upper Egypt with Strachan. Once more, Powell was fatalistic about a close friendship. He told his parents that when he and Strachan returned to Cairo. 'I parted from him possibly, indeed more probably than not, for ever.'[94] Yet his new posting did not help his desire to see action, to take his share of the responsibility for actively fighting the war, to fulfil his destiny of dying in combat, and, above all, to do the right thing by Thomas. Earlier in the year Powell had told Strachan that 'I do not expect to see England for some years more, nor do I want to, until Singapore (and several other places) are again British.'[95] Such was Powell's desperation to fight the Japanese that, when he heard that General Orde Wingate was in Cairo, shortly before Wingate was due to go to India, Powell set off in search of him. He found him on his way to Heliopolis airport, and stole a ride in his taxi with him in which he made the case to be allowed to be transferred to his outfit. Like Powell's previous attempts, it did not work: Wingate 'was killed before I could cash the cheque'.[96] Even had Wingate lived, the reality was that the army would not let Powell's intellectual strengths be scattered on a battlefield.

IV

Powell reached Delhi on 26 August 1943; he slept his first night there on a bench at the railway station, having arrived at two in the morning and realised it was too early to report to General Headquarters. When he woke with the dawn he found the air and the environment 'intoxicating'.[97] His romantic nature asserted itself instantaneously; here was a new object for his passions, and a truly worthy one at that. He was overwhelmed by his surroundings: 'I soaked up India like a sponge soaks up water.'[98] He went out and bought as many books as he could manage on his new love-interest, and set to reading them omnivorously. By the end of his two and a half years there, he would feel as much Indian as British.

'Its disadvantage', he wrote to his parents of his new posting, 'is that I must reconcile myself to continued existence at a GHQ and that migration onward to China must be deferred until at least some time next year when the next leap becomes possible.'[99] Powell was convinced the great fight to the death between British and Japanese forces would be in China; it was a consolation that from his new position he could influence the strategy that would lead to that denouement. He resolved to add Chinese to his arsenal of languages, and, on a less taxing level, realised the necessity of learning to ride a bike. Another consolation was that the pay was excellent: £1,530 a year, or what he termed 'Regius Professor standard'.[100] Throughout the war, most of his earnings were salted away in his bank at Cambridge, or invested for him by his parents: they would give him, if not financial independence after the war, at least a cushion while he orientated himself.

He was allowed relatively near the Arakan front – though not allowed to go forward of battalion HQ – for a fortnight's acclimatisation shortly after he reached the sub-continent. The ulterior purpose was to discover how many Japanese speakers the army had at the front. He promptly went down with jaundice. Throughout his life, Powell had an aversion to admitting defeat in the face of illness, and carried on with his tour of the front irrespective. 'Picturesque incidents', he told Strachan in a letter from Delhi afterwards, 'included the descent of a river by sampan and the ascent with a half-section of Gurkhas and a mule of a pass which extinguished the Col de Chrea forever from my memory. The impressiveness of this last was heightened by coming out with jaundice that night at the summit.'[101] He told his parents he was 'bright yellow all over', but hoping for a quick recovery that would prevent his having to go to hospital.[102] His mother wrote to Strachan of Powell's illness on 10 October 1943, nervously saying that 'I hope I have his permission to admit to you that he has been "sick" – by the way.'[103]

While recovering he was mistaken for a Japanese spy. A young major in Intelligence called James Allason – who would later sit alongside Powell in the Commons as Conservative MP for Hemel Hempstead – was at his desk in Delhi one morning when, without ceremony or greeting, a lieutenant-colonel came into his office and demanded to see the plans for the invasion of Burma. Suspecting, from the curt manner, the hair *en brosse* and above all the yellow skin that something was wrong, Allason stalled until a senior officer arrived. Powell repeated his request for the invasion plans. The senior officer agreed, and Powell scanned them for a few minutes. Uttering a sharp 'thank you', he left, and the two men lamented that they had just been hoodwinked into showing these sensitive documents to a spy. It was not the first time in his military career Powell had come under suspicion; in his excellent biography, Andrew Roth tells of how a guard at Guilsborough had put Powell in the guardhouse having heard him approach the camp singing the 'Horst Wessel Lied'.[104]

He was immediately given a seat on the SE Asia Command planning staff.

Among his early responsibilities was the development of plans to invade Burma. He worked extensively on one part of them, for the capture of the island of Akyab, with Glyn Daniel, who later became Disney Professor of Archaeology at Cambridge; their efforts were pointless, as the island turned out to be undefended. Nonetheless, it was the next best thing for him to being at the front. 'At least,' he wrote to Strachan on 23 September, 'if I can't give British policy a twist from here, it will be my own fault.'[105] Daniel claims in his memoirs that Powell and Wingate, with whom he was occasionally working closely in planning operations, did not get on; and that Wingate once said to Daniel: 'One day I want to beat the brains out of that stupid man Powell. Will you restrain me? Will you see I don't make a fool of myself?'[106] Daniel's memoirs are not, though, reliable; elsewhere, he claims to have met Powell in Cambridge in May 1938, at exactly the time Powell was 11,000 miles away delivering his inaugural lecture in Sydney. Powell also remembered only having met Wingate once, in the taxi in Cairo.

Powell's days were divided between committee meetings and routine intelligence gathering. He discovered the library of the Imperial Secretariat within his headquarters building, which gave him 'the first opportunities for serious military and political reading that I have had since Camberley'.[107] His childhood interest in ornithology was reawakened by the stunning bird life of India: he wrote home of the joy of seeing weaver birds, mynas, drongos, kites, vultures and paroquets on his morning walk from his bungalow to his office. It was a compensation for the bureaucracy in which he found himself being swallowed up, and the unremitting twelve- or thirteen-hour days. His senior officers, recognising his superior skills, encouraged him to make suggestions, and involved him closely in their work and decision-making, which gratified him. Inevitably, though, his mind returned to its usual course: by 15 October he was complaining to his parents that, after four years in the army, he had 'never yet seen a dead body and, apart from air raids, only once heard shots fired in anger'; and this while Thomas was 'perishing like Oates in the blizzard'.[108] He told his parents categorically that he would not be going to the post held open for him at Durham, and sought their advice on when 'fairness' required him to tell the University this. As he had made up his mind, his parents told him to advise them quickly.

He also wished to know what his parents thought of his making a 'liaison visit' to England, if, as seemed likely, the opportunity arose. He stressed he would not seek the opportunity, presumably because he could not endure the emotional distress it would cause him to see his parents, and to see England again, before the war and his part in it were finished. However, he hinted that he would come if they wished it, and sought their opinion. His father replied: 'We feel we must leave the matter entirely in your hands: you know all the attendant circumstances and their probable bearing on your future progress and conditions. So far as we can, we should prefer to leave you unfettered by sentimental considerations.'[109] His mother, in the same letter, added that she didn't want to give her son the idea that they didn't want to see him – 'the mere possibility naturally caused quite a lot of heart flutter'. She, too, said that they would leave the decision up to him, while making it clear how she longed to see her son again despite her 'mental contentment of attitude to your now prolonged absence'.

The following month he met, by chance, a major who had been second-in-command of the volunteer battalion in which Thomas had enlisted, and who told him that only two of the five officers in Thomas's company had come back alive from the front after the fighting of 7/8 February 1942. Powell's instinct that Thomas was dead was not, naturally, altered by this conversation. Nevertheless, he was glad when the major offered to write to another survivor, then in West Africa, to see what he could tell: hope was not yet finally extinguished, but this new line of enquiry revealed nothing. In November he related to his parents 'a strange thing' that had happened to him. 'Amongst some officers newly arrived I saw someone I remembered but could not place. He bore a striking resemblance to the "ghost", and I remembered having remarked this resemblance before, whenever it was that I met him. I shortly afterwards ran into him in a corridor and we stopped. He said "I dare say you don't remember my name." I admitted I didn't. "Thomas!" he said. It was a weird and supernatural sensation and I remained under the impression of it for some hours before it wore off.'[110] This Thomas had been a captain on the staff at Guilsborough, but the event was indicative of the almost permanent torment Powell felt, and the half-formed death wish he harboured.

He realised that his lack of knowledge of Urdu would hinder the pursuit of his affair with India. He set about trying to correct it, embarking wholeheartedly on yet another language. That was not the only skill he sought; he had to learn to ride a bicycle, which he had concluded was the only satisfactory means of locomotion in Delhi. After many initial tumbles, he acquired the knack. He confided this to Strachan, though begged him to keep the news from Curtis: 'I once promised Curtis that if ever I learnt to ride a bicycle, I would thereupon also learn to swim; so these facts must be kept from him.'[111] Powell's main ulterior motive for learning to cycle was so he could tour Delhi in search of a horsed unit, where he could learn to ride as the preliminary to his taking up hunting after the war: or, as he put it to Strachan, pursuing his 'discipleship of Jorrocks'. In fact, within a few months Powell would find the motivation to teach himself to swim too. In helping to plan a landing on Sumatra, he saw one more opportunity to get into the front line. At the age of thirty-two he literally took the plunge – though, by his own admission, not very well – thinking it would be useful in helping him to persuade his superiors to let him in on the actual landing. Again, he was turned down. Learning to ride, which he eventually did, was scarcely better, to begin with, for his *amour propre*: he found it a struggle and recalled that 'learning to ride is a humiliation for a grown man'.[112]

He became used to the discomforts of India. 'The climate here is abominable,' he told Strachan. 'In his first moments the victim thinks it an English spring – trees, singing birds, morning dew, mild sunshine – but before he has proceeded 100 yards through this English spring, he finds himself soaked through and half exhausted ... Lying in bed in my bungalow before turning out the light I often amuse myself by trying to find some part of the floor, walls or roof on which something is not hopping, running, crawling, walking, flying; and there never is. The worst is that the crawlers often turn out to hop and the runners to fly.'[113] In the extreme heat he still always wore his full military uniform – tunic, collar, tie, Sam Browne – while others dressed for the climate; he would always work in the afternoon after a heavy lunch because no one else worked at that time; and he would offer visitors a whisky because, as he would say with Wildean irony, 'that's what an English gentleman usually takes after a journey'.[114] He was determined to be himself and make no compromises.

By mid-November 1943 boredom set in; Powell had not spent a day outside the office in the grand Government Buildings since 16 September, absorbed in deciding whether to bomb the Burma–Siam railway. However, he got on well with his immediate colleagues, which made life bearable until his hoped-for posting to more exciting climes. His progress in Urdu was such that he put in to take a lower-standard examination in it the following January. He had hoped that learning the language would solve some of India's riddles: but, as he told Strachan, his acquaintance with it 'does not alter first impressions of utter and fundamental incompetence which lies at the bottom of so many problems here'.[115] His sense of humour had not deserted him: he signed this letter to Strachan 'Almost affectionately, your own Mongol warrior'. His Christmas greeting to his parents, though, talked of a 'present protracted period of inactivity and despondency' and he claimed that he lacked 'the surplus energy that I could wish for improving myself'.[116] Christmas Day he divided between working, walking, studying Urdu and reading a book on Curzon's viceroyalty. A month later he told his parents that he was not bored, but he was lonely. He had found it relatively easy to make friends in Cairo, helped by the fact that Curtis and Freeth were already established there, and that he had Strachan shipped out to him. Women were still not an option.

As before, he used any spare time to write out his thoughts on the progress of the war. His obsession with the anti-British activities of the Americans continued undiluted: he cut out and retained in his papers an item from the *Statesman* newspaper of 13 November 1943, in which it was reported that the American radical Clare Booth Luce had told an audience in America that 'Indian independence peacefully consummated would mean that the USA will really have won the greatest war in the world for democracy'. It confirmed Powell's belief that Britain was as much an enemy in America's war as Germany, if not more so. He had the previous month sent a brother staff lieutenant-colonel, R. P. Fleming, his latest analysis of war aims, in which he stated categorically that America was one of Britain's two biggest potential enemies in the Far East – the other was China, or someone operating from South China. He saw an American threat to Australasia, and quite possibly to China too. He reiterated the point in '1943' about the need to preserve the Japanese Navy as a counterweight to American aggression, and of the need to secure a base in Indo-China, with Britain assuming the protection of Annam, Laos and Cambodia.[117] Fleming responded to this grand strategy somewhat curtly, saying it was 'OK as chess but lousy as strategy', and that to keep the Japanese Navy afloat was 'surely to ignore the facts of life and the lessons of history'. He felt the likelihood of an attack by America was 'remote'. 'If you have a man-eating tiger in the compound I can't see the sense of basing your precautions on the possibility of your being savaged to death by either the cow or the cockroaches.'[118]

Powell's duties were now entirely within the India Command, not South-East Asia. When Mountbatten decided to move SE Asia Command from Delhi to Kandy in Ceylon Powell refused a transfer to his staff. The spell of India was upon him, and he was determined to stay there. In a letter of 13 January 1944 he admitted to Strachan that 'though you will despise me for it, I have increasing distaste for employment with a formation on active service. My mind turns more and more to the political side; and though we are a long, long way from peace with Japan, war and peace at this end of the world are less sharply divided than in Europe and strategy merges more insensibly into policy.'[119] On 27 January he sent his letter of resignation to Durham, and began to plot how he could serve and further the interests of the Empire in India. He told his parents that the defeatism he detected among the British about the future of their rule in India reminded him, painfully, of their attitude towards Hitler in 1938–9.[120]

Having passed his first examination in Urdu, he continued to study to a higher level. He had an Urdu teacher, a poet and nephew of one of the greatest Urdu poets, Hali. Powell would read aloud to him and the two men would discuss the scansion and prosody of Urdu poetry; and, when the time came for Powell to study for his interpretership, his teacher prepared him for that too. He had an ambition – never realised – to produce a critical edition of *The Rise and Fall of Islam*, the story of the Moslems in India as told by Hali. He also continued to read exhaustively in the history of India, inspired as much by the sudden effect on him of the visual splendour of its relics as by his desire to look into the background of his current political interests. Where once he had walked about with regard only to landscape, now his eyes were focused mainly on architecture. Buildings spoke to him as the monuments of 'our own ... legal predecessors'; he began to understand the building as a symbol of a people's continuity.[121] The greatest personal legacy he would bring back from India was this love of architecture; it became a consuming passion once he was in England, and forced him to see his own country as if with new eyes. It was started by a visit with a brother officer to Humayun's tomb in Delhi. They went on their cycles, 'and as I approached Humayun's tomb I realised what a building was about'. Powell was given to such moments of revelation. Thereafter, on short leaves, he and his bearer would take a train to a new site, packing their bicycles in the luggage van and taking them out at their destination to ride solemnly round the Uttar Pradesh or Gujerat, with the bearer riding dutifully a few yards behind Powell Sahib.

Yet, for all the new forms of mental stimulation Powell was experiencing, he still felt the need to write to Strachan on 20 May 1944 that 'my own life at present is one of almost unrelieved drudgery with less responsibility than for two years past – editing intelligence summaries, attending like some person or a general practitioner to the woes and wants of nearly 30 officers ... I say all this in no tone of complaint.'[122] Powell thought the war would last several more years, and had conceived a plan, which he shared with Strachan: 'The plan roughly is to grit my teeth and stick it out in this backwater till I get a little more rank, then go flat out for certain key positions that I visualise existing in a set of circumstances which most would consider chimerical but I do not.' Although his study of the history and language of India was absorbing, he admitted to Strachan he missed three things: 'I miss music; I miss verse and the freedom of mind to read and write it; and above all I miss Alcibiades. Dialogues between Socrates and Socrates are dull and inconclusive.' By that, he meant he missed the intellectual companionship of Strachan. He asked him to put 1950 in his diary as the time he had chosen for them to traverse Asia from west to east as they had done North Africa – '1950, or as soon afterwards as the restoration of international tranquillity may permit'.

Powell was promoted colonel at the end of March 1944, as Assistant Director of Military Intelligence. Throughout that spring and summer he worked longer hours even than in Cairo. It was often seven days a week, rising at 4 a.m. and being at his desk often until ten in the evening, helping direct the intelligence operation behind the attritional campaign in Burma of Lt-Gen William Slim, later Viscount Slim, Commander of the 14th Army. He reported to his parents on 16 April, two months short of his thirty-second birthday, that he had counted three grey hairs on his head.[123] Strachan wrote to him in June 1944 asking whether a post could be found for him in India Command: Powell advised him against it, on the ground that if he came he would probably spend 'four barren years' there.[124] Yet he would have liked nothing more than to have Strachan with him again, for he still had found no close companion to replace him; 'the acquisition of friends', he wrote, 'is laborious and painful and the loss of them once acquired represents a loss of capital that is never made good again'.

That month also marked a significant watershed for Powell: 'it was the day the monsoon broke ... when I suddenly said to myself: You're going to survive. There'll be a time when you won't be in uniform, painful though it may be, you've got to face it ... and I opened the door, as it were, this was the opening of the door from one mental room to another and there was the answer.' The answer, as he stood being soaked in the torrential rain, was: 'Of course you'll go into politics, in England.'[125] It was perhaps the most important moment of revelation of all, and one conducted in appropriately mystical and romantic terms. He reported it obliquely to his parents in a letter of 5 July, though he warned them they might think he was 'raving'.[126] Before receiving this letter his mother, alarmed at the depressed tone of some of his recent missives, wrote to him that 'often things have been a bit heavy going – as it was revealed unto me on 16.6.1912 that they would. To say the least you have always taken life very seriously and made us do the same, though we have often been happy, even hilarious together ... yet I have sometimes wished for your own sake as much as ours that you had found life more light hearted and joyous and that your "daemon" had not been such a stern monitor and your self-examination so rigorous.'[127] She added, 'Most people would think we had a son to be proud of; then how much more do we who know most appreciate *all* that you are.'

For almost the first three weeks of August 1944 Powell had a long-overdue leave, which he spent at Darjeeling. He travelled with a new friend, James Wickenden, an officer on his staff, whose existence he had mentioned to his parents earlier, in a letter about a visit to the Taj Mahal at Agra.[128] He had also, in telling them in June of his hopes of going to Darjeeling and thence trekking towards Tibet, said that the trip was 'very uncertain. Perhaps it will be better if it is not so, as it hangs together with what I fear may prove the saddest of my sad romances.'[129] Wickenden, who had fought through Burma against the Japanese and was something of a buccaneer, had become the new figure for Powell's still-adolescent hero-worship. This was the latest example of Powell's 'Boys' Own Paper' fascination with the glamour of adventure, such as had manifested itself at Cambridge and in his poetry as a Housman-like adoration of youth. Patently exhausted by weeks of unremitting hard work – 'I do, of course, overdo it: I have now got to the stage of being efficient on 5 hrs sleep a night' – he wrote a letter to his parents about this 'sad romance'.[130] That he did so was prompted partly by his loneliness, to which he would now at last own up, and partly by their concern for his happiness.

A few weeks earlier, in the bizarre context of his disregard for his life assurance policies, he had spoken of his 'conviction, deepened by further experience and observation, that a certain peculiarity of which you are aware is so strong, real and deep-seated as to render the eventuality of marriage very improbable'. This is most likely to be evidence of his deep misogyny (for which there are many other proofs, such as a description of married men as 'that great nation of the dead') than of his acceptance – let alone his parents' acceptance – that he was at that time in any way homosexual.[131] It is inconceivable that he would have written to his parents in this way, especially bearing in mind the conventions of the day, if there had been any hint of a homosexual relationship. His feelings would develop greatly after the war, once he overcame his shyness and inhibitions about women out of which he had, somewhat childishly, manufactured this aversion, and once he matured emotionally. He was desperate for companionship more than anything, and there is no evidence of any sexual impulse – nor, from Wickenden's letters to Powell, any suggestion that Wickenden regarded their friendship as anything out of the ordinary, or that it had had anything like the emotional impact upon him that it had had on Powell.

In his letter home of 30 July 1944, Powell gave evidence of a more reflective and deeper feeling for his new friend. Referring again to how this might be the 'saddest of my sad romances', he wrote:

> it may be, and certainly will be if certain events of war take their course, yet I now think it need not be. One driving, compelling and overwhelming impulse, in addition to a thirst for achievement, I shall always have, whether I like or not; and that is the impulse to give affection and if necessary sacrifice to courage and manliness manifested in a form in which I recognise and imagine I can help it. This need is, I realise, a weakness; but I can only say that other men have others. There is also this, that though time and experience may not change the force or even the direction of our impulses, they do at least impart gradually some skill or cunning in diverting, palliating or escaping the attendant evils and pitfalls: a man learns in the end to outwit himself.

Wickenden's health had been damaged by his time in combat, and he was ill with asthma. It brought out an almost fatherly concern in Powell, who took Wickenden into his own quarters and effectively became his nurse.

His parents, knowing both how highly strung and how overworked he was, were unfailingly sympathetic. His mother wrote to him that 'I hope by the time you receive this you will be feeling less keenly the wrench of losing what must have been a great help to you – but of course you knew it was inevitable. I also hope it was some help to you to be able to express yourself fully to us on paper, as you were wont to do of old, when we were together, and to feel that owing to our past talks, we should be able to understand as well as possible and certainly to give dispassionate sympathy. I hope you will always feel able to use us, as you have done, as a kind of overflow exhaust safety valve.'[132]

The wrench was indeed severe. Shortly after his return to Delhi he had an agonising duty. Wickenden asked him, as his senior officer, to secure him a posting to the front. Powell, understanding better than most the imperative of fighting, and further recognising the heroic and self-sacrificing qualities that had drawn him to Wickenden in the first place, duly obliged. He wrote home on 1 September of the trauma this had caused him, and at last revealed to them something about his new friend. He apologised for a delay in writing, caused, he said, by the fact that:

the last fortnight has been the conclusion of a brief phase, the significance of which I feel unable to measure till I am at a somewhat greater distance from it. Two days ago I saw off to the Burma front, at which, by his own request, I had obtained for him an appointment, one of my officers, whom since 13 May I had not passed any period longer than three days (and usually less) without seeing; we went to Agra and Darjeeling together and since we returned till he left he lived in my quarters.

Over nine years younger than I am, with an ailing and not strong constitution already somewhat impaired by two Burma campaigns, with features as near as I can describe like Shelley's and the courage of a tiger. Enlisted at under 18 in Aug. 39 after an irregular schooling and a futile year at Edinburgh University, it appeared that his natural mental capacity had been able to extract from war and experience the education to make him a man in whom I recognised an equal. From the moment on 13 May that he told me he was going into hospital . . . to 30 August when his train left, the thing was an incomprehensible wonder to both of us. To me it seemed there had never been anyone to whom I could to such an extent give. But giving is not the easy thing people imagine, but harder than receiving.

The letter concludes: 'What will come of this thing which has occupied the last three-and-a-half months of our lives I think neither of us knows: the marks, I believe, will in any case be lasting on both.'[133] Powell seems sure he had found a heroic figure for his devotion, with the 'courage' and 'manliness' he had already told his parents were magnetic to him. It was a classical ideal, but all the more painful because his loneliness led him to pour out his affection on the few who were his genuine friends.

He now awaited, with a mixture of hope and dread, a letter from the front in Burma. He could not think of the future at all; having now resigned his chair at Durham, he still had no plan of what to do instead, and was in no condition to make such a plan. 'Somewhat ungraciously', as he told Strachan, Durham had accepted his decision. 'Those boats therefore are burnt and that Rubicon crossed.'[134] Within a few weeks he had pulled himself together, and he told his parents on 24 September that 'my future (if I have one) is likely to be bound up with the object of preserving, consolidating and extending His Majesty's power and dominions in the East'.[135] While this might be accomplished from home, he advised his parents to resign themselves to the fact that he might live in India for the indefinite future. He was deeply affected, in his thinking about India and Britain's role there, by the example of Curzon; and quoted to his parents Curzon's observation of 1904 that 'to me the message is carved in granite, it is hewn out of the rock of doom – that our work is righteous and that it shall endure'.[136]

He had embarked on this line of thought in a letter to Strachan some three weeks earlier. Powell told him that the tumultuous events taking place in Europe were barely perceptible to him, because in his view 'the Far East was in the beginning, is now, and ever shall be the only source of world power'.[137] He had been in India exactly a year, and professed himself 'more ignorant and baffled than at the beginning, despite much earnest endeavour to learn and understand'. He wished he had had the chance to begin in India as a subaltern in an Indian regiment. Events in Europe had made some impact on him, however much he denied it. During that summer a change of perception had overtaken him; he now told Strachan that 'my situation is gloomy, especially as I fear the war may not be prolonged beyond about 1946'. Meanwhile, as he put it, 'I vegetate and labour at self-improvement.'

He had begun to feel a massive affinity with the Indian people, and a deep sense that Britain and India were made to be together, to extend civilisation together. India had begun to humanise him, to take him out of himself. He was driven by the need for Britain and India to stay together: the romantic in him surged uppermost, and he resolved that he wanted to be viceroy. His immersion in India, as a result, became more complete. He now spent an hour and a half each day talking Urdu, and the same amount of time reading and writing it. On his Sundays off he would ride around the environs of Delhi on his bicycle, exploring the country in ever greater depth.

His social isolation became more intense, and he knew it. He told Strachan (who had written to him of his thoughts about marrying a woman with whom he was serving) that he had absolutely no knowledge of such things and could not comment on them; that, in Milton's phrase, he was 'from the cheerful ways of men cut off'.[138] He made no mention to Strachan of the latest cause of his emotional distress. When, the next year, Strachan wrote to him of his engagement Powell replied that he would expect him to send congratulations on it 'which it is hard for me to do, not comprehending such things'.[139] He felt that a spiritual death accompanied marriage, which was partly why he refused to attend Freeth's wedding, or to approve of Curtis's marriage later in the war. His friends chose not to hold this priggishness against him. Writing to Strachan to express her delight at the news of his impending marriage, Powell's mother said that 'although our son has some very odd inhibitions about offering congratulations on engagements or marriages (knowing him you will perhaps have understood his seeming discourtesy), I am very certain that he will in truth be very pleased when he hears that I have offered them very sincerely from all of us'.[140]

While Powell's main motive for his commitment to India was, in the long term, his ambition to be viceroy, in the short term he wanted to work for the recovery of Burma, Siam, Malaya and Indo-China by a predominantly British force, in the interests of securing Britain's place there in the post-war world. His distrust of American intentions towards that region and, more to the point, towards British power had not abated. He was, the following month, given a position that would help him achieve his ambitions; he was promoted brigadier to have appropriate seniority on a committee of two other brigadiers and a lieutenant-general – Willcocks, after whom the committee was named – charged with drawing up a plan for the post-war defence of India. With the promotion came the matter of the bet he had made with Strachan in Cairo, so on 4 November he sent him a telegram which read simply: 'I PAY FOR HUNTING – POWELL'. His was one of only two instances during the whole war of a private soldier rising to the rank of brigadier; and for a few weeks he was the youngest holder of that rank in the army.

The appointment was sprung on Powell, and there was nothing he could do about it. 'I am out of the war probably for good and all,' he told Strachan in a letter the following month.[141] The only way he could have tried to evade it would have been to protest to the Commander-in-Chief, Sir Claude Auchinleck, in person; but Powell, despite or perhaps because of his willingness to take on his superiors in the past, decided against it. The committee set up its base at Dehra Dun, north of Delhi, which Powell described as 'a semi-hill station'. From there it could tour India by aircraft and private railway coach, making observations and collecting information before it made its final deliberations. With Thomas probably dead and Wickenden in the jungle, Powell told his parents that this travelling around India in 'pomp' was 'one of God's little jokes; and I consider it to be in outrageously bad taste'.[142] His consolation was that 'the "private in the Warwicks" now sets out on the last long lap to General'.

The Willcocks Committee's work was dominated 'by a single, almost obsessive idea. In the First World War the Indian Army had expanded from 155,000 to 573,000. In the second war it had expanded from 150,000 to 1,800,000 ... the Indian Army was never again to go to war unprepared for rapid expansion and for facing the most advanced military opponents.'[143] The work was not, to start with, particularly demanding, but did allow Powell to expand his knowledge of India, both by practical experience and by using his additional spare time for reading; he also passed his higher-standard examination in Urdu and started to train for an interpretership. All this 'unwarlike' activity, he told Strachan, exacerbated his feelings of fraudulence. 'But I suppose I can be considered as fighting the next war, to which, as you know, I have always been strongly attracted.'[144] With a view to prospecting for his post-war career he cultivated some of the civil servants he met, and learned about their work. 'The result is a feeling that at any rate so far as I am concerned that is not the answer,' he told his parents on 10 December 1944. Hinting at his eventual decision, he asked them: 'Was it not Burke who said in the Commons: "The keys of India are not in Calcutta, nor in Delhi; they are here in this House"? I wonder if that is not after all still true.'[145]

His new routine gave him time to resume writing poetry; from January 1945 he allowed himself an hour a day to indulge this long-unpractised pursuit. He told Strachan the verse was the 'working off' of 'the products of a week of "violent excitement" (to use Housman's expression) last May, which at the time I was not able to put to writing'.[146] This was an oblique reference to his captivation by Wickenden, who used a leave from the front in January 1945 to visit Powell at Dehra. They spent what free time Powell could muster on architectural tours, both in the vicinity and on a return trip to Agra. Powell was relieved that Wickenden's asthma had improved. When Wickenden went back to the front his departure caused Powell 'the usual heartache and, as before, utter astonishment at the fate, which for no apparent reason selected us to be the causes to each other of consequences not yet foreseeable but which exceed any previous experience of mine in this order'.[147]

The time at Powell's disposal also allowed him to think more clearly about the future: 'The form and outline of my "third life" is now perhaps taking shape in my mind.' He would begin that third life at the bottom, as he had the other two; but he felt it was his last chance, because 'if I fail, I fail for all eternity'. His committee was returning to England in May to have meetings at the War Office. Powell chose not to go, but to stay in India and, at his own request, write the first draft of their report. It was in keeping with his stated desire not to set foot in England until the war was over. He had also not abandoned hope of getting to the front, and felt that only by taking control of the report could he have the work finished early enough to allow him that chance. He had also used his time at Dehra for serious daily training in the saddle, under an Indian sergeant instructor. By the end of January he had mastered the canter and trot; travelling then intervened, but on his return he resolved to gallop and jump.

On 5 February Powell and his colleagues left for a six weeks' tour of India. By the middle of the month he had reached Bombay via Lahore and Karachi, interviewing provincial governments, politicians and military personnel. He was exhausted by the constant round of inspections that, as a visiting dignitary, he had to carry out, and by the entertainments to which he, as a profoundly anti-social man, had to be subjected. The provisional date for the completion of the report was November 1945, and even one with an appetite for work the size of Powell's began to feel intimidated by the amount that had to be done before then. He added to his own workload by getting up early in the morning to draft the next paragraph of the report his colleagues would be considering. That way he ensured that he retained control over the contents of the report, as none of his colleagues had the determination to challenge in depth what he had done.

His fascination with India grew the more he experienced the country, and the people. He had worked out the importance of the events that would be unleashed once the war was over, and told Strachan they would be as significant as those of 1936–9 had been in Europe. The committee included a senior Indian officer, Brigadier Kariappa, and segregation was operated between whites and Asians when it came to accommodation. Powell, who had struck up an especially cordial friendship with Kariappa, objected to his being denied admittance to the Byculla Club in Poona, where Powell was billeted. He insisted on staying in the same place as his Indian colleague. It was something of which Kariappa reminded Powell when he visited England thirty years later, after the furore about Powell's immigration speeches, and of which Powell had no recollection.[148]

As Germany fell, Powell watched with awe from afar the final resistance the Reich put up, which he described to Strachan as 'a wonderful performance ... I think only Germans are capable of such a feat.'[149] He doubted the sense of Britain's strategy, in regard to her long-term interests, but said that 'a more hopeful event is the removal from the scene of Roosevelt [who had recently died] which gives some prospect of assisting a return to American isolation or, alternatively, to a cruder and therefore (to us) less dangerous form of American imperialism'. He sent some newly written poems to Strachan for his consideration, and held out hopes of publishing some soon.

Once the war in Europe was over, the fighting in Powell's own theatre of war began to reawaken in him feelings he thought he had suppressed. Apologising to Strachan in a letter of 17 July 1945 for not having written earlier, he excused himself by saying he had been 'in a certain distress of mind' for two or three months: 'I have, in fact, been living mentally on the Mandalay road and the Siltang, much more personally than I had lived July–Oct 1942 at Alamein; and I have been fighting a losing battle to escape, of which the anxiety felt in July 1943 is a very pale and distant idea.' Though he was not more explicit to Strachan, Wickenden – still in Burma – was the cause of the distress. He continued: 'One result is that I find myself, even at this late hour, hatching plans of a sort which I thought I had long forsworn, and wondering by what device I can be present in the fall of "Jerusalem, where Christ was slain".'[150] He had, at least, managed to convince himself that Wickenden would survive, so much so that he was now writing to former colleagues at Cambridge to try to secure him a place to finish his education after the war, and guaranteeing the money to fund it there if no government grant were available. In early June 1945 Wickenden turned up unannounced in Powell's office, much to Powell's delight, and the two men set off for the Himalayan foothills for a week's leave spent yachting, rowing and playing billiards. Writing to his parents, Powell explained Wickenden's attraction for him: 'W is more like myself in capacity and aspirations than anyone else I have had dealings with, and in that, the whole wide scope and implications appear to be realised fully and instinctively grasped, without fears or doubts or tragic elements or reservations.'[151] Powell heard that Trinity would almost certainly take his protégé in October 1946; but then Wickenden was, to Powell's intense anxiety, posted back to the front – 'the very front' as he told his parents –

having had, in the days before he left, 'a presentiment that he would be killed'.[152] Their parting was horrible for Powell, not least because of the similarities with an earlier one in another life: 'the thought is naturally with me that before I can see him again he will go where Thomas is and where I ought to be'. He fell into a spiral of mental torment, 'tortured', as he told his mother and father, 'by my own impotent imagination. It is like seeing Thomas bayonetted [sic] in front of me. Please forgive my inflicting this upon you: I write it to relieve my mind, having no one in whom else I can confide.'[153]

At the end of July 1945 the torment reached its worst. He had been trying to secure a staff posting for Wickenden, without success: an ironic thing for a man who himself wished to die to be trying to do. He confided to his parents that he had been undergoing 'a period of mental torture unique in my experience hitherto. Anything I felt about Thomas either in 1939 or since is a jest compared with the monstrous chain of events, like the deliberate working of a malignant will, which, with the responsibility for opposing it resting solely on me, inexorably placed him in the most exposed position in the most heavily engaged battalion at the precise period of the one battle which was being fought anywhere.'[154] One of the strands of this tangle of emotions was his belief, in his shame at not fighting himself, that if Thomas were to rise from the dead he and Powell would be 'mortal enemies'. When the Americans bombed Hiroshima, Powell, writing a few days before the Japanese surrender, told his parents of his fear that the enemy would 'let him down': he would never have his chance to fight.[155] When the end came, he frankly told his mother and father that it was 'a shock'.[156] He had 'missed the war – every bit of it', and had been denied the consolation of a general's 'sword and baton'.

He was still, apart from all this, struggling to get his committee's report finished. The twelve hours a day he devoted to it at least spared him from complete self-destruction. After VE Day his main concern other than for Wickenden, as expressed to his parents, was that 'the time will in due course come when His Majesty will have no further need of me'.[157] His hopes rose when a superior officer suggested that the regular rank of brigadier in the post-war Indian Army, though not at home, was 'not ruled out'. He told Strachan not to expect him back in England before mid-1947, and suggested to his parents in April 1945 that the war in the East would last at least another year, 'and then there will be much to do, quite apart from starting in with preparations for the next'.[158] Yet the knowledge that he would survive had, predictably, an extreme effect on him. A thirst for life presented itself. In middle age he recalled that 'I used to play the game of deciding, if I had ten lifetimes, what I would do with each of them.'[159] In mid-July he told his parents categorically that his 'third life' would be 'a life of affairs amongst men of affairs, for objects of temporal ambition but at the same time in the service of King as Emperor. And it must begin at the bottom.'[160] He begged for their support.

He found the last three months' work on the report 'nightmarish in their intensity and personal tension'.[161] He finished on 12 October 1945, and the following month was spent editing and proof-reading. The result was two volumes, one of 320 and the other of 150 pages, which Powell called 'the most comprehensive report ever made on the Indian or, I believe, the British army'. He told Strachan: 'Every word, from title page to index, and 95 per cent of the meaning, is mine.' It was a stupendous achievement, not diminished by what would soon emerge as its painful futility. He had dominated his colleagues, one of whom said later: 'He would cut into waffle without caring a damn who was talking. I've seen him humiliate a vastly senior officer by destroying his argument with just one telling point. He didn't bother about doing it gently either.' When he received the report Auchinleck immediately saw that the application of Powell's remorseless logic to questions of the military control of disturbed areas meant that some of Powell's ideas were probably unworkable, for they had taken little or no account of human nature.

Having finished this immense task, Powell was unsure what would happen to him, but began to realise he might well get back to England in 1946. Auchinleck, who for all his criticism of the Willcocks report had a high regard for Powell, offered him the post of assistant commandant of an Indian version of Sandhurst. Powell refused it. Glyn Daniel recalled a dinner in Delhi in December 1945, at which Powell asserted again a determination not to return to the academic life. He shocked Daniel by saying, no doubt ironically, that 'having achieved what I have achieved in this war, I should be the head of all military intelligence in the next'.[162] He allegedly added that 'the next war will not be between America and the West versus Russia. It will be between Russia and Europe versus America. Therefore the key area to understand is Central America. I shall go underground for a year or so and get to know everywhere from Mexico to Peru.' Certainly, Powell told his parents that he hoped to return home, for, it seems, reconnaissance purposes, via 'South, Central or (at the worst) North America, because having got so far round the globe it seems a pity not to finish the job and have a look at some of the battlefields of the *next* war'.[163]

After seeing the report through the press in Delhi he had a month's leave from 15 November to 15 December, which he had wanted to spend in Malaya; Wickenden had been posted with his unit to Singapore, and Powell hoped to see him. However, the turmoil of that region made such a plan impossible, even though the Supreme Allied Commander reluctantly gave him permission to go. So he chose, instead, to relax in Delhi, studying for a Hindustani interpretership examination the following January. He was informed that the authorities would decide at the end of his leave whether he would stay in the army or be demobilised. He told Strachan that 'my own object is, if possible, to stay in India until April and then return as a civilian via Australia and South America'. He was beginning to formulate how he would enter Westminster politics as a prelude to his viceregal ambitions. He was, though, becoming aware of the difficulties his country would have in trying to govern India. Kariappa told him, 'We don't have to drive you out by force. We four hundred millions would only have to lean on you and say, "Get going, little people, get going".'[164]

Powell now felt as Indian as any native. The romance of the Raj, of its places and its people, would never be evacuated from his soul. In later years he would see this as 'a shared hallucination', shared between the rulers and the ruled. In that last November of his there, he was cycling by himself along an open road near Muttra:

> when a young Brahmin drew alongside me and after some conversation in Urdu between us, pointed to his home some hundred yards from the road and suggested I go there with him for a drink of water. While my hosts used a brass vessel, I drank from a rough earthen tumbler, which, on thanking them and taking my leave, I smashed on the ground to show that I knew it could not anyhow be used again. 'He is a Hindu,' they said to one another with a smile. There is a sense in which it had been true: the British were married to India, as Venice was married to the sea.[165]

The authorities told him to go home for demobilisation after his interpreter-ship examination. With the signal that the King had no further use for him, he was now impatient to get home and see what could be done about launching his 'third life'. With the end of hostilities, the heat of his concern for Wickenden had passed: it was with easy resignation that he accepted he would not see him before beginning the journey home. Powell's plan to go round the world was thwarted, since it could be accomplished only by securing a passage on an American troopship, something even he was prepared to do in these circumstances, but which proved impossible. One can only conjecture what the effect would have been on him had he endured several weeks on a ship in the Pacific unable to escape from the American psyche. Instead, he made plans to fly back to Britain in early February. 'I shall leave India with real reluctance and regret,' he told Strachan, 'partly because every Englishman in India has *ipso facto* a certain value, partly because it seems caddish to leave others of one's countrymen to be shot at, but mainly because of the unending fascination of this incredible Empire in which potentially we have in our hands power and wealth that would make America seem insignificant, and where nevertheless an evil spell seems to bind both the land itself and us.' So it was all at an end: he signed off his last letter from the sub-continent to Strachan: 'Perhaps no longer your own Mongol warrior, Enoch'. His bearer, who had been with him throughout his two and a half years, burst into tears as the Brigadier left for home; there was an equally sad parting from his Urdu teacher. Contrary to his then wishes, Powell would not leave his bones in India.

4

THE THIRD LIFE

Long after the war, Powell told an interviewer: 'I went into the war expecting to be killed. I came out alive. All my assumptions of life had to start again. I went into politics. I can explain the mechanics of this action, every step leading up to it, but I have no power to analyse the inner compulsion.'[1] In the winter of 1945–6, in fact, the compulsion was clear. Powell wanted to be viceroy. He knew he would first have to do what most viceroys had done: distinguish himself in politics. Nietzsche had said that 'scholars who become politicians are usually given the comic role of having to be the good conscience of a policy', which would become almost self-parodically accurate in Powell's case.[2] However, a more political philosopher influenced him this time. Burke had said that the keys to India were to be found not in Delhi or Calcutta but on the dispatch box at the House of Commons; so Powell planned to enter Parliament. His parents were divided on whether it was right for him to do this. His father had reservations, but his mother was sure that if he applied himself he would succeed; and, despite having been a professor and a brigadier, he was still not thirty-four: there was time enough for him to apply himself.

At the 1945 election, Powell had appointed his father to vote as his proxy. In December 1944, when the issue first came up, he had instructed him to cast his vote 'against the candidate who undertakes to support Churchill. A coalition may be needed for winning the war; it is a hindrance in winning the peace. On their prewar record the Conservatives are every bit as nasty traitors as the Labour party and they will have the additional disadvantage of tending to be bound by some of their pronouncements during the war.'[3] He thought his fellow countrymen had made the correct decision in electing Attlee. He regarded Churchill as 'erratic', his greatest weakness his willingness to propitiate the Americans.[4] However, all Powell's intellectual and social instincts propelled him towards Conservatism: 'I was born a Tory ... a Tory is a person who regards authority as immanent in institutions.'[5] The Conservative party badly needed him. Indeed, in those days immediately after Labour's landslide victory – its majority was 146 over all the other parties – the Conservatives needed almost anyone they could get; someone with Powell's credentials was a supreme luxury. Churchill was sensible enough to see that the way in which the pre-war party had run itself, with candidates generally having the independent means needed to help fund a Conservative machine in the constituency, was outmoded. A committee was established, under David Maxwell Fyfe, that would report in

1948 that the money a candidate would be expected to put into his association would be severely restricted. Thus was it made possible for Powell and others like him, without a personal fortune, to contemplate life as a Conservative MP.[6]

It was widely perceived that the party had lost so heavily in 1945 because it had nothing original or compelling to offer; it had completely missed the radical reforming spirit of the time, and as a result had allowed that spirit to be tapped in a socialist direction. This deficiency in ideas had quickly to be rectified; and a sense was needed of what, after effectively fifteen years of coalition, it meant to be political. One 'well-born Tory' was quoted as saying in 1946, as the Government began its programme of nationalisations, welfarism and retreat from Empire: 'I do not mind what the Labour Government are doing ... but I do mind that they and not we should be doing it.'[7]

This was a mentality Powell, with his philosophical sense of absolutes, would set out to break. It would be long after he left the Conservative party before he could be seen to have succeeded. The financial slump of the 1930s had been blamed on neo-liberal laissez-faire economics, and had buried them; years of coalition had given Conservatives a taste for state control and intervention. This legacy, feeding upon and distorting the party's paternalist tradition, would exert itself until the late 1970s. Whatever Powell would feel about the Conservative party in the future, he had not had an especially high regard for it in the past. He would never entirely overcome this absence of blind loyalty to it as an institution. His romantic devotion to the nation always gave him higher loyalties to observe. 'I had not only no sympathy, but deep hostility during the 1930s towards the Conservative Governments of the United Kingdom, which I regarded as having been purblind to the situation in which the United Kingdom found itself and having pushed to the extremity of danger the safety and survival of ... the British Empire.'[8]

However, it was still the party for him. It was, he thought, 'the party of the maintenance of acknowledged prescriptive authority' and 'it would be a party which did not believe in always starting afresh over and over again, it would be a non-innovatory party, a party which chimed in, therefore, with my own prejudices and nature'. It was also, to be entirely pragmatic, the only machine through which Powell would be able to achieve his goals. So, intellectually, he would let bygones be bygones. In any case, the party he had so detested in 1938 was under new management – Chamberlain dead, Baldwin history, and their antagonist, Churchill, still at the helm. More to the point, the stated aims of the Attlee Government provided one with Powell's innate political beliefs and logic with the perfect targets: state control of large swathes of industry, the virtual nationalisation of building land and cheap housing, the creation of a largely indiscriminate welfare state and constitutional reform being the main provocations.

In the last week of February 1946, twenty-four hours after arriving at Brize

Norton by transport plane from India – 'I remember weeping when I saw green fields' – he looked up the number of Conservative Central Office in the telephone directory, dialled Whitehall 8181, and demanded to speak to the chairman.[9] Unable to get through, he made do with a conversation with a deputy chairman, Marjorie Maxse. It was a time of opportunity: within two weeks the Brigadier was on the staff of the Parliamentary Secretariat, on the 'speaker's panel', and on the official candidates' list. Having made contact with the party, Powell was directed to a basement in Wilton Street, Victoria, the headquarters of the Conservative Political Centre, the party's policy discussion organisation. That operation was being run by 'Cub' Alport, who would enter the Commons in 1950, and who remembered Powell's arrival vividly.

> One day a brigadier in full uniform arrived, said his name was Powell. He wanted to join the Conservative party because his object was to ensure the continuance of British rule in India, and he thought that we were the people most likely to do this. He wasn't the sort of brigadier I had been accustomed to in my own army career. For all the shine of his buttons, I noticed his shoes were dirty ... but he told me he had been a fellow of Trinity, which always impresses someone like myself. I was very anxious to recruit intellectuals, who before the war had been alienated from the Conservative party. So I sent him along to David Clarke of the Research Department, phoning Clarke first to tell him a strange bird was on the way who might be of use to him.[10]

Alport was also struck by Powell's 'piercing eye and authoritative manner'.[11]

His application for a job caused some curiosity, not least on the part of the party chairman, Ralph Assheton. Most recruits had had a connection with the party, either on the voluntary wing or in local government. Powell had neither, had not been a part of the party 'network', and was unknown to those who would have to decide whether to hire him. Assheton, impressed by the history of this unusual young man, asked to meet him, and recalled a quarter of a century later: 'He came into my room with his short-cropped hair standing on end. Rather a startling apparition, but when he started talking he was immediately impressive. I remember I had allotted him 15 minutes, but we went well over that. I put him through old Disraeli's test, you know, "Uphold the Constitution, Defend the Empire, Improve the lot of the people". I gave Powell an Alpha Plus. He was clearly a man to be watched, even then.' Assheton was so impressed that he had Clarke immediately appoint Powell to the party's Parliamentary Secretariat at a salary of £900 a year, briefing front-benchers who, in many cases for the first time, found themselves without the resources of the civil service to call upon.

The Secretariat – which would in 1948 be merged into the Research Department – was based in 24 Wilton Street, and Powell soon found himself sharing a large first-floor room with two other new boys. The first to arrive had been

Reginald Maudling, who had spent the war in the Air Ministry and who now, at the age of twenty-eight, was looking to lay the foundations of a parliamentary career; he would soon become candidate for the conveniently close seat of Barnet, for which he would sit until his death. Next in, shortly after Powell, was Iain Macleod. Before the war Macleod, a brilliant bridge player, had earned most of his living as a professional gambler. Wounded while with the British Expeditionary Force in France in 1940 he had, like Powell, developed political interests as a result of staff work, and had fought the Western Isles for the Conservatives in 1945. He, Maudling and Powell became good friends, though the closest partnership was between him and Maudling, who had more in common temperamentally and in their social ease than either had with the buttoned-up Powell. They represented a notable departure from the ethos of the Conservative Research Department before the war; then, research officers had been hired on the strict understanding that they would not use their experience as a route to the Commons. However, the demands of finding the talent to ensure that the party did not go into the next election with the dearth of ideas that had characterised its approach to the last meant the notion of emulating the civil service had to be jettisoned.

Initially – because the Secretariat was not, unlike the Research Department, under the immediate control of R. A. Butler – the received wisdom that Powell, Maudling and Macleod were Butler's private political kindergarten was wide of the mark. However, Powell soon came to Butler's notice because of his interest in India, and, once the Secretariat was merged into the Research Department, worked directly to him. Butler had a stark first impression of the Brigadier: 'there was nothing languid or easygoing about Enoch Powell',[12] he wrote, comparing him with Maudling. Butler, no fool himself, judged Powell to be 'probably the most intellectually formidable of the men who have passed through the Research Department. He took an interest in almost every subject, and on almost every subject he had strong and pungently expressed views. Only some of these were eccentric.' Powell would have his differences with Butler, and be well aware of his politician's faults, but he would back him for the leadership of the party in 1963 to an extent that forced him to end his own ministerial career. It was ironic that Powell should feel such affection for a man who, as an arch-appeaser before the war, was the very embodiment of the mentality he had felt shameful, and which he had flown home in 1939 to fight and expunge.

Maudling and Macleod both played their part in conditioning Powell for the real world; they were not entirely successful. 'I tried to persuade him that he was too logical,' Maudling recalled in his memoirs, 'a concept which he could neither accept nor understand.'[13] The men would share an office for two years, an experience Maudling, after the vicissitudes of the next thirty years, nonetheless still looked back upon with 'considerable affection'.[14] Maudling gave an insight into Powell's methods: 'I do not recall meeting anyone else with a mind that had such a power of acquiring knowledge. At one stage when Enoch was detailed to become an expert on town and country planning, he acquired the standard textbook and read it from page to page, as an ordinary mortal would read a novel. Within a matter of weeks he had fully grasped both the principles of the problem and the details of the legal situation. Within a matter of a few months he was writing to the author of the textbook, pointing out the errors that he had made.' Macleod's role was less elevated: Powell recalled that the great contribution Macleod had made to his life was introducing him to the films of the Marx Brothers, which he came to love.

Powell had gone to stay with his parents at Seaford on returning home, but now needed a base in London. He set himself up in a spartan flat at 34a Earl's Court Square, which his future mother-in-law would describe as being like the Potsdam military academy, just as others had regarded his room at Trinity; there was a spare room in which Macleod would camp when in London too late to get back to his family home in the northern suburbs. The flat soon became less spartan: Michael Strachan, who had just completed his degree at Cambridge, sold some furniture from his rooms there to Powell for £30. He and Powell had renewed their acquaintance in the spring of 1946, having attended together a performance of Handel's *Messiah* at Easter before going on a walking holiday from Shrewsbury to Hereford; and Powell saw Strachan again in Cambridge on 5 May, when he made the first of many visits to the University to address the Conservative Association.

The system by which the Secretariat then operated was that each front-bench spokesman was assigned a member of it as a 'private secretary', to help compensate for the lack of civil service support. Conservative MPs could call on the Secretariat's resources if a brief was required for a debate, or material was needed to put down a perplexing question for a minister. Powell was deputed to carry the bags of W. S. 'Shakes' Morrison, who had been Minister of Town and Country Planning in Churchill's coalition Government. Of necessity, Powell took on responsibility for policy in the areas of local government and housing. It suited him, as the question of how to rebuild Britain, and provide homes for the millions who needed them, was of deep and absorbing interest, not merely from the perspective of improving social conditions, but because of his belief that the virtual nationalisation of building land the Government had imposed was wrong. Powell's instinct then, as later, was to maximise the role of the private sector working through the market.

In this capacity, he had to spend part of his first few months in the Secretariat preparing a brief on the New Towns Bill. He also acted as secretary for the party's backbench Housing Committee, important at this time of reconstruction. As Maudling recalled, Powell set to work on reading all he could about the subject, and was ready by late April to start briefing. He was instinctively revolted by the Government's plans, which he felt proposed too much indiscriminate subsidy and too much central planning. In his first brief of 3 May 1946, he said he was worried that the need to attract employers to the new towns would be difficult to fulfil 'without dictatorial powers on the part of Government to control and direct both population and employment'. This meant a high level of government control over private industry 'with all that that implies'.[15]

His other main policy responsibility was to be defence. However, as soon as he had settled into the Secretariat he set about writing a lengthy memorandum to Butler on the subject closest to his heart – India – and of which he had the most recent, direct experience of anyone in the party machine. Other than furthering his own claims as an expert, the memorandum also had a sound political purpose. The Government's policy was felt to be weak and dangerous, and was something that most united the Conservatives against them. Powell soon became secretary of the parliamentary party's backbench committee on India.

His memorandum, sent to Butler on 16 May 1946, is more than 6,000 words in length. It starts from the solidly imperialist premise that 'the continuance of India within the British Empire is essential to the Empire's existence and is consequently a paramount interest both of the United Kingdom and of the Dominions'. The reasons for this interest were 'strategic, political, economic and moral'.[16] From this first substantive paragraph the answer to an apparent paradox about him is made immediately clear. Powell was a fervent imperialist so long as India was within the Empire. His anti-imperialism, which by the time he entered the Commons in 1950 was quickly growing, was simply a function of India's leaving the Empire and thereby devastating it.

He began by outlining the strategic value of India. Only, he said, by controlling the Indian Ocean and South-East Asia could Britain and the Empire guarantee security and the liberties of Australia and New Zealand: that was why those countries retained their tie to Britain. Were India to go, Britain could not guarantee those nations' security in time of war; the same was true of other parts of the Far Eastern Empire. He added that 'control of the Indian Ocean and unimpeded access to the Far East and to Australasia imply and require control of the whole Indian sub-continent'.[17] It was not enough simply to have air, sea or land bases there: 1942 had shown how the country could be defended only with 'full co-operation from the communications, resources and administration of the whole country ... it is a dangerous delusion to suppose that the Empire's interests in India could be covered by a military treaty of the type of the Anglo-Egyptian and Anglo-Iraq treaties ... for strategic purposes there is no half-way house between an India fully within the Empire and an India totally outside it'.

He felt that the next phase of imperial development was for countries populated predominantly by non-Europeans to achieve self-government within the Empire. As India was by far the largest and most important, what happened there would set the tone for all the other nations. 'Should it once be admitted or proved that Indians cannot govern themselves except by leaving the Empire – in other words, that the necessary goal of political development for the most important section of His Majesty's non-European subjects is independence and not Dominion status – then the logically inevitable outcome will be the eventual and probably the rapid loss to the Empire of all its other non-European parts.' This was exactly prophetic; and Powell voiced another fear that makes a mockery of the allegations of racialism flung at him twenty years later. 'It would extinguish the hope of a lasting union between "white" and "coloured" which the con-ception of a common subjectship to the King-Emperor affords and to which the development of the Empire hitherto has given the prospect of leading.'[18]

Powell said that to contemplate an Indian state or states independent outside the Empire was 'a betrayal for which no legal or moral justification can be cited'. There was no compulsion on Britain to recognise such a future for the country. 'Indeed, it is doubtful if His Majesty's ministers have the right to take deliberate steps calculated to result in a body of His subjects renouncing their allegiance.'[19] He lamented that the powerful arguments for remaining within the Empire had not been advanced 'to the majority of even educated Indians'. There is an obvious parallel between these sentiments and his later views on Ulster.

He sought to justify Britain's retention of her Indian, and African, empires on sound economic grounds: the might of the United States and the Soviet Union would 'crush' Britain as an economic power unless that power was countered with the help of the massive populations of the Empire. 'In discussion of the wealth of India,' said Powell, 'it is usual to forget the principal item, which is four hundred millions of human beings, for the most part belonging to races neither unintelligent nor slothful.'[20] Lest this seem too utilitarian, Powell added that there were strong moral arguments for the maintenance of India within the Empire: 'If India, becoming independent, falls prey, as it almost inevitably must, to internal strife and foreign intervention – becomes, so to say, a second China, the reproach of this cannot but fall on Britain,' he wrote.[21] It would be a sign that Britain was losing self-confidence and could not handle her responsi-bilities, particularly the responsibility of giving equal citizenship to 400 million people – an embarrassment the Labour Government, once it had given away India, was to feel so keenly that it framed the 1948 British Nationality Bill in the way it did, causing the legacy of problems that was to have so startling an effect on Powell's political career.

Powell set out a clear definition of Britain's duty: 'to create the preconditions of democracy and self-government by as soon as possible making India socially and economically a modern state'.[22] He also dictated why the need would remain for a viceroy; in accordance with the British constitutional practice, all executive power had to proceed from the King, having taken advice from his ministers. Therefore 'the people of British India, if self-governed within the Empire, must be governed by the King-Emperor's representative, acting on the advice of ministers responsible through a parliament or parliaments to an Indian electorate or electorates'; though he did concede that the King's representative could be elected rather than selected[23]. India could not be self-governed without a system of cabinet and parliamentary government. It was not merely a matter of historical logic that India should have this Westminster-style system; it would be morally impossible for Britain to allow her to have anything else, because of the catastrophe that would result.

Until democracy could be achieved, a 'caretaker' government, directly responsible to Westminster, would need to be established. There would also need to be a halt of the policy of Indianisation while this transition took place. 'There is clearly a limit', Powell wrote, 'to the reduction of the British element in the Government of India itself, in the officering of the Indian Army, in the troops of the Army of India, in the officering of the Police and in the Civil Service which is consistent with the British government being sure of its intentions and decisions being carried out.'[24] Given that no cabinet responsibility could yet exist, the appointment of Indians to senior posts would merely be tokenism, and would not help the essential discharge of British responsibility.

The main legacy of Powell's own time in India was his optimistic view of what could be achieved by Europeans and Asians working together. 'The political campaign against Britain', he wrote, 'has no relation to the actual feeling or behaviour of the peoples of India towards the individual Englishman or the British in India collectively. It is possible for an Englishman, in or out of uniform, to move freely up and down India, its industrial cities and its rural areas, from one year's end to another without encountering a single case of hostility, while, on the other hand, he will still be met with innumerable marks of his acceptance as an integral part of the structure of the country.' This was because 'modern India is so much a creation of Britain'.[25] He claimed that 'even the so-called nationalists' did not contemplate the 'literal removal' of British influence and control. Also, he believed from his own experience of talking to Indians that none of them would expect Britain to leave India in her present state: there was an expectation of the discharge of certain responsibilities, an expectation that Attlee and Mountbatten were shortly to explode.

Among the educated classes in particular, he argued, there were fears that the accepted structure of order would be broken down once the British left, and replaced by something far less desirable. However, while even the most extreme anti-British view was guaranteed a hearing within India, Indians who wished to advance the opposite viewpoint had little or no opportunity to do so. This was, he said, hardly surprising, since the British themselves were unwilling to advertise their own virtues: it could scarcely be wondered at that Indians were reluctant to do it for them. He made, too, the fundamental constitutional point that the King of England was the only person ever to have ruled over the whole of India; British rule had created the very conception of India. The monarchy in India, since the proclamation of November 1858 when the Government of India had been transferred from the East India Company to the Crown, had been identified with racial equality and political progress. This was not a link it would be wise to break, and its strength should be better advertised.

Now, in his memorandum, Powell moved to an assessment of the present crisis in India. He warned that 'the forces of disorder are endemic'.[26] He had the evidence of the Royal Indian Navy mutiny three months earlier as 'the infallible precursor of the coming storm'. The police force was unreliable, and the withdrawal of the British made civil administration a hit-and-miss affair. In another prophetic statement, he said that if there were an attempt to force the Indian parties to take on the Government 'an outbreak of violence in India such as will dwarf 1857 is not only likely but certain ... the scene is set for a tragedy which can probably no longer be prevented'.[27] The tragedy, and the clearing-up after it, would, he said, be Britain's responsibility. He drew a parallel with the aftermath of the Mutiny in 1857, when India had looked to Britain to restore order, and he wrote that 'it is surely not unreasonable to imagine that after witnessing in India the catastrophic outcome of recent policy, opinion in Britain would be prepared to back the measures necessary to restore order and administration throughout the sub-continent and thereafter to initiate and pursue a policy of bold and vigorous social and economic reorganisation as the preliminary to renewed constitutional advance'.

That meant, Powell said explicitly, that 'for some two generations ahead ultimate responsibility for the government of India will continue to be with Britain.' He was not, though, too explicit about the amount of military manpower that would be needed to restore, and maintain, order: 'There is no reason why in military resources the burden need be more onerous than in the past; indeed it may well prove less so.' He conceded that administrative manpower might have to be expanded, but said that was preferable to having a chaotic India outside the Empire. In the belief that Britain could shoulder this responsibility for years to come he was, for the first but not last time in his political life, engaging in a wishful thinking rooted in his failure to understand the willingness of the British political class to wash its hands of trouble as quickly, and as shamelessly, as possible.

He made some recommendations for Conservative policy. The priorities were these: 'to ensure that discredit for the impending catastrophe in India falls as fully and directly as possible upon the present Government: and to prepare the way for the Conservative Party, if called upon to do so, to take positive measures in the right direction when these become possible'.[28] Powell felt there were various 'helpful' statements the party could make in the interim, such as about the benefits of Dominion status within the Empire. The party should also urge the consultation of other Dominion governments about India's future, as they too would be affected by the loss of India; and it should not endorse any of the Government's Indian policy over and above anything that had been pursued by the coalition Government and which, therefore, it would be embarrassing to depart from now. He said the party should call for extensive parliamentary debate on any policies affecting India, as a transfer of responsibility was a transfer from the British people, whose representatives should be consulted on the matter so that they could be satisfied that any power being transferred was going to people able to discharge it properly. 'The constitution of a self-governing India is an act not of His Majesty's Government, but of the King in Parliament.'

He accepted that, in public, the party might have to take a non-committal attitude on the future of India, so as not to be opened up to accusations of exacerbating trouble, but that should not stop policy being developed in private. He urged Butler to allow research into a plan of social and economic reform, to go hand in hand with a more flexible political plan. Powell was sure that revolution and civil war would come to India, and equally sure that Britain's response would be to go in and assume full day-to-day control of the country. Butler read and considered his memorandum and, at the end of June – eight months before Mountbatten's appointment as Viceroy and the seismic events that sprang from that – asked Powell to go ahead and prepare an outline of the plans he had suggested were necessary.

<h2 style="text-align:center">II</h2>

In the late spring of 1946 David Clarke, who had recruited Powell, was moved to the Research Department, and the Secretariat came under the control of Henry Hopkinson, Clarke's deputy. It was the first important change in Powell's working regime; in the autumn, the Research Department would move to the premises it had occupied before the war in Old Queen Street, much nearer the Houses of Parliament, and the Secretariat would move with it. The bringing together of the two related functions under one roof was the obvious prelude to their eventual merger.

During his first year working for the party, Powell broadened his political interests and started to develop a better grasp of domestic issues, one of the most pressing of which was the housing crisis. This provided his first public entry into political battle, through the letters column of the *Sunday Times* in September 1946. He attacked a speech made by Aneurin Bevan, the Minister of Health, as 'an authoritative confession of the Government's failure in housing'.[29] He was provoked by Bevan's claim that the Government would be hard put to built the 750,000 houses it had promised as speedily as it would have liked because 'frivolous-minded people' were sidetracking labourers on black-market repairs. Powell asserted that, like everyone else, Bevan should have known of the existence of the black market and built it into his calculations. Powell's thirst for detail was also offended; he ridiculed Bevan's vague claim that 'in a few years' time we will have broken the back of the housing programme'.

Following the interest Strachan had awakened in him, Powell duly set about taking up hunting during the winter of 1946–7. His friends suspected that it was, in fact, a way for him to have some of the experience of physical danger denied him during the war – in keeping with Jorrocks's view. Powell had learned, after a fashion, to ride; but, typically, once back in England, he read all the most authoritative books on hunting before taking his first foray into the field.

He discovered the Old Berkeley East, a hunt on the edge of the Chilterns he could reach by the Underground. He would take a workman's ticket out on the Metropolitan Line dressed in his full kit, changing trains and picking up a hired horse at Gerrards Cross. Strachan's instruction had not been thorough enough; Powell told of how one of the 'bravest' things he had ever done was to turn up for cubbing in the wrong clothes, dressed as if going for a day's hunting. Nonetheless, allegedly, meeting the master after his first day out on a hunt he said: 'You're doing it all wrong.'[30] He revelled in the danger, his frequent falls simply spurring him on to take bigger risks. Ian Beddows, who rode with Powell often and would later chair his constituency party in Wolverhampton, said that 'he was a brave rider rather than a polished one'.[31]

Throughout the autumn of 1946 he continued to work on his second Indian memorandum, as requested by Butler. This involved, in the first instance, extensive research into the published government and viceregal papers about the conduct of Indian policy, and also investigation of the welter of statistics about the country's economic standing. The writing of the paper took several weeks, and Powell finally submitted it to Butler on 3 December 1946. It is a massive document, of more than 25,000 words, dealing in detail with Powell's plans for economic and social improvement in the country. Lord Wavell, the Viceroy, had already drawn up for the Government his own plan of withdrawal, which had failed to impress Attlee; and Attlee had begun the process whereby, a few weeks later, he would arrive at the choice of Mountbatten as Wavell's successor to complete a rapid exit from the sub-continent. It was felt by Attlee that the imperialist wing of the Conservative party had no plan for what they would do in lieu of withdrawal, but there was such a plan, and Powell had drawn it up. It was not, of course, a plan merely to enable Britain to discharge her historic responsibilities towards India, but one that would allow Powell the opportunity to accomplish his own ambitions.

The assumptions behind the second memorandum are outlined immediately: 'A general collapse of law and order in India, accompanied by a mutiny of the armed forces, has occurred and . . . Britain has interposed to restore the situation by force of arms.'[32] He assumed that the revolution had affected most of the country and that India was mostly under military administration; and he set out to answer the question 'what, on general principles, would be the right organisation to give to the country?' Starting from scratch, as it were, in these circumstances gave Britain and India a massive opportunity: 'At the end of a period of disorder, when previous institutions and habits have been shaken or broken, the minds of men are prepared for changes and innovations which at other times the strength of custom, the hostility of vested interests and the general inertia of an existing condition would render impossible.'[33] Above all, to start afresh brought with it 'the advantage of breaking once and for all through the atmosphere of hallucination which surrounds Indian politics'.[34]

Powell's main priority was developing means of economic advancement for the Indians. Showing still the senior staff officer's grasp of strategic imperatives, he argued that the opportunity would exist only for a short time; and the governors of India must have ready a clear plan to implement decisively as soon as the circumstances presented themselves. However, he felt the India Office at home was crippled by the half-belief (actually, it was more than that) that Britain was about to relinquish her responsibilities on the sub-continent; and the Government of India was paralysed and incapable of administering anything. The work of planning for the future, therefore, 'remains to be done, if it is done at all, by unofficial hands; and the present paper is an essay at the first phase of it'.[35]

Much of Powell's paper is given over to expositions and explanations of basic economic theory: he was manifestly under no illusions about the economic literacy of his masters for whom the paper was intended. He envisaged moving trade by trade, industry by industry, throughout the nation's economy, striving to improve efficiency and to redirect labour to other, more profitable occupations. The obvious starting point, as he saw it, was to improve productivity in agriculture, thus freeing up labourers to go and work in industry. He went into great detail about the rebuilding of infrastructure, the need to provide agricultural capital from sources other than usurious money-lenders, and a control over the land and its cultivation which might, in some extreme cases, involve nationalisation. It was important, in particular, that land was parcelled up into and farmed in economic units, and this would have to be achieved by state compulsion if necessary. The state could also take control of the marketing of crops, to ensure it was done with maximum efficiency. Constantly, and despite his excuses in the matter, one is struck by the contrast between Powell's view on salvaging the economy of India and those he would later seek to have implemented at home – though, as he also pointed out in his paper, state ownership of land in India was a long-established fact.

Having discussed similar programmes of increased efficiency for both industry and services, Powell said that the social improvements many Indians wanted would have to be postponed if the country were to prosper economically. There was a danger in expending the new profits from greater efficiency on welfare, social services and other social improvements, when it would have been better if they were ploughed back as capital into the industries that generated them. There were examples close to home of this disease: it was exactly what the Labour Government was doing with its American aid money, whereas defeated powers such as Germany were, instead, setting as a priority the re-establishment of an efficient industrial base.

The erudition and scope of Powell's paper are breathtaking, but even if they had been properly comprehensible to many in the party leadership – though Butler and Eden, the shadow Foreign Secretary, would certainly have both had the grasp needed to understand what Powell was saying, and to make the necessary challenges to some of his assumptions – time was running out. Attlee announced the appointment of Mountbatten as Viceroy ten weeks later, and Mountbatten proceeded to wind up the Empire in a little under six months. It is hard, in the light of the level of violence that tore through India in the following two years, to believe that the British Army would have been able to restore order as Powell had assumed: for, without that, the rest of his plan fell to pieces. In his memoirs, Butler recalls – as usual somewhat vaguely – the policy being outlined to him by Powell as being 'with ten divisions we could reconquer India'.[36] Butler goes on to say that, at Powell's request, he submitted the memorandum to Churchill, 'who seemed distressed and asked me if I thought Powell was "all right". I said I was sure he was, but explained that he was very determined in these matters.' Powell regarded this story – also retailed by T. E. 'Peter' Utley, who had it from Butler – as 'curious'.[37] He felt that Butler had misremembered his – Powell's – last activities in India, when he had been investigating the size of an army the Indians would need to defend their country, and not the army the British would need to hold the country against the wishes of the Indians.

Powell found time amid all his other activities to develop his Urdu, studying part-time for a diploma of the School of Oriental and African Studies at London University. What still drove him on was the indispensability such fluency in the language would have in his quest to be viceroy. He tried to cram all this into his day by arriving at his office early – rather as he had in Egypt and India – and dictating all his letters and memoranda in order to leave the rest of the day free for more creative work. His secretaries found this something of a strain, but he commanded their loyalty.

III

Powell's first chance to enter Parliament came in the arctic winter of 1947. A by-election was caused in the south Yorkshire seat of Normanton after the appointment of the sitting Labour member, Tom Smith, as labour director of the North-East Regional Coal Board. Powell's Labour opponent was a miner, George Sylvester. A miner's representative had held the seat since 1885, and Sylvester was defending a majority of 19,979. On 1 January 1947 – the day the coal industry was taken into public ownership – Powell volunteered to fight the seat, and was selected almost at once. He adopted the traditional optimism of the doomed by-election candidate. 'The important thing', he told the *Evening Standard*, 'is to get the case against Socialism heard from every platform, as often as possible.' The *Standard* further reported that 'Dominion and Indian affairs especially concern him', and he added: 'I have turned my back on academic life. My future is in politics.'[38] Although Central Office, realising the hopelessness of their candidate's task, sent up relatively few supporting speakers, Conservative activists swarmed in to help from the rest of Yorkshire. There were ten pits in the constituency, and Powell visited most of them. He held public meetings in every part of the division and made a heroically energetic canvass, considering the weather. 'I'm a believer in the canvass. The only real power base in politics is the doorstep, the only place where reality meets the candidate or member,' he would say later.[39] He would apply the logic of this throughout his career, scouring new electoral registers for details of newly registered voters, and then visiting them, to be aware of the changing nature of his constituency.

The local area agent, Colonel Bill Urton, devoted himself to help Powell put up the best possible performance: the two men began a lifelong friendship. Powell's chief volunteer helper was Mrs Charlotte Wainwright, who remembered a rather diffident candidate.

> He was very quiet and rather bewildered, I think, to find himself among a lot of miners. Rather sick-looking, but brilliant. He had to find his way in company, but he talked very straight to the miners and they seemed to get on with him. But he was so very quiet that I thought to myself: 'Now what on earth can I do with this man here?' I suppose it was because he was so shy. You could see his eyes roving about assessing everybody within range. His dress was rather too quiet and punctilious, but my goodness how he worked. It was hard work in hard weather with the two of us snatching meals at a local British restaurant.[40]

Powell's election address invited the public to cast a vote of censure against the Government by voting for him. He said that the well-laid plans of the coalition for national recovery had been ignored by Attlee, thereby driving down the standard of living and intensifying rationing. He railed against nationalisation, and the expansion of the public payroll, and argued that policy abroad, in Egypt, Palestine and Burma in particular, was leading to massacre of civilians and 'danger and humiliation' for British soldiers and policemen.[41] Although Powell was never going to win, it was perhaps a mistake to concentrate so much on 'Dominion and Indian affairs', of little interest in the West Riding coalfields. In his adoption speech on 30 January he warned that the difficulties Britain faced in Palestine and Egypt were nothing compared with 'graver dangers, notably in India and Burma'. In full imperialist mode, he warned that the socialist approach 'has threatened the eclipse of the whole Empire'.[42] In a further affirmation of faith, he said that the Empire 'is the structure on which we are dependent for our very existence', a claim he would start, inwardly, to repudiate within weeks. The Brigadier appealed to the 1,500 ex-servicemen in the constituency to support him. His main slogan was 'Had enough of not enough? Vote for Powell on February 11th'.

The weather closed in again at the start of the main campaign on 29 January. If it were not bad enough that so few senior Conservative speakers were scheduled to come to Normanton, some who did were stranded on snowbound trains. When bad weather prevented the arrival of R. S. Hudson, the former Minister of Agriculture, Powell – who had already made one speech – promptly made another. The Yorkshire Post reported that 'Although Mr Powell had spoken once, he faced the contretemps imperturbably. For a second time, he expounded Conservative policy, and his audience of mining folk listened with obvious interest.'[43] The weather did not improve. A shovel became an essential canvassing tool, to clear snowdrifts. Power cuts hindered the candidates' organisations. Powell estimated that only one house in four of those he wanted to visit could be reached because of the weather. He struggled on, often addressing three meetings each night, outnumbered and outgunned by his socialist opponent and his supporters. There was some recognition in the press of Powell's efforts. Towards the end of the campaign, the Yorkshire Post's special correspondent wrote, 'Mr Powell is a fluent speaker with the vigorous personality one would expect from a man who, joining the army as a private in 1939, rose to the rank of brigadier. Although he admits he has a formidable task in this Socialist stronghold, it is evident he has made a favourable impression on the electorate.'[44]

On 7 February Powell stepped up his rhetoric, saying that his impression of Nazi Germany on his visit there in 1938 was similar in one respect to that of Britain in 1947:

> People are already in many parts of the country reluctant to disclose their political views for fear of jeopardising their employment or livelihood under the State or a public authority. Parliament is treated more and more like a rubber stamp Reichstag, while the real legislative powers are translated to Ministers of the Crown. The Gestapo, as yet in a mild form and under the reassuring title of inspectors or enforcement officers, pry into our private affairs to see if we are breaking any of the multitudinous orders and regulations by which our lives and actions are restricted, and actually try to tempt us into committing offences so that they can prosecute us.[45]

Powell manifestly had no qualms about echoing Churchill's own controversial comparison between Labour and the Gestapo, which was felt to have contributed to his party's heavy defeat in 1945.

Butler wrote privately to Powell on 5 February, mainly to console him for what he called the 'flop' of a visit Powell had made to speak for him in the village of Great Bardfield in his constituency. He also said, 'I want you to know how much I value this friendly act. I hope you are looking after yourself.'[46] Churchill sent him a public letter of support. 'Thus we hope', the former Prime Minister wrote, 'to create by enterprise and good national housekeeping that property-owning democracy without which individual freedom cannot be enjoyed by the mass of the people. I hope that the electors of the Normanton division will by now have had their eyes opened to the hollowness of Socialist pretensions, to the fallacies of their doctrines, and the incapacity of their management.'[47]

They had not. Sylvester held the seat with a majority of 14,827, polling 19,085 votes to Powell's 4,258. A local doctor had entered the race at the last minute as an independent and took 579 votes, mostly, Powell suspected, from him. Powell was unperturbed: 'The Socialist vote, compared with the General Election, has fallen 32 per cent, whereas the Conservative has fallen only 19 per cent. The Socialist majority in the General Election was 55 per cent of the electorate, and that has fallen to 34 per cent.'[48] This concealed, though, the obvious truth that it is hard for a party in possession to get its vote out at a by-election because of complacency; it was, despite the appalling weather, not a great result for Powell. He was, though, upbeat when he reported the outcome to Strachan on 12 March 1947. 'Though everyone competent to judge was pleased with Normanton, it was bitter that the weather, the lunatic of a third candidate and the fuel crisis (yes!) prevented it from being what without those factors it could have been. However, that is all forgotten; and I wait with the patience of deep impatience for the election that I shall win.'[49] The consensus in the press was that the Conservatives could take no great satisfaction from the outcome; the *Yorkshire Post*, though, did say that Powell 'proved to be a thinker as well as a man of action. Many even of those who voted against him will foresee for him a great political career.'[50]

Powell sent a memorandum to Jim Thomas, the MP in charge of the candidates' list, on his return to London. He said that but for the third candidate and the shocking weather he could have polled up to 5,500 votes.[51] He criticised the shortage of speakers from the front bench, made worse by Hudson's accidental absence at the start of the campaign. Also, with the exception of the *Yorkshire Post*, no newspaper except the *Daily Herald* had given any coverage to Powell's effort. Above all, he was upset by Lord Woolton, the party chairman: 'The fact that the Chairman of the Party gave no indication of being aware that there was a by-election, either by private communication with the candidate or the association or in any other way, was noticed in the constituency and tended to increase the impression that little interest was taken in the result by London,' he told Thomas. It contrasted with the effort from the Conservatives' local area organisation and constituency associations which, Powell said, was exemplary. The Normanton association unanimously congratulated Powell on the way he had fought the seat, saying that 'no candidate could have done better'.[52] At least he had convincingly passed the first main test in his political career.

This was, though, a difficult time for him. On 20 February Attlee announced the appointment of Mountbatten, with the intention of bringing India to independence as soon as possible. Powell's hopes were shattered. The whole basis for his entry into politics had been removed. It was 'a shock so severe that I remember spending the whole of one night walking the streets of London trying to come to terms with it'.[53] So traumatised was he that he could recall the exact details of his shock forty-two years later, in a conversation with Peter Hennessy. During that night 'occasionally I sat down in a doorway, my head in my hands'.[54] He believed that the Americans, as Britain's *de facto* economic masters, had been the main influence behind the policy, and had now fulfilled one of their main war aims. One of Powell's biographers, Humphry Berkeley, without much exaggeration described this moment of catastrophe as 'a spiritual amputation from which Powell has never recovered'.[55]

When, in June 1947, the Conservative party decided not to oppose the Government's Indian policy, Powell was so distressed by Churchill's decision that he made his first political resignation, from the secretaryship of the party's India Committee. He asked to be relieved of it rather than support what he felt to be a sham and a mistake. In his letter of resignation he argued that by pledging unconditional support of the legislation to grant India independence, without yet knowing what the new Indian legislature would be, the party had agreed to support a Bill that was 'a blank cheque, signed in the dark'.[56] He felt the party had repudiated its previous, principled stand that authority for India could be transferred 'only to a Government or Governments capable of exercising it'. Churchill had restated this in a Commons debate on 5 March; it was a breach, Powell warned, that 'if I were a Member, I should find myself obliged to oppose'. He felt the debacle that would attend upon independence was one the Conservatives would be well advised to stand clear of, and there was no obligation for them to support this latest twist in the Government's policy. It was a first, and uncomfortable, lesson to him of the compromises expected in the career he had chosen.

The letter was typed for him by his new secretary, Pamela Wilson. The daughter of an Indian Army colonel, she had been born in Liverpool, educated at Wycombe Abbey, and had spent two and a half of the first five years of her life on the sub-continent. Now twenty-one, she had started three years earlier as a shorthand typist in the War Cabinet and the Ministry of Defence, with the Chiefs of Staff Secretariat, after a year's training at a secretarial college. She had just returned from New York, after a year working for the United Kingdom delegation of the Military Staff Committee of the United Nations. She was hugely interested in and excited by politics, and a natural Tory. Highly efficient, with her service upbringing she had been considered an ideal secretary for the Brigadier. Nor, before long, was she intimidated by him, and had a competition with the other secretaries to see whether any of them could get this normally curt man to return a cordial greeting of 'good morning' on the way into the office. She was determined to break the ice, even though for some time the relationship remained formal.

Powell vented his feelings about India to Strachan in his letter of 12 March. He said it 'is not as appalling as it sounds – it is much more so. The fate of British honour is now in the balance again as in 1938–9. The consequences, as then, will be terrible one way and fatal the other. But I do not trust myself to write on the topic.' He forced himself to make an immediate psychological break with what was soon to be the past. Writing to Strachan on 9 August, days before the Union flag was run down for the last time over India, he rebuked his friend for not having come to visit him in 'the capital of our former Empire'.[57] For the first time, but not the last, Powell had invested effort and emotion in a cause that turned out hopeless, though other causes that looked that way did, like his economic doctrine and his view of the dangers of Europe, turn out less hopeless than had once seemed the case. Among those senior members of the party with whom he shared his anger was Harold Macmillan, who came to see him in June 1947 about housing. After their meeting, Macmillan wrote to Powell, 'I quite understand your point of view about India and admire it.'[58]

Although the loss of India had apparently removed Powell's reason for becoming a Member of Parliament, new reasons replaced it. He had frequently to attend the Commons, then sitting in the House of Lords while its own bomb-damaged chamber was rebuilt, and had become deeply attracted to it as an institution. 'The House of Commons took possession of me. It seemed to me the most wonderful thing that here was this assembly, and it alone made the laws, it alone sustained the Government of the United Kingdom.'[59] He saw this as the essence of British nationality, and admitted it had made the question of nationality 'an obsession' with him. He realised that, hitherto, he had been 'woefully ignorant and unreflective' about the Commons, a deficiency he was now eagerly rectifying.[60] As he watched the proceedings of the House, Powell felt 'an immensely strong affinity in myself with this institution'. That was reason enough, now, for him to wish to be a part of it. For the next forty years, 'to be and to remain a member of the House of Commons was the overriding and undiscussable motivation of my life as a politician'. As he said in an interview almost fifty years later, 'I fell head over heels under the spell of the House of Commons. I said, "this is wonderful, this is what I want" … the vision of this place whose decisions and words are hung upon by a nation; it was the incarnation of a nation to me.'[61]

IV

When Powell had been appointed to lead the Secretariat's defence studies it had been hoped he would soon move on to some other area; but the summer of 1947 found him still engrossed in this subject. He was still researching and writing briefs on town and country planning, but defence was of more importance to the party than the use of land – whatever the principles at stake – and Powell had to brief Eden for the army debate at the end of July. Numbers were being run down badly and recruitment was a problem, which gave the Conservatives ample scope to score points. As when Powell himself was defence spokesman twenty years later, financial stringencies mocked a Labour government's attempts to have a defence policy based on national strategic needs.

Powell attended the Conservative backbench Army Committee, where he found himself in the comfortable presence of several other former soldiers; he still chose to be known in the Secretariat and among those with whom he came into contact professionally as 'Brigadier Powell'. He struck up a good relationship with Anthony Head, the committee's chairman, who like Powell had served as a brigadier in Intelligence, though unlike him had been a career soldier. Throughout the winter of 1947–8 Powell briefed Head on the failures of army recruitment policy, indicating questions that could profitably be put down. Head was grateful for Powell's input on the Army Committee, writing to 'Dear Powell' on 30 December 1947 that 'you have been its main prop and stay ... As a Parliamentary spiv I salute the workers of Old Queen Street and hope they don't start a union.'[62]

One great advantage to Powell of his job was that it provided him – and, for all his accomplishments, he was in the context of the immediate post-war Conservative party at a social disadvantage – with an entrée to the higher reaches of the party. This was not just through his day-to-day contact with Butler, or his occasional assistance to Eden or even Churchill. He could also meet Head, and the other MP brigadiers who consulted him on matters of policy, like Otho Prior-Palmer or Toby Low, on a level of equality. Immediately after the 1947–8 Christmas recess Powell was closeted with Head's committee again, this time discussing the reform of the court-martial system.

In his spare time he was reviving an intellectual life. He had brought out his Herodotus again, with a view to completing the translation of it into biblical English that he had devoted the first hour of each day to at Cambridge, and which had been three-quarters finished at the outbreak of war. He finished it in 1948, having it published the following year by the Clarendon Press. He argued that the eccentric choice of prose style was appropriate: 'the simple and flowing language of Herodotus needs least remoulding for modern English ears if presented in the style and cadences rendered familiar by the Bible, and that a certain quaintness and archaism thereby imparted make an impression not dissimilar from that which the Ionic original must have made upon Attic readers in the twenties of the fifth century BC'.[63] He had been thinking about writing a book on Disraeli; but above all was attracted to the idea of embarking upon a history of the House of Lords, to the point of looking round for a publisher prepared to give him a contract. The stimulus was the research he had undertaken for briefings on Labour's plans to reform the Lords; it also turned him from one with a casual liking for history to one with an almost obsessive interest in it, particularly in constitutional history. He spent much of his spare time over the years ahead reading many of the classic Victorian historians – Green, Macaulay, Froude and the like.

He also had an active winter hunting with the Old Berkeley, though he admitted to his mentor, Strachan, that his experiences were 'chequered'; they managed to go out together on Boxing Day 1947. Three weeks later Powell had what he described to Strachan as 'a disastrous day' with the Old Berkeley: 'quite my worst performance ever; but perhaps my riding has to get worse before it gets better. The moment of "getting its goat" has apparently not yet arrived.'[64]

Part of the problem – and it would get worse – was the lack of time Powell had for his new recreation. He had attended the Conservative party conference in October 1947; and, also that month, as head of the local government secretariat, he made a speech stating that the first task in any local government reorganisation was to constitute councils so they could deliver a wide range of services and yet remain genuine communities. Such speechmaking was becoming a more usual part of his routine as a prospective candidate. On Secretariat business, he had spent much of December 1947 and January 1948 in rural Wales, collecting information for the party's policy on the Principality – it had been asked by the party conference to devise one to encourage a Conservative vote there – and speaking engagements arranged for him took him away from his hunt on other days. 'How can a fellow improve his riding with three week gaps?' he asked Strachan plaintively. 'You really will have to take me in hand again – you are neglecting your duty, having entangled me in this pursuit, to enable me to follow it with competence.'

As well as assisting the party's Commons Army Committee, Powell found his services being called upon more and more by the Conservative peers' committee on the same subject. This was run by Lord Bridgeman, a major-general who had held high military office during the war. He and Powell soon established a good relationship, though inevitably one less familiar and more deferential – on Powell's part – than that with Head. During the spring of 1948 Powell regularly attended the peers' committee too, and wrote briefs for Bridgeman on the Army and Air Force (Annual) Bill, for Lord Long on Territorial Army accommodation, and for Lord De L'Isle on married quarters for servicemen. Yet he had to write sternly to Bridgeman on 15 March 1948, rebuking another peer, Lord Mancroft, for a speech the previous weekend. Mancroft, who was then in his early thirties and whose enthusiasm exceeded his experience, had said 'most of the blame' for the failure of the Territorial Army to recruit properly 'rests with the Trade Unions' for discouraging ordinary men from 'siding with the bosses'. Powell told Bridgeman that this assertion was 'grossly unfair' and 'also extremely inexpedient'. He was afraid Mancroft had given the impression that the Conservatives wanted to urge some form of compulsion on the unions when it came to recruiting for the reserve.[65]

Wales took up more and more of Powell's time. In his first report, on rural matters, delivered on 20 January 1948, he said that ministerial representation for the Principality was a 'sine qua non'.[66] He followed this with a report on industrial Wales, submitted on 26 May 1948, and based on conversations between 23 April and 5 May with representatives of twenty-two constituencies. This, too, was a full survey of conditions. In it, Powell recommended a new housing policy, urging that a statement of Conservative policy be issued 'without delay'. He suggested a pressure group of peers be formed to ask questions in the Lords – the Commons being too busy.[67] A note of realism crept into his conclusion: 'It would be idle to pretend that without sustained and generous financial support, to start and keep up agents and offices and to fight elections, the grip of Socialism on South Wales can be loosened or the foothold of Conservatism in the valleys extended.'

One of Powell's other main duties that spring was to research the effects of the British Nationality Bill. Lord Simon, who had served in governments since the Edwardian era and was an eminent lawyer, told Powell not to be concerned about what he feared were the implications of the proposed law on citizenship, which would allow massive entry of ethnically non-British 'British subjects' from the colonies. Similarly unconcerned was David Maxwell Fyfe, the party's main home affairs spokesman. Powell, though, was worried, his concept of nationhood being romantic in practice but logical in principle. He took every opportunity to denounce the measure both before and after its passage in law. He regarded it as a legal fiction.

The situation before 1948 was relatively unreal, since it defined all those born within the Dominions of the Crown as within the allegiance to the Crown. There had been no attempt at mass immigration, so there was little practical relevance to this widespread citizenship. Powell argued that the law would become more unrealistic as more and more countries followed India's lead and quitted the allegiance. Also, in the brief he sent to the shadow cabinet on 5 July 1948, in advance of the second reading* of the Bill two days later, he pointed

* After a Bill has been published and made available to every MP and Peer, a formal debate usually lasting at least most of a parliamentary day takes place, followed by a vote or 'division' of the House. Provided the Bill is approved by a simple majority of those voting, it moves on to the Committee Stage.

out that there was no reason for the Government to be rushing the measure at the tail-end of a session; but, with Labour's large majority, and given the widespread indifference of the Conservative party, the Bill passed serenely on its way. Appropriately, its after-effects were to dog Conservative cabinets throughout almost the whole of the thirteen years of their rule after 1951.

The 1948 Bill substituted a new definition of citizenship – or, to be more accurate, subjectship – for the old one. Citizens of a list of self-governing countries, and not just of countries directly governed by Britain, were to be designated 'citizens of the United Kingdom and Colonies'. As Powell said in a speech more than twenty years later, this was the moment when United Kingdom citizenship law became divorced from reality: 'It recognised a citizenship to which no nation of even the most shadowy and vestigial character corresponded; and conversely, it still continued not to recognise the nationhood of the United Kingdom.'[68] It was a matter of months after the passing of the Act before its main consequence – the mass immigration from what became known as the 'New Commonwealth', began. Powell's view followed on from his recognition of the change in his outlook after the surrender of India the previous year. He now felt Britain should be unchanged by the passage of Empire; that, as a nation, she had never depended on the Empire for her self-awareness or identification – an idea he would be forced publicly to contradict at the next two elections. He exorcised from his spirit the idea of the nation he had formerly held. As he said nearly forty-five years later: 'If somebody had asked me in 1939 "What are you coming home to fight for?" I would have said "the Empire". By the end of the forties I had worked myself through to the perception that what really mattered was the way in which the English, here on this piece of island territory, managed their affairs.'[69]

The measure had been partly provoked by a decision of the Canadian Government in 1945 to create a separate citizenship for its country, which had been established by its Citizenship Act of the following year. The Canadians chose to define the term 'British Subject' differently from how it was defined in Britain; the Bill was supposed to regularise the definition. The need to revise the notion of imperial citizenship was discussed after the Commonwealth Prime Ministers' conference of the same year, and given new impetus by the end of the Raj. The Government accepted advice from civil servants that, despite the creation of separate citizenships, the inhabitants of those Dominions (including India and Pakistan) should become 'Commonwealth Citizens' while those still under British rule should become citizens of 'the United Kingdom and Colonies'; that would give these citizens, who were mostly of non-British descent, the right to come into the United Kingdom. It was this notion that Powell, the former imperialist, wanted to stop.

As Paul Foot has pointed out, in his detailed analysis of this Nationality Act, it did not introduce a right of free entry, but merely rationalised it.[70] As Foot

also says, much Conservative opposition to it was based not on Powell's fear
that the door might be opened to unrestricted immigration, but on the fear that
the differentiation between Commonwealth citizens and citizens of the United
Kingdom and Colonies would lead to many of the King's subjects being denied
the traditional hospitality of the Mother Country – from whose people most of
those in the self-governing dominions were descended. However, Maxwell Fyfe
clearly said that 'what I am asking for is the maintenance of the old basis of
subjecthood, based on allegiance': which, had it been the case, would soon have
eliminated India when she became a republic, Pakistan in 1956 when she ceased
to be a monarchy, and the West Indian colonies during the 1960s when they
achieved independence.[71]

The 'problem', as Powell would define it twenty years later, would not have
been eliminated, but it would have been reduced in scale. It was the subsequent
divorce of nationality from allegiance that was to fuel his antipathy to immigration policy until the explosion of 1968, though he would keep his own counsel
on the matter for years yet. Foot is wrong to say Powell opposed the Bill in 1948
because it 'wrote into British subject law the distintegration of the Empire'. His
letter to Strachan of the previous August confirms that Powell knew the Empire
was disintegrating without any help from the Nationality Bill; with his logical
mind, all he wanted was to ensure that the prize of citizenship was not conferred
on those who had lost the right to it by going outside the allegiance. The
difficulty with the Bill was that its provisions, as outlined at the second reading
in the House of Commons by the Home Secretary, Chuter Ede, on 7 July 1948,
were soon expanded to cover those who owed no allegiance to the Crown. The
Bill was ambitious: Ede told the Commons its 'essential feature' was 'that each
of the self-governing Commonwealth countries shall determine by its own
legislation who are its citizens and shall declare those citizens to be British
subjects; and shall recognise as British subjects the citizens of all the other
countries of the Commonwealth'.[72] In other words, the creation of a person's
right to enter the United Kingdom was to be taken out of the hands of the
British Government.

Ede also categorically set the Government against any notion that 'it would
be a bad thing to give the coloured races of the Empire the idea that, in some
way or other, they are the equals of people in this country'.[73] He said that 'we
believe wholeheartedly that the common citizenship of the United Kingdom
and Colonies is an essential part of the development of the relationship between
this Mother Country and the Colonies'. Thus the door was opened, and Powell,
in the officials' box in the House of Lords, could only watch. Maxwell Fyfe, in
the same debate, argued for a Conservative amendment made in the Lords to
alter the notion of citizenship of the United Kingdom and Colonies: not for
the reasons Powell had advanced, but because the distinction thereby created
impaired Maxwell Fyfe's wish to 'maintain our great metropolitan tradition of

hospitality to everyone from every part of our Empire'.[74] These notions, rooted in sentiment rather than reality, were underlined by Maxwell Fyfe's assertion that 'it is through that ability to improve through change that our Commonwealth and Empire has lasted while other similar institutions have gone with Nineveh and Tyre'.[75]

V

Although Powell was trying to spend more time on home affairs, defence still occupied much of his attention. He was constantly asked to field inquiries from Conservative MPs' constituents about the terms and conditions of military service, and more often than not he was able to bring his own experience to bear. In reply to one query about whether the punishment for desertion should be reformed, Powell stated simply that it was important it remained 'for the sake of discipline in the services'.[76] Many MPs were swamped by complaints about the new policy of conscription, often from mothers seeking exemption, on nebulous grounds, for their sons; Powell's replies were as stern and incomprehending as one would expect from a man who had rushed across the globe to join up and, he hoped, be killed in action.

There were many complaints, too, about officers' pay, a recurrent theme being that with the decline of the private income many soldiers could not survive on what the Government paid. Powell was firm on this too. He answered one, passed on to him by a colleague, thus: 'It is public policy that there should be no inducement to a Regular Officer to marry in the early twenties, and I have no reason to suppose that the Party is in disagreement with this policy. Nobody obliged Lieutenant Johnson of the King's Dragoon Guards to marry at the age of 20 or less when he was perfectly aware of the financial consequences and was intending a career as a Regular Officer. He has therefore no complaint.'[77]

Powell was less adept than more clubbable colleagues – notably Maudling – in being taken up by party grandees, not least because of his reserved and austere manner. However, in time he visited Chartwell (where Maudling was soon a veritable habitué) to brief Churchill, and saw much of Eden, particularly on defence. Butler was his main link with the top table, better able than most, no doubt, to handle Powell's radical divergences from the party line. Other senior spokesmen were less fortunate. When Oliver Lyttelton asked for a brief about Labour's plans to introduce conscription, Powell provided it with his customary efficiency and thoroughness. 'He [Lyttelton] came into the office and said to me: "But this is a brief against it! We're supporting it!" '[78] Eden had a similarly quizzical impression, relayed years later to Andrew Freeth, who was painting him. When the conversation turned to Powell, Eden apparently said: 'Ah, Enoch, dear Enoch! He once said something to me I never understood. He said, "You know, I've told you all I know about housing, and you can make your speech accordingly. Can I talk to you about something that you know all about and I know nothing? I want to tell you that in the Middle East our great enemies are the Americans." You know, I had no idea what he meant.' The conversation with Freeth took place after Suez, and Eden ruefully added the observation: 'I do now.'[79]

In July 1948 Powell was again on the attack against Bevan, accusing him of misrepresenting Lord Woolton in the matter of the number of houses private enterprise should be allowed to build, in which Woolton seemed to be at odds with other senior Conservative spokesmen. Again, Powell harried Bevan for his failure to determine the facts: he had accused Woolton of wanting one house in four to be allowed for the private sector; in fact Woolton had said one house in three. Powell did not, though, clear up the question of why Walter Elliott, a Conservative former health minister, had called for a ratio of one in two. Even as early as then, Powell was in constant conflict with what he saw as incorrect thinking by less rigorous adherents of the anti-statist line than he was. On 31 March 1949 he wrote to David Clarke complaining that it had been advocated by some Conservatives that tribunals should continue to assess 'fair rents'. Powell said this mechanism was 'arbitrary' and 'unsound in itself' and 'hardly one to which the Conservative Party should give assent gratuitously'.[80]

During 1948 some of the defence workload was taken off Powell by a younger man, Peter Hodgens, a former army officer. However, there were still some thorny issues Powell had to deal with himself. Lord Long told Hodgens – who passed the problem up to Powell – in August 1948 that he was concerned by Churchill's reluctance to support a new recruiting campaign for the Territorial Army that had been launched by Manny Shinwell, the Minister of Defence, and which had the declared support of many Conservative MPs. Long had surmised that Churchill's behaviour was prompted by a detestation of Shinwell, but Hodgens told Powell that 'the position is that action, if any, rests squarely with you'.[81] On this occasion, Powell decided for once that discretion was the better part of valour.

After a short further trip to Wales, to meet industrialists in Wrexham and Holywell at the end of August 1948, Powell went to Porlock in Devon for a fortnight's riding holiday. He told Strachan that 'I have never enjoyed any holiday, not even with you, so much in my life. I came second in the school jumping competition.'[82] The break, although the Secretariat were in regular contact with him while he was away, preceded an intensification of his political life. In November 1948 Butler merged the Secretariat with the Research Department. The new body had four sections, and Powell and Macleod were jointly to control home policy; Maudling was given economic affairs. David Clarke, who assigned Powell to his new post, did so because of the capacity he had shown for mastering intricate detail in the preceding two years.[83] Clarke was one of the few to discover the best way of taking Powell on: not to question his arguments and conclusions, since they were always so well composed logically, but to question the hypotheses and assumptions from which they were drawn.

Powell's next main task, though, was to research and help write a pamphlet on party policy for Wales – the *Charter for Wales* – published on St David's Day 1949. He had been travelling around the Principality again during the preceding months, and returned that autumn for further consultations on policy with Conservative activists. Once the pamphlet was published, depending on which end one started from, one could read it in either English or Welsh, though Powell did not bring his own linguistic talents to bear on this – the translation was done by a Welsh clergyman. Pamela Wilson had to type the translation, and Powell gave her a Hugo's *Welsh in Two Weeks* to help her; it was to no avail, and in the end it had to be typed by a native Welsh speaker.

The notion of the 'charter' was a political fashion among Conservatives at the time, keen as they were to find an easily comprehensible way of setting out the improvements they planned to make for the people. Powell was also engaged on another, the Industrial Charter, but with less happy results. After weeks of preparation the charter was due to be published; but, to his and his colleagues' horror, Powell read that the essence of its proposals had been delivered, unsanctioned, in a weekend speech by Macmillan. 'An act', Powell recalled half a century later, 'of what Rab Butler called political kleptomania . . . typical Harold Macmillan'.[84]

Although his campaign in Normanton had done no discredit to Powell, throughout 1947 and 1948 he approached nineteen other constituencies without finding a seat for the general election. They did not all reject him: he was quite choosy, and rejected some of them himself, such as seats in Coventry, Birmingham and London that he deemed too marginal. By late 1948 he was becoming tense about the matter: he was now thirty-six, about five years older than many others who were looking for seats, and beginning to feel in a hurry. If he could not place himself well for the next election, he might be forty-two or -three before having a decent chance of being elected. He had close shaves at Beckenham, Nottingham Central and Oswestry in the autumn of 1948, but just could not find the right formula to be selected. His next opportunity was an invitation to meet the selectors at Harrow Central. Macleod, who had secured a winnable seat at Enfield two years earlier, now came to Powell's aid. He sent him a draft speech that he, with Maudling's assistance, had drawn up for Powell to use when before a selection committee. 'I personally (so would Reggie) would absolutely guarantee to win H[arrow] C[entral] with it just as it stands,' Macleod told him.[85] He invited Powell to add to his draft some personal reminiscences 'humourous [sic] if possible', and added: 'If you use any or all of it for God's sake don't rewrite it into what you call English. Where I'm ungrammatical I mean to be. Where I'm (slightly) dishonest I mean to be.' Powell was, certainly

later in life, an infinitely more amusing man than his public demeanour suggested, but it is hard to imagine him delivering some of Macleod's jokes, such
as: 'You will have heard (and heard I expect with some alarm) that I was a
Professor of Greek in Sydney University at the age of 25. I plead in defence that
I can speak fairly good English as well.' More plausible would be Powell's
agreement with the view that, having been both, 'it's a damn sight easier to be
an efficient Brigadier than an efficient private soldier'.[86] The draft speech ends
with the stage direction 'prolonged applause'.

Either Powell did not use it at Harrow Central, or it did not work. However,
in December 1948, shortly after what he thought had been a good interview at
Ealing, he arrived at Wolverhampton South-West, a compact, entirely urban
seat, to try his luck there. Ostensibly, the sitting candidate, Patrick Stirling,
had decided to withdraw; this was a euphemism. Stirling said that 'it is impossible for me to afford the time apparently looked for by the new divisional
executive committee'. In fact, he was forced out because the executive, which
was badly split, simply did not feel he had the necessary qualities to wrest a
highly marginal seat from Labour, whose sitting member, H. D. Hughes, was
a much respected and assiduous MP. This would have been a difficult manoeuvre at the best of times, but was made harder by the fact that Stirling was
the son-in-law of the president of the association. It reflected a keenness for
politicking among the activists that would cause the new candidate some
problems too.

On the night of Powell's selection, one of the association's activists, Mary
Westwood, was sitting in the same room as those waiting to be interviewed. Her
job was to try to break the ice and relax the candidates, one of whom, she
recalled, was 'this rather unusual looking man called Enoch Powell'; another
hopeful and his wife were also in the room. Miss Westwood recalled that
'suddenly the central heating pipes started making an odd gurgling sound . . .
the other candidate's wife made some remark about it – adding, more to make
conversation than anything else: "I wonder why heating pipes make that noise?" '
Powell, of course, was not one to go in for the mere making of conversation. He
had heard a question asked, and he was able to answer it, as Miss Westwood
noted. 'Enoch Powell at once launched into a full-scale explanation. It went on
for several minutes and by the time he had finished there wasn't much left to
know about central heating pipes. He even made it quite interesting. I remember
being quite astonished by this man called Powell.'[87]

Inside the committee room, the selectors were warned by their chairman
before Powell made his entrance: 'Don't be put off by appearances.' Clement
Jones, who was covering the event for the Wolverhampton *Express and Star* – of
which he would later become editor – and who would later become a close
friend of Powell's, recalls him then as being 'not the candidate the smart money
would have been on'.[88] Stanley Tatem, a member of the committee and a future

mayor of Wolverhampton, recalled: 'It was as well [the chairman] warned us. Powell came in with his short hair on end and his bulging eyes ... but as soon as he opened his mouth we knew we were on to something. I think we felt, even then, that we had a potential prime minister on our hands.' The rest of the committee were equally impressed, and told the press it would unanimously recommend the association to adopt Powell, a local man of high accomplishments with whom the committee felt far more comfortable than they had with their last candidate. Powell returned to London overnight by train, to find he had been offered the candidacy at Ealing as well, on the unanimous vote of the committee there; but Wolverhampton had it, for Powell had accepted their nomination, and he was formally adopted on 17 December 1948.

Stirling took his replacement by Powell badly, so much so that he wrote in petulant terms on 12 December to Woolton, as party chairman, to complain. His main grievance was a promise Powell had given to spend four days a week in the constituency – far more time than Stirling had been able to devote; and Stirling felt Powell had been given an unfair advantage by the party. He admitted to Woolton that he felt 'rather sore' at being 'unhorsed', saying Powell had been 'authorised' to work four days a week in the constituency while on the party's payroll. 'Here, apparently, is a man employed by the Conservative Party and paid largely from funds subscribed by supporters, saying that he will be able to leave his desk in London for three days out of five and be in Wolverhampton for four. While we less fortunate devils have to earn our livings during most of the week.' Powell, he argued, was being paid a week's salary for two days' work – allowing him to 'unhorse' Stirling.

Hopkinson told Woolton that, when Butler had offered Powell the joint headship of the Internal Affairs Section, Powell had wanted to decline on the ground that he was looking for a seat and might have to spend much time doing so. Butler said that 'he was sure arrangements could be made so that he could devote whatever time was necessary to the constituency'. Powell had told the selection committee that, if necessary, he would give up all or part of his present work; pressed, he said he would give four days a week averaged out over the year. He was angry that Stirling had been told of an exchange at a private meeting, and Hopkinson advised Woolton to reply in those terms. One of Woolton's assistants was told to 'send a very strong letter to Stirling, who is behaving abominably'. Stirling was suspected, too, of having leaked the story to the *Daily Telegraph*'s Peterborough column, which further stoked up anger at Central Office. He was duly rebuked for his 'monstrous conclusion' made 'without knowledge of the facts' that Woolton had asked for another £200,000 so that he could pay people for work they were not doing: 'I hope that you regret making it.'[89]

VI

Initially, Powell was restrained about his prospects. Telling Strachan of his selection, he added that it was 'not a matter for much congratulation for, although certain to be won, there may not be as much margin as I should like, and it is in any case a hard constituency inconveniently situated'.[90] The Conservative area agent for the West Midlands told Powell he was stunned he had accepted Wolverhampton South-West; he had been offered, and turned down, the Brierley Hill seat in the same area, which was thought to be much safer – but which was not, in fact, won by the Conservatives until 1955. Powell was becoming bored with the Secretariat, which he confided in Strachan he was minded to give up, the election being expected before too long. He had started to dabble on the fringes of journalism, but progress on his House of Lords book was 'fearfully slow', and his restless, romantic temperament was struggling to remain within its usual confines.

He reported that his outings with the Old Berkeley that season had been 'a great improvement on the first, I having at last found a hunter who really suits me'. He still could not hunt often enough. Quoting Surtees, he reminded Strachan that 'ALL TIME IS LOST WOT IS NOT SPENT IN 'UNTIN. How can I thank you sufficiently for having shown me the way to the only true source of unalloyed human happiness?' He was able to combine this new enthusiasm with his work, drafting a memorandum in February 1949 to Hopkinson on proposed anti-field-sports legislation. It was entirely philosophical in tone: 'No objection', he wrote, '... is felt to trawling for fish or hanging up fly-papers, though logically considered the "pain" (if such an idea were transferable to non-humans) of a fish slowly suffocating under a mass of other fish or of a fly straining and starving itself to death in a blob of gum is far greater than the discomfort to a dog of being killed by a blow on the head instead of a humane killer.' Powell said that if field sports were to be treated like a perversion it would have to be proved that the pleasure taken in them was sadistic. Any offence caused by, say, fox-hunting was due to 'indirect and incorrect representation of the nature of the sport to persons not immediately concerned'. Only total abolition would placate these people; and it was, he concluded, irrelevant in this context to talk about the amount of suffering by a fox or, on the other hand, the indispensability of hounds to vermin control.[91]

Having acquired, as he told Strachan in a letter in January 1949, a constituency and a good hunter called Lucky in the same week, 'I am now looking for a girl called "Fortune" to do the hat trick.'[92] By this Powell meant he was looking for a run of good luck to speed him on in his various projects. Although taking up hunting was, eventually, to lead to the most important act of socialisation yet in Powell's life – his recognition of the purposes of women – at this stage it was still only metaphorical girls in which he was interested. Strachan had sent Powell a draft of 'Teaching the Professor' for his comments, of which Powell had many. One in particular revealed that he had softened his image; the hair was no longer *en brosse* in the Germanic manner: 'I have imitated the ancient Spartans and grown my hair long.' There was also a further insight into the psychological effect of Powell's going on to the hunting field, reflecting his relief at coming through unscathed. 'Is this a normal phenomenon?' he asked his mentor. 'When hunting or even riding, I find that, if anyone meets with an accident, especially a pretty serious one, it always heightens my pleasure afterwards and also my willingness to take risks. I have observed this so regularly that there must be some rational cause; but I have failed to hit upon it.'

The textual criticism of Strachan's article gives a clear insight into Powell's mind. The Professor could now, at last, assert his expertise over the man who had taught him hunting. He rebuked him for the 'cliché-ridden' nature of parts of the text. 'Try going through your writing and deleting every adjective and adverb; you will find you not only don't miss them but that the tone of the whole is strengthened and improved.' One sentence in particular served as an example. 'The word "grim" is pure *Daily Mail*, and ruins the attempt at pathos. Almost any sentence will yield parallels.' There was a lower blow yet. 'Incidentally, if you are going to quote Surtees, quote him right, and hunting kit should be described by the correct names.'

Once Powell had been selected for the Wolverhampton seat he started to reorder his life. He took a two-bedroom flat in the town in the Chapel Ash district and, while nursing the seat, would spend most weekends there. Mary Westwood remembered that 'when he first arrived I think he was a bit out of touch with people. It was a bit of a shock having so many women around him in our constituency office. We started the job of humanising him.' Nonetheless, he soon became popular with the women in the association who, as in so many others, were and still are the backbone and driving force of the voluntary section of the Conservative party. This was not least because of his shyness and apparent loneliness, which it seemed prompted the normal feminine instincts in many supporters.

Powell started to get to know his largely industrial seat, mainly by thorough canvassing, repeatedly walking the streets from one side of the constituency to the other. Courtaulds and Goodyears were the two main employers, and most of the breadwinners in Powell's constituency were employed (mainly in white-collar, managerial or clerical capacities) in manufacturing, either with those firms or outside the seat in the steel industry at Bilston. The amount of effort he needed to put in led him, in the early summer of 1949, to resign from the Research Department; there had been tension between Powell and Hopkinson about just how much time he should spend on constituency duties. He not only intended to keep his promise to spend four days a week in Wolverhampton; he knew he had to keep it if he was to stand any chance of winning so marginal a seat. Having maintained the frugality of his early life, he had saved enough to sustain him until the election, which he knew must come within a year.

According to Robert Rhodes James, who spoke to some of Powell's contemporaries from Old Queen Street, his departure occasioned 'mixed feelings' despite his 'formidable record of work'.[93] He had never lightened up, or proved particularly easy to work with. Rhodes James reported that Powell had demonstrated a gift for sincere friendship; 'But – and this was particularly true before his marriage in 1952 – he has also a strong capacity for alienating people. In this early period his ambition was itself so overwhelmingly evident that it had, for some, a positively repellant quality.' Nonetheless, he was soon missed; a colleague, Philip Bremridge, told Hopkinson soon after Powell's departure that 'There is no doubt that the quality and value of papers on defence questions have deteriorated since Brigadier Powell gave up these subjects.'[94] At about the time of his leaving, Powell went to Essex to speak, as he had done several times, for Butler. In writing to thank him, Butler added the typically double-edged comment, 'I was much comforted to feel that you are on the way towards your proper destiny as an independent MP.'[95]

'Brigadier' Powell had, in fact, agreed to drop his military title in Wolverhampton, whence the area agent, Colonel Ledingham (who kept his rank), forwarded a request to Central Office that all correspondence be addressed, and all documentation refer, to 'Mr J. E. Powell' in future. Ledingham was pleased with the performance of the ex-Brigadier. In his annual report to Central Office on 9 August 1949, he described Powell as 'a very enthusiastic and hard-working candidate. His keenness tends to make him tense and that, coupled with a rather shy personality, does not make him a good mixer. His political knowledge is brilliant and he puts his case across well in a very convincing manner. He is canvassing every house in the constituency.' His conclusion was that 'this seat should be won'. There were 4,925 members, and 595 Young Conservatives on the strength.[96]

Powell's early excursions into journalism – a craft from which he would come to earn a substantial living from the 1960s onwards – were at this stage mainly in the local press. An article of July 1949 had remarkable longer-term significance, foreshadowing a belief almost heretical in his party that he was to expound throughout the cold war: that the nuclear threat was not real. His argument, prompted by a discussion of the best form of provision for civil defence, was that, in the light of the demand for massive concrete reinforced shelters against a nuclear blast, some clear thinking was necessary about the nature of the threat. The population could be dispersed from cities; factories and other essential plant could be built into hillsides; and at the immense cost of all this disruption partial protection could be given to the people. However, it was not worth it: 'When atom bombs are a stock line in the principal arsenals of the world, the absolute certainty of reprisals reduces the likelihood of their being used, though it cannot, of course, eliminate the possibility. Nevertheless, the atom bomb in World War III may be like poison gas in World War II – a constant potential menace, but never an actual one.'[97] It was a line from which he would not deviate, but one to which governments of both colours would pay no heed.

His partial relocation to Wolverhampton also gave him an opportunity to join a new hunt, and he went out with the Albrighton in Shropshire. He would hire a grey mare from a farmer, John Downes, who remembered Powell's intellectual approach to the sport rather than his horsemanship. 'The thing that struck me was his interest in every detail. He was a town man by our reckoning, but he soon was able to talk about the same sort of things as us country people. Every time he went riding he would come back to our house for a cup of tea and spread out an Ordnance Survey map and go over where he had been riding. He was particularly interested in old buildings.'[98] Powell told Strachan – whom he tried to tempt from his home in Edinburgh to hunt with him in December 1949, just before the election – that the farmer 'breeds show-jumpers by thoroughbreds out of shire carthorses: they jump like fleas, look like carthorses and gallop as near like the French cavalry at Agincourt as anything you ever saw'.

He felt the Albrighton offered him stronger challenges than the Old Berkeley. 'Only since I came here', he told his mentor, 'have I known what foxhunting is. As I remarked to myself last week when we cleared a rasping fence with a good deep ditch *from*: "John Enoch," said I, "I never expected to see you well over one of those." '[99] In the same letter, he rebuked Strachan for further etymological inexactitudes, this time in the naming of his infant son. 'I can't make out your son's first name: it appears to be HEW; but of course there is no such name. HUW, the Welsh form of Hugh, exists and would be perfectly suitable for use by parents afflicted by an objection to ENOCH.'

His new routine in Wolverhampton also coincided with a seismic change in his life, and one typical of the way in which his mind worked. Powell had felt little conscious urge in the preceding years to revert from atheism. However, one winter's Sunday in 1949, walking from the railway station to his flat, he felt – in a particularly Housmanic flourish – that he heard the bells of St Peter's Wolverhampton calling him. He believed himself drawn into the church. He entered quietly and 'sat down in a dark corner, just by the south door, hoping I wouldn't notice myself, because I didn't know what I was doing and I was rather ashamed of it'. It was the first time Powell had gone into a church to worship for twenty years. He took up the prayer book and began to participate in the ritual. 'And I thought to myself, "This is wonderful" and I came again and again and again … and I realised a necessity upon me which I couldn't refuse.'[100] It was, as with his introduction to architecture, a moment of revelation that would precede a lifetime of attachment, though it was a revelation not about God, but about religion.

He found himself attending on the next few Sundays, and within a year was as committed a High Churchman as he had, only a little earlier, been a committed unbeliever. After twenty years of struggle, it was an important rejection of one of Nietzsche's fundamentals, and done as a direct contradiction. Powell had heard the bells, but his mentor had mocked them: 'When we hear the old bells ringing out on a Sunday morning,' he had written in *Human, All Too Human*, 'we ask ourselves: can it be possible? This is for a Jew, crucified two thousand years ago, who said he was the son of God. The proof for such a claim is wanting ... are we to believe that such things are still believed?'[101] It was a struggle for Powell; 'the intellect still works ... but it doesn't fight any longer with the rest of the personality which worships'.[102]

Powell's decision to repudiate Nietzsche was taken instinctively, neither as an intellectual nor as a romantic, and it was to have important consequences for his life, thought and work. When asked whether he was a Christian, the shade of Nietzsche seemed never entirely to have passed from him: 'I am an Anglican.'[103] It seemed as though participation in religion were more a conscious social act, of participation in a central part of the English national culture and communion with it, rather than just an exercise of spirituality. 'As I now perceive in retrospect,' he wrote a quarter of a century later, 'the atheism had become a dogma, a closed and fixed conclusion, and my mind and attention had moved elsewhere.' The war had been 'an intellectual hibernation', but now he had, instinctively, sought to come out of that hibernation, and to open a book he had believed would stay closed for ever.[104] He never entirely repudiated his earlier conclusions about religion, but 'began to perceive that the assertions which the Church was making were not vulnerable to the weapons with which I had thought them demolished'. He realised that just because he could demolish the Gospel as a textual critic, proving it was historical nonsense, this did not mean the Anglican faith was a nonsense too.

On Christmas Eve 1949, in what was to prove a lull before the start of the campaign for the 1950 election, the women in the office of Powell's constituency association learned that he intended to spend Christmas Day alone in his flat in Chapel Ash, which contained little more than a rug and an iron bedstead. They made a collection to buy him a Christmas tree, which they hung with jelly-babies and took to him. Miss Westwood remembered that 'he was so touched to find that we were concerned about him that he was near to tears'.[105] The austerity in which Powell was living reflected the sacrifice he had been prepared to make to nurse and win his seat. He had had no income for several months since leaving the Research Department, and was running down his savings. Unlike many who would be entering the House with him the following year, nothing was made easy for him. He was not, though, helped by his unremitting earnestness. When Jim Thomas visited Wolverhampton in the summer of 1949, he told Powell he 'had heard on all sides how very successful you were as a candidate. They told me you were quite outstanding and they had only one small grouse – that your smile would win many votes but was far too rare!! This, surely, could be easily remedied!'[106]

When Parliament had risen for the Christmas recess on 16 December the Leader of the House, Herbert Morrison, told the Commons he expected a new session to be opened on 24 January. In fact, Attlee decided in the first week of the year that, as there was little that could be achieved before he was forced to go the country when his five years were up that summer, he would call an election for 23 February: the country was told on 11 January. The main thrust of Labour's campaign was the maintenance of full employment and the welfare state, but there were also promises of further intervention in the workings of private capital if deemed necessary to propel the economy forward. By contrast, the Conservative manifesto was a document Powell could feel at ease with: it spoke up for private enterprise, sound money – the Government had devalued from $4.03 to the pound to $2.80 the previous September – the need to cut both public spending and taxation, and a halt to nationalisation. His party did, though, also commit itself to full employment, and to a minimum level of social services.

Powell planned the election campaign in military fashion. To take one example, Labour was unconcerned about collecting postal votes. Powell attempted to track down every one, something which had to be done early in the campaign. He used a car, a 1935 Austin Seven acquired from Freeth and named Gabriel, to tour the constituency. The campaign was fought throughout in cold, wet and inhospitable conditions. It made no difference to Powell, and he expected his workers to take the same attitude. However ruthless he was with them – and he had to be careful, since they were only volunteers – he could not be accused of not leading by example. He did, however, find the time to hunt on two of the three Saturdays after the election was called: once with Strachan, having tempted him down from Edinburgh.

He had a short, but intense, programme of nine public meetings in the constituency in the ten days before the election, speaking at 7.30 every evening, foregoing the hustings only on the Sunday before the poll. His eve-of-poll meeting was a rally at the Wolverhampton civic hall. His election address was a mixture of the standard Central Office edicts – 'The Conservative Party – for King and Empire' – and enunciated the five main points of policy. With four of them – cutting taxes by bringing down spending, reducing prices through competition and enterprise, building more homes by deregulating the building industry, and extending the rights of the private citizen by abolishing state controls – Powell would have been in wholehearted agreement. The fifth, 'Make Britain strong again – by uniting the British Empire', was something he had been unable to take seriously since the loss of India; indeed, in his view, it was now a phrase that was literally meaningless.[107]

He undertook a thorough campaign aimed at getting out the maximum vote – Wolverhampton 'was canvassed like it had never been canvassed before, and probably as it has never been canvassed since'.[108] At the association head-quarters, and in each branch, helpers were assigned specific tasks; it was a regimented organisation of a sort so striking, compared with many Conservative campaigns, that *Picture Post* went up to Wolverhampton to report it. A picture showed a group of volunteers in a garage holding up labels signifying what their roles were. Nothing was taken for granted. Having devised what he took to be the best system for getting the vote out, Powell wanted it used in every branch. Most branches were happy to comply, in the interests of victory; one, though, was to resent what its members regarded as his high-handed attitude, and the resentment would explode against him later.

The election address included his letter to the electors, in which he put the most emphasis on the failure of the socialists to control inflation and to stop shortages five years after the war. He endorsed the Conservative party's plans to denationalise the iron and steel industry and road transport, to reopen the commodity exchanges and to break the state's monopoly over land. The one sign of a faint heart – compared with his later ideological zeal – was in his claim that 'where it is too late to denationalise, we shall see that the State monopoly is run on sound, competitive lines'. Powell declared his special interest in housing, and his commitment to slum clearance and the removal of state control from the building industry. Even in his letter, though, he was compelled to utter the belief that 'the United Kingdom can only be prosperous and safe as part of a great Empire. To preserve, strengthen and extend our Empire is the mission of the Conservative Party.'

He won by just 691 votes, by 20,239 to 19,548, with a Liberal candidate in the distance with 4,229. The postal votes, of which there had been 1,200, had been crucial after all. As with much of what Powell had done, and would do, it was an achievement attributable principally to remorseless hard work and 'sheer drudgery'.

INTERLUDE

POWELL AND GOD

'Worship and intellectual activity', Powell reflected at the age of eighty, 'are manifestations of different aspects of the person, and they serve different – God forgive me, I was going to say biological purposes – no, they correspond to different aspects of that extraordinary animal, *Homo sapiens*. Religion must have been very important for his survival, because he has it everywhere.'[1] A decade earlier, interviewed by John Mortimer, he had been asked, in response to his assertion that he was a High Tory, ' "does that mean you're a Christian?" "I am an Anglican," said Mr Powell carefully.'[2] In many of Powell's theological pronouncements there is an undercurrent that his spirituality is partly that of a creed of nationalism, and that the Church of England's value to one of his intellectual disposition is that it is a national church. 'Once got within the walls, physical and liturgical, of the Church of England,' he recalled, 'I was proud enough and English enough to see that it was a goodly inheritance from which, like a prodigal son, I had so long deliberately exiled myself.'[3] Although he claimed he had entered into the Church Universal, it was the church's part in English life that, as much as anything, pulled him back, and this same national idea would inform his politics for ever. 'For us alone,' he wrote of the English in 1974, 'the identity of nation and Church survives in the symbolism of historical forms, and the link between spiritual and secular sovereignty is still, despite everything, a living reality.'[4]

Powell's embracing of the Conservative party in 1946 was a precursor to his return to the church. He viewed the Conservative party as a Tory party, and took to heart the Tory belief in 'Church and King'. In an undated essay found in his papers after his death, but seeming to belong to his active One Nation period in the early 1950s, Powell said it was an 'absurdity' that his party had had nothing specific to say on the church for decades past.[5] 'Much of what we think about our country is bound up with what we think about the Church,' he wrote. 'We cannot conceive the future which we hope for our nation unless it can become identical with the Church in a true and lively sense.' The established church, in both England and Scotland, represented the unity of the nation – despite the historical accident of there being two separate established churches. 'It may appear an unpractical assertion, but it is an arresting and undeniable one, that if everyone were a full member of the Church, the class war and that mutual envy and fear which is socialism would instantly be inconceivable.'

Explicitly linking the church to the root of his political credo – the nation –

Powell wrote in this essay: 'The existence and the welfare of the national depend upon an opinion or faith shared by its members; for the nation is neither the product of reason or deliberate human creation, nor does it correspond to any objective reality ... this super-natural character, if it may so be described, of the most important of human relationships is exemplified and inculcated by the Church, in which men join in order to make assertion and to pursue ends which are frankly, even defiantly, supernatural.' That seems to be a clear statement of why Powell himself had joined it. The church and the nation were 'the two supreme and complementary means of fulfilment for the human being'; and this 'community of nation and church ... lies at the heart of Toryism'.

In the same way that Powell's view changed in 1949 from atheism to belief, there was a development of the nature of his belief throughout the rest of his life. One of his closest friends, himself deeply religious, believed that Powell had never stopped being an atheist; but that he had come back to the church because its power as a social and national institution was too overwhelming for him to stay away. His friend and archivist Richard Ritchie, similarly, recalled Powell telling him in old age that he did not believe in life after death.[6] The restoration to him of religious belief did nothing to diminish his certainty of final extinction, the reason for his brooding about 'the sadness of spring'.[7] His highly sceptical commentary on St Matthew's Gospel, published in 1994, in which he would suggest that Christ was stoned to death and not crucified, and that much of the Gospel was invention and embellishment, helped mark him out as a deeply unorthodox Christian. To those who knew him better it seemed to confirm their belief that, however religious he was, he was not really a Christian at all. However, in an interview at the time, Powell protested that 'I am an obedient member of the Church of England. I am not trying to demolish. I am just reading the documents, which I cannot help reading as documents and treating as I treat other documents – critically.'[8] He said his discoveries had not shaken his faith: 'the statement that God became incarnate as man is a theological statement and not a historical statement'. The Gospel, he added, had been rewritten for political reasons – hence its inaccuracy – to take a pro-Roman, anti-Judaical stance. A note in his commentary about the 'implied lifetime of Jesus' was picked up by the press. In an interview, Powell said, 'I was trying to avoid the issue of whether Jesus really did exist historically. There are some questions I thought it best to duck.'[9] The close study Powell made of the Gospels during the 1970s and 1980s prevented him from taking the biblical texts at their face value. It had been a process started in his teens at King Edward's, when he had realised on first reading the Greek Testament with a critic's eye that it was 'not true'.[10] The textual critic in him seemed, despite his return to the church, to be determined to continue to prove it.

Although to many Powell seemed to be an Anglo-Catholic, his refusal to accept the authority of the church over his own intellect marked him out as an extreme Protestant. Christianity was, he insisted, 'an intellectual religion'; and it had to be made subject to the same examinations, challenges and disputes as any other matter of the intellect.[11] However, the Christian religion could, as he had realised when he returned to the church in 1949, continue to matter irrespective of the historical accuracy and textual integrity of the Gospel. For all his fierce Protestantism, so often revealed in later years in the context of the authority of the Queen as Supreme Governor of the Church of England, he adopted many of the rituals of the High Churchman or Anglo-Catholic, such as crossing himself.

Most of Powell's contributions in ecclesiastical debates in the Commons were about the relationship of the church to the Crown in Parliament; his interest seemed to be essentially about the constitutional position of the established church, rather than reflecting the concerns of the churchmen in the Synod. His fellow MP Frank Field, himself a serious churchman, said of Powell that 'the mission of the Church was not his concern at all'.[12] This would seem to bear out further the suspicion that Powell returned to the church for cultural or sentimental reasons. The power of Nietzsche and Frazer on his well-formed intellect never entirely wore off. Yet, of all the known influences on Powell, the most direct parallel with his religious thought seems to be found in Carlyle, who believed in God but could not bring himself to believe in the Christian miracles. In the matter of the resurrection, for example, Powell argued that the texts had been so distorted, first by Matthew and then by Mark and Luke who had derived their accounts from him, as to be meaningless.[13] Far from being a matter of historical fact, it becomes one of personal mysticism. The 'gulf between crucifixion and resurrection', Powell wrote in 1974, 'is the gulf between historical time and timelessness'.[14] Space and time were, in Powell's view, irrelevant to Christianity: as a religion, its concepts were set solely in the moral world.[15]

Like Carlyle, Powell seems to have become what the Tory historian and philosopher Maurice Cowling called 'a post-Christian' by which he meant one who believed in God but could not accept the truth of the Christian miracles.[16] Also like Carlyle, while Powell would concern himself largely with matters of social and political philosophy, theology became a main and underpinning intellectual activity. This was partly because of its emotional importance to him; partly because of the challenge the Gospels would come to present him with not as a believer, but as a textual critic; and partly because of the provocation he felt when others wrongly tacked on Christianity to politics. Yet Powell, when in his sixties, came to emphasise the limits of factual knowledge. 'Faith', he wrote, 'is believing something which, though not provable, so takes possession of us that it is impossible afterwards to imagine living without it. It has the force of inevitability. If I am asked why I believe in the Trinity, I reply: "Because it is inevitable." '[17] This pro-Christian view was, though, to be moderated sub-stantially towards the end of his life, twenty years later, when his thinking had become if not Nietzsche's again, then something more akin to Carlyle's. However Donald Gray, the last clergyman to minister to him, testified that Powell regarded the sacrement with great seriousness and devotion, right to the end: 'He was not prepared to give up on Christianity.'[18]

Cowling, in his own study of Powell's religion, said that 'its bases are Anglican, whatever other confusing ingredients it may also happen to include'.[19] The most crucial use of religion by Powell in his political career would be in the repudiation of churchmen who had accused him of lacking Christian feeling in his statements, from the late 1960s onwards, on immigration. However, as Cowling also observed, 'Powell asserted three main principles – that Christ's Kingdom was not of this world, that Christ's pronouncements called men to salvation, and that church leaders had authority only to prepare men for the Kingdom of God. Since Christ had provided no guidance for an earthly kingdom, the modern clergy had no authority to do so either.'[20] Thus in his religious views Powell would prove as controversial as in his political ones; and, whereas in politics his views were to be conditioned by his own rigorous interpretation of the gospels of Toryism, in religion they were shaped by a frighteningly exact, unrelenting, textual critic's interpretation of the Gospels of Christianity.

Powell's conviction about the impossibility of linking the misguided assumptions of modern Christianity with the demands of the real world would lead him into wholesale denunciation of the church later on: not just prompted by the immigration question, but also in what he saw as the naive and economically illiterate attempts of Christian leaders to combat such problems as poverty, hunger and crime. In 1965 he said the proper conception of Christianity had been hijacked by welfarism and had had grafted on to it the welfarist's 'shibboleth of "equality of opportunity" and its idolisation of "fair shares"'. Such a religion would be one 'in which every story had a happy ending, here or hereafter. There may be, and no doubt are, such religions; but Christianity is not one of them. Christianity is not for us unless we are able to face the fact that failure exists.'[21] He relished rubbing this point in, such as in 1973 when he preached at St Peter's, Eaton Square, on the text 'Many are called, few are chosen'. Also, he condemned the 'social gospel', particularly in its treatment of the story of Dives and Lazarus, which was that 'the rich are punished for having been rich, and the wretched rewarded for having been wretched ... no wonder people are afraid to read the Bible'.[22]

His religion became more and more politically combative. When, that same year, Canon Paul Ostreicher invoked 'am I my brother's keeper?' to urge intervention by the West in the war in Mozambique, Powell repudiated him both for a misreading of the Bible and for a complete failure to understand the political difficulties of sovereign nations going around interfering in each other's affairs. 'The moral instruction conveyed by the passage', Powell wrote, 'is that one ought not to murder one's own brother.'[23] Any wider interpretation would be 'nonsense', a 'prescription for paternalist tyranny'. In this and in his other assaults on the 'happy ending' school of Christianity, it is almost as though Powell, resigned to his own disbelief in the Christian miracles, is taunting those with weaker minds who still look to them as a 'means to cushion and shield themselves against having to meet this truth [of death and judgment] face to face'.[24] This shows how little he had forgotten of his Nietzsche after he found himself drawn into St Peter's Wolverhampton in 1949.

Although some of his doctrines were seized upon by his critics – including, later on, Edward Heath – as unChristian, religion in fact gave Powell a sense of perspective, and a deeper humanity. He believed that on controversial issues more harm would be done to humanity by his not speaking out, but he resisted any notion that he was self-righteous. 'Over and over again, and often in the course of a day,' he would tell Malcolm Muggeridge in 1970, at a time of the greatest self-doubt in his political career, 'I am conscious in my life as a politician of committing the sins of hatred, of envy, of malice; and I am conscious of the command operating, to some extent at any rate, upon my nature which not merely forbids these things but equates them with death.'[25] There was a strong streak of Calvinism in him: his doom was completely in the hands of a higher force, and there was nothing he could do to temper it. It was this fundamentalism that informed his belief that the church could not sensibly apply itself to social and political questions, and which – like, for many years, his economic views – put him at odds with many experts in the field. This became more apparent when, from the mid-1960s onwards, he received and accepted an increasing number of invitations to preach in churches; and he fulfilled such invitations with an intent just as earnest as his political speechmaking. Indeed, in both tone and content it would often be hard in the years ahead to see where one discipline ended, and another began.

5

A PUBLIC LIFE

Attlee's massive mandate of 1945 had vanished. His new majority was just six. Four times in the first month of the new Parliament the Opposition tried, and failed, to have the Government turned out, three times on votes of censure. It was clear the Government would not last five years, and much of the socialist intent of the manifesto would remain unfulfilled. The result was a relief for Powell, and a surprise to many observers in Wolverhampton, such as Clement Jones, who believed the sitting Labour Member was too formidable to lose.[1] Writing to Michael Strachan just before polling day, asking him to come out with the Albrighton again during March, Powell said that if he was elected he would 'therefore not require to be fished up out of the Birmingham–Wolverhampton canal'. He added, tempting providence, 'I have bought a silk hat, more or less as one buys a crown when anticipating promotion to field rank.'[2] Two days after his election he was out with the Albrighton again, though he chose not to wear the new hat.

Powell's election meant an absolute change of life, undertaken with the ruthlessness he customarily employed on such occasions, just as when, in September 1939, he had laid aside his classical studies, expecting never to resume them (which, with the exception of completing his translation of Herodotus, he had not). The one work in progress, his history of the House of Lords, was not ditched: it was too relevant to his new life, and the access he now had to the Commons library was invaluable. Otherwise, it was a time for concentration on his new role. He would shortly stop writing poetry and, with the exception of occasional visits to the opera, stop listening to music – though, as we shall see, his new career was not the only reason for these emotional breaches. Years later Powell told an interviewer why he avoided music: 'I don't like things which interfere with one's heart strings. It doesn't do to awaken longings that can't be fulfilled.'[3]

He was one of several former party officials elected. Henry Hopkinson won Taunton, Maudling won Barnet and Macleod Enfield West; and Central Office's former broadcasting liaison officer, Jack Profumo, was returned for Stratford-upon-Avon. Powell remained conscious that he, like the Government, had a small majority, and faced an early second election. It was urgent for him, therefore, to do all he could to get the vote up in Wolverhampton South-West. The insecure hold the Government had on power also created opportunities for bright young men to distinguish themselves in making the process of governing difficult; and that was precisely what Powell and Macleod, operating as a partnership because of their shared recent history and shared interests, in particular set out to do.

Powell continued the military organisation he had put to such good effect in the campaign itself. He started a card index, in the minutest detail, of everyone who had visited him at a constituency surgery, so that he could follow up any case presented to him. He kept highly personal details about constituents in Greek, so no one else could read them. He was meticulous. If invited to a constituency function he would always turn up on time, irrespective of how far he had to travel and how inconvenient his attendance was. He would canvass almost every weekend, and make a point of personally visiting new constituents. He told his helpers he had canvassed in all six languages he spoke fluently: English, French, German, Italian, Greek and Urdu. He soon struck up a friendship with Clement Jones at the *Express and Star*, a friendship that became based as much on his and Jones's shared interests in literature and topography as on his political needs. Jones was an indispensable aid to Powell in getting his message over to his voters, and taught him much he would need to know about the art of self-publicity.

Powell rose at 6.21 p.m. on 16 March 1950 to make his maiden House of Commons speech in a debate on defence, in which Churchill had spoken earlier. He began with the customary imprecation to his fellows: 'There is no need for me to pretend those feelings of awe and hesitation which assail any hon Member who rises to address this House for the first time, but I trust I shall receive the indulgence which is usually accorded to one undergoing that ordeal.'[4] He argued that Britain had been obliged to double her burdens in defence by having conscription. As so many conscripts were at any one time under training, the army's manpower was being put to relatively inefficient use: 'I think it more than fair to say that the 150,000 or 160,000 conscripts in the Army are fulfilling the demand of approximately 100,000 Regulars.'[5]

The speech was packed with detail and closely argued: setting a standard for the contributions he would make in the next few years while he sought to impress and win office. He spoke about how the army would have to adapt to Britain's new responsibilities following the loss of the Indian Army, and the need to remain an army of occupation in Germany. Predictably, he lamented the loss of the Indian Army, and the Indian empire, a rare moment of retrospection. There was a practical purpose: 'If we are an Empire defending the Empire, we must draw far more than we do on the vast reserves of Colonial manpower which exist within the Empire. The virtues which enabled British officers and British administrators to create the Indian Army are not dead. The virtues which made the Indian Army so great an instrument, although some of them are perhaps peculiar to the martial races of India, are paralleled in other parts of the world ... it is imperative that we should create from other parts of His

Majesty's Dominions a replacement for that which we have lost.'[6]

He was sad that, in this light, colonial manpower in the forces outside Europe had fallen by 15,000 in the previous year. He said the duty of defence was incumbent on the Dominions and the United Kingdom together. Were it not seen as such, the Empire's defence would be too heavy a burden for Britain alone to bear. Powell was followed by the Labour MP Reginald Paget – with whom in later years he would ride to hounds – who congratulated him and called his speech 'very good and thoughtful', and welcomed him to the House as a fellow ex-serviceman.[7]

On 24 March Powell spoke in the committee stage* of the Diplomatic Privileges Bill, and showed an early grasp of procedure and of the potential abuses of parliamentary power. In one part of the Bill the Government, in seeking to confer diplomatic immunities on members of the consultative committee of the Council of Europe, had 'taken the power to do almost anything by Order in Council and have justified it by the declaration that they intend to do practically nothing. It is a steam roller, admittedly to crush a gnat, but it is a steam roller.'[8] In another part of the Bill, he foreshadowed his objections three years later to the change in the Queen's titles by arguing against the conferral on Commonwealth high commissioners, representatives (as he saw it) of parts of the Queen's realm, of the privileges of ambassadors, who were representatives of foreigners. He was soon noticed by colleagues, and his skills learned in the Research Department were quickly put to use; he became secretary of two Conservative backbench parliamentary committees, one on legal affairs and the other on town and country planning. It was not a glamorous start to his parliamentary career, but it was a start. His main political interest – one that would colour his thinking throughout his career, and dominate his thoughts until other matters overwhelmed him in the late 1960s – was to halt and then reverse the socialist state. That was how he intended to make his name.

Away from politics, Powell felt his religious life intensifying. A year after his return to the church he found himself, at six o'clock in the morning on Easter Sunday 1950, taking Communion for the first time since he left school. His non-communicating attendance at church had confused him, and he had felt the urge to intensify his worship. 'I said to myself,' he recalled, ' "look, you can't stay here, you either go back or you go forward," and back I knew I couldn't go, so forward I went.'[9] He made a little more time for recreation, and during his first parliamentary recess he drove through the night in his car, Gabriel, to Edinburgh to see Strachan and his wife. Reporting to his host his successful

---

* At this stage the details of the Bill are examined. Either a committee of a small number of MPs, their political allegiances reflecting the proportionate strength of parties in the House of Commons as a whole, meets in a separate room in the Palace of Westminster to discuss a Bill clause by clause, voting where necessary. Or, in the case of major Bills such as constitutional Bills, the Committee meets in the Chamber and consists of the whole House.

return, he said the 290 miles from Edinburgh to Wolverhampton had taken him nine and a half hours. He was triumphant about having done the trip on just five and a quarter gallons of petrol. 'The only mishap was that the speedometer cable broke – less significant than it sounds.'[10] He could at last afford some little indulgences like this; his salary as a backbencher was £1,000 a year, an improvement on what he had made in the Research Department. He told a newspaper interviewer that he managed to save £100 a year out of this modest sum.[11] The principles of austerity were never relaxed. He did not bother with the expense of a secretary. He found that, rather than endure cramped, shared office space he could more happily work in the Commons library. It was from there he would answer, by hand, much of his constituency correspondence.

This was the time of the birth of two great love affairs for Powell. The first, and more enduring, was with the buildings of the countryside as a romantic embodiment of the continuum of England and her history. His love of architecture, awakened in India, had been further fuelled by the awareness that several years abroad had given him about the special place England held for him; and in buildings, in particular, he saw embodied the humanity of the generations who had created and lived in them.

His second love affair was with a woman: the first who had captivated him. He met Barbara Kennedy while they were both hunting with the Albrighton in the winter of 1949–50. She was then twenty-four, a colonel's daughter from Yorkshire who was, at that time, working as secretary to her uncle, a Major Monckton. He was the Albrighton's Master and owned a large estate in Staffordshire. Monckton was a committed Conservative, and a strong supporter of Powell's association. Miss Kennedy had seen Powell at Conservative functions and had, occasionally, driven the candidate to some of his meetings. Though he and she appeared to have interests in common, they were in fact poles apart. A man, albeit a brigadier, professor and Conservative candidate, who had to hire his horse was still, in 1950, looked down upon by the county set. They, in turn, could not conceive of the breadth of Powell's intellect, interests and knowledge. 'In a funny way,' she recalled, noting why Powell could not have been more than a friend to her, 'class is printed into you and you can't escape it. He was such a dedicated career man and I don't think I thought I was up to it. I couldn't begin to speak at his level, he was intellectually so above me.'[12]

This, in terms of Powell's courtship of her, was the root of the problem. 'John,' she recalled many years later, 'was very nice, highly intelligent, rather quiet, very reserved, desperately shy, very musical: we used to go to musical highbrow performances in Wolverhampton. This is what I found difficult. I had other friends, I went out with a lot of people.' What follows she described as 'a short romance'. It had begun when riding back from hunting one evening, when she felt the attraction of an opposite as they talked to each other. After that, 'I went out with him quite a lot; I wouldn't have done that if I didn't care.' She found him 'very good looking with piercing, absolutely piercing, penetrating eyes'. In the spirit of the times 'we didn't have a sexual relationship. It was much more of a very attractive companionship: we just got on frightfully well together.' However, she could not attune herself to Powell's wavelength and he, being rather undemonstrative, did not make matters any easier. He would meet her out hunting, or would ring and ask her to go with him to musical recitals or to party functions. It was, in that respect, a conventional courtship; but, for a man of thirty-seven, Powell was utterly inexperienced with women, and in the normal social conventions that underpin such a relationship.

Her attraction for him was devastating in its suddenness. Giving an interview to his local newspaper in the run-up to the 1950 election, at the time he was pursuing Barbara, he seemed to have no inkling there was about to be revolution in his life: 'A wife? I suppose I've been too busy for courting – but I'm still an eligible bachelor.'[13] Immediately he was elected he started seeing her regularly, hunting with the Albrighton so long as the season lasted, and then making social plans that took him into that hunt's country once spring came. When Barbara felt Powell was 'getting serious' about her, she could not understand it; but then she also admitted that much of the fascination Powell held for her was that, half the time, she could not make out what was going on in his mind. She liked his impeccable manners, and the way in which he did not patronise her, though she was far less educated than he was: her parents had not even sent her to school until she was twelve, but Powell gave her Greek books to read.

By early March 1950 Powell seems to have decided that Barbara was an appropriate wife. While taking Strachan out hunting he confided in him, and Strachan soon after wrote to him sagely: 'With regard to the possibility of a matrimonial project, may I repeat my advice not to rush your fences before you have done your best to get an idea what is on the other side.'[14] Powell then planned a strategic campaign, like the good intelligence officer he was. He attended to his constituency on Saturdays once hunting was finished, and attended to Barbara on Sundays. He appears not to have been so naive as to have missed noticing that various other suitors – one in particular – were attending to Barbara as well.

Because she had always taken hunting for granted, she was amused by the almost adolescent thrill with which Powell approached it, as a relative newcomer. It certainly never occurred to her that he was contemplating marriage with her; but he felt he had, in what must have been a rather roundabout or tangential way, put the question to her, while out walking one day in the appropriately Housmanic setting of Clee Hill. He also thought she was considering his proposal before giving him an answer. She, though, claimed not to have interpreted anything he had said as a proposal, nor felt she had given him cause to hope. She believed she and he were so different that she would never have accepted a proposal. 'I don't think I'd have been very good at politics. I'm much too indiscreet.'

So when, in July 1950, she announced her engagement to Paul Hawkins, a local tile manufacturer, Powell was stricken. Her letter to him telling him of the event was matter of fact, though she clearly had a suspicion he might be disappointed. 'I have always said that we are friends, John, and I do hope that we will continue to be so. I do very sincerely value your friendship,' she wrote.[15] 'John was very upset,' she remembered, 'and said he understood that he had proposed to me. I have always thought it must have been in his mind and he never actually said it.'[16] John certainly was upset. He had telephoned Barbara routinely, after she had written her letter but before he had received it, and when he made no mention of the engagement she had not been able to bring herself to tell him. Then the letter arrived: his reply was extraordinary. 'As to its contents,' he wrote on 1 August, having thanked her for it, 'I will only say that (a) I don't really believe the fact which it purports to announce and (b) I can't approve the manner of relating it even if true.'[17] He said he would be in Wolverhampton the following weekend – the August bank holiday – and he expected her to come to see him to explain herself; or, as he tactfully put it, 'we might meet and you could tell me how I can forgive you'.

It is hardly surprising that she took some offence at this. 'As to whether you wish to believe it or not, that is entirely up to you.'[18] She sidestepped his suggestion of a meeting by telling him that the marriage would be on 8 September, that she hoped to get away to the Riviera before then, and that she was 'desperately busy'. She could hardly have been more crushing, but Powell had not quitted the battle yet. He turned up at Major Monckton's house, Stretton Hall, 'very, very irate . . . He desperately wanted me not to go ahead. He thought I was making a terrible mistake. And he thought it was very unsuitable.' He kept himself under control at this difficult meeting: he did not raise his voice. He walked out of her uncle's house and she never saw him again; there were, though, two more letters from him before the wedding day. On 27 August, still not having abandoned hope, he wrote that 'you know how absurdly slowly my mind works . . . Barbara, I beg you to forgive me for anything on my part which may have seemed unkind or harsh, especially lately . . . I reproach myself bitterly for my stupidity, when if I had been less blind, I might have been some help to you. I would be, if I can, even now.'[19]

He came to the point.

You remember my saying to you that there was nothing I would not do for you regardless of return or consequences. I say it again. Barbara, I am as sure as that I write these words that you did not really want to marry Paul – or at the very least, not at present. What the compulsion is which made you nevertheless persuade yourself to act against your wishes, I do not know. I imagine it must be a strong one, whatever it is, and I realise the extreme difficulty of altering course at the last moment. But whatever the difficulties it must be wrong to do this, of all things, against one's true wish and conscience. It is so wrong that none of the consequences of avoiding it can be as bad. If you decide to take what I now know, and you know, to be the right course, there is at any rate one person who is ready to help, whatever is involved – your John.

She replied that 'your conclusion was mistaken ... I realised that I did in fact love him [her fiancé] very much ... I have never been happier in my life and I feel sure that it is only the beginning of many happy years for us both, and please believe me when I say that although I deeply appreciate all your concern, it really is unfounded.'[20] His last word to her – on this subject, and indeed on any subject for forty-five years – was sent on 5 September, three days before the wedding. 'No-one could have written a kinder letter ... for one human being to understand another is an infinitely difficult thing. Perhaps it is never fully possible; we have to fill the gap by having faith that the best which we want to believe about one another is true, though we cannot see how. That is what I must now do.' In a conclusion of studied ambiguity, he said: 'Barbara, I wish you nothing but well, now and for ever, Goodbye, John.'[21] He was invited to the wedding, but did not attend. Piling the torture on to himself, he cut out and kept the report in the local newspaper, complete with its photograph of the bride and groom. Peculiarly, he compiled a table of occasions on which he had seen Barbara, and those on which he knew Hawkins had seen her, in the preceding six months. It was as if the matter was susceptible to some sort of logic or rational assessment, which, as he of all people should have known, it was not.

When, a few years later, some mutual friends in Staffordshire tried to arrange a dinner party including the two couples – Powell had by that stage married, and Barbara 'would very much like to have met his wife, who everybody says is charming', Powell was adamant that he would not see her.[22] He would also ignore a direct attempt by her, after his own engagement, to resume a social relationship. To her, their relationship had just been another one of the many mild and innocent flirtations she had had in her life; she never understood the depth of Powell's feeling for her, a feeling that had all the undiluted irrationality and fervour typical in those twenty years younger than he was, but not to be expected in one who has been both a professor and a brigadier.

As with so many things in his life that had gone – like India and the notion of Empire, on a grander scale – the break with the past had, for him, to be absolute. With his last letter he sent her copies of all the poems he had written since he had met her – which he would publish the following year as *The Wedding Gift*, and most of which he had written on train journeys between Euston and Wolverhampton – and a gold cigarette case with what she described as 'a snarling fox' engraved on it. She thought he was having a dig at her: she thought the present 'absolutely horrible'. It was not so intended; it cost Powell £50, a fortune to him in those days. It was years before he could bring himself to talk to anyone of his disappointment, and when he did it was to the point: 'I failed. I was not satisfactory. That's it.'[23]

He was glad to have the heavy commitment of his marginal seat to distract him after the disappointment of Barbara; he had not yet found anyone else to occupy his affections. He had kept Strachan informed of his courtship, at one stage – before the end, but when he was clearly failing to elicit the response for which he had hoped – using an appropriate metaphor. 'With that determination which is characteristic of fox-hunters, I hung around after my mount was killed, caught a loose horse and went on. Hounds are still running. I never imagined it was possible to suffer so much: the country is deep and terribly strong, and of course quite strange to me. *Miserere mei.*'[24] Yet in the same letter he showed that his sense of humour had not entirely been extirpated. He took a civilian driving test, but failed it at the first attempt. 'The Ministry of Transport examiner', he told Strachan, 'gave what seemed to me a deplorable exhibition of cowardice.'

He threw himself into his constituency life, not least because by being there he was near to Barbara. He had told Strachan he would be unavailable for social activities outside Wolverhampton from June to September as he planned to spend every weekend there. He continued to keep Strachan informed: 'I am beginning to think that this is the second part of Faust,' he wrote to his friend on 13 June.[25] His next letter to his friend, on 5 July, lamented that they had not seen each other for exactly four months: 'I do not recollect any equally short period which has produced any comparable revolution in my mind and outlook.' This was not merely due to Barbara, but also because of the growing hold religion was having on him. When the catastrophe of her engagement came he could not bring himself to tell Strachan the full details, but merely hinted at them; after that, as far as the world could tell, a sort of peace appears to have descended on him. As well as his obsessive identification with Faust, he was also pouring out his grief in poetry. There was, though, a discipline about this, and by the autumn of that year he had arranged with the Falcon Press to publish *The Wedding Gift*, in a joint volume with *Dancer's End*, the poems of his service years: they appeared in the summer of 1951.

Ever since his return to England in 1946 Powell had tried to find a publisher for the collection he had named *Dancer's End*, after a brother officer's house in Buckinghamshire that he had visited during 1940–1. He had sifted and changed the content and order of the collection, leaving some fifty poems from the period unpublished. He had started by approaching Faber and Faber, of which T. S. Eliot was a director, in July 1946, but that had brought the first of many rejections. To be fair to Powell, the shortage of paper after the war meant that many publishers were forced to be even choosier than usual. When, in January 1947, he offered the poems to Jonathan Cape, Cape himself replied with a constructive critique – 'these strike us as being too much in the A. E. Housman manner for us to want to publish them, we being the publishers of Housman'.[26] Cape did, though, invite Powell in for a talk and to be offered advice, and had been keen for Powell to send him 'an autobiographical work, in which you would have the opportunity of a statement of your social and political convictions'. When the two men met a few days later, Cape promised to reconsider *Dancer's End*, but nothing came of it.[27] When Powell eventually did the deal with the Falcon Press, he had to pay for the privilege.

Powell had found that his war experience created 'a new and powerful sensation demanding to be released'.[28] The poems in *Dancer's End* were a psychologically important vehicle for him to express his 'sensation . . . of self-reproach' at having survived, though some of the poems had been written as early as 1938. Those who went into battle had been estranged from him: 'a veil had been drawn between them and us, between friend and friend. It must be my own fault. I must be guilty.'[29] He was now aware his whole life had changed: 'The *Götterdämmerung* world before 1939 was not a world of living and dying old, of getting and begetting, but a world of killing and being killed, destroying and being destroyed. I had walked out of one world and into another, out of a crazy world into a sane world, out of a nightmare world into a waking world, an unnatural world into a natural world, a world in which there would be "marrying and giving in marriage", children and the rearing of children.'

With his growing maturity as man and poet, Powell became more metaphysical in his writing; but his is a metaphysics with a habit of turning sharply into the concrete, as in this poem, written when home with his parents at Seaford for Christmas in 1938, and under his obsession with the war to come:

> Sweet child, you need not fear
> Lest spring be lost,
> Nor think of autumn sere
> And winter's frost.
>
> Fear not lest suffering bow
> Or age betray;
> Holy and fair as now
> You still shall stay.
>
> The Gods will set their guard
> To shield you well:
> Flame, and the flying shard
> Of bursting shell.[30]

The book is dedicated to Thomas. The Greek inscription translates as a salutation to him as the noblest and most beautiful of men: Powell still could not come to terms with his death, and in many respects never would. A guilt-ridden preoccupation with the deaths of others dominates the poetry, lending it a tone of bitter realism not so obvious in Powell's earlier writings. Perhaps the finest example was, though, written in April 1939, on a sea-voyage from Brisbane to Sydney, and which Powell told Ted Curtis at the time was 'the best stanza I ever wrote'.[31] Though it cannot be about Thomas's actual death, it is eerily prophetic both of the event and of Powell's reaction to it, and confirms the certainty with which he knew that the two of them, who had parted just a few weeks earlier, would never meet again:

> Over your grave in far Japan
> Do almond trees, I wonder, grow,
> Or does the palm-frond lift its fan
> When the Pacific breezes blow?
> I wonder; but I cannot think
> That you in truth are buried there,
> Beyond imagination's brink,
> Too far for even grief to dare.
> But when at home I see the red
> Of poppies in the ripening corn,
> Then I shall know that you are dead,
> And then at last I'll mourn.[32]

In a similar vein there are, too, signs of Powell's political awakening, the reflection in his poetry of his disgust, when still in Australia, at the policies of appeasement. In a poem dedicated to R. M. Tinkler, bayoneted by the Japanese at Tientsin on 6 June 1939, Powell asks:

> Who then the murderer?
> England, that would not stir,
> Not though he died for her;
> England, the slumberer.

However, he concludes:

> insensate fear
> Had stopped the mother's ear;
> But now revenge is near,
> For while his land forgets
> And bends the knee to threats,
> His vengeful spirit whets
> The German bayonets.[33]

The obsession with what was, at the time he wrote it, Thomas's apparently impending death is brought out in a poem Powell wrote at Singapore, on a stopover on his way home in September 1939. The force of his certainty is, once more, disturbing:

> Four figures on the cliff's edge
> Were standing where I came
> To watch the sunset tingeing
> The Timor Sea with flame.
>
> I went and stood beside them
> And two of them I knew
> But the other two were strangers -
> And one of them was you.
>
> But I shivered in the stillness,
> And the hair rose on my head,
> For I thought, but I dared not ask you:
> 'Are you alive or dead?'[34]

Several of the poems were written while Powell was at Guilsborough in 1941, but it is a period he does not see so clearly until more than two years later when, at Cairo in August 1943, waiting to leave for India, he reveals his mounting impatience at his inactivity. He tells how while walking one August evening from Guilsborough to Northampton – an imaginary walk, it seems, as he was not at Guilsborough in August – he had felt the ghosts of the old English rising into the air around him and brooding on England's destiny; and, in another, written at Camberley in the summer of 1941, how the cuckoo 'winged in his gloom / He flies away, / And death is nigh'.[35]

At Dehra Dun in August 1945, Powell shows he is still haunted by the battle to which he came closest – El Alamein – and his failure to be able to make the sacrifice in it. The night before the battle, the poet fancies he sees storms raging across England and, like him,

> many a man that night,
> Lying abed and hearing on the air
> The tumult of the rain and tempest, thought
> Of Henry and the host at Agincourt,
> And knew himself accurst he was not there.[36]

In an interview in 1986, he still found himself breaking down when reading the poem in which he tried to come to terms with his feelings, written at Delhi just before his return to England after three years of torment:

> I dreamt I saw with waking eyes the scene
> So often in imagination wrought,
> The flame-wall in the night at Alamein
> Before the attack. And I was glad, and thought:
> 'My sorrow and despair was after all
> Some evil dream. It is still not too late,
> My friends who passed before me through that wall
> Not lost, nor I forever separate
> From them condemned to live. I break to-night
> As they did through the fire, and so again,
> Knowing and known, shall pass into their sight.'
> But then I woke, and recollection came
> That I for ever and alone remain
> On this side of the separating flame.[37]

Egypt has her happy memories, too: the journey across the desert in *Pinafore* with Strachan, and the moment they saw the pyramids, and sang 'Rule, Britannia':

> The skyline suddenly fell sheer away
> And showed the smoky Delta; to the right
> Rose sharp and blue against the desert's brown
> The pyramids; and our astonished sight
> Described, above it all, the Imperial Crown.[38]

Dancer's End is about the war: its last poems were written before Powell embarked for home. *The Wedding Gift* is about after the war, about the vital life-force of Barbara, seen through a prism of agonised loss tempered by the reawakening of religious faith, but recalled longingly as a source for strength and hope. The volume was, as Powell put it with some understatement, 'the response to a brief period, no more than a few weeks, of intense emotional excitement'.[39] This was what he had meant by the world in which there would be 'marrying and giving in marriage'; it was a world that 'sprang upon me' when he met Barbara.[40] 'For a period incredibly brief in retrospect existence was transformed into an epic struggle where the prize was eternity, eternity graspable at one leap. Like a powerful hallucinatory drug, it unsealed again the necessity and the capability to write poetry. Dawn after dawn the stuff rose in my throat and would have choked me, had I not got it down and licked it into shape in *The Wedding Gift*, a shape much more undisciplined than I had permitted myself before.'[41]

As is clear from the poems themselves, though, it was not merely Barbara who had inspired them. Powell's new devotion to the church, and emotions stirred by his return to religion, were scarcely less powerful. He appreciated a link between these two, to him strange, emotions: 'Without venturing into the speculative territory of the hidden relationship between religion and sexuality, I can note objectively the influence of that turning point in my life upon the vocabulary and the imagery of the poetry which was forced from me when "like Lucifer" I leapt to grasp the hallucination of eternity.'[42] His experience of Barbara had taught him that, if he wanted to find a means to grasp eternity, it would need to be one that was in spiritual, and not human, form.

The tone is set from the start, in the poem 'Faust's Gift'. Faust was, as Powell had told Strachan, much on his mind during this episode:

> Here in this golden case the very quill
> I send you from my place among the dead.
> And at its hollow point the black speck still
> Of blood with which I signed my soul away.
> Raise, take it from your writing desk, and show
> To husband, friends or children; toss your head
> And with the well-known gesture laugh, and say:
> 'See, here is blood! This made I once to flow!'[43]

Until resurrected by religion, the Powell of these poems is dead, though not without a fight with his rival. He is occasionally soothed by memories of Asia, the mysteries and phenomena of India the only appropriate complement to the ordeal he has just endured. When he looks back at Barbara, she takes on aspects of the miraculous, such as in the poem in which he recalls taking her to Lincoln's Inn, and seeing the tulip-tree (which 'Scarce once a century / Puts on its blossoms white') in bloom: Barbara 'had brought / This thing to pass, who wrought / The like for me'.[44] Without her, the situation is bleak. Out hunting, at the end of the day,

> I face the darkened road alone
> And hear, like echo of griefs past,
> The chill wind's rising moan.
>
> Of all the living hang upon,
> Of love, of fear, despair, delight,
> The day's imaginings are gone;
> Remains now but the night.[45]

He writes in several poems of the prospect of eternity, though it is 'the eternal solitude'.[46] Life takes on a sense of decay, with the old huntsman, for example, seen now as 'an empty skull with grinning chap'.[47] The fighting Powell now wishes to do is not in war, but in his quest for Barbara, for the eternal prize:

then vanquisher
Return to walk earth's flowery ways
Alone with her,
While he, the other, falls like Lucifer
To endless dark.[48]

The religious poems proclaim Powell's belief in the resurrection of his spirit, if not also his body; and show explicitly the putting of his faith in God rather than in the human form. In the most intense of these, he signals a new 'Everlasting Yea', a moment of moving from an emotional dependence to a spiritual one:

Now to the altar-rail draw nigh
All who beneath affliction break –
The live that sorrow for the dead,
The maimed and palsied, halt and blind –
And in their midst come also I,
Her image in my mind.
But stretching out my hands to take,
I see her pattern on the Bread,
I see her shadow in the Cup;
And as I leave the hallowed place
And lift my heavy forehead up,
She greets me face to face.[49]

The mental agony of his affair with Barbara still intrudes undiluted, how at their last parting 'words not those I purposed / From lips and heart impassioned broke', and how the very world was darkened by his grief:[50]

Dark over Staffordshire lie bent
The heavy clouds;
By banks of Penk, and Sow, and Trent
In dank, dim shrouds
Dawn mists are creeping
Out of the gloom
Where she is sleeping
Whose heart is keeping
Hidden my doom.[51]

Perhaps because he stopped publishing poetry, his brother politicians failed to make allowances, in their estimates of him, for his romantic motive. It did not, though, diminish: all that changed was the medium through which it was expressed. The ghosts of the old English still rose up to confront him, and the search for eternity was still on.

II

Powell's first letter to the editor of *The Times* as a Member of Parliament was to correct an assertion in a leading article that the Convocations of the two provinces of York and Canterbury were in any way linked to the division of Parliament into two houses. It was the fruit of his House of Lords researches, bound up with his romantic interpretation of the historical facts surrounding the nation and its Parliament. He saw Parliament clearly for what it was: as he wrote later, 'a monarchical institution, the parliament of a monarchy'.[52] He added, with the fervour of a jealous husband, 'This is the one thing which makes the miscalled "Mother of Parliaments" unique: she has in fact neither daughters nor peers; for there are long since no other ancient monarchies, only despotisms and republics (crowned and uncrowned).[53] Powell was never ashamed of his nationalism, to him 'the nation is the ultimate political reality. There is no political reality beyond it.'[54] The parliament was the focus of the nation; he would fight for its sovereignty. As his anti-imperialism developed, and as his reluctance to have Britain interfere in the affairs of other nations became more marked, these ideas too led on from his concept of nation.

His love of Parliament was rooted in its preservation of the historical thread of monarchy without absolutism: 'Parliament and the House of Commons are not sovereign. They stand over against sovereignty, criticising it, checking it, thwarting it, and yet maintaining it. There never was a more dangerously misleading phrase ... than "parliamentary government". Parliament does not govern, never has, and as long as it remains, Parliament never will.' He saw the Commons as 'this meeting place ... where the two [monarch and subject] talk to one another. For a thousand who know that parliament has to do with *parler*, not one remembers that it was not a speaking of the subjects amongst themselves, but a speaking of the king with his subjects, and of them with him – a dialogue, a debate, but a debate between government and governed.'

In Parliament Powell never saw himself as lobby-fodder, doing what the Whips desired, but almost always as a man exercising his independent judgment. He had been in the House barely four months when he engaged in his first rebellion, or what he termed 'my first manifestation in the House of Commons of my opposition to the loss of British self-government': abstaining on a three-line whip when Churchill moved a vote of censure against the Government for not having joined in the European Coal and Steel Community established under the Schuman Plan – the forerunner of the Common Market and, eventually, the European Union.[55] The Government had been presented with a short-notice ultimatum about whether or not to join, and, given the gravity of the question, had acted sensibly, not least because the intention of Robert Schuman, the French Foreign Minister, was to call Britain's bluff in the hope of neutering her in this industrial context. For Powell, it was a matter of principle. He objected to the notion of the removal from British control of the policies on production of coal and steel, and noted that Churchill, when he returned to power a year later, did nothing to pursue the notion of pooling sovereignty on this issue himself.

His rebellion – explicitly, as twenty years later when the Common Market debate was dominating politics, about sovereignty – put an immediate blight on what was supposed, by his superiors, to be a glittering career. Powell remembered the Chief Whip, Patrick Buchan-Hepburn, 'sadly and solemnly' telling him: 'I don't think we shall be able to put you in the government, at any rate not at first, after what you've done' – for it was expected that the Conservatives would be in power within months. Powell recalled, 'I was quite prepared for that, and quite unsurprised by it.'[56] Another of his contemporaries, Edward Heath, chose the debate to make his maiden speech in passionate defence of the Plan. He, too, had been marked out for promotion, but unlike Powell would do nothing to prevent it.

The 1950 intake would be celebrated in years ahead as rich in ability, though it might more accurately be said that it was one which provided more than its share of senior cabinet ministers, for the government in which most of them participated at the highest level – Heath's, from 1970 to 1974 – hardly reflected ability to govern. There were many ambitious men among Powell's contemporaries. They knew they needed to position themselves if they were to take advantage of their – and their party's – forthcoming opportunity. The self-appointed cream of the intake formed what would be known as the 'One Nation' group partly as a vehicle for their ambition. It arose out of a discussion between Angus Maude, who would be one of Powell's closest friends and supporters, and Cub Alport about their party's failure to consider properly the development and funding of the social services. They recruited another new MP, Gilbert Longden, and the three of them decided to invite other new colleagues to form a discussion group. Robert Carr, Richard Fort and John Rodgers were the first three; Rodgers then brought along Heath, and Macleod was the eighth to be invited. The group had an inaugural lunch at which Macleod suggested that Powell, with his specialist knowledge of housing, be asked to join.

Powell's membership completed the group. When, after the 1950 summer recess, it agreed to meet every Thursday, he was asked to keep the minutes. It was a great opportunity for him, not just intellectually but also socially, since it was clear he was not the sort to frequent the smoking room. Alport remembered Powell being relatively quiet at the group's dinners, 'not throwing his weight about', but saving comments for a particularly telling moment. 'I remember him telling us', Alport recalled, 'that there was no such thing as social justice.'[57] Lord Carr remembered that Powell was very different then from what he would become: 'As a man, he changed ... the great thing about Enoch then was that he would give ground as well as taking ground. He did more taking than giving, but there was never really any edge to it. He would laugh and say, "Well, I never expected to get you the whole way, but I have moved you, haven't I?" He punctured one's platitudes and made one think, and he did move us. He could laugh at himself."[58]

The first publication of the group, which dealt with the conflict of ideas between Labour and the Conservatives over social reform, was trailed in the press in late August 1950. It had its origins in a pamphlet on the social services that Macleod – who quickly 'emerged' as chairman – had been asked to write by the Conservative Political Centre, before the foundation of the group. This project developed into a joint exercise, with most of the members contributing a chapter, each chapter being discussed at meetings during the summer of 1950. Macleod coined the title 'One Nation' for the pamphlet, and from that the group took its name. When the pamphlet appeared in early October it set out a programme somewhat at odds with the subsequent interpretation of 'one nation' once the term was appropriated in the 1980s by those opposed to Thatcherism. For example, it proposed charges for some NHS services, saying Labour was right to insist that no more money could be spent on the service. It called for food subsidies to be withdrawn but family allowances to be increased. It argued that, in the economic condition of the time, there could be no case for increasing National Insurance benefits in line with the cost of living, as that would merely assist inflation; the 'apparently uncontrollable expenditure' on the social services would have to stop.[59] Productivity would have to be increased if Britain were to compete, which might mean working longer hours.

To help with provision for an ageing population, it argued for the retirement age to be raised, if necessary compelling firms to employ a certain proportion of elderly people; and, for the elderly who could not work, voluntary provision rather than help by the state would be their main support. To improve prosperity for everybody's benefit, it argued for a system of competitive free enterprise. The group did commit itself to the Keynesian ideal of full employment, describing this as 'a first responsibility of government'. However, it added that the ideal 'depends on the competitive power of British industry in the world markets. No devices within the power of Government can counteract a failure in this respect.' Clear though it was from this that it was up to business, not to the state, to maintain the ideal, the wording was sufficiently ambiguous to sow the seeds of one of the great ideological battles that Powell would have with his One Nation colleagues on the front bench in the 1960s. Less ambiguous was the pamphlet's chapter on housing, advocating a massive building programme stimulated by a return to free-market principles: this was written by Powell.

The main principle of the group was set out in the pamphlet's first paragraph: 'Socialists would give the same benefits to everyone, whether or not the help is needed, and indeed whether or not the country's resources are adequate. We believe that we must first help those in need. Socialists believe that the State should provide an average standard. We believe that it should provide a minimum standard, above which people should be free to rise as far as their industry, their thrift, their ability or their genius may take them.'[60] The group believed that the point at which redistribution of income became harmful to the interests of the poor, by so handicapping the better-off that the prosperity of the country was restricted, had been passed. In what would later be recognised as utterly Powellite – or Thatcherite – terms, it lamented that the normal civic duties of charity, once exercised by individuals, had now been transferred to the state. 'Perhaps this is the millennium of "fair shares for all"', the pamphlet said. 'It is certainly the death of human society.'[61] It called for 'those features of taxation and other policy which are promoting the fragmentation of property and hindering its accumulation and transmission' to be 'checked and to some extent reversed'.[62]

Powell's chapter on housing – which Macleod told him was 'really brilliant' – was set in an explicit historical context.[63] He endorsed the precept of the reformer Octavia Hill that all housing 'must be self-supporting, and that the tenants should pay an economic rent'.[64] These principles formed the core of his own ideas. He attacked Bevan's record as minister in charge of housing, pointing out as an example that, under his control, the construction industry had completed fewer than 15,000 houses and flats in April 1950. The output per man was less than half that of 1939. Slum clearance was at a virtual standstill. Often branded a hard man later in his career, Powell revealed his instinctive humanity in this argument; and he showed he had never forgotten the advantage his own simple but secure and happy home as a child had given him.

'These conditions', he wrote of the perpetuation of the slums,

> touch on many aspects of our national life: health threatened by overcrowded and insanitary homes; education retarded when children have no room in which to do homework, or arrive tired at school after sleeping in a room with several others; marriages broken up through the strain of sharing a home or making do in cramped and uncomfortable quarters; Borstal institutions, remand homes and approved schools filled by the products of an unhappy home life. A home of the right size and in the right place and at the right rent is everybody's first need. Less would need to be spent on the other social services if housing conditions were drastically improved.[65]

He argued that the main limiting factor in building quickly enough was the way in which Government planning interfered with the laws of supply and demand; those industries producing building materials were concerned that changes in Government policy would leave them with huge unsold stocks. In particular, the Government's interference in the timber market had resulted in less timber than Britain's builders needed coming into the country, and at a price far higher than it should have been. The building industry, whose activities were controlled by the grant of local authority licences, had to be opened up to the free market. The licensing system meant productivity could not be maximised, and that the building-supplies industry had to try to respond to levels of demand set in the most arbitrary way. Powell called, therefore, for licensing to be abolished, and for the 1947 Town and Country Planning Act to be subject to 'drastic alteration'.[66] Abolition of licensing would also lower the price of existing houses by expanding supply, and would make new ones relatively cheaper too; reform of the 1947 Act, especially in ending the nationalisation of the right to use land for house building, would also make more land available and bring down prices. Above all, a culture of private building had to be restored, with rent controls and other housing subsidies removed in both the public and private sector to encourage supply.

In terms of its detail, its grasp and the nature of its prescriptions, Powell's chapter was the intellectual heart of the pamphlet. Indeed, the fact that the pamphlet embodied such radical thought as it did – radicalism most of the group's members would steer away from subsequently – was a tribute to Powell's immediate didactic influence and the strength of his convictions. However, another section he had drafted, on rights to private property and the iniquity of taxing inheritances, was criticised by Macleod. He told him it 'has all Enoch's faults. It is hopelessly romantic and arrogant and packed with unanswerable unemotional damn silly logic' – something of which Macleod, as a supreme pragmatist, was ever to hold against him.[67] Macleod also, however, asked him in the same letter: 'May I sometimes see your poems? And scrap the one you showed me. The woman hasn't been whelped yet who would act like that.'

III

Powell drove to Edinburgh at the end of August to stay with the Strachans. He fell asleep at Gabriel's wheel and crashed it into a ditch fifty miles short of his destination. No harm was done to him, but the car needed extensive repairs that resulted in its staying in Scotland for the winter. It became a legend in the Freeth family that the letter informing Andrew Freeth of the news of what had happened to his car began, 'Dear Andrew, at least the chassis is recoverable.' 'They were the sort of friends', Freeth's son Martin recalled, 'who could happily have written each other's cars off.'[68] Powell was spotted in the ditch by passengers on a bus, who disembarked and helped haul him out. When one told him he was lucky to be alive, Powell replied, 'That is a matter of conjecture.'[69] His visit to the Strachans did, however, give further evidence of his humanisation: he gladly took their infant son Hew out for walks in his pram at a time when no self-respecting Scotsman would be seen doing such a thing.

Early that autumn Alport, Powell and a few other new Members went to lecture at a weekend school in Northern Ireland. Powell spoke on the importance of the Union, and received a massive ovation; no one could then have seen the wider significance of what he said.[70] In September he went again to Porlock for another riding holiday, shunting his loneliness to one side. He felt he had acquitted himself well, by jumping a five-bar gate on a 'refuser', as he put it to Strachan.[71] It was soon the hunting season. After Barbara there could be no return to the Albrighton, so he set about looking for another hunt, and found one near Bridgnorth, the Wheatland, where he was made welcome. However, his new duties crowded in on him so much that he managed only three days out by the end of the year.

He returned to his constituency from Porlock to find a new distraction: what he called a 'rebellion' was brewing in Wolverhampton, a direct legacy of the way he had imposed his will at the election. One of his constituency branches, Graisely, had passed a resolution on 18 September criticising him. The censure had been concerned with the way Powell had given orders to members about how they were to occupy themselves at the next election, expected within months; the branch was angry that directions for building up an election fighting organisation had come from the candidate and not, as they felt proper, from the executive via the agent. The area agent, Colonel Ledingham, told Central Office that the resolution had been couched in 'unfriendly terms' and was 'probably inspired' by a prominent local Conservative who had not warmed to Powell, James Beattie.[72]

There was a long history to these events. The old Wolverhampton West division had been fought in 1945 by Major Beattie, whose family ran a department store in the town, and were large employers. He had lost badly – but then so had many Conservatives in 1945 – and had not been selected to fight Wolverhampton South-West, as the seat became after boundary changes. Beattie had not left politics, but organised the Graisely branch and generously funded it, to retain a power base. By no coincidence, the officers and members of the branch were mainly senior employees of Beattie's, or ex-employees, or their relatives. They did not necessarily live in the ward. Beattie had made the branch, in Powell's words, 'a fortress within a fortress', and took exception to the way in which the MP regimented the operation, and maintained so personal an interest in it.[73] For his part, Powell admitted that his style of organisation was a little heavy-handed and unduly reminiscent of the staff officer's methods; but then, in his defence, the majority he had to overturn – notwithstanding the boundary change – had been over 7,000. A candidate had, in the end, to be responsible for having the campaign fought in the way that most suited his purposes. In the years ahead, the style would become more relaxed, but now a feud threatening Powell's career was started. For the moment, the matter was kept 'in the family', with neither side alerting the press while Ledingham tried to broker a compromise. However, once Powell's rigid sense of principle and his *amour propre* were brought into play, no truce appeared possible.

On 30 October 1950 he wrote to the association chairman, J. C. Mills, telling him that he would not be standing again because of the 'severe and deliberate censure' on him. The press, inevitably, latched on. *The Times* on 13 November reported: 'It was announced on Saturday that Mr J. E. Powell, Conservative MP for South-West Wolverhampton, has declined the candidature of the division at the next General Election. Sir Robert Bird, president of the divisional Conservative association, has refused to disclose the nature of a vote of censure sent forward from a ward committee which led to Mr Powell's decision.'[74] Bird said that the executive had repudiated the vote of censure and passed a unanimous vote of confidence in Powell; but Powell did not see how he could co-operate with those who had passed the censure.

The press followed the story closely and reported it at length. The executive, acting in accordance with Powell's basic demands if he were to stay their candidate, announced that it would dissolve the Graisely branch and dismiss its officials; then the branch would be re-formed by the constituency chairman, and those dismissed could hold office only when permitted by the executive. The decision had, however, been close: four votes to three. The branch, moreover, refused to submit. It issued a statement that said: 'The executive council had no power to dismiss their freely elected officials, ban them from future office, dissolve their branch or appoint one outside man to reform it. It was incorrect to say that their officials had censured Mr Powell. The executive made themselves look ridiculous by trying to dictate to electors who [sic] they could or could not elect as officials. The officials only did their duty in expressing their opinions in a courteous manner.'[75] In the face of this assault, the executive failed to hold together. The association vice-president, Councillor T. Williams, resigned, accusing his former fellow executive members of 'undemocratic unconstitutional conduct akin to Socialist dogma'. He also expressed regret that Powell 'had not acted in a more statesmanlike and reasonable manner'.[76] Councillor Williams, leader of the Conservative majority on the town council, had been elected vice-president only a week earlier, in recognition of his 'outstanding services to the Conservative cause'. He said that the decision to dissolve the branch was 'entirely contrary to Conservative principles'. Calling for a special general meeting of the association to resolve the issue, he added that 'it is the infliction of a penalty on officers and committee members who considered they were doing their duty. It is wrong democratically and constitutionally and may be of great detriment to the Conservative cause.'

This view found an echo in Central Office. On 15 November Jim Thomas, vice-chairman of the party and with twenty years' experience in the Commons, wrote to the chairman, Woolton, that Powell had been 'far too dictatorial', but that as only one branch had complained a reconciliation should be possible.[77]

'I am dealing very firmly with Mr Powell at this end.' On the same day he wrote to Powell: 'I do beg you to be reasonable. So far as I can make out you have a vote of confidence from your Association and the offending ward has been censured but you still insist that the officers of that ward should be dismissed by the Association. This, of course, is quite impossible as the Association have not the constitutional powers to do so and no Member of Parliament has the right to make this demand.'[78] Telling Powell that he himself had had similar difficulties in Hereford, but had been content with the backing of his association, Thomas added: 'You really are not justified in digging your toes in.' As well as firmness, he tried flattery: 'The party in the House of Commons is most anxious not to lose you as I am sure you have a big future in front of you and are already of immense help to us all.' He also warned Powell that it would be 'awfully difficult' for him to be adopted elsewhere as associations would regard him as troublesome.

Woolton, on receiving Thomas's memorandum, told the Chief Whip and Eden about the problem. In a memorandum to Thomas on 16 November headed 'Brigadier Powell' the chairman was scathing:

> There is a point of principle involved. Neither Members of Parliament nor candidates must be allowed to determine who shall occupy office in the constituencies. If Powell is so lacking in political sense as to do this when he has only been the Member for a few months, and with a majority of only 600, he is likely to cause us trouble in many ways. He is brilliant, of course, but it does not follow that he has common sense. My advice to the constituency would be to accept his resignation, since I regard this particular sort of threat as more than a little uncooperative.[79]

Thomas advised Woolton he had told Powell that 'he is an unmitigated fool' for ignoring 'my perpetual instructions that candidates ... should not interfere in local organisations', and reported that the Graisely officers had been sacked. Thomas was receiving letters from would-be candidates asking to be notified when Powell's seat became available; he was in no mood to mess about.

In response to the Graisely dissolution order P E. Morrell, the branch chairman, told the association chairman that neither he nor his fellow officers would resign. Justifying his refusal, Morrell stated that the association executive had acted unconstitutionally; rule 15 of the association stated that such a dispute should be referred to Central Office. He repeated that the motion passed concerning the fighting of elections was not a censure, and announced that the branch would call its own special general meeting within a week. Morrell had support from Miss Betty Twentyman, who had recently retired as vice-chairman of the association. For some time,' she said, 'I have considered that a large section of the public have felt indignant at the attitude of Mr Powell. It appears that the Graisely ward branch committee has had the courage to voice opinions shared by other ward branches. I consider it would be wrong and shameful to allow any disgrace to fall on that branch.'[80]

Alderman Henry Bowdler, who had just become chairman of the association, responded to Morrell's throwing the rule book at him by picking it up and throwing it back. 'My reading of the rules governing the association leaves no doubt in my mind of the executive council's authority to replace the officers and committee of Graisely ward. To ask for arbitration on the interpretation of those rules seems purposeless … In courtesy to you I will place your letter before the executive council when they next meet.'[81] Powell, who had kept a tactful silence following his upbraiding by Central Office, made a move of peace. Thanking Bowdler and his colleagues for their 'generous expressions of support and confidence', he declared: 'It is my firm hope that the steps the executive council have taken will result in conditions which would enable me to be their candidate at the next election if the association then desires it.'

Powell was confident his threat of resignation would have the desired result. 'I think I am winning the Wolverhampton battle,' he told Strachan, 'which had in any case to be fought out, and shall emerge with increased authority. Certainly, there is nothing to compare with smashing up one's association and burning it as firewood: it makes a blaze one can see to read by.'[82]

Powell involved his parents in his parliamentary life every bit as fully as he had involved them in his previous activities. Sadly, relatively few letters between them from this period survive. As a result we see less of Powell as an ordinary man and more of him as a political figure, a balance that would not be altered until after he left the Commons. His letters to them in the first year of his election to Parliament invite them to share his achievements not just in the chamber, but as a broadcaster and journalist. He also retailed to them his slow but steady progress on his book on the Lords and, most extensively, his thrills in the hunting field.

He told his parents on 2 December, 'I am well satisfied with the new chairman and the arrangements being made,' and reported to them a conversation overheard between two socialist MPs: ' "He's a stiff-necked sort of cuss, this Powell, isn't he?" "Ah, don't you believe it, he's a sly b——r and you'll see, he'll get what he wants." I have.'[83] Nonetheless, Graisely went ahead with its appeal to Central Office, with Morrell the prime mover against Powell. Undeterred by his dusty answer from Bowdler, he wrote to Powell on 13 December, copied to Ledingham, to say that 'the Executive Council are not entitled to prohibit a Branch from electing whatever Officers and Committee it wishes'.[84] He warned Powell that unless he backed down a situation would exist in Graisely that might prevent a Conservative being re-elected. However, Morrell said that 'practically every member of the Association would welcome a reconciliation', and offered to make one last gesture – the exact nature of which was up for negotiation – that would allow Powell to withdraw his opposition to the committee. He sought a private meeting at which this could be discussed, and the 'gesture' agreed upon. Ledingham advised that no action should be taken by Central Office in light of this letter. Thomas simply commented, 'I wish I could be present to watch Brigadier Powell and the Graisely Ward "gesturing" at each other.' Powell did not reply to the letter either.

A meeting on 2 January 1951 gave Beattie and Morrell a 75–25 vote of confidence, and re-elected them; and then, in accordance with the 'gesture' agreed with Ledingham, they stood down in favour of Powell's nominees, a deal fixed by Bowdler. Nervously, Central Office – horrified by the precedents being set – waited to see whether the ward would accept its new officers. The crunch came when Powell addressed the ward branch on 'the situation abroad' on 19 January. The new chairman, assailed by complaints from members, refused to accept a vote of confidence in himself, or to question the election of the imposed officers. In the words of Ledingham's report 'there was renewed uproar and boos when he invited Mr Powell to address the meeting. When the Member started to speak the majority of the audience, approximately 150, walked out, leaving approximately 25 to hear Mr Powell.'[85] Ledingham, who had not attended at Powell's request, as he did not wish for higher intervention, reported that Bowdler and Powell had now fallen out. Bowdler's predecessor, Williams, then wrote to Ledingham begging for Powell to be found a safe seat somewhere else as he could not win Wolverhampton again.

Bowdler, however, was still doing all he could to placate Powell. He wrote to him after this latest debacle to apologise for the behaviour of those who had walked out, saying they had mostly been from outside the ward, and in many cases from outside the association. On 24 January the divisional executive also apologised to Powell for the disorder, and Powell, according to Ledingham, said he was prepared to 'forgive and forget'.[86] That was not everyone's view. The following week Councillor Brian Baylis, a Graisely man ejected from the branch on its dissolution, resigned from Wolverhampton council. He said his position had been made untenable by his ineligibility to serve on any of the ward committees, and that his enforced ineligibility was a 'personal insult' to him.[87]

On 2 February Powell saw Ledingham for the first time in six weeks. The area agent appears by this point to have taken a dislike to Powell. Writing a report on 29 January to his masters, Ledingham brought up ancient history, claiming that Powell had 'pretty well frozen out' his officers before and during the 1950 campaign, and had 'forced the resignation' of Williams as chairman the previous March. When Ledingham and Powell met on 2 February, the MP told him all was now quiet in the constituency, a surprising statement in the light of the fuss created by Baylis. Knowing well what was going on, Ledingham said he did not agree with his judgment; it was a confrontational meeting. The area agent maintained that the association was seriously split and that 'there was a very strong and dangerous under-current operating against him. He [Powell] bridled at this and said he had got what he wanted. After some further comments his tense, almost fanatical intransigence changed. He admitted that the present calm was surface deep. He asked me what I thought of the situation.'[88]

Ledingham, in response to this solicitation, told Powell that his unbending attitude made it hard for him to help the MP. Powell had, he claimed, left him without a negotiating position. He urged him to conciliate both Beattie and Williams. Powell, for all his earlier talk to his parents of having resolved the situation successfully, agreed. Now he wrote to them of the 'peace offensive' he was conducting towards his officers, Beattie's imminent appointment as mayor providing an opportunity.[89] Ledingham also advised him to urge the executive to lift the ban on the ex-Graisely people serving in officerial positions. On 5 February Powell wrote a 'Dear Jim, Yours Enoch' letter to Beattie, inviting him and his wife to lunch at the Commons, to meet on 'friendly terms'. On 25 February he wrote to 'Dear Bowdler' saying that the ban on the Graisely officers need no longer pertain. A resolution to that effect was passed on 14 March.

A long and largely unnecessary conflict was over, and would have no local long-term effects. However, the involvement early on of Woolton, and the alerting of the Chief Whip to the difficulty, cannot have helped Powell's promotion prospects. In the Conservative party of the 1950s troublemakers were unwelcome, however talented. In his annual report to Central Office, Ledingham wrote on 7 May 1951 that Powell was 'an able and most hard working Member but quite inhuman and arrogant in personality with little or no knowledge of human psychology. His political worth is esteemed in Wolverhampton but his real friends are few. He considers the Association his own personal appendage and constantly intervenes in its affairs. "They must be disciplined" is a phrase of his which is a true reflection on his outlook towards the voluntary worker.'[90] In the same report Ledingham criticised the agent, Miss V. E. Norrington, as 'incapable of doing other than sitting on the fence', which he felt had exacerbated the problems of the previous autumn. Saying she was 'dominated' by Powell, 'to whom she has given unswerving loyalty', Ledingham felt that a 'firmer and more constitutional attitude would have been wiser'. He said that 'an uneasy armistice' now prevailed in the association, but he feared that many volunteers would not be there at the next election. Happily for Powell, Ledingham was overdoing the pessimism.

IV

Powell did not allow these difficulties to deflect him from his parliamentary activities. He continued to speak on many subjects – having been helped to a precocious understanding of them in the Research Department – and, as ever, to do so in great depth. He was on his feet in the House on 15 November 1950 on the matter of colonial development and welfare, showing a faultless grasp of the relationship between taxation and jurisdiction. Later that month he revealed the historical underpinning to his approach to the House and its business while speaking on the apparently prosaic Rivers (Prevention of Pollution) Bill. 'I think that it is particularly incumbent upon Tory members of this House, when we are repealing and replacing ... an Act of the Disraeli administration – one of that constellation of Acts which made that administration a landmark in the social history of this country – to ensure that what we are putting in its place is something that is decisively better.'[91]

In an industrial constituency like Wolverhampton South-West, such matters were important, and Powell had also been made aware of a particular problem in the Black Country with tuberculosis. He urged in the Commons on 23 November that steps be taken to advertise the worthwhile nature of TB nursing as a speciality; in March 1951 he and Macleod returned to the subject, when Macleod proposed and Powell seconded a move to have tuberculosis registered as a prescribed disease under the Industrial Injuries Act. There was a widespread view that nurses in sanatoria were liable to contract the disease as a result of their duties, and Powell called for more statistical evidence, lest the anecdotal evidence get out of hand and recruitment be harmed.

On 5 December he made the first of several speeches on Welsh affairs – 'like very many Black Country people, I come of Welsh stock on both sides and I have since my earliest years been connected with the Principality by ties of both study and affection' – in which his expertise, ironically, would lead to his first refusal of office.[92] He argued that, as it was a United Kingdom parliament, all Members should share responsibility for all parts of the Kingdom, even if, like him, they sat for a constituency outside the area under discussion. His main argument was that although industrial Wales currently enjoyed near-full employment – in stark contrast to the pre-war years – there was still apprehension among the workforce because they knew that the pressure the socialist Government had put on firms to open factories in the region was 'of a quite exceptional and temporary nature'.[93] Powell doubted – as those who followed his intellectual lead would do under another Labour government a quarter of a century later – whether the work brought to South Wales was 'as firmly based as it should be'; they were jobs created not by the market, but by a government that thought it could bypass the market and create jobs as a social service.

In his speech Powell quoted a Welsh proverb he had learned as a child: '*Pan gyll y call, fe gyll ymhell* – when a clever man goes astray, he goes far astray.' It was quoted back to him by George Thomas, a future speaker of the Commons, who claimed that Powell himself had gone astray. Thomas did, though, pay him a compliment that showed how rapid had been the creation in the House of the impression of Powell's own ability: 'there are few men on the other side of the House who are more clever than the hon. Gentleman'.[94]

Powell spent much of the Christmas recess in Wolverhampton, maximising his non-parliamentary time in a thorough canvass of the constituency in preparation for an election that could come at any moment. His Black Country origins and freedom from snobbery helped him communicate with his electors. He made a point of accepting invitations into their homes to see the often straightened circumstances in which they lived. There was no repeat of his lonely Christmas of the previous year; he went to stay with his parents and thence, bravely, to a Fabian weekend in Bognor to debate the motion 'Has socialism lost its appeal?'[95] He was also developing a practice as a freelance journalist. His first article for the *Spectator* – for which he would become a regular contributor and, during the 1970s and 1980s, one of its main book reviewers – appeared in December 1950, arguing for the building of 300,000 houses a year. Powell argued that it could be done, provided 'socialist planning and control' were removed.[96]

There was still too little good housing, as he had seen in his own constituency. The slums were being cleared at a rate far below what Labour had promised. The war damage had still not been made good. Such older property as survived was, in the private rented sector, subject to heavy regulation and restrictions. At the end of January in a debate on the reform of leasehold property he argued again that restrictions had prevented the development of new housing; he also pleaded for the principle of *caveat emptor* to apply to those who had bought leases in the immediate post-war period, in the full knowledge of the restrictions a socialist government would place upon them, and who now complained about them. He moved various amendments to the Bill, some of them highly technical, such as when he pointed out that the distinction between property owned by the Duchy of Cornwall (which was, in theory, separable from the Crown) and the Duchy of Lancaster (which was not) was not covered by the Bill.

Powell's research into the history of the Lords helped him intervene in matters well outside his main specialisms. On 13 March 1951 he spoke on the Bishops (Retirement) Measure, showing such self-confidence in his understanding of the workings of the prelacy and its role in the constitution that he could criticise the form in which the Church Assembly had sent the Measure up to Parliament. He was especially vexed by an apparent self-contradiction in the text about the removal of bishops once a complaint has been made against them, being unclear about whether this step could be taken, and a vacancy declared in the bishopric, with or without an inquiry and report. He said, rather pompously, 'I hope that, in future, means will be used to ensure that the drafting of these Measures is up to the high standard to which we in this House are accustomed.'[97]

We gave an erudite account of some of the more celebrated examples of the removal of a bishop, showing how various forms of tribunals through the ages had dealt with this task. He was unsure from the case of Bishop King of Lincoln, for example, in 1888 whether the Judicial Committee of the Privy Council had admitted the 'propriety of an appeal' from the tribunal that removed him. The question of the House of Lords' jurisdiction over a bishop was yet more complex.

> The bishops are indeed Members of the Upper House for a reason which originally would have entitled them to trial by peers, namely, that they held of the King-in-chief under feudal law. Since then, they themselves waived their privilege of peerage before the end of the Middle Ages, and they have never since that time been treated as peers. Indeed, the very appellation "House of Peers" applied to the Upper House is not fully accurate, and there are no grounds for supposing that an original jurisdiction upon the bishops vests in the Upper House.[98]

Powell complained that the new Measure did not take the opportunity of clarifying the question of jurisdiction over miscreant bishops; there was still the prospect of appeal to the secular courts and, from there, to the House of Lords. In the end, to compound the confusion, the Measure allowed an archbishop sitting with three bishops to decide a case, but the archbishop, in seeking to deprive a bishop of his see, was not obliged to take any notice of those sitting with him; and there was an appeal to the King in Council anyway, which effectively bypassed the Judicial Committee of the Privy Council. Having politely pointed out these complexities, and warned that they had 'for centuries' caused 'severe acrimony and debate', Powell sat down.[99]

In the first three months of 1951 he hunted more frequently, and rode in the hunt point-to-point in early April, having returned from a short post-Easter visit to the Strachans in Edinburgh to collect the newly restored Gabriel. For Powell, like Jorrocks, the hunting season was too short; so, to extend it through the summer, he joined a pack of otter hounds, the Hawkstone, whose country ran from the Severn Estuary up through the Welsh border and marches. He contrived to spend almost every other weekend that summer out with the Hawkstone, reporting to Strachan on 4 June his satisfaction at having seen six otters dispatched in five outings thus far. There was still the sense that Powell had an excess of restless energy to be used up by whatever means were available; his political work was not enough.

In his first years in the House, he ranged widely not merely into the obscure, but also into many other areas of more routine importance. On 13 April 1951 he spoke in the debate on the Elderly Persons (Employment) Bill, arguing for more incentives to keep men working beyond sixty-five. Three days later, he pointed out the absurdity of including overheads in the charge for school meals because, he said, if the price of the meal was more than it would cost a parent to provide at home, fewer children would take them up, possibly harming their nutrition. On the report stage* of the Leasehold Property Bill he argued again for deregu-

---

* A Bill comes back to the floor of the House after its Committee Stage, and amendments made by the Committee are discussed. Also, Members who did not serve on the Committee have an opportunity to move their own amendments.

latory provisions to be inserted. With Macleod he operated the now familiar double act on two other measures: a debate on 17 April, on the private building of housing, and, almost constantly for the last week in April and the first week in May, the National Health Service Bill.

In the housing debate Powell's grasp of detail allowed him to score points off the under-secretary, George Lindgren. Defending the Government's record, Lindgren stated that 'we lost one-fifth of the houses in the country from enemy action during the war'. Powell jumped to his feet. 'That is an absolute mis-statement, and the Minister knows it.' Lindgren refused to acknowledge this, claiming, 'I think it is true.' Powell rounded on him. 'It is completely untrue. The Minister should know perfectly well that the number of houses lost by enemy action during the war was less than half a million. Four million were damaged to a slight extent.' Lindgren modified what he had said, while claiming not to do so: 'I repeat that one-fifth of the houses in the country were either destroyed or damaged to such an extent as to require war damage repair.'[100]

Both Powell and Macleod took a keen interest in the health service: both saw the difficulties of continuing to finance the socialist scheme, while recognising its popularity among the public; and both knew the importance of good and available health care to the 'one nation' idea. Also, for ambitious men conscious of their own abilities, so prominent an issue as health provided a perfect platform to impress. On 15 March Hugh Gaitskell, the Chancellor of the Exchequer, had proposed in the cabinet committee dealing with the NHS that its costs be limited to £382 million in the year ahead, the same as in the present year. It was proposed to help do this by imposing prescription charges. Labour was split; Bevan, who had until January that year been Minister of Health and had acted as midwife for the NHS, threatened to resign as Minister of Labour if charges were imposed; so did Harold Wilson, the President of the Board of Trade. Both men – Bevan in particular – felt that Gaitskell had overstated his case when arguing of the need to engage in rearmament, and disputed the taste of his finding part of the money to do this from the health service.

In the Budget on 10 April charges were announced, with a Health Service Bill needed to implement them. Bevan and Wilson duly resigned rather than vote for the Bill, and the parliamentary secretary at the Ministry of Supply, John Freeman, went with them. On 24 April Powell spoke in the second reading debate, the day after Wilson's and Freeman's resignations and two days after Bevan's. In his speech, he discounted the idea fostered by the Government that the introduction of charges was 'of minor importance and . . . introduces nothing which is really new or fundamental'.[101] It was, he said, a whole change of principle, 'a turning point in the history of the development of the social services in this century'. Specifically, health was passing from being a totally free social service to one in which, in part, a means test was applicable. Under the means test in this case, some who had paid for prescriptions could apply to the

National Assistance Board to be reimbursed, even if in some cases that person was not receiving National Assistance. This would, he warned, overload the board to the point where 'sooner or later, almost inevitably, it will become rigid and bureaucratic, and will tend towards inhumanity'.[102] Worse, he said, many of the most deserving, such as pensioners, would not bother to try to get their money back from the National Assistance Board, but would pay up and have to make financial sacrifices. Powell felt there must be a better way – as did many others, which was how the system of exemption from prescription charges developed. He also argued that charging should have been extended more widely across the NHS, so that it fell less heavily on prescriptions.

The Bill went into committee almost immediately, on the floor of the House. Powell and Macleod busily moved amendments. On 2 May Powell suggested one to remove the National Assistance Board from the Bill to prevent it being used in much the same way 'as the Poor Law Commissioners regarded poor relief in 1834, when they conceived it to be their duty so to organise poor relief that as few people as possible would apply for it'.[103] He also criticised the illogicality of free medicines for in-patients, the assumption having been that they were unable to earn money. Powell pointed out that many trades and professions continued to pay staff who were hospitalised, at least for a time; and the free service would even go to those in pay beds and amenity beds. He felt this decision had been made to remove the need for those in hospital to apply to the NAB for reimbursement; it made his point that use of the NAB did not help achieve his main aim, which was to help those who most needed it.

In April 1951 he widened his attack on socialist iniquity, complaining about the over-regulation of Coal Board land, and asking for import duty to be taken off wood so that more timber houses could be built (as was happening in Europe) to help alleviate the housing shortage. In early June he spoke again on the health service, arguing that the treatment of the elderly sick (who accounted then, as now, for a disproportionate amount of NHS resources) should be conducted outside the hospital service: something which, if implemented, would, he said, be 'the truest economy we can carry out' as it would assist the turnover of patients.[104] Later that month the Leasehold Property Bill came back to the Commons, and Powell was again active; and on 25 June there was another opportunity with Macleod to harry the Government, this time on its attitude to men injured at work, and the compensation they should receive.

On 10 July, in what turned out to be his last significant contribution of the Parliament, he spoke on what he felt was the harmful effect National Assistance 'pocket money' of £1 a week was having on those institutionalised with tuberculosis. The Government had announced that the numbers receiving assistance of this sort had, since July 1948, been rising by 100 a week; Powell felt this ran counter to the frequently expressed optimism about the decline in the tuberculosis death rate, since it meant an extra 15,000 cases in three years. He also wondered why the 'pocket money' was being paid at so low a rate; it had been designed in 1948 as an incentive to those who had the disease to give up work and receive treatment for it. It seemed to him now, with the rate of illness apparently still rising so quickly, that more inducement was needed, for the benefits of the individual and the community, for those with TB to have proper treatment. He also argued that the extra assistance given to the blind, to help them meet the additional expenses of their disability, should be raised – there was no intention to do that by the Government – because of inflation since 1948.

More significant, in the light of work Powell was undertaking with Macleod under the auspices of One Nation, was his exposition of his theory about how the insurance principle of the welfare services had been eroded by the cost of living. Beveridge had estimated the subsistence level for a man and his wife in 1938 at 32s a week, including 10s rent. When the Government made its proposals for the post-war welfare system in 1944, it raised the figure to 40s. After the National Insurance Act of 1946, Attlee's Government had increased the sum to 42s; that was the basic figure for the purposes of calculating all insurance benefits. Whenever new measures were introduced calculating the subsistence figure, they were out of date even before they came into force; the latest figures were 50s excluding rent, which was calculated at 14s. The total of 64s doubled Beveridge's 1938 assessment, which Powell called 'a staggering and alarming story'.[105] The cost of living index for the present year showed an alarming inflation of 9.2 per cent, which the Government explained as the effects of the Korean War. The increase in the cost of living was something people were not insured for, and there would be serious long-term consequences if that were not altered.

As with the calling of the last election, the House of Commons had embarked on a recess from which it had expected to return for another session of business. However, Attlee, by the novel means of broadcasting on the BBC after the nine o'clock news on 19 September 1951, announced an election for 25 October. His sudden decision did not help his party, as the faction around Bevan and Wilson chose, coincidentally, to publish a pamphlet the day after the announcement critical of Government policy. The Conservatives had a wide-open split in their opponents' party to capitalise on; the wind was set fair for victory.

Powell canvassed exhaustively, as before. He made nine speeches in the ten days before the election, taking off just the Sunday. His election address put more emphasis than in 1950 on the imperial theme; its first main point was 'I BELIEVE IN THE BRITISH EMPIRE. Without the Empire, Britain would be like a head without a body.'[106] Whatever his private reservations, Powell used imperial policy as a weapon against the socialists. 'In six years, nearly all our Empire in Asia has been lost; our position in the Middle East is gravely under-mined; Africa threatens to go the same way; and our links with the Dominions are slighter than ever. Everywhere Socialism has wrought chaos and brought us into contempt.' He spoke of 'the determination to restore our prestige throughout the world' that his party had; he attacked nationalisation but did not advocate denationalisation; he promised lower taxes, and maintenance of the social services. He concluded with a Tory promise to maintain the things the Conservatives were supposed to maintain – 'our hereditary Monarchy and House of Lords; our freely elected House of Commons; the Rule of Law, our right to own property, small or great, and to leave it to our children; and last, but not least, our faith'.

V

The Conservatives won, with a majority over all other parties of seventeen. In a two-way fight with Labour, Powell was returned by an increased majority of 3,196. He was still not safe, but the Government's majority was large enough to suggest that it would be more than twenty months this time before he had to fight another election. It was good news for him, too, given the interests he had established, that Churchill should announce that housing would have a priority second only to defence. He renamed the Ministry of Local Government and Planning the Ministry of Housing and Local Government to make this point more forcefully, and put Harold Macmillan in charge of it. For all the talent and dedication he had shown in his first Parliament, Powell was not offered office: his black mark for rebelling over the Schuman Plan, and his behaviour over Graisely, had been insufficiently countered by his role in irritating the last Government.

Others of the 1950 intake were luckier. James Clyde, the Lord Advocate, and Lionel Heald, the Attorney-General, were special cases: both in their early fifties, they were distinguished lawyers in jobs with a restricted list of applicants. Brigadier John Smyth, who was fifty-eight and had won the Victoria Cross in the Great War, became parliamentary secretary at the Ministry of Pensions. Henry Hopkinson, Powell's former chief in the Research Department, was made a parliamentary secretary at Trade. One of a comparatively small band of Welsh Conservative MPs, David Llewellyn, became, at thirty-five, under-secretary at the Home Office with responsibility for Welsh affairs. George Nugent, five years older than Powell, was made a parliamentary secretary at the Ministry of Agriculture, and Charles Hill, the 'radio doctor', who was eight years Powell's senior, became parliamentary secretary at the Ministry of Food. The stars of the intake appeared to be Anthony Nutting, still only thirty-one, and under-secretary at the Foreign Office, and Patricia Hornsby-Smith, at thirty-six parliamentary secretary at the Ministry of Health. Of Powell's other contemporaries, Edward Heath and Dennis Vosper both became junior Whips. For the Research Department trio of himself, Macleod and Maudling, there was as yet no recognition, so guerrilla activities on the backbenches had to continue. For his part Powell, despite his relative youth and inexperience, stood for election to the executive of the 1922 Committee of backbenchers; one of thirty-nine candidates for twelve vacancies; he failed. It attracted attention to him, though, and he would serve on other backbench committees.[107] On 14 November, in recognition of his expertise, he was elected vice-chairman of the Housing and Works Committee; a week later he called for the Government to have a housing survey, the first since 1936.[108]

During the election campaign constituency workers in Wolverhampton had noted how frequently Pamela Wilson, Powell's former secretary, was visiting, and how when Powell gave groups of ladies lifts home in Gabriel after a meeting he would undertake the most enormous detours in order to ensure that she was the last to be dropped off. Miss Wilson had gone to work in Strasbourg after the 1950 election, but being 'hooked on politics' had willingly gone to see how Powell was faring in his new seat. She had noticed a change in his attitude towards her when, on one of her visits, her train had been badly delayed from a fog-bound London. Expecting that he would have other matters to attend to, she found Powell still waiting for her on a rain-lashed platform at the station when her train pulled in four hours late. He decided after his re-election not to renew the lease on his flat in Wolverhampton, but to base himself permanently in London. The truth was that a different sort of accommodation would be needed in the constituency.

On 10 November 1951 his engagement to Miss Wilson was announced. She later recalled that at the time of his proposal to her – made on bended knee on an eiderdown in his London flat – he had said, 'Life with an MP has to be hard.'[109] He remembered, 'I promised her two things. I promised her grinding poverty and my whole life spent on the back benches.'[110] It was a remark Powell would later cite as proof he had not gone into Parliament in pursuit of office. She had long been captivated by her ex-boss: 'his eyes were very blue, and he was great fun.'[111] Although she had been engaged to someone else, she was now available again. In one respect especially she was made for Powell: someone of his single-mindedness needed constant support if he was to succeed, and needed, above all, someone to be his bridge to the real world. In his fiancée he had found someone prepared to be totally and utterly loyal to him throughout the great vicissitudes that would befall them; it was one of his luckiest moves. She had known, after dinner at a Chinese restaurant three days earlier, that he would propose, and was prepared. She did not hesitate to accept; her only conditions were that she would not be expected to cook tripe, one of Powell's favourite dishes, or to jug hare.[112]

His wife would have a profound effect on him. 'I think especially before I was married, that there was a certain reserve and concentration about me. Perhaps intensity is nearer the mark.'[113] Now that would change. Clement Jones, who was getting to know Powell well, saw this as a crucial transition: 'Pam took over the mantle of his mother.'[114] Powell had found a new most important person in his life. His friends and colleagues quickly came to admire his new wife, not least because she immediately set to work on mellowing him. 'I thought it was a marvellous marriage for him,' said Alport, 'and I thought she was a marvellous girl. We all admired her, and, knowing Enoch as we did, we admired her all the more for taking on such a task. We felt she would have a tremendously good influence over him.'[115] She changed her husband in some respects: he did not hunt for twenty years, now that he had domestic responsibilities. Pam was philosophical about the task, and never wavered. Later, she would tell friends that 'living with Enoch is fun, especially if you like being blown up politically, so to speak, every five years'.[116] There was already a more developed human side to Powell than many knew. Macleod told Robert Carr, 'I wish you could come and be at home one weekend when he comes and stays with us. You should see him with our children. They absolutely adore him. He's light and easy with them, he comes and sits on the end of their beds and spins them stories entirely of his own invention.'[117]

When the news of Powell's engagement was broken, one of the many letters of congratulation he received was from Barbara Hawkins. She bore him no ill-will, and congratulated him sincerely on his engagement, making it clear that she and her husband would like to be friends with the future Mr and Mrs Powell. 'Is your fiancé [sic] still in Wolverhampton? If she is do give me a ring one of these days and bring her over for supper one evening.'[118] Powell marked her letter next to the observation: 'Have you written any more poetry lately. I heard that you had a collection published the other day. Were they old ones or new ones?' She apparently had no idea they were her wedding gift. 'Dear John,' she concluded, 'I do hope that you are really very happy. I think that you will have understood why I haven't come to see you before, but now after a year has elapsed and in view of your engagement the situation is altered, and I would love to talk to you.' There can be no doubt of her sincerity, but she – like, perhaps, Thomas and Wickenden before her – plainly had no idea of the intensity with which Powell threw himself into his romantic friendships. He never replied.[119]

In the five years since Powell had first been confronted with the shock of Britain's decision to withdraw from India he had, to meet this new reality, revised completely his view of imperialism. An empire was one thing: a sham-empire, which was how he had quickly come to view the Commonwealth, quite another. He would admit, nearly forty years later, that although he had made the intellectual break, he would never completely make the emotional one with the past era of British glory: 'I also know that, on my deathbed, I shall still be believing with one part of my brain that somewhere on every ocean of the world there is a great, grey ship with three funnels and sixteen-inch guns which can blow out of the water any other navy which is likely to face it. I know it is not so ... but that factor – that emotional factor ... will not die until I, the carrier of it, am dead.'[120] When the Diplomatic Immunities Bill had its second reading in the Commons on 5 December 1951, Powell used the occasion to sound some unemotional notes that would resonate in his thinking and oratory for decades. The Bill clarified the status of diplomats from the Dominions and the Republic of Ireland, ostensibly at the wish of Commonwealth countries: Powell, though, said that 'the Government cannot shelter behind the real or alleged wishes of what is called the Commonwealth'; it had to make up its own mind about the nature of diplomatic privileges to citizens of these nations.[121]

He described the Bill as 'one of the progeny of that most evil Statute, the British Nationality Act 1948'. Powell's objections to the Act were rooted in the fact, as he reminded the House, that it had 'effected a complete revolution in the basis of British subjecthood', eradicating the old basis – 'our duty of allegiance to our common Sovereign' – and replacing it with citizenship as created, and as liable to be varied by, various Commonwealth legislatures. Hitherto, the Foreign Office had resisted conferring diplomatic immunities on British subjects in Britain; this Bill sought to alter that, and could do so only as a result of the 1948 Act. What concerned Powell was that:

> the Bill makes a differentiation in the eyes of the law between two categories of British subjects, between those who are what is called 'citizens of the United Kingdom and Colonies' and those who are not; for a person to whom the description of High Commissioner or any of the servants of a High Commissioner applies, who is also a citizen of the United Kingdom and Colonies, is placed in a different legal position from that of a similar person who is not such a citizen. It therefore effects a distinction in this country in the eyes of the law between the rights of two British subjects.[122]

Powell recalled that it was the fear of precisely such distinctions as these that had provoked some Conservatives to object to the British Nationality Bill when it had gone through three years earlier. He referred to his party's 'Imperial Policy' statement of 1949, in which the desire to return to the old concept of common citizenship had been expressed; and he asked that the Government design a new Nationality Act to replace that of 1948, rather than legislate for the old Act's unfortunate consequences. He also protested against the Bill because he could find no evidence that the diplomats it sought to protect had suffered by not being protected in the past. He said legislation should be undertaken only when clearly necessary, which was not so in this case.

Although Powell voted with the Government, his independence of mind was glaringly apparent from the force with which he had argued against what most of his colleagues regarded as a harmless measure. He was making a reputation for attention to the smallest detail: two days earlier he had detained the House on the subject of the statutory number of matches in matchboxes, and the price controls on this commodity. At the end of February 1952, when the Diplomatic Immunities Bill came back to the House, he pulled up James Duncan, a fellow Conservative, for suggesting that the concept of immunities had started when the Czar of Russia, visiting Queen Anne, had been attacked by the mob in London. 'I think it was the Czar's Ambassador, and not the Czar in person,' Powell interrupted, omnisciently.[123]

With Ted Curtis as his best man and the Macleods in the congregation, he married Pamela Wilson at Christ Church, Lancaster Gate, on 2 January 1952. Each year he would mark the anniversary by a gift of red roses – one for each year of their marriage – and a poem. 'They will be your pension,' he often told her. Writing to Strachan – who could not be present – on the morning of his wedding, Powell said he had sat up the previous night 're-reading Ovid's *Ars Amatoria*. This and Catullus have already stood me in good stead.'[124] The honeymoon was spent driving through France and Spain in Gabriel, with a small excursion to Majorca. Never one to dilute his standards, Powell submitted to having a paddle in the sea, but declined to remove any part of the three-piece suit he was wearing at the time. There were no plans, once they returned to London, to move from Earl's Court Square, and Powell went to an auction and bought the marital bed – a four-poster. Once his parliamentary life resumed, Pam began to work for him as his secretary, from the Earl's Court Square flat. Thus he was freed of some of the routine administrative work he had been doing since his entry to the Commons, and had more time to devote to policy matters.

On 19 February 1952 Powell wrote to Strachan: 'Dear Michael, We have today purchased an electrically heated oil-filled three-bar aluminium towel rail for the (in the circumstances not immoderate) sum of £10 16s 10d and are complying with your wishes by informing you of the fact. *Dein schamlosestes*, Enoch.'[125] The Strachans had asked the Powells what they would like as a wedding present; the electric towel-rail was their choice. They had been told to buy it and send Strachan the bill. The towel-rail was christened Fritz, and Powell, reporting on its progress, proclaimed that 'for no more expense than a small light bulb he keeps bathroom warm & clothes and towels aired throughout the day'.[126] He added, tactfully, that 'Pam was shocked by my barefaced impudence in taking you at your word & sending you the accompt. I know better.'

In late 1951 Powell and Macleod had written jointly a pamphlet called *The Social Services: Needs and Means*, which they described as 'having had its origins on the benches of the House of Commons during the passage of the National Health Service and National Insurance Bills of 1951'.[127] The authors explained that, during the debates on those Bills 'it became increasingly clear to us that the feature they had in common – the application of a means test to social services hitherto without it – was of more than minor significance'. They added that it had seemed neither party had thought out the relationship between the social services and the means test, nor had defined either term. The result of Powell's and Macleod's attempt to do so was published by the Conservative Political Centre in January 1952. Macleod claimed, in a lecture two years later, that he had only 'a very minor share' in writing the pamphlet, a claim supported by the fact that Powell felt little scruple, in 1954, in revising it himself for a second edition.[128] The pamphlet gave a potted, but remarkably thorough, history of social service provision in Britain from the time of the Poor Law Acts of the nineteenth century and, having detailed how matters had reached their present state, came to conclusions that should have been, but were not, obvious to the rest of the parliamentary Conservative party.

The main argument was that the original purpose of National Insurance had been lost, and that contributions to the fund would have to be increased. The contributory principle was, instead, being eroded by National Assistance; because of the growth of welfarism under the Attlee administration fewer people received poor relief in 1900 than received its successor, National Assistance, in 1950. The principle Powell and Macleod wanted to return to was this: 'not "Should a means test be applied to a social service?", but "Why should any social service be provided without a test of need?" '[129] The conclusion was that a crisis had been reached in the social services, 'a crisis all the more dangerous for being unrecognised'. This was blamed on the Labour Government; and the authors claimed that 'the plans laid down by the Coalition Government which sprang from the Beveridge Report are becoming a patchwork'.[130]

Means testing was, they argued, 'imperative'; and Conservatives – principally, though they did not say so, themselves – had tried to apply the principle by amendment during the passage of the National Health Service Bill the previous year. They warned that if the value of money kept falling, the National Insurance benefits, spread thinly as they were, would become derisory. To restore their value, there had to be an increase in contributions – spread by whatever means between the employer, the employee and the Exchequer. The argument would rumble on, unresolved, for the rest of the century, despite attempts by Conservative and Labour administrations after 1979 to restrict welfare benefits to those who needed them.

When the Diplomatic Immunities Bill had its committee stage at the end of February, Powell had another opportunity to advertise his dissatisfaction with the use of the term 'Commonwealth', and what he regarded as the casual and inexact way in which it was used. The Bill included the phrase 'being a country within the Commonwealth', to which Powell took particular exception. He said that the term 'Commonwealth' had not appeared in British statute law until, peculiarly, the 1950 Finance Act. That Act had not bothered to define the term it used, 'Commonwealth Territories', though Powell himself had put down an amendment to ensure that it did so. The definition had been for the purposes of that Act, and that Act only. Now the term 'Commonwealth' was being used, on its own, for the first time, and without definition: so he asked for the words to be taken out, not just to avoid problems of definition, but because they were not necessary to the meaning of the Bill, its purpose not applying to diplomats from 'foreign' powers in any case as such people already enjoyed the immunities it sought to confer. His advice was taken.

An attempt by a Labour backbencher, Geoffrey de Freitas, to bring in a Bill in April to compel any cabinet to have two out of every three of its members chosen from the Commons also attracted Powell's constitutional eye. He protested, unsuccessfully, to the Speaker that it was out of order for de Freitas to try to bring in the Bill unless a Privy Councillor had first signified to the House that the Queen consented; this was because the Bill, in his view, affected the royal prerogative: 'The selection of the Ministers and advisers of the Crown is, beyond doubt or dispute, a matter of the Royal Prerogative, and any Bill which seeks to ensure that the advisers of the Crown shall be selected from a specific range of persons is, upon the face of it, a limitation of that Prerogative.' The Speaker told him that he felt the passage without royal assent at the earliest stage of the Ministers of the Crown Act 1937, which had limited the number of ministers who could sit in the Commons, was sufficient precedent for this Bill proceeding. He did not agree with Powell that the 1937 Act was totally different in that it dealt merely with disqualifications from sitting in the Commons.

Powell had concerned himself with the constitutional position of the Sovereign and her family in another regard a few weeks earlier. King George had died on 6 February, providing Britain with a queen regnant and consort for the first time in ninety years. On 26 February that consort, Prince Philip, came to watch a debate in the Commons from the Peers Gallery – as was his right as Duke of Edinburgh. Powell mentioned to the Chief Whip that he found this objectionable, and wrote to Churchill to explain why. 'Owing to this closeness to the Sovereign the impression can too easily arise, however unjustified, that his attendance and behaviour convey the Sovereign's own wishes and feelings and that a new and unconstitutional means is created of acquainting the Sovereign with what passes in the lower chamber.'[131] Powell did not deny the Duke's right to attend but argued that, like the Sovereign's right to veto Bills, or the Duke's own right to vote in the House of Lords, exercising the right was not necessarily advisable. He pointed out that Prince Albert, the last consort, had attended in January 1846, to watch Peel introduce the resolution to repeal the Corn Laws. Disraeli had commented unfavourably on his attendance, and Lord George Bentinck had openly criticised it in the House. The Prince never attended the Commons again. Churchill, though, would have none of it. 'It seems to me a good thing that His Royal Highness should understand how our parliamentary affairs work,' he wrote.[132] As for Prince Albert, there was no comparison because 'in those days the contact of the Crown with political issues was much more direct than it is today'.

VI

The alliance between Powell and Macleod – Powell seems already to have learned the truth of his famous dictum that there is no such thing as friendship in politics – had a setback in the spring of 1952. On 27 March the House gave a second reading to the National Health Service Bill, and for it Powell had put in extensive work preparing a speech he had hoped would display his intellectual credentials in all their glory. However, the speaking order of the backbenchers was rearranged at the last minute, and instead it was Macleod, who Powell had understood would follow him, who spoke first. He followed Bevan, who had denounced the idea of further charges – the Minister of Health, Harry Crookshank, had made a poor defence of them as a means of stopping the abuse of resources. Macleod and Powell both knew that Bevan relied on emotion rather than reason, and it was easy for disciplined intellects to take him apart. Not that Macleod confined himself to the *argumentum ad rationem*, as his opening words – 'I want to deal closely and with relish with the vulgar, crude and intemperate speech to which the House of Commons has just listened' – made clear.[133] Churchill, on his way out of the chamber, stopped and listened to the first part of the speech; he was impressed by Macleod's guts in taking on Bevan, and noted him. Powell's speech stayed in his pocket.

His belated chance to make an impact on the subject came the following week, at the committee stage. He took on Hilary Marquand, who had succeeded Bevan as Minister of Health, and who was demanding that a limit after which there would be no charges should be set. 'The rt hon Gentleman came down to the House a year ago and presented a National Health Service Bill in which charges comparable with those in the present Bill were embodied, without any qualification, proviso or terminal date whatsoever. He, therefore, is the last person who ought to get up in the committee and complain now that there is no proviso in the present Bill.'[134] Marquand countered that he hoped Powell would do him the honour of remarking that, in that second reading debate, Marquand had said the Act was not meant to be permanent. Powell simply replied: 'Of course. No Acts of Parliament can be permanent. It may be that hon Members opposite are not aware that Parliament cannot bind itself.' He also pointed out the harmful effects of setting such a date limit, for it would mean patients postponing treatment, in some cases with disastrous effect, until it became free.

However, for all Powell's efforts, Macleod had won this round. Within six weeks of his attack on Bevan he had, at the age of thirty-eight, replaced Crookshank as Minister of Health. Bill Deedes, who had heard his speech, said this was like 'a decoration in the field ... promoted on the strength of just one speech'.[135] For all his undeniable ability, Macleod had performed the politician's favourite trick of being in the right place at the right time. Powell's pride was wounded. Once on that inside track, Macleod never left it, his own resignation in October 1963 notwithstanding. Powell could never quite, in sheer terms of office, catch up.

His hurt impaired his social relationship with Macleod. This mattered to Macleod very much for, like the good politician he was, he did not like having enemies. Late at night on 27 May 1952, three weeks after his appointment, he wrote in friendly but exasperated terms to Powell:

My Dear Enoch

Let us get at least two things clear.
1. (although like you I don't write these things) You know, or bloody well should know, that to me your opinions on health or anything else are worth those of ten other men.
2. Being where I am I need you more – much more – and not less than I did.
These things being so for the love of heaven stop being twelve years old and come and see me every single minute you can spare from the House of Lords.
I won't expand this: why should I?
    Ever Iain.

PS. Show this to Pam and she (sensible girl) will hammer your silly head in.[136]

There is no trace of Powell's reply, if there was one; his wife did not doubt he was jealous of Macleod's success, because he believed he was just as capable.[137] Robert Carr, who knew them both well, recalled an incident in the division lobby when Macleod, who was with Carr, saw Powell ahead of them. 'Iain said: "I must get hold of Enoch. We can't go on like this." And he sidled up to Enoch, who proceeded promptly to turn his back on him, and refused to speak to him.'[138] At the end of June 1952 Macleod's wife Eve was taken into hospital, gravely ill with polio and meningitis from which she gradually made a recovery. The Powells took Macleod in for the duration, and Pam Powell – who found Macleod 'lovable and a charming man' – looked after him in his wife's absence; the invitation had, though, been on her husband's initiative.[139] The gesture was made with Powell's usual repressed emotion. Macleod recalled that 'Enoch strode into the room and threw a key on my desk. "There's a room ready in my flat," he said, "come and go as you wish." And the door banged behind him.'[140] However, the Powells noted a cooling off in Macleod's interest in Powell, an interest only revived shortly before Powell joined the Government at the end of 1955. There was talk of Macleod's being hurt not to have been asked to become godfather to the Powells' first daughter. He had cause to be irritated by Powell's behaviour towards him, and towards his success. Also, though, there seems to have been an element of Powell's having, for the moment, served his purpose for Macleod. However, Ian Gilmour recounts that, during the froideur in 1954, Macleod was still trying to persuade the leadership to give Powell a job, writing to Butler, not perhaps entirely helpfully, that 'his ability of course is not in doubt, only his judgment'.[141]

That spring and summer Powell spoke on two important Bills. On the Housing Bill on 22 April he argued for a system that would encourage the building of economic dwellings, with more cottages and fewer flats. Two months later, on 24 June, he spoke on the Pensions (Increase) Bill. It was a highly political speech – more populist than some of his earlier, more detail-laden efforts, perhaps as a result of his noticing how such a tone had worked for Macleod – condemning Labour for its accusations of parsimony against the Government when the party itself had not raised pensions from 1947 until leaving office less than a year earlier.

Being political did not, of course, always mean being popular; but Powell's economic rigour was ever to the fore. That summer he defended the Government's transport policy, which sought to relate rail fares to real costs rather than to operate the railway as a social service, and to decentralise management and financial control. He also engaged regularly in public point-scoring against Labour, such as when exposing again the hypocrisy of Marquand in pledging to abolish the NHS charges that Labour itself had had to introduce. Marquand had said, again, that Labour ministers had pledged the party to end charges for dentures and spectacles in 1954. However, as Powell pointed out in a letter to *The Times*, the 1951 National Health Service Bill (in the course of whose passage Labour had made the abolition promise) actually allowed charges to be renewed simply by an Order in Council*. 'So far', he said, 'from pledging themselves to end the charges in 1954, the Labour Government deliberately provided the machinery for continuing them.'[142]

With married life began the routine, seldom departed from for the next forty years, of an annual holiday to France. The holidays were never that protracted: throughout his time in Wolverhampton, Powell would try to spend much of his recess in his constituency. The main activity in France would be exploring architectural jewels, but he also made a point of reading a French novel each year. He started with Zola, and then advanced into Proust. On his return, his high-profile political activity was noticed by the press, and he started to appear in diary columns tipped for promotion. 'Tory MPs often discuss among themselves

---

* An order made by the Sovereign at a meeting of the Privy Council under the Royal Prerogative (acting on ministerial advice) or, more usually, as subordinate legislation already allowed for by an Act of Parliament. Northern Ireland was governed in this way following the imposition of Direct Rule in 1972.

"How far will Enoch Powell go?" ' noted the *Daily Mail*. The paper concluded that the journey would end at 'the top' but only after he had corrected faults in his personality. 'His logical thought and his mastery of any subject on which he speaks are so overwhelming that they have done him more harm than good. The House does not like to be lectured. He lacks the human touch and has up to now failed to evoke the members' sympathy. With his somewhat lofty, ascetic air, he gives the impression at times of not caring very much what the rest of the world thinks about him. Intellectually, he is utterly sure of himself.'[143]

Powell did not have to wait much longer for recognition. Churchill offered him the post of under-secretary for Welsh affairs at the Home Office in the autumn of 1952. It was an obvious choice for the Prime Minister to make: Powell had rather asked for it, by participating in many debates on Welsh affairs, being so supportive to Government policy, showing such erudition about the culture, history and current state of the Principality, and proclaiming his Welsh ancestry. The Chief Whip, Buchan-Hepburn, had decided that Powell deserved to be forgiven his abstention on the Schuman Plan. Yet Powell had wanted either an economic ministry or the parliamentary secretary's job at the Ministry of Transport, where he could get his teeth into the deregulatory Transport Bill for which he had been leading backbench support in the Commons. Therefore, he turned Churchill down, telling him that the post, if discharged properly, would take him away from his constituents at a time when his seat was still so marginal it needed to be nursed – which he also believed. After he had left, Churchill's private secretary, Jock Colville, rushed in saying there had been a horrible mistake; a miscalculation of the numbers meant there was no vacant post within the Government left to offer.[144] Churchill was relieved, saying it was just as well in that case that Powell had refused.

He would have to wait three years for another offer, and at times he would find it a depressing and demoralising wait. His wife was 'surprised, and a little fed up' that he had turned the job down.[145] Nonetheless, for Powell his rejection of office was a relief. He would recall that on this and the two other occasions when he would refuse office, and on the one occasion he would resign, he had a distinct sensation on re-entering the House of Commons after he notified his decision to the Prime Minister: 'It was like coming home to one's mother. It was as though I said, "I am back again; I am back where I belong, I have not gone away, I am back." '[146]

A few weeks later the Powells were invited to a tea-party in Downing Street at which, to their joy, the Prime Minister came up to Powell and told him: 'I do understand.'[147] There would, it seems, be another chance. However, Powell had come into the House with clear ideas of what jobs were or were not desirable; Bill Deedes recalled meeting him during a reshuffle early on in their parliamentary careers and being told, the main ministerial posts having been reallocated, that there was 'nothing left worth having'.[148] Powell was re-elected vice-chairman of the Housing Committee, and threw himself into a close scrutiny and critique of the Town and Country Planning Bill. There is one other question mark over his commitment at this time: with the Korean War at a critical phase, an old obsession seems to have returned. Powell wrote to the War Office in October 1952 to say that, in the event of general mobilisation, 'it is my present intention to hold myself immediately available for military service'.[149]

In the second reading debate on the Transport Bill on 17 November he spoke in praise of the decentralisation of road and rail transport, and of the breaking up of the Road Haulage Executive. He was contemptuous of threats made by Labour of union action if and when the Government broke up transport monopolies, talking of the overriding need for competition. As he mocked suggestions made by Labour for consolidating and improving the monopoly, as made in various pamphlets by which some of the Labour leadership had been embarrassed, he joked that 'I find study of the Fabian and Labour pamphlets so fruitful that I have hardly time to read the Tory ones.'[150] Labour was divided on what to do with road haulage, which many of them recognised had been about as far from a natural monopoly as it was possible to get. When the Bill went into committee in December, Powell exploited the inconsistencies of his opponents, and dissected the failure of rail nationalisation. He cited a letter from an engine-driver in his constituency who told of the bureaucracy and over-centralisation of the railways since the advent of state ownership, and, to Powell's delight, how the experience had turned many ordinary working men against Labour.

Powell's own economic stringency did not prevent him, at this stage, from accepting that an element of support by the state might be needed. 'I ... recognise', he said during the committee on 17 December 1952, 'that in any system of transport there is bound to be some degree of internal subsidy. The question is: how much? Under the present charges system it is fantastically excessive; it is keeping in use entirely uneconomic forms of transportation and suppressing the development of economical forms.'[151] The next day he made an impassioned plea for the Government to protect the passenger against the abuses of transport monopolies.

Having turned down office there was, however, another important post for him to fill. The vacancy was, ironically, created by Macleod's promotion. The London Municipal Society was the Conservative electoral machine for London and a rallying organisation for the party's London councillors. Macleod had chaired it, and Powell succeeded him in the late summer of 1952. Since another of the society's functions was to assist councillors in much the same way as the Secretariat had helped shadow spokesmen, Powell was in his element; and the post, supposedly five mornings a week, brought with it an additional salary of £500 a year, helpful in providing for his new wife and the family they hoped to start. The Society's offices were in Bridge Street, by the Palace of Westminster and opposite County Hall. He soon acquired a reputation there quite unlike that fostered in the Secretariat, leading by example: as Roth puts it, 'if there was a big mailing to be done, everyone pitched in. If there was a big clean-up, then Powell rolled up his sleeves and joined in.'[152]

It was a crucial time to assume these responsibilities. London borough council elections were scheduled for May 1953. In April the campaign started with Powell addressing the metropolis's Conservative candidates. Speaking to the *Evening Standard* afterwards, he was sanguine. 'I started by being pretty pessimistic, but a different spirit has arisen among candidates and the general public in the last few months,' he said. 'There is a kind of grim determination among Conservatives which there was not last year.'[153] Powell threw himself into politics. 'I never open a classic nowadays,' he told the *Standard*'s diarist, who had quizzed him about the apparent incongruity of the world's leading scholar of Herodotus masterminding a municipal election campaign. For all his efforts, Labour enjoyed the gains in local elections that are so often the benefits of national opposition, winning two boroughs and 129 seats. Their success was no fault of Powell's.

His work at the Society was not confined to running local elections; one aspect of it would provide a long-term legacy. He applied his mind to the question of strategic local government in the capital, and would submit to Duncan Sandys, the minister responsible for local government, a report suggesting how it could be made more effective. He envisaged breaking up the London County Council, replacing it with strong county boroughs; this was the genesis of what, in 1964, would become the Greater London Council. The plan was at first regarded as too politically divisive to be acceptable, but was looked at again later in the 1950s, with dramatic consequences.[154]

VII

On 3 March 1953 Powell made a speech in the Commons that he would, for the rest of his life, regard as his finest ever. Maxwell Fyfe, the Home Secretary, moved the second reading of the Royal Titles Bill, the fourth measure authorising a change in titles to have been introduced since 1901. Each had reflected first expansions, then reductions, in the British Empire. The question of the new Queen's title – she would not be crowned for three more months – had been discussed by Commonwealth leaders at an economics conference in London the previous December. There was agreement that, according to Maxwell Fyfe, 'the existing title of the Queen did not reflect the existing constitutional position under which other members of the Commonwealth are full and equal partners with the United Kingdom in our great family of nations'. He went on: 'The existing title is incorrect in its reference to Ireland and in that it does not reflect the special position of the Sovereign as head of the Commonwealth.'[155]

He further defined the Commonwealth countries and the United Kingdom as 'full and equal partners, united in their allegiance to the Crown; and the Sovereign is Queen of each of them'. As the Commonwealth countries' position had, therefore, gone beyond that set out by the 1931 Statute of Westminster – which recognised the legislative independence of parliaments elsewhere in the Empire – it would now be up to the legislatures of each to 'take the action appropriate to its own constitutional requirements' in defining the Queen's titles as relevant to them. All that had been agreed between the Commonwealth heads of government was that each country would include in its version of the titles 'a reference to Her Majesty's other realms and territories and her title as head of the Commonwealth'.[156] However, as Patrick Gordon Walker, welcoming the measure on behalf of the Opposition, put it, after the legislation had passed in all the Commonwealth parliaments, 'the Queen will be as much the Queen of India and of Ceylon as she is of England or of the United Kingdom'.[157] Although Gordon Walker realised that some would be upset by the apparent acceptance of the principle of the divisibility of the Crown, he took solace in the fact that every country in the Commonwealth recognised the Queen as head of that body. 'Never before has there been this express and explicit recognition of the Crown as such a unifying factor.'

For two hours constitutional argument of a mild nature occupied the House, with pedantic points made about the accuracy of the new royal title: the Scots, for example, objected to the Queen being named Elizabeth II, as they had not had an Elizabeth I. Then, just before a quarter-past six, Powell rose and immediately confessed to his sense of embarrassment at having to agree with those speakers who had opposed the Bill. He said the Statute of Westminster had, in fact, imposed two limits on what the Dominion parliaments could do; alteration in the law regarding the succession to the throne or the royal style and titles would require the assent of all parliaments as well as Westminster's. The unity of the identity of the monarch, which the Statute of Westminster had been designed to protect, was now explicitly removed by this Bill.

Powell said that in the proposed change of style for the United Kingdom he noted three changes, 'all of which seem to me to be evil'.[158] One, as had already been pointed out, was the divisibility of the Crown. The second was 'the suppression of the word "British" both from before the words "Realms and Territories" where it is replaced by the words "her other" and from before the word "Commonwealth", which, in the Statute of Westminster, is described as the "British Commonwealth of Nations"'. The third was the invention of the title 'Head of the Commonwealth'.

On the matter of divisibility, he did not like the term 'realms'. In statute law all the Dominions of the Crown constituted a single realm, and not separate ones. Gordon Walker tried to pull Powell up by saying that Henry VIII, by contrast, referred to his 'Imperial Crown' when he had meant just of England. Powell gave him a sharp history lesson: 'When he used the word "empire" he meant it in the mediaeval sense and was proclaiming the independence of this country from the Holy Roman Empire.'[159] Within the unity of the realm had grown up the British Empire: the unity of the Empire had been equivalent to the unity of the realm. There was one Sovereign; one realm. In the course of constitutional development, indeed, the Sovereign began to govern different parts of that realm upon the advice of different ministers; but that in itself did not constitute a division of the realm. Indeed, the realm's unity had been preserved by the unity of the Crown. He feared that by recognising divisibility of the realm, Parliament would open the way to recognising the divisibility of the person who ruled them.

On his second point, Powell described the notion that the Queen was Queen of 'her other Realms and Territories' as 'literally meaningless.'[160] A monarch had to be designated, he said, by reference to the territory of which he was monarch. 'To say that he is Monarch of a certain territory and his other realms and territories is as good as to say that he is King of his Kingdom. We have perpetrated a solecism in the title we are proposing to attach to our Sovereign and we have done so out of what might almost be called an abject desire to eliminate the expression "British".' He ridiculed this notion. 'Why is it that this "teeming womb of royal Kings", as Shakespeare called it, wishes now to be anonymous?'[161]

In referring to his third point, Powell said he had found the answer to his second. The 1948 British Nationality Act had revolutionised the nature of subjecthood and nationality, replacing allegiance to the Sovereign with nine separate citizenships combined together by statute. When India chose to become a republic the following year the rest of the Commonwealth had been happy to see her remain as a member, recognising the King as head of the Commonwealth but owing no allegiance to him. 'The status of India resulting from these changes and declarations is an ungraspable one in law or in fact. The Indian Government say that they recognise the Queen as the Head of the Commonwealth. Well, I recognise the right hon Member for Walthamstow West as leader of the Opposition, but that does not make me a Member of Her Majesty's Opposition.'[162]

Powell claimed it was always intended that the relationship between India and the rest of the Commonwealth should be 'uninterpretable', a precedent enforced by the vagueness of the new title. The essence of unity, as he saw it, had to be a willingness for the parts to sacrifice themselves in the interests of the whole. The entity being created did not have that unity, and could not therefore be described properly as a Commonwealth. 'I therefore say that this formula "Head of the Commonwealth" and the declaration in which it is inscribed are essentially a sham. They are essentially something which we have invented to blind ourselves to the reality of the position.' What Powell saw as the underlying evil of the changes, though, was that 'we are doing it not for the sake of our friends but of those who are not our friends. We are doing this for the sake of those to whom the very names "Britain" and "British" are repugnant ... We are doing this for the sake of those who have deliberately cast off their allegiance to our common Monarchy."[163] Rebuked by Godfrey Nicholson, a fellow Conservative backbencher, and asked to 'measure his words' because of the affection felt for, and the sacrifices made by, India in the past, Powell retorted that as one who had served with the Indian Army he was hardly likely to be unmindful of them. Nor, he said, was he under any delusion that his words would have any practical effect. He reminded his colleagues, that however high or low they were in the House, 'we have a meaning in this place only in so far as in our time and generation we represent great principles, great elements in the national life, great strands in our society and national being ... It is because I believe that, in a sense, for a brief moment, I represent and speak for an indispensable element in the British Constitution and in British life that I have spoken. And, I pray, not entirely in vain.'

Winding up the short debate, Maxwell Fyfe's only answer to Powell's complex points was that 'it is easy to make difficulties, especially verbal difficulties'.[164] In other words, no attempt would be made to consider them properly, or to acknowledge the consequences of marked changes in precept that the Bill would usher in. It completed its remaining stages that same day, Powell abstaining in the division on the second reading. His speech confirmed the disillusion he felt in his transition from imperialist to nationalist. Unable to delude himself, he could not abide the delusions of others. He saw, several years before the move to independence in Africa and elsewhere, the inevitability of the process and its implications, and did not wish Britain to be saddled with this 'sham' that would make coming properly to terms with the post-imperial state difficult, if not impossible. It was an argument he would propound, in different contexts, for the rest of his life, and one in which the force of his logic could not, despite compelling empirical evidence, triumph over those delusions. In his reply, Maxwell Fyfe showed the lack of intellectual grip, or the avoidance of reality, that would typify the actions of the Conservative Government until it lost office eleven years later, and which would ultimately assist in its destruction.

The speech had, though, confirmed Powell's authority, and consolidated the reputation he had not just for mastering detail, but for spotting implications of detail where others supposed they did not exist. It also brought him a large mailbag from those who had read reports of his dissent in the papers and who, like him, felt that their British patrimony was being undermined and threatened. The expression of such intellectual independence did not go unnoticed or unadmired among his peers either. Macleod, still keen to be friends, wrote to him after the debate to say that 'you may have been foolish to say what you did, but it was nobly said. And that is enough.'[165]

Powell was not, though, above engaging in relatively low politics when the need arose. He spoke on 5 May in a censure debate tabled by the Opposition after what Powell described as a 'little tantrum' by Herbert Morrison, who had hoped for two days' further consideration of Lords' amendments on the Transport Bill, but instead had been given only one. He claimed that the outrage of Morrison and others was manufactured, since the Opposition had known for three weeks what the amendments were, and had raised no objection to their timetabling. He sought to show that the Opposition actually agreed with many of the amendments – as their members in the Lords had not voted against most of them – but were objecting to them purely to obstruct the House by mounting a filibuster. He ended with the magisterial observation: 'I believe that Parliament and this House consults its dignity most, and preserves its own rights and privileges and the spirit of the Constitution best, when it talks least about them.'[166] He was immediately criticised by his friend Reggie Paget, who imparted the eternal truth that just because Labour peers had not objected to something did not mean that Labour MPs would take the same line.

On 20 May, after a relatively short fight against cancer of the liver, Powell's mother died. He had rushed down from London on hearing that her health had deteriorated, and arrived at her bedside shortly before she died. He, like his father, was devastated: 'she was everything to him ... it was terrible, really terrible, he was distraught', Pam Powell remembered.[167] They had remained intensely close spiritually even during his long absences abroad; the blow was hard. She was buried at Worthing three days later, after which Powell wrote to Strachan that she had 'suffered less than had been feared'. His concern shifted to his father, who 'seems temporarily unbalanced – I am afraid at present my absence helps him more than my presence'.[168] The event had also had an unpredicted effect on him: 'I had never expected that my mother's death would force upon me so inescapable a sense that there is an immortality.' Powell later recalled that his wife had noticed a tension growing up between him and his father after Ellen's death: 'There was an actual jealousy between us for the position of her memory.' The death was 'a great disaster'.[169]

Powell's main legislative interest that summer harked back to the original 'One Nation' pamphlet, a new National Insurance Bill. Early on in the Bill's consideration he had made sure to warn against plans to expand social service provision without properly planning how to pay for it: there was still a marked tendency on the part of the Government and the civil service to discount what the actuaries were telling them. In a separate debate in early July on the long-term unemployed, he once more warned the House that the principle of paying out benefits on the insurance principle was essential, and any policy that threatened to weaken it 'must be rejected and resisted', even if some had to suffer hardship in the process.[170] This was, though, a losing battle: even after just seven years, the insurance principle was already shaking.

After the summer recess, during which the Powells holidayed in Touraine, he spoke on foreign affairs for the first time in his Commons career, during the debate on the Queen's Speech. The tensions that would lead to the Suez crisis three years later were boiling up. Colonel Nasser, the Egyptian leader, was putting pressure on Britain to come to a new agreement about the Suez Canal Zone, and, although ministers had not yet commented on Nasser's demands, Powell noted how all the information that had leaked out concerned the complete evacuation of the zone by British troops. He said he believed any such move to negate the existing treaty of 1936 'would not only be a fateful, but a fatal step'.[71] He could neither support nor assent to it. Even a new agreement that allowed a right of re-entry by British troops in certain circumstances, and which did not prevent Britain from carrying out her obligations under the Suez Canal convention, would be a 'fatal self-deception'. He suspected that an agreement would also allow for a few thousand British technicians to stay in the zone, but he argued that, without 70,000 fighting men to protect them, they would be hopelessly vulnerable to terrorism, and would soon be driven out altogether.

His main message was that the word of the Egyptian Government, in this or any other agreement, would not be 'worth the parchment on which it is engrossed'. The Egyptians had signed, but then unilaterally failed to respect, the treaty of 1936. They were already routinely violating a treaty made with Britain about the Sudan just twelve months earlier. In the matter of the canal itself, the Egyptians were frequently, and without any legitimacy whatsoever, stopping shipping passing through it. Since the Egyptian Government could not be trusted, British troops had to stay. To remove them would imperil all other British bases in the Middle East and the Mediterranean. It would also, he argued, have severe implications for Britain's relations with Iraq, Jordan and Persia; and, throughout the rest of Africa, it would encourage those hostile to Britain to step up campaigns of terrorism to force Britain out. In this regard, he dismissed the argument that Britain could no longer afford to keep so many troops at Suez: by pulling out from there the need to send troops to all the other colonies and protectorates where trouble would flare up would prove far more costly than Suez was.

This speech was also significant as the first public statement of Powell's anti-Americanism. Many older members of his party took the view that America had never understood Europe, and the historical forces at work there, and that the Second World War could have been avoided had there not been such strong American pressure to 'modernise' the continent by removing the Hohenzollerns and the Habsburgs. Powell had not stopped believing that the principal aim of America's foreign policy in the twentieth century had been solely to diminish the power of others, including her nominal allies, to establish herself as the leading world power. Above all, he still blamed her for the loss of India, and for his personal disappointment as a would-be viceroy.

Dismissively, he said that 'I believe a second factor which has weighed heavily in this matter is the attitude, or supposed attitude, of the United States. I confess that I am not greatly moved by this. Whatever may be the attitude of the American Government and public to the United Kingdom as such, my view of American policy over the last decade has been that it has been steadily and relentlessly directed towards the weakening and the destruction of the links which bind the British Empire together ...' This was too much for one of Powell's fellow Conservatives, Cyril Osborne, who shouted out a plaintive 'No!' Powell was unstirred. 'We can watch the events as they unfold and place our own interpretation on them. My interpretation is that the United States has for this country, considered separately, a very considerable economic and strategic use but that she sees little or no strategic use or economic value in the British Empire or the British Commonwealth as it has existed and as it still exists. Against that background I ask the House to consider the evidences of advancing American imperialism in this area from which they are helping to eliminate us.'[172]

He listed them: a new naval base on Crete, more men stationed on Malta, positions being taken up on the Spanish peninsula – and all the time America was, too, 'assisting the process of eliminating us from a base which we have maintained, for American as well as our own interests, with the blood of Imperial troops in two wars'. Osborne formally intervened, and asked Powell to justify this 'very serious charge'; Powell replied sarcastically that 'no doubt when my hon friend the Joint Under-Secretary of State for Foreign Affairs replies, he will be able to repudiate it'. In concluding, Powell reminded his own front bench of the very words the Queen had used from the Throne when opening Parliament: that her Government would try to settle the differences between Britain and Egypt 'while safeguarding the security of the Middle East and the Suez Canal'. Powell had left them in no doubt of what would be required if that were to be achieved.

He returned to this subject a fortnight later, in a speech to his constituents. Egypt had, twice in the preceding ten days, breached the 1952 agreement with Britain respecting the territorial integrity of the Sudan. Powell argued:

it almost passes belief that we should contemplate discussions with the same Egyptian government for another agreement, this time about Suez. Yet indications are that the agreement would remove all British troops from the Canal and base almost immediately and British personnel in a comparatively short time. A Government guilty of allowing Britain to be eliminated from the isthmus of Suez, in the conditions which exist there and in the Middle East today, would be judged at the bar of history and condemned. We hold our position at Suez by right. The treaty of 1936 remains in force till replaced by another to which both parties freely agree. By its own terms no replacement of it is valid which does not provide for the fullest alliance between Egypt and Britain.[173]

Powell's view on Suez was, inevitably, coalescing with his radical view of Britain as a post-imperial power with delusions about her place in the world. In 1958, not long after the event, he explained over his dinner-table to Anthony Wedgwood Benn – as he was then known – what had gone on in his mind at this time: he had seen that Eden, as Foreign Secretary, had tried to pretend that Britain could exert military power in Egypt without bases, which Powell recognised as a sham, and so it was to turn out.[174] Yet he had for some months been attending meetings of the Suez group of Conservative MPs, forty or so strong, who were leading the internal resistance to an evacuation. In the privacy of those meetings throughout 1953 and the first half of 1954, Powell's emotional belief that Britain had to stand up and fight was taken to his customary logical extreme. Leo Amery, a spiritual driving force behind the group of which his son Julian was one of the leaders, noted in his diary in December 1953 that only his son and Powell felt sufficiently strongly about the issue to 'go to the point of risking the Government's existence'.[175] Powell saw the British position not as imperialism for the sake of it – he had long since ceased to believe in that – but as a need to retain national credibility by honouring obligations, particularly in the face of American power. He attended the Conservative Foreign Affairs Committee on 2 December 1953, intervening to say that, in the light of Eden's strong protests against the Egyptian breach of faith in the Sudan elections, British negotiations with Egypt over Suez had changed: to conclude an agreement now would be in the face of evidence that they could not be trusted.[176]

He had now been in Parliament almost four years, and there was still no sign of his being offered a job he would have felt commensurate with his abilities. He had, in mid-November 1953, succeeded at the third attempt in securing a place on the 1922 executive, so his voice was being heard in the higher counsels of the parliamentary party. He was also invited by Butler to sit on a committee reviewing policy for the next manifesto, and attended its meetings until 1955. Yet after his rare excursion into questions of great international importance over Suez he spent the bulk of the 1953–4 session on matters of domestic interest. On 1 December 1953 Macmillan, the minister responsible, announced that the goal of 300,000 houses built in a year – announced at the previous year's party conference – had been achieved. At the time the House was considering the Housing Repairs and Rents Bill, aimed at improving the existing stock.

In a speech in the second reading debate on the Bill on 30 November, Powell made a wide-ranging assault on socialist housing policy, and on the importance of the operation of the free market: something not all of his colleagues, including at ministerial level, appreciated as keenly as he did. Sparring again with Reggie Paget, he stigmatised Labour's policy as one that would bring all rent-controlled housing into local authority ownership, which would lead to less new housing being built while local authorities concentrated their resources on repairing the existing stock. The Government's Bill envisaged the rent-controlled stock remaining in private hands, with help given to landlords to improve it by decontrolling some rents to reflect the costs of improvement.

He pointed out that the effective nationalisation of the private rented sector would be a huge and continuing task, with seven million houses coming under that definition. Labour simply could not, he said, achieve that aim. He also took on Bevan, who had recently said housing could never be afforded by lower-income groups, and therefore should be put into the field of the social services. Powell challenged the core Labour idea that rented accommodation could be provided only by means of subsidy – again, something many on his own side of the House would have found themselves inclined to agree with. He presented the classic supply-and-demand argument: that if housebuilders did not build to rent they would find no market for their wares, and if they did not rent at a market price they would find no tenants; that, in his view, dealt with the matter of the need for subsidy, as otherwise all the housebuilders would go out of business. Bevan interrupted Powell, reminding him it had been an assumption shared by socialists and conservatives alike immediately after the war that local authorities would have to provide housing. Powell agreed that had been the case immediately after the war, but the war had ended eight and a half years ago. Rent controls were still depressing the building industry, creating an unfavourable price differential between the existing housing stock and the new. Not only would Labour's policy result in the nationalisation of rented housing, it would also destroy the efficiency of the building industry, which would be 'substantially working everywhere under contract for subsidy ... that is the absolutely classic prescription for destroying the efficiency of an industry, and for depriving it of the incentive and of the opportunity to improve'.[177]

The Bill was vehemently opposed by Labour, as it believed it would make housing more expensive for the working class and was, in effect, an anti-working-class measure. Powell repudiated that claim not just on the basis of the laws of supply and demand, but in proposing that the housing subsidies saved by rents rising and the private sector improving its own stock could be channelled into slum clearance. However, in the privacy of the Conservative Housing Committee on 18 November 1953 he had expressed reservations about slum clearance taking place at the top of the market instead of the bottom, as had been the case in the 1930s. He found himself outnumbered, though: his colleagues insisted it had to be done.[178] Throughout the winter he took a close interest in the Bill, arguing at the end of February for more time to be allocated to it in committee, and speaking during the committee stage. His defence of the measure, and the detail in which he spoke, helped mark him out once more for promotion, this time in a field that he would find acceptable.

The Powells' Christmas holiday was spent partly in Wolverhampton, with the usual heavy canvassing of a constituency he still did not regard as safe. It was a time of intense activity: he had agreed to write, with Angus Maude, a short book entitled *Biography of a Nation*, about the emergence of British national consciousness; his part of it was due for delivery in January 1954. So, too, was something of more importance. Pam Powell was in the last month of her pregnancy with their first child; she was born on 13 January 1954, shortly after the Powells' second wedding anniversary, and was christened Susan Mary, Ted Curtis being one of the godparents. Powell had wanted a son – whom they would have called David – and whom he had already put down for Eton. He justified the choice of school because he had discovered at Cambridge that 'although the Old Etonians . . . weren't as good as I was at Greek and Latin, they were *nearly* as good. But they knew so much else! They were able to handle the situation of being an undergraduate with more confidence than, as an ex-grammar school boy, I was able to.'[179] Jonathan Aitken, himself an Etonian, recalled that Eton was not, however, a school lighted upon easily. He remembered the Powells coming to stay with his family in Suffolk at about this time, and taking the opportunity to visit a local public school to investigate the quality of its classics teaching in the event of it being better for the son destined never to be.[180]

According to Pam Powell, in a letter of 29 January to Andrew Freeth's wife Roseen, Powell swiftly overcame his disappointment. 'Both Enoch and I are thrilled with her . . . once "it" has arrived, the sex doesn't matter.'[181] Pam also noted that the baby 'has got E's forehead and certainly his way of using eyebrows'. He turned out to be a capable father, particularly adept at changing nappies and feeding. He was popular with children, and not just his own: he became god-father to Freeth's son Richard, whose brother Martin recalled an 'incredible warmth' from Powell towards them as children.[182] One with Powell's interest in genealogy was bound to look fondly on the prospect of a son; if it was a disappointment that, when his family was complete, he had none, his devotion to his daughters certainly did not betray it.

VIII

In May 1954 One Nation published a 104-page pamphlet entitled *Change Is our Ally*. It was edited – and mostly written by – Powell and Maude. It argued for a retreat from the planned economy and towards a more competitive system in order to help create wealth. It comprised a detailed historical review of the encroachment of the state on the private sector ever since the Great War, and of how as a result the presumption had shifted from individual action towards central control; the review was entitled 'The Retreat from Laissez-Faire'.[183] There are many foretastes of Powell's subsequent economic doctrine: a repudiation of subsidies and price controls, and, above all, the futility of economic planning in trying to predict the free will that motivates the laws of supply and demand. These were almost heresies, even in the third year of a Conservative government elected to undo socialism. The pamphlet's radicalism was deeply conscious: 'Unfortunately, one of the main human characteristics is a resistance to change. The devil you now is better than the devil you don't. This natural resistance is reinforced by the time lag in public comprehension of events. Opinion today is conditioned to a large extent by the circumstances of the 1930s, instead of by the quite different dangers of the 1950s.'[184] As would be the case when he was in government, indeed when he was in the cabinet, Powell would regard his own senior colleagues as those most needing to learn this lesson. He felt that once the presumption about the role of the state was altered, so too could taxes be cut, more money be made available for investment, more risks taken, more innovations made. From his place on a party committee on policy he had been arguing for a commitment to denationalisation, but had been ignored.

Two months later Powell brought out a revised edition of *Needs and Means*, the revisions all his own now that Macleod was a minister. Most of the changes took into account developments in policy in the preceding two years. However, Powell argued for increased National Insurance contributions to cover all welfare benefits except for the retirement pension, and for a system of increments for pensioners if they delayed retirement – and taking their pension – beyond the age of seventy, reflecting the reality of an ageing population. He included more factual detail about the inadequacy of the pension ever since it had been introduced in 1908: it was, he said 'never intended to be at subsistence level', nor a state substitute for the normal practice of thrift.[185]

He claimed that the retirement pension alone should not be subject to a means test, though people should be encouraged to view it as merely a part, and not the whole, of their support in old age; nor could it be financed by the National Insurance scheme, realistically, so it would have to be paid for out of revenues from income tax. When he repeated this philosophy a few months later, he won a plaudit from an unlikely source. Michael Foot, in his column in the *Daily Herald*, praised Powell 'for preaching socialism'; to drive the point home, a photograph of Powell in a grey top hat and morning dress accompanied the column.[186] In a considerably more provocative and urgent conclusion than the first edition had contained, Powell argued that the position the Government now maintained in the social services was 'illogical'.[187] From this position there were only two obvious exits: to abandon the principle of insurance, and use the revenue-financed National Assistance scheme alone to support the poor and needy, something close to the hearts of some in the Labour party.

The other course was to restore insurance benefits to above subsistence level, something Powell argued was more practicable in 1954 than when he and Macleod had first broached it in 1951. This was because the fall in the value of money had ceased to be so rapid as under Labour, and the benefits had, under the 1952 Family Allowances and National Insurance Act, been uprated in real terms to their 1948 level; so a small additional re-rating was all that was needed to take them back to the level at which they had been putatively set in 1945. Both main parties had committed themselves to this, but Powell argued that higher benefits would have to be financed not out of revenue, but out of higher National Insurance contributions. The longer-term problem for social security financing – which Powell was one of very few to see as early as 1954 – was that an ageing population would have to finance its own supplementary pension, and the state pension would have to be regarded as not a substitute for thrift, if a truly prudential approach were to be taken to the problem.

The Suez debate was still fermenting. In June 1954 Powell wrote to *The Times* lambasting a report it had carried suggesting that forty Conservative MPs, of whom he was one, were the obstacle to an 'advantageous' new agreement between Egypt and Britain. He said that a new agreement that allowed Britain neither 'the right to station troops and air forces in the zone during peace' nor 'almost unlimited use of the facilities of Egypt during war' could not 'conceivably be "advantageous" '.[188] Despite his membership of One Nation, Powell was still not by nature a joiner, and his association with the Suez Group was about to founder. The agreement with Egypt threw the group into confusion, heavily outnumbered as they were by mass opinion in the parliamentary Conservative party. He stuck to his principles, being one of twenty-six Conservatives to vote against the Government when the policy was the subject of a division in the Commons in July. Over thirty years later he explained that he had done so 'not in the belief that indefinite British occupation of the Zone was practicable but in protest against a treaty which purported to give Britain rights of re-occupation and a policy which proclaimed that Cyprus, Jordan and Kenya afforded adequate geographical alternatives'.[189]

For Powell that was the last, and absolute, extinguishing of his imperial notions. 'Well, Enoch,' a colleague in the group is reported to have said to him at this time, 'what's the next move?' 'I don't understand,' he answered. 'Well, how do we go on fighting for the Empire?' Powell replied, 'I don't know what you mean. It's over.'[190] He told Paul Foot fifteen years later that, in November 1954, he went to one last meeting of the group to tell them 'our work is done'.[191] He explained that 'our attitude had been that Suez was a key position; its strategical significance was such that a withdrawal from there was a sign that we could no longer maintain an imperial presence. I told them that if they were going to go on as we had done over Suez over other places in the area like Cyprus and Malta, I could not join them.' Foot notes, however, that to his constituents a few days before that meeting Powell had said that 'the Cyprus question is entirely different, because Cyprus is British soil and the Cypriots are British subjects'.[192]

Lecturing at the Conservative Political Centre summer school earlier that year, Powell had provided further evidence of the absolutism of his anti-imperial view, in a talk on 'the Empire of England'. Defining sovereignty as 'a group to all of whose members, but to no others, a single authority is able to give commands', Powell pointed out how this process had been defied by the creation of the British Empire; many of those colonies, as Burke had noticed with North America, had no direct representation in Parliament.[193] In time, it would be seen that authority could not extend over those who did not contribute to the election of that authority. Both a domestic and an imperial parliament would have been needed to sustain this Empire; a federation would have had to be constructed, but federation was 'a dream'.[194] His conclusion was that the end of Empire had been inevitable right from the start of Empire, that no political miscalculation had brought it about, and that nothing could have prevented it. All that surprised him was that it had taken so long. It was time, he urged his fellow Conservatives, to shake off their 'self-delusion'.[195]

A year later, in another CPC lecture, he went further, arguing that in just the same way that Dominions and, in time, colonies would assert their own nationalism, so too should the Mother Country, stripped of her Empire, assert hers. A similar philosophy, realistic about the declining state of British power, imbued *Biography of a Nation*, published that summer. The book also embodied what Powell would make one of his main theses during the rest of his career: that the British could find a new basis for their sense of nationhood if only they were prepared to make the effort.

The dismantling of the socialist state was still not being pursued with the vigour he would have liked. In early July he spoke again in the Commons on the wisdom of breaking up the road-haulage network, in the interests of a better service for the consumer. Then, three days later, he argued for a reform of the structure of gas and electricity prices, and for the capital structure to be made more like that in the private sector – arguments that would be adduced thirty years later when these utilities were being prepared for privatisation. Unsurprisingly, Labour Members disagreed with Powell. One, Ernest Davies, regretted that 'the test as to how capital investment was to be used would be not the national interest but the profitability of the use of that capital investment'. Powell interjected: 'How does the hon Gentleman distinguish between the national interest and the most advantageous use of the national resources?' Unfortunately for Davies, he could not.[196]

The arrival of their first daughter, and growing concern about Powell's father – who was in his eighty-second year – had prompted the need to establish a larger and more permanent base in Wolverhampton. The flat the Powells had had in Wolverhampton since their marriage had proved simply too small for the family on their weekend visits there; and he and his wife worked out that if they bought a house in the constituency it would provide not just the space they needed, but also somewhere for Albert Powell to live and receive regular visits from his son and daughter-in-law. In the summer of 1954 they found a large semi-detached house in Merridale Road, a quiet, Edwardian suburb of Wolverhampton, for which they paid £1,500. Powell, who had acquired a penchant for woodwork and do-it-yourself from Ted Curtis in the 1930s, set about building shelves, cupboards and generally redecorating the house, and took pains to maximise the potential of the small plot at the rear. He turned it into a vegetable garden, from which in later years he would supply some of his family's needs. Visitors to the house remembered it as being gloomy and somewhat spartan, but it was in frequent use: however safe his seat would become, Powell would never neglect Wolverhampton, and would continue to devote much of his recesses and many of his weekends to visiting it.

Powell's vote against the Government over Suez meant that, once more, he had ground to make up if he was to be considered for promotion. As a means of helping re-establish his loyalty he undertook a substantial programme of speeches around the country during September and October 1954, and was back in the Government's defence immediately the House resumed after the party conferences. On 21 October he spoke again on housing, attempting to show in detail how existing subsidies were still too generous and were harming the supply of housing and the interests of the taxpayer. This speech drew him to the attention of the minister responsible, Duncan Sandys, who wrote to him to say that it had been 'splendid': 'I think everyone was impressed with your obvious mastery of the whole subject ... I think it would be a good thing if you and I had a quiet talk together about all these matters. Perhaps you would care to lunch with me one day?'[197]

Later that month he spoke on the price of coal, which, as he had already said of other power supplies, was unrealistic in its structure and furthered 'a price system which will retain in production the uneconomic pits' – another complaint that would resonate down three decades. Powell pleaded with the House to take the long view: 'In the long run, the social welfare of this country and its economic welfare are bound up together. The public interest, socially and economically, is one and indivisible, and the public interest, with all our social progress, rests upon an increase in the productivity of the nation.'[198]

He continued his assault on the lack of commercial realism of the nationalised industries in a speech in his constituency on 7 January 1955. He argued that wages in state-owned industries – specifically the railways, whose workers were for the second successive year engaging in industrial action – could not be subsidised either from taxes or from the profits (if there were any) from the rest of the public sector. 'Unless the payment of "fair and reasonable" wages is coupled with the requirement that the industries which pay them shall be commercially viable,' he said, 'we shall get into the nightmare situation of everybody subsidising everybody else's wages.'[199] On the same tack, he spoke the following month in Birmingham of the absurdity of the continued inefficiency of the Coal Board, relating it (as he had earlier done) to the financial structure of the board and to the fundamental fact that 'the prices at which coal is sold have no necessary relation either to demand or to cost of production and transport'.[200]

Also in early February he had the opportunity, with a debate in the Commons on British Railways, to develop his criticism of that service. Observing that under the present dispensation the railway would never be able to pay its way, he dismissed, once more, the notion of an integrated transport policy where the profits of one part were used not to reward the workers and shareholders in it, but to subsidise workers elsewhere. Labour was advocating this, and Powell said of the party: 'I hope they will make it perfectly clear to the country that they want to see the wages of the workers in road haulage subsidising the wages of the railways workers – for that is what it means.'[201] Well ahead of the Government's decision to order the review of the railways by Dr Beeching, which would devastate the network, Powell called for a 'drastic' and 'ruthless' modernisation plan. The following month, speaking in Walsall, he said that the rail unions should learn a valuable economic lesson: that demand for their members' services had been overtaken by supply; they had learned, too, the disadvantage of being an industry in which pay claims are settled according to political and not commercial considerations. It would have been better, he said, for them to work for concerns ruled by the profit motive if they really wanted scope to increase their earnings.

In February 1955 the House gave a second reading to the Clean Air Bill, of which Powell – like most MPs representing industrial areas – was a keen supporter. He was attracted by the Disraelian public health aspect of the Bill, and also believed that the need to develop smokeless fuel would promote greater efficiency in the coal industry. Referring to the practice in some American cities, he said he wished the local paper in Wolverhampton would publish the names and addresses of those who owned particularly offensive chimneys, so that pressure could be put on them to make improvements. 'The time is ripe now for a drastic step which within a measurable period – let us say, of 10 or 15 years – will make the description "Black Country" once and for all obsolete,' he said.[202] An aside during the debate gave an interesting insight into Powell's capitalist fervour. His colleague Michael Higgs, in talking of the costs the legislation would present to industry, observed that 'there must be a limit to the amount of wealth one can produce', to which Powell retorted, 'Why?'[203]

Another local issue caught Powell's attention at this time. He read a news report that two local bishops, of Lichfield and Birmingham, had called on bus drivers in West Bromwich to stop industrial action caused by the refusal of their employers to operate a colour bar. The bishops said that it was unChristian for the men to behave in this way. Powell wrote to the Bishop of Lichfield, whose diocese covered his constituency, to question their action. He did not deny that the main cause of the strike was 'the employment by the Corporation of a single British subject of Indian origin'. However, he added, 'It is impossible to separate that narrow issue from the wide one of the influx of British subjects not of European race into the United Kingdom during recent months. I feel sure that it is only because of this background that the employment of an individual non-European by West Bromwich has assumed such importance in the eyes of those on strike.'[204]

Anticipating quarrels he would have over a decade later, Powell continued:

this wider issue of coloured immigration is one which I find it difficult to decide on religious grounds. It is most certain that Christ died for all men whatever their colour, and for that reason and many others black and white are equal in the sight of God. But so are Englishmen and Frenchmen: yet we do not allow Frenchmen to obtain employment on the West Bromwich buses, nor do we condemn the Durham miners as irreligious when they strike against the employment of Italians.

It may be said that the French and the Italians are not British subjects, whereas the Indians and the Jamaicans are. In saying this, however, we have quit the ground of religion and entered upon that of law. Christianity can know nothing of the British Nationality Act 1948. But an amendment of the Act would put the Jamaicans in the same category as the French and the Italians or at any rate would distinguish them from citizens of this country.

Powell argued that the workers were not acting because of racial motivations, but simply because of their anger at a large foreign influx, irrespective of race. He concluded his letter, vainly, 'in seeking to prevent while it is still possible the creation here of perhaps insoluble and intractable political problems, I hope one is not necessarily in breach of any obligation of humanity or Christianity'. The Bishop politely refused to accept that this was the reason for which the men were striking, but agreed with Powell that 'if the flood of foreign immigrants reaches proportions which might threaten to become unmanageable action may have to be taken by the Government'.[205]

Having been taken up by Duncan Sandys, Powell had, the previous December, succeeded to the chairmanship of the Housing Committee. On 15 February he supported the Requisitioned Houses Bill, arguing that with over 200,000 homes still being built a year the need for requisitioning was over. The following month he welcomed the London County Council Bill, which among other things tried to stop the LCC appropriating land for development and then using it for other purposes, when Powell felt that it should be sold on the open market if not needed; and on 6 April he spoke on the Rating and Valuation Bill, criticising only the discretion given to local authorities for the rating of the premises of charities which, he said, put those charities at the mercy of the councils.

The day before Powell's speech on the Rating Bill had marked the end of an epoch in British political life. Churchill, who had celebrated his eightieth birthday the previous November, resigned as Prime Minister. He advised the Queen to send for Eden, who had been increasingly debilitated by the uncertainty of when, rather than if, he would succeed. Eden had a limited reshuffle, in which Macmillan followed him as Foreign Secretary. On 15 April the new Prime Minister announced that there would be a general election on 26 May. On 19 April Butler delivered a Budget that included tax cuts, much to the delight of his party. It gave Powell's, and his Conservative colleagues', campaigns the flying start they needed.

For Powell, it was an opportunity to consolidate his seat to the point where it could be regarded as safe. He did not open his campaign of speeches until 17 May, just over a week before polling, and then on five of the next nine days spoke at least once in Wolverhampton. The usual thorough canvass preceded all else. On 14 May he sent out his election address, trumpeting the achievements of the Government since 1951 and urging its re-election. The main element of the previous election address was absent from this one: there was no mention of Britain without the Empire being like a head without a body – ironically, it had been under a Conservative government that the new realities had been observed. Instead, Powell concentrated on asking for support for the policies that had allowed the expansion of prosperity in the preceding four years.

On polling day he held his seat by a majority of 8,420, obtaining exactly 60 per cent of the vote. The Government was returned with an overall majority of sixty seats, theoretically enough to forge ahead with the process of undoing socialism after existing on a small majority since 1951. However, the opportunities apparently created by the victory were, in the light of the tribulations to come in the next four years, quite deceptive.

6

MINISTER OF THE CROWN

Powell had made his marginal seat relatively safe. This should have consoled him after being overlooked for office again. Others of his vintage were surging ahead: Macleod stayed Minister of Health, but would soon be in the cabinet as Minister of Labour. Maudling was Minister of Supply, Nutting Minister of State at the Foreign Office; Heath had been Deputy Chief Whip since 1953 (having been made Joint Deputy a year earlier, after just two years in the House). Powell's dedication and intellect were not enough; his unwillingness to ingratiate, and his reputation as a loner and a 'difficult' man – as well as his various assertions of his independence – ensured the door stayed closed. For his part, though he liked the new Prime Minister, Powell saw Eden as merely 'an arrangement of coloured lights' and felt 'disconcerted' by his 'apparent superficiality and lack of analytical power'.[1]

He continued to try to impress from the backbenches. On 11 July he spoke in the debate on the Transport Commission report and accounts, and once more objected to the notion of an integrated transport policy. The Labour MP Bob Mellish, who followed him, made a point about Powell that would have been endorsed by many in the House, and not just on the Opposition benches. 'The hon Member', said Mellish, 'is a well-known warrior in these debates. He becomes very technical and learned, very much as if he were addressing a class of rather young school boys. He always forgets the human aspect of the transport industry. He is never very much concerned with the individual.'[2] Ironically, in ideological terms, the individual as against the corporate was precisely what Powell was concerned with: though the human consequences of the transition from the socialist state to one where the individual once more held sway were not allowed for in his logic. This caused him to develop the reputation for a lack of humanity, which Auchinleck felt he had noted in India in 1945. That, as much as his rigid independence, had kept him out of office while others less gifted won startling promotions. He showed his ferocious anti-statism again two days later, chairing a meeting of the Housing Committee, at which he called for rent control to be reconsidered and for an end to 'indiscriminate all-round subsidy'. He wanted the private sector, and not the state, to pay for slum clearance, which was not presently the case.[3]

During the summer recess, Powell did some serious broadcasting. It had been an increasing sideline since 1950, when the BBC producer Archie Gordon 'discovered' him as a presenter of *The Week in Westminster*. Powell would sporadically approach Gordon with ideas for talks or discussion programmes, many of which were taken up as a result of the high esteem in which Powell was held by those in authority at the BBC. He had occasionally, also, used his languages in the BBC's Overseas Service, notably in Urdu to Pakistan. Now, for domestic consumption, he recorded a series of three programmes on the House of Lords, a profitable offshoot of his work-in-progress. Then with Tony Benn he attended the three main party conferences, and together they presented a nightly programme *Live from the Conference*, a good-natured – as the transcripts show – political debate between the two men, lasting a quarter of an hour each evening. This, too, was an initiative of Gordon's. That year the Conservative conference, at Bournemouth, preceded Labour's, at Margate; and on the opening night Powell told Benn that the gathering was one not of 'yes men' but of independent-minded Conservatives 'interpreting to the Government the real opinions and feelings of what is today the majority of the country'. He also put up a robust defence of Butler, the Chancellor and his own mentor, in using the 'methods of freedom' – in other words, restraints on public spending – rather than 'physical controls' such as an incomes policy to fight inflation.[4] At the Labour conference, Powell and Benn – whose own friendship was properly forged at this time – argued about the respective internal democracies of the two parties, Powell never quite overcoming his amazement at the chaotic way in which the conference was managed. They were gentler times; the calm and earnest debate was ended each evening with the sign-off: 'Good night, Benn.' 'Good night, Powell.' 'I found him a very charming companion,' said Benn, 'quite unlike the public image of this grim-faced man.'[5] Powell reciprocated the feeling, and the Benns were invited to Earl's Court Square for dinner later in the autumn.

Powell continued to signify, in speeches outside the House, his interest in housing and local government. At Shrewsbury on 23 October he spoke with what sounded like almost ministerial authority, telling his audience that reform of local government would have to wait until the next year, because of the delay in the rerating of England and Wales; there had been no such exercise since 1934, which Powell attributed to the 'blundering legislation of our socialist predecessors'. He emphasised that, in his view, it was right for ratepayers rather than central government to bear the burden for local government finance: 'you cannot divorce powers from financial responsibility'.[6] He was also careful to give the Whips wider demonstrations of his experience. The next day, at Halesowen, he made an early display of his attachment to the free-market economics of the nineteenth century Manchester liberals, denouncing subsidy and praising the price mechanism. If any other course were followed – and he claimed his party was not so stupid as to do that – 'freedom and self-discipline will fail'.[7]

That autumn a measure came before the Commons that would prove crucial for Powell's future. The Housing Subsidies Bill had its second reading on 17

November, and provided for the reduction of subsidy on houses that were not replacing slums, while maintaining it on those that did. In his work with the London Municipal Society Powell had become greatly absorbed with the question of slum clearance in London, and had written in *The Times* the previous March about the lamentable failure by Labour councils to do the job. In July 1951 the London County Council had adopted a five-year plan of slum clearance, designating 8,160 dwellings to go. Powell pointed out that by the end of 1954 only 262 had been demolished, and earlier programmes had not been fulfilled either; even some designated for clearance before the war, and which had survived the Luftwaffe, were still standing.[8] In August 1955 he had written in the *National Review* that housing subsidies and rent controls were 'as direct a route to socialism as anybody could wish' and would have to go – another ideological edict that would take thirty more years to be implemented.[9]

During the second reading debate Powell intervened repeatedly, pulling up other speakers on points of detail as they sought to harry the Government, and proving far more effective in doing so than the Government front bench. Then, as the Bill went into its committee stage a few days later, on 21 November, he was presented with an opportunity to impress of the sort so brilliantly taken by Macleod three years earlier: the chance to follow Bevan. Powell, while not nearly so cocky and seething with mock outrage as Macleod had been, nonetheless went for Bevan direct. He accused him of having entirely ignored the issues – which was true – and said that Labour was merely seeking to have housing nationalised. He was interrupted with a shout of 'Municipalised!' from the Labour benches, to which he retorted, 'Brought into state ownership, or under state control, in some form or other.'[10] He quoted Bevan back at him, that he had agreed in 1946 to 'a progressive reduction of the general housing subsidies' having said subsidies were of 'a temporary nature'.[11] Powell called the Bill 'the first step in a new phase of enabling the British people to improve their own conditions', and sat down to approval from his front bench at having put Bevan once more in the shade. It would, at last, trigger an offer he would feel able to accept.

In December 1955 the twenty-four MPs who had opposed withdrawal from Suez were summoned to a secret meeting to discuss Cyprus. Powell had ceased to be active in the group after the agreement with Egypt of July 1954, and now made it clear he could no longer associate himself with their activities. He had, shortly after the election, succeeded to the vice-chairmanship of the 1922, a reflection of the high esteem in which he was held on the backbenches, but which had put a further demand on his public loyalty; yet his new distance from his former allies caused press speculation that he was keen to be offered a job. He was offered one, within days. Eden had been branded weak by the press for not having substantially reconstructed the Government earlier. Shortly before Christmas he moved at last. Sir Hugh Lucas-Tooth, under-secretary at the Home

Office, was irritated to be told he was unlikely to be promoted further, and so resigned. His place was taken by Bill Deedes, parliamentary secretary at the Ministry of Housing under Duncan Sandys. This job – tailor-made for Powell – was the one he was offered. This time, he was pleased to accept, at a salary of £2,000 a year. He called it 'the best ever Christmas box'.[12] In the same reshuffle Heath, still only thirty-nine, enjoyed another phase in his meteoric rise by becoming Chief Whip.

Eden appointed Powell from his bed: not because his health had already broken down but because, like Churchill, it was a favoured place from which to conduct business. Powell was intensely grateful, and in this somewhat bizarre setting made a point of telling his leader how conscious he was of Eden's kindness, given that he had been one of the rebels in the vote on the Suez Canal Treaty; but the store Eden set by that was far less than Powell did. He attained office, it seems, in spite of Heath. As Deputy Chief Whip in November, Heath had written to Eden confidentially to ask him to see John Morrison, who had just been elected to the chairmanship of the 1922. Heath seems to have been worried that the post might have gone to Powell. 'I was alarmed about Enoch Powell as he was very heavily canvassed; but happily the danger passed.'[13] If Heath was seeking to influence Eden's opinion about Powell, he failed; to give him the benefit of the doubt, he may just have been reflecting the orthodoxy that Morrison had been the leadership's 'official candidate', and there may have been nothing personal against Powell.

The Powells enjoyed a happy family Christmas with their baby daughter, Pamela Powell's mother and Powell's father, who was eighty-three and in apparent good health. However, directly after Christmas Albert Powell collapsed with an aneurysm of the aorta, was taken to hospital, and died on New Year's Day. He had at least lived long enough to see his son on the first rung of the governmental ladder; but Powell, who had planned to spend that week after Christmas preparing himself for his new post (though, in terms of the detail of what the department he was joining was doing, he was probably already as well briefed as any minister would have been), instead had to spend it arranging his father's funeral. Albert Powell was buried with his wife at Worthing, his funeral having taken place, like hers, in St Mary's Church at Goring-by-Sea. In memory of his parents, Powell presented the church with a font-cover, on which he had inscribed: 'Given by John Enoch Powell in memory of his mother, Ellen Mary, and his father, Albert Enoch, to the church they entered last for those who will enter it first.'

II

Powell valued the time he spent working for Duncan Sandys. He saw his chief being 'horrific' to civil servants, but noted that he was always generous with colleagues, and keen to share out the credit for success. He taught Powell how to be a good minister – 'never put anything before the House of Commons until you have read it openly, in the presence of civil servants'.[14] Sandys would admire Powell immensely for his command of policy and of the detail of the legislation they would be bringing in, and ensured word travelled upwards about his deputy's abilities. Sandys's adviser, Kenneth Post, recalled that Sandys and Powell 'got on really well'.[15] Powell was still something of a stickler, however, and retained some of the *amour propre* of the senior officer. 'He was never an easy man,' Post recalled. 'He was always conscious of his own status.'

The other benefit Sandys enjoyed with the appointment of Powell was the signal it sent out about the Government's readiness to be radical about housing. Powell first spoke from the front bench on 25 January 1956, during the committee stage of the Housing Subsidies Bill. The clauses under discussion included one allowing subsidies in areas where labour was needed, so the incoming workers could have houses. It was something which, had he been on the backbenches, Powell would have felt best left to the market. There were particular representations made by MPs for mining areas, which allowed him the chance to observe, 'I represent a constituency under which coal is mined,' and to assure them that if new houses were needed for more miners a subsidy would be paid. The following week he was back in the committee again, dealing with the question of unfit houses, and repeatedly having to answer jibes from Bevan, whom he succeeded in grinding down – along with much of the rest of the House – with relentless, dispassionate technical detail of the sort Bevan would not normally have allowed to interfere with his arguments. On 14 February, at the Bill's report stage, Powell made a speech on slum clearance, urging the House to reject an amendment that would have hampered this aim. By this stage he had already successfully undergone initiations into two other parts of ministerial life: his first adjournment debate*, on the Sheffield Development Plan, on 6 February, and his first questions in the House, also on 14 February.

The next day, 15 February, he opened the debate on the third reading of the Housing Subsidies Bill. It was a dry, highly technical speech with a detailed historical sweep, precisely the sort of lecture not geared to winning the House's sympathy and which caused Powell, even after six years in the Commons, still

* The most usual form of adjournment debate is a debate at the end of the day on the motion that the House do adjourn. It allows a backbencher time to make a short speech on a subject of his choice, and to be replied to by the Minister responsible for that subject.

to be regarded as something of an outsider. In his speech he repeated the justification for the winding-down of subsidies except for slum clearance, and agreed that the Government's record in that area, so far, had been unimpressive. 'The Government accept the challenge. They do not believe that 10 per cent for slum clearance will do for 1956 and the following years. This Bill puts the emphasis where, in our opinion, it ought to be – upon the earliest removal of unfit houses; and it gives the local housing authorities the incentive and the means to do the job.'[16] Powell quoted his party's own 1955 manifesto commitment to have a slum-clearance drive to match that of the late 1930s, and promised to honour the pledge.

Once the Housing Subsidies Bill was dealt with, Powell threw himself into preparation for the second reading of the Slum Clearance Bill, on 28 March. It allowed him a further chance to consolidate his reputation in what remained a high-profile department. He introduced the Bill, saying slum clearance was now under way 'on a large scale'. The first provision of the Bill was to make an exception to the rule that when a house unfit for human habitation was purchased compulsorily only the site value was paid to the owner, on the ground that the building itself was worthless. This had, said Powell, been the case since 1919, so no owner need have been under any illusion that to buy a derelict house would result in little or no profit. However, because of a combination of rent control and the housing shortage, derelict sites on which there was vacant possession were of unusually high value. Many people, notably ex-servicemen, had bought such properties out of desperation, unaware that they could be compulsorily purchased at only site value. So the apostle of the free market told the Commons that 'this is a case where a too strict insistence on the principle of *caveat emptor* would be harsh on the individual concerned and, what is more ... it would attach a taint of arbitrariness and unfairness to that process of slum clearance which we want to command universal support'.[17] Therefore, anyone who had bought such a property after August 1939 and had still occupied it – or it had been occupied by a member of the same family – in December 1955, when the outline of this Bill had been announced by Sandys, would be entitled to full compensation, not just site value.

Powell dealt firmly with questions from Opposition spokesmen about those who had bought freeholds after August 1939, but had had them compulsorily purchased before the Bill had been outlined: there had had to be cut-off dates, and that was that. He then moved back to generosity: many houses unfit for human habitation also had business premises attached that were suitable for that use. In those cases, proper compensation would be paid. Finally, there would be better compensation for those houses in a relatively good state of repair. He criticised Labour for opposing the Bill because it made no allowance for a direct subsidy to be paid to those compensated by the Exchequer, rather than through the rates. Powell argued that the additional cost, because of grants already available to local authorities, would be slight and easily met out of the rates; a new, separate subsidy would be 'ludicrous'.[18]

In his role as a housing minister, Powell sat on a cabinet sub-committee in the spring of 1956 to consider the desirability of immigration control. It was, though, to be over five years before a Bill would be introduced on this subject. The committee comprised Kilmuir (as Maxwell Fyfe, now Lord Chancellor, had become), Lord Salisbury, Macleod, Gwilym Lloyd-George, the Home Secretary, Lord Lloyd, under-secretary for the Colonies, and Allan Noble, under-secretary for Commonwealth Relations. The committee had been told, in a memorandum, that the rate of increase in 'coloured people' entering Britain had been rising steeply since 1953; also, the numbers of Irish were growing sharply, with about 250,000 having immigrated since 1950. Despite this, the cabinet had decided not to introduce a Bill to control numbers, but had asked this committee to consider the question further. At the second meeting of the committee two months later, a draft report was presented in which a warning was given on pressure on housing in industrial areas if the rate of inflow continued, and it was suggested that it was better to introduce controls at a time of full employment. While discounting the possibility of race riots or colour-bar incidents, the committee thought that, in time, the 'coloured vote' could become significant in twenty or twenty-five constituencies; and it concluded that opinion was 'much less exercised' than a year before. The long-term consequences of coloured immigration were regarded as not serious. The committee stressed its concern about the shortage of housing, which suggests that Powell made some impression.[19]

Powell's own recollection was that he had gone far further than that. In 1971 he wrote to Salisbury, reminding him of the committee's conclusion that 'it was the general view of the Committee that steps to impose controls would not be justified at present'. 'The words "the general view of the Committee" conceal the fact,' Powell continued, 'which I clearly remember, that you yourself and, in my junior capacity, I also spoke and gave our voices against this conclusion and in favour of the imposition of control forthwith.'[20] Salisbury replied that, though his memory was declining with age (he was then seventy-eight), 'for what it was worth it entirely coincides with yours'. So, twelve years before his most inflammatory speech on the question, Powell had already marked out his position. The committee had recommended keeping the question under review, but Macmillan, on becoming Prime Minister in January 1957, had disregarded this wish. Powell noted in June 1971, after a meeting with Salisbury, that Macmillan's refusal 'was one of the causes of his [Salisbury's] resignation [from the Government in 1957] and was mentioned by him when he spoke to Macmillan on resigning'.[21]

Although the legislative workload kept Powell in the House more than many ministers – the committee stage of the Slum Clearance (Compensation) Bill was in the Commons during May 1956 – his job also required him to travel the country to inspect the rebuilding of England. In June he went to Northamptonshire, to see land reclaimed from ironstone works; later that month he went to Folkestone to address the Urban District Councils' Association, where, in a portent of things to come, he urged them to hold their borrowing down as part of the fight against inflation. In July he spoke in the House in a debate on new towns and overspill. The Conservatives' success in building new homes – one and a half million in the preceding five years – had led to the spread of built-up areas and the destruction of countryside, as well as to an increase in commuting time for workers. Powell said that the Government was doing all it could to move employment to the new towns – the Stationery Office had gone to Basildon and the Meteorological Office to Bracknell – and rejected suggestions by Labour that the Government should build more new towns. The eight built to serve London were only a third full, with room for another 200,000 Londoners if they chose to move there. He also noted that new-town projects did not have to be undertaken by the state, as Labour seemed to think, but could be started by private enterprise – as with the original new towns, like Port Sunlight and Bournville.

At the end of August, Powell addressed a branch meeting of the Institute of Personnel Management in his constituency, and was asked about immigration. In the preceding two years sizeable numbers from the colonies and the New Commonwealth had started to arrive in Wolverhampton, and the matter was becoming one of keen concern to his constituents. Powell, remembering well the events of 1948, told his audience that 'a fundamental change in the law is necessary before there can be any limit to West Indian immigration. It would be necessary to define a citizen of the British Isles by his place of birth and his race. Such a definition would put in the category of "the rest" many British subjects, white, yellow and black, and would bring with it the necessity to discriminate against classes of citizens and to accord this or that class certain privileges. There might be circumstances in which such a change of the law might be the lesser of two evils.'[22] As with his committee interventions, these remarks are consistent with the stand he would take in the late 1960s. However, he added, 'There would be very few people who would say the time had yet come when it was essential that so great a change should be made.' Powell told Paul Foot in 1969 that the statement was, inevitably, made 'out of loyalty to the Government line'.

The growing crisis in the Suez Canal Zone cut short all MPs' holidays that year, Parliament being summoned back for a special debate on 12 September. Powell, having realised two years earlier that Britain's bluff would be called, was watching the mounting anguish of his colleagues with 'amused detachment'.[23] He had other, less world-altering, duties to discharge that month: a three-day Welsh tour, visiting Swansea, Aberystwyth and Dolgellau and, later, a visit to

Bournemouth to address the conference of the Sanitary Inspectors' Association. He suggested to them that individual towns might start pilot schemes for smoke-controlled areas as specified under the Clean Air Act. He developed this theme at Southport the following month, when he spoke to the conference of the National Smoke Abatement Society. He used his speech to announce the appointment soon of a Clean Air Council, which would monitor the new law once it came into force in April 1958.

At home, Pam was about to have their second child. The *Evening Standard* rejoiced in the news that she was to have a £4 14s 6d a week 'amenity bed' at Lambeth Hospital, where Susan had been born two and a half years earlier. 'You have a private room,' said Pam, 'yet it comes under the National Health Service. Being a Minister, my husband is no longer able to make extra money by broadcasting or writing.' More expense, though, was on the way. 'We shall soon grow out of our flat,' Pam added.[24] The *Daily Sketch*, picking up the story, sneered that 'even £2,000 a year doesn't go far these days', referring to Powell's ministerial salary. A private room would cost between £16 and £20 a week.[25] For Powell, the main difficulty of his wife's confinement would be administrative. Though a minister, he still answered most of his constituency correspondence by hand, so his burden of work increased.

On 11 October 1956, at the Conservative party conference in Llandudno, Powell wound up a debate on local government, in which calls for the reform both of its finances and of county councils – issues that would dog the party for the next forty years – predominated. He said the Government's guiding principle had to be to give local authorities more, not less, financial responsibility. He also attacked bad local authorities, saying there was no need for them to vary in efficiency and effectiveness from the best; and pledged that the Conservatives would abolish rent control. Introducing legislation to carry forward that promise would be his main task that autumn, embarked upon as soon as his wife was safely delivered of their second daughter, Jennifer, on 17 October – the birth took place while Powell was on the train to London from a speaking engagement in Hereford.

Later that month Powell had to stand in for Sandys at a speaking engagement – his chief was at an emergency cabinet meeting prompted by the Suez crisis – and volunteered to answer off-the-cuff questions about his department's policy from the floor of the National Housing and Town Planning Council's annual conference at Brighton. It was made clear to him that the slowness of slum clearance (which he himself had attacked before achieving office) was causing problems. Powell denied that the Government was at fault, shifting the blame instead on to local authorities. With those authorities now free to borrow on the open market, there was less excuse for them to proceed slowly. Interest rates were not the problem; and, when told by the chairman of the conference that rates would 'no doubt' rise, Powell responded that 'you must have access to sources of information, divination, and prophecy which are absolutely closed and unknown to me'.[26]

The concentration of the slums was a problem: 26 per cent were in Manchester and Merseyside alone; and, even in an area where the difficulty was as acute as that, all other building work could not be stopped to allow all resources to be channelled into clearance. Moreover, the formation of new and stable communities could not be achieved instantly, and nor could those communities be comprised entirely of those who had lived in the slums. The overriding problem was financial: no sector of the economy and no aspect of consumption could contract out of the consequences of inflation. Powell rejected, categorically, demands from the floor for specially subsidised housing loans at a time of credit squeeze, as such an indiscriminate subsidy would defeat the agreed policy of giving first priority to slum clearance, and more building work would be begun than the nation had the resources to complete.

Britain's bluff having been called by Nasser – as Powell had known it would be – he put his private views aside. On 2 November, addressing his constituents, he said that within hours British and French troops would be occupying the Suez Canal Zone. 'Those troops', he said, 'deserve a united Parliament behind them, but that possibility is gone. They still deserve to have behind them a united country, and it is the duty of the British people to give our soldiers that backing in the action which is to come.' Drawing a parallel with the Panama Canal, he said: 'Does anyone believe that the United States would not have felt it was its moral duty to intervene physically to prevent an international waterway from becoming the target of two opposing armies?'[27] By his position in the Government, he was disabled from venting his feelings on the issue in any more controversial sense. He believed, justifiably, that American financial blackmail was responsible for what he later termed the 'disastrous reaction' Britain had made to Nasser's nationalisation of the canal, a reaction which at the time 'startled and mystified' him.[28]

However, as he made clear to Tony Benn in a conversation two years later, he was not, in private, remotely behind the policy Eden was following; he told Benn that Britain had forfeited the means to maintain overseas possessions or influences, and therefore an attempt to invade and regain the canal was wrong.[29] Having mentally closed the door on imperial longings, he could not engage with the furore going on around him in the parliamentary Conservative party. As he sat, as he recalled, 'hunched in a remote and subordinate cranny of government – devising a rent bill ... I was not disposed to go overboard'.[30] Like other politicians on other occasions, he could have been forgiven for calculating that this was not an issue on which to throw aside a career that was, after so long, only now taking off. Powell later commented that he was merely 'a spectator' at Suez, watching 'an incomprehensible drama ... in which I played no part'. He also rationalised that, if Britain controlled the canal, she would have to take Cairo; and, if she took Cairo, she would have to govern Egypt: which was impracticable. It was, therefore, 'a drama to which there was no intelligible conclusion'.[31]

The following week he spoke on slum clearance during the debate on the Queen's Speech. He had also discussed the reform of local government finance, saying it had to be kept separate from any reform of local government – which, he said, should in any case be 'not a revolutionary alteration in the system but a modernisation and overhaul of the structure'.[32] A fortnight later he had more extensive work to do, moving the second reading of the Rent Bill that would achieve his long-held aim of ending rent controls. He told the Commons that controls had been 'essentially an emergency measure' brought in with the war. He argued that supply and demand in the housing market were now coming into balance, with between two and a half and three-quarters of a million new houses built since the war. Aware of intense socialist objections to lifting controls, Powell cited in his defence the *Manchester Guardian*, which had condemned rent controls for the way they accelerated the rate at which houses became uninhabitable, because it was not in the landlord's economic interest to improve or repair them. Also, the anomalies of the control system led to injustices to both landlords and tenants.

To support his and the Government's case, Powell outlined how other costs had risen in the period during which rents had been controlled: building costs were at three and a half times the level when war broke out, average earnings at more than three and a half times that level, and the cost of living overall at two and a half times the level. So, he contended, if rents rose as a result of the freeing of controls – and they probably would – there was no doubt such rises could be afforded. However, given the huge number of empty controlled tenancies on the market, additional supply would, he hoped, help keep costs down. He did, though, concede that as there had been a seventeen-year 'freeze', any rises would have to be phased in. The Government's proposals were, therefore, that controlled tenancies would become decontrolled only once the existing tenants had moved out. The exception would be 'luxury' tenancies, categorised by high-rateable-value houses – more than £40 in London and Scotland, more than £30 elsewhere. Smaller rent rises would be permissible in the other four and a half million controlled properties. Gilbert Mitchison, the Labour spokesman, sympathised with Powell for having been 'put up to argue an unarguable case' for this 'preposterous Bill'.[33]

Meanwhile, American objections had led to Britain being wrongfooted at Suez, forcing a reversal of the policy. Eden was stricken by illness; so it fell to Butler to address the 1922 Committee on 22 November, the day after Powell's speech on the Rent Bill, the day upon which Butler had made a Commons statement on the imminent withdrawal of troops from the canal zone. The parliamentary party was in a frenzy at the Government's handling of the crisis, and the '22 meeting was designed to cool tempers. Such was its significance that, as an extraordinary measure, ministers outside the cabinet were invited, which is why Powell, unusually, found himself there to witness Butler's act of restoring calm. Butler had taken Macmillan with him for moral support, an act which, as Butler's biographer Anthony Howard points out, 'turned out to be a highly expensive mistake'. Butler made a short and lacklustre appeal for unity. Macmillan, following him, performed (in Howard's words) 'a veritable political organ voluntary lasting thirty-five minutes – pulling out every stop and striking every majestic chord in his well-practised repertoire, including a *tremolo* on his own advancing years'.[34] To Powell it was 'one of the most horrible things that I remember in politics ... seeing the way in which Harold Macmillan, with all the skill of the old actor–manager, succeeded in false-footing Rab. The sheer devilry of it verged upon the disgusting.' Thus Powell had established the roots of a lifelong dislike of Macmillan before he even came to serve under him. Writing immediately after Macmillan's death, Powell went to the heart of the problem. 'Macmillan was a Whig, not a Tory ... he had no use for the Conservative loyalties and affections; they interfered too much with the Whig's true vocation of detecting trends in events and riding them skilfully so as to preserve the privileges, property and interests of his class.'[35]

Macmillan's opportunism was, though, to provide an opportunity for Powell. In his year at the Ministry of Housing and Local Government he had taken through some of the most important deregulating legislation passed by the Conservatives, and had done so in a way that had won him respect on both sides of the House, and a reputation for competence and thoroughness. The talk, by that autumn, was that Powell had already proved to be an obvious candidate for promotion. On 23 November, two days after his speech on the Rent Bill, he took a short break from parliamentary duties to have Jennifer christened in St Stephen's Crypt. He had, though he did not know it at the time, just one more important front-bench duty to discharge in his post, when he wound up a debate in the Commons on 13 December on the Draft Housing Subsidies Order, which abolished general housing subsidies and promoted slum clearance. It was an appropriate place for him to sign off as a housing minister, for the tumult in the higher reaches of the Conservative party, that would shortly bring about Eden's resignation, would result further down in the promotion which all had been sure Powell would receive.

III

Ironically, the job realistically within his grasp that he most wanted – the post of Financial Secretary to the Treasury – was given to him by a man who, before

Edward Heath assumed the mantle, would represent to Powell all that he found regrettable about the principle-free conduct of politics. Harold Macmillan became Prime Minister after Eden's resignation on 8 January 1957, the Queen having been advised to appoint him rather than Butler on the advice both of Churchill and of Lord Salisbury. Salisbury, famously, asked ministers and grandees individually, 'Well, which is it, Wab or Hawold?' It was Harold; though Powell, who should have been asked his view by at least a Whip, said that 'I was never polled at all.'[36] Macmillan began to reconstruct the Government immediately, hoping to avoid the taint of weakness Eden had attracted by not acting with similar ruthlessness on his accession in 1955.

On 14 January he sent for Powell and, on the recommendation of the outgoing incumbent, Henry Brooke (who had succeeded Duncan Sandys, the new Minister of Defence, at Housing), asked him to become Financial Secretary. Powell would be unable to see his beloved Rent Bill on to the statute book. Instead, the task went to Brooke and his new deputy, Reginald Bevins. They were, perhaps, less ideologically suited to this task than Powell. On 18 February the Labour-supporting *Daily Herald* reported gossip that Brooke and Bevins were 'saying bluntly' that they had been 'saddled' with the Rent Bill, which they were finding it hard to defend. They were said to be receiving 250 letters of protest a day.[37]

The offer of an economic post was perfect for Powell: the fulfilment of all his immediate ambitions. The Financial Secretary's job was at the heart of government: every spending proposal by every department came across his desk. Eden wrote to him to say that Macmillan had made 'an excellent choice'.[38] Powell was now the Chancellor's deputy, and the most important minister not in the cabinet. Given this seniority he asked Macmillan, on his appointment, whether he might join the Privy Council. Macmillan wrote to him two days later to say he had investigated the matter, but 'I find from all precedents that this honour does not accompany the appointment, and indeed that there is often a substantial delay. This was so in the cases of your two immediate predecessors. But of course I will have this matter very much in mind in future.'[39]

Powell's promotion threw him together with two personalities radically different from his own. The new Chancellor was Peter Thorneycroft, who had been President of the Board of Trade for five uneventful but competent years, and had started off in 1951 as the youngest member of Churchill's cabinet. An Old Etonian and former regular soldier, he was highly popular and considered genial and kindly. Another Old Etonian, Nigel Birch, became Economic Secretary, demoted from the job of Air Secretary, but with the promise of a more influential role in government. Although Birch had family wealth, and had married money, he had made his own fortune as a stockbroker. He was completely independent, both financially and intellectually. His sharp tongue had made him many enemies, but he was also feared and respected for his blunt honesty and probity. He was suffering increasingly from deteriorating eyesight, to the extent that he had to memorise his speeches in the Commons as he could hardly see to read his notes. His experience of the City had given him a close understanding of the economy and he was, like Powell, a rigid advocate of sound money. Powell soon became an almost unqualified admirer.

Powell's economic outlook was, as we have seen, already well developed, and of a strict laissez-faire variety. During his time in the Research Department he had met Diana Spearman, first wife of the Conservative MP Alec Spearman, and an enthusiast for the ultra-liberal economic philosophy of Friedrich von Hayek. She had communicated this enthusiasm to Powell; and Powell had kept sporadically in touch with an acquaintance from his Cambridge days, Dennis Robertson, who had been an associate of Keynes but had turned against him at the time of the publication of the *General Theory* – the bible of deficit financing – in 1936. Mrs Spearman was also close to Lionel Robbins, the London School of Economics' liberal economist, and to Michael Oakeshott, the Cambridge Conservative philosopher.[40] These, in particular, were the influences brought to bear on Powell by the time he went to the Treasury, though he had provided himself with others by applying his own powers of logic to questions of money. His attachment to liberal economics had, though, been evolving throughout his time in Parliament, and would continue to evolve further long after he had left the Treasury. In 1954, reviewing a collection of essays on the British economy in the nineteenth century edited by Hayek, Powell had raised a sceptical eyebrow at two of Hayek's assumptions: 'the freedom of economic activity which in England had proved so favourable to the rapid growth of wealth', and 'the undeniable wealth which the competitive order has produced'.[41] These were, wrote Powell, 'connections of cause and effect without proof'; but, as his immersion in the theology of the market deepened, these were not views he would question for much longer.

With the Budget preceded by a period of 'purdah' in which Treasury ministers said little in public and did not talk to the press, Powell had a quiet few weeks on entering his job. The economy was not, in the immediate aftermath of Suez, healthy. Cameron Cobbold, the Governor of the Bank of England, had met Eden days before his resignation to recommend a Budget surplus in the forthcoming financial year, to restore international and domestic confidence in the currency.[42] Butler and Macmillan, the Chancellor, had also been present. The ministers doubted whether such a surplus was either possible or desirable. Thus was a theme set for the coming year, for which the change of Prime Minister would make no difference.

The aftermath of Suez meant the pound was still suffering from a loss of international confidence. Macmillan's last act before leaving the Treasury had been to call for £200 million savings in the defence budget and between £80 and £100 million cuts in social security; Thorneycroft intended to pursue these economies. Powell and Birch entirely supported him, as, at first, did his main officials. The chief economic adviser, Sir Robert Hall, said after meeting all three ministers at the first Budget Committee of Thorneycroft's rule, in the third week of January, that 'the main thing is that all three of them feel that they had better do what they believe in and don't try to hold votes too much, which I am sure is the right line'.[43] The story of the year to come, though, was to be of the ministers holding to this zealous line, and the officials – who were to a man Keynesian – looking on with mounting horror.

Powell's first speech in his new post was made in an adjournment debate on 18 February, on the unlikely matter of the impounding of supposedly obscene books. Denis Howell, a Birmingham MP, complained that customs officers – for whom the Treasury was responsible – had impounded two books by Jean Genet, ordered by the library of Birmingham University, for their explicit homosexual content. Howell appealed to Powell, as a former don, to recognise the dangers of what had happened. Powell said that the matter would have to be referred to the courts and decided there: it was not for him to say. This was three years before the *Lady Chatterley* trial. One of Powell's few other outings before the Budget was on an equally arcane subject, the question of what to do with a treasure trove discovered in Cheshire. In it he admitted to a rare gap in his growing antiquarian interests: he said he was no numismatist.

Soon after assuming office Macmillan had been persuaded by Butler of the need to have a committee of the party's brightest men considering what should be in the next manifesto, even though the election was, theoretically, over three years away. Macleod was invited to chair this group, and in February 1957 asked Powell, Maudling, David Ormsby-Gore (a Foreign Office minister of state) and Jack Simon (a Home Office minister) to join him on it. Michael Fraser, the director of the Research Department, and Peter Goldman of the Conservative Political Centre also joined the group. Powell quickly sent in a position paper on 'what seem to me to be the main pieces of mental work before the party'. The first was external relations: 'The Tory Party must find the means to interpret its membership of international organisations in a manner which shall not be repugnant to its deep sense of nationhood and shall also not be verbiage and humbug.'[44] He attacked the 'mad theory of universal democracy' as preached by the United Nations Organisation, and said that 'the Tory Party must be cured of the British Empire'. Finding patriotism not in Empire but in 'this England' would, he said, 'be a salve to the wound of Suez'. He wanted reform of social security, with a Ministry of Labour and Social Security, and one of Health and Local Government. He wanted no radical change of system in schools or the NHS, but said, 'Wanted: a Conservative theory of Higher Education.' Before the work of this committee was even half done, Powell would cease to be part of it.

Thorneycroft delivered his first, and only, Budget on 9 April. Although the Treasury was still reeling after Suez the Chancellor was able to find £98 million for tax cuts – which, controversially, he gave to British firms operating abroad and to surtax payers. With the Bank still pressurising him to adopt a firmer monetary policy, Thorneycroft announced the appointment of a committee – under Lord Radcliffe – to examine different ways of operating such policy, with a view to settling the best methods. However, Cobbold's plea for firm measures fast had been ignored. Powell took part in the debate on the Budget on 11 April, his job being to explain further the reasoning behind Thorneycroft's proposals. He told the House that his chief had been confronted with an overall balance in the books, and that the country would be going hardly any further into debt thanks – ironically, in the light of Powell's future thoughts on the matter – to the success of the National Savings drive. Given this prudence, Powell said, Thorneycroft had been entirely justified in making the tax cuts.

He also commended the decision to reform entertainments duty, a move made to help the revenues of cinemas and theatres that were closing down unable to bear competition from the newly flourishing television channels. Powell made the political point that the tax had last been increased by a Labour government in 1951. The Budget also reduced purchase tax on some domestic goods, which Powell praised. His main challenge, though, was to defend the tax reliefs for companies trading overseas, which the Opposition felt would be open to abuse by businesses claiming more overseas trade than was actually the case. Powell could only tell Harold Wilson, the Shadow Chancellor, who brought the question up, that he would like him 'to see our shot at it and then we will see how watertight we can make this alteration in tax law'.[45] When Powell came to defend the tax cuts and alterations in child allowance – which would mean a man on £600 a year with two children would now pay no tax, whereas hitherto he had paid £35 – Wilson challenged him about the effects of inflation on those wages, saying that £600 now would not buy what £565 had in 1951, when Labour left office. Powell refused to engage in that argument, but instead defended his policy against two other Labour charges. Surtax payers had had, he said, no additional relief since 1920, and were in equity long overdue for it; and, although the tax cuts would not favour pensioners whose income was below the tax level, their pensions had risen in real terms to far above where they had been when Labour ruled.

The argument Powell was having with Labour was one which successive Conservative Treasury ministers would have with their opponents in the decade ahead. Wilson said the Budget had been inflationary, and he spoke of the need for personal consumption to be 'held back'. Powell disputed that the Budget was inflationary, given the tightness of the control of the money supply and indebtedness, and asked the Opposition to outline what its checks on personal consumption would be, and whether they would include higher taxation: he was met with silence. He continued to goad Wilson, who had spoken on television the previous evening about the need to enforce vague 'controls'. These, said Powell, were 'associated with reserves slumping, first, to a convertibility crisis, then to a devaluation crisis and, finally, to a run-away-from-Government crisis'.[46] He concluded by saying, proudly, that the proportion of gross national product taken in taxation was now 26.5 per cent; it would fall as a result of this Budget to 25 per cent. In 1951 it had been 31.3 per cent.

Patrick Gordon Walker, one of Labour's principal foreign affairs spokesmen, replying to Powell, ridiculed his defence of 'the downtrodden Surtax payer'. He said the Treasury was now operating 'Powell's law, which is: the bigger the share of income kept by anyone the better for him'.[47] Gordon Walker's colleagues loved the joke; Powell would not have found it either remotely funny, or remotely offensive. That was exactly how he viewed the correct operation of the tax system. A sharper point made by Gordon Walker, and one Powell did not leap up to challenge, was that instead of fretting about 'the plight of the Surtax payer' they should be fretting about the slump in the reserves. These were down to £789 million, more than a quarter of which was borrowed money on which the taxpayer was having to pay interest. He tried to defend the notion, which Powell had ridiculed, of a controlled economy, claiming that the Treasury team's 'doctrinal attachment to the laissez-faire ... leads the Government into an inextricable dilemma. They are always either curing a balance of payments crisis by inducing stagnation, or curing stagnation by inducing a threatened balance of payments crisis.' The smell of hypocrisy caused by this assertion was too much for one Conservative, Douglas Glover, who called out: 'Is the hon Gentleman talking about 1947 to 1951, or since then?'[48]

A month later Powell moved the second reading of the Finance Bill, which would legislate on the intentions of the Budget. In a long and detailed speech, in which he was frequently interrupted, he spelled out exactly the technical details of what the Bill proposed – a more exact version of his speech on the Budget proposals a month earlier. This time when following him Gordon Walker observed, in response to Powell's claim that the Bill was shorter than usual, that it was 'no less complicated ... I have a feeling that Finance Bills are becoming more and more unintelligible and more and more difficult to follow in their details.' Powell, whose grasp of detail was legendary, was unprepared to make compromises. Ministers less gifted would have made the details more intelligible, not so much to help their audience as to help themselves. Powell's style in the Commons was encapsulated by the *Telegraph's* sketch writer during the debate on the Finance Bill. 'Competence on a financial and economic brief, and Mr Powell is very competent indeed, often soothes Members to sleep. But the slumber created by Mr Powell was not warm and comforting. It was as frigid as any spell woven by some ice maiden of a Nordic saga. Under his chilling touch the Finance Bill was laid out like a fish on a slab.'[49]

The monetarist orthodoxy, as far as the ministers were concerned, was in place by May 1957, when Powell went to address the Conservative women's conference. He pointed to the fall in the rate of increase in the cost of living, down to just 1 per cent in the previous twelve months, and told them nothing would contribute more directly to pushing it up than heavy borrowing by the Government. The small amount of borrowing in which the Government intended to indulge in the present year would, as he had told the Commons, be covered by National Savings. Unknowingly, the parameters were set for the collision that would come just over six months later. However, the Bank of England was still not satisfied that sufficient rigour was being imposed. Cobbold wrote to Thorneycroft at the end of May 1957 to warn him about the continuing decline in international confidence in sterling.[50]

It was an intensely busy time for Powell. Earlier in May he had spoken on a measure affecting NHS contributions; a few days after his second reading speech he was in committee on the Cheques (No. 2) Bill. For the last week of May he was almost constantly in committee on the Finance Bill, which became bogged down for days on the reform of entertainments duty and the addition of a small levy to the television licence. Those proceedings were interrupted after the Whitsun recess, though there was still no respite for Powell: he had to move the second reading of the Superannuation Bill, which had started as a Private Member's measure and improved pension terms for certain classes of civil servant. At the end of June and into early July the Finance Bill committee reconvened, and this time Powell and Wilson were locked in combat over the company taxation measures, and exemptions from stamp duty.

Nor was it just in his professional life that Powell was busy. With two children, the flat in Earl's Court Square was now too small; and with Powell's income improved by his ministerial job and a pay rise, taking his earnings to £3,250 a year, the family could afford to look for somewhere more substantial. They settled on a tall, narrow late-Georgian terraced house on the southern fringe of Belgravia, 33 South Eaton Place, having coincidentally driven past it and seen it for sale. As well as being handy for Westminster, it was close to an ideal school for the two girls: it was Powell's job, which he enjoyed, to take his daughters to school each day before attending to his political duties. Number 33 would be the Powells' home for the rest of their life together. In what little spare time they had, Powell put his handyman's skills to good use in trying to renovate their new house. In the 1990s, when leasehold reform would have enabled the Powells to buy the freehold of their property from the Grosvenor Estate, Powell refused. 'I wouldn't steal from a duke,' he said.

The Finance Bill's proceedings did not exclusively show Powell at his most desiccated. At the report stage on 16 July he spoke for the Government on an amendment that would exempt from taxation in the United Kingdom compensation payments made by the German Government to victims of Nazi oppression. There was all-party support for a move that would stop the Government profiting from the suffering of these people, and Powell said 'it is impossible to approach the subject matter of the new Clause without emotion and without evoking associations which, in our different ways, we all have in our minds'.[51] However, he argued, emotion alone could not govern the question. He said that one class of the compensation given was for loss of pension rights: and, therefore, it was logical this should be taxed as a normal pension. 'I add, however,' Powell was careful to say, 'that this class of case has not actually been referred to the Inland Revenue and that, therefore, is a provisional view.' In other cases, there was the invidiousness of discriminating between widows of victims of German persecution and widows of men who had died on active service and whose war widow's pension was taxed in the normal way. To do so would, he said, cause ill-feeling. Nor was he prepared to make an allowance for the fact that the German Government, in setting the levels of compensation, had assumed no tax would be levied on it: 'It would be impracticable for us to treat incomes received and enjoyed by British taxpayers differently according to the tax law of the country in which they originated, even where, as here, those tax laws have been deliberately and for political and possibly moral purposes framed in a special way.'[52] Powell said he hoped the House would not vote to change the law, but he assured members that every payment received by individuals from the German Government would be taxed no more heavily than any comparable payment from British sources. There were immediate expressions of understanding from the Opposition benches; he had argued a difficult case well.

The following Friday, 19 July, the Finance Bill at last had its third reading. Moving it, Powell noted that it was three short clauses longer than originally, and conceded that 'in some respects it is certainly a more efficient and correct Bill for the purposes for which it is designed, thanks to the co-operation of hon Members on both sides of the House'. Its basic thrust remained, though, unchanged. The tax reliefs intended had risen by just £100,000, and were still under £98 million. National Savings receipts were still on course to match Government borrowing. In his reply, Wilson observed that the Bill was having its third reading only three weeks before the last date specified by law, largely because of the wrangles over company taxation, which Labour still believed had not been scrutinised sufficiently, even then, to prevent exploitation of loopholes. He did, though, praise Powell for having made 'the most courteous and full replies' to points raised to him – a contrast with the abrasive Birch, whose answers, Wilson said, had been 'perfunctory in the extreme'.[53]

IV

During that summer the three Treasury ministers found themselves talking to each other about the nature of the main problem over which they were presiding – inflation running at between 3 and 4 per cent, despite the clearing banks, at the behest of the Bank of England, operating a 'self-denying ordinance' about levels of lending, to try to restrict the supply of money in the absence of Government action to do so. Years later, Powell recalled that 'Nigel Birch started to drop into my room to talk about the causes of inflation, I started to drop into his, and when we conferred with the Chancellor, we found we'd all come to the same conclusion.'[54] This consensus was one of such absolutism that no other remedy would be worth considering: that the inflation was caused by something over which the Government had complete control, namely the supply of money. Powell had, of course, already said this publicly, and it was assumed (not least by Macmillan) that he had driven the policy. They agreed that this truth should be propagated, and that the appropriate policy – which would come to be called monetarism – should be pursued accordingly. Inflation was not, as Sir Stafford Cripps had argued, a moral issue, to do with the immorality of people accepting large pay rises. Powell came to this conclusion, he said, not because of anything he had read in Adam Smith, but through the simple application of logic to the problem.

His extensive parliamentary duties having ended, he took up the political fight again outside before allowing himself a summer holiday, this year spent in England with his wife and two young daughters. He returned aggressively to the theme of monetary prudence on 3 August, when he spoke at Sheringham in Norfolk of the Opposition behaving, on economic matters, like 'Satan rebuking sin'. He claimed that the plans coming out of transport House would add £1000 million a year to public spending, and several times that in Government money bills on the market. The plans 'might have been deliberately designed as an attack on the value of money. The two undoubted causes of inflation are excessive Government spending and excessive Government borrowing. The Socialist Party is pledged to both.'[55] The warning signs he was sending to colleagues in the Government could not have been clearer. Speaking at Gloucester on 11 September he repeated the point, saying that socialism equalled inflation, whereas the Government had tried to maintain the value of money, and had saved the taxpayer £800 million a year. Thorneycroft was already taking action. In July 1957 he had asked officials in the Treasury 'to consider possibilities of checking inflation by taking firmer control of the money supply'.[56] He had sent out a memorandum to cabinet colleagues on 17 July warning that, unless checked, present spending plans would 'far outstrip the rise in revenue'.[57] On 7 August he requested that 'a study should be made in the Treasury of the possibilities of bringing about a measure of deflation in the economy'.[58] This was a blow to the senior Treasury mandarins, several of whom had to cancel their summer holidays to manage the problem.

Thorneycroft had warned Macmillan, after an Opposition Day* debate on inflation on 25 July, that the Government had merely 'survived' it. He had left the Prime Minister in no doubt that sterner measures, principally credit controls, would need to be implemented.[59] For the first time Thorneycroft told him that 1958's civil estimates would have to be at 1957's level. Before going on holiday, he told senior officials that while he was not pursuing a 'full blooded deflation' such as had happened in 1930, a new way of doing things had to be found. Throughout August, officials worked on various policy proposals for limiting the credit created by the banks, and looked at other ways of restricting the supply of money. Late that month the Bank of England signalled that compelling the clearing banks to limit their advances would be unacceptable: so 'the only action left in the monetary field was a drastic increase in bank rate'.[60]

Matters were aggravated by a *de facto* devaluation of the French Franc in August, which set up sterling as the next target on the foreign exchanges; there was a sudden fall in the reserves of £80 million.[61] In the continuing search for a solution, a committee was set up to examine prices, productivity and incomes, and the Treasury ministers argued for Lionel Robbins, the most prominent anti-Keynesian, to take charge of it. The mandarins were aghast and, in a stand that damaged relations between ministers and officials, effectively ruled Robbins out; as Hall noted in his diary, 'I felt strongly that the whole left wing of the country would regard this as the choice of a notorious reactionary to do the work of a Tory Government. It is not true ... but it would be said.'[62] Thus, at the very moment the matter started to become ideological, so too did the normal relationships between ministers and mandarins begin to break down.

When it was announced in September that Lord Hailsham would become party chairman, speculation arose that Powell would succeed him as Minister of Education. The *Manchester Guardian* pointed out that Powell's promotion at the start of Macmillan's administration had been prompted by his impressive record at Housing; 'and nothing he has done since has lessened his reputation for being master of his subject, courteous, and yet thoroughly committed to the policies he advocates'.[63] However, such a promotion – which might have had vastly different consequences for Powell's subsequent career – did not materialise. The job went instead to Geoffrey Lloyd, who had been Minister of Fuel and Power in Churchill's last Government.

It was as well Powell was not moved: he was enjoying his job immensely, finding at last the mixture of severe intellectual challenge and position at the heart of Government he had always desired. This was, too, a time of deep personal philosophical reflection for him. It was eight years since he had

---

* Formerly known as Supply Days, these are days in the Parliamentary timetable – normally twenty in each session – when the Leader of the Opposition, or the leaders of other main opposition parties, can choose the subject for debate.

returned to the church, and had felt a deepening attachment to religion through-out that time. He recalled that, during that late summer, aged forty-five, he was digging his garden in Wolverhampton when he seemed to feel a hand on his shoulder and to hear a voice: 'My boy, you're getting older.' From then on he held no reservations about his faith, nor entertained the notion that death was to be feared.

By the end of August the rest-starved Treasury officials were beginning to have severe doubts about Thorneycroft's approach, Hall complaining in his diary on 27 August that the Chancellor, in his view, did not adequately dis-tinguish between bank deposits and cash in pockets when theorising about the money supply, and Sir Roger Makins, the joint permanent secretary, Hall reports as being 'bewildered'.[64] It is quite likely that Makins was bewildered for reasons other than the crisis: by breeding a Foreign Office man, he knew little about economics and understood less. In his turn, Thorneycroft 'took against all his officials' – Hall's words again – and called in Robbins for monetarist advice.[65] At the cabinet meeting on 10 September 1957 Thorneycroft said the reserves had fallen by more than $200 million during July and August, and would probably continue to fall during September. This was a result of speculation after the fall in the Franc and the undervaluation of the Mark; and he warned that the speculation would be 'aggravated' if the Government did nothing to shore up sterling. He added that, when he went (as he was imminently to do) to the International Monetary Fund in Washington, he would state the Govern-ment's intention to maintain the $2.80 exchange rate, but that would be credible only if he could also outline the measures he intended to take. 'The key to the problem', the cabinet minutes record, 'lay in restricting the supply of money.'[66]

The main proposals he had to advance were credit controls, holding bank advances at 5 per cent below their level of previous years. He also reiterated, however, that ministers had been asked to keep expenditure next year at this year's limits, and would be expected to do so. Butler raised concerns about restricting investment, though agreed it might be prudent to raise Bank Rate; David Eccles, the President of the Board of Trade, concurred that Bank Rate should be adjusted, as did Macleod. The idea of floating the currency was discussed, to be rejected because of its perceived resemblance to devaluation. On 22 August Cobbold had sent Thorneycroft a memorandum arguing that a drastic rise in Bank Rate was the only option left; in a discussion with Makins, the governor had been 'strongly discouraged from believing that any short-order cuts in public expenditure were feasible', a position entirely at odds with that of his ministers, and from which Makins would not resile.[67]

Macmillan was worried about the effects of 'disinflation', and at the next cabinet meeting, two days later, announced the creation of a sub-committee to discuss its effects. By the time of the meeting after that, on 17 September, the committee had considered Thorneycroft's proposals to restrict investment in the public and private sectors, and had concluded that 'although these measures were drastic, they were realistic and practicable'.[68] Worries were still voiced that 'the Government were now departing, for the first time, from the objectives of the 1944 White Paper for Full Employment'. However, no alternative could be devised, though the cabinet was told the proposed rise in Bank Rate from 5 to 7 per cent 'was probably unprecedented except on the outbreak of a major war'. The agreement to raise the rate was made on the understanding that it would be reduced again as soon as possible.

On 19 September 1957, the rate was raised. Cobbold had put the case for a 2 per cent rise to Thorneycroft a few days earlier, but the Treasury team wanted only 1 per cent. The Chancellor demanded measures to force the clearing banks to restrict lending further, but Cobbold and his deputy, Humphrey Mynors, successfully argued the practical and political difficulties of such an intervention. However, since Thorneycroft was told that, in the circumstances, it would be difficult to sack the Governor because he wanted to be tougher on interest rate policy than he did, the 2 per cent rise was agreed. Thorneycroft's success in convincing the cabinet of the need for stringency aggravated the already serious strain with Hall, who shared none of the Treasury team's monetarist principles. Hall complained that the 19 September measures were 'done by Ministers and they would not listen to any suggestion that what they were saying did not make much sense as economics'.[69] In this and subsequent observations by Hall, there can be no measure of objectivity. To a Keynesian, the measures would be nonsense, as Keynesian theory repudiates the relationship between the supply of money and inflation. To a monetarist, though, the sense was utterly clear. If the Government could not get the banks to restrict their own lending, the Government would restrict it by the simple expedient of limiting its own borrowing from them.

So far, the Government was determined, through the credit squeeze and by other means, to maintain a policy of honest money. Yet already Macmillan, who had only reluctantly agreed to the rise in Bank Rate, was aware of the dangers of the policy, and, concerned as always to avoid confrontation if at all possible, told the cabinet two days later that 'the Government's decision to restrict the supply of money should not ... be represented as a challenge to organised labour. On the contrary, the Government should emphasise that the strength and stability of sterling were a pre-condition of the maintenance of a high level of employment.'[70] Hall, in his diary, writes of Thorneycroft and Macmillan having believed that the deflation 'would cure the wage/price spiral without forcing the Government to face a row with the Unions or a strike'. There is no evidence that any of the Treasury team held this view; it was not remotely a consideration for Powell. Macmillan's moral cowardice – or what his adherents would term the scarring of his personality by the spectre of unemployment in pre-war (and pre-welfare state) Stockton-on-Tees – would be the guiding light of the months ahead.

The statement put out on 19 September to accompany the interest rate rise was heavily Powellish: 'There can be no remedy for inflation and the steadily rising prices which go with it which does not include, and indeed is not founded upon, a control of the money supply. So long as it is generally believed that the Government are prepared to see the necessary finance produced to match the upward spiral of costs, inflation will continue and prices will go up.'[71] Since January 1956 – that is, over the previous twenty months – inflation had risen by 7 per cent, and wages by 11 per cent. On television that night, Thorneycroft said that 'no longer will more and more money be issued to enable prices to go on getting higher'.[72] Hall, as chief adviser, said he did not object to the policy 'as such', but 'felt that the words chosen to announce it were dangerous as far as economists were concerned'.[73] Hall twice offered to resign during these weeks; he may not have objected to the policy, but he still records Thorneycroft telling him that 'it was nonsense to say it [the cause of the inflation] was not the supply of money because everyone knew it was'.[74] In addition to the 2 per cent rate rise, it was announced that the clearing banks would try to observe a new voluntary ceiling on lending, and there would be a freeze on public sector capital expenditure.[75] In the briefing offered to the press, it was stressed that the main aim was to keep the value of sterling at $2.80, though Powell, then as later, was personally more concerned about the anti-inflationary effects than about maintaining the virility symbol of a certain level of the currency.

Macmillan's doubts about the policy were sustained by urgings from his Keynesian economics adviser Roy Harrod. Harrod wrote to him from Oxford on 7 October telling him that 'the present policy can easily be reversed without loss of face in the next month or two'.[76] He told Macmillan that Thorneycroft was edging towards a policy that would be understood by the public as keeping down wage demands by restricting investment which 'would lose you the election in a very big way indeed'. Harrod was not qualified to make such political judgments, and his economic ones were scarcely better:

> The idea that you can reduce prices by limiting the quantity of money is pre-Keynesian. Keynes spent half his energy inveighing against precisely that idea. Hardly any economists under the age of 50 would subscribe to it. If it were supposed that the Conservatives were associated with any such idea, that might drive many middle-of-the-way economists into the ranks of Labour, and, what is more, Gaitskell would probably succeed in galvinising them all into lambasting and ridiculing the policy. I do sincerely hope that no Govt. speaker would use words implying that the Govt. subscribes to such an antiquated doctrine.

Macmillan made sure the note was copied to Thorneycroft.

In fact, Macmillan had already gone far further than Harrod would have liked, in a secret note to the cabinet issued on 30 September. Stressing the 'vital importance' of no doubts being cast on the determination to enforce the policy, he said that 'whatever the theoretical arguments for or against a particular course at a particular time, we as a Government have now nailed our colours to the mast. I trust, therefore, that we shall not show any wavering in our own ranks, or allow idle or foolish talk among those whom we have the power to influence, whether officials or unofficials. It is of course an attractive intellectual exercise to discuss alternative policies; the moment is certainly not opportune.'[77] In another minute sent round on 6 October, Macmillan was defensive about the policy, claiming that it would safeguard rather than damage the principle of full employment. 'We are looking for a pause, not a retreat.'[78]

The Bank Rate rise had a tedious by-product for Powell. The Shadow Chancellor, Harold Wilson, complained that news of the rise had leaked out in advance, on an afternoon when £4 million worth of business – a quite normal amount – was done in gilts. The documents covering the subsequent inquiry show that some prominent journalists, notably the City editor of the *Daily Telegraph*, knew of the likelihood of a Bank Rate rise on the Wednesday evening before the rise on the Thursday.[79] It also looked as though the leak had come through the chairman of one of the clearing banks, all of whom had been consulted by Thorneycroft on the terms of the strictest secrecy the week before the rise took place.

It fell to Powell to investigate Wilson's claims, made in a letter on 24 September. Two days later Powell had a half-hour meeting with Macmillan, after which he wrote to Wilson refusing the public inquiry the Shadow Chancellor wanted. A private, internal Treasury inquiry, which had reported to Powell, had found no evidence of a leak, having interviewed everyone who knew: notably the Governor of the Bank, the chief Government broker and the chairman of the Stock Exchange. Wilson responded that he was 'astonished' by Powell's reply, referring to press claims that £10 million worth of business had been done shortly before rates went up.[80] Wilson's next step, on 4 October, was to suggest that it had been 'a political source' that had disseminated the leak. The Treasury inquiry had been well aware that Thorneycroft had, on the day before the rise, seen Central Office officials, among them Oliver Poole, the deputy chairman of the party, whom Wilson was trying to implicate. He also asked for an inquiry into why it had taken seventeen hours for Powell to read his letter after he had handed it in at the Treasury, and insisted that an inquiry would be justified 'if only £40,000 or £40 changed hands as a result of a tip-off'.[81] He also cited Attlee's response, ten years earlier, to the leak by Hugh Dalton, when an inquiry was immediately constituted. '*Prima facie* evidence has been brought to my attention suggesting that the leak emanated from a political source. I am prepared to arrange that that evidence be made available to any tribunal the Prime Minister may appoint.'

Macmillan, responding in Powell's absence in his constituency, said that if Wilson could provide this evidence he would put it before Kilmuir, the Lord Chancellor. Eventually, an inquiry, which met in December 1957, was set up under Lord Justice Parker, but by 12 October the focus of suspicion had moved from the clearing banks to Central Office.[82] It was strongly maintained that Poole had not been told; but it turned out that he had, when he left Thorneycroft's office, been given a copy of the press release to be issued the next day – except that a Treasury official had 'doctored' it with a pair of scissors to remove the offending detail. It was not, though, found by the inquiry that this act of amateurism had done anything to alert Poole's suspicions, or that Poole had leaked anything.

Meanwhile, Powell returned to his theme of the debauch of the currency. In Wednesfield the week before the Conservative party conference in October he spoke of 'the inescapable necessity of the decisions to spend less, many of them harsh and difficult decisions, which the country must face in the coming months'. He praised Thorneycroft for announcing limits on Government borrowing and bank advances. However, he warned: 'Neither will succeed without a limitation of public expenditure.' This was, of course, a political decision for the cabinet; Powell, for reasons of tact, put the point somewhat differently: 'the public have got to make up their minds which way they want it. We could go ahead and spend on all the desirable things a Government can think of, from power stations to pictures, and pay the price with roaring inflation and a devaluing of the pound. If this is not the result people want, and it is certainly not the result which this Government is prepared to contemplate for a moment, then public spending and public borrowing must be limited to what we are prepared to finance by real savings and real earnings and not just by printing extra bank notes.'[83] There was an ambiguity about whether it was the public, or his fellow ministers, to whom he was referring when he said: 'It is very easy to call for limitation of Government expenditure in the abstract: few prove ready to demand and support it in the concrete case.'[84] He explicitly expounded the monetarist doctrine: 'If inflation with its evil consequences at home and abroad is to be stopped, this increase in the money supply must be halted and halted without delay. He concluded that 'roaring inflation and devaluation of the pound' was 'not the result which this Government is prepared to contemplate for a moment'. Not for the last time, Powell was badly overestimating the judgment and resolve of his colleagues.

On the opening morning of the party conference, following Thorneycroft's speech on financial policy, Powell spoke on taxation. He said that in the six Budgets since his party had come to power the proportion of national income taken in taxation had fallen by 20 per cent. He wanted further reductions, and said that 'the only true means of reducing taxation was to spend less'. He added that cutting spending was so hard that 'without clear comprehension of what is involved and determined support from those wide sections of the public of which this conference is the sounding board, I would describe it as impossible'.[85] In Newbury ten days later he repeated this warning, reminding his audience that 'upon the measures the Government are taking depends the future of our currency and the future of our country'.[86] The Government, as he would warn in a speech at Halifax in December, could not be diverted from an elementary duty: 'the duty to secure and preserve the integrity and stability of the medium of exchange, on which depend all the economic dealings of man with man'.[87]

Once the House returned after the State Opening in November, Powell resumed his intense activity on the front bench. On 11 November he answered an adjournment debate on the prosaic matter of purchase tax on heat pumps; two days later he moved a measure to repeal a provision of the 1947 Finance Act that provided tax relief on tobacco duty for pensioners. Powell argued there was no need for this discrimination between smokers and non-smokers, and in any case other allowances for pensioners had been increased in lieu of this reduction; for his pains a Labour backbencher, Harry Hynd, said that 'this is the meanest thing that the Government have done yet and ... they ought to be ashamed of themselves'.[88]

In the next week Powell had to introduce debates on the second readings of two Bills. The first, on 15 November, concerned the trustee savings banks, and put forward measures which, Powell said, 'will further ease the inconsistencies between the present practice and the present circumstances of the trustee savings banks and the legislative framework within which they are required to operate'.[89] In practice, this meant raising the maximum amounts of money the National Debt Commissioners could pay the banks, as their existing sums were not meeting running costs, and paying a lump sum to the banks to make up for past shortfalls. The Bill would also extend the range of investment opportunities the banks could offer. Powell had an easy ride, as this was a Bill with which the Opposition agreed. Then, on 21 November, he moved the second reading of the routine Public Works Loan Bill, to renew powers for the raising of loans by state agencies. What turned out to be his last speech from the dispatch box in his post as Financial Secretary occurred on an Import Duties Bill on 18 December. By this time, other events were moving out of his, and Thorneycroft's, control.

V

That autumn Powell relentlessly toured the constituencies hammering home the anti-inflationary, monetarist message. He spoke most prominently on it at Newcastle on 29 November, shortly before the final storm actually broke. Still under the impression that his non-Treasury colleagues would support the policy, he referred to the 'Government's declared intention to reduce the burden of taxation still further', and therefore, as a result, to reduce spending. The nation would move, he said, by 'self-discipline' to 'honest money'.[90] This was not, though the philosophical level at which anyone outside the Treasury was prepared to conduct the debate.

Indeed, not everyone inside the Treasury was prepared to conduct it at that level either. Powell's determination to save money began in a rigorous but good-humoured way. He called his campaign to cut spending 'Operation Caesar's Wife', and wrote at the beginning of December to the second secretary, Sir Thomas Padmore, about where cuts could be made, following his perusal of a list sent him by a junior official. On the matter of nature conservancy Powell wrote that 'Mr Nicholls tells me that, if I like, I can successfully insist on no increase here. I do like.'[91] As the process continued, Powell would drop round most evenings to 11 Downing Street to discuss strategy and tactics with Thorneycroft; Pam Powell recalls hardly ever seeing him at this time.[92] It was typical of that age of a more deferential press that no one noticed him doing so, and therefore no one started to come to conclusions about the difficulties the spending round was throwing up.

Things soon, though, became more serious. Powell imbibed the details of the submissions for money from the various departments, and was horrified. In a memorandum to Thorneycroft which he copied to Birch, Padmore and Makins, Powell said that if the demands were met they would constitute 'the biggest increase ever recorded in peacetime' in public spending.[93] It was, he submitted, the direct result of bad governance. 'The main increases', he continued, 'are overwhelmingly due to the operation of the Government's own policies, and ... in the cost of these policies price and wage increases play only a minor part: the major part is either inherent in the nature of the commitment (e.g., agriculture subsidies, national insurance, education) or actual expansion deliberately decided on (e.g., roads, war pensions, universities).'

That was not all:

Following the disastrously large supplementaries which are inevitable, I do not see how the Government can come forward with increases of this order in its own expenditure.

Are the Government prepared:

(a) to face the farmers?

(b) to cut out civil defence (£21 million)?

(c) to put new charges on the health services (£12 million)?

(d) to cut drastically Britain's colonial, Commonwealth and foreign grants and services (totalling over £60 million)?

(e) virtually to halt public building at home and abroad (total £33 million)?

Even if we do all these things on a grand scale we can hardly limit the increase to the size of last year's increase.

His conclusion was stark and, while it may have been uncomfortable for his colleagues, it stunned his officials: 'We cannot go blundering on as we are at present.'

Padmore immediately sent a memorandum to Makins saying that, whatever Powell thought, there was 'no real alternative' to 'blundering on'. Makins replied that what was happening was not, in fact, 'blundering' but flowed from precise policy decisions – a point Powell had also made and which, in the context of good governance, he regarded as 'blundering'.[94] Makins was a friend of Macmillan's, having been a colleague in the Mediterranean during the war; he would come to regard the stand the Chancellor and his two ministerial colleagues were to make as 'incomprehensible'.[95] Makins owed his appointment directly to Macmillan, who had had him brought back from Washington, where he had been ambassador, to the Treasury in the autumn of 1956, when Macmillan himself was Chancellor. Makins had no Treasury or economic background whatsoever. Sir Leslie Rowan, a senior Treasury mandarin, had told Macmillan that the appointment of Makins, a Foreign Office man, to the Treasury was 'the biggest blow the civil service had ever received'.[96] There was never any chance, either personally or ideologically, that Makins would take the part of his ministers in this battle with his patron.

Then, as throughout the dramas of the next four weeks, Thorneycroft was entirely in support of his Financial Secretary. On 9 December he sent Makins his own memorandum, in which he described as 'grave' the situation Powell had outlined. It could not, he added, 'be defended in terms either of economics or politics'. His officials had pointed to the buoyancy of the inflow of revenue in seeking to defend the proposals; but Thorneycroft, under Powell's constant tutelage, had countered that this was irrelevant as that buoyancy was caused by inflation – and therefore would have no impact on cutting the deficit. The Chancellor warned there would have to be 'an agonising reappraisal' in which nothing, the social services included, would be considered 'immune'. 'I do not believe', Thorneycroft continued, 'that it is impossible to save £200 million out of a proposed spending of £2926 million. I do not believe there is a single department which could not within 18 months be in a healthier condition as a result of such a policy.'

The hand of Powell, and of the strict moral code that would come to be known as Powellism, are blatantly apparent in those words, despite Powell's own repeated protestations that he had not egged Thorneycroft on or written his script for him. Such unbending determination not to compromise – not to pay lip-service to the usual expediencies of politics – was Powell's trademark, and until now he had practised it almost uniquely among his colleagues in the Macmillan Government. It was apparent, too, in the 'warning note' Thorneycroft sent on 8 December to Macmillan, alerting him to the impending crisis over what the Chancellor called the 'grim picture' of the estimates.[97] With a deeply Powellish touch, he reminded the Prime Minister that he himself had sent a minute, on 10 August 1957, to all ministers saying that expenditure would be held at 1957–8 levels – not the projected levels either, but the out-turn, which was significantly higher. The ministers had ignored him. 'This', the Chancellor observed, 'at a moment when we are claiming to be in control of the supply of money.'

Macmillan was scheduled to begin a long Commonwealth tour on 7 January, so the matter had to be resolved swiftly. Thorneycroft immediately applied pressure, saying that the estimates did not represent 'a position which I could defend'. On 11 December the two men met, and Macmillan ordered a paper to be prepared outlining how the Treasury proposed to make the cuts. Powell was given the responsibility of writing the paper, and one of his officials, Ewan Maude, wrote to Padmore on 12 December warning him about which areas of spending Powell would pay particular attention to: the Board of Trade and Ministry of Labour estimates as a whole, the Foreign and Colonial grant, the capital programmes of the ministries of Transport and Civil Aviation, agricultural subsidies and the cost of drugs in the health service. Over the next few days, Powell had meetings with colleagues from those departments.

On 16 December, once the meetings were over, he sent Thorneycroft a report of what progress he had made, but introduced it in a way that seems to confirm he really was the driving force, supplying Thorneycroft with the intellectual underpinning of the policy the senior man, because of his position, had to discharge. 'The object of this minute', Powell wrote, 'is to set out (a) the reasons for the reduction which you demand in the Civil Estimates as put to the Treasury; and (b) the scope for securing that reduction – in order to serve as the basis, if desired, of a note for your colleagues.' He warned Thorneycroft – so that Thorneycroft might pass it on with interest to the rest of the cabinet – that he had 'no right' to expect more non-inflationary lending to be available to the Government in 1958 than had been the case in 1957; indeed, an additional £100 million of debt would mature that year. In this context, the 1957–8 out-turn really was the 'outside limit' of spending.[98]

The solutions Powell advocated were severe, but would, as he knew, certainly cause the cabinet to understand the seriousness of the position. The Government could, for a start, remove family allowances from the second child, which would save perhaps as much as £70 million a year. It could introduce basic charges for board and lodging in hospitals, which would raise £11 million; and it could increase the price of school meals by 6d to 1s 6d and abolish all the subsidies for school milk and 'welfare' foods, saving £50 million a year. For good measure, if the cabinet felt it could not face this, it should be reminded of the Government's statement of 19 September 1957, that it was no longer prepared to finance inflation.

Inevitably, Powell's remarks caused consternation even before they went outside the Treasury. A senior official, A. T. K. Grant, noted Powell's assertion that 'the Government decided and announced in September that there should be no increase over this year's out-turn on the *capital* side of the budget'. Grant was horrified, complaining to his superiors that the capital funding for the nationalised industries was already 'artificially low' and they would have to be made an exception.[99] Thorneycroft, though, remained firm, not just in the face of this attack, but in the face of alternative proposals of a less provocative, and less adequate, nature than Powell's from five senior mandarins. Powell's economic rigidity was such a shock to the officials that some of them seem to have been confused about what he really meant: Hall wrote in his diary that, by 'inflation', Powell meant 'government borrowing': which was not what he meant at all.[100] Undeflected, Thorneycroft returned from his Christmas holiday on 27 December and circulated a minute, largely based on Powell's submission to him of 16 December, underlining the crucial importance of agreeing to the cuts. In a meeting with Macmillan on 23 December he had given the Prime Minister reason to believe he was in a 'resigning' mood, so Macmillan would have no cause to feel surprised when events unfolded as they did.[101]

It was of this meeting that Powell wrote to Birch on Christmas Eve. 'Peter failed to get agreement to any of the major economies proposed in his paper,' he informed his colleague, 'though the Prime Minister the day before had agreed that the family allowance ought to be cut.'[102] He told Birch that without £70–£80 million of economies, the policy would be frustrated and would 'make certain a repetition of the lamentable slide into further inflation. I think Peter ought to fight this on resignation. I have told him that I shall go if he does, and I believe that is your own position.' This was a gamble, and would not be the last time Powell would misread the character of other politicians. 'I hardly see', he continued, 'the cabinet, on the eve of the PM's departure, facing the resignation of all three Treasury ministers because their colleagues refused the necessary co-operation in reducing expenditure; but even if they do, the three of us have no business to acquiesce in what we know to be a drift to disaster.'

While apparently certain of Birch's steadfastness, Powell seems to have harboured a doubt about Thorneycroft's. 'It will be necessary to screw the Chancellor to the sticking point and, this done, to present the pistol at the right moment. It seems to me this will need to be concerted not later than Monday 30 December, and I hope you would think it worthwhile coming up for Monday, or even perhaps on Sunday, if there were an occasion to talk to Peter that evening.'

Thorneycroft did not, however, waver. His ultimatum to this colleagues remained, and the cabinet met on New Year's Eve to consider it.[103] He repeated the basic facts Powell had put to him and which he had put to them in his note of four days earlier: £153 million had to be saved, and they would have to save it. He suspected that the application of the usual Treasury scrutiny could prune

£40 million; £40 million to £50 million could go from health and welfare, and £65 million if the second child lost family allowance. He admitted that this would be politically unpopular, but economies were, he said, 'unavoidable if the Government were to succeed in imposing an effective check on inflation and averting the threat to the stability of sterling'.

At this, the cabinet assumed the posture it would occupy until this matter was resolved: looking both ways at once. The cabinet minutes record ministers' complete agreement with Thorneycroft's strictures about the need for economies, but also the doubts raised about the practicability of 'some of the more drastic measures envisaged'. Some of his colleagues argued that, as the deflationary policy had only been launched the previous September, it could not expect to be seen to work that quickly, but would have to wait to have its effect by 1959–60. This incomprehension of the immediacy of the problem was merely the intellectual deficiency against which Thorneycroft was battling; there was a greater one still of moral and political courage. Whatever suggestions were made for savings were quickly repudiated; the idea – Powell's idea – of cutting overseas expenditure would, the cabinet felt, provide 'further openings for penetration of friendly countries by hostile influences'.

Macmillan led the two-faced approach. He agreed that economies would have to be achieved, 'but the precise amount of these reductions was less important than the ability of the Government to demonstrate that they were adhering to their aim of limiting the quantity of money in circulation' – as if the latter could be achieved without the former. Above all – and this was his overriding concern – the economies could not be allowed 'to involve the Government in a politically indefensible position'.

The cabinet agreed that Macmillan would tell his colleagues to look for further economies; the matter was not settled yet. The next day, 1 January 1958, the Prime Minister sent his own memorandum to his colleagues, commenting that it was 'essential that the Government should be seen to be applying to its own expenditure the same disinflationary discipline as it is imposing on the rest of the economy'.[104] Later that day, after further talks with Thorneycroft, he sent personal memoranda to the ministries of Health, Transport and Agriculture urging them to look again for savings. While this was going on, Powell was meeting colleagues to try to persuade them to find savings.

The next day, he reported to Thorneycroft on the outcome. Cuts had been agreed in the civil estimates of £84 million, and in the defence estimates of £42 million. Now, having done his sums again, Powell introduced a new factor into the equation. 'It now appears', he told Thorneycroft, 'that the target of £153m may (confidentially) be revised downwards to about £141m, leaving a gap of £15m only. Thus, if we can get the above £126m, we are in practical reach of your objective. I am not, however, suggesting that at this stage your full demand should be abated or your preference for the family allowance cut altered.'[105]

The revenues had been better than expected; hence the revision downwards. However, this last £15 million would prove more than Macmillan, loyally supported by his cabinet, was prepared to swallow.

On 3 January the cabinet met twice. At eleven in the morning Thorneycroft, now with only three days in which to achieve an outcome before Macmillan left the country, announced that discipline had to be asserted now. Yet the main ways of doing this were all quickly rebutted by the ministers present: family allowances were a non-starter, and there could be no question of defence cuts. The 'least objectionable' option was an increase in National Insurance contributions.[106] Macmillan, summing up after a circular discussion had revealed little stomach to fight among his colleagues (the spending ministers found themselves pressured by the non-spending ones not to give way) spoke theatrically of the 'grave decision' that had to be taken at a 'critical point' in the Government's fortunes; the need to survive in office was firmly being placed above responsible management of the currency.

The Prime Minister came, though no one realised it then, to his final position. He could not be bothered to look any further. If £100 million could be saved, 'the residue of £50 millions, representing an increase of no more than about one per cent in Government expenditure, could perhaps be regarded as defensible in itself and consistent with the Government's broad purpose of maintaining a firm control over the supply of purchasing power in the economy'. This was nonsense, though loyally assented to by all except Thorneycroft, whom Powell had taught well. The cabinet adjourned, and agreed to meet later that day at 4.30 p.m. to consider the matter further, though Macmillan's mind was made up. He was fed up with his Chancellor, whom he described in his diaries as having that day behaved in 'such a rude and *cassant* way that I had difficulty in preventing some of the cabinet bursting out in their indignation'.[107]

At that afternoon meeting, Thorneycroft was attacked by Sandys, the Minister of Defence, when he suggested that pay and allowance increases in the services could be delayed for three months, thereby saving £9 million.[108] Sandys was worried about the effect on morale; Thorneycroft said it would set an example across the rest of the public sector. There was a brief adjournment, suggested by Macmillan, for 'reflection'. On resuming, Thorneycroft opened a new front, proclaiming that, in principle, any extra defence cuts must be matched by cuts in the civil estimates. In a last desperate attempt to get agreement, the cabinet concluded that Macleod, the Minister of Labour, would consult John Boyd-Carpenter, the Minister of Pensions, and Derek Walker-Smith, the Minister of Health, about trying to find £30 million more savings out of the welfare budget.

The crunch came two days later, on the evening of Sunday 5 January 1958. Powell had spent the weekend in London, and had had no further contact with Thorneycroft before the meeting. Macmillan told his colleagues, when they met at 6.30 p.m., that the collective view must now be formed about whether the rigorous discipline being advocated by Thorneycroft should be applied and, if so, how.[109] The discussions about cuts in the welfare budget had been fruitless; nor was any more to be found from defence. Thorneycroft was furious: he minuted his frustration that the 'cabinet were not agreed, as he had hoped, on the importance of eliminating this increase'. That morning he had had a private meeting with Macmillan, who had asked him 'on personal and public grounds' not to push the disagreement to its logical conclusion.[110] Again, the Prime Minister received the impression that the Chancellor, 'pushed on by the Treasury Ministers', had made up his mind to resign. Part of his belief was based on information from Makins, who had, along with his fellow joint permanent secretary Sir Norman Brook, been deputed by Macmillan to talk to the three ministers and to try to persuade them not to make the stand that, eventually, they did. This political activity, at the behest of the Prime Minister, by civil servants was odd enough, but Makins – whom both Powell and Thorneycroft regarded as 'unsympathetic' – was out-argued by Powell, who was intellectually more than his match, which led the Treasury mandarin to draw conclusions about his influence over Thorneycroft.[111] On 3 January Hall and Makins had discussed the growing impasse, with Makins telling his colleague that Thorneycroft 'was being egged on by Birch and Powell, who in their different ways are both rather mad'.[112] Thorneycroft was equally dismissive, in private, about Makins: 'He only comes in one day in three,' he told Powell, 'and when he does he's against me.'[113]

With stalemate persisting, Macmillan called another brief adjournment. He continued to pirouette in a fashion preposterous for a man whose own mind was made up. Solemnly, he told colleagues on the resumption that they all had to share Thorneycroft's 'heavy burden'. That said, however, he added that 'disinflation, if enforced to the point at which it created a stagnant economy or provided a new outbreak of industrial unrest, would defeat its own ends'. During the adjournment Macmillan dined with his wife, and with three close colleagues – Butler, Macleod, and Heath. Macmillan recorded in his memoirs, with his usual regard for the truth, that he still felt the situation was 'confused' as 'the Chancellor had left the door open'.[114] The Chancellor had done nothing of the sort: he was simply waiting for Macmillan to force further cuts, or to force him to resign. Macmillan recalled Macleod saying, over dinner, that Thorneycroft was 'obsessed and dominated by Powell'. Although Macleod and Powell were still friends Macleod was no free-marketeer and, according to his biographer, would dismiss Powell's near-religious devotion to the free market as 'Enochery'.[115] Macmillan believed that Thorneycroft 'would retreat, if I could get him a few more economies to save his face'.[116]

At the resumed meeting – it was by now 10.30 p.m. – Macmillan returned to the position he had adopted on Friday. He said the Government should pledge to achieve 'as nearly as possible' the Chancellor's objective. Achieving it completely might be accomplished only at the price of an 'injury' to the Government's other purposes – by which he meant not provoking the unions or the Labour party. He demolished the possible solutions he had willingly discussed two days beforehand: taking £30 million out of the welfare budget would be 'unreasonable'; abolishing family allowance for the second child was 'neither politically or socially desirable' and, for good measure, was 'contrary to the tradition of the Conservative Party'. The hospital boarding charge was 'open to serious objection'. Defence could not be cut.

Having made his objection to any further economies absolutely clear, and safe in the knowledge that none of his colleagues would take Thorneycroft's side against him in seeking to avoid an end to the quiet life, Macmillan summed up that 'the Chancellor of the Exchequer could feel assured of the wholehearted determination of his colleagues to support him in his disinflationary policy' – a statement of pure flannel in the light of what he had said only moments previously. All he was asking for, he added, was a 1 per cent leeway – that mere £50 million – for to let that through 'could not fairly be represented as indicating any weakening in the Government's resolve to resist inflation'. All that was in question were the methods. Apart from that, in a conclusion of the most breathtaking hypocrisy, Macmillan said that Thorneycroft had the 'unreserved support' of the cabinet.

The Chancellor knew he was beaten; even if he could succeed in making Macmillan and his colleagues see the issue, he would never make them see that the political furore caused by treating it responsibly would be worthwhile. With dignity, Thorneycroft merely said that 'he must consider his own position in the light of the Prime Minister's summing up of the issues at stake'. The meeting ended. Macmillan claimed that, afterwards, he reflected that the pursuit of further economies would lead to so many resignations from the cabinet that the Government might be brought down. It was not to be. Powell went into Thorneycroft's office on the Monday morning to be shown the details and be told: 'Well, that's what I've got. Will it do?' Powell said to Thorneycroft: 'Shall we follow the former practice in the House of Lords, where the junior peer votes first?' And Powell put his hand on his breast and uttered, 'Not content.' 'I don't think it will do,' said Birch. 'I don't think it will do either,' said Thorneycroft. 'I'm going,' added the Chancellor, 'but that doesn't mean you have to.'[117] However, there was no question of what they would do. At 10.30 that same morning Macmillan was handed the three resignation letters.

VI

The Prime Minister accepted their resignations not least, as Butler recalled, because he 'had a feeling that the strict puritanical application of deflation was in danger of being developed into a sort of creed'.[118] Now out in the open, the dispute caused a seismic shock; no one outside, least of all in Fleet Street, had had an inkling of what was going on – it had been said the flurry of cabinet meetings had been about Cyprus. 'The differences', the press reported, busily catching up on the story, 'proved irreconcilable at the long cabinet meeting on Sunday night.'[119] The Downing Street briefing was that cuts in vital services, notably the family allowance, would need to take place if the original estimate were to be held to; and, displaying the fundamental ignorance of economics that underpinned the whole problem, Macmillan was said to feel that such cuts would lead to wage claims that, in the words of the *Telegraph*'s lobby correspondent, 'would endanger the whole economic front'.

If the nature of the crisis – provoked as it was by Macmillan's refusal to adhere to the policy he himself had set out the previous summer, and then by the pretence that, in fact, failing to adhere to the policy was nonetheless a fulfilment of it – shows one of the weaknesses of the Conservative party at that time, the way in which the aftermath was handled brings an even higher degree of discredit. It went, insidiously, beyond mere briefing of the press. The public pronouncements at the time showed the nature of the establishment against which Powell, though he could not then have known it, would spend much of the rest of his political life fighting.

Derick Heathcoat Amory, the new Chancellor, issued a statement saying that 'the change of Chancellor means no change in the Government's economic or financial policy'.[120] On one level, that was a direct lie; the policy had changed in principle from the statements made in August and September 1957, in that the Government was again prepared to finance inflation. On another, it was a sort of truth; Macmillan had decided on the change of policy before forcing out his previous Chancellor. Other statements in Amory's bulletin – 'the measures which have been successful over recent months in improving our economic position will be maintained as long as necessary without relaxation', 'public expenditure, both capital and current, will continue to be sternly restricted' and 'the Government will adopt the same criteria in regard to its own expenditure as it had been urging others to adopt in relation to theirs' – were pure fiction. The sheer dishonesty of the Macmillan style – for Amory was not to blame for these sentiments – could be seen in the remark that 'there have been no divisions between us in the Government at any time on these objectives'. What was not stated was that, however the objectives might have been agreed to, they could not be achieved by following the line the majority of the cabinet, led by Macmillan himself, chose to pursue.

The exchange of letters between Thorneycroft and Macmillan also illuminated this point. The ex-Chancellor – in a letter the Prime Minister described as 'a formal and somewhat contemptuous document', and which offended him for coming with no private covering note expressing personal regret – honestly stated his reasons for leaving; he had gone because Macmillan and his colleagues were not prepared to support the principle that expenditure be held at the same level as in the previous year.[121] Macmillan, shocked that Thorneycroft should give in his letter the entirely accurate impression that 'he alone in the cabinet stood against inflation', tried to load all the blame on him, when all Thorneycroft had been doing was to have the Government conform to the same standards of restraint urged on the private sector. 'I particularly regret', Macmillan wrote, 'that you should think it necessary to take this step when the difference between you and the rest of the cabinet is such a narrow one.'[122] Macmillan conceded that controlling spending was vital, but added that 'we must regard the policy as a whole'. This view was supposed to support Macmillan's subsequent contention that the 'rigid application' of Thorneycroft's – or, rather, Powell's – doctrine 'would do more harm than good' because of the cuts that would be needed in 'vital services'. Macmillan said this had nothing to do with popularity – 'we have never shrunk from unpopular measures' – a point entirely given the lie by his private remarks that the demands for cuts had come at such a sensitive time in the Government's progress.

That, though, was not the limit of Macmillan's mendacity. Because the cabinet had, as he pointed out, agreed to reduce spending to within 1 per cent of Thorneycroft's target, and because promises had been made about looking again at the structure of spending during the year ahead, the Prime Minister asserted that 'I therefore cannot accept that there is any difference of principle between the rest of the cabinet and yourself ... your resignation at the present time cannot help to sustain and may damage the interests which we have all been trying to preserve.' Whether this is obtuseness or dishonesty is a matter for conjecture; but, given the detail with which the Treasury team had spelt out to ministers the essential importance of not financing inflation, obtuseness seems the unlikelier option. Birch, in what Powell called his 'fulminatory' letter of resignation, hammered home the point that 'the Chancellor's demands for reductions in expenditure were the minimum necessary' and declared that ignoring them showed the Government to be 'lacking in courage and clear thinking'.[123] This brought a fierce rebuttal from Macmillan; but, in a measure of the distress the events had caused in Downing Street, the reply to Birch was put in an envelope addressed to Powell. He had merely sent a short, formal note that said: 'For the same reasons as are given by the Chancellor of the Exchequer in his letter of resignation of today, I find myself unable to continue as Financial Secretary and must ask you to accept my resignation.'[124]

In response to Thorneycroft's and Birch's unembroidered accounts of the situation Hailsham, the party chairman, decided instead to maintain the posture traditional to those of his office of insulting the intelligence of and patronising the public. 'Nothing could be further from the truth', he argued, than the impression given by Thorneycroft that the Government was weak on inflation.

It had been agreed to take 'unpopular decisions'; and 'none of my colleagues would shrink from such decisions'. In a particularly foul and dishonest insult to Thorneycroft, he added that 'although the Chancellor has decided to abandon the struggle on which the Government is embarked, his colleagues in the Cabinet are all determined to carry on the responsibilities of Government'. It was yet another complete lie: Thorneycroft, Powell and Birch had stuck to the struggle; it was their colleagues who, whether obliviously or not, had abandoned it. In the management of the party at this time Macmillan was greatly assisted by his Chief Whip, Heath, who when himself Prime Minister would show a similar disdain for economics. Heath's biographer, John Campbell, thinks the events of January 1958 were the origins of the Heath–Powell feud, though Powell himself said there was no evidence to suggest this was so. 'Heath treated that episode', said Campbell, 'purely as an attempted coup against Macmillan and never ceased to regard Powell from then on as congenitally disloyal.'[125] It did help Powell line up Hailsham as another antagonist for the years ahead. In his memoirs Hailsham wrote that he saw the resignations as being 'unreasonable to the point of being perverse' and a 'betrayal of the common cause'.[126]

In his memoirs, published thirteen years later, Macmillan suggested that the resignations had been planned, as Thorneycroft's resignation letter had 'clearly' been written days earlier – 'the date of the month was typewritten, the day filled in by hand'. As The Times had reported this, Powell wrote to the newspaper pointing out Macmillan's error: it was standard practice in government at the time for the month to be typed on the letter, with the actual day filled in by hand by the minister when he signed it.[127] In his memoirs, Macmillan said that although Powell and Birch were 'nominally subordinate to the Chancellor of the Exchequer' they 'were, in my view, largely responsible for leading him, by their powerful advice and influence, to this final step. Although I had great personal admiration for their gifts, I distrusted their judgment, since they seemed to have introduced into the study of financial and economic problems a degree of fanaticism which appeared to me inappropriate. If they did not actually welcome martyrdom, they did nothing to avoid it and seemed rather to seek and enjoy the crown.'[128] Powell dismissed Macmillan's notion that he had pulled Thorneycroft's strings: 'Anybody who thinks that a junior minister can force a minister of the cabinet to resign is a fool.' They had arrived at the same conclusion, and taken the same decision.

Macmillan, as he showed in his apparently flip – but in fact laboriously scripted – comment about 'little local difficulties' as he boarded the plane for his Commonwealth tour the next morning, just could not see the matter properly.[129] It was for moments like this that Powell dubbed him an 'actor-manager'. In a secret telegram to Hailsham, the Prime Minister said after the event that 'from what I can judge the situation is improving, and other subjects and personalities from Bulganin to Fuchs superseding the notoriety of Thorneycroft'.[130] To his relief, a difficult confrontation with economic reality that was to have consequences stretching over the next twenty years had, fortunately, been avoided at a cost merely of three members of Her Majesty's Government of whom he, fortunately, was not one.

The resignation provoked much ignorant comment, most of it in a Conservative press still, at that stage, slavishly loyal to Macmillan. Like the Prime Minister, the leader writers had no adequate grasp of what caused inflation. 'It seems inconceivable', said the *Telegraph*, 'that such a grain of dust should become a mountain ... one is tempted to conclude that Mr Thorneycroft has suffered a reaction from the special strains to which he has been exposed during recent months.'[131] It pronounced, reassuringly, that 'the character of ... Mr Heathcoat Amory is in itself a guarantee that the battle against inflation is still very much on'. For, after all, had not 'the Prime Minister and the chairman of the Conservative party ... made clear [that] there will be no taking of the hand from the anti-inflationary plough?' By the time those loyal sentiments were written, it was already too late. The cowardly attitude that underpinned Government thinking was, no doubt unconsciously, well expressed by the Minister of Power, Lord Mills. While uttering the usual anti-inflationary mantras, Mills nonetheless claimed that policies 'which had received general approval' could not be altered overnight.[132] At the first cabinet meeting after the resignations, on the same day the three ministers went, the cabinet loyally expressed its appreciation to Macmillan for his attempts to persuade Thorneycroft to do what, unsurprisingly, all the cabinet wanted him to do. There was similar relief in the Treasury, Hall recording in his diaries his dismay at the 'silly things' Thorneycroft had said about the money supply, and how 'uncomfortable' he had felt about the ex-Chancellor's 'rigidity on things like social services and aid to underdeveloped countries'; he sneered at the 'bad errors of judgment ... presumably based in the end on a sort of laissez-faire morality'.[133]

However, a number of Powell's ministerial and backbench colleagues wrote to him privately to express their sorrow at his leaving, and their admiration for what he had done. A typical letter came from Thorneycroft's parliamentary private secretary, Willie Whitelaw, who told Powell, 'I must write to you to say how much I admire your courage. I need only add that my faith in Peter and in you has if possible been strengthened by your actions. I feel very depressed about the future of the country and even our party under present circumstances ... Assuredly the battle for courageous handling of our national finances will be won *in the end* and that will be your reward.'[134] As one of Heath's closest lieutenants during the monetary explosion of 1970–2, Whitelaw would not always find himself on the same side as Powell in that battle, though he did, eventually, help Mrs Thatcher to fight it.

In the succeeding days all three ex-ministers explained themselves to their constituents; Powell was first, on 9 January, having already told the press he agreed with every word of Thorneycroft's letter of resignation. It would not be a difficult ride for Powell, at least once he reached Wolverhampton to address his meeting: his car broke down between Birmingham and Wolverhampton and he very nearly missed it. His association agent, H. S. Bendall, had already said that 'there is no question of the meeting being invited to consider a resolution of confidence on Mr Powell in the present circumstances. We have every confidence in him as our MP and recent ministerial changes do not affect the position.'[135] In front of 200 activists, Powell made a robust defence of himself and his colleagues, stressing that the issue over which they had resigned was not £50 million, or any other sum. 'The issue was whether Mr Thorneycroft felt he had the necessary minimum support from his colleagues for the policy to which he and they were committed.'[136] He pledged his continuing support to the Government; but read out Thorneycroft's letter of resignation and, measuring his words 'as I have never measured them before,' added that 'it is not only to the Chancellor's responsibility that the level of Government expenditure is central. Constitutionally the Financial Secretary to the Treasury has a direct responsibility for the Civil Estimates. It is his initial, not the Chancellor's, which they bear. It is in his name, not the Chancellor's, that they are presented to Parliament.'

Most telling of all, Powell said: 'I do not personally regard £50 million or 1 per cent of the national expenditure as a triviality.' He added: 'To be Financial Secretary of the Treasury was one of my aspirations, and I felt proud to occupy that place. I did not decide to give up quickly, lightly or hastily.' He sat down to loud applause, after one last shaft or irony: 'It will be my endeavour by word and deed and, perhaps more important, wherever possible by silence, to give my utmost support to the Government, despite all that has passed.'[137] It had been a year of intense fulfilment and joy for him as Financial Secretary; he looked back on it as a post in which had 'gloried'.

Whether or not one believes that Powell and his colleagues were sensible in taking the stand they did depends on two things: first, whether it is right to resign on principle in any circumstances; and, second, whether the policy they were following was the right one. The first is a matter of taste; the second is too, though the point of taste is more specific. If one believes in the theory of the money supply causing inflation – as even Labour governments now do – one must see that the Treasury ministers' view was right. If one feels, like Keynes, Harrod and Macmillan, that control of the money supply is a low priority or even has no bearing on inflation, then one will feel that the resignations were futile. The evidence suggests that, since 1958, when the money supply has been loosely controlled the inflationary consequences have been stark; when tightly controlled, inflation has fallen. On that evidence, Powell was right.

A recent biographer, Robert Shepherd, suggests otherwise, claiming that the official papers now available under the thirty-year rule prove his point. However,

Shepherd's proof seems to rest upon the assertion of Bruce Fraser, a Treasury mandarin, that it was 'difficult for anyone to pretend that Government supply expenditure has been leading the inflationary gallop'.[138] This misses the point that the Government was already over-borrowed, and to meet the projected expenditure more money would need to be brought into circulation. The mandarins, steeped in the post-war consensus, were at one with Macmillan in fearing confrontation with any section of society, particularly the working class. Yet, as the historian Mark Jarvis has pointed out, the new Chancellor found the financial position of the country was even worse than the three ex-ministers had thought: monies due from the Federal German Government showed a £16 million shortfall, the deficit on the National Insurance fund was now scheduled to be £23 million and not £14 million; and other items took the total deficit to £90 million, not the £50 million it was thought the Treasury Three had resigned over.[139]

Whatever theoretical or empirical evidence the mandarins may have sought to adduce to support their cowardice, cowardice it was. It was the thin end of a wedge that grew into a disaster by 1973. When the correction had to take place in the 1970s and 1980s it was on a far worse, far more confrontational scale than would have been required in 1958. With great self-righteousness, Hall noted on 8 January 1958 that Powell was 'a very queer man indeed, fanatically holding principles of economy and austerity which he does not understand in the least'.[140] This was another way of saying that Powell was not a Keynesian; it was typical of the superior assessment made by inferior minds about Powell that he had no 'judgment' – the essence of 'judgment' being to fall in with the crowd, however unprincipled or wrong the crowd was, rather than to do something inexpedient. Hall himself was a Keynesian to an extent that can only be interpreted as *plus royaliste que le roi*. It is clear from his diaries that he was prepared to go along with any policy so long as it did not lead to confrontation; in that, he was at one with the managerialist tendencies of the Government.

Powell himself, in a private memorandum written for his archive on 22 January 1958, was in no doubt that it was weakness among the senior mandarins that had caused the difficulty. 'If the Official Treasury had been headed by a strong personality, the Departments – and through the Departments, the departmental Ministers – might have been permeated for months past with a different attitude towards the prospective level of expenditure in 1958–59,' he wrote.[141] He could not pinpoint one wrong action that had led to the problem: rather, in reference to Makins and Padmore (whom he did not name), he refers to 'the general attitude of cynicism or defeatism which characterised senior levels of the official Treasury, especially on the Supply side. Though that attitude in the last year or two may have strengthened with the weakness of the official head, it must itself be of longer growth.' He also condemned lack of support from former Treasury ministers – by which he meant Macmillan and Butler, the last two Chancellors – and a 'guilt complex' about Treasury policy between the wars, at the time of the great depression.

The 'unco-operativeness' of Treasury officials had, Powell said, 'not only left Ministers to devise and apply the policy of September 1957 practically to themselves. It meant that the implications of that policy were never analysed or understood as they should have been inside, or consequently outside, the Treasury. It never got to be realised how violent a revolution in thought and policy the statement of 19 September heralded.' He admitted that even the three ministers had lacked the time to analyse the policy and its implications completely – implications for the nationalised industries, for local authority spending and for the Bank's interest rate policy which, if allowed time to work through, would have caused the 'revolution' that only happened between twenty-five and forty years later. Powell had also seen that adopting a monetary theory of inflation would alter the whole aspect in which wage claims were viewed, and the nature of the relationship between employers and the unions. He felt there had, in the end, been a 'gulf' between the three Treasury ministers and their colleagues made up of 'incomprehension – in not more than one or two cases did it amount to conscious rejection – of these consequences of the policy of September'.

As well as blaming Macmillan and Butler for having 'not outgrown their own past as Chancellors', Powell wrote that 'the Prime Minister in particular is by disposition an inflationist (see Stockton-on-Tees passim)'. He regretted that the Government had, the previous September, embraced a policy it did not understand. 'It poses the question: how is a Chancellor to educate his colleagues?' Powell believed that the Chancellor had been addressing his colleagues, effectively, 'in a foreign tongue. The recent Ministerial discussions revealed some of the ablest Ministers as innocent of the rudiments of public finance.' Nonetheless, if one other factor had been present, that need not have mattered. 'The proximate cause of our resignations', Powell wrote, was 'the First Lord of the Treasury's failure to support the Second Lord'. Having gone along with the policy, Macmillan had double-crossed his Chancellor – as Harrod (though Powell was not to know this) had told him he could.

Bruce Fraser, the senior official who would become Powell's permanent secretary – and friend – at the Ministry of Health in 1960, told him privately over thirty years later that 'Makins was certainly very seriously to blame for what he did (or, rather, didn't do) during those events ... I thought then, and think still, that Peter Thorneycroft ... was wrong both in his political judgment and in his ministerial tactics. But at least he was trying to do his job. Makins wasn't. He had no interest in the management of expenditure and made no attempt either to give leadership to officials or to frame sensible advice for the Chancellor. In the early stages of the crisis he did nothing; in the later stages he went on leave.'[142] Fraser also criticised Makins for not having verified the figure in Macmillan's published response to the resignations, which claimed a gap of just £50 million. 'The true figure was much bigger then £50m. So we had to go through the most ridiculous contortions before publishing the estimates, so as to make £50m look plausible.'

Powell would say of his and colleagues' adherence to what would become known as a radical new economic doctrine: 'We didn't know how distinguished we were. We didn't know that others were to get the Nobel Prize and not share it with us for the monetarist theory.'[143] Not having a share in that prize, he would joke, was 'the chief grudge I have against Milton Friedman'.[144] Powell had acted in accordance with his own conception of honour, which was more highly developed than most politicians'; but he had also acted in accordance with his own philosophical certainty about the rightness and truth of the doctrine he was advocating, and did not believe that what he had done would be in vain. He might have remembered Nietzsche: 'All philosophers are tyrannised by logic; and logic, by its nature, is optimism.'[145]

7

THE WAY BACK

Powell's speech at Wolverhampton on 9 January was closely analysed for any threat of trouble: some felt they found it in the remark about 'minimum support' for Thorneycroft. A Commons debate on the economy was scheduled for 23 January, and it was leaked to the press that in the annual 'economy' circular on 1 October 1957 Powell had used 'the strongest terms' to demand reductions in spending. In this, so Government sources let it be known, he and Thorneycroft had had rather more than minimum support from Macmillan and his colleagues. Selwyn Lloyd, the Foreign Secretary, told his constituents there had been 'no differences of principle or outlook between Mr Thorneycroft and the rest of the Cabinet. It was confined to method.'[1]

There were few public plaudits from Conservatives for the three resigners. Boat-rocking was never welcome, then as now, in the 'natural party of government'; and it caused special irritation that the three had chosen to go on the eve of what was supposed to be the unalloyed triumph of Macmillan's Commonwealth tour. Powell was most touched to receive, at the time, a telephone call of support from Tony Benn, who immensely admired Powell's integrity; Benn had the impression that hardly anyone else had bothered to give Powell any moral support for what he had done.[2] Eventually, some courageous backbenchers put their heads above the parapet. Replying to a letter in the *Daily Telegraph* from Sir Godfrey Nicholson, who had claimed that the Conservative party was united and should not air any differences it might have for fear of letting in a socialist government, Angus Maude wrote that 'the assumption that so long as the Conservative party remains united it must be right in what it does only needs to be stated for its absurdity to become apparent. This is the fatal solidarity of the Gadarene swine ... even if the Treasury Ministers had not resigned and if every Tory Member of Parliament were to keep his mouth permanently shut, the Conservative party as a whole would still not be united.' Birch, whose post-resignation statements were more flamboyant and less tactful than Powell's, stated baldly that the majority of the Government were not resolved to win the battle against inflation.[3] When the parliamentary debate on the Government's economic policy came the Government won the vote comfortably, with the ex-ministers all, predictably, voting for it.

Powell's behaviour hardly suggested he was one who should aim for or desire office. Out of government, he had not just new freedom, but a higher profile and new weight. Addressing prospective Conservative candidates in Eastbourne on 3 February, he urged the Government to 'get back to economic realities'.[4] The basic tenets of the Powell manifesto were spelled out: the value of money had to be preserved and the burden of taxation reduced. Power and responsibility had to be decentralised. He also made it clear to friends in the City that he would welcome the chance to pick up some directorships, and the word was put round on his behalf: it was to be a slow process, but one that would eventually bear fruit.

The first exercise of his independence came on 14 February, when he abstained on the second reading of the Life Peerages Bill, on which the Government had a majority of fifty-four. On the first day of the two-day debate, Powell had spoken defending the hereditary principle, and opposing the notion of life peerages. The Labour opposition was against the reform too, thinking it insufficient; no one else thought to argue from Powell's atavistic standpoint. His views were not merely the manifestation of his Tory instinct, but also reflected his years of work on his book on the Lords. Butler, the Home Secretary, had moved the second reading, arguing that the prerogative power to create life peers, unused since the fifteenth century and further rejected in a specific case in 1857 when Queen Victoria had tried to create a life peerage with a seat in the Lords for a law officer, should be given new meaning. He said that lack of means was no longer a bar to entry, with peerages being conferred not according to social clout but because of public service.

Butler tried to justify the life peerage as something to enable those reluctant to take hereditary peerages to sit in the Lords. It would widen the field of recruitment, as there could be more peerages created in the knowledge that no one in future generations could succeed to them, thereby raising the number of peers to an unmanageable level. It would allow women to sit there, though Butler ruled out, at that stage, including a provision in the Bill for hereditary peeresses to take their seats in the Upper House. He commended it as just the sort of moderate, sensible, evolutionary step that should be taken in the development of the constitution.

Powell came straight to the point. 'I believe', he began, 'that the House will make a mistake if it passes the Bill into law.'[5] He said there was no possibility of arguing that the existing composition of the House of Lords could be justified by logic. 'It is the result of a long, even a tortuous, process of historical evolution. Its authority rests upon the acceptance of the result, handed down to our time, of that historical process. It is the authority of acceptance, of what Burke called "prescription".' The Lords had this in common with trial by jury, or with the institution by which 'it comes about that a young woman holds sway over countless millions'.[6] Even the House of Commons was not that logical, but rested on the acceptance of it by the people.

He stressed he was not saying that such institutions should never be interfered with; but interference with this sort of prescriptive authority should not be undertaken unless plainly necessary to remove an evil. That was not so in this case. It was a serious interference with the hereditary principle, 'for here is an institution of which, ever since it has been recognisable as the House of Lords, no temporal Lord has been a member except by virtue of a heritable dignity, and that basis it is proposed to alter'.[7] Powell discounted the provision made in 1876 for Lords of Appeal to sit as life peers, for they were there purely and specifically to allow the House of Lords to discharge its appellate jurisdiction, and be the highest court in the land. As for Butler's point that the prerogative had been used to create life peers 500 years earlier, Powell said that to resurrect it after so long a lapse was, *de facto*, an innovation that would alter what had, since then, become the prescriptive principle.

He asked whether the two main reasons advanced for the change – that the socialist case would be better put in the Lords, and that a wider range of people might be available to go there – were sufficiently compelling for so fundamental an alteration to the constitution. He doubted it. For all Labour's alleged resistance to the hereditary principle, Attlee had prevailed upon no fewer than eighty-six men to accept peerages. It had been calculated that fifty-four of these were political creations: 'So the party opposite, when in power, found the necessity of conferring a hereditary peerage no insuperable obstacle to what it regarded as the necessary manning-up, in quantity and quality, of the then Government bench in the House of Lords.'[8] Powell also pointed to an admission by Gaitskell that Macmillan had not even made preliminary inquiries of him about whether he would accept more hereditary peers, or whether only life creations would do. Until such inquiries had been made, Powell argued, it would be difficult to decide whether fundamental change was called for.

In any case, the arguments about a proper opposition in the Lords had come about, he said, as a result of a misconception of what the Upper House was supposed to be: 'We make a great mistake when we figure to ourselves another place as a kind of replica of what we are here.'[9] The House of Lords was, he argued, at its least effective when dividing and debating on party lines. The greatest influence on the Government, Powell felt, could be detected from its own benches in the Lords, who worked then – as later, during the Thatcher and Major governments in particular – as an effective internal opposition. Similarly – and this was a point made earlier by Butler, not by Powell – Lord Salisbury (then Lord Cranborne) had promised in 1945 not to use the notional Conservative majority in the Lords to stop legislation getting through, provided the Labour Government had a specific manifesto commitment to honour. This had made the Lords more, not less, effective during the period of Attlee's administration.

Nor did Powell accept the argument that, without life peerages, the House could not be properly representative of the diversity of national life. 'I invite any hon Member', he said, 'to take a list of the creations since the end of the war and look down it to see the variety, the width and the scope of the interests which those creations cover – science and the arts, the professions, medicine, the law, agriculture, the Press, the trade unions, the Services, both fighting and civil, industry, trade and commerce in every branch.' Such recent evidence made this argument for life peerages nonsense, and it disposed of the assertions made by ministers in the Lords that, otherwise, there would be too few peers, particularly on the opposition benches, for the Lords to function effectively. Powell added, caustically, that there 'is no greater guarantee of regular attendance in the recipient of a life dignity than of a hereditary dignity'.[10]

His conclusion was unequivocal. There was no pressing need for change; and it was, he pointed out, such a non-issue that this was the first time in thirty-one years that the House had debated the matter of the composition or the reform of the Lords on a substantive motion. 'This Bill is one which is clearly not desired by the parties opposite. I believe that it is not desired by many of my hon Friends on this side of the House. I suspect – it would not be right for me to say more than suspect – that it is not greatly welcomed by many Members of the Government. In that case, the best thing is not to pass it.'[11]

It was an early example – Powell's assault on the Royal Titles Bill had been another – of his scenting what he regarded as the craven submission to mounting progressive constitutional opinion, this time about the validity of the hereditary principle in the legislature in the second half of the twentieth century, and acting in an illogical and profoundly unConservative way in response to it. Frank Bowles, the Labour MP who followed him, praised Powell as 'a man for whom we have very great respect. He is a very learned man and also a great historian.' He hoped that the next day, when the vote took place, Powell would vote against it. However, Powell had large, and justified, hopes of a return to office. He abstained. The previous evening, winding up on the first day of the debate, Sir Reginald Manningham-Buller, the Attorney-General, conceded that of all the criticisms of the measure (not all of which had come from the Labour benches) Powell's had been the most serious. However, Manningham-Buller was not prepared to take it seriously, going on to dismiss what Powell had said as 'somewhat exaggerated'. He also took care to make Powell look ridiculous by quoting back to him things he simply had not said – as in 'all members of the House of Lords had always been hereditary'. Powell had said nothing of the kind; indeed, he had acknowledged that life peerages had been created up until the fifteenth century, and peerage law was something he knew infinitely more about than Manningham-Buller, by general consent a spectacularly third-rate lawyer. His casual, constitutionally illiterate and ill-informed defence of the Bill was typical of the careless approach taken to constitutional measures by Conservative governments in the second half of the twentieth century.

II

For all the energy of this diversion into the constitution, Powell's main concern was still economics. In April, in the *Banker*, he argued for reform of the way the Treasury dealt with public spending, moving away from an annual review. Later that month, seeking to make concrete suggestions for how spending might be kept in check, he advocated cuts in health service bureaucracy, specifically regional hospital boards. Also in April he used his new freedom to speak in the debate on the Budget, not fearing the raking over of matters of all too recent history. The previous year, he told the House on 16 April – the day after Heathcoat Amory's first Budget – expenditure had been expected to be lower than in the year just ended. However, an international loss of confidence in sterling had made it harder for the Government to engage in non-inflationary borrowing from the public to cover its new debt.

The floating debt then was £400 million up on the previous year; at the last Budget it had been £600 million down. Expenditure was rising. Borrowing was forecast at £236 million, compared with a forecast of £125 million in 1957 and an out-turn of £212 million. Powell's strictures about the need to prune spending, which had forced his resignation, had, in the light of that variance, been justified; and he praised the Chancellor for having resisted the temptation to cut taxes at a time when stringency was needed. He warned against printing money to cover the debt if borrowing proved insufficient – nothing could justify the inflation that would result. The most essential thing was 'the reduction of the dangerously high amount of the floating debt'. His prescription was simple. 'If we are to fund, if we are to reduce the total of the floating debt, and so get a greater control over the monetary system, it must mean that we borrow more from the public in total than is necessary to cover our requirements. It must mean that we borrow not only to cover the overall deficit on the Budget, but also in order to fund.'[12] Such concepts, commonplace thirty years later, were intensely foreign in 1958, when Macmillan was taking his economic advice neat from Roy Harrod.

Powell said he longed for tax cuts, but these had to be earned. Until the looseness of the policy of preceding years had been atoned for, none would be possible. However, the process of atonement had to be started. 'We shall ill-serve the nation if we flinch from the harsh reappraisals which such a reduction of our commitments demands, and if we suggest to others or to ourselves that there is some soft option, some easy trick or some excuse to be found in changing economic conditions for not doing this difficult duty.' He addressed directly the paradox that, despite the long period of full employment enjoyed in the country, and the rise in prosperity, there still seemed to be in Britain 'a deep-seated public malaise, an anxiety, a sense of insecurity, a sense of uncertainty – even of discontent'. He attributed this to the fact that 'we seem never as a nation, or as a Government of either complexion, to have pursued any one objective long enough or with sufficient determination or firmness'. This had led to a profound lack of self-belief, which he hoped would be rectified by Amory's 'stubborn reaffirmation of the stability of the value of our money as his primary objective'.[13] In this, Powell foreshadowed his main political message of a decade hence, something akin to the economic equivalent of liberation theology.

He argued against the notion that one could have either stable money or growth. The one, he said, was the precondition of the other, another assault on the orthodoxy of the times. When Powell sat down Douglas Houghton, a Labour backbencher, put his party's own construction on the speech: 'I infer ... that he wanted to go on doing something to the bitter end and that his right hon Friend would not allow it. It is not very clear from what he has said what precisely he wanted to do and what the bitter end might have been.'[14] The Opposition capitalised on Powell's analysis of the malaise, and drew further comfort from what he said, that the Conservatives were still riven on the question of economic management. It could have been worse: Powell wrote to Thorneycroft on 19 April to say that the real figures, comparing the present Budget estimate with that of April 1957, were so bad that he had not used them in his speech 'because they are too damaging to the Government, but I have drawn the attention of one or two journalists to them'.[15] They showed that compared with Thorneycroft's estimated reduction in expenditure of the previous year of £127 million, the estimated increase now was £262 million. Within a week Powell wrote to Thorneycroft again to say that newly reported higher costs for supporting Germany – still being reconstructed, and with an army of occupation still present – took the figure up to £297 million.[16]

After his speech on the Budget, Powell went into a long period of parliamentary silence. He was busy in the Commons library, working on his House of Lords book. He spoke occasionally in the country, and brooded upon other projects connected with his interest in parliamentary history – one of which would bear fruit two years later as *Great Parliamentary Occasions*. For the time being, he chose to communicate his main political messages through the written word. In an article in the *Daily Telegraph* on 9 June he returned to the theme of Treasury reform, necessary, he said, to cut taxation. He said the present taxing and spending system afforded neither 'timely decision [nor] efficient policing'.[17] He wanted spending estimates made not just for the next year, but for two and three years hence; presently, decisions were made with only three months' notice, and once made an insufficient check was kept on their execution. In January 1959 Powell was still playing the same tune: he wrote that Government borrowing must be held where it was, even if this meant there could be no tax cuts – an unlikely scenario in an election year.[18]

The diligent way in which he continued to conduct his public life, and the energy he was putting into writing privately, may have concealed some dark doubts about his situation. On 19 January 1959 the Powells dined with Tony and

Caroline Benn, together with the Richard Crossmans. Benn recorded that, although his guest was 'nice and friendly as ever', 'Enoch is really very depressed. His resignation now looks to have been fatally ill-advised.'[19] Powell denied ever having harboured such feelings, but his wife was not so sure.[20] Benn held his view because the policy Powell had been urging in January 1958 was even tougher than the one that had already caused higher unemployment, and a certain amount of distress for the Government: 'so he is in the wilderness of wildernesses as far as the Tories are concerned'. Powell wondered aloud at Benn's dinner-table about what the future would hold for him; Benn, whose fondness for Powell was sincere, 'told him that . . . his sheer ability and lucidity would carry him upwards'. Benn also reported concern that Powell, who lacked the City connections of so many of his colleagues, had not been offered any directorships since his resignation, and had as a result taken a drastic fall in his standard of living, despite his journalistic work. Within days, though, it was announced that Powell – and Thorneycroft – were both to join the board of a new unit trust.

Powell was still monitoring the financial situation, being determined to prove the stupidity of the course the Government had taken the previous year. He wrote to Birch on 22 January 1959 complaining that 'our colleagues in the party, and indeed opinion in the country' seemed prepared to tolerate rising expenditure because of the belief that the increased spending had 'minimised the "recession" and assisted "recovery" '.[21] Powell wished to make a political point: 'If this belief can be proved, or plausibly argued, to be baseless, then greater sympathy would be felt with those who have opposed increased expenditure, and less with a policy which bids fair to produce Budget estimates showing a record increase in each of two successive years.' He sought Birch's views, before going on to propound the points publicly. However, the following month he reported to Thorneycroft – who had been on an extended trip abroad – that 'the climate of opinion has, to my feeling, deteriorated further from our point of view since you left. The majority inside and outside the House take it as axiomatic that we were wrong, because everything has gone well since then – retail price index, reserves, balance of payments – and the danger has appeared to be recession rather than boom. Even to the small minority who do not share this oversimplification, the issues which divided us from our colleagues seem of little more than historical interest.'[22]

This was partly about Powell's self-justification, but he was also keen for Thorneycroft to defend himself. 'I believe that it would now be a mistake to refrain from comment and criticism of financial and economic policy as occasions arise or can be made. Above all, I submit that it would be mistaken for you now to appear to make foreign affairs your concern, either in Party meetings or in public. The interpretation would be put on this that you admit you were wrong as Chancellor and are trying for a fresh start in a different field.' He told Thorneycroft that Birch had seen the letter and agreed with its sentiments: and that the two of them would continue to find opportunities to assert the line of January 1958.

Powell's absence from office, and his relatively light activity in the chamber, allowed him to concentrate on his book, and make great progress. He did not break his parliamentary silence until 20 January, on the second reading of the Electricity Bill, which he and Birch both used as one such opportunity to attack plans for greater borrowing for this utility – successfully, as it happened, as the borrowing powers sought were reined back after the ex-ministers' attack on them. Powell was then drafted, at Macleod's personal request, back on to the policy studies group, now urgently trying to put together a programme for the next manifesto. Macleod was relieved when Powell accepted 'as we are coming into the drafting period'.[23] Powell was scrupulous to be seen to be doing nothing to make waves, and in this respect his work with Macleod was a valuable part of his rehabilitation. He was too late back on the committee to have the radical impact that might have been possible had he been inside for the previous year, but he tried his best to make a difference. Soon after accepting the invitation to rejoin he drafted a paper on National Insurance, advocating 'supplementation' of retirement pensions to an agreed national minimum income, with a means test, saying that growth in occupational pensions would reduce the supplement over the years.[24] Later that year, on 15 July, when Macmillan attended the group's regular dinner, Powell advocated cutting taxes as an important policy, not least since it could not be expected from the other side.[25] On 1 August he argued that, in the interests of a free society, there should be a commitment to denationalisation, though he accepted that the economy would need to improve, and that coal and the railways would have to come last. All this thinking was twenty, or in some cases thirty, years before its time.

His appetite for participating in the Commons – he had always been an assiduous attender – returned that spring, with a speech on the situation in Cyprus, where Britain was about to act as a guarantor of independence following the agreement between the Greek and Turkish factions on the island. It was another opportunity to pursue his theme about the illusions of the Commonwealth. He welcomed the fact that the notion of a Republic of Cyprus, dismissed as 'fantastic' but a few years earlier, was now the basis of the settlement the Government was proposing. Even Labour, in a document setting out its colonial policy in 1957, had viewed Cyprus as a territory that 'will neither be capable of national sovereignty nor anxious to attain it'.[26] He said the lesson of Cyprus was that there were many countries in the Commonwealth assumed incapable of exercising their own sovereignty, but which would, in fact, be perfectly able to do so. 'I believe that we have made these assumptions', he said, 'because of the difficulty of conceiving how territories of this kind can both be independent and still within the Commonwealth. I suggest that a good deal of rethinking may be necessary in this respect about the composition of the Commonwealth.'²⁷

The other difficulty Powell said Britain had to overcome was the notion that only by retaining sovereignty in her territories could she exercise her responsibilities in the region. He pointed out that the United States had air bases in Britain without any share in British sovereignty; Britain could retain bases in Cyprus by similar means. 'We have to divest ourselves', he said, 'of the notion that sovereignty in itself confers any advantages or gives any security which does not rest upon the real circumstances in the places concerned. Sovereignty itself is a mere form. The realities within it are the will of the people and the power of the sovereign.' This was an argument which, in the context of Europe, would come back to dominate Powell's thinking more than a decade later, but for the moment he adduced it as the epitome of another national problem.

In the preceding twenty years, he argued, 'the reality inside our sovereignty has gradually been hollowed out. Both the physical and the moral or sentimental reality of sovereignty have gradually fallen away – the physical reality by the loss of Britain's absolute and relative economic and military preponderance in the world, and the moral reality by the spread of what we ineffectually call "national-ism", but is really the projection of all that Europe has given over the last two centuries to peoples of different races and circumstances throughout the world.'²⁸ All that was left was 'the shell of sovereignty', together with responsi-bility for the peace and well-being of those who, in the past, had served the Crown.

Powell said Britain's colonial position then was 'a tragedy', and a defiance of the logic that there can be no responsibility without the power to discharge it: 'but that is logic and not reality'. A moral duty remained, and he said Britain had to avoid the extremes either of giving guarantees, for the welfare of min-orities and such like, which she could not keep, or of simply ignoring her responsibilities altogether. This meant that in the withdrawal from colonial power – which Macmillan would not formally set in train until after his visit to Southern Africa the following year – 'wherever humanly possible our presence should not be withdrawn until there is a reasonable possibility that the rights of minorities will be provided for, that there will be peace and justice when we have gone, and that those for whom we have been responsible have a reasonable opportunity and a rational likelihood of survival and of well-being'.²⁹ There was no trace of imperialism left in him.

In 1959 Anthony Fisher, the founder of the Institute of Economic Affairs – a free-market think tank set up in 1957 – had the general director of the Institute, Ralph Harris, make an approach to Powell about doing some work for them. Fisher, a Battle of Britain hero who had made a fortune out of broiler chickens, had been attracted to Powell both by the nature of his resignation from the

Treasury and by his obvious sympathy for monetarism and the free market. Harris, who had met Powell shortly before Fisher's suggestion to him, proposed to Powell he should write an economic monograph on a subject of interest to him, which the Institute would publish. After some reflection, Powell agreed to research and write a book on the theory and practice of saving, though the IEA had most wanted Powell to write on housing. From the middle of 1959 work on this dominated his spare time, and he kept at the task throughout the winter of 1959–60. Harris was pleasantly surprised to have a politician writing for him who took the rigorous approach of a scholar.[30] Powell was strongly attracted to the ideas of Harris and his co-director, Arthur Seldon, and took the trouble to commend their work wherever possible, as in the *Spectator* in March 1959, when he wrote in praise of a Harris and Seldom pamphlet on the benefits of advertising; he observed, hopefully, that laissez-faire was no longer the dirty term it had once been in the Conservative party and that 'a lot of people in a lot of places have been rediscovering uses and even beauties in the laws of supply and demand'.[31]

Before embarking on his own work for the IEA, Powell had a more immediate task. The editor of the *Lloyds Bank Review* asked him to write about the procedure for raising and spending revenue, and when he published the results in his April 1959 number explained to his readers that, while it was not normally the policy to ask party politicians to write for the *Review*, this expository work did not descend into politics. In fact, though, it did. Powell's main task was to outline how it came about that the British government planned how it would spend its money two or three months before it had a clear idea of how much it had raised in revenue. Having outlined the historical reasons for this – mainly of custom and practice, and rooted in the keen desire of the Commons in Georgian times to know how much it could spend, with far less urgency about knowing how much could be raised – Powell made a suggestion about procedure that would be taken up by a Conservative government more than thirty years later: having a Budget and a Finance Bill that considered both parts of the equation simultaneously, and which therefore allowed for better budgeting.

His opening paragraph, though, read very much like the settling of a score: 'That expenditure should be considered in relation to revenue is a dictate of common sense which applies no less to a nation than to an individual. The present British system of Parliamentary control over public expenditure might have been devised deliberately to defy that dictate and to ensure that the public and Parliament, the government and the Chancellor of the Exchequer consider expenditure in the greatest possible detachment from revenue.'[32]

In the debate in the Commons on the 1959 Budget Powell followed Hugh Dalton, the former Labour Chancellor, and teased him for his commitment to further tax reliefs, and further increases in Government spending: 'one felt, rather nostalgically, that he was the same old inflationist as ever'.[33] There were more serious matters. The deficit, which had risen to £721 million, was the central issue of the Budget, according to Powell. It was, though, a central issue to which the Chancellor, in his Budget speech, had deliberately not drawn attention, or discussed. The increase in expenditure in the year just ended had been only 2 per cent against the 5 per cent predicted in 1958, largely because of the decline in the cost of financing the national debt; but a pre-election boom would now ensure that that situation did not last long.

If the forecasts were correct, the year ahead would be the first for seven years in which the share of the national income taken by the Government rose instead of fell. Small tax cuts and pension increases, in advance of the election expected for later that year, had boosted the deficit, only £355 million of which was planned to be met by borrowing. Powell called the total £721 million deficit 'a stupendous sum'; it was 'an increase, in one year only, of no less than two-and-a-half per cent of the whole National Debt'.[34] The deficit was four times that of the previous year. Powell said that if the Chancellor tried to borrow money to fund it from the public, he would defeat his other stated aim of boosting demand in the economy. If he did not borrow most of it from the banks he would have to expand the money supply, and cause inflation. Sternly, Powell added that this all went to show 'the danger, and the difficulty, which attach to the engineering of economic expansion by increases in Government expenditure'.[35] He said the moral was that the economy could not be expanded by those means; it could be expanded only by people and their increasing productivity, and their willingness to take risks. His one consolation was that the Conservatives were not trying to expand by a mixture of both inflation and state control, as Labour had promised to do. What he had, however, identified was the economic fallacy that would dog his party until the removal of Heath as its leader fifteen years later, and whose wrongness few, apart from himself, recognised at the time.

III

An incident at the Hola prison camp in Kenya, in which eleven Mau Mau terrorists were beaten to death by warders in March 1959, gave Powell the chance to make one of the finest speeches of his career, and one of the finest heard in the Commons since the war; indeed, Denis Healey, who sat in the House for forty years from 1952 to 1992, described it as 'the greatest parliamentary speech I ever heard ... it had all the moral passion and rhetorical force of Demosthenes'.[36] Powell had not contributed to a debate in the House on Hola on 16 June, when the Opposition put down a censure motion against the Government. Originally, it had been reported that the fight at the camp had been over the distribution of water to the prisoners, but subsequently it had emerged that the uproar had been provoked by beatings by warders trying to enforce a regime of forced labour. This regime had been deemed necessary by the Kenyan authorities to break the remnants of fanaticism among the Mau Mau, most of the other prisoners having been successfully rehabilitated. Powell felt particularly provoked by a remark by a fellow Conservative MP, John Hall, who said the victims had merited no better treatment because they were sub-humans. He also felt that those responsible for the outrage were not being brought to account, and this caused him intense unease. He wrote to Alan Lennox-Boyd, the Colonial Secretary: 'I am sure you do not think that I could have feelings towards yourself but those of admiration and the warmest goodwill. It is not in spite of this but because of it that I believe the matter of Hola Camp must not remain where it was at the end of Wednesday's debate. A large share of responsibility for this administrative disaster lies at a high level in Kenya, and I trust that it is going to be accepted publicly and in the only possible way. If I have the opportunity, I feel I must say this in the 1922 Committee.'[37]

Powell also made his views known when the matter was raised a second time in the Commons, on the night of 27–8 July, after the publication of a White Paper on colonial policy arising directly out of the incident. It was already 1.15 a.m. when he rose, but the House was relatively full. He said the killings had been the culmination of 'a great administrative disaster', but acquitted Lennox-Boyd of blame for it; that rested, instead, with two ministers of the Government of Kenya – the Minister of African Affairs and the Minister of Defence. They, while apparently aware of the possible ill consequences, had devised and pushed through a plan for the treatment of the fanatical prisoners that would almost certainly lead to trouble.[38] The governor of Hola had warned his superiors that he did not have enough warders to impose a new regime within the camp if order was to be maintained; he was ignored.

Powell said that, while some culpability had to fall on the officials at the camp, the ministers in Nairobi had a case to answer. 'That responsibility', he said, 'has not been recognised; but it cannot be ignored, it cannot be burked, it will not just evaporate into thin air if we do nothing about it.'[39] Powell said that 'it cannot be within administrative convention that these matters could be brought to his [Lennox-Boyd's] attention before or during the execution. When I say my rt hon Friend was in this matter utterly and completely blameless, that is of a piece with the administration of his high office generally, which has been the greatest exercise of the office of Colonial Secretary in modern times.' However, he continued: 'It is in the name of that record, it is in the name of his personal blamelessness, that I beg him to ensure that the responsibility is recognised and carried where it properly belongs and is seen to belong.'[40] Later in his speech, Powell stated that the morale of the prison service in Kenya would hardly be improved by punishing those in the camp while those who brought about the policy that they were implementing went uncensored. Similarly, the morale of the whole colonial service would be damaged if there was so much as a 'breath or blemish' left on its reputation because of this incident.

Powell immediately went on to make a point that would sit ill with the accusations of racialism made against him a decade later. As well as Hall's branding of the men as 'sub-human', others had said they were 'the lowest of the low'. 'So be it,' he said. 'But that cannot be relevant to the acceptance of responsibility for their death. I know that it does not enter into my rt hon Friend's mind that it could be relevant, because it would be completely inconsistent with his whole policy of rehabilitation, which is based upon the assumption that whatever the present state of these men, they can be reclaimed.' The responsibility could not, Powell said, be different from the responsibility for the death of anyone else. 'I would say that it is a fearful doctrine, which must recoil upon the heads of those who pronounce it, to stand in judgment on a fellow human being and say, "Because he was such-and-such, therefore the consequences which would otherwise flow from his death shall not flow." '

In his peroration, Powell brought not just compassion, but his remorseless logic, to bear. 'It is argued that this is Africa, that things are different there. Of course they are. The question is whether the difference between things there and here is such that the taking of responsibility there and here should be on different principles.'[41] It looked bad, at a time when Britain claimed to want to leave representative institutions behind her wherever she gave up her rule, that she should be seen to be shirking important responsibilities, 'the very essence of responsible Government'. He concluded:

> Nor can we ourselves pick and choose where and in what parts of the world we shall use this or that kind of standard. We cannot say, 'We will have African standards in Africa, Asian standards in Asia, and perhaps British standards here at home.' We must be consistent with ourselves everywhere. All Government, all influence of man upon man, rests upon opinion. What we can do in Africa, where we still govern and where we no longer govern, depends upon the opinion which is entertained of the way in which this country acts and the way in which Englishmen act. We cannot, we dare not, in Africa of all places, fall below our own highest standards in the acceptance of responsibility.

The *Daily Telegraph* reported that, 'as Mr Powell sat down, he put his hand across his eyes. His emotion was justified, for he had made a great and sincere speech.'[42] It was a great triumph for him: both sides of the House cheered him while he made it, and Lennox-Boyd, understandably relieved to have been unequivocally endorsed by so powerful a backbencher, congratulated him afterwards. When Lennox-Boyd himself spoke later, he said Powell had made 'incomparably the best critical speech' of either of the debates on the matter, but he refused to accept Powell's point that the change of regime in the camp was likely to have 'serious' results; he did admit, though, that there had been 'an error of judgment', and agreed to appoint a special commissioner to oversee detention camps in the future.[43] The Labour MP Leslie Hale, who followed Powell, said that 'when an hon Member has spoken with the effect and the sincerity which the hon Member for Wolverhampton South-West showed, I realise that felicitations from the other side of the House are, sometimes, a little tactless. I beg the hon Member to believe that I convey them with the same spirit that, I am sure, many hon Members on both sides feel.' A Liberal MP, Mark Bonham Carter, wrote to Powell to say that the speech 'was by far the most impressive, the most intellectually convincing and the most moving speech I have heard in the short time I have been here'.[44] Bonham Carter would later become a senior figure in the race relations industry, and one of Powell's most bitter opponents.

Observers felt the Hola speech was a turning point for Powell personally, and that he could not be excluded from the Government much longer after such a performance. Bill Deedes, who was present, admired Powell's courage: Macmillan's success was at its peak, and the climate was not one in which backbenchers were routinely taking on senior ministers and criticising their conduct of policy. The speech confirmed Powell as a leader rather than a follower of opinion. A general election could not be far away – the present Parliament was now into its fifth year – and this was felt sure to be the point at which Powell would come back. With the public mood about Macmillan and his policies looking propitious at the time when Parliament rose shortly after the Hola debate, few expected it to return before an election was called. Indeed, Macmillan announced on 8 September that the Queen had granted a dissolution, and the election would be exactly a month later.

Macmillan's main election theme was continuity: he invited voters to endorse the policies they had been prospering under at home, and to be represented abroad by the same leaders. Trumpeting the achievement of 'stable' prices and low unemployment, the party put out the line that 'life is better under the Conservatives'. The nation agreed, returning the Government on 8 October with a majority of 100. Powell held eight speaker meetings in his constituency, concentrating on propounding his belief that his electors faced a choice between a free or a planned economy. In his election address he explained his personal vicissitudes since the last election, proudly proclaiming his support over Suez for Eden, 'whom I believe the nation will remember with gratitude in years to come, as a gallant and upright Englishman who served them well'.[45] He defended the measures of September 1957, and said of his resignation the following January that 'if I had the decision to take again, it would be the same one. There could be no faith in public life if it were thought that Ministers hesitate to prefer the national interest, as they see it, to their own.' In a straight fight with his Labour opponent, Powell recorded his greatest majority yet, 11,167; the marginal seat he had wrested from Labour just under ten years earlier was now completely secure.

During the campaign Powell had endured the irony of a visit by Macmillan. A press report said that Macmillan 'greeted Mr Powell, perhaps the most respected Tory in the West Midlands, with a fervour that made one doubt whether Mr Peter Thorneycroft...had ever existed'.[46] A minor issue in the campaign, though one which was apparently brewing up among many of Powell's voters, was the influx of immigrants into Wolverhampton. Powell, who so far had shown a reluctance to become involved in a campaign about the problem in the hope that a quiet approach would bring about the need to legislate for control, had said nothing could be done short of a reform of the citizenship law: he made no further comment. He would do what he could during the next Parliament, but to little avail, to try and bring such a change about. The victory of his party, securing a third term in office, seemed at the time to have vindicated Macmillan's stand against the Treasury team, but that would be to mistake the winning of a battle for the winning of a war.

As Macmillan reconstructed the Government on 21 October 1959, he saw Powell at Downing Street. He offered him the parliamentary secretaryship to the Ministry of Education, a lowlier post than he had resigned from – he was patronisingly told he would have 'work his passage' back.[47] He refused it on the ground that his former chief, Thorneycroft, was not asked back. This reasoning was not made public, but when his name did not appear on the list of ministers it was assumed, as the *Telegraph* put it, that this was down to his 'quixotic code of honour'. 'His evident self-sacrifice', the paper went on, 'will enhance the respect in which he has always been held in the House of Commons.'[48] What he had said to Macmillan, citing the celebrated case of the resignations over appeasement, was: 'Is Thorneycroft coming back?' Macmillan said, 'No.' Powell replied, 'What would you have thought of Lord Cranborne if he'd gone back as assistant postmaster-general after Eden resigned?'[49] There was a further compensation other than that of honour: Powell was appointed a director of the Bestwood Company the following month at a salary of £3,000 plus fees, and also became a director of an engineering company, Plowright.

He continued to use his freedom widely, arguing in the debate on the address the following month that the Government's £100 million subsidy of council housing should be abolished as part of the process of removing the state from the lives of individuals. Powell had been thinking increasingly of the ideological concepts of the free economy and its indispensable link with the free society since his time at the Treasury, and particularly in his work-in-progress on saving. He said the Conservative party's success at the election had proved that 'an increasing number of our fellow citizens are disposed to seek their own interests and the national interest within the framework of a free society and a free economy'.[50]

He called for taxes to be reduced, and for the money supply to be better controlled to help suppress inflation, for the same reason, but did defend the continuing subsidies on agriculture. 'There is a case', he said, 'for the producer subsidy where an industry is in a state of transition from a condition where it was subjected to pressures and distortions to a condition where it can take its place in a free competitive world.'[51] His clear message was, though, that, as soon as that transition was over, the subsidy should be ended too. His conclusion was uncompromising: 'progress' should be measured by 'how far we progress in realising ever more fully the advantages of a truly free economy, and how far we make progress in discerning and fulfilling those needs which, in the present and the future, the community should, and alone can, perform for its members'.[52]

If this was Conservative policy years ahead of its time, the conclusion drawn by astonished Labour MPs was even closer to the mark. The one who spoke after Powell, Fred Bellenger, said he inferred from what Powell had said that he had also wanted the denationalisation of all the state-owned industries, putting them back 'into what the hon member calls a free economy'.[53] Powell would have agreed, but recognised that the party, and the Government of which he was keen to be a member when his conscience allowed him, was far from ready for that radical step. The Macmillan years, thus far, might have brought more prosperity, but they had also brought the firmest acceptance yet by the Conservative party of a consensus whose agenda was largely dictated by Labour, and in which the cornerstones could be moved only with the most ruinous of shocks to public opinion. Powell's call can be interpreted only as the recognition by him that the new, large majority of the Government provided a rare opportunity to forge the free society he wanted; but no one with power, least of all Macmillan himself, was willing to do anything more daring than manage decline, while dressing that decline up as economic success.

This was a theme to which Powell returned a month later, when the Commons debated the report of the inquiry by Lord Radcliffe into the monetary system. The Radcliffe Committee had reached its conclusions unanimously, and there was general agreement with them in the Commons; but Powell, who had just been elected chairman of the Conservatives' backbench Finance Committee, said this agreement had led to 'ambiguity, to blurring and to downright contradiction'.[54] He said the problem in assessing what should be the monetary policy and monetary system was not so much that different schools of economists did not agree with each other as that the 'great divide' between those who believed in a planned, controlled economy and those who believed in a free one 'does not skirt the frontiers of monetary policy, but runs slap through the middle'.

Powell took as an example the report's section on interest rates, which he said was a form of price; and he declared that those who thought as he did had considerable respect for the price mechanism, which is why they were so concerned when a government did something to fix or manipulate a price. However, because of the political importance of the interest rate, he admitted that 'no

Government can just "pass by on the other side" and leave this price entirely unaffected and untouched by their own behaviour, however much they might be devoted to working a price mechanism'.[55] The fact of the Government being such a large customer of the money markets would mean its own activities would affect the supply of and demand for funds, and therefore the interest rate. The ambiguity of the wording of the report made Powell feel he could not tell which side it was on; the power the Government had in influencing the interest rate either gave it massive scope to control the economy, or it might make the Government regard that power as to be used always with regard to preserving the rate of interest as a proper market price. The report did not pass judgment on which of these views was the more correct.

However, there was one 'centrally important' paragraph on to which Powell latched, and which he took as proof of illiberal thinking: 'The authorities ... should take a view as to what the long-term economic situation demands and be prepared by all the means in their power to influence markets in the required direction.'[56] He paraphrased this as 'it is the business of the Government ... to decide what the rate of interest should be; and see that that is the rate of interest'. However, he then quoted another paragraph that demonstrated how the committee had got 'cold feet' over this prescription. If demand were to be suppressed unduly by interfering with the market price of money for borrowing or saving, measures to influence the rate differently would be 'appropriate'.

'So there one has it,' said Powell. 'The planner's prescription: make up your mind on your objective; resolutely pursue the measures which will take you there; be ready at any moment to abandon them; but never abandon them – unless you think that you ought to abandon them. It is a perfect description of the planner's dilemma, a perfect description of the situation in which an Administration attempting, by the manipulation of the interest rate, to operate a planned economy inevitably find themselves.'[57] The objectives and the escape route as described by Radcliffe were, ironically, exactly those pursued and then used by a supposedly free-marketeering Conservative government during its disastrous experiment with the fixed exchange rate in the European Monetary System in 1990–2.

Powell drew comfort from the fact that the Government, as it was currently operating monetary policy, did not take the *dirigiste* view of Radcliffe's committee; he quoted a letter written recently by the Chancellor of the Exchequer on the subject of War Loan, a gilt-edged stock which was then paying a poor rate of return. Amory had said categorically that it would be wrong for the Government to seek to bring about a rise in interest rates artificially, since the rate was the product of 'fundamental conditions in the capital market'. Powell said that those remarks, and particularly Amory's conclusion that any attempt to influence the rate would bring great discredit on the Government, should be 'inscribed in golden letters – or should I say in gilt-edged letters? – over the portals of the Treasury in Great George Street'.

However, he felt it followed from Amory's remarks on the interest rate that Government action in other spheres, which impinged on that particular price, should also be examined carefully. The relationship between the Government and the Bank of England could not be allowed to move in a direction that divorced decisions about Bank Rate from what was happening in the money markets. Radcliffe had suggested that the interest rate should become an entirely political decision, and Powell praised Amory for having rejected that notion when he had spoken earlier in the debate. Equally, Powell felt that the committee's Keynesian view of the Government's relatively high levels of borrowing as a 'national blessing' was wrong, and all the factors contributing to that high borrowing deserved to be kept under 'ceaseless criticism'.[58]

He also wanted new accounting methods to take the capital investment for the nationalised industries out of the mechanism for central government borrowing, and attacked the report's suggestion that borrowing by local authorities should be loaded on to the Government, when councils were perfectly able to borrow the money by other means. He concluded by praising the Government for bringing the country back into contact with reality by observing 'the real balance between savings and investment, between the supply and demand for investible funds'.[59] Harold Lever, the Labour MP and businessman, who followed him branded Powell as 'one of the unfortunate trio – unfortunate but honourable and sincere – whose elimination made possible the victory of the Tory party at the last General Election', since the economic policies advocated by the former Treasury team would have been too austere to be popular; and said that Powell was even more extreme on interest rates than his 'boss' in the House of Lords, by which Lever meant the recently ennobled Lionel Robbins.

However much Powell professed to be in agreement with Government economic policy, he still courted serious reservations of a sort he was not prepared to expand upon in the House of Commons for fear of attracting accusations of disloyalty. In the press he was less guarded, but still not so outspoken as he would become after his resignation in 1963. In mid-1959 he had written in the *Financial Times* that the alleged action being taken by the Government to help growth – a Budget deficit – was not what had stimulated the perceived recovery. That, he claimed, was caused by a natural upswing in the trade cycle. Because this had brought in higher revenues, Powell argued, 'the Government have taken out of the economy by taxation and borrowing from the public as much extra as they have put into it by increased expenditure'.

So, with irony, he lamented in January 1960: 'Once again we have been denied the privilege of observing at first hand a British Government coping with recession on orthodox Keynesian lines. We still do not know experimentally what would be the result if, in the face of a persistent fall in propensity to spend, a British Government equally persistently increased its expenditure, and financed it by the creation of money through the floating debt ... we must await some other opportunity to ascertain by experience whether the prescription is beneficial, poisonous – or simply neutral.'[60] He was not to be kept waiting indefinitely. Also, the continuing bad conduct of economic policy by Macmillan was fuelling Powell's disdain for his leader. At dinner with the Benns just before Christmas 1959 he and Pam revealed their disillusion with Macmillan's political conduct, which Benn found somewhat surprising.[61]

IV

During the 1959–60 session Powell was far more active in Parliament than he had been during the previous year. He was still working on his writing – not just *Saving in a Free Society*, but also preparing for publication the texts of twelve radio broadcasts on the history of Parliament, which he had made in the summer of 1959, that would be the book *Great Parliamentary Occasions*. He also found the time for some modest business activity; on 21 December it was announced that he had joined the board of AEG Unit Trust (Managers), his second such sideline. His attention to detail never slipped, however busy he was. He wrote rebuking *The Times* in February 1960 for announcing that General de Gaulle 'will address jointly both Houses of Parliament in Westminster Hall'. As he added: 'He will not, because he cannot. He can, and probably will, address members of both Houses in Westminster Hall; but that is something entirely different. Neither House of Parliament, nor Parliament itself, will be sitting in Westminster Hall; nor, if they were, could the French President address them.' *The Times*'s justified response, printed underneath, that 'the phrase was printed as given in the official announcement' was neither here nor there.[62]

On 18 February he spoke on the second reading of the Iron and Steel Bill, on the question of accounting for loans to the industry. Powell hoped the Government would allow the business to develop in a way that would allow it, as a denationalised industry, to be financed more like the rest of the private sector and not like a state-owned one. The following month he took part in a debate on housing, again denouncing the existence of subsidies and calling for their early reform. Much of his theorising was economic in nature, but in a speech to Conservative women in March 1960 he expressed his horror that the Government was thinking of developing policies for how people used their leisure time. The following month, writing in a publication by the Bow Group, an association of ambitious younger Conservatives, he explicitly said that 'there have lately been signs that Conservative leaders either themselves lack clearly defined ideas about the limits and conditions of such Government action, or else have not been willing to reveal them to their followers'.

Powell was particularly impatient with his party's tolerance of state own-ership, and with the failure of many of its leaders to feel any conviction about the issue. He was not yet recognised as a troublemaker in voicing such criticisms; the *Financial Times*, predicting his early return to office, said that 'he is not by any means the leader of the dissident Tories when they are making a nuisance of themselves. He tends to become their leader when there is constructive work to be done of a high intellectual character.'[63] His reputation as a thinker would shortly be consolidated by *Saving in a Free Society*, the manuscript of which he delivered to the IEA that March.

In pressing his case for office – though that commodity was very much histo acquire, since Macmillan had made it clear he was a willing seller – the annual Finance Bill was a superb platform. His chairmanship of the Conservative Finance Committee gave him a new prominence when the House considered Amory's 1960 Budget. Powell spoke in the debate on 7 April, and was an assiduous attender at all the proceedings during the Bill's committee stage, actively moving amendments. In his speech on 7 April, he said that the 'central point' of the Budget had, once more, been the level of borrowing.[64]

He supported Amory for instituting a modest tax increase – £13 million – that would bring the level of borrowing down from £331 million to £318 million. He rebuked those who felt that Amory had been over-cautious; Powell could not see where extra money would come from if borrowing were not cut. National Savings, indeed, were the only way he could see of meeting the Budget deficit. He had, of course, been researching this question for his book, and told the House that government borrowing financed by National Savings had begun only in 1957, and was expected to reach record levels in the year ahead. Relatively high, tax-free rates of interest on those savings made the scheme attractive. 'We should be clear about what we are doing,' said Powell. We were 'meeting our budgetary deficit by borrowing for which we pay at very high effective rates of interest.'[65]

The danger of this, as he went on to say, was that if interest rates generally rose – and they were on an upward trend – money could flow out of National Savings and into other investments quite quickly, leaving the Government looking for somewhere else to borrow from. That was why he thought Amory's caution admirable; to borrow more, with this danger lurking, would invite trouble. Some had argued that to give tax cuts would lead to greater investment, and boost savings, but Powell said there was no evidence that tax cuts would do anything except boost the money supply to dangerously inflationary levels. Then, there was the 'fallacy . . . that personal savings are somehow a withdrawal of that amount of purchasing power. Of course they are not . . . they represent a transfer of purchasing power from one type of spending to another type of spending, namely, investment spending.'[66] Only a small fraction, he prophesied, would help the Government by coming back into its coffers as National Savings which it could, in turn, borrow.

He lamented that, for the first time since the Conservatives had come to power nine years earlier, public expenditure had increased faster than the growth in gross national product. This unfortunate development had to result in higher taxation – either now, or in the future. Powell rubbed it in by telling the House that the percentage of personal incomes taken in tax had risen to levels not seen since 'the great taxing year' when Gaitskell had been Chancellor, in 1951. He gave Amory credit for being 'honest' in his way of dealing with the problem of high borrowing, saying that it should ensure stability for the future.

Once the Finance Bill went into committee, Powell's main concern was to have the Government amend proposals to counter tax-dodging by granting discretionary powers to the Inland Revenue to cancel tax advantages gained by dividend stripping and bond washing. Amory agreed to compromise when Powell, acting on behalf of the Conservative Finance Committee, raised objections to the breadth of this discretion. During the committee stage on 25 May Powell said that while no one wished to see tax-dodgers getting away with their activities, 'vigour and effectiveness' in preventing it 'are not the same as arbitrariness and unfairness in the methods by which the House of Commons attempts to do so'.[67] He sought to move an amendment that would limit the circumstances in which the new discretionary powers could be used by reducing the onus placed on taxpayers to substantiate claims or assertions they made for tax advantages. The Chancellor said that, instead, he would have any cases for investigation put before an independent tribunal, and only then could the discretionary powers be used.

Two days earlier, Powell had taken a break from his work on the Finance Bill Committee to object to one conclusion of the Peppiatt Report on Gambling, whose recommendations would lead to the liberalisation of betting and the availability of off-course bookmaking. He said the cost of receiving a permit to practise as a bookmaker was far in excess of the cost of issuing it, and was therefore a tax imposed by the authority of the House of Commons. The tax was, though, to be assessed and levied by a Levy Board, and applied for the benefit of racing by a Control Board. 'It is, therefore,' Powell said,

> an assigned revenue, that is, revenue designated in advance for a specific purpose or application; it is, moreover, a revenue which is both raised and applied otherwise than under the direct control and authority of this House. That is a departure from what I might call the principle of the Consolidated Fund, upon which the public control of finance by this House basically rests – the principle that all revenue which is raised by the authority of this House shall be paid into the Consolidated Fund and that all payments which are made by the authority of this House shall be made out of the Consolidated Fund.[68]

Powell added that it would be hard, as well, to find a logical case for subsidising racing out of these funds, when other activities were not so fortunate. However, if bookmaking were to be taxed, and the revenue from it used to subsidise racing, then the subsidy should be made by an annual vote of the House of Commons, as with other such grants. The departure from this principle, and the authorisation by Parliament of a monopoly, Powell found distasteful. However, his plea to tax betting and subsidise racing by conventional and precedented means was ignored.

On his forty-eighth birthday on 16 June there was a party in the Commons for him, not to mark that event but to celebrate the publication of *Great Parliamentary Occasions*, the first of his two books to be published that year. By the end of June the Commons had moved on from the Finance Bill to broader issues; and Powell, showing the social liberalism that had been noted the previous summer in his speech on Hola, was one of only two ex-ministers to vote for the implementation of the Wolfenden proposals on homosexuality. His parliamentary activities since the summer of 1959 had helped him and his reputation greatly. It was after the Hola speech that his name, seen by colleagues on the annunciators around the precincts at Westminster that stated the name of the Member speaking in the chamber at that time, would guarantee an influx into the chamber to hear him; it was to be thus until the end of his career. His work on the Finance Bill, seen to be critical, expert and constructive, had done him even more good. The following winter the *Observer* commented: 'Others have hailed him as the only MP (including the Chancellor of the Exchequer) who understood the technicalities of the 1960 Finance Bill; if it had been left to a free vote of the Parliamentary Party, he would probably have succeeded Heathcoat Amory last July.'[69] Powell was still hungry for a challenge, and not for the usual reasons of self-gratification. When Cub Alport, his former One Nation colleague, was sent that year to Rhodesia as high commissioner, Powell told him at a drinks party given by Duncan Sandys to mark the occasion: 'You know, Cub, this is the most romantic thing that has happened to any of us.'[70]

Throughout that July speculation about a reshuffle began to take hold. Bank Rate had risen again, and Amory, who had wanted to stand down at the election, was now thought to be in the last stages of his Chancellorship. There was internal dissent about Macmillan's perceived squandering of the advantage the party's 100 majority the previous year had given him. Word went round that the Prime Minister would shortly embark upon a major reconstruction of the Government. However enthusiastic Powell's colleagues might have felt about him and his abilities, the promotion of colleagues on the ground of sheer talent was not Macmillan's style.

Downing Street was careful to brief lobby correspondents in late July that, in the faithfully reported words of the *Telegraph*, 'any suggestion that he [Thorneycroft] or Mr Powell would be brought in merely to bolster party unity and stifle backbench criticism is wide of the mark'.[71] In fact, the question of these two men had been exercising Macmillan for some time. He had referred in his diary on 5 July to 'the problem of Thorneycroft and Powell', a problem Powell had put to him in clear terms the previous year when refusing office. 'On the whole, I am in favour of making them an offer,' Macmillan confided in his diary, 'but I must carry the cabinet and the party with me.'[72] In fact, agreement between Macmillan and Powell that he would become Minister of Health was reached by mid-July, though the appointment was not announced for a fortnight, a maintenance of secrecy almost unimaginable today. Powell engaged in his own subterfuge about it, mischievously spreading a rumour that Dennis Vosper, who had been Minister of Health for eight months in 1957 before resigning because of illness, would be returning to his old post: 'I got it into the press!'[73]

The reshuffle was finally announced on 27 July, after what Macmillan some-what inaccurately described as 'delicate and protracted' negotiations over the 'problem'.[74] Ten posts changed hands, with Selwyn Lloyd's replacement of Amory at the Exchequer and Lord Home's succeeding Lloyd at the Foreign Office the most prominent. Heath was chosen to speak for the Foreign Secretary in the Commons, and given special responsibility for handling Britain's attempts to enter the Common Market. Thorneycroft returned in the relatively junior pos-ition of Minister of Aviation, but with a seat in the cabinet; and Powell, freed of the moral obligations that had stopped him from taking office the previous year, took up his new ministry, without a seat in the cabinet, but on a salary of £5,750, equivalent to a cabinet minister's. To those who thought it a reversal of principle to rejoin the Government, when that Government had done nothing to alter the policy over which he had left, Powell simply answered: 'Life goes on. One makes one's point. One makes one's point firmly and dramatically; but life goes on and government goes on and Parliament goes on. You remain a member of it. And one cannot be a non-juror … for ever.'[75] Now he was a juror and, ironically in the light of the nature of his resignation, in one of the main spending departments of the Government. It was to be a happy time in his and his family's life: his wife said, 'I enjoyed Enoch being Minister of Health and *not* in the cabinet more than any other years in politics.'[76]

He had resigned in 1958 – as he maintained to his constituents at the time with more tact than candour – not in support of a policy, but in support of Thorneycroft. Thorneycroft was back, and that was the end of it. He was under no illusions about Macmillan, but reasoned that 'you do not accept or refuse office in the light of the supposed moral characteristics of a Prime Minister, unless those moral characteristics are operating in a field with which you are at that moment concerned'.[77] What in Macmillan's character he had earlier attri-buted to ignorance he now attributed to duplicity, but he believed he could discharge the office he had been offered without being impeded by that. He was to be proved largely justified in that belief.

The next day, as an additional recognition of his new status, Powell was sworn of the Privy Council by the Queen in an audience at Buckingham Palace. Maybe his and Thorneycroft's return had nothing to do with maintaining party unity, though the Lord Chancellor, Lord Kilmuir, thought somewhat differently. Writing a few years after the event he noted that, 'although they had behaved with great restraint and loyalty, no Prime Minister could feel pleased with a situation whereby two men of such talents and a natural focal-point for back-bench dissatisfaction were outside the Government'.[78] If Macmillan had seen the danger of Powell remaining outside the tent, it was a testament to his wiliness as a political operator, and a lesson at least one of his successors would not learn.

8

POWER

Powell reflected, in an article published twenty-five years after he left the Ministry of Health, that he would have preferred another office. 'An organisation', he wrote, 'which had absorbed and amalgamated all the previously existing channels of health care was not the area of choice for a politician identified with the limitation of public expenditure and already interested in exploring the scope for the restoration of market economics.'[1] He realised he could not refuse the challenge, and suspected he would find enough to stimulate his hungry intellect. For all his free-market passion, he believed there were limits to what the laissez-faire doctrine could deliver (though these were far broader limits than accepted by almost all of his colleagues). He saw the social and economic benefits of a health service, but from the start was determined that the NHS should be funded with the maximum of economy commensurate with humaneness. Ralph Harris wrote to Powell on 29 July, ostensibly to congratulate him on his appointment, but also to urge him not to forget the IEA or its principles: 'I hope your new work will not preclude an occasional meeting with some of us, who will miss you rather badly.'[2] Powell replied the following month that his contacts with the IEA would not end with the publication, due in September, of *Saving in a Free Society.* With due regard to the proprieties, he added, 'I should like to continue exchanges of ideas – *sub rosa*, as far as may be necessary.'[3] Also in this letter, Powell revealed a crucial intellectual influence, Hayek's newly published *Constitution of Liberty*, which was to assume almost biblical significance for many of Powell's and the IEA's free-market outlook. 'I have virtually appropriated your copy (spare, I believe) of Hayek, and hope I may hang on to it. I do not remember when I read a book with so much enthusiasm.'

He had two great advantages awaiting him at the Ministry in Savile Row. The first was his permanent secretary, Sir Bruce Fraser, who had assumed his post a few weeks earlier. Like his minister, Fraser was a Trinity man – two years Powell's senior – and a classicist with a double first. He had come from a glittering career at the Treasury and was regarded as one of Whitehall's Rolls-Royce minds; above all, he always saw the need for innovation, and had while at the Treasury contributed to the review of public financing that would help predicate funding years ahead in a way that would help with Powell's plans to rebuild the NHS. Ironically, it was a system Powell would, once introduced the following year by Selwyn Lloyd following the report of the Plowden Committee, come to criticise as wasteful. Initially, Powell was dismayed to find that he would be working in tandem with Fraser, who had had a minor, supporting role against the Treasury ministers during the 1957–8 crisis, but he showed complete loyalty to Powell, and the two men became lifelong friends. On the evening of Powell's first day at the Ministry he and his wife entertained the Frasers to dinner at South Eaton Place, and the bond began to be formed when Fraser appreciated the compliment of being served crème brulée for pudding, the dish known as 'Trinity Cream' that the College always serves to a visiting monarch.

Powell's second advantage was the relatively new chief medical officer of health, George Godber, whose principal role was to maintain good relations with the medical profession and to provide the Minister with such clinical advice as might be needed for the proper discharge of his duties. Powell described Godber's role as that of 'a bodyguard and a lightning conductor', there to protect the minister against the frequent prickliness of the medical profession.[4] Godber, too, was a radical, but unlike Fraser was an old Ministry of Health hand, having been there since just before the war. He would enjoy a close friendship with Powell that would extend after their professional contact ended, and would be vital in the strategic planning Powell, after looking over is new empire with the eye of a senior staff officer, saw he would have to undertake at the Ministry if the health service were to be brought up to scratch.

One of Powell's private secretaries, Bryan Rayner, recalled the immediate impact the new minister had. He 'asserted his authority from the very first day.'[5] On the afternoon Powell's appointment had been announced his new private office provided him with a detailed briefing and papers for a cabinet committee the next day. The main paper was, according to Rayner, 'on an abstruse, complex and detailed area of public health legislation'. His civil servants were stunned to be told the next day that Powell had asked leave to withdraw the paper as there were some areas of it with which he had disagreed. That same afternoon, he talked to the experts who had drawn up the paper, and explained to them why he had rejected it. The officials found themselves agreeing with him. 'News of that shot round the department,' said Rayner, 'and had a profound effect on his future relations with it.' 'He could be prickly,' another official, Bernard Harrison, recalled, 'but he was absolutely straight. He initiated ideas and he responded to ideas. He wanted to know the detail. He put a lot of time in.'[6] His staff were struck by his formality, notably that he would always wear a black jacket and striped trousers when performing in the Commons.

Aside from his civil servants, Powell also had an experienced and dedicated parliamentary secretary, Edith Pitt. Notwithstanding his reservations – most forcibly expressed later on in the context of Mrs Thatcher – about women fitting into the House of Commons, Powell's regard for Miss Pitt was high, and they would work together effectively. Powell thought her the best woman MP he had ever known, and 'the perfect parliamentary secretary.'[7] She, too, came from

Birmingham, the daughter of a manual worker, and Powell felt a deep affinity with her.

Thus blessed in his most important colleagues, the new minister tried to start his tenure by establishing a good relationship with the professions who worked in the NHS – something, as he would reflect later in his book *Medicine and Politics*, that would be increasingly hard to do as more and more of those workers used the weapon of embarrassing the Government in order to secure more resources. He soon learned, from his officials and from direct experience, that 'the politicians responsible for the National Health Service can accomplish anything (humanly speaking) *with* the medical profession and *nothing* against it'.[8] He quickly won the respect of his civil servants. 'We thought we were getting someone who would slow things down materially. We didn't,' said Godber.[9] His officials soon worked out that, for all the emphasis Powell had already put on free markets and limiting the role of the state, he regarded the NHS as an essential social service and not as an economic good. His civil servants soon found he had no preconceived notions. Above all, they liked the way he would return to his Ministry early each morning having done all the work he had taken home in his red boxes the night before. 'He tried to find out as much as he could as quickly as he could,' said Godber. 'He worked very hard indeed.'

On 1 August Macmillan had sent Powell a memorandum on 'some of the many problems which you will have to face as Minister of Health', his main concern being the annual drugs bill.[10] 'I know', said Macmillan, 'that you will set about this question with the energy and integrity of mind which are your characteristics.' He regretted the fact that he did not see as much of ministers outside the cabinet as he would like, but said he hoped Powell would not hesitate 'to come and see me from time to time for a general talk'. Powell, back from his holiday three weeks later, replied in a tone of similar courtesy, but relations between the two men would never be warm.

At the end of August Powell met doctors' leaders. The official report of the meeting had it that both he and they dedicated themselves to forging 'a real partnership of the profession and the Ministry in the National Health Service'.[11] However, this spirit of amity was short-lived, for at talks held immediately to try to resolve a doctors' pay dispute new proposals were made by Powell to raise standards in general practice, something disingenuously branded irrelevant by the British Medical Association's negotiators. The Government proposed a modest scheme of payment by results, rewarding the best family doctors for their excellence through a points system according to their skills, attendance at refresher courses and services offered. The BMA unequivocally rejected this, even though the recent Royal Commission on the NHS had suggested a fund be set up to reward good doctors.

Powell's budget for his first year was £546 million, but he was determined to try to prune excess expenditure. He let it be known that he wanted higher

National Insurance contributions to reflect the more sophisticated treatments the NHS could now offer. On taking up his office, he said that 'if the people have willed a National Health Service it is because they desire it and are prepared to pay for it'.[12] He also wanted a more competitive structure of pricing in the drugs industry, and to have that industry cut the huge budget it spent promoting its products to doctors. The annual drugs bill was £86 million, and the Ministry was already engaged in talks with the industry for voluntary regulation of the prices of most proprietary drugs. There was also pressure in the Conservative party to raise prescription charges; these were a shilling, at a time when the average actual cost of a prescription was 6s 11d. A National Insurance Bill would be included in the Queen's Speech, which would raise more in contributions for the NHS and for a larger retirement pension.

Predictably, it was not long before some enterprising journalist dredged up *First Poems*, and found in it 'I hate the ugly, hate the old / I hate the lame and weak'. At least when the *Daily Mail* did so it claimed that 'many people will be surprised at the benevolence with which Mr Powell is overhauling the NHS'.[13] Powell took a similarly puritanical view of his own comforts as a minister as he took to the rest of his departmental expenditure. Unless on an official visit, he hardly ever used his car, preferring to take the tube from Sloane Square to Westminster. 'I know it's silly,' he said, 'the car's there anyway. I just have a feeling about public property.'[14] He would send his chauffeur home early if he was going to be working late in the evening, which further helped his popularity among the other ranks.

Once special permission had been granted by the Cabinet Office, a loose end was tied up – the publication, on 26 September, of *Saving in a Free Society*. In the foreword to it he enunciated a principle that would be further and further left behind by the Government of which he was a member, and by its successors of both parties: 'I happen to believe that when a society's economic life ceases to be shaped by the interaction of the free decisions of individuals, freedom is in a fair way to disappear from other sides of its existence as well. The terms "free economy" and "free society" are to me interchangeable.'[15] Powell believed that saving could be regulated only by free decision, and signalled that he felt this to be so of all economic decisions. In the months he had spent researching and writing his book he had had, for the first time, extensive and detailed exposure to the great liberal economists: it confirmed the impression he had formed earlier, from previous, more limited acquaintance with economic thought. His views would set him apart from almost everyone else in the parliamentary Conservative party, at least for the next fifteen years.

His basic argument was that saving was beneficial provided, eventually, it was matched by 'dis-saving'. Radically, Powell described gambling as a form of saving, redistributing lump sums to others. He argued that failure by companies to redistribute profits was undesirable, since it forced shareholders to reinvest in a company that might not deserve it; and governments were sometimes prone to see taxation as a form of compulsory saving, even though that money was usually spent by the government on dubious enterprises. Powell argued that all the government should do to influence saving was keep taxation as low as possible, take as little from the individual as possible, and allow the individual to make the decisions about what to do with his disposable income.

Powell felt few writers on this subject had properly attempted to define what saving really was, so he sought to rectify the omission. He defined it as being the same use of capital as consumption, differing from it only in time. He did, though, distinguish between various forms of saving – such as buying a house for sale later on at a profit – that others might simply regard as consumption. There was also saving by those who did not need to do so, but who simply loved accumulating wealth; and unintentional saving, where people simply could not manage to spend their whole income. Corporate saving, by companies, was obviously different, and often longer term, and was divorced from the sort of motive that operated in the case of an individual.

The final form of saving was by the government, or the state. Governments, he said, tended to redistribute rather than save. The state saved when it added to its gold and foreign currency reserves; it dis-saved when it ran them down. Despite his own puritanical reputation, Powell questioned the orthodoxy that 'the practical benefits of saving to the individual are, and always have been, almost an article of religious conviction among whole classes of citizens'. He said that, in reality, the subject 'is complex, difficult and full of paradox'.[16] For the benefits of saving as widely understood were largely in the moral, and not in the economic, sphere. Powell said bluntly that 'economic benefit lies in consumption; and saving is a good thing (economically) for the individual precisely in so far and only in so far as it gives him the most desirable level of consumption over the span of his existence'. It was knowing how and when best to dis-save that was the key: otherwise 'there is a certain absurdity in describing as a good thing what is economically harmful to the community'.[17]

Similarly, he argued that the tax regime that militated against the distribution, as opposed to the retention, of company profits was undesirable: an attack on the policy of the Government he had just joined. As for the state, there was no point in inflating the reserves to unnecessary heights. In a free society, the money the community spent had to judged as right if it satisfied the desires of the community 'as expressed by it spontaneously'.[18] This was difficult to define, since it relied on an amalgam of individual decisions, but it was superior to the alternative, which was for the government to make the decisions on its own.

He renewed his critique of the National Insurance Fund, showing how, with each year that passed, it went more and more deeply into deficit, and diverted from its original purpose. This, too, was controversial, given his new job. However, the main controversy was in Powell's attack on National Savings, which he said had merely diverted money that would otherwise have gone, directly or indirectly, to the government in any case; and that this was not really saving at all, but another means for the government to borrow. He knew this empirically from his own justification, in the Commons after the 1957 Budget, of the limited borrowing Thorneycroft was indulging in, all of which would be financed by National Savings. Now he argued that better means could be found. This provoked the director of the National Savings Scheme, Viscount Mackintosh, to say that 'Mr Powell is as out of touch with the real situation of the small saver as I am in touch.' Mackintosh evangelised about the opportunity National Savings gave to 'the ordinary man and woman to participate in the economy of the country for their own and the country's good', which missed Powell's point entirely. Helpfully, he added, 'I have not read the book.'[19]

Having analysed the different forms of National Savings – the Post Office and Trustee Savings Bank, Defence Bonds, National Savings certificates and Premium Bonds – Powell provocatively concluded that he was confirmed in his 'initial impression that National Savings have now remarkably little connection with saving',[20] as opposed to the redirection of assets that would have been saved anyway. Also, interest rates paid on long-term National Savings bore little relation to market rates and could be expensive to the taxpayer. Powell said he felt the aim should now be, 'over the years, to convert more and more National Savings into other less liquid forms of Government debt. ... the evidence of recent years suggests that the costly and not entirely risk-free effort to increase the total of National Savings could be reserved without diminishing such opportunities as they afford for genuine "small saving" in the traditional sense'.[21]

Powell also set out his objections to inflation, saying that the phenomenon distorted the market for savings:

> It is scarcely going too far to say, for example, that in recent years the saver has not enjoyed the traditional choice between retaining the capital value of his savings at a relatively low reward and accepting an element of capital risk in return for higher reward. This distortion makes serious inroads into the efficiency of the 'market' for savings and, if carried beyond a certain point, could damage the case for the spontaneous, as opposed to the centrally directed, determination of the application of the community's saving. It is one of the grounds for ascertaining that the acceptance of a state of inflation is basically irreconcilable with the acceptance of a free economy.[22]

He also warned the Government not to mitigate taxes on investment, partly because it was discriminatory, and partly because the direction of policy – towards the encouragement of saving – perhaps needed to be rethought, not further consolidated.

This highly technical and original work showed that Powell was determined not to stop philosophising. In a speech at Barry, Glamorgan, on 10 September he had sounded a broad ideological warning: 'The battle for freedom is still on. Almost daily the exploits and achievements of communist countries receive publicity, and we are invited to draw the conclusion that these are the fruits of state control and state planning.' He said that 'it would be easy for Conservatives to be misled by the massive change-over in votes between 1951 and 1959 into imagining that Socialism is a danger of the past and that the choice between a free Britain and a Socialist Britain has been made once and for all. Our opponents' present disarray could all too powerfully reinforce this delusion.'[23]

Powell knew well the seductive hold statism had over some of his colleagues, and added, 'Nor is the enemy only outside the gates; he is inside as well, a fifth column wearing sometimes the most disarming and unsuspected of disguises. Here at home it is not only avowed or conscious socialists who can be heard arguing for more state action, clamouring in every difficulty for the Government to intervene, making the case for subsidy here, control there, restriction somewhere else.'[24] He also uttered a statement that would, within months, compromise him badly. He proclaimed that inflation had been dealt with without 'direct and physical controls which opponents and others urged upon us', and concluded that 'that is the right pattern of policy'. This cast his resignation of 1958 in an interesting light, but such an avowed belief would also leave Powell badly placed when the Government of which he was now a member chose an incomes policy to try to dampen the economy the following year.

Being in government inevitably put constraints on Powell. At Manchester, later that autumn, he spoke about the export drive, and had to choose his words carefully so as not to be seen to condemn a policy contrary to all his beliefs. In some intellectual pain, he observed that the system of the fixed exchange rate was 'a policy which commands general support and of which the advantages are generally held to outweigh the disadvantages'.[25] To assuage his own feelings, he added that the system could only work provided the government maintained the internal value of money by not inflating; but his ideological isolation was apparent. Macmillan, in a minute to the cabinet on 27 September, had warned that 'unless we can secure a substantial and sustained improvement in our overseas earnings, many of our policies, internal and external, political and economic, will be in jeopardy'. Powell's subsequent expositions on this theme would show he regarded such a view as utter rubbish.[26]

II

Powell ruthlessly pursued ways of cutting NHS spending. He told the Conservative party conference at Scarborough on 16 October 1960 that he 'wholeheartedly associated' himself with demands that the NHS should not be exploited by foreign visitors, even though Powell's own doctor, Brian Warren,

Ellen Mary, John Enoch and Albert Enoch Powell, 1913

Jack at his books, 1927

Undergraduate, 1931

In the country, 1933

A thoughtful family, 1934

Master of pasta, Turin, 1935

On the eve of his professorship, 1937

In Italy, 1936

With topee to
Australia, 1938

A guided tour of the Acropolis for his fellow passengers, 1939

In battledress,
by Freeth, 1939

Michael Strachan, 1942

The Brigadier in India, 1945

Above Left: The candidate for Normanton, hair *en brosse*, 1947

Above Right: 'I have imitated the ancient Spartans and grown my hair long.' 1949

Left: The candidate for Wolverhampton, 1950

The Wolverhampton machine, 1950

VOTE CONSERVATIVE

Vote for **ENOCH POWELL** YOUR CANDIDATE

CAMPAIGNERS

VOLUNTEER CLERKS

WARD CHAIRMAN

WARD CHAIRMAN

WARD CHAIRMAN

WARD CHAIRMAN

WARD CHAIRMAN

ORGANISER

FILE

ORG

WINDOW CARD

ELECTION ADDRESS

SECRETARY

ELECTION AGENT

With wife and parents, 1952

Miss Wilson becomes Mrs Powell, 1952

On honeymoon in Majorca, maintaining the standards expected of an officer and a gentleman, 1952

speaking from the floor, said reports of such abuse were an exaggeration.[27] In his speech to the conference, Powell said that improved treatment for mental patients would mean that the way they were regarded by the service would have to change, and he would make them a higher priority. Hospital building was another theme: £100 million would be spent in the years ahead on a programme of improvements, and Powell would ensure that value for money was obtained. He emphasised that the NHS had not been designed to seal off voluntary effort, and he would now seek to encourage it further.

His speech did not please everybody. A Conservative backbencher, Geoffrey Hirst, said he was 'shocked beyond belief' that Powell had not addressed the subject of private patients obtaining prescriptions at NHS rates, namely a shilling.[28] He was one of eighty Conservative backbenchers to sign a Commons motion calling for private patients to be allowed to benefit from the NHS in this way. In fact, Powell – who was personally in favour of allowing private patients these cheaper prescriptions on the ground that they had contributed towards them – had been called into the cabinet meeting on 6 October where, inconclusively, this had been discussed. He had written to Macmillan on 29 August that 'the only ground on which the concession can now be delayed or refused is cost, it having been virtually admitted for a long time past that there is no objection of principle'.[29] However, the cost was only £3 million a year, and Powell said that failure to act would mean the matter would 'continue to bedevil relations between the Health Ministry and the Party inside and outside the House'. He argued privately that the concession should quickly be made, not least to get Conservative MPs on his side when further economies had to be made.

Powell was invited to cabinet at the end of October to attend a further discussion about prescriptions for private patients, but a prior engagement in Wales prevented him attending. He wrote to Macmillan on 25 October to say that 'I am sure that it would be a mistake to make any promise or half-promise at this moment'.[30] He added that he would be prepared to say in the Commons that 'in the Government's view it is not possible to make the concession against the background of the rising gross cost of the National Health Service'. On 31 October he wrote to Butler, saying that when he addressed the Conservative party's Health Committee the following month 'I intend to tell them that the Government regard it as politically impracticable to make the concession when the rising gross cost of the service may at any time call for unpalatable decisions. I shall tell them that if asked for reasons in public, I shall be obliged to refer in general terms to the rising cost of the service, but that, as it could be embarrassing to have this argument against the concession on the record, I hope I shall not be pressed.'[31]

On 15 November, after further informal consultations, Powell made his appearance – his first – before the Health Committee, at which sixty MPs were present. He told them that, even though he agreed with the principle of what they were arguing, there was no hope of their wish being granted, which only provoked more to sign the motion, given the low cost of the concession. Powell had added that he had not signed a motion calling for the concession the previous year because, as chairman of the Conservative parliamentary Finance Committee, he had agreed not to put his name to anything that might lead to higher spending. However, while he had hoped to do something, it was now clear that 'the present rate of increase in the cost of the National Health Service indicated that it would be necessary for the Government to take some far from palatable steps before long to restrain it'. These steps could not, politically, be taken in the light of a 'sectional concession' to private patients.[32] He was 'disappointed' to have to say this, as he did not agree with the notion, but there it was. There was widespread sympathy, but widespread disagreement. Powell emphasised that 'he could make no promises, or half-promises, in private or in public in this matter'.

In the pursuit of economies, the notion was gaining ground that the level of the NHS contribution could be raised while the levels of service were, in some respects, cut, making those cuts, or the increases, seem unjustified. The arguments of January 1958 were turned on their head; now it was Powell uttering words of caution. Invited to cabinet on 18 October, he told the meeting he was 'hoping to be able to put before the cabinet certain proposals for effecting economies in the NHS, and it might be more difficult to ensure general accept-ance of these if the prospective increase in the cost of the service had already been largely met by increased contributions'.[33] Powell's words were heeded; the cabinet appointed a committee of officials to examine alternative ways of financing the service. The discussion was resumed at the next meeting, and centred upon the level of an increased contribution. An extra shilling would, Butler said, raise £50 million. The meeting was moved to agree, but no decision was made.

Powell's debut at the dispatch box as minister was on 25 October, when he spoke on the Professions Supplementary to Medicine Bill, which conferred certain disciplinary powers for these groups of workers on to their professional bodies. He had a broader canvas three days later in Llandudno, addressing the Executive Councils Association on his vision of the NHS. He agreed that, by its very nature, the health service had to be centralised, but he was determined to avoid the dangers of rigidity. These were principally of the slowness in changing policy when such change was necessary, because of new circumstances or changes in demand. 'The great machine', he said, 'is bound to have a one-track mind, to be cumbrous and unresponsive, to abhor variations, to be insensitive to the world around it.'[34] He said he wanted to encourage pioneers in the NHS, a reflection of what he hoped he, Fraser and Godber were doing in Savile Row. For this reason, he said he welcomed the independence of the professions within the NHS, and the separate representation they had in hospital and executive council services, so they could act as a counterpoise to the bureaucracy: 'I shall be as jealous of the independence of the professions as they are themselves.'[35] The voluntary organisations, too, were part of this counterpoise, and he again praised their role. He ended with three pioneering pledges: more community care, more preventive medicine and a more intensive use of hospital accommodation. It was this innovative spirit, coupled with a correct philosophical understanding of how the NHS operated, that was to underpin Powell's undoubted success as Health Minister.

The serious political consequences of running the NHS were kept from him for the first few months in his office, allowing him time with officials to put together his strategy for the service's future. In November, he returned to his theme of voluntary help in the NHS when addressing the Women's Voluntary Service. 'I refuse to contemplate', he said, 'the hospital service, let alone the National Health Service at large, as some great monolith or as a kind of granite pyramid, built with public money, composed of public employees, and rising majestically and mathematically to a ministerial summit. I want to think of it rather as a live and growing and changing thing, in which the fibres of central government, and of voluntary effort, are all knit together.' He was particularly keen for voluntary workers to play a part in his reform of mental hospitals.[36] He also, that autumn, embarked on the first of a series of tours around his empire, visiting and walking the corridors of hospitals and assimilating data and experiences to shape his thinking. He would gather doctors, nurses and other staff at the end of a visit, often in the sluice room at the end of a ward, where nurses would gather while carrying out various medicinal tasks, and talk to them about what the service needed. He learned better to understand the people he was working with as a result, and hoped they better learned to understand him. He also ordered a quarterly meeting with the chairmen of all fifteen regional health authorities, who were not used to consultation by the minister. His officials had feared the meeting would be taken up with incessant arguments and disagreements. Powell ignored them, and the meetings became a fixture, and something of a success.

On 29 November he sent the regional health authorities costing returns that showed an 8 per cent increase during 1959–60 of keeping patients in 350 large hospitals; and asked each regional board to carry out deeper costing investigations. The average cost of an in-patient per week in a London teaching hospital was £36 6s 8d, £1 13s 2d up on the previous year. However, the question of spending in the hospital service was about to undergo a revolution. As Powell came into office, two health authorities, Wessex and Oxford, submitted prototype plans for capital spending over several years ahead. The chairmen of the two authorities came to talk to Godber about it; Godber alerted Powell, who immediately saw the attractions of translating it to a national framework. It was not that he invented a hospital-building programme: one already existed, but it was incoherent, uncoordinated, and ripe (as Powell saw it) for putting into a shape where it and its resources could be properly harnessed and driven forward more impressively. Powell had not always been so attracted to such long-termism in the NHS. Speaking as a backbencher seven years earlier, at a meeting of the party's Health and Social Security Committee, he had on 22 July 1953 argued that a four-yearly 'block grant' for hospitals would be wrong as it would put them in a 'privileged position'.[37] The armed forces would, he said, want the same treatment. An 'annual overall check' on expenditure was vital.

Also on 29 November he had told his backbench colleagues, at a meeting of the Health Committee, of his long-term plan; and, for the next eighteen months, the notion of NHS forward planning was to occupy much of Powell's and his officials' time. When a White Paper came to be drafted, Powell did most of the drafting himself, something his civil servants regarded as highly unusual; but when they looked at his draft they found few areas in which they could improve it.[38] His critics would find it odd or even hypocritical that one so opposed to state planning should embark on such a scheme, but that is to forget two things. First, much to the frustration of his friends in the IEA, Powell felt the people wanted the National Health Service and it therefore had to be provided. Second, since the money would be spent year-on-year in any case, it made sense to plan for its spending so as to maximise utility. All he was striving to do was to make the inevitable more efficient and coherent in its execution.

The first meeting with the regional chairmen took place on 20 December. Powell explained that the gathering was meant to avoid 'conflict between his own detailed responsibility for the hospital service and the necessity that many decisions should be made by the board with delegated powers'.[39] He outlined to them the fact that he was thinking far ahead: he invited them, by the end of May 1961, to send him their 'basic views on planning for the next 10 years'. He let them into his secret that he wanted to publish a White Paper by the end of 1961. Because of the extent to which Powell wanted to take the chairmen into his confidence, he told Fraser on 29 December that he did not want minutes of their meetings circulated to them 'even confidentially' as the 'risk' was 'too great to be taken'.[40]

The financial side of the NHS was central to Powell's work, though he did not neglect other important issues concerned with medicine. On 20 December Edith Pitt moved the second reading of a Bill legalising the removal of parts of corpses for therapeutic purposes and medical research. Advances in medical science, notably in transplant surgery, had made the Bill essential, as otherwise life-saving procedures would be illegal. Kenneth Robinson, Labour's health spokesman, welcomed the Bill, for which Powell thanked him in his winding-up speech; and Powell concluded by saying that he felt objections to organ donation were rooted in 'solemn and even irrational emotions' that, he hoped, would pass during the ensuing years.[41]

The following day he attended cabinet and, in advance of the next spending round, told his colleagues that the next year would be the fifth in succession in which there had been increases of 8–10 per cent in spending on the NHS.[42] Unlike a typical spending minister he was unhappy with this rate of increase; and outlined a series of proposals to slow it down which, if they received approval, he was planning to announce in February. The measures would lead to the suspicion that he was only notionally a minister of health, and really a Treasury minister across the water. However, since he had already settled on the concept of a massive plan of capital spending to begin immediately and last ten years – what he would announce the following month under the title of the Hospital Plan – inevitably some current costs would have to be reduced. The cabinet approved his spending and revenue-raising plans; he made sure to tell them that, since the prescription charge was last fixed in 1956, the cost of medicines had risen by 50 per cent. The one concern the cabinet had was over the plan to reduce the availability of subsidised welfare milk for children; Powell was asked to go away and think further about that.

The whole business of saving money in this way was grievous to Macmillan, who told his diary that at a 'long and difficult' cabinet Powell had proposed various economies that were 'not real economies – they are old stagers – welfare milk, prescription charges, and all the rest. I do not like this "regressive" taxation very much – nor do some of my colleagues ... But the enormous increase in the Estimates makes one feel that something must be done.'[43] Nor was Macmillan alone. When Macleod, who was somewhat distant from Powell at this time, heard what he was preparing to do he was upset at the potential for trouble. Butler was detailed by Macmillan to calm Macleod down, and a minute to Macmillan from his private secretary on 20 December 1960 reports that 'Mr Butler telephoned this evening to say that he had spoken to Mr Macleod about the National Health Service, as a result of which he (Mr Butler) was sure that Mr Macleod would not make any bother in cabinet tomorrow on this subject except (to quote Mr Butler's words) "perhaps to utter a few philosophical words".'[44]

In January 1961 Powell was ready to unveil the consultation process that would lead, the following winter, to the Hospital Plan, the most significant initiative of his tenure of the Ministry of Health. The ten-year plan was costed at about £500 million. The idea was to have the service fully modernised by the early 1970s, with the old remote psychiatric and tuberculosis hospitals replaced by a concentration of general hospitals in urban areas. Powell sent a circular to hospital boards on 17 January 1961 asking them to submit, by 31 May, proposals for building works to be started in the next ten years. At that time there were already 180 major projects, including forty-three new hospitals, either being planned or built. A programme of renewal was desperately needed: since 1948, when the NHS had been founded, only £157 million had been spent on capital projects, with not a single new hospital project approved until 1956.[45] In keeping with his philosophy of decentralisation, Powell announced that the maximum cost of projects hospital boards could undertake without ministerial approval would be doubled from £30,000 to £60,000. The *Daily Telegraph*, for one, noted that this largesse came from a man who when at the Treasury 'was noted for his Puritanic refusal to countenance increased Government expenditure'.[46]

Also on 17 January Powell was called in to the cabinet, prompting press speculation that he was party to Budget discussions about raising the National Insurance contribution. In fact, the matter under consideration was the more prosaic, but no less politically sensitive, one of welfare milk. Powell was still keen to reduce the subsidy by 2d a pint, but conceded that the full subsidy would still be paid to families with four children or more, or with three children where the mother was expecting a fourth. The concession would cost an extra £2.5 million a year. John Boyd-Carpenter, the Minister of Pensions, argued that the full subsidy should be paid to families with more than three children, and to widowed mothers. Powell did succeed in persuading the cabinet to agree to abolition of all subsidies on welfare foods, but could not convince them about milk. Even Boyd-Carpenter's policy was more radical than most would tolerate. It was not merely a question, Powell found, of upsetting the mothers of Great Britain; the cabinet was more concerned about the Milk Marketing Board and the National Farmers Union. Christopher Soames, the Minister of Agriculture, argued that to remove the subsidy – putting up the price from 4d to 6d a pint and saving £12 million a year – would destabilise the market for milk.

No decision was taken, so Powell was called back on 24 January, this time prompting more accurate speculation that the health estimates were under discussion. Rumours arose that he was holding out for increased charges against a cabinet determined not to frighten the horses. At the 24 January meeting the only part of the package the cabinet had objected to – the removal of milk subsidies – was finally buried, with worries about the political effects of falling consumption the main sticking point, but Powell had long had almost everything else settled. He attended the cabinet on 31 January, where he won approval for plans to increase charges for amenity beds and lenses.

The next day, 1 February, Powell announced all the raised charges for health care, which he argued would make the individual rather than the Treasury bear more of the burden of improving the service. His Ministry's estimates had shown a likely increase of 11 per cent in the year ahead, and he was determined to finance that without cutting the service. The weekly Employed Man's contribution would rise by a shilling, of which the employer would pay 2d; this alone would raise an extra £49 million a year. Prescription charges, unchanged for five years, would double, to 2s; in that time the average gross cost of a prescription had risen from 5s 1½d to 7s 4d. Payments for dentures would rise, the maximum going up to £5 from £4 5s. Spectacles would rise by 5s, 'welfare' orange juice would rise from 5d a bottle to 1s 6d, and cod liver oil and vitamin tablets would no longer be free.

Although liberal commentators agreed that the increases were justified – in a generally fair profile the *Observer* described Powell as 'an honest man, who will act in any situation as he thinks best' – Labour's outrage was immediate.[47] Gaitskell called the charges a 'major assault' on the NHS. A censure motion was tabled, and debated in the Commons on 8 February. George Brown, Labour's deputy leader, moved it. In a rambling, undisciplined speech lasting over an hour (but which nonetheless cheered up his backbenchers after months of in-fighting over nuclear disarmament) he called Powell's policy 'monstrous', and one that had offended even hardened Conservative supporters.[48] Brown said he had had a larger postbag on the new charges than on anything since Suez – a comparison invoked by the *Telegraph*'s sketch writer, who described the last hour during the winding-up speeches as the ugliest scene in the Commons since 1956.[49] Brown read out a letter from an elderly doctor who claimed to be a lifelong Conservative supporter, in which he had written that 'after a lifetime of helping others and healing the sick, my considered opinion is that anybody supporting the increased charges is a wicked old—' Here Brown paused for effect, before continuing, to the amusement of his colleagues: 'Here, I am afraid, I am in some difficulty. I think that the word he meant to type was "beggar", but that is not, in fact, the word that he has typed.'[50]

Brown said the NHS was in need of a great architect but had, instead, 'a quantity surveyor'. He took Powell's repeated calls, while on the backbenches, for an end to housing subsidies as proof he was anti-welfare, and even managed to construe the One Nation pamphlet on welfare Powell had written with Macleod as a call for the restoration of the Poor Law. Guilty of conscience, Brown also repudiated, in advance, the usual allegation that Labour had been the first party to introduce prescription charges. He said it had been necessary to raise money to help pay for the Korean War, and in using those means to do it Labour had been supported by the Conservatives; so it ill became them to have made political capital out of it ever since. Brown's basic plea was for more money: 'What are we telling our people – that we cannot put 2 per cent extra a year into the Health Service? Is that too much for us? Is that a disaster?'[51]

He worried that the principle of charging would be extended to other public services – particularly education. He saw the whole thing in class terms: the determination by the Conservatives to deprive people of what he called his 'background' – 'any of us who grew up in circumstances where reliance upon a public health provision was essential' – of a proper free-at-point-of-use health service.[52] He concluded that in order to support the proposals one would have to be capable of writing, 'I hate the ugly, hate the old, I hate the lame and weak.'

Powell's speech was infinitely more temperate, in the face of sustained bar-racking from the Labour benches. He began by illustrating the improvements in the service: a 10 per cent increase in the number of doctors over the previous five years, a 13 per cent rise in the number of full-time nurses and a 35 per cent rise in the part-time ones. There had been large rises in the amount of treatment carried out. He presented himself unequivocally as a moderniser, not just in terms of newer buildings, but of new routines within those buildings; and he expressed particular interest in reforming care of the mentally ill. He emphasised that the national plan was the first time the health services had ever been asked to think ten years ahead; and he hoped that by planning and modernisation the costs of running the service could be brought down further.

He took up Brown's point about the Korean War, and said the real issue then was that there had been reached 'a point beyond which the increased net cost could not be borne upon general taxation'. That, he reminded the House, had been in the year when taxation levels were last at the pitch they had now reached again.[53] Action was needed to take some of the burden directly off the Exchequer. Before coming to the debate, Powell had justified the increases by saying that the 1961–2 health estimates would show an increase of about 11 per cent on the current total of £867 million. The increases reduced the share of the cost the Exchequer had to find from 76.3 per cent to 70.7 per cent. In 1956–7 the Ex-chequer's burden had been 82.8 per cent. He had started to pursue his aim, expressed in *Needs and Means* nearly ten years before, of relating the insurance system more directly to the welfare state. He had been keen to spend more on the NHS, but he believed the growing prosperity of the insured population could be used to finance it directly. This was in direct ideological opposition to Labour, which believed in a service financed not by the user, but by progressive taxation. There were some consolations. Children's spectacles and dental care were to be made cheaper, as was dental care for expectant and nursing mothers.

However electorally difficult the economies Powell was proposing to make might be, many of his colleagues – and others in the press – gave him credit for trying to reverse the one-way traffic of increased public spending. The Government avoided censure by a majority of ninety, and then tried to move the Order needed to enforce the higher charges. This led to uproar, since the Deputy Speaker effectively cut short the debate when Labour was preparing to prolong the sitting through the night and use every obstructive method it could to stop Powell getting his way. It was not until nearly 1.30 a.m. that the House finally rose, and then only after a confrontation between Gaitskell and Butler, and the threat of a vote of censure against the Deputy Speaker.

The day after the Government won the censure debate the civil and defence estimates for 1961–2 were published, and Powell was shown to have made a significant contribution to better economy. His saving of £50 million, just under 1 per cent of total spending, was recognised as having helped towards a predicted

Budget surplus which, while not allowing tax cuts, would maintain a proper sense of control.

III

Labour bitterly opposed further proceedings to raise NHS charges on 15 February, the sitting lasting until 6.30 a.m. Then Kenneth Robinson, Powell's shadow, moved a prayer* in the Commons that the charges be annulled. Powell, who admired Robinson and thought him a sincere and thoughtful man, charitably said in his reply that the opposition to the charges had been 'inspired by concern for the well-being of the National Health Service', and particularly by concern – which Powell shared – about the cost of the pharmaceutical services.[54] He emphasised that in the year ahead the cost of the NHS would rise by the enormous sum of £79 million, from £807 million to £886 million, and that £50 million of that increase had been made possible by the higher charges to which Labour so fiercely objected; and he asked Jennie Lee, Bevan's widow, who had made an emotional attack on him, whether she would rather leave prescription charges where they were or have another £12 million to £13 million to spend on the service. Miss Lee retorted that there was money to do both, and it was an 'insult' to pretend otherwise.[55]

Powell concluded by making the fundamental point to Miss Lee, and her friends, that 'the Opposition have never realised that neither the National Health Service nor the society in which it exists stands still. They are both living, changing things reaching out to new aims as people are able to meet old needs for themselves.' Labour, he said, was 'a party for which time stood still in 1951'. Again, the Government won the vote easily; but the fight continued. Just under a fortnight later, on 1 March, Brown used a party political broadcast to attack Powell and his reforms, quoting yet again from 'I hate the ugly', but the attack backfired. Brown said in the broadcast that 'when you hear in the morning that we on the Labour side have been keeping the Commons up most of the night, you will now know what the struggle is really about'. In fact the House rose at 10.26 p.m., not long after the broadcast ended.[56]

On 6 March a majority of eighty-two rejected a Labour motion to prevent the guillotine on the two NHS Bills to allow the higher prescription charges and higher contributions. Powell, himself an adept parliamentary tactician, said in winding up that 'the Guillotine has a function to perform and is recognised as such by both sides'; this was in response to Brown's theatrical closing remarks about 'the arrogance of the Treasury Bench'.[57] Powell said the duty of the Government to discharge the business the country expected it to do overrode all other

* A motion praying the Queen that a statutory instrument be annulled, i.e., pass out of law.

considerations, and the Opposition were clearly trying to frustrate that business. He added that in the recent censure debate, in the second reading debate and during the committee stage of the National Health Service Contributions Bill the principle had been extensively debated and supported by majorities of the House. No one could argue that the measure was being steamrollered through.

After the guillotine had been secured, the Labour MP Peggy Herbison brought up *Needs and Means*, claiming that the Government was full of ministers who, secretly, approved of a means test. Powell intervened and asked her: 'Will the hon Lady, for the sake of the record – the Colonial Secretary's as well as my own – go on to tell the House that in the rest of the book we went on to say why health and education should be comprehensive and universally available services?'[58]

Powell attempted to move to other items on his Ministry's agenda. Speaking to the National Association for Mental Health on 9 March, he argued that within fifteen years 75,000 beds used for mental patients – half the total – would be freed for other uses; and beds for such patients should be in general hospitals, not isolated asylums.[59] He made a pioneering call for more community care, saying the old asylums would be pulled down: 'A hospital is a shell, a framework, however complex, to contain certain processes, and when the processes change or are superseded, then the shell must probably be scrapped and the framework dismantled.'[60] A historian of the welfare state, Nicholas Timmins, has called the policy enunciated in this speech the 'second great memorial' of Powell's time as minister, after the Hospital Plan.[61] George Godber said the initiative was typical of Powell's close personal involvement with, and commitment to, his own responsibilities.[62] Once the Hospital Plan was launched, Powell would deal with community care in greater detail: not merely out of compassion, but because of his recognition that although most of his Ministry's budget was spent in the hospital service, the hospital service was but a small part of the general health services.

There had been warnings made to Parliament ever since the NHS's foundation in 1948 that a scandal would erupt out of the mental hospitals, and there had been urgings to look at the wider possibilities for the treatment of such patients in the community made possible by the development of new drugs that could suppress the symptoms of mental illness. The Government had already committed itself to community-based care, but no action had been taken – even though, as Timmins records, the population of the asylums had been falling ever since 1954, when the main new drug, Largactil, became available.[63] Powell's advisers projected that by 1975 that population would halve to 75,000; this gave him the scope needed for resolute action.

He had been to some of the institutions, and announced, in typically arresting language, what the problem was, and what would be done to overcome the 'sheer inertia of mind and matter' causing it: 'There they stand, isolated, majestic, imperious, brooded over by the gigantic water-tower and chimney combined, rising unmistakable and daunting out of the countryside – the asylums which our forefathers built with such immense solidity. Do not for a moment under-estimate their powers of resistance to our assault. Let me describe some of the defences we have to storm.'[64] Using a metaphor that would serve again in his most apocalyptic speech, he spoke of the 'funeral pyre' to which the 'torch' had to be put. He added that he wanted the buildings pulled down rather than put to an alternative use, as if seeking to wipe from the earth a symbol of society's neglect and shame. 'If we err,' he added, 'it is our duty to err on the side of ruthlessness.' Timmins reports that his speech divided the audience of psy-chiatrists, administrators, volunteers and social scientists 'down the middle. There was a mix of enthusiastic backing and of horror at what he proposed.'[65] Nor was it just mental patients whose lot Powell sought to improve. He endorsed a report by senior nurses to make hospitals more like home, with an end to five o'clock waking and a more flexible routine, including afternoon naps, rather than relentless activity.

Although Powell's regime was itself one of relentless activity, he still saw the importance of recreation. At least, now, he could indulge in it against a background of success and career fulfilment. He spent the Easter recess of 1961 fulfilling a long-held ambition to walk the length of Hadrian's Wall. Though such prolonged rest was rare, Powell still kept Sunday as a day off, and made the most of it. With the coming of spring (which he defined as late February) the Powell family – his daughters were now five and seven – began a regular ritual of 'Powell picnics', usually with friends. These were Sunday excursions meticulously plotted with the aid of an Ordnance Survey map and including visits to churches and other buildings of architectural interest. When in Wol-verhampton, the Powells' most regular companions were Clement Jones and his family, the most popular destinations Shropshire and the Marches. Since his conversion to the joys of architecture Powell had educated himself in the subject with his customary thoroughness. He would scrutinise guidebooks and leaflets sold by churches and stately homes and, when detecting an error, would write and inform the incumbent or the owner. On one picnic, the participants became guinea-pigs for a new health policy; George Jones, Clement Jones's son, remem-bers a new chewing gum being handed round after the food because medical advice had decided it would be good for cleaning and protecting the teeth.[66] Occasionally favoured members of Powell's private office would come, though George Jones remembers the agony of one junior civil servant gasping for a cigarette but not daring to light up in front of his disapproving chief. Edith Pitt, Powell's parliamentary secretary, was sometimes asked too.

At the annual dinner of the Association of the British Pharmaceutical Industry on 26 April he returned to his theme of driving down the drugs bill. 'Each of us has a weakness in his bargaining position which, to the other, is a corresponding source of bargaining strength,' he told his audience. 'My weakness is that the Health Service must have the drugs you supply. Your weakness is that virtually your only home market for your ethical drugs is the National Health Service.'[67] The press, ever alert for hypocrisy, could only find Powell practising in his private life the economy he preached in his public. The *Daily Express* found out that Powell was a secret handyman, saving money on home repairs. 'It's his hobby – but goodness me it's a useful one,' Mrs Powell told the paper. 'The saving involved is quite considerable, apart from the pleasure he gets. And that's a consideration these days. He makes the most magnificent fitted cupboards,' she said. 'Really very professional.'[68]

Powell finally started to tackle the drugs bill – by now running at £110 million a year – on 17 May. In a move aimed at the hospital bill (which accounted for £14 million of that figure), he said he would apply Section 46 of the 1949 Patents Act, which enabled the Government to use patented goods for the service of the Crown, a measure hitherto applied only for defence purposes. It would prevent hospitals buying their drugs from unlicensed sources, and the Ministry would invite tenders for central buying – something of a contradiction of Powell's earlier policy of decentralisation. This would allow him to negotiate royalties direct with patent-holders, thereby driving prices down. The Association of the British Pharmaceutical Industry immediately said it viewed the action 'with grave misgivings', as lower prices would limit the money available for research.[69]

Powell then resumed his agenda of humanising the NHS. He told the Association of Hospital Matrons at their annual meeting on 10 June 1961 of his objections to finding, at a maternity hospital he had visited, a large hand-bell to be rung when a birth was about to take place, in order to summon students. 'I have no wish to pillory the particular hospital which, at my request, replaced this ancient instrument of torture within a week with electric bells at a distance. But what volumes of insensitivity it speaks that such a thing could not only continue, but not be felt to be intolerable.'[70] He said he wanted to root out unnecessary noise in hospital, and repeated his objections to the five o'clock waking. 'The hospital day exists for the convenience of the patient and not of the staff,' he said, going on to describe some visiting hours as 'downright cruelty'. He also initiated the removal of noisy, metal fittings on curtain rails around hospital beds, and their replacement by quiet, plastic ones. Three months later, addressing the Royal College of Obstetricians and Gynaecologists, he said the NHS needed a good bedside manner, not the sort that concealed ignorance of and contempt for the patient, but the sort that conveyed a proper understanding of him by the doctor.

Before the Commons' summer recess, Labour tried once more to inflict political damage by debating the NHS. On 11 July Robinson observed that a similar debate the previous summer had been followed within hours by Derek Walker-Smith's resignation from the Government. 'There can be no certainty', he continued, 'that the present Minister will be guided by that precedent.'[71] He went on to claim that all that Labour had predicted would be the result of the higher charges introduced earlier in the year had come true – far fewer prescriptions were being fulfilled, the conclusion being that some were no longer able to afford the care their doctors advised; there had, he said, been a fall in prescriptions of 21 per cent in the first month of the new charging structure alone. He also produced anecdotal evidence of poor service for out-patients, excessive delegation by lazy consultants, too many overseas doctors and short-comings in the treatment of mental patients.

In answering this charge sheet, Powell agreed that the 'human relations' of NHS staff with patients could do with improvement, as could the regime in certain hospitals – points he had tried to deal with in the preceding months.[72] Continuing his campaign to reduce noise in hospitals, he said a special study would be published on it the following month. He renewed his criticism of inflexible half-hour visiting times. He hinted that, unless the professions showed some leadership on the issue, he would be giving central direction on a liberalisation of the rules governing it. Above all, there was a 'blind spot' in the communications between hospital officials and patients and their families, and Powell would see to this, too, if the professions did not instigate an improvement. He wanted 'a much more general understanding of how important it is that the patient, his relatives and those concerned with him should never be left in ignorance about what is going on, what is intended to be done with him, why he is where he is, and all the obvious questions which any sentient human being will want to know about himself and those for whom he cares'.[73] This exposition of a policy to 'humanise' the service took some of the sting out of Labour's attacks, and allowed Powell to defer some of the other serious questions to the province of his parliamentary secretary's winding-up speech.

IV

Since the end of 1960 Powell had, at his own urging, sat on the cabinet sub-committee considering the changes needed to citizenship law to control the inflow of immigrants to the United Kingdom, and which would result in the 1962 Commonwealth Immigrants Act. In a minute to Macmillan, the cabinet secretary Sir Norman Brook had said on 24 November 1960, 'it is understood that the Minister of Health would like to be a member of the Committee (because the problem arises in a particularly sharp form in his constituency)'.[74] While Wolverhampton had reinforced his feelings, Powell's view on the need to restrict citizenship had remained unchanged since the 1948 Act, on which he had briefed the then Conservative front bench, notably Maxwell Fyfe – who as Lord Kilmuir was now Lord Chancellor, chaired the committee on which Powell sat, and had to endure the mistakes of 1948 being thrown back at him. Powell felt vindicated by events, and had had plenty of opportunity to observe the effects from the close quarter of his own constituency. Although the NHS relied heavily on overseas staff, Powell was not responsible for recruiting them – that was left to health authorities – and many clinical staff were in Britain temporarily, to acquire extra skills and training to take back with them to their own countries. He was still reluctant to speak in public on the matter, but in the privacy of the sub-committee left no one in doubt of his feelings.

The Commonwealth Migrants Committee's terms of reference were 'to consider and keep under review the problems caused by the uncontrolled entry into the United Kingdom of British subjects from overseas'.[75] Its first meeting was on 16 February 1961, with Macleod, John Hare (the Minister of Labour), Henry Brooke (Minister of Housing), Charles Hill (Chancellor of the Duchy of Lancaster) and Manningham-Buller (Attorney-General) also present. That meeting raised the main concern that slum clearance would be difficult if the immigration continued, and there was a danger of large-scale unemployment among the immigrants in a recession. However, it was also agreed that 'the present level of coloured immigration raised problems which could not be ignored'.[76] The theory was advanced that a new United Kingdom citizenship, to replace the UK and Colonies one, was an option. Before the meeting Powell had circulated a letter sent to him by the Wolverhampton town clerk, R. J. Meddings, telling him that the immigrant population were making 'a disproportionate claim on the Health Services of the Town'.[77] Because of the poor home conditions in which many of the immigrants lived, 'their women folk . . . frequently receive priority for the allocation of hospital beds for confinements'.

On 11 April Powell wrote to Kilmuir, at the Lord Chancellor's invitation, 'to expand in writing what I then said about the legal change which seemed to me a precondition of measures to limit the right of entry of British subjects into the United Kingdom'. He argued – as he had done thirteen years earlier – that there was under the existing law in effect no distinction between citizens of the United Kingdom and Colonies, and British subjects. 'If therefore we desire to impose limitations or conditions on the entry of coloured British subjects into this country, it is not sufficient to do as the other independent countries have done in restricting the full privilege of citizenship to their own citizens. We should also need, within the "Citizenship of the United Kingdom and Colonies", to carve out a new "United Kingdom citizenship", and then attach the full privileges of citizenship to this.'[78] He argued for a United Kingdom citizenship and a Colonies citizenship, with distinct privileges. 'I do not see how any of the members of the Commonwealth – all of whom make the same distinction *mutatis mutandis* – would cast a stone.' Harking back to 1948, Powell rubbed it in by adding: 'Indeed, from the beginning the "Citizenship of the United Kingdom and Colonies" was an artificial and rather absurd entity, being merely a residuum left in the course of transition from subjecthood based on allegiance to citizenship based on statute. The recognition of a United Kingdom citizenship is a natural further development.'

At the second meeting of the committee, on 17 May, new urgency was added to the deliberations. Butler reported that the immigration figures for the first four months of 1961 were much higher than for the same period in 1960: he projected an out-turn of 150,000–200,000, compared with 58,000 in 1960. 'It was now accepted', Butler is reported as saying, 'by Government supporters generally that some form of control was unavoidable if we were not to have a colour problem in this country on a similar scale to that in the USA.'[79]

Powell was not present – he was represented by Edith Pitt – at the last meeting of the committee in October 1961, at which the draft Bill that would be the 1962 Act was considered. As a memorandum circulated before the meeting said, 'The broad effect ... is to enable an Immigration Officer to refuse admission to any Commonwealth citizen not belonging to the United Kingdom or to admit him subject to conditions.'[80] It claimed, too, that British subjects without citizenship – such as Asians in Africa and Pakistanis in India – would be controlled, but that was to prove not the case in practice. The Bill stated that to secure entry a person had either to be born in the United Kingdom or to have a passport issued by the United Kingdom Government – a passport from elsewhere in the Commonwealth would not do. The loophole left open was that British high commissioners could, and would, issue such passports in the future.

That summer, events were taking place elsewhere in the Government that would resonate in the party for the next twenty years and lead to Powell's own estrangement from his colleagues in the field of economic policy. The country was running a massive balance of payments deficit, widely interpreted as a function of excessive demand. On 24 July the cabinet had a lengthy discussion about the economic situation, to which Powell, as one of the main spending ministers, was invited. Much of the discussion was about the balance of payments crisis, which Powell, if his later response in similar circumstances is any guide, would deny existed. There was not then any detailed discussion of an incomes policy. Selwyn Lloyd, the Chancellor of the Exchequer, made a statement the next day that contained within it the germ of two ideas aimed at reducing demand by keeping pay under control. The first was the formation of what would become, the following winter, the National Economic Development Council, where both workers and management could talk about targets for the economy with Government ministers; and Lloyd also called for a 'pause' in pay settlements while productivity caught up with existing levels of pay.

For the moment, Powell did not feel strongly enough about this form of interventionism to raise objections from his post outside the cabinet. On 3 August the cabinet considered the pay pause specifically, and Powell was called in for that item only. The cabinet agreed the public sector would have to give a lead, a policy Powell would have to enforce with his staff in the NHS. The minutes of the 3 August meeting do not record his raising any objection to a policy he would subsequently, after the experience, come to dismiss as 'dangerous nonsense'.[81] The next day the cabinet met again for a meeting that discussed nothing else; again, there is no minuted objection by Powell.[82] There is incontrovertible evidence, from Powell's grasp of monetarist principles in 1957–8, that he understood well that pay rises did not cause inflation. Yet he kept his own counsel – although, to be fair to him, protocol carefully circumscribed what a non-cabinet member could say when invited to attend cabinet deliberations. Also, he saw that by keeping down pay awards in the public sector – and no minister would interpret the policy more rigidly – he was fulfilling his aim of not contributing to growth in the money supply, as parsimony would help restrict that growth.

This was not the only economic matter with which Powell concerned himself at this time. In August 1961 Lloyd had written to all ministers seeking views on the recommendations of the Plowden Committee on public spending, which were that targets should be set for years ahead to include growth. Almost all the ministers, confronted by this technical detail, wrote back to say they had no special comments to make. Powell, however, did. He sent Lloyd a lengthy letter on 16 September detailing his objections. 'I believe', he told Lloyd, 'that the central recommendation of the Report (that public expenditure decisions be taken in the light of prospective total expenditure and resources over a period of years) is destructive of Treasury control and will strongly tend to the increase of public expenditure and to inflation.'[83] He said that for political reasons there would always be a tendency to overestimate both resources and expenditure, 'given the current preoccupation of politicians and the public with "growth"'. Low estimates risked taunts from the Opposition, and it was impossible accurately to predict demand for services in the future. Additionally, forecasts were made 'in real terms', which allowed for 'a built-in inflationary mechanism'. He concluded that 'the Plowden exercise, as a public policy, is an exercise in escapism. There is only one key to the control of expenditure. That is for the Government to wish it, and to wish it more than they wish anything inconsistent with it.'

Appropriately, as he ended by using the language of December 1957, Powell found himself answered by his old adversary from those days, Sir Thomas Padmore – to whom a discomfited Lloyd turned for an answer to Powell's tirade. Padmore said that 'this is a case in which I would recommend the Chancellor to send Mr Powell a note coming from us instead of writing a long and complicated letter himself'.[84] Padmore said that all Powell's points had, of course, been taken on board when the policy was developed – 'I would have hoped that he would have given us credit for a little more commonsense.' He agreed that Powell's conclusion about the need for Government to wish control was 'true enough', and asserted that this was unlikely to happen. Padmore said Plowden had felt that 'the forces of public opinion which formerly kept public expenditure under control are no longer able to do so ... In my own view, Mr Enoch Powell has allowed his sense of realism to desert him.' The defeatist mentality Powell had fought against four years earlier was more entrenched than ever.

By the time Powell had his regular meeting with the regional chairmen on 19 September 1961, he was sufficiently optimistic about the Hospital Plan to hope it might be mentioned in the Queen's Speech, though the date for publishing the White Paper had slipped back to early 1962. A draft of the plan was sent to chairmen in early November, and discussed at a meeting with Powell on the 21st of that month. Throughout the autumn, he was greatly concerned to maintain secrecy: not for fear of compromising his own good publicity, but because some hospitals would have to be closed as a result of the planned concentration of services on district general hospitals. He was keen to forestall the threat of industrial unrest.

It was Powell's grasp of theory and principles, rather than practice, that most impressed the party. He was invited to give the Conservative Political Centre address that autumn at the party conference at Brighton, in succession to Butler, Hailsham, Macmillan, Macleod and Salisbury. His scope for ideological pronouncements was constrained by his job, to an extent, but this did not stop him observing, in a speech at Oxford on 30 September 1961, that 'one often finds that those who profess least confidence in any particular government have the most unbounded faith in the possibilities of government action in general'.[85] In this speech he prefigured the doctrines he would spend the mid-1960s spelling out, of the effect of individual free will in negating attempts by the state to regulate public behaviour. 'The level of demand for labour, the fluctuations of trade and economic activity are attributed not only to governmental policies generally, but to specific acts and omissions of government inside each country, though all the evidence shouts out that deeper forces are at work.' His conclusion was clear: 'Delusions of grandeur about the Government's role as regulator of the economy may easily obscure its duty, and obstruct the fulfilment of it, to preserve the honesty and validity of the nation's money.'[86]

At the party conference Powell made a routine speech, praising the work done by health authorities and in hospitals, and previewing the ten-year Hospital Plan, the most puritanical of spenders highlighting that the total capital outlay on building in 1958–9 had been £6 million, but next year it was expected to be £22 million. His Conservative Political Centre lecture was on 'The Welfare State'. He started from a statement in the Plowden report on public spending, which had suggested that because of the social changes since the foundation of the welfare state fifteen years earlier there was likely to be an excess of help to certain people and insufficient to others. He felt it was the changes not of the preceding fifteen years, but of the preceding thirty, that Plowden should have taken into account, for it was the world of the depression that the Beveridge report, on which the welfare state was based, took as its starting point.

He was under no illusion about the difficulty of removing benefits from those who did not need them: 'In politics it is more blessed not to take than to give.'[87] He added that 'the termination of a benefit or a payment or a service is a sharp, specific assault upon identifiable individuals; it gives political opponents something solid to talk about; they can actually produce the bodies and point to the wounds.' Those for whom a benefit had not been introduced were harder to identify, and to identify with. Above all, the resentment of losers outweighs the gratitude of winners: 'The beneficiaries thus regard themselves as having received no more than their due, to which they were entitled anyhow, while those whose benefits are discontinued regard themselves as cheated of what they had a right to and had been encouraged to expect.'[88] These eternal truths would haunt Powell's successors, of both parties, for years ahead.

That was not, he argued, all of the problem. Social services became quickly institutionalised. He gave, at length, the example of housing subsidies – a social service which, he claimed, happened by accident – and how difficult they had been to undo, even after forty years. He called for the reform of other social service institutions – such as state pensions, which he hoped would be replaced by private provision, though he realised the unlikelihood of that happening soon. He drew attention to the growing numbers of elderly, and hoped society would harness a new sense of purpose to caring for them. His conclusion was that the question for his party 'is whether, having seen this, we put the file into the "Too Difficult" tray and "pass by on the other side". I can see the expediency of that course. . . . however, I confess that I do not believe a party, any more than the society which it serves, can fail to suffer if it knowingly allows institutions to fall more and more out of correspondence with contemporary needs.'[89] If, he said, Plowden was right in theory – a mischievous assertion, since he believed he was not – that theory had to be given recognition in practice.

Powell was concentrating heavily on reflecting social change by what he was doing to the National Health Service. In January 1962, after an autumn of intense thought and analysis of the submission sent to him by the health authorities, he finally released a White Paper confirming details of the Hospital Plan, with the closure by 1975 of up to 1,250 smaller or specialist hospitals. These would be matched by the promise – still costed at £500 million – to build ninety new general hospitals, remodel 134 more and have a further 356 improvement schemes each costing more than £100,000.[90] He and Fraser had not succeeded in getting a guarantee of money for the duration of the plan, but had secured a guarantee of capital spending in each financial year – something that had more often than not been absent from the NHS.

Part of the plan, too, was a scheme to boost the status and role of general practitioners, allowing more of them to work in the new district general hospitals part-time and allocating them maternity beds there for their patients. The White Paper also pursued other of Powell's main interests as minister – the modernisation of the infrastructure, better food and more consideration for patients. A special booklet about food was sent out during February, ordering that a choice of menus be made available and the 'take it or leave it' attitude of the health service hitherto be scrapped. In the leaflet Powell made the charge that many hospital kitchens were unhygienic.

'Humanisation is a vital part of the programme and must march hand in hand with modernisation,' he said in an interview at the time of the White Paper. 'I think we have made progress in the past 12 months – and we certainly do not intend to stop at this point. There has been a great change in the attitude of hospitals to patients and I can see nothing but good coming out of this.'[91] The plan was regarded as a success by Powell's senior colleagues, and did much to boost his standing in the Government. It also received a warm endorsement from backbenchers, who congratulated him formally when he attended the Health Committee on 25 January. It would, in retrospect, be the crowning achievement of his ministerial career.

Hoping to complement the modernisation plans, Powell made new calls for the voluntary sector to mobilise itself in support of the health service, whether in hospitals or in the community. Further economies would also have to be found from current spending; and Powell attended cabinet on 13 December 1961 to ask, once more, that consideration be given to reducing the subsidy on welfare milk.[92] He found the cabinet more willing to agree now that many were receiving this expensive subsidy who had no need of it. If, as he had urged before, the subsidy could be targeted on families with four or more children, £20 million of the £26 million total cost would be saved. Even if it were targeted on families with three children or more, as Boyd-Carpenter had argued, the saving would still be £14 million. For good measure, Powell also asked for the price of school meals to be increased from 1s to 1s 6d. The cabinet asked him to go away and take further advice; and to come back after Christmas and let them know whether there really was no other way round this.

Powell presented his proposals again on 8 January 1962, at the second of two cabinet meetings held that day. In the morning, as a result of the large workforce for which he was responsible, he had been present at a discussion of the incomes policy, and had heard Macmillan utter sentiments that, within a couple of years, Powell would repudiate unequivocally. Macmillan said the 'main objective ... was to secure the co-operation of the TUC in long-term planning directed towards economic growth'.[93] It was such beliefs that would make it so hard for the Conservatives, once in opposition, to take on the Wilson Government effectively. It was Powell alone who was prepared to ignore the decisions to which, at this stage only in a minor way, he had been implicit, and to propound the truths as they had seemed to him after a revelation.

At the second meeting that day, Powell reported back on welfare milk. He said he had consulted a departmental advisory committee of doctors and nutritionists about the effects of limiting the subsidy. The committee had told him it would back restricting the subsidy to families of four or more children provided it was still given to families of just three children if all those children were under five. On this basis, Powell said, the policy could be defended nutritionally. The cabinet, though, was still reluctant to proceed, and no decision was reached that day. Finally, on 15 February, it agreed that the money for the subsidy could be 'better used', and considered announcing its removal during the summer.[94]

On 26 February 1962 Powell made a party political broadcast on the wireless, stepping outside the confines of his portfolio. 'What matters most about Government expenditure', he said, 'is not the size of it in millions of pounds, but the rate it grows at compared with the rate our production grows. If the two keep in step, with production preferably in the lead, then in Mr Micawber's words "result happiness". We can do the things we want to do without this either causing inflation or calling for more taxation.'[95] This was his consistent economic doctrine; but there was one sentiment he would come to repudiate. Making the sound point that 'all of us will be losers if we try to increase our incomes faster than the nation increases its output', he said that was why 'last year the Government called a temporary halt to increases in incomes'. That month Lloyd had published a White Paper asserting the principle that wages should not rise by more than the 2 to 2.5 per cent rate by which productivity was rising. Powell was not yet ready to protest that such higher rates could be paid only if the Government continued expanding the money supply above the rate of increase in productivity.

His signing up, under collective responsibility, to the pay policy was one of the acts that would conflict most with his subsequent career. It would also, as soon as the policy was breached – as it soon would be – cause him direct political problems over his stringency with the nurses. The following month, addressing a group of manufacturers in the West Midlands, Powell returned to the inflationary theme, saying that inflation made a mockery of pay bargaining, particularly when those party to the bargain knew it would be financed by inflation. 'The annual round of wage and salary increases', he said, 'has become so established a feature of our way of life that we have almost lost the power to perceive what an extraordinary institution it is. So rooted has this idea of a vested right to an annual increase become that the increase is pressed for and insisted on even when those concerned realise that the increased money income will not, and cannot be, accompanied by correspondingly increased purchasing power.' The shortfall was, of course, made up by the money-manufacturing power of the state.

It is this that in reality carries – or earths – the responsibility for the bargains which are struck. The employers are relieved of responsibility for the effect of paying increased wages on the demand for their output, and the employees are relieved of responsibility for the effect of receiving increased wages upon the demand for their services, as long as both of them know that any excess of incomes over productivity will be balanced by the creation of additional money. Inflation knocks the reality and the economic meaning out of collective bargaining.[96]

That spring an interruption to the purely political side of Powell's job – or so it seemed – came in the form of the first apparently conclusive scientific evidence that smoking was a direct cause of lung cancer. Powell had always found smoking disgusting; when he first arrived at the Ministry of Health, and occasionally found officials preparing to light up, he would issue a warning of his sternest disapproval. This objection was rooted in Powell's natural fastidiousness rather than in any empirical observation of the damage smoking could cause. He had also been alerted by Godber, on his arrival at the Ministry, that the Royal College of Physicians was investigating the effects of smoking, and would soon report, he suspected, that it was dangerous. On 6 March the cabinet authorised Powell to issue a statement about the effects of smoking, and there were discussions about the desirability of raising taxes on tobacco and restricting its advertising.[97]

Powell, always scrupulous in accepting his chief medical officer's clinical judgments, told Godber that, if tobacco were able legally to be sold, it would be illogical to make it illegal to advertise it – a purely political matter on which Godber disagreed, and which the next Government would act upon by abolishing the television advertising of cigarettes from 1965.[98] It was agreed that the cabinet would have to consider the matter further, and this delay helped stay the warning to the public, for at the cabinet's next meeting, two days later, Selwyn Lloyd warned that for the Government to issue so fierce a warning as was planned about smoking would inevitably prejudice the discussions it was about to have.[99] Lloyd's views were heeded, and the public were left incompletely informed by the Government about the nature of the threat.

As his fiftieth year drew to a close, Powell was now sufficiently eminent and successful to command the attentions of television interviewers. Malcolm Muggeridge, who put him under the spotlight on 9 March 1962, asked him about his ambitions. 'Ambition is the stuff of politics and it is what makes the clock tick,' Powell answered. Asked whether he would like to be Prime Minister, he said, 'Every politician would,' but added, 'I should think the chances are very heavily against it.'[100] He elaborated: 'There is no politician, from the beginning to the end, who in some remote cell in his mind, has not built up a picture of the day when he will be sent for and asked to form a Government as Prime Minister.'[101]

V

Five days after this interview, the ground began to shift under the Conservative party. In a by-election at Orpington in Kent, a 15,000 Conservative majority was turned into an 8,000 Liberal one. This phenomenon, commonplace in the 1980s and 1990s as an electorate became more sophisticated in the exercise of the protest vote, was startling then. It was not as if the party had put up a bad candidate; Peter Goldman, who had that honour, was one of the stars of the Research Department and just about the best the party could produce. He fought what was deemed to be a near faultless campaign. The blame was entirely the Government's. The full measure of its unpopularity, the implications for the future and the urgency of making wholesale changes were all brought home with a crash by the result.

The Opposition rapidly cashed in on the most vulnerable areas of Government policy, of which manifestly the NHS was one. On 27 March, shortly before the House rose for Easter, it had a debate on recruitment to the NHS that lasted until after seven o'clock the following morning. Powell was teased by Robinson for what the Labour spokesman construed as his attempt to 'alter his brand image' – the interview with Muggeridge, a difficult appearance on a special programme to cover the (as it turned out) disastrous by-election, and being photographed bouncing round Eaton Square on a pogo-stick as part of a campaign to improve public fitness (a photograph made the more magnificent by Powell's being clad in a black coat, striped trousers and the regulation Homburg, and with his equally impeccably dressed wife and daughters looking on). More seriously, Robinson had claimed that the shortage of doctors in the service in particular had brought staff morale 'to its lowest ebb', adding that 'resentment in the service at the Minister's conduct is intense'.[102]

Powell was on the front bench for most of the debate, but made his main speech just after seven in the evening. He claimed there had been a steady increase in the numbers of doctors both in hospitals and in general practice, and nor was this increase down to the numbers of overseas doctors – doctors who, it was feared, would train and gain experience here before returning to their countries of origin, leaving the NHS with gaping holes. Similarly, he said, the professions supplementary to medicine had expanded too, with only physiotherapy standing still – at which the veteran Labour MP Fenner Brockway intervened with the observation that Powell could not have expected the numbers to rise 'unless he increases the appalling rate of pay which they now receive'.[103] Powell's response was that more were now coming forward to train, and he expected the service would retain them. Finally, he said, there were more qualified nurses in the NHS than ever, with much better use of part-time nurses and midwives – so nurses who had left the service to start and bring up a family need not be lost to it. There were still not enough: accused by Bessie Braddock, a

Labour MP, of saying 'we are not short of nurses', Powell replied, with instinctive honesty, 'I have not said that we are not short of nurses.'[104] He felt the indication by the Government of its clear intentions for the future in the Hospital Plan would help recruitment.

Again, as Minister, Powell was speared on the ideological spike of the incomes policy. Taunted for having singled out the nurses for harsh treatment under this policy, he replied that 'the nurses and all the other sections in the National Health Service are not being called upon to take part in a policy which does not apply to the nation at large. They are only being asked to accept the same common sense of the incomes policy as the whole of the nation is being asked to accept.'[105] Soon, that 'common sense' would become 'dangerous nonsense'. For now, he was content to praise the Government's handling of the economy; in a speech a few days earlier at Birmingham he had made a plea for wage settlements to be kept low, but had added that, if they were not, 'an invisible third party' would provide the money for them – meaning the printing capacity of the Government, with its resultant inflation. He was, in the midst of his necessary support for the incomes policy, determined to reaffirm the principles of January 1958. However, he added, 'I know it is difficult. Do you imagine it was easy for me to limit the pay offer to the nurses to two-and-a-half per cent or to refuse an independent inquiry into the salaries of physiotherapists and others?'[106] He was also facing pressure from backbenchers to be more generous, and had had a difficult time at a meeting of the Health Committee the night before the debate. There had been some voices of support, however, and he was not prepared to be shaken.

A committee, again chaired by Macleod, was considering proposals for the next party manifesto, and Powell was invited to a session on 19 March. He hand-wrote a paper which he sent to Michael Fraser, the director of the Research Department, for circulation. It was highly political, and went outside the simple departmental remit. He said that 'the inherent dilemma' for the party was that 'the record of our past achievement and the pejorative comparison of socialist achievement and policies have become boring to the point of irrelevance'.[107] It was twelve years since anyone had had to vote on the socialist record; what were needed instead were 'the momentum and attraction of bold and new policies'. Yet he understood that the longer the Government remained in office, the harder it was to propound such policies. 'The question "why have you only just thought of this" grows increasingly embarrassing, and the practical admin-istrative problem of disengaging from policies in force becomes more and more intractable.'

Social service reform was especially difficult, he argued, for these reasons. He was pessimistic about NHS reform. While insisting he would do nothing to obstruct the growth of the private sector, he said it was 'impossible to imagine how this could be more than very limited'. There was little scope for change. At the election, the 'improvement, rather than the supersession' of the NHS would be the main electoral demand. He drew attention, for the longer term, to the inadequacy of old-age pensions and of care provision for the increasing numbers of elderly. The idea grew up out of this for a 'new Beveridge report'; but apart from discussions between Powell and Boyd-Carpenter about possible redistribution of responsibilities between their two ministries, so one minister would have sole responsibility for all questions facing the elderly, nothing came of it, symptomatic of the retrenching attitude of the time.

At the dinner meeting in the Commons on 19 March Powell, praised by Macleod for coming up with 'new policies', admitted that his paper was 'in some ways an essay in escapism' as he had nothing new to suggest in respect of his own Ministry. However, he stressed the electoral importance of a new policy for the elderly, now society was becoming more prosperous. He wanted a means-tested pension for the over-seventies, with the richer getting less and the poorer more. The committee were nervous of the means test, and of Powell's proposal for the wider availability of private pensions.[108] Powell rebuked Sir Keith Joseph, then a junior trade minister, for saying that pensions would cost more if pro-vided through the market.[109]

The dinner took place in the gloom after Orpington. Goldman, who was present, was greatly commiserated with. Interestingly, Powell made a rigid defence, at this private meeting, of the pay policy, the rough minutes stating him as saying: 'I am all for the Chancellor's policy. I have just antagonised all the nurses in the country, and all those who go to the physiotherapists, and all the doctors and civil servants throughout the country, and the universities.'[110] He added that 'having settled on this line we have got to stick to it ... until it is seen and proved to be right'. Just before the meeting adjourned he advised: 'I think we should be very slow in the constituencies where there is not a by-election pending to acknowledge that there is any opponent except a socialist. I never acknowledge by thought, word or deed that there is such a thing as a Liberal.'

Powell spent the spring of 1962 mainly in routine administration. Eventually, he secured cabinet approval for the first government circular about the dangers of smoking. It was put out jointly with Hailsham, the Minister of Education, who warned in cabinet that the Government should avoid at all costs any suggestion that it was adopting 'a paternalist attitude' to the problem.[111] Hail-sham also said there was no evidence about any danger from what would come to be called passive smoking, and the Government should say nothing on this subject.

Another difficulty for Powell was a public perception that there was a problem with doctors emigrating. He denied it existed even though 40 per cent of junior medical posts in hospitals were now being filled from overseas; and he denied, too, claims by Dr John Hunt, the secretary of the Royal College of General

Practitioners, that he had taken out private medical insurance. His most difficult problem was a pay claim by the nurses, to whom he had offered 2.5 per cent, in line with the Government's policy. Even that offer had been delayed, and the nurses were, in some cases, seeking rises of 49 per cent. When, on 12 April, Powell visited Napsbury Hospital in Hertfordshire, his car was surrounded by nurses brandishing placards, who banged on his windows. While trying to placate this feeling, Powell got on with other initiatives: finally announcing incentives for GPs to go on refresher courses, and to reward practices where list sizes were kept down by the formation of partnerships, thereby giving a better service to the patient. Also, continuing his themes of more voluntary service and the liberation of mentally ill patients from asylums, he sought volunteers to act as 'godmothers' to such patients in the community, escorting them to the shops or the cinema and helping them live normal lives. He also attacked the 'lie' of waiting lists, which he believed were statistically entirely inaccurate and included patients who were dead, already in hospital, recovered or no longer in need of treatment.

After Orpington backbenchers began to let it be known, both to the 1922 Committee executive and to the newspapers, that they felt a widespread reshuffle was necessary. In the last week of March Major John Morrison, the chairman of the 1922, had seen Macmillan to relay to him formally the feelings of the rank and file. Backbench feeling had it that four men in particular – Hailsham, Brooke, Joseph and Powell – should be promoted, and Powell was mentioned as a possible successor to Selwyn Lloyd if the Chancellor's political fortunes did not improve. However, Powell was having to sustain increasing heat from the nursing unions about pay, and a debate was scheduled in the Commons to discuss the matter. A wave of sympathy strikes for the nurses started, pre-empting the Commons debate on 14 May. At the cabinet meeting on 10 May Powell, who was invited to attend, was authorised to make a statement that the management side of the nurses and midwives Whitley Council – the profession's negotiating body for pay – would resume negotiations about a new pay struc-ture – an apparent sign of flexibility creeping in.[112]

Throughout 1962 Powell regularly attended the cabinet's Wages Committee, chaired by Lloyd, to discuss strategy for the pay claim being made by nurses and midwives. The main strategy – if so it can be termed – was that 'it would be undesirable to take up a firm position on nurses' pay at a time when Government policy on incomes for 1962 was still developing.'[113] On Sunday 13 May – the night before the debate – Macmillan convened a meeting of eight ministers, including Powell, to take into account what effect a dockers' pay settlement, announced the previous day and at 8 per cent well above the 2.5 per cent limit, would have. Powell said he would argue that, as recruitment to the nursing service was rising, 'there was no such situation as would justify him in agreeing to a breach in the Government's incomes policy'. Macmillan, deeply embarrassed by the unilateral action of the dock employers, stressed that there was little he could do in a democracy to command the employers in the docks not to pay a certain rate to their employees.[114]

Starting off for the Opposition in the debate, Robinson argued that, following a caving-in to the dockers on the pay policy there was now no excuse not to raise the offer to the nurses. In any case, he reminded the House that the nurses were not simply after a policy-busting pay rise, but after a whole restructuring of the pay scales of their profession. Powell himself knew the absurdity of the Government's position, and was not helped by the intervention in Robinson's speech by Hare, the Minister of Labour, who claimed that all he had done was to bring the two sides in the dock dispute together – the subsequent negotiations had been up to them. In trying to wash the Government's hands of the whole business, Hare had merely demonstrated the futility – of which Powell, privately, was well aware – of it trying to intervene in the private relations between an employer and his staff.

The only way Powell could cope with such an attack, and such a dilemma, was to make a speech of such stunning aridity that much of the heat was taken out of the debate. He could not, though, depart at all from the party line on the pay pause. 'The basic proposition of that policy cannot be challenged,' he said. 'It is that a rise in incomes which outstrips production has consequences from which all are bound to suffer, not least professions like that of the nurses themselves, which will always be at the tail of the rat race of inflation.'[115] As he said that the Government had to stick to that precept, he was assailed by cries of 'What about the dockers?' and he was forced into using the Government's let-out that the White Paper on Incomes Policy had said that 'only the clearest and strongest reasons could justify increases which are appreciably in excess of two to two-and-a-half per cent'. Wisely, he did not try to justify the inclusion of the dockers in that definition. It was a deeply uncomfortable moment for him.

As in the debate of 27 March, Powell did not deny that there were fewer nurses than would have been ideal, but he claimed that the statistics were not reliable in making a judgment. Now the Hospital Plan was in place, it would be possible to work out the exact needs in terms of numbers of nurses for the new, modernised service. He said the levels of recruitment in the NHS – which he had defended as encouraging – would not be used by him as an argument that the levels of pay were necessarily right, but he did use them to argue that no great exception could be made for NHS staff in the current pay policy. These were not sentiments that impressed the Opposition, and they also failed to excite Powell's own side in their new, post-Orpington depression.

Predictably, Powell remained under fierce attack from Labour; Gaitskell, speaking at Swindon on 19 May, claimed that 'we only manage our hospitals on the basis of a great deal of foreign labour. We cannot get the girls to go in, which is not surprising when you consider the wages and conditions. But in spite of this situation we have the Minister of Health simply saying "No, no, no." We used to think of Mr Molotov as the great negative, but I think Mr Powell is catching up.'[116] Even the Conservative press was urging him to find more for the nurses, who, in extreme cases, earned £6 a week. The *Daily Telegraph* argued that 'the Government must stop falling into the obvious trap of making the whole burden of its pay policy fall on its own relatively underpaid employees'.[117] According to his assistant private secretary, Bernard Harrison, Powell became angry at what he perceived to be the lack of support from colleagues on nurses' pay. Hailsham, who had said that the Government had to 'get off the hook' on the issue, particularly excited his wrath. 'We are *not on the hook* on nurses' pay!' a livid Powell told a meeting of officials.[118]

Later, at the Oxford Union to debate a motion about the Liberal party, Powell was rebuked by the undergraduates for his stance. The house, by an overwhelming majority, adjourned temporarily before the main debate in support of the nurses. The Government's policy was one that Powell, in direct contradiction to his subsequent behaviour, found himself forced to grin and bear. At cabinet on 28 May, which he attended, he found himself hearing Macmillan utter the virtually socialist mantra that 'no policy on wages would command the support of the trades unions unless the Government had pledged themselves to take action to keep profits down to an acceptable level'.[119] This was one stage in his life when Powell made a calculation to keep quiet and not, for once, to resign. He was as aware as everyone that Macmillan would soon be forced to reconstruct the Government, and that he stood to become a beneficiary – and would, at last, have the authority and the influence to try to remake Conservative policy in a way he found ideologically acceptable.

Powell relished the challenge of his job. 'I was a lucky man to come to the Ministry of Health at a critical time – when there was room for big thinking and long vistas,' he told an interviewer from the *Daily Mail* in late May.[120] He added that it was the job of a minister 'to lean against the wind. He is there to see things are done differently. Otherwise he is nobody.' He somewhat surprised his interviewer by telling him that, even in the midst of all this pressure, he was still working away at his history of the Lords. He also had a big Commons debate to prepare for, when the House at last discussed the Hospital Plan on 4 June.

He found himself, in winding up the debate, having first to defend not his own record, but the record of the Government's stewardship of the NHS – it had, after all, been in power for eleven of the fourteen years of the service's history. In that time, Powell said, the equivalent of fifty new district general hospitals had been added. For the future, the British Medical Association had claimed that £750 million was needed to modernise the service; Powell said that the plan in fact earmarked £800 million for the task. He promised there would be further investment beyond that, as the plan would be reviewed and carried forward year by year, always planning ten years ahead. He reassured those who worried that parts of the plan would fall behind schedule that it would be policed from the centre, and quick remedial action would be taken. Standardisation of new fittings and equipment would take place, enabling both time and money to be saved.

From Powell's personal point of view, the most important feature in the plan was the provision for community care. A quarter of the plan was devoted to the subject, and he had asked separately for all local health authorities to prepare their own ten-year community care plans. It would, he hoped, be the mechanism that put into practice the promise he had made to close the asylums, a plan professionals had told him would be impossible to implement because of the fiction of community care. Powell would not be deflected. 'The principle upon which we approach this', he said, 'is that the prevention of illness and the care of illness should take place in the community, except where the specialised services of the hospital are necessary.'[121] He hoped that within the context of a ten-year plan proper provision could be made for the aged and the mentally ill outside institutions. These two main plans would, in time, be complemented by a third, on the general practitioner services. The result of the first of those plans, he affirmed, would be 'an environment which will challenge comparison with that available anywhere in the world'.

Later in June Powell undertook what was supposed to be a five-day hospitals tour, and met protests wherever he went. After a particularly noisy one in Sheffield he cut the tour short by a day, missing out hospitals in Nottingham and Leicester. However, it turned out that this truncation had been caused by his summons to a cabinet meeting at Admiralty House (where Macmillan was staying during a refurbishment of Downing Street), and not out of despair. At a hospital in Derby he had to get in through a back door, and found when arriving at Lincoln the next day that protesters had all entrances to the hospital covered. As he tried to leave Lincoln a protester drove a van in front of his car, which was forced to brake sharply, and was then surrounded by nurses with placards. Powell made no comment to the press following him, and at Sheffield declined to meet a delegation of fifty nurses who demanded to see him. 'I refuse to comment on nurses' pay,' he said. 'I think my tour has been well received.'[122]

The cabinet Powell was asked to attend featured yet another surreal discussion of the effects of the incomes policy, and showed Macmillan out of his depth in dealing with economic theory. Virtually none of his colleagues, as the minutes record, was any better equipped to understand why the policy was failing, and it was becoming apparent that the old men of the cabinet would soon be under threat as Macmillan tried the time-honoured remedy to give a Government in decline a sense of refreshment. At the 22 June meeting he told ministers that 'only a successful incomes policy' could stop reflation being inflationary.[123] However, the minutes also reveal one who has learned nothing since January

1958: 'He [Macmillan] considered that too much had been made of the dangers of inflation; the real danger not merely to the United Kingdom, but to the Western position as a whole, lay in the opposite direction.' If the seeds of the debacle of 1970–4 had been sown in early 1958, they were now properly germinating.

VI

On Friday 13 July Macmillan carried out his cabinet purge, an event known as the Night of the Long Knives. The intellectual state reached by the cabinet at its meeting the previous day was symbolised by the fact that there was serious discussion about setting up a Royal Commission on Incomes, a move so interventionist that even the next Labour Government did not do it. In 1980, reviewing a book on Macmillan, Powell recalled this scene, and especially the Prime Minister's fondness for reading out to the cabinet his own neo-socialist thoughts on this and other policies redolent of 'the middle way', the measures being seen as a 'quid pro quo to the workers for co-operation in an inflation-free planned economy. I still relish recalling how the heads which were to roll not long after nodded like cuckoo clocks in sycophantic approval.'[124] The key to the reshuffle, as Macmillan saw it, was that Lloyd would have to go, principally for his refusal to contemplate an inflationary pre-election boom of the sort he felt necessary to redress the effect of Orpington.

Macmillan, who was ripe for panic anyway, was bounced into the reshuffle by an indiscretion of Butler's. He had had lunch with executives of the *Daily Mail* on 11 July, with the result that Lloyd's fate was spread across the front page the following morning. Macmillan sacked Lloyd that evening. Hearing that Hare was threatening to resign out of disgust at the treatment of Lloyd, Macmillan's panic reached gale force: he dealt with the rest of the appointments the following morning at a ferocious rate. Seven ministers went – a third of the cabinet. Powell remained Minister of Health, but was made a cabinet minister, the word relayed to him by his private secretary while he attended a coffee-morning in Wolverhampton. 'The mood was rather like Henry VIII's Privy Council reassembling after several of their number had been beheaded,' Powell recalled. He could not erase from his mind the image of an axe by the side of Macmillan's chair.[125]

It was good for the Ministry of Health, as well as for Powell, that the minister now had cabinet rank. As well as sending him a formal note of congratulation on behalf of the Ministry, Sir Bruce Fraser wrote privately to 'Dear Enoch' to say 'how very warmly Audrey and I congratulate both of you. Whatever the office, the rank of cabinet membership is so very obviously your due that pleasure is entirely unmingled with surprise ... the cabinet will be powerfully reinforced by the special qualities of mind and character which are your distinctive contribution to public life.'[126] Tony Benn wrote of how 'Caroline and I were absolutely delighted to hear of your promotion into the cabinet. After all of the ups and downs of the last few years you are at last where you should have been a long time ago.' Ted Heath wrote to 'my dear Enoch' to say 'Welcome – and many congratulations.'[127] His assistant private secretary, Bernard Harrison, recalls Powell's being most amused by a letter from an ordinary Black Countryman, Herbert Peplow, written in dialect to 'Dere Aynuck'.[128] Powell replied, in his own hand: 'Dere 'Erbert, Yo am decent ter write. Ah day know as 'ow the cabinet am much moer than cabinet rank (wot ah 'ad befoer). There ay moer pay! Yoers truly, Aynuck.'[129]

The reshuffle was badly received on the backbenches, notably the execution of Lloyd, who was popular; when he took his seat in the chamber for the first time after his sacking, he was loudly cheered. On the night of his sacking the Powells were at a dinner with Eden – now Lord Avon – at Birmingham University, of which he was Chancellor, and Avon, who did not know about Lloyd, was 'shattered' when Powell told him.[130] The act of panic was one from which Macmillan's reputation would never recover – his premiership was now doomed. However, the traditionally loyal press was largely approving. The *Daily Telegraph* said that 'Mr Macmillan may be seen to have rendered his greatest service to the Conservative party: to have made it clear that there is room for brains at the top.'[131] Other newspapers seized on Macmillan's panic and had sport with what they, remarkably accurately, regarded as the beginning of the end for a weak and vacillating government. The minutes of the cabinet meeting immediately after the purge show, too, a masterpiece of Butler's command of ambiguity. After Macmillan's opening remarks, the First Secretary of State (as Butler had become) observed that, 'despite the misrepresentations in the press, the new cabinet fully understood the purposes for which the Prime Minister had reconstructed the Government'. Rubbing more salt in, he added that Macmillan could 'be assured of their full support in the difficulties which lay ahead'.[132]

In a typically courteous and considerate action after his own promotion, Powell wrote to Lloyd, and in doing so gave a further indication of his sympathies with the pay policy. After thanking Lloyd for his help over the preceding two years – without which, Powell said, the long-term planning of the NHS would not have been possible – he added, 'How warmly I have agreed with your wages and expenditure policies, and tried to further them in my own department, I think you know. All this cannot go for nothing.'[133] The point Powell was making, of course, was not one in support of an incomes policy, but in support of the restraint of public spending which, when applied to the public sector, the incomes policy achieved. He had sympathies to extend closer to home, too. Macmillan had wanted to replace Edith Pitt with someone younger – Miss Pitt was twelve years the Prime Minister's junior – and sacked her without consulting

Powell. Powell, angry not just at this slight but also at the insult to a colleague whose hard work and dedication had done nothing to merit her sacking, was at least allowed to influence the choice of her successor. He and Martin Redmayne, the Chief Whip, agreed on Bernard Braine, an admirer of Powell's, and one with whom Powell worked happily for the remainder of his time in office. Miss Pitt, who broke down in tears when told of her dismissal, wrote to Powell to praise his 'kindness and understanding', and to say that 'when you came to the Ministry of Health you said you intended I should be happy in working with you. It has been so – completely.'[134]

Powell made his debut at the dispatch box as a cabinet minister on 20 July, moving new NHS superannuation regulations. Robinson congratulated him on his elevation, noting with irony that Powell would be able 'to argue on more equal terms with the Chancellor of the Exchequer for an even greater share of our national resources to be devoted to the NHS'.[135] Powell replied that he had 'the hope – though it is none of my business – that this may perhaps have made him a shadow cabinet minister'.[136] He soon started to take mild pot-shots at the incomes policy. When the cabinet was reminded on 24 July of the limits by which pay in the public sector could increase, Powell curtly reminded his colleagues of the existence of the entrenched structure of review bodies: the professions governed by these bodies expected them to act independently, and not in accordance with what the Government wanted. Now Powell had a pre-scribed seat at the cabinet table, Macmillan, opposite whom he sat, became discomfited by the gaze of the man he still regarded as a 'fanatic'. He told his official biographer, Alistair Horne, that he had the cabinet secretary move Powell's place around the table because 'I can't bear those mad eyes staring at me a moment longer.'[137] Macmillan also said that 'Powell looks at me in cabinet like Savonarola eyeing one of the more disreputable popes.'[138]

In the preceding year or two the casualties of the Thalidomide drug – pre-scribed to some women as a sedative to counter morning sickness – had become painfully apparent, with the birth to some of them of terribly deformed babies. The matter was raised with Powell in the House for the first time at Questions on 23 July. 'I am not anxious to draw a veil over any aspect of this matter,' he protested.[139] He said there had been no clinical trials on any other sedatives being prescribed to pregnant women, as he had been assured by his expert advisers that the taking of no other sedative had resulted in the birth of afflicted children. He was being pressed by a Conservative backbencher, Sir Hugh Linstead, to say whether better testing in the past could have prevented the unhappy experience. Powell told him that 'it is always impossible to answer on "might have been" with complete certainty, but I think it right to say that there is no machinery which could guarantee to detect in advance all the long term side-effects of a drug'.[140]

Powell's entry to the cabinet gave him an involvement in party and Govern-

ment policy outside his own brief of the sort he had craved for years. It also
sealed the good relationship he had developed with Fraser, for they now had
'real meat to chew on together', as Powell's assistant private secretary put it.[141]
The big issue that immediately confronted the cabinet was the negotiation to
enter the Common Market, which had been entrusted to Edward Heath. Powell
had abstained on the Schuman Plan twelve years earlier; now, under collective
responsibility, he fully subscribed to the notion of negotiating with a view to
securing entry. The discussion at cabinet level is not minuted as having been
focused at all on the question that would obsess Powell a decade later – sovereignty. It was all about maintaining prices, and about the effect on trade with
the Commonwealth. Powell is not minuted as having argued against the cabinet
line either on the principle of continuing negotiations despite disadvantages to
the Commonwealth (discussed on 31 July 1962) or on the general level of farm
prices (discussed on 22 August).[142] 'I didn't raise dissent,' he said later, 'because
at that stage it was presented as a free-trade exercise.'[143] Those are certainly the
terms contained in the minutes of the discussions. Nonetheless, his acquiescence
would be held against him bitterly when the battle was fought to a finish in
1971–2.

Shortly afterwards, Powell took his family to Spain for a holiday, having first
ensured that they had all had an anti-typhoid injection – there was a campaign
under way to educate travellers to Europe about the dangers of the disease.[144]
Soon after his return to England, he embarked on the execution of one of the
main promises in his programme: better care for the elderly. Opening a new
residential home in Worcestershire on 13 September, he said that the old surviving workhouse accommodation for the elderly was 'a blot, and an inadequacy,
and they must go'.[145] The cost would, he said, be £60 million, and there was a
growing ageing population to be housed in the future in proper conditions.
'The paramount need of the old, almost to the very last, is for a home; a home
which gives privacy, comfort and dignity, but also, as infirmity increases, a home
in which there is increasing support and care to meet that infirmity and make
it tolerable.' The new regulations also gave local authorities the power to inspect,
and enforce standards in, privately run establishments. This departure was,
two months later, criticised by the Commons Select Committee on Statutory
Instruments, on the ground that it thought the regulations appeared to make
unexpected use of powers conferred by the Acts under which they were made.

Powell's talents were put to wider use in December 1962, when he defended
Government plans for the creation of a council for Greater London. The *Daily
Telegraph*'s sketch writer said he had 'transformed or even reversed the whole
debate with a blistering counter-attack'. He continued: 'Mr Powell has none of
[the] superficial attributes of a great speaker. He appears grim and humourless,
his voice flat, dull and Midland. Even his logic, though impeccable, can seem at
times petty, almost mean. What lifts him out of the rut is his courage, his

combative spirit, his appetite for victory, his blazing conviction that what he says is both relevant and right.'[146] He began by countering George Brown's surprise that he should be chosen to wind up the debate for the Government, saying that, 'as Minister of Health, I am happy and proud to wind up this debate and to commend the Bill to the House because I know that in the whole range of the Health Services there is no more important element, no element which is changing and developing more rapidly, than the health and welfare services of the local authorities which are part of that growing body of what are known as the community services'. No other services, he added, 'stand to gain more than these from the reorganisation of the government of Greater London which is enshrined in this Bill'.[147]

He asserted – and it was an assertion discounted by a Conservative government less than a quarter of a century later, when it abolished the Greater London Council – that to extend the benefits of co-ordinated metropolitan government to the whole of inner and outer London was unquestionably sensible. New, larger boroughs – which the reorganisation of 1986 retained, while removing the umbrella council that superintended them – would be created of a size ideal to discharge important educational and welfare functions, and would develop services more rapidly and deliver them more efficiently than was the existing case. Health, children's and family services could be brought under the same control as education, which, Powell argued, was manifestly right. He attacked Labour for opposing the proposals, claiming they were backward-looking to want to retain the old borough system, in which they had a large political investment. That system was, though, designed for the needs of 1889; the Royal Commission on the future government of the capital had unanimously reported that the old London County Council was simply too small to discharge all its necessary functions effectively. When the time for debate about the abolition of the GLC came in the mid-1980s, it was Labour that repeated the points which, in 1962, Powell made against them as he concluded his speech: 'The continuous built-up area, inhabited by 8 million people, calls for a single administration of the strategic and planning services ... within this Greater London there is the potentiality and the opportunity for unified administration of all the personal services by authorities which can bring the pressures of local opinion, local ambitions and local vision to bear upon the development of local services.' He ended with a stunning anachronism, given his unromantic post-imperial view: 'I ask the House not to deny these benefits to the capital city of the Empire.'[148] Roth reports George Brown answering cries of 'What Empire?' from his colleagues with the retort: 'Maybe he means the Holborn Empire.'[149] Despite this strange end, the speech demonstrated the ease with which Powell could command a brief alien to him, and the range of his political intelligence: it is the most tantalising sight of what might have been had he ever discharged any other cabinet office.

In January 1963 the negotiations to join the Common Market threatened
to break down because of de Gaulle's threat to exercise a veto over British
membership. At a meeting on 22 January the cabinet considered how Britain
would react if the veto were exercised; in the discussion of the contingencies,
Powell is again minuted as having said nothing.[150] He was similarly reticent two
days later when the cabinet discussed reform of the House of Lords, an issue
upon which, like his abstention on the Schuman Plan, he had already expressed
strong views, the month after his resignation from the Treasury in 1958.[151] It was
also an issue on which he would express the most violent opposition to the
party line once freed from collective restraint.

As well as continuing his intellectual life by working on his history of the
House of Lords, he gave readers of *The Times*, in March 1963, a clue to other
cerebral recreations, in a contribution to a series entitled 'Critics Under Review'.
He wrote that 'I am a devotee of reviews. I like reading them; I like writing
them – signed or unsigned.' He admitted that he experienced a 'little instant of
happy surprise when the early morning mind discovers that it is Thursday', the
day *The Times* published its book reviews.[152] 'Every single review – even the
reviews of the novels, though I never read novels themselves – will have been
read before I so much as peep to see if the *Times* has reported my winding-up
speech on the middle page or dismissed my policies with paragraphs of por-
tentous ambivalence in a third leader.' Powell wrote that he enjoyed witnessing
the meeting of minds between reviewer and author, and the collection of
'effortless gobbets of information'.

For him, the newspapers only skimmed the surface of the intellectual possibilities of the review. The specialist journal was far superior in this respect, and
he noted with longing that 'something departed for ever from the pleasures of
specialist review reading when A. E. Housman gibbeted his last victim'. He
confessed that his reason for liking writing reviews was 'terribly crude. I like to
be given books.' He could not understand those reviewers who sold their books
once the reviews were done. To him, 'almost any book, however remote its
subject, seems to me worth shelf-room'. Most revealingly, he claimed to like
reviewing because it gave him an excuse to read; at bottom, he liked the challenge
with which reviewing presented him. 'The knowledge that one has to write a
review fixes the salient points of a book upon the mind, like the landmarks
along a route by which the traveller must return.' Another opportunity to display
his intellectual leanings came when he had to follow the tradition of new
ministers in the cabinet by contributing a book to the Cabinet Room library
in Downing Street. Keith Joseph, for example, gave a copy of Karl Popper's
The Open Society and its Enemies; Powell gave *Dancer's End* and *The Wedding
Gift*.

Some of the heat went out of the NHS debate in the spring of 1963, partly
for financial reasons. The funding for the hospital service was set to rise from

just under £427 million to just over £451 million. Powell was able to write on 8 March to the Royal College of Nursing, pledging that 'in the new financial year about to begin regional boards will have additional spending power which will enable them to continue to increase nursing staffs where necessary'.[153] The hiatus in militancy allowed him to concentrate more on preventive medicine, particularly in capitalising upon the mounting evidence that smoking caused lung cancer. He launched a film for schoolchildren on the theme in early April, after releasing the statistic that 23,383 people had died of lung cancer in 1962, a rise of 1,095 on 1961. However, the Poster Advertising Censorship Committee, the regulatory body governing that type of advertising, forbade Powell to launch a campaign on billboards that would have carried the slogan 'Cigarettes cause lung cancer', on the ground that the case – to the delight of the tobacco industry – was not proven. Powell was also, at this time, trying to promote the fluoridation of water supplies, and railed against the 'cranks who are trying to hold up fluoridation by scaremongering and mis-representation'.[154] He had assured his cabinet colleagues at the end of 1962 that the treatment was perfectly harmless.[155]

On 17 April he published the latest projections for the Hospital Plan, detailing capital spending of £220 million over the next ten years, and based on sub-missions from health authorities. The plans included a projected staffing increase of 45 per cent by 1972, principally to service the planned growth in community care. The elderly, the mentally disturbed and mothers with young children – three groups in which Powell had taken a specific interest – would be the principal beneficiaries of the spending. He announced 63,000 new places in old people's homes by 1972, with seventy-five new homes for the elderly planned in London alone. He also asked health authorities to review urgently their casualty provision, with a view to replacing casualty departments with twenty-four-hour accident and emergency units.

Yet for all this planning for the 1970s – a specific theme of a special cabinet summit held at Chequers on Sunday 28 April in an attempt to reinvigorate the party – Powell appeared dismissive of the concept. He accepted it in the health service as a matter of almost military necessity; he could not see it was needed anywhere impinging upon the private sector. He had found much of the meeting (the idea of Martin Redmayne, the Chief Whip) distasteful because of the enthusiasm many of his colleagues showed for the adoption of neo-socialist policies and their lack of enthusiasm for the free economy. The discussions were, in any case, somewhat superficial, as the Conservative Research Department's secret record of the proceedings shows. An hour and a half before lunch was spent discussing industrial and economic questions; an hour and twenty-five minutes afterwards was spent on social questions; and the last hour and three-quarters, after tea, was devoted to Government reorganisation.

In the first session, chaired by Maudling, Powell did not participate in the discussion. Its platitudinous nature is apparent from the report: 'There was a great desire in the country to see Britain strong.'[156] Some round the table urged that the state should take a more active role in the 'mixed economy', providing funds for research and long-term investment, and to encourage sectors deemed 'lagging'. 'The profit motive was not always enough,' it was agreed.[157] 'To the public,' the report continues, 'an active planning policy of this kind could be made to appear very sensible . . . there was in fact a long tradition of Conservative thought that we should, when necessary, use the power of the State to shape the economy.'[158] No wonder Powell bit his lip in the face of such consensus. The alternative arguments were made too. It was agreed, after some debate, that private enterprise was a good thing. There was no attempt to reconcile this with the apparently more enthusiastic support for the opposite view. The conclusion drawn was that 'partnership' between the state and the private sector was possible.

After lunch, Powell opened the discussion on social issues. He outlined how the party's policies for the social services could adapt to modern times and provide a means of helping people out of poverty and hardship rather than trapping them in those conditions. He emphasised the 'bogus' nature of the National Insurance scheme, an actuarial problem he had been expounding for more than ten years, but faced pragmatic objections from colleagues that 'the present position was difficult to reverse without upsetting people's expectations and the belief that pensions should at least keep pace with the cost of living'.[159] When the discussion moved on to housing, Powell was unable to persuade colleagues to have remaining rent controls removed; 'creeping' decontrol was all they would settle for. On his own health service, Powell was categorical: 'There was no practicable alternative to the present structure of socialised medicine, though private arrangements like BUPA had a useful subsidiary role.'[160]

The view of the 'summit' leaked to lobby correspondents afterwards by party functionaries and ministers was that most who spoke made contributions that were shallow and intellectually limited: Powell and Joseph were the two main exceptions. Indeed, the party's press spokesmen were unstinting in their praise for Powell's vision of the years ahead, their views obediently reflected in an article by the *Sunday Times*'s political correspondent, who wrote that 'in sheer intellectual dynamism ... he towered over most of his colleagues, including some more senior figures whose contributions to the pool of ideas struck many as pedestrian and trite'.[161] This was certainly a time when even Macmillan – whose close colleagues and advisers were forever thinking of better ways to project him and run the Government – was prone to consider a better use for Powell's talents even than the important job of Minister of Health. His press secretary, Harold Evans, recalls that Powell's name was the only one canvassed –

by Oliver Poole and Macleod – for what would have been a revolution in the way Downing Street operated: the appointment of a chief of staff. 'On closer consideration,' Evans adds, 'the advantages were seen to be outweighed by the disadvantages.'[162]

Powell's objections to the drift of his party's policy, under the increasingly feeble and out-of-touch leadership of Macmillan, were rooted in his belief in the absurdity of economic planning (as opposed to the specific, strategic planning he had followed in the health service, which was not dependent for its accuracy on the exercise of free will by individuals). After the best part of a year as a full cabinet member, he began to start to advance his radical views around the cabinet table. At the meeting on 16 May, when the question of housing subsidies directed through a national housing corporation was raised, Powell rebutted this piece of socialism with the view he had taken with him into the Ministry of Housing in 1955. 'He doubted', the minutes reported,

> the wisdom of measures which might be held to run counter to the normal operation of the machinery of supply and demand. The case for the proposed Housing Corporation rested on an assumption that philanthropy would provide the enterprise which elsewhere required to be rewarded with profit.
>
> This was a questionable assumption, which did not justify the creation of a new agency, guaranteed by the Government. Moreover, the proposal that the improvement of existing houses should, if necessary, be affected by compulsory powers was alien to the Government's political principles. Finally, it would be dangerous to announce a target figure for the new housing programme, since the majority of houses were built by private firms or individuals over whom the Government had no effective control.[163]

Having registered this detailed objection, he assented to the cabinet view that a White Paper on the subject be published.

Speaking at Bournemouth in late May, he said the phrase 'Britain in the Nineteen Seventies' had become 'the cliché of the year'; the lunacy of predicting how things would be ten or fifteen years hence could be demonstrated by thinking back to how difficult it would have been to predict the present ten or fifteen years earlier. 'The possibilities open to us are always far more varied, the opportunities infinitely wider, than the cleverest economists and the wisest planning committees suspect,' he said.[164] 'The nation will find them for itself, the people will sense them and work them out, if only they are given the freedom to do so, if only they have the courage to keep that freedom. For Britain the one fatal course would be a policy which put all the decisions that really matter into the hands of a little group of men who think they know best. Socialists make no secret that this is what a Labour government would mean.' Yet it was not merely Labour Powell was castigating; he was also castigating a large element in his own party.

Earlier in May he had participated in what would be his last set-piece debate on the NHS. Robinson had observed 'how Conservative love for the National Health Service grows with the approach of a General Election', a love he found ironic since, as he reminded the House, the Government that now loved it so much had voted against its creation in 1946.[165] He alleged that, far from it being true, as Powell claimed, that the service had expanded, his economy drive was now undermining it – essential repairs and maintenance were not being done. Robinson added that Powell's elevation to the cabinet – which had been met with hopes in the NHS that it would be easier to fight for more resources for the service – had failed to accomplish anything of the sort.

Powell noted that Robinson, in his understandably negative view, had failed to mention the Hospital Plan except in passing: 'I cannot feel that the hon Member's selection [of topics in his speech] was entirely unmotivated.' Powell signalled that he would, instead, 'fill out the picture'.[166] First, though, he digressed into the vexed subject of Thalidomide, and elaborated on the new Committee on the Safety of Drugs that he, with the Scottish Secretary, had decided to appoint. He promised that the committee would have 'teeth', and would be so authoritative that no consultant would lightly ignore its recommendations. Having outlined a range of safeguards, he added that 'when we use the word "safety" in this context we should not be understood to mean absolute safety. Safety in this field is relative, whatever be the arrangements, whatever be the law.'[167] Powell said that, even had these arrangements been available before Thalidomide was first prescribed, it was unlikely that 'disaster' could have been averted; there had been casualties, he said, in countries that had operated such a system.

VII

The following month the routine events of government were overtaken by the greatest crisis Macmillan would face: the scandal surrounding the Secretary for War, Jack Profumo, following his association with a prostitute, Christine Keeler, who herself had had contacts with a Soviet military attaché in London. Allegations had been made both in print and in the Commons in March about Profumo's relationship with Miss Keeler. The Secretary for War had, after consultation with senior colleagues in March, made a statement to the Commons about the innocence of his friendship with Miss Keeler; it was a personal statement, and therefore could not be challenged. However, Miss Keeler had sold a letter from Profumo to a Sunday newspaper, but before even this was known Profumo decided to make a clean breast of things, and resigned both from the Government and from Parliament on 5 June, to spend the rest of his life blamelessly and heroically in work for the underprivileged. Powell objected strongly at a cabinet meeting when Macmillan said he would be removing Profumo's name from the roll of the Privy Council, because he felt that 'an evil and dangerous precedent' was being created.[168] Sensing that the matter might become unseemly, Macmillan said that the question was not, in fact, one for the cabinet at all, but that he would deal with it in his own personal capacity. He cited no authority for this action, which caused Powell to suspect he had no right to take the action against Profumo that he did.

A cabinet meeting on 12 June considered Macmillan's general handling of the affair. At the end of it the press was told there would be no ministerial resignations, and none was expected: implying that the Prime Minister had the support of his colleagues. However, Macmillan had been subjected to close questioning by Powell, supported by Brooke, the Home Secretary, Joseph, the Housing Minister, and Edward Boyle, the Education Minister, which led some of their colleagues to think they might be contemplating resignation. The detail of such questioning is not reported in the minutes, but Lord Deedes, who was present, remembered Powell questioning the competence of those ministers, led by Macmillan, who had handled the affair when it had blown up. Powell had said to his wife, when reading Profumo's statement to the Commons the previous March, that he had not believed it; and he felt that Macmillan, far more of a man-about-town than Powell was, should have been sceptical. The briefing after the meeting was, though, that Macmillan's colleagues had merely demonstrated arguments that would be used against him in the Commons when the matter was debated the following Monday. The Attorney-General, Sir John Hobson, and the Solicitor-General, Sir Peter Rawlinson, also attended, to give accounts of the meeting with Profumo that preceded his statement to the Commons of 22 March, and to testify to his plausibility.

There was a strong feeling in the Conservative party that, even if Macmillan won the vote after the debate, his position as a leader would still be threatened; and he would need to move on within months to allow a new leader to play himself in before the election. The cabinet was scheduled to meet again the next day, 13 June, but its members were assured that no further discussion of Profumo would occur: the problems in Central Africa were the main item for discussion. After the 12 June meeting Powell and Brooke had stayed behind for half an hour, and emerged with Dilhorne (formerly Manningham-Buller), the Lord Chancellor. To lobby men watching the proceedings this suggested that the two men had been less than convinced about Dilhorne's report into the crisis. He had concluded, and the cabinet accepted, that no breach of security had been caused by Profumo's association with Miss Keeler. Powell then went off to Wolverhampton for a meeting of his constituency association.

Attempts to draw from him after the cabinet meeting an assurance that he would not resign were not answered directly. The *Daily Telegraph* reported the next morning that 'Mr Powell, Minister of Health, a stickler for high standards in public life, is believed to be gravely disturbed. He resigned from office once before on an issue of principle.'[169] The report went on: 'Two or three others' – referring to Joseph, Brooke and Boyle – 'are said to question whether any Government under Mr Macmillan's leadership can have the moral authority to survive the Profumo scandal.' The *Daily Express* carried a more sensational version of the same story, saying that Powell led a cabal within the cabinet against Macmillan. Macmillan may not have liked Powell, but he knew enough about his abilities and influence to realise that if he had reservations about the handling of the affair they would have to be taken seriously. Despite being one of its newest members, Powell was one of the cabinet's most heavyweight figures. 'I think Macmillan was conscious that people might see through him,' Deedes recalled. 'And I think of all the ministers around him, Enoch was the most likely to do so ... Enoch was the sort of figure who would worry Macmillan.'[170]

The meeting on the morning of 13 June passed without providing any further proof of dissent, and Hailsham, in an unfortunately over-excited mood, was wheeled out on to BBC television to defend Macmillan's integrity. There was still a fear, though, which grew over the weekend before the debate, that Powell was (in the words of the *Telegraph's* political correspondent) 'holding the resignation pistol to the Prime Minister's head'. At the cabinet meeting, despite the earlier indications given to the contrary, Profumo was discussed, and Macmillan was on the defensive. He maintained, for the record, that 'the fact that two members of the cabinet, the Chief Whip and both Law Officers of the Crown had felt able to accept Mr Profumo's statement as a true and honest record of his relationship with Miss Keeler should suffice to convince any reasonable individual that it was not lack of experienced judgment on the relevant day that had contributed to the unfortunate sequel'.[171]

Powell went straight from the meeting to lay the foundation stone for the North East London Centre for the Jewish Blind at Stamford Hill. He refused to answer questions from reporters about whether he would resign, and when asked to make a statement simply replied, 'No.'[172] He confined himself to saying, when laying the stone, 'I am delighted that this occasion should have attracted the attention which it deserves.' Brooke, Joseph and Boyle, all horrified to read reports of their alleged intentions to resign, issued heated denials; Powell did not. Macmillan's friends began to brief against Powell, saying that, if he did resign after a delay, the less this would look like a resignation on the grounds of conscience, and the more like a calculated move to bring down Macmillan – who, in the meantime, let it be known to the cabinet that if three ministers were to resign he would have to advise the Queen to dissolve Parliament. In fact, Powell had been asked by Redmayne, the Chief Whip, to delay a public statement of his support for Macmillan until nearer the time of the debate, in the interests of news management, and because of the significance such a statement would have when it was made. That was why Powell, who had made up his mind, kept quiet.[173]

The Prime Minister also invited John Morrison, as chairman of the 1922 Committee, in for a half-hour talk on the Thursday afternoon, and arranged to meet him again on the morning of the debate to allay any new fears. To safeguard his position, Macmillan invited all non-cabinet ministers to see him on that same morning too. However, Powell's persistent refusal to give a categorical declaration of support for Macmillan continued to suggest, with mounting urgency, that he was about to bring him down. He received, and ignored, a telegram that evening from the editor of the *Daily Sketch*, sent to South Eaton Place, saying 'other ministers mentioned in Express have categorically refuted that they are to resign. Your silence makes it difficult to maintain that cabinet holding together. Do you say you are not resigning?'[174] Three doctors from Bedford, having read the same report, wrote in different terms. 'We were delighted to read in the *Daily Express* this morning of your possible resignation, and hope very sincerely that you will allow nothing to delay you in tendering this as soon as possible.'[175]

Powell, having made his compact with Redmayne, was determined not to be drawn on his feelings, so much so that when Donald McLachlan, the editor of the *Sunday Telegraph*, called by appointment to see him at his office on 13 June he was offended that Powell asked his private secretary not to leave the room, so that no 'intimacy of conversation' could take place.[176] McLachlan – who had wished, privately, to ask Powell how dispensable Macmillan was to the Conservative party – was particularly upset because he thought Powell might have leaked the details of his feelings to the newspapers, and was behind the stories about him that morning. Powell had denied this to McLachlan in front of the private secretary, saying he intended to have no contact with the press before the debate on the Profumo affair, having assumed McLachlan was coming to see him on a matter connected with health.[177] Still maintaining his silence, Powell went to Wolverhampton on Friday 14 June to go about his constituency business as best he could, trailed by journalists. First at a ladies' coffee morning, then at a Conservative ball that evening, he remained silent. 'There is no chance', he told reporters at the ball, 'of my opening my mouth.'[178] This was entirely in keeping with Powell's conduct: he never even told his wife what passed at cabinet meetings, despite her often begging him to do so.

The next day, Saturday 15 June, Powell finally broke his silence, while attending a fête at Narborough in Norfolk. He toured the attractions for half an hour, picking up a doll that was a prize in the raffle and grinning at photographers, saying, 'I'm holding the baby.' His mood changed from flippancy to intense earnestness when he rose to speak formally. 'I am convinced', he said, 'that from beginning to end of the Profumo affair, and in every aspect of it, the personal honour and integrity of the Prime Minister, Harold Macmillan, are absolutely unsullied and untouched. I look to be in my place on the Treasury Bench on Monday to support him.'[179] He went on to abhor the concentration by the press and other politicians on the matter of personalities in politics, and made a plea for a return to an emphasis on principles.

Powell said of the distinction between the politics of personality and the politics of principle: 'There is no doubt which of the two kinds of politics matters more in the life history of a nation. It is the ideas by which that nation is guided and governed, it is the deep beliefs about itself and the world around it which influence that nation's decisions at moments of crisis; it is the standards and judgments which slowly mould that nation from generation to generation.' He wanted the next election fought on the 'supreme issue' of the matter of 'the free society versus the Socialist State'. It was, for him, a time above all for the reassertion of fundamental personal principles. 'If you ask me why I am a Tory,' he told the writer Peter Utley, who would later write a book on him, 'the best answer is that when I look at the Government benches and then at the Opposition benches, I see two kinds of men, both admirable, but I know instinctively that I belong to one kind, and not the other.'[180] He would return to the theme three weeks later at Bromsgrove, where he said that 'we uphold the capitalist free economy as a way of life, as the counterpart of the free society. It guarantees, as no other can, that men shall be free to make their own choices, right or wrong, wise or foolish, to obey their own consciences, to follow their own initiatives.'[181]

His decision to declare his public support for Macmillan should have been, but was not, the end of the matter of his personal position. Redmayne was keen to know how the newspapers had learned of the doubts, after the previous Wednesday's cabinet meeting, of Powell and his three colleagues. There was a suspicion in the Whips' Office that the dissemination of this view was the work of an anti-Macmillan faction in the party that had hoped to force a revolt against his leadership. One prominent rumour was that Butler had spread it, via the commentator Henry Fairlie. Powell was told the following October by a ministerial colleague, Lord St Oswald, that Butler had leaked the story, a view also held by Macleod.[182] Leading on from this was the rumour, denied by Powell, that Nigel Birch had promised to raise supporters for him for the party leadership had he resigned and forced Macmillan out. Powell said he 'never remembered' Birch discussing the matter with him.[183] Powell's belief that Macmillan had been taken for a ride, rather than been dishonest, was sincere, sufficiently so that he went round to see some who doubted Macmillan had behaved properly, like the future cabinet minister John Peyton, to persuade them to support the Government in the vote on 17 June. Powell and his wife, talking over the issue at the time, agreed that the circumstantial evidence of Profumo's involvement with Keeler was strong: but it was not conclusive, and therefore there was no reason for Powell to condemn Macmillan.

Powell was in his place on the front bench for the debate. It was a debate that even at the time was seen as fatal to Macmillan's premiership. Of course, Powell was silent – Macmillan opened and Macleod had the painful task of winding up. Many Conservatives known to be unhappy with Macmillan's handling of the case, and who felt they had seen their anxiety represented in Powell's behaviour, had continued to express doubts to the Whips about whether they could support the party line; and word leaked out that, in return for their support on a three-line whip, potentially dissenting Conservatives had been told that Macmillan would choose his time, but step down soon. Embarrassed by this revelation Hailsham, who had lost his temper on television in a famously self-righteous outburst, had emphatically maintained that the three-line whip was merely a summons to attend the debate.

Whether or not there was any truth in the notion that Birch was prepared to rally support behind Powell, it was he who delivered the hammer-blow to Macmillan. In a spectacular speech of little over twelve minutes, laden with irony, laced with jokes, reinforced by intellectual rigour and bereft of cant, Birch took his final revenge on the Prime Minister he despised. He began by asserting that 'as far as the moral health of the nation' – a subject with which the debate thus far had been extensively concerned – 'can be affected by any human agency, it is affected by prophets and priests and not by politicians. But this certainly has been one of the best field days that the self-righteous have had since Parnell was cited as co-respondent in O'Shea's divorce case. In all these miseries, the fact that so many people have found some genuine happiness is something to which, in all charity, we have no right to object.'[184]

Having administered that implicit rebuke to Hailsham, he turned on the editor of *The Times*, whose 'activities', he said, he viewed with 'some distaste'. 'He is', Birch continued, 'a man about whom it could have been predicted from his early youth that he was bound to end up sooner or later on the staff of one of the Astor papers.' He said he accepted Macmillan's claim that security had not been affected by the affair, but that was not the point. The point, he contended, was whether it had been right to believe Profumo's personal state-ment; and it was his belief that Macmillan and his colleagues, in accepting it, had been guilty of incompetence. For a start, they had all known Profumo well: 'I must say that he never struck me as a man at all like a cloistered monk; and Miss Keeler was a professional prostitute ... On his own admission, Profumo had a number of meetings with her, and, if we are to judge by the published statements, she is not a woman who would be intellectually stimulating.'[185] Profumo's word that he had not had a sexual relationship with her was accepted because, Birch said, he was accorded the special loyalty reserved for a colleague.

He said that while Macmillan had a duty to support colleagues, 'that comfort and that protection must stop short of condoning a lie in a personal statement to this House'. And, if – as the press had reported – a special weight had been given to Profumo's words because he was a Privy Councillor and a Secretary of State, Birch reminded the House that 'I am a Privy Councillor and I have been a Secretary of State, but when I sustained the burden of both offices I did not feel that any sea change had taken place in my personality. I remained what I was, what I always had been and what I am today; and I do not believe it reasonable to suppose that any sea change took place in Mr Profumo's personality.' He did not doubt Macmillan had absolutely believed what his colleague had told him; but that he had done so had shown a deficiency of competence and good sense. It would have made little odds had Macmillan sacked Profumo when the news first broke. 'I absolutely acquit my right hon Friend of any sort of dishonour,' he said of Macmillan. 'On the other hand, on the question of competence and good sense I cannot think that the verdict can be favourable.'[186]

Therefore, he told Macmillan that he 'ought to make way for a much younger colleague'. He said he would not quote the 'savage' words of Cromwell at him – by which he meant the words Leo Amery had quoted to Chamberlain on 7 May 1940, and which Cromwell had used to the Long Parliament – 'You have sat too long here for any good you have been doing. Depart, I say, and let us have done with you. In the name of God, go!'[187] He had something far more devastating instead:

Perhaps some of the words of Browning might be appropriate in his poem on 'The Lost Leader', in which he wrote:

> let him never come back to us!
> There would be doubt, hesitation and pain.
> Forced praise on our part – the glimmer of twilight,
> Never glad confident morning again!

'Never glad confident morning again!' – so I hope the change will not be too long delayed.

That was not the end of Birch's assault. 'Ahead of us we have a Division. We have the statement of my right hon and noble Friend Lord Hailsham, in a personal assurance on television, that a Whip is not a summons to vote but a summons to attend. I call the Whips to witness that I at any rate have attended.'[188] Macmillan had turned round to his backbenches when Birch called for him to go, hoping to see signs of disapproval. He was disappointed. As Birch sat down the Prime Minister stalked out of the chamber, his face in the words of one observer 'flushed with anger'.[189]

As expected, though, the Conservatives won the division, in which Birch abstained. Macmillan tried to defuse anger about his role by announcing the following Friday a full judicial inquiry by Lord Denning, the Master of the Rolls, into the security aspects of the scandal. However, this also backfired and further weakened him. His critics in the party could not understand why this inquiry was not, from the outset, given powers to compel witnesses to attend or to produce documents. All Macmillan had conceded was that Denning could request Parliament to grant these powers if necessary. Macmillan's reluctance to grant extra powers to Denning had been because of the outcry, and political damage, caused by the jailing of two reporters by the Vassall tribunal the previous year. Talk of the leadership resurfaced, with newspapers helpfully carrying out private polls that showed Maudling as the hot favourite to succeed Macmillan. The 1922 executive privately agreed that between 60 and 70 per cent of the party was ready to support Maudling in the event of a vacancy. The talk did not go away during the summer, and Maudling seemed to maintain, indeed strengthen, his position. By early August the strength of the anti-Macmillan faction in the party – defined as those who were actively working to bring about his demise – was estimated at seventy-five. Its leaders claimed to have three supporters in the cabinet: Lord Home, the Foreign Secretary, Boyle and Powell.

Powell, meanwhile, returned to the day-to-day matters of his Ministry. His concern for the mentally ill manifested itself at the end of June with an announcement of a £1.25 million modernisation scheme for Broadmoor, announced at a lunch he attended to mark the secure hospital's centenary. He also announced that his former army comrade, Hardy Amies, had been commissioned to design new uniforms for the staff: Powell felt they looked too much like warders, and wanted them to look more like civilians. Once Amies had designed the uniforms the staff loathed them, feeling they made them look less authoritarian, which was exactly what Powell had asked him to do. His other big programme of the year, fluoridation, was going slowly. By August, eight months after he had announced the scheme, only 60 of the 146 health authorities in England and Wales had agreed to fluoridate, despite Powell's enthusiasm.

When on 28 June Macmillan fulfilled a long-standing engagement in Powell's constituency, the Minister of Health led the standing ovation after a speech in which Macmillan had promised to lead the party into the next election if his health and strength permitted. However, Powell started to sound a more apocalyptic note in his speeches, and seemed to be trying to urge his colleagues to face up to some obvious realities. 'There come from time to time moments in the life of a party when it needs to talk politics again; when it once again needs to tell itself and others, loud and clear, what it stands for; when it needs to say plainly what it wants and aims at and what kind of future it wishes for the nation,' he said at Bromsgrove on 6 July 1963.[190] He was in no doubt what this meant, though he remarked later that he was astonished no one picked up

at the time what he said: 'We are a capitalist party. We believe in capitalism ...
we honour profit competitively earned; we respect the ownership of property,
great or small; we accept the differences of wealth and income without which
competition and free enterprise are impossible ... we believe that a society
where men are free to take economic decisions for themselves – to decide how
they will apply their incomes, their savings, their efforts – is the only kind of
society where men will remain free in other respects, free in speech, thought
and action.' Powell had spotted the weakness at the top of his party. If there was
to be a new leader, he was determined to lay down his intellectual marker well
before any change of policy.

He continued, in what spare time he had, with his books on the Lords. 'I find
writing the book an interesting and academic amusement,' he said. 'I may finish
it this year. Or it may take another five years. After all, a politician never knows
when he's going to get time to spare for such things.'[191] Asked to name his
favourite poem for an event at the Cheltenham Festival of Literature, he chose
Tennyson's 'Ulysses', 'because of the limitless undefined possibilities in life and
this world and the spirit of bloody-minded determination not to be cheated of
exploring them.'[192]

VIII

Powell seemed in doubt, by September 1963, about how long the Government
would last. Addressing party activists in Somerset on 20 September, he said in
reply to a question about the timing of the next election, 'I would advise you to
be ready any day from now on,' a remark that greatly excited the press.[193]
Now almost self-consciously the ideological conscience of an apparently non-
ideological party, he warned again of the 'choice between a free society and a
society in bondage.'[194] If he thought the moment to make the choice were so
close, it might explain the detached tone of a philosophical interview he gave
Peter Utley in the *Sunday Telegraph* on the eve of the 1963 party conference. He
reiterated his by now familiar anti-statist line that the essence of Toryism, as he
saw it, was the conviction that salvation was in the hands of individuals and not
of the state. He further defined this view with reference to his own activities
over the preceding years. 'Today,' he said,

> the Ministry of Health is perforce the central spending authority; I must try to
> use the power that falls to me as Minister as rationally as I can and with what
> little foresight is ever vouchsafed to a planner. But I do claim that I have used
> this power in a way different from that in which it would have been exercised by
> one of other convictions.
>
> I have tried to build up and strengthen local agencies within the national

system; I have done all that lies in me to strengthen and encourage voluntary effort and the voluntary bodies. I have gone, some would say, to the length of adulation in commending the activities of such independent bodies as the King's Hospital Fund and the Nuffield Trust; I have jealously guarded the frontiers between administration on the one side and the territories of professional knowledge and skill, of scientific research and of commercial enterprise on the other.[195]

In the light of imminent, but then unknown, events the tone was highly appropriate.

In the tumult of the events of the next fortnight, a proper judgment on Powell's tenure of the Ministry of Health was never made. The reasons for his leaving his office having nothing to do with his conduct of it, but with unrelated matters; hardly a proper assessment has been made since. Sir George Godber, who worked in the Ministry and its successor Department for more than thirty years, felt that only Bevan and Macleod were comparable as ministers with Powell.[196] Powell unquestionably laid the foundations of a modern health service; he was the first occupant of his office to see the need to make the NHS an evolutionary beast, rather than one rooted in the climate of 1948. He also succeeded in winning the funds to do this. He ran the NHS in a way his predecessors, for many years hence, would find no cause to divert from. He made the Ministry one of immense political importance, and one which would always now be led by a cabinet minister. 'On many issues we were fighting for the same things,' his opposite number, Kenneth Robinson, wrote to him on his resignation. 'I only hope you realise that this did not altogether make things easier for an opposition spokesman.'[197]

During the night of 7–8 October 1963 Macmillan found himself in excruciating pain, a development of discomfort he had experienced for several days while trying to urinate. Prostate trouble was quickly diagnosed. On 8 October he presided over a three-hour cabinet, the first to be held in Downing Street since its renovations and, as it turned out, the only time Powell ever attended a cabinet meeting there. Macmillan said nothing to colleagues about his illness, but they noticed he looked ghastly. Their suspicions were confirmed when a glass of medicine was brought in for him during the proceedings, and when he twice had to leave the room. Eventually he sent the Cabinet Secretariat, with the exception of the secretary himself, Sir Burke Trend, out of the room and explained what his illness was. He then told his colleagues he still planned to lead them up to and during the election; his doctor had given him 'no reason to think ... that my trouble would be very serious'.[198] He believed he could go to Blackpool the following Saturday to deliver his speech to the party conference.

Having announced his intentions, Macmillan withdrew to allow his colleagues to discuss his plans in an unencumbered way. Thus was initiated the chain of events that would culminate, eleven days later, in Lord Home's assumption of the Prime Ministership. At the end of the period Powell wrote a memorandum of his view of the events, which has remained closed in his papers until now. As Macmillan withdrew, Powell recalled, 'Lord Hailsham impulsively exclaimed, with tears starting into his eyes: "Prime Minister, wherever you go, you know our hearts go with you." ' Powell says that 'I was struck by the valedictory note of this outburst; in fact I scribbled to Mr Deedes, my neighbour, a note to the effect that I had never heard a more effective *coup de grâce*. I was afterwards to realise that Lord Hailsham already knew that the Cabinet were never again to see Mr Macmillan as Prime Minister.'[199] Once Powell heard the words 'doctors' uttered by Macmillan, he concluded it would be the Prime Minister's means of escape.

Macmillan was well served by his Chief Whip, Redmayne, as he had been by Heath before him. Redmayne told Macmillan, as the Prime Minister noted, that in his absence 'the cabinet had (with one exception) agreed to back me to the full if I decided to go through the general election. (The exception was "Aristides" – Enoch Powell, who thought I ought to resign).'[200] Macmillan's nickname for Powell referred to an Athenian statesman, Aristides the Just, who was never wrong. Powell was, simply, ahead of the game. As he recalled later: 'You lose the public, you lose the press, you lose the party in the House, but the men whose heads you can cut off before breakfast you lose last. The most difficult operation there is for a cabinet itself is to depose a Prime Minister. So it was everything else that slipped around Harold Macmillan before the cabinet itself.'[201] Powell told his colleagues that the interests of the party and the country would be best served by Macmillan's telling the rally the following Saturday that he would be standing down.[202] 'No one hastened to express a contrary view,' Powell recalled. Indeed Home, who described himself as 'not a contender', admitted that in the preceding days he and Butler had emphasised to Macmillan the difficulties he would face if he carried on. Macleod said that Macmillan should carry on, and then Hailsham stunned the meeting by announcing he had all but decided to disclaim his peerage. 'When the Cabinet ended,' Powell continues, 'I three times walked to the door of No. 10 and back again ... wondering whether I should speak to Lord Hailsham before I too left for Blackpool in the early afternoon. I am sure that but for his being surrounded at that time by other ministers and the shortness of the time at my disposal, I would have asked to see him in private there and then and told him not to be a fool.'

That afternoon, as most of his colleagues headed to Blackpool for the opening of the conference, it was announced that Macmillan was ill. He was admitted to the King Edward VII Hospital for Officers for an operation, and a scrap began for the succession, even though Macmillan had yet to say he would resign. On Wednesday 9 October, when it was clear Macmillan could not address the rally, Butler (immediately on his arrival at the conference) insisted to the senior members of the National Union of Conservative and Unionist Associations –

the conference organisers – that he, as Deputy Prime Minister, would make the speech instead; this was seen as an important advance by him towards the leadership. The chairman of the National Union, Mrs T. C. R. Shepherd, rang Lord Home, the president of the Union, to seek his approval for Butler's move, which he gave. An *ad hoc* meeting of the eight other cabinet ministers in Blackpool, including Powell, was held at five o'clock that afternoon in Butler's suite – the leader's suite, which he had insisted on using. Butler said that he and Redmayne had both seen Macmillan, and he had asked Butler to pass on to colleagues the word that they should feel free to consult among themselves about his successor, though he had not yet decided whether to stand down.[203] 'This astonishing message', Powell noted, 'caused Mr Soames to query it, and Mr Redmayne repeated it again with evident embarrassment and consciousness of its contradictory nature.' Powell, Macleod and Hare all argued that the rally was personal to the leader and should not take place if the leader could not address it. Brookes and Deedes dissented, and Butler took their side; it was agreed he would address the rally.

Immediately, a group in the party started talking up Home as a possible successor to Macmillan, taking advantage of it still being within the initial twelve-month period of the Act that allowed all hereditary peers to renounce their peerages. Home's biographer suggests that a decision that the Foreign Secretary should run had been taken much earlier in the summer by leaders of the 1922 Committee; and that Home had been spoken to about the prospect by Morrison on 31 July, the day the new peerage law went on to the statute book.[204] Powell suspected more advance planning was taking place than met the eye, not least because Macmillan's admission to hospital had, he was sure, been arranged before he took the cabinet meeting the previous morning.[205]

In the light of what would happen, Home was helped by the fact that he stayed in London, in close contact with Macmillan, during the first two days of the party conference. He did not reach Blackpool until Thursday afternoon, and on doing so read out, in his capacity as president of the National Union, a letter from Macmillan announcing his intention to resign. Powell received a message warning him of this from Home's private secretary moments before the public announcement was made. The private secretary clearly thought that the ministers had already been told Macmillan would stand down, but they had not. At once, the message conveyed by Butler and Redmayne became clear. In one regard, the atmosphere among the party's leaders was not surprising, since most of them were in shock. Butler and Macleod had been told the news in advance, and one or two other cabinet ministers were aware of it; but to the rest, including Powell, it was a surprise. Wisely, he kept quiet.

From that moment near hysteria gripped the conference. One of its principal casualties was Hailsham, who publicly made a histrionic promise to disclaim his peerage and seek the leadership. This and other acts of self-promotion –

notably asking colleagues and others to come to his room in the Imperial Hotel to watch his baby daughter being fed – effectively did for him. Powell was one who witnessed the infant's feeding: 'She at least was an innocent figure in the drama.'[206] There were other elements of farce: some of the rooms being used by ministers were being repainted, and the bustling grandees came and went with the painters.

In his famous *Spectator* article three months later, Macleod would rubbish suggestions that Home was an obvious candidate at Blackpool, attributing such statements to hindsight. But, in fact, the Sunday lobby were briefed to this effect, as loyally reported by the *Sunday Telegraph*'s political correspondent immediately after the conference had ended. Writing that 'a decision on a successor to Mr Macmillan is likely to be made within the next few days' because 'the Conservative party leadership ... are determined to end as rapidly as possible the confusion and speculation of the last week', he reported that the choice seemed to have narrowed to two men – Butler and Hailsham. Home was, nonetheless, described as 'universally acceptable', Hailsham as 'backed by a powerful group in the party's hierarchy', and the main conclusion of the report was that Home could well become leader.[207] Maudling, who had been clear favourite among backbenchers to take over, was felt to have behaved with diffidence and a lack of leadership during the crisis at Blackpool. That particular caravan had moved on; he was no longer, by that stage, a serious contender. Powell himself had favoured Maudling, but felt his stock had dwindled since the Profumo affair. Thus, in Powell's view, 'Mr Butler was emerging as the only answer I thought acceptable.'[208]

Macmillan's official biographer states that he had on 9 October made up his mind to resign. He had communicated this immediately to Home, and had at the same time asked him to consider taking on the leadership.[209] Home immediately expressed his reluctance, having no desire to leave either the Foreign Office or the House of Lords. Macmillan told Home it would be his duty to disclaim his peerage and accept the commission if no one else 'emerged'. It was the last thing Home wanted.

It was that Thursday evening that the old alliance between Powell and Macleod was re-formed. Relations between the two of them had been chilly for years, despite frequent efforts by Macleod, who minded about lack of approbation by Powell, to heat them up. 'I went to Mr Macleod's room,' Powell recorded, 'and congratulated him on the success of his speech that morning, observing that it was "the first time for many years that a success of his had given me pleasure". It was the first mark of resumed friendship to pass between us.' Powell told Macleod of the nature of the message he had had from Home's private secretary, and of his belief that the most important part of the message had been withheld by Butler and Redmayne from their colleagues. 'The motive on Mr Butler's part', Powell wrote, 'was obvious – to be accepted speaker at the rally, before the Prime Minister's resignation became known and so enhanced the importance of the occasion to such an extent that the decision might well have been to hold no rally or to have it addressed by someone other than a potential successor.'[210] The next day Macmillan's private secretary, Tim Bligh, tried to convince Powell that there had been a misunderstanding. He failed.

Powell and Macleod talked about what they thought should happen, and found themselves in complete agreement, now Macmillan had decided he would not go on as Macleod had hoped. 'Lord Hailsham was impossible and we would neither of us contemplate serving under him. It seemed unthinkable that Lord Home should be brought down from the Upper House at this juncture for this purpose; we agreed that Mr Maudling's star was not in the ascendant; and we concluded with cordiality that the remaining choice, Mr Butler, was the only one which we personally wished to see realised and believed could be the means of restoring the party's fortunes.' For the last two days at Blackpool two camps emerged: one around Hailsham, and the other around Butler. It was the violence of the opposition to each of these candidates by adherents of the other that would provide the means for Macmillan to execute, from beyond the political grave, his otherwise unlikely scheme to have Home succeed him. By the Friday, Home had agreed to stand if his supporters could prove there was sufficient backing for him. Nigel Birch went around Blackpool pronouncing: 'I'm an Alec Home man. There aren't any other possibilities. He's *going* to get it.'[211] Though a maverick, Birch had the antennae of a well-heeled, well-connected Old Etonian, and had read the situation correctly long before anyone else outside Macmillan's close circle. Powell was told categorically, by Birch and by others whom he respected, that Home would be chosen. From that moment, he decided to do all he could to stop it.

Powell spent most of the Friday away from Blackpool, addressing meetings in Liverpool and Preston. On the Saturday morning, before the rally, he went to see Macleod to find out what had happened in his absence. Macleod reported that Hailsham 'was eliminated'.[212] The conference, with its concentration of politicians and activists, had been the worst possible place for the party to realise it faced a leadership succession, and had destabilised that succession. The decision by Macmillan to announce his resignation when he did inflicted a week or so of indignity and ridicule on his party, but it helped him achieve his aim of having Home succeed him – as Hailsham's self-immolation proved. Macleod and Powell affirmed their objections to Home 'both practically and ideo-logically'.

That lunchtime Dilhorne, the Lord Chancellor, invited Powell for a formal consultation about the succession. 'I began by ruling out Lord Hailsham as lacking the self-control, stability, patience and prudence which was essential to a Prime Minister, and I stated flatly that I would not serve under him,' Powell wrote. Dilhorne stood up for Hailsham and intimated that Macmillan backed him, an intervention Powell regarded as 'judicial' and designed merely to test Powell's feelings further. Powell indicated that he had no objection to serving under Home on personal grounds, 'but I could not conceive that it would be a wise or even a practicable operation'. He told Dilhorne unequivocally that he was for Butler as a man who 'would unite and represent the talent and the youth on the Treasury Bench; I believed (as I had believed in January 1957) that if given the opportunity he would soon appeal to the public; and while he and Mr Macmillan were approximately equal in duplicity, there was in Mr Butler what I had never discerned in Mr Macmillan, an ultimate sub-stratum of faith in things which I myself believed in.' Dilhorne told Powell that Macmillan felt Butler 'lacked decision in a crisis and was liable to be suddenly deserted by willpower and no need to be sustained by others'. Powell assured him that such support would be forthcoming if Butler were Prime Minister, but did not, apparently, challenge the main assertions.

Dilhorne and Powell then argued about Home, whom Dilhorne persisted in saying was Powell's second preference: Powell had to impress upon the notoriously unintellectual Lord Chancellor that that was not at all what he had said. Then Dilhorne said he intended to put the results of his consultation to the cabinet, which horrified Powell. 'I hoped we might be spared so embarrassing an occasion: it was surely best to arrive at the upshot by informal consultation, as the Crown itself had hitherto done, when the post was already vacant.' After his consultation Powell saw Boyle and Freddie Erroll, the President of the Board of Trade. Both said they were Butler men, though Dilhorne confidently noted in a memorandum on the views of the cabinet that Boyle was supporting Home.

On Sunday 13 October, once the grandees had returned from Blackpool, the various campaigns swung into operation. Julian Amery took charge of Hailsham's; Macleod let him know that same day that he would not be supporting Hailsham, Powell having already told him in Blackpool. Lord Poole, the chairman of the party, went to see Macmillan on the Monday, leaving by the back door of the hospital, and Butler's supporters, now including Maudling, declared themselves. On Tuesday, after an unofficial canvass, it emerged that half of backbench MPs would support Hailsham; and, since no clear candidate was in front, on Wednesday the whips began soundings about Home's suitability. In the meantime, Macmillan, on his sickbed, had seen a number of cabinet colleagues: he lists Butler, Home, Macleod, Heath, Maudling, Hailsham, Thorneycroft, Boyle, Soames, Lloyd, Hare, Brooke, Joseph and Sandys.[213] Powell did not bother to invite himself in. There had never been any warmth between the two, and Powell would not manufacture it now. He was, though, 'a little surprised not to be called' to see the Prime Minister. It was a calculated act of discourtesy by Macmillan towards a cabinet colleague, albeit the only one who had the previous week felt he should resign.

As Home's biographer illustrates, the soundings by the Whips about Home were not just another act of casting about for a solution. On Tuesday 15 October Macmillan had written the first draft of his resignation memorandum to the Queen, in which he outlined his view of how events should develop. In it, he plainly came down on Home's side, for predictable reasons: 'Lord Home is clearly a man who represents the old, governing class at its best ... had he been of another generation, he would have been of the Grenadiers and the 1914 heroes.'[214] As with his decision not to follow through the economic hard line in 1957–8, what was going on outside Macmillan's mind was purely for show. Three days before the Queen would invite Home to see whether he could form a government, Macmillan had decided the succession. Now, all procedures and strategy would be bent to ensure that his personal wish was fulfilled.

On the crucial day – Thursday 17 October – Powell went about his ministerial business, busily engaged in not plotting. In this, he was almost alone. It was also his daughter Jennifer's seventh birthday, and he was preparing to be master of ceremonies, and film projectionist, at her party that afternoon. Powell's way with children had continued to develop since having his own two daughters. The cartoons he hired to show them were silent, and he would do the characters' voices himself. If any children misbehaved – and the most awful misdemeanour was putting their dirty hands on the wall – their 'punishment' would be to recite the dates of some of the kings and queens of England.

Macleod had been told by his wife that morning – her information having come from Lady Monckton (wife of a former cabinet minister), who had had it from Lady Dorothy Macmillan – that the decision would be made that day. Such a source was utterly reliable, and Macleod knew at once it must be true. He imagined this swiftness must mean it would be Butler, and he believed he had confirmed this view in a meeting with Maudling later in the day. Dilhorne was again canvassing cabinet opinion, following a morning visit to Macmillan. Neither Macleod nor Maudling had any idea of the other manoeuvrings, prompted by Macmillan's belief that only Home could stop Butler, which were going on to put Home in the job, or that the cabinet soundings were being taken long after the mind of the man who mattered – Macmillan, who, whatever the constitutional properties, would tender the appropriate advice to the Queen – had been made up. Redmayne acted as Macmillan's main man of affairs. 'It is some measure of the tightness of the magic circle on this occasion', wrote Macleod, 'that neither the Chancellor of the Exchequer nor the Leader of the House of Commons [Maudling and himself] had any inkling of what was happening.'[215]

As well as seeing Dilhorne, Macmillan had summoned the Chief Whips in both Houses, the chairman of the 1922 Committee, and the chairman of the party. He states in his memoirs that 'the remarkable and to me unexpected result' of the 'soundings' of these people was '(rather contrary to what I expected) a *preponderant first* choice for Lord Home (except in the constituencies, who hardly knew he was a serious candidate but agreed that he would be universally acceptable if *drafted*.[216] He claims the cabinet was divided ten for Home, three for Butler, four for Maudling, two for Hailsham; more MPs supported Home than supported anyone else, he claims, and the Lords were two to one for Home. The constituencies were 'sixty per cent for Hailsham, forty per cent for Butler, with *strong* opposition feelings for both'. He stresses that his opposition to Butler – and Hailsham – was rooted in the strength of 'violent' opposition to them, a violence of opposition Home did not attract. That was, and was to remain, his justification for the advice he would give the Queen. That it seems, in terms of the cabinet factions alone, to have been based on an entirely inaccurate, or perhaps even wilfully dishonest, view would not stop him.

Macleod was told that afternoon by William Rees-Mogg of the *Sunday Times* that the choice had been made, and that it was Home. Bill Deedes, who as Minister without Portfolio was responsible for the presentation of policy, had been told by Redmayne to see Home to discuss the programme for the day he became Prime Minister. He went to the Foreign Office by means of the tunnel connecting it to Downing Street – 'it was all fairly cloak and dagger'.[217] The Whips had just told Macmillan that Home was an acceptable compromise candidate; Butler would be informed he would not be the next leader and had until 11.30 the next morning to decide whether he would serve under Home. Soon the story was all over Fleet Street. 'News management,' Macleod observed, 'can be taken too far.' He rang his two oldest colleagues, Powell and Maudling. Powell took the call at 3 p.m., just as he was about to start the film-show. Macleod warned him that 'things were moving at incredible speed'.[218] Powell abandoned Jennifer's party and went to Macleod's room at Central Office.

Once Macleod had briefed him, Powell said that 'I thought the essential thing was for as many people as possible to tell Lord Home at once that he was "not on", and not to wait until events moved further; but we decided to await some further confirmation before doing this.' Powell paid a flying visit back to Jennifer's party, then went to meet both Maudling and Macleod at Macleod's flat in Chelsea at 4.45 p.m. The meeting was repeatedly interrupted by telephone calls from journalists asking Macleod to comment on reports of Home's imminent appointment. Despite this evidence of Macmillan's intentions – it seemed the story had been deliberately planted by someone close to him – Macleod and Maudling were still reluctant to approach Home on the basis of rumour. Maudling solved the problem by ringing his private secretary and asking him to get confirmation from Macmillan's office that this was the case. Maudling was almost immediately asked to go to the Treasury to see Bligh. He returned to Macleod's flat to tell his two colleagues, and Lord Aldington, the party's deputy chairman, who had joined them, that the rumour was true.

Powell and Macleod decided to talk to Home directly about their opposition to him rather than operate behind his back; Maudling 'as a potential successor' decided not to come with them. Powell eventually got through to Home at 8 p.m., and was told he would be glad to see him and Macleod between 10 and 11 p.m., but warned that his house in Carlton House Terrace was under surveillance by the press, and they were bound to be spotted. Macleod went to South Eaton Place at 10 p.m., and they decided to ring Home to assess the chances of their getting in without being spotted. Before they could do so Hailsham, 'deeply shocked' and 'plainly much upset', rang Powell having heard the news, and asking what could be done about it.[219] Powell said that, like him, Hailsham should without delay bring all his personal influence to bear on Home.

Convinced of the impossibility of going to Carlton House Terrace, Macleod and Powell spoke to Home on the telephone. Macleod, in his *Spectator* article, recorded the conversation thus:

> I spoke first. I told him that there was no one in the party for whom I had more admiration and respect; that if he had been in the House of Commons he could perhaps have been the first choice; but I felt that those giving advice had grossly underestimated the difficulties of presenting the situation in a convincing way to the modern Tory party. Unlike Hailsham, he was not a reluctant peer, and we are now proposing to admit that after 12 years of Tory government no one amongst the 363 members of the party in the House of Commons was acceptable as prime minister. I felt it more straightforward to put these views to him tonight rather than perhaps have to put them in other circumstances tomorrow.
>
> I did not hear what Powell said to Lord Home, but I believe that he spoke to him on similar lines.[220]

Powell did not record what exactly he said to Home. Aldington arrived at South Eaton Place, and the three men 'decided that the essential requirement was that Mr Maudling and Lord Hailsham should both formally agree to serve under Mr Butler. If this could be done, the major factions could be re-united and a virtually agreed successor would have emerged.'[221] Calls went out for Butler's other supporters to congregate at South Eaton Place – at what became known as 'the midnight meeting' – to discuss their options. After Jennifer's party, the place was festooned with balloons.

As well as Powell, Macleod and Aldington there were Maudling, in black tie after dinner – fetched from a neighbouring street by Pam Powell as his telephone was permanently engaged – and Erroll. While the conclave continued, Pam Powell and Beryl Maudling went out to buy the first editions of the newspapers at a railway station. The meeting did not remain secret for long. Maudling had, foolishly, given his daughter Powell's telephone number in case anyone wanted him. It was recognised by the journalist Henry Fairlie, who put two and two together. A picket of press men arrived within minutes, and stayed outside until long after the new Prime Minister was in office. The photographers were in time to record the arrival of Redmayne, invited by the ministers to hear their views and to relay them to Macmillan.

Redmayne tried to persuade the men to accept the magic circle's decision, but met with fierce resistance. Powell warned him against making the mistake of relying on second preferences – such as the one Dilhorne was sure Powell held for Home – in making his calculations. It was impressed upon Redmayne that the warm regard most ministers had for Home was not to be confused with a desire to see him as leader and Prime Minister. Crucially, Redmayne was told that, as Hailsham and Maudling had both agreed to serve under Butler, he 'had emerged by the due processes as the acknowledged successor'. Redmayne gave further evidence of the ruthlessness with which Macmillan was acting in saying there was a plan to defer the opening of Parliament for a fortnight to give Home time to win the pending Kinross by-election and have a seat in the Commons, the incumbent candidate having agreed to stand down. Macleod was 'dumb-founded' by this, since, as Leader of the House, he should have been among the first to know.

Redmayne agreed, after this 'long wrangle', to go away and report the ministers' views to Macmillan. Aldington took Redmayne back to Downing Street. To be on the safe side, Aldington himself rang the Queen's private secretary, Sir Michael Adeane, to tell him about the midnight meeting and what had been agreed. Meanwhile, back at South Eaton Place, his three old lieutenants from the Research Department rang Butler, staying with his wife at St Ermin's Hotel in Victoria while their town house was being treated for dry rot. Powell wrote: 'First Mr Macleod and then I assured Mr Butler that he was accepted to our certain knowledge by Mr Maudling, there present and approving our words, and to the best of our belief, based on telephone conversations that night, by Lord Hailsham also. We expressed the view that the party was thus in effect united behind him, and our own conviction that in this it was right. His words to me, before I replaced the receiver, were: "Thank you for telling me. The Prime Minister must be told of this." '[222] Butler was going to bed to sleep on what he had been told. The meeting broke up at 2.30 a.m., at which point Powell drove Macleod home. 'Well, we have placed the golden ball in Rab's lap,' he said to Powell on the journey. 'If he drops it now, he does not deserve to be Prime Minister.' Powell, in an even more graphic image, felt they had handed Butler 'a loaded revolver'.[223]

However, the meeting would have the opposite effect to that intended by those who had participated in it. Once Macmillan learned that a substantial minority in the cabinet were moving against his choice, he acted more speedily than he had planned. On Friday morning Butler tried to telephone Macmillan, but could not get through. He could have intervened in a more determined way, but chose not to fire the loaded revolver. At 9.45 Macmillan's resignation was formally tendered to Buckingham Palace, and at 11.15 the Queen arrived at the hospital to see him, staying for half an hour. Home had telephoned Macmillan that morning, aggrieved that, having come forward as a compromise candidate in the interests of the party unity, he now had several colleagues rounding on him from different directions. He wanted to withdraw; Macmillan, successfully, urged him not to, saying that 'if we give in to this intrigue, there would be chaos'. Macmillan was determined that only one intrigue would be successful, and it would be his. He told the Queen, as he read her the memorandum he had drawn up containing his advice for deposit in the Royal Archives, that 'I thought speed was important and hoped she would send for Lord Home immediately – as soon as she got back to the Palace.'[224]

This tendering of advice by a Prime Minister who had resigned was to lay Macmillan open ever afterwards to accusations – well founded – that he had played fast and loose with the royal prerogative. When Macmillan published details of his dealings with the Queen in his memoirs ten years later, Powell was quick to condemn his 'gross impropriety' in doing so. He claimed that the action Macmillan had taken in manipulating the succession before he resigned as Prime Minister, rather than waiting to be asked by the Queen whether he had any advice to tender, informally, once he had resigned, had destroyed the royal prerogative. The nature of what had passed, though, would also ensure that no leader of the Conservative party would ever 'emerge' again.[225]

Powell and Macleod had met in Macleod's office at the Duchy of Lancaster at eleven that morning. They knew Macmillan had sent in his resignation and had persisted in his advice for the Queen to send for Home. They decided it was imperative that Maudling and Hailsham should be brought together with Butler so that they could reaffirm their allegiance to him. 'After some prima-donnaish objections on protocol, Mr Butler agreed to see them both, and they met him at the Treasury at noon, while the Queen was with Mr Macmillan.'[226]

At 12.21, with the speed Macmillan had counselled, Home arrived at the Palace to be asked to form a government – the advice Macmillan had given the Queen, as opposed to advice that she should appoint Home as her Prime Minister. It was crucial to see whether Home could command the necessary support from his colleagues before being formally appointed. Powell was summoned to the Treasury at 2 p.m. to meet Maudling, Macleod, Erroll and Boyd-Carpenter, who told him Butler was seeing Home at 2.45 p.m. It was agreed that Maudling and Powell would see Butler at 2.35 p.m. to make final entreaties. Initially, Powell saw Butler alone.

I said to him that as I looked back over the 18 years since I came into politics, over all that had been thought, written and done in those years, largely under his guidance, I was convinced that this could be carried forward and successfully presented again to the country by my generation under his leadership. No-one else in my opinion could do this, and I appealed to him 'not to let us down'. He replied 'You think I ought to handle him (i.e. Lord Home) pretty carefully?' I said that if I were in Mr Butler's position, I would tell Lord Home that I, not he, enjoyed the confidence of the majority of the cabinet, having the adherence of the two principal rivals and of other Ministers, and that it was I, not he, who would form the government.[227]

This meeting, like that with Hailsham and Maudling, failed to stiffen Butler. He told Home he would serve only if he was sure it was necessary to maintain the unity of the party. Home assured him it was. Although Butler asked to have a final meeting with Home the next morning, the golden ball had been dropped. Hailsham and Maudling, who had said they would serve only if Butler did, were thus enabled to continue their careers. Once Butler agreed to serve, it was certain Home would succeed in forming a government. Home, naturally, was determined to maximise party unity. The first blow came that afternoon when Macleod refused to serve. Then, at 6 p.m., Home saw Powell, explaining that he had not yet accepted the Queen's commission. Powell recalled, 'I told him that in my opinion it would be a disastrous error for him to be Prime Minister, and that to my knowledge Mr Butler, whom I regarded as the right successor, had the support of his two main rivals as well as of others. He certainly had mine. Lord Home then formally enquired whether this meant that if he asked me to serve under him I would decline. I replied that this was surely the inevitable implication of what I had just said.' After the meeting Powell spoke to Boyle, who was about to return to London from Manchester. Boyle told him he was as opposed as ever to Home becoming Prime Minister, and that he would decline to serve under Home when he saw him later that evening – to do otherwise, he told Powell, would be a breach of 'moral integrity'.[228]

   Powell had intended to head off Joseph before he, too, saw Home, but hearing a report that Joseph had said Home would be as good a prime minister as any other, he decided not to bother. He and Macleod contented themselves with the reflection that with the two of them and Boyle refusing to serve, and Hailsham and Maudling reserving their positions, their hand was strong. They informed Butler of the position and of the stand they had taken. The next morning Powell and Macleod sat by their telephones to hear the outcome of the interview between Home and Butler. 'By 12 o'clock Mr Macleod and I learnt that Mr Butler had capitulated, and accepted the Foreign Office, and that in consequence Mr Maudling had accepted the Treasury. Consequently, Lord Home had gone straight to the Palace and kissed hands as Prime Minister.' Powell told Maudling he had not acted inconsistently, having reserved his position. He was less impressed with Boyle, who was pressurised by Butler to continue to serve at the Ministry of Education, and who rang Powell to try to explain his volte-face. 'The importance of handling the Robbins Report [on the expansion of higher education] now seemed to him at least as great as the maintenance of "moral integrity".

Home asked both Powell and Macleod to see him that afternoon, to see whether they would change their minds. Powell told Bligh, now acting as Home's private secretary, that he had no intention of serving unless Macleod did, and that Macleod should therefore be seen before him. Before Powell reached Downing Street he had two calls from colleagues: the first was from Brooke, who told him 'in his most unctuous manner that it was a terrible tragedy, and that it would never be understood. He himself could not understand it. However, when I told him that I had not expected him to understand my action, he appeared to know well enough what the implication was.'[229] Thorneycroft, who rang a little later, said Butler's decision to serve had created a new situation, but Powell replied that he had been asked a straight question by Home and had given a straight answer: 'I saw no justification for attempting to take back a card which had already been played.'

Powell and Macleod went to Downing Street at 4 p.m., and Macleod went in first. His was a brief interview. Powell then went in. In a phrase which encapsulated the relationship between his principles and his actions, he looked Home in the eye and said: 'Well I don't expect, Alec, you expect me to give you a different answer on Saturday from the one I gave you on Friday. I'd have to go home and turn all the mirrors round.'[230] Home accepted this, and admired Powell for his integrity. 'For myself and Powell it had become a matter of "personal moral integrity",' Macleod recalled in his *Spectator* article, cruelly quoting the unnamed Boyle. Macleod wrote that from his personal knowledge eleven members of the cabinet wanted someone other than Home to be leader, and only two were positively in favour of him. Certainly, only Powell and Macleod felt strongly enough to stand by their original decisions. Butler, Powell believed, had not betrayed them by choosing to serve. 'If he wasn't prepared to fight for it he wasn't letting me down, he was letting himself down,' Powell observed.[231] He conceded he had overestimated Butler's willingness to make a stand.

A week later, Pam Powell said to her husband, 'Every one of you behaved exactly like himself.' She knew her husband's quality lay precisely in his readiness to make such sacrifices, and there was no complaint from her about them. She would, though, tell friends later on that she was glad for her husband's spell in the cabinet, glad to have had the fun of being on the inside: she is a woman who loves politics, perhaps even more than her husband did. Powell himself recalled that 'after years, after decades even, of patience and of waiting, there comes the moment to "draw sabre and charge". When the moment came to Rab, he turned his horse and trotted slowly away.'[232] Powell's last illusions about Butler had been dispelled. The common view among his colleagues was that if Rab's first wife, who had died several years earlier, had been alive still, she would have given him the gumption to pursue the quarry right to the end. That, though, was not to be.

Throughout that Saturday, a week after Butler's address at Blackpool, intense pressure was put on Powell and Macleod to change their minds. Powell refused to make any comment to the Sunday press about his position, having been asked by Bligh and Home's press officer to say nothing. Sunday was fraught for him in other respects; he had two motor accidents during it. First, bringing back his daughters from St Peter's, Eaton Square, he wrapped the rear nearside bumper of his green Morris Traveller estate car around the rear bumper of a maroon Citroën next to which he was trying to park. He did not, apparently, notice what he had done. His neighbour, whose car was undamaged, alerted Powell to the mishap later when he found a section of Powell's Morris on the ground, and returned it to him. Powell was being chased by photographers and reporters all day, and had driven around the houses on his way back from church in an effort to shake them off. Then, four hours later, he reversed into a car on Putney Bridge; this was less of a problem as it was driven merely by an irate photographer from the *Daily Telegraph* who was pursuing him. He did, though, find the time to receive at home his successor as Minister of Health, Anthony Barber, and brief him about the Ministry he was taking over.

That evening Home announced his cabinet. Both Powell and Macleod stayed silent. Home, when pressed, simply replied, 'You will have to ask them ... I am sorry, they just don't feel they can accept office.'[233] The press was unclear why Powell had resigned. The *Daily Telegraph*, in a leading article, teased him for having enunciated as his only objection to Government policy the recent Act that had allowed Home and Hailsham to renounce their peerages; and, as for his principles, the paper could not understand how a man who had talked so vividly of the contradiction between the free society and the socialist state could have been so wedded to the health service, which relied on the state for its existence. 'Mr Powell', the paper said, 'might make the voice of conscience a bit less muddled.'[234] Powell kept his reasons to himself, regarding them as so self-evident as to require no explanation, and knowing that his own explanation was secure in his archive and would one day be known. Kenneth Robinson, his shadow, at least understood, writing to him 'to salute an act of outstanding political courage. It must have been a most difficult decision, but however painful in the short run it will, I believe, prove justified by events.'[235]

Selwyn Lloyd, reporting a conversation with Home, said that 'Enoch had told him he would very much like to join the Government, but felt himself pledged not to. In other words, it was quite obvious that he had promised Iain that if he stayed out he Enoch would also do so.'[236] Macmillan, in his memoirs, said he was sad that 'Macleod, for whom I had the highest regard, did not feel able to join' the Government.[237] He made no mention of similar regret for his Minister of Health, something that minister noted, and for which he had his revenge, when reviewing the memoirs in 1973. As well as glorying in the fact that, unlike Macleod, he was alive to put the record straight, Powell also described Macmillan's literary style as creating 'a recurrent sensation akin to that of chewing cardboard'.[238]

On the Monday evening Powell went to Buckingham Palace, surrendered his seals of office, and took his farewell of the Queen. His career in office was over.

INTERLUDE

'BACKWARD TRAVELS OUR GAZE'

On St George's Eve 1961, nine months into his time as Minister of Health, Powell was guest of honour at the annual dinner of the City of London branch of the Royal Society of St George.[1] He delivered a speech which, with hindsight, embraces all the main themes that would dominate his thinking and his actions from the moment in 1963 when he was freed of collective responsibility, and in the years leading up to the climacteric of his breach with the Conservative party in February 1974. It also demonstrated how his peculiarly deep affinity with England would, in the years ahead, allow him better to appeal to the often undiscovered feelings of the people, who were less excitable when addressed in purely political terms. It was a defining expression of belief in more ways than one: not just for how it clarified Powell's deep personal motivation, but also for how it defined a romanticism and a profound sense of destiny that would rule out for him the conventional successes of a political career.

The dinner was emphatically not a political occasion, though the Society of St George is, by its very nature, a conservative organisation, and an overtly patriotic one. For Powell, patriotism was the big issue. The main impulse he had always felt as a politician, and which he wished his fellow Conservatives to feel, was to do what was right for his country. That involved imbuing people with an idea of their individual worth and responsibility, of enterprise and freedom; it also involved fostering within and among them a well-developed sense of nation and of cultural identity. Above all, as Powell would say specifically in his uncompromising speech to the 1968 Conservative party conference, what was right for one's country was always possible. This speech, made seven and a half years earlier, is his concise manifesto as a visionary for a decade in which vision was often lacking.

Powell would, in the years ahead, continually tell his fellow countrymen not to believe it when they were told how hopeless their country had become, and that all politics had to be an exercise in damage limitation. Though wedded to the British nation, he saw England and the English as the overwhelming force within that nation. He began his St George's speech with the insistence that 'from time to time an Englishman among other Englishmen may without harm, and even with advantage, seek to express in spoken words just cause to praise his country'.[2] He evoked, immediately, a period of supreme national self-confidence, the mood after which he was once more hankering:

There was a saying, not heard today so often as formerly, 'What do they know of England who only England know?' It is a saying which dates. It has a period aroma, like Kipling's *Recessional* or the state-rooms at Osborne. The period is that which the historian Sir John Seeley, in a now almost forgotten but once immensely popular book, called *The Expansion of England*. In that incredible phase, which came upon the English unawares, as all true greatness comes upon a nation, the power and influence of England expanded with the force and speed of an explosion.

For Powell, Englishness was a set of values and a state of mind. The sowing abroad and flowering of these had been the point of the Empire, and he had seen it at first hand and been enraptured by it first in Australia, then, far more potently, in India:

> The strange and brief conjuncture of cheap and invincible seapower with industrial potential brought the islands and the continents under the influence, I almost said under the spell, of England; and it was the Englishman who carried with him to the Rockies or the North-West Frontier, to the Australian deserts or the African lakes, 'the thoughts by England given', who seemed to himself and to a great part of his countrymen at home to be the typical Englishman with the truest perspective of England.

Of course, 'spell' was what he meant. His vision was mystical, and unequivocally romantic. The love of England and of nation was not a function of the intellect alone.

When Powell became shadow defence spokesman and, more to the point, when he delivered the speech that stopped him continuing in that post, he made the most ruthless and unsentimental statements of modern realities in the light of the imperial legacy. On defence, it was to be his unshakeable belief that Britain could no longer engage in a role as world policeman, and in particular should abandon any idea of a continuing function East of Suez: this was in direct contravention of what almost all in his party, still clinging to the glories of Empire, wanted. In the controversies about immigration, he argued that the perceived imperial debt that required any former colonial subject to have the right to settle in Britain could no longer be called in. He used the St George's Day speech, long before any of those controversies were stirred by him, to set out his position. Referring back to imperial glory and responsibility, he said unflinchingly: 'That phase is ended, so plainly ended that even the generation born at its zenith, for whom the realisation is the hardest, no longer deceive themselves as to the fact.'

This was a typical Powell rhetorical device, to become familiar in many of his speeches in the years ahead. An audience would be lulled by a clear exhibition of sympathetic thoughts into an implicit trust in Powell the speaker, and he would then make a statement with which they were unlikely to agree, but with which he would credit them complete, and intelligent, agreement, even though they had almost certainly not reached that stage. Now, in language more ornate and poetic than he would ever use in one of his political speeches, and which set out precisely the conflict between romantic and steely intellectual that was to occupy his mind ever more openly in the years ahead, he hammered home his unpalatable point: 'That power and that glory have vanished, as surely, if not as tracelessly, as the Imperial fleet from the waters of Spithead – the eye of history, no doubt as inevitably as "Nineveh and Tyre", as Rome and Spain.' The romance of Empire had died, but the people needed romance, and Powell would replace it with the romance of nation. He wanted to make them realise that England had never depended for her character or strength upon the Empire she had just lost. The myth of Empire had a short history, having originated in late-Victorian England, within the memories of many still alive.

He had shrewdly identified the constituency that would provide him with his support in the years ahead, a group of decent, conservative-minded people of all political parties and none, whose main aim was to be left alone to get on with their lives, to have their way of life left intact, and who felt that no politician or group of politicians recognised their needs and concerns. Having identified them, Powell saw the need to educate them out of some of their own unrealistic beliefs. But he also saw that, once he had led that change of opinion, he would have an invincible bedrock of support. What he did not manage to do – and here Margaret Thatcher learned from his mistake – was to get the parliamentary Conservative party to go with him, so that popular support could be translated into legislative success. For Powell, in leading his people, his main message had to be that England, however reduced, was still a land of hope.

> And yet England is not as Nineveh and Tyre, nor as Rome, nor as Spain. Herodotus relates how the Athenians, returning to their city after it had been sacked and burnt by Xerxes and the Persian army, were astonished to find, alive and flourishing in the midst of the blackened ruins, the sacred olive tree, the native symbol of their country. So we today at the heart of a vanished empire, amid the fragments of demolished glory, seem to find, like one of her own oak trees, standing and growing, the sap still rising from her ancient roots to meet the spring, England herself. Perhaps after all we know most of England who only England know.

When Powell made his speech on immigration at Birmingham seven years later almost to the day, it seemed to some he was inventing, for the sake of political expediency, a divided notion of citizenship, allowing him to argue that citizens from the New Commonwealth could be treated differently from those whose families had been here since before the 1948 British Nationality Act. Yet in the St George's Day speech he had already defined this notion of separateness between the two groups of citizens.

> There was this deep, this providential difference between our empire and those others, that the nationhood of the mother country remained unaltered through it all, almost unconscious of the strange fantastic structure built around her – in modern parlance 'uninvolved'. The citizenship of Rome dissolved into the citizenship of the whole ancient world; Spain learnt to live on the treasure of the Americas; the Hapsburgs and the Hohenzollerns extended their policy with their power. But England, which took as an axiom that the American Colonies could not be represented in Parliament and had to confess that even Ireland could not be assimilated, underwent no organic change as the mistress of a world empire. So the continuity of her existence was unbroken when the looser connections which had linked her with distant continents and strange races fell away.

How Powell saw this was not, in the years immediately ahead, to be the way most of his party saw it, and that would be at the heart of many of the conflicts in which he and they would participate. For him, the imperial episode had left a legacy that was mental rather than physical, or should be. It was just another transient part of a long and largely distinguished history. Once the sentiment was stripped away from the imperial memory, the clock could be put back, and England could be found in a predicament mostly unchanged from that in which the imperial acquisitions had begun. He had made his speech on the Royal Titles Bill, and issued his plea against the divisibility of the realm, in a different world just eight years before. He had forced himself to accept the end of that world. Yet he made for himself the consolation that the England he now lived in, or wanted to live in, was one that bore distinct resemblances to the pre-imperial phase: one whose predominant moral and intellectual features, of individualism, enterprise, freedom and a small apparatus of the state, would be emulated if Britain was to be at the head of nations in terms of prosperity and freedom. They were qualities far even from those practised by the Conservative Government of which Powell was a member, further still from the Labour administration that would shortly succeed it.

> Thus our generation is one which comes home again from years of distant wandering. We discover affinities with earlier generations of English, generations before the 'expansion of England', who felt no country but this to be their own. We look upon the traces which they left with a new curiosity, the curiosity of finding ourselves once more akin with the old English.

Here, the romantic took over, with Powell rhapsodising about the continuity of the English people and the nation, setting out his own understanding of the mature Anglo-Saxon culture and its integrity, and trying to put himself and his audience in mind of the legacy of England on which he, and they, would have to build:

> Backward travels our gaze, beyond the grenadiers and the philosophers of the eighteenth century, beyond the pikemen and the preachers of the seventeenth, back through the brash adventurous days of the first Elizabeth and the hard materialism of the Tudors, and there at last we find them, or seem to find them, in many a village church, beneath the tall tracery of a perpendicular East window and the coffered ceiling of the chantry chapel.

It was not an abstract idea of the past with which Powell was communicating, it was with the individuals who made it:

> From brass and stone, from line and effigy, their eyes look out at us, and we gaze into them, as if we would win some answer from their inscrutable silence. 'Tell us what it is that binds us together; show us the clue that leads through a thousand years; whisper to us the secret of this charmed life of England, that we in our time may know how to hold it fast.'

The supreme part of Powell's conception of himself was as a parliamentarian: parliament was the gift England had given to the world, and it was to his rights as a Member of Parliament, with a right and duty to speak for his constituents and entitled to a hearing in a free country, that he would appeal again and again during the attempts to marginalise and silence him in the late 1960s and early 1970s. It was Parliament that had maintained the peace and the quiet, non-revolutionary continuity of England down the centuries; it was the model of parliament that had civilised such large stretches of the globe during 'the expansion of England'. As Powell gazed at the brasses and the effigies of the feudal lords of the middle ages, he could well imagine what they would tell him.

> What would they say? They would speak to us in our own English tongue, the tongue made for telling truth in, tuned already to songs that haunt the hearer like the sadness of spring. They would tell us of that marvellous land, so sweetly mixed of opposites in climate that all the seasons of the year appear there in their greatest perfection; of the fields amid which they built their halls, their cottages, their churches, and where the same blackthorn showered its petals upon them as upon us; they would tell us, surely, of the rivers, the hills and of the island coasts of England. They would tell us too of a palace near the great city which the Romans built at a ford of the River Thames, a palace with many chambers and one lofty hall, with angel faces carved on the hammer beams, to which men resorted out of all England to speak on behalf of their fellows, a thing called 'Parliament', and from that hall went out men with fur-trimmed gowns and strange caps on their heads, to judge the same judgements, and dispense the same justice, to all the people of England.

This was not simply an indulgent prose-poem; the point Powell was making, at length, was of the continuity of English institutions, the rock of his faith as a Tory. It was this over-arching desire to maintain the integrity and supremacy of those institutions that would fuel his campaign against the Common Market. At the head of all the institutions was the monarchy, the notion of British sovereignty, of the King in Parliament, in parley through his ministers with the representatives of his subjects, the Parliament sovereign. The intellectual roots of Powell's campaign against Britain's accession to the Treaty of Rome may not have started in this speech, but they are, for the first time in his career, publicly apparent here.

> One thing above all they assuredly would not forget, Lancastrian or Yorkist, squire or lord, priest or layman; they would point to the kingship of England, and its emblems everywhere visible. The immemorial arms, gules, three leopards or, though quartered late with France, azure, three fleurs-de-lis argent; and older still, the crown itself and that sceptred awe, in which Saint Edward the Englishman still seemed to sit in his own chair to claim the allegiance of all the English. Symbol, yet source of power; person of flesh and blood, yet incarnation of an idea; the kingship would have seemed to them, as it seems to us, to embrace and express the qualities that are peculiarly England's: the unity of England, effortless and unconstrained, which accepts the unlimited supremacy of Crown in Parliament so naturally as not to be aware of it; the homogeneity of England, so profound and embracing that the counties and the regions make it a hobby to discover their differences and assert their peculiarities; the continuity of England, which has brought this unity and this homogeneity about by the slow alchemy of centuries.

Powell would look with dismay during the years ahead at attempts to dilute this particular way the English had of doing things, not just in the move to have Britain assimilated into European institutions, but in the apparent corruption of the British way by American influences. His belief was that, by nature of her history, England was simply not like anywhere else, and, if left to her own devices, that history proved that the country could not but flourish. 'For the unbroken life of the English nation over a thousand years and more is a phenomenon unique in history, the product of a specific set of circumstances like those which in biology are supposed to start by chance a new line of evolution. Institutions which elsewhere are recent and artificial creations, appear in England almost as works of nature, spontaneous and unquestioned.'

The first great institutional defence Powell would make in the years ahead was his triumphant defeat of the plans, jointly agreed by both front benches in the Commons, to reform the House of Lords by dealing with the hereditary element. This was nearly eight years away, and Powell could have no inkling of it when he spoke. Yet one phrase in particular summed up the tenacity and zeal with which he took on that apparently hopeless case, and won. 'The deepest instinct of the Englishman – how the word "instinct" keeps forcing itself in again and again! – is for continuity; he never acts more freely nor innovates more boldly than when he is most conscious of conserving or even of reacting.'

Above all, for the future, Powell would urge his fellow countrymen not to lose their natural self-confidence, not to lose their belief in England. When the Labour Government, and then Heath's own, took to blaming the British people for what were, in fact, the failings through mismanagement and stupidity of governments themselves, Powell saw that confidence coming most under attack and, to his distress, replaced by defeatism. He would argue that Britons had done nothing, either domestically or in the world, of which there was any need to feel ashamed; and they had their long history, rich in examples of achievement, on which to draw for comfort:

> From this continuous life of a united people in its island home spring, as from the soil of England, all that is peculiar in the gifts and the achievements of the English nation, its laws, its literature, its freedom, its self-discipline. All its impact on the outer world – in earlier colonies, in later *Pax Britannica*, in government and lawgiving, in commerce and in thought – has flowed from impulses generated here.

There was the one, ultimate national institution that 'symbolised and expressed' the 'continuous and continuing life of England' – 'the English kingship'. Whatever the Stuart and Hanoverian constituent of the British monarchy, and notwithstanding the Irish, Welsh and Scottish over whom the Queen reigned, hers was, he maintained, an English kingship: 'The stock that received all these grafts is English, the sap that rises through it to the extremities rises from roots in English earth, the earth of England's history.'

In his peroration, Powell urged careful stewardship of 'the parent stem of England, and its royal talisman', for there were dangers likely to be ahead: not of war, as so often in the past, but the peril of 'indifference and humbug, which might squander the accumulated wealth of tradition and devalue our sacred symbolism to achieve some cheap compromise or some evanescent purpose'. It was a clear, but perhaps unconscious, recognition of the carelessness with which his fellow Conservatives would surrender what he believed should be their principles at the time of the great debate over Europe ten years later. It was right that there should be, he concluded, the urge to 'renew and strengthen in ourselves the resolves and the loyalties which English reserve keeps otherwise and best in silence'. In his own defence of those resolves and loyalties, he would find increasingly that silence was no option.

9

POWELLISM

With nice irony, Powell's first public pronouncements after refusing office were made in Bromley, to Macmillan's constituency party. Macmillan, of course, was not present, but had said of Powell, in talking of the meeting, 'One day he will be back in the Government, like Selwyn Lloyd.'[1] This was in dubious taste, given Macmillan's earlier judgments on Lloyd, whom Home had brought back. Powell used his speech to confirm that, at fifty-one, he had not given up. 'I certainly have no intention of going out of politics. I would have to be carried out feet first. I live and die a politician.'[2] He sidestepped a question from his audience about why he had refused to serve, stating simply that 'the party, and the principles on which we stand, are greater than any individual or group of individuals. They, and loyalty to them, embrace all of us.' Powell would not believe that for much longer.

The significance of his speech – which was largely about what he called 'socialist delusion' – was that he used it to promise to use his new-found freedom from collective responsibility to set out the starkness of the alternatives facing Britain, and to raise the curtain on his abomination of Labour's intended 'national plan' for the economy, and other ideas of state control. He delivered the sort of lecture he no doubt felt Macmillan needed: 'We are a capitalist party. We believe in capitalism ... that system of competition and free enterprise, rewarding success and penalising failure, which enables every individual to participate by his private decisions in shaping the future of society.'[3] Yet he spared some apparently kind words for his ex-leader: 'As I look back upon those years in time to come, I am sure that one impression will remain dominant in my mind above all others from observation of Mr Macmillan in counsel, in cabinet, in the Commons. It's the sheer, cold, dauntless courage of this man, a courage which one senses is the combination of personal gallantry and steely determination.' This assessment was at odds with what Powell would say and write about Macmillan only a few years later. Like his remarks about loyalty to principles with which he did not agree, it smacks of observing the form of such an occasion.

The latest renunciation of office by Powell was a crucial point in his career, and the speech at Bromley a symbol of the way he had marked out ahead. He had always treated audiences with respect, never talking down to them, but as a result often speaking over their heads. Yet the sight of Powell permanently 'on the stump' campaigning would become the central part of his public image.

The hundreds of speeches he would make in the next decade would, like an evangelical mission, become the means of communicating the creed of 'Powellism'. If audiences were nonplussed by a speech, the press would usually report it, with added commentary, the next day. He was one of the last senior politicians successfully to use a regular programme of public meetings as the prime means of appealing to the electorate. He knew, too, that his willingness to speak in a way that did not inevitably reflect the party line would ensure his efforts did not go unnoticed. His individualism was not merely a means of securing a press. Whereas his fellow resigner, Macleod, used the next year to consolidate his position on the centre-left of the party, for Powell it was the start of a period of yet deeper thought, the pursuit of a more ruthless logic. This would not only make the mainstream Conservative party something with which he was incompatible, but would begin the process of making him incompatible with politics as it would now be practised. For him, it was the end of compromise.

After the resignations the party's grandees went to the usual lengths to advertise that, despite two of the cabinet's most talented men refusing to serve, the party was united and all was well. Heath, now President of the Board of Trade, described the unwillingness of Powell and Macleod to serve as 'a matter of great regret' to him.[4] However, he added, 'The important thing is that they were offered office in this administration. They knew what the Prime Minister's views were through serving with him as colleagues. From that point of view I do not think they should have had reservations.' That was absolutely true. 'If you differ on a matter of principle,' he went on, alluding to the men's as yet unrevealed support for Butler, 'you should resign.' Heath's remarks were made in a television interview in which he was asked why, as a fellow founder of One Nation, he had not felt the need to go too in support of his friends. That was not, as he knew, the issue, but he reiterated that the policies Douglas-Home (as he had become) would follow would be entirely consonant with the One Nation creed. The trouble for Powell in particular – whose record of refusing or resigning office required many more offences to be taken into consideration than did Macleod's – was that this walk-out seemed to confirm the view of his more pragmatic colleagues that he was not really a politician at all. It would, however hard he strove, place him under a handicap. It would put him behind in the race with others of his generation to shape the party, and to challenge for its leadership. Heath, who had seemed to take second place to Maudling, was already busy trying to pull ahead.

The Sunday after his resignation Powell gave a genial interview to the *Sunday Times*, sounding like one relieved to be shot of a burden. Referring to this limerick:

> There once was a man who said 'damn!
> It is borne in upon me I am

An engine that moves
In predestinate grooves,
I'm not even a bus, I'm a tram,'

Powell said that 'a minister is like a tram, a backbencher is like a bus, with no predetermined lines to run on. It does a man no harm to run like a bus for a while, to disengage his mind from the things he's been thinking about for some years – and just to see what happens.'[5] The interviewer taxed him about his image as a 'man of conscience', to which Powell replied, 'It's no good being embarrassed by an image because you can do nothing about it. Anyhow, public images are but little connected, and that by accident, with the real man. As for conscience, that's a word I never use. Beware the man who says he is honest.' Powell said he had no regrets – 'except some things I regret not having said'.

Later, he would recall that his liberation from office was:

as if a spring in my mind snapped back into action. I had lived through years in which the Government to which I belonged had been engaged in the business of attempting to create governmental control over essential prices, including the price of labour. It was the age of Franco-Macmillanite planning, it was the age (the early age) of prices and incomes policy. I had found this profoundly repugnant, repugnant because it jarred with another Tory prejudice, the Tory prejudice that, upon the whole, things are wiser than people, that institutions are wiser than their members and that a nation is wiser than those who comprise it at any specific moment.[6]

This explains why Powell would embark with the zeal he did on his personal ideological campaign over the next year; and also why, once he held shadow office, he would not be confined again as he had been during the Macmillan years. His view of the freedom accorded to a man in his position was long-standing, and would create great difficulties for him as the party moved, in the years ahead, under more doctrinaire management. 'The fact must be recognised', Powell had written in 1953, 'that a political party, especially in a two-party state, is immensely embracing and can include within its limits diametrically opposite opinions on almost all subjects except the one or two which happen to be the immediate ground of party conflict at the particular time.'[7] Even that last qualification would become dispensable in Powell's view as his confidence about his position in the party rose.

In his new-found leisure Powell returned to work on his history of the Lords, mostly in the library of the Commons. For the rest of his parliamentary career he would be found, if he was in the Palace of Westminster, either in his place in the chamber or at his regular desk in the library – which his friend John Biffen noted, ironically, was by the shelves that stored the complete works of John Maynard Keynes. To help him on his Lords book Powell engaged a young

American assistant, Keith Wallis, to try to finish the project in a reasonable time. Powell came to regard Wallis as indispensable, and paid him generous tribute in the book when it came out. Wallis became devoted to Powell, though a fellow guest on a Powell picnic remembered the American, who was a chain-smoker, disappearing into the bushes every fifteen minutes for a cigarette, not daring to smoke in Powell's presence because of his deep disapproval of the habit.

Powell also undertook more journalism, though he ignored an offer from Richard Ingrams, the editor of *Private Eye*, to join the editorial board of that publication at the unlikely sounding salary of £5,000 a year.[8] His speech-making continued unabated, its theme predominantly that of the fallacies of the socialist state – fallacies, he was never slow to point out, that were not confined to the socialist party alone. He did not, then or later, resent the hours spent travelling all over Britain, usually by train, to put his message over at Friday and Saturday evening functions, or the many hours of preparation that went into each speech. For one thing, he had for years made it a rule that he spent the time on trains reading for intellectual stimulation rather than in the line of business, and there would be much opportunity for that ahead. His family, however, saw scarcely more of him than when he had been a minister.

Three weeks after Douglas-Home's appointment Powell finally made a public protestation of support for him, after a meeting with officers and committee members of his constituency association. He said his reasons for not serving were 'individual and private', and implied no disagreement with the party, its policies, the Government or personalities in it. He was taxed by his association about how, if Butler had felt able to take office, he had not. He told them that 'it is not in the least surprising that two individuals in different situations should make different decisions'. He also denied that his failing to serve had any detrimental effect on party unity.[9] He had a relatively hostile postbag from Conservative activists, in whose eyes he had for the second time in five years publicly violated the unwritten creed of blind loyalty. Powell was having none of it. When, for example, the chairman of the Leicester Conservative Association wrote to him somewhat pompously that he was 'dismayed, deeply' by the 'inexplicable reactions' of him and Macleod, and that it was 'unfortunate' Powell had behaved as he had, Powell replied curtly that 'as to what is unfortunate, that is a matter of opinion'.[10]

When the new session of Parliament opened in mid-November Powell was unanimously elected chairman of the Conservative backbench Education Committee. In a speech the following month, to the annual dinner of the Working Men's College in St Pancras, he sought to define the real purpose of education. He said that 'the facility with which not only politicians but people who should know better argue for education in the name of economic growth is frightening'. By contrast, education was 'a good in its own right, something which men desire because they are men, and which they will therefore spend their effort and their riches to procure for themselves and bestow upon others'.[11] He also knocked an emerging, fashionable view about education, and the value of vocational studies: 'The silliest and the most sinful of the many heresies of pseudo-democracy is to pretend that all studies and all learning are "created equal". They are not. It matters just as much to a person's education what he learns and is taught as it matters to his salvation what he believes.' This truth, he added, 'does prevent us from assuming that students are being educated because they are at a university'.

Whereas the previous Prime Minister had greatly favoured Macleod over Powell, entirely for personal reasons, so his successor favoured Powell over Macleod, also for personal reasons. Douglas-Home had always distrusted Macleod, largely, it seems, because of an intuition that Macleod was 'on the make' as much as for any political action.[12] There had never been any hostility between him and Powell; in fact, according to Douglas-Home's biographer, he 'respected the reasons' for Powell's refusal to serve.[13] As a gesture of his support for Powell, he invited him to attend, as an observer, the party steering committee on policy, and to help with the manifesto. Macleod, who had far more experience of such matters than Powell, was not invited.

In the middle of January 1964 cover was broken on the events of the previous October. Macleod, who had just been appointed editor of the *Spectator*, wrote his account of events. Macleod had been provoked by the deeply partisan, and selective, account published by Randolph Churchill in his book *The Fight for the Tory Leadership*, which had specifically exonerated Macmillan from a charge of asserting any undue influence to steer the succession away from Butler and towards Home. Macleod wrote to Redmayne on 6 January to warn him of the impending article, saying that what 'horrified' him most was that Macmillan, and, on his instruction, certain friends, had supplied Churchill with the most significant material. 'I regard this as most improper,' wrote Macleod.[14] He continued: 'As you know, Enoch Powell and myself have been at great pains (and may I add at great cost to ourselves in our constituencies) to say nothing and to refuse interviews to the press and television. Obviously this now becomes an impossible position to maintain.' Powell's only comment on Macleod's article was: 'I can confirm the accuracy of Mr Macleod's narrative on all matters within my knowledge, and I agree with his general assessment of those events.'[15] Powell had an agenda concerned solely with the future, and was not prepared to be sidetracked into arguments about the past. When the Conservative defeat came nine months later, Home blamed Macleod, and this article, in large part for it.[16]

Apart from a couple of brief interventions in debates in the autumn of 1963, Powell said nothing in the Commons from the moment of his resignation until 27 January 1964. The Robbins report on higher education, which would promote the foundation of new universities, had recently been published, and Powell made his own observations on why more children wished to stay in full-time study after passing the school-leaving age. It was not down to the Government, nor any other politicians, nor the local education authorities, but was the expression of free will by parents: 'This is the expression, the self-expression, of a national will for progress in education'.[17] He said the main aim of the Government had to be to secure that 'there is no-one with an aptitude for higher education who, by reason of the organisation of our school system, fails to have that opportunity turned into reality'.[18] In a move that would set no precedent, Powell's remarks were warmly endorsed by the Minister of Education, Quintin Hogg – as Hailsham, having renounced his viscounty, had become – in his winding-up speech.

Powell's emphasis on individual motivation was the clearest sign of his growing philosophical impulse. He planned an assault on the corporatist institutions a Conservative government had done nothing to countermand. Breaking his virtual silence outside Parliament since his resignation, in the course of one week in the winter of 1964 he redefined what, as he saw it, should be the economic orthodoxy of the Conservative party and the British nation. In doing so, he set himself intellectually apart not merely from most of his former Government colleagues, but from most of his parliamentary party. His first target was the NEDC, or 'Neddy', the employers' side of which had recently talked about the need to keep prices and profits down, and the possible establishment of a prices commission. Powell attacked this as 'nonsense', saying such plans 'will not work. We do not know how to make them work. In fact, they cannot work in any society which we are prepared to contemplate. Wages, profits, prices are determined, always have been determined, and always will be determined, until we go communist, by the market – by supply and demand working through the market'.[19] It was not his first assault on the NEDC, set up by the Government of which he had been a member. Writing in the *Observer* at the end of 1963, Powell had warned that by setting up this body the Conservatives had forged a weapon for Labour to use against them, particularly in the sphere of economic planning.[20] He exposed the futility of trying to allocate resources to an industry so it could grow in line with government plans; it could only properly grow in line with demand for its goods.

He branded these anti-market ideas as 'nonsense in massive doses, solemnly swallowed by large and representative bodies of men, and commended, without the flicker of an eyelid, to the nation at large'.[21] He sought, in barely restrained language, to express his amazement at the way in which the supposed forces of capitalism were behaving. 'When you find management – the representatives of enterprise and risk capital – standing up in public and saying that they have a responsibility to keep prices stable or lower them, that individual prices ought to be reported on by a commission, and that profits ought to attract special tax penalties if they exceed a certain level, then it is a sign that either the millennium has arrived or else something is going very seriously wrong indeed.'

This was the germ of Powell's great onslaught against the national plan

Labour was promising. He set out his basic, and for those times intensely radical, ideas about the responsibility of the forces of capitalism, and would not veer from them again. Of the notion that managements should accept responsibility for prices, he said:

> Managements have no business to accept any such responsibility. The duty of every management is to conduct the business, including the price policy of the business, in the way which, in the opinion of the management, is likely to maximise the return on the capital invested in the business. A management which does not do this betrays more than the shareholders in the business: it betrays the employees and the nation as a whole. In some circumstances, returns will be maximised by keeping prices stable or by reducing them. But in other circumstances returns will be maximised by raising prices. Wherever that is so, it is the responsibility and duty of the management concerned to raise its prices, whether in the home or in the export market.

Scarcely had he drawn breath after this than, in an article for the *Sunday Telegraph* the following weekend, he turned his attention to wages and productivity. He stated the direct relationship 'between our total income as a nation and our total productivity', and said that 'if total money incomes outrun total productivity, there is trouble ahead'.[22] Relating the incomes of individuals to this national productivity was problematic, and an incomes policy (such as Lloyd had practised two years earlier, when Powell was in office) was no answer. Even if it could be enforced, it 'would freeze the economic pattern for ever and stop all progress. It would be the prescription for stagnation.' Powell argued that increases in productivity should not determine increases in earnings; the level of earnings would always have to be set according to the supply of and demand for labour. He knew this was an unpopular truth, unpopular because of 'the widespread, emotional, almost instinctive desire to see wages and salaries as a kind of reward for intrinsic merit, related somehow to the ethical deserts of the recipient'.

He made his point by referring to the pay of two of the more emotive groups of workers. He cited the 'nonsense' of politicians trampling the rights of teachers and nurses underfoot, but claimed, 'the political decision is how many, and what, teachers and nurses the state is to demand; the right pay is then that which equates the supply with this demand'. With this, Powell came to the heart of his argument, indeed to the heart of his economic programme as he would outline it in the months and years ahead: 'Supply and demand, working in a market, will, and indeed do, determine the distribution of incomes. They do the job, as no-one else can do it, of determining the respective shares of the national total – which incomes shall increase faster, which slower.' Individual free will, in a free society, was the only mechanism that could work. State intervention, such as by the incomes policy, was hopeless and illiberal.

This attack on his own party's economic policy – for that is what it amounted to – was sustained in speech after speech until the general election the following October. Powell's views were only the natural extension of what he had manifestly believed in during his spell as an economic minister in 1957–8, but were the more shocking for being expounded when the Government was so obviously vulnerable, and when he had so recently left it in such controversial circumstances. He attempted to defend himself at a press gallery lunch at the Commons on 12 February. He knew, he said, that people were going around saying, 'Just listen to Enoch – he seems to think he's living in some economic wonderland.' He added, of his newly expounded philosophy, 'I don't know if this is old Toryism or new Conservatism.'[23]

He said he wanted Conservative policies to be distinct, and not a compromise with socialism, and to inspire a less timid approach by British capitalists to world markets. 'We are full of fears and anxieties about the changes which rapid economic progress brings. We are more fearful of automation than welcoming of it. We are fearful of the big movement of population and of industry without which industrial progress is not possible. We are timid in the face of change in every form. We are fearful of affluence itself. We have allowed it to be made a dirty word in recent years.[24] He tried to disarm his critics by saying his creed did not contradict welfarism. On the contrary, greater wealth creation would improve the social services, a point Mrs Thatcher would make during her premiership twenty years later.

Powell, at this time, took steps to play his own role in capitalism. He accepted an offer to become a director of the National Discount Company, one of the select group of a dozen discount houses then doing £1 billion a year worth of business with the Government. Powell's stipend of £2,500 a year was an improvement on his £1,750 parliamentary salary, and he reassured reporters that his departure into finance did not portend an impending retirement from politics. Far from it; in a Third Programme broadcast on 11 March he pointedly advised Douglas-Home that his cabinet was too large, and might benefit from being reduced to fifteen people. He also opposed the expansion of the payroll vote by having more junior ministers in a department, mainly because to have more than the traditional one in the average department would prevent them from exercising their historic role as the understudy of the minister.

A few days later Powell, his philosophical drive apparently unstoppable, was in the public prints again, attacking a staple of economic policy. This time his target was regional planning. The Government had expressed a desire for economic growth to be 'channelled away' from the south-east of England. He argued that the free will of individuals, the markets for residential and business property, and labour market would dictate where and how economic growth happened, not the Government; and he attacked the continuing housing subsidies, principally rent controls, and the subsidising of public transport fares in

London for distorting the appeal of the south-east. 'The country as a whole is made to promote the growth of London employment by making the costs of living and working there appear lower than they really are. The nation is subsidising London's congestion.' The idea of replicating these subsidies in other regions to tempt people away from London was, he argued, absurd. He also believed that the concentration around London, for all its congestion, was an essential concomitant of economic progress, which it would be stupid to dilute.[25]

A little later, on 3 April, Powell developed this attack in a speech in Glasgow. He wondered why the party of free enterprise, when confronted with areas of high unemployment, threw its principles overboard instead of harnessing them to deal with the difficulty. 'The fault is not that there is an excess of "Tory freedom"; there is a deficiency.'[26] Rather than removing obstacles to mobility of labour, the Government instead seemed determined to impose more of them. He attacked, again, the idea of incentives for firms to set up in areas where there were particular economic problems, and argued that, in the long run, this was an anti-capitalist move that would cost jobs rather than create them. Mobility of labour, and of businesses, was, he argued, essential to economic progress. Regional incentives would simply trap labour and businesses in areas unsuited to them rather than encourage them to move and expand, and, of course, their financing would drain the productive sectors of the economy. Moreover, it showed complete contempt for British management, in concluding that they could not be trusted to make a proper economic decision without the assistance of bribes and other inducements from the Government.

His party's growing appetite, as he saw it, for state intervention he called 'an axe laid at the root of a fundamental principle'. He repeated his call for people in depressed areas to be helped by an end to housing subsidies that favoured more affluent areas, by less intervention rather than more; and the workforce needed to adopt the mentality that it might need to move if it was to work, to marry supply with demand. There also had to be an end to national pay bargaining, which meant depressed areas could not attract business by lowering wage rates. To ignore the need for such reforms was to contradict capitalism, but Powell seemed to imply that his party was doing just that. 'We cannot', he told his audience, 'fight the battles of freedom if our faith in it is half-hearted.'[27]

That, at least, was the interpretation Thorneycroft, still in the Government as Minister of Defence, put on it. In a speech at Harrogate the day after Powell's Glasgow outburst, Thorneycroft expressed mystification that Powell talked 'as though the Conservative party must offer the capitalist system to the public, or nothing'. In Thorneycroft's bizarre view – and he was not alone in his party – 'the Conservative party is a great deal bigger than the capitalist system'. He emphasised the need, through the social security system, to put compassion before 'any of the economic isms'.[28] However, Powell had made clear his support for social security, financed by greater wealth creation. In that regard, Thorneycroft had entirely missed his point.

II

Powell's high-profile campaign was taken by commentators as evidence of the growing disunity in his party between its radical intellectual wing and the much larger group who explicitly accepted an element of socialist doctrine. By coming out into the open like this, in a way he had not had the clout to do after his 1958 resignation, Powell effectively drew up battle lines in the party for a fight that would not be resolved until after Mrs Thatcher's election to the party's leadership in 1975. There was, it seemed to many, further evidence of his belligerence in three articles in *The Times* in the first week of April 1964. Written under the pseudonym 'A Conservative', these three pieces sought to set out exactly what was wrong with the party. Though pseudonymous, some observers recognised that the content and style were pure Powell. He refused, at the time, to confirm or deny authorship; indeed, he refused publicly to confirm or deny at any time subsequently. Stylistically, the clues were plain – most notably in the description of Macmillan as a man who 'enjoyed aristocratic poses',[29] a phrase anyone who knew Powell knew him to have used often about his former chief. The historical sense of the pieces, the rooting of the first article in the work of the Conservative Research Department after the war and the betrayal of the radical agenda during the years since 1951 also led back to Powell.

In addition, the articles showed a coming-to-terms with the new realities of life as Powell saw them: post-imperial realities, the notion of the Commonwealth as 'a gigantic farce',[30] the ridiculing of the idea that Britain was still a power in the Middle East, the abjuration of the concept of overseas aid, the urging on the Government of a foreign policy that protected British access to world markets above all other considerations, and a resounding call for the Conservative party to be inspired by patriotism, but a patriotism based on reality and not dreams. These were themes Powell had been expounding in public since the early 1950s, and most notably in the St George's speech. The last of the three articles, published on 3 April 1964, seemed to conclude the case. It is a microcosm of Powell's protracted assault on the socialist economics now practised by both main parties, and which he would propound in Glasgow that very evening. The article, like Powell in his speeches, railed against the socialist attempts to eliminate 'choice, initiative, competition, profit', and pointed out there was no need to wait for the coming of a Labour government to see these malign forces in action. The article illustrated the damage done by the subsidy culture, regional planning, incomes policies and the NEDC. The *Guardian*, the following week, concluded that Powell had written the third article only, with the first (the historical overview) written by Angus Maude, and the attack on the Commonwealth by Nigel Birch.[31]

Around Westminster and Fleet Street the assumption that Powell had written the three articles was otherwise universal. Peter Utley, writing in the *Sunday Telegraph*, asked the obvious question: 'how can a man with such views have sat comfortably in any Tory cabinet since the war – indeed, one might add, in any Tory cabinet since 1918?' That was not the only contradiction that presented itself. How, Utley asked, could Powell have presided 'with a clear conscience' over the massive spending department he had run for the last three years? How could he have sacrificed his career in protest at Butler's failure to become Prime Minister? (That, Powell would have told him, was not an ideological point.) Utley, who knew Powell well, summed up his doctrine of politics as being that 'nine tenths of it is governed by necessity, but the remaining tenth is a crucial area in which decisions of principle can and ought to be made. It is, he holds, about this tenth that the election is being fought, and the only way to fight it effectively is to dramatise the issues it presents even at the cost of giving the literal-minded the impression that the battle of principle is ranging over the whole area of politics.'[32] In that, Utley was guilty of wishful thinking; Powell had more widely to range yet.

It fell to Robin Day, who interviewed Powell on *Panorama* on the Monday after the articles appeared, to be the first to question him about their authorship. Powell made his first of many refusals to deny he had written them, though he did claim, perhaps with self-mockery, that the author of the article about the Commonwealth was 'extreme'.[33] Powell had talked earlier of his own policies and views with assurance and self-confidence, but became less assured and self-confident when asked outright by Day whether he had written the three articles. 'I have got my own ideas, but unlike some people I am naming no names. But you know there is no monopoly in the things I have been saying, in the things I have argued.' Powell told Day, as he persisted in his line of interrogation, that 'I am averse to people who ask impertinent questions,' and that Day's questioning came into that category.

As Powell and his wife confirmed to me in 1997, he wrote all three articles. The series had been the idea of Sir William Haley, *The Times*'s editor. Powell had agreed to write the series on the express condition that his anonymity was respected. Haley did not let him down. Corrections to the articles were handled by Haley himself, from his home and not from his office. Powell and his wife drove to Haley's home in Blackheath after dark to deliver the articles; and the typescripts were destroyed afterwards. When Powell was paid it was in cash, so no transaction went through the newspaper's accounts. The secret has remained safe to this day.

In the *Panorama* interview, Day had also asked how Powell's conscience could have allowed him to serve in the Macmillan cabinet while that cabinet was

introducing regional policies; Powell retorted that, in private, no minister was
expected to agree with every policy, nor to flounce out of the cabinet whenever
his own private views were dissented from. In fact, Douglas-Home was far more
relaxed about Powell's activities than was thought to be the case, and far more
relaxed than his successor would be. There were no rebukes when Powell
attacked the Government, in another newspaper article in April, for its foundation of six 'little Neddies' – offshoots of the NEDC whose function was to
construct plans for individual industries – with a promise of three more to
come.[34] Once again, the Government was doing the Opposition's work for it;
Labour had already promised (and Powell cruelly quoted its promise) to set up
such further bureaucracies. What is more, as he warned a fortnight later in a
speech at Maldon, the industry-by-industry approach was exactly how Labour
intended to undertake its planning of the economy.

Yet Douglas-Home, and those who made policy in the Conservative party,
were in no doubt about Powell's genius for radicalism, or for coming up with
arresting ideas. For this reason Sir Michael Fraser, the Central Office official put
in charge of the steering committee on the manifesto, sent Powell a draft for
suggestions. When the suggestions came back – and they were all of a radical
piece with Powell's programme as set out in his speeches in the country, aimed
at breaking the post-war consensus – traditional caution overcame Fraser and
his committee, with the result that the party would fight again on the principles
of 1959.[35] A suggestion by Powell that capital spending on schools should increase
was ignored, as was a commitment to producing more, and better-trained,
teachers.[36] While the party trumpeted the success of the Hospital Plan, it
bypassed Powell's desire to encourage, as he had always sought to do, an
enhanced role for the voluntary sector in health care.[37] Douglas-Home was,
however, sufficiently impressed to earmark Powell to take charge of what he
regarded as the most important task if the Conservatives were returned to
power: a reform of the civil service and of Whitehall, with the aim of cutting
down the workload of ministers and officials in the interests of better government. Powell had no idea of this until years later.[38] It was a job for which his
supreme staff officer's mind was ideal, and which to judge from his work at the
Ministry of Health he would have done successfully. After that, his entire career
would have been different. But it was not to be.

In the debate on the Budget Powell, speaking on 15 April, turned his attention
to monetary policy in the light of the boom Maudling was stoking up for the
election. He noted that, the previous year, the Chancellor had said he would
have to increase net borrowing by 'a substantial amount' – £260 million – to
achieve the desired rate of growth, 4 per cent.[39] However, the additional borrowing had not been made; growth had nonetheless been at 5 per cent; and
Maudling's critics had been proved wrong. Powell discounted the assertion,
which Maudling had not made himself but which some of his officials were

making, that the economy had grown so well in response to fiscal and monetary stimuli. He preferred, consistent with his philosophy, to attribute it to 'a spontaneous movement and reaction not of the economy only – for that is a cold, callous, abstract term – but of the nation as a whole to its opportunities and circumstances. Forces deeper, wider and more embracing than anything in the Budget, forces partly external, but also partly internal to this country, swept forward, obliterating the landmarks of the intended net borrowing requirement ... this was expressed by an increase in the velocity of circulation ... in short, this was a reaction to circumstances, to opportunity, by the nation as a whole.'[40] Expansion would now be governed, he said, by the use to which resources were put, and helped if they were put to more valuable and effective uses.

He stressed, though, that this expansion could not be exceeded by the growth in the money supply; and he was nervous of Maudling's decision, in the interests of a pre-election boom, to increase borrowing now by £300 million to £800 million: 'I will say only this of that decision, that it certainly represents the utmost limit to which prudence could possibly go.'[41] He concluded with a stern lecture that will have embarrassed those of his former colleagues on the Treasury Bench literate enough to have understood it:

It is not only false, it is also dangerous, to inculcate into a nation, as many do today ... the idea that prosperity is something which can be engineered for it by financial arrangements; that its economic progress and development wait upon the acts and upon the nod of Governments, and that it is within the power of any Government to set a specific rate of advance and guarantee by their policies that it will be achieved. The creative forces in a nation lie in the people themselves – in their determination, their effort, their hopefulness, their thrift, their readiness to venture and to change.

Even this hard-edged economic logic, it should be noted, was set in a romantic, almost mystical context of nationhood: it put Powell on a different plane from his colleagues.

His sentiments would not be embraced by his party for another decade. His final words were the template for what would be known as Thatcherism. 'Only in proportion as they show and apply those qualities can the economy advance. The truly creative policies are the policies which enable the nation to put forth the effort and to take the decisions upon which, alone, the rate of its advance depends.' Thinking perhaps more wishfully than he knew, Powell added, 'It is this conviction which unites all hon Members on this side of the Committee. Between this conviction and the converse, which is represented by the party opposite, lies the battlefield on which, this year, we shall be contending for the mind and for the heart of the nation.'[42]

With an election so close – it had to be held within just over six months – Powell's freelance philosophising was becoming a source of the utmost irritation

to some in the leadership who lacked the courage of his convictions. In a speech
in Stirling on 22 April Hogg branded Powell 'a sort of Mao Tse-tung of Toryism'.[43]
Hogg was especially wounded by Powell's assault on regional policy, because
Macmillan had, earlier, made him the minister responsible for devising a policy
to regenerate depressed areas in the north-east. Powell had been in the cabinet
when that policy was formulated, and Hogg felt it odd he should start to attack
it now. Hogg said that to believe it was 'not so much wrong as useless to interfere
with the so-called laws of supply and demand ... is plain nonsense'. Hogg's
remarks were indicative of the level of economic sophistication with which
Powell, on his new crusade, would have to contend.

Such attacks started to have an effect on Powell. With an election so near,
even his zeal would have to be tempered by the tact needed to ensure his party's
chances of re-election were not harmed further. He undertook a speaking tour
of East Anglia, and at Fakenham on 21 April broke relatively new ground by
attacking Labour rather than his own side, asserting that the Opposition were
seeking 'an unrestricted mandate for nationalisation. Although in their programme they only specify steel, road transport and water supply the terms in
which they are seeking the mandate cover the nationalisation or public ownership or control in one form or another of any business or industry.'[44] He
rebuked socialists for claiming that their policies were 'humane'. He could see
nothing 'humane' about limiting the creation of wealth, and the good that could
be done with it.

Then at Maldon in Essex the following day Powell launched what would be
his greatest, and most damaging, specific campaign of the months ahead: the
absurdity of Harold Wilson's view that a Labour government could plan economic development. This would, Powell pointed out, require government to
control and direct private investment, and the public had not yet paused to
think how this would change their lives. 'This, of course, is just what the Labour
party want. Herein lies the mortal peril, that people will wake up one morning
and find themselves saddled with something they had no idea they were voting
for and had no desire to have.'[45]

Powell quoted an NEDC model of the gas industry, which a year earlier had
made what turned out to be wildly underestimated forecasts of the use of gas.
He said it was as well these forecasts were purely an academic exercise, rather
than the means to gauge the planned investment in the industry the state would
control. Otherwise the industry would have had too little capacity to respond
to demand, and insufficient funds to develop that capacity. 'In a Socialist Britain
where the planners had the power to make their forecasts come right we should
never know till too late, if at all, how wrong the forecasts had been.' Powell's
wider point was that such absurdities were a gift to Britain's competitors, even
in a natural monopoly like the gas industry. Industries would have investment
directed away from them so that funds could be available for those chosen by

the planners; thus industries that might otherwise flourish would have their growth cut back. Labour's immediate response was not to attack Powell, but to attack his party for its earlier assaults on him. Patrick Gordon Walker, the shadow Foreign Secretary, described Powell as 'chief whipping boy in the Conservative party', adding that he was 'the most able and prominent of the honest Conservatives. He expresses what is in the Conservative heart.' Gordon Walker came close to the truth when he said Powell stated 'ideas that Conservatives only act on after they have an election safely behind them'.

Powell's turning on Labour did not mark an unconditional repentance. On 3 May he wrote in the press mocking those – Hogg – who had compared him with Mao Tse-tung. All he had called for, notably in his attack on regional policy, was more 'Tory freedom' and not less. 'Instead of trying to reverse economic trends, might it not be better to reinforce them by helping and encouraging the man who needs a job to move to the place where someone is anxious to employ him?' Powell was annoyed that his view had been represented as 'inhuman', when all he was trying to do was improve mobility of labour and allow people to fulfil their potential. He said it might involve just 50,000 people moving from one region to another to bring the level of unemployment in the so-called depressed regions down to below the national average. More than ten times this number of people made such a move every year anyway, so it would hardly constitute a great or painful social upheaval. Unlike a generation later, some areas of the country suffered immense skill and manpower shortages; therefore Powell was justified in arguing that paying to entice people to certain regions was wasteful. But he admitted it might seem, to some, tactless for him to advocate an end to this waste so close to an election. He argued, though, that because his policy was self-evidently right, and promised an expansion of 'Tory freedom', he would be unjustified in keeping quiet about it, whatever the time – an argument he would use to defend himself after making more controversial outbursts in later years.[46]

He was also, that spring, engaged on a substantial philosophical excursion. The previous summer *Encounter*, under the editorship of Arthur Koestler, had published a special number somewhat overdramatically entitled 'Suicide of a Nation', in which various writers had argued for stronger state controls throughout the economy and in welfare provision. The challenge was taken up by Powell's friends at the Institute of Economic Affairs who, organised by Arthur Seldon and Ralph Harris, arranged to publish a symposium pointing out that the real need was for further economic liberalisation. Powell's contribution to the book, published later in the summer of 1964 shortly before the election was called, was entitled 'Is it politically practicable?'

Powell began with an autobiographical note, in which he quoted from his last work for the IEA, *Saving in a Free Society*, where he had said that 'the terms "free economy" and "free society" are to be interchangeable'. He added, 'I still believe that, though some people seem to think it tactless to repeat it just now.'[47] He said the writers in *Encounter* had fallen into the trap of believing myths about the past inevitably being better than the present, with the only hope for the future being that decline would continue.

The harm was, though, that the left harnessed this myth to call for change, and in this case change that would limit personal freedom and economic efficiency. The massive possibilities and potential of the millions of individuals who made up the nation would be exploited only if those people were allowed to flourish as individuals. 'What is politically practicable', he wrote, in relation to this, 'is not a constant; it changes, not necessarily predictably and sometimes swiftly, while the validity of the arguments and principles remains. Indeed, the enunciation of "politically impracticable" thoughts and proposals has itself often made things "politically practicable" which were not so before.'[48] Powell denied the existence of the trend towards state control, which was then the main political practicality as acknowledged by the left.

He was able to point to some of the anti-statism of the Conservative Government, not least to measures in which he had had a direct hand in the 1950s, such as the reduction of rent control and housing subsidies; and even during the apostasy of recent years, with regional plans and the like, the abolition of resale price maintenance, the brain child of Edward Heath, had shown there was still the instinct to deregulate. The main problem with capitalism, though, was that those charged with prosecuting it – namely, the Conservative Government – had lost the public-relations battle about it: the left had succeeded in gaining public acceptance for the notion that capitalism was 'unfair'. Powell proceeded to lay down some hard truths about capitalism.

First, he said that 'a market need not be perfect in order to be superior to no market at all'.[49] However imperfect competition might be, it will still tend to a better use of the resources than none whatsoever. Second, capitalism would work even in an economy with a nationalised sector: just because some industries were nationalised did not mean they all should be. Third, there was no contradiction between a welfare state and a capitalist one; indeed, a capitalist state should be better able to provide welfare than one that is not. Fourth, capitalism is about giving power to individuals: 'respect for humanity and tolerance for the individual are implicit in the capitalist system as in no other: it is the planned economy which insults people – by producing, for example, consumption goods that they do not want.'[50] Fifth, and finally, those who thought capitalism unfair should reflect that 'there can be no worse unfairness than to deny people the chance to put whatever assets they have to what they judge the best use', which is what the market does.

He said clearly – as he had in *Saving in a Free Society* – that capitalism had on its side the 'powerful emotive idea' of freedom, something he felt should be popular with the British; 'political practicability' was therefore dependent on successful public relations about capitalism, and linking it to the public's desire for greater personal liberty. With an eye obviously, but for the moment just implicitly, on the election, he said the time had come to go on to the offensive, and to develop more and more radical ideas to further the free economy. It was an argument to which the Conservative party would be deaf for another decade, while it lost four of the next five elections.

At Bridgnorth later in May he returned to the evils of planning, pointing up the continued failure by many in his own party to understand the realities of what the struggle against Labour should entail. He did not tone down his rhetoric in addressing his fellow Conservatives. 'Here is a party', he said, 'engaged in a life-and-death struggle with political opponents who are pledged and dedicated to Socialism and whose very policy is aimed at eliminating the processes of capitalism from our economy and our society. Yet the same nation and the same party will stop their ears and turn the other way if they hear mention of the very word capitalism. ... It is the Socialists and the economic planners who are the ptolemaics and the flat-earthers of the modern world. They have not moved on beyond capitalism. They have moved back before it.'[51]

In June, Powell turned his fire directly against the economic claims of the trade unions. He told an audience at the London School of Economics that the notion that the unions had been responsible for rises in the standard of living was 'the kind of absurdity which people entertain only when desperately determined to do so, for fear of the consequences of disbelief'.[52] Powell made the obvious point that, instead, living standards had risen only because of greater productivity. The following month, shifting back to his line of attacking a Conservative administration for being insufficiently Conservative, he made a wider-ranging speech on the evils of syndicalism, arguing that the damage done by restrictive practices in the labour market had been an issue governments had avoided for years, but could avoid no longer.

> If the restrictive practices of labour are as wasteful and unjust as other restrictive practices and attended by no compensating advantages to the workers themselves or to the public in general, then sooner or later the law will have to recognise this, and a new framework of law and practice will have to be found for those many functions of the modern trade union which do not depend upon restrictive practices. It is a task of formidable dimensions, which may well take years to accomplish fully. That is no reason for not putting it in hand; still less for pretending that the task is not there at all.[53]

Powell was right about an attempt at reform taking years to accomplish. It was twenty years before the Thatcher Government made any headway on his agenda.

He justified his attack on two counts. First, there had been a spate of legislation aimed at controlling the monopolistic practices of employers and producers; and, second, there had been the first rumblings of opposition in the courts in the matter of union immunities. In February 1964 the House of Lords, in the case of *Rookes* v *Barnard*, had ruled that if a union forced an employer to sack an employee who would not join the union, then the union had to pay that employee damages.

Powell's overriding theme, as always, was the contempt being shown by the state for the freedoms of individuals, judged by the casual way in which the state regarded the infringements of those liberties by third parties such as unions. He said that to maintain restrictive practices 'the individual citizen has to be coerced into withholding or restricting his labour against his own judgment and wishes, and into joining associations to which he does not desire to belong'. He stated baldly that the immunities the unions enjoyed made them 'a state within a state' and were 'not compatible with the rule of law'. He ridiculed as a fantasy the notion of collective bargaining securing higher wages, arguing that in a market economy enjoying full employment firms who paid too little would soon find their staff, if up to the job, going elsewhere. And he scorned the idea of the strike. 'It is a sad spectacle to see deluded men standing idle or parading with banners and slogans, unaware that they can no more affect the demand schedule for their services than they can vary the phases of the moon.' He argued, with empirical justification, that unions followed each other in making their demands, and ended up, therefore, back exactly where they had started before machinating for pay increases, the result being that the unions were pointless.

Just before Parliament rose for the summer, Powell put on a stunning demonstration of the breadth of his expertise, this time as a churchman. On 30 July the Commons considered the Vesture of Ministers Measure, concerned with the rights of parochial church councils to authorise changes in vestments. Powell said this issue had only ever been discussed in Parliament in the course of the Bill that became the Act of Uniformity 1558, 'when the fires of Smithfield were barely out', and in the Act of Uniformity 1662.[54] The Judicial Committee of the Privy Council had said in the 1870s that the only lawful vesture at time of ministration was the surplice, 'an absurdity and stumbling block', as Powell put it, that the Measure they were debating would remove in its 'spirit of tolerance and comprehension'.[55] He said it was not a breach of the Reformation Settlement for, had it been, he would have voted it down.

He returned to the subject of the unions in an article for the *Sunday Times* in early September. Entitled 'Are the unions necessary?' it once more ridiculed the idea that anything other than the laws of supply and demand could affect workers' pay-packets. He said that *Rookes* v *Barnard* had alerted people who had hitherto taken the power of the unions at face value to the fact that those powers were damaging and could be challenged. It was now the job of a responsible Tory party, on the eve of an election campaign, to commit itself to review union law.[56] In reality Douglas-Home's party was too timid to take on such large vested interests and to break the post-war consensus, whatever moral and economic damage Powell could prove it was doing.

III

The election was called for 15 October. In his native West Midlands, Powell saw an issue emerging that had a significance altogether different from that of the agenda he had been pursuing for the preceding months. Since the 1959 election there had been a massive influx of immigrants from the New Commonwealth, to the point where it was estimated there were 80,000 in Birmingham alone, with smaller concentrations in nearby towns, including Wolverhampton. There were already acute housing problems, and in some constituencies the question took no time at all to become an election issue. In Wolverhampton the Indian and West Indian immigrants had come in principally to do dirty jobs in heavy industry, such as the steel mills. Before their arrival, some parts of inner Wolverhampton had been badly run down; and, given economic necessity, it was these cheap and depressing areas that supplied the housing stock for them. Whole streets, then whole districts, turned black, the remaining white residents moving out to newer, but scarcely less depressing, council estates on the edge of town.

Ostensibly, there were no great social problems. Observers from as far away as America had come to Birmingham to see how successfully it had assimilated its immigrants, and, with a huge demand still for labour in a tight market, there had been no trouble finding most of them unskilled or semi-skilled jobs. Yet the resentment among whites was boiling up, particularly among those who lived in areas that had attracted the bulk of the immigration. In council elections earlier that year immigration had been a prominent issue, its most offensive manifestation being in a leaflet put out in Smethwick by alleged Conservative supporters: 'If you want a nigger neighbour, vote Labour'. The Conservatives had made substantial gains in local elections in Smethwick since 1962; and results in the 1964 general election at such places as Eton and Slough and Perry Barr suggest it was the only seat where the race card promised to be profitable for the Conservatives. The Conservative candidate for Smethwick at the general election, Peter Griffiths, a junior school headmaster, was taking on the shadow Foreign Secretary, Patrick Gordon Walker. Griffiths committed himself to a complete ban on unskilled immigrants. Such was the feeling locally that he was reported to be 'confident that the only question to be decided on October 15 is the size of his majority'.[57] He was right. He won the seat from Labour by 1,774 votes, putting a torpedo through Gordon Walker's political career in the process.

Powell did his best to avoid raising the temperature, or to predict how the immigration issue might benefit his party. By comparison with the rest of the region, Wolverhampton was relatively quiet. However, in his election address, published at the end of September, he had said that 'in my opinion it was essential, for the sake not only of our own people but of the immigrants themselves, to introduce control over the numbers allowed in. I am convinced that strict control must continue if we are to avoid the evils of a "colour question" in this country, for ourselves and for our children.'[58] A young reporter from *The Times*, Norman Fowler – later a Conservative cabinet minister – remembered interviewing Powell during the campaign, and asked him what was the biggest issue on the doorstep. 'I expected to be told something about the cost of living but not a bit of it. "Immigration," replied Enoch. I duly phoned in my piece but it was never used. After all, who in 1964 had ever heard of a former Conservative cabinet minister thinking that immigration was an important political issue?'[59]

Although it would be another two or three years before Powell would start raising the immigration issue nationally, locally he could not but encounter it, and its effects on the people of his constituency and on the town of Wolverhampton, wherever he went about his duties as a Member of Parliament. He had now discerned 'an influx to which there was apparently no end', and was beginning to worry deeply about it.[60] 'Wherever I went, it met me.' Nor was it a product of the Smethwick campaign; Powell had seen it in Wolverhampton from the late 1950s, and this had been one of the factors in his lobbying to be included on the sub-committee considering the Commonwealth Immigrants Bill in 1961. He had long had it on his conscience that he had not done more to air the issue earlier. When a colleague, Cyril Osborne, had raised the question in 1958 at a meeting of the 1922 Committee, and had broken down weeping at the end when no one seemed prepared to take any notice of the gravity of the problems the country would face, Powell kept silent. But he admitted later that he looked back 'with regret ... I always felt that having failed to support him vocally, I'd let him down.'[61] He told Paul Foot that he had 'deserted' Osborne because he felt that immigration control would be better achieved by a softly-softly approach than by causing a great stir.[62] It was a tactic on which he would claim to be forced by circumstances to change his mind within a few years. Just before polling day 'nigger neighbour' stickers started to appear around Wolverhampton, prompting the Labour candidate for the North-East division, Renee Short, to denounce these 'fascist tactics'. Powell, determined to play it down, said, 'I have not seen nor heard of these.'[63]

Yet Powell would make one of his most definitive public statements yet on immigration before the campaign was over. At Clement Jones's invitation, he wrote an article in the Wolverhampton *Express and Star* on 10 October saying that better integration of the various communities in Wolverhampton and elsewhere was the only long-term route to happiness. It was a view he would reject within a couple of years because of his belief that the sheer weight of numbers still immigrating would make integration impossible. Powell said he estimated that 10 per cent of his constituents were coloured immigrants, and that he had served them as their MP as diligently as he had served anybody else: 'I have set and I always will set my face like flint against making any difference between one citizen and another on grounds of his origin.'[64] He said he believed the overwhelming majority of Conservatives and others would agree with him that the integration of the immigrants into British life – as had been the case with the Jews who had come at the end of the nineteenth century – was the most desirable option. He admitted such assimilation would not be easy, and could take 'generations'. He added that it would be possible only if the rate of increase were to slow down dramatically; and he would soon see that, despite the 1962 Act, that just was not happening.

In his adoption speech in Wolverhampton on 25 September, Powell had warned again of the hand of the state threatening to disregard the free market, and all that meant for individual liberty. He distinguished the planning of things the state had to do – like his own Hospital Plan, or a roads plan – from the total planned economy Labour was intending. He pointed out that Wilson, if elected, might attempt to stop the market working at home, but he could not prevent it from working abroad – 'what sheer nonsense and utter hypocrisy it is of a country dependent on selling a fifth of its product abroad to pretend not to "be ruled by market forces"!'[65] In his election address he had spelt out the essential nature of such material progress if the public funds were to be raised to improve schools, hospitals and the social services. He praised the 'wind of change' that had dismantled the Empire, and added that 'the fault is not ours if the economic unity with Britain which most of Europe desired has not yet been achieved. But it will come.' He said this in the context of the pursuit of 'wider and freer trade', but it was the sort of remark that would be hurled back at him when, five years later, he began to campaign against entry to the Common Market. Urging a Conservative vote, he said Labour wanted to create a state 'where all the decisions that govern our lives would be taken, and forced upon us, by a little group of planners in Whitehall'.

Having established a reputation as the hammer of socialism, Powell was stung by an accusation made by Colin Welch, the deputy editor of the Daily Telegraph, that in his stewardship of the NHS he had 'looked, for a time, a socialist'. Less then a fortnight before the election he broke the silence on his old Ministry which he had observed for the year since leaving office to reply to Welch's criticisms on his own newspaper. He claimed in his defence that the NHS was being run more efficiently and to a higher standard than ever before, but acknowledged that many Conservatives 'doubt whether we have not been perfecting what we ought rather to have been altering. I believe there are good reasons for this doubt; but I also believe there are equally good reasons why we are right to live with it.' Lest this appear unduly socialist, he qualified it with 'I have never made any secret of my conviction that universal state responsibility is not the ideal organisation for medical care.'[66]

Powell conceded that without nationalisation of health care the new hospitals he had planned would have been built faster, since they would not have had to compete for resources with other state priorities, such as education and housing. He also regretted that a centrally controlled system worked to eliminate spontaneity: a euphemism for the mechanisms of supply and demand to which he was wedded in the rest of the economy. He doubted that denationalisation was a practicable proposition 'and cannot be bought out with a dubious reduction in taxation', by which he meant that the greater disposable income created by a tax cut could be used to pay for privatised health care: 'People's outlay and people's expectations have now set in a different mould.' The problem was of human nature, making people pay highly for something they have been used to receiving free. Even for a visionary like Powell there were limits. The furthest he would go in applying the free-market vision to the NHS was to argue for greater decentralisation to allow better 'spontaneity' – an end sought by the creation of hospital trusts nearly thirty years later.

That done, Powell immediately went back on to the attack against Labour. He mocked the party's land policy, which had at its heart a notion of owner-occupied houses held perpetually on Crown leases administered by a proposed Crown Land Commission. Speaking at Aldridge on 2 October he dismissed Labour's belief that it could buy land at less than its market value, and then lend money to would-be leaseholders at below-market rates; this would mean either the printing of money or an increase in taxation. If there were not rationing of houses, demand would rise to such an extent that mortgage rates would have to go up to restore equilibrium. 'Either way, it is fraudulent to say that the result would be more homes at prices that ordinary people can afford. ... it is the price of houses, goods and services which governs the price of land, and not the other way round. Consequently, if the Commission buys land and lets it below the current market price, the only effect would be to add the same amount on to the profits of the developers.'[67] The idea the houses so occupied could be passed on to the heirs of the original leaseholders 'as long as the houses stood' seemed to Powell a sure way of creating new slums, as there would never, under those terms, be any incentive to pull old houses down and build anew.

Housing was an issue Powell concentrated upon in the campaign. It was a symbol of socialist interference in the freedoms of individuals that electors could readily grasp, and an unfortunate gaffe by George Brown, to the effect that Labour would subsidise mortgage interest rates by 3 per cent, gave him further evidence of the economic incompetence of that party. 'When a man offers to sell you something at less than its market price, it is a pretty good sign that you are about to be swindled,' he said in his Aldridge speech.[68] Three days later, at Romford, he ridiculed Labour's sudden attachment to 'hereditary principles' in the passing on of property by the Commission's leaseholders. As a means of curing the housing shortage this was, he said, 'like the Swedish king who tried to put out the fire in his house with kegs of brandy'.[69]

Throughout the campaign, and even throughout the counting of the votes, the result was too close to call, for although Wilson was felt to have had a better campaign than Douglas-Home, and had attracted much favourable press comment, the signs were that the country was still reluctant to entrust the governance of Britain to Labour. In one of his last big speeches of the campaign, Powell said Labour's talk of modernising the economy was a 'cant phrase', there being 'no substitute for the system of competitive free enterprise by which the Tory party stands'.[70] The public were almost convinced. Despite Douglas-Home's image as a loser, he took his party to within fourteen seats of Labour. Wilson had an overall majority of just four. The battle was still on.

IV

If the election defeat on 15 October was a shock to the cabinet, it seemed a tonic to Powell. He held Wolverhampton by a majority of 9,856, reduced from 1959 thanks to the intervention of a Liberal. With his party out of office, he could pursue his own private manifesto with ever greater zeal. Upsetting the Government was no longer to be avoided; upsetting his own party was merely a minor inconvenience. On the Sunday after the defeat, when the shock of opposition after thirteen years of rule was still sinking in, Powell was already on the attack. In an article in the *Sunday Telegraph* he defined Britain now as a nation 'which has one foot over the brink of Socialism and pauses on the other'. He claimed that during the campaign what really divided the two parties had started to become apparent: Labour had 'proclaimed liberation for the community from "market forces beyond its control" and therefore were obliged to define the alternative to those forces, namely determination by the state itself of the activities of all its members – Government decision ahead of private decision'; the Conservatives had 'sharpened their antithesis perceptibly during the last 12 months and quite rapidly during the campaign itself: a society ... where private decision is superseded by state decision can be neither efficient nor, what is more, humane or just. Those market forces which the socialist rejects are the safeguard not only of progress but of individual freedom and of justice between man and man.'[71]

Powell was too modest – or too ironical, or too mischievous, or all three – to note that much of the 'sharper antithesis' had been down to the disproportionate amount of noise he had been making since the beginning of the year. The unfortunate reality beyond this was that he, and with the exception of Keith

Joseph probably he alone of the front rank of his party, understood the philosophical distinction that should have existed between the two main parties. The
rest of what was now the shadow cabinet – which Powell would imminently be
rejoining – were either oblivious to the real nature of the distinction or preferred
not to address it.

However, Powell was undaunted. 'The Conservatives in opposition will grow
freer, as time passes, to develop the inherent and devastating strength of the
case for the free society. That case is as strong in humanity and justice as in
efficiency; and in the election just passed there were signs of a new opportunity
for the Tory party, congenial to its nature and traditions.' Citing the swing
to his party in his own constituency and in others with large working-class
electorates, he said it was down to the working man appreciating the growth in
prosperity that could be enjoyed in a free society, and resenting the growing
above-the-law attitude of the unions; fifteen years later this would be the electorate that put in the Thatcher Government. 'In the end,' wrote Powell in 1964,
'the Labour party could cease to represent labour. Stranger historic ironies have
happened than that.'

He also used this article to comment on 'the sounds of self-righteous unction
which arose after the defeat of Gordon Walker at Smethwick'. Peter Griffiths,
before even arriving to take his seat in the Commons, had been branded a
pariah by Labour for the alleged racialist tone of his campaign. That many
Labour supporters, in Gordon Walker's old seat and elsewhere, fully agreed with
the anti-immigration stance was an irony lost on the party. In the light of what
would happen three and a half years later, it is worth quoting in full what Powell
had to say on this question:

> Immigration was, and is, an issue. In my constituency it has for years been
> question number one, into which discussion of every other political topic –
> housing, health, benefits, employment – promptly turned. It is not colour preju-
> dice or racial intolerance to say that only if substantial further addition to our
> immigrant population is now prevented, will it be possible properly to assimilate
> the immigrants already here, which in turn is the only way to avoid the evils of
> the colour question.
>
> I said this in my own election address; I said it in speeches; I wrote it in the
> press. The only difficulty was to explain the reasons why Parliament delayed so
> long to change our law so that, like every other country in the world, we could
> control immigration. A politician who says these things – in the Black Country
> or elsewhere – does no more than his duty; and he is entitled to impugn the
> sincerity of the Labour party, who hastened to affirm at election time that they
> would keep the very Act which they had voted to end 10 months before.
>
> To perceive this is not peculiar to Smethwick. The new Foreign Secretary is
> not a martyr; he is much more like a humbug. Conservatives will have only

themselves to blame if they acquiesce in a taboo being placed on issues which are live and real to millions.

On 28 October Douglas-Home announced his front-bench team. Both Powell and Macleod were back, Powell as transport spokesman and Macleod as steel spokesman; Labour was pledged to renationalise the industry. Powell explained why he had decided to serve. He admitted he had made it clear the previous October that he would not serve under Douglas-Home if he became Prime Minister: now he was no longer Prime Minister that objection no longer arose. However, word went round that he felt 'insulted' at having been offered so lowly a portfolio.[72] In his illuminating study of Powell four years later, Peter Utley adduced his own reasons for Powell's decisions: 'Having refused office twice and resigned once, he may well have calculated that a third refusal would confirm the deadly criticism already privately formulated by his former patron R. A. Butler that he was a "natural resigner".'[73] Utley was right: it was precisely the calculation Powell had made.[74] Certainly, there was a risk that the leadership would have lost patience with Powell had he refused again, and would have been entitled to draw the conclusion that he had lost interest in office, and, indeed, in playing the game by rules everyone else was happy to follow. Also, as Utley says, the radical programme and philosophy Powell was determined to continue setting out would have more impact if enunciated by a member of the shadow cabinet. He devoted himself to politics full-time at some cost: his reputation as a writer and thinker was such that, once the Conservatives were defeated, he was made several lucrative offers of press contracts that would have made him a relatively rich man.

Home appointed Maudling deputy leader in all but name, making him shadow Chancellor and giving him charge of co-ordinating all domestic policy. Heath was the other senior figure in the team, shadowing George Brown, the Secretary of State for the new Department of Economic Affairs. Brown's job was to implement the very 'liberation' from market forces of which Powell had been so critical. It was not, therefore, Heath alone who would be shadowing him. The idea of Brown's new department was to separate strategic management of the economy from the Treasury, which, in theory, would be left with little more than a book-keeping role. It was doomed from the start by a combination of Brown's caprice and the civil service's entrenched resistance to the notion of this separation of functions; and from the intellectual onslaught Powell would launch, unremittingly, against it.

On 4 November 1964 he spoke from the front bench as transport spokesman for the first time, complaining that the Government's policy of implementing rail closures more slowly than its predecessors had intended would merely pile additional burdens on the taxpayer; it was a complaint he repeated a week later. On 13 November he led the Opposition's response to the Travel Concessions

Bill, which allowed free or cheap fares for certain classes of persons on public transport. He did not advise a vote against the measure, even though it created anomalies – for example, pensioners would have free travel irrespective of means, whereas widows would not – as 'it is no part of the customary function of Opposition, if the Government choose to offer benefits at public expense to any particular section of the community, to seek to veto those benefits however ill-conceived or inappropriate the method chosen may be'.[75]

Douglas-Home's shadow cabinet – or Leader's Consultative Committee as it was officially known – met once or twice a week. Having been out for a year, and being, unlike Macleod, largely out of step with the feelings of most of his colleagues, it took Powell a while to make his presence felt. On 18 November he 'asked if we [the shadow cabinet] were really committed to a pension for Members, as he thought it a most unfortunate innovation which could change the whole character of membership of Parliament'.[76] His point was taken, but there was no willingness among his colleagues to share the hair-shirt with him; and Butler finally put paid to Powell's atavism, saying that the existing Members' Fund (which helped ex-MPs in financial straits) could simply not go on as it was. For the most part, Powell kept his own counsel at these meetings, through his three and a half years on the Consultative Committee. As when he had been in the cabinet, he reserved his contributions for special occasions. Peter Utley said that when Powell did speak 'it is to announce and defend with precision conclusions at which he has already arrived in private. Most men's minds are formed in conversation with their peers; Powell's is not.'[77]

Before long Powell's shadow cabinet colleagues would have cause to be infuriated by him. He demonstrated later that month his unwillingness, or inability, to be confined to his own portfolio, when at a Young Conservatives' meeting in Birmingham he launched a full-frontal charge against Labour's intention to try to secure an incomes policy. He said it was no surprise the incoming Government had realised just how difficult its original economic policy would be to implement; what was a surprise was that it had taken just six weeks to come to that conclusion. With the pound under pressure, a deteriorating balance of payments problem and Bank Rate having to be increased, Labour had understood the impossibility of trying to boost demand 'to get the economy moving again'. An incomes policy, he argued, was no answer.

'Before more months or years are spent by ministers, industrialists and trade unionists in a pursuit which is as foredoomed to futility as filling a sieve or making a rope of sand, it is time to call a halt,' he warned. 'It is time to declare in round and unmistakable terms that an incomes policy, in any relevant or useful sense, does not and cannot exist, except perhaps in a communist dictatorship.'[78] Saying that the very idea was 'a dangerous nonsense, because the nation is invited to drug itself as if with a narcotic', he added that 'in the modern state there is no automatic mechanism which will keep the level of monetary demand continuously in unison with the level of production'.[79] He noted that wages were not the only form of income – there were rents, profits, dividends and so on; and was the Government proposing to lock up employers and employees who agreed pay rises above the Government's ordered level?

Two of Powell's backbench friends, Nigel Birch and John Biffen, had earlier in the week expressed doubts about the efficacy of such a policy. However, other than Powell's intervention no firm line had been taken against the notion on his front bench, a matter he felt would require his colleagues to be given a push. But then, since many on the front bench had dedicated themselves in the preceding two years to the pursuit of just such a policy as Powell was denouncing, it would have been difficult for them to make such a leap.

Inevitably, his speech caused Labour to accuse the shadow cabinet of being split. The Conservatives' own manifesto had said clearly that 'an effective and fair incomes policy is crucial to the achievement of sustained growth without inflation. We shall take a further initiative to secure wider acceptance and effective implementation of such a policy.'[80] A briefing was given to lobby correspondents reminding them forcibly that Powell was not a front-bench economics spokesman, but spokesman on transport; and Maudling reaffirmed immediately that the Government was right to continue to try to persuade the unions to accept an incomes policy.

At a shadow cabinet meeting two days after the speech, Powell found his outburst the main talking point. Macleod, who had been especially annoyed by Powell's freelance activity, told his colleagues that the incomes policy speech was a specific example of why the party in opposition needed better to co-ordinate its activities. A discussion of the germ of Powell's argument concluded that it would not be adopted as shadow cabinet policy, but that no other firm policy would either. On the philosophical question of what freedom should be accorded to shadow cabinet members discussing ideas in public there was, as the minutes put it, 'some difference of opinion'.[81] Only Powell and Hogg came out in favour of such open debate; the great majority of the shadow cabinet wanted an agreed line to be adhered to at all times. The problem was, though, finding a line upon which all could agree. Powell took his rebuke like a good soldier, but he would not show in the future that he was minded to make compromises of personal political principle in order to salve the sometimes confused consciences, or pander to the ignorance, of his colleagues.

The moment the Conservatives had gone into opposition, Powell's already strong links with the Institute of Economic Affairs had been renewed. The IEA sought first to demolish the intellectual background to the socialist economic policy, and to influence a new and more radical Conservative policy in opposition to it. Powell was the natural political leader for the IEA, and was widely recognised as such by other economic liberals. No less than Friedrich von Hayek, writing to Ralph Harris in January 1965, told him that 'it seems all our hopes for England rest now on Enoch Powell'.[82] The IEA took various initiatives to boost Powell, arranging a programme of City lunches for him, and having John Wood, one of its officers, begin to compile the first collection of Powell's thought, which would emerge in 1965 as *A Nation Not Afraid*. Powell also had the chance to meet and talk to the leading liberal economists of the day at the IEA's monthly lunches, to which he would often be invited. 'He fully understood the automatism of the market,' Harris recalled.[83]

Powell was not inclined to rein back on controversy. On 10 December he dismissed aid to underdeveloped countries as 'both futile and harmful', arguing that the greatest gift that could be given them was not capital, but capitalism. Even if the West were to give everything it had to the poorer countries, he said, it would disappear 'like a snowflake on boiling water'. The next day he called on the Postmaster-General, Anthony Wedgwood Benn, to denationalise the telephone system, saying it was the duty of the Conservative party to start to dismantle the legacy of nationalisation inherited from the 1945 Labour Government: 'A whole new theoretical framework has to be worked out within which these enterprises can resume their proper, integrated place in a free economy.'[84] A week later he argued, in a speech in his constituency, that the whole Conservative party organisation needed a facelift: 'How can a party with its paint peeling off persuade people it is selling a more prosperous future?'[85] Powell argued for more staff in the party both locally and centrally, and for them to be paid more in order to attract a higher calibre of official.

Defiantly, he returned to the most vexed issue of all – the efficacy of an incomes policy – in two widely noticed articles in *The Times* on 17 and 18 December. The first was a summary of the history of such policies, the second a detailed exposition of why they could not work. The series was entitled 'In Pursuit of a Mirage'. He recalled how the July 1961 statement by Selwyn Lloyd had been designed to take excess demand out of the economy, an excess made evident by the large balance of payments deficit. NEDC had been set up the following December; the White Paper on the pay pause in March 1962 had been followed by open defiance from the dockers and Lloyd's own removal from office. Maudling had taken up the policy and he, too, had failed. Powell's second article, the following day, sought to explain why.

He said there were nine reasons why one could not work. First, total income was an abstraction, the sum of all individual incomes. 'They are not derived from it, but it from them. Any mechanism must therefore operate in particular, and not in general.'[86] Second, different types of income, such as profit contrasted with wages, behaved in different ways. Third, wages in different industries needed to move in different ways according to specifics of supply and demand. Fourth, there could be no way of knowing how a rise in a certain group of incomes would affect a rise in the total of all incomes. Fifth, to achieve a certain overall figure, some wages would have to rise by more than that figure, and others by less, because of the different levels of income and their uneven spread. Sixth, relativities were constantly altering, and it would be difficult to persuade a group whose incomes had lagged behind to wait before they caught up with the rest. Seventh, many incomes were not set collectively, but individually, according to supply and demand. Were employers to be punished for allowing above-average rises? Eighth, income was not wholly monetary, but included fringe benefits. How were these to be controlled? Finally, these difficulties could not be shrugged off by the assertion that, even if the policy only half worked, that was better than nothing; the policy had to be equally rigorous across the whole economy, or it would be unjust.

These were reasons why a policy could not work, assuming one was necessary. But Powell saved the most fundamental point until last. No policy was necessary, because incomes policies did not stop inflation. Governments, by the control of the money supply, did – or could do – that. That, he said, was his rejoinder to those of his colleagues and opponents who asked what, if he found incomes policies so objectionable, he would put in their place.

His party had greater problems even than this to deal with. Douglas-Home's first couple of months as Leader of the Opposition had not been a success. He, personally, was no match for Wilson, and the calibre of his front-benchers was not universally high. At the end of a two-day debate on defence and foreign affairs on 16 and 17 December, Wilson crushed Douglas-Home in demonstrating that there was no such thing as an independent British nuclear deterrent; Wilson was negotiating a joint one with the Americans, much to Conservative disquiet. Douglas-Home's humiliation prompted a wave of dissent among backbenchers, who began to whisper that it was time he went. Powell's savaging of the party organisation was timely in that it compounded this problem of credibility. The stark fact was that Labour was presiding over an economic crisis, but the Conservatives were still 10.5 points behind it in the pre-Christmas Gallup poll.

There was no agreement about a successor. Maudling, for all his powerful positioning, had singularly failed to capitalise on the economic crisis. Also, the understanding was seeping out that part of the crisis was down to the economic mismanagement Maudling, as the last Chancellor, had been responsible for before losing office. Heath was, then as later, perceived as cold and uninspiring. Powell began to see an opening for someone who knew not just when to take an initiative, but also how to take it. Douglas-Home nobly told the shadow cabinet early in 1965 that proposals would shortly be brought forward for a new, and more democratic, means of choosing the leader. The assumption soon took root that, once such a mechanism was in place, there would be an early opportunity to test its efficacy.

V

At one of the first clear signs of unacceptable state interference in the workings of the market, Powell went into action, and did so in a way that personalised the campaign against George Brown. Addressing the Edinburgh University Conservative Club on 15 January 1965, he denounced Brown for sending letters to firms that had recently put up their prices asking them why they had done so. He said the only correct reply to such a letter was 'mind your own business', adding that 'what, in effect, they are doing is to put the private citizen into the dock, to answer questions publicly about the conduct of his private affairs in order that authority, if it thinks fit, may hold him up to obloquy and create prejudice against him. This is government by smear. It is clean contrary to the rule of law.'[87]

Powell justified this assertion by saying: 'The citizen is entitled under the rule of law to know what it is that by law he is entitled to do or not to do. If there are particular ways in which he ought now to act in regard to prices, then those must be defined by law, law made by parliament in the proper way and interpreted and applied by the courts in the proper way.' No such law had been passed. What the Government was doing was nothing more than hounding. Such behaviour would, he added, 'be intolerable even if what these gentlemen are saying about the prices were economic sense. As it is, they are talking economic nonsense.' Powell attributed the policy to a loathing of profit, as well as to basic ignorance of how the laws of supply worked in a free society. No one seemed to understand that, if a price went up too far, customers would stop buying the overpriced good. As usual, this was a criticism he applied as much to his own side as to Labour. Only a handful of his colleagues had appreciated the logic and importance of what he was saying.

He then went on, in the February issue of the *Director*, to upbraid the self-appointed 'representatives' and 'spokesmen' of British industry for their response to the Government's interference in their affairs. Claiming that the leaders of industry had 'all the pathos of the baby in the presence of the ruthless candy stealer', Powell said it would be best if industry had none of these spokesmen or representatives at all – he referred not just to trade federations, but to the even more vulnerable CBI and Institute of Directors – as their concentration simply provided the Government with an easier target to nobble. 'Remember Caligula,' he said, 'who wished the Roman people had one neck, so that he could cut it off?'[88] Predictably, industrialists themselves were outraged by what Powell said, denying that their mimicking of the organisational behaviour of trade unions could in any way be interpreted – as he had interpreted it – as being 'at least half way to being anti-capitalist'. Powell found it objectionable that businesses, instead of concentrating on competing with each other, were busy trying to make accommodations with the Government. He did not hesitate to attribute base motives to them: 'It would be disingenuous not to add that cold terror and pseudo-political prudence are sometimes reinforced by self-interest' – not least the self-interestedness attached to receiving the knighthood or the peerage that the years of 'representation' of industry had usually merited, but which could be denied to someone considered to be a troublemaker.[89]

Labour was highly sensitive to Powell's charges, and sought to return his fire. A group of MPs, including the future cabinet ministers Shirley Williams and Merlyn Rees, tabled an early day motion* in the Commons deploring Powell's call for non-cooperation by industry with the Government, and maintaining that his attitude 'would strike at the very roots of our democratic institutions and way of life' – an odd assertion, since the most recent thrust of Powell's attack had been on the anti-democratic nature of Brown's prices policy. Sir Eric Fletcher, Minister without Portfolio, claimed that Powell was 'untiring in his efforts to take Britain safely back into the eighteenth century', and wondered what his attitude would have been had the unions disbanded a year earlier, refusing to co-operate in the NEDC and to assist the Conservatives in their version of planning.[90]

This was a cogent criticism. Fletcher called on Douglas-Home to clarify whether Powell, as a shadow cabinet member, was outlining orthodox party policy when he called for non-cooperation. It was not credible for most of Powell's colleagues to come to his aid because of their own recent support for the principles of planning through NEDC. Labour lost no opportunity to expose divisions between Powell and his fellows. On 2 February Douglas-Home had moved a no-confidence motion in the Government. Defending his administration, Wilson had compared Maudling's claim that an incomes policy was 'essential' with Powell's view: Wilson said that Powell 'has, if he was correctly reported, described an incomes policy as being a nonsense, a silly nonsense, a transparent nonsense, and, what is worse, a dangerous nonsense'.[91] Never one to prevaricate, Powell, sitting on the front bench opposite, nodded his assent, which Wilson welcomed.

However much disquiet Powell was causing by his statements about issues outside his portfolio, he was not neglecting to make radical statements within it. That spring, when chaos took hold of the docks, he argued that the whole dock labour scheme and the management of the ports should be reformed, for the operations were not functioning like a business. Speaking in Wolverhampton on 12 February he attacked the criticism that there was much 'wasteful competition' in the provision of transport services, arguing that just because there was competition between the various forms of transport, and waste in its

---

* A motion put down by a backbencher for debate 'on an early day', but which is in practice never debated. Other MPs add their names to the motion on the Commons' Order Paper to give a sign of how much support a particular motion has.

provision, did not mean the competition was wasteful: 'on the contrary, waste continues because there is not enough competition, because operations are carried on which are not competitive'.[92] He feared that the Government would not fulfil the programme of closures and reductions in rail services recommended by the Beeching report, that, instead, Labour still subscribed to 'the object of maintaining a nationalised industry as a permanent pensioner of the public, not required to justify itself in open competition for capital and traffic, but feeding like a parasite on those parts of the economy which are competitive'.[93]

Unimpressed by the unease among his colleagues on these high doctrinal issues, Powell's next step was to make his most violent attack on Brown yet, in an article in the *Sunday Telegraph*. Entitled 'The Trouble with George', the article ridiculed Brown for his belief in so many wrong-headed economic notions, suggesting that he was somewhere between naive and downright stupid. Powell argued that even the TUC was not as optimistic as Brown about the success of Government-inspired policies to increase demand, and the effects of incomes policy, but was too tactful to tell him so. To point out the truth to Brown 'seems almost a wanton cruelty, like disabusing a child of its belief in Father Christmas'.[94] He hammered home the point that prices and incomes could not be set by governments, only by the market; and Brown simply could not know what those markets would decide. 'But he thinks that other people are going to find out and tell him. That is where he is wrong.'

Powell's article in the *Director* was used by the Labour-controlled council in Wolverhampton to attempt to humiliate him. To celebrate his fifteen years as MP, Powell offered to present the town with some silver candlesticks. A resolution had been passed by the council to accept the silver on behalf of the town, but a sub-committee of the council then tabled an amendment to delete the words 'with gratitude' from the resolution. The resolution was carried by thirty-two votes to twenty; the leader of the Labour group said they could not prevent Powell from presenting the gift, but whether they received it gratefully was a different matter. The Labour party in the town held a meeting at which it demanded Powell's resignation for 'sabotage'. Nor was it only Labour who felt aggrieved at Powell's recent behaviour. A Mr W. Gibbs, chairman of the Merridale Ward of Powell's constituency association, resigned from his post on the grounds that 'Mr Powell is turning the clock back ... he is way off beam. He is not doing the party any good at all.'[95] Most Conservatives in Wolverhampton, though, were totally loyal to Powell, and outraged by the behaviour of the Labour group.

He withdrew his offer of the silver, telling the Mayor of Wolverhampton that if the gift was not welcome he would respect the council's wishes. A formal presentation was cancelled; the Mayor expressed his deep personal regrets that the embarrassment had occurred. The matter would, eventually, have a happy conclusion: in February 1971, with the council under Conservative control,

Wolverhampton took the gift 'with gratitude' to mark Powell's twenty-one years as an MP. However, the candlesticks were stolen in a burglary at the town hall two years later.

That distraction over, Powell returned to his usual agenda. In a speech in Aylesbury on 25 February he called on his party to abandon its ideas and commitments left over from its thirteen years in office, and instead to rethink its entire political approach. He was, essentially, trying to address the problem of colleagues who had gone along with the type of policies Labour was now embracing being unable, without facing charges of hypocrisy, to go on the attack against the Government.

Because of the link the party felt with 1951, and because of collective responsibility, it seemed:

> nothing which has once been said or done can ever be openly changed or disavowed. The increasingly absurd fiction has to be maintained that it has all been perfectly consistent and perfectly right. Meanwhile the world around is altering swiftly and continuously. Political parties, no less than individuals or the nation itself, need to be able from time to time to put behind them all that is past and make a fresh start. What we as a party ought to want to say and do today should be as fresh in spirit and as different as the world of 1965 is from the world of 1951. We cannot be tied to statements, attitudes and policies which Conservative Governments and Ministers happen to have espoused in years gone by just because they were Conservative.[96]

As a further help to his colleagues, Powell also summarised the main points on which he was fighting: he was opposed to regional policy and other forms of subsidy, price-fixing, state ownership, wealth and profits taxes, planning and trade union immunities. It was an agenda he had made his own. Powell, though nominally transport spokesman, was already becoming apparently uncontrollable as the main voice of a new Conservative policy. As Douglas-Home continued to flounder, he was filling the policy vacuum his party, embarrassingly, still had. His exhortation to colleagues 'to eat that most disgusting of meals, one's own past words', was largely ignored, mainly because of the intellectual and political paralysis taking firmer and firmer hold on the party.

This speech came at the end of a week in which Powell had put, in the privacy of the shadow cabinet, strongly dissenting views on a main area of policy. He observed, in response to a paper on pensions and care of the elderly drawn up by Sir Keith Joseph and his deputy spokesman, Margaret Thatcher, that there should be 'a graduated social security tax and abolition of the state graduated scheme, the place of which should be taken by private provision'.[97] The minute records that Powell 'felt that the conditions which needed a state flat-rate benefit no longer existed, and proposed a guaranteed minimum income in its place'. Such measures were too radical for Joseph and Mrs Thatcher, who, along with

John Boyd-Carpenter, argued for the importance of retaining the basic pension 'in an inflationary world'. Among Powell's other colleagues there was no appetite whatever for boldness, an attitude further exemplified the next day when, at another meeting of the shadow cabinet, Thorneycroft, as defence spokesman, put forward a paper in which the astronomical costs of maintaining the British presence East of Suez were admitted. Powell had already come to the conclusion that, now the Empire had gone, such a presence was largely pointless, as well as expensive. But, without examining the issues, his colleagues obediently endorsed the view that, despite the cost, 'it appears to be common ground that we should sustain this role'.[98]

In the face of this spirit of deadened acceptance of the status quo, Powell continued to stir things up outside. On 26 February he told the Bristol University Conservative Association that schemes to stimulate exports – such as the embryonic Queen's Awards – were misguided. He said he did not share the assumption that exports were 'inherently desirable'; the only point of them was to raise the foreign exchange to pay for imports, so if a measure of greater prosperity were sought it would be just as apparent from a rise in demand for imports. To make a fetish of exports was, as usual, to misunderstand the basic laws of supply and demand. All that was required was for the Government to do its job and maintain the value of the currency. If that was done, there would be no need for export drives; they were a means of trying to repair the damage done by inflation. 'This ballyhoo about exporting is only a smoke-screen to hide the reality, a cloak for the evasion of responsibility by the Government.'

In case that message had not got home, Powell reiterated it on 8 March at a Young Conservatives' conference at Folkestone. He shared a platform with Heath – whose job as Brown's shadow Powell had been doing more effectively than its incumbent – and Heath seemed to have been pushed into an admission that there would have to be changes. 'There were parts of our manifesto in which people felt we were out of tune with the times,' he said. 'This we have accepted and I have been given the job of putting it right.' Heath's remarks could, though, be read more than one way; and he was not prepared to take any risks in making changes, instead asking for policy submissions from Conservative associations before making up his mind. Powell was the polar opposite: he had made up his mind and was seeking to bend others to his will.

One of the most difficult plates of words to eat concerned capital gains tax. Powell was bitterly opposed to it, but it had been put on the statute book while he had been in the Government in 1962. He argued that a tax on capital or capital gains was simply an income tax by another name; it was a tax on income that was being saved, in the same way that a tax on alcohol or petrol was a tax on income that was being spent. He said that, at a time when Britain had to be more competitive, it was wrong to levy a further tax on entrepreneurs, since the capital sum being taxed had already been taxed once, when it had originally been income.

Two weeks after the Folkestone conference the shadow cabinet discussed the capital gains tax. Heath had drawn up a paper on it, taking no view in particular, and asking his colleagues what they thought the party's line should be. In the face of those colleagues being apparently unable to see any point of principle attached to the question, Powell forcefully set out what he believed. 'The presumption', the minute records him as saying, 'should be that Conservatives opposed the tax, in whatever form and at whatever rate it was introduced.'[99] He added that 'it was no business of an Opposition to approve new taxes', and concluded that CGT was 'an inherent nonsense'. Most of his colleagues remained confused or reticent. Joseph said he could swallow CGT provided it was accompanied by a cut in surtax. Heath had declared in his paper that 'if the Government proposes a harsh rate of tax it will be necessary to vote against it even though we may not oppose the form of the tax itself'.

Frustrated by such thinking, Powell circulated his own memorandum, outlining exactly why CGT was wrong. If the capital gain had been made because of inflation, or because of alterations in the pattern of supply and demand, then taxing that gain was 'confiscation of existing property'. Taxing gains due to investment was 'double taxation of the same income'.[100] However, Powell's colleagues were still prone to make more of an effort to see the Labour Government's case than to see his. When the discussion was resumed a week later, the consensus view was that it was 'difficult to oppose capital gains tax in principle', and, more to the point, if the Conservatives regained power 'it was unlikely we would abolish it'.[101]

At two other shadow cabinets that spring Powell was minuted as saying nothing on two issues that would come to dominate his thought and action. On 9 March the committee discussed immigration; and on 30 March the desire to enter the Common Market was reiterated, if only the opportunity would arise for the country to do so. It may be that Powell said nothing on immigration because he and Douglas-Home had already privately corresponded on the matter. Powell set out his views in a letter of 26 January, which he said he had been asked to write on behalf of 'a number of us, including Reggie Maudling and Edward Boyle'.[102] He continued:

> There is good reason to think that the rate of inflow of immigrants, both legal and illegal, alarms the Government, and that they will shortly have to announce restrictive measures – probably linked with proposals (unlikely to be acceptable to us) against racial discrimination. If so, much would be gained by our Party striking the note first, and words in an early speech by yourself might be the right way to do so.

Powell advocated three measures the party might like to support: power to repatriate illegal immigrants, limitation of the right entry of dependants of immigrants already here, and power to assist voluntary repatriation. The first he said was 'surely non-controversial'; as for the other two 'it is at least time [they] were seriously canvassed. There would be widespread support for them. Without them those of us who live with this thing at close quarters are increasingly fearful that integration will never be achievable: instead, an intractable racial problem will have become endemic in many parts of the country.' It was a clear statement of Powell's own non-racialist approach to the problem, and his belief – waning, but still there – that integration could still be achieved. Douglas-Home, in a reply of 28 January, told Powell, 'I entirely agree with the views you express.'[103] In a speech at Hampstead the following week, referring to the 1962 Act, Douglas-Home said:

> although this considerably affected and arrested the flow, further action is now required. We believe that power should be taken to repatriate immigrants who come to this country illegally. We also believe that we should have the power to assist voluntary repatriation and that the dependants must be counted against the limits on numbers and that the total should be further reduced.[104]

Powell took this henceforward to be his party's policy on the matter.

In the light of the bad press he was getting personally, and the effect this was having on an already strategically inept party, Douglas-Home raised the question of his own position at a shadow cabinet meeting on 31 March. He told his colleagues that if it would improve the fortunes of the party he would stand down at once. He was popular, and his colleagues, perhaps aware of their own not insignificant role in the party's bad standing, protested that he should not think of leaving. Lord Carrington complained of the 'vulgar abuse' to which the leader had been subjected, but Thorneycroft suggested that, to settle the matter, Douglas-Home should submit himself to a vote of the parliamentary party, now that such a mechanism was in place. Powell disagreed with this fundamentally, saying that there was a risk of 'getting over-excited about the whole situation'. For once, Powell prevailed. Douglas-Home wrapped up the discussion by saying, wearily, that he was 'beyond the point of suffering personally'.[105]

For all the trouble Powell had caused by his campaign against the new orthodoxies, he was also boosting his stature and commanding greater attention from the press. 'He has the taut, pale face of a missionary, and the zealous energy of a man who is not afraid of the stake,' wrote the *Sunday Express*. 'At Westminster he is treated by both sides with nervous respect.'[106] In an interview with the paper, Powell insisted: 'I am a party man. Not a revolutionary or rebel or anything like that. A party man – a professional Tory.' He said he was not bothered about crazes ('I've got nothing against the Beatles'), nor about fashion ('I shall continue to wear a waistcoat to the end of my days'). He was a conventional man, and would stick to conventional politics.

That week he also revealed a further part of his character by writing an article in the Advertising Association's *Quarterly* entitled 'Truth, Politics and Persuasion'. 'The professional politician', he wrote, 'can sympathise with the professional advertiser. They inhabit similar dog houses. Both must resign themselves to a low public estimation of their veracity and sincerity.' Powell went on to say that, because of the on-the-record nature of politics, politicians rarely lied; and most people technically lied all the time, for reasons of tact and in order to be courteous. In politics, whips – whom he called, on another occasion, the sewers of Parliament – were hired to lie: that was their job. For any other MP 'his business is to bring out the strong points of the course of action he proposes. He is not required to tell "the whole truth".' This should be well understood and was, therefore, 'morally neutral'. But this line of Powell's was one that would harden up to the point where he made the breach with his party in 1974 for reasons of its 'fraudulence'.[107]

Also in early April an event occurred that would be used as ammunition against him when he led the Conservative minority against the Common Market. One Nation published a pamphlet, mostly written by Nicholas Ridley, enthusiastically advocating membership of the EEC, and saying that entry must be a priority of a Conservative government when one was returned to power. Powell did not sign the pamphlet because of the convention binding him, and other One Nation members, as members of the shadow cabinet; but he did not dissociate himself from it, and did not seek to correct the impression given explicitly in the press that he was sympathetic with the pamphlet's views. He had, in fact, offered his journalistic and textual critical skills to Ridley, who had offered him up what Powell considered to be an insufficiently literate first draft. There are whole phrases, indeed, in the pamphlet that sound like Powell and seem to embody what would soon become seen as the Powell doctrine: such as 'Our nuclear arm is both our trump card in Europe and our greatest problem as a nation.'[108] Whatever Powell's views at the time, that pamphlet was within four years to become the antithesis of what he publicly stood for.

On 13 April he had his own chance to put, formally, his views on the incomes policy to the shadow cabinet. Rather than adduce any new arguments, he simply circulated the committee with his articles on the subject from *The Times* of the previous December. In the discussion, Powell amplified his fear that some Conservatives might think an incomes policy 'a useful educational exercise', which he felt would be nonsense. He was almost as worried that his colleagues might accept that an incomes policy was not practical, but that they would think that if it were practical then it would be a wonderful thing. This he branded 'an inherent nonsense which would stand up to no examination'.[109]

At this, Heath rounded on Powell. He said his arguments were an over-simplification and that the incomes policies of the last Conservative Government had achieved something: though what that was either Heath did not say or the minutes did not specify. Above all, Heath felt that the shadow cabinet should not be seen to undermine the Government's incomes policy. That did not stop them agreeing with Powell that it was a failure, but it was important to Heath that, when it eventually failed, that failure was not seen to be the Conservative party's fault. So Powell's radical impulse was defeated again, and the Conservatives chose not to attack, but to be associated in the public's mind with complicity in the policy the Government was following; or to seem to have no ideas of their own – a strategy that would, within a year, help secure another, and much heavier, electoral defeat. The minutes of the discussion concluded that 'the Government was being shown to have failed in their promises that they could achieve an incomes policy. It would be a good idea if the cry of failure could come from the back benches rather than our front bench.'

Powell maintained his high-profile campaign against Brown and the incomes policy, which he continued to denounce as 'dangerous nonsense'. When Brown announced, at the end of April, a five-year economic plan, Powell went into overdrive. He told a meeting at Wolverhampton on 1 May 1965 that the private sector should refuse to co-operate with Brown by not sending back answers to the detailed, bureaucratic questionnaire he had sent out to businesses. The plan was, in any case, doomed 'to utter futility' and would be 'a monumental edifice of fatuity and folly'.[110] There was still no legal obligation for individuals to comply, any more than there had been for them to answer Brown's earlier inquiries about their prices. Powell's impact continued to grow. Geoffrey Howe, then a junior backbencher, wrote in the *Sunday Telegraph* that Powell's economic doctrine 'has won many converts'. However, another future minister, Michael Spicer, then chairman for Pressure for Economic and Social Toryism, said that Powell's attempt to pull the party to the right was 'both tragic and subversive'.[111]

For a moment, though, Powell was distracted from his crusade; the immigration issue bubbled up again. A report was published which showed that in 1961 the birthrate among immigrants in Wolverhampton was eight times higher than among the rest of the town's population. Conservative councillors lost no time in drawing the report to Powell's attention. They formally asked the Government to prevent further immigration to the area so that the local culture could be preserved. Further information came to light that, in 1964, some 24 per cent of the births in Wolverhampton were to black or Asian mothers. The immigrant community was only about 5 per cent of the population. Powell finally made a statement on 21 May, asking that Commonwealth immigrants should be treated the same as all other aliens when seeking entry to Britain. He specifically rejected the argument that Commonwealth immigration was justified on the grounds of cheap labour. He described as 'almost inconceivable' the notion that the previous year's inflow – 75,000 – could be allowed to continue, as in twenty years it would mean an extra 1.5 million, excluding their natural increase.[112] This was the first recorded instance of Powell using the tactic that would mark out most of his future speeches on this issue: spelling out not just the consequences of a year's immigration, but the effect of it were it to continue at the same rate over a given period.

His immediate concern was not, though, that the numbers might lead to racial strife, though he did say that stopping the inflow would take the heat out of some issues where discrimination was undoubtedly occurring. His was primarily an economic point. 'It is a mistake to think that because immigrants are willing to be hewers of wood and drawers of water they are increasing productivity by releasing indigenous workers for more productive tasks. The actual effect is probably that some mechanisation, reorganisation, capital invest-ment, which would otherwise take place does not happen and consequently our productivity all round is lower than it would have been.' He attacked the Government for being concerned with 'irrelevancies' such as nationalising steel when this desperate problem remained unaddressed. His remarks caused scar-cely a flurry. Throughout the summer, as the Race Relations Bill went through Parliament, the shadow cabinet discussed it several times. Powell is not minuted as saying anything.

That was, perhaps, because he had already stated his views in another party forum. On 30 April 1965 he had given evidence to the party's Immigration Committee, chaired by Selwyn Lloyd. Powell outlined the situation in Wol-verhampton, and warned of his feeling that there could be a 'flashpoint' over maternity beds rather than schools – which were popularly considered to be the main problem, as some classes were now more than half made up of the children of immigrants. He was minuted as saying that 'he thought the time had come for the virtual termination of net immigration. This was the absolute *first* priority required – both from the point of view of the immigrants and the local population.' Commonwealth citizens, he added, should be admitted only on an aliens basis. He continued: 'We should open the door in the reverse direction and encourage a backward flow.' He said that many immigrants found life in Britain 'a misery' and longed to return home; he said too that 'it was the hope of most immigrants to obtain an honoured position in the community. What *they* feared most was that they might be swamped by fresh arrivals.'[113] Powell felt, and had good reason to feel, that Douglas-Home supported him on this, and wrote to his leader, before a debate on the Commonwealth in early June 1965, to advise him that he could in his speech 'go far to free us from the humbug, insincerity and self-delusion of what we have said for years on this subject in Government'.[114] It was not advice Douglas-Home chose to take, and his and the party's stance on the Commonwealth remained the same.

It was also at this time that Powell started to look from a distance at the social situation in America, then in the midst of turbulence from civil rights and anti-race-discrimination protests. In a curious speech to the American Chamber of Commerce in London on 11 June, he attempted to reconcile his own distaste for America with the fact that the country, broadly, followed an economic programme of the sort he had been advocating in Britain. He cited reports of unemployment and the effects of the colour bar in America being interpreted by socialists as proof of the failure of capitalism and of the need to persist with the socialist experiment in Britain. Powell repudiated the notion that capitalism and enterprise had caused the evils of America, but he pointedly steered clear of disquisiting on what had.

Another political action by Powell at this time gives the lie to the stereotypical impression of him as a hard-line right-winger. He was one of only four Conservative front-benchers to vote in favour of legalising homosexuality between consenting adults in private. Most others abstained, but a small number – including Heath – voted for the status quo. Later that year Powell would vote to suspend the death penalty; the last hangings in Britain had been carried out the previous August. He had taken the abolitionist line consistently, being one of only a handful of Conservative MPs to vote in 1955 for Sidney Silverman's Bill to suspend the death penalty for a five-year period. It was one of the attitudes that confounded attempts to categorise him as a right-winger. It was also, perhaps equally surprising, one of the notions he had imbibed from another great believer in the liberal reforming ethos of penology, Nietzsche.[115]

VI

In mid-July Powell published the first of several influential collections of his speeches and writings, *A Nation Not Afraid*, edited by the IEA's John Wood. The word 'Powellism' – whose first use is stated by the Oxford English Dictionary to have been in the *Economist* of 17 July 1965 – had been a vogue term around for some months; and this book was taken to be the first gospel of the testament. In fact, in one of the most cited profiles written of Powell, Iain Macleod mentioned Powellism in his references to the book in the *Spectator* of 16 July. He spoke of Powell as 'the finest mind in the House of Commons and, by the normal touchstones of what differentiates left and right wingers, a "progressive" ': he cited Powell's support for homosexual law reform and his opposition to both capital and corporal punishment.[116] 'He does not fit into any political slot. He is just Enoch Powell.'

Macleod asserted that Wood, in editing Powell's thoughts, had found a consistency where none existed. He claimed that, during Powell's year in the Treasury, the scourge of the incomes policy had, in fact, advocated a variant of one. The Treasury papers, now available, do not support Macleod: while Powell may not have challenged the orthodoxy, then or in his later spell in office, with quite the vigour he was later to adopt, he did make the basis of his opposition to expansion of the money supply his belief that it was the 'onlie begetter' of inflation. For him to have advocated an incomes policy too would not just have been intellectually wrong-headed, it would also have been otiose. However, Macleod's other observations about Powell were germane: how his speeches were designed to provoke; how he 'detests the cult of the personality' and would therefore sit with his arms folded at party conferences when a colleague received the statutory standing ovation, preferring to congratulate him privately afterwards; and how the key to his personality was his religion. In the most famous passage, Macleod said he admired Powell's work, but entered a reservation. "I am a fellow traveller but sometimes I leave Powell's train a few stations down the line, before it reaches, and sometimes crashes into, the terminal buffers. I am certainly less logical in my political approach, but I would argue that Powell sometimes suffers from an excess of logic.' Macleod concluded, optimistically as it turned out, that much of the next Conservative election programme would be based on Powellism. Perhaps if Douglas-Home had remained in charge, he might have been right.

William Rees-Mogg, in a review on 18 July in the *Sunday Times* (headlined 'Powellism is not enough'), was among those bemused by the book. Saying that Powellism 'is claimed to be a coherent political doctrine' he said he was struck by a conflict that could be sensed even in the title, 'a title which is concerned with nationalism and emotion and not with the main economic themes which dominate Mr Powell's political philosophy'.[117] Rees-Mogg was feeling his way towards an understanding of how Powell's economic doctrine of the individual relied, nonetheless, on support from the framework of the coherent nation state. He wrote that 'Mr Powell turns out to be involved in two systems of ideas. One is a stark black-and-white apology for capitalism, an apology which is almost as absolutist as the Marxism of a good Marxist. The other is a more complex and perhaps therefore more sympathetic nationalism, which combines a strong sense of Britain's national identity with a distrust of imperialism.' Shrewdly, Rees-Mogg, writing that 'Mr Powell is not in favour of unfettered immigration into Britain,' pointed out that for all his interest in mobility of labour within Britain, Powell was not in favour of mobility internationally. This was because Powell put the coherence of the nation above the free market.

Rees-Mogg felt that Powell's philosophy was 'inadequate'. Other reviewers were more sanguine. Donald McLachlan, the editor of the *Sunday Telegraph*, said that 'those who buy the first edition may one day find themselves owning a volume of historic importance', and that Powell was 'trying to cure the Tories of what I would call the Butlerian blush, the party's embarrassed reluctance to use with any conviction the vocabulary and arguments of capitalism'.[118] The psephologist Robert McKenzie, writing in the *Observer*, found the book remarkable for the evidence it presented of how far Powell was divorced from the thinking of the Conservative cabinet in which he had served, and, indeed, from the shadow cabinet of which he was a member. McKenzie stated baldly that

Powell 'has been engaged in a massive one-man campaign to convert his party into (what it has never in fact been) an utterly uncompromising exponent of "free market" economics'. McKenzie wondered, in this light, how Powell could have served in a government that embraced an incomes policy, and which had used Neddy to engage in half-hearted economic planning.[119]

Almost immediately, Powell would have the chance to test the level of support for him and his doctrine. On Thursday 22 July 1965 Douglas-Home resigned after twenty-one months as leader of the Conservative party. He had advised William Whitelaw, the Chief Whip, and other close colleagues of his decision on the Wednesday evening, but most of the shadow cabinet had no idea until shortly before the announcement was made. When he told Powell, Powell told him he regretted the decision: 'I remember saying to him ... that, whatever happened in 1963, having joined his shadow team in 1964, I would be "the last man to leave the ship" if he decided, as I hoped he would, to remain in command.'[120]

A ballot was called for the following week: the first time the party leadership had ever been chosen other than by a candidate 'emerging'. The new system was a direct result of the outrage caused by the manner of Douglas-Home's succession to the premiership. Getting such a system in place, and appointing a new chairman, Edward du Cann, to reform the organisation of the party, had been Douglas-Home's main priorities after the defeat. Now those things had been done, he could leave with a clear conscience. He emphasised that the decision had been 'mine, and mine alone', though at a genial press conference at which he announced his departure he also revealed, with some under-statement, that 'a considerable number of people genuinely felt another leader would be better able to win a General Election'.[121] The ballot to find the successor was scheduled for the following Tuesday, 27 July.

It was immediately obvious that Maudling and Heath would be the main contenders, with Maudling the favourite. Both had performed in a lacklustre fashion since the election, which had helped Maudling to make up some of the ground he had lost during the Douglas-Home premiership; however, Heath, who had taken over Maudling's economic responsibilities in February, was again in the ascendant after some good performances in the Budget debates. Macleod said at the start he would not stand; both Thorneycroft and Hogg had their supporters. The *Daily Telegraph*'s political correspondent reported, on the morning after the contest was called, that 'in the lobbies last night one found what was described as "a strong ground swell" for Mr Enoch Powell, in the hope that he might be persuaded to stand. It was argued that no-one in sight is better equipped to imbue the country with faith in sound Conservative principles, which might have more relevance than "personality" when the election comes.' The report suggested that Powell could come through as a compromise can-didate if Heath and Maudling dead-heated on a second ballot, though it is hard to see, even in retrospect, what element of compromise there was in such a candidacy. The most prevalent view of Powell in the party at this time was that he was the most likely Chancellor of the Exchequer in a future Conservative government.

The mood in the party was predominantly one of wanting to change the perception of the Conservatives: an end to the 'grouse moor image', with, instead, an apparently ordinary middle-class man like Maudling, Heath or Powell to take over. Others, though, felt that a trap had been set for the party by Wilson, who had shortly before announced that there would be no election in 1965. It had been felt that Douglas-Home had not resigned sooner in case a snap election were called; now there was no call for him to stay on that account, although equally there would be no call for Wilson not to change his mind and call an election before the new leader had had a chance to make an impact.

On the very day Douglas-Home announced his decision, Powell was at the dispatch box leading an attack on the Government's handling of a rail dispute that was disrupting journeys for London commuters. He quoted a remark of Wilson's the previous week, in which he had said that if working to rule meant crippling essential services, then the rule had better be changed. He said the public wanted to know whether this was mere rhetoric, or whether something would be done to improve the situation. The grievance that had brought about the work to rule – a productivity scheme – had been rumbling on for eight months, which led Powell to impugn the Government's competence in handling the matter. He ended up questioning, as he had before, the Government's ability to run the railway in a commercial way. But it was a short, relatively unimpressive speech that simply asked one question: what was the Government proposing to do? The Minister of Labour, Ray Gunter, who answered him, had little difficulty putting the blame squarely on the unions. For Powell's part, it was the speech of a man looking forward, patently, to giving up the tedious portfolio with which he had been saddled, and in which he seemed unable to generate much interest.

Heath and Maudling formally declared themselves for the leadership race. Powell stayed his hand, prompting speculation that he was waiting to see whether a second ballot provided him with a better opportunity. Reports over the weekend before the contest suggested that he might have as many as sixty supporters: a substantial exaggeration, as it turned out. On the Sunday, returning from a weekend with friends in Sussex, he let it be known he would stand; and the feeling in the party was, peculiarly, that his decision made it more likely that Maudling would win. One of Heath's leading supporters, speaking without attribution, told the press he estimated Powell would take two votes from Heath for every one he took from Maudling. Maudling's people saw the matter the same way, and were jubilant. Estimates of Powell's support quickly took on more realistic proportions as the ballot neared. On the morning of the contest, reports had it that Powell would 'do well to get into double figures' and that his vote would be ten to fifteen at the most.[122] On the night Powell's decision to stand was announced, Eve Macleod rang Pam Powell to ask why on earth he had chosen to do it. Powell's motives were clear: it was to show that he considered himself *papabile*.

Powell was widely perceived as representing the younger, more intellectual section of the party, including such future Thatcherites as John Biffen, Nicholas Ridley and Jock Bruce-Gardyne. Biffen, who seconded the nomination, had been under Powell's spell longer than the others, having, as an undergraduate, first met him when Powell addressed a meeting of the Cambridge University Conservative Association in 1951. The effect on Biffen had been instantaneous – not so much for what Powell said as for the style, wit and certainty with which he said it – and as a Conservative activist in the West Midlands in the 1950s he had taken care to get to know Powell better.[123] Ridley was perhaps the most energetic in his espousal of Powell's economic convictions, and also helped bring him into contact with a wider circle of junior backbenchers through the frequent lunches he would give for colleagues – to which Powell was often asked – in his house near Lambeth Palace.[124] Another early adherent was Geoffrey Howe. He recalled having had a fierce argument with Michael Alison, like him a new Member, just before the poll in which Alison advanced reasons for supporting Heath and Howe advanced reasons for backing Powell. 'When we met again just after the result had been announced,' Howe wrote in his memoirs, 'we found that our mutual advocacy had been so successful that we had both changed sides,' Howe having voted for Heath.[125]

Powell's campaign – if such it can be termed – was low-profile, and was aimed merely at securing recognition of his and his ideas' small, but significant, influence in the party. Neither he nor any of his supporters believed he would win; the plan was to put down a marker for the next time. Powell's nomination was proposed by John Hay, who had entered the House with him in 1950 and had come to know him well when chairing the party's Housing and Local Government Committee during Powell's time in that Ministry almost a decade earlier. Harry d'Avigdor-Goldsmid, a fellow West Midlands MP, was another prominent supporter, as were Ronnie Bell, the MP for Buckinghamshire South, and Victor Goodhew, who sat for St Albans. The highest-ranking adherent, who did not at the time publicly declare himself, was the former War Secretary, James Ramsden.

Quietly, and not particularly successfully, Powell's men embarked on a canvass of the parliamentary party. When the contest was held Heath came top with 150 votes; Maudling, who had told friends he expected to win, had 133; Powell recorded just 15. A fortnight later the *Times Literary Supplement*, noticing *A Nation Not Afraid*, wrote that 'fifteen votes in the leadership election nowhere near reflect the influence he is having on Conservative thinking, especially among younger meritocratic Tories these days'. So Powell had established what his constituency was, and had founded, with his book and his campaign, Powellism. In an interview three years later he memorably described his part in the exercise as 'I left my visiting card,' giving a clear indication that he would try again more emphatically in the future. He later confided in Richard Ritchie that he would not have stood had he known his vote would be so small; but it was not until the process was well advanced, and withdrawal not an option, that he realised how poor his showing would be.[126] He went to see Maudling after this first ballot; and, although Heath had not won what the rules of the contest regarded as a conclusive majority, Maudling put it to Powell that it would be best if they both conceded defeat. Powell agreed.

Powell had not expected to win; Maudling had. Powell recalled the scene: ' "What went wrong?" he kept asking. "Why did I lose?" I told him; perhaps I shouldn't have done.' The two men had been friends for nearly twenty years, so Powell did not equivocate: Maudling's decision to take on three significant directorships, one of them full-time, when the Conservatives lost the 1964 election had caused his colleagues to conclude, as Powell put it, 'that you weren't really interested any longer'.[127] It was not a truth Maudling enjoyed hearing. He told Powell he 'really didn't like' Heath; yet he served him loyally. For the second time, the leadership went in a way that would not serve Powell's interests. His whole career would probably have been different had Butler succeeded Macmillan, and it would have been different again had Maudling succeeded Home. Powell felt no dislike for Heath, but the two of them would soon begin the most bitter period of struggle between a party leader and a senior colleague the modern Conservative party had ever seen.

10

THE SILENT MEMBER

Heath began his leadership with magnanimity towards Powell. His rival may have secured only fifteen votes, but he knew the following Powell was building in the party. He offered him a choice of shadow portfolios. Powell chose defence, having conceived the ambition to be Defence Secretary. Macleod took the job Powell might have been expected to want, shadowing the Treasury – Powell did not ask for it because, typically, he felt it would have been 'like returning to one's own vomit'.[1] Maudling became the first formally designated deputy leader in the party's history.

Powell's choice was quixotic, but also pragmatic. He felt there were great, and as yet largely unseen, challenges for Britain in shaping her post-imperial role. Most would affect her deployment of military power, and would hinge on the question of the concentration of that power in Europe and for home defence. Such power was, in the 1960s, the real nature of the conduct of diplomacy. From the defence job Powell could have an influence. He also realised that the other subjects of concern to him – notably the economy – could be addressed from wherever he was in the shadow cabinet. In this, though, Powell would be at odds with Heath. Powell understood the difference between a shadow cabinet and real cabinet; collective responsibility did not apply in the same way, and the Conservative party, when last in opposition from 1945 to 1951, had not demarcated areas of responsibility for shadow spokesmen. Powell had seen this at first hand from his place in the Secretariat and the Research Department. Heath had not; perhaps as a result, he was determined to run his team like a government, and he was not prepared to indulge Powell's freelance activities in the way Douglas-Home had.

The new defence spokesman was more than aware of the disagreements he would have with Heath over policy. Not, at that stage, setting out to provoke, he was keen to take a portfolio in which the scope for disputes was as limited as possible. When he discussed the possibility of defence with Heath, he formed the impression that he was as realistic about Britain's post-imperial role as he was, and would be as reluctant to cling to old notions about the nation's power in the world. He also believed that Heath had a properly cynical view about the United States. 'I didn't accept the role of defence spokesman', Powell recalled, 'until I had thought I had satisfied myself that the leader's outlook on the world and my own were similar – that is to say that East of Suez had ceased to exist politically, and that we were a European power without obligations to or dependence upon the United States.'[2] Not for the first time, Powell's estimate of a colleague was wrong, particularly since Heath did not remotely share the view now underpinning Powell's political outlook – that the nation state should be the new focus of political activity. Writing to Andrew Freeth on 6 August, the day before his departure for the family holiday in France, Powell said he hoped his friend was 'not too dismayed by the outcome on 27 July: I was not at all, and defence is exactly what I would have chosen to shadow. So (for once) your friend has had his wish.'[3] For a time, Heath and Powell were on good terms, Heath coming to a successful dinner-party at South Eaton Place, the high point of which was one of Jennifer's hamsters choosing to come and sit on the leader and wash himself during the evening.[4]

Powell especially underestimated two things: first, how keen Heath was to appease the sentiment, still widespread in his party, that Britain had a world role far in excess of what was in fact the case. Powell had long ago ceased to be shocked by imperial decay; many of his colleagues, and more to the point much of the Conservative party in the country, were however still reeling, and Heath was not prepared to confront them. Second, he failed to appreciate just how little sympathy there was among his colleagues for his view of America. Powell was aggrieved that Britain had – while he was a member of Macmillan's Government – chosen to adopt a nuclear strategy that depended on America's selling Polaris missiles to her. He felt the strategy was wrong, and the reliance on America wrong too. In this he would be more in sympathy with the Labour left than with anyone on his own side. Fundamentally, Powell was only just realising that Heath was a bureaucrat and not a politician. It was a problem that, as much as any differences in ideology, would provoke the conflict between the two men.

Powell signified that he would do the job in his own way. The shadow defence spokesman had always been offered, on Privy Council terms, briefings from the Government on areas of sensitivity that it might be inappropriate, for reasons of national security, to exploit politically. Powell believed that such knowledge would compromise him, and he declined to perpetuate the arrangement.[5] He took his responsibilities intensely seriously, and organised them to maximise trouble for the Government. He convened a weekly meeting with members of the backbench Defence Committee, to settle what difficult questions could be asked, what traps could be set, what lines could be pursued. Powell would come to the meeting with copies, appropriately marked, of Hansard, and would give out carefully prepared questions to his team. The arrangement worked well, and created a new group of supporters for Powell on the backbenches, impressed by the care he was taking over his portfolio and the consideration with which he handled them.

His Commons debut as defence spokesman was a Private Notice Question*

---

* A question on the matter of urgency put down by an MP to a Minister, with permission of the Speaker, to secure an immediate answer from the Government.

to Denis Healey, the Defence Secretary, on cuts Healey planned in the forces, and which had been mentioned in a debate the previous day. Healey, who was as near to being Powell's intellectual equal as anyone in the Commons but who mixed his intellect with verbal thuggery, would be one of the more effective opponents of Powell's dry, logical style. He started with him as he meant to go on, congratulating him on his appointment and hoping he would last longer than his predecessors had: 'I must say that three shadow Defence Secretaries in a year beats even the record that the party opposite set when in office.'[6]

In his spare moments that summer Powell completed a detailed work of historical research, published by *History Today*, about a beautiful late-four-teenth-century tomb in the church at King's Langley in Hertfordshire, which Powell claimed he could prove had been intended as the tomb of King Richard II and had been originally meant for Westminster Abbey. The article is a perfect example of the brilliance of Powell as a historical researcher, his activities all the more remarkable for their being carried on at a time of heightened political activity. It displays not just his grasp of history, but also his command of the details of heraldry and architecture; and how, when faced with any building or part of a building, he would treat what he saw as the conclusion of some sort of detective story, which invited him to trace backwards the sequence of events that had led to the result he saw. In this case, it was the concealment of royal arms on the tomb that marked its conversion from a king's tomb into that of a subject. There were to be many such articles in learned antiquarian publications in the years ahead.

Powell's next prominent public speech was nothing to do with defence, but a direct attack on George Brown. Speaking at Shotton on 6 September, he argued that the tone of some of Brown's recent remarks on a prices and incomes policy hinted at a move to compulsion, with dire results. 'I daresay it is with prices rather than incomes that the Government will prefer to make a start. That in itself is formidable enough, with all the apparatus of officialdom, verification, inquiry and regulation which it would necessitate. But, formidable though all this is, it is only the beginning. Control of prices and incomes themselves are one kind of control, and must be accompanied as night follows day by control of things and people. Price control and rationing are inseparable twins.'[7] Powell also savaged Douglas Jay, the President of the Board of Trade, who had rebuked British manufacturers for concentrating on making easy profits in home markets when they should be exporting and trying to sell their wares in difficult markets. Powell told Jay it was the main responsibility of business to make as much money wherever it could. 'If British businessmen and industrialists worked on this principle, picking the hardest and least profitable markets, our economy would be a madhouse, and incidentally a poorhouse.'

That spring, Douglas-Home had set up policy review groups in preparation for the next manifesto. Powell had chaired one on the rating system, which had concluded that £230 million of the money currently raised from rates should be funded by central taxation, with a large transfer of funds for the education budget in particular. At the first shadow cabinet meeting after the recess, on 15 September, Heath announced that a draft document had been drawn up by the Research Department based on the conclusions of the policy groups. Powell, alert to the need to maintain his own intellectual freedom, asked whether the document would be binding upon members of the shadow cabinet or would merely be a basis for discussion. His colleagues, more accommodating than was perhaps good for them, agreed that the document should not be seen to be 'the last word', but that there should be a clear commitment to the policies contained in it.

Powell made the specific request to Heath that a commitment to airline denationalisation be included in the document, a request Heath squashed by saying that no work had been done on such a policy. In response to further protests of his on other subjects, Powell was asked, and agreed, to redraft sections on housing subsidies and transport. When the committee met again to consider a later draft – now entitled 'Putting Britain Right Ahead' – on 28 September one thing still missing was a clear statement about an incomes policy. It was agreed that a form of words would be thrashed out between Macleod, Maudling and Powell. By the time the manifesto came out six months later the pledge was worded, 'Our new economic programme will make a prices and incomes policy really effective,' a statement so nebulous as to be literally meaningless, which is presumably why Powell felt he could sign up to it.[8] Macleod, ever the pragmatist, had some sympathy with Powell, but felt his absolutism was utterly impracticable. The general view of the shadow cabinet was that, although the incomes policy might not be right, the alternatives could not be pursued until the trade unions were brought within the framework of the law.[9]

Although Powell lost the battle against an incomes policy in the shadow cabinet, the very fact that he fought helped him compose a formidable legacy. Margaret Thatcher, who had admired him from afar for some years as 'integrity writ large', noted ruefully in her memoirs that by the time she joined the shadow cabinet in 1967 Powell had lost the fight about market economics.[10] 'But Enoch was right. He had made the two intellectual leaps in economic policy which Keith Joseph and I would only make some years later. First, he had grasped that it was not the unions which caused inflation, but rather the Government which did so ... consequently, incomes policies ... were a supreme irrelevance to anti-inflation policy.'[11] Speaking of the tenor of those shadow cabinet meetings, Lady Thatcher said that there 'was not a lot of discussion', and 'Enoch did not deploy the full basic arguments there.'[12] Older colleagues, like Robert Carr, who had known Powell for fifteen years, noticed a change in him: 'to those not close to him, he ceased to have this ability to laugh with you, let alone laugh at himself.

He seemed steadily to be taking himself so much more seriously. There was no give and take. It was all or nothing.[13]

He was never part of Heath's inner circle. The decisions were made elsewhere, and Powell was not part of that process. At the business meetings that gatherings of the shadow cabinet had become, Powell said increasingly little. 'In Ted's shadow cabinet,' Carr recalled, 'he was the silent member. He upset some of us sometimes because he was such a loner.'[14] Of his relationship with Heath, Lady Thatcher observed that 'it was not good. I think that is why Enoch did not get into the nitty-gritty of argument at those meetings. I think that Ted was not really prepared to listen to ... arguments. I suppose there are some people who do not like an opponent in argument to be that strong.' Powell's problem was that, when he did break loose, it was with a combination of passion and remorseless logic Heath simply could not match, and so chose to ignore.

Powell continued to chip away at Brown and the economic strategy. At Meriden on 18 September he urged Brown to admit what a waste of time the national plan was – not least because many businesses had taken Powell's advice and not bothered to return their questionnaires, so the information upon which it was founded was incomplete – and warned what excuse the Government would make when the plan started to go horribly wrong. 'They will cry out that they are being let down, sabotaged by unpatriotic people who will not do what the nation requires; and so, with a show of reluctance, they will proceed to compulsion.'[15] This stung Brown to a response. Speaking at Doncaster the next day he claimed that 'the moment you start compelling people in the field of industrial relations, in the field of work, or in the field of management and unions, you are going well down the road away from democracy ... I am too long a democratic socialist to be the man to put that kind of operation into practice.'[16] Later that month, though, Powell rejoiced at one of the first signs of the failure of the Brown method. Brickmakers had been told by Charlie Pannell, the Minister of Public Building and Works, that they should increase stocks from 200 to 300 million bricks in 1965 to cope with an expected boom in building. No boom came, and manufacturers were left with huge unused stocks. They complained to Pannell, who shrugged his shoulders. Powell said that this was the inevitable consequence of allowing fiats, rather than the market, to rule supply and demand. Throughout the autumn, as examples of reality not matching up with Brown's prophecy came thick and fast, Powell did not hesitate to highlight each one, and pile on the mockery.

The Conservative party conference at last found Powell addressing his own portfolio, and doing so with what, initially, seemed conspicuous success. Speaking on 14 October, he began by referring to his most fundamental philosophy, defining the nation and the national interest. He seemed to launch a new defence policy, calling into question Labour's continued commitment East of Suez. Powell defined Britain as a power only in the European context; success in trade was no longer contingent on military might, and communism an abstract theory that could not be shot down with bullets. So measured and logical was his speech that the great policy leaps he was making caused barely a stir, even when he hinted there might not be a permanent need for an independent nuclear deterrent.

The key point – which at the time, like so much he was wont to say of significance in public speeches, went straight over the heads of his audience – was this:

> However much we may do to safeguard and reassure the new independent countries in Asia and Africa, the eventual limits of Russian and Chinese advance in those directions will be fixed by a balance of forces which will itself be Asiatic and African. The two Communist empires are already in a state of mutual antagonism; but every advance or threat of advance by one or the other calls into existence countervailing forces, sometimes nationalist in character, sometimes expansionist, which will ultimately check it. We have to reckon with the harsh fact that the attainment of this eventual equilibrium of forces may at some point be delayed rather than hastened by Western military presence.[17]

David Howell, a future Conservative cabinet minister then working as a leader writer on the *Daily Telegraph*, went up to his colleague Andrew Alexander and said, 'I understand Enoch's just withdrawn us from East of Suez, and received an enormous ovation because no-one understood what he was talking about.'[18]

Powell's speech alarmed American diplomats in London. A transcript was sent to Washington, and the American embassy let it be known that it would take an early opportunity to ask Heath for more details about the 'Powell doctrine'. The Americans were mainly worried about Powell's desire to stop policing commitments in Asia, where the Americans thought they had a joint deal with Britain; and they were not sure whether Powell's desire to have Britain withdraw was prompted by philosophical or economic considerations. American resources were becoming heavily stretched by Vietnam, and there were fears that Britain would start moving away just when she was needed most – a point to which Powell was alert, as he saw no possible British interest being served by the commitment of British troops to that theatre of war. Healey challenged Heath to say whether he supported Powell's thinking, hoping to locate a split. Within days, though, the Labour leadership saw that Powell had provided them with a trump card. As Richard Crossman, the Minister of Housing, recorded in his diary on 19 October, following a private meeting with Wilson: 'Harold and I agreed that pressure from our left wing and from Powell on the Right would have value since it would leave him free either to withdraw from East of Suez or to extract a higher price from the Americans for standing staunchly by them.'[19]

The *New York Times* reported Powell's speech as 'a potential declaration of independence from American policy', all the more worrying since its London correspondent confirmed, not entirely accurately, that Powell had the full backing of the party leadership.[20] Certainly, Powell's speech contributed to a conference theme of the demolition of imperial nostalgia. Heath and Douglas-Home, who had assumed overall charge of external affairs, both made distinctly unromantic noises about Rhodesia. The Tory commentator Peregrine Worsthorne saw clearly what Powell was getting at: his 'proposals for withdrawing British power from Africa and Asia ... which seem so defeatist and un-robust, so un-Tory, spring in truth from an almost de Gaulle-like national conceit – a willingness to take risks in areas where Britain can only play a poor second fiddle to America so as to be able to concentrate more on the one area where Britain still hopes to be able to cut a major figure: Europe'.[21]

After the conference, Powell returned to more familiar ground. In a speech at Weston-super-Mare on 20 October he urged his party to look intently at trade union reform. Labour was seeking to end unofficial strikes by making collective agreements enforceable by law, a notion Powell said would be practicable only if both employers and workers belonged to the same union, and were controlled by it, because the unions could not otherwise be made accountable for what those in industry did. Provocatively, he said this was exactly how matters had been ordered in fascist Italy, and – taking a swipe at some colleagues who were cautiously welcoming the plan – added that 'such a system is inconsistent with all that the Conservative party has ever said about the right of a man to belong to any union or to none'.[22]

This, after Powell's defence radicalism, was more than one Conservative MP could stand. Aidan Crawley, speaking in his constituency of West Derbyshire, called for Powell's resignation from the shadow cabinet, since he appeared at odds with most of its thinking. Referring to a Labour maverick, he said Powell was 'in danger of becoming the Frank Cousins of the Conservative Party'.[23] Crawley spoke for a growing group within the party. The initial support from the leadership for what Powell had said at Brighton was now checked, as word crept in from the constituencies that activists were not yet prepared to accept such post-imperialism. Heath became concerned at the volume of disapproval from America, upon which he had not reckoned. For all his own lukewarmness about America, he believed that Britain could not sit by and watch an ally defeated in Vietnam – a view Powell simply did not share. Crawley's belief was that the independence of small countries in Asia could be guaranteed only by British involvement; and, on the matter of Powell's views on the unions, Crawley maintained that the Conservative party was simply not the party of laissez-faire, and that was that. Powell, who that same day was at Oxford claiming that Crossman secretly wished to ration housing, refused to comment on what, coming from a backbencher not known for flippancy, was an attack of unprecedented seriousness. As dissent grew, Heath ensured that lobby journalists were briefed that Powell had, in fact, in his speech been posing questions to stimulate discussion about very long-term defence policy. Like most lobby briefings, that was only a partial truth. Powell, for his part, was shocked by Heath's retreat from a position he had thought they both occupied.

The issues raised by Powell at Brighton – of which he had given his shadow cabinet colleagues a broad, though not exact, outline in advance at their meeting on 5 October – were discussed at greater length at another meeting on 27 October. Jointly with Christopher Soames, the foreign affairs spokesman, Powell submitted a paper on what the party's attitude should be towards wider global defence commitments. As joint papers go, this was rather comical, Soames entering in brackets at the end of several paragraphs his dissent from Powell's position on withdrawing from East of Suez. Powell's line had been that specific obligations had to be honoured, but that a scaling down, without committing Britain to a timetable or to any detail, had to take place as quickly as possible. Soames, on the other hand, said the main priority should be to safeguard oil supplies, and to give no encouragement whatever to Nasser. Powell's view – not expressed in the paper – was that there were plenty of other sources of oil, and whether Nasser felt encouraged or not was of no long-term interest to Britain.

The paper highlighted Powell's intellectual isolation within the shadow cabinet, and in the discussion on it he was further marginalised. As the official minute reported: 'It was considered that Mr Powell's speech at Brighton had been misunderstood and misrepresented in some quarters.' It also spoke of confusion on 'time scales'; above all, colleagues feared upsetting 'our American allies and … our Commonwealth friends'. There was a strong view that the record had to be put straight, and that it should be put straight in the Commons, not in speeches in the country. Powell was being out-manoeuvred; only he, as defence spokesman, appeared to disagree with one of the principal defence policies of his own party. Lord Carr remembered this initiative of Powell's as being one that chimed most deeply, and uncomfortably, with his colleagues. 'I hoped he was wrong, but I had an uncomfortable feeling that he wasn't wrong. I felt I was being made to face up to something that I didn't want to face up to, but that I really ought to.'[24]

It may have been the collegiate wish that the damage be put right in the Commons, but Powell raised the subject, obliquely, in the country nevertheless, in a speech on 4 November at Hemel Hempstead. He called for a 'rethink' of the way in which the West tried to control the advance of communism in South-East Asia, and, using terms already outlined in his shadow cabinet paper, emphasised that he was seeking not to resile from existing commitments, but to avoid making further commitments for the future. Heath, unsurprisingly, stuck to the cabinet line. Interviewed for the next weekend's *Sunday Telegraph*, he claimed that while he understood the furore which Powell's comments at Brighton and after had created, the furore was the result of a misunderstanding.

Sticking to the briefing, he said Powell was 'posing questions, not formulating policy. He was thinking ahead over a period of years.'[25]

The sternest test for Powell came the following Wednesday, when he faced an audience of 120 Conservative backbenchers at a joint Defence, Foreign Affairs and Commonwealth Committee meeting, also addressed by Douglas-Home and Soames. Dame Patricia Hornsby-Smith, the MP for Chislehurst, tore into Powell for the effect his speech had had on American opinion; and several other MPs protested that, now Powell was a senior shadow spokesman, he should adapt the unguarded way he had addressed policy issues while on the back-benches. Of all those who spoke only Angus Maude, typically, came out in support of what Powell had said. Powell reiterated the points he had made the previous week about the need for 'rethinking', claiming that, in a fast-changing world, such a process was both right and inevitable. In his summing-up, however, Douglas-Home said that Britain must remain a force in the Far East, which was interpreted as a rebuke to Powell.

II

Even in the Commons, Powell was reluctant to stick to his portfolio. On 18 November he made a weighty speech on the Government's pensions policy, in which he scolded ministers for having broken pledges made in opposition. His excuse for doing so was that former members of the armed forces were particularly unfairly treated, in his view, as some pension increases the Government planned would not be paid until an age usually long beyond that when most servicemen retired. In quoting back to ministers words that they had uttered in opposition about their generous plans for pension provision, he showed he was far more effective at undermining their case than the Treasury spokesmen on his own side nominally responsible for doing so.

In the shadow cabinet it was not merely East of Suez that was a cause of dissent. The unilateral declaration of independence on 11 November 1965 by Ian Smith on behalf of Rhodesia was a direct challenge to British authority. Many Conservative MPs openly supported Smith, since he and his colleagues were self-evidently better equipped to run Rhodesia than the majority native population. This was never Powell's view; he abjured the illegality of the regime, and saw the inevitability of democratic rule. However, he entered a strong objection, at the shadow cabinet meeting of 29 November, to the Opposition's supporting a request from neighbouring Zambia to be sent British troops for protection. Heath said troops had been sent in in such circumstances in the past by Conservative administrations. Powell, though, warned of the likelihood of British troops being involved in fighting, and of arriving to find other troops, under various commands, being sent in simultaneously. Once more, Powell was alone.

The rest of the committee said that the Government should send troops, but with a clearly limited role. In the event, only the most marginal military advice was given, and the RAF made a brief visit to Zambia.

His remarks of the previous May about the need for stricter immigration controls had gone unheeded. Powell made no apology for returning to the theme in a speech in Birmingham on 20 November. He said he feared that the issue was being downgraded as unimportant or not urgent, something his own experiences as a constituency member had shown him was not so. He quoted the latest figures – 33,000 entrants from the New Commonwealth in the first half of 1965 – and said the steps the Government had supposedly taken to control this inflow were not working. 'Even after the further limits on vouchers announced in the White Paper of August were in force, there was an inflow of more than 10,000 from the West Indies and the Indian sub-continent alone in the two months of August and September. It will be realised that these figures, being official, can take no account of illegal entries or entries through Ireland.'[26] He repeated his call not just for strict controls on Commonwealth immigrants, but for voluntary repatriation. Again, he was unheard. So he would simply have to go on repeating his demands, reflecting the views of his constituents, more and more stridently until someone did take notice.

In December Powell wound up for his party in a debate on Labour's Territorial Army policy, for which Heath himself had opened the attack. The Conservatives were angered that a decision on the future of the TA had been taken in isolation from the rest of the defence review – which Powell dismissed as illogical. An urgent move had been made to cut the size of the reserve because of the effects of the Government's economic policy, and the need the Treasury felt to prove that it would act in a way to prevent further pressure on sterling. Accused by a Labour backbencher of having done a similar thing in January 1958, Powell replied, 'I have no objection at all to the Chancellor of the Exchequer endeavouring to sustain the value of sterling by a proper control of Government expenditure, but in this case his action had the result of precipitating the disastrous decision which we are considering and are condemning tonight.'[27]

He alleged that this desperate need to save money reflected a panic that the Government had tried to 'dress up' by a statement by Healey that the TA was no longer a 'realistic' force when it came to defending the United Kingdom, or much use in the preparations for a major conventional war. It was not just that discounting of the reserve that worried the Conservatives: it was that the destruction of the TA would also, as Powell put it, destroy 'the territorial framework of the Army, with all the effects that has not just on recruitment of the Regular Army – which is a comparatively narrow aspect – and not just upon the manpower ready to come forward for service in many parts, including the rural parts, of our country ... It means the tearing of the connection between the Army and the country which here at home has always been provided, both in the time of the Territorial Army and long before that, by citizen volunteer forces.'[28] Healey said Powell's analysis had been 'very remote from reality', but he was not as ebullient in his defence as usual; there was disquiet on his own backbenches.[29] In the division that followed, the Government had a majority of just one.

Powell gave a pre-Christmas interview to the *Sunday Express* (his interviewer, Marshall Pugh, realised that they had last met at the Gurkha depot at Dehra Dun in 1945 when Powell was 'the intense young brigadier with the incandescent eyes who might have served as the hero – or the villain') in which, after a taxing few months, he engaged in a bout of introspection. 'I happen to know that I have to work hard to keep my emotions under control. If I found myself at the Ministry of Defence I should have to be careful that my heart didn't take charge of my head. I'm naturally impulsive, impatient, even hasty. Perhaps overcompensation by years of control has produced a superficial appearance of the opposite.'[30] Powell also denied that, in his ostensible puritanism, he had ever felt the slightest envy for those wealthier or of higher status than himself. 'I'm like a stone deaf person being told about music, it's an emotion I don't share ... When I see success in any form I like it and I'm glad to know there are rich people about. It affects me like looking at sunsets and snow-capped mountains.' He dismissed the idea that this attitude was due to any great feeling of philanthropy. 'Perhaps it reflects a kind of arrogance. I've always felt confident that I'd be able to go out and get anything I wanted sufficiently badly.'

For a while Powell tried to tread more cautiously on the territory of others, but his impulsiveness would get the better of him. Following an outbreak of typhoid in Aberdeen the Government had ordered the withdrawal from sale of 200 six-pound tins of Argentine corned beef, since there was a belief they might have been a source of the outbreak. Powell thought this outrageous, and, in his capacity as a former Minister of Health, issued a statement through Conservative Central Office on 1 January 1966 saying so. He objected to the interference of Fred Peart, the Minister of Agriculture, in the matter by summoning the managing director of an import firm and telling him to stop selling the beef when no issue of health (by the Government's own admission) was at stake; and to the insistence of Wilson, holidaying in the Scillies, that the press be told about it to make capital out of the panic. What the businessman had been doing was perfectly lawful, said Powell: 'Ministers have no right to arraign private individuals and bully and browbeat them into doing what the Government happens to like.'[31]

More established areas of internal conflict soon flared again. In a speech at Wellingborough on 5 January Maudling said an incomes policy was 'essential', but the one the Government was running was so structured as to be ineffectual. The speech – which included a wider, if intellectually bereft, attack on the principle of laissez-faire – was a direct contradiction of Powell's beliefs, and was seen to be so.[32] Powell retaliated a week later in Manchester, asking why those who attacked socialism nonetheless supported some of its core concepts, such as the prices and incomes policy. He was uneasy with the view, held by Maudling and others, that the unions were an autonomous force in the economy which would have the main effect on levels of demand. 'From this belief is drawn the deduction that a kind of formal treaty must be concluded with these powerful, independent principalities, much as one would sign the terms of capitulation with a victorious enemy or of alliance with a predominant partner,' he said.[33]

Powell was once more starting to concentrate on attacking the intellectual weaknesses of his own side rather than the philosophical shortcomings of his opponents. Returning nearer his own brief at Camborne on 14 January he called for more realism about the Commonwealth. 'There always comes a time', he said, 'when the kissing has to stop. In my belief, it has come.' Referring to tensions between India and Pakistan, which Britain had been powerless to ease, and internal strife in Africa, he scorned the notion that 'all these countries form with us a great Commonwealth, which is the world's best hope and model for international and inter-racial co-operation'.[34] Nor, at this stage, was he the only agent of disunity in the upper reaches of the party. Angus Maude, one of his closest friends and supporters in the House and a junior front-bench spokesman, wrote an article in the *Spectator* in which he condemned the ineffectuality of the party organisation under the chairman, Edward du Cann, and expressed his opposition to the consensus-laden nature of party policy.

Heath, taxed by Robin Day in a *Panorama* interview about this and about Powell's activities, said: 'Of course there is room for discussion. We are not autocratic. We are a very democratic party. Never before has there been such an opportunity for members to put their views and have their views thoroughly discussed. I believe in this.'[35] Nonetheless, Maude was sacked the next day. He went with good grace and protestations of loyalty ('We are a very gentlemanly party. We don't want to make things too awkward for each other'),[36] but with dark references to the split between Powell and Maudling on incomes policy. A rumour, entirely unsubstantiated, did the rounds that Powell had put Maude up to his article.

Powell returned from a three-day trip to Paris, where he had meetings with and was briefed by senior NATO officials at Fontainebleau, just as the Maude affair reached its climax. His response was almost satirical. Speaking in Fulham the night after his return from France he made a call for party unity, claiming that discussion within the party about policy could be achieved without 'fouling one's own nest':[37] his words can only be interpreted as being aimed at Heath rather than Maude, but that is presumably not what he knew the non-textual critics of the press and his own party would read into them. He himself was not inclined to hide his own dissent. On 27 January a junior minister, Richard Marsh, speaking in a Commons debate on the cost of living, spoke of Powell's own opposition to incomes policies by way of indicating how split the Conservatives were. Rather than sit in silence, Powell nodded vigorously in assent.

The subject came up again at the shadow cabinet meeting on 31 January. The form of words in 'Put Britain Right Ahead' had been an appropriate precursor to the fatuity of the line in the manifesto, saying that the whole economic policy was, in effect, an incomes policy. Again, Powell had not been affronted by this because of the latitude it give him to interpret it. In this latest discussion, he said he entirely agreed with the economic policy, since it expressed a commitment to make control of inflation paramount. However, there was plenty of scope still to discuss the best means by which that control would be operated. The party remained unwilling to oppose the principle of an incomes policy; but, in what those present obviously regarded as an important theological distinction, it was prepared to say that the 'machinery' being used by the Government was wrong.[38] Powell had minuted his own belief that no Government should attempt to control prices or wages, and that the laws of supply and demand should be paramount. There was to be no hint of unity on the issue.

The matter was, though, becoming urgent. At the beginning of February it became known that Labour would soon publish a Bill embodying its own prices and incomes legislation, and the press began to speculate on the efficacy of Conservative opposition to such a step, given the known disagreements. It was speculation out of which Powell emerged well, for at least all knew where he stood. The failure of the Conservatives to be seen, in public, to stand for anything in particular was becoming damaging. However, the press concentrated on the main objection to such a policy being that it would not work without compulsion. Powell had long moved beyond this point, knowing that the main problem was its irrelevance to the true causes of inflation.

III

In the winter of 1966 there was plenty in Powell's own sphere of responsibility to occupy him. He teased Healey about Labour's complete retreat, in less than eighteen months, from the principle of a shared nuclear deterrent to stay with an independent one. Then, when controversy arose about whether Britain should choose the new F-111A bombers, the Conservative backbench Defence Committee tabled a motion claiming that the Government's dithering over whether or not to have these bombers was causing 'alarm and uncertainty' in the services. Powell issued a statement on 15 February saying that the procrastination had created a 'state of ferment', and that Healey's paying two visits to the United States in three weeks to consult Pentagon officials about the decision was 'undignified'. Powell's objections were rooted on this occasion not in his distaste for the American way, but in his feeling that Healey was showing disrespect for Parliament.[39] The Conservatives had a further bonus in their belief that the Navy Minister, Christopher Mayhew, was prepared to resign if the F-111As were purchased at the expense of the existing aircraft-carrier programme. Healey decided on the bombers, and, immediately, Mayhew went, saying the Government's policies were 'dangerously mistaken'; he also talked of the need to prepare to disengage East of Suez, a view that put him closer to Powell. When the First Sea Lord, Sir David Luce, resigned too, the Conservatives looked to have the Government on the rack.

However, within days of Mayhew's resignation Healey came to Commons and made a statement on the defence review, justifying the need because of what he described as the 'runaway growth' in defence expenditure under the Conservatives.[40] He said Labour had found the forces over-stretched and under-equipped, but nonetheless would work to limit the budget in 1969–70 to what it was in 1964–5: some £2 billion in 1964 prices. This meant cutting £400 million, three-quarters of which Healey said could be done by securing better value for money; the other quarter necessitated a reduction in military capability. He announced that Mediterranean deployments would be greatly reduced, that the base at Aden would be given up in 1968, that forces would be cut in the Far East, and that within a few years there would be no forces at all in the Caribbean or Southern Africa. Nor, in the future, would Britain undertake any overseas commitments without the support of allies.

Much of this, embarrassingly, was consonant with Powell's doctrine. It was the beginning of a phase that Peter Utley, in his book on Powell, would recall with the sentence: 'No feat of tightrope walking in recent British political history has been more remarkable than Powell's handling of his double function of educating the Conservative Party about defence and representing its official policy against Labour.'[41] However, another announcement of Healey's, that Britain would buy 'the smallest possible number' of F-111A aircraft from the Americans to tide the RAF over until an Anglo-French aircraft project was ready, was something Powell could object to.[42] The Defence Secretary also said there would be no new carriers for the foreseeable future. When he replied, Powell began by reminding Healey that, a week earlier, he had said he expected no resignations because of the review, and yet had lost Mayhew and Luce. He added that it would not be 'practicable nor appropriate to reply point by point at this stage to his long and tendentious statement'. He confined himself to the observation that the policy had been forced upon the Government by 'their own absurd preoccupation with fudging a figure of £2,000 million in 1969–70 regardless of the consequences for the morale of the services or the defence of the country'.[43]

Powell's failure to press Healey about the detail – detail with which Powell would have been in large agreement – and the nature of what he did say allowed Healey off any hook the Opposition might have hoped to hang him on. 'I am surprised that the right hon Gentleman should have made the last point,' he said, 'since he himself resigned from the previous Government because they did not fix a limit for defence expenditure' – a point not strictly accurate, but accurate enough to leave Powell no comeback, as he was normally the last to endorse the failure to set strict financial targets. Healey continued: 'On the question of resignations, on which the right hon Gentleman is, indeed, an expert...' It was not Powell's day. Heath intervened in the questioning of Healey shortly afterwards, and compounded Powell's difficulties – even though he berated Healey for having 'reduced such a statement in his answers to supplementary questions to the level of personal attacks' – by going into detail with a series of sharp and difficult questions about finance and diplomatic obligations that would be sundered by Healey's policies in the Middle East.[44]

These events were seen almost entirely in the context of what was expected to be an imminent calling of a general election. The Opposition wanted a two-day debate on defence, concentrating on the threat to the carrier fleet and the withdrawal from Aden, but feared that Wilson would call an election to avoid being pinned down on the question. Such a debate would put Powell in a difficult position, for the same reason he had been compromised during Healey's statement on the review. However, speaking in Manchester on 25 February he called for an extensive debate, and expressed the hope that an election would not come before the matter could be properly aired. 'The more we dig under the facts,' he said, 'the more disagreeable creatures will be able to crawl out from underneath the stones.'[45] It was not clear to whom the creatures might be disagreeable. The Commons debate was then promised; Powell would have to make the best of it.

The same day, in Bolton, with an eye on the impending contest, he returned to his main theme of the Government's attacks on individual freedom, and the failure of the economic policy. This would be Powell's main weapon during the campaign, once the election was called for 31 March. At Eastbourne on 4 March – two days after the shadow cabinet had agreed the text of the manifesto, which made no mention of this specific aim – he called for a repeal of the 1906 Trades Dispute Act, from which the unions drew their legal immunities. He repeated the call in Staffordshire ten days later, strengthening it with an implicit rebuke to his side for having tolerated this law for so long. 'Intimidation is not accidental nor incidental to our trade union law; it is written into the basic law itself.'[46] He was distressed, he later revealed, by the Conservative manifesto, entitled *Action Not Words*, which he said was just about the silliest title a manifesto could have. 'A politician's business is with words. With words as opposed to action.'[47] However, as his friend Andrew Alexander noted, one of Powell's abiding weaknesses was to overrate the value of argument.[48]

Before Parliament was dissolved the Commons had its debate on defence, which Powell led. The specific motion he proposed stated that the estimates as published would 'impair the ability of our forces to carry out the duties required of them'.[49] He rooted his concerns in the resignations of Mayhew and Luce, and described the justification Healey had made for his new policy as 'without foundation'. He said, 'I intend to show that both the suggestion that defence costs have been engaged on a runaway course, and the notion that they have been brought under control by decisions taken in consequence of a careful review of commitments, are mere mystification, and that the only reality was the financial panic into which the Government were plunged in the early days of their administration.'

He began by reading out a list of the percentages of the proportions of national income spent on defence since 1957–8; and, in contrast to Healey's claim that it had been spiralling out of control, he showed how, with the exception of one year when there had been a slight increase, it had fallen steadily from 7.3 per cent to 6.5 per cent in 1964. The percentage had started to rise only under Labour. There had been a claim – which he said was groundless – that expenditure would, under the Conservatives, have risen in real terms by £400 million by 1969–70, and it was this imaginary figure Healey was so proud of having eliminated; and he mocked, once more, the fact that the elimination had come after 'a recurrence – I think it was the third recurrence but I tend to lose count – of a loss of international confidence in the value of sterling'.[50]

He also accused Healey of being unwilling to specify the 'value for money' savings referred to, at least until the election was out of the way, for the effect of such cuts might be serious in some parts of industry. Mayhew had, after his resignation, referred to the absence of detail in the White Paper. Powell suspected another reason for this reticence was that it would prove that the decision not to have a new carrier would be shown to have turned on a very small saving in the target year. He pointed out that while the military withdrawals Healey had referred to might amount to eight or nine battalions, which was a substantial force, this 'involves no saving at all in budgetary expenditure if those men are still to be maintained under arms . . . any saving . . . can come about only through a reduction in the size of the standing Army'; and Powell referred to leaks from Healey's own department that such a reduction, amounting to perhaps 16,000 men, was planned by 1970.

Although Powell was not wedded to the concept of British forces remaining in Aden, he did state the nature of the commitment Britain had made to stay there, and accused Healey of being prepared to repudiate it. There had been a request, in 1964, from Aden that Britain should maintain her place there after independence, and it was clearly stated in a White Paper of July 1964 that the Government agreed. 'One can hardly imagine a more direct breach of the undertaking,' said Powell, which prompted Healey to intervene. He asked Powell whether the promise – made by Duncan Sandys – could constitute a binding commitment on a future government, especially when a base was no longer required and when the local population no longer wanted it. Powell, taunted by Healey's colleagues, said the commitment had been made and was binding. He said that if the Conservatives won the election, they would regard it as binding. More seriously still, he accused Healey of giving comfort to Britain's enemies by making the promise of withdrawal. Violence had flared in Aden as soon as the news was made known.

Powell then turned to the confusion he felt Healey and the Government were in over the Territorial Army, saying that they wanted to destroy not just the spirit but also the volunteer tradition of the TA at a time when the running down of the Regular Army would, inevitably, put still more pressure on the reserves. He spoke, too, of the danger of creating a gap in British capability by not building any more aircraft carriers. At this point he was interrupted by a Labour backbencher who asked hi how he reconciled such a statement with one made in February 1958 by Sandys on the unaffordability of carriers. 'Very simply,' Powell replied. 'It was a great mistake to have scrapped the aircraft carrier under construction.'[51]

When it came to the Government's plans to have the F-111As, Powell asked what the purpose was of buying, at great expense, aircraft that would allow Britain to mount operations on her own and strike at a range of 1,500 miles when such a policy was disavowed by the rest of the defence strategy. He asked Healey what sort of circumstances he imagined occurring, therefore, where such a capability would be necessary. Then Powell ridiculed the long-term replacement for this aircraft (the Anglo-French 'variable geometry' – swing-wing – project), which he pointed out did not exist 'even on the back of an envelope'.[52] He claimed that 'the whole thing is a structure of spoof', covering up the mess caused by the Government's cancellation of its own earlier projects and the obligations entered into with America. In taking the American option, Powell claimed, the Government had damaged the British aircraft industry.

At this stage Woodrow Wyatt, a Labour MP, attempted to derail Powell, who had been speaking for over an hour – one of the longest speeches in his parliamentary career. Wyatt said Powell had been making 'a very powerful case against the Government's defence cuts. Could he reconcile that case with his often repeated statements that our commitments east of Suez ought to be reduced drastically and more quickly? Where is the consistency' Powell brazened it out. 'I should be very obliged to the hon Gentleman if he would do me the honour to draw my attention to the place and circumstances in which I have used either those words or anything like them.'[53] Wyatt had not chapter and verse to hand, and was in any case relying largely on what many of Powell's parliamentary colleagues thought – rightly – to be his view rather than upon any direct statements he had made on the matter.

Powell's was a typical Opposition Day speech, with him doing what he was best at, attacking and denouncing and highlighting hypocrisy and humbug, but offering no clear alternative strategy that the Government should follow. In a speech that lasted an hour and a quarter that was a great weakness, made greater by his own private views on the post-imperial role and on the use of public money. However, Healey's case was riddled with hypocrisies, and Powell had done well to pin down so many of them.

Healey, though, was more than a match for him. He derided Powell for failing to explain the Conservatives' policy, and for failing to clarify the contradictions apparent since the last Conservative party conference, with one wing of the party wishing to spend more and another less on defence. He also renewed Wyatt's accusation that Powell was committed to a strategy built on Europe, and as such was merely a faction within his own party. Powell's speech had, he said, contained 'equivocation on every important issue in the hope of maintaining the facade of solidarity until the election is over'.[54] As for Powell's key point, that expenditure as a proportion of the total had fallen until the end of the Conservative government, Healey said that was only the out-turn: the estimates had always been higher, and the Government had failed to meet its own programme, postponing further expenditure until later in the decade – which was the situation created by the time Labour came to power. More to the point, he teased Powell for not having given a judgment on whether the new target of £2 billion in real terms for the rest of the decade was too low, too high or right; and he wanted to know how the Conservatives would have found the money to maintain spending at the levels they had predicted, which, if fully serviced, would have required – he claimed – either severe cuts elsewhere or 1s 6d in the pound on income tax.

Here, Powell interrupted them: 'Does not the Secretary of State realise that what he is saying now is that he does not anticipate any growth in the national income in the next five years?'[55] Healey claimed quite the contrary: that the growth expected in national wealth would mean that defence spending could be maintained while falling, as a proportion of national income, from 7 to 6 per cent. Later, he repeated the taunt that Powell had resigned in 1958 because of a refusal to set a target for defence spending. Thorneycroft had just left the chamber, so Powell rose and stated that 'As he is not here, perhaps I should say that the issue of defence expenditure was not involved in the issue over which he and I resigned.'[56] Healey was assailed by cries of 'Withdraw!', but refused to do so. He read extracts from Thorneycroft's resignation speech, in which the former Chancellor stated as a fact – not as a cause of his and Powell's going – that defence expenditure had grown. Spotting this weakness, the cries of 'Withdraw' continued, and Heath rose to make a formal request for Healey to set the record straight. Healey said he would leave it to the country to judge what interpretation should be put on the words of Thorneycroft's that he had quoted. For once, his combination of intellectual weight and bluster could not see him through.

Inevitably, defence came back to the fore of the campaign. Powell attacked the Government on 16 March for its subservience to America, a point with which many in his own party would have disagreed, but which many on the Labour left would have silently cheered. Powell claimed that in foreign affairs Britain's voice had been an indistinguishable echo of the State Department's ever since Wilson had come to power. 'This presumably is what Harold Wilson meant in 1964 when he said: "You can get into pawn, but do not then talk about an independent foreign policy or an independent defence policy." These were prophetic words. Within six weeks of Labour coming into office Britain was in pawn and today we have not got an independent foreign policy or an independent defence policy. We shall not have them until it is clear that Britain no longer means to be in pawn but means to get out of it.'[57] For that, Powell reminded his audience, economic strength was essential, which was why he also believed the value of sterling was the most crucial issue of the election.

Thanks to Powell's refusal to conceal his own beliefs the issue of British independence of policy would dominate the end of the campaign. But, first, he returned to matters of more parochial importance. In his election address he had referred briefly to the importance of immigration controls. Speaking in his constituency on 25 March he described immigration as an issue 'which forces itself upon our attention'. There was a conspiracy between politicians of both parties, for reasons of self-interest, to keep the subject off the agenda during the campaign, not least because of the nasty taste the defeat of Gordon Walker in 1964 had left in some mouths. Powell was having none of it. 'It is absolutely absurd', he told his electors, 'to say that immigration either is not, or ought not to be, an issue at this election, especially for Wolverhampton and other parts of the Black Country ... It would be quite wrong that the policies on this matter of those presenting themselves for election to Parliament should not be known to their prospective constituents.'[58]

He outlined the two sides, as he saw it, of the problem: the problem of those immigrants already in Britain, and the problem of those still seeking to get in. For the former, he said he would fight for them to have the same rights as any other citizens, and would help them in the same way as he would help any other of his constituents. There were some not happy in Britain, and they should be enabled to return whence they came if that was what they chose. He said he regretted that controls had not been enforced earlier and added, in a phrase that was a harbinger of his most famous speech, that 'even after the measure we introduced in 1962 and which Labour by a remarkable about turn reluctantly accepted, the rate of inflow is far too high'. He claimed that, at the present rate, there would be another two and a half million Commonwealth immigrants by the end of the century: 'We say therefore that the rate of admission must be further and greatly reduced.'[59] This was not, he argued, merely to benefit the indigenous population, but to benefit those immigrants already in Britain.

In 1962 the Government of which Powell was a member had at last introduced restrictions to the notion of British nationality, for immigration purposes, as defined by the Attlee Government's 1948 British Nationality Act. The right to enter had been restricted to those born or naturalised in the United Kingdom, and to their immediate male descendants. There were two loopholes: no restrictions applied to movement between the United Kingdom and the Irish Republic, and high commissioners could – and frequently still did – issue 'UK and Colonies' passports to applicants in Commonwealth countries; this had been allowed in order to protect the interests of 'white settlers', but this racial dispensation was not something the Government of the time had boasted about. Powell admitted that, even had he sat in the cabinet at the time (and he had, it will be recalled, sat on its immigration sub-committee nonetheless), he did not know whether he would have spotted the 'fatal blunder' that created these loopholes.[60]

This apparently controversial stand was, however, nothing compared with the effect of remarks he made at Falkirk on the Saturday before the election. Saying, 'I am going to voice an apprehension which is better voiced now than when it will be too late,' he claimed that he would not be surprised if the Ministry of Defence did not have contingency plans for sending at least a token force to Vietnam to assist the Americans, their arm twisted to make such a provision by the need for economic help from America.

> The American administration have made no secret of desiring this, for reasons which are understandable from their point of view in terms of internal politics and of military power. But it would be intolerable if such a step on Britain's part, with all the large and unforeseeable consequences which would ensue, were to come about as part of a package deal arising from pressure on sterling, or a bout of short term insolvency. If such a step is even remotely in contemplation, the Prime Minister ought to confirm or deny it now. He ought to tell the country one way or the other before polling day.[61]

There was more to this than met the eye. On the previous evening, Powell had received a message to call Michael Fraser at Central Office. When he did, Fraser told him word was going round about Wilson's intentions to send a token force to Vietnam, and suggested to Powell that he, as defence spokesman, might like to ask, publicly, whether this was so. Furthermore – remarkably, in the light of subsequent events – Fraser told Powell that he would be acting on Heath's specific wishes. Powell was delighted to take up the challenge, for it allowed him to make, in what he was told were the interests of his party, a speech that clearly reflected his own views – though in making what developed into a definitive text of Powell's Americo-scepticism, he went too far in the eyes of some colleagues who were avidly pro-American.

He derided the notion of a 'special relationship' between Britain and America, saying that whereas Churchill might have been able to sustain it by the force of his personality, 'in later days it has often been more imaginary than real, a product perhaps as much as anything of our own wishful thinking. But it has been reserved for a Labour government to give the "special relationship" a precise and definite meaning. Under the Labour Government in the last 18 months Britain has behaved perfectly clearly and perfectly recognisably as an American satellite.' As evidence, Powell cited the fact that when, soon after his election, Wilson had decided that the Government would levy a 15 per cent import surcharge, it was the Americans alone whom he had troubled to inform of this impending breach of international treaties. Powell said that the rest of Europe had concluded that Britain felt she could act as she liked provided she had American permission.

In Vietnam, he continued, every American action had received British endorsement, with Britain acting like an 'obedient commentator'. Wilson had agreed with the bombing of North Vietnam; he had agreed with its cessation too. When the bombing was resumed, the Foreign Office rapidly issued a statement of continued agreement. This was, Powell said, just how the Soviet Union expected her satrapies in Eastern Europe to respond to her own excesses. He quoted Mayhew's resignation statement, in which the ex-minister had described Britain 'not as a power in our own right, but as an extension of the United States power, not as allies but as auxiliaries of the United States'. Part of the deal had been the purchase of American defence equipment on 'buy now, pay later' terms. 'With grim humour an American source hoped that United States industry would make no difficulties over these concessions, since it was getting in return the elimination of Britain's "once proud" military aircraft industry.'

With stunning hypocrisy, Central Office's first reaction was to distance itself in the traditional way from what Powell had said. 'Mr Powell was speaking on his own behalf,' said a spokesman. 'His speech does not reflect any change so far as party policy is concerned.'[62] Healey immediately took a swing at his opposite number. 'Mr Enoch Powell tried hard to keep his real views hidden once the election was announced. The strain has evidently been too much for him. There is, of course, no truth in his delusion that the Ministry of Defence has made contingency plans for a British contribution in Vietnam.' He added that it was Heath's 'plain duty' to sack Powell; Wilson dismissed the allegation as a 'last minute scare'. In fact, he would admit in the 1970 election campaign that President Lyndon Johnson had asked him whether he would supply troops.[63] It was reported at the time from Washington that the public reaction to Powell's revelation of Wilson's intentions was such as to make the Prime Minister realise he could not go through with it. 'The greatest service I have performed for my country, if that is so,' Powell reflected thirty years later.[64]

Heath was not happy, and when taxed on the speech by reporters icily repeated the Central Office formula about it being Powell's own view. However, when asked whether Powell might have been acting on background information in expressing this view, Heath guardedly replied, 'It is possible.'[65] He added, though, that if Healey said there were no plans, he was prepared to take his word for it. In sheer policy terms, though, Heath was not too compromised. He had already stated his opposition to troops going to Vietnam, partly because the services were overstretched already in the Far East, and partly because Britain was co-operating with the Soviet Union to try to find a settlement in South-East Asia.

Powell felt badly let down by Heath, on whose orders he had been told Fraser was operating; and it was the penultimate straw in his relationship with Fraser. Andrew Roth, Powell's biographer, says Heath was not aware of the instructions given to Powell in his name.[66] Powell was not, though, to be deflected. On 27 March he returned to the subject for the second day running, this time in Derbyshire, demanding that Wilson give a categorical assurance that troops would not be sent. British newspaper correspondents in Washington were reporting that the administration planned to 'turn the heat on' for assistance, and that Wilson's ambivalent denials were still not enough; but they were all Powell would get. He let the matter drop, and ended his campaign relatively quietly, his last two speeches in Wolverhampton being devoted to attacks on overseas aid, since the money was wasted on corruption, and to the need to resume negotiations with the Smith regime in Rhodesia, since Britain could not realistically use force to intervene. On 31 March the election took place, and Labour was returned with a greatly increased majority of ninety-seven. Powell's own result reflected the swing away from his party: his majority, in a two-way contest, was cut to 6,585, making the seat look far less safe than since 1951. He would need to look carefully at constituency issues in the coming Parliament; and he did.

IV

Immediately after the election Powell went into print, in the *Sunday Telegraph*, outlining the precious opportunity so heavy a defeat had given his party – hardly tactful in the light of the gloom and shock of his colleagues, but he knew no other way. Wilson's previous majority had been so slender that the Conservatives had always had to act with a caution bred of the possibility that they might be in office within twenty-one days. Now, as Powell rightly observed, Wilson's new majority meant that it would be four or five years. Indulging in wishful thinking, or bravado, he praised the intellectual changes that had already, to judge from the campaign, taken place in the party, and wrote in a tone that assumed the battles against collectivism in his own party had already been won, itself something of an illusion. He said Conservatives could now think and act radically with one clear message: 'Freedom they can have from none but us.' He advocated the clearest possible break with the past. It was, finally, time to bury Macmillan and his legacy, and to pursue the politics of principle rather than those of naked opportunism, with their inflationary and destabilising consequences. 'The path lies at first through criticism, continuous and unsparing, of every aspect of government, no matter how fashionable or seductive, which cannot be reconciled with our belief. We need not fear. Whatever contortions or contradictions we were to submit ourselves to, we should still not be mistaken for Father Christmas or the Labour Party.'[67]

One main responsibility of his party in opposition, he told City of London Young Conservatives on 6 April, was to consider how best the nationalised industries could be put back into the private sector. Such philosophical issues were, though, for the moment put to one side. Wilson had a resolution tabled at the United Nations to allow the use of force, if necessary, to blockade the port of Beira in Mozambique to prevent oil shipments from reaching Rhodesia. He had, the previous December, ruled out force in such circumstances; in a statement Powell asked, inevitably, where such a volte-face left Wilson's assurances on sending troops to Vietnam. The statement was not issued through Central Office, and Maudling, in charge of the Opposition during Heath's absence on holiday, was furious about it, even though Powell was not stepping outside the already agreed limits of policy. He had not been consulted.

Powell's fighting talk of radicalism, and his freelance action on relations with America during the campaign, had deeply unsettled Heath, already feeling vulnerable in the aftermath of such a defeat. The Rhodesia statement, and the cavalier regard he and Maudling felt it showed for the normal courtesies, forced the issue. On 13 April, as the dust was beginning to settle, Heath let it be known he was inviting Powell to see him to discuss how much freedom a member of the shadow cabinet should have to develop policy without general consultation of senior colleagues. Heath had his own, more modest strategy for opposition, and wanted to be sure Powell accepted it before he announced him as a member of the new shadow cabinet. The marketplace of ideas and internal debate to which Powell had committed himself simply did not chime with Heath's measured view of a framework for government. One passage in Powell's speech in the City of London had particularly grated with Heath:

> The levers of power have been removed from our reach or even our remote control ... 'Words not Action' describes with precision the role of the Conservative Party as this new phase opens in its and the nation's political life ... some of our words will be harsh, fierce, destructive words, aimed in defiance and contempt at men and policies we detest ... we have liberty to question and propose, without fearing the jealous scrutiny for pedantic consistency to which the words of a party in office or on the brink of it are forever of necessity obnoxious.[68]

Powell rejected the rumours about Heath's threatening him with an ulti-matum as 'nonsense'. He gave an interview to Llew Gardner of the *Sunday Express*, in which the interviewer had hoped to clarify the position, but Powell refused to talk about politics, only about himself. He rejected Gardner's claim that he was austere: 'Not fair at all. I think you should ask my children about this. My younger daughter especially thinks I am the funniest man she knows. If you explain the meaning of the word austere to her she would be astonished to learn that it would ever apply to her father. Austerity is not one of my outstanding qualities. One of my sayings is that Toryism is about enjoyment.'[69] Yet, having refused to comment on politics, what Powell said about himself could be interpreted as a specific warning to Heath. 'As a Tory I have great respect for authority, for traditional instruments of authority. But intellectually speaking there is no such thing as authority. Someone may have the right to tell me to do something but that cannot be authority for a view. The mere fact that 60 or 60 million people happen to think something is so is neither here nor there. You cannot have anyone else's ideas but your own – or at least I can't.'

He admitted he would enjoy a further spell in opposition, which prompted a question about how healthy such an attitude was. 'I know there is a division within myself here. I do enjoy the despatch of business, but there is a critical slant to my mind. However, I like to think that I am not engaged in breaking down but in breaking open; but in saying here is a stone, let us see what is behind the stone.' Powell recited his main influences – Housman, Carlyle, Nietzsche:

> but if you ask who I would most like to be in all history I think the answer is Charles XII of Sweden ... he had a fantastic career. He was born a military genius. He drove his way across Europe to the edge of the Black Sea. He was captured by the Turks. Finally he was released and marched his tattered little army back across a hostile Europe to Sweden. Then he plunged into new cam-paigns, only to be killed, shot from behind curiously enough, in Norway. I think what I admire is the bloody mindedness of it all. The application of cold intellect to apparently unsolvable material, the endless pursuit of the impractical. I do like blood-minded people ... I owe any success I have had partly to an ability to go on thinking about a subject beyond the point where other people might feel they have taken it to the limit. I am conscious that I have a habit of saying: 'This isn't bloody well good enough. Therefore it cannot be right.'

Heath announced his new shadow cabinet on 19 April. Partly because several of his colleagues, like Thorneycroft, Brooke and Soames, had lost their seats, he was forced to make changes, though these were fewer than they might have been because he decided to shrink the size of the group from twenty-one to seventeen. Powell retained his post shadowing defence, to the general approval of the press, but only after going to Heath's London flat in Albany for an

interview with him. He made it clear to Heath – and was as good as his word –
that he would continue to speak outside his brief; Heath was not prime minister,
and the notion of collective responsibility that applied to a cabinet could not be
made to apply to a shadow one. Heath's parliamentary private secretary, Jim
Prior, had warned him not to include Powell in the team, as his recent record
on East of Suez and Rhodesia suggested that he had not lost his capacity to be
a troublemaker. But Heath told Prior that 'the view was that he was too dangerous to leave out'.[70] Some of Powell's shadow cabinet colleagues continued to be
irritated by what they felt was his discourtesy in speaking on their portfolio
subjects without telling them first. This was, in its most magnified sense, to be
the cause of Powell's downfall two years later.[71]

The press approved Powell's and Heath's apparent concord. 'It is right',
observed the Telegraph, somewhat pompously, 'that his great gifts should continue to be recognised and their occasionally wayward expression tolerated.'[72]
In fact, the concord was hardly what it seemed; the mistrust was heavy on both
sides, but especially Heath's. Powell had been aware of the problem for some
time, and before the election Pam Powell had tried to do something about it.
At a party she buttonholed Heath and started to tell him that, in fact, Powell
did not want his job, and he need have no fears that he was plotting to get it.
However, before she could make her main point Heath's gaze went elsewhere,
and he walked off as if in a trance. He had seen the editor of the Daily Express
enter the room. He knew the paper was publishing an opinion poll the next
morning, and had gone to find out what it said. As a result of his rudeness, the
pre-emptive peace overture failed.

The session of Parliament after the election was busy for Powell. On 26 April
he wound up the section of the debate on the address dedicated to defence and
foreign affairs. But there was little to add to what had been said in the two day
debate before the dissolution, Powell confining himself to saying that 'remorseless care and detail' would be needed in following up the implications of the
defence review.[73] Also, Douglas-Home, who had led off that day, seemed – in
Healey's words later on – to have conducted the 'ceremonial burial of Powellism
as it was defined in a famous speech at Brighton not long ago' by sticking to the
traditional party policy on East of Suez. This 'rebuff', as Healey also put it, was
adduced by him as the reason Powell avoided specific policy issues in his own
speech – though Powell interrupted him and said, somewhat disingenuously,
that there was no conflict between what Douglas-Home had said and what he
had said.

One event leading from the election campaign – the question of whether the
Government, contrary to its claims, had any intention of sending British troops
to Vietnam – did allow Powell to take the debate in a fresh direction. He tried
to tempt Healey by quoting press reports from Washington which seemed to
suggest that the Government had not disabused the Johnson administration of

the idea that, at some stage, troops might be sent. There was, in particular, a report that troops now no longer required to help carry out Britain's responsibilities in Malaysia might be sent to Vietnam. Powell said he was prepared to believe that there was a misunderstanding between the two governments, but he made it clear he did not believe this for a moment.

The following month Powell led another – unsuccessful – assault against the Government's plans for restructuring the Territorial Army, and on 11 May moved a vote of censure against the Aviation Minister, Fred Mulley, for having misled the House in March by concealing from it that the value of a Saudi Arabian contract, announced the previous December, had been included in the dollar offset arranged with the Americans for the cost of the F-111As. The White Paper of the previous February had said the Government would ensure 'that the foreign exchange cost of the F111A would be fully offset by sales of British equipment'. In other words, the Commons had been told the Americans planned to buy an equivalent amount of defence goods from Britain, or to facilitate sales of those goods to third countries; and Mulley, giving an example, had said that such sales would be 'of a kind similar to that we have recently arranged with Saudi Arabia'.[74]

The Saudi Arabian deal was not an example of what was promised: it was, in fact, part of it, though – as Powell argued -this would not be the construction most people would have put on Mulley's words. Becoming, once more, the textual critic, Powell reminded the House that Healey had said the United States '*will* co-operate with us', and Mulley had used the past tense about the deal 'arranged' with Saudi Arabia. Powell was careful not to impugn Mulley personally. He suggested that he had said what he had on 7 March – and the truth had only been dragged out of Healey two months later – because he had not been in on the secret. However, Mulley interrupted Powell and said he had known. That prompted Powell to say that 'in that case I have to say that the gravest censure and blame rests upon the right hon Gentleman himself and upon all his colleagues who were concerned with this matter for not insisting that the record was brought into agreement with the facts which they knew, but which no-one else suspected until weeks afterwards'.[75]

Powell urged Mulley to make a full apology and restore his personal reputation, even though the Government's would be irretrievably blotted. Mulley thanked Powell for the personal generosity towards him, but said that he had never intended to mislead the House, and that the motion against him was unjustified. He sought to explain that the chronology of the deal was complicated, and that no sinister motive should have been read into the statements made by him and Healey. With a Government majority of 100 the censure motion was never going to succeed, but Powell had performed a ruthlessly forensic task with strict attention to the facts, avoiding the personal element that usually characterises such motions. Though personal censures were rare,

Powell had to take a lead role in another one barely six months later, when he wound up the attack by the Opposition on Roy Jenkins, the Home Secretary, for the escape of the spy George Blake from Wormwood Scrubs. That, though, was less successful, the element of blame attaching to Jenkins far less obvious than that incurred by Mulley.

If Heath had used his meeting with Powell after the election to warn him off Vietnam, it did not work. Later that summer, reviewing a book by Lord Avon – as Eden was now styled – on the means of securing peace in the region, Powell took issue with his former chief for repeating the 'familiar assertion' that 'the United States cannot be beaten'.[76]

> This is one of those statements which look precise and definite, but in reality are both ambiguous and vague. Such statements are apt to be dangerous, just because they escape examination. Of course the United States cannot be beaten in the sense in which Germany was beaten in 1945. But where lesser interests than the supreme national interests are at stake in a war, the effort to attain them may at a certain point appear to be more than they are worth. In this (very different) sense it undeniably *is* possible for the United States to be beaten. There can come a point where even the importance with which the Americans themselves – and largely, as a matter of historical fact, the Americans alone – have endowed South Vietnam is exceeded by the cost, in moral and physical terms together, of the Vietnamese war.

It was, as it turned out, one of his more exact prophecies.

Having tried to establish a new *modus vivendi* with Heath, Powell adopted a lower profile for much of the summer of 1966. He did have a new, extra-curricular distraction. With the help of Keith Wallis he started the final heave on his history of the Lords, which he had now, on the advice of his publisher, decided to terminate at 1540. Meanwhile Heath, visiting America, was asked at a press conference on 3 June whether he had Powell 'under wraps' and intended to keep him there. Heath, being jocular, replied, 'Yes to both questions – at least he was when I left, and I think he has talked about nothing since but milk and the Co-ops.' It was hardly the epitome of tact. What specifically stung Powell into breaking his silence, however, was a comment in *The Times* in July 1966 that 'all Conservative front benchers since Mr Macmillan have accepted the need for an extension of economic planning, and in public and in private they have boasted that "we are all planners now" '. 'Not so,' maintained Powell in a letter to the editor, pointing out that, in the 1964 and 1966 Conservative mani-festos, 'economic planning is not so much as mentioned'.[77] His uncompromising line on the matter was apparent again a few days later, during a debate in the Commons on economic affairs. Brown, for the Government, was taunted by Conservatives about the prices and incomes policy, which prompted him to observe that 'some, like the right hon Member for Wolverhampton South-West, hoped it would fail'.[78] Powell interjected: 'I knew!'

'All right,' retorted Brown, 'the right hon Gentleman knew that it would fail and he has taken a lot of pleasure—' Powell interrupted again, 'No, I knew!' Brown resumed, determined now to drive a wedge between Powell and Maudling: 'But this afternoon the right hon Member for Barnet regretted that it had failed, and when I interrupted him at his express wish, and asked whether the right hon Member for Wolverhampton South-West went along with him, I was jeered at by hon members opposite for daring to ask such a silly question. We now have an answer.' At the shadow cabinet on 25 July, two days earlier, the question had come up again, and the election defeat had done little to clarify thoughts about it. The official minute summarised the discussion thus: 'Our line would be that we approved of a voluntary wage freeze for a limited period ... but we were opposed to compulsion.'[79] At the next meeting, on 1 August, Heath made it clear, at last, that it was time to 'refute the impression to which the country was inclined that there was little to choose between the parties' economic policies and methods'. The minute goes on to record that Heath and his committee were opposed to the Prices and Incomes Bill 'in principle', though what exactly that principle was is not minuted.[80]

Powell ended his purdah and took up the fight for Powellite economic doctrine on his return from holiday. At Chapel-en-le-Frith on 3 September he undertook an anniversary review of the national plan, observing that 'all the figures in it that are of any consequence – even those for 1966, let alone those for 1970 – are known already to be hopelessly wrong'.[81] His main regret was that Brown, who had become Foreign Secretary, was no longer in his old, now emasculated, Department to answer for the 'pyramid of rubbish' he had created. Powell was not slow to remind his audience how he had been proved right about the futility of the plan. He had more to be proud of than his colleagues, whose own lack of opposition to the plan had been marked by their decision not to divide the Commons on a motion welcoming its publication.

Then, in Wolverhampton three days later, he sought to demonstrate that in its interference in the business of private companies the Government was violating the rule of law, abetted by industrialists who did not understand what the rule of law meant. The Government's programme of intervention had been almost entirely conducted by exhortation or duress, not by passing and enforcing laws. He cited the case of Lord Renwick, an industrialist, who had written to *The Times* defending himself and his board against an imputation of having broken faith with shareholders by holding the dividend down to the level of the previous year, in compliance with the wishes of the Government. Renwick had claimed that a 'state of national anarchy' would result if no one did what the Government told them, and so all his company had done was subscribe to 'the overriding constitutional principle of recognising the authority of government as such'.[82] Powell said that this view would, if it took hold, be fatal to the rule of law, under which 'there is no such constitutional principle as "the authority of government as such". Government "as such" has no authority: it has only that authority with which the law at the time endows it.'

Powell's new campaign was complemented by an attack of breathtaking candour on Macmillan, the first volume of whose memoirs, *Winds of Change*, was published that month. Reviewing the book in the *Glasgow Herald*, Powell violated all the normal conventions of respect by a front-bencher discussing so recent a leader. He dismissed the book's claims to be an autobiography, saying it was merely a popular account of political history between 1914 and 1939. He then proceeded to dismember Macmillan's character. 'More supremely than any other political figure of our time he possessed the quality which Roman historians called "dissimulation", the art of concealing his real intentions by suggesting others.'[83]

He brought up the events of January 1958, implying that Macmillan's sentimental rather than rational approach to politics – conditioned by his Stockton years – had led to his failure to think correctly. 'To an observer, like myself, the gulf between a vanished past and a real present seemed to be reproduced in the cabinet room. It was a gulf which Macmillan almost studiously emphasised and sharpened, as he does in this book. Reading it, I found constant difficulty in remembering that the writer was a man only half a generation older than myself.'

He then moved to the real case against Macmillan.

> Conservatives in 1955 would have been more incredulous than indignant had anyone told them that, in seven years' time, their political platform would consist of national economic planning, regional economic planning, planning of incomes ('incomes policy'), rationalisation of industries by state intervention, more subsidised housing, and higher public expenditure generally. Those whom these policies shocked could be heard to say that Harold Macmillan had 'debauched the Tory Party'. Debauch or not, he certainly performed one of the largest mass baptisms in history.

Over the next twenty years Powell would be much in demand by literary editors to review memoirs by and biographies of Macmillan, and, if anything, he became more vicious as the memories faded. Noting, in 1982, Nigel Fisher's observation in his life of Macmillan that there was 'no truth' in the claim that he had married Lady Dorothy simply because she was the daughter of a duke, Powell added, 'One envies the ability to be so sure – and so innocent.'[84]

He moved back into the economic field. In a speech in his constituency on 6 September he advised the trade unions, meeting for their annual conference at Blackpool, that any moves by the Government to force them to acquiesce in a pay freeze would be illegal. The Prices and Incomes Act, which would have made such compulsion legal, had been enacted but had not come into force;

and Powell told the unions that, until the Government had the courage to invoke this controversial measure, they should seek whatever rises they wanted. Then, on 8 September, he published a second edition of *Saving in a Free Society*, in which he once again questioned the point of the National Savings movement. As in 1960, his view was that the movement encouraged no additional saving, but merely redirected a level of saving that would have been made anyway. He also called on the Government to stop trying to influence the interest rate, an unspeakably radical doctrine for the 1960s.

The director of National Savings, Sir Miles Thomas, was incensed by Powell's thesis, describing his conclusion as 'absurd'.[85] Hoping to land a killer punch, Thomas quoted Powell's address to a National Savings assembly 'a few years ago' in which he had spoken warmly of the benefits of individuals participating in the scheme. Powell replied to Thomas immediately, saying that he had made the speech as Financial Secretary in 1957, and had undertaken his research into the question of savings in 1959–60, before writing the first edition of his work: 'Which seems to show that even politicians sometimes learn.'[86]

On 24 September, addressing Young Conservatives at Blackpool, Powell sought to destroy the notion that the economic problems were a moral question. At least, he said, they were not a question of personal morality, rather the morality of the Government ministers executing the policy. He denounced the 'moralising sermons' being preached at the British public, rebuking them for 'idleness, fecklessness, inefficiency, greed and selfishness'.[87] His attack on politicians cited actions by Labour ministers, but did not exclude Conservatives who shared the consensus view. He condemned Wilson for allowing public expenditure to grow at 4 per cent a year – twice the rate of the increase in national income – thereby causing inflation; to blame it on workers, employers and manufacturers was simply dishonest. 'The individual citizen cannot help himself,' he said. 'The flood of rising demand which the Government has fed and maintained left no option to customer and supplier, to employer and employee. The prices and incomes policy and the prices and incomes freeze are cynical manoeuvres designed to transfer blame from the guilty to the guiltless, by pretending that inflation happens because people are "greedy" and put up prices, or "selfish" and obtain more wages.' He added that the Government had spent £354 million more than it had earned in 1965, all of it borrowed abroad and subject to interest payments. That was not the fault of the workers either.

Then, at Bristol on 29 September, Powell condemned both employers and employees for boosting state socialism by participating in the incomes policy. He lambasted the 'trooping off to Whitehall' by workers' and managers' representatives 'to work out with a socialist Government the principles on which the prices of people and things are to be controlled in a socialist Britain'.[88] The people had been made to feel guilty about the inflation, which had really been caused by the Government, and in order to assuage their guilt made themselves

quite willing to co-operate with the socialist plan of control. The next day, at
Bridgwater, he ridiculed the recent National Productivity Conference, saying
there was no point striving to produce with maximum efficiency things no one
wanted to buy. 'Look after profits,' he said, 'and productivity will take care
of itself.'[89] However, all the Government manipulation and regulation of the
economy in the preceding two years had made profits difficult to achieve and
profitability an apparently unhealthy concept.

Powell's conference speech was more low-key than the previous year's. He
confined himself to two main precepts: that expenditure on defence had to be
related to returns in terms of security; and that only military obligations that
could and should be performed should be undertaken. He pledged the Opposition to watch that the Government honoured its NATO commitments, on
which 40 per cent of the defence budget was spent. There was one hint at a
return to his speech of 1965, when he warned against Britain's taking on more
than she could successfully manage in the East. Capabilities there, he said, had
to be looked at 'realistically'.[90] In a nod to his colleagues, however, he did specify
that just because Britain's physical presence in the world might be shrinking,
that did not mean her influence had to shrink too.

He saved his most controversial outburst for the evening the conference
closed, when he spoke at Lancaster. He returned to his point that the prices and
incomes policy was still being implemented on a voluntary basis, the Act of
Parliament that would have enforced it still not having been invoked. He urged
the country to wake up to this, and to stop rolling over whenever urged to
reverse some act deemed contrary to the policy – as the directors of Great
Universal Stores had done the previous week when told by the Treasury, without
any right in law, to rescind a dividend. It was a speech made in the knowledge
that many Conservatives, inside and outside the parliamentary party, still saw
little wrong with the policy.

His rehabilitation in the party machine was such that he featured in a party
political broadcast on 26 October, spelling out his doctrine to some Young
Conservatives (of which movement he was the national president) in uncompromising terms. 'The word "competition" sounds good, but whenever you talk
about competition you must ask yourselves whether you realise that this means
not only that some people win, but that some people lose. It means that the
weakest are not going to be propped up by the Government. They are going to
go under.'[91] He echoed his uncompromising message of the period immediately
after the heavy defeat of that spring: 'Young Conservatives ... have got to ask
straight questions and they have not got to be afraid of the answers. They have
not got to be afraid to be seen arguing.'

He followed his own precept immediately, in the wake of the Aberfan disaster,
in which a slag heap crushed a school in South Wales. The Attorney-General,
Sir Elwyn Jones, had warned the press and politicians about comment on

the disaster, which had horrified the nation. There was manifestly (to the embarrassment of the Government) great state responsibility, not merely for the school that was destroyed, but for the Coal Board whose tip had collapsed. Powell called Jones's announcement 'preposterous', adding that 'some of us have had experience before the war and since, of countries where government did regulate the behaviour of the citizen by this kind of method. We do not intend to live under such a regime here.'[92]

On 3 November Powell went to the Cambridge Union to speak in a debate against incomes policy, and against Dick Crossman. Crossman records in his diaries how confident he was at taking on Powell, since he had assembled the evidence of Powell's complicity in the policy operated by the Macmillan Government, not least in the matter of nurses' pay. He accused Powell of only having opposed incomes policies once out of office, and made what he reckoned was 'a pretty effective debating speech'.[93] 'But it was followed by a tremendous oration. Without the faintest inhibition Powell turned the whole audience against the concept of any kind of incomes and prices policy, demonstrated that it was complete intellectual nonsense and concluded that it was an insult to the intelligence of the Cambridge Union to ask them to support it. He got a standing ovation, which made me grind my teeth a little.' Crossman gave Powell a lift back to London afterwards, and asked him what Heath would have made of his speech. Powell, he said, answered: 'Oh, it's only Reggie Maudling who's the problem and Reggie is so busy with his business affairs that he's hardly ever with us. If it wasn't for him I think Iain Macleod would go along with us.'

The next day, Powell opened up a new economic front. He accused the Bank of England of 'behaviour one hardly expects from a fifth-rate hire purchase company' in requesting, without any legal right, information from private companies about overseas investment activities. The Government, worried about falling investment levels at home, had requested a voluntary programme of refraining from investing abroad over the next three years. Powell regretted that some chairmen of big companies, afraid to upset either the Government, the Bank or both, were co-operating, when, as he had observed before, the only correct response was 'mind your own business'. He said the fear that 'modern Chancellors of the Exchequer make very powerful enemies' would pass for 'a description from Germany in the 1930s. It is certainly a description of a Government outside the law.'[94] He added: 'If a Government can get its way simply by making its wishes known, then we have said goodbye to Parliament and the Courts. A method has been discovered, which the Stuart monarchy sought in vain, to by-pass legislation and substitute the arbitrary will of authority, uncontrolled in direction and application.'

The Bank made no official response to Powell's attack, but claimed its inquiries into the activities of some of its customers were, in fact, the action 'of a first-rate hire purchase company'. Powell, seeing a report of this claim in *The Times*, fired off a letter to the editor, pointing out that the people about whom the inquiries had been made were not the Bank's customers, and the Bank still had no legal right to do what it had. Then, a week later, he told the Cambridge University Conservative Association that the Bank was still assisting in the principle of 'government by intimidation'. He reserved special condemnation for Sir Maurice Parsons, the Deputy Governor, saying it was 'the proverbial stone-throwing of the glass-house dweller when the Deputy Governor of the Bank criticised British wage-earners for their "apparent lack of common sense" in "engineering" unjustified pay increases. Quite apart from the inappropriateness of the quarter from which it comes, this sort of statement is blatantly absurd.'[95]

A week later he developed the theme further at Bognor Regis, where he was given a hero's welcome at the largest political meeting in the town since the war. He said the Government's revolution – an 'enormous and exceedingly swift extension of the ownership, power and influence of Government' – was being assisted by 'collaborators' from among the representatives of capital.[96] The collaborators – seduced by patronage – sat on committees in Whitehall, or on boards, or advised on nationalisation, or agreed to operate government controls, and Powell depicted this as a brand of treachery. 'Then they discover that it is impracticable to denounce, attack and oppose the very Ministers and policies with which they are co-operating. Reluctantly at first – but habit is a wonderful healer – they come to recognise on which side their bread is buttered. It is now buttered on the state side, so they turn advocates of the state.' As always, it was his fellow Conservatives most in his sights, such as his former ministerial colleague Aubrey Jones, who the previous year had become chairman of Wilson's Prices and Incomes Board. Those former 'capitalists' who had betrayed their principles would continue to betray them because 'they have a vested interest in the new order, the state order, continuing.'[97] He claimed that Conservatives were accepting as fact many expressions of opinion about the new responsibilities of the state that led to pure socialism, and regretted that, in contradicting them, he would make some Conservatives 'extremely angry'. Powell was, presumably, speaking from his experience of shadow cabinet meetings.

Later that autumn, on 1 December, he addressed a luncheon of the Institute of Chartered Accountants, and accused it of having turned itself into a subordinate instrument of government. He had been provoked by a letter, sent out by the president of the Institute six weeks earlier, to all its members telling them that the Council of the Institute 'would deprecate action by members which was contrary to the spirit of the prices and incomes standstill though not legally in contravention of it'.[98] Powell's remarks were greeted by prolonged applause. He was then attacked by the Institute's president, Sir Henry Benson, who accused him of 'distortion' and of quoting remarks out of context. Benson received only polite applause from his audience, which provoked Powell to shout at him:

'There is your answer. You have it. Your members are against you.'

Powell gave only the most cursory public attention at this time to his own portfolio, but one speech in particular – to the Young Conservatives at Llandudno on 6 November – was curious in the light of one of his subsequent obsessions. He warned against the consequences of reducing British forces in Europe, not least because to do so would make a mockery of Britain's anxiety to join the Common Market. To cut the British garrison in West Germany, then comprising 55,000 troops, might send a message to the West Germans that they had better take more of their defence upon themselves, or even make a new accommodation with the East. Although Powell remained concerned about sacrifices of sovereignty in entering the EEC – as he had since his rebellion on the Schuman Plan in 1950 – he had still not fully focused on the issue.

V

That autumn Powell went back to an earlier interest, borne of his three years as Minister of Health. With the help of the Institute of Economic Affairs he published a short book – not much more than an extended pamphlet, at 30,000 words – entitled *Medicine and Politics*, explaining how the NHS and the doctors in its front line had a battle of constant tensions with the politicians responsible for the service. He had written it during the spring and summer of 1966, greatly helped by Arthur Seldon and Geoffrey Howe, who had lost his seat at the election and was an expert on the NHS. Both Seldon and Howe had taken issue with Powell's defeatism about the NHS, Howe having thought that more radical, market-based solutions could be tried. Powell was unconvinced, then and for ever, about the political wisdom of such a thing.

At the book's launch Powell, like every minister before and since, was questioned about the phenomenon of the waiting list. He said he had tried to do away with it, 'but I discovered that this was like filling a sieve'. He said his book was a warning that one could 'never take medicine out of politics'. He also dispelled the notion that a department secured more money and legislative time when its head sat in the cabinet; that had not been his experience. He said that although a minister needed eighteen months in post to be able to have a reasonable command of his portfolio, after three years 'a Minister ceases to be capable of contributing significantly. When a Minister begins to think like his officials and understands before they explain, his work in that office is done.'[99] Medical opinion on the book, as expressed through the *British Medical Journal*, was uniformly unflattering. One critic, Professor Henry Miller, said that 'Mr Powell is remembered by the profession chiefly for his sponsorship of an ambitious plan for rebuilding the nation's hospitals which was soon whittled away as impracticable and unrealistically costed. The profession remembers him without enthusiasm and it is clear from his book that the emotion is reciprocated.'[100] In fact, the concentration of hospital facilities on big district general units was continuing, though not as quickly as Powell had hoped. But it was now out of his, and his party's, hands.

Early in 1967 Powell broke new economic ground, and pulled away from the party line. In a speech to the Institute of Export in Birmingham, he called for a floating exchange rate: he said politicians had jammed the normal market mechanisms. 'They have decreed that the international price of our money is not to behave like other prices, moving up and down with supply and demand. It is to remain stationary, immutable, what Sir Stafford Cripps in September 1949 said it should be.'[101] Powell pointed out that, because of this contravention of normal economic laws, 'frantic adjustments' had to be made elsewhere in the economy. He implicitly attacked his own side, in power for thirteen of the seventeen years since the parity with the dollar had been fixed at $2.80, and, without naming him, mocked Macmillan's phrase that 'exporting is fun'. He observed that 'so long as the price mechanism is out of action ... there will always be balance of payment troubles every few years, simply because there is nothing to keep exports and imports in balance'.[102]

What especially upset the various exporters' organisations – more of Powell's 'collaborators' – was his likening of the plea from the Government to exporters to that of the convicted embezzler who says he would not have plundered the company's funds if only his salary had been a little higher. Powell reminded them that 'anybody who knowingly exports, because the politicians have told him they would like him to do so, when on a just and prudent business view he could make more money in some other way, is not really serving the national interest any better than his fellows. He is helping to divert attention and under-standing from the real causes of our predicament, and so is helping to prolong them and delay or prevent their removal.' The exporters, who had been told for years that they were practising a high form of patriotism, lined up to denounce Powell. Crossman used his outburst to attempt to portray a split Conservative party. 'It makes me ask', he said, 'what is happening inside the Tory leadership. Who is running the Opposition? Certainly not the titular leader who sits ner-vously strumming on his piano in the Albany while our latter-day Savonarola rampages around the country summoning devout congregations of the faithful to reject as heretics those Conservative leaders all of whom, in his view, have departed from the straight and narrow path of 19th century laissez-faire.'[103] Jim Prior recalled that Powell's demands for a floating pound 'only helped streng-then Ted's commitment to a fixed parity'.[104]

Before the shocked sensibilities of the business classes could recover, Powell was off, the very next day, on a new crusade. Addressing the Wolverhampton branch of the National Union of Bank Employees, he told them that the very existence of trade unions was contrary to the interests of their members, and had no beneficial effect on their wages. He said Parliament had a moral obligation, for that reason, to end the unions' immunities. Despite all this, and an attack on the 'superstition of collective bargaining', he received a warm ovation.[105] Two days later, in Chesterfield, he took the argument one stage further, urging immediate repeal of the unions' immunities. Wilson himself, angered by restrictive practices in the newspaper industry, had a few days earlier called for managements to act to curb them, remarks Powell condemned as 'humbug'. 'Until the politicians, and the Government in particular, are prepared to withdraw the statutory privileges and immunities from collective action which is restrictive in its intention, method or effects, they have no right to preach at either the employers or the workers – still less to call them cowards, when the cowardice lies in a very different quarter.'[106]

Between his anti-union speeches, Powell denounced government interference in the housing market in a speech at a homes exhibition in Birmingham. He admitted that all political parties had engaged in this vice, with a result that there was a permanent housing shortage. 'Give me a year or two and I guarantee to organise you an equally squalid shortage of anything else you care to name by applying the same methods as have been successful with housing. Control the price, subsidise the product, and wait for the scarcity to come along.' Powell said there was a clear choice between charging market rents and having a shortage. 'Which do you prefer? Myself, I vote for houses.'[107]

His attack on the export drive prompted Douglas Jay, the President of the Board of Trade, to write a letter of complaint to Heath, and to ask him to confirm that Powell's feelings did not represent the official view of the Conservative party. It was a shrewd move. It had been Heath who, in the last government, had set up the British National Export Council, and he was not now going to repudiate its aims. In what could only be construed as a rebuke to Powell, he told Jay that 'I have always welcomed anything which the Government does to make exports a commercial proposition and I have criticised the Government when it has placed additional burdens upon our exporters. I shall continue to do the same.'[108] Powell, as usual, was unrepentant, and issued a two-part challenge to Jay: 'If Douglas Jay does not think people ought to export for profit, for what does he think they ought to export? And how does he think they ought to decide what to export, and when, and how much? Secondly, why does he suppose his colleague, the Chancellor of the Exchequer, has been trying for the last two years, though alas unsuccessfully, to make exports more profitable and the home market less profitable?' Heath sent for Powell and the two men had a frosty meeting, at which Heath told Powell that the floating pound was 'not the policy'. Powell replied that he knew well it was not, but he had merely been making the intellectual case for it. He gave no promise of good behaviour. If Heath had thought he could contain the problem of Powell's single-mindedness, that meeting should have convinced him otherwise.[109] However, Powell was resolutely not acting like a team player, exploiting Heath's unwillingness to let him loose outside the team.

The shadow cabinet devoted much of its meeting of 23 January to a general discussion on defence, with Powell saying that his own activities would be devoted to proving the 'fallacy' of the 1966 review: namely, that it could not make sense to decide policy according to financial targets. He endorsed the nuclear deterrent as a 'defence against blackmail', but warned his colleagues about the running down of the navy. 'The assumption that America would act ... had had a numbing effect on British Maritime defence thinking,' he said.[110] He urged the party to adopt a policy of building up naval defences, based on a new submarine fleet. Also, though, the army would have to be built up, because he did not believe there would be anything other than a conventional war in Europe, if war broke out.

On East of Suez, Powell outlined the very strategy Healey was now, for reasons of financial stringency, coming round to himself. 'He felt it was beyond question', the minute records, 'that in a few years' time British land forces would have no role east of Suez.' Powell was alert to the need to pander to some of the party's susceptibilities about this part of the globe, and argued for British power in that region to be maritime, with an Australasian-based air force, in order to maintain British influence. Of those present, only Lord Harlech broadly agreed with Powell. Maudling criticised Powell's notion of dividing the forces of the free world, with European powers looking after Europe and America looking after everywhere else. Supported by Carrington, he said that the idea of rebuilding the navy was prohibitively expensive, and Britain would simply have to rely on America. Hogg criticised Powell for his comments about war in Europe, saying he was certain such a conflict would go nuclear. Also, he believed the British Army would have to sort out what seemed to him to be the inevitable conflicts brewing up in the Middle East.

The discussion was not completed at that meeting, but continued a fortnight later. Powell was annoyed at the way in which some of his views had been represented in the minutes of the previous meeting, and asked for corrections to be put on the record. He said he had not 'denied' that European war could escalate into a nuclear conflict, but had said it was important to build up proper conventional forces for the likelihood that it did not.[111] As for finding the money to make the improvements he wanted, he counselled bringing home almost all British forces, and argued that the end of the British Army on the Rhine was 'inevitable'. The establishment of a home-based mobile force could, he contended, reduce overall manpower by 50,000, while still providing a proper defence in a European war. These notions of washing the Conservative party's hands of any responsibility for the wider world still stuck in the insufficiently post-imperial throats of Powell's colleagues. When, a fortnight later, Powell advised a vote against Healey's latest White Paper, the committee agreed, subject to such a vote not compromising any past commitments by the party.

In between the two shadow cabinet discussions, Powell did nothing to help ease the tensions, using a review in the *Spectator* of Christopher Mayhew's new book about East of Suez to speak with typical candour about the realities of the policy. 'When Britain has quitted Southern Arabia next year, there will be nothing physically left on the ground east of Suez except small forces in the Persian Gulf, a few islands in the Indian Ocean – which nobody thinks could ever be more than staging posts for aircraft – and a force of (presently) about 30,000 men located in Malaysia and Singapore,' he wrote.[112] He said everybody, not least the Government, knew that Britain was 'phasing out' in those areas, and that her troops were only 'guests' in the Far East. He said the Government's aspiration, in Mayhew's phrase, to have a 'world role east of Suez in the 1970s' was 'inherently meaningless'; and Mayhew, before resigning, had said as much to his colleagues, knowing that money would simply not be there to sustain the 'role'.

This conduct of shadow cabinet warfare through the columns of the press was precisely the sort of thing that built up resentment of Powell among his colleagues, and not just because he used the press, under cover of an attack against Labour, to goad those Conservatives who were, in his view, guilty of similar doctrinal lapses. Few of them could match him as a writer, and fewer still had the courage or intellectual arrogance to be as straight about policy as he was. The resentment he created would not immediately explode, but was stored away in the arsenal for the future.

Heath was anxious not to provoke Powell into a confrontation, the more so when Ernest Marples, who had been in charge of reorganising Central Office, resigned the following month. Heath told a rally of Young Conservatives on 12 February that Powell and his views were not an embarrassment; rather, Powell had proved he was invaluable at stimulating thought. As if to take Heath at his word Powell immediately made another attack on export councils, and the way the export drive was being used to make up for Government incompetence, which prompted Jay to complain to Heath again, demanding once more to know whether Powell enunciated official party policy.

Even if Heath was playing it coolly, others no longer concealed their irritation with Powell. Ivan Rowan, compiling a hostile profile of him for the *Sunday Telegraph*, found no shortage of colleagues willing to stick in the knife. There was a general view that he was having little impact in his shadow portfolio, something at odds with the ferocious reputation he was acquiring as the party's potential iron man as he tramped the country repudiating old doctrines. One colleague told Rowan, unattributably, 'there's a streak of calculated self interest in everything he does'.[113] It was said of him – and this more than a year before the so-called 'Rivers of Blood' episode – that his abiding failure was his concrete-like logic coupled with 'a total misjudgment of the business of politics'. Above all, there was ridicule for Powell's line on the free market: 'he discovered economics late in life'. However, later that year another economic thinker whom Powell's critics would despise, Milton Friedman, wrote that Powell was the only man in Britain who understood what had to be done with the economy.

Inevitably, some of Powell's fellows were jealous of the publicity he commanded; but then his energies were prodigious. In the first seven weeks of 1967 he made twenty-six speeches, sixteen in public and ten in private. Only three were in Wolverhampton, and the others ranged from Dundee to the Isle of Wight. After the Government's latest Defence White Paper on 17 February Powell scaled down his movements a little, but still managed to speak every Friday and Saturday. He remained keen to work behind the scenes for the development of Conservative policy in his direction. He had never stopped being a regular attender of One Nation dinners – and, despite strains with his colleagues and his growing reputation as a loner, never would stop until he left the party – and contributed that spring to a One Nation policy paper on denationalisation.

Against the often shallow and prolix contributions of some of his colleagues, Powell's was a concise exposition of the essential detail of the policy: 'It is . . . necessary to convert a sufficient block of the public debt, representing the value of the nationalised undertaking, into privately held stocks and/or shares,' he wrote, 'because . . . private investors will not put capital into an undertaking of which they do not control the management.'[114] He also argued that the proportion of privately held shares would have to be high, and the debt ratio low. These basic points had not been mentioned in the first draft that he had seen, indicative of the amateurishness with which supposedly the finest brains in the party were embarking on this activity.

At about this time, the Conservative Political Centre asked Powell to write a pamphlet on the future of defence policy, which he duly did, not diverging from his own long-held views about the importance of the British defence capability being set in a European, and not a global, context. In July 1967, some time after it was submitted, Powell had a call from Michael Fraser, now deputy chairman of the party. Fraser simply told Powell that the pamphlet could not be published because 'Heath will not wear it.'[115] Powell invited Fraser to reconsider, but Fraser wrote to him on 21 July to say, 'I have now read the proofs again as I promised to do but have come to the same conclusion.'[116] He added that he had asked the CPC not to proceed with publication, 'at least for the time being', and concluded with the sort of nonchalance that would have irritated Powell in the extreme: 'sorry if I am a bore'. He asked Fraser whether Heath had seen the pamphlet, and Fraser said he had not.

In fact, he had, as Powell learned from Russell Lewis, who had been handling publication for the CPC. When Lewis told Powell this, on Powell's return from his summer holiday on 29 August, Powell immediately wrote to Heath saying that 'I am sure there must be some misunderstanding.'[117] Powell acknowledged that his leader had the right to stop publication, but added, 'If you decided that something which a colleague had written – in this case, on his own subject and at their [the CPC's] request – should not be proceeded with, I am sure you would always go direct and tell him so. This makes it evident that something has gone wrong which can be cleared up.' He also told Heath that Fraser had told him that 'no judgment or decision other than his own was concerned – which suggests there may be some confusion where he too is concerned'. If Heath replied formally to Powell, no copy of his reply survives in the Powell papers; but this act by Heath was one of the few by him that Powell resented. Powell and Fraser had had good relations over the years, but this incident, coming after the Falkirk episode of 1966, ended them. So angry was Powell that when, in 1975, he was told that Lord Fraser (as he had by then become) would very much like him to attend his retirement dinner, he replied to an intermediary, 'I am afraid that, since certain events in 1967, which I expect will not have slipped his memory, it would be merely hypocrisy for me to be present on such an occasion.'[118]

VI

On 16 February Powell made his first substantial contribution to the debate on immigration. In an article in the *Daily Telegraph*, entitled 'Facing up to Britain's race problem' – Powell would not have liked the headline, for he was always careful to point out that his concerns lay with immigration, and not with race – he said that for the preceding ten years immigration had been the main political problem in Wolverhampton: 'entire areas were transformed by the substitution of a wholly or predominantly coloured population for the previous native inhabitants, as completely as other areas were transformed by the bulldozer'.[119] He said he was amazed at the complacency with which this had taken place: people had been 'driven from their homes and their property deprived of value', and 'those were the years when a "for sale" notice going up in a street struck terror into all its inhabitants'.

He said that, before the 1962 Act that imposed some control, when asked by constituents why this immigration was allowed, he replied that the law could not distinguish between one British subject and another; this had been 'a romantic fiction, but one which could only be maintained if no practical effect was given to it'. He had begged colleagues to change the law to bring it into consonance with reality, but most MPs had no direct experience of the problem, and would not take it seriously. He said the average annual inflow of 50,000 a year would lead to 1.75 million by the end of the century, but the problem was deeper than that. Perhaps as many as 120,000 British citizens – mainly whites –

would leave the country each year during that time, with the new immigrant population reproducing quickly enough to leave the total coloured population at 5 per cent of the total by the end of the century.

He called for a policy of 'virtually terminating net immigration', and thought net emigration might ensue, especially if people were given financial incentives to rejoin their families in their countries of origin. He hoped that, by adopting such a policy, the 'moment of national aberration' that had allowed the immigration would pass. He wished the chance would be taken, but added, 'I fear it will not be.' The language of the article, and its content, are scarcely less provocative or plain-spoken than those of the speech fourteen months later; but there was no outcry.

Powell had a heavy schedule in the Commons throughout the winter of 1967. A debate on pay in the armed forces at the end of January was followed by an intervention on Malta on 2 February, in which he accused the Government of having made a 'terrible hash' of Britain's relations with her former colony.[120] Then, on 24 February, there was another debate on the Territorial Army, followed on 27 February by one on the new Defence White Paper. Criticising it, he argued that the assumptions of the defence review the previous year – that a growth rate of 3.8 per cent would enable expenditure on defence to remain constant while falling as a proportion of the national income – had collapsed entirely, since in the first of the years for which that projection had been made the rate of increase had been only 1 per cent. He quoted, with amusement, a recent paper by the Ministry of Housing and Local Government which included the admission that 'over the two years ahead the rate of growth of the economy will fall short of that postulated in the National Plan'.[121]

Not only had income not grown as expected, but the savings planned – on what, Powell reminded the House, was the entirely 'bogus' figure that the Conservatives would have spent, of £2.4 billion – had not been made either. As he and his colleagues had predicted, the policy was in disarray. There was now the additional pressure of the West German Government's no longer being willing to help pay for the British Army on the Rhine, a point that gave Powell great sport. However, Michael Foot – then on the backbenches and himself no admirer of the Government's conduct of affairs – asked Powell exactly what his policy would be. Powell said that his party would not unilaterally abrogate the country's obligations to NATO.

The fighting in Aden was then adduced by Powell as further evidence of the stupidity of the Government in announcing, so far in advance, that it would be pulling out of that protectorate. Aside from civilian casualties, there had in the year since Healey's announcement been 375 British military ones, more than 150 per cent higher than in the preceding year. Then, coming to each of the services in turn, Powell illustrated how no progress appeared to have been made with any of the rationalisations Healey had outlined a year earlier. Although

Powell still did not reveal what the Opposition thought would be a sensible level of expenditure, his demolition of Healey's claims was so thorough – unquestionably his best performance in the eighteen months he had been shadowing him – that he was heard in near silence on the Labour benches. By the time of his conclusion – 'in the view of this side of the House, the reduction of commitments, forces and expenditure overseas is not the end of national defence policy. It is not the supreme, let alone the sole, criterion by which a defence policy ought to be judged' – the case he had made was so hard for Labour to answer that the Conservatives' own absence of firm commitment was irrelevant.[122]

Powell soon had another pressing matter to address within his portfolio, in formulating the response to the Government's plan to reduce the Rhine army. At Llandudno on 4 March he made clear the party line: that such a reduction would (as he had said personally before) threaten stability in Europe and compromise British chances of entering the Common Market. France had already shaken NATO by withdrawing, and America was looking more and more to her commitments in the Pacific. In this context, 'the pulling out of British troops would be felt by our allies and by the world as a deliberate turning of our back on Europe'.[123] It was a line of argument he himself would repudiate within two years.

The annual debates on the defence estimates allowed him an early opportunity to renew his assault on Labour's mismanagement of the defence review. On 6 March, in the discussion of the army estimates, he concentrated on Healey's failure to give any firm commitment about the future size of the army. He also attacked the Government's intention to bring home 30,000 troops from overseas postings that were no longer considered essential, without any idea of where to house them or what to do with them once they returned, and with no attempt having been made to cost the exercise.

More significant for the long-term development of Powell's own theories, this was the first time that he, as defence spokesman, put on record in the Commons his notions about what he called 'the nuclear assumption'.[124] As he put it, 'stated in bald terms, this assumption is that there can never again be a war which threatens the safety of this nation, because if such a war were ever to commence it must speedily be terminated by the inconceivable catastrophe of the nuclear exchange'. He said that acceptance of this assumption was the taking of 'a decision of the utmost gravity for the future of our country'. This was, he explained, because 'if our military preparations were based on it – and logically they must be, if it is accepted – then in the event of its proving to be wrong, we should have thrown away the means of rational self-defence and stand, like Wolsey, "naked to our enemies" '. Powell urged that this assumption be 'examined and re-examined, and, at the end, that any benefit of the doubt be given against rather than for it'.

His wider argument was that the navy in particular, but also the army, would be run down because it was not 'realistic' to imagine that the tasks for which they had traditionally been envisaged could be discharged after the expected nuclear exchange. Powell accepted that so long as the weapons existed there was a chance of their being used, and that the holding of them by other countries was the fundamental deterrent against their use. However, he cited the dictum of the military historian Sir Basil Liddell Hart that 'the nuclear weapon is a deterrent to nuclear war, but not to war'. Powell had gone to see Liddell Hart, whom he regarded as a great sage, immediately upon his appointment to the shadow defence job, and the two men had kept in touch.[125] Powell's point was that a conventional European war could still occur, and Britain would be severely disadvantaged in trying to take part in it. He accused Healey – though Healey denied it – of believing that 'every European nation has resolved to choose nuclear annihilation rather than fight to win or lose'.[126]

Powell said that, had the European powers had a nuclear capacity in 1939–40, it probably would not have been used; a conventional war would still have been fought. This prompted him to assert that 'in making and being seen to make preparations to fight with reasonable prospect of survival and victory lies the longest hope of peace'. He accepted that the old British Army had gone for ever, but urged that the debate about the nuclear assumption be carried to a conclusion, so that it could be better judged what sort of army would be needed. It was a debate he would conduct, with views almost unique on the right of British politics, for the next twenty years.

Such concerns, though, were at that stage a subsidiary feature of Powell's agenda. His anger at public indifference to the damaging effects of socialism could not be contained, and his language became more florid. He warmed up by telling a meeting at Wheatley in March that the sort of socialism practised by the Wilson Government was beginning to smell like fascism. Then, speaking in Stratford-upon-Avon a couple of days later, he likened the Government to a dictatorship, berating James Callaghan, the Chancellor, for resorting too frequently to terms like 'the battle for economic survival' and an economic 'Dunkirk'. 'Dictators talk like that. I lived in Italy during the 1930s and I remember Mussolini was always getting tired of one battle and starting another. This is not the language of people who believe what we believe in.'[127]

Nothing, though, irritated Powell more than what he had already termed 'collaboration'. On 31 March he denounced a firm in Bath whose management had written to employees stating that it would have to sack any of them who did not authorise it to deduct union contributions from their pay packets; this was because the firm had signed trading agreements with other firms whose unions had refused to let them trade with companies that did not operate closed shops. Powell said he would oppose the closed shop 'as long as there is breath in my body' and attacked 'the great firms who allow themselves to be used by the union as the lever to impose the closed shop upon the customers'. He urged shareholders in such companies to take action.[128]

He warned, too, of the potential for squandering the benefits of the newly discovered resource of natural gas. He ridiculed the Government, in the face of this boon, for acting swiftly to 'ward off the threat to coal-mining; for we regard it as a criterion of our national happiness that as many Britons as possible earn their living underground. Better educated than their Victorian forebears, the miner's tearful wife and children now cling around him, sobbing: "Don't come up the mine today, daddy!"' The Government had protected the mines by banning imports where it could, and taxing heavily those where it could not; and a penal taxation was being levied on the speculators whose risk had paid off, and who had found the gas. Powell mocked the effect this commercial success would have on the socialist conception of 'social justice', and wondered when the Government would use 'the weapon of nationalisation' to impose control on this industry. 'Happily,' he wrote, 'we have a Government imbued with the true spirit of Dunkirk that will not hesitate to use this ultimate weapon.'[129]

Ever present in his speeches and writings was the notion that the Conservative party was still not equal to the challenge presented by the socialists, and could easily procure far better weapons than it was using. 'The policies of the Conservative party', he warned in a speech at Nottingham on 17 April, 'can ... never be thought of in static terms, because society as we understand it is neither a static thing, nor tends to a static goal, but is endlessly dynamic and changing. Neither the next parliament, nor the one after, nor the one after that will see the end of our work, the completion of the programme. There will always be barriers to remove, assumptions to challenge, laws, organisations and institutions to alter because they preserve past limitations and constrict the freedom of a new generation.' It was restless, visionary talk of the sort that made his shadow cabinet colleagues, few of whom would even think of speaking in such terms, clutch the edge of the table in apprehension.[130]

Powell stepped up the personal element in his assaults on Labour, comparing Wilson in a speech on 3 April to a street urchin who believed there was no argument so effective as a dead cat: the longer it had been dead, the stronger the argument. 'In every difficulty or embarrassment, we invariably find that his instinctive reaction is to throw some filth at his opponents or, better still, at a section of the bystanders. He then makes good his escape during the confusion.'[131] He accused Wilson of operating by smear and innuendo to cover up his own policy shortcomings, such as in his rush to use the oil slick from the tanker *Torrey Canyon*, wrecked off Cornwall, as an implicit condemnation of the profit motive. 'I have never considered that mere personalities have any place in politics, but when the Prime Minister indulges in the face of the world his habitual pattern of dead-cat-slinging, the matter has passed beyond personalities. The nation itself is lowered when its representative exhibits the reactions of the gutter.'

At a shadow cabinet meeting later that month, Powell made a rare expression of his feelings about immigration, feelings which the experiences of his constituents were making it impossible for him to play down. Hogg had drawn up his own paper on race relations, due to be presented to the committee at its next meeting. Powell – who had barely missed a single shadow cabinet in two and a half years – could not be present, so was allowed to put his own views early. He said he felt that 'the present liberality of outlook' among the people generally would not last for ever; this was as a direct result of what he saw in his constituency.[132] He added, specifically, that when it was realised that there could be three million blacks in Britain by 2000 there might be a new 'wave of emotion' on the issue. He said – and was not contradicted in this assertion by any of his colleagues – that the net annual intake of 50,000 was 'an excessively high figure'. Sir Edward Boyle, the shadow cabinet's arch-liberal, said he agreed with Powell that the climate could easily change.

Some of the Government's activities were breaking new ground in peacetime in a supposed free society. Jay, as President of the Board of Trade, launched an inquiry into the economic effects of advertising, the hidden agenda, as Powell saw it, being that if there was less advertising of goods their prices would come down. 'Tell them to try it on the marines or on anybody who can believe that prices will be lower if there is less competition,' he said. 'It is advertising that enthrones the customer as king. This infuriates the socialist.'[133] In another move to try to keep prices down, Jay had announced the start of consultations about standardising packaging for detergents. Powell called this intervention 'the crossing of the boundary between West Berlin and East Berlin. It is Checkpoint Charlie, or rather Checkpoint Douglas, the transition from the world of choice and freedom to the world of drab, standard uniformity.'

Even when things started to go better for his party – such as after good local election results at the beginning of May – Powell was on hand to warn of the creeping menace of socialism. At a Conservative lunch in London he said, with much justification, that the great triumph of the socialists in the preceding two years had been to have many of their anti-freedom assumptions accepted by ordinary people as the new conventional wisdom. 'This', he said, 'is the most dangerous of all the fifth columns, to infiltrate unobserved into one's opponent's own mind.' Powell said this had happened for two reasons: a spirit of national masochism, which told everyone that the growing economic crisis was their own fault, and a backs-to-the-wall mentality that the British were rather good at. 'So many of our national epics have been hours of heroic resistance that we cannot wait to feel the comfortable pressure of the bricks against our backs, and to start striking patriotic and defiant attitudes.'[134] For this reason, he added, even senior clergymen and judges were swallowing the

Government's propaganda about the great sacrifices needed in this time of struggle.

Similarly John Davies, the director-general of the CBI and a future minister in Heath's government, had made a speech in California telling Americans that the Government's measures to keep prices and wages down were working. Powell was angered not just because a representative of the forces of capital was collaborating with the enemy, but also because what Davies said was not true. He had been 'brain-washed', according to Powell. 'If I were a socialist and could listen to the very spokesmen of capitalism thus doing my work for me, I confess I could bear the present election reverses with a light heart.'

Powell's trumpeting of uncomfortable truths with flawless certainty continued to irritate his opponents, both at Westminster and in the press. Hugo Young, writing in May 1967, said of Powell's speeches that 'they are heard with more hypnotic attention than is given to any other politician on the circuit. Audiences are mesmerised by the crisp beauty of his logic, the daily press entranced by the ever-widening chasm between him and any accredited political philosophy – certainly any endorsed by his own party.' Young said Powell had become 'a mythical figure', who got away with peddling nonsense because, delivered with 'the unfamiliar tongue of the scholar and the logician', people thought it must be true.[135]

In one part of his intellectual life, though he himself did not then fully understand it, as he would later admit, Powell reached the end of a chapter that month. The Commons voted on whether Wilson should make another application on behalf of Britain to join the Common Market. Powell voted for the application. It would be the last gesture of support for that institution he would ever make, for he would soon be unable to believe that the EEC was merely a free-trade area. Knowing that a main reason for the desire to join was to find a post-imperial role for Britain, Powell broadened his attack on modern attitudes to the country. In a speech at Hanwell he branded Britain 'a nation with a split personality, rent between illusion and reality, withdrawing ever and again like the schizophrenic into a dream existence peculiar to ourselves'.[136] He ridiculed the new notions that made the British feel comfortable with their post-imperial lot:

> In our imagination the vanishing last vestiges, south and east from the Straits of Gibraltar, of Britain's once vast Indian Empire have transformed themselves into a peacekeeping role on which the sun never sets. Under God's good Providence and in partnership with the United States, we keep the peace of the world and rush hither and thither containing Communism, putting out brush fires and coping with subversion. It is difficult to describe, without using terms derived from psychiatry, a notion having so few points of contact with reality.[137]

He addressed this theme even more candidly in a speech on 24 June, in which he inveighed against the 'dangerous illusion' that Britain was still a world power. He blamed politicians for perpetuating this idea, and did not except those on his own side. Only five days earlier Heath had congratulated Brown, the Foreign Secretary, for rejecting in the wake of the Six Day War between Israel and Egypt 'the argument that the Middle East experience has shown that Britain is incapable of taking action there or ought to be incapable of acting there'. Powell issued his speech through Central Office, so his views were at least being tolerated.

The view at the time was that, in calling for Britain to observe new realities, Powell spoke for about a third of the parliamentary Conservative party, though for hardly any of his front-bench colleagues. 'World events in recent weeks, and especially those in the Middle East, could be a blessing in disguise for Britain,' he said. 'For any country, but perhaps above all for ours at this stage in our history, the most essential and often the most difficult condition of success is to recognise the truth about oneself.'[138] He referred to the way in which the Middle East crisis, taking place as it had in an area supposedly of British influence – with bases in Cyprus, Libya and Malta – had unfolded without Britain being able to take the slightest part in it, for all the remnants of her local power. He said the British presence had proved powerless to defend her interests either in oil or in sterling. 'From the Government of Iraq to the Sheikh of Abu Dhabi, those who wanted to just turned the oil taps off and we – of course rightly – never dreamt that we could do anything to prevent it by our military presence, any more than we could have used force in the area to prevent it by our military presence, any more than we could have used force in the area to prevent sterling deposits from being withdrawn.' Powell preferred the attitude Britain had, perhaps unwittingly, taken towards Nigeria, a country she had created where she had extensive commercial interests, but in whose increasingly troubled affairs she had gone out of her way to remain neutral.

His remarks caused further ructions among his senior colleagues. Perhaps as a result his next high-profile outing, in Ripon on 8 July, was studiously loyal to the party line. He held that Britain should meet her obligations to NATO, and under that alliance do what was expected of her in the Middle and Far East. The shadow cabinet discussed defence in two respects at its meeting on 19 July: first, to consider its opposition to Healey's latest White Paper, driven even more than its predecessors by the problems Labour was having with the economy; and second, to examine a paper which a study group headed by Powell had produced on the future of the army. He repeated his previous assertion that the assumption 'cannot' be that Britain would never have to fight a major conventional war. The forces presently in Europe could not be reduced; and it was important, for the moment, that those based in Europe stayed there and trained there, 'for no such army' as might be needed 'can be trained in the United Kingdom'.[139]

On 27 July, just before the summer recess, there was a debate in the Commons to approve the White Paper. Healey advertised it as marking 'the end of a process which has taken three years continuous hard work. It does not mark the end of the Government's review of defence.'[140] He repeated that the plans the Government had inherited from its predecessor bore no relation to changes in foreign policy, nor to the new realities of the world, and claimed that £750 million had already been saved to use to other ends. He outlined how British troops had been successfully withdrawn from various parts of the globe, and how manpower cuts would be managed: 75,000 men would go by the mid-1970s, mostly by natural wastage. Above all, he repeatedly called Powell 'pedantic' for his insistent illustration of how Healey had misrepresented him and of how Labour had reneged on commitments, and he taunted Powell for not having tried to show what the Conservatives would have done instead.

Healey devoted the last section of his speech to a demonstration, using Powell's own words, of the differences between Powell and Douglas-Home over policy in the Middle East, something Powell would struggle to contradict. Most damagingly, he quoted from an article written by Maudling a few days earlier, in which, without naming Powell, he had said that 'we must not indulge in the fashionable sport of belittling our own role in the world'. Healey added, 'I agree with the right hon Member for Barnet. It is about time that the official Opposition spokesman on defence stopped it or that the Opposition got another spokesman.'[141] He mocked Powell for wanting an army 'capable of fighting and winning a conventional war against the whole might of the Red Army. He wants us to be able to achieve command of the sea and command of the air on our own. Has he ever thought what this would cost?'[142]

At several points in the speech, Powell had invited Healey, when quoting his words back to him, to supply the source of the quotations, or admit they had been made up or distorted. At this particular remark – which Powell called a 'bit of fiction' – he pounced. He had to hand the passage Healey had just quoted against him, and read it out, including the statement that the sort of forces Powell wanted would 'be able ... to play an important and continuing part in continental warfare'.[143] Healey, who had relied as much on bluster and assertion in his speech as on fact, had been caught out. He was howled down by cries of 'Withdraw!', and a formal – but pointless – protest was made to the Speaker by Stephen Hastings, a Conservative backbencher, to have Healey withdraw and apologise for the 'three occasions' on which he had 'grossly misquoted' Powell. Healey did not withdraw, but the continuing protest from behind Powell was silenced by the Speaker, who urged that the debate move on. The episode allowed the Opposition to regain some ground after the headway Healey had made earlier, and Healey seemed to know it. He ended without keeping his promise to Powell and to another Conservative member to supply evidence of quotations as he had attributed to them, closing instead with a volley of puerile insult against Powell – 'the high priest of humbug, the bishop of bogus, the Savonarola of spoof himself'.[144]

The tone of Healey's speech, and the fact that the only hit he scored was concerned with shadow cabinet divisions – and not during a compelling defence of his own policy – pointed directly to the weaknesses of his case. Powell, when he spoke, immediately highlighted another: that this crucial statement had been rushed out at the very end of a parliamentary session, so that attention would not linger on its shortcomings. However, Powell still had no agreed shadow cabinet policy to outline: he focused his attack on Healey on the 'crazy process of picking a distant budgetary figure and arguing everything backwards from it' as a means of making policy. The new cuts announced in the White Paper, he said, were because the budgetary figure had had to be moved a notch lower, thanks to the Government's mismanagement of the economy. He proceeded to quote broken promises and contradictory statements that bore out his case that the growing pressure for savings meant that defence policy had to be reinvented almost month by month. Powell was given an easy ride by Labour backbenchers. What his argument lacked in policy proposals it made up for by its closeness to the uncomfortable truth of why Healey had acted as he had.

Before going away for the summer, Powell corresponded with Heath about the party's immigration policy. Central Office had prepared a standard letter on the subject, outlining the party's belief in 'the firmest possible control', and the integration of those immigrants already in Britain.[145] It added that the party favoured government assistance for those who wished to be repatriated, and equal treatment for all under the law. Powell, who thought the letter 'excellent', sent Heath some correspondence he had received on the subject following an article in the *Sunday Express*.[146] Heath replied, 'I certainly agree that we must make sure that our immigration and race relations policies are framed to avoid the development of racial violence in this country.'[147] Powell wanted more emphasis in the policy put on control and repatriation, but Heath disagreed: such an emphasis, he argued, 'would encourage the racial intolerance which undoubtedly lies below the surface in many parts of the country; and this could only exacerbate the problem'. He also told Powell he doubted whether his figure of 3.5 million coloured Britons by 1985, which Powell had quoted, was 'really valid', since he did not believe the rate of immigration would continue to be so high.

Powell told Heath that the figure was the Home Office's, not his. He also warned that 'I find in my constituency in the last few weeks an ominous deterioration, which is taking the form not of discrimination by white against coloured but of insolence by coloured towards white and corresponding fearfulness on the part of white. It is this which will be exacerbated by the projected legislation on discrimination and which we shall have to take into account in making up our minds on our attitude.'[148]

VII

After the summer holiday, Powell went briefly into hospital for a minor operation on his foot, and to have the remains of his tonsils removed – the operation had not been done properly when Powell was a boy. Shortly beforehand he returned, once more in the *Glasgow Herald*, to the dissection of the reputation of Harold Macmillan. In August, in a review in the *Evening Standard* of Anthony Sampson's *Macmillan: A Study in Ambiguity*, he had spoken of Macmillan's 'absolute changelessness of ideas over a span of 30 or 40 years, in one whom observers saw as a politician of exceptional flexibility and awareness. This is the realisation which startles and depresses.'[149] This assessment was delicately subtle, however, compared with the *Herald* review.

The second volume of Macmillan's memoirs, *The Blast of War* ('it is to be assumed that a sufficient number of wind metaphors for the whole series has been worked out in advance'), covered the author's activities during the Second World War. Powell's criticism started at the dust-wrapper, part of which included a photograph of de Gaulle and Churchill with the author 'wearing a grotesquely exaggerated version of his Eton-and-Guards grin. How on earth, where on earth, the reader wonders, could such a picture have come into existence?'[150] Powell finds his answer on page 337, where Macmillan appears in a group photograph with the two leaders from which, when it appears on the wrapper, all the others have been rubbed out and a new background painted in. Macmillan is left 'presiding like a beneficent magician over Winston and de Gaulle. How could he have done it? The question merges into the other one, with which the reader lays the volume down: how could he have written precisely this book? In the end the picture seems to express the answer.'

As with the first volume, Powell was savage about the book's literary merit: 'fearfully dull'. His main purpose was to attack Macmillan's personality: 'How wrong we were. All that stuff about the "crofter grandfather", the publisher in politics, the historical sentimentality – we used to mistake it for a pose. He took it, we thought, no more seriously than we did ourselves. But here it is, the genuine thing; unselfconsciously bourgeois, snobbish, ingenuous. . . .'

Out of hospital, Powell went back into the fray with his usual forthrightness. George Brown had, as Foreign Secretary, been behaving badly in public: often drunk, often embarrassing, to many unintentionally entertaining. He had clashed with photographers outside a dance-hall, causing new indignities to be heaped upon him. On 6 October Powell attacked him as 'a sick joke', saying that 'little more than a year ago, if an author had written a novel or a farce with the British Foreign Secretary talking and acting as George Brown talks and acts, he would have had the manuscript rejected by every publisher and producer to whom he submitted it. First incredulity, then astonishment, then disgust have successively greeted George Brown's performances since he has been Foreign Secretary.'[151]

In his war against regulation and the erosion of liberties, Powell used a speech in Aberdeen on 13 October to argue for an end to the tight restrictions on overseas travel for Britons, and on the amounts of money that could be taken abroad. He had, he said, been alerted to the full iniquity of these restrictions – no more than £50 could be taken abroad on holiday, a business trip had to be authorised on receipt of proof that it was a business trip, and a trip for reasons of health needed 'a pretty drastic doctor's note' – on a recent visit to Berlin.[152] The absence of liberty he had seen symbolised by the Berlin Wall was thought impossible in Britain, but it was in fact there in the travel restrictions, whose cause was the same. 'It is that the Government are determined to manage affairs at home – in this case, the economy – in a manner which is inconsistent with the individual citizen's freedom of movement for himself and his goods ... this is no more than a mild version of the Communist system which will only work if those within it are not allowed to make comparisons with the outside world.'[153]

On 19 October he made his third – and, as it turned out, last – speech as shadow Defence Secretary at a Conservative party conference. Rather than get into the internal debate about Britain's role – a representative who, shortly before Powell spoke, called for a withdrawal from all commitments East of Suez was treated to cries of 'rubbish' – he concentrated on the shortcomings of the Government, claiming that it had left Britain under-prepared for a possible crisis in the future by concentrating too exclusively on the nuclear deterrent. Cuts in the army and the territorials had severely undermined Britain's ability to defend herself. Powell received a handsome ovation. It would be as good a way as any to make his exit.

The issue that would lead to his loss of shadow office was boiling up. On the eve of the conference Powell, in a speech at Deal, called for an urgent review to close the loophole in the immigration laws that had allowed 87,000 British passports to be issued to Kenyan Asians, entitling them to settle in Britain; the Kenyan government had just excluded Asians from citizenship. Powell asserted that, even without this, half a million new immigrants would arrive in the next decade, and, with another 170,000 Kenyan Asians entitled to ask for passports, that number could increase by half. 'It is quite monstrous', he said, 'that an unforeseen loophole should be able to add another quarter of a million without any control.'[154] Having argued for a proper definition of British citizenship to be forged when he sat on the cabinet's Immigration Committee in 1961, he felt vindicated, even though he at the time had not noticed the loophole either: the complacency then about the take-up of United Kingdom and Colonies passports by those who had not wanted Kenyan citizenship was, as he saw it, the chickens of that particular evasion coming home to roost.

His increasingly apocalyptic view of Britain's failure to control immigration was then given its most profound boost. At the age of fifty-five he made his first visit to the United States, then in the midst of great civil rights tensions. Powell instinctively loathed America. It was not a nation as he understood the term; it was a conglomerate of huge power whose economic doctrines he admired, but whose diplomatic activities and conduct of foreign policy he abjured. He had recognised in its governing class, and among many of its people, an arrogance and a vulgarity that he – occasionally accused, as he was, of arrogance and vulgarity himself – found utterly inimical. Above all, America had done all she could during and immediately after the war to ensure that Britain was rendered a debtor nation incapable of maintaining her imperial obligations, and into the vacuum left by that failure America had been ready to step. Yet he also saw a country whose internal tensions, because of the race problem, could so easily be mirrored in Britain. America's problems, stemming from the legacy of slavery, were in his view far less tractable than those in Britain needed to be, provided action was taken soon. Not long after his return he told an American visitor to England: 'Integration of races of totally disparate origins and culture is one of the great myths of our time. It has never worked throughout history. The United States lost its only real opportunity of solving its racial problem when it failed after the Civil War to partition the old Confederacy into a "South Africa" and a "Liberia".'[155]

Powell and his wife – who had worked in New York in the 1940s and had fond memories of the country – left on 29 October for a tour of just under three weeks. New York, Washington and Los Angeles were the main destinations. For all his animus against the country, he was excited by New York, which his wife showed him round.[156] Powell's position as shadow Defence Secretary meant he was keenly awaited at the Pentagon and the State Department. He was also scheduled to give a seminar at Harvard on exchange rates and liquidity, and to debate at the University of Virginia either with J. K. Galbraith or Senator Paul Douglas – 'they're both socialists, you know,' he said before he left.[157] Of his reasons for having delayed so important a visit so long, Powell was coy. Admitting that he was unusual in never having been to America, he said, 'I should disembarrass myself of this peculiarity.'

Once in the United States, Powell recalled that 'I kept getting the weird impression of *déjà vu*. I soon realised why. . . . It was Australia that kept coming back to me after the lapse of nearly a generation, forgotten scenes reviving, forgotten conversations recalled, forgotten sensations felt again. Once more, after nearly 30 years, I was in a colonial country.'[158] He thought he detected the physical and cultural isolation he had felt at Sydney. He found America 'saturated with exile. Though the Americans do not call Europe "home" as the Australians, at least until yesterday, called Britain home, they know a sensation that no dweller in Europe can know, the sensation of being remote.'

He sought the answer to one question in particular, which lay at the heart of his feelings about America: 'You are an enormous power, inconceivably endowed with all that man could want. Moreover, unlike us British and our 21 miles of salt water, you are protected on either side by an anti-tank ditch thousands of miles wide. You are not only rich, but safe, beyond our power to imagine. Why, in the name of wonder, do you fuss about Europe at all, or for that matter, about Asia? Nobody can invade you and conquer you. What's your worry?'

He said he had heard three justifications: first, that in the two world wars America had been dragged in, and the country was acting now in a way that might prevent it having to enter a third; second, the notion of the 'missionary motivation' of the country; and third, 'we are afraid of having nobody to talk to'. Powell dismissed the first notion as 'the fallacy about history repeating itself', the second as 'a myth which easily degenerates into a slushy sentimentality', but with the third he found much more to get his teeth into: 'It expresses the deep yearning of the exile still to belong, to be wanted, to be a participant in the world's conversation.'

He felt that Americans could not avoid the assumption that 'the earth is inhabited either by Americans or by those whose manifest destiny, however long or laborious its achievement, is to become a passable imitation of Americans. This, too, is the voice of the colonist, the frontiersman in the empty or inhospitable land.' It was also, he warned, the 'source of all their mistakes and disillusionments'. He found the officials in the State Department and the Pentagon sophisticated and of high intellectual quality: 'One is at home, on the same wavelength, with men literally "of the world" until, just at the last, the goal, the objective, the ultimate vision is mentioned or implied; and there it is again! Even for them the only world imaginable is a world made in America's image.' Powell was frustrated by the simplistic American fashion of dividing the world into good and evil, darkness and light, and categorising dissent from their views as 'anti-Americanism' or thinking that 'anti-Americanism' meant complete dissonance with the American view.

He was also struck by the contrasts between the political life and institutions of America and those he was used to at home. In a meeting with service chiefs at Fort Bragg it was suggested to him, tongue in cheek, that he might like to make his first parachute jump. Someone said, 'The British Government wouldn't like that.' Powell replied, 'So far as the Government are concerned, they would be happy enough, I dare say, if I broke my neck; but anyhow, I'm just a private citizen.' A worried aide-de-camp took Powell aside and asked whether there had been some misunderstanding: wasn't he a Member of Parliament? Powell realised that American conceptions of what constitutes 'government' were very different from British ones. America was a democracy, Britain a monarchy, but America's representational institutions did not have the same power to debate that the British Parliament did.

VIII

The economic crisis that had put such pressure on the Government's defence policy came to a head on 13 November 1967, when Wilson and Callaghan decided to devalue the pound by 14 per cent, from $2.80 to $2.40. The decision was announced the next Saturday, 18 November, and the following Tuesday the Commons debated the issue. Tony Crosland, for the Government, used an extract from Powell's Hanwell speech the previous May to show that the Conservative party had been no more wedded to a fix at $2.80 than Labour. He spoke of how Powell had referred to the 'great national totem, the pound sterling. It is a matter of great national honour, we declare, to uphold the decree of Providence that the pound was created equal to two dollars eighty, give or take two cents.'[159] He then quoted the passage in which Powell had said 'it is difficult to describe, without using terms derived from psychiatry, a notion having so few points of contact with reality'.

This was embarrassing for the Opposition, because it made their own assault on Labour's humiliation seem hypocritical. However, the next day, Powell himself sought to undo the damage. He rose in the Commons and read out the full extract from his speech – which Crosland had taken badly out of context – showing that the 'psychiatry' remark had been made 'in a context wholly unconnected with the pound sterling'.[160] Crosland did not deny this, but tried to argue that to 'any objective reader' the phrase would be taken as 'a summary of the entire argument', even though a reading of the speech shows that it manifestly was not.[161]

All this time, tensions between Heath and Powell were rising to the point where colleagues began to wonder whether they could be contained. It was not, though, incomes policy, or East of Suez, that would provide the flashpoint; their first blistering argument at shadow cabinet was about, of all things, the function of Black Rod. During November 1967 this parliamentary official arrived in the Commons in the middle of a debate on the Common Market to summon MPs to the Lords to hear the royal assent being given to a Bill. This particularly irritated Heath among many others, and he told the shadow cabinet that he would support a move by Wilson to have the procedure stopped. Powell's historical and constitutional sensibilities were aggrieved. He lectured Heath on the history of the procedure, the form of words Black Rod used dating back to the Parliament of Carlisle in 1307, and of ancient usage even then. Heath snapped back that this was just the sort of useless ceremonial of which the people were sick, and which he intended to have a hand in modernising. The change went through. Another nail was knocked into the coffin of the Heath–Powell relationship.[162]

Because of the quantities of foreign exchange needed to buy defence equipment, the devaluation had a specific effect on Powell's area of responsibilities.

A debate on this was held in the Commons on 27 November, and Powell led the proceedings. Jenkins, the new Chancellor, had already signalled a net reduction of £100 million in the defence budget for 1968–9, though Healey told Powell in an intervention that the £100 million reduction was after increased expenditures due to the devaluation. Powell repeated a remark by Healey, made to journalists the previous week, that 'the forces are now to be working to closer margins, involving a risk that would normally be unacceptable'.[163] He contrasted this, to cries of 'shame' and 'betrayal' from the Conservative backbenches, with Healey's earlier pledge that the forces would be 'capable of meeting all the demands that may be made upon them'.[164] He asked Healey to promise that there would not be further withdrawals, and made a wider ideological point: 'What a triumph for the principle of long-term planning!' Healey was not in a strong position, and, with irony, thanked Powell 'for a speech of exceptional moderation as far as I have come to recognise his way of speaking', accusing him, as a former textual critic, of following the old adage: 'When in doubt, always take the most difficult interpretation of any disputed text.'[165]

For Powell, the devaluation was a primary opportunity to advance again the case for a floating exchange rate. For want of a floating system the country had, in the form of the devaluation, 'added a new thong of exquisite torment to the economic cat-o'-nine-tails with which we flagellate ourselves'.[166] Speaking to a conference in the City of London a fortnight after the event, he denounced the whole Bretton Woods arrangement of 1944 that had established the fixed exchange rates as an 'attempt at mass self-deception' on which 'reality keeps on bursting in'.[167] He made a blunt call for the price of the currency to reflect, at any given time, the fluctuating demand for it. But few, yet, were listening.

Sensing the disarray in the Government over defence since the devaluation, he told a dinner of the right-wing Monday Club in London on 7 December that 'a Britain which concentrated its defensive investment overwhelmingly upon the means of victory in the areas of its natural strength, the Eastern Atlantic and Western Europe, would find itself, relative to its situation, a military power not inferior to any. We should not need to buttress our self-esteem by talking about its role and importance in the world. It would have them.'[168] Powell's argument was that in the twenty years since Britain had left India she had forgotten or denied the axiom that military power is relative to distance. Israel had defeated Egypt and Jordan earlier in the year because her resources had been concentrated on self-defence; five years earlier, Kennedy had faced down Khrushchev because of the United States' military might around Cuba. By contrast, America could not be so effectual in Vietnam, which was too geographically remote; and, likewise, Britain had proved ineffectual in the Rhodesian crisis, because force was not a realistic option. At a shadow cabinet meeting at this time Powell, reporting on his visit to America, voiced his opinion that the Americans would be driven out of Vietnam without a victory. His authority for the statement had been none less than Robert Macnamara, the Secretary for Defense, who had 'expressly admitted to me that he knew the Americans had no choice but to disengage'.[169]

Health told Powell 'angrily' in response that 'you are absolutely mistaken. The Americans will stay in South-East Asia twenty or thirty years if necessary, and leave only when they have transformed the society and the economy of those countries.' He did not have a high opinion of the Brigadier's grasp of military strategy. 'Earlier, much earlier, when Britain's Foreign Office, with Conservative approval, had lifted up its voice to approve the American bombing of the Vietcong supply lines and I had advised my colleagues that this would prove futile, I had been told [by Heath] that "someone who had been a General Staff officer in the war ought to know better." ' In 1966, at a private dinner-party, Powell had advanced his opinion of the inevitable consequences for America to Henry Kissinger, the future Secretary of State, advising him to look at the British drill for evacuating a country. When Kissinger returned to America he sent a note telling Powell not to imagine that he had disagreed with what he had said.[170]

Powell's American lessons in immigration were having a greater influence. When, on 7 December, he addressed the annual general meeting of his constituency party, immigration was the main topic. He lamented the effect it had had on Wolverhampton, altering for many of his constituents 'the circumstances in which they live and in which they had expected to spend the rest of their days'. The rate of inflow was still 'far, far too large'; and, increasingly aware of the lid that polite society was keen to place on the issue, he warned that 'no amount of misrepresentation, abuse or unpopularity is going to prevent the Tory party, my colleagues and myself from voicing the dictates of common sense'.[171] For himself, at least, that was true. He protested vigorously to the BBC the following week when the Corporation showed an interview with the Black Power leader Stokely Carmichael, in which Carmichael was asked by the interviewer, Patricia Philo, what he thought 'we Black people in Britain should do liberate ourselves' and whether strikes or 'killing or something like that' would help.[172] Powell claimed that the broadcast would 'have the effect of wounding and inflaming feelings'. The Corporation denied any intention to incite racial hatred but admitted that showing the interview had been 'an error of judgment, which we regret'.

The devaluation had given Powell an opportunity to move back to his more familiar agenda in matters unconnected with the effect on defence. Within three weeks of it he brought out a pamphlet entitled *Exchange Rates and Liquidity*, designed to point out the shortcomings of the Bretton Woods system and to argue for floating exchange rates. Although the devaluation had been meant to lift British exports and suppress imports, the air of economic crisis persisted. Typists at a Surrey firm, Colt Ventilation, started a campaign entitled 'I'm Backing Britain': they would drop their tea-breaks in order to work harder for company and country in the hope of boosting productivity and prosperity. Their managers saluted their example. Even if it not been so economically wrong-headed, this was precisely the sort of Dunkirk-style behaviour, or collaboration with economic traitors, that Powell so despised when undertaken by the forces of capital. Heath sent Colt Ventilation a telegram of congratulation when the campaign was launched at New Year 1968, complying with the Wilsonian metaphor of national uplift to get Britain out of the mess the Government was trying not to admit it had created. 'The action of your staff and your board', Heath told Colt, 'is a fine example of the spirit needed in this country today. Will do all possible to help positive proposals.'[173]

Whatever his leader thought, Powell could not have been more unimpressed. Addressing the Institute of Management in Wolverhampton on 10 January, he said the real slogan of the movement should be 'Help Brainwash Britain'. He continued: 'I can find no better word than "hysterical" to describe the state into which discussion of economic policy in Britain has got itself. The so-called Backing Britain campaign is not only ineffably silly, but positively dangerous.' Powell pointed out to the typists that, if the Government chose not to adjust the exchange rate further to help exports, they could have 'no tea-break at all for perpetuity' and it would not make a blind bit of difference to the balance of payments. This public display of his isolation in the shadow cabinet encouraged Maurice Cowling, a fellow of Peterhouse at Cambridge, to write with a suggestion: 'would you absolutely forbid me to suffer your name for the Mastership of Peterhouse?' Powell scribbled on the letter 'no, categorical'.[174]

Although he felt isolated, Powell was starting to draw immense strength from the letters he received from members of the public telling him of their gratitude for the way in which he enunciated their feelings and reflected the realities of their lives. In reply to one such, two days after he rejected Cowling's interesting suggestion, he spoke of 'how cheering and encouraging' it had been to have such a letter of support. He added, 'We have got to support the Tory Party and its leader through thick and thin, but we are not only entitled but in duty bound to emphasise those parts of what is being said on its behalf that seem to us truest, deepest and most important and to draw out what seem to us the conclusions from the basic principles we all share. This is what I have been trying to do, especially in these last four or five years; and I do not know how others can help except by doing the same.'[175]

The Commons debated public spending on 17 January, Powell winding up for his side – the First Secretary of State, Michael Stewart, wound up for the Government – illustrating the great impact that the new, urgently needed controls on spending would have on defence. Powell attacked the Government's complacency, given the importance of the issue, in not putting Healey up to answer for the consequences of the new stringency for his Department. Having endured Healey's bombast and looseness with the facts over the preceding two and a half years, Powell took his own chance to hit back. Commenting on Healey's reluctance to take part, he surmised that 'even his self-confidence and effrontery might shrink back from examination of the turning upon its head of all that he has said, promised and offered by way of policy and intention during the three years that he has been in office'.[176] As one who, himself, had not been reluctant to leave or refuse office in the past, Powell wondered aloud how Healey could remain in office 'amid the wreckage of assertions, pledges, plans and policies'.

Powell went over the history of policy changes, reversals and broken promises through the three White Papers of the preceding two years. He said that Healey's behaviour towards the Royal Air Force alone ought to be enough for him for offer his resignation, with the assumptions about the Anglo-French variable-geometry aircraft and the importance and numbers of F-111As having been proved wrong again and again; and he cited Callaghan's removal to the Home Office from the Treasury as an example that should be followed. He said Healey had made Britain 'a laughing stock' and, more seriously, that 'we are getting to a point where cancellation charges are forming a rising proportion of the defence expenditure of this country'.[177]

Healey was provoked to intervene, reminding Powell that he had in recent months 'sneered at our presence in the Persian Gulf, and has said to a meeting of his own party that we have and can exert virtually no influence in the Far East'. He said that Powell's support of his party on this matter was 'humbug and hypocrisy'; but Powell retorted that he would have no charge to answer unless Healey and his side could 'find that I have advocated that, having accepted commitments, we should break them'. The debate became bad-tempered, as Powell went into more detail about Labour's hypocrisy, and defended the reputation of the former Conservative Defence Minister, Duncan Sandys. Healey, angrily, intervened and said that Sandys (like him) had recommended the Government to withdraw from Singapore, prompting Sandys to shout out, 'That is a complete lie' – a remark Sandys had to withdraw, and amended as 'it did not correspond with the truth'.[178] Powell listed more of Labour's retreats, proving his point that 'the authentic voice' of the party had spoken in the desire to milk all the savings needed in the economy from defence. Indeed, he quoted one minister, Jennie Lee, as refusing to resign over cuts in the social services because she felt the defence cuts were 'real, drastic, and permanent'.[179] It made for him, he said, the point that Labour had dismembered the secure defence of Britain. Once more, Powell had exploited the opportunity Labour's mis-management had given him, and was putting behind him the memories of the difficulties he had experienced in taking on Healey at the start of their antagonism.

At the Cambridge Union in early February Powell met J. K. Galbraith in a return match, Powell proposing the motion that 'the true function of government is to regulate, not intervene'. Galbraith was unfortunate in seeking to defend socialist policies after three and a half years in which they had led to economic failure. Powell won a standing ovation – the first seen in the chamber for two years – for his defence of anti-statism, but lost the vote by 498 to 263. The zeal with which he attacked Galbraith was something most of his colleagues could not understand. Part of the problem between Powell and Heath was not so much that Heath had a different view of economic policy as that he held his view for what Powell considered to be reasons of political convenience, whereas Powell held his for reasons of theological conviction. Soon after his joust with Galbraith he told a luncheon of lobby correspondents: 'Often when I am kneeling down in church, I think to myself how much we should thank God, the Holy Ghost for the gift of capitalism.'[180]

Powell would later say that one of his mistaken beliefs in politics was that the 1962 Commonwealth Immigration Act would have a substantial effect in reducing the future immigrant population. 'I began to realise about 64/65 onwards that this was mistaken.'[181] At the shadow cabinet of 7 February 1968 Heath had expressed concern about the spectacle of Kenyan Asians arriving in Britain 'on privately chartered VC10s'; and Macleod, sharing his leader's anxiety, suggested that Heath write to Wilson privately about it.[182] Powell confined himself to the suggestion that the party should look at how other former imperial nations had handled similar problems elsewhere.

The Kenyan Asians episode was just another example of Powell's, and his party's, 'mistake' over the 1962 Act. He could no longer resist the need to speak out about it. At Walsall on 9 February he called for the 'virtual termination' of work vouchers and the end of unconditional right of entry for dependants.[183] He repeated his prediction that there would be a million new immigrants in the next twenty years if controls were not imposed, saying that by the end of the century this would leave Britain with a problem of similar magnitude to that of the United States. Powell was supported by his former chief at the Ministry of Housing, Duncan Sandys, who said that if necessary he would introduce a Private Member's Bill* to implement controls. Sandys said that the Government's Race Relations Bill, then going through Parliament, could be postponed and replaced by a Bill that addressed causes rather than effects.

Some on the liberal wing of the parliamentary party were beginning to become unsettled by the force of Powell's opinions on immigration, and the liberal-left press condemned him, the *Guardian* – not disputing the figures – saying that the numbers were 'by no means excessive'.[184] Yet in the West Midlands Powell's views were welcomed across party lines. A Labour activist in his con-

---

* A certain number of Fridays in each session are given over for the debating of Bills proposed by backbench MPs. In practice, these Bills rarely become law unless the Government either adopts them, or makes time available for all their stages to be completed.

stituency and member of the Wolverhampton Council for Racial Harmony, Peter Bentley, told the press: 'Mr Enoch Powell is absolutely right on immigrants. We cannot go on taking them here.'[185] It was estimated that in the spring of 1968 one in twenty of the borough of Wolverhampton's 262,000 inhabitants was an immigrant, or the dependant of an immigrant. The birthrate was still well ahead of that of the white population, so a freeze on immigration would only have eased, not ended, the problem. In an early biography of Heath, the opinions of an unnamed shadow cabinet member were reported as suggesting that the leadership's patience with Powell was running out. The anonymous member recalled that the shadow cabinet meeting the week after the Walsall speech was the only one in which there was 'a good deal of ill feeling. Enoch sat there absolutely like a sphinx and never blinked an eye.'[186] This account is uncorroborated, unsourced and bears no relation to the minutes of the meeting concerned.

One statement in the speech would have particular repercussions. Powell said that 'only this week a colleague of mine in the House of Commons was dumbfounded when I told him of a constituent whose little daughter was now the only white child in her class at school. He looked at me as if I were the Member of Parliament for Central Africa.'[187] The local branch of the National Union of Teachers questioned the truth of the allegation, and on 14 February the Sun published a report suggesting that Powell had admitted that the situation he had described could be achieved only by absenteeism of other white children. The following week the chairman of the Wolverhampton Education Committee, Walter Hughes, confirmed that on one day there had, because of the absence of the other white children, been only one white girl in the class, but that was not normally so. Clement Jones, who had had the forces of the Express and Star searching fruitlessly for the school, felt that Powell had been misled. There were many myths about the immigrant population doing the rounds in Wolverhampton, according to Jones, some of which ended up in Powell's constituency correspondence and which he would treat with his usual sincerity.[188] For the moment the public argument died.

In private, at least one of Powell's friends was disturbed by the tack his thinking was taking. Ralph Harris, for whom Powell had much respect, wrote to him on 1 March arguing that his views on immigration were inconsistent with the general libertarian philosophy he had applied in other areas. Powell replied on 8 March, saying it had not occurred to him that anyone could think his views inconsistent. 'It does seem to me right and necessary that any country should have the legal discretion whether or not to admit within its boundaries those who wish to settle there, and, for this purpose, to distinguish between "its own people" and the rest of the inhabitants of the world.'[189] Powell justified his perceived illiberalism by telling Harris that many inhabitants of former colonies who had no connection with Britain had UK passports, and no promise had ever been made to accommodate them in Britain. The Kenyan Asians were a case in point, even though at the time of independence Britain had specifically exempted herself from a responsibility to take them. He listed, broken down by nation, examples of how more than another two million Commonwealth citizens could have a similar right to settle in Britain, even after the 1962 Act, if the precedent of an implicit pledge were honoured in the case of the Kenyan Asians.

The next few weeks were intensely busy for him in the Commons. There was a big debate on defence on 4 March, in which he repeated the usual charges against Healey. Powell still, though, had his own difficulties and did not, for example, answer a straight question from the Labour MP Tam Dalyell about when the Conservatives would withdraw from East of Suez. Indeed, there were still few signs of what the Conservatives would do. Powell had just circulated the shadow cabinet with a paper on defence, in which he observed that the forces of NATO and the Warsaw Pact were about equal. It was, though, insufficiently noted – though he had done so before – that Russian naval strength was increasing, and he reiterated his belief that Britain should build up her navy too.

He echoed these points in his speech to the Conservative Central Council at Bath on 15 March, when he said that 'the assumed alternatives of no war or nuclear suicide' were simply not true, and the Americans themselves had recently abandoned them. According to Powell, the United States 'now officially envisages the possibility of what they call "an all-out war at sea", lasting months if not years, which would be fought, and could be won, without going nuclear at all'.[190] This should, he argued, make the British realise that the prospect of a war at sea should 'be recognised to be still in the future the supreme contingency of British defence policy'. In the Commons the following week he took part in two debates on the navy, though he adhered firmly to the party line. At a shadow cabinet meeting on 25 March he said that, if the rumour then circulating about the planned abandonment by Britain of the Falkland Islands were true, it would be 'utterly wrong and harmful'. For once, Powell's colleagues agreed with him wholeheartedly, and it was settled that 'guidance' would be issued, stating that the retention of the Falklands was party policy. Also at that meeting the shadow cabinet discussed plans to reform the House of Lords, plans for which cross-party support was necessary if they were to have a chance of success. Though a year later Powell would be fighting these plans bitterly, he remained silent on the question when it was raised.

The Conservatives were in good heart as April started. They had just won four by-elections on one day, and Wilson was facing a crisis within his party. For Powell, however, the immigration issue and the anger it was causing his constituents was becoming all-consuming. When on 10 April the shadow cabinet had its last meeting before the Easter recess, and the question of how the Race Relations Bill would be approached was raised, Powell stayed silent.[191] The Bill, which would outlaw discrimination, was due for its second reading on 23 April. Conservative liberals wanted the party not to oppose the second reading. There was no consensus in the shadow cabinet on the matter but Heath, conscious of the need to make a concession to the right, led his colleagues to a decision to table a reasoned amendment declining to give the Bill a second reading, in order to preserve some sort of party unity. This gravely affronted some of Heath's main supporters and should have placated those like Powell, who with Carr and Maudling helped draft the amendment. 'Enoch didn't contribute, as far as I can recall, but nor did he disagree,' Carr said.[192]

Powell would have been – or should have been – happy with what Heath stated at the meeting to be the party's policy on immigration: 'limitation of immigration into Britain; equal treatment for everyone in the country once they were here; and financial help for those who wished to return to their countries of origin'.[193] Hogg, in discussing what he thought was a flawed Bill, said there needed to be a distinction between individuals who, say, chose not to sell their house to a black man because of feeling for the neighbours, and great commercial concerns that systematically discriminated. He said he hoped to move amendments in committee. He also opposed a right to damages for those discriminated against, saying this could exacerbate racial feeling, and was opposed to special race relations courts. The reasoned amendment would be couched in terms that explained that the Bill as it stood would harm, not improve, race relations. Boyle, Carr and Keith Joseph all said they would have to decide their positions once they had considered the terms of the amendment.

Powell's silence would lead to the hostility with which Hogg would treat him for the rest of their lives. With hindsight, Hogg took the silence as a sign that Powell could not be trusted. Many other shadow cabinet ministers felt the same. Hogg remembered Powell as the only colleague who had neither offered advice nor criticised him during his discussion of the policy. But this should not have been unusual because Powell, accustomed to feeling isolated during the meetings of the shadow cabinet, was still usually, in Carr's phrase, 'the silent member'. Margaret Thatcher remembers that by this time he had 'largely with-drawn into himself'.[194] Also, Powell was happy with the line being taken in not giving the Bill a second reading. The discussion had not covered the wider areas of the problem, on which he was already forming more radical views than those of his colleagues. Whitelaw, too, would regard Powell as a double-crosser on account of this meeting, and, as with Hogg, it set the two men apart for the rest of their lives.[195]

Hogg claimed to have been determined to check where Powell stood. 'I therefore asked him, after we had left the room, if I had explained the situation fairly. "You could not have been fairer," was his reply. That was all he said.'[196] The recollection of that meeting by another colleague, though, is different. Jim Prior records in his memoirs that 'Powell was very restive and pushing for much tougher controls, but Macleod, Boyle and Hogg were not prepared to accept them. The left wing of the party was not yet digging its heels in, but there was a beginning of a feeling that no compromise with Powell would prove possible.'[197] Prior, who may have confused the last shadow cabinet meeting before Easter with an earlier one, also says it was 'agreed' that no one would say anything out of doors on the issue. That apparently important agreement is not in the minutes.

Powell felt that, whatever concessions were made by Heath, and however much he agreed with the policy, his party and the political establishment still simply had not understood the nature of the problem. It was, also, yet another frustration to pile on the many others he felt in a shadow cabinet where he was isolated, and in which his personal and ideological ambitions seemed likely to be thwarted. That he was under some strain seems to have been clear to Heath, who wrote to him, considerately, on 16 April to say that 'I hope you are getting some break this Easter.'[198] For Powell, however, there was no break. Though he went to Wolverhampton for the holiday, he spurned rest and instead set his mind to what had to be done to meet the growing concerns of his constituents about immigration. His Walsall speech had had little effect on the public's consciousness. His former policy of integration of immigrants into British society no longer seemed viable, given the sheer weight of numbers. He realised he would need to shake the Government by stirring up the people. It would require an act of brinkmanship, as many of his speeches since 1965 had been. He seems not to have realised, this time, that his luck could run out. So he decided to say once more what he had said at Walsall: only this time he would see to it that people would take notice.

'THE GREAT BETRAYAL'

The platform Powell chose for his detonation – which he referred to ever after as 'the Birmingham speech', but which everyone else knows, with poetic licence, as 'the Rivers of Blood speech' – was a gathering of the Conservative Political Centre in his native city on 20 April 1968, in a small upstairs room in the Midland Hotel. He put the speech out through the West Midlands Area CPC rather than through Central Office, which had already circulated three of his tracts in the previous week. This, he maintained, was his normal practice when addressing such a group, and he happened to be its chairman. He had, according to Clement Jones, an idea of the likely effect. Without confiding in him the subject matter, Powell told him earlier that week that 'I'm going to make a speech at the weekend and it's going to go up "fizz" like a rocket; but whereas all rockets fall to earth, this one is going to stay up.'[1] Jones took the blame for the speech's not being distributed through Central Office. He had advised Powell that personal and selective distribution of his speeches, with embargoes timed to make them fresh for the six o'clock evening news, would create more impact and more publicity.

The Central Office area agent, to whom Powell had given the speech for distribution, commented that it would be useful to have it to put out over what, being a bank holiday, promised to be a quiet weekend. When the Birmingham-based television company ATV saw an advance of it that morning, a news editor instantly appreciated its news value. He sent a camera crew to the Midland Hotel; they captured the few rare clips of Powell's defining moment that survive. Pam Powell, who typed out the speech, said later that 'I agreed with every word of it but when I heard it I thought of it as just a good speech, a forceful speech. I never thought it would cause so much controversy.'[2] Heath and his shadow cabinet colleagues had no idea what he was up to. Powell should have realised the trouble he would cause: in the past, when Heath had had advance notice of his speeches, he had sent Whitelaw, as Chief Whip, to talk Powell out of saying contentious things. Powell had, he claimed, always been willing to oblige. 'Oh, that's all right, Willie,' he remembered having said on these occasions. 'Tell me what Ted's upset about, and I'll change it.'[3]

Ted would not have the chance this time. Powell was determined to make his point, and, sincere though he was about the immigration issue, he was determined also to prove that he could not continue to be sidelined in the shadow cabinet. He would succeed in that, but not how he expected. His fault was to believe he could use such emotive language to treat such an emotive subject, and remain a member of a shadow cabinet run on authoritarian lines that favoured a liberal social policy. He should have recognised the inevitable, and resigned first. He gambled, as it turned out, once too often on Heath's need to tolerate his freelance activity.

Aficionados of Powell's oratory could tell this was a speech like few others, and not merely because of its content. Mostly, Powell made vigorously theoretical speeches on matters of ideology which, however much he illustrated them using examples of socialist folly, often defeated his audiences. This was different. There was scarcely any element of theory; it took its text from the real anguish of Powell's constituents, whose experiences, controversially, he adduced in evidence. This gave the speech a drama and momentum lacking from some of his other more academic exercises. He said what he said plainly, and in terms that would be universally comprehensible. Powell was, for sure, acting on unquestionably the main concern of his electors, but it was also apparent from the passion and force with which he spoke that he was acting, too, to relieve his own pent-up anger that an issue so closely affecting almost every great urban area in the country was suppressed by politicians of all parties, including his own, and by the press and the broadcasters.

His message was the same as at Walsall, but Walsall had not had a reaction, and some of Powell's friends felt he framed his Birmingham speech as he did precisely to change that. It was also clear from the opening of the speech that he was conscious, moreover, of his place in the continuum of history: it is a speech as much about Powell's sense of history and nation as about anything else. Sadly for him, it would be interpreted, by supporters and opponents alike, as being racial in motive. In fact, as he would say less emotively a decade later, the issue was entirely political: 'It is the belief that self-identification of each part with the whole is the one essential pre-condition of being a parliamentary nation, and that the massive shift in the composition of the population of the inner metropolis and of major towns and cities of England will produce, not fortuitously or avoidably, but by the sheer inevitabilities of human nature in society, ever increasing and more dangerous alienation.'[4] Individuals could identify with the nation, but whole communities of millions could not.

'The supreme function of statesmanship', he began, portentously, that Saturday lunchtime, 'is to provide against preventable evils'.[5] With immigration, the attitude was, instead, 'if only people wouldn't talk about it, it probably wouldn't happen'. However, Powell knew reality was inescapable. A week or two earlier, he said, he had fallen into conversation with a constituent, a middle-aged working man. Suddenly, the tone of their conversation, and of Powell's speech, changed radically. 'After a sentence or two about the weather, he suddenly said: "If I had the money to go, I wouldn't stay in this country . . . I have three children, all of them been through grammar school and two of them married now, with family. I shan't be satisfied till I have seen them all settled overseas. In this country in 15 or 20 years time the black man will have the whip hand over the white man." '

Powell knew what would come.

> I can already hear the chorus of execration. How dare I say such a horrible thing? How dare I stir up trouble and inflame feelings by repeating such a conversation? The answer is that I do not have the right not to do so. Here is a decent, ordinary fellow-Englishman, who in broad daylight in my own town says to me, his Member of Parliament, that the country will not be worth living in for his children. I simply do not have the right to shrug my shoulders and think about something else. What he is saying, thousands and hundreds of thousands are saying and thinking – not throughout Great Britain, perhaps, but in the areas that are already undergoing the total transformation to which there is no parallel in a thousand years of English history.

He repeated the projections – not his, but the Registrar-General's – for future numbers of immigrants and their descendants; three and half million by the end of that fifteen- to twenty-year period. Saying there was no comparable figure for the year 2000, Powell estimated it at between five and seven million, 'approximately one-tenth of the whole population, and approaching that of Greater London'. He warned that by 1985 the majority of that community would have been born in Britain, which was why action was so urgent, or else a future parliament would have greatly magnified difficulties to cope with. The nature of that action was plain: 'stopping, or virtually stopping, further inflow, and by promoting the maximum outflow'. Powell was careful to add that 'both answers are part of the official policy of the Conservative party'.

He adopted an increasingly apocalyptic tone. 'It almost passes belief', he said, 'that at this moment 20 or 30 additional immigrant children are arriving from overseas in Wolverhampton alone every week – and that means 15 or 20 additional families a decade or two hence.' The news film captures an intensity of anger in his manner at this point of which the simple words are a poor reflection:

> Those whom the gods wish to destroy, they first make mad. We must be mad, literally mad, as a nation to be permitting the annual inflow of some 50,000 dependants, who are for the most part the material of the future growth of the immigrant descended population. It is like watching a nation busily engaged in heaping up its own funeral pyre. So insane are we that we actually permit unmarried persons to immigrate for the purpose of founding a family with spouses and fiancées whom they have never seen.

Powell stressed that he was merely talking about people coming to Britain to settle. Remembering his time as Minister of Health, he said he had no objection to anyone, from the Commonwealth or elsewhere coming for training or education.

He then talked of the urgency of re-emigration, which could be tackled only 'while a considerable proportion of the total still comprises persons who entered this country during the last 10 years or so'. He was not advocating forcible repatriation, but the encouragement of re-emigration through 'generous grants and assistance'. He said immigrants in his own constituency came to him asking whether such a scheme existed. Nor was he talking about splitting families: 'but there are two directions in which families can be reunited'.

Powell specifically endorsed Heath's view that immigrants should be equal before the law, and that there should be no first-class and second-class citizens. 'This does not mean', he added, however, 'that the immigrant and his descendants should be elevated into a privileged or special class or that the citizen should be denied his right to discriminate in the management of his own affairs between one fellow-citizen and another or that he should be subjected to an inquisition as to his reasons and motives for behaving in one lawful manner rather than another.' He attacked the *bien-pensants* of the press for their continual urging of the Government to pass anti-discrimination legislation, swiping particularly at *The Times* – which would swipe back viciously – in a reference to 'leader-writers of the same kidney and sometimes on the same newspapers which year after year in the 1930s tried to blind this country to the rising peril which confronted it'. He warned that if such legislation were enacted it would aid discrimination against the indigenous population, and the social effect would be like 'throwing a match on to gunpowder'.

He drew a distinction between the black population of America – descended from slaves who lived there before the United States became a nation – and Commonwealth immigrants, who came to Britain with fully fledged rights of citizenship. The impact upon the existing population was therefore very different, the problems created, and the reasons for them, very different too. He spoke up for the white population:

> For reasons which they could not comprehend, and in pursuance of a decision by default, on which they were never consulted, they found themselves made strangers in their own country. They found their wives unable to obtain hospital beds in childbirth, their children unable to obtain school places, their homes and neighbourhoods changed beyond recognition, their plans and prospects for the future defeated; at work they found that employers hesitated to apply to the immigrant worker the standards of discipline and competence required of the native-born worker; they began to hear, as time went by, more and more voices which told them that they were now the unwanted. On top of this, they now learn that a one-way privilege is to be established by Act of Parliament; a law which cannot, and is not intended to, operate to protect them or redress their

grievances, is to be enacted to give the stranger, the disgruntled and the *agent provocateur* the power to pillory them for their private actions.

He said he had been used to receiving anonymous letters, and most MPs knew what sort of person the typical anonymous correspondent was. However, following his Walsall speech he had started to receive letters on immigration from 'ordinary, decent, sensible people, writing a rational and often well-educated letter, who believed that they had to omit their address because it was dangerous to have committed themselves to paper to a Member of Parliament agreeing with the views I had expressed, and that they would risk either penalties or reprisals if they were known to have done so'. To illustrate this sense of persecution Powell read out a letter to him from a woman in Northumberland, who had given her name and address, but which he did not disclose. It was about an elderly woman living in a 'respectable' street in Wolverhampton, in which a house had been sold to a black man eight years earlier; now the woman was the only white person left in the street. She had been widowed, and lost both her sons, in the war. She turned her home into a boarding house to make a living.

However, once the immigrants moved into the street her white lodgers moved out. She lived in fear of attack. One morning at seven o'clock two black men had knocked on her door demanding to use her telephone, and when she refused she was abused. She had asked for a rates reduction, but was told by a young woman council officer to let out her rooms to make ends meet. When the woman had replied that the only tenants she could find were black, the council official said: racial prejudice won't get you anywhere in this country'. The last part of the letter was, though, the part of the speech most seized on by the press:

> 'She is becoming afraid to go out. Windows are broken. She finds excreta pushed through her letterbox. When she goes to the shops, she is followed by children, charming, wide-grinning piccaninnies. They cannot speak English, but one word they know. "Racialist," they chant. When the new Race Relations Bill is passed, this woman is convinced she will go to prison. And is she so wrong? I begin to wonder.'

Those words were not Powell's, but his decision to broadcast them convinced the liberal establishment that he was a racialist himself. Even some of his closest adherents – such as John Biffen, who supported him on this issue – felt that to use this letter was a grave mistake and could not but be inflammatory.

Powell did not deny that some Commonwealth immigrants wanted to integrate, but he called the notion that the majority of them did 'a ludicrous misconception, and a dangerous one to boot'. Small communities, in the past, had come under irresistible pressures to assimilate, but the new immigrant community was sufficiently large to ignore such pressure. Instead many immigrants were working to maximise racial and religious differences 'with a view to the exercise of actual domination, first over fellow-immigrants and then over the rest of the population. The cloud no bigger than a man's hand, that can so rapidly overcast the sky, has been visible recently in Wolverhampton and has shown signs of spreading quickly.'

His peroration sealed the speech, depending on one's point of view, either as a masterpiece of incitement, or as the sincerest and most eloquent testimony to a grave, and so far ignored, social problem. Describing the Race Relations Bill as 'the very pabulum' that dangerous and divisive elements needed if they were to flourish, he warned that, if it were passed, the law would allow the immigrant community to 'agitate and campaign against their fellow citizens'. The apocalypse was in sight. 'As I look ahead, I am filled with foreboding. Like the Roman, I seem to see "the River Tiber foaming with much blood".' The allusion was to the Sibyl's prophecy – not, ironically, a Roman's – in Book VI of the *Aeneid*, to Aeneas about his return to Italy: 'I see wars, horrible wars, and the Tiber foaming with much blood.' He quoted it in Latin, and then translated for the assistance of those in his audience who had a poor grasp of Virgil. Powell's only regret, later, about the speech was that he had not stuck to the Latin in his press release too; those news editors who had been able to translate *Et Thybrim multo spumantem sanguine cerno* might not have done so with such a poetic, and such an emotive, rendering as Powell. 'My fatal decision', he reflected long after the event, 'was not to be pedantic and leave it in Latin ... at the last minute I said "I can't put that out in Latin, that's pedantic" ... In Latin, it would have been lost.'[6] Another MP, telling Powell that the quotation was an error of judgment, was told by him: 'The expression came easily to me as I am a classical scholar and you are not.'[7] Jonathan Aitken, later a Conservative MP, recalled being present at a lunch later in the year, given by Selwyn Lloyd to bring together Powell and Whitelaw, where the matter of the 'foaming with much blood' remark came up. An attempt was made at reconciliation, but Powell was unrepentant. He was put on the defensive, though, pointing out repeatedly that the remark was a quotation, not a phrase of his. Aitken remembered Lloyd and Whitelaw agreeing that Powell was too powerful a talent to be left outside, but nothing could be done about it. Whitelaw told Pamela Powell at this lunch how sorry he felt for Heath, whom he described as 'all alone and a difficult personality'.[8]

Powell's American visit had seemed to set off his train of thought, with its inevitable logic, and to have made him think so keenly about the British predicament compared with the American which was then, as the civil rights protests escalated, so much in the public consciousness. 'That tragic and intractable phenomenon which we watch with horror on the other side of the Atlantic but which there is interwoven with the history and existence of the States itself, is coming upon us here by our own volition and neglect ... only resolute and urgent action will avert it even now. Whether there will be the public will to demand and obtain that action, I do not know. All I know is that to see, and not to speak, would be the great betrayal.'

'Looking back,' recalled one who was present, C. Howard Wheeldon, 'it is fascinating to note what little hostility emerged from the audience. To the best of my memory, only one person voiced any sign of annoyance.'[9] Elsewhere, though, the explosion was instantaneous. 'It is doubtful', wrote Robert Rhodes James, in a review of the Wilson years, 'whether any British political speech in peacetime had had an immediate effect comparable to that created by Powell's Birmingham speech of 20 April 1968, since Joseph Chamberlain had flung down the gauntlet of Tariff Reform, also at Birmingham, in May 1903.'[10] Hogg, on whose toes he had trodden the hardest, had been walking in the Lake District with friends. He was alerted by his host's family on his return to their house that Powell had said 'some very odd things about immigration'.[11] Hogg put the television news on to see what this was, and saw footage of Powell delivering his speech before what Hogg regarded as 'a somewhat unsuitable audience'. Because he had had no inkling of it, he was 'outraged'.[12] 'The speech obviously rendered my position the following Tuesday [the second reading of the Bill], already difficult, almost impossible ... I fully intended to resign from the shadow cabinet if my own estimate of the speech was correct.'

Hogg rang Whitelaw, who lived near his hosts, and asked him to watch the news and see what he thought. Hogg does not say whether or not he made his threat of resignation to Whitelaw. Whitelaw's own recollection – he himself was 'totally outraged' and 'knew then that I could never bring myself fully to trust him again' – was that the only threats of resignation he received were from Macleod, Boyle and Carr.[13] Carr told Heath that 'we have only been putting up with this lonerism because it's Enoch, but this is going too far. You either get rid of him or you get rid of me.'[14] As far as Carr, one of the mildest of men, was concerned, his patience had run out with someone who had become 'a bad colleague' – it was, for him, as much that Powell had spoken outside his ground, and without warning his colleagues, that caused offence as anything he said.

Whitelaw contacted Heath, who asked him to come to London the next day for urgent consultations. Heath should have been alert to what was happening. He had written an article for that Sunday's *News of the World* outlining the official position on the Race Relations Bill; but when his press officer rang the newspaper on the Saturday morning, a few hours before Powell spoke, he was told confidently by the editor that whatever Heath was saying would be pushed aside by the 'shaker of a speech' Powell would make – and of which the editor had seen an advance.[15] As Peter Utley, in his analysis of the event, concluded: 'It would be a bold man who altogether rejected the idea that Heath's decision to dismiss him on April 21st had nothing whatever to do with the interest aroused in that Sunday's papers by Powell's speech and the almost complete neglect accorded to an article on the same subject by Heath.'[16]

The next day Powell did not go to ground, as was usual for him on a Sunday, but defended himself on the BBC's *World This Weekend*, saying he had merely spoken about a great problem he knew to exist. He went to Communion at St Peter's Church in Wolverhampton, and as he left a member of the congregation came up to him and announced, 'Well done, Sir. It needed to be said.' Before he had spoken, the view of him by his constituents was, as Clement Jones put it, 'one of great respect, great admiration, but not matched by great understanding of his philosophy'. Now he had said something they could all understand, and which sealed him as a hero in their eyes. When Jones, who had been so shocked by the speech that his long-standing family and business friendship with Powell was finished by it, went into the *Express and Star*'s office on Monday morning he found it deluged by letters, a deluge which continued for days and disrupted the whole town's postal system. (A generation later Jones, while still disapproving of Powell's language, said he did not doubt that Powell had acted sincerely in what he thought to be the best interests of his constituents.)[17]

Powell stuck to his rule of not reading the Sunday papers, and asked waiting journalists quizzically: 'Have I really caused such a furore?'[18] Interviewed on ITN later in the day, he claimed he had chosen his words carefully and said, 'I didn't wish to be misunderstood, and I believe there is no room for misunderstanding.' The received wisdom was that Powell wanted to be sacked, and was determined to go in style. In fact, he believed Heath could not sack him for what he had said. This belief was of a piece with an observation he had made about himself, and which was later quoted about him: 'I deliberately include at least one startling assertion in every speech in order to attract enough attention to give me a power base within the Conservative party. Provided I keep this going, Ted Heath can never sack me from the shadow cabinet. But I never assert anything so extreme that I could not put it into practice in office – allowing of course for the inevitable compromises of power.'[19] Powell later denied ever having said this, though no retraction appeared at the time. Whatever the truth of that, this time Powell had gone too far. Having had several run-ins with Heath in recent months over his economic speeches, Powell did not feel the level of provocation in this speech would prove exceptional. He was wrong.

One of Powell's longest-standing parliamentary admirers, Tony Benn, was dismayed by what he had said. 'He has never been accepted by the Tory party,' wrote Benn in his diary on 21 April, suggesting that a sense of class inferiority had been at the root of Powell's motivation.[20] 'He has got to have someone to look down on and this is the way he does it.' Benn, whose anger with Powell would not be permanent (though it would become worse before it became better) subsequently refined this view to see Powell as the natural representative of the large working-class element in the Conservative party in the struggle to have their voice heard. Another of Powell's old political alliances was finally destroyed by the speech: that with Macleod. Thereafter, Powell recalled, Macleod's dealings with him were 'those of one's dealings with a pariah. There was nothing in it for him to be in any way associated with me.' What hurt Powell in particular was that Macleod 'knew what I said was not motivated by what is crudely called racialism, but he behaved as if he did not know'.[21] For Macleod, the speech at least meant that a close rival was out of the way.

However upset Labour MPs, and even many moderate Conservatives, were by Powell's comments, they had to accept that he spoke for the majority of the country, however unsophisticated that majority may be. It was a case of Powell's apparent provincialism clashing head on with the metropolitan political establishment. Therefore, the press furore was unstoppable, and fed on itself and on the reflex hysteria of polite opinion. Liberal opinion queued up to denounce him publicly, from the cricketer Sir Learie Constantine to Baroness Gaitskell, who termed the speech (or what parts of it she had read) 'cowardly'.[22] Jeremy Thorpe, the Liberal leader, felt there might be a *prima facie* case against Powell for incitement; and Ted Leadbitter, a Labour MP, said he would refer the speech to the Director of Public Prosecutions. The best Central Office could do, while Heath kept what the lobby was told was an 'infuriated silence', was to concur that what Powell had said had been in line with party policy.

For much of Sunday Heath, who drove up from his weekend retreat in Broadstairs to Albany, awaited Whitelaw's arrival from Cumberland. Both knew what would have to be done to forestall division in the shadow cabinet. Heath told his biographer, George Hutchinson, that he was 'deeply upset . . . saddened and offended as well as angered'.[23] For him, the timing was not merely painful because of the imminence of the debate on the Race Relations Bill. He was also committed to a short tour of the West Midlands, Powell's heartland, the next week. As his Chief Whip records, Heath was under no illusions about the strength of support there would be for Powell in the party and in the country.[24] Long before Whitelaw arrived, Heath had made up his mind. He saw the importance of distancing himself from Powell's view by sacking him. Also, quite simply, he had had enough of Powell. Powell was unequivocal in his view of what had motivated Heath. 'He was frightened out of his wits . . . and scenting danger, ran for cover.'[25]

Margaret Thatcher, who knew nothing of Powell's speech until she read of it in her Sunday papers, was telephoned by Heath at eleven o'clock that morning. He said to her: 'I am ringing round all the shadow cabinet. I have come to the conclusion that Enoch must go.'[26] Lady Thatcher recalls this as being 'more statement than enquiry', an impression confirmed by Carr, who remembered Heath's telling him that Powell was sacked.[27] Although she felt that some of Powell's language was 'strong meat', she also sympathised with the point he had made, and told Heath that 'I really thought that it was better to let things cool down for the present rather than heighten the crisis.' She also pointed out that Powell had made the speech before. Yet 'Ted was having none of it. "No, no," he said. "He absolutely must go, and most people think he must go." ' Lady That-cher, who knew Powell to be 'a deeply Christian gentleman' and 'not a racist', said she regarded this outcome as 'a tragedy', though she admitted that, outside the confines of the shadow cabinet, Powell was able to shift the balance of Conservative policies to the right in a way that would not otherwise have been possible. Keith Joseph, perhaps the man closest to Powell ideologically in the shadow cabinet, told the Powells at a dinner-party to which he asked them the following July that Heath had not bothered to consult him at all before sacking Powell.[28]

The initial briefings to lobby correspondents were that Heath would see Powell on the Monday at the next scheduled shadow cabinet meeting, and that Powell would be 'carpeted' for intruding in the responsibilities of others. Heath also confirmed that neither Hogg nor Maudling, both of whom would have a part to play in the debate on the Bill, had been told by Powell of his speech, and he took into account the Walsall speech of two months earlier, which had angered him. The initial view, by those unaware of Hogg's threat, was that Powell was too significant to let loose on the backbenches. Friends of his briefed that he was unrepentant, and would make no apology. He himself said he had not cleared the speech with Heath. 'No, one doesn't. It was a speech entirely on the lines he has set out.'[29]

He did not survive in his job until the shadow cabinet met. Heath, his discussions with Whitelaw complete, and contemplating the growing assault from Fleet Street and Parliament, sacked Powell (who was still in Wolverhampton) that Sunday evening by telephone. It was, Powell would recall, the last conversation they ever had. Heath had been trying to ring him for much of the evening, hoping to have the deed done in time for the first editions of Monday's papers. However, Powell – who had only recently had the telephone installed in his constituency home – had been so inundated with calls of support that he had asked the Post Office to put a block on the line. Heath was reduced to ringing Powell's agent, who drove to Merridale Road to see Powell and ask him to ring the leader.

Powell rang at nine o'clock to be told of his dismissal. An hour later Heath put out a statement saying he considered the speech 'racialist in tone and liable to exacerbate racial tensions'. He had sacked Powell 'with the greatest regret'.[30] The press was told, for good measure, that Heath felt the timing of the speech deliberate, and a strike directly at his authority; and it was put about that Powell had behaved 'shabbily' by not letting those colleagues who would have to put the party's policy to the Commons of 23 April know of his intentions.[31] The moderation with which Heath had charged his spokesmen to present the rea-soned amendment in that debate would sit oddly with Powell's tone.

Heath's friends also said that he and his colleagues had found Powell's claim that he was only echoing party policy 'disingenuous': the language and tone of the speech could not, they said, be considered consistent with the party line. Powell would be accused of having double-crossed his own colleagues by not having raised his doubts with them at the last meeting of the shadow cabinet. His claim that he was merely – albeit colourfully – expounding party policy was central to his defence against that accusation, but it was not one his colleagues would accept. Journalists went to the Powells' house in Wolverhampton to be told by Mrs Powell: 'My husband has gone to bed. He will write to Mr Heath tomorrow and has no further comment to make.' Right-wing MPs, especially from the West Midlands, immediately began to express outrage that Powell had been sacked. Duncan Sandys, Gerald Nabarro and Teddy Taylor were among the first to come out in his support. Peter Farmer, who had been Powell's constituency chairman, said that 'it is entirely wrong that a man who is seeking to represent the views of his constituents not only now but in the future should, because of a speech made by him, lose his position in the shadow cabinet'.[32] In fact, the Powells had not gone to bed. Correctly expecting a siege by the press the next morning they woke up their children, explained that Daddy had made a big speech that might cause the press to be interested, and drove back through the night to London. Jennifer, his younger daughter, would recall that this 'was the first time it dawned on me that perhaps he wasn't the sort of father that most children had'.[33]

II

Though there can be no doubt Heath felt that the way Powell had handled this issue made it impossible for him to stay in the shadow cabinet, the events did provide an opportunity for him to sideline the man who had slowly become the main threat to his authority in the party. Whether this would be good or bad from the point of view of Heath's leadership, only time would tell. One shadow cabinet member, speaking unattributably, told the *Guardian* exactly what would happen with Powell on the backbenches: 'he will create hell'.[34] In the short term, though, Hogg's and Maudling's tasks as front-bench spokesmen were eased by the fact that Powell was no longer with them, and they did not have to reconcile their reasoned amendment with his views. The rumours began about whether Powell had engineered his dismissal in an appropriately spectacular way, seeing how he was losing important arguments about defence, the economy and other matters close to his heart in shadow cabinet. Certainly, given the passion with which Powell would fight against other matters of party policy, had he not gone then he could hardly have remained beyond the agreement over the reform of the House of Lords.

When Monday came most of the press was against Powell – a detail Heath had, through his press officers, taken care to ascertain before deciding to sack him. *The Times* attacked him in a leading article entitled 'An Evil Speech', congratulating Heath and arguing that the dangers of having Powell as an enemy were far less than those of having him as a friend. The paper, too, pronounced the speech 'racialist' and therefore 'disgraceful' and 'shameful'.[35] The *Daily Telegraph*, by contrast, while not approving of Powell's tone, deplored the sacking, pointing out that he represented a far wider band of Tory opinion than some, like Sir Edward Boyle, who took the opposing view and supported the Bill. It also deplored, as possibly 'the most serious encroachment on freedom of speech and on the authority of the Commons for two centuries', the threat to have Powell prosecuted for airing the fears of his constituents.[36] The press's main preoccupation was to find the old lady in Wolverhampton; they were unsuccessful, leading some to doubt the veracity of Powell's story. After Powell's death, when the controversy was aired again, a Wolverhampton solicitor, Kenneth Nock, wrote to the *Express and Star* in April 1998 to say that his firm had acted for the woman in question, and to confirm that she had existed; because of rules concerning client confidentiality he could not name her.

Powell wrote a 150-word letter to 'Dear Ted', promising to support him from the backbenches 'as I have done from the day you were elected', a remark Heath could have taken in more than one way. He continued:

> I believe you will be Prime Minister of this country, and that you will be an outstandingly able Prime Minister, perhaps even a great one. There is one cause of anxiety which I hope that time will dispel. It is the impression you often give of playing down and even unsaying policies and views which you hold and believe to be right, for fear of clamour from some section of the press or public.
>
> I cannot help seeing in this light the fact that you took occasion to stigmatize my speech at Birmingham as 'racialist' when you must surely realise that it was nothing of the kind.[37]

Heath, who received the letter by a messenger sent from South Eaton Place, felt it did not merit a reply, not even to clarify whether he did, really, share Powell's views. He then chaired the shadow cabinet meeting, at which preparations were made for the following day's debate: it was reported that his decision to sack Powell had unanimous support. Hogg called the Bill a 'curate's egg' that would do more harm than good. He also told the committee that, had Powell not been sacked, he would have resigned, and said Powell's speech made it all the more imperative that there should be a party line on the reasoned amendment.[38] Still highly emotional, he added that, if colleagues did not agree, he might have to go after all.

One of Hogg's colleagues was not, however, prepared to support the line: Boyle announced that he would not be voting with his colleagues. Because his objections were the opposite of Powell's and therefore not able to be construed as embarrassing, he was indulged. He told his colleagues he would abstain, and would 'explain himself' to Hogg. Hogg did not resign. Finally, the committee agreed that front-bench speakers would take pains to point out how greatly in favour the party was of immigration controls. This was hardly surprising. The avalanche of hostile mail from the public to Heath, not least from Conservative supporters, was only just beginning, and had already caused some disquiet.

Heath then stepped up his public defence of Powell's sacking. Appearing on *Panorama* on 22 April, he told Robin Day, 'I dismissed Mr Powell because I believed his speech was inflammatory and liable to damage race relations. I am determined to do everything I can to prevent racial problems developing into civil strife.'[39] Elaborating on his earlier statement, he said he had acted 'with the greatest possible regret, but I have the full support of my colleagues'. When Day suggested to him that he had sacked Powell because Powell had had the courage to speak up for mainstream opinion, Heath replied, 'I don't believe the great majority of the British people share Mr Powell's way of putting his views in his speech.' Day also referred to Heath Powell's point that the Tory leader was afraid of pursuing any policy that might provoke a section of the press or the public. Heath rejoined that if Powell thought that he should say so specifically, not by innuendo.

One part of the British people that did support Powell totally was his own constituency party. On 22 April it put out a statement which said: 'We deeply deplore his unjustified dismissal from the shadow cabinet because he has had the courage to express the true facts which exist in his constituency and in other parts of the country. We pledge our support to Mr Powell and place on record our appreciation of his magnificent service to the constituency over the past 18 years, during which time he has rendered notable assistance and service to constituents of every race, colour and creed with equal dedication and energy.'[40] The shift of public opinion against Heath – indeed, against all the established political leaders – from a hitherto silent, and large, section of the population, and the lionisation of Powell, were only just beginning. As Utley put it: 'Powellism, or at any rate something thought to be Powellism, had ceased to be the eccentric profession of a few sophisticates and become a strong popular movement.'[41]

Because of the growing anger from the grass roots at Powell's dismissal, the front bench went to lengths in the debate on Tuesday to point up just how grave the internal politics of the party would have become had Powell not been sacked. In his speech, Hogg made public the fact that he would have resigned. He also attacked Powell for the way he had publicised the speech without having told close colleagues first, accusing him of having primed television crews to be there. Powell wrote to Hogg immediately, releasing his letter to the press, to say, 'Whoever told you that I "summoned the two television networks" to my speech last Saturday did you and me a wrong. I took no step of any kind to call television to know that I was speaking at all, let alone of the speech. Incidentally, my speech was issued at their request by West Midlands area, as often happens when I am speaking in my own area.'[42]

The anecdotal evidence of anti-immigrant feeling after the Birmingham speech is plentiful, and would be held against Powell not just until his dying day, but beyond it. It was the reason why several senior clergymen objected to his body resting in Westminster Abbey the night before his funeral. They claimed then, as others had done from 1968 onwards, that immigrant communities were pitched into terror by Powell's speech, as he seemed to be legitimising racial attacks on them. That was certainly not Powell's intention. He contended that such feelings were present anyway, which was why he had spoken as he had. However, the way events developed was out of his control and, in this respect, it was he who had thrown the match on to gunpowder. As Parliament assembled for the debate on 23 April, 1,000 dockers walked out in protest at what they termed Powell's 'victimisation'. They marched from the East End to Westminster in his support, some carrying placards demanding 'Don't knock Enoch' and, ironically, 'Back Britain, not Black Britain'. Three hundred of them, still in their working clothes, went into the building, 100 to lobby Peter Shore, the MP for Stepney, and the other 200 to lobby Ian Mikardo, the MP for Poplar. Both MPs were shouted down, and Mikardo was kicked, by men who could normally be relied on as firm Labour supporters. Baroness Gaitskell shouted at them, 'You will have your remedy at the next election'; they shouted back, 'We won't forget.'[43]

Powell met a deputation of eight dockers who delivered a petition to him that claimed his sacking violated the right of free speech. The rest chanted 'We want Enoch' and sang 'For He's a Jolly Good Fellow'. Another 600 dockers at St Katharine's Docks, plainly unaware of Powell's views on union immunities, voted to hold a one-day strike in support of him the following day. Many smaller factories across the country, but particularly in the West Midlands, experienced similar walk-outs; men at the Wolverhampton and Dudley Brewery marched on Wolverhampton town hall. Speaking on Tuesday morning, before going to the Commons, Powell said, 'I have received several hundred telegrams and the ticker tape at the House of Commons was on the go all day yesterday, mostly with messages of support for me, and today it is at it again. About 4,000 letters have been received already at my home – so far only six have been against.'[44] He took no part in the debate itself, other than to vote with the Opposition at the end of it; the Government had a majority of 104. Powell was waiting to gauge the full extent of his support before making any further statements, in or out of Parliament. According to Crossman he sat 'in the third row back, glowering, with everybody eyeing him and only Gerald Nabarro up in the front giving him overt support'.[45] Many on the Conservative benches who knew Powell was right nonetheless regretted the effect of what he had said. Bill Deedes, now prominent in the party's Home Affairs Committee, felt that by speaking as he had Powell had made it impossible for the Government to take the necessary action, because to do so would make it look as though it was supporting him.[46] This was true, and would apply as much to Heath as to Wilson. 'He made it impossible for those using other language and other means to do what had to be done,' said Deedes, who admitted that Heath and his front bench were still largely oblivious to the realities.

By Wednesday 24 April Powell had received 20,000 letters, four or five sackloads arriving at each delivery; the Post Office assigned a van to make a special run several times a day. By that stage, Powell had found just a dozen letters against. Those for him included many Labour supporters, and some who described themselves as anti-racialists. On that day, emulating the dockers, 600 Smithfield meat porters walked out, marched to Westminster, and delivered a ninety-two-page petition to Powell supporting him. Becoming embarrassed by this unrest, Powell advised them not to take industrial action, but to write to Wilson, Heath or their Member of Parliament. Among the letters he received was one from thirty-nine immigration officers at Heathrow Airport, saying they were tired of the 'corruption and deceit' used for years to get immigrants into Britain. They released their letter to the press. Callaghan, as Home Secretary responsible for the officers, was outraged, and had the ringleader suspended pending disciplinary action. Powell was greatly buoyed by this public recognition, and moved by the thousands of individual stories of fear and sadness that poured through his letter box. It made him all the more determined to press on with his campaign.

One letter must suffice as an example of all those tens of thousands, still retained in his papers, that Powell received in his support. It was written by a woman in Kent, whose origins were in the West Midlands, and the concerns she expresses are typical:

Congratulations from my Mother, myself, and many friends on your speech last Saturday. We admire you for speaking up for us all. Other Members of Parliament in the Midlands know the situation as you do, but either will not, or dare not say, especially places like West Bromwich, Dudley, Smethwick and Wednesbury – there have been complaints from all these districts but we hear nothing, and we have come to the conclusion they are afraid of losing votes.

We know people cannot help the colour of their skin, but they can change their uncivilised way of life by conforming more to ours.

My Mother, who lives in West Bromwich, spends most of her time here with us as life is made a misery for her in her terraced house. The noise from the adjoining house is unbearable at times, but even this is better than their filthy habits which she has to contend with, i.e. urinating against her front door so that she has to clean up after them each time. My Mother is a widow and lives alone. It is for people in the same situation that I feel so strongly for [sic]. Also I feel the crowded rooms should not be permitted.

How dare Mr Heath sack you for your courage?

Believe me, sir, you have not only support from the Midlands but all the country.

Good luck sir, in your efforts to save our country.[47]

However valuable and inspirational to him mass support was, Powell had his most heavyweight endorsement on 24 April through the letters column of the *Daily Telegraph*. A leading party elder statesman, the Marquess of Salisbury, who had resigned from Macmillan's cabinet partly over immigration, wrote that Powell's only offence had been to fail to clear his remarks with the leadership; indeed, he felt that for that reason alone Powell should have resigned without waiting to be sacked. Salisbury argued, correctly, that all Powell had been trying to do was to shock his party out of its complacency about a problem 'fraught with dire peril for the future of our country'.[48] He added his conviction that 'Mr Powell is clearly not a racialist. He is merely a very worried man; and it would be hard to imagine anything more calculated to split the party – as we are told it has done – from top to bottom than to use the kind of words that Mr Heath did.' He dismissed the 'vague general phrases' used by Heath and his colleagues to conceal the inadequacy of their response to the problem, and ridiculed the notion that Hogg had given Powell a 'trouncing' in his speech on Tuesday. Salisbury demanded to know what Heath intended to do; and, referring to the licence given to one member of the shadow cabinet to abstain in the vote, Salisbury warned: 'It is not only Sir Edward Boyle who has a conscience.'

Despite Powell's pleas, strikes in the docks continued, spreading as far down river as Tilbury by 25 April. That day he received his 30,000th letter, now with a mere thirty against. His life had changed dramatically. One feature of it for the few years ahead was that he would be dogged wherever he went by protests, particularly from students. He did not waver in the face of these, but in the immediate aftermath of his speech, in order to give the authorities time to plan for the security measures now necessary, he did cancel some engagements. That week he was due to dine at Queens' College Cambridge and lecture at Clare on the history of the Lords in the middle ages; but when the university authorities realised they could not guarantee his safety, he cancelled at the last minute to avoid, as he put it, embarrassment to his hosts.

Heath started to defend his actions more vigorously. Speaking to party members in Rugby on 25 April, he said no one witnessing the events of the previous few days could think it had been wrong to sack Powell. He was referring to the visceral reaction from those who, unlike Powell, were undoubtedly racialist, and which he had seen too plainly in his own postbag. Heath was applauded, but so too was a woman in his audience who asked whether Powell should not rather have been given a suspended sentence. The next day, pressing on into the West Midlands, Heath condemned the 'nasty, vicious reaction' to Powell's speech, and appealed to people to remain 'calm and sensible'. At Dudley on 27 April he found himself heckled by some in an otherwise utterly loyal crowd, but 1,000 people gathered outside to chant 'Heath out, Enoch in'.[49] Maintaining Heath's own *de haut en bas* tone Douglas-Home, speaking in York on a day when 4,500 dockers were now on strike, said their action should be 'a salutary warning' to Powell of the latent prejudices he had stirred up, 'the dangers of which he has no doubt already appreciated'.[50] Few Conservative MPs were prepared to be seen to support Powell, sensing it might harm their careers; it was only those with a record of opposition to Heath and of loyalty to Powell, such as Maude, Nabarro and Ronald Bell, who were willing to take the risk. The grass roots were less quiet. The York University Conservative Association sent Heath a telegram saying: 'Disgusted by treatment of Powell. We fully support his speech as realistic, and view of majority of British people. You ignore such at peril to yourself, party and nation.'[51]

A clear gap was opening up between the leaders and the led, and not just in the Conservative party. Three thousand of those dockers marched to Parliament again that Friday to deliver a petition. Powell flew to Montreal to attend the three-day Bilderberg conference, an international economics meeting. As he boarded his plane at Heathrow 100 airport workers shouted, 'Good old Enoch!'[52] On Sunday 28 April, while he was away, 1,500 people marched to Downing Street chanting, 'Arrest Enoch Powell.' They then signed copies of a letter to Powell pledging themselves to combat 'your racialist views', which they went to South Eaton Place to deliver; they found the house well covered by policemen. Two days earlier the house had been approached by students from the London School of Economics shouting 'Oswald, Powell, Adolf' and 'Powell is foul.'[53] The police kept them, too, at bay.

At the same time, another demonstration was happening at the Bilderberg meeting. A busload of blacks went from Montreal to the ski lodge in Mont Tremblant in Quebec Province, where the meeting was being held, surprised guards and managed to march to the entrance with placards proclaiming, 'Go home, racist monster.' Prince Bernhard of the Netherlands, chairing the conference, consulted Powell about how best to handle the problem. Powell agreed to meet a deputation of four leaders of the group. They gave him a petition and urged him to stop his campaign to restrict immigration. That evening he returned to London, where he was met by a protection squad of six Special Branch men and ushered into the VIP lounge, where normally only politicians of cabinet rank were accorded the privilege of bypassing the normal immigration procedures. 'It was not my decision to use the lounge,' Powell said to waiting reporters.[54]

In his absence the Sunday papers, having had a week to digest events, mused on whether Powell had been motivated purely by ambition, whether he had realised he was losing arguments in his party, had relatively few of his colleagues on his side on economic questions, and as defence spokesman was compromised by his own disbelief in his party's East of Suez policy. Certainly, whatever his motivation, he could now speak with complete freedom. Crossman, summing up the whirlwind of the preceding week in his diary for 27 April, noted that Powell had 'stirred up the nearest thing to a mass movement since the 1930s. . . . Enoch is stimulating the real revolt of the masses . . . he has changed the whole shape of politics overnight . . . it has been the real Labour core, the illiterate industrial proletariat who have turned up in strength and revolted against the literate.'[55]

By early May more than 43,000 letters and 700 telegrams had been sent to Powell, four of the telegrams and 800 of the letters disagreeing with him. He promised to reply personally to every one from a constituent, and to every one posing a serious question; the rest he acknowledged through an advertisement in the *Daily Telegraph*. He maintained a policy of not giving interviews or writing elucidations of his views in the newspapers, but arranged for a copy of his speech to be sent to every MP. Many who had been loudest in their comments against the speech had still not read it, and Powell was determined to stand by what he actually said rather than by any subsequent interpretation others might want to make of it.

On 2 May the Attorney-General, Sir Elwyn Jones, issued a statement saying that after consultations with the Director of Public Prosecutions he had decided not to prosecute Powell under the terms of the 1965 Race Relations Act. Such a prosecution could proceed only on the Attorney's authority, and Jones was not prepared to take that step despite having received twenty-five separate representations from individuals and bodies urging a prosecution. He and Sir Norman Skelhorn, the DPP, were mainly influenced by the difficulty of proving Powell's intentions in making the speech. The wording of the Act clearly stated the need for the offender to show 'intent to stir up hatred against any section of the public in Great Britain distinguished by colour, race or ethnic or national origins'.[56] The other main concern was whether a prosecution would be in the public interest. Seeing how Powell had divided the nation substantially in his favour, the decision Jones made was of a sensible politician and not of a lawyer. The circus that would have attended such a prosecution would have made it impossible to have justice done. Also, the political establishment, at odds with Powell's views, would have had to endure endless further publicity being given to those views during so high-profile a prosecution, and it was unlikely that Powell, to judge from his parliamentary reputation, would have given anything other than the performance of his life in the witness box.

Powell opened his own defence, at last, in an interview in the *Birmingham Post* on 4 May. 'What I would take "racialist" to mean', he told the paper, 'is a person who believes in the inherent inferiority of one race of mankind to another, and who acts and speaks in that belief. So the answer to the question of whether I am a racialist is "no" – unless, perhaps, it is to be a racialist in reverse. I regard many of the peoples in India as being superior in many respects – intellectually, for example, and in other respects – to Europeans. Perhaps that is over-correcting.'[57] Perhaps it was: Powell was reported at this time by friends to be increasingly alarmed at the sort of people who were climbing on his bandwagon, and at the things they were saying. Although in the continuing furore his self-absolution from the charge of racism was barely noted, to make it was wise and necessary. Powell also maintained his steadfast loyalty to Heath and to the party in his comments. 'I cannot believe that any actions of mine have reduced the chances of the Conservatives winning the general election – reduced what at present appears to be a virtual certainty.'

The day the interview appeared Powell took his first surgery in Wolverhampton since the speech. 'How happy I am to be in my constituency,' he told waiting reporters, continuing to frustrate their desire to have a comment from him about immigration, or about his sacking. 'There is no happier place for any MP to be, particularly when he is such a popular member.'[58] A protest march of local churches, students and communists arrived to find him and his workers locked in to the constituency offices, but the march, of fewer than 150 people, was too small to pose any threat. One of Powell's first clients was a constituent of West Indian origin, Herbert Maclean, a fifty-six-year-old labourer. He told Powell he had a sick wife and four children in Jamaica, and wanted to be repatriated. Powell said he would do all he could to help. When, just before lunch, he left for home he was cheered by a group who shouted, 'Good old Enoch.' He stopped to talk to them, moving on as soon as the press came into earshot.

At the end of April, Gallup had undertaken a survey that showed beyond question that Powell had spoken for Britain. Of those questioned, 74 per cent agreed with what he had said and only 15 per cent disagreed; 69 per cent felt Heath was wrong to sack him and only 20 per cent felt he was right. Before the Birmingham speech only 1 per cent of those questioned had felt Powell would be the right man to replace Heath were there a vacancy; the favourite by far had been Maudling, with 20 per cent. Now Powell, with 24 per cent, was the clear favourite, with Maudling having dropped to 18 per cent. As well as having an effect on his own standing, Powell had also had an effect on the perception of the immigration issue. An already significant 75 per cent of those questioned had, before the speech, felt immigration controls were not strict enough; after it, that figure rose to 83 per cent. The survey also seemed to show that support for Powell could not be explained by accusations of racial prejudice. Some form of anti-discrimination legislation was felt by 65 per cent of those surveyed to be desirable; only 19 per cent said they would move if immigrants came to live next to them; only 17 per cent said they would object to having to work with immigrants; and only 12 per cent would object to non-white children being in the same class as their children at school. The foundations of Powell's reputation as a tribune of the people had been laid.

There was an immediate electoral test that seemed to bear out his claims of how he had helped, not harmed, his party. The local elections, due on 9 May, were a triumph for the Conservatives in the West Midlands. Officially, the main parties steered clear of immigration. Unofficially, it dominated the campaign. Conservative candidates and their helpers encountered mass support for Powell, and found it helping their cause. The official line they were told to take, though, was 'while not necessarily agreeing with Mr Powell, I think he has done a service by airing the issue'.[59] Roy Jenkins, another Birmingham MP, belatedly joined in the attack on Powell, making the allegation that he had invented the stories about the school with the one white child in a class (from his Walsall speech of February) and the old lady. The story about the child he described as 'almost certainly falsely based'.[60] He said the story about the old lady was a 'dreadful kind of propaganda' of the sort used by the Nazis against the Jews in the 1930s. Jenkins was immediately challenged not by Powell, but by Walter Hughes, chairman of the Wolverhampton Education Committee. Hughes said – as he had done to the press weeks earlier, which Jenkins had not noticed – that Powell had been correct about the school, and that he would tell Jenkins the name privately if he chose to get in touch with him. Meanwhile David Winnick, the Labour MP for Croydon South, wrote asking Powell about the old lady. Powell replied, 'I never disclose, except at their request, particulars likely to assist in the identification of constituents.'[61] Winnick said that still did not answer his question, about whether she was personally known to him.

Powell did, though, respond sharply to an attack on him in a letter from Sir Robert Birley, a former headmaster of Eton and chairman of the United Kingdom Committee for Human Rights Year. The letter included the remark that 'speeches in the tone of the one you delivered are an affront to the dignity of Commonwealth immigrants'. It went on to criticise Powell's desire to limit the rights of dependants to immigrate into Britain, saying that 'we cannot feel that this disregard for the sanctity of the family should be accepted in a Christian country'.[62] Powell, whose equanimity was beginning to be strained, replied, 'I resent it as an impertinence that you and your committee take it upon yourselves to imply that I should do otherwise than show discretion and a proper feeling for the interests and human feelings of any group in the community, either in my constituency or generally.'

III

Powell did not regret what he had done, but equally strongly he wished to return to the rest of his agenda, particularly economic issues. At Belfast on 10 May, where he had gone to address the Institute of Directors, he tried to get a hearing for his view that the Government was blaming the people for the economic crisis that it had created, but he found that the press, who had attended in strength, were under orders to prise more statements out of him about immigration. He refused to oblige. At Chippenham the next day, in his first speech in England since Birmingham, he secured a better hearing. He referred to the immigration issue obliquely, discounting the 'laughable and far-fetched' explanations provided for the massive support given him by trade unionists.[63]

He went on to try to disabuse the union movement of the notion – which it appeared to have accepted uncritically – that it was responsible for rising prices and the falling value of money. He said trade unionists had been brainwashed rather in the style of victims of the Soviet secret police, and had had to endure their leaders talking of the need for their members to be 'restrained', the sort of language normally applied to a dangerous madman. 'Who shall complain, then,' he asked, 'if even the sturdy commonsense of the British working man gives way at last under the onslaught?' He told them categorically that 'inflation, with all its attendant consequences, comes about for one reason only. The Government causes it.' Looking forward to the Prices and Incomes Bill, which would be published the following week, he said it should be called 'An Act for blaming the British people and interfering in all their affairs in order to distract attention from the real causes and the true remedy of this nation's financial predicament'. He added that the way the Government was blaming the people was akin to 'stealing a man's wallet and then locking him up for theft'.

As so often, Powell's real concern was to stop his own party from playing the socialists' game; he could be less inhibited about that now he was out of the shadow cabinet. He set the tone for his internal opposition of the next six years: 'This is the Tory Party's opportunity to speak out for the people as a whole. It is not a time to hum and ha, or to blur the issue by talking about "voluntary" this "non-statutory" that. These subtleties are not understood, and for the very good reason that they are not intended to be understood and are not capable of being understood.' In case his own party did not understand, he supplied a script for them: 'What we have to say is that the Government ought to conduct its affairs, and that we as a Government will conduct our affairs, in such a way that the excessive demands of public expenditure, the sole ultimate cause of inflation, cease to plague the people of this country and interfere with all their plans and all their actions.'[64] This was a long way from the Birmingham speech, but had one important thing in common with it. Beneath the ideology and economic doctrine was, ever clearer, the populist message: what is wrong is the

Government's fault, not the people's; the so-called wage–price spiral was a chimera. All taken together, it began to look like a calculated bid for power. Powell would, though, spend the rest of his career denying he was a populist. 'A populist', he said in 1981, 'is a politician who says things because he believes them to be popular. I have never been that. My worst enemies wouldn't say that.'[65]

Powell's life changed suddenly beyond recognition, despite his and his family's attempts to retain a sense of normality. A death threat resulted in the stationing for several weeks of full-time police protection at South Eaton Place, and a Special Branch man accompanied Powell wherever he went. Heath, too, received additional protection as a result of the feelings expressed against him since the Birmingham speech. To clear the immediate avalanche of mail the Powells took on extra helpers, but Powell's new position as one who spoke for the millions disregarded by the political establishment would require a greater support system than had previously been necessary. Writing to Michael Strachan on 13 May he put a brave face on the upheaval: 'We are all well, and I think the daughters regretted going back to the quiet of school after the "rumpus", which they had enjoyed in a truly adult fashion. Pam is weary, but has never been more in support, and as for me, as you knew it would be, I think it all good fun, and half as good as foxhunting.'[66]

This was not a pose. He told John Biffen, who was concerned about the pressure he had put himself under, 'You mustn't worry about me. I was brought up to be alone. You often stand apart from the class for good reasons. I have no fear of heights.'[67] Biffen felt Powell did not like the way he had lost friends over the speech, but was prepared to accept it as a price that had to be paid. He felt that Pam Powell, by nature more gregarious than her husband, took this part of the after-effects less well. She would not, though, have been too surprised by the events: she told friends afterwards she had never expected Powell to go into the next election as a loyal member of the shadow cabinet, but had thought that, because of his tensions with Heath, it would always end in a row. It had: it was only the exact nature of the row that she had not predicted. 'I was worried stiff about it,' his unswerving wife recalled later. 'It was a terrible time for me.'[68]

Powell had finally learned the value of publicity from the experience after Birmingham. He was aware the press and broadcasters now hung on his every word, and was determined to supply them with those words more efficiently than in the past. Startled by the mass support he was receiving, he was made aware too of the strong political position he had carved out for himself, and was determined to maintain it. He had always been a good administrator; now he had to become a more ruthless and professional politician. To these ends, one by-product of the Birmingham speech was to prove invaluable to the Powells, not just then but for the rest of Powell's life: this was the sudden arrival of Greville Howard, a twenty-seven-year-old advertising executive. Powell and

Howard could not have been more different. A descendant of the dukes of Norfolk and the earls of Suffolk and Berkshire, Howard had left Eton nearly a decade earlier with few qualifications. His main recreation now was back-gammon, at which he made a handsome living, and which he sat up most of the night playing in West End clubs with the likes of 'Lucky' Lucan and John Aspinall. Howard had first met Powell in the winter of 1967–8 at his uncle's, Harry d'Avigdor-Goldsmid's, and had been instantly enthralled by Powell's intellect, charm and political views. Howard was at a loose end and wanted a new challenge. When Powell was sacked, Howard wrote to him expressing his outrage and volunteering his services, if 'some idiot buffoon who knew nothing about politics' could be of any use.[69] Somehow, from among the tens of thou-sands of letters – there were nine volunteers and two unemployed actresses at one stage opening them around the Powells' dining-room table – Howard's surfaced. Powell made inquiries of the d'Avigdor-Goldsmids, after which Howard received a reply inviting him for an interview. He was engaged, initially at a token salary – Howard had not wanted to be paid at all, but Powell insisted – to work for Powell for three months.

He in fact worked for Powell for the next two and a half years. He was chiefly responsible for monitoring and replying to some of Powell's mail, and ensuring that the texts of Powell's speeches were copied and taken to Fleet Street news editors and political correspondents – a specific list Powell had drawn up with the help of Andrew Alexander, a close supporter from the *Daily Telegraph* – on a Friday afternoon. He received, not unsurprisingly, an education in politics, but in other things as well. Referring letters on to Powell, he would receive from him short lectures on the derivation of the name of the place whence the letter came, and on the origins of the surname of the correspondent. Somewhat overawed by his new responsibilities, Howard was mortified when, early on, he spilt a bottle of ink all over a carpet. Powell took it well, asking his assistant 'where's the ink?' whenever finding him at his desk, just to be on the safe side. Eventually, Powell had his revenge. Staying in Howard's cottage a few years later, and finding that new carpets prevented the doors from closing, Powell removed them from their hinges – without Howard's permission – and cut the bottoms off.

Howard, like the young men who followed him, helped Powell not merely to maintain a grip on the mass media that even Heath, at times, could not manage, but also to establish a publicity machine independent of that run by the Con-servative party. This would be vital to Powell when, within a few months, Central Office became wary of distributing some of his speeches, and he became increasingly wary of letting Central Office have them. Powell's long-standing association with the Institute of Economic Affairs also helped: he established a business relationship with the IEA that allowed him to have many of his speeches typed and duplicated by staff at the Institute's nearby headquarters.

For all Powell's attempts to shift his agenda to other matters he could not get away from immigration. Some parliamentary colleagues had sent him to Coventry, including Heath (in Heath's case it was permanent), and the word had gone out to some Conservative wives that they were not to speak to Pam Powell. In the country Powell was still welcome at Conservative associations, the more so since his speech; but at some universities hostility to him was such that far-left groups, sometimes supported by dons, acted to prevent his fulfilling speaking engagements.

The first of these was the decision by a Canadian, Professor Henry Ferns, head of Birmingham University's department of political science, to cancel an invitation to Powell to speak on 19 June on 'Britain in Europe' because he feared that Powell would be at risk of assassination. Powell was outraged. He wrote to Ferns saying that 'the reasons you give for cancelling the invitation to address a private conference ... are untruthful and you know them to be so'. Powell's evidence was a letter Ferns had sent to the meeting's organiser, Neville Brown, in which Ferns told Brown that the real reason he wanted Powell's visit stopped was because of hostility among students and teachers to his views, particularly on immigration. 'The fact, therefore,' Powell told Ferns, 'is that you have taken it upon yourself to exclude from the university a person invited to address a private conference there and, incidentally, a member of the Senate because a section of students and staff disagrees with what they believe to be his views and dislike his expression of them on a particular subject. I must tell you that this is scandalously at variance both with the nature of a university and with your functions as a university teacher.'[70]

Ferns stuck by his original story, saying that 'if Mr Powell wants to make political capital out of something done in his own interest, let him do so. But he is a fool to try.' Stirring up hysteria further, Ferns also defended himself by referring to the recent assassination of Robert Kennedy. While he was sure no one at the University would want to kill Powell, he could not be sure whether someone from outside would not come and do so. 'You can't exclude the possibility of an individual being pushed over the brink and doing something bloody and violent. There is always the determined individual moved by hatred and resentment. My view was better safe than sorry.' Even the University's vice-chancellor, Sir Robert Aitken, was not prepared to defend free speech on his campus. 'This is a matter entirely between Professor Ferns and Mr Powell,' he said. 'The only thing that could be said from a university point of view is that we are not in a position to guarantee personal safety in these days.'

This brought unexpected support for Powell: the former Labour minister Christopher Mayhew cancelled an engagement at the University. 'People who believe in free speech and practice it should stick together whatever their other differences. If Birmingham University won't have Enoch Powell they can't have me.'[71] Stung by Mayhew's decision, Ferns announced that he would be writing to Powell again to explain further his withdrawal of the invitation. However, embarrassed by the adverse publicity, the University had a change of mind. Ferns said that, if Powell was prepared to take the risk of coming, he would be happy to chair the meeting. Needless to say, Powell accepted, and on the afternoon of 19 June delivered his private lecture on British policy towards Europe.

Despite the earlier protestations of the vice-chancellor, a heavy contingent of uniformed University security staff ensured the lecture theatre was open only to the 200 or so students holding tickets. Powell was met by a demonstration of about 500 students and dons outside the arts faculty building, but the visit passed off peacefully; there was no attempt to assassinate him. Nonetheless, Ferns tried after Powell had left to justify his original attempt at censorship, referring once more to the Kennedy assassination and to unrest in Paris. There could be no assurance, he maintained, 'in this age of instant communication when a senator of the United States can become a casualty of the war in the Middle East' that 'a conspicuous and controversial British politician cannot become a casualty in the war on the banks of the Niger or a war on the banks of the Seine'.[72]

Meanwhile, the Race Relations Bill was continuing its progress through Parliament, and splitting the Conservative party comprehensively. On 3 July the shadow cabinet agreed unanimously that the party should abstain from voting against the third reading*, largely because it was satisfied with changes that Callaghan, the Home Secretary, had agreed to make. However, eight members of the executive of the 1922 Committee tabled a reasoned amendment against a third reading. In the closing stages of the debate on the Bill at 4.30 in the morning on 10 July – the ridiculous hour at which it came on was the result of deliberate collusion between the Whips, Whitelaw having hoped that most of his malcontents would have gone home – Hogg, attempting to state the Opposition's case and to distance it from what he called the 'ugly' manifestations of sentiment that had followed the Birmingham speech, was shouted down by his own backbenchers. Cries of 'rubbish' and 'disgraceful' came, in particular, from Gilbert Longden, a member of the 1922 executive. This prompted Hogg to turn on them petulantly and self-pityingly, exclaiming that he had given up a peerage and a career at the Bar 'for my party' and – according to press reports 'near to tears' – adding that 'I will not be put down by unmannerly people who cannot even hear in silence views with which they disagree.'[73]

This performance was greeted with howls of 'Shameful!' and 'Sit down!', with one backbencher, Maidstone MP John Wells, reported to be 'incoherent with rage'. Whitelaw, at Hogg's side on the front bench, was powerless. There was a general feeling that, while the behaviour of Hogg's internal opponents was

---

* The final debate on any Bill, happening after the Report Stage. A vote is taken at the end, after which the Bill will have been passed or defeated.

appalling, Hogg had asked for it by seeming, in his remarks, to equate any opposition to the Bill with 'ugly' racialist feeling. A supporter of Powell's, Ronnie Bell, forced a division, and forty-four of his colleagues, including Powell (who did not speak), voted with him. Whitelaw's and Heath's hopes of burying the issue had been wrecked by Hogg's histrionics, and the legacy of division in the party over immigration was destined to continue.

Later that day Powell gave an interview to the *Daily Mail* directly on immigration, in which he denied having created the division now rending his party. 'It was already there. Is the exposure of a division a good thing? There is no general answer, but I think it is dangerous that the great anxiety of the people should be suppressed and equally dangerous that in a matter so deep the divisions in the Tory party should be smothered.' Presaging the arguments he would use six years later when refusing to stand as an independent candidate, he added, 'I have a strong sense of team. A politician by himself is nothing. He is unlike a doctor who should never take collective decisions.'[74] He denied he had any regrets about the Birmingham speech. 'My speech was a thing that had to be done ... when I do something, I suffer no agonies of indecision. Deciding does not come hard to me. Decisions appear to present themselves fully dressed at the door. There is a knock at the door and I open it, and there is a decision. And so it was with the speech.' Asked whether he was a racialist, he answered, 'We are all racialists. Do I object to one coloured person in this country? No. To 100? No. To 1,000? No. To a million? A query. To five million? Definitely.'

He also denied whipping up feeling among the people, and in doing so gave the clearest definition of how he saw his role: 'A politician crystallises what most people mean, even if they don't know it. Politicians are word-givers. When they have spoken, individuals recognise their own thoughts. Politicians don't mould societies or determine destinies. They are prophets in the Greek sense of the word – one who speaks for another and gives words to what is instinctive and formless. Winston did this in the war. He crystallised a will which existed.' Powell also described the dichotomy of his personality: 'I can see two persons in myself living together. There is a scientific person. I get great joy in logical deduction and I used to love lexicography and textual criticism. But I am also aware of a passionate person, but not sentimental or romantic.'

Immediately, Powell found another burning interest to deflect attention from immigration, and it was one that would lead to his greatest parliamentary triumph: his campaign, with Michael Foot, to block Labour's plans to reform the Lords. At a press conference on 18 July to mark the publication, at last, of *The House of Lords in the Middle Ages*, Powell announced that if, as promised, the Government introduced a reform Bill, he would be its 'resolute enemy'. He added, however, that 'I would like to bet that the House will survive this rash of reformism as it has survived many before.'[75] Wilson's main aim was to end the hereditary element in the Lords, and Powell said he hoped a Conservative government would once again advise the Queen to create hereditary peerages (counsel Heath chose not to act upon when he became Prime Minister). He said the Conservatives could afford to repeal such a Bill even if one were passed because the effects of a democratically elected chamber or one nominated by governments would be 'intolerable conflict' between the two Houses of Parliament. Powell was asked whether he would like a peerage, to which he replied, 'I have lots and lots to do in the Commons. There will be time enough to think of other things.'

The book was the result of twenty years of study by Powell. Keith Wallis, his co-author, had helped him for seven years to cross-check every word in it, and then to rewrite it and make it ready for publication; but notwithstanding Wallis's particular expertise in fifteenth-century baronies, the intellectual input is largely Powell's. Reviewing the work prominently in the *Daily Telegraph* the novelist Anthony Powell said it should be 'compulsory reading for everyone, in or out of Parliament, who ventures to hold forth on what is to be done about the contemporary House of Lords' and was 'a prodigious work of scholarship'.[76] There was a similar encomium in the *Sunday Times* from the Conservative party's historian, Robert Blake, who hoped Powell would one day find time to bring the history up to date. Powell's method is that of a man schooled in textual criticism; there is page upon page of evidence that parliamentary rolls have been scrutinised for changes of nomenclature or procedure, and the description of the development of the rights and duties of the peerage is given in the minutest detail. As well as being a work or scholarship, it is a work of love that exposes Powell's devotion to the institution. Any who would feel the weight of his opposition in the coming debate over Lords' reform would have done well to read it, just to measure the force of will Powell would bring to bear behind his own historical arguments against reform. To the party to launch the work, Powell invited all peers whose titles dated from before his book's cut-off point of 1540.

On 25 July he made his first speech in the Commons since Birmingham, in a debate on yet another supplementary statement of defence policy. It was of a piece with the attacks he had made on Healey when shadow spokesman, Powell arguing that the latest changes of policy had been forced on the Government by the arbitrary budgetary process Healey had agreed to at the start of his tenure. He told Healey, as he had done when they last met across the dispatch box, that he had failed; but it was Powell who had been sacked, and Healey was still there.

Restored after his summer holiday, Powell came back into battle with his customary lack of compromise. He mounted his campaign through an assiduous round of meetings with small groups, without the modern aids of the television cameras, teams of assistants or a sophisticated public relations machinery. The force of his charisma, and the certain knowledge the press was hungry for everything he said, however recondite and in however select a gathering, ensured that he commanded wide publicity. There was also the drama of what many in the press perceived to be his determination to force a showdown with Heath, and no stage in that drama would pass unreported.

In a speech at Market Bosworth in Leicestershire on 31 August he dealt with a wide range of issues, and appeared to be making a high-profile attempt to hijack the agenda for the Conservative party conference six weeks later. In a breathtaking assault on the household gods of his own party, he said Conservatives had to decide whether they wanted to go on tinkering at the edges of the national consensus, or to make great changes: 'Do we need a shake-up, a shock, a revolution even – or don't we?'[77] He said this question was more important than that of the survival of the Wilson Government, on which he felt the country had made up its mind, for it dealt with what sort of government would follow Wilson's. It was also a question his party had a duty to answer before the election.

He renewed his old themes in definitive fashion:

> If we decide that we want the brains, energy and enterprise of our people to create wealth and power in the forms which they wish it to take; if we decide that we want success, as the world judges success, to be rewarded and failure penalised; if we intend that profit and price and preference shall guide the direction of people's efforts and provide the expression of their desires; then tremendous deductions follow.
>
> We could no longer be satisfied with the limbo of semi-socialism – with the 'semi' continually diminishing and the 'socialism' continually advancing – which has been our consensus system for more years than most of us care to remember. We should not be able to put up with the state ownership and management of our industry, from coal mining to civil aviation, from atomic energy to steel production, a system which is the direct negation of the basic principles of private enterprise and capitalism, but must set to work at once to dismantle state socialism in industry and re-organize it on capitalist lines.

Unfortunately for him, this prescription – the Thatcherite manifesto of a decade later – found few takers in the Conservative party of 1968, even among some famous future Thatcherites. One such, Jonathan Aitken, then prospective parliamentary candidate for Thirsk and Malton, said that 'Powellism is not a credible political philosophy at all. It is merely a rag bag of contradictory discontents. . . . the wholesale adoption of all his present ideas would be a grave mistake.'[78] Aitken had supported Powell's economic thought, but had been distressed by the Birmingham speech. It mattered little what junior players like him thought; however, even those around the shadow cabinet table like Keith Joseph and Margaret Thatcher, who would embrace Powell's ideas, were cautious in deviating from the Heathite orthodoxy. Some speeches Joseph made in the winter of 1969–70 about a more laissez-faire approach to industry helped ensure Heath did not make him Industry Minister after the 1970 election.

For good measure, Powell also used the Market Bosworth speech – delivered at a party rally on a bank-holiday weekend when almost every other senior politician was observing a saturnalian silence – to attack Heath's continued obsession with East of Suez, which (without naming his leader) he branded 'the post-imperial delusion of being all things to all men all around the world'.[79] Heath had just committed his party to rebuild Britain's role East of Suez, during a speech on a tour of Australia. Powell also indirectly attacked Macleod, who had been talking about reshaping the tax system. Powell said that was a good thing to do, but it sidestepped the fundamental point that, whatever system was used to raise taxes, the state was still spending too much and the individual was being left too little. 'The main point is public expenditure itself, and the key issue is the proportion of the national income spent on public account, whether it is to go on rising, or remain stationary, or fall. If the decision were that it must fall, that would mean curbing and reversing the automatic growth of public provision and of income redistribution in our social services.'[80]

Later that week, at a meeting of the free-market Mont Pelerin Society at Aviemore, Powell called for exchange rates to be allowed to float, to try to avoid the humiliation of the previous year when Britain had devalued. He ridiculed the cries of the Labour left to be rid of the control of international bankers when, as he pointed out, they had only to agree to let the market decide the value of the currency to have those very shackles cast off. He argued that the system Britain chose to follow would even cripple the powerful Swiss franc. 'Give me control of the exchange rate of the Swiss franc and I will reduce Switzerland within six months to the appearance of snivelling incompetence with which Britain is often presented to the rest of the world. I will make them a deficit nation. I will make their bankers incompetent. I will make their workers idle and I will do it all by altering the international price of their money.'[81]

Feelings among the Conservative rank and file about the greater desirability of Powell leading their party than Heath were stimulated again by remarks made by Edward du Cann, who the previous year had resigned from the chairmanship of the party after a disagreement with Heath. Describing the party workers as 'devoted, loyal and hard-working as ever', he added that 'the country has every reason to expect leadership and inspiration from the Conservative party, and I hear it too often said that this has been conspicuously lacking in recent months. We must be more specific about the principles that the Conservative party stands for. There are too many people who genuinely think there is little difference between the parties. Our party's preoccupation with the so-called middle ground of politics has led us too often to fail to present to the nation our theme in a sufficiently distinctive form. We must be clearer about policy.'[82]

Asked afterwards whether he was advocating a more right-wing course for the party, du Cann claimed he simply wanted some distinction between his party and Labour. Asked whether he was moving towards Powell's position, he said, 'I am certainly arguing for more right-wing policies in some respects, particularly in home affairs. But I certainly do not go all the way with Enoch Powell in many respects.' Heath was livid, saying icily after he had heard du Cann being interviewed on the wireless about his views, 'I have no comment to make.'

The populist tone of Powell's own personal campaign continued to deepen, as if he were setting out an unashamed stall for the leadership. His self-confidence, having grown steadily since his refusal to serve in 1963, was unstoppable. On 7 September his association in Wolverhampton published its yearbook, for which he wrote an address to his members. He told them:

> I have never believed it was the duty of a Member of Parliament to say and do on every matter what the majority of his constituents thought or wished, just because it was what they thought or wished. I hold to the assertion that a Member is a representative, not a delegate; he owes to his constituents the service of his own judgment.
>
> On the other hand, it is equally the duty of a Member of Parliament not to refrain from saying what a great number of his constituents wish and think, even though he agrees with them, just because it runs contrary to fashionable opinion or to the consensus of the elite or possibly to the current policy of the party. People rightly look to see their wishes and views voiced and discussed in Parliament and if, over a long period, they feel this is not happening a dangerous estrangement can set in between electorate, Parliament and Government.
>
> I believe this has increasingly happened in recent years. On a whole range of subjects – Commonwealth, overseas aid, free trade, crime and punishment, inflation, taxation, immigration – people feel that their voices are simply not 'getting through' – the astonishing reaction that followed my speech at Birmingham in April on one of the subjects was to me evidence of how deep and widespread was this pent-up frustration. To 'trust people', which is the essence of Toryism, means for a Member of Parliament not to be afraid to voice their anxieties, their instincts and their aspirations. That is what he is for.[83]

Other remarks of Heath's, this time about the whole anti-interventionist creed represented by Powellism, provoked Powell to further not-so-veiled attacks on the leadership. Heath had talked about Conservatives who opposed interventionism as having theories that were 'out of date'. Powell responded, at Watford on 12 September, with a further elaboration of what would become one of the cornerstones of Thatcherism: privatisation or, as he called it, denationalisation. The Conservative party had been conducting a feasibility study into denationalisation. For Powell, though, it was a question not of feasibility, but of moral necessity. 'Our purpose', he said, 'cannot be less than to convert to private enterprise that great block of British industry which accounts for 10 per cent of the annual product and over 20 per cent of the annual investment.'[84]

Referring to the party research into the question, he added, 'My purpose is not to try to guess or anticipate the conclusions of that study, nor the leadership's conclusions upon it, but to destroy the principal fallacies upon which the superstition that denationalisation is impractical is founded.' He himself said he disliked the term 'denationalisation', as 'it suggests a going back or undoing, whereas denationalisation is actually a going forward to a better method which some of these industries have in fact never enjoyed before'. What he set out was not the pre-nationalisation structure, which he said would be irrelevant to the 1970s, but a system remarkably like the eventual privatisation of those concerns in the 1980s and 1990s: a system whose foundation was 'to convert the title deeds of the physical assets from public debt into equity shares, thus transferring responsibility for the future management, replacement and renewal of the assets from the public and its political and administrative servants to the equity owners and their agents'. This is exactly what happened, at a net gain to the Exchequer, with the privatisations of twenty years later. Powell further argued that the resultant cut in public debt would suppress inflation, as opposed to the way that phenomenon had been fed by the nationalisations themselves. He referred to the squandering of money in the public sector since 1964, but admitted that the Conservative administrations from 1951 to 1964 had been just as culpable as Wilson.

IV

The Conservative leadership had by now worked out what Powell, and his followers, acting for the most part independently of each other and without specific co-ordination, planned to do at the party conference. The Monday Club, self-appointed Praetorian Guard of Powell and the Powellite interest, arranged to hand representatives attending the conference at Blackpool a badge proclaiming Powell as their 'Man of the Year'; judging from how many wore the badge, the various factions would be able to tell how much support Powell had among the hard core of the faithful. The move by the Club, under the patronage of Lord Salisbury, was not merely aimed at boosting Powell. It was also aimed at having them do for the Conservative party what the Tribune group of left-wing MPs, with its conference rally, had done for Labour. The Club booked a large hall for a rally on the Friday night of the conference, the night before Heath made the leader's traditional speech, and invited Powell to speak. He refused to do so, intending to concentrate his efforts on a speech in the conference itself, and having a prior engagement. He was also determined not to be seen as leader of an organised faction.

When, on 19 September, the agenda for the conference was published, the extent of Powell's influence became clear. The leadership found itself facing scores of motions, most of them strongly worded, on immigration; many called for the reinstatement of Powell. The total number of resolutions on all issues was, at 1,031, a third higher than the previous year. Of these, eighty were on immigration and sixty-nine on the future of the party. Powell had not intended his Birmingham speech to provide a means of drawing attention to the rest of his agenda, and to his wider critique of what was wrong with modern definitions of Conservatism and of the Conservative party, but his new fame had achieved just that, for him, helpful end. Typically, the motion chosen for debate praised Heath for his statements on immigration – notably his wish that all Britons should be equal before the law, which avoided the real issue – and urged the party, when it returned to power, to take 'effective steps to promote racial harmony'.[85] More indicative of mass feeling were motions from Folkestone and Hythe claiming that 'Conservative leaders are not sufficiently in touch with the people,' and from Dover, urging Heath to appoint more right-wingers to the shadow cabinet, 'thus making the Conservative Front Bench truly representative of the views of the great mass of party workers and voters'.

On 18 September Powell had reopened another front against his party, on East of Suez. In terms he could not have used six months earlier, he said in a speech to the Royal United Services Institution that a military presence in South-East Asia would be 'an exorbitant premium against a risk so remote that it cannot be identified'.[86] He asked why Britain alone of European powers felt it was essential to have this presence. 'One might have thought it suspicious that none of our continental neighbours thinks so. Yet it no more occurs to them to exert themselves militarily for the stability of south-east Asia than South America or Central Africa.' It was, he added, 'a mirage' to suppose Britain's economic ends could be furthered by such a presence. 'We are by no means so much dependent as a number of other nations on overseas trade and investments for out standard of living; but we are the only one that dreams of protecting them with garrisons.' Now the Empire had gone, the military role of the future was defence of the British Isles. He mocked the strategic thinking of his party's leadership: 'Twice in our lifetime we have been all but overwhelmed by a military power located 200 miles away, yet the best service brains in the country are still engaged on how best to stage the opposed landing of a brigade group in the Far East.' It was not a speech designed to heal the rift between him and his former shadow cabinet colleagues.

Hogg, who would have the difficult task of leading the debate on immigration at the party conference, did not wait until then to start his assault on Powell and his supporters. On 27 September, in one of the few front-bench responses to Powell's autumn offensive, he made a speech at Monmouth, in which he attacked those who were seeking to split the party. 'A divided party always loses elections,' he said. 'You do not unite a nation by dividing a party. You do not win elections by intrigue and back-biting.'[87] Hogg's speech indicated the fear that Powell's latest campaign had instilled in the already beleaguered leadership, and their determination to try to neutralise him before the conference. Airing a theme that would form the burden of his own conference speech. Hogg, tilting at Powell, said that 'extreme policies seldom pay dividends. They may sound grand on the platform. If they are tried out in practice they usually prove unworkable. They also lose elections almost quicker than anything else.'

Hogg, as some other Conservatives had done, sought to draw a parallel between Powell and Barry Goldwater, the right-wing Republican who had fared badly against Lyndon Johnson in the 1964 American presidential election. The Republicans, he said, 'had embraced a programme and selected a leader who inspired a section of their own party and lost by a landslide precisely because he tried to oversimplify issues and exaggerate differences.' For Hogg, the fact that Johnson had promised a continuation of the ideals of the recently assassinated President Kennedy was not, apparently, material to his argument. Turning directly to what he believed were Powell's divisive qualities, he said (in an allusion few in his audience would have understood) that 'to hear some people talk one is reminded of the situation described by St Paul when some said "I am for Apollos", some said "I am for Cephas" and some "I am for Paul" – or was it Powell?'

That evening Hogg was interviewed on television by David Frost. He made an emotional attack on Powell, saying his speeches had 'tended to alienate the party leadership from the rank and file', and that Powell had been foolish to use some of the phrases that he had. 'I think a person of his eminence – and he is very distinguished and eminent – ought to be very careful when making speeches.' Some of Powell's supporters were in the studio audience and turned on Hogg, saying he was ignoring the likelihood that the British race problem could become as bad as America's. Hogg's remarks, though, went to the heart of the leadership's fears about Powell. It seemed to some party managers, on the basis of both anecdotal evidence and more systematic surveys of opinion, that it was only the high command of the party, and various ingratiating young activists who hoped for candidacies, who were energetically supporting Heath at the time; the rest were for Powell. One ambitious younger man not tarred with this brush, though, was Geoffrey Howe. Reviewing Peter Utley's book on Powell, Howe praised him for his determination to attack the Conservative party's obsession with the 'middle way'. Howe, who had lost his seat in 1966 but would be back in 1970, was prepared to be more supportive of Powell than any of the other future Thatcherites. 'Surely,' he wrote, 'most Conservatives now share Powell's overwhelming conviction that the Tory party – which sometimes in its history has emphasised authority – must now emphasise liberty. In our present economic state the case for the free market cannot be too often or too clearly stated.'[88]

Naturally, the faction-fighting was a gift to Labour, which itself had not had the best of years. Wilson, addressing his own conference on 1 October, attacked what he called 'the virus of Powellism'. Powell had an instant response. 'Yes, I am a virus. I am the virus that kills socialists.'[89] Powell's opponents inside and outside his party consoled themselves with one thought above all: however much Powell tried, with some degree of success, to shift the agenda away from immigration, his ideas on the paramountcy of free will in a market economy were beyond the comprehension of most of his supporters. They had come to him over immigration, and that was why they stayed with him; and it also explained why many Conservative activists, despite their infatuation with Powell, remained slavishly loyal to the party's leadership.

Heath, aware he had a fight on his hands not just with Labour but with the Powellites, went on television the Monday before his conference to give an interview to Robin Day on *Panorama*. Day challenged Heath with the notion that the party's own policies were not a patch on Powell's. 'Mr Powell has put forward his own ideas from time to time,' Heath replied dismissively. Asked whether he ought to have Powell back in the shadow cabinet, Heath outlined what he termed Powell's 'sins': disagreements with the party line on East of Suez, immigration, regional policy, floating the pound – it was a long list. 'I don't think Mr Powell would want to rejoin,' said Heath.[90]

As the conference started on 9 October the chairman, Sir Theo Constantine, announced that Powell would be called to speak in the debate on immigration, and had asked for no favours: he would have the same five minutes as any speaker from the floor. Powell and his wife arrived, having to push their way through a throng of sightseers to get in. Attempting to keep a low profile, he went to sit in a relatively dark corner of the hall, where he was greeted by the sight and sound of Anthony Barber, the party chairman, loyally knocking Powell's policy of withdrawing from East of Suez.

It was on the second day of the conference that Powell spoke. His supporters were much in evidence in the Winter Gardens and cheered whenever any of the preceding speakers mentioned Powell's name. They had given a rough ride to Stephen Milligan, an Oxford undergraduate who would become an MP before dying in unfortunate circumstances after less than two years in the House. Milligan had been jeered for urging his audience 'not to degenerate into emotional hysteria' in response to his call for them to go forth and spread 'the gospel of the multi-racial society'. He said that, were the party to move further to the right on immigration, he and others like him would be tempted to follow the path of Humphry Berkeley, who had resigned from the party over the issue earlier that year. Milligan drew some applause for these remarks, but also a storm of booing as he left the rostrum, which transmogrified into a rapturous clamour for Powell as he approached the microphone – though the few that did not join in the clamour added an undercurrent of boos.

The platform party made a point of looking studiedly unconcerned, or, in Heath's case as captured by the television cameras, somewhat uncomfortable. The atmosphere, according to Richard Ritchie (who would later become Powell's archivist and close friend), who was present, was 'electric'.[91] Ritchie had seen Powell at a reception the previous evening and remembered his being 'in a really good mood', buoyed up by the excitement of the attention he was receiving. Once the tumult had subsided, Powell – who, in good Conservative conference style, had indicated he was speaking in support of the motion – delivered a measured speech about the effects of mass immigration. 'We deceive ourselves if we imagine, whatever steps are taken to limit future immigration, that this country will still not be facing a prospect which is unacceptable.'[92]

When he spelt out that the immigrant community, even if it were only 4 or 5 per cent of the population, would be in concentrated communities he was greeted (in the words of the *Daily Telegraph*'s correspondent) by 'immediate and loud cheers'. As a result, 'the character of England itself will be changed and changed in a way which its people neither chose nor expected nor desired'. To further cheers he proclaimed that, whatever the previous speaker had wanted, Britons did not want to live in a multi-racial society. The only sensible solution, he said, was to pursue a humane policy of assisted repatriation and resettlement, such as adopted by Douglas-Home when he had led the party. Powell concluded that 'to proclaim that policy and, when we have the opportunity, to put it into effect with generosity, with humanity, with determination and hope is a duty which we owe to all, white and coloured. Too often today people are ready to tell us: "This is not possible, that is not possible." I say: whatever the true interest of our country calls for is always possible. We have nothing to fear but our own doubts.' He was rewarded with another prolonged ovation, the stamping of feet almost masking renewed booing from his opponents.

Hogg, given the temper of his audience, was not lacking in courage when he replied to the debate. He told colleagues during that week that he was convinced Powell would prove a great danger to the party, and he was determined to do what he could to fight that danger.[93] Without setting out any new policies, he urged the Government to see that the problem of those from independent Commonwealth nations who came and settled permanently, without restriction, was a problem that had to be addressed. Hogg was given a fair hearing; he relied on, and was not disappointed by, the traditional loyalty and good manners of his party. He helped himself by stressing that Britain was not an under-populated country, and had a right to erect a fence around herself to protect her standard of living; and that independent Commonwealth countries should realise that Britain was entitled to independence too.

He did not mention Powell until the very end, when he said he wished to offer 'just one word to Enoch', on the point that nothing in the interests of Britain was impossible. 'I agree,' said Hogg, 'but exactly what significant numerical contribution to the problem does he expect from the policy of repatriation to which he is committed and to which we are committed? He did not tell us. But he deceives himself if he thinks that the kind of demographic situation that he was discussing will be significantly altered, though it may be ameliorated by a policy of repatriation. That is if he means, as I assume he means, a policy of voluntary repatriation and not compulsory repatriation.'

Having cast this innuendo, whose import was contradicted by everything Powell had said, Hogg turned his argument directly *ad hominem*, and, typically, did so in a way that trumpeted his own erudition:

> He and I like to think of ourselves, I hope justly, as men of integrity, courage and principle. He and I have been brought up and nourished on the ancient philosophy of Europe enshrined in the Greek and Latin literature, now alas almost forgotten studies in our modern age. Let him remind himself of one principle which has come down to us from ancient times, a gem of perennial wisdom uttered by the Greeks before the coming of the Christians: 'Meden agan'. Do not be an extremist – moderation in all things. Moderation is the hallmark of our country, and the guerdon of our Conservative faith.

He, like all other shadow cabinet members who spoke that week, received a standing ovation. The motion, like all others that week, was carried by an overwhelming majority. Yet it was Powell around whom the journalists crowded at the end of the debate – not least, one recalled, to check the spelling of Hogg's Greek quotation.

Hogg's point about the limits that might be expected of a programme of voluntary repatriation was well taken by the press, a sign of the recognition of the huge numbers that were contributing to the problem. Nonetheless, the *Daily Telegraph*, whose political correspondent Harry Boyne had been one of Heath's most devoted supporters, still said of Powell in a leading article the next morning that 'his proper place is in the shadow cabinet'. That, though, was the last thing Heath intended; and, as if to make certain of his disfavour, Powell chose to upstage his leader by making a controversial and radical speech on the economy the night before Heath's keynote address to the conference. Thus when the newspapers, that Saturday morning, should have been trailing Heath's rallying message, he once more found himself shunted off the front pages by reports of yet another direct challenge to his authority by Powell.

The thesis of what would become known as the 'Morecambe Budget' was that income tax could be cut from 8s 3d to 4s 3d in the pound, or a basic rate reduction from 41 to 21 per cent. Capital gains tax and selective employment tax would go too. Although the timing did not help Heath, it was greeted with glee by many of his supporters, who felt Powell had exposed himself to derision by suggesting so large a cut in direct taxation – a cut almost as large, in fact, as that made by successive Conservative governments after 1979. Powell's opening remarks in Morecambe picked up the climax of his speech to the conference itself: 'The trouble with this nation is that we have been brainwashed for years into believing that "it can't be done".'[94] Before, he had tried to argue that easing the problems of immigration was not impossible; now he applied the same doctrine to massive cuts in public spending, the abolition of numerous state agencies and the denationalisation of industry, all of which would enable a massive tax cut.

Powell argued that the public simply had to reject the notion that there was nothing that could be done about high taxation. He quickly came to attack his own party: only the previous day the conference 'chose to debate not reduction of taxation – oh dear, no; nothing so wild and irresponsible as that – but taking a bit of taxation off some people and putting it on to other people'.[95] He recalled that, after falling as a proportion of national income until the time of his resignation from the Treasury in 1958, public expenditure under the Conservatives rose again, so that by 1964 it was at the same level as when Labour went out in 1951. 'It begins to look', he said, 'as if there were some law of nature behind it all and that one might as well try to eliminate gravitation as reduce taxation.' Such a mentality was 'the perfect breeding ground for socialism'.

He asserted, in advance, that some of the cuts he wanted to make would not be painless: 'but if you are going to get big results, you must take big decisions'.[96] To make all his tax cuts required a saving of £2,855 million. As well as selling off the nationalised industries, and saving their running costs, he proposed to end the system of investment grants and assistance to development areas that were a central part of the state's regional policy. All the apparatus of the corporate state – the NEDC, its offshoots, the Prices and Incomes Board and other corporations whose job was to intervene in the private sector – would go too. Agricultural subsidies would be slashed, overseas aid abolished, housing subsidies ended and responsibility for housing entirely transferred to the private sector. All this, and the sacking of civil servants who would no longer have anything to do, would, he argued, save far more than his £2,855 million.

He argued, too, that the great reduction in taxation would enable the Government to borrow from the public again for capital projects in the essential services, like hospitals and roads. So highly taxed had the nation been that raising funds in this way had been nearly impossible in recent years. He drew attention to the fact that he was not cutting a penny from the social services – he did not count housing subsidy as a social service, because of its indiscriminate nature, and promised that his reforms would allow for a system of housing benefit to assist those genuinely too poor to afford to finance their own housing. Although his aim was to reduce the size of the state, he accepted that there were things only the state could do, and which it should have more resources in order to do properly. Reminding his audience that he had always been liberal on matters of penal policy, he argued that the firm and humane treatment of criminals could not be provided by services that were 'scandalously under-nourished', and that they were undernourished because the state chose, instead, to spend its money fouling up private enterprise.[97]

It could, he said, be different if only the nation had the will make it different. Almost immediately, Powell came under a deluge of execration from econ-omists, a typical headline being the *Observer*'s 'why Enoch's budget is such utter rubbish'.[98] In the article under the headline Alan Day, a professor of economics at London University, said Powell's views reflected 'astonishing depths of economic stupidity'. Day's main charge against Powell was that, by undertaking denationalisation, the transfer of so much economic activity into the private sector, and a tax cut, would cause 'unmanageable inflation'. Defending himself against this and similar attacks, Powell merely pointed out that the new demand created in the private sector would replace that no longer occurring in the public; and there would be no inflation unless the money supply were, coincidentally, expanded.

In his end-of-conference speech the leader, without mentioning Powell by name, repudiated the central Powellite doctrines on taxation, defence and econ-omics, and rejected the growing right-wing call for compulsory repatriation, which was interpreted as another snub to Powell even though this was not a policy Powell supported. Heath was uncompromising. 'At the end of the day,' he told the conference, 'it is upon me personally as your elected leader that the responsibility for policy rests. I accept that responsibility in full.' Heath also attacked Powell's notion of ending regional policy, said that housing subsidies had 'a vital part to play in helping with the housing of the unfortunate members of the community', and reiterated his party's determination to allow Britain 'to honour our obligations and to defend our interests' East of Suez.[99]

Heath received a seven-minute ovation from his audience, but commentators at Blackpool estimated that two-thirds of the representatives had been sup-porters of Powell. That Heath, who had made an impressive speech, attracted such support as he did was attributed to the desire of the party to avoid another leadership battle before the general election. Powell, though, let it be known that he was not seeking the leadership, but simply wanted the party to adopt his policies. As he put it in a radio interview, 'I plead guilty to wishing to influence the way in which the Conservative party moves and is led.'[100] By the end of the conference, though, there seemed little doubt that if there were a battle for the succession Powell would be powerfully placed to participate in it.

Heath's supporters may have found the thesis of Powell's Morecambe speech beyond their imagination, but they recognised, too, that Powell, for all the power of his logic, exerted a largely emotional appeal over the rank and file; and such an appeal would be all the more difficult to counter. In a perceptive analysis of the week's events Peregrine Worsthorne wrote that 'it is fairly clear that, barring some unforeseeable upheaval, Enoch Powell cannot capture the Conservative party leadership. But it is equally clear that, barring a miracle – such as Mr Powell being struck dumb – the leadership is going to have to follow in his wake ... Mr Heath will certainly stay put in the saddle, but Powellism will go galloping on.'[101] The massive display of support for Powell at Blackpool, however emotionally driven, had reflected his real strength in the party. It could not be explained away as an act of loyalty by the representatives, as the support for so many ministers could. The road to Heath's ill-fated Selsdon experiment, in which the party would be taken temporarily and unconvincingly to the right, was now mapped out. For all the disdain with which he and his associates had treated Powellism, Powellism would have to be part of the blueprint for the next election. Worsthorne categorised Powellism as 'National Capitalism – that is to say, capitalism made palatable to the people by mixing it up in the popular mind with national regeneration.' There was nothing Heath could do to counter such a phenomenon.

Worsthorne also suggested that Powell had re-established his credentials on the Thursday as a heroic figure to the working classes before, on the Friday, offering up an economic programme that envisaged the sort of cuts in state provision that the working-class electorate would, otherwise, find entirely inimical. There had been an echo of his conference peroration in his Morecambe speech: 'We are surrounded all day long by the great throng of those who lecture us on what we cannot do, until in the end John Bull is replaced as the national type by Mr Can't ... only that is impossible which you have not the will to do.' Powell, through an appeal to nationalism and patriotism, seemed to have found a way of making naked capitalism attractive to the mass electorate. For Heath and his friends, this was a terrifying prospect, whereas it should have been seen (as Mrs Thatcher would see it) as a unique opportunity.

V

Yet, immediately after the conference, Powell was on the road again wishfully, or mischievously, proclaiming that his party was undergoing precisely the shift in attitudes he had been advocating. At Welwyn on 18 October, addressing Young Conservatives, he said that 'gone, one hopes never to be exhumed, is the sterile, stay-put phrase "We shall call a halt to nationalisation." In its place are now different and dynamic formulae. If they discount none of the real obstacles, they at any rate imply the general aim of reconverting to private enterprise, competitive management and the capital market this whole, great sector of our economy which nationalisation has withdrawn into isolation.'[102] His evidence for this was his party's treatment in the Commons that week of the Transport

Bill, in which spokesmen had said that the nationalisation of the peripheral trappings of the state railway – coachbuilding, hotels, land development and travel agencies – would not be acceptable to Conservatives. The party would take them away from the nationalised industry, even though they were the sort of functions into which a private railway company would have diversified. This implicit recognition of the need to move away from, rather than simply stop, nationalisation gave Powell great heart.

The new university term being under way, Powell began a programme of visits to student bodies, and met demonstrations of predictable ferocity. At Exeter on 23 October he was howled down; at Reading two days later he was heckled by some in an audience of about 500 students, but managed to keep his composure despite dropping his portable microphone and knocking his watch off a lectern to the ground, where it shattered. He defended his Birmingham speech, saying that 'maybe in the long run it will be found to have done no harm and much good', and, according to press reports, received more cheers than boos when he finished. He took questions, and the meeting ended in a good-natured spirit, despite his maintaining that if the tide of immigrants continued 'I fear it will be impossible for them to be integrated.'[103]

From there Powell moved on to Cambridge, where his appearance had been the subject of controversy for weeks. At the same time – the afternoon of Sunday 27 October – a big anti-Vietnam War demonstration was scheduled for London, and left-wing groups at Cambridge were faced with an interesting choice about where to demonstrate. The Cambridge University Conservative Association, Powell's hosts, initially could find no building prepared to have the meeting because of fears of damage to the fabric and injuries to staff. They had hoped the Mill Lane lecture rooms, which were due to be demolished, could be used, but the police ruled against that. The police's favoured location was the Union Society, but as it was a private building, not a University one, CUCA would be left with a bill for any damage, and they might not have had the funds to meet it. The Union's president, Ken Jarrold, said Powell was welcome there. 'We feel that whatever happens to the building we have a duty to allow the meeting to take place here.'[104] As usual, the University authorities were less concerned about maintaining the principle of free speech in the face of self-important posturings by potentially violent students. However, CUCA settled on the Union.

A crowd of 500 demonstrators awaited Powell, with all five entrances to the building guarded by police and stewards. Just after four o'clock loud applause erupted from inside the building; to the demonstrators' fury, Powell had been smuggled in earlier. When a black car sped up to the rear entrance of the building 300 or so demonstrators rushed to meet it, only to find it did not contain Powell. Inside, Powell spoke for forty minutes on the relationship between the state and the individual and was given a lengthy standing ovation when he finished. The questions from the audience were mainly about immigration; Powell stayed in the building until 7.15 p.m., leaving under escort of a dozen policemen to a waiting car. Despite roving with megaphones to try to marshal their troops, the organisers of the demonstration failed to trap Powell into a confrontation. It was, though, the only occasion in all the demonstrations against him that Pam Powell was to admit to feeling worried about his safety.

The next week he went, on the same day, to Bath and Cardiff universities to be met, again, by demonstrations. Bath went relatively quietly, Powell commenting: 'It was a very good meeting. If we were ever to get into a position in which public meetings could not be held and disturbance was general we would be on a very slippery slope indeed.'[105] Cardiff, later in the evening, was a rougher ride. There was a walkout by eighty students, mainly African and Asian, when Powell began his speech, though around 1,000 stayed to listen while 500 stood outside. A few in the hall hoisted banners proclaiming 'We are all foreign scum' and 'Some of my best friends are foreign scum'. After the walkout, Powell was heard in relative silence; boos and jeers turned to cheers and, eventually, good humour. When the ritual shouts of 'Fascist' and 'Nazi' went up Powell countered: 'I hope those who shouted "Fascist" and "Nazi" are aware that before they were born I was fighting against Fascism and Nazism.' When he tried to leave, the lane down which his car was travelling was blocked by students sitting down and linking arms; the police put him in a BBC Land Rover further on that drove him away, evading the protest. Earlier that week, at Orpington, demonstrators had tried to throw themselves in front of his car after an otherwise peaceful meeting had ended with a group of them shouting, 'Black and white unite and fight.'[106]

Powell may have become one of the most celebrated men of his day in the preceding months, but his adherence to principle caused a blow to his personal finances that autumn. After nearly five years on the board of the National Discount Company, he resigned on 3 November following the board's decision to comply with the Prices and Incomes Board's inquiry into the pay of top executives, in accordance with the stated policy of the CBI. Powell told Lord McCorquodale, National Discount's chairman, that his position would be 'impossible politically' if he stayed after the company had taken such a move, given his position on the PIB and its operations.[107] The decision cost him £2,000 a year, which he strove to make up by more journalism and broadcasting.

With the publication of the Bills for the new session of Parliament, Powell found himself provoked by Heath further than ever before. The Conservative leader had said he would accept the Government's plans to reform the Lords, a notion that incensed Powell for its complete contradiction of what he understood by Conservative principles. The plan had been drawn up in collusion between Macleod and Richard Crossman, so Heath was always going to favour it; and the idea of expanding the patronage he hoped to enjoy as Prime Minister will also have appealed. Powell argued that only a hereditary House of Lords could be effective as a revising chamber, because only it could have the authority to exercise delaying powers over the Commons. Such a chamber could not be one that 'Harold Wilson, Ted Heath and Jeremy Thorpe made, not a chamber that Harold Wilson and Harold Macmillan made'.[108] Across the floor of the Commons the very plans that so enraged Powell – the elimination of the rights of hereditary peers to vote, and the creation instead of a smaller chamber in which the government of the day would normally have a majority – equally incensed Michael Foot, tribune of Labour's left, who felt they betrayed what should have been his party's principles too. Only complete abolition would suffice for him.

Thus were Powell and Foot drawn together, from their polar opposites, in the fight against the Bill. Foot had criticised him strongly for the Birmingham speech, but had never doubted the truth of Powell's statement that he had not, in making the speech, been motivated by racial prejudice. Powell was an unqualified admirer of Foot's; indeed, he had said he admired him more than anyone else in the Commons. 'I suspect he likes me too,' he had told an interviewer a few months earlier, 'for we have many similarities. I admire Michael Foot because he speaks beautiful English. He is through and through devoted to the House of Commons. I think he has the same combination that I have of logic and passion.'[109]

Powell revealed his intentions in the Commons on 14 November, asking Fred Peart, the Leader of the House, to consider the argument against Lords reform being debated in both Houses simultaneously. The Commons debate was set for the following Tuesday, five days later; but, before joining battle on that issue, Powell returned, with a typical lack of repentance, to immigration. In a lengthy and detailed speech to the Rotary Club at Eastbourne on 16 November, he referred back to the Birmingham speech, noting that in the seven months since he made it 'I have been the target of endless abuse and vilification. No imputation or innuendo has been too vile or scurrilous for supposedly reputable journals to invent or repeat.'[110] He also noted the 'astonishing manifestation, from among all classes of people and from all the areas of the community, expressing relief and gratitude that the speech was made'. Nonetheless, apart from his five-minute intervention at the party conference, and replies to questioners after speeches, Powell had made no further mention of the subject: until now. He felt the Rotary Club provided an appropriate platform, being a non-party organisation and existing solely to further the public interest. He also made sure to trail the speech well in advance to selected lobby correspondents, and tipped off Bill Deedes, a former cabinet colleague and regular contributor to the *Daily Telegraph*'s Peterborough column. Since the events of the previous April, Powell had learned more about press management than most of his colleagues grasped in a lifetime.

He said he wished to discuss the future rather than the past, though asked for one moment of indulgence to defend himself. He had been accused of disloyalty to his party line and to colleagues, particularly Hogg, but said that 'there is no substance in this charge. No rule or convention forbids front benchers to advocate or defend, even before parliamentary debate, the line which the leadership of the party has publicly decided to take. There is none which requires them before doing so to consult or even inform their colleagues. Such speeches are continually made and indeed expected.' Powell reiterated that he had stuck to the party line and broken no rules; he had merely offended taste, and threw in, in the original Latin, *de gustibus non est disputandum*; 'and a leader is entitled to be guided by his own taste in the choice of his colleagues'.

He talked of the gulf he had witnessed, not between black and white – 'On the contrary, over the months and years the pressure upon me to oppose the growth in the number of immigrants has come as much from my immigrant constituents as from the rest, if not more so' – nor between those with direct experience of mass immigration and those without, but between 'the over-whelming majority of people throughout the country on the one side, and on the other side a tiny minority, with almost a monopoly hold on the channels of communication, who seemed determined not to know the facts and not to face the realities and who will resort to any device or extremity to blind both themselves and others'. He cited as evidence the fact that when the chairman of the Wolverhampton Education Committee had confirmed his story about the one white child in a class no one wanted to report it until well after the event, and Roy Jenkins had branded him a liar when all he had to do was pick up the telephone to ascertain the facts. Now 'the very newspapers which had attacked me had the ignominy of having to report the existence not only in Wol-verhampton but in Birmingham of such classes . . . so quickly does the incredible turn into what everybody knew all the time'.

Powell amplified his claim, made at Birmingham, that the Race Relations Bill had been a measure of reverse discrimination, leaving the Briton feeling himself 'the toad beneath the harrow'; and he recalled his mention of the old lady, and the assertion that as no one had been able to find her he must have been inventing the story. He still refused to betray the confidence in which his correspondent had written to him, but said that 'as I have been traduced and defamed, I will select one out of the numerous witnesses who wrote and offered me their own evidence for the truth and typicality of what I described. It is, I repeat, not something rare, not something abnormal, but something which is part of the daily life and experience of fellow countrymen of ours who happen to be less fortunately situated than Mr Rees-Mogg or Mr Bernard Levin.'

He chose a letter written to him by Dr W. E. Bamford of Wandsworth, who described visiting a woman patient of eighty-four living on the second floor of a house owned by an immigrant landlord, and said the police had to provide him with an escort each time he visited her. Because the landlord wanted her out he had engaged in a campaign of intimidation which had led to the old lady begging, successfully, to be put in a residential home. Bamford outlined other acts of intimidation perpetrated upon another elderly woman, on a young couple and on a widow with two children.

Powell said he did not dispute that there were foul British landlords too. He had never implied that immigrants were worse in this respect; that was not his point. We had to deal with malefactors who were part of our own society, but 'it is something totally different when the same or similar activities are perpetrated by strangers, and above all when they occur in the course of an increase in the number of those strangers and an extension of the areas which they occupy – an increase and an extension to which the victims perceive no end in sight. Surely only very clever people could fail to understand so simple a point.'

It was not, he repeated, a question of not treating people equally before the law irrespective of their colour; it was a question of numbers. He repeated the statistics, and the point that no one had been consulted: 'the people of Britain are faced with a *fait accompli* . . . all sorts of excuses are invented and we are told in terms of arrogant moral superiority that we have got a "multi-racial society" and had better like it'. So tolerant were the English, he reasoned, that if the present numbers were all the problem could probably be contained; but the present numbers were not all. Even if the immigration fell from the 1968 level of 60,000 by a steady rate to nil by 1985, that would still leave three million in Britain. Then there was the birthrate. Powell did not doubt that those who integrated into the host community would adopt the birthrate of the host community. He did, though, warn that because sheer weight of numbers would make such integration impossible those immigrants would tend to live in their own communities, and have a higher birthrate: this had been indubitably the case in Wolverhampton. The immigrant community there, which was 5.13 per cent of the population, accounted for 23 per cent of the live births: 'and before anyone calls me a liar, I might mention that the figures are those of the borough Medical Officer of Health and may be found reprinted, among other places, in *The Lancet* for 26 October'. Even if the birthrate fell after 1985, on the lowest estimates there would be an immigrant-descended population of four and a half million by 2002. So Powell stuck to his earlier estimate of between five and seven millions for that community by 2000; and it would not be spread evenly across the country.

So far, his speech had been almost entirely factual. As he neared its end, he ventured into the philosophical, and seemed to re-adopt the 'tone' of seven months earlier that had not been to everyone's taste. 'My judgment then is this: the people of England will not endure it. If so, it is idle to argue whether they ought to or ought not to. I do not believe it is in the human nature that a country, and a country such as ours, should passively watch the transformation of whole areas which lie at the heart of it into alien territory.' He returned to his two earlier solutions: that immigration from the New Commonwealth should virtually cease – 'I say "virtually cease", because of course no-one would wish an absolute veto on the settlement of individual Afro-Asians in this country in future, any more than of other aliens' – including a ban on the settlement of dependants of existing immigrants. As he had said at Birmingham, there were two ways in which a family could be reunited.

The second solution, leading on from this, was the voluntary, assisted repatriation that was already party policy. Hogg, of course, had said such a policy would be inadequate and make little difference. Powell disagreed. 'I believe that ignorance of the realities of Commonwealth immigration leads people seriously to underestimate the scope of the policy and thus to neglect and despise the chief key to the situation.' He said that, while individuals had uprooted themselves, there were many more cases in which it was more realistic to see the new communities as detachments from their communities back home, 'encamped in certain areas of England. They are still to a large extent a part, economically and socially, of the communities from which they have been detached and to which they regard themselves as belonging.' Thus voluntary repatriation, or re-emigration, was not the outlandish idea some had branded it; and a Ministry of Repatriation should be established to undertake this 'national duty'.

Time, though, was of the essence. The sense of belonging to their native community would diminish rapidly with time, and a new tragedy would overtake the immigrants:

> The West Indian or Asian does not, by being born in England, become an Englishman. In law he becomes a United Kingdom citizen by birth; in fact he is a West Indian or an Asian still. Unless he be one of the small minority [who had successfully integrated] ... he will by the very nature of things have lost one country without gaining another, lost one nationality without acquiring a new one. Time is running against us and them. With the lapse of a generation or so we shall at last have succeeded – to the benefit of nobody – in reproducing 'in England's green and pleasant land' the haunting tragedy of the United States.

He ended by echoing his conference speech: that seemingly insurmountable obstacles could be overcome, if the will were there.

Powell's decision to speak again caused further fury, not on the scale of the April explosion but with pockets of comparable intensity. Heath was swift to condemn him, arguing that the character assassination of a particular racial group led to 'tyranny and it must be fought wherever it raises its ugly presence. It had to be fought in Germany in the 1930s, in America in the 1950s. Wherever it happens today, it must be fought.'[111] The determination by the political establishment to keep facts suppressed was at odds with a speech that had had less emotion and more fact than that of 20 April. What Powell had said was a cause of grave discomfort, and Labour politicians acted immediately to put up a smokescreen. Renee Short, whose constituency adjoined his, asked Elwyn Jones whether, this time, a prosecution could be brought under the 1965 Race Relations Act. But, as before, the difficulty was proving Powell's intent. Powell had sent out the speech in advance to all Members of Parliament, helped by financial assistance from the Earl of Warwick, long an admirer, who was already meeting the costs of some of Powell's office staff. The purpose of this exercise had been 'to guard in advance, as far as possible, against distortion'.[112]

This time, Central Office had distributed the speech, and the Conservative high command was nervous lest any prosecution of Powell for uttering it might be matched with a prosecution of the party chairman for allowing Central Office to propagate it. Several complaints about Central Office putting out such a speech worried Tony Barber, the chairman. It is thought that Heath was one of those who complained to him.[113] Perhaps as a result of that, Barber wrote to Powell to say the usual practice was that, when the Central Office press department thought a passage in a speech might cause problems, they referred it to him. If Barber agreed he would suggest that the Member concerned might put the speech out through some medium other than Central Office, and this usually happened 'without embarrassment of any kind'. Barber said that, 'with someone as senior as yourself, it would be best, if possible, for you to consider whether it is appropriate for you to ask for a particular speech to be distributed through Central Office or for you to decide that it should be handled otherwise'.[114] Powell saw what Barber was trying to do, and telephoned him to say that his strictures were not, for the moment, applicable.

Wilson, answering a question in the Commons the following week, described Powell's proposals as 'utterly evil'; he was aware many Labour MPs wanted to see Powell prosecuted.[115] In response to a question from John Biggs-Davison, a supporter of Powell's, about the threat of violence from enemies of free speech against Powell, Wilson gave what seemed, at best, an equivocal reply: he claimed to be in favour of free speech but said he was 'not surprised that he [Powell] does provoke some reaction'. Wilson, ignoring Powell's ample protestations to the contrary, reiterated that he would not have people treated unequally before the law; and when he said 'no party in this House is going to let Mr Powell drag the politics of this country into the gutter', Heath, on the front bench opposite, nodded. Powell was not present to defend himself.

Outside Parliament, the liberal establishment was again mobilised. Mark Bonham Carter, who held an archiepiscopal post in that establishment as chairman of the Race Relations Board, condemned the speech as 'one long excuse'. He also found the tone distasteful though, this time, it was in his view a tone that was 'somewhat self-pitying and self-righteous. But it is just as prejudiced.'[116] In fact, Bonham Carter contradicted himself. The speech was open to the construction that it was self-pitying and self-righteous precisely because Powell had sought to defend himself by recourse to fact. It was hard that in the same breath he should be accused of prejudice. However, the speech confirmed Bonham Carter's supposition that Powell was racially prejudiced. 'It now seems clear that Mr Powell is the chief victim of his own preconceptions,' he asserted, 'and this is the most common characteristic of a prejudiced mind.' In Bonham Carter's eyes, Powell's principal offence was to quote evidence of racial harassment by blacks against whites, 'the evidence of single witnesses and particular cases from which he then proceeds to generalise'. Had Bonham Carter been able to read the tens of thousands of letters Powell had received since 20 April, accusing him of generalisation would have been something even one as anxious to exert censorship as Bonham Carter was would have hesitated to do. He attacked Powell for appearing to scale down his estimate of the immigrant population by 2002 by citing the figure of four and a half millions as the lowest number there was likely to be; though Bonham Carter was subject to the same erroneous Government-collected information as Powell, stating that there would be seventy million people in Britain by 2000 (the figure on the eve of the millennium is in fact nearer fifty-eight million). Bonham Carter assumed there would be a 'total coloured population' of 2,500,000. Powell said it would be at least 4,500,000 by 2002. An estimated figure for 1996 was 3,500,000.[117]

VI

It was Richard Crossman, Secretary of State for Social Services but architect of the plans for Lords reform, who opened the debate on it on 19 November. He defined the Government's five main aims: to eliminate the hereditary element, to prevent any one party having a permanent majority in the Upper House, to allow a government, in normal circumstances, to have a reasonable working majority there, to restrict the Lords' powers to delay public legislation, and to abolish the Lords' absolute power to withhold consent to subordinate legislation against the will of the Commons. He announced a formula for the composition of the House: 'If we assumed a total voting House of 230, the Government would have 105, the Opposition 80, the Liberals 15, and there would be about 30 cross-benchers, excluding those law lords and bishops with voting rights.'[118] This would be the root of much of the trouble the Government would have with the Bill. On the matter of the cross-benchers, Hugh Fraser, a Conservative MP, asked Crossman: 'Will the 30 be appointed as stooges of my Front Bench or of the Government Front Bench?'[119] In reply, Crossman played down the notion – advanced even more forcefully by his own colleagues than by Conservative MPs – that Prime Ministerial patronage over this new, unelected chamber would be deeply undesirable.

Maudling, for the Opposition, said the more he had thought about the proposals, 'the more difficult it is to find any better solution'.[120] He discounted the idea that abolition of the hereditary peerage would in any way compromise the hereditary basis of the monarchy. He did call for safeguards on patronage, but admitted he saw no viable alternative to a nominated house. All, in fact, the Opposition did take issue with was the timing of the implementation of the reforms, which it felt should be delayed until after the next election. From the moment the two opening speeches had been completed, it was clear the House was preparing to exercise its traditional scepticism, if not hostility, to any matter on which the two front benches agreed. It was Powell, the next speaker from the Conservative benches, who did this best of all.

He made one of his most brilliant speeches, exposing the absurdities of the proposals, and had even hard-line left-wing opponents of the measure – and, in normal circumstances, of him – laughing along with him. He began by calling the reform 'unnecessary and undesirable', and said there was no substance in the assertion that the Upper House, as it was constituted, 'can check or frustrate the firm intentions of this House'.[121] He pointed out that, if the present composition of the Lords by prescriptive right were to be altered, one of only two methods could replace it: election or nomination. In an elected system, the question would be which of the two chambers was truly representative of the electorate. No amount of rigging, he said, could remove the dilemma: which was 'how can the same electorate be represented in two ways so that the two sets of representatives can conflict and disagree with one another?'[122]

He then moved on to nomination, saying nominees would merely be 'the deposit not only of the last general election but of the last few general elections'; and they would have this life after political death because they had taken 'a sort of oath', binding them to the wishes of the Chief Whip of their nominating party – 'and what sort of men and women are they to be who would submit to be nominated to another chamber upon condition that they will be mere dummies, automatic parts of a voting machine?'[123] Powell called the notion of picking thirty cross-benchers 'a grand absurdity', saying such nominees would receive their posts 'upon the very basis that they have no strong views of principle on the way in which the country ought to be governed'.

He said it was better to describe the Lords as having 'prescriptive' rather than 'hereditary' authority, and conceded that there might be no case for it in its then form. He added, though, that it would be unwise for the Commons to sneer at the prescriptive institution. Alluding to the contradictions of the first-past-the-post system at general elections, in which an opposition could win more of the popular vote than the government did, Powell asked how MPs would answer the question: 'By what right do you so often install and support a government against whom a majority of the electorate have just voted at a general election?' And what, he asked, about the answer to the question: 'How comes it that you in this House continue to support a Government when you

With the infant Susan, put down for Eton before she was born, 1954

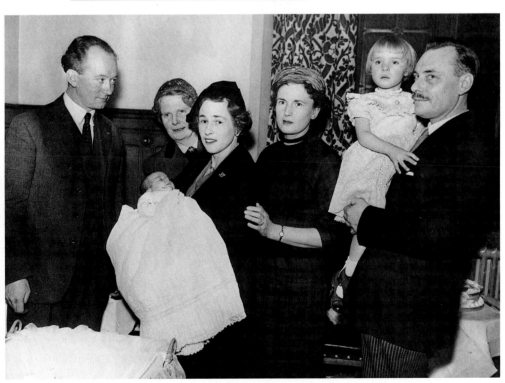

At Jennifer's Christening, 1956 with (left to right) Andrew Freeth, Barbara Brooke, Pamela Powell with Jennifer, Ursula Rodman, Susan Powell.

Financial Secretary, 1957

Minister of Health, 1961 with (left to right) Edith Pitt, Sir Bruce
Fraser, Sir George Godber

The Minister gives a practical demonstration of the benefits of exercise, 1962

A man who always did it himself, enlightening his daughters, 1962

With Pamela after refusing to serve Home, 1963

'Whatever the true interest of our country calls for is always possible.' Peter Walker, Sir Alec Douglas-Home, Reggie Maudling, Ted Heath, Quintin Hogg and Tony Barber listen unimpressed: Blackpool, 1968

Selwyn Lloyd bestows a
benediction, c. 1964

A target for satire, 1968

The politician, by
Freeth, 1966

In the saddle with Susan and Jennifer, 1970

With some friends in Wolverhampton, 1973

Left: A prophet in a pulpit, 1969

'Judas was paid! Judas was paid! I am making a sacrifice!' Saltaire, 1974

are morally sure that the majority of those who put them into power would no longer do so if they had the opportunity?' He said that 'our reply to such questions can only be: "It has long been so, and it works." Prescription is just as much the basis of the authority of this particular House, the House of Commons in this Kingdom, constituted as it is, as it is the basis of the authority of the other place, constituted as it is.'[124]

There was, he said, no provocation at all for the Commons to prepare itself to spend so much time in this session on Lords reform: the Lords was not holding up Government business or imperilling the national good, and there was no 'widespread public indignation' that led for calls for reform. Indeed, he quoted a recent survey of working-class voters showing that only a third of them favoured reforming or abolishing the Lords, while another third felt it an intrinsic part of the national traditions of Britain. 'As so often,' Powell commented, 'the ordinary rank and file of the electorate have seen a truth, an important fact, which has escaped so many more clever people – the underlying value of that which is traditional, that which is prescriptive.'[125] His conclusion on the reform was categorical: 'we ought not to do it'.[126]

For all the approval voiced from the Labour benches of what he had said, he found the immigration issue suddenly intruding. The moment he sat down Willie Hamilton, a deputy chairman of the parliamentary Labour party, rose to move an amendment. He observed, sarcastically and to cheers from his own side, how glad he was to see Powell speaking in the House for a change. He hoped he might come and speak on certain other matters there too one day (Powell had been silent in the House on immigration ever since Birmingham). Hamilton said it might interest Powell to know that some, like him, who opposed the Government's plans were dubious about going into the division lobby against them in case it was 'soiled' by the presence of Powell. This raised a few protests from the Conservative side. Andrew Faulds, a West Midlands Labour MP, started yelling 'Coward!' at Powell, but was ordered to control himself by the Deputy Speaker. That done, the Deputy Speaker ordered Hamilton to withdraw his remark. Hamilton said he would, but he was merely reflecting the facts of the matter. Throughout, Powell sat still showing no trace of emotion.[127]

The decision by the Chair to call Hamilton's amendment posed great difficulties for the Government. Numerous backbenchers on both sides showed, in the course of the debate, how widespread was the irritation that the two front benches had joined together on plans for reform that included so large a boost to front-bench patronage. Hamilton had the support on his own side of Manny Shinwell, a former cabinet minister and ex-chairman of the parliamentary party, Walter Padley, another former minister, the Tribune group, and the right-wing Labour MP David Marquand. Whips on neither side had believed that the amendment would be called; as a result, Labour had imposed a one-line whip on what was originally a motion to take note of the proposals in the Government's White Paper, and the Conservatives no whip at all. Now, to force the issue, a three-line whip was imposed by both sides.

The following day Labour went for Powell again, demonstrating that the left on the backbenches appeared to have developed a policy of hounding him whenever he rose to speak. When he attempted to ask a question about the absurdity of fixed exchange rates, Faulds, an actor with a finely developed voice, once more roared 'Nice to see you back.'[128] The Speaker told him to control himself, but, as Powell carried on, Faulds shouted out, 'Pariah! Pariah!' One of his colleagues, presumably addressing Powell, yelled, 'Monster!'[129] The main effect was to rally support from the Conservatives, many of whom had been cool or even downright hostile to Powell since 20 April. A group of them, led by Sir Charles Taylor, the MP for Eastbourne, amended an early day motion signed by 140 Labour MPs condemning Powell's Eastbourne speech to call for the upholding of an MP's right to express his views freely and publicly 'however many people may find them objectionable'.

In his constituency, Powell never received less than complete support from Conservatives. Julian Dallow, his association chairman, defended him against the clamour caused by his Eastbourne speech. 'The gulf', said Mr Dallow, 'is not between white and coloured but between politicians and people.' He emphasised it was objections not to immigrants themselves, but to such large concentrations of them, that was causing the problem, and he addressed himself directly to Heath and Hogg: 'Stop blaming Enoch Powell for having the courage to state the facts as he saw them.'[130] On 24 November fifty members of the Young Communist League marched to South Eaton Place and stood outside Powell's house chanting, 'We want you, Enoch.' To their astonishment he went outside to greet the four leaders of the group with a 'Good morning, gentlemen.'[131]

He was handed a beautifully illuminated scroll, bearing the fictitious first decree of his 'Ministry of Repatriation'. It decreed that his ideas be sent back 'to their spiritual home, which was Nazi Germany, and is now in South Africa'. Accepting the scroll, Powell said, 'Thank you very much. It's very nicely done.' His petitioners told him, in case he had missed the point, that his ideas were evil. He told them, 'The only way to refute that which is unreasonable is by reason.' They replied, 'The Jews could reason with the Gestapo, but it didn't stop them being killed.' Powell thanked them for their courtesy, and went back in. As a farewell gift, they draped a swastika flag on the railings outside. Powell was less tolerant that week of remarks made by Mervyn Charles-Edwards, the Bishop of Worcester, who in a diocesan newspaper had said Jesus Christ was 'a dark-skinned Palestinian. No doubt if he grew up here, a certain politician would like him to be expelled from England.' In a letter, Powell told the Bishop, 'These words are false as well as blasphemous. I have at no time proposed that anyone should be expelled from England. It would be bad enough for a layman to be guilty of this imputation, for a priest and a bishop it is scandalous.'[132]

The following day he had to endure an attack from much closer to home. At the weekly One Nation dinner, after a discussion of whether or not the pound should float, Geoffrey Rippon, who had succeeded Powell as defence spokesman, 'launched a vicious attack on Powell for a flagrant breach of honour with his shadow cabinet colleagues' over the Birmingham speech.[133] The words are those of Tony Royle, a Whip who sent an account of the meeting to Whitelaw the following day. More remarkably, Royle claimed in his note that Powell – who 'was shaken and confessed that he had no idea that the shadow colleagues felt he had betrayed them' – was 'pinned down' by James Ramsden, who extracted from him 'for the second time at a One Nation dinner that he favoured compulsory repatriation'.

If this happened as Royle reported, it would have been sensational. Powell never, at any time before or afterwards, advocated compulsory repatriation. Although many at this private meeting have since died, Ramsden, fortunately, is still alive. In a letter to me in April 1998 he denied any knowledge of having pinned Powell down – 'pinning people down is not the sort of way I go about things ... what I am quite sure of is that a kind of boat people compulsory operation never for a moment entered my head, nor I should have thought Enoch's either' – or of Powell having said what he was reported to have said. Ramsden thinks it might have been a misunderstanding, or even Royle's seeking to curry favour on Ramsden's behalf with the leadership by depicting him as a persecutor of their hated Powell. Heath had discovered that Ramsden had voted for Powell in 1965, and Ramsden was in some discredit as a result.[134] Ramsden also recalled telling Heath, who stayed with him in December 1968, 'Enoch is not a racist.' Heath replied, 'Of course he is a racist.'[135] Heath was used to being blunt with Ramsden about Powell. He had told him when Powell was still defence spokesman, that one of the papers he had circulated about defence and the need for it to be seen in a national and European context was 'Balls. Total and utter balls.'[136] To judge from Ramsden's memory of what really happened at that meeting, such a view could well apply to Royle's secret account of it, written as it was for a highly specialist audience.

At the end of that week Powell was a panellist on *Any Questions*, with the writers Auberon Waugh and Marghanita Laski, and Lord Wigg. As Colonel George Wigg he had been Jack Profumo's nemesis, and, as one of Wilson's leading toadies, one of the most unpopular men in the Commons. He was now fulfilling that function in the Lords, where his self-righteous pomposity would continue until pricked by his arrest for kerb-crawling. The programme was originally supposed to be broadcast from a factory near Oxford, but the management feared demonstrations and asked the BBC to go elsewhere. The ultimate venue, the concert hall at Broadcasting House, was kept secret until the time of transmission, and an audience was chosen from a cross-section of BBC audience research panels and from correspondents to *Any Answers*.

Almost the first half of the programme was dominated by immigration, with Powell using the opportunity to pay tribute to the British people for their 'tolerance' in the face of the massive wave of immigration. 'It does them enormous credit,' he added.[137] However he repeated his point that tolerance would break down unless the measures he had been advocating were taken. Wigg accused Powell of having ignored the immigration question until 1964, and of only dealing with it now in such inflammatory terms because he sensed that, electorally, he was 'on to a winner'. Powell interrupted him by saying 'you are talking as much rubbish now as you did when you were in the House of Commons'. He also denied that it was a question of skin colour: 'If the immigrants were Germans or Russians the problems would be as serious, and in some respects more serious, than with West Indians and Pakistanis.'

Slowly, a few senior Conservatives were putting their heads above the parapet to defend Powell, in defiance of the leadership. It was not a good time to do it, as Powell, in a *Panorama* documentary about his life on 2 December, acknowledged that he had stood for his party's leadership when there was last a vacancy and would reserve the right to do so when there was next one. Two who prominently endorsed him were former cabinet chiefs of his: Sandys, who put out a statement after the Eastbourne speech calling for a tightening of controls and more assistance for repatriation, and Thorneycroft, who, on a tour of Australia in December, said Powell was 'certainly not a racist. He is a very liberal-minded and humane man. I think he is right to draw attention to the scale of the problem. I do not think his is an emotional approach. It is an intellectual approach and very clear. His speech on the subject was not a racist speech on any ground.'[138] Probably the greatest triumph for Powell was when his fellow Wolverhampton MP, Renee Short, called on the floor of the Commons for a halt to the issuing of work vouchers for immigrants wishing to go to Wolverhampton. A fortnight earlier, Mrs Short had been calling for Powell to be prosecuted; now, she rebuked him for not having spoken on the issue before 1964, when the Conservative government was presiding over the immigration that had caused the problem. She said that fifteen to twenty children of school age were coming into her constituency each week. 'It is quite clear that we cannot really continue to take people into the Wolverhampton area, or, indeed, into the West Midlands, at this rate.'[139] In a poll of white adults commissioned by *Panorama* for their programme, 82 per cent thought there should be further controls on immigration, 74 per cent agreed with Powell's call for voluntary repatriation; however, 35 per cent thought repatriation should be compulsory, and 55 per cent thought Powell had worsened race relations. A survey of immigrants found that 38 per cent would like to return to their country of origin if given financial help, 47 per cent favoured more immigration controls (only 30 per cent did not) and only 8 per cent said they had been treated worse by white people since Powell's Birmingham speech.[140]

On 6 December Powell found a new point of confrontation with his own party. For the first time, Central Office refused to distribute one of his speeches: one to be made in his constituency, in which he called for the Government to admit that it could not coerce Rhodesia, and should acknowledge it as an independent republic. 'To recognise the fact is neither shame nor dishonour. It is a wise and manly act. We should be recognising that Rhodesia is an independent, albeit a foreign, country by successful rebellion.'[141] His party workers gave him a standing ovation for the speech, a contrast with his reception earlier the same day at the Wolverhampton College of Technology when a meeting in which he was taking part had to be abandoned after twenty minutes. Powell had a tomato, paper darts and streamers thrown at him, and a black man twice jumped on to the platform, once seizing the microphone.

The decision not to distribute the Rhodesia speech was taken by Barber, following consultations with Douglas-Home. The excuse was that the speech could prejudice the success of negotiations for a settlement. It little mattered. Powell, who by now had worked out how best to have the press do his work for him, distributed it separately to them, and its contents were therefore far more widely available than they would otherwise have been. Powell had already spoken to Douglas-Home, as the front-bench spokesman for external affairs, during the drafting of the speech, and had been advised not to take the line he did. Powell chose to ignore the advice, as he had every right to do. Central Office also had every right not to distribute the speech, but its decision was viewed with alarm in the party, and not just on the right, as an attempt to impose a new and ever more rigid orthodoxy on debate among backbenchers.

Douglas-Home, who had not thus far joined the front-benchers lining up to rebuke Powell, was provoked into doing so by this. Although as we shall see, Douglas-Home would later claim to sympathise with Powell's views, he had been saying privately that he deprecated the Birmingham speech; now his criticism became more public. In a speech in Glasgow on 7 December he referred to Powell's having done him the 'courtesy' of consulting him, and reiterated that 'I had hoped he would not find it necessary to proceed. I thought it much too early to conclude that the political position of Britain and Rhodesia were "irreconcilable" ... Mr Powell, by inviting Rhodesia to become a republic, does so because he claims to be a realist. I hope that Rhodesians will pause and recognise the harsh realities of their situation should they take his advice.' Those realities, according to Douglas-Home, were for Rhodesia to cease being a colony of Britain and to start, instead, to be one of South Africa.

Powell was becoming used to attempts by students to deny him a platform at universities – he had even been caused to abandon a visit to his old school in early December to talk about monetary policy because of a threat by students from other institutions to invade the meeting – and now had the unpleasant sensation of his own party seeking to suppress his views. What appalled him most of all, though – he admitted more than a quarter of a century later that 'it hurt me more than anything that has happened to me in my political life' – was a decision to censor him by Major-General Erskine Crum of the 4th Division of the Rhine Army.[142] Crum withdrew an invitation to Powell to lecture to his officers on 'Britain in the 1970s', something he had heard Powell speak on the previous year at the Imperial Defence College. Powell revealed the move in a speech at Thetford on 13 December, in which he said that the new joint fears of intolerance and violence had created a climate in which those who – like him – expressed strong views contrary to receive opinion 'can now with impunity and even with approval be silenced and insulted'.[143] He read out the letter Crum had written to him, after reading reports of the Eastbourne speech, in which he said that 'from this distant and ill-informed viewpoint, your speech yesterday will be so likely to connect you primarily in some quarters with race relations problems that your attendance in a speaking capacity at an official Army study period may be open to misinterpretation; particularly because it is important, in my belief, that this topic should not become controversial within the Army. I must make it clear that the withdrawal of my invitation is my personal decision.'

Powell was furious. 'On the fitness for active command of officers who take decisions from "distant and ill-informed viewpoints" when there is ample time for mature thought and information, I will not comment,' he said. He had delayed publicising this matter because he had written to Crum inviting him to reconsider. Then Powell had received a letter from Healey, the Defence Secretary, saying that while the decision had been Crum's, he fully supported it. 'We have, therefore,' Powell continued,

> got to the point where in the British Army a Member of Parliament and Privy Counsellor, holding Her Majesty's commission, is banned from a private engage-ment to address a division study period because of the light in which his public statements on a particular topic of public controversy have been widely rep-resented. You will notice that the general did not even seek to exclude that particular topic from anything I might propose to say. No, I had *ipso facto* become unacceptable, and that was that. And that, in the view also of Her Majesty's Government, was that. It is that aspect which relates the individual case to the common danger. If intolerance is publicly approved and supported in one case, so will it be in others.

He warned that the government of a free country could not wash its hands of responsibility for free speech, and nor could individual members of the public. He also used the opportunity to rail against the heads of universities, who had allowed the campaigns against him, and against freedom of speech, in the preceding months. 'The first duty of the institutions was the maintenance of internal order, since on that everything else must depend. Whatever the excuses and explanations may be, the heads of the universities and colleges which have been characterised by disorder have fallen down on the most basic part of their job: they have no business to be in charge of institutions provided wholly or mainly by the public unless they can render at least that account of their stewardship. By any standards, the performance of some of them has been deplorable, and several are clearly unfit for their posts.'

VII

Whatever the difficulties, Powell maintained his policy of confronting opinion critical to him. He as still attracting massive coverage in the media, and editors had used the thin days over the 1968 Christmas break to look back at the effect he had had on politics in the year ending. Typical of these assessments was one by the academic John Vincent in the *Listener*, where he wrote: 'What Mr Powell has done is not to create right-wing opinion, but to make it matter.'[144] Perceptively, Vincent spotted that Powell had turned the tide in Conservatism, and – although the domination of the party by the centre-left was to have its most historically serious consequences in the five years ahead – that the right were on their way to significance. Vincent said that 'what Mr Powell has added is that force of soul which turns an unnoticed majority into a superiority'. He added that Powell was the best leader the right had had since the war, mainly because he was the least right-wing by the traditional terms: not a hanger or flogger, not an imperialist, not a reactionary. The same week, reflecting in his diary, Crossman said the latest symbol of failure in England was 'the nationwide acclaim of Enoch Powell as the great unspoken leader in the nation's revulsion against what had happened, first of all under Macmillan's Tory regime and now under Wilson and our regime. That is to say, racialism is a protest against the decline of Britain as a world power, and this semi-fascist reaction has been accompanied by a general lack of credibility in the whole establishment.'[145]

Powell accepted an invitation to appear on David Frost's evening television programme on 3 January 1969, where Frost tried to provoke him by asking whether he would dissociate himself from undesirables who claimed to support him, specifically some thugs who had beaten up an Indian student while shouting, 'We want Enoch.' Powell told him, 'I am not going to start condemning the behaviour of people who are condemned by their own actions. It is not for a politician to be a preacher.'[146] However, Frost pressed him: 'But do you dissociate yourself?' Powell replied, 'I am not going to be put in the absurd position of dissociating myself from people who have nothing to do with me and whom I have never met and do not know.'

Frost, nonetheless, asked his question again. 'I won't have you putting words in my mouth,' Powell snapped back, 'words which dissociate me from or make it appear I should be associated with such actions. Good heavens, you could put me in the dock and ask me to dissociate myself from all kinds of weird behaviour.' Frost then changed his tack: 'A lot of people say you are a racialist: will you admit to being this?' Powell sat silently for a moment, and then replied: 'It depends on how you define the word "racialist". If you mean being conscious of the differences between men and nations, and from that, races, then we are all racialists. However, if you mean a man who despises a human being because he belongs to another race, or a man who believes that one race is inherently superior to another, then the answer is emphatically "No".' The interview became so heated – and therefore made such good television – that the programme controller of London Weekend Television, Cyril Bennett, rang the studio from his home to order it to be extended for half an hour. It was a set-piece of Powell's now titanic self-belief. Interestingly, one of the many notes of congratulation Powell had about his performance was from Tony Kershaw, Heath's parliamentary private secretary. He wrote to Powell promising that the standard letter Heath's office sent out to those who wrote to him on immigration would include a reference to the fact that the measures Powell had called for at Birmingham and Eastbourne were specified in the 1966 manifesto, but added the postscript: 'Bravo *re* Frost. He was out of his class. I haven't enjoyed a programme so much for years.'[147]

Despite Powell's clear denials of racialism, the wave of student protests continued unabated. At a technology college in Newcastle on 16 January, students occupied a lecture theatre where Powell was scheduled to talk on 'Gold, money and politicians'. They left after being told by the authorities that the talk had been cancelled. However, immediately they were out of the way Powell entered through a rear door and delivered his lecture – about the continuing march of the power of the state – to an invited audience of 500 people, while the thwarted students outside banged on the windows. Commenting on the meeting afterwards, Powell said that 'the students there showed they would stand no nonsense. It was a very good show.'[148] He had a further reason to be pleased. The publicity generated by the visit almost completely wiped from the local newspapers and television news coverage of a visit to the north-east by Heath. The *Newcastle Journal*, on the morning after Powell's visit, devoted half its front page to the story, complete with a picture of Powell surrounded by his Special Branch minders. A small story about Heath, reporting some remarks he had made about industrial and retailing estates, was relegated well inside the paper. Heath and his publicity men were furious; it was just how Powell, and the Morecambe Budget, had trumped them at Blackpool three months earlier.

The next day only a few students picketed the Merchant Taylors' hall in York, where Powell spoke to the constituency's Conservative women's group. However, that evening 400 students marched from Sheffield University to the city's Grand Hotel, where Powell was addressing the University's Conservative Club. One hundred policemen surrounded the hotel and twenty more were inside, but it was the effect of standing in the rain for an hour and failing to get anywhere near Powell that finally persuaded the demonstrators to give up and go away. At Oxford, though, a bigger argument was brewing. A group calling itself the 20th January Committee – after the day on which Powell had been invited to address the University's Conservative Association – called for towns-people and undergraduates to prevent the meeting taking place by civil action; and the University authorities were asked by local race relations activists to ban the meeting.

Some of Powell's colleagues – not all of them committed supporters of his by any means – were increasingly worried by the failure of university authorities to foster free speech. A fellow MP, Eldon Griffiths, said that if the administrators could not guarantee such freedoms, they should be replaced. Powell's views, said Griffiths, 'are of a great deal more interest – and importance – than those of a rabble of downy-faced youths with the marks of the cradle still upon them'. One of Powell's closer associates, Sir Keith Joseph, became the first member of the shadow cabinet to speak up for Powell since his sacking. He said in a BBC radio discussion, 'Thank God, Enoch Powell is a member of the Conservative party. I am proud to be a colleague of his.'

Joseph – bravely in the circumstances of the prevailing view in the high command – went on to defend Powell, and to blame his own party for the problem Powell had highlighted.

> The fact is that the honourable short-sightedness of the last Tory Government in allowing a flood of immigrants, exacerbated by the passion of the Labour party to allow floods of immigrants in, built up a problem where popular demand was violently against what the politicians were doing ... for five or six years the Conservatives ignored this. When in 1962 the Conservatives closed the door partly, there was uproar in the House from the Labour Opposition. Now, the last embers of this flame have been rekindled by Enoch Powell, simply because the Tory leadership hadn't spelt out clearly enough their own perfectly well thought out policy.

Challenged afterwards by the press on his words being construed as a support for Powell's view of immigration rather than the official party line, Joseph reiterated that he had long been a friend of Powell's and was close in particular to his views on economic policy. However, he added diplomatically, 'In my opinion he did a service by speaking out as he did on immigration, though I would never adopt his phrases or his anecdotes.'[149] Joseph was on safe ground, for Heath had just made a speech at Walsall advocating legislation to prevent immigrants from settling permanently, but to allow them to have 'a specific job in a specific place – for a specific time'. According to Paul Foot, who recounts the anecdote, there was 'thunderous applause' when a member of the audience stood up and said, 'May I say how delighted we are that Mr Heath appears to have adopted many of the views expressed by Enoch Powell?'[150]

Such gradual rehabilitation for Powell made no odds with the left. When he made his visit to Oxford town hall as planned, about 1,000 people marched against him, charging a three-deep cordon of 100 policemen in an attempt to force entry. As was now usual, Powell entered and left by a back door, and delivered his speech, on the importance of setting up a free university, independent of state funding, and of the need for the Conservatives to support such a venture. He deplored the nationalisation of higher education, saying that radical student demands for control over the teaching and curricula of universities were, ironically, 'an instinctive attempt to re-assert the sovereignty of the consumer, which the state financing of higher education was bound to obliterate and was intended to obliterate'.[151] Meanwhile, outside, the mood of those radical students was turning ever uglier. Demonstrators started to chant, 'Disembowel Enoch Powell,' but the charging of the police turned some of the demonstrators against each other. Some of the demonstrators threw tear gas. To complicate matters a rival demonstration turned up, called the Group for Order and Democracy, whose aim was to defend Powell's freedom of speech.

Powell continued, in the face of such disturbances, to try to maintain the profile of his campaign against state socialism. At Albrighton on 8 January he denounced the recent reference of the level of wages in the building trade to the Prices and Incomes Board. Barbara Castle, the First Secretary of State, had legal powers to make such a reference, and intimated that she would. The employers, threatened with this, agreed to make a new, lower offer, and the threat was dropped. Powell called this a 'lawless' use of power; he said the Government might as well threaten to levy income tax at 12s in the pound but then say 'we shan't collect it provided you pay up voluntarily at 8s 3d'.[152] As a result, he argued, responsibility for interfering with the laws of supply and demand as they should have operated in the private sector was now shifted from the Government, where it belonged, to management, where it did not. This operation of the prices and incomes policy was therefore carried out, thanks to threats rather than legislation, by private individuals, who could not, unlike the Government, be held to account for their actions in Parliament.

Nor had Powell lost sight of his old defence brief. In his speech at York on 17 January he criticised Healey for having said that the Falkland Islands 'have no contribution to make to our future strategy'. Powell saw the Falklands as the south-western Atlantic's equivalent of the British base at Simonstown in South Africa. He believed, still, that the nuclear stalemate would lead to a conventional war being fought if Russia attacked the West, and the Falklands would become of supreme naval importance. If the Russians owned them, he said, they would never give them up. He also condemned the Government for leaving the islanders to make a decision about whether or not they should be handed over to Argentina. 'The effect of this', he said, 'is to put the islanders in the jaws of the nutcracker. That handful of isolated British people are thereby made the sole impediment to a settlement with the Argentine and to compliance with the decolonisation mania of the United Nations. To tell them in these circumstances that they should not be sold up against their will is a cynicism suitable for a nation bent upon demolishing its own assets.'[153] The themes he set out would return, with more potent force, thirteen years later.

On 25 January 1969 Powell attended a party rally in Walsall, which Heath, on a tour of the West Midlands, was to address on the subject of immigration. The previous day Heath had told a press conference in West Bromwich that 'public opinion polls seem to show that a majority of people feel he [Powell] has not helped race relations in this country'.[154] Some polls did show that, but Heath chose not to mention the paradox that they also revealed massive support for Powell's stance and somewhat less for his leader's. When Powell – who, as a prominent local MP, was invited to join the platform party – met Heath at the rally the two men were seen to exchange superficially cordial greetings. As far as Powell was concerned the mood stayed cordial. Heath told the rally that the Government should bring in urgent legislation to give it complete control of immigration, for without it 'the fears of our people will multiply and problems will increase'.[155] He called for the issue to be stripped 'of its emotional overtones', though claimed that he recognised the 'genuineness' of the fears of ordinary people. There were four specific measures he wanted taken: to prevent Commonwealth citizens, once admitted, from settling in Britain permanently; to make those who were allowed to stay for longer apply for renewal of their permits each year; to stop the automatic right of future immigrants to bring their dependants to Britain; and to verify the credentials of potential immigrants in their country of origin, and not on their arrival in Britain. Heath was given a standing ovation, in which Powell conspicuously joined. There was, though, even greater applause when a member of the audience rose and said, 'We look forward to Mr Heath inviting Mr Powell to rejoin the shadow cabinet.' Heath, who had listened impassively, replied, 'The question of members of the shadow cabinet is a matter for me, which I do not discuss in public.' Heath further smarted when another questioner expressed delight at his views having moved so closely to Powell's. 'Do me the kindness of reading our 1966 manifesto, for which I was responsible,' he snapped back.[156] As Powell had always maintained, the Birmingham speech had merely followed party policy.

The question of whether Powell would be brought back was being ever more keenly debated. There was, simply, no way Heath would have him back, because he believed – rightly, as it turned out – that he could win the election without him. Then, if he became Prime Minister, he would owe Powell nothing. If he did not, he might not be in a position for long to offer Powell any front-bench responsibility. Two days after his Walsall speech Heath was interviewed on Independent Television News, and seemed once more to be distancing himself from Powell. 'I don't say one should stop all immigration. I think Mr Powell does. I don't say that no dependants should come in. I think Mr Powell does.'[157] Nonetheless James Callaghan, the Home Secretary, described Heath's speech as 'shifty' and said the Leader of the Opposition was 'dancing to Powellite tunes'. In a statement put out before Heath's interview, Callaghan said that 'he wishes to appease the Powellites and be all things to all men. He tries to convey the impression that he has a formula which would result in a huge cut in immigration. He knows this can be done only by stopping wives and children from joining the men already here. Yet in the same speech he argued that it would be inhuman not to allow families to be united. This is hypocrisy.'[158]

A newspaper article about Heath's speech provoked Powell, for the first time in the aftermath of the controversy stirred up by his Birmingham speech, to sue for libel. On 2 February the *Sunday Times* discussed whether Heath had shifted his and party's position, and in the course of it said: 'This does not make Mr Heath indistinguishable from Mr Powell. He, after all, has a genuine desire to see race relations improve – a very important difference. And he refuses to spout the fantasies of racial purity.' It was the last phrase that incensed Powell and caused him to instigate a suit against the newspaper, notice of which the *Sunday Times* received on 13 February. It took over a year for the action to be settled in Powell's favour: his counsel said in court in April 1970 that Powell 'took the strongest possible exception to those words ... however, the *Sunday Times* has informed Mr Powell that the reference to "fantasies of racial purity" was never intended to suggest that Mr Powell had ever held or advanced doctrines of the type put forward by Nazi leaders before and during the Second World War. The *Sunday Times* has agreed to repeat this assurance in open court.' The paper also expressed its regret at the distress caused to Powell. He received no damages: he accepted that the rest of what the paper had said was the paper's sincere opinion, genuinely held; and there was the problem of the construction that could have been put on a phrase from his Eastbourne speech when he had said, 'The West Indian or Asian does not, by being born in England, become an Englishman.' The phrase was the product of Powell's logical mind: Englishness was an ethnicity, not a citizenship. One could become British by law, but not English. As so often in consideration of Powell's view of the profound issues attendant on the immigration question, logic and emotion had become confused: and the emotion was not always his.

12

AN ENEMY WITHIN

For Powell, the question of stopping reform of the Lords now became paramount. The Conservative Whips, sensing that their party had nothing to gain by ordering support for a Government measure, announced a free vote on the Parliament (No. 2) Bill. By early 1969 Powell had joined forces with three others to organise Conservative opposition: Nigel Birch, Sir Lionel Heald and Hugh Fraser. The Labour Whips were still ordering their MPs to support it, but those opposed to it, led by Michael Foot and Robert Sheldon, were already planning an impossible weight of amendments for the committee stage. This began in the Commons on 12 February, with half an hour of points of order, and it did not take long before Labour realised the depressing predicament it was in.

On that first day Powell spoke twice. Sheldon had spoken earlier about the iniquities, as he saw it, of the hereditary system; and Powell was therefore given the opportunity to deliver a short history lesson to the Commons about how Sheldon had based his argument 'on an entirely false assumption'.[1] This was 'that the so-called hereditary principle on which the House of Lords is at present constituted is the principle of heredity'. He said that if this principle did operate then a peerage would not descend to the eldest son but to all sons, and to females as well as males. He reiterated that the House was composed by prescription, 'because prescriptive right to succeed in a certain way to a seat and to a writ of summons to the upper chamber has come down in the course of our history'.[2] Primogeniture was merely a convention, and an 'arbitrary' one at that; and there had been confusion in the fourteenth and fifteenth centuries, when the parliamentary barony was succeeding the feudal barony, which had allowed some peerages to descend through the female line, a convention that had also taken on the status of prescription.

He dropped dark hints about the preamble of the Bill – in which Crossman's various formulas were set out – and warned that this would need severe scrutiny later on. Later in the day he spoke again about the status of royal peers, and attacked the notion of a non-parliamentary peerage – the idea of which 'outside Parliament after its function in Parliament has been destroyed is an abomination'.[3] The reason, he said, that the British aristocracy was held in far higher esteem than its continental counterparts was that it was a functional aristocracy. He added that it would 'pervert' the peerage if it were allowed to survive as 'an effete floating institution with no roots, no standing place and no function'.[4] Crossman replied immediately, saying that such matters were outside the scope of the Bill. If future prime ministers wished to create hereditary peers, that would be up to them.

The committee wound slowly on the following week, Sheldon taking two and a quarter hours to discuss the exclusion of peers by succession. Powell offered his views on that, and, later on, spoke at length on the question of nomenclature. He spoke after a fine speech by Foot, who even at this relatively early stage was urging his own front bench to observe reality, to see the level of opposition across the House to the Bill, and drop it at once. Powell urged the Government to listen to Foot, but his main point was that if the Bill were to become law, which he believed it would not, the members of the new assembly should not be called peers, since the historical term was inappropriate to the new, non-historical body that was envisaged. His preferred term, which had a historical parallel in the fourteenth century for such placemen, was 'Lords of Parliament'. He then turned to the question of the length of tenure of the nominated peers, saying prime ministers would be bound to appoint them for the shortest possible time, so as to ensure they were 'to the maximum extent subservient' to the executive in the Commons.[5] Discussing the various suggestions for the nominating body – such as a committee of the Privy Council – Powell reiterated that the present chamber seemed perfectly well constituted, and should be left alone.

What he, and his comrades on both sides of the House, had spotted was that the Government had not made clear, because it did not itself know, what the legal effect of the preamble was. Powell harried the Leader of the House, Fred Peart, about this later that day, until Peart begged him not to press him any further. 'I will do all that I can to help,' the flustered minister said.[6] However, the next day Powell turned specifically to the question of the preamble, saying that it bore on one of the most important issues of the time, 'the future of the rule of law'. He explained that 'one of the most dangerous trends in recent years has been the breakdown of the rule of law by the continual obscuring of a distinction which should be absolute and upon the absoluteness of which the freedom of the individual depends, between that which is law and is, therefore, binding and that which is opinion – even be it the opinion of a Government or some other exalted body – which is not binding'.[7]

Powell said that the effect of the preamble, which outlined aims for the legislation that were not specified in the rest of the Bill, had been to blur that distinction further. As far as he was concerned, the preamble was not within the statute. The Government's own legal opinion seemed to confirm this, contradicting Wilson and Peart, who had both maintained that the preamble gave 'statutory recognition' to what it contained.[8] He was especially critical of the vagueness with which the preamble referred to the composition of the reformed House, and said it was no good the Government claiming that the royal prerogative prevented them from being more specific, because much legislation down the ages had diluted that prerogative, so no precedent would be set by such a move. Indeed, as Powell reminded the House, the Queen had formally placed her prerogative at Parliament's disposal for the purposes of the Bill, so it was no obstacle at all. The fact was not that the number of peers created was up to the monarch; it was that the Government did not wish to include details like that in the Bill for fear it would make the measure even harder to get through than it already threatened to be. It was also the case that a deal had been done between the two front benches as to numbers, so there was no need to put the matter into the statute – which angered backbenchers on both sides who had not been consulted about, nor taken into the secret of the results of, the deal.

So poorly drafted, and such a provocation to the backbenchers, was the Bill that even after three days in committee hardly any progress had been made; and the Government, embarrassed and angered by this, and not least by the guerrilla operation from its own side, began to show the first signs of cracking. Callaghan came to the dispatch box later on 19 February to complain about progress, citing the 'lot of drivel' that had held things up so far. Powell rebuked him for this; and when, moments later, Callaghan talked of the 'frivolous opposition' to the Bill, Powell cut into him immediately. 'Those who have sat through this debate, as he has not,' he said, 'will be aware that the vast majority of speeches have been very far from frivolous and have gone to the heart of about the most serious matter, the constitution of Parliament, that the House of Commons could possibly debate.'[9] The Government's complacency and contempt for the opposition to the Bill began to turn to deep anxiety, and Callaghan had to listen as both Powell and Foot warned him of the difficulties the Government would experience. Callaghan let out a cry of despair: 'Two and a half days on one clause!'[10]

Later that day, Powell found another issue that annoyed him, and made another speech, this time on the 'two-tier' nature of the proposed assembly, under which existing peers could sit in it, speak in it, but not vote unless they were one of the nominees. He said it was hard to believe that those who were told they could take part in the debate but not in the decision would turn out to be very useful contributors to the deliberations. 'The fact', he said, 'that our vote must follow our voice is a tremendous discipline. It gives a responsibility which nothing else can give to one who speaks in an assembly.' A chamber where this was impossible would be 'an abortion'.[11] He dismissed the notion as having been merely a 'sweetener' for those in the Upper House who were anxious not to lose the right to attend the Lords, and he surmised that the support which that House had given the measure was largely because of this inducement.

This was a particular cause of anger for Powell, and he spoke on it with more than his usual passion: 'I cannot, within the rules of order, be offensive, either individually or collectively, to members of another place,' he said.

But I wish to say that no member of another place, nor another place collectively, has the right to sell out valuable elements of our constitution for the sake of advantages which they may hope personally to enjoy during their lifetime. The British Constitution is not the personal property of any particular generation of members of either House of Parliament. We who sit here are not in the possession of the fee simple of the House of Commons, so that if sufficient inducement were offered to us we might agree to barter it away, to dispose of it in job lots, perhaps.[12]

He felt some peers, conscious only of their own situations, had already participated in this bargain, being 'prepared to swallow the consequences for the future and the inherent absurdities and obscenities of the scheme. *Après moi le deluge* – it is a good, aristocratic rule.' Callaghan, who replied to Powell's point, was at his most managerial, and refused to outline the 'bargain' that had taken place. His view, and that of the Government, was that the points Powell had made were interesting, but nothing more. It was to be this obdurate refusal to take on board the important points raised by Powell and others that helped the Government, and its collaborators on the Opposition front bench, to slip deeper into the mire.

By 20 February – when Powell spoke again, this time on the restriction of peers' rights to vote – the committee stage was eating up parliamentary time and holding up the entire legislative programme. It was still thought, though, that the Government would try to bring in a guillotine rather than drop the Bill altogether, as an increasing number of Labour MPs were urging. Callaghan, for all the brave face he was putting on things, was prominent among those keen to drop it. Because of his commitment to stopping the Bill, and also because there were other matters in Parliament that interested him – notably the Government's attempts to reform industrial relations – Powell cut down his speaking in the country and spent more time in the chamber. He had been heavily criticised for neglecting Parliament, but the behaviour of left-wing socialists after his Birmingham speech had meant his presence was disruptive and counter-productive. Their anger with him gradually abated, and many could not help agreeing with him on his critique both of the Parliament (No. 2) Bill and of their party's plans to reform the unions. By the spring of 1969, there were signs that, at last, his life was returning to normal, or at least to being as normal as it would ever be.

On 25 February the Parliament (No. 2) Bill had its fifth day in committee on the floor of the House, and Powell spoke on the 'squalid manoeuvre' by the Government – endorsed by the Conservative front bench – to pay the nominated peers a salary. The history of this was, though, typical of much of the Government's manoeuvring on many issues. From an initial commitment to pay, Wilson had moved to the point where he ruled out paying, but then, under pressure, moved back to say that payment could occur at some time in the future: it was, it seemed, to be left until after a general election for a decision to be taken. Powell mocked this vacillation, and asked whether the prospect of pay was part of the 'bargain' the Government had done with peers – not least Conservative peers – to give the Bill a quiet passage. If payment were given, he said, the subservience of the chamber – about which he had already warned – would be compounded. It was, for him, another sign of the 'absurdity' of the proposals.[13] When Callaghan spoke later Powell pressed him to admit what promises had been made. The Home Secretary refused. It was yet another embarrassment.

This was one of four long speeches (there were several more short interventions) Powell made in the course of a sitting that lasted until 1.29 p.m. the following day. It was not all earnest. When, in the early hours, a Labour Member said that all the peers who came from the Lowlands of Scotland were 'bloodthirsty', Powell jumped up. 'Is it in order', he asked the chairman of the committee, 'to refer to noble Lords and members of another place as bloodthirsty?' 'I think it is to be deprecated,' the chairman replied, 'but it is not unparliamentary.'[14] At 7.30 a.m. Powell analysed the problem of the voting rights of Scottish peers, dismissing the notion that the Scots needed any special representation in the Lords as they already had it specifically in the Commons. This brought him back to the danger of the imprecise preamble: 'we are also shown the value of that prescriptive chamber which we are proposing to destroy in order to replace it with something we cannot explain, nor show how it would work at all intelligently or tolerably'.[15]

Before the House rose at lunchtime he contributed once more, on the matter of retirement ages of the nominees. He was back in his place just after four o'clock, when the committee resumed for its sixth day. As usual, little progress was made, the whole day being spent discussing amendments about the retirement ages. Once that sitting was complete the Bill was put on ice for over a fortnight. This was not merely to allow the Government to rethink its strategy, but also to allow some other important business: the publication of, and debate on, the industrial relations White Paper, *In Place of Strife*.

The House debated it on 3 March. Barbara Castle, introducing it, acknowledged the discontent it was causing on the benches behind her. 'I am not', she said, 'the first woman in history to offer a poisoned package to those whom I would seduce.'[16] Powell spoke early on, praising the Conservatives' employment spokesman, Robert Carr, for the clarity and candour of his attack on Mrs Castle's proposals, but taking an early opportunity to restate his fundamental belief about the unions: that no action of theirs could cause inflation, and that to be seen to act against them in the belief they could was wrong. He also argued that the impact of strikes on the economy was immensely small – though he accepted that certain forms of strike action could be extremely 'dislocative' – and that it was the level of the exchange rate, and not any union activity, that caused balance of payments deficits.[17]

However, he agreed reform was needed, for two reasons. The first was efficiency, the second justice. He argued that collective bargaining prevented an efficient use of resources, because it did not allow for the reward of those who by their merits might deserve more than others. The labour market was also distorted by closed shops, which could not be justified morally. He called, too, for the law to reform the many immunities and privileges under the law which had been accorded to the unions, and which had, as he put it, caused them to fall 'progressively out of touch with reality and out of touch with public opinion'. Accused by a Labour MP of thinking that the unions were to blame in all disputes, Powell affirmed that poor management was as likely to be the cause. Finally, he argued that, if recourse to the courts were allowed in trades disputes, it would not only help employees suffering from what was effectively a breach of a hitherto unenforceable contract. It would also help unions who were being held responsible for unofficial action. He argued that the existing law 'permits, renders lawful and protects that which a great majority of the public, indeed in many cases the great majority of trade unionists, regard as unjustifiable'.[18] Sensing the trouble that might be ahead with the measure, he appealed for Parliament to act to end this insupportable state of affairs, but to do so slowly.

In one of his now less frequent outings, to speak at Farnham in Surrey on 7 March, he once more criticised defence policy. Powell had been amused by the spat between Healey and the Labour unilateral disarmers, who had been told by the Defence Secretary that if they did not accept – as Powell tactfully put it – the 'big bang' option in defence, they would have to put up with conscription to make the conventional forces big enough to counter Russia. Powell argued that nobody took nuclear weapons seriously, and said it was not a foregone conclusion that America would commit national suicide to ensure that Western Europe was 'frizzled instead of conquered'.[19] He added, 'Not one of the Governments in Western Europe really believes that the Americans are likely to destroy the world if Russian tanks reach Bonn, for the simple reason that no rational human being can believe it.' Powell was convinced that, since neither side would use nuclear weapons, Russia could be beaten conventionally, but only if someone took a political lead to build up the conventional forces. The Conservatives, with an eye on spending priorities, showed no inclination to do this.

A Gallup poll, conducted the week before this speech, showed that the public thought Powell was the most admirable man in Britain. Having overcome the initial handicaps brought by his Birmingham speech, the attempt to deny him public platforms and to disrupt him in the Commons, he had in the eleven months since Birmingham made over 100 public speeches, and, through his new and explosive fame, secured a hearing for his other views on the economy, defence and the philosophy of the state. Reviewing this success – the more remarkable since Powell had accomplished it almost single-handedly – the commentator David Watt correctly observed that 'his most obvious achievement is to have captured the news media', something Powell had managed by 'sheer quotability'. A Powell speech may have been over the heads of its audience on many occasions, but it was never boring or irrelevant. The very fact of Powell's enormous following now invested anything he said, on any subject, with the most conspicuous relevance. It had caused his polar opposite, Sir Edward Boyle, to note in a lecture at Reading Powell's 'baleful genius' in inserting 'certain Iago-like words and phrases' strategically during any speech he made. This may have caused Powell to be quoted out of context, but at least it caused him to be quoted.[20]

In his assessment, Watt made a definitive analysis of why a Powell speech was successful: 'He starts with some simple, essentially romantic idea such as patriotism or economic freedom, or Natural Man. On this basis a dry suprastructure of logic is then raised. And finally this suprastructure is adorned with irony, emotive allusion and adjectival embellishments. The embellishments catch the eye and the rationalisations satisfy the conscience of some intelligent men. But what makes Mr Powell an important figure is not the brilliance of his mind or his style but the emotional attraction to many people of his own emotional assumptions.' This was not entirely fair: Powell had, most notably at Birmingham, made emotional assumptions about the feelings of the British people. They had, however, turned out to be manifestly correct. Nor, as Watt accepted, was this merely true about immigration. The Wilson Government had behaved in a way that had caused the British people to come to detest the idea of big government: this feeling prevailed in all sections of society, for different reasons. As Watt said, Powell's success 'shows that extreme Manchester school economics and Conservative vocabulary, if cleverly deployed, are one way of exploiting the national mood'. The stage was, indeed, being set for the election that would come the next year, for Powell had his own, massive constituency and, at that stage, neither of the main parties or their leaderships could be seen to be reflecting its views.

Powell never lost sight of the general sense of the concern in the country, nor ever imagined that, for all the popularity it had brought him, it was simply a matter of the immigration issue. On 9 March he spoke at Sussex University – where stink-bombs were thrown in the audience – and related the story of a woman from whom he had bought a newspaper at an Underground station. She had said to him, 'We have gone wrong. We seem to have gone mad.' He had replied, 'I think I know what you mean, but in that case we must put it right.' 'She said: "But Mr Powell, is it not too late?" That woman's voice is, I believe, the voice of millions in this country. Somehow, it seems to have gone wrong. Somehow, to put it in her terms, we have lost touch with reality. We have become mad. That is how millions of people feel. People are asking: "Is it too late? Has it gone too far?" ' Ostensibly, Powell was talking just about immigration; but, as with many of his speeches, he spoke in ways that left his message open to more than one interpretation: he was also alert to the general malaise, and to the general failing of politicians to recognise it. He felt the need to clarify his speech later, and said there were three examples of the 'madness': mass immigration, the delusions of British influence over Rhodesia, and defence, the policy for which was now built around the 'unbelievable assumption' about the use of the nuclear weapon.[21]

With so many fronts now open against his party and, by extension, its leadership, it was hardly surprising the party machine should be taking steps to distance Powell from it. He was, however, aggrieved to hear from a supporter that a letter had been sent out by Barber to him saying, 'I cannot agree with many of the policies which Mr Powell has been proclaiming recently.'[22] Powell took this up with Barber, asking him 'if you would not wish to reconsider at any rate the word "many" '. He added, 'I am aware of course that on immigration there is a minor difference of substance and a major difference of emphasis. I know, too, that what I said about Rhodesia in December was, in your view, at best premature. But I am at a loss to think of any other policies I have "proclaimed" in the last eleven months that I had not "proclaimed" during the previous $3\frac{1}{2}$ years when a member of the leader's consultative committees, if not even before.'

Barber replied that, 'in answer to those who have criticised you, I have frequently stressed our common ground in fighting Socialism and pointed out that this has been obvious from your help at by-elections'.[23] He said that, as chairman, he was caught in the middle of complaints from people who accused Powell of ' "disloyalty", "rocking the boat", "racialism" etc', and 'those who believe that your approach – particularly on immigration – is the answer'. However, he said, 'I am afraid I do disagree with much that you have said, quite apart from your immigration policy. I have in mind such major subjects as defence, sterling, important parts of your speech on the economy made during the Blackpool Conference, some of your ideas on de-nationalisation, your basic attitude to incomes policy and, as you realise, the important subject of Rhodesia ... I have ignored a number of, I suppose, comparatively minor matters on which I also strongly disagree.' Barber said he would rather not have to spend his time fielding letters for and against Powell, but concluded with the gratuitous reflection that 'happily, there are not many nowadays'. This should have made it clear to Powell what a horror a Conservative government would be for him. He replied with the double-edged comment, 'I know you do defend me whenever necessary; and of course I do the same for Ted.' He congratulated Barber on having taken the point that his policy pronouncements were consistent with what he had said when they were both in the shadow cabinet, though there is no evidence from Barber's letter that he had come anywhere near accepting such a point.

On 18 March the Parliament (No. 2) Bill returned to the Commons, the earlier momentum being recaptured by the opening of the proceedings with more than an hour of points of order. Retirement ages, pay and attendance criteria were discussed, as well as the plans to have a chamber of 230 members, with a retirement age of seventy-two. Powell spoke at length, but his main message was in his peroration: 'How much longer do we have to go on before the Government admit that the thing is grotesque nonsense and take it away?'[24] The same grind continued the next day, this time introduced by over an hour and a half of points of order. The recognition that the Bill would be lost was now endemic, but not yet accepted within the cabinet.

II

While he was aggravating the death throes of Lords reform, Powell was also preparing to embark on his next, and in many respects most crucial, great crusade. On 21 March he began the process that would make him leave the Conservative party. In a speech to a Conservative women's meeting at Clacton he announced it would be best for Britain to withdraw her application to join the Common Market. Her second attempt to enter had failed in 1967, and Powell conceded it had been better to leave the application on the table then rather than withdraw it, as it would have seemed like international pique. His reasons were not the explicit ones of retention of sovereignty that had prompted him to rebel on the Schuman Plan nearly twenty years earlier, and which would dominate his argument against the EEC in the years ahead. He confined himself to saying that 'with the progress of time ... and the movement of events, this is fast becoming an absurdity and a humiliation and for my own part I believe the time has come to call it back and resume an independence and freedom of action which suits the present reality both of our own position and that of the Common Market'.[25]

Powell would quietly have accepted entry had it been possible earlier. He admitted he had backed Macmillan's decision to seek entry because, as he later wrote, 'I was prepared to accept it, on the grounds of trade, as the lesser evil, compared with being excluded.'[26] In 1966, on the BBC programme *Any Questions*, he had answered a question about the pros and cons of Britain's joining the Common Market by saying, 'there aren't any cons provided we can get ourselves into the Common Market'. The most important argument for, he continued, was 'that it gives this country access to a very much greater market than we could otherwise enjoy'. He believed British agriculture could 'make a killing' and that 'the time for hanging back is past'.[27] When Wilson had sought to renew the attempt, 'I was far less sure of either the wisdom or the prospects; but I did not see how Edward Heath and the Tory Party could creditably do other than wish him success. Now, however, the failure of the attempt has long been perfectly manifest.'[28] He suggested more than a quarter of a century later that his unease was of long standing, but it was not until leaving the shadow cabinet that he had been free to describe it.[29]

This absolute change of mind would be thrown at Powell by pro-marketeers consistently during the battle that followed. As a member of the Government when Macmillan tried to get Britain in, and as a shadow cabinet minister when Heath had supported Wilson's attempt, he would have had to resign in order to oppose the policy with the vehemence he later did. It seems either he did not feel the principled objection to loss of sovereignty as keenly until after 1967, or he had been too preoccupied with other issues to treat it with the seriousness it merited. Either way, his volte-face provided his opponents, inside and outside his party, with a weapon to use against him; and they did.

His turn against Europe seemed to have been provoked mainly by the failure of the six member countries of the Common Market to respond to Britain's overtures. He was certainly most concerned, as he told his audience, by a record of international humiliations for Britain dating back to Suez, and which he was anxious to stop: otherwise, such supine failure fed a mood of dejection and desperation. However, Powell then made a definitive statement of his belief about Britain's place in the world. He wanted to make 'a unilateral declaration of independence', and said, 'We do not need . . . to be tied up with anybody. When we consider the various arrangements we might make with other countries we are not a drowning man clutching at a rope or screaming for someone to throw him a lifebelt. We are no more drowning than these islands are sinkable; and we can take our time and pick the alternatives over with deliberation, if also with an eye for bargain opportunities.' He simply did not believe Britain had to choose between America, Europe or the Commonwealth: she did not need any of them.

He did, however, pick up on words General de Gaulle had used, notoriously, to Christopher Soames, now Britain's ambassador to Paris, when he had said that the market might evolve into 'a looser form of free-trade area' – which he said was the type of arrangement that would have suited Britain best all along. Thus he defined the parameters of the debate that would rage over the issue for the rest of his life. The speech was noted keenly by Labour, and not forgotten. At a cabinet meeting on 22 July, four months later, when the subject arose of whether Wilson should try to reopen negotiations, Healey made a shrewd observation. Benn, in his diary, recorded that the Defence Secretary 'said it was better to wait in the hope that Enoch Powell would make an issue of it with Heath and split the Tory party rather than us'.[30] It was not the last time Labour would see Powell as their agent of destruction.

By the end of March the cul-de-sac into which the Parliament (No. 2) Bill had been pushed was now the subject of widespread press comment, the assumption being the Government would have to ditch it. Powell and Foot, still emphatically denying collusion, had not only wrecked the Government's legislative timetable and helped, but for the formalities being pronounced, to put an end to this reform; they had also shown that backbench MPs were not there merely to do the bidding of the front benches. Normally, when besieged by such a filibuster, a government would introduce a guillotine. However, although the front benches had colluded, this was one issue on which even Heath was not prepared to indulge the Government. A guillotine on a constitutional issue was – at that stage – anathematical to the Conservatives, and they would not back it. The measure would not therefore get through the House. Although the rebels were close to achieving their aim, they were beginning to suffer from the resentment of loyalist backbenchers who had been sitting up until all hours to vote as their whips directed. Powell, typically, was unaffected by this, but the pressure was beginning to tell on Foot.

As the inevitable defeat of the proposals came nearer, Powell returned to a programme of speaking on a broad agenda. He began with education. Starting at Thornaby-on-Tees on 29 March he said that he felt, as a vigorous defender of selective education, there was no logic, if there were to be a comprehensive system, in letting it operate side by side with grammar schools. His party should either abolish all selective schools – including direct grant and public ones – or, given what he full well knew to be the impossibility and ideological unde-sirability of that action, they should create more selective schools.

A fortnight later he returned to attacking his leader. Heath had announced that, if he won power, he would develop a scheme to allow wage-earners to save £3 a week tax free. The greater national savings would, he had said, allow taxation to be cut by £250 million a year. Powell dismissed this, in a speech at Widnes, as economically illiterate: savings had nothing to do with taxation. 'It is irrelevant whether personal savings are increasing or diminishing. All that matters is whether more is being lent to the Government. One form of lending to the Government is called "national savings". This is one of those maddeningly misleading expressions which summon patriotism to the aid of deception.' The best way to get taxation down for wage earners, he argued, was to cut public spending. 'To play about now with new national savings schemes is to behave like a spendthrift trying to pay his debts by borrowing at more and more exorbitant interest. So let us hear nothing, or let us protest loudly if we do hear it, about increasing savings to reduce taxation.'[31]

For this uncompromising assault on Heath, Powell was immediately attacked by Macleod. Describing him as 'the acknowledged master of paradox', Macleod said that 'even his admirers must have found his latest excursion into the realm of economic policy a trifle bizarre'.[32] He maintained that the more was saved the more would be invested, the more national wealth would grow, and so the more taxation would be reduced. However, Macleod did agree with Powell that public spending had to come down. Other of Macleod's colleagues made it known that they were even angrier than the shadow Chancellor was. It seemed to some of Heath's friends that Powell was waiting for Heath to ally himself with certain issues – as he had with the savings question – and then going directly for him. The timing of Powell's Widnes speech had also irritated them: that same day Macleod made a speech on taxation that went largely unreported. They feared that Powell was creating a situation in which Heath would have to choose between excluding him from any government he formed, thereby increasing the rank and file of the party, or giving him office on his own terms.

Meanwhile, the Parliament (No. 2) Bill was still not out of its misery. On 1 April, despite the belief that it would have to be killed, the Commons devoted the first of another two-day session in committee to it. Powell complained vigorously, when proceedings opened, about remarks made in the Lords by a Labour peer, Lord Shackleton, to the effect that the debate in the Commons had not always been relevant to the Bill – which Powell argued was a reflection on the Chair of a sort that, had it been uttered in the Commons, would have resulted in a censure. Later that day he made his longest speech during the proceedings – one of his longest speeches in his parliamentary career – of more than an hour in length on the absurdities of the nomination system and what the average attendance of the new chamber would be, and how they would be regulated. He spoke on this again the next day, asking, at length, whether law lords would be included in the Government's proposed figure of 230 members attending, and later moved an amendment concerning the right of ex-ministers retaining their places after they had left office. The Easter recess then intervened, and when the Bill came back to the floor of the House of 14 April, Powell picked up where he had left off, on the absurdity of the new chamber's voting qualifications.

Now, though, the end really was imminent. That day the Government suffered its greatest humiliation yet on the Bill. It managed to win a motion to put the debate on a clause affecting the role of bishops in the reformed House to the vote, but by only ninety-two votes to forty-nine, and the motion could not be effected without 100 in support. Callaghan, deeply embarrassed, was left with no option but to move the adjournment. By this stage the Bill had spent nine days in committee, and only five clauses had been disposed of; fifteen remained. In the seven and a half hours before this debacle, only two minor amendments had been debated. Foot's and Powell's supporters continued to table amendments, raise prolix points of order and make interminable speeches.

The denouement was swift. At cabinet on 16 April there was what Benn recorded as a 'tremendous row' about the Bill, with which he and Michael Stewart almost alone of ministers in the Commons wanted to continue.[33] Crossman, the main architect, had realised that no guillotine would be obtained, no massive amendment of the measure was credible, and so it would have to go.

Wilson was determined to scrap it, and prevailed. On 17 April he came to the Commons to announce that the legislation was being dropped, to make time for the measures arising out of *In Place of Strife* and a merchant shipping Bill – a formula cooked up in cabinet to try and save his face and the Government's authority. He did so in a short statement which, as was his wont when faced with a humiliation, he gabbled in order to get it over and done with as swiftly as possible. Powell, on the Opposition benches, mordantly interjected, 'Don't eat them too quickly,' which caused such hilarity that Wilson was thrown off course.

The destruction of the Parliament (No. 2) Bill was perhaps the greatest triumph of Powell's political career, and it served largely to rehabilitate him in the Commons. At a Primrose League dinner on the evening of the abandonment, he once more criticised Heath who, in an attempt to save face, had given the impression in the Commons that the Opposition front bench had had no responsibility for the measure. Powell knew how untrue that was: Macleod's and Maudling's collusion in the plans had been one of the reasons why Heath and his close colleagues had not stood in the way of the Bill.

He took the opportunity to attack not just Heath but also 'my good friend and colleague Quintin Hogg', who (with no conscious irony) had just issued a pamphlet on the future of the constitution – one framed, Powell added, 'with that freedom of personal expression our party traditionally happily allows to its front bench spokesmen'.[34] Much to Powell's amusement, Hogg had spoken dramatically of Parliament becoming 'an elective dictatorship', in which debate had dwindled to mere ritual. However, the two colluding front benches – of one of which Hogg was a prominent member – had known all along that the Commons as a whole did not want the Parliament (No 2) Bill. 'This is what made it possible', Powell said, 'for a relatively small number of Members, who constituted themselves the spokesmen of that general feeling, to use – not to abuse, but use legitimately – the proper procedures of the House so as to render progress so slow that the Government had to conclude that the game was not on.'

Also, Powell maintained, the public had no desire for reform of the Lords. 'There was an instinct, inarticulate but deep and sound, that the traditional, prescriptive House of Lords posed no threat and injured no interests, but might yet, for all its illogicalities and anomalies, make itself felt on occasion to useful purpose. The same sound instinct was repelled by the idea of a new-fashioned second chamber, artificially constructed by power, party and patronage, to function in a particular way. Not for the first time, the common people of this country proved the surest defenders of their traditional institutions.'

III

In the same week that Wilson abandoned the Parliament (No. 2) Bill, Powell had another victory: the Government ended its prices and incomes policy. For good measure, Jenkins announced in the Budget that rather than borrowing more money, the Government would be increasing its repayment of the national debt – just as Powell had been advocating it should do to reduce inflation. This reduction in debt had been achieved by increasing taxation rather than cutting spending, but it was a reduction nonetheless, and sterling would be strengthened. In the debate on the Finance Bill, on 16 April, Powell interrupted a Labour speaker to proclaim that 'the international so-called system of fixed rates of exchange is an institutionalised nonsense'.[35] On 21 April he attacked Jenkins for offering a new, higher rate of interest that, he felt, was far above what the market would dictate, to attract National Savings; and he called again for the exchange rate to be allowed to float, professing that the gold standard was the precursor of the Bretton Woods system of fixed exchange rates then being used, and had culminated in the crash of 1931. Britain had, he said, been forced to abandon it then, and would be forced to do so again.

On 23 April – 'purely a coincidence that this is St George's Day', he said – he held a press conference to mark the publication of what would endure as his most influential collection of speeches, *Freedom and Reality*, edited by his friend John Wood of the IEA.[36] As well as containing his provocative tracts on immigration from the previous year – one of the main reasons why it was reprinted even before it went on sale – it outlined almost the whole Powell thesis: it included his demolitions of the national plan, his expositions of the fallacies of socialism, his belief in the supremacy of markets as an expression of individual free will. At a Foyle's lunch, he said he had published it because 'the spoken word is the politician's supreme instrument'; and if the word was not merely relevant to the immediate present 'the need arises for a book'.[37] What he had, in effect, done was publish his own personal manifesto, well before the election. It was now up to his party to produce theirs, and see how it measured up.

One policy Labour still had not mastered was defence. In a speech early in June Powell ridiculed the notion, gaining currency in the wake of de Gaulle's departure, of a joint Anglo-French nuclear deterrent with a curt 'One nation, one button. It is as simple as that.'[38] Two days later he wrote in the *Sunday Express* of the problem facing America and her allies over Vietnam, still a difficult issue with the Government. Offering unsolicited advice to President Nixon, he said most Americans now realised their country must disengage from Vietnam, and the sooner the decision was taken, the better. He talked of the need, too, for Nixon – in office for only just over four months – to ditch the Democrat economic legacy, float the dollar and cut spending. The allegorical message to British Conservative leaders who might, soon, emulate Nixon by gaining power was obvious.

On 9 June Powell made a calculated return to the immigration question. In a speech in his constituency, he called for a £300 million programme of organised repatriation and resettlement to be set up, with an inducement of £2,000 per family. He said the plan was in line with party policy, and accused Heath not of humbug, but of 'something more alarming: sheer incomprehension of the very magnitude of the danger'. He condemned the leadership for having played down voluntary repatriation as if they were 'almost anxious to represent it as of no significant importance'.[39] He told his constituents that at the beginning of 1968 the proportion of immigrant and immigrant-descended children in the town's infant schools had been 17.1 per cent. At the start of 1969 it had grown to 21 per cent.

He called for admissions for settlement to be reduced to 'negligible proportions' and to end the inflow of dependants, as well as for the setting up of the new voluntary repatriation scheme. The £300 million cost would, he estimated, cover between 120,000 and 140,000 families of five, and the funding would be the same as eighteen months of the overseas aid budget. He repeated his earlier claim that it was still early enough for those being repatriated to reintegrate into their native communities; another decade and this would no longer be so. He also mocked his critics, hinting that they were mainly of the hard left or anarchist fringe who wanted a race problem in order to destabilise society. 'It is impossible to contemplate without astonishment and indignation the sheer inhumanity of those who have been, and are, working night and day to make that tragedy inevitable. There are some whose intention is to destroy society as we know it, and "race" or "colour" is one of the crowbars they intend to use for the work of demolition. What a glorious chance if a permanent and growing "colour problem" could be riveted upon Britain! Naturally those who would avoid or minimise or reverse it have to be howled down.'

Powell was careful to refer to copper-bottomed statistical sources, and to avoid, almost entirely, language of the sort that had characterised the Birmingham speech. He contrasted figures suggesting a 3 million immigrant population at the end of the century, produced in a study at Sussex University, with the estimate of 1.4 to 2.1 million produced by the Conservative Research Department which, he said, was partly responsible for the party's inadequate response to the problem. This time his only classical allusion was to Themistocles, and he applied it to himself: 'I say to my colleagues and to my countrymen, strike me if you must, but hear me.' His hard-core opponents on the Labour benches made, as he had predicted, their Pavlovian reaction. A group of them put down an early day motion calling on Heath to withdraw the whip from Powell 'as a mark of his contempt for the evil, racialist and alien doctrines expounded from a Conservative platform in Wolverhampton'. However, another almost equally fierce critic, the editor of *The Times*, commended Powell for his restraint in making the speech in the way he had, but advocated, rather than voluntary repatriation, a policy opposed to the creation of ghettos, settling families of immigrants around predominantly white council estates.[40]

Most Conservative MPs maintained an embarrassed silence, principally because of Powell's attack on Heath. Only one, Ronnie Bell, publicly commended the idea. Trevor Huddleston, the anti-apartheid campaigner and Bishop of Stepney, wrote to Powell condemning his speech as 'evil', a charge Powell repudiated immediately and in full. 'In judging my words and actions,' he wrote to the Bishop, 'you have mistaken not only what I am saying but also what is much more important – the real circumstances in this country, so utterly different from those in other places where your own courage has won worldwide admiration.' Powell said he would not be doing his duty as a Member of Parliament if he did not speak on the issue, and offer a constructive solution to it. 'I cannot see that such a course tends, as you say, to "lower human dignity". On the contrary, it can often be a denial of human dignity to fail or refuse to take into account the differences, often profound, between one individual, group or nation and every other.' Huddleston, in a reply to this, conceded that Powell regarded what he had said as a matter of principle. However, he did not agree with the argument, and invited Powell to debate the matter in public with him. Powell agreed: a date, in front of the television cameras, was set for the autumn.

Powell then found the heavy guns of both front benches turned on him. Hogg, writing to *The Times*, derided him as being either 'one of the greatest philanthropists of all time, albeit one who may have allowed his idealism to outrun his financial discretion' or 'the purveyor of nonsense so strange that it requires a very clever man to persuade himself that it is even worth serious consideration'.[41] Hogg, parodying Powell's arguments to an extent in saying that he believed 'the great mass of Commonwealth immigrants desire nothing so much as to go home', said that if that really were the case there was no need to pay them to do so. He also said that if Powell was right about this desire, then his frightening figures about the immigrant-descended population for 2000 would need to be revised. This was Hogg, intentionally or unintentionally, missing the point, as Powell knew that as things stood the immigrants did not have the means to go home. He also claimed that the £300 million 'increase in taxation' needed to pay for the repatriation scheme was 'rather out of tune with his general approach to public expenditure'.

This was a gross distortion and misrepresentation of what Powell had actually said: he had suggested the money be diverted from the overseas aid budget, not any additional expenditure. Hogg had not read the Birmingham speech before exploding about it, and he may have followed the same policy with the Wolverhampton one. He sought to wound Powell for the criticism he had made of the Opposition front bench and its attitude to the problem. Hogg, ever petulant in his own defence, wrote that 'since 1966 I suppose I have made not less [sic] than 50 and perhaps more separate interventions in Parliament or Standing Committee on various aspects of immigration and race relations. So far as I recollect Mr Powell has made one.' Whatever the circumstances that had prevented his participation in the House, Powell's reputation as a parliamentarian who preferred to get his message across outside Parliament was one colleagues less adept at commanding the mass media would continue to trumpet. Most astonishing about Hogg's remarks, though, was the unprecedented level of hostility they represented from a front-bencher to a backbencher of the same party, in public. It showed how far Heath and his closest colleagues had placed themselves from Powell in the fourteen months since his sacking, and also how much they feared him. Those who talked of Powell rejoining the shadow cabinet were simply not observing the realities.

The party's Research Department, which Powell had explicitly criticised, was immediately thrown on the defensive by his allegation of inaccuracy. It fell to one of its staff, Patrick Cosgrave, a future sympathetic biographer of Powell, to write a memorandum to Heath and Hogg. Cosgrave told them it was necessary, in order to repudiate Powell, to question his statistics as closely as possible, and, even where the statistics were found to be accurate, to examine the projections he made from them. Cosgrave took comfort from the fact that Powell's Birmingham prediction of 3.5 million immigrants by 1985 was based on a parliamentary answer given by Julian Snow, a junior minister, in the Commons in 1967. David Ennals, another minister, had then revised this figure downwards, something Powell had seen no cause to emulate; and, as was clear by the mid-1970s when the erroneous basis of Ennals's calculation was exposed, Powell was right to be sceptical.

Cosgrave was content that Dr David Eversly, who had led the Sussex University survey, was now revising his figure, expressed to Powell in private correspondence, of a 3 million population; he now thought it would be 2.5 million, still some way above the Research Department's estimate. The Research Department was working on new projections, and Cosgrave said he believed that 'at the outside' the immigrant population would be 2.5 million by 2000 – still a substantial upward revision of the previous figure of 1.4 to 2.1 million. Cosgrave also said that the Kenyan Asians' immigration of 1967–8 was a 'once and for all inflation of the figures', an assertion unsupported in fact when the figures for the first half of the 1970s had been formulated a few years later, and which seems to assume the immigrants would not reproduce.[42] 'It is quite clear', Cosgrave told his masters, 'that Mr Powell's suggestion that immigration is not on the decline has no basis in fact. We can look forward to a dramatically decreasing intake, the extent of which will be controlled mainly by the number of vouchers issued.' He did concede, though, that it might be sensible to 'encourage' further research into the efficacy of repatriation.

Hogg's opposite number, Callaghan, was equally fierce. He called Powell's plan a 'fantasy', and urged him to 'rid himself of the taint of racialism' by coming out in favour of an equal opportunities policy in housing, education, jobs and human rights. 'I ask a direct question of Mr Powell,' said Callaghan. 'Do you agree that they [immigrants] should have the same rights when they bear the same responsibilities? This is the crunch for Mr Powell. These are the questions he has never answered. He can be clear when he likes, only too clear. Why then does he remain silent on this fundamental issue? Is it because he fears that if he gives a non-racial answer he will lose some of his support?'[43]

However, Powell did not remain silent. Interviewed by Robin Day on *Panorama* the following Monday he said unequivocally that 'all who are resident in this country should have equal rights before the law ... there should be no first-class citizens and second-class citizens'.[44] He added, though, that if the policy were allowed to persist that fostered the ghettos in towns and cities, and if the white indigenous population felt no one cared about this development, 'then the danger will be that there will be a tendency for people to be treated differently'. It was a point he had made several times since Birmingham, but still the question would continue to be asked.

On 18 July Powell went to Bradford, one of the cities most heavily populated by New Commonwealth arrivals, to speak on immigration. He defended himself against the accusations of cowardice levelled against him for not speaking on the issue in the Commons: 'but the House of Commons will not debate immigration ... debates on whether the controls imposed in 1962 should be maintained, on what appeal there should be against the decisions of immigration officials, on whether this or that loophole in the 1962 Act should be closed, on discrimination, real or alleged, between one citizen and another – these are no substitute for looking the facts and consequences of immigration as a whole direct in the face'.[45]

That such an opportunity had not arisen was not just the Government's fault; the Conservatives, he said, had had days at their disposal when they could have censured the Government, but had chosen not to do so: 'It is not I, but others, who shun parliamentary debate.' He promised to go on speaking outside Parliament, and added, with typical defiance, that his only mistake had been not 'to have spoken louder, oftener, sooner'. He told the Bradfordians that they were like his own constituents, people who had shared an anxiety 'which until recently was like a private grief, something of which the rest of the world knew nothing and wished to know as little as possible ... at least we have been heard of at last'. He went on to argue that there were strong lobbies concerned with keeping the issue suppressed: ' "Race relations" is one of the fastest growing sectors of British industry, and with its rise goes a vested interest in assuring the maximum raw material for the race relations industry by way of immigrant population.' That, he said, explained the intemperate way in which he had been abused and insulted for outlining the truth as he had seen it.

In his support Powell cited remarks by a prominent judge, Lord Radcliffe, who in a lecture earlier that year had talked of the difficulties of 'inserting into a fairly complex urban and industrial civilisation a large alien wedge', creating 'a menacing problem which has climbed the sky in so short a space of time'. Powell, who given the provenance of this remark was greatly encouraged by it, said the judge had reminded the public 'of the two key factors, size and alienness, of which of course each increases the significance and effect of the other'. His concept of the word 'alien' contrasted in his mind with the

> horrifying passage in the first report of the Community Relations Commission, where it says, of the so-called 'second generation': 'They are English in all respects other than the colour of their skin.' It is not so much that such a statement is factually untrue which is shocking. It is the sheer insolence and contempt for human dignity which it expresses; for the true mutual respect between human beings rests upon the recognition, without any implication of superiority or inferiority, of differences – differences between one individual and another, differences between one society and another.

That was the Powell of India talking, the Powell none of his vociferous critics knew, and were still determined not to know.

One determined to know him was the newspaper magnate Cecil King, who collected grand politicians and had been curious about Powell ever since the Birmingham speech. The two men would lunch in September 1969, but King invited himself to South Eaton Place on 23 July for a preliminary discussion. Expecting a demagogue, he instead was surprised to find Powell 'very polite; said my calling on him was a great compliment!'[46] Powell told him he expected politics to become more 'normal' over the next year or so: 'He assumes a Tory victory in the election when it comes. I think he thinks his chance may come at some date after that. He explained that he is not the sort of man to lay a plot which will reach a climax at a given point of time.' King came away looking forward to their lunch.

During Powell's summer holiday, in the middle of August 1969, civil strife in Northern Ireland reached a pitch where Wilson and Callaghan decided to send the army in to keep the peace. Powell was alert immediately to the dangers of the situation, in terms of the constitution and the nation's security. He fired off a choleric letter to *The Times* on 20 August having read a report by one of the paper's future editors, Charles Douglas-Home, from Belfast. Douglas-Home had quoted a conversation with a senior officer in the Province who had expressed a number of views about the political situation, the level of military intelligence, and fears that the army itself would soon become targets. Powell said he hoped the 'impropriety' of the officer's remarks would be brought to the attention of the General Officer Commanding and that such an outburst would not be repeated.[47]

A few days later, he made a speech at Bridgnorth in which he said the time might come when citizens of the Republic of Ireland had to be treated as aliens in the United Kingdom. He was prompted to say this, paradoxically, by the arrest in Londonderry of two students, one French and one German, for throwing petrol bombs. 'We simply must have more control', he argued, 'over the admission, the movement and the activities of aliens in this country than is exercised at present: the foreign students with the petrol bombs are the tip of the iceberg, but one is obliged to wonder how much material of future danger lies below the surface and beyond the limits of surveillance.'[48] From this, it was a small leap of logic to address the question of Eire citizens in the United Kingdom.

It was already, he continued, his party's policy that all who were technically British subjects but did not belong to the United Kingdom should be treated as aliens. 'I doubt', he said, 'if it will be possible indefinitely to balk the question why the same principle ought not to be applied to the Republic of Ireland, whose citizens, though nationals of an independent state, are treated in the United Kingdom for all purposes except military service as if they belonged to it. There is a contradiction here which I believe will sooner or later have to be resolved.' The land frontier between the two countries counted, he said, for nothing, any more than that between Canada and the United States caused all Canadians to be treated as American citizens.

He saved his most provocative point until last, though. 'No ground is more favourable for the new techniques of political destruction than that where substantial elements are present which do not identify themselves with the rest of the institution, or community, or nation ... as in opposing aggression from outside, so in resisting destruction from within, the corporate sense of a people is its strongest safeguard.' These sentiments inflamed Hogg to fever pitch, and also to his usual orgy of self-reference, almost immediately: 'I think Mr Powell is perpetually talking about subjects which he does not know as much about as other people. I have lived with this problem all my life. I am a man of Irish extraction. I married a wife of Irish extraction, and I think if Mr Powell did know as much about it as I do he would have made a very different speech.'[49]

It was Europe, though, that Powell had chosen as the opening and principal theme of his autumn campaign. Expanding and developing the themes of his Clacton speech, he called at Smethwick on 5 September for a whole new mood on the issue. Mischievously, he began by quoting (with apparent approval) recent remarks of Heath's, who had said that after the two failed attempts at entry to the EEC 'it is natural that people should want to look again at the whole argument from the beginning'. Powell said that 'Mr Heath never more accurately hit off the instinctive feeling of the great majority of his fellow countrymen than in those words.'[50]

He reiterated that the departure of de Gaulle had prompted new consideration about Britain's place in Europe and the world. He felt it was not just de Gaulle who had kept Britain out; he had merely voiced the views of several others, who could leave their own feelings to be expressed by him. Now he had gone, Powell said, others would voice the same objections. He argued that there had, in Britain, been a massive change of view since 1961–2. 'If the negotiation had succeeded, I believe the outcome would not have been rejected by the electorate as a whole but accepted with the general feeling that this was the way of the world and would give us an impetus, a challenge, even a shock, but at least a kind of new start such as was vaguely felt to be needed.'

Now, he said, there was a demand that 'a clear, definite and cast-iron case be made out before Britain is again committed to accede to the Treaty of Rome. People are prepared to listen to argument. They are no longer prepared to be led blind, as they might have been seven or eight years ago, on a general hunch.' That was Powell's way of saying he had looked into the matter more closely than before, and had felt the need to change his mind. He said the performance of the Six in the seven years since Britain's first application had done nothing to promote faith in their institutions. He claimed that his party would have to announce, unequivocally, in its next manifesto where it stood on the question of European unity. There were two main considerations for it to take into account: the economic and the political.

On the first, Powell admitted that at the time of the first application 'it was assumed – and I shared and argued the assumption – that that there was a positive and negative economic gain for Britain in membership of the Common Market'. The positive gain was the widening of the market for British goods; the negative was that Britain would not be excluded by the tariff barrier of the Six, and would be better off inside it even though that then put up a barrier between Britain and the rest of the world. Powell felt that those assumptions had since been discredited. 'The disastrous results that were predicted from our exclusion have not presented themselves.' Powell also pointed to higher growth and incomes in some European countries, like Switzerland and Sweden, outside the Common Market. The argument was not for the EEC, but for 'free, or freer, trade all round'.

He looked at the Common Agricultural Policy and found it appalling: artificially high prices punishing first consumers and then, because the consumers could not afford to buy as much as was produced, punishing consumers again (this time as taxpayers) in having to fund the surpluses. This, he reminded his audience, was to be the model for other common policies, and was the bridge to the political consideration.

When advocates of accession to the Treaty of Rome find the economic argument difficult to sustain, they commonly shift the ground by saying: 'After all, the real justification is political,' and in the next breath we begin to hear about European unity. Both words in this phrase are liable to be grossly misused. The word Europe is rarely, if ever, intended in its only precise sense, which is the geographical area delimited by the Atlantic, the Mediterranean, the Black Sea and the Urals. The word unity fares still worse: for unity is an absolute – as the mediaeval song says, 'One is one, and all alone, and evermore shall be so' – and in a political context is being abused if it conveys any less connotation than in 'United Kingdom' or 'United States', namely, that of a single, independent, sovereign state.

Powell said the main political argument seemed to be that only a big country could have influence in the world. To him influence was unlinked to physical size, and depended strictly on military might. If the argument were put that it had nothing to do with military might, then the size of a country was irrelevant also. 'Influence must mean persuading others to do what one thinks they ought. I question anyhow whether this is a proper ambition for one nation in relation to others ... but as good and laudable an example can be set by a small nation as by a large one, and history to this present day is full of the instances which prove it.' He identified the issue that was to hamstring proponents of 'unity' into the 1990s: 'Whatever is meant by unity in the context of Britain and the European Economic Community must imply that, within that meaning, the views and wishes of the majority are accepted by the minority or minorities.'

If agreement to operate like this were not to be obtained by force, he argued that it could be obtained only by the complete conviction of all those taking part in the union; otherwise, democratic and other institutions would become unworkable. Without those institutions working, 'the acts of sovereignty, which a political unit must perform, on behalf of all its members and binding upon all its members, would be intolerable and unacceptable'. He had, correctly, identified the Achilles heel of the movement to complete European union. He asked whether the British people could really foresee themselves as part of a single electorate for such pan-European institutions as would be needed, with their nationality and national wishes counting for nothing if in a minority of other nationalities and their wishes. 'If the answer to that question is no, then we cannot envisage democratic institutions; and if we cannot envisage democratic institutions, then we dare not advocate on political grounds the accession of Britain to the European Economic Community.' He already knew the answer.

Anti-marketeers in both parties welcomed Powell's speech. It provided them with a coherence and leadership they had hitherto lacked. Thus far, Labour politicians had made all the running in the campaign against entry; now, at last, Conservative opponents of the EEC had someone to follow. It was still an issue of relative unimportance in the party. At the time Powell spoke, 384 motions had been submitted for debate at the next month's party conference, and only one was about the EEC. It was equally clear that Heath and his shadow cabinet colleagues would not be shifting an inch from their agreed position to support a new application for membership. However, in terms of Powell's philosophy and the effect on his followers, the Smethwick speech had done for the EEC issue what the Birmingham speech had done for immigration, and it had set up what, in the end, would be an even more destructive collision between Powell and his notional leader. Again, Powell infuriated the leadership with his timing. Some had seen, from his Clacton speech, that he was warming to the issue, but had thought he would wait until the party conference before going into detail. Now, though, he had ensured that any discussion at the conference on the issue would be on the agenda he himself had set.

Powell's lunch with Cecil King took place on 16 September, and much of the discussion at it was about his new crusade against the Common Market. The 'main impression' his host formed of Powell, though, was 'the contrast between his very reasonable and rational conversation and his apparent fanatical personality'.[51] King flattered Powell by saying that, if there were a straight presidential fight to be Prime Minister, Powell would win it. 'He said he agreed,' King notes in his diary, 'but what was the use of that?' King then developed the point that Heath would become Prime Minister, would fail, and Powell would be positioned to succeed him. Powell was not so sanguine, reminding King that Wilson had failed for years and nothing had been done to remove him – he was not to know that King himself had privately advocated a coup to depose Wilson. Discussing Ulster, Powell wondered aloud whether 'an answer would be to detach Fermanagh, Tyrone and southern Down from Stormont and let them go ahead with an overwhelmingly Protestant three and a half counties' – something King felt would lead to the sort of scenes, on a smaller but still bloody scale, that had affected India at partition.[52] Powell was not to know that one of the areas he was considering for removal from the Union was one he would, five years later, represent in Parliament.

Later in September he also marked the leadership's card on local government reform. A Royal Commission under Lord Redcliffe-Maud, Master of University College Oxford, had been sitting on the question since 1967, and had just reported. The Commission proposed that Britain be divided, outside London, into eight provinces, fifty-eight unitary authorities and three metropolitan areas, each containing metropolitan districts. When, the following February, the Government published its own White Paper, it had dropped the idea of provinces, but added two new metropolitan districts. Speaking on 25 September, Powell branded the findings 'an exercise in socialism', and added that he hoped his party would not touch them with a bargepole. He would be disappointed, for the White Paper would form the basis of the reforms that Heath and his

Environment Secretary, Peter Walker, imposed on local government – only they did not take the opportunity of abolishing a tier of government by creating unitary authorities.

Powell was angry that there had been no commitment by his party on the issue. The time when it would have to make up its mind was drawing near. 'Descent from the fence is growing imperative,' he said. 'We must soon take our line and stick to it.' He said he found the proposals farcical, but experience had told him that just because they were absurd did not mean they would not be put into practice. 'For a lifetime the socialists have hankered after regional or provincial government as one of the instruments of socialism,' he added, saying that his party should be actively fighting against this. The eight provinces were going to be used by the Government as eight separate economic units, with separate plans and strategies, and Powell was shocked that his own party had not seen the offensiveness and stupidity of this. 'The future economic life of this country, both in total and in detail, is something which the people are going to work out for themselves in the only way that this can come about – by individual freedom and competitive enterprise. If anything could be worse than one economic plan it would be eight economic plans, all going at the same time. The very idea is hair-raising. It would be bureaucracy run amok.'

With his profound sense of nation, Powell could not but find the idea of provincial government ludicrous. Referring to the fact that one of the intended provinces ran from Cheltenham to Land's End, he asked: 'What in the name of sanity can be meant by planning the economic and social development of huge slabs of England such as these, with no coherence or common characteristic, except such as are shared with the kingdom at large?' He also found distasteful the idea of 'paid full-time officials to whose operations they are intended to add a veneer of representation'.[53] However, such bureaucracy and patronage were increasingly attractive to the Conservative leadership, which is partly why they had been so compliant with Wilson's plans to reform the Lords. Powell would not find a sympathetic hearing.

IV

At the grass roots, though, the clarity of his message was all too apparent. Marcel Everton, an industrialist from Halesowen in Worcestershire, sent a telegram to Powell at the end of September to say that a group of fifteen businessmen, of whom he was the chairman, had raised £10,000 to fund a challenge by Powell for the Conservative leadership. Everton refused to name the members of the group, but said they included a millionaire and several who were not members of the party. He did, though, tell the press that the initial sum was for the establishment of a fighting fund, and felt sure other donations would pour in once Powell agreed to stand, perhaps as much as £1 million. 'A leader is needed who would make a positive challenge to the Government,' Everton added. 'Unfortunately, Mr Heath has not achieved this. But Mr Powell would be a brilliant challenger.'[54]

Needless to say. Powell rejected the offer, and fiercely. He rebuked Everton for having told the press of the plan before he himself had learned of it, and added, 'The leader of the Conservative party has been duly elected by a known and accepted procedure and it is the duty of all members to acknowledge and support him.'[55] Having received his refusal, Everton wrote back begging him to reconsider, saying that, by 3 October, £40,000 had been raised. 'We can only ask Mr Powell to look at the response we have had in such a short time as an indication of the support he has in the country,' he lamented.[56]

Powell maintained again that his aim was to influence party policy, not to topple Heath. Indeed, he had done none of the things a leadership challenger (declared or undeclared) would have to do. He was not cultivating a group in the Commons; he was not even making himself more accessible to and gregarious among his colleagues. In short, he was simply not playing the leadership game: and it was the votes only of his parliamentary colleagues that would matter in such a contest, not of activists in the country. However, Powell was clearly keeping his options open about how he would act after a possible election defeat for Heath. Yet at that stage it was widely believed in the party – correctly – that Heath would win the election. A matching assumption at the grass roots, less well founded, was that he could not but bring Powell into the cabinet after doing so. The liberal establishment harboured a growing fear of Powell's potential, so much so that, in a leading article that seems embarrassingly hysterical in retrospect, the *Observer* of 4 October 1969 said that the press should make a voluntary agreement not to report him.

However, for all his earnests of loyalty to Heath, Powell was not planning to retreat from his headline-grabbing tactics. He had arranged to speak at Worthing on the day the party conference opened at Brighton, and again at Portsmouth on the Friday evening before Heath made his rally speech on the Saturday. Even before that, though, on the Saturday before the conference, Powell raised his anti-Common Market banner again, in a speech at Preston, ensuring the right tone was set for the conference itself. He ridiculed the pro-marketeers' assertion that it was 'vital' to join, noting that Wilson had said that British trade with the market from which we were 'excluded' had, in fact, risen by 40 per cent in the preceding two years. 'It hasn't been vital for the last ten years. It won't be vital for the next ten years. So who is kidding whom?'[57] He tied the mood of national defeatism, which had fuelled the longing to be part of the Common Market, to the emigration figures, which seemed to reflect that mood of despair. In 1968 over 138,000 Britons had emigrated, to be nearly replaced by 70,000 Asians and Africans, 24,000 aliens and 25,000 from the Irish Republic. He left unanswered, deliberately so, the question about what sort of future such movement portended.

As the party gathered in Brighton, those who wanted Powell to become prime minister would not go away. A group of businessmen from Sussex took out a full-page advertisement in the town's *Evening Argus* newspaper, calling on Heath to stand down 'and make way for a man better suited to handle the tasks ahead'. It went on: 'We believe that the best interests of all the people of this country – irrespective of colour, nationality or political party – will be better served if Enoch Powell is our next prime minister.'[58] When Powell left the conference hall at lunchtime on the first day he found himself cheered by a small group, some of whom had banners proclaiming 'Powell for Prime Minister'. As it turned out, his profile during conference week was nothing like so high as it had been the previous year. He chose the debate on economic policy and taxation in which to make his main speech of the week, and devoted it to a call for floating exchange rates.

The Powells were coping well with the profile and attention that his activities in the last eighteen months had brought him. His speechmaking and policy campaigning was a full-time job. Mrs Powell recounted that she had a chance to talk to him only when he came home to go to bed, when he would fill her in on what was going on. 'Life', she told an interviewer, 'is never dull.'[59] Powell would work more from home than before, and the telephone and doorbell would ring continuously. There were usually Greville Howard and two secretaries in the house, often supplemented by Richard Ritchie. Like Howard, Ritchie (who was not much older than Powell's daughters) was soon absorbed into the family. The postbag they had to process was between 70 and 150 letters a day: thousands came after a big speech. Powell tried to reply to all of them. Mrs Powell remained resolute in her complete support of and agreement with her husband; she was upset only by criticism of him in the press. She was his main sounding-board, a point of contact with the real world – a function also undertaken by Howard and Ritchie. In the end, though, Powell's decisions were his own.

Immediately after the conference, Powell had his television debate with Trevor Huddleston. The Bishop defended his description of Powell's Wolverhampton speech as 'evil' by saying he felt it had been calculated to increase racial tension, which was evil. Powell responded that he had thought Huddleston had meant 'evil' in the religious and not the political sense, and he had not seen any way in which the immigration issue could be considered specifically religious. This left him and Huddleston as merely two citizens comparing their views outside the religious sphere. The Bishop, though, said the threat that racial strife made to human dignity was something on which the Christian church had to speak out. The contest was for a time evenly matched, until Huddleston made an error that let Powell trump him. He asked why Powell objected to the presence of a coloured immigrant group, to which Powell gleefully retorted that colour had nothing to do with it. He had said that the presence of five million Germans in the country by the end of the century would probably bring even greater risks of violence and disruption than a similar body of Commonwealth immigrants.

Powell made two controversial speeches in the House shortly after the summer recess. In the first, on 16 October, he rehearsed his objections to Britain's maintenance of sanctions against Rhodesia. He referred to the fact that the debate was about renewing part of a statute 'which begins with the statement that Her Majesty's Government in this country have jurisdiction in and over Southern Rhodesia, and responsibility for Southern Rhodesia. I do not believe that there can ever have been another statement on our Statute Book which is so completely unrelated to the facts of the real world.'[60] This was not Powell, as his critics would have caricatured him, the white supremacist defending a racialist regime; this was Powell the vigorous post-imperialist, seeking to outline the realities of British power in Africa in the late 1960s. To make it clear, he stated, 'I could not vote for any legislation which would legalise a constitution for Southern Rhodesia under which there would not be evident and relatively early advance to majority rule.'[61]

However, he also stated, plainly, that the Queen's writ no longer ran in the former colony. The sanctions, while they were law in Britain, were a legal fiction; and it was self-deception, he added, for anyone to imagine they would bring Rhodesia to her knees. He felt that in the preceding year the chance of a settlement with Ian Smith, the Prime Minister, had receded further. The Rhodesians had decided to proclaim a republic, realising they could not maintain their loyalty to the Queen while ignoring the laws made by her Government. It was, therefore, nonsense to claim, as supporters of sanctions did, that their continuation held open the possibility of a settlement. He also asked why, if sanctions were so appropriate for Rhodesia, they were not being applied to other countries in 'a world half full of tyrannical regimes of various kinds. Half Europe groans under a kind of tyranny which we are happy to think has nothing in common with the liberties we ourselves enjoy.'[62]

A Labour backbencher interrupted him to say that Rhodesia was different, because Britain had responsibility there. Powell retorted, 'I have pointed out that there is no meaning in responsibility where there is no power – that we cannot be responsible for doing what we cannot do.'[63] He was similarly caustic about the claim that Britain had to maintain sanctions because of an obligation to the United Nations; if it was true 'that a mandate of the United Nations is in that sense binding upon this nation, binding to oblige this nation to maintain an evident absurdity ... then responsible government is lost'. Powell concluded with a call for the 'self-deception' to be ended, and sanctions to be removed. He was followed by Foot, who praised his stand on majority rule, but disagreed with his view on sanctions.

However, it was the second of Powell's speeches in the Commons that autumn, on 11 November, that was of the greater significance. He used the annual debate on the expiring laws Bill to raise the subject of immigration in the House for the first time since the Birmingham speech, since one of the laws being renewed was the Commonwealth Relations Act. In doing so he countered one of the main accusations Labour MPs had been making against him, that he was afraid to raise the matter in the Commons. He was preceded by Callaghan, who challenged him to substantiate the prophecies he had made since the Birmingham speech. As Callaghan had claimed that immigration was falling, a woman in the public gallery cried out a plea for it to be stopped, and scattered leaflets before she was marched out.

Powell accepted Callaghan's challenge. He spoke for an hour, to the irritation of the Labour party, who felt such a speech had no place in the debate. Although he was subject to the usual haranguing from the hard core – especially Faulds – he was for the most part heard in silence. It soon became a statistical lecture, though Powell did repeat his standard call for an urgent voluntary repatriation programme, which he urged the House to hear. He agreed with an earlier speaker from his own side who had said that the tensions and fears of 1969 were far less than would have been the case had the 1962 Act not been passed; but he said those fears and tensions 'are nothing to the fears and tensions which are portended by the future which we see today arising out of the circumstances that already exist as a result of the last 20 years'.[64]

Citing the level of net increase in the immigrant-descended population, he disputed a prediction, which had been used against him by Bonham Carter, that the entire coloured population would be 2.5 million by 1985. To cries of 'so what?' he stated that, in eleven London boroughs, one birth in five was a coloured birth, and in some boroughs coloured births accounted for as much as 30 per cent of the total. As Powell's flow of statistics continued, several Labour Members rose and said his remarks were out of order; the Chair disagreed, and he continued. In his peroration he rebuked Callaghan for having asked him to use his influence with the country to call for tolerance, restraint and patience. 'The right hon Gentleman has it exactly wrong,' Powell said. 'It is not to the people of this country that we in this House should be appealing for tolerance, restraint and understanding. The people of this country have shown tolerance and restraint in a way which could not have been anticipated ... the appeal is from the people of this country to this House – and this House has not heard them yet.'[65] He was cheered by many on his own side when he sat down, though Hogg, conspicuously, was immersed in gloom on the front bench. Several later speakers, including his fellow Wolverhampton Member, Renee Short, and David Steel attacked what Powell had said; but the occasion had little of the drama and tension that had been expected of it.

A unique insight into Powell's private mood at this time can be gained from notes by Michael Strachan of a breakfast with him at South Eaton Place on 6 November 1969. Mrs Powell had gone to Funchal as part of a convalescence after an operation. Powell opened the door to Strachan in his dressing gown, and took him downstairs to the kitchen to cook him bacon and eggs. Powell began by talking about his family, not least about his daughters' satisfactory progress at Wycombe Abbey, and especially about how Susan, the elder, had been said by the Staffordshire county tennis coach to be capable of reaching Wimbledon standard if she applied herself. For all the distractions of his political life, Powell never devoted himself any less thoroughly to his family than he did to political issues.

He told Strachan he was able to cover half his staff costs from his parliamentary allowance; the other half was met by well-wishers, notably Lord Warwick, a fact he would confide only to close friends. His wife's main complaint was that so much of their house was taken up by office space since the events of the previous year. Looking forward to the next election, Powell told his friend that 'I am driving blind, but it is foggy in any case.' Strachan interpreted this to mean that, if power were offered to him, he would seize it.[66]

His personal security was of some concern to him, though he said there were 'not many murder threats through the post'. The police had him, his home and his family under constant surveillance, and he believed the main threat to his safety was not from extremists at home, but from the American Black Power movement. He confessed his surprise that the movement had not, so far, emerged in Britain, but felt sure it would. He told Strachan he wanted to stay in the Commons long enough to be Father of the House – which he suspected would take another twenty years – rather than go to the Lords, which 'isn't fun any more'. Grinning, he said that the only worthwhile honour left was the Garter.

The new parliamentary session was characterised by a common assumption that it would be the last before an election: an assumption Powell shared. Once more, therefore, he broadened out his campaign. He spoke in the country between the end of October and Christmas on matters as diverse as the bogus nature of the balance of payments equation ('payments do balance, always, automatically, and inevitably, because payments are made by buying and selling pounds and the number of pounds bought is always, automatically and inevitably equal to the number of pounds sold'),[67] the evils of the Industrial Training Act, the Government's working party on allowing council tenants to buy their own homes, the support of the teaching profession for the sort of anarchy that he was experiencing when he tried to speak, and a renewed call for an expansion in the provisions of further education, using the private sector to fund universities and colleges. Whenever he said anything he thought might bring disapproval from Central Office – such as his speech on anarchic teachers, or one at the end of the year on the stupidity of incomes policy – he put the speech out himself, with Greville Howard taking it to Fleet Street on what Powell termed the 'milk round'.

His workload in the Commons that session was lighter than in the previous year, and more eclectic. He spoke on 18 November in a debate on the regulation of casinos, arguing that the regulatory regime being proposed by a new Gaming Clubs Bill was too stringent. He emphasised that he spoke with complete independence: 'I wish to declare a disinterest. I have never entered a casino, and I may never well do so. As a matter of rare prejudice, I have a certain distaste for gaming.'[68]

On 17 December he was on more familiar ground in the debate on the Government's new prices and incomes policy White Paper, the latest effort in its five-year attempt to sort out the deteriorating economy. Heath, opening in reply for the Opposition, talked – ironically, considering what would pass in the next three years – of the Government's 'obsession' with the prices and incomes policy, and reaffirmed his party's opposition to 'state control of prices, wages and dividends'.[69] Heath also demonstrated his lack of grasp of the causes of inflation, something that would have terrifying consequences for the economy once he came to power: he taunted Wilson for finding himself 'landed with a spiralling wage-cost inflation' because he had not had 'a real incomes policy'.[70] That was the intellectual background, at the head of his own party, against which Powell a little later made his own contribution.

In a definitive analysis of the pointlessness of a prices and incomes policy, he began by emphasising how difficult it would be to run such a strategy, even if that policy could be relied upon to work. 'It implies upon the part of the Government virtual omniscience and ubiquity ... the essential impossibility is to define the way in which individual prices and incomes have to behave in such a manner that anyone can apply the policy in practice.'[71] Mischievously, he referred to the fact that, since he had been Chancellor, Jenkins had been doing the one thing that should keep inflation down: controlling the expansion of domestic credit and of the means of financing the net borrowing requirement – in short, the money supply. Callaghan had failed to do this, and, while he was failing, the first part of the prices and incomes policy had been imposed with no real effect as a result.

'In fact,' said Powell, 'the Government have been using a prices and incomes policy not as an economic instrument – it is not an economic instrument because it is not intelligible and it is not applicable – but as a political instrument. They have been using it as a guilt transfer mechanism, as a means of transferring to the public at large the blame for the consequences of what they themselves were doing or had in the past failed to do.'[72] This White Paper, he added, was no different. The idea that individual restraint could make a difference was, he said, 'humbug'.

Addressing his constituents in Wolverhampton early in 1970 he predicted that the return of a Conservative government would be ideal for the housing market, since he trusted (somewhat optimistically) that rents would be restored to market levels, and more building would take place. Once market rents were charged, he said, 'shortage of housing would be as non-existent as shortage of clothes or bread or bicycles or television sets or mink coats'.[73] In advocating the change, Powell pointed to a political phenomenon that would later characterise the reforms of the Thatcher Government. He said he remembered how, at the start of the Conservative Government in 1951, 'blue murder was screamed over the abolition of food subsidies and price controls and the disappearance of rationing – not to mention the disappearance of the television monopoly of the BBC. I also remember that when the next election came, not a mouse was stirring to attempt to put into reverse a process which was proving itself in practice.'

Also in Wolverhampton, on 7 January, he gave the town's Rotary Club a clear insight into his quixotic ideas of justice. He condemned proposals to restore capital punishment for the murders of policemen – he was opposed to the death penalty altogether – because it 'would mean that the punishment for the offence would vary according to the professional status of the victim, which seems to me to be utterly repugnant'. In the same speech he also condemned the operation of the recently-introduced breathalyser (Powell himself drank so little as to be only a few shades off teetotalism) as being a battering ram directed against one of the principles of British justice – it represented a means of self-incrimination. This could not, he said, be justified even in the name of reducing casualties on the roads because of the fearsome precedent it set.

At Kingston-upon-Thames the following week, in a meeting packed with 1,200 supporters, he once again raised the question of Europe, demanding that searching questions be asked about the implications of a single currency and British participation in Community-wide institutions before a further application was made to join. He also took a serious swipe at Heath, in asking where the British people would seek redress if governed not as hitherto by national, but by supranational institutions: 'And what should we say? "We will turn you out, you horrid European Labour Party, at the next election, and put in the European Conservative Party, under its leader, Mr Edward—" Sorry, the needle slipped.'[74] This meeting, like so many others, was besieged by demonstrators, which caused Pam Powell some work the next day. Writing to Roseen Freeth to thank her for an evening at the theatre – the Powells and the Freeths saw each other regularly, and the theatre was a favoured recreation – she explained how she had spent the morning scraping egg off a hat and sending a coat to the cleaners because 'the aim of one demonstrator last night was better than usual'.[75]

On 17 January Powell returned again to immigration, and his doing so was a prompt for the leadership of his party to estrange him further. Indeed, his estrangement was almost without parallel or precedent, in terms of the language

front-benchers were sanctioned to use against him. In a speech to Young Conservatives at Scarborough – a speech distributed by Central Office – he said that
programmes of assistance for predominantly immigrant areas, or to promote
integration, were 'positively harmful' unless complemented by voluntary and
assisted repatriation, because they helped deceive everyone concerned about
the scope of the problem.[76] He repeated his insistence that it was not too late to
act. Referring specifically to his quotation from Virgil about the bloodshed he
foresaw, he commented that 'huge notoriety has been fastened upon these
words, as if the anticipation were something unique to me. But of course it is
not. It is those who imagine such a future exempt from civil strife who are
indulging in the personal flight of fantasy.'

He urged his fellow Conservative MPs to force the matter to be debated, in
the open, in the Commons – 'let us have it out into the open as a party, without
prevarication or excuse' – and he spoke of the way in which cities such as
Wolverhampton, Birmingham and the inner suburbs of London were already
one-fifth black, with the proportion being further enlarged by the migration of
whites from those areas. He also quoted from local newspapers prominent
reports – reports which, he noted, had for some reason failed to make the
national newspapers – of racial skirmishes in Gloucester and in Brixton in the
second half of 1969, justifying his earlier claims that civil strife would break out.
He mocked the attitude of other senior politicians: 'It will be all right after all,
provided we can just alter human nature.'

Still contemptuous of his party's own projections, Powell again outlined the
basis of his own. The proportion of coloured births of the total in Birmingham
had risen from 6.8 per cent in 1958 to 21.2 per cent in 1968; that meant that 15
per cent of children aged under twelve in the city were immigrant-descended,
and to that figure had to be added those not born, but settled, in the city.
Around forty children of school age were arriving in the city each week, an
average of 2,000 a year, taking the proportion up to 20 per cent of those under
twelve. In Wolverhampton the proportion of coloured births had risen from 23
per cent in the inner area in 1963 to 26 per cent in the newly enlarged borough
in 1968. He claimed that, even allowing for a decline of 1 per cent per year,
Wolverhampton's coloured births would be an average of 20.5 per cent a year
over the next ten years, and this ignored all further net immigration, and ignored
children of those born in Britain. He also assumed the fertility rate was the same
in both the indigenous and the immigrant populations.

His main point, though, was the waste of money on aid to immigrant areas.

It is the hoariest of fallacies, which experience has refuted over and over again,
to suppose that the morals of a society will improve, individually or collectively,
if that society is better housed or better educated or consumes or produces more
per head. Neither crime nor violence nor war has yielded to improvement in any

of these conditions, and there is as little reason to suppose them relevant to the causes of communal strife. It is a perilous delusion to talk about the consequences of Commonwealth immigration in terms of council housing or school building, as though they would be altered or removed if only sufficient public money was expended.

Both Heath and Hogg immediately dissociated themselves and the party from Powell's remarks. Heath said that to cut off aid to immigrant areas would be 'an unChristian act', and added that if the money were instead used for a programme of voluntary repatriation it would be 'an example of man's inhumanity to man which is absolutely intolerable in a Christian community'. He also said categorically that he had no plans to bring Powell back into the shadow cabinet, or into any cabinet he might form after an election victory. 'His views clearly do not accord with the policy of the whole party and this is one of the facts of life.' As far as Heath was concerned, the party had a policy on immigration with which it was quite happy, and it did not intend to change it.[77] It was the formal statement of Powell's detachment from the party of which he was nominally a member. However Heath, interviewed on television, said he was not going to withdraw the whip from Powell, despite this further provocation: he had a right to express his views.

Hogg, as usual, was more hyperbolic. 'If he goes on bellyaching like this, he will lose us the election,' he said. He resumed his attack on Powell's failure to raise the issue more than twice in two years in the Commons. 'It is Mr Powell's habit to make these speeches to an audience which has not the necessary information to apply serious criticism to them. He selects his audiences to get the minimum criticism. He is, in fact, doing the very thing which he falsely suggests the Conservative party is doing.' Powell immediately rebutted the distortion of his views. He did not want aid ended. He reiterated that he had said it would be harmful unless part of a policy that included voluntary assisted repatriation. Again, Heath and Hogg seem to have read the headlines, not the speech. However, when on 19 January Powell attended the backbench party Home Affairs Committee, Hogg – who tried in private to maintain the good relations that had long since disappeared in public – wrote in his own hand to Powell to say, 'I was delighted to see you at the Home Affairs Ctte tonight. You were most welcome. I am sorry we had nothing much on the agenda for you. But we run our business v. informally, & I hope you will not only come often, but raise any subject within our terms of reference, with, or without, notice.'[78] Of course, Hogg was trying to make Powell speak on immigration in a parliamentary context, where his views could be subject to the scrutiny of colleagues, but Powell seems to have taken his invitation kindly. Later in the year, the two men corresponded briefly on some classical references, so there was no obvious private hostility.

On 23 January Powell went to St Andrews, to the annual dinner of the University's already famously free-market Conservative Association. Among friends and sympathisers, he made a rapturous defence of market economics. Reflecting specifically on the continued complaints about pay, he observed that 'it is not possible, for any significant length of time, for anybody to be either overpaid or underpaid'.[79] No business could survive if it failed to pay a market rate for the job – an astonishingly heterodox assertion in those days. He warned, though, of the state's ability to ignore some of the laws of supply and demand through its raising of taxation.

Before he left Scotland, Powell opened up another controversy. He lamented to an audience in East Lothian on 24 January that so many of the country's brightest young people wanted to emigrate. A survey of 1,000 Cambridge under-graduates had just found that 27 per cent of them intended to emigrate per-manently; the proportion was higher among science than arts students, highest of all among those wanting a career in industry. 'If we are not shocked by this,' Powell said, 'we ought to be'.[80] He said that in the age of Empire it had been normal for bright young people to think of working abroad, but now the Empire had gone it was 'a sign and a portent' that so many wanted to leave. Powell said it was up to politicians to ask whether they could do anything to reverse this trend, and added, 'Wherever in Britain a young man looks to the future, he finds more and more that the shadow of the state lies across his path.' It controlled so much of industry and what should have been enterprise; it was eradicating the last vestiges of independence from professions such as medicine and education; and in business, 'the highest and most necessary skill is to know how to live on terms with the state, in all its ramifications from industrial training boards through exchange control to the ever more ingenious and ubiquitous tax collector'.

Powell had, since 1964, been outlining what had to be done to make Britain a country the well qualified would not want to leave. Now, he issued a veiled challenge to Heath, saying the country would become completely unattractive to anyone of ability 'if for another four or five years the state were to extend and strengthen its grip as it has done in the last four or five: or if – and this perhaps is the nearer and more hidden danger – the opportunity to roll back the state were proffered but not taken'. He cited, as one of the other needless intrusions by the state, the maintenance of rent controls, saying that rents were too low in Scotland. This was greeted with a cry of 'Fascist!' However, Powell told a young man who had pressed him on the issue that 'you can provide yourselves with cars, food, clothing, television sets and the rest. Is there something peculiarly wrong that you say you cannot provide yourselves with houses?'

In early February Heath took the shadow cabinet to the Selsdon Park Hotel in Surrey for a much publicised brainstorming session that would set the tone of the party's forthcoming election campaign. It was, ironically, to cast Heath –

until his U-turn in 1972 – as what Wilson sneeringly termed 'Selsdon Man', the embodiment of a form of sub-Powellite anti-statist economic and industrial policy that put, to use a later phrase, clear blue water between the Conservatives and Labour. It seemed to represent a victory by the much derided forces of Powellism in the battle for the soul of the Conservative party. To Labour, this action by Heath seemed to confirm Wilson's suspicion that, ever since he had sacked Powell, Heath was now 'on the run in terms of policy' and 'on some issues following Mr Powell's line with a delay of three to four months'.[81] It was ironic, then, that this was the moment when Powell chose to distract attention from this great act of purpose and vision by his leader by writing to him to complain about his wilful misinterpretation of the Scarborough speech.

Powell had been especially angered by Heath's assertion on the BBC the day after the speech that he had advocated an end to aid for immigrant areas. Not wanting to make too much of a scene, but determined to have the record put straight, he negotiated with Whitelaw an exchange of letters with Heath in which Heath could, without eating humble pie, agree that Powell had not said what he was accused of saying. Whitelaw, who had been trying to patch up the quarrel between the two men, agreed. Powell told Heath in a letter issued to the press – he no longer saw any reason not to follow the leadership's example of washing whatever dirty linen it had in public, and Whitelaw agreed to the correspondence being published – that 'no-one who has read the speech could reasonably understand the conclusion or implication of it to be that which you are recorded as asserting'.[82]

Heath, however, was not so charitable towards Powell as Whitelaw was. He was convinced, not least by some of his advisers, that Powell was laying a trap for him.[83] Livid, too, that once more Powell had rained on his parade, he replied as follows:

Dear Enoch
    Thank you for your letter of 2nd February about my broadcast on *The World This Weekend*. My remarks were based on a careful reading of the whole of your speech at Scarborough, and I have nothing to add or alter.
        Yrs ever, Ted[84]

As had been agreed, the letter was released to the press, and the usual supporters of Heath were primed to make sycophantic noises about its wit and brilliance to obedient lobby correspondents, notably Harry Boyne of the *Daily Telegraph*, who reported it – and the Central Office brief on immigration that accompanied it – without dilution, criticism or amendment. Unfortunately, it did not acknowledge the key fact that Powell had not called for aid to immigrant-dominated areas to be cut off; and even Boyne, while suggesting that Powell had asked to be misquoted by using 'tortuous sentences' to get his message over, suggested that Heath may have gone too far in using the adjective 'unChristian'. (It was a supreme irony that when, in 1976, Boyne was finally knighted for services rendered it was by Wilson, not Heath.)

Powell's customary serenity was dented by Heath's reply. Just when most of his party hoped the controversy would end, and allow them to pull together for what they now believed was an imminent election, he issued a further, unusually hostile, statement. 'When someone says that his words have been mis-understood, it is usual to accept this, even between opponents, let alone col-leagues in the same party. I am sorry that you have chosen not to do so.'[85] The two most prominent Conservative politicians were now, therefore, in a state of publicly declared mutual enmity, at a time when the party could most have done without it. Heath was clearly in the wrong but, even had he not been, Powell's massive support at the Conservative grass roots would not have been impressed by Heath's attack on their hero. On cue, the 'Powell for Prime Minister' campaign erupted again, Marcel Everton announcing he had now raised £92,000 and was seeking to establish a national federation of groups wanting to achieve that aim. One letter from a donor of £500 was typical: 'It is essential that a massive campaign is mounted to bring Heath down before the election. It is better for everyone to vote Labour than give Heath any chance. If he loses, the Tory Party will fall into Enoch's lap like a ripe cherry.'[86] For all their intentions of being organised, and for all their money, the group was still hopelessly unsophisticated politically: Everton's latest idea was for a 100,000-strong march from the Powell heartland in the West Midlands to Central Office to demand his appointment as leader. Yet, however naive they were, they represented a current of opinion Heath and his supporters could not afford to ignore, for it would live on after his election victory.

Meanwhile, Powell went on television to talk, guardedly, about his strained relations with Heath, and the campaign against him in his party. 'You know how the game is played,' he said. 'One word from me and I am rocking the boat.' He also said he would like to be Minister of Repatriation in a future government.[87] He hinted that he would welcome a return to office. 'I am on the boat all right that is going to sail into Parliament with a Tory majority. But whether I am on the bridge is not up to me.'[88] Heath had, however, that very day signified again that Powell would not be on the bridge. Speaking to the Young Conservatives' conference at Llandudno, he said, 'I understand Mr Pow-ell's position. He has different views from the whole shadow cabinet on almost every item of party policy. My job as leader is to ensure that the cabinet, when formed, is a united cabinet. I am determined to have a shadow cabinet which knows exactly what it is going to do – there are going to be no differences amongst us.'[89] Macleod was also reported as having said some harsh things about Powell, which stung Powell to write to his former friend. That letter cannot be traced, but Macleod's reply is extant: 'Dear Enoch, On personal grounds I too regret what I said, but I'm afraid now that on all the key issues of economic affairs, defence and now immigration our views are so different that we simply don't belong to the same team.'[90]

The Selsdon exercise succeeded in rattling Wilson, who showed signs of his concern – and of the fact that he was considering an election before too long – at a Labour party reception on 6 February. In a phrase that would have cheered Powell, Wilson described the Selsdon agenda as 'back to the free for all'. He said that Heath and his colleagues 'seek to replace the compassionate society with the ruthless, pushing society. The message to the British people would be simple and brutal: "You're out on your own." '[91] Closer to home, he pointed up the debt that the new agenda owed to Powell. 'Of course, I know Enoch is *persona non grata*, but despite these highly publicised governessy slaps on the wrist he gets from time to time for speaking out of turn, the last two years show that what Enoch says today Edward will be proclaiming as Tory policy anything from three to six months later.' Wilson said the Conservatives were casting back to 'the Britain of the 1930s, that halcyon era when the workers were kept firmly in their places and there was no shortage of housemaids at 15s a week . . . it is an atavistic desire to reverse the course of 25 years of social revolution.' Wilson was convinced – or, rather, claimed he was convinced – that Heath would set about the wholesale dismantling of the welfare state. Yet he professed to take little notice of Heath, who was not now the true voice of his party. 'Enoch has put it with blunt clarity: restore all rents to market level and shortage of housing would be as non-existent as shortage of clothes or bread or bicycles or television sets or mink coats.' Wilson went on: 'In a free market there is no shortage of mink coats because only those who can afford them can buy them.'

At that very moment Powell was in Northern Ireland, speaking at Enniskillen. His main theme was that, as he had said the previous summer, the 'fiction of the Ireland Act 1949 must disappear': this was the act that accorded citizenship to people from the Republic of Ireland in Britain. Mischievously, Powell brought Hogg into the argument on his side, since he had just developed the policy that decreed there would be no difference between alien and British subjects not belonging to the United Kingdom – that is, those from Commonwealth countries – for the purposes of entry to the United Kingdom and residence and settlement there. Powell praised Hogg for this policy, calling it 'of historic importance', adding that 'it will be impossible, and soon be seen to be impossible, to treat an Australian, a Frenchman and a Russian on the same basis for the purposes of admission and settlement to this country but differently once they are here. It is blankly impossible that an Australian seeking to enter the United Kingdom should be no different from an alien, while a citizen of the Republic of Ireland should be treated as something which he has persistently disclaimed any desire or intention of being, namely, a citizen of this nation.'[92]

He, somewhat disingenuously, skated over the fact that the land border between the Republic and the Six Counties would have to be sealed if such a policy were to be effectively implemented: a point on which Hogg, embarrassed by his association with these remarks, was not slow to pick up. As usual, he claimed that Powell did not know what he was talking about; as usual, he made no effort to repudiate the substantive point Powell had made. However, Powell's visit to Enniskillen had a longer-lasting relevance than simply his remarks about citizenship. He was asked about the future of the assembly at Stormont, and replied: 'I think there could come a time, and I think perhaps it would be right for our fellow-citizens in Northern Ireland to be reflecting on this, when their assertion of oneness with the rest of the United Kingdom, which they clearly and passionately want to make, would be at odds with their assertion of Parliamentary independence, which is a relic of a period when a different solution in Ireland was being looked to.' It was an unequivocal statement of the creed he would take with him to Ulster in 1974, and an indication that, whatever his critics were to say at that later time, he did not start to think about the Ulster problem only when he left behind the electors of Wolverhampton and the Conservative party.

There were still occasional opportunities for Powell to turn on Labour. He condemned a Bill giving equal pay to women for three reasons: it would raise the price of women's labour and therefore reduce the demand for it, creating fewer opportunities; it would raise the price of all labour in the market, which would have to be corrected either by bringing down the overall level of employment or by inflation to lower the price in real terms; and, finally, the changing of a price – in this case of labour – by law brought with it an element of compulsion that in turn entailed that employers would try to avoid it, with unfortunate effects for women workers. This was one of the issues Powell misjudged: over the next quarter-century the labour market's operations led to more women and fewer men being employed, for with the 'price' of both sexes now equal, and the doctrines of feminism making women as keen on careers as men historically had been, it made sense for employers simply to hire the best candidate, irrespective of gender. At many levels, women were better qualified than men because they had higher records of achievement in education. Powell's sympathy for the ideas of feminism, or of equality between the sexes, was no more advanced than it had been at Sydney in 1938.

V

At a supposedly secret meeting on 17 February 1970 of the Conservative Foreign Affairs Group, a row broke out between Powell and his friend Julian Amery on the issue of the Common Market. The Government had just published a White Paper that, in the main, tried to cost the exercise of entry and weigh up the benefits for Britain. The meeting, of more than 100 MPs, was more or less equally divided on the merits of entry; the divergent views expressed at it did not stay secret for long. Powell attacked the political aspects of entry, and warned of the sacrifice in sovereignty that would be needed if Britain were to go in. Amery, however, countered that the political arguments for going in were stronger than ever, because of hints of America withdrawing from Europe. In the end, the consensus seemed to be that Britain should enter if the terms were right; but, typical of the fog coming down in the party on the issue, few had any clear idea of what 'right' terms would be, though Heath was seen to be more enthusiastic for entry than Wilson, and was thought, by Powell and other anti-marketeers, to be willing to accept almost any deal to get in.

A week later, Powell spoke in the Commons on the issue, placing himself prominently at the head of the anti-market faction. He dismissed the economic arguments for entry, as he had done ever since Smethwick, and said the market in which Britain had to operate could not be confined simply to Western Europe. He did not believe the assumption that, just because the existing EEC countries had a certain growth rate, Britain, too, would enjoy an identical rate were she to join them. Turkey, he argued, had a 6.9 per cent growth rate, far higher than that in the EEC. 'It is a good NATO country too,' Powell added. 'So what is wrong with having an economic community with Turkey, and growing at 6.9 per cent per annum?'[93] He sought to prove that growth was not dependent on the countries one joined up with, and said he was not 'frightened' by the prospect, raised earlier in the debate by Roy Jenkins, of Europe and America slugging it out in a trade war. 'The existence of that tremendous economic unit in the Western Hemisphere does not damage this country,' he said, referring to the United States. 'If I were put to it, I would rather argue that it assists than that it damages this country.'[94]

The real issue, Powell went on, was whether Britain wished to be embodied in 'a Western European unit, compact "economically, legally, commercially and politically"', something far wider than the free-trade area to which Conservative adherents of entry were already alluding.[95] Public opinion had, he asserted, recently swung against entry precisely because some of these wider implications were becoming known: the White Paper had spoken of the aims of the other members as including progress towards economic and monetary union, a common social policy and political unification. 'We are now told', he said, 'that whatever be the form – federal, confederal, or whatever – that is what the Common Market is about. Whether or not we are to be compacted with it, it is to be a unit which increasingly has common monetary, economic and social policies.' He quoted from a report from the existing heads of EEC governments, which had proclaimed that there had to be 'meaningful harmonisation of policies'; this the report defined as requiring 'that such things as growth targets, rates of inflation, unemployment, budgets and taxation must eventually all conform to a community standard'.

Powell then came to what would be the central argument between pro- and anti-marketeers, in their various forms, for the rest of the century.

> Are not social policies, growth targets, unemployment, development and taxation the very stuff of politics, about which we in this House argue day and night? Are they not subjects about which we compare our differing opinions and objects before the electors, seeking to bring them to our point of view? This is what politics is about, what this House is about, what the electoral system of the country is about. ... All pretence is now aside. All the words with which we amused ourselves two or three years ago, eight or ten years ago – I confess that I also amused myself, along with the rest – that this was really an economic matter, a matter of trade, and that the rest was pure theorising ... that is all stripped aside. The question we are deciding is whether we can and will enter into a political unit that deals with all the major matters of political life affecting the daily lives of all the people in this country, under a Government sustained by a European elected parliament. Elected it must be: nothing else would be imaginable or acceptable.[96]

He wondered whether even that would be acceptable, or whether, to the British people, it would merely be a nonsense: 'An electorate which sustains a true parliament has to be an homogeneous electorate. By that I mean that every part of the electorate has consciously to say, "We are part of the whole; we accept the verdict of the majority as expressed at the polls and then, somewhat curiously, reflected in the composition of this House." That is why this Parliament works.' He could not imagine the electorate feeling that way if they were just part of an electorate of 200 to 250 million others. 'I do not believe', he said, 'that in that sense, which is the necessary sense, they identify themselves, as part of a whole, with the electorate of Western Europe.' To demonstrate this further he moved on to the question of European military alliance and its relationship with political unity, and said it was only because British servicemen were under British command in 1940 that they had saved Britain. Had they been under the political control of an extraneous body, they would have been thrown into another battle elsewhere and 'swallowed up in defeat'. Other MPs were outraged by this, and cried out, 'Not true!'[97] Powell, though, said that this perception was the reality. He added that when the other reality, of what the Six intended Europe to evolve into, was comprehended 'it will be rejected by the people of Britain'.

The next week he took a further shot at his party's orthodoxy in the Commons' defence debate, in which he stated baldly that 'the whole theory of the tactical nuclear weapon, or the tactical use of nuclear weapons, is an unmitigated absurdity'.[98] He said that 'it is, if not quite inconceivable, remotely improbable that any group of nations or any alliance, particularly an alliance on both sides of the Atlantic, at the stage of a continental war which is envisaged, would decide upon general and mutual suicide'.[99] Powell was calling not for nuclear disarmament, but for there to be in Britain 'a continental army in being, of high quality in armament, in training and in philosophy,' with the easy possibility of expansion by professional soldiers and by the sort of volunteer reserve the Government had been running down for the preceding five years. He also implored Healey to recognise that the 'nuclear falsehood' had deflected attention from the importance of the navy, and from the concept of 'the maritime defence of these islands'.[100] However, Julian Amery seemed to misunderstand him and, when speaking later on, rebuked him for his apparently anti-nuclear sentiments. Powell corrected him. 'I have always regarded the possession of the nuclear capability as a protection against nuclear blackmail. It is a protection against being threatened with nuclear weapons. What it is not a protection against is war.'[101]

That month, Powell had an early triumph in his battle to prove that the immigration statistics were wrong. To the embarrassment of those – not least in his own party – who had been attacking his unreliable data, the Registrar-General published immigrant birth statistics that led Powell to issue a statement demanding that official Government estimates be 'revised drastically upwards'.[102] The Government had been working on estimates that the number of births in which one parent was from the New Commonwealth were around 35,000 a year; but, using the new figures, Powell had calculated that in the six months from April to September 1969 some 23,514 babies had been born to immigrant mothers, and a further 4,968 had had fathers from the New Commonwealth. To reinforce his point, Powell said that figures showed that in any of the five preceding years the number of births in those six months was no more than 51 per cent of the annual total: so the true figure was not 35,000, but 59,000. Crossman, the Social Services Secretary, was incandescent at Powell's remarks, saying that they were 'untrue, alarmist and totally irresponsible'.

While Crossman was not prepared to be honest in public, he did confront the truth in his diaries. Less than a month earlier he had attacked the Registrar-General.

We have always had a worry with this fellow. For some reason the Registrar-General is never a trained statistician but a sort of squashy humanist from the Ministry of Health, who is perhaps good at Latin verse. The person who really runs the thing is a tough, ruthless lady, whom we must check all the time because these two are hell-bent on providing Powell with the statistics he really wants. We had only just stopped them doing this four months ago. Now they were producing the new draft of their projections of immigrant figures. I must say we had got a lot of our own way. True, they had described one of the lines, the one which showed the greatest number of coloured children, as the most realistic projection, but that was easily taken out.[103]

To counter this suspected deceit, Powell immediately tabled four parliamentary questions to Crossman, aimed at making him confirm his calculations. The figures were not easy to deny, and were a huge embarrassment
to Labour. So, instead, Crossman's deputy, David Ennals, tried the tactic of
saying that Powell was 'brilliant, inexhaustible and ruthless. Above all, he is
ambitious. The great question is, can Heath tame him?' Similarly, Merlyn Rees,
under-secretary at the Home Office, did not deny the truth of Powell's figures,
but argued that his 'grave and irresponsible error is to forecast what he thinks
will happen over the next 15 years on the basis of a single statistic relating to a
period of only six months'. This was not a matter Labour was keen to have a
debate on. Crossman, in turn, was unable to answer Powell's questions about
the status of the fathers of some illegitimate children born in 1969. Nor could
he answer a question about the proportion of births in that period where one
parent or another was from the New Commonwealth as 'information on origin
as distinct from birthplace is not collected'. As usual, many in Powell's
own party were distressed by his bringing up this issue. Even Rab Butler, for
whom he had given up office in 1963, said on a tour of India that week that he
would resign from the Conservative party 'if it swung over to the extremes
of Mr Powell's policy'.[104] In his memoirs, published the following year, Butler
was more charitable about his former supporter, saying he regretted Powell's
Birmingham speech because it belied the fact that he had a 'warm heart'.
He added that 'Powell could be a most valuable lieutenant instead of a lost
assailant, and this is a pity'.[105] He also apologised to Powell privately for the
remarks, when urging him to come to Trinity – where Butler was Master –
to dine on High Table, 'since you have always been loyal to me and I value your
friendship'.[106]

Relentlessly, Powell swung back to the economic front. He had already made
an enemy of the CBI by vilifying them for advising their members to co-operate
with Government by giving prior notice of price increases, even though the
request did not have the force of law. Now, in a speech to Young Conservatives
at Eastbourne on 21 March he vilified them further for advising non-cooperation
in future since the CBI had taken exception to the proposed Commission on
Industry and Manpower. He drew a wider ideological point, that fear rather
than obedience to the law was more and more influencing the actions of the
British people, which was the essence of the police state 'whether it comes under
the jackboot or on the feet of doves'.[107] A month later, at Sevenoaks, he rebuked
the CBI again, this time singling out its director-general, Campbell Adamson,
for expounding the heresy of incomes policy. 'Only a week ago Mr Adamson
told the Lincolnshire Iron and Steel Institute that a voluntary incomes policy
was a necessity in our society, and that something more than voluntary methods
may be necessary if the situation is not to get out of control. How many times
round do people have to see the horror film before they remember how it ends?'

For now, the Selsdonised Conservative party showed no signs of listening to its friends in the CBI.

In the Commons on 7 April Powell laid down his guiding principle in relation to the Ulster troubles. 'It is of the nature of all internecine violence that it lives on hope. Violence feeds upon the hope of success ... violence will not continue indefinitely where the objects which it proposes to itself appear to be unattainable, or at any rate unattainable within a predictable future.' He did not deny that the nationalist community in the Six Counties might have complaints against the authorities there, 'but it seems to me perfectly clear that such grievances as there are have been exaggerated out of all proportion to serve the purposes not of reform but of anarchy itself'.[108]

His point was simple: 'The Government in Northern Ireland and the Government in this country actually assist violence and strengthen it in so far as they appear to act and appear to reform under the pressure of violence.' He urged the Government to see to it that 'neither by word nor deed do we treat the membership of the Six Counties in the United Kingdom as negotiable. Every word or act which holds out the prospect that their unity with the rest of the United Kingdom might be negotiable is itself, consciously or unconsciously, a contributory cause to the continuation of violence in Northern Ireland.'[109] He went on to argue, as he would for years ahead, that the best way to insure against this was a policy of integration of the government of Ulster with that of the rest of the Kingdom, and removing the citizenship rights in Britain of Irish nationals.

In a speech a fortnight later on Jenkins's last Budget – as it was to turn out – Powell, in praising him for bringing about a debt repayment for the third successive year, referred to what would become the main items of disagreement between himself and the Conservative government that would take power within two months. He congratulated Jenkins on the 'profound change of philosophy' that had allowed him to achieve this probity: 'He based his policy upon control of the money supply and control of domestic credit.'[110] Yet inflation was still roaring ahead, in defiance of logic – and of Powell's own beliefs. Powell urged Jenkins to stick with the policy, and not imagine that, after all, a return to incomes policy might be necessary. The time-lags in the economy, he argued, were longer than generally assumed. It was the credit expansion, and the growth in the money supply, of Callaghan's last disastrous year as Chancellor that, he said, had caused the present difficulties, not the policies Jenkins was pursuing.

Powell still had to put up with heckling and offensive remarks against him in the Commons, and became angry when the Speaker did not act to prevent unparliamentary attacks on him. One such was a self-advertising speech by the Labour MP Leo Abse in a debate on the permissive society on 4 May. Abse had said, 'the language of the Birmingham racialists reveals their mad fear of the potency of the black man – the sexual rivalry felt by those uncertain of their own Wolverhampton virility ... Let there be no doubt – if we had fewer eunuchs we would have less Enochs. The speeches of the right hon Member for Wol-verhampton South-West are really about how many times a week a coloured man copulates, not about the birth rate.'¹¹¹ Powell was not present to hear this, and nor was the man who wrote to the Speaker, Horace King, to complain most vehemently about it, Sir Edward Boyle, who took a polar-opposite view of the immigration question to Powell. Boyle said he did not think such language had ever been used by one member about another, and that it was especially deplorable of Abse to make the attack without notifying Powell in advance – a courtesy, as he pointed out, Powell always scrupulously observed.¹¹²

Boyle alerted Powell to the remarks, and Powell wrote to ask Peart, the Leader of the House – who had earlier in another context reminded a Labour backbencher of the 'decencies' to be observed between MPs – what he would do about Abse's behaviour.¹¹³ Peart replied that, while he could understand Powell's feelings, it was a matter for the Speaker.¹¹⁴ Powell told him that 'it is not a question of my feelings. It is a question of the credit and good repute of the House as a whole, which is damaged when its Members cast obscene aspersions on one another on the floor of the Chamber.'¹¹⁵ Other Conservative Members raised with King their disquiet at there having been no rebuke to Abse from the Chair at the time. Powell himself raised this point with King, whom he regarded as the weakest Speaker he ever knew.¹¹⁶ King replied to Powell that he did not think at the time any unparliamentary language had been used, and that 'I cannot think I would have been on firm ground if I had attempted to intervene.'¹¹⁷ Powell, who had put up with much in the chamber since April 1968, was furious. He told King, 'I wish to place on record my belief that Mr Speaker's responsibility is not limited to requiring the withdrawal of words which are technically "unpar-liamentary", or to maintaining observance of the rules of order.' He cited an incident in 1967 where the Chair had protected Norman St John-Stevas, a Conservative MP, 'in substantially similar circumstances', and concluded that 'most of us, I believe, feel that the standard of decency in the House has deteriorated in the Parliament just ending. I do not think that in retrospect the Chair can hope to be clear of responsibility.'¹¹⁸ King replied that, if Powell and others felt so badly about his conduct, it was their duty to oppose his re-election. He concluded, 'Your letter is the most distressing one that I have received since I took office.'¹¹⁹

Before the election campaign actually started, Powell took one last oppor-tunity to set himself apart from his party – indeed, in many respects, from the national consensus – when he spoke in the Commons on 5 May in a debate on Vietnam. Following on from several idealistic speeches – Powell's preferred adjective was 'visionary' – about how Britain and America ought to be in harness together in the defence of freedom, he told his peers that there was, in fact, 'a very practical, precise and instant question before the House this afternoon'.¹²⁰ It was not, he said, 'whether Her Majesty's Government should associate themselves with or disassociate themselves from the policies and the actions of the United States Administration. If there was ever a time when we still had that choice, that time has long gone past.' It was, because of what the Labour administration had been saying for years about Vietnam, 'impossible for us now to be silent without being associated ... we have to accept that the option of neutrality in word is no longer open to us'.

He said that if it were certain American military action could bring 'independence, security, self-determination, self-government' to the people of South Vietnam, then all would support it. But he stated bluntly that 'American military power cannot secure any specific political result in South-East Asia ... this is a war in which the United States can win, if it wishes, every battle; but it is a war which the United States is bound to lose.'[121] He reminded the House that, from the moment he had become shadow defence spokesman, he had warned his colleagues privately, and then publicly, that America could not win, and that in the years since nothing had happened to make their victory look any more likely. Even if their military might were used to eliminate all enemies, the 'ultimate fact' would then reassert itself, for 'the Americans do not live there; everyone knows that their presence there, long or short, is destined to be temporary; everyone knows the realities that will prevail over them'.

He concluded that there was nothing in the friendship and alliance between Britain and America 'which requires that we should encourage a friend or an ally in a course manifestly self-defeating, a course destined to end in ignominy and failure'.[122] President Nixon had just escalated the conflict by sending US combat troops into Cambodia to attack communist bases, and Powell said this provided a suitable moment for Britain to re-evaluate her support for the course America was taking. 'We should say to our friends and allies: "At last, at length, enough!" '[123] The discomfort such heretical opinions caused the Conservatives was seized on by the next Labour speaker, Alan Lee Williams: 'a characteristically brave speech' was how he described Powell's remarks, 'as one can see from the look of his hon Friends sitting alongside him'.

VI

On 18 May Wilson went to ask the Queen for a dissolution of Parliament: the election was set for 18 June. This was a minor irritation for Powell. He had agreed to undertake a short lecture tour of the United States, sponsored by the Foundation for Economic Education and arranged with the help of the IEA, and this would now have to be cancelled. It also represented something of a financial blow. Powell was now able to command an honorarium of at least $1,000 a lecture, plus expenses.

Though standing again as a Conservative he was almost a freelance operator, the front bench putting as much distance as they could between themselves and him from the moment the campaign started. He began on 18 May, at a meeting in a school in Wembley, by assaulting Labour in general and its plans for further nationalisation in particular. With the election under way, so too was there a return to high-profile demonstrations against him. He had to run a gauntlet of several hundred shouting 'Sieg heil!' as he went into the school, but was given a rapturous reception once inside. He said the demonstrators signalled 'the beginning of the loss of freedom . . . tyranny always threatens. Liberty can never be taken for granted.' He repeated his earlier calls for the establishment of more grammar schools and the ending of public housing: he was still a long way ahead of his party.[124]

Just how far was shown when, ten days later, he published his own election address. It was immediately seen as an alternative manifesto, and he announced that almost nightly until the election he would be speaking in his heartland in the West Midlands, consolidating his power base almost in the manner of a latter-day Joe Chamberlain. The main point of the address was 'halt immigration now', but he also laid out the principal point of enmity in the Parliament to come. 'I do not want to see this country give its political independence away. The Conservative party is not yet committed to Britain entering the Common Market. I shall do my utmost to make sure we never do.'[125] His promise to counter the advance of state control under socialism can, in retrospect, be seen to apply as much to his own party as to Labour. The layout of Powell's address also caused some comment. 'You may notice one word missing,' said a senior local party official. 'The word "Conservative".'[126] This was unfair, but only just: the word was there, but inconspicuously. In inch-high letters, once the document was unfolded, the voter was urged to support 'ENOCH POWELL'. It was almost as if a contingency plan had been formed, to promote Powell rather than his party, in case the party repudiated him during the campaign. Powell had not sent his election address to Central Office for their information, and Richard Ritchie recalled being with him in Wolverhampton when Central Office rang up to ask to see it, because they were receiving press inquiries. Ritchie remembers Powell admitting he should have sent it beforehand, but believes this was a genuine oversight, not an act calculated to deceive or to cause embarrassment.[127]

Talking of the Birmingham speech, the address said it had caused Powell's dismissal from the shadow cabinet 'but evoked overwhelming approval and support for him throughout the country'.[128] Powell told his constituents that Britain faced three great dangers, 'at least as great as any she has faced before'. The first was immigration, and he asked for three specific actions: the halt of immigration, a new law of citizenship, and voluntary repatriation. The second danger was the Common Market; stressing his long-standing commitment to free trade, he stated baldly that what the Six had in mind was 'a single government, and therefore a common parliament based on one electorate. For my part, I do not believe the British people should consent to be a minority in a European electorate.' Socialism was but the third of the three dangers. But it was the promises Powell finally made on behalf of the party of which he was still a member that he was to feel a personal sense of betrayal about in the years ahead: 'Only a Conservative government, which cuts back the share of the state in our income; reduces taxation; protects the value of money; reverses the rush into state ownership and control; and gives price and profit a chance to work will lift from the people of this country the fear of a future without freedom and without pride.'

Such sentiments appealed to many in the party. A group of Conservatives in Surbiton, disenchanted with the Heathite views of their sitting member, Nigel Fisher, split off and put up their own candidate, Dr Bryan Hill, as an independent Powellite. Rumours had circulated for some time, causing Central Office to make threatening noises to anyone in the party thought to be associated with the move – though Health later denied any pressure had been put on Powell to dissociate himself from independent Powellites. Hill told the press at his adoption on 28 May: 'Pressures which have been brought to bear on myself, on my supporters, the Monday Club and even Mr Enoch Powell himself since rumours first started concerning my candidature have only increased my determination to stand in Surbiton.'[129] The Powellites in Surbiton, however, quarrelled among themselves; and a few days later Hill, who was from Cardiff, withdrew and was replaced by a local baker, Edgar Scruby.

Powell became a dominant figure in the campaign, rivalling Heath and Wilson. Labour speakers noted with amusement that, at some open meetings, home-made 'Enoch' posters outnumbered official Conservative ones among their opponents. An analysis of the column inches Powell commanded showed that in every daily paper except the *Guardian* he had more coverage than the whole Liberal campaign – usually twice as much. He attracted between a quarter and a half, depending on the newspaper, of the amount of publicity of the whole Conservative campaign.[130] It was further evidence of widespread dissatisfaction with the main parties, and of Powell's genius for tapping into a vein of national sentiment those parties failed to represent. From the start, the Conservative leadership wondered whether he would do something to torpedo them. He did not intend to give them the satisfaction of soothing their worries, and for the whole four weeks manipulated both them and the press with his customary skill.

The campaign gave him a special platform to put his views and his personality over to the public. Terry Coleman of the *Guardian* recounted how the request for an interview was handled: 'He requires to see cuttings of your previous interviews with politicians. Having examined the texts, he says you had better come to his house, rather than to the Commons, so that you can have a chance to put in the usual touches about ormolu clocks and so on. Asked for two hours, he says: "No, I think we ought to transact our business in one hour." At the door he says: "Upstairs, and let's go to work." Upstairs he asks: "How much of my published work have you read?" "[131] Aware that the press needed him more than he needed them, Powell was always able to play, and enjoy playing, these games of intellectual intimidation with reporters.

In his interview with Coleman, Powell explicitly defined his role, saying that politicians were concerned with prophetic utterances: 'And I am using the word in its basic sense, in the Old Testament sense; a speaking forth, not a telling in advance. Not a telling of the future, but putting into words a sense of what is striving to become.' He said that Parliament, like the Athenian dramatists, interpreted life: 'It is a dramatisation of the life of the nation, giving its life an intelligibility which it doesn't inherently possess.'

Having raised immigration in his election address, it was inevitable it would be used in an attempt to injure him and, more particularly, his party. It was done by one with whom Powell had been friendly, Tony Benn. Addressing an audience of 200 left-wing students in London on 3 June, Benn said that 'if we don't speak up now against the filthy obscene racialist propaganda still being issued under the imprint of Conservative Central Office, the forces of hatred will mark their first success and mobilise for their next offensive. Enoch Powell has emerged as the real leader of the Conservative party. He is a far stronger character than Mr Heath. He speaks his mind. Heath does not. The final proof of Powell's power is that Heath dare not attack him publicly even when he says things that disgust decent Conservatives.' The phrase that incensed the Conservative and Labour leaderships alike, and did nothing to help Wilson, was that 'the flag hoisted at Wolverhampton is beginning to look like the one that fluttered over Dachau and Belsen'.[132]

Benn attempted to justify his remarks by saying he had been brought up in the East End of London and had seen Mosley in action before the war; he felt the sort of following Powell was getting was in the same vein. He further challenged Heath to repudiate him. Powell, for his part, was dismissive when told of Benn's remarks while speaking at Smethwick. 'All that I will say is that in 1939 I voluntarily returned from Australia to this country to serve as a private soldier in the war against Germany and Nazism. I am the same man today.' At that meeting he had made it clear he was opposed to discrimination before the law in Britain: 'It does not follow that because a person resident in this country is not English that he does not enjoy equal treatment before the law and public authorities. I set my face like flint against discrimination.'[133] Instead of being smuggled out through a back door, as was the normal practice, Powell strode out through the body of the hall, the audience patting him on the back and shouting 'Good old Enoch!' Ritchie remembers Powell was annoyed at having to enter the campaign nationally at this stage: he had planned to stay silent until the last week or so, building up expectations through his silence and then guaranteeing headlines and the attention of the media when he started to speak. Having to come out in the open so early was an irritation, but did not in the end undermine his plan.[134]

The next day Heath – who reiterated he would not have Powell in the cabinet if he won – said he had taken the strongest action he could against him after the Birmingham speech, and felt there was no cause for Benn to criticise him. Douglas-Home was the only member of the leadership who defended Powell, saying he was a man of wide human sympathies and it was unfair to brand him a racialist or fascist. It would be another five days before Heath, speaking to a rally in Bristol, was applauded for saying of Benn, 'he has impugned the patriotism of the whole of the Conservative party, in addition to that of Enoch Powell, with whom I have differences of view but whose patriotism cannot be doubted'.[135] Wilson was furious, and Healey admitted he would not have used Benn's language himself, despite his own detestation of Powellism. The whole focus of the Labour campaign had been altered by Benn's speech, and with Powell so popular the specific assault on him by a cabinet minister could only harm Labour's prospects. As a result, Wilson ordered all ministerial speeches to be vetted before delivery, and told Benn to keep off race.[136] 'Wilson was absolutely furious', said Benn, 'and thought I had lost the election.'[137] He also had doubts afterwards about whether he should have been so personal about Powell, whom he still liked. In fact, according to Crossman, Benn should have been well aware of a Labour Campaign Committee directive to avoid making Powell an issue.[138] When, in 1974, Labour was discussing its tactics for the first of that year's two elections, Wilson told Benn to 'ignore Enoch Powell because the last time the attack on him lost five seats' – something Benn maintained was not true.[139]

Heath had an uncomfortable time defending Powell, whom all the press knew he loathed. He would state simply that Powell was the Conservative candidate for Wolverhampton South-West, and he wanted Conservative candidates elected. 'I hope', he said on 4 June, 'no-one is going to say that because I want Conservative candidates elected my views or my approach is the same as Mr Powell's.' Maudling, too, was forced to support him. Asked by a member of the public in Exeter 'why don't you expel Enoch?' Maudling replied, 'Why should we? He is a Conservative and has his own views. He is entitled to hold his own view.'[140] Hogg, though, questioned before Benn's speech about whether he supported Powell, answered simply: 'No.'[141] On the evening of 4 June, the day after the Benn attack, Heath was in Birmingham addressing a rally of 2,000 supporters, and, being in Powell's heartland, it was sensible for him to round on Benn – which he did, demanding that Wilson repudiate his remarks. He did not defend Powell. He claimed that Benn had 'made a crude attempt to smear the whole Conservative party'.[142] For the rest of the campaign after Benn's attack, Powell received about 500 letters a day; only 1 per cent were against him.[143]

In Wolverhampton, threats from extremists caused Powell's headquarters to have all their identifying marks removed, though this low profile was not assisted by having the windows taped as if against a blast. A round-the-clock guard was put on the Powells' house. Pam Powell, however, painted a picture of serenity in the household, despite the raised temperature. Her husband – who, she admitted, still felt nervous before a speech, and who would speak on a full bladder to maximise tension – had found time during the battle to mow the lawn and tend the dahlias, and to read political biographies aloud in bed to her every night. Of herself, she said: 'You can get used to almost anything, but there are still things which one does not like and things which hurt me, especially when they are said by people who ought to know better. It does not bother Enoch at all. He sleeps like a new-born baby every night. He has got terrific courage and once he has made a decision he does not look backwards and worry.'[144]

That courage would be further tested in the closing days of the campaign. On 6 June he faced the first organised demonstration against him in his constituency, when fifty people picketed a school where he was speaking. Two nights later, also in Wolverhampton, police had to keep apart demonstrators against and for Powell. When one opposed to him gave him a Nazi salute, Powell shouted over a chorus of chanting and booing:

> You may think what you are seeing here is an exhibition of youthful exuberance and bad manners. It is not. You may think it is harmless. It is not. You may think it is aimed at me. It is not. It is aimed at all of you. They are after you. All of you are their target. Its aim is to see the day to day way of life, the decent things of life, that the majority want, demolished and destroyed. It is a movement that is in its infancy in this country. It is world wide but no mistake about it, it is spreading.

Pointing at the youth who had given the Hitler salute, he said, 'Some of us personally witnessed what was done on the continent under that sign and it is a symbol we shall never forget.'[145]

Most of Powell's speeches in the campaign were on economics. When questioned about immigration, he dismissed the subject as tersely as possible, despite having highlighted it in his election address. It was an irritation to him that a three-day national newspaper stoppage during the penultimate week of the campaign disrupted the public perception of his momentum, but he ploughed on. In the West Midlands constituencies where he operated Heath was hardly on the map: one reporter noted that of all the halls Powell had spoken in during the second week of the campaign, only one had a picture of the leader. In this region Powell was the *de facto* leader, and Powellism the creed; but on public platforms, to try and keep order, Powell avoided immigration. When one candidate for whom he was speaking was asked by a middle-aged West Indian whether, after twenty-six years in Britain, he should volunteer to repatriate himself, Powell told the candidate not to answer the question, as it was really meant for him.

It seemed to some of the press observing him towards the end of the fight that Powell was beginning to lose his customary composure. He was genuinely distressed that, in an election campaign, anti-democratic elements were trying to impede his freedom of speech as a parliamentary candidate. He was feeling worn down by the dangers to his wife, who accompanied him devotedly around the constituency. Also, he knew from his own observation of the growing Conservative support in the West Midlands that the election was going to be close, and that Heath could well win, despite a rash of polls showing a Labour lead. He knew that if Heath won, he was, for the moment, finished. His high-profile campaign was a gift to the mass media – a *Daily Telegraph* cartoon had a television executive saying that 'the three party leaders are demanding equal coverage with Enoch Powell' – and in one respect it did not exaggerate his significance. The swing to his party would be higher in the West Midlands than anywhere else, and so Powell could take credit for helping his arch-enemy win the election. However, his great pyrotechnic display was soon to be snuffed out, and Powell began to have forebodings of this. Perhaps as a result, his temper frayed more easily, his speeches became more Cassandra-like than ever, and his tone more caustic. He also started to lose his voice, forcing his wife to minister to him with patent remedies to keep the message coming.

In a series of speeches culminating at Birmingham on the Saturday before the poll, Powell spoke of 'a hidden enemy within', saying the future of Britain was in as much peril now as it had been before the two world wars, because the enemy was invisible or disguised. At a school in Birmingham on 11 June, to an audience of 400 with 1,000 listening outside, he attacked what would later be called the cult of political correctness. 'Have you ever wondered', he asked, 'why opinions which the majority of people quite naturally hold are, if anyone dares express them publicly, denounced as "controversial", "extremist", "explosive", "disgraceful" and overwhelmed with violence and venom? It is because the whole power of the aggressor depends upon preventing people from seeing what is happening and from saying what they see.'[146]

Later that day in his own constituency he rounded on civil servants who had concealed the truth about immigration. 'If I have been guilty on this score it is understatement that has been my offence. On this subject, so vital to their future, the people of this country have been misled' – there was a pause while his audience cheered – 'cruelly and persistently, till one begins to wonder if the Foreign Office was the only Department of State into which enemies of this country had been infiltrated.'[147] It was right he should return directly to the theme of immigration in Wolverhampton, since it was his experience there that had prompted him to make the Birmingham speech. He told his audience that the scale of immigration was already higher than it had been in the previous thousand years of the nation's history.

He went on to give evidence of the Government's perfidy – and that of the civil servants who administered it – in detail, alluding to his questioning of Crossman earlier in the year. He referred again to the net emigration of whites, alleging that, as a result, the net increase in the black population had been as high, in the previous year, as the white, which greatly overshadowed it in proportion: by 98 to 2 per cent on official figures, by 96 to 4 per cent on Powell's estimates. He was, though, greeted with a cry of 'Rubbish!' when he said that 'there are at this moment parts of this town which have ceased to be part of England, except that they are situated within it geographically'. It did not deter him from saying, immediately, that if matters were not taken in hand 'the prospective growth in this country of the Commonwealth immigrant and immigrant-descended population will result in civil strife of appalling dimensions, and that institutions and laws, let alone exhortations, will be powerless to prevent them'.

Heath was badly rattled by Powell, and these latest speeches had pitched him and his entourage into confusion and dismay. Despite advice from wiser hands to play down Powell's new, heightened tone of doom, Heath chose to go directly for him at his press conference on the morning of 12 June. He attacked Powell's views on immigration, on help for dependants of immigrants, and on notions that civil servants were bending the truth. To the deepening chagrin of Heath's aides, the press conference, which should have been devoted to attacking Labour, was thereafter dedicated to Powell, and the question of whether Heath wanted to see his ex-shadow cabinet colleague back in Parliament: he replied, 'Er, yes.'[148] As one observer, Powell's friend the prominent *Daily Telegraph* journalist Andrew Alexander, put it: 'The message that went out from Smith Square that day was unequivocal. The leadership was in a state of war with Powell.'[149] However, there were strategic limits outside which Heath was not prepared to pursue the fight. Goaded by the press to acknowledge the precedent of a candidate in the 1950 election who had been repudiated after expressing anti-Semitic views, Heath clammed up.

Leaving his power base briefly that day, Powell went to Erith in north Kent, to speak for a supporter, John Jackson. At a meeting disrupted by demonstrations, he again attacked the civil service, stating that 'people are entitled to wonder what is the reason why year after year vital facts were either withheld or were distorted or were played down'. Embarrassingly for him, the far right continued to attend and support him, and cause trouble. As the *Sunday Times*'s report of the Erith meeting said, 'after the satisfactory dispatching of a demonstrator, a steward called to Powell: "It's all right sir. The skinheads have got him."'[150] Powell went from Erith to St Albans to speak for another supporter, Victor Goodhew, and sought to answer 'the $64,000 question' about why so much criticism of him had been voiced in the press and so little attention had been paid to the support he enjoyed. It was, he said, because the media had become his enemies. They were 'part of a brainwashing process whereby the morale and good conscience and self-confidence of one democracy after another is broken down, so that the mass of the public, the majority, are delivered over helpless ... This is what Maoism is. This is what anarchy is. This is the thing we see spreading. ...'[151]

The 'enemy within' theme reached its culmination at Birmingham the next day. 'Other nations before now have remained blind and supine before a rising danger until it was too late for them to save themselves. If we are to escape the same fate, then it is high time we opened our eyes.'[152] Powell listed the portents: the anarchy of students; the need to send the army into Ulster to prevent civil disorder; and the capitulation by the Home Secretary to the anti-apartheid demonstrators who had tried, successfully, to stop the South Africans' cricket tour that summer. 'When in 1942 the *Repulse* and the *Prince of Wales* disappeared beneath the waters of the Gulf of Siam, at least we knew that Britain had suffered a defeat. We suffered no less decisive a defeat when Britain's Home Secretary surrendered the rule of law in order to buy off demonstrators; but do enough of our fellow citizens know that it was a defeat, or do they suppose that such an event is the end of a humiliating story, and not rather the beginning?' He added that the continued huge inflow of immigrants was meat and drink to the subversives, who saw in them the raw material of future conflict and division.

For good measure, he spoke too of enemies within the BBC and the press. His old enemies on *The Times*, predictably, denounced Powell as 'hysterical' for saying these things, and took it as final proof he had gone mad, reserving for use against him the familiar patronising phrase of the self-assured, complacent establishment that 'he never seemed to have good judgment': in other words, the good judgment to agree with them. On one thing, though, the editorial was woundingly accurate. 'It is ludicrous to suppose that any British political party could be led by Mr Powell.'[153] *The Times* was not alone in overreacting to Powell's words; one of Heath's aides, having contracted the same paranoia about Powell from which his master suffered, told a journalist that the speech was 'real fascism'.[154]

Denis Healey, however, said in public what many of Powell's colleagues were saying in private: 'Mr Powell's main purpose was obviously to stake his claim to leadership of the Conservative party after the election.'[155] Powell himself knew how difficult it would be to persuade the small electorate – the parliamentary Conservative party – who would, in the event of a vacancy, have the power to choose, that he should be chosen. Few more than the fifteen who had voted for him in 1965 supported him to that extent; and they would not be mandated by their associations, however strongly grass-roots feeling was in favour of Powell. Yet some of his parliamentary colleagues were prepared to stand up for him:

Angus Maude, naturally, who said, 'I believe he is doing the party more good than harm,' Sir Gerald Nabarro, Victor Goodhew and a few others. They were, though, an endangered species.[156]

The leadership were incensed by Powell's 'enemies' speeches, feeling they had shifted the focus of the campaign just as Benn had ten days earlier. In his travels about the country Heath had been haunted by Powell – or, rather, by Powell supporters heckling him and waving placards. In a speech in Newcastle Heath, talking about the new power of the British housewife, had said that 'there is a new voice in this election', at which someone interjected, 'Yes, Enoch Powell!' This sort of thing had been doubly dispiriting for Heath, whose attempt at a relaxed meet-the-people approach had been hammered out at an emergency council of war held in his rooms in Albany on 7 June, when it was obvious the party's campaign was – unlike Powell's – completely failing to catch the public's imagination. In terms of charisma, Powell was the only thing the Conservatives had to match Wilson. Heath had been particularly distressed that his morning press conferences seemed always to be hijacked by questions about Powell, putting the leader permanently on the defensive. Over the weekend before the election, Heath's aides forced him to the obvious conclusion about this: that, after his self-inflicted wound in bringing up Powell on the previous Friday, he should, on the Monday morning, refuse to answer any more questions about him.

Macleod, according to his friend and biographer Sir Nigel Fisher, 'was furious about the part played by Powell in the closing stages of the campaign. We talked about it on the telephone and he was outspoken in his condemnation of what he regarded as a dangerous distraction and of Powell's disloyalty to the party and its leader.'[157] Fisher adds that Macleod chose not to make any public comment in case it split the party, a demonstration of his shrewdness in recognising the size and power of Powell's following. Privately, relations between the two men were not completely barren. Powell appears to have sent a message of condolence to Macleod shortly before the election, when Macleod's mother died. Again, he kept no copy of it, but Macleod's brief reply, dated 16 June, does survive. 'My dear Enoch,' it reads, 'Thank you. I am so glad you wrote. Ever, Iain.'[158]

At Tamworth on 15 June Powell – who had lost his voice the previous day and had to croak through his speech – said that many voters were frustrated because they felt the main parties were so similar that they did not offer them a proper choice. He went on to say that the voters 'find, in a way that perhaps has never happened before, that they cannot use their vote to express their wishes on what seem to them the most important political questions'.[159] His main concern was the apparent unanimity of view on the Common Market: 'The party system seems no longer to do its work of offering a choice between policies, and it is not surprising to hear so many demanding that the parliamentary system itself should be short-circuited, and the people offered the direct opportunity to say

Yes or No by referendum.' He warned that the Six had already committed themselves to a single currency by 1980, and said that if Britain were to participate in such a programme it would reduce general elections to the level of municipal ones. 'A single currency means a single government, and that single government would be the government whose policies determined every aspect of economic life.'[160]

Then, two days before the election – on Powell's fifty-eighth birthday – fighting broke out at a meeting in Wolverhampton Grammar School, a few hundred yards from his home. There were 300 in the audience, and another 1,000 heard his words relayed outside. The meeting started in a surreal good humour, the crowd singing 'Happy Birthday, dear Enoch'. Soon, though, stewards fought with demonstrators who were chanting, unoriginally, 'Sieg heil!', and the police had to separate them. Powell was able to finish his speech, but chairs were thrown across the hall as he and his wife left. He intervened to stop one over-enthusiastic steward throwing out a television cameraman; however, he then went to the front of the platform, pointed at the ranks of cameramen and said, 'The BBC and other media are now photographing trivialities with which they are concerned, not being concerned with political reality ... this is the sort of people who are in control of the channels of communication in this country – now in this room you have a very fine idea of the nature of the channels of communication upon which you are dependent.'[161] He added, in reply to a questioner, that 'despite the massive and monumental misrepresentation to which I have been subjected over the past few years, the great majority of the people in this country know perfectly well what I have been saying and agree with it'.

Yet there were more dark notes of his recognition of his own deepening isolation in his speech. He admitted he had become an outcast from his party, saying his colleagues had turned their backs on him. In telling his supporters to 'vote, and vote Tory' he said, 'I have at least one accidental advantage ... I have no personal gain to expect from the outcome other than that of any citizen ... whatever might have been obscure or undefined about the policies of the Conservative party, this at least has been made crystal clear, over and over again by the leader of the party – that if there is a Conservative Government after Thursday I shall not be a member of it.'[162] On cue, that very evening, Hogg went on the BBC and, rather than attack Labour, vilified Powell as one who liked 'to roar around the country like a rutting stag and not to play a part in parliament'.[163]

Meanwhile, Powell made his appeal to electors to vote Conservative not, pointedly, on the basis of a presidential contest between 'a man with a pipe' and 'a man with a boat'. Although he said he resented not having received the 'normal loyalties and courtesies' from Heath and his colleagues during the campaign, and felt that the leadership should better have repudiated attacks made on him which they knew to be unfounded, he was still putting Britain's freedom first in making the call. 'You'll have us in tears in a moment,' yelled a middle-aged heckler, only to find himself grabbed by four stewards and ejected.[164] 'You dare not entrust it', said Powell, returning to his theme of freedom, 'to any government but a Conservative government.' His meeting ended in uproar. A police car patrolled outside broadcasting from a loudhailer, 'Clear the streets, please.' The fifty or so demonstrators, who included a number of Sikhs, then marched towards Merridale Road, to be intercepted by police, who tore their banners and flags from them and broke placards over their knees.

The next morning – the day before the election itself – those on both sides who wanted Wilson to win were cheered by the final opinion polls. There seemed to have been a sudden, sharp swing back to Labour. Marplan's poll, in *The Times*, showed a Labour lead of 8.7 per cent: perhaps, after all, Heath was about to be defeated, allowing a chance for Powell to replace him. That day Powell gave an interview to the Press Association, in which he claimed that former Liberal and Labour supporters had said they would vote Conservative thanks to his presence in the party. 'Now no doubt there must be the odd one or two electors somewhere – odd in more than one sense of the term – who react the opposite way. I am sure they are very few, so that on balance I am confident that I have done what any Conservative would wish to do – help his party.'[165] He denied that his speeches in the preceding weeks had heightened divisions in the party, and even seemed to contradict his statement about Heath made the previous evening by denying that the two of them were 'at daggers drawn', saying that 'I have never had any but a courteous and friendly intercourse with Mr Heath on a purely personal level. What has passed between us in public life is on the record, and I no more propose to comment upon it than he does.' When asked whether he would be ready to seek Heath's job if the Conservatives lost, Powell snapped, 'Politicians do not answer hypothetical questions, even those that contain a less obvious trap than that one.'

Yet it did seem to many grass-roots Conservatives that Powell had overstepped the mark during the campaign. Powell's behaving as though the election were already lost, and the assumption implicit in that behaviour that he would then oppose Heath for the leadership, simply confirmed the loathing the front bench had for him. Central Office reported that telegrams and other messages of support had been sent to Heath expressing dismay at Powell's conduct at a time when Heath was desperately fighting for victory. A sort of panic broke out among Conservative candidates the weekend before the election, when it looked as though Heath could not close the gap. As the *Sunday Times* reported on 14 June, 'Mr Powell, many Tory candidates believe, has changed the prospect of defeat into calamitous disaster.'[166] There were calls for the whip to be withdrawn from Powell once Parliament resumed, and the adjective 'unforgivable' was freely put about by Powell's colleagues to describe his actions.

Given this sense of betrayal among mainstream Conservatives – and most of the party continued to support Heath – it is likely that, even if Heath had lost the election, Powell would not have replaced him as leader, though many of the new intake of MPs would be well disposed towards him. His best chance of achieving that would, ironically, have come four years later, when he was no longer in the party. The view from inside Heath's private office of Powell's effect on the proceedings was unequivocal. Douglas Hurd, Heath's political secretary, said that Powell had given the impression 'of a solitary prophet, filled with scorn for his former friends and colleagues, waiting for the nation to turn to its real leader ... what is certain is that he thoroughly disrupted the campaign of his own party'.[167]

Having finished in Wolverhampton, Powell was the speaker at the eve-of-poll meeting on 17 June in the Wrekin, before a packed all-ticket audience of almost 800. He said he would, whatever the outcome of the election, continue to raise the issues on which 'others dared not speak'.[168] He added, 'I think the only assurance that one can have about a man's future behaviour is his past behaviour. And therefore I am content to leave the answer in your own hands.' He reiterated the importance of electing a Conservative government. Asked what would happen if his party lost, he said it would simply have to offer the people the opportunity 'to regain the path of sanity, reason and self-advancement. Patience is the great law for politics, and patience in adversity is one of its great virtues. I only hope we do not have to show it after Thursday.' His party would not; he would.

As the first results came in on the night of 18 June, it became clear that Wilson would lose. Powell himself won Wolverhampton South-West by a majority of 14,467, his largest ever, reflecting the massive identification with him his constituents had made since April 1968; but he was less than unrestrained in his jubilation when interviewed at the count, saying he was 'not surprised' by his own success. He did not agree that the results were a vindication of his views: 'I cannot say that, even after studying the results of the whole country, since it is not possible to attribute specific causes to electoral movements, local and general.' Asked whether he had helped the swing to his party, he replied laconically, 'I am pleased to see that a lot of people are saying that. But would not anybody be pleased to hear people saying that he has assisted in the success of his own party?' Someone then asked him whether he would like to serve in the new Government, to which he answered, 'Not as Assistant Postmaster-General.' Later that night he observed, 'I have noticed that during the last few days I have been seen to help my party more than to hinder it.'[169] At the same time Heath, exalted by victory, told reporters, in answer to the obvious question and contradicting recent evidence, that he felt no personal animosity towards Powell.[170]

Nonetheless, there would be no way back.

13

UNFINISHED VICTORY

Once the consequences of the Conservative victory hit Powell he was, for some weeks, disconsolate. For days after the result he sat around on his own with his head in his hands, deep in gloom. He had realised immediately that, after Wilson, he had been the great loser of the election. His personal success in Wolverhampton was no recompense; nor was the share he could take – paradoxically – in the party's success, thanks to his influence in the West Midlands and, to a lesser extent, elsewhere. The influence was not always constructive: in Tavistock, successfully defended by Michael Heseltine, 'forty ballot papers . . . were spoilt by having "Powell" scrawled across them'.[1] Richard Ritchie, who had observed him during the campaign, believed that Powell expected the Conservatives to lose, and actually wanted them to lose: Ritchie interpreted Powell's call to vote Conservative as a reflection of his sincere belief that a Wilson victory would be bad for Britain, however much it might benefit him privately if Labour won. Seeing Powell in London on the Saturday after the election, Ritchie found him deeply and uncharacteristically depressed, and making plans to take an extended holiday.[2] 'It was the end,' his wife recalled. 'We just had to put a brave face on it.'[3]

He received a touching letter just after the result, sent by one from whom he was politically estranged but who bore him no ill-will. Though meant well, it summed up how the gamble Powell had taken with public opinion appeared to have failed. It was from Lord Alport:

My dear Enoch

Just a note to say that at this moment when One Nation has reached the top of the greasy pole, I am sorry that you are not with them, and that you have had such a rotten time during the last few months.

While I profoundly disagree with you in some respects and need all my Christian charity to forgive you for torpedoing the House of Lords Reform, the comradeship of earlier days should, and does as far as I am concerned, enable friendships to survive.

Yours ever

Cub[4]

The next day another, closer friend wrote: Thorneycroft. He told Powell he had 'watched from the wings your immense solo effort and it was tremendous to dominate the election the way you did . . . your majority was a tribute to your performance'.[5] He wanted to offer Powell some advice, consoling him on being 'the one man with cross-society and cross-class support and no power to do anything about it'. He warned Powell that, for the moment, the Government could do no wrong: 'it should be left severely alone to take its first steps without comment or interruption'. This was advice Powell took. Thorneycroft spoke of Powell's ability to 'pack so much inside himself', and said he hoped this would enable him 'to find fulfilment even at a time of what I believe to be temporary frustration'.

It took Powell the best part of a fortnight to deal with the enormous mailbag he had received after the election. He wrote to his wife, who was away in Sweden, nearly two weeks after the election to say that the letters were still pouring in, and that he had not yet been into Parliament: a sign of his sense of futility.[6] In keeping with the Thorneycroft doctrine, Powell's normal round of frantic, messianic speech-making was halted. He had taken an immediate decision not to react publicly to the result, or to any of the policy announcements or ministerial appointments made by Heath. Due to speak in Dover on 25 July 1970, he told his hosts – the local Conservative Political Centre – that he would not be coming. The chairman, Alec Stanley, told the press that 'Mr Powell has told me he sees no point in coming to Dover because he is unable to make a political speech at the present time, and has nothing useful to say.' Powell promised he would come at a later date, but it was clear that, for the moment, it would look too much like sour grapes to go on the attack against Heath. He would bide his time.

Powell's effect on the overall result was beyond doubt. This was not all helpful to the Conservatives; many seats with substantial immigrant communities, such as Smethwick (where Andrew Faulds had a 1.6 per cent swing in his favour), showed a strengthening of the anti-Conservative vote; in others where there was a large immigrant community, the swing to the Conservatives was kept down to below the national level. However, in seats where Powell campaigned actively on behalf of supporters, and in Wolverhampton itself, he helped his party: Renee Short's majority in Wolverhampton North-East was cut from over 8,000 to under 2,000. Labour reckoned the 8.6 per cent swing to the Conservatives in Birmingham Northfield and the 9.2 per cent swing in Dudley were directly down to Powell. His effect in the West Midlands was held to be particularly potent. Jennie Lee, Bevan's widow, lost her seat in Cannock on a massive swing, since she had held it previously with an 11,000 majority. 'I blame it on Powellism,' she said. 'This is a different Cannock to the one I fought in 1966.' Others blamed her indolence as a constituency MP.

Donald Stringer, the Central Office agent in the West Midlands, said that 'in the immediate environs of Wolverhampton, where his word is law, he did have a considerable effect. But in some places I feel his influence may not have been advantageous.'[7] A week later, a poll showed that Powell had created mixed feelings among the electorate: while he had overshadowed Heath and Wilson during the campaign, in the eyes of those surveyed, and while 78 per cent felt he had 'great courage and sincerity', only 19 per cent thought the Conservatives would have done better had he led them, and only 27 per cent thought he would make a good prime minister. However, only 26 per cent thought Powell 'a fanatical and dangerous man', and just 18 per cent thought he had damaged the party by his attacks on Heath.[8] Nonetheless, in exhaustive research carried out in 1974 on this election, the American pollster Douglas Schoen and the Oxford academic R. W. Johnson found it beyond dispute that Powell had attracted 2.5 million votes to his party. As Johnson later wrote: 'It became clear that Powell had won the 1970 election for the Tories . . . of all those who had switched their vote from one party to another in the election, 50 per cent were working class Powellites.' Moreover, 'Not only had 18 per cent of Labour Powellites switched to the Tories but so had 24 per cent of Liberal Powellites.' The 2.5 million estimate was conservative: Johnson believed the figure was 'quite possibly four or five million'.[9]

Powell's friend Diana Spearman analysed his postbag, and confirmed the influence he had exerted over a section of the electorate. During and immediately after the campaign, she recorded, he received between five and six thousand letters, only about sixty of which were opposed to him.[10] They came from every corner of England, and some from Wales and Scotland as well; they were varied in age group and the social class of the writer. She quoted dozens of typical comments in her analysis, such as: 'during canvassing here in Bedfordshire, I can assure you that hundreds of people voted for the Conservative party, indeed it must be said thousands of people, in support of yourself'.[11] Or: 'It was my intention never to vote for the Conservative Party again . . . but in view of your recent appeal, I shall vote Conservative.'[12]

Powell's life after Heath's victory need not have been desolate. Richard Crossman had become editor of the *New Statesman*; and Harry Creighton, the proprietor of the *Spectator*, was heavily lobbied to make Powell his editor in succession to Nigel Lawson, who had been sacked. Andrew Alexander was enlisted as go-between, but Powell refused to play. It was not, he said, a job for a politician; and he had, it turned out, been one of those who had sought to dissuade Macleod from taking the job six years earlier, on the grounds of inappropriateness.

Macleod's sudden death on 20 July stunned British political life. Powell heard of it when a news agency rang at three o'clock in the morning to ask for a comment on the death of his 'friend'. The statement he issued – composed, his wife recalled, on the spot, as he walked solemnly around the bed to the telephone on her side – said that 'I am sad to think that when Iain Macleod and I entered the House of Commons together, 20 years ago, no two members of our generation were closer politically or personally. When he left it, no two were further apart.'[13] The comment, according to Macleod's friend and biographer

Sir Nigel Fisher, 'greatly distressed Iain's family, but he might himself have considered it a compliment'.[14] Pam Powell thought it 'rather wounding for Eve', Macleod's widow.[15] One of Macleod's most lapidary comments on Powell exemplified the gulf between them, and was reeled out by profile-writers of Powell for the rest of his life: 'Poor Enoch! Driven mad by the remorselessness of his own logic!'[16] For all that, Powell was one of the contributors to the £15,000 fund established by the Conservative party for Macleod's widow, who was left in straitened circumstances – though in 1973, when approached for a donation to a Macleod memorial, he replied that it would not be 'appropriate or sincere' to subscribe.[17]

Powell was genuinely upset by Macleod's death, despite their recent distance from each other, and what he had felt to be Macleod's hurtful behaviour towards him since 1968. Although not one to make politics necessarily the basis of friendship, Powell's divorce from Macleod had been rooted in the divergence of their political view. At this time, when his political battles were at their height, his friends were his supporters: one of them recalls that disagreements over fundamental issues could put strains on friendships with Powell, because of the absolutism of his views. His friends were mainly there for support, or at most for tactical advice. On the great questions he would seek no advice but his own, and trust no one else's intellect.

The political by-product of Macleod's death was that Heath needed a new Chancellor of the Exchequer. He had appointed Tony Barber, who had succeeded Powell as Minister of Health in 1963, Chancellor of the Duchy of Lancaster, with specific responsibility for the Common Market negotiations. As party chairman since 1967, Barber had shown unquestioning loyalty to Heath. Having been a Treasury minister for the last four years of the Macmillan government, he was an ideal choice for Heath. Nonetheless, his appointment was a surprise, not least to Barber. Legend has it that he was suffering from a gallstone at the time, and facing the prospect of having to take leave of absence from his duties in order to have surgery. Such was his shock on hearing of his promotion that, it is said, he passed the stone.[18] Barber's loyalty to Heath would remain exemplary. It would also allow Heath to be his own Chancellor, with disastrous results.

Powell maintained his low profile for weeks. If he was mentally regrouping after Heath's victory, some of his supporters were taking the initiative in his name. David Carr, a London businessman, and Bee Carthew, who had become friends with Powell in the aftermath of the Birmingham speech, formed an organisation called Powellight, which began publishing a monthly newsletter in the summer of 1970. The tone was one of uncritical adulation of Powell and his works; but the group also served the useful function of distributing to what became several hundred members full transcripts of Powell's most important speeches, and details of meetings he would be addressing. It set the seal on Powell's personality cult within the Conservative party, and acted, with his arm's-length co-operation, as a guerrilla movement among Conservative acti-vists for Powellite ideas. Unlike most such political fan clubs, it could be seen, over the next four years before Powell's departure from the Conservative party made the group unworkable, to have done constructive work in building Powell up against the party machine.

More than halfway through the parliamentary recess, on 11 September, Powell announced that he and his wife would be taking a Mediterranean cruise until the beginning of November. This would preclude his attendance at the party conference, a delayed victory rally at Blackpool. The Powells went to stay with friends while awaiting the departure of their ship, delayed by a dock strike. However, at the end of September, when the ship had still not sailed, they decided to abort, though Powell said he would nonetheless not be going to Blackpool. He was home in time to make his first condemnation of an act by the Heath government: the decision to release and fly to Egypt the twenty-four-year-old Arab guerrilla Leila Khaled, who had been held for three weeks at Ealing police station after hijacking an aircraft. Powell called this an 'unconstitutional interference with the course of law', and a blow against one of the central principles of British justice.[19] That done, the Powells went to Milan and Rome, where they stayed with Powell's friend and benefactor Fulke Warwick.

In his absence, he was much discussed at the party conference. Andrew Roth's comprehensive biography of him had just been published, to deserved acclaim, and the *Spectator* – which had found a new editor in George Gale – devoted much of its conference issue to the cult of Powellism, and saturated the rep-resentatives with free copies. Powell maintained his silence until after the Black-pool event was over, and then, the lustre beginning to wear off the Heath Government, began to emerge from his self-imposed exile – or, as his opponents saw it, sulk.

He was first provoked by a letter from a constituent, Jack Bradbury, who ran a car dealership. Bradbury had received a letter from the Prices and Incomes Board demanding information about charges and earnings. He wrote to Powell complaining, saying that the information would be outdated and useless by the time it was analysed. Once Bradbury had refused to comply with the request, the Board had written urging him to do so, reminding him of its statutory powers under Wilson's three Prices and Incomes Acts. Powell, responding to Bradbury, said the Board was 'bluffing', as he had no statutory duty to comply. Heath had made no statement about the Board, whose existence Powell felt anathematical to a Conservative government; the form was not filled in, and care was taken that the press were made aware of the details of the case.[20]

On 19 October he made a more controversial re-entry into politics still, writing an article for the *Daily Telegraph* on the occasion of the twenty-fifth anniversary of the United Nations. He spoke of that group of politicians who 'are living out their lives with a bad conscience about the United Nations'. He admitted he was one: having attacked almost everything else, he had never attacked the UN. He had never been specifically civil about it either, but that was not the point. He, like many others, had never argued against the UN because it was about peace, and peace was 'a good thing'.[21] The UN embodied a 'superstition' that protected it from attack: a notion of 'peace' unknown to politicians, but known to philosophers, in which – unlike all human experience – the possibility of war was not envisaged. Powell said, in a comment that applied more widely to his range of views, that 'the Lucretian argument "that gods there are, *for all men so believe*" is daunting to all but those few stout hearts who are always a minority; and the politician's business is, if possible, with majorities'.

He said he could maintain his 'guilty silence' no longer:

> The United Nations is, always has been, and always will be, an absurdity and a monstrosity, which no lapse of time and no application of ingenuity and effort can remedy. It is so because it embodies a contradiction. The United Nations, as its very name declares, adopts as its basis the nation, the sovereign, independent, self-conscious nation. If anything, this basis has become more pronounced over the past 25 years, during which no sooner has the tiniest group been recognised as a nation than it has been enrolled in the company of the elect. As between these entities the United Nations purports either to maintain what those ignorant of Latin imagine to be the *status quo*, or to regulate its alteration without the use of force (which must of necessity include the prospect of the use of force).
>
> Here lies the fatal contradiction; for the very nature and existence of the nation itself are inseparable from force, which is why the rise and growth and disappearance of nations is mediated by force. A nation is unthinkable without the prospect and the intention of defending itself and its territory, and this necessarily implies the prospect and possibility of being attacked. Without war the sovereign nation is not conceivable.

Thus the UN, 'which denies the most fundamental fact about the units of which it is itself composed', was an absurdity. Powell concluded with the thought – again one of wider application to his philosophy – that 'we are not permitted to ignore the conditions of our existence just because we choose to find them distasteful ... Perhaps the urge which again and again impels men – and sometimes politicians, at that – to denounce folly and absurdity, however strong the prudential reasons for silence, is in the last resort only a working of the instinct for self-preservation, not of the individual but of the race.'

Later that week Powell went directly on the attack against Heath. The Prime Minister had just appointed John Davies, the former director-general of the CBI as Secretary of State for Trade and Industry before, as Powell put it in an article in the *Spectator*, he had learned 'the parliamentary arts' – he had been elected for the first time only four months earlier.[22] He added, 'Mr Heath has given his silent but effective verdict' on parliamentary government. 'When

Caligula made his horse consul, he was telling the Roman senate what opinion he held about them and about government; and the Roman senate understood perfectly what he meant.'[23] Heath was manifestly of the view that government was not about what Parliament was about; it was about professional knowledge or experience, not about politics and persuasion: 'for him, in the last analysis, government is about means and not ends'. It did, though, allow Powell to pay tribute to Macleod, whose death had precipitated Davies to the cabinet. It had taken Macleod five and a half years in Parliament to reach that pinnacle, after he had repeatedly proved himself with distinction in debate. The contrast with Davies could not have been more stark. Moreover, Powell pointed to the lack of success that Frank Cousins, a minister in the previous administration, had had after being catapulted in from a post as a trade union official. He could not understand Heath's 'propensity' to repeat some of the most blatant mistakes of Wilson. What had driven Heath, Powell feared, was 'the determination to de-politicise government'.

Powell co-operated with ATV, his local television station in the West Midlands, in an hour-long documentary about him broadcast on 10 November. The programme received immense pre-publicity, prompting both Central Office and the House of Commons library to ask for transcripts in advance. The documentary was most noticed for its footage of Powell as a horseman, but also for his clear statement that he had further ambitions in politics: and that he thought Heath feared him. 'I think he's afraid of me. He generally seems to exhibit the symptoms of fear. It seems to be the only thing which really rationalises his behaviour where I am concerned. I don't wish to be unkind. I'm not being unkind at all. We all have things which we fear, and we all fear things which we don't fully understand and forces which we apprehend may perhaps be bigger than ourselves.'[24]

He admitted he had engaged in great introspection about his Cassandra-style behaviour, trying to ensure he was not wrong in making the forecasts he had about immigration. 'A lot of people wouldn't believe that. A lot of people wouldn't believe the figures and projections for the future, how often I've started again and said: "Now look, Enoch, you've got this wrong: just get this into your head and start again, and work it out again, reason it through again," because I had wanted not to see, but I had to.' Naturally, Powell was pressed on his immigration speeches, and said the settlers from the New Commonwealth in Wolverhampton were 'part of somewhere else'. Looking back, he said the Birmingham speech had been 'a seismic event for me personally and, if it is not too large a claim, perhaps for politics'.[25] He was asked whether he felt anyone else in British politics occupied a similar special role to his own, and replied obliquely: 'I was profoundly obliged when one distinguished political commentator during the weekend of a party conference drew a parallel between me and Harold Wilson. Because to be compared with one of the most astute politicians of the time, whatever else one might have thought of him, seems to be the one thing I was missing. I welcomed that with both hands.' He was able, too, to shoot some of his own complex personality into the interview, saying he had a 'nil return' of friends in the normal sense of the word. 'I sometimes think I would have made a good monk. I don't feel it would have got on my nerves.'

He was still waiting for a real issue he could pick up and use against the Heath Government, and in so doing attract more public support and not risk marginalising himself. The Common Market would soon provide it, but for the moment he returned to an older agenda, the economic arguments that had dominated his political life since 1963, and the theory of the role of the state. For nearly a fortnight after Barber's Budget on 27 October he held fire, knowing that all Budgets look profoundly different once the excitement and hyperbole have died down. He welcomed the sixpence cut in income tax, and the Government's decision to abolish industrial grants and the regional employment premium as a token that they were serious about letting industry run itself without state interference, but lamented that public expenditure was still expected to rise by 3 per cent in the next year, at a time when he did not expect the national income to do so.

Even he, though, did not predict the huge inflation, without precedent, over which the Heath Government was about to preside. With regard to his own position, he remained cautious at this stage in his criticism. 'The deduction is clear: it is no criticism of a Government so new in office, but it is clear nevertheless. The policies which can bring about the major reductions of taxation expected of a Conservative government are still in the future. We have not heard them yet. No doubt they have not been decided yet.' His warning, too, was clear.[26] The months ahead would see a substantial rebuilding of his position, based on his correct analysis of the problems facing the Government against Heath's false one. He would also attract more support and sympathetic coverage in the press, many of whose luminaries, according to Maurice Cowling, 'needed Powell to persuade them of what they had only half-believed, that the conclusions of a pessimistic sub-section of the intelligentsia were in many ways the opinions of the people'.[27]

Powell resumed his customary level of parliamentary activity that autumn. On 9 November he spoke in the debate to renew sanctions against Rhodesia, which were now, for the first time, being imposed by a Conservative government. He was one of twenty-one to vote against their renewal – demonstrating the size of the right-wing hard core on the backbenches, though Powell's reasons were not the same as what might politely be termed the old colonialist views of most who voted with him. The next day he found another element of new policy to oppose, though this time he voted with the Government – Powell always believed he could only handle so many rebellions at a time. This was the Family Incomes Supplements Bill, which introduced, effectively, a subsidy for the low-paid. Powell invoked the Speenhamland system, invented in the village of that name in Berkshire in 1795, when the subsidising of wages had driven them down and pauperised the workforce. He said the same would happen with FIS, and that it would not liberate people from poverty, but would entrench them in it. He ridiculed assertions by other Conservative speakers that wages at the lower end of the labour market would not be affected by the subsidy, as it was bound to distort the system. 'Many of those who vote for it or let it go through will live to regret what we have done,' he warned his front bench.[28]

On 12 November he made more detailed, and more prophetic, suggestions for the future of his party's policy. He was playing a gentle game with Heath, determined to be seen to be constructive: it was an attitude that would not survive long. Speaking to Conservative women in Southport, and knowing full well that the manifesto had promised no further nationalisations, he sought to persuade the Government to go even further, and start the process of denational-isation. He wanted it done almost immediately, though he did not address the political difficulties such a move would entail since, there having been no mention of it by the leadership in the recent campaign, it was hard to see how Heath could have claimed a mandate for it. However, Powell's main purpose was to set his party thinking. He said that the 'commanding heights' of socialism were still crowned by a fortress whose name, on the map, read 'NATIONAL-ISED INDUSTRY'. Using a phrase that would become common by the end of the decade, he added, 'Unless we advance to their assault, we shall have done little to roll back the state and socialism will easily regain sooner or later the outlying ground which it had temporarily lost.

'We have to show at an early stage in this parliament,' he went on, 'that we are able and determined to make serious inroads into nationalised industry.'[29] He wanted it done soon because the legislation would take time, and would be contentious. The other arguments against, though, he dismissed one after the other. 'When the public have had it dinned into them for so long that denational-isation is impossible – the silly metaphor of "unscrambling eggs" is perennial – it is desirable that as soon as possible there should be live examples of denation-alised industries working in practice.'

He dismissed as 'absurd' the notion that no one would want to buy the industries while they were making losses: the evidence of the private sector showed this was not the case, otherwise few mergers and takeovers would occur. The value of a business was the value of its future profits, so there would be no shortage of takers. Indeed, many shareholders in the pre-nationalised com-panies would still have the gilt-edged securities given them as compensation by the government of the time: no new asset was being created, and the money was there to buy the industries back. Moreover, the sooner they were bought back, the sooner the drain on the taxpayer ended. Powell was particularly alert to one of the problems of the privatisation process that would reach its height fifteen years later: the substitution of a private monopoly for a state one. There would have to be 'mortal competition' between the denationalised industries and other providers, and it was important that the first denationalisation was chosen carefully as a test bed on which his theories could be proved: he recommended the two state-owned airlines, BEA and BOAC, as obvious candidates. When, that autumn, Rolls-Royce collapsed Powell hailed it, for related reasons, as a great opportunity for the company and its workforce, and an end to the nonsense of state involvement in the enterprise. He denounced the Government's willingness to take the enterprise over, to allow completion of the RB-211–22 engine project. He was a lone voice.

The annual debate on the Expiring Laws Continuance Bill on 25 November gave him another chance to talk about immigration in the Commons. The main burden of his speech was that it had not fallen. He warned once more of the shock the real figures contained, and of the proportion of the black population of some inner cities. He was attacked by the Labour MP Stanley Clinton-Davis for not having talked about 'community relations', which provoked Powell to ask him what he thought he *had* been talking about. 'What does he think is implied in a Birmingham one-half coloured but the future of our society?'[30]

It was a bad-tempered debate. Callaghan, now shadow Home Secretary, had tried to make political capital out of the Government's planned deportation of Rudi Dutschke, a student extremist with a record of violence. Maudling, the Home Secretary, could not answer him frankly because the case was *sub judice*, but this did not stop Callaghan. When Callaghan accused Powell of 'tilting at windmills', Powell interrupted him with unusual severity: 'Since the right hon Gentleman has referred to me now directly, I take the opportunity to say that just now he has treated this chamber to the dirtiest performance that has been seen here for many years.'[31]

That same week, at Eastbourne, he attacked something the Government was setting out to do: the Industrial Relations Bill. Powell's ideological sensibilities had been struck by remarks made by the Employment Secretary, Robert Carr, accepting the right of the trade unions and employers to fix wages by collective bargaining. Powell argued that no Conservative would stand for prices being fixed in this way, so Carr's assumptions were outrageous. He argued that, therefore, legislation would be inappropriate. 'How can the same party and government which condemns and attacks collective buying and selling of everything else legislate about the collective buying and selling of labour?'[32] Powell said that in a free society the unions performed a social function, and as such it would be improper to legislate about that function, as it would constitute state intervention in the voluntary activities of individuals. If the Government chose to legislate it was because it was, equally improperly, assigning an economic function to the unions that, in a free society, the unions should not have. His disagreement with the Bill gave Labour another means to point to divisions within the Conservative party. When the Bill came to the floor of the House on 18 January, Powell was taunted by Stan Orme, a Labour MP, for not having voted against the second reading, given his well-known objections.

Christmas in the Powell household took on a particular routine during these years – though Powell spent one of them gallantly unblocking the drains of a lady neighbour. The Powells would give a lunch party on Christmas Day, which would last well into the evening, and to which they would invite close friends, especially any without family of their own: Diana Spearman and Keith Wallis were regular attenders, and, later, Ted Curtis, Bee Carthew and Richard Ritchie. Another young devotee, Jonathan Denby, a Monday Club activist, succeeded Greville Howard as Powell's private secretary at the start of 1971. Ritchie would still go in during the evenings, two or three times a week, engaged in the business of putting Powell's archive in order. Howard remained part of Powell's inner circle until the end. When his wife was killed in an accident in 1980, Powell did all he could to console his former assistant, showing a compassionate human side the public seemed unable to believe existed.

This Christmas holiday was a last lull before Powell's longest, and most intense, campaign. He opened his new front on Europe immediately the New Year began. In an article in the *Sunday Express* on 3 January, he attacked the Government for financing inflation by failing to cut back on public spending, and said it should be looking for cuts in indirect taxes too in order to get prices down. He said that, like Chancellors of the previous century, Barber should be actively seeking ways to make the family budget go further, rather than seeking ways to keep prices up: and this brought him to Europe. 'If there is one thing that millions of British people would be glad to see dead, buried and forgotten before 1971 is out, it is British entry into the Common Market. They look with apprehension to the possibility of a decision reached over their heads, a decision without real debate, a decision which they have not taken part in – and yet a decision which they feel, with a true instinct, commits them and their descendants irrevocably.'[33]

Powell predicted that by the end of the year the vital economic questions of prices, balance of payments and contributions to the community budget would have been properly aired and debated – an easy prediction to make, since he was about to undertake a massive programme of such airing and debating. However, it was the constitutional issues that concerned him more. He said the pro-marketeers – the Conservative cabinet not least – were guilty of 'dishonesty' when they implied that the great economic benefits they were advertising would result from membership could be achieved without 'a common government, a common parliament, and a common sovereignty', notions the would-be joiners would 'pooh-pooh ... as things almost infinitely remote and theoretical'. He said that, in reality, 'there can indeed be a European economy and a European world power, but only if and when the ingredient nations cease to exist as nations', and the British must be told that this is the price they would have to pay for membership. It was, he added, a fantasy of statesmanship similar to that of the Commonwealth, and the British people were becoming sick of the humbug of their political leaders on the question.

Powell's thinking about the concept of nationhood now dominated his intellectual life. It surfaced again on a two-day tour of Ulster, where he went better to acquaint himself with the troubles there. In Londonderry on 15 January he branded as 'petty' the highly contentious issues of the local government franchise and council house allocation, saying they had come to enjoy 'the spurious significance of civil rights, not to say human rights, only because of the relevance to the question: 'Which nation? What nation? Ulster's experiences have been a warning that her people cannot forever, like Laodiceans, halt between two opinions.'[34] He was annoyed that the Heath Government, like its predecessor, kept on about 'learning to live together': 'The assumption that people start fighting in Ulster and throwing petrol bombs at one another because they have suddenly lost their senses or their tolerance or become foolish, or conversely that trouble stops because they have mended their ways, become tolerant and wise and "learned to live together" is more insulting to the intelligence of those who use this sort of talk than it is to those about whom it is used. Its danger is that, being foolish, it is bound to obscure the real causes and therefore the real remedies.' He then came on to the parallel, obvious to him, with what was happening in England: 'That issue is, in one sentence, to decide who we are; to establish or re-establish our identity as a nation.' There was no doubt in his mind, he concluded, that the people of the Six Counties were British, and the Six Counties themselves were part of the British national territory. For his pains he was described by the Stormont Social Democratic and Labour Party MP for Foyle, John Hume, as 'an undesirable alien as far as the Northern Ireland Catholic is concerned'.

The next day Powell went to Banbridge in County Down, to speak about the Common Market. He complained about the trivial level of the debate thus far, and noted, as he would continue to do with growing disbelief, that the Government having received its mandate to negotiate at the election, the principle of entry seemed to have been settled. 'The answer of the electorate', he said, 'and of the people was assumed to be yes, subject only to tidying up a few details.'[35] He disputed the truth of this, observing that 'the people whose future is being decided in perpetuity are well aware that they have not spoken yet'. His most controversial statement, though, was when he conjectured on the use to which British taxpayers' money would be put after entry: it would fulfil 'the political intention to keep in being large numbers of farm units of low efficiency; for the three major countries of the Common Market have large, though diminishing, peasant elements in their populations'. What was meant was 'a British subsidy to the Continental peasantry'.

Returning to the mainland, Powell was affronted by news of a Treasury memorandum, sent as evidence to a court of inquiry into rates of pay for electricity workers, which had stated that the current inflation was the result of an acceleration in labour costs. This went to the heart of his economic doctrine: that only governments, by printing money, cause inflation. He had put this doctrine directly in a speech in his constituency earlier in the month, on the anniversary of his resignation from the Treasury in 1958, saying that 'ever since 1957 Government expenditure has continued to increase. not only in terms of money but as a proportion of national income; ever since 1957 Britain has continued to be plagued with inflation, even beyond the general experience of the Western world'.[36] However, he noted that in Heath's first six months in office 'there has been a scrupulous silence about money supply and about the relevance to it of government expenditure'. It was, as he had said before, 'the cause and not the consequence' of inflation. All that had changed was that he was now blaming his own leader for negligence in the matter.

Determined to prove his point in the context of the argument about the effect of higher wages, he wrote to Lord Wilberforce, the chairman of the court of inquiry, volunteering to give evidence in which, he said, 'I believe it can be conclusively shown that a rise in labour costs neither is, nor can be, the cause of inflation. As the point could be material to the conclusions of your court, I would be happy to place myself at your lordship's disposal for the purpose of giving evidence to this effect, if desired.'[37] For good measure, he also sent Wilberforce a copy of *Freedom and Reality*.

Powell was taken up on his offer, and appeared before the court on 20 January. As his evidence he read out an extract from a speech he had made at Johnstone in Renfrewshire the previous November, in which he had said that 'the most powerful union or group of unions which was ever invented is powerless to cause prices to rise, even if that were their intention, which manifestly it is not', and in which he repeated his oft-made point about the government's responsibility for inflation as the controllers of the money supply.[38] Speaking in Birmingham two days later he delivered a stern economic lecture to the Government, referring back to his appearance before Wilberforce, and making it clear that he did not believe Barber and Heath understood what the real cause of inflation was. As tactfully as he could – 'the Government are still in a state of hesitation' – he said that in trying to engineer a boom 'the Chancellor has now openly abandoned the policy which his predecessor at least professed of trying to limit the rate of increase in money supply to the rate of growth in goods and services'.[39] However, he added that Barber had also professed that he would not provide the 'amount of money needed to underwrite the going rate of inflation', which caused Powell to pounce on him: 'This must mean that, in his view too, inflation cannot occur unless the Government underwrites it by providing money, and that a reduction in the increase in the money supply is the means by which the Government intend to slow the rate of inflation down.' Gleefully exploiting the confusion of his former close colleagues, Powell pointed out that this was irreconcilable with the view that inflation occurs because of 'militantly secured pay increases' (again the Chancellor's words) which the Government by exhortation and obloquy intend 'to work to de-escalate'.

The Commons debated the EEC on 20–21 January. No vote would be taken; the purpose was to allow the subject a parliamentary airing in the light of the negotiations now under way. Powell spoke towards the end of the second day, and argued that Geoffrey Rippon, the Chancellor of the Duchy of Lancaster and the man whom Heath had put in charge of the negotiations, had in his speech the previous day given the game away about the long-term agenda: 'the Community is now beginning to work gradually towards an economic and monetary union'. Moreover, Powell said Rippon had also made it plain that the intended union 'is not purely economic and monetary, that the economic and the political cannot be separated'.[40] What had especially horrified him was Rippon's quoting, with approval, the remarks of President Pompidou of France that the object was a union that would 'be able to have its own policy, its own independence, its own role in the world'.

Having clarified the objectives – or, rather, used the words of his own front bench to clarify them – Powell emphasised how this showed that the argument had moved on since the 1960s (when he had approved of the idea of negotiating for entry) from being merely the question of joining a wider free-trade area. It was now about political union, and all that that entailed. Powell used this development to explain his own change of mind. He said he understood the desire to have Europe's higher growth rate – though, as he said before, that was illusory. He said, too, that he understood the allure of becoming part of a body that had a great voice in the world, though this 'emotional attraction' was not sufficient to merit the high price – that of political union – being demanded.[41]

Pro-marketeers had argued that Britain had already accepted certain surrenders of sovereignty, such as by joining NATO, and that entry into the EEC would be on the same principle. Powell rejected this: it was, he said, totally different from deliberately giving up for all time the freedom in future to take a decision. It is essentially different from the merging of sovereignty or "pooling" of sovereignty ... in a political and economic union of Europe it would be contradictory to speak or think of national sovereignty in the sense in which that exists at present.'[42] Britain would, after such a union as was envisaged, be in the same position as Scotland after the union of 1707. He made mischief about Rippon's inability, at this delicate time, to go to Brussels and tell Britain's would-be partners of the constitutional convention that a parliament could not bind its successors, though Powell warned darkly that 'the nature of the act [of entry] is intended to lead to an irreversible alienation of our separate sovereignty and the merging of our decisions in the decisions of a greater political whole'.[43]

He mocked the notion of Britain's exerting 'leadership' in the Community, since that was a view already taken by the other members about their own roles. He asked what British 'leadership' would amount to: it would, he repeated, be about the same proportionate influence as the Scottish members had over the Commons. The basic question of whether the British electorate wished to be subsumed into a wider one consisting of much of Western Europe could not, he said, 'be answered by sarcastic references to "Little England". It cannot be answered by transposing . . . the phrase "Little England" into "tight isolationist island". In order to answer it, we have to envisage profoundly what we as a nation are.'[44]

There were few in the Commons better intellectually equipped to make the point that Britain was, culturally, a European nation than Powell. In doing so, he stressed that it was not culture, religion or race that were the issues, but whether British nationhood could or should be subsumed into a wider political and economic entity. He defined that nationhood as 'the thing for which men, if necessary, fight and, if necessary, die, and to preserve which men think no sacrifice too great'. In that respect Britain was not part of Europe:

> The whole development and nature of our national identity and consciousness has been not merely separate from that of the countries of the Continent of Europe but actually antithetical; and, with the centuries, so far from growing together, our institutions and outlook have rather grown apart from those of our neighbours on the continent. In our history, both recent and earlier, the principal events which have placed their stamp upon our consciousness of who we are, were the very moments in which we have been alone, confronting a Europe which was lost or hostile. That is the picture, that is the folk memory, by which our nation has been formed.

He argued that at other crucial times in her national development Britain had, successfully, stood with her back to Europe 'and her face towards the oceans and the continents of the world'. The British, he felt sure, understood instinctively that they should not join an entity where their wishes as an electorate would be reduced to merely a small part of a whole; and he believed that was the right instinct, and that the House of Commons should be speaking for it. Freer trade with Europe, or military alliance, these were acceptable; the merging of political destiny was not. 'We cannot. We will not.'[45]

II

Having formally declared his opposition to his party's European policy, Powell now declared it over economic policy too; and the more his former colleagues seethed in fury, the more he teased them and played with them. On 6 February

1971, in a speech at Swindon, he claimed that his doctrines about inflation were now winning converts in unlikely places, notably with the Chancellor. He again quoted Barber's statement about 'underwriting inflation', saying he was sure the truth was now recognised by some in the Treasury. However, this was not what the Treasury had, he remarked, told Lord Wilberforce; they had submitted evidence that made no reference to the money supply at all. 'If the Chancellor was right, and I am sure he was, these statements are either false or irrelevant, and the Treasury were gravely misinforming and misadvising the court.'[46]

Some fun was had at Powell's expense at this time and about his own rates of inflation. A report appeared in *The Times* saying that he had been due to participate in a BBC documentary about the Common Market, but had failed to agree terms with the Corporation's contracts department. They had offered £75; Powell, well aware of his uniqueness and pulling power, asked for £100. The BBC, however, chose to do without him.[47] Before the 1970 election a story had appeared in the *Guardian* about Powell making a regional talk programme with a Labour MP. During a lunch break, he had allegedly been disappointed to be offered just a buffet lunch as, when he had done the programme before, he had had a full sit-down meal. So (according to the anonymous Labour MP who retailed the story, and who may not have appreciated Powell's well-developed sense of irony) he had gone to a telephone and negotiated a higher fee.[48] Stories such as this would crop up over the succeeding years, but Powell was not inevitably so sharp when it came to taking the performer's fee. When, in December 1970, he was offered fifty guineas for a talk in St Mary-le-Bow church in London, he insisted on giving it all to the restoration fund, as he felt it improper to profit from something done in a church.[49]

Powell quickly moved up a gear in his anti-Common Market campaign. He embarked on a series of visits to the six member countries, to make speeches about why the British people did not wish to enter. Ralph Harris's contacts with sister organisations of the IEA in Europe proved invaluable in finding Powell significant audiences to address. Out of courtesy, he wrote to Douglas-Home, as Foreign Secretary, to inform him of his intentions. Douglas-Home replied, 'I do wish that instead you would concentrate on making speeches on immigration, because that is so vitally important and you are so right about it.'[50] Powell would remark that this 'friendly candour' was typical of Douglas-Home, as was the fact that no hint of what he really believed on immigration ever reached the public.

On 12 February Powell began his foreign campaign, going to Lyon to address the Association of Leaders of Free Enterprise. Unlike Heath – whose French was poor and whose French accent risible – Powell spoke the language fluently, and agreed both to speak and answer questions in it. Much was made in the press of his polyglot abilities: fluency was now claimed in English, French, German, Italian, Urdu, Modern Greek, classical Greek and Latin, with a reading knowledge of Welsh, Russian, Spanish and Portuguese. Mrs Powell told the press, 'His German is the best – the people always ask him what part of the country he comes from. And the only thing wrong with his French is that the accent is on the English side. He would like to learn Persian, but I don't see how he will ever get the time.'[51]

Powell told his French audience that it was a principle in British politics that politicians did not attack the Government while abroad, there being more than sufficient opportunities to do so at home. However, this was an exception. He was not, in the conventional sense, abroad: 'the arena of this debate forms a single arena bounded only by the frontiers of what would be the enlarged community if Britain accedes'.[52] He went on to say that 'it seems to me ... wholly right and necessary, not to say urgent, that the British case against, as well as for, accession to the Community should be placed before the peoples of the Community, who are to decide, together with us, what the limits and membership of their community are to be'. He did not equivocate. 'The greater part of the people of Britain are profoundly opposed to British accession to the Community.' He dismissed the claim that those in Britain in favour of membership had made on the term 'European' to describe themselves, saying they would better be described as 'anti-Europeans'. It is a European among Europeans that I claim to speak to you.'

He outlined his credentials to support this statement. As defence spokesman, he had always stressed the importance of Britain's continental alliance as second only to the defence of the British Isles themselves. He described himself as 'passionately Francophile', and mentioned his devotion to the study of the ancient European cultures and more recent history. 'The truest European, in my opinion, is the man who is most humbly conscious of the vast demands which comprehension of even a little part of this Europe imposes upon those who seek it; for the deeper we penetrate, the more the marvellous differentiation of human society within this single continent evokes our wonder. The very use of the word "Europe" in expressions like "European unity", "going into Europe", "Europe's role in the word" is a solecism which grates upon the ear of all true Europeans: only Americans can be excused it.'

Powell said that when de Gaulle had put an end to Britain's ambitions in the EEC eight years before, the issue had been regarded in Britain as commercial, not even economic. The 'pedants' who had insisted on reading the Treaty of Rome and pointing out the commitment it had to political unification – of whom, at the time, Powell had not (as he admitted) been one – had been ignored, largely because the notion was dismissed as one of typical continental theorising of the sort that would soon be dealt with by British pragmatism once the British were on board. 'Of course,' he said, 'we were wrong.' Now, it was clear that the advantages the British pro-joiners claimed for membership were only likely to be there in a state of full and complete union. This was what had shocked the public, not the widely reported economic costs of membership. 'The motive is political. In a word, it is nationalist.'

He said that British proponents of entry were being forced to argue against their own case, dismissing the likelihood of the political union they knew was inevitable and which, secretly, they wanted to achieve. Powell warned that no British parliament could bind its successors: any decision to cede sovereignty could be regarded as only temporary. He dismissed arguments that France proved that a nation did not have to lose sovereignty through membership, as they referred to the past, not to the future, and said a key sticking-point for the British would be the loss of control over the raising of taxes, of which the proposed introduction of VAT would be the symbol. His final point against British membership was his understanding that, in one community, all had to stand or perish together – but Britain was distinct from any other European power except Russia in that she could suffer defeat in the decisive land battle and still survive: 'this characteristic Russia owes to her immensity. Britain owes it to her ditch.' As a result, Britain's commitment to the continent could never be total. The Community, he warned, should not want and would not benefit from an unwilling partner, but that is what they would get if they got Britain. He ended by reminding them he was in France 'to leave no-one in doubt that those who seek to make the United Kingdom a member of the European Economic Community are not speaking for the people of Britain'.

He spoke hours after Heath had made the opening speech of the Parliamentary Council of the European Movement at Lancaster House in London. On his way back, at Paris, Powell arranged to give a press conference at which he could illuminate his own views and respond to the points Heath had made the same day: much to the fury of Central Office, who saw Powell more and more as a leader of an internal opposition.

Heath was also promising a new immigration Bill, and Powell signalled his intention to put forward his views again. He had, the previous week when the Government put through the Commons the Bill to take Rolls-Royce into state ownership, shown his determination to go his own way in Parliament by accusing the Minister for Aviation, Fred Corfield, of 'humbug': he had been prevented from voting against the rescue package only by the fact that no other MP shared his view – or was prepared to be seen to share it – and without at least two tellers and one to vote against, there could be no division. The Rolls-Royce nationalisation was the first big sign that the Government was prepared to act in a socialist way towards industry; it was a portent that Powell was the only man to admit to seeing. Once this rescue was effected, it would prove politically harder to resist effecting others. Heath and his ministers deluded themselves that this was not a change of strategy, merely a change of tactics. Like all delusions, that was nonsense.

As a precursor of his stand on the Immigration Bill Powell spoke on the

subject at Carshalton in Surrey on 15 February. On arrival, he found two factions
outside having to be separated by fifty policemen: 200 anti-apartheid demonstrators on one side and, to the delight of Powell's opponents, 100 National
Front protesters on the other carrying banners proclaiming 'Powell is right'. He
called for a massive programme of voluntary repatriation to start immediately.
He also claimed that the figures were still inaccurate, and added, 'I do not
believe that the Government and public could have been misled so persistently
and gravely without a certain determination in some quarters to leave facts
unascertained, or to play down for as long as possible those that were known,
so that when the true situation could no longer be concealed, it should
be irreversible.'[53] Alert to the difficulties of repatriating so large a part of
the workforce, he said he did not see why a system of 'guest workers' –
such as operated in Germany – could not be established in Britain. When
the Immigration Bill was published the following month it made none of
the provisions Powell had wanted, and it coincided with the publication of
revised figures from the Registrar-General's office about the birthrate among
coloured immigrants that further fuelled his arguments that these statistics
had been greatly underestimated. The Government estimate of 35,000 births
in this community in 1969 and now been revised upwards to 52,000, which
Powell still claimed was not high enough, since he felt that the Registrar-
General had subtracted too high a figure for whites born in the new
Commonwealth.

Powell's Lyon speech prompted interest in when, exactly, he had become so
anti-Common Market, and why he had only just started to create such a furore
about the negotiations for entry. He had put down his marker two years earlier,
at Clacton; but in an interview in the *Guardian* he explained how his mind had
been changed. He had supported Macmillan's first attempts to join in 1961
because of his belief in free trade, and he had thought that 'the political aspects
weren't of practical importance'. He admitted he had not been concentrating
on the matter: 'A member of a Government, not in the cabinet, who has his
own department, does not commonly apply his mind fundamentally to the
other things the Government is doing. I know one is not supposed to admit
that, but it is a fact of life, and so it might as well be said – and I suppose that
even then I had the odd twinge.'[54]

He said he had given little thought to it at the time of Wilson's application
because 'I think probably most of us thought that to use Alec Home's famous
words this was a dead duck, and one doesn't give much thought to dead ducks.'
He suggested that it would have not have made sense either intellectually or
politically to say no on the issue just because Labour had said yes, 'so I dare say
my name can be found in the division list in '67 approving the initiative taken
by the then Labour Government'. Since 1968, when Powell had had time to
concentrate on the issue, he had seen the economic emphasis receding and the

political ones advancing, with the Community viewed 'as an embryonic political unit'; and that, as he had said before, seemed to be something he could not bear to see Britain join.

Accused of over-emotionalising his arguments against membership when he should have been more rational, Powell replied that 'a nation is not a rational thing. There is no rational basis for nationhood. What a nation is is what it feels itself to be, instinctively and emotionally.' He denied he was an isolationist: 'One is not isolationist just because one does not want to be amalgamated with another country or countries ... I am a free trader. I want the maximum intercourse between this nation and other nations; but I don't want to see this nation drowned in other nations. I don't believe it will allow itself to be drowned, anyhow.' He rejected the assertion that he was seeking to convert public opinion. 'Politicians rarely alter people's opinions. Politicians articulate, crystallise, dramatise if you like, render intelligible and therefore render capable of being turned into action, legislative or administrative, something which is present already in people's minds. If this were not so, I can't think of what would be the meaning of democracy.'

He made a prediction in this interview on which he would be proved wrong – though only just. 'I believe that at the end of the day it won't be possible in the House of Commons to secure either an adequate majority or perhaps a majority at all for the proposal to enter the Common Market.' He said this because of what he saw of parliamentary opinion growing against it, but he was content to continue striking out against it on his own rather than joining any formal anti-market grouping. He said the purpose of his speaking on the continent was to alert negotiators from other countries of the reality of the British position, to enable them to drive a bargain so hard that Britain would not be able to accept it. He said he intended to be 'yet another nail in the coffin of Britain's bid for entry'. When it was pointed out that this would not endear him to his own party, he said, 'I cannot say that it is my prime objective in life, for which I work day and night, to endear myself to anyone, front bench or back bench, top or bottom.'

By this time Powell felt that the Heath Government was conducting itself in sufficiently provocative a fashion to merit his going more prominently on the attack against it. He raised his profile among his non-Conservative-voting supporters by giving a series of long interviews to Tony Shrimsley, the political editor of the *Sun*, which appeared in the first week of March 1971. Shrimsley's first inquiry was whether Powell still wanted to become Prime Minister, which he answered by saying: 'I can't see how anybody can take a serious part in politics for the greater part of his life, without putting what he is doing to himself in the form of the lead which he thinks he might give to his party, and to his country. There's nothing to be ashamed of in that, and there's nothing to conceal. But while one's person and one's outlook and one's basic ideas remain constant, the circumstances in which the opportunity – to use a trite expression – to speak for England might arise cannot be foreseen.'[55]

Powell said that he felt his main contribution had been to articulate the feelings of ordinary people, such as those who came up to him in the street to shake his hand and thank him for what he had done. 'And I think to myself: "Done! What have I done?" Then one understands that saying is doing.' He continued to make a virtue of his isolation, saying he had 'the comfortable capacity to be alone. I don't mean solitary – going and shutting yourself up in a room – but being able to take one's own line. That, I think, is inborn. If others don't, at any given time, agree with me, I note the fact, but it doesn't undermine my self-confidence. And this is perfectly consistent, I hope and think, with being a good fellow. I wish as a human being to be very much a member of a team. But my mind climbs mountains by itself, without any vertigo.'

In the second part of the interview, Powell was trenchant about foreign affairs. He described the continual words of support by Britain for what was going on in Vietnam as 'a symptom of a very highly imaginative view of the relationship between Britain and the US'. Asked what Britain's relationship should be with the Commonwealth, he retorted, 'There is no such thing.'[56] The next day, he took a longer view of Britain's domestic policies, setting out the full long-term Powellite agenda: a Britain in which the old-age pension was no longer automatically paid because people or their employers would have invested for the future; one in which the activities of unions negotiating pay deals were not subject to legislative restraint, but in which they were prevented from doing harm to the public or their members; and one in which it was clearly seen as the duty of all workers to extract the highest price for their labour that the market could bear. He said he regretted the 'monolithic, compulsory, rigid character' of the health service, but could not see his way out of it. He was similarly pessimistic about altering primary and secondary education, but wanted to eradicate council housing, and to end tax relief on mortgage interest: 'I've never been able to convince myself that a person who pays as he goes ought to be taxed more heavily on the same income than the person who borrows as he goes.'[57]

When, later that month, the Immigration Bill, which aimed to provide new controls over permanent immigration and to enable more help to be given to immigrants who wished to return to their country of origin, went into its committee stage, Powell was one of the MPs chosen to sit on that committee – appropriately, since no one could doubt the high level of interest he had shown in the subject in the preceding three years. He had spoken in the debate on the second reading on 8 March, and said that this would, inevitably, not be the final immigration law the House considered because it still omitted to define a law of citizenship; and explained that this was because 'this country, alone I think of all countries, has never known in its law a status which defined its own people. We have never had a citizenship of the people of this country.'⁵⁸

The British had, he reminded the House, simply had the status of subject, which they had shared with hundreds of millions elsewhere in what was the Empire. He teased Maudling for being confused about this, and allowing himself sometimes to refer to something called a 'United Kingdom citizen'. Even in the days of Empire Britons had been unable to enter many British Dominions and colonies without being subject to immigration control, while the reverse was not true; and the chance to define that citizenship had been passed up in 1948, at the time of the British Nationality Bill. Powell described his own status, as a result of the way in which the question of citizenship had been addressed, as being 'a British subject, citizen of the United Kingdom and Colonies by birth, to whom the provisions of the Commonwealth Immigrants Act, 1962, as amended in 1968, do not apply. I must confess that, on the whole, I would rather be an Englishman.'⁵⁹ Because of the terms of this Bill, Powell protested that 'once again we are shying away from putting ourselves in the same position as any other nation of being able to recognise ourselves, the people of this kingdom, for what we are'.

What particularly angered Powell about the Bill was the, to him, illogical clause that allowed entry to anyone from the Commonwealth with a British grandparent. Someone from America with four British grandparents would not be allowed in; someone from Australia with no British grandparents, but who – as Powell knew from his own experience in that country – regarded Britain as 'home' would also be barred. He compared it with the old Nazi saying, *Grossmutter nicht in Ordnung*, or 'grandmother not in order', applied to those with a Jewish grandparent in order to justify the discrimination visited upon them.⁶⁰ However, Powell applauded Maudling for using the Bill to withdraw the statutory right of entry into Britain of dependants of those already immigrated, though he urged him to justify to the House why, in an interview at the time of the presentation of the Bill he had said that large-scale repatriation was impossible 'in practice'.⁶¹ Powell's criticisms were ironic, since the massive Labour opposition to the Bill – and the disquiet about it on parts of the Conservative benches – was largely caused by a belief that it was aimed at appeasing the emotions stirred up by his own speeches on the subject. Certainly, it is hard to believe the 1971 Immigration Act would have happened but for the Birmingham speech.

With Powell on the committee examining the Bill, it received far more attention than might otherwise have been the case. He did not limit his objections to what became known as the 'patrial' clauses. On 23 March he offered his view on what Britain's obligations were to Asians holding United Kingdom passports in East Africa who had not taken out Kenyan citizenship, and were now in larger numbers seeking entry to Britain. He said that 'where a section of citizens of a country are so treated that life becomes intolerable, and they are literally or in effect driven out, there is a general obligation on the rest of mankind'.[62] He said Britain did not have a special obligation, beyond that general one, to help such people, and blamed a 'drafting error' in the 1962 Commonwealth Immigrants Act – creating a loophole which had in fact been closed by the successor Act in 1968 – for having left millions of Commonwealth citizens with the idea that holding a United Kingdom and Colonies passport provided a right of entry to Britain.

Meanwhile, Powell resumed his European anti-marketeering. He went to Frankfurt at the end of March to address the Hessian Circle, and the press learned that this famously frugal man was paying his own expenses for this trip and for his other similar forays. In response to inquiries about his willingness to fund his own campaign, Powell replied, quoting from Corinthians: 'Who goeth a-warfare any time at his own charges? Who planteth a vineyard, and eateth not of the fruit thereof? Or who feedeth a flock, and eateth not of the milk of the flock?'[63] Powell admitted he could have found someone to fund him, but asked, 'Why should I? After all, I am doing this for myself. I am doing it because I think it is a thing that should be done and doing it as an individual.'

The tack he took in Frankfurt was that, even if there were parliamentary approval for entry, it would be by a majority insufficient to justify so significant a constitutional step. Even the Government's present majority of thirty would not be enough: approval would need the support of 'the bulk of both major parties'.[64] Powell also said that entry could take place only if the majority of the British people understood what the implications of it really were, since none of these true political implications was being reported to them. He said that this was the construction he put on Heath's own statement that 'entry would be impossible unless it was supported by the British parliament and people'. He was in no doubt that approval, in the terms in which he had defined it, would not be given. Heath had said that, although he would call on Conservatives to support entry in the lobbies, no one would be thought the worse of for not doing so. It was a pledge by which Powell set far too much store.

He spoke of the 'paradox of the British government riding at a fence at which the probabilities seem to be that they must fall'; a point in the negotiations had to be found at which a 'negative conclusion' could be reached with minimum embarrassment. Needless to say, his activities angered the Government. The following month Geoffrey Rippon, Heath's chief negotiator, went to The Hague to try to win Dutch support. Hearing that Powell would soon be in Holland preaching his anti-market message, Rippon claimed that the negotiations were being conducted on a basis approved by Powell when he had been a member of Macmillan's Government. He reminded the press that Powell had always talked of defence needing a European basis (something to which the Heath Government had still not, ironically, committed itself, and which Powell would have deemed irrelevant to the matter in hand). 'The tragedy of Mr Enoch Powell', said Rippon, 'is that he is a brilliant man who has just ... I must be careful what I say.' He dismissed Powell's changes of mind as 'curious', even though Powell had so recently gone on the record, in great detail, to explain them.[65] Rippon lost his cool sufficiently to reel out the entirely bogus claim, made down the years by Hailsham (as Hogg had once more become) and others, that Powell had encouraged immigration to fill nursing vacancies when Minister of Health.

Rippon also told journalists that Powell's objections to the Anglo-French Concorde project, which he had raised a few weeks earlier because of the state's involvement in the enterprise, were inconsistent, since he had not earlier objected to the notion when Macmillan's cabinet discussed it in 1962. Rippon had not been a member of the cabinet in 1962; and Powell wrote to Sir Burke Trend, the cabinet secretary, to ask whether, unusually, Rippon had been given access to these papers, which were subject to the thirty-year rule. Powell also wanted to know whether Rippon had been allowed the appropriate clearances to disclose who had or had not spoken, and what had or had not been said, on any particular topic. It seemed to him that, simply so that Heath and his friends could attack an internal opponent, the normal conventions binding cabinet discussions had been flouted. Powell also wrote to Rippon challenging him to verify the various assertions he had made about him.

Powell used a speech in the Budget debate on 5 April to launch, in the parliamentary context, his assault on Heath's economic policy. He was fortunate to follow Tony Benn, who had accused the Government of causing inflation by having given tax cuts in the first Budget the previous year. Powell corrected him, and his own side: it had been the decision not to fund the growth in public expenditure fully that had caused the inflation, then starting to boil up from the already high rates inherited from the Wilson years. Barber, in his Budget speech, had mentioned in passing the steep rise in the money supply; Powell rubbed this in. Knowing what the answer would be, he asked whether the Government was powerless to stop this rise, or whether it could, perhaps be avoided. He had his answer: he found the speech by Barber, delivered the previous winter, in which Barber had said that the policy should be 'one that does not passively provide the amount of money that is needed to underwrite the going rate of inflation, but something less'. Powell pounced upon these words. 'If ... they mean what they say, they mean that the Government, if they chose, could provide less money – could finance not "the going rate" of inflation, but a lower rate of inflation.'[66]

This was not all. He quoted back part of Barber's own Budget statement to him, in which the Chancellor had said that 'the policy I have pursued has been to allow an increase in money and credit sufficient to support a rise in the level of economic activity but not so large as to compound the pressures of cost inflation'. Powell interpreted this for the benefit of the House: 'It means that if the Government do not "compound the pressures of cost inflation", we do not have so much cost inflation, and if perhaps they sufficiently refrain from "compounding" them, we do not have cost inflation at all. My only observation on that policy is – and I am sure that my right hon Friend shares this regret with myself and with all of us – that that was not what actually happened.'[67] The rise had not just covered a 'comparatively modest' rise in economic activity, it had compounded a very substantial inflation. By way of a final warning, he made another quotation from the Budget statement, in which Barber had said that 'I intend the growth of the money supply simply to accommodate the going rate of inflation.' That, he emphasised, was Barber yet again admitting that the Government had it within its power, by determining the supply of money and the increase in credit, 'to determine how much inflation there is'.

This, though, was not the end of his torture of Barber, for the Chancellor had also talked of a rise in costs and prices being moderated, and that leading to a slowing down in the growth of the money supply. So now, Powell observed, cause and effect appeared to have been reversed. If, as the Government had said, the money supply would be expanded by 3 per cent per quarter, it was effectively saying to the country:

> We will go on inflating the money supply at a rate equivalent to 12 per cent per annum. But we should like you to understand . . . that it is your business to act as though we were not doing so. It is your business to act as though, instead of increasing the money supply by 12 per cent – and thus underwriting 12 per cent inflation, presumably – we were only increasing it by 10, 8, 6 or 4 per cent.
>
> Then, when we find that you have listened to us; when we find that you have behaved as you would do if we were acting in the way that I have explained we shall not be acting; when we find that you have behaved as you would be behaving if we were only underwriting an inflation of 10, 8, 6 or 4 per cent; then we shall come along afterwards and slow down the growth in the money supply.[68]

The joke over, Powell said that this was 'a grave contradiction . . . which goes to the root question of the cause and, therefore, the remedy of inflation. It is in no carping spirit that I have sought to expose this contradiction, because it is one which I believe not only the Conservative Party or the House but the country as a whole has to face and to resolve.'

He knew why Barber was buried in this contradiction: he did not want to cause unemployment. Heath, who was dictating the policy, was obsessed with a desire to avoid, at whatever cost, the unemployment he remembered from the Britain of his youth in the 1930s. Powell called it 'a crude and dangerous superstition' to link unemployment with the control, or otherwise, of inflation: there was just 'a certain connection between employment and the cessation or reduction of inflation'.[69] This was because, in a period of inflation, business was carried on as though the inflation would continue; and so, when it did not continue, those who miscalculated would have to adjust accordingly, and this could mean 'It is like a game of musical chairs. When the music of inflation stops, there will always be somebody who, for the time being, is without a chair until a new pattern of activity, behaviour and expectations is attained which corresponds either with a reduced rate of inflation or with stable money values.' He said that Barber had admitted the problem, and had admitted the severity of the problem: he had, therefore, to do something about it.

Powell felt that Barber could act, by warning people to scale down their expectations now. That would not obviate the unfortunate consequences of inflation control, but it would help limit them. He stressed he was talking not about deflation, but about a reduction in the rate of inflation. The money supply problems had been aggravated, he argued, by the continuing large balance of payments surplus, which, if the pound had been allowed to find its own level on the foreign exchanges, could have been eliminated. He was stern, too, about the way in which the £540 million tax cuts had been purchased in the last Budget – by an increase in borrowing of a similar amount, which had in turn led to further inflation. Powell was followed by Jo Grimond, the former Liberal leader, who said that in the light of what Powell had said he wondered why he remained a supporter of the Government. 'This is where Enoch was ahead of all of us,' Robert Carr would later admit.[70] The merciless attack Powell had made on Barber was one thing, but the devastating quality of his critique would only properly be seen a year, or two or three years, later, when, as a result of Barber and Heath not following the course he had outlined, the disasters of which he had warned had happened.

III

The Immigration Bill Committee ran on through April, and Powell enjoyed some success. He managed to lead a group that struck out, by nineteen votes to sixteen, the clause which would have given right of abode to Commonwealth citizens who had a grandparent born in the United Kingdom; and it was only by the casting vote of the Conservative chairman of the committee that the Bill retained a clause granting a right of free entry for people who had a parent born there. Maudling was faced with a decision about whether to restore the grandparent provision when the Bill came back to the floor of the House. For the moment, he was nonplussed, not least because it had been the Foreign Office, and not he, who had been keen on the provision. Powell had won his victory with the unlikely support of the Liberal Chief Whip David Steel, a left-wing Conservative and the Labour contingent: two other Conservatives abstained.

As a sideline to his European activities, Powell used a businessmen's lunch in Worcestershire on 16 April to condemn the existence and activities of the

Metrication Board. He said that in 1965 the President of the Board of Trade had expressed merely the 'hope' that the country would have adopted the metric system within ten years. This hope had, without any reference to Parliament, become an assumption when the Board had been founded in 1969. It had stated on its foundation – somewhat optimistically, as it turned out – that 'Britain will be a metric country before 1975'. What had especially provoked Powell was the statement by the chairman of the Board, the Labour peer Lord Ritchie-Calder, that 'going metric is no longer a question of whether but when. We in Britain have made our decision.' Powell commented, 'I am very much concerned with usurpation of power, and Lord Ritchie-Calder and the Metrication Board are engaged in just that.'[71] Metrication had not been a general election issue, and Parliament had not been consulted; the Government had taken no such 'decision', and had only the previous month said that 1975 would not be the date of British metrication.

'Yet', he continued,

> here is Lord Ritchie-Calder telling us that 'we' have decided. And his board, masquerading as Government and spending public money, goes ahead pushing, cajoling, browbeating, presuming, and all the time allowing no-one to suspect that there is not true authority behind it. This, I say, is usurpation. This is government by assumption. It is not to be tolerated in a country which still claims to live under the rule of law and the authority of parliament. Moreover, it is an insult to Government itself that Lord Ritchie-Calder should announce and implement decisions which the cabinet have not taken.

Such attacks soon looked mild, though, by comparison with what Powell was building up to against his own front bench. Speaking in Wolverhampton the day after his metric onslaught, he said that 'the British people will not submit to become part of the European Economic Community as the result of a trick, and they will never forgive any person or party who they feel has got them there by sleight of hand'. He reminded Heath of what the last manifesto had said: 'Our sole commitment is to negotiate.' Therefore, the question of joining had not been an election issue.[72]

'But the electorate turns out to have been misled. Anyone who read the manifesto could not have supposed but that the negotiations would be about the terms on which Britain would agree to be a member of the Community.' Instead, he implied that Heath was preparing to accept the terms of the Community exactly as they stood; the other words of the manifesto, that there was 'a price we would not be prepared to pay' were meaningless, as the Government had agreed to the price before the talks had started. 'Those who in present circumstances talk about "breaking the back of the negotiations" by the summer are talking about breaking the compact of Government with people.' Directly attacking Heath's authority, he added, 'This is not only not what the Conservative party led the country to believe ... the electorate will not forgive a party or a government who treat them in that way.'[73]

In a swift but extensive diversion, Powell flew to New Orleans on 20 April to have a public dialogue at Tulane University with the conservative commentator William Buckley, on the causes of error in past political decisions – appropriately enough, on the tenth anniversary on the Bay of Pigs crisis, when armed Cuban exiles had attempted an invasion of Cuba. It was an exhausting week for Powell. After a lengthy session in the Immigration Bill committee he flew to America overnight, snatching an hour's sleep at his hotel before a day of interviews and discussions culminating in the dialogue with Buckley. He then flew back to England overnight, via New York, arriving back on 22 April. He made a speech in Croydon during the evening and then, the next morning, went to Scotland to make three speeches. On May Day he was in Merthyr Tydfil, attacking Heath's conduct of the economy, and then went to Turin, on the Italian leg of his Common Market tour. After his personal setback of the previous year, he had recovered his momentum.

On 7 May Powell's constituency association gave a dinner for him to mark his twenty-one years as their MP. He mischievously used the occasion to take credit for his party's victory the previous year. He told the 200 guests:

> It is a cause of permanent, indeed historic, pride for us in Wolverhampton to know that without what was done and said here and from here a year ago, Edward Heath would not be Prime Minister and there would still be a socialist government in office. The Conservative party in the country knows that this is so and in parliament many more acknowledge it than just the marginal handful whose election turned the scales. We understand and respect the reasons for the public reticence on this subject on the part of members and party officials, but it was right that once, at least, and on this occasion above all, the truth should be told out loud.[74]

It was a happy night for Powell: he was presented with a fourteen-volume edition of *The Complete Peerage*, the full historical and genealogical account of all peerages.

There was another twenty-first anniversary to be marked: the original One Nation pamphlet was also republished that spring, and Powell was upset by a paragraph that appeared in the *Daily Telegraph*'s diary column referring to it, and to the fates of the 'eight' original members. There were, of course, nine, and the one who was not mentioned was Powell, as if confirming the way that many in the upper ranks of the party were now rendering him a non-person. He wrote to Bill Deedes, the diary's parliamentary correspondent and his fellow Conservative MP, to tell him that the paragraph – which he stapled to the top of his letter – was 'strange, but cannot be intentional; yet it is a grievous hurt and I am sure you will prominently put it right'.[75]

Another hurt was being put right at the same time: Powell finished exacting his revenge upon Rippon. The Chancellor of the Duchy replied to Powell's earlier letter admitting he could not verify the statements he had made about him at The Hague, saying that his remarks were 'based on my recollection of the view which I believed you to have held . . . no doubt you will let me know if this recollection was mistaken.' It was. Powell wrote him a letter – which, since Rippon had made the 'personal attack' on him publicly he did not hesitate to release to the press – in which he particularly upbraided him for having said that Powell, in 1962, had claimed that nurses' pay could be kept down because enough coloured nurses in need of jobs could be found to fill them. 'I immediately wrote asking you to refer me to the occasion of this statement. I am obliged to you for admitting in your reply that you had no knowledge of any such occasion or any such statement or any such views.' Powell added, 'I take this opportunity to put on record that your purported revelation at the same press conference that, as a member of the cabinet, I did not express opposition to the adoption of the Concorde project was equally unfounded.'[76]

Powell reached The Hague himself on 17 May, and sarcastically told the Netherlands Society for Foreign Affairs that he had no doubt that, when Heath met the French President Georges Pompidou later that week, he would tell him that Britain could not enter the Common Market. 'Regardless of whatever ballyhoo accompanies his visit,' Powell said, 'Mr Heath will do his duty.'[77] Powell said that what Heath should tell Pompidou was that 'even if an arrangement could with your assistance be contrived at Brussels, I would lack the right to conclude it. To do so would be to mislead the countries of the Common Market whose partners we became and, even worse, to betray the confidence which the British people have given me. I will not do it.' What Powell did not know at the time was that his former shadow cabinet colleague, Christopher Soames, now ambassador in Paris, had been engaged in secret talks with Pompidou's officials to ensure that he did not repeat the veto of his predecessor, de Gaulle. The assurances given included a commitment on behalf of Heath that Britain would, if allowed to enter, participate fully in the development of a European Union, including complete economic and monetary union. This was not the version Heath at the time gave to the British people or to Parliament.

Powell, ironically, said he was sure Heath would be straight with Pompidou because his leader had 'absolute honesty and transparent sincerity'. It was these qualities that, naturally, led Powell to assume that Heath would tell the French President that public opinion in Britain was growing more and more hostile, the majority of the Labour Opposition in Parliament was antagonistic, and a substantial minority on the Government side would not support the measure. 'The prospect, therefore, which faces the Government is of carrying a proposition to join the Community by only a narrow majority and without the bulk of the opposition party.' On this, Powell was uncannily accurate. For good measure, he said Heath would no doubt also remind Pompidou of statements he had made at the election about the need for widespread support for entry. Repeating his earlier arguments about the realities of the sacrifice of political sovereignty, Powell said that the reality of the Common Market was what a later generation would come to call the 'Franco-German axis'; and he warned that, in the future, whenever West Germany had to choose between policies that would benefit the whole of Europe, and policies that would benefit the process of German reunification, she would choose the latter.

Powell's exposition of the logical and historical flaws in the arguments of the pro-marketeers did not, however, stop him from taking a more demotic approach to the subject. Two days later, in another newspaper article, he went even further in widening the breach between him and his party, saying that the Conservatives were suspected of trickery and stood 'on the brink' of being accused of it. He was provoked by what he saw as Heath's increasingly high-handed attitude about Europe, and his attempts to squash dissent in his parliamentary party. One reason for the sense of impending trickery, as he had said before, was the liberal way in which Heath was interpreting his promise not to take Britain into the Common Market without the support of the people, coupled with Heath's willingness to accept the terms offered to him by Brussels. 'Today we hear no more about the support of the British people. Instead Mr Heath lectures the House of Commons on Edmund Burke and the duty of a Member of Parliament to use his own judgment – not, by any chance, the judgment of his Government, perhaps, or his Whips – rather than to be a mere delegate of the electors.'[78] Powell reminded Heath that the exercise of judgment could cut both ways: and that the time to tell the voters that their wishes could be ignored by their elected representatives had been at the election, not now. He also cast doubt on the political wisdom of Barber's statement that those who opposed entry – according to opinion polls, most of the public – were 'flat-earthers', and said that the leadership had not been honest with the public in 1970 because they would have been 'hooted off the hustings'.

The question of the Kenyan Asians, which Powell had raised in the Immigration Committee two months earlier, now prompted him to write a lengthy article in *The Times* justifying his belief that their passports gave them no right of entry, a point that became yet more important the following year, after the mass expulsion of the Ugandan Asians. Maudling had admitted to Powell that no specific pledge had been given to Asians who had not been given Kenyan passports after that country's independence in 1963, but he had also told Powell it had been the 'intention' at the time of the 1962 Act that that 'they should be able to come to this country when they wanted to do so. We knew it at the time. They knew it, and in many cases they have acted and taken decisions on this knowledge.'[79] Powell put his own gloss on these words: 'When the 1961 Bill was drafted and passed through parliament to become the 1962 Act, nobody realised the consequences of the definition of "United Kingdom passport". By the end of 1963 these consequences had been spotted: but the Government of the day – or the ministers concerned – decided to stay mum and hope for the best. When the worst happened, they afterwards claimed that they intended it all the time. Yet they had not told parliament – nor anybody else.'

This gloss provoked a furious response from Humphry Berkeley, who had left the Conservative party in 1968 over immigration – he considered the policy far too illiberal – and now believed that Powell was rewriting history. In a letter to *The Times*, he said Powell had become 'careless'. Any Asian born in Kenya, and with one parent born there, became a Kenyan citizen automatically at independence.[80] First-generation Asians had become eligible for passports issued by the British high commissioner in Nairobi – which, being government passports, allowed a right of entry – unless within two years the Asian opted for Kenyan citizenship. Powell was, he added, 'grossly inaccurate' to say that a drafting error in the 1962 Act had caused the confusion. The Act acknowledged identical policies that were already operating in Uganda and Tanganyika, so the intention was plain and nothing had been concealed. Also, Berkeley said that the assurances which Powell claimed (at, though Berkeley did not say though, Maudling's behest) had never been given had, in fact, been made 'between 1961 and 1963 ... by successive colonial secretaries' in Berkeley's presence. He also claimed that Powell set such store by his assertion that the error had been detected by 'the end of 1963' because by that time he was no longer in the Government. 'I cannot ... permit him', Berkeley concluded, 'to re-write history in order to satisfy his particular whims and fancies of the moment.'

Powell kept up the pressure in the Immigration Bill Committee, arguing on 16 June that it was irrational to impose a five-year time-limit on the deportation of non-patrials. This was revised, a revision Powell welcomed the next day at the Bill's third reading, along with the survival of the clause that denied automatic entry to dependants. A young Conservative backbencher, Kenneth Clarke, told Powell triumphantly that dependants would still be let in; Powell told Clarke he was aware of that, but now it would no longer be necessary to alter the statute in order to alter the policy. At the end of the committee stage that day Powell had the opportunity to put on the parliamentary record his response to the allegation, most recently made by Rippon, that he had brought in immigrant labour to work in the NHS.

Rippon's remarks were repeated, slightly inaccurately, in the Commons by the Labour MP Sydney Bidwell, who had earlier described Powell as 'wicked', and who had mentioned Rippon's claim earlier in committee. Powell rose and said that 'since the hon Member has sought to place on the record of the House the same falsehood as he sought to place upon the record of the Committee, I will again state that my right hon and learned Friend, the Member for Hexham, admitted that he had no foundation whatsoever for the statement which he attributed to me in that interview'.[81] Bidwell said Rippon had done no such thing. Powell said, further, that 'I asked him to refer me to the circumstances or occasion on which I made that statement, and he admitted that he was unable to do so.'[82] Despite howls from the Conservative benches of 'Withdraw!', Bidwell refused to do any such thing, saying that all Rippon had admitted was that he could not recall the exact words. Even if this had been a true interpretation of what Rippon had said – and it was not – Rippon never did find those words. Sir George Godber, who worked more closely than most with Powell during his years at the Ministry of Health and who was no supporter of Powell's immigration policies, described the allegation as 'bunk ... absolute rubbish. There was no such policy.'[83]

By the end of June it was clear that, in just three months since the Budget, the economic situation was deteriorating badly. The Retail Price Index, the usual measure of inflation, had risen by 9.8 per cent in the year since the Conservatives had assumed office. Labour put down a censure motion against the Government on 28 June, which Jenkins, as shadow Chancellor, moved. The motion spoke of the Government's 'gross betrayal of their election pledges and ... their mismanagement, or lack of management, of the nation's economy'.[84] Powell rose early in the debate to make his contribution, which, if it was in anything like the tone of his assault on Barber during the Budget debate, could only have compounded his party's problems.

Pausing only to brand Jenkins's speech as 'remarkably devoid of positive content', Powell did indeed continue his ferocious attack upon his own side: 'If anyone at the General Election a year ago, friend or foe, had predicted 10 per cent inflation in the year 1970–71, he would have been scoffed at as a dishonest scaremonger.'[85] Such a rate was not something the country ought to feel it could get used to. Urgent attention had to be paid to what had caused it and how it could be remedied. He reiterated the arguments he had made in the House on 5 April about the money supply, and used them to help exonerate the unions, who were becoming a target of blame again by his own side. He repeated, too, that the high currency inflow caused by the balance of payments surplus in the preceding twelve to eighteen months had been the most aggravating factor; it was now running at £4 billion per year. The effect could have been neutral had the Government used the foreign exchange to finance its debt, but it had not. Nor, as he had said on 5 April, had it floated the pound against most currencies in order to bring the size of the surplus down.

Powell said there was a 'pervasive dislike' of putting the blame for the inflation where it belonged, and a deep resistance to owning up to the causes as being mechanical rather than moral. He stressed that it could no longer be sensible to ignore the fact that floating the currency would remove one of the great inflationary pressures. He then proceeded to examine why the economic impossibility – or so many had seen it – of high inflation coexisting with high unemployment had happened: there were then three-quarters of a million out of work. He highlighted the absurdity of Jenkins's having called for 'reflation' when it was clear the Government was in the middle of roaring inflation. 'What does he want?' Powell asked. 'Another 2 per cent? Is he saying that 12 per cent instead of 10 per cent inflation would do the trick? If 10 per cent inflation is consistent with three quarters of a million unemployed, then it is not for lack of inflation or of monetary demand in the economy, nor for lack of money supply matching the rate of increase in prices and wages, that we are suffering from unemployment. It is not merely thoughtlessness, it is a stupid abuse of language, to talk about "reflation" when face to face with those facts.'[86] Powell defended the Government, saying that the unemployment was structural, caused by the shaking-out of men in old industries which had lost their markets, and it had been right for the Government not to intervene in the face of that reality. He concluded by calling again for a separation in the minds of the Government of inflation and unemployment, and for the currency to be floated. By Powell's standards, the speech had been loyal indeed.

In July 1971 Heath reached agreement about EEC entry with the Six. The issue was debated in the Commons on 22 and 23 July, but Powell made only the briefest intervention. Within a few days he had collected his thoughts, and raised the matter elsewhere. On 31 July, speaking in Scotland, he said the Government could not, 'without indelible breach of honour, purport to accede to the Treaty of Rome if Her Majesty's Opposition were against'.[87] He put this construction on Heath's words at the general election, which he said amounted to a 'binding affirmation of principle': he sought to make it clear that Heath could not go back on his earlier statements without standing accused of a massive breach of faith. Nor was the leadership able to isolate Powell entirely. After reaching agreement with the Six Heath had suffered the first ministerial resignation on the issue, that of Teddy Taylor, who had been a junior Scottish Office minister.

Powell argued that without massive Labour support the decision to go in could not be seen as having been taken with 'the full-hearted consent of Parliament' as Heath had promised in a speech to the British Chamber of Commerce in Paris on 5 May 1970. Heath had also said, on television on the 27th of that month, that 'no British government could possibly take this country into the Common Market against the wishes of the British people'.[88] Powell said that 'the full-hearted consent of the House of Commons can be given only by a House of Commons overwhelmingly united. Anyone who sought to pretend otherwise would deserve ill of the Tory party, because they would be seeking to equivocate away the plain words and the personal affirmation of its leader.'

The irony of another statement Powell made was lost on some who reported it. The Conservative Whips were already making it clear that dissent on what would now be the Bill to secure entry would not be tolerated. Powell said:

We have read a good deal recently about what is called 'arm-twisting' going on in the Conservative party, meaning the Conservative Members of Parliament are being subjected to pressures of various kinds, varying from threats and blackmail to promises and cajolery, exerted by or with the knowledge and countenance of the Government Whips, by the local party organisation or by local officials and associations. It needs to be understood that there is not a word of truth in such assertions. They are, no doubt, like the paper pinned to Norfolk's tent in *Richard III*, a thing devised by the enemy, with the purpose of discrediting the Conservative party and its leader.

There is no ambiguity at all about the considered statement which Mr Heath made during the General Election: 'We recognise', he said, 'that some members of the party hold opposite views on European policy, very often on grounds of principle, such as sovereignty. These people would be absolutely free to vote in the way they so decided.'

Laying on the sarcasm even further, Powell said he was sure that Heath would be issuing an order to officials of the party at all levels to respect what he had stated to be his wishes in this matter, and not to seek to limit the freedoms of individual members. In case Heath thought about making the issue into a vote of confidence in order to force the support of his party, Powell had a warning on that too:

Many would probably consider the issue of British entry so great, intended, as it is, to be irreversible and to change in course of time the whole status of Britain – a question, as some have said, concerning our children and our children's children – that it succeeds any other consideration in importance, and that in this context the call of party cannot override the call of country. Fortunately we need not appeal to that principle; for Mr Heath has faced and answered the question in advance. A question of confidence is one in which the leader of a party considers he has a right to the support of its members. It cannot be one in which he himself deliberately and in advance accords them 'absolute freedom' to vote according to their individual opinion.[89]

Powell's distaste for Heath was now at new heights, and the acrimony touched upon more than just the European question. The Government had introduced internment of suspected terrorists in Ulster in August, which had led to violence on a scale not seen in Ireland for fifty years. Beatings, shooting, bombings and burnings of houses and shops became routine. After his summer holiday Powell went to Omagh in County Tyrone and addressed a rally of 900 Unionists. He received standing ovations before, during and after his speech, and every remark he made critical of the governments in both London or Dublin was greeted with foot-stamping and applause. He complained that few of his colleagues at Westminster bothered to visit Northern Ireland. He said that, as a former staff officer, he knew that during the battle a commander's proper place was normally at the centre where his headquarters were: a comment immediately interpreted, correctly, as an attack on Heath, and one which appeared to some to be in dubious taste given the security implications of a Prime Ministerial visit to Ulster at that time. 'The fact remains', Powell said, 'that the people of Northern Ireland are in the front line. An assault upon the United Kingdom is in progress, and the men and women of Ulster have for months been the forward troops in an exposed position under increasingly heavy attack.'[90] As before, Powell made little differentiation between the terrorist attack on the nation and its values in the Province, and the attacks to which he had been subject on the mainland from those whom he had identified as wanting to destroy the nation and its values on the mainland.

'In such circumstances,' he went on,

> front-line troops have a right to expect from time to time the presence and encouragement of their commander in chief, no less than of his principal sub-ordinates. Otherwise they may too easily get the idea that they are being left to their own devices and that somebody somewhere does not want to know. What is more dangerous still, and is beginning to happen, is that the impression is conveyed to friend and foe alike that Her Majesty's Government does not really regard Ulster as the front line of defence of the United Kingdom – does not really regard the war as their war, our war, at all.

Although not all of Powell's audience might have been alert to the nuances of what he was saying, it was hardly surprising in the light of such high-profile visits and remarks as this that he was, three years later, regarded so seriously as a prospective Unionist MP; and they further gave the lie to the assertion of his critics at the time that he had, hitherto, shown no interest in Ulster.

Powell's theme was that the people responsible for the violence in Ulster were not to be found in either Belfast or Dublin but at Westminster, where the Government and Parliament had failed to demonstrate a belief in the import-ance of the unity of the realm. He claimed that, in reality, the Government (with the collusion of the Labour front bench) wanted to push the Six Counties into the Irish Republic, a claim he would make consistently for the rest of his life. He condemned Heath for recently having held talks at Chequers on the Ulster question with Jack Lynch, the Irish Prime Minister, an event which had made it look as though 'the British are wobbling and preparing to get out'. Nor was he impressed by talk of reforms or initiatives to bring peace: the only reform the IRA sought was the capitulation of the Government. Returning home, Powell was taken to Belfast airport by a senior Unionist official, who asked the visitor whether he would give more time to Ulster in the future. The Unionists were well aware of what a man of Powell's stature could do for them. 'If I get the call,' Powell replied, 'I will not ignore it.'[91]

Before visiting Ulster, Powell had outlined in a newspaper article what further steps he would take to safeguard the future of the Province. He had branded Lynch's Government as one 'which agrees with the gunmen on aims and only quibbles about means', and said the weakness with which the Heath Government addressed the question was typified and explained by its failure to stop Irish citizens being treated as British subjects once entering this country, allowing them to vote, sit on juries and, of course, enter without restrictions. To continue to do this was to pretend that the past had not happened: 'So long as we continue to treat the republic and its citizens as we treat ourselves, no-one, whether friend or foe, will believe us when we proclaim that Ulster is unalterably part of this realm. Our deeds contradict our words; and people conclude "Britain is not in earnest; she means to give up." '[92] He disregarded claims that because of the land border with the Republic such immigration control would be impossible to enforce: it could be done, he said, without resorting to a variant of the Berlin Wall; and, what is more, the Government had recognised it could be done by excluding the Republic from the 'common travel area' of the British Isles in the recent Immigration Bill. If such a step were taken, it would make the Republic and Ulster see that Britain was serious about the integrity of the United Kingdom including the Six Counties.

Beyond that, though, Powell argued for an end to the contradiction of a United Kingdom with a separate parliament at Stormont for the Six Counties. 'It is a standing admission that Britain is in two minds, a standing invitation to disbelieve her when she says Ulster is inalienably part of us.' He said the change in the status of Irish citizens could be made overnight, but the end of Stormont could not. In that, as events were to show within two years, he was wrong.

IV

Although Powell always tried to avoid fighting on too many fronts at once – and the Common Market, the economy and Ulster provided a handful for him even by his standards – he was drawn once more into the immigration debate. In a speech at Smethwick on 8 September he attacked the Home Office for its 'propaganda' about immigration, which it claimed was falling. Not so, said Powell. 'You may wonder who these men are who are so determined to present a false picture, and what may be their motives,' he added.[93] He said that in the three and a half years since the Birmingham speech there had been a net inflow of 180,000, and that was only recorded entries: illegal immigration boosted the figure far higher. 'It was widely expected that a Conservative government would reduce the rate at which immigration had been running under their predecessors, and certainly nothing was said (to put it mildly) to counteract that expectation. On the contrary, net immigration in the first year of Conservative administration has been substantially higher than in the last year of socialist administration, over 17 per cent higher in fact. At 41,300 it was not far below the rate being recorded in the mid-1960s.'

The Home Office, he said, based its 'propaganda' on figures for those immigrants granted permanent settlement rights immediately, and even these excluded the Asians from East Africa. Yet the same officials knew well that many of those not admitted for permanent settlement nonetheless did settle in Britain permanently; nor did they take into account the outflow of Britons, now running at 150,000 a year. The Immigration Bill was scheduled to receive the royal assent during the autumn after having its third reading in the Commons directly after the recess, and Powell said this would give the Government power to control immigration absolutely. If it stopped immigration, the rate of increase of the coloured population would, he said, be almost halved, 'if I may coin a phrase, at a stroke', referring to a remark authorised by Heath about reducing prices contained in a press briefing document before the 1970 election, and which was now haunting the Prime Minister. Powell had grave doubts whether the Government would use the provisions of the Bill to do as he suggested.

Maudling, the Home Secretary, was stung by Powell's comments, though could not refute the charge that immigration had risen by 17 per cent in the first year of the Government. He did, though, maintain that the use of net immigration figures was unreliable because they included people in Britain temporarily. Home Office officials briefed the press after Powell's speech to the effect that many of those he included in his figures would by now have left the country. Others, though, would have arrived to replace them; and there was no denying, either, that some allowed in for a limited period did stay longer than they should have done.

On 13 September Powell published a paperback entitled *The Common Market: The Case Against*, a compendium of speeches made in the two years since Clacton. That evening, at East Ham, he provoked Heath again by saying that 'the first and most important thing to say about British entry is that it is not going to happen. I cannot undertake to tell you precisely how or at what stage or date that will become self-evident, nor when the statement I have just made will pass across the boundary between the realm of bold and speculative prophecy and the region of what everybody knew all along. Of the fact, however, I have no doubt.'[94] His belief, as usual (and as usual with an underpinning of irony), was based on Heath's promises about only going in with full-hearted support. Powell was not, though, the only one making rash predictions that evening. Geoffrey Rippon, speaking in Newcastle, said that the increase in food prices in Britain as a result of joining the Common Agricultural Policy would be about 15 per cent over six years; within three years they would be increasing by more than that in a year alone.

Powell's remarks inevitably provoked derision. One of Heath's strongest backbench supporters, Sir Tufton Beamish, offered to take a bet of £10 with Powell at odds of five to one that he was wrong; but Powell was not a gambler, and nor was he deterred from his thesis. Speaking at Sutton Coldfield on 16 September, he concentrated on the specific question of whether membership would help trade. He did not doubt Britain would do more trade with the other Common Market countries, but felt that that would only mean it did less with the rest of the world. He compared those advocating entry with the man selling earthquake pills who, when asked whether they would prevent earthquakes, said, 'Well, perhaps they don't, but what's your alternative?'[95] Powell was reaching new heights of belligerence. Asked that week by a Swiss journalist whether it was he or Heath who truly represented the people of Britain, he replied, 'It is I.'[96]

The rising violence in Ulster over the summer recess led to a special recall of Parliament on 22 September. Speaking ten days earlier on a BBC news programme, Powell had directly accused Heath of making things worse in the Province. 'Reform will not satisfy those who are causing the violence,' he had said. 'Their object is not reform; their object is annexation.'[97] Speaking of 'a general and growing opinion' on the part of the gunmen that they would succeed, he had added that 'nothing encourages this opinion so much as the behaviour of the British government'. In the debate, Powell was the first to speak after Heath and Wilson. He agreed with them that what was now going on in Ulster was a 'war', but it 'is a war which at present is being lost'.[98] The paradox of a numerically small number of terrorists being able to take on 'some of the finest regiments and forces of any country in the world' was because 'terrorism feeds upon the growing hope that, somehow, it will be successful'.[99] Powell said it had to be brought home to the enemy that they could not win: 'we must deprive terrorism and violence of that hope upon which it feeds'.

He had constructive suggestions about how to do this. It was 'militarily absurd' to leave the border with the Republic open. He did not argue that it should be closed, but that it should be 'controlled', for there was no doubt that the motorisation [sic] of terrorism had allowed it to flourish, and that it could be practicably limited. Second, while he shared the abhorrence most Britons felt at carrying an identity card, it was now, for the citizens of Ulster, the lesser evil, for this was a time of war. Finally, it was bad for the morale and efficiency of the army for it to be used for police duties, so the police force in Ulster had to be built up to the point where it could do its own work properly. To do all these things, he claimed, would show the terrorists that their hopes were misplaced.

Powell feared that the country was entering upon 'a new and dangerous phase ... of either self-deception or deception of others, if we imagine that by tinkering now in one way or another with the Constitution in Northern Ireland we shall do anything to lessen the incidence of violence'.[100] On the contrary, all such ideas suggested to the terrorists that they were achieving their aims. Heath had been to Dublin for a summit with Lynch, the Irish Prime Minister. Powell called this 'a profound miscalculation', even though he credited it with 'the best intentions'. The Government with which Heath had been treating not only retained in its country's own constitution a claim on the Six Counties; it also 'for its own safety and existence – perhaps its personal existence – dare not effectively do anything to counter what is going on in the North'.[101] The responsibility for the bloodshed, he affirmed, rested with the British Government. If there were no change of policy endorsed by the House of Commons, he concluded that 'the guilt will rest with us'.

At the end of September Powell went to America, for a short economics lecture tour, elated by the fact that a dollar crisis had recently forced a temporary float of the American currency. He told journalists at Heathrow that he was 'a very happy man', and said that 'in a few hours the great advocate of floating currency will be among them in Washington. I am very happy about the situation. Currencies are as buoyant as the Dead Sea.'[102] On his return, though, he would face a heavy, though predictable, defeat. On 13 October at Brighton the Conservative party debated Europe at its conference, and voted by a majority of eight to one to support entry: but then it has never been the habit of the Conservative party conference to do anything other than support the leadership. Powell spoke in the debate, winding up for the opponents of entry and given extra time by the conference chairman in order to do so. He was booed by some representatives when he said his party was displaying the will to give up national independence.

He was heckled with a cry of 'That's laughable' when he said that 'it is not in Western Europe but in the rest of the world that we have already found compensation and more than compensation for our declining trade with the Commonwealth'. However, he was cheered when he said, 'Today the voice with which Britain speaks in the world, be it weak or strong, heard or unheard, is Britain's own.' That would not be so after entry. 'Political unity, right or wrong, good or bad, is incompatible with national independence. The will to bring Britain into the Community is the will to give that independence up. Each one of us must take his own resolve. I can only say what is mine. I do not believe this nation, which has maintained and defended its independence for a thousand years, will now submit to see it merged or lost. Nor did I become a member of our sovereign parliament in order to consent to that sovereignty being abated or transferred. Come what may, I cannot and I will not.'[103]

Powell had only one in three supporters among the speakers – though one, the future Trade Minister Neil Hamilton, then vice-chairman of the Federation of Conservative Students and a member of Powellight, said that Heath would 'betray the trust placed on him as prime minister if he carries on with this policy'. Douglas-Home, winding up for the leadership, confirmed many of Powell's fears about Britain's motivation for entry when he said that, for the first time since the end of Empire, joining the Community would provide an opportunity for the exercise of British talents in wider fields. The resolution to support entry was passed by 2,474 votes to 324.

In a speech from the floor, Sir Tufton Beamish brandished a copy of the 1965 One Nation pamphlet *One Europe*, of which Powell had been joint editor, and in which the phrase 'to be excluded means eventual isolation' had appeared. Powell's opponents in the Conservative party became immensely excited about this, and the rumour flew round that Powell himself had not merely jointly edited the pamphlet, but had written it. The pamphlet had also said – interestingly in the light of the nature of Powell's campaign – that Britain 'should not be frightened of political union'. The document was endorsed by nineteen MPs but not by five others, including Powell, who were members of the shadow cabinet at the time. The rumours of Powell's involvement stemmed from Nicholas Ridley – another who would change his mind on Europe – telling a journalist that he had written the first draft, which he had submitted to Powell who 're-wrote it almost completely'.[104]

Immediately after the Brighton debate Powell went into print to stress that the fight went on. 'Just below the level of the blatantly obvious, reality was quite otherwise,' he said. 'Below the surface the result of the conference has been to reinforce the fears (or, as the case may be, the hopes) that the thing cannot be done.' He said it would reinforce Heath's own view that dissent was allowable, and that there would have to be an end to 'arm-twisting'.[105] He paraphrased Heath's statement of 2 June 1970, made during the election campaign, that 'members of the Conservative party who hold opposite views on European policy, very often on grounds of principle, would be absolutely free to vote in the way they so decided'. He said that the vote in the Commons on the issue on 28 October, which would either approve or reject the White Paper on the question, would be 'a beginning, not an end', since he believed that Government business managers were concerned about 'the unlikelihood of getting through the legislation in the subsequent session'. As in 1968–9 on the Parliament (No. 2) Bill, Powell hoped this constitutional measure would be taken in a committee of the whole House and that no attempt could be made at a guillotine. On that, too, he was wrong.

On 18 October he spoke in Cardiff on the impending Commons debate. He made an appeal for the issue to be seen not, as it inevitably was, in economic terms, but in political ones, which was nearer to the reality. He added that even if it were economic, it was impossible to predict future patterns of trade; but, if those patterns were to be set, it would mean that a 'vital principle of commercial policy – the ability to seek through the free choices of her citizens, that pattern of external trade which at any time accords most nearly with her own best interest' would be lost.[106] He moved on to more delicate ground at Newport, Monmouthshire later that week, highlighting the wrongness of his party's policy

in the light of the overwhelming evidence of public opposition to joining the
EEC. The opposition was, he said, the more impressive since 'the great majority
of people are under the impression that, whatever their own opinions and wishes
may be, British entry is a virtually accomplished fact'.[107] However, bolstered by
his memory of what happened with the Parliament (No. 2) Bill Powell made a
fatal miscalculation: he told his audience that, since there was so little support
for entry, that entry was highly unlikely ever to be 'a fact at all'. And, though he
did not say this, the defeat of the plan would be the end of the Heath leadership,
and would destroy his own chance to take the party in what he thought was the
correct direction.

Powell told his fellow Conservatives they did not need to worry about
harming the Government by opposing its policy on this issue. Heath had 'greatly
helped' them by announcing that the principle of British entry would not be
considered as a matter of confidence. Therefore, 'at a stroke that issue is completely divorced from the survival of a Conservative Government'. Of course –
as Powell himself suspected – the notion of Government supporters being able
to act in accordance with their consciences and principles on this question was
not to be treated with the freedom that might have been expected. That illusion
would be well and truly scuppered by the time of the second reading. To
compound the mischief, Powell said, 'I have for months past repeatedly drawn
attention to Mr Heath's unequivocal assurance of absolute freedom for Tory
Members to form their own judgment and (in his own words) "To vote as
they so decided"'. Yet another of Heath's promises in advance of the European
Communities Bill was about to be shredded; and, highlighting another that
would go the same way, Powell made sure to advertise Heath's famous phrase
about entry being obtained only with the 'full-hearted consent of parliament
and people'. He concluded with what was tantamount to a threat: 'This is
certain: The Conservative party cannot for long cease to speak for Britain
without ceasing to be the Conservative party that we know.'

The great debate on the Common Market ran in the Commons for six days;
and Powell, brooding on the Conservative benches for most of it, was the last
backbencher to speak, at twenty to nine on the evening of 28 October. A sign of
the alliances this issue was forging was that, on the morning before he spoke,
Tony Benn received a letter from him congratulating him on a speech he had
made in the debate the previous day. From the opening of his own remarks,
Powell directed his comments against his own front bench; he taunted them for
the accusations they had been hurling against the Opposition, which now –
with some notable exceptions – opposed entry, for having changed their mind.
Powell told his own leadership of the very good reason why some people –
including himself – had thought again. 'What has changed is that for the first
time a proposition has been put to the people of this country.'[108]

He put on the record himself Heath's words, already quoted in the debate, 'about the necessity for the full-hearted consent of parliament and people'. He added his interpretation, also for the record, that this meant that the Government could not take the country into the EEC against the wishes of the people; and Powell knew that the opinion polls showed the people were against. He said these words 'have been quoted because they are manifestly true. They are not true because my right hon Friend says them. Rather my right hon Friend said them because they are true.' Such full-hearted consent was, he stressed, essential because 'it is an unprecedented act of renunciation which this House is called upon to make'.[109] It was an irrevocable decision, and was about – as Maudling himself had said earlier that day – political unity.

Full-hearted consent was, he said, manifestly not there. Whatever the result of the division, 'we know before the Question is put that this House is deeply and, indeed, passionately divided'.[110] In his peroration he quoted Burke's letter to the Sheriffs of Bristol of 1777, in which he had said that 'to follow, not to force, the public inclination, to give a direction, a form, a technical dress and a specific sanction to the general sense of the community is the true end of legislature'. He ended: 'Anyone who, tonight, knowing that the necessary conditions to approval of these proposals have been withheld, that they do not command the full-hearted consent either of the House or of the Country, nevertheless votes for them, casts his vote against the vital principle by which this House exists.'

The Government won by a majority of 112, thanks to the support of sixty-nine Labour MPs; but thirty-nine of its own, including Powell, voted with the Opposition. There was uproar when the result of the division was announced, principally Labour MPs recriminating against those who had voted with the Conservatives. Powell, rarely for him, became emotional in the chamber, shouting at his own front bench: 'It won't do! It won't do!'[111] Shortly afterwards, he told Andrew Alexander of the likely implication for him of Heath's policy succeeding: that if the Conservative party took Britain into Europe, he could not in conscience stand at the next election as a Conservative.[112] The full extent of his personal investment in this issue, the inevitable culmination of the marriage of his remorseless logic to his nationalism, was only now becoming apparent. The issue became an obsession. He had hardly any time for his favoured recreations, or for his favoured friends. He never lived his political life as intensely as in these months.

Ten days later, having assessed the defeat, he told a party dinner in Nantwich that the vote had been merely a preliminary stage. He said the Commons had never recognised the notion that, once an idea had been debated, those who disagreed with it must accept it as 'binding them to limit debate and division thereafter to the means of applying the principle'. Had it ever done so, the nation's liberties would never have been secured. 'On the contrary, some of the most important and glorious episodes of the history of the House of Commons have been those in which every stage of procedure and every tactical device were used to prevent what a section of the House disagreed with from coming to pass.' Powell repeated his warnings that the Commons was preparing to legislate away its own authority, to become subordinate to another body as it had never been.

'For the first time in history the electorate could not call the Government of this country to account in parliament for the policy by which their lives and perhaps the very existence of their country would be governed. For the first time they would be powerless to change the Government's policy by changing the Government.'[113] Having said so often that that decision would be irreversible, Powell now seemed to find some consolation in the hope that the opposite was true.

While waiting for the European Communities Bill to have its second reading, Powell returned to some older preoccupations. When the Immigration Bill had been enacted, allowing a provision for assisted repatriation, the Home Office minister Lord Windlesham had said the scheme would be administered if anyone wished to take it up. Powell felt the clause in the Immigration Act that said expenses would not be met 'unless it is shown that it is in that person's interests to leave the United Kingdom and that he wishes to do so' effectively emasculated the measure. He immediately sent Maudling 300 letters he had had in the previous three years from immigrants asking to be repatriated, and published to the press passages from a few of them showing the desperation some felt in their desire to go home. He said the Government's attitude was 'all in all, as nice a little job of sabotage as you could wish to meet'. He hoped the receipt of the letters would spur the Home Office into action.[114]

Maudling sat on the letters for six weeks, writing to Powell after Christmas to say that the Government's policy was that any immigrant who wished to go home should contact direct the agency handling the service, rather than have their application forwarded by a third party. Powell was outraged that the Government would not facilitate assistance, available under the law, when asked to do so by someone with the *bona fides* of a Member of Parliament. However, Home Office officials briefed the press that many of the letters were simply requests for information about a repatriation scheme, not specific requests from people to be repatriated.

The winter of 1971–2 saw new depths achieved in the breakdown of the relationship between Powell and his party, almost to the point where the breach that would come in February 1974 was anticipated. But Powell's guerrilla actions would also start the final undermining of Heath, who was now facing trouble on other fronts as a result of following policies his chief critic found insufficiently Powellite. Although Heath would secure his aim of having Parliament support entry to the EEC, by the summer his position as leader of his party would be coming under threat as a result of the disunity within it – disunity Powell would do more than anyone to exacerbate.

In the last few weeks of 1971 Powell had several opportunities in the Commons to develop his critique of Barber's increasingly wayward command of the economy. As the Chancellor prepared to attend the Group of Ten meeting in Rome on 30 November, Powell asked him whether it was not the case that 'the only realignment of currencies which can be lasting and satisfactory is one which is continuously worked out by a free market'.[115] Barber replied that 'if we lived in a completely pure and theoretical world I should be somewhat inclined to agree with my right hon Friend'. Later that day Powell had a longer opportunity to expound his economic theories, when the House debated an Opposition censure motion on unemployment.

Speaking in Coventry three days later, Powell pronounced 23 November 1971 – the day of the censure debate – as historic, for it was the day 'the British House of Commons formerly recorded that Keynes is dead'.[116] He was stirred to this observation after Robert Carr, the Employment Secretary, announced that the old principles of demand management based on Keynes were no longer functioning as politicians of all parties had expected. Carr would have to eat his words, and Powell's optimism would prove misplaced, within months; but, for the moment, Powell was joyously prepared to welcome another convert to the fold. In his Coventry speech he referred to the debate as 'like an old-fashioned Oxford Group meeting: everybody was confessing their mistakes'. Governments had realised that they did not have the power to cause full employment, so they no longer felt an obligation to promise it.

In the debate, Powell carefully avoided putting all the blame for the rise in unemployment on the Government. He said the election had been a political, not an economic, watershed: the policies that had fostered unemployment had been in play since the mid-1960s. The most remarkable factor had been that, during that period, inflation had stopped going down while unemployment increased; since 1969 both had been going up together. Powell expected that the floating of the dollar would have reduced the balance of payments surpluses and slowed down the growth in the money supply. This mild deflation would, he said, have a temporary effect in putting up unemployment, but it could not explain why there had been such a large rise as the House was debating.

What had been proved was, as he put it at Coventry, that Keynes was dead. There had been attempts at reflation since after the devaluation; and unemployment had, nonetheless, continued to rise. He ridiculed Labour calls for 'reflation', and declared that the 'monetary myth, upon which a whole generation has been reared – that an injection of money into the system is the automatic cure for unemployment – has collapsed in the face of the experience of the past four or five years'. His explanation for the new phenomenon was simple: 'We are in a new period when the rate of technological change of increase in productivity, has, at any rate for a time, outstripped the rate at which we are producing new needs, new demands, and new methods of fulfilling them.'[117]

The remedy for this was, in his view, equally simple: an economy in which resources and labour could move from the obsolete to the new as easily as possible. He felt that, thus far, the Government had pursued 'policies which give the maximum encouragement and reward to the successful exploitation of new forms of production and the meeting of new forms of demand'.[118] It had, he said, declined 'to use public money to maintain processes which are obsolete or obsolescent' and had encouraged change and innovation. The Government was, he concluded, doing as much as it could to minimise the duration of the transitional unemployment he had always maintained was inevitable at a time of change.

After this conciliatory interlude, Powell went to Rugby on 27 November and made a nakedly populist speech that emphasised his role as leader of an internal opposition within the Conservative party. It was an outright challenge to Heath's moral authority, as he made clear in his opening paragraph. 'With every post,' he said, 'I get letters from people all over the country in all walks of life who write to me because they agree, or think that they agree, with what they understand me to be saying ... nearly all the writers declare themselves convinced that their own wishes and opinions count for nothing.'[119] He related that these people felt that writing to their own Members of Parliament was a waste of time, that they regarded the media as in a conspiracy against their best interests. Powell made it clear he agreed with this analysis. Talking of the public's frustration, he said, 'I do not believe there has been anything on the same scale in British politics since manhood franchise, and quite possibly not for long before. The formerly normal phenomenon of the suppressed and disregarded minority has been inverted; people have settled down to a dazed or irritated acceptance that they are living in an age when the majority is always wrong.'

He said this was 'perilous' for the Conservative party, and knew too well that change would only come from the bottom up. 'This is why tirelessly, to scores of correspondents day by day, I commend what is an act of faith: "If your Member of Parliament does not agree," say I, "all the more reason to tell him so, and to assure him and not me of the strength of your opinions and the depth of your feelings." ' He said his individual supporters could make a difference, if they mobilised themselves, to the way the party was being led. Indeed, in a sentiment more familiar from the left of British politics, he called upon them to organise. 'Sometimes, to some correspondents, I go further and say: "Are you a member of the Conservative Association in your constituency? Do you take part in its work? Do you even subscribe to it? If you do, you have a right, along with the others and in the proper ways, to make your opinions known. If you do not then have you not yourself to blame?" ' In a phrase aimed more at Heath and his colleagues than at his audience, Powell added, 'A national party is an organisation of the nation's opinion or it is nothing.' Reporting this speech, Powellight drove home the message, telling its members to join their local associations, if necessary overcoming in the process their distaste for the views of their MP or Conservative candidate, in order to spread the true gospel.

On 9 December the Commons debated public spending, and Powell renewed his attack on Barber and Heath. He referred to the two White Papers on the subject, of October 1970 and January 1971, that had projected public spending as increasing at a rate, over the following four years, of less than the growth in national income. This he had found commendable. However, a new White Paper showed that spending would increase not at the rate of 2.6 per cent specified earlier, but at a rate of 3.2 per cent; and no promises were made about whether this was likely to exceed or lag behind the growth in income. Powell judged it would be the latter, and thundered that 'the prospect is no longer, subject to certain qualifications, one of our being able to look forward to progressive, however gradual, limitation of the sphere of the state in the economy as a whole, or to a reduction in the burden which that represents on the public in terms of taxation'.[120] He cast doubt on the 'optimism' of the Treasury in expecting a 3.3 per cent growth rate, which he dismissed as 'highly improbable'.

Drawing on his experience as a Treasury minister, he warned his successors that, in any case, their estimates of what would have to be spent in the foreseeable future were almost certainly too low. 'The reason is simple: it is that in the immediate future we see what there is to be done; we see the expenditures that are needed; we know the circumstances. But try as we may to insert contingency items ... we never, and experience verifies this, dare insert sufficient contingency items to grasp the reality of what comes along as the later years arrive.'[121] To make his point, and to show his consistency, Powell read from the letter he had written in September 1961 to Selwyn Lloyd, then Chancellor and now Speaker, to argue that the Plowden Committee's projections for spending years ahead would destroy Treasury control and lead to inflation. As Powell had written at the time, 'Every service has to be allowed to "expand"; otherwise there would be a terrible outcry.'[122] He had called Plowden 'an exercise in escapism', saying that 'there is only one key to the control of expenditure. That is for the Government to wish it. If this condition is not fulfilled, no amount of long-term planning and forecasting will give control.' The effect of the Treasury's present exercises in trying to plan spending for years ahead would, he feared, suffer from precisely the same futility.

Powell's financial puritanism extended to his own life. On 20 December he spoke against the Ministerial and Other Salaries Bill, having earlier given written and oral evidence to a committee on the subject, saying that there should be no increase in MPs' pay and allowances. He had also told the committee that 'the facilities available were already larger than conduced to the best possible discharge of their duties'.[123] He now added that to pay MPs more would help change their status into that of 'paid, salaried and pensioned employees', infringing their independence.[124] When he said that some who could earn twenty times as much elsewhere would still aspire to the job of Member of Parliament 'because of the honour in which it is still clad', Whitelaw, the Leader of the House and a far wealthier man than Powell, asked whether Powell's policy would not merely favour the rich. Citing the example of himself, Powell said it would not.[125] He rigidly applied his own standard to others: it was simply not 'fitting or dignified' to vote such sums; and, speaking as a man who worked out of the House of Commons library and answered much of his constituency correspondence himself, he said that the clerical and secretarial duties for which extra allowances were being demanded were exaggerated.[126] His was, though, almost a lone voice.

The new year brought with it the immediate prospect of dealing with the European legislation. Powell had given the Commons a brief hint of the belligerence with which he intended to address the subject when on 13 December he questioned Geoffrey Rippon on his return from a meeting in Brussels where Britain had agreed to certain concessions on fisheries policy. 'As the Government have shown that they are prepared to go back on their General Election pledge not to enter the Community without the full-hearted consent of the British parliament and people,' he asked, 'was it really necessary for my right hon and learned Friend to make such heavy weather over breaking the pledges on fisheries?'[127] Rippon replied, 'I must say, with respect, that I consider my right hon Friend's question wholly unjustified.' Yet the facts were not in the Government's favour, and that was the main theme Powell would hammer home, fruitlessly, for the months ahead.

In a speech in his constituency on 12 January 1972 he set out his position unequivocally. He said the Government had no moral right to sign the Treaty of Accession to the Community later that month, and declared that he would vote against all the legislation formally securing entry. He also warned that the action Heath was taking 'would have the most damaging and incalculable effects not least on the future of the Conservative party'. He pointed out that the conditions Heath himself had set for entry at the 1970 election had not been fulfilled, and that no one could contend that the seven-to-five majority for entry in the House of Commons on 28 October represented the wholehearted consent Heath had said was necessary. He reminded his activists of his election address from 1970 in which he had said he would do his utmost to ensure that Britain did not enter the Community. 'I have grievously misjudged my friends and supporters if there is one among them who would suggest that I ought to break my public word. I can carry out my undertaking without the shadow of a question of breach of loyalty to our leader and Prime Minister.'[128] Powell's chairman at the time, Ian Beddows, recalled that the weight of opinion in the association was against Powell on this issue; but such was the reservoir of support he had built up, not least over his stand on immigration, that his own dissent was respected. He told Beddows he was prepared to bring the Government down on the issue, and meant it.[129]

Three days later Powell went to Liechtenstein where, speaking in German, he forecast that public opinion would keep Britain out of the EEC. He said the majority of 112 on the matter of principle the previous October was deceptive, and that when specific issues came to be debated it would shrink. It had been 'no more than the overture; the real play or opera begins next week', when the legislation itself would be debated.[130] He based his belief on his conviction that the result had been a 'freak' caused by the internal power-plays of the Labour party, and that 'we shall not again witness a mass of 69 Labour members who by not merely abstaining but voting with the Government converted into victory what would otherwise have been a substantial Government defeat'. The fundamental fact about Parliament was that, in the end, Oppositions opposed. Yet again, he reminded an audience of Heath's commitment not to enter if backed by anything other than wholehearted support.

On 24 January he was in Brussels, where he told the city's branch of the Lions Club that Heath's signing, with senior colleagues, of the Treaty of Accession two days earlier was an act for which 'the conditions necessary to impart reality to it were not available'.[131] He added, 'They can sign, and they did sign, the treaty; but they cannot secure for it that consent of the British people which is necessary to validity.' Of Europe he said that 'the English have never belonged, and they have always known that they did not belong to it'. Of legislating away British sovereignty – something no member of the Government at home was prepared to admit was the case – Powell said: 'The House of Commons will not do it; and the people of Britain will not suffer it.'

In between his two continental trips, Heath had had to face an Opposition motion in the Commons calling for him not to sign the Treaty of Accession until the full text had been laid before Parliament. He had tabled an amendment to the motion saying that the Treaty had to be ratified by Parliament, and would, obviously, be published before it was. It was a sign of the growing awareness on both sides of the House that the sort of support the Government had won on 28 October was unlikely, as Powell was saying, to be repeated. The Whips even consulted some of the party's anti-marketeers – though not, needless to say, hard-liners like Powell – before the amendment was drafted, in the hope of framing a form of words that would not entice them to vote with Labour. In this, they were successful, though Heath had said that, in accordance with what he claimed was normal diplomatic practice, he would go to Brussels to sign the treaty even if the Labour motion were carried. Only treaties that became effective immediately upon signature – which this one did not, as it had to be ratified – had to be published in advance, the leadership claimed.

In that debate, on 20 January, Powell harried Rippon for breaching what he termed the 'usual rule' that treaties were laid before Parliament before signature. 'Is it', he asked Rippon, 'his contention that the Parliament were obliged to sign the treaty before it was published or that they chose to sign the treaty before it was published?'[132] Rippon replied that it was not possible for one Government to make such choices with a multilateral treaty. Powell countered by asking him whether this was true in all the other countries who were party to the treaty; Rippon hedged by saying that it was 'only a draft treaty'.

The following week Powell used a speech at Chester-le-Street to urge every man and woman in Britain to do all in their power to prevent entry taking place, for he claimed no government and no majority in Parliament, however large, could ignore the clear will of the people. 'Governments, majorities and Members are all, at the day's end, the potter's clay – they cannot forget their makers. Let people therefore not say "We can do nothing." They can, if they will, do everything.' He added, 'If the House of Commons, in the name of the British people, gives up the authority and independence which it has exercised on their behalf for so long, and the people of this country henceforward are to be taxed, governed, judged, and ruled elsewhere, let there be no doubt by whose fault it happened. Do not blame the whips; do not blame the members; do not blame the patronage machine; do not blame the pressures, the threats, the promises, the bribes that will be brought to bear. It is the nation itself that will have judged itself.'[133] Powell's attempts to motivate the public by telling them how they would no longer be able to hold their parliament to account for the way they were governed and taxed was, though, of limited success. His only hope was that, when the battle came to the floor of the Commons itself, he would be heard more keenly.

14

A BATTLE FOR BRITAIN

A vote on the second reading of the European Communities Bill was scheduled for 17 February 1972, after three days of debate. By way of warming up, Powell said two days before the debate started that the Government was already putting 'utterly immoral' pressure on some MPs to support the Bill, notably threatening Ulster Unionists – six of whom had voted against entry on 28 October – that, if they opposed the Government, it might be less sedulous in defending their interests. He had not entirely grasped the nature of the pressure on the Unionists, though; there were fears among them that, if Heath were defeated, their fate would once more be in the hands of Wilson, whom they then trusted less than Heath to defend their place in the Union. While Powell conceded there were circumstances in which the party machine could be pushed beyond what was normal by 'the rough and ready standards of political life', and even beyond a point that was wise for Government and Parliament itself, the present playing upon 'the basic human emotions of hope and fear' was unreasonable, given that the House of Commons was more or less equally divided and was seeking to oppose the 'preponderant will of the electorate'.[1]

Nor was he just talking about the usual threats to withhold honours, or promises to confer them. Central Office was, he said, going 'behind the backs of MPs' who had quite properly made up their minds on matters of principle to 'cajole and suborn' constituency officers into challenging their Members' behaviour, often despite those Members having made promises of opposition to the Common Market to electors in 1970. 'It is something different when the apparatus of patronage and the system of bribes and threats is exported from Westminster to the country to constrain MPs to vote against what they know to be their wishes, and believe to be the interests of their electors.' He ended with a direct attack on Heath – 'once a chief whip is always a chief whip'. However, 'there are greater things in politics than are dreamt of in the whips' office, and Edward Heath was speaking from a higher standpoint when he declared the truth that nothing but the full-hearted consent of this nation could authorise British entry into the Community'. Certainly, it was Heath the ex-Chief Whip who ran the Bill, and ran it with the utter contempt for individual MPs that had always characterised his approach as a Whip. When, as Leader of the Opposition, he had appointed one of his backbenchers to the Whips' Office in 1967, Heath had told him: 'there are three sorts of people in this party: shits, bloody shits, and fucking shits.'[2] Such an attitude would explain much about the way in which Heath would lose touch with opinion in the years ahead.

The Bill itself had come as a shock to Labour and the anti-marketeers on the Government benches. They had hoped for a long and complex measure that could be bogged down in the same way the Parliament (No. 2) Bill had been. Heath was too sharp for that. Thanks to some cunning drafting by his Solicitor-General, Sir Geoffrey Howe, the Bill had only a dozen clauses, which would limit, though by no means remove, scope for obstruction. When the debate started on 15 February Powell intervened to make a lengthy point of order as Rippon rose. His argument was that the Ways and Means Resolution* tabled for the taxation implications of the Bill was defective; nonetheless, it should be passed, he argued, before the debate could proceed, such was the Resolution's importance. He was followed by Michael Foot, who said that Powell 'has made a most formidable case to the House'; he, too, advocated postponement of the debate.[3] The Speaker, however, ruled that the Bill 'does not need to be founded on a Ways and Means Resolution'.[4]

Normally, Powell was so reverent in matters of the Speaker's authority that he would not have dreamed of taking the matter further, but this was an extreme case for him, almost of constitutional life and death. With a hint of intellectual menace, he conceded that it would be improper to carry on disputing the ruling in the light of what Selwyn Lloyd had said; but added, addressing him, that 'it will by no means be the last [time] in the course of proceedings on this Bill when you and the House will find themselves faced with unprecedented questions ... I hope that in that light you will do as your predecessors have done and not hesitate to make precedents.'[5]

Powell himself spoke on the last evening of the debate. Conscious of the large majority the Government had had on 28 October, he reminded the House that this was the first time it had ever been called upon to decide the specific question of entry: White Papers were merely theoretical, and argument about their contents, eventually, futile. The Bill was, he contended, a clear statement what stood to be lost by entry: the legislative supremacy of Parliament, the exclusive control of the Commons over taxation and expenditure, and the surrender of the country's judicial independence. There was, apart from these, another consequence not so explicitly set out in the Bill: the strengthening, as a result of all the other changes, of the power of the executive relative to that of the House of Commons.

He then moved to counter the arguments used to palliate the costs he, and the Bill, had outlined. 'The first', he said, 'is the *de minimis* argument – "Don't worry; it's not very important, because it will not refer to many subjects or very important matters." The second is the remonstrance "Don't worry, because, at any rate in the future, we" – whoever "we" is – "will be participating in whatever

---

* A vote on a motion to allow the raising of revenue to pay for the effects of legislation.

decision results from the overriding authority of the Community being exercised in this country." [6] Powell dismissed the first argument by saying the present arrangements were but 'a receptacle which is intended progressively to contain more and more external powers, legislation and decisions. It is a receptacle created to be progressively filled.' [7] This had to be the case, if the admissions by Rippon and others that the aim was political union were remotely true. 'This surrender begins as minimal,' Powell warned. 'It is intended to become maximal.'

As for the question of Britain's participation in the decision-making, as the receptacle was filled, Powell mocked the assertion that the Commons would remain in charge of the process as far as Britain was concerned. In fact, he said, the intention was merely that the House should be 'apprised' of what was going on in the Community – 'but it is not by being "apprised" of what is proposed that this House exerts its control or ever has done'. [8] He suspected he knew what would happen: 'The views expressed on both sides of the House would be taken into account "with great interest". One can almost rehearse the wind-up speech which would be heard from the Government Bench.' The decision would be 'the common decision' of all the partners; and to defy the executive would, it had been candidly admitted, be a breach of the treaty.

In this case, the assertion that the House could continue to control the executive took on a new gravity in its likely consequences. 'Of course all treaties can be broken,' said Powell. 'In that sense no parliament can bind its successors. All agreements can be scrapped, all engagements can be reneged upon. Is that the dishonour that this House intends – to enter into this with the *arrière pensée* that if we do not like anything that comes out of it we can always break the treaty?' [9] He defined the power of the Commons as the power to reverse decisions; no House could, he said again, bind its successors. 'What meaning', he asked, 'has the right of the electorate to send hon Members here unless, so far as legislation and administration can bring it about, what has been done in the past can, if the electors desire it, be reversed?'

He contended that another problem for the Commons was that the executive, in the European context, had no right of initiative; that lay with the Commission, and there would be no point attacking a government for not taking certain actions when it had no power to take them. 'So it remains a fact', he said, 'that, as the Community develops with this country as a member of it, so the control of this House and of the people of this country will diminish and shrivel.' He said there might be circumstances in which a surrender of sovereignty was in the national interest; but it had to be willed, in this case, 'by the overwhelming majority of the people', for 'what is given up, what is paid, is not the personal property of hon Members of this House or of any one parliament, but comes from and is held as a trust for the entire people of this country'. [10]

Naturally, Powell used this assertion to raise the famous words of Heath again, about full-hearted consent: Heath, Powell suggested, had recognised the truth of what he had just said, which underlined the significance of his promise. 'Those words were not plucked up as a verbal infelicity for which he was to be held to account,' he continued. 'They have become so famous because they enshrine a manifest and necessary truth.'[11] This was, too, the crux of Powell's argument. 'That condition does not exist.' The people were manifestly not in favour; they had not been asked at the election, and very few Conservative MPs had said in their election addresses that they supported entry. They had not been told about the sacrifice of sovereignty. At this point, Rippon interrupted Powell, claiming that the people were aware of the sovereignty issue, which prompted Powell to observe that if Rippon believed that 'he belongs to a very small number of exceptions'.[12]

As for the full-hearted consent of Parliament, Powell continued, that would require a far larger majority on second reading than had been obtained in the debate on the White Paper – 112 – four months earlier. This prompted another interruption, this time from Sir Tufton Beamish. He demanded to know why Powell had not 'answered the question' of why he had voted for the 'principle of entry' when the House debated the matter in 1967. 'That vote was in favour of negotiation,' Powell snapped back. The White Paper, and the specific proposals of the Bill, were all that now mattered: 'None of us can shelter behind the past. We each have to take our decision in the open upon the proposition that is now before the House.'[13]

In his peroration, Powell struck a powerful blow. He looked at the 'full-hearted consent' as it was likely to manifest itself that evening. The Conservative Whips had been using all manner of threats for days to get rebels into the lobbies behind Heath; Powell himself would say later that grown men had been seen leaving the Whips' Office in tears. 'In order to secure a narrow majority in the Division tonight, they [the leadership] have brought to bear upon hon Members of different views, despite my right hon Friend's [Heath's] assurance that they would have an absolute right to vote as they so decided on this question, every available form of pressure. Is that a sign of belief?' His conclusion was magisterial:

> For this House, lacking the necessary authority either out-of-doors or indoors, legislatively to give away the independence and sovereignty of this House now and for the future is an unthinkable act. Even if there were not those outside to whom we have to render account, the very stones of this place would cry out against us if we dared such a thing. We are here acting not only collectively but as individuals; and each hon Member takes his own responsibility upon himself – as I do, when I say for myself, 'It shall not pass.'

Heath simply did not care about Powell's constitutional arguments; and nor did he care about his breaches of promise either on consent or on allowing the party a vote according to conscience. He had not finished with the pressure yet.

In his own, uninspiring speech winding up the debate two hours after Powell had spoken he was sufficiently rattled by the falling-off of support in the Commons for the measure that, in complete contradiction of his earlier assurances, he warned those in his own party planning to vote against that if the Government was defeated he would call a general election. Another plan, to truncate the parliamentary session, start a fresh one and introduce the Bill again had been considered but dismissed. Powell and his supporters decided that Heath was bluffing. In the end, the Government majority was slashed to eight, with thirteen Conservative MPs, including Powell, voting against, and two Ulster Unionists. Four other Conservatives abstained, and the Labour pro-marketeers simply did as they were told, with the exception of four abstainers. The *Sunday Telegraph*'s political correspondent, present in the press gallery, described the look on the faces of the front bench as being of 'devastating shock' at the size of the rebellion, given Heath's threat to ask for a dissolution.

It had been a horribly close call for Heath. He had summoned almost all the rebels – though not Powell, to whom he could not bring himself to talk – to his office to be threatened privately, when it finally came home to the Whips just how narrow any victory was likely to be. Heath had been relying on support from the Liberals, but had upset their leader, Jeremy Thorpe, a few days earlier in a row about Rhodesia: Heath had accused Thorpe of wanting to 'bomb Africans'. When told this might prevent the Liberals from supporting him, an unprecedented and not especially gracious letter of apology was dispatched to Thorpe. More worrying, though, for Heath was the way this great argument had brought Powell out of isolation. Though he was not formally the leader of a faction in his own party, he was now certainly pre-eminent among a group of like-minded MPs who might, in extreme circumstances, bring the Government down. Future attempts to marginalise Powell could not be as successful as some in the past had been. He and Heath were now formally polarised against each other, and the Conservative party was properly beginning the process of tearing itself apart that would culminate in the events of February 1975, when Heath was removed.

Immediately the result was known – the actual numbers were 309 to 301 in Heath's favour – Wilson jumped up to make political capital out of Heath's discomfort. He echoed Powell's words and reminded him of the earlier promise about proceeding with 'full-hearted consent'.[14] He told Heath that not only did he not have the full-hearted consent of Parliament, he did not even have the full-hearted consent of his own party; there were not enough Conservative votes to get the measure through. Heath remained impervious to such assaults. His determination to get the Bill through – not least as Powell was the symbol of the opposition to it – overcame all other moral and intellectual considerations.

So bucked was Powell by the narrowness of the vote on the second reading that he went straight home in glee to tell his wife, and they drank a toast to the result before going to bed. They both agreed that the Bill now could not get through.[15] The next day Powell wrote to the French ambassador in London advising him that entry would not now take place; and he told him to let his Government know this, so that the French could make their diplomatic plans on the basis that Britain would not join the Community in 1973. Already, though, Powell's optimism was beginning to look misplaced. Labour's pro-marketeers were now prepared to defy their party line as the second reading had been given: for example, the financial resolutions contingent on the Bill had been passed by majorities of around thirty. Powell had spoken in that debate too, on 22 February, and had denounced the plan to pass a Ways and Means Resolution to raise unlimited taxation for the financing of Britain's contribution to the Community. He quoted Rippon attacking a Labour plan to do something similar on a less contentious Bill in 1966. The hypocrisy in which the Government was having to engage was mounting by the day.

Powell said the resolution was so worded as to mean there was 'literally no limit' to the future taxation that could be raised.[16] It would be raised 'without the normal parliamentary procedures' or further Ways and Means resolutions; it was taking taxation in this respect entirely out of the control of the House, and without the people, at the preceding election, having been asked to give a mandate for such fundamental action. Again, he illustrated that the powers being surrendered were 'of the essence of Ministerial responsibility to this House and of the responsibility of this House to the country'.[17] He said that even those who supported entry should see the danger of such an open-ended resolution, and vote it down. Again, he was ignored.

Heath's other problems were mounting. Douglas-Home was trying to secure a settlement in Rhodesia, now in its seventh year of rebellion; and Powell, speaking at Weybridge on 20 February, chipped in with the advice that sanctions should be abandoned whatever the outcome of the talks. This issue, though, was of small significance compared with industrial unrest boiling up at home, and in the coal mines in particular. Heath capitulated relatively quickly to the demands of the National Union of Mineworkers, an act Powell branded 'unconditional surrender'. Speaking at Malvern on 26 February, he warned Heath not to be tempted to fund the pay rise by expanding the money supply and, therefore, inflating.

He said the miners may not have realised it – indeed, it is certain they did not – but they were embattled against the idea of nationalisation itself, for in taking on their employers they were also taking on the state, and because they were a nationalised industry the normal disciplines of the market that would have dictated the acceptable size of the settlement were not applicable. By not resorting to the market, the state was attempting to exercise its power arbitrarily over the miners, which was unacceptable in a free society and had led to confrontation. He argued that the rise awarded did not have to be inflationary:

'It is a misuse of language to describe any single wage or price increase as inflationary.'[18] What worried him most was the heretical talk among some Conservatives about a prices and incomes policy, something not foreseen in the manifesto of 1970: 'It is as absurd as if someone, having dropped a heavy article on his toe, were to say: "I really must get down at last to altering the law of gravitation." ' He said that the large balance of payments surpluses in recent years, caused by the undervaluation of the pound, had caused the inflation then being endured. 'These huge surpluses are inevitably translated into an increase in the money supply inside Britain and have been the principal means of financing the inflationary explosion we have experienced.' A floating pound would, he said, have helped solve this problem, a further reason to regret the planned entry to the EEC in which, he said prophetically, 'the right to take our own decisions on the management of our currency is part of that economic and political independence which must progressively be parted with, as the cost and consequence of membership'.

When the European Communities Bill came back to the Commons for its committee stage on 29 February the Government immediately suffered an unexpected defeat, though merely of procedure, before any detail could be discussed. Two and a half hours of points of order began the proceedings, mainly about the selection of amendments by the Deputy Speaker, Sir Robert Grant-Ferris, at which stage the Government felt it had no choice but to accept an Opposition call for a vote of censure on Grant-Ferris; a decision that seemed to lead to an altercation on the floor of the House between Whitelaw, the Leader of the House, who had dug in against it, and Francis Pym, the Chief Whip, who saw it as the only way out of an impasse. The committee was adjourned until after this, which meant that the first two days allocated for it had been wiped out.

Michael Foot had started off the points of order, to nods of approval from Powell; it had looked to the Government's business managers as though history was about to repeat itself. Foot succeeded in making a twenty-five-minute speech about the Chair's selection of amendments, even though technically he was not allowed to challenge this. Grant-Ferris said he had disallowed the amendments Foot referred to because they were out of order: he said the Bill was not to approve the treaty itself, and therefore amendments designed to vary the treaty's terms were out of order. This provoked uproar, since there seemed little point in debating the measure at all in that case and, in any event, the Government had promised that the Bill would be opened to amendments. Powell rose to say it was with reluctance that he criticised Grant-Ferris's selection – or, rather, non-selection – of amendments, but the Deputy Speaker's ruling would mean the House was unable to debate a whole series of proposed changes to British law. The earlier assurances should be abided by.

Grant-Ferris protested in response, 'I have to take the advice of the learned clerks,' which brought further uproar. He corrected himself, saying instead, 'I have to listen to the advice of the clerks,' but the damage was done. First, Whitelaw agreed to a censure motion on the Chair, but only on condition that the amendments could be proceeded with until the motion was debated; but that was shouted down too, and he had to retreat. Powell was seen, in the words of one sketch writer, 'heaving with mirth' as the Government went into reverse.[19]

When the censure motion was debated the following day Powell was the only Conservative to vote with Labour, while thirteen others abstained. It was moved by Sir Elwyn Jones, the shadow Attorney-General, and Powell spoke early on. He stressed that the censure was not intended personally; it was an attempt to alter the 'intolerable position in which the House has been placed by the quite unprecedented character of the nature of accession to the European Community and of this legislation interacting with the normal rules and procedures of the House'.[20] The problem, as Powell saw it, was the expectation of the Government that the Treaty of Accession had to be taken as a whole – 'we cannot unpack the parcel and look at each item separately, with a view perhaps to rejecting or accepting or, more likely, to attaching conditions'.[21] This was not how the House normally operated, and Powell could see no reason why this Bill should be such an exception.

'If', he continued, 'it is allowable during the Committee stage to propose the question, that the clause stand part of the Bill, then it must be conceivable that the decision of the Committee should be in the negative – that the Clause should not stand part of the Bill.' This, were it to happen, would conflict with the multilaterally agreed terms of the Treaty of Accession. Powell accepted that the House could not amend a treaty; and it was not a treaty that was before the House, but a Bill. The Bill could be amended, 'though certain consequences for the Government in their relations with their treaty partners may follow from the House doing that'.[22] Given the unprecedented provisions of the Bill, he said it was 'monstrous' that the Commons should be told, 'you are also prevented from debating, discussing, examining in detail, let alone amending the terms and conditions upon which your sovereignty is given up'. He said he could not believe that 'this is a humiliation to which this House will submit'.[23] As with his protest on the Ways and Means motion, he said the principle at stake was important whether one wanted or opposed entry to the EEC. As before, the Conservative leadership demonstrated a complete lack of concern for the points he was making.

Speaking in Montgomeryshire the following weekend, Powell charged up his rhetoric about what was happening in the Commons. It was 'a life and death struggle for its independence and supreme authority', he said, adding that 'with other weapons and in other ways, the contention is as surely about the future of Britain's nationhood as were the combats which raged in the skies over southern England in the autumn of 1940. The gladiators are few; their weapons

are but words; and yet their fight is everyman's.' Beneath his romantic nationalism he had a serious constitutional point to make about the way in which the
Commons was being made to debate the treaty.

> With breathtaking effrontery the sovereign legislature of this country is informed
> that it will not be allowed to debate anything but the details ... of the surrender
> of its own powers: the big matters, it is told, cannot be altered and therefore
> cannot be discussed. Why? Because they say it is all in the treaty which has been
> signed; and the treaty cannot be altered, and you knew all about it in advance.
> Every one of these assertions is false. It is an impossible affront to the House of
> Commons, and through the House of Commons to the electorate, to be told, in
> the very moment when it is being invited to legislate its own sovereignty away,
> that it has already lost that sovereignty without so much as a by-your-leave and
> has no alternative but to accompany its captors in handcuffs and fetters.'[24]

The question of inability to amend the Bill would not go away. Labour put
down a motion of censure against the Government on 6 March. It was moved
by Peter Shore, the shadow Leader of the House, who said the Bill had been
framed 'with the intention of removing the possibility of substantial amendment'; this had been 'a gross breach of faith'.[25] Powell said that, whatever predicament the House found itself in, it was not because of ill faith or misleading
of the House by the Government. He referred back to the speech made earlier
by Rippon, in which he had said that the Government had fully expected the
Bill to be open to amendment. The matter was one for the Chair; the House, he
felt sure, would find a way to debate the wider issues contingent on the Bill.
And, indeed, amendments were allowed, but the Whips were under the strictest
orders to avoid any being passed, as the leadership did not want a report stage;
it was soon possible to carry out these wishes, thanks to the collusion of Labour
pro-marketeers with the Government they were supposed to be opposing,
taking a leaf from Powell's book and voting according to their consciences.

Powell was active throughout the committee stage of the Bill. He was ever
alert to the ploys being used by the Government's business managers to prevent
the Bill's enemies from wrecking it. On 7 March he complained that he had
been able to attend the committee stage only by abandoning his important
duties on the Committee of Privileges, sitting upstairs at the same time. That
afternoon, Powell estimated, between 150 and 200 Members were supposed to
be doing something else. The Government had promised that committee work
upstairs would be restricted on Wednesdays; but it would still take place on
Tuesdays, the other day the Bill was on the floor of the Commons, which meant
that for about half the time it was in committee a large portion of Members
could attend only by neglecting duties elsewhere.

In his fiercer and fiercer assaults on his own party, Powell was now, consciously or unconsciously, preparing the ground for his renunciation of it in

1974. In the first three months of 1972 he made fifty speeches in private or in public outside the Commons. Almost all, whatever their ostensible targets, could be interpreted clearly as attacks on the Heathite orthodoxy. At Edgbaston on 10 March he noted that the Wilson Government had been undone by its retreat from the principles upon which it had been elected, and the same fate now threatened to befall Heath's. On economic matters he listed the nationalisation of Rolls-Royce, the rescue of the Mersey Docks and Harbours, and the pouring of public money into the Upper Clyde shipyards. Public spending was rising, not falling; new examples of state largesse were promulgated as achievements. It was a malaise that went wider than the European question. Indeed, he said it often seemed as though Wilson were back in Downing Street, 'or even the more elderly might reflect, Harold Macmillan'.[26] Nothing, he added, could be more dangerous for an administration 'than to be thought or seen to have abandoned or, worse, inverted the principles on which it was believed to be elected'. In advance of the Budget later that month, when most were calling for reflation, Powell called for the opposite, noting that the money supply in the last quarter of 1971 had expanded at an annualised rate of 25 per cent. The inflationary spectacle of the years ahead would prove him right. Barber and Heath did not listen.

In the early stages of the European Communities Bill's time in committee, Powell described the evil of allowing, under the treaty, legislation by prerogative. 'By the simple prerogative act of making a treaty, a future Government could make the domestic law of this country.'[27] The first clause of the Bill, he said on 7 March, 'means prerogative legislation, and prerogative legislation is a contradiction in terms. It is a contradiction of the very nature of the House. Under the innocence of a Short Title and Definition Clause we are presented with an invitation to legalise prerogative legislation once and for all and to end, in an every expanding sphere, the central function of this House.' The next day he returned to the theme: 'If the Bill is passed, the balance of power between the Executive and parliament shifts dramatically and permanently ... on all matters which concern the community and Executive which the House will confront will no longer be alone the Executive of this country. Over and behind the Executive of this country, like a shadow standing behind the Minister at that Box, will be an Executive power which the House cannot get at.'[28]

A week later, Powell and Foot complained about the grouping of amendments, demanding smaller groups and more divisions. It was clear by now that Powell was assuming the same leadership role for the opponents of the measure as he had with the Parliament (No. 2) Bill. A Labour backbencher, William Molloy, no admirer of Powell's, said that in his defence of the rights of the Commons and of the electorate Powell had 'shouldered the responsibility of pointing out these grave dangers'. Powell moved amendments – which were unsuccessful – to restrict the ability of the Bill to allow the legislation in advance on matters which parliament did not know. The secret co-operation between Labour supporters of the Bill and the Conservative Whips ensured that this safeguard was not adopted, and Rippon remained utterly insouciant about Powell's attacks on him for allowing these erosions of sovereignty to take place.

As the European Communities Bill dragged on, even so experienced a parliamentarian as Powell continued to be amazed by the tactics the Whips were using. As a result, he said, 'not even the most fervid apologist of British entry dares to claim the consent, let alone the full-hearted consent, of the British people', he told a party dinner in Staffordshire on 8 April.[29] He said it was 'an insult to the intelligence of the public to offer such a pretence' that the narrow vote on the second reading, or even the seven-to-five support for the motion on 28 October, represented full-hearted consent. 'So conscious is the Government of not having even the bare consent of the House of Commons that no device of political pressure and thuggery has been omitted to constrain Conservative Members to vote on this issue against their opinion and conscience – a fine commentary on the meaning of "full-hearted".'

Referring to the anodyne formula of the last manifesto, with its promise merely to negotiate, Powell said, 'the Government and the nation are set on a collision course. I repeat: if this thing comes to pass, our Government and our party will not be forgiven by the people whom they have deceived.' Powell said he was still hopeful of having the measure stopped. If he could not, he said it would be fatal to Heath, and he went further in contumely against his leader than he had ever publicly done before, actually naming him rather than speaking in more coded terms. 'For him it would be no compensation to have received the plaudits of Europe and the congratulations of commentators. Nor would any of the other acts or achievements of his government be weighed in the balance against this. He would go down in history bearing with him the indelible brand of broken faith and trust betrayed.'

This attack on Heath led to immediate briefings of lobby correspondents by party managers that, if this sort of thing continued, the whip might be withdrawn from Powell. Yet his popularity in the country was scarcely less than at the time of the Birmingham speech; to martyr him by removing the whip would have been a disastrous mistake for Heath, as most MPs knew, suspecting that it was what Powell most wanted. 'He'd love to play Becket to Heath's Henry II' was how one anonymous MP put it.[30] Others felt that the new levels of vituperation were the clearest sign that Powell knew he had failed. He had distributed the speech himself to the press well in advance to ensure it made the appropriate impact; he had sent a copy to Central Office, but without any request for them to send it on the media, as was normally the case.

Powell's hopes of a new means to defeat the Government over Europe were boosted when the Ulster Unionists, affronted by the imposition that spring of direct rule of the Province, said they would consider resigning the Conservative whip. Powell's relations with the group, after four years of close involvement with their cause, were good. When it had been announced, the previous month, that an 'initiative' was impending, he had said that what that word really meant was 'abdication, the confession that lawful authority was blameworthy, and that violence and terrorism were, not maybe exactly right in themselves, but substantially in the right all along'.[31] He denounced, as he had done before, the civil rights movement in the Province as 'a tissue of trivialities and untruths' before which the Government 'made haste to worship and bow down to confess its faults'; it was merely a front for the removal of the Six Counties from the Kingdom. On 23 March the initiative came. Heath, deciding he had no confidence in the Northern Ireland Government's ability to control the situation, abolished Stormont. The action confirmed two of Powell's beliefs about him: it was made not least because of international unease, with Heath inordinately concerned about the opinion of other states; and the solution he implemented was that of the bureaucrat, and showed little care for the political sensitivities. Powell had advocated full political integration into the Westminster system himself the previous year, but this did not achieve it. Northern Ireland was still to be governed separately, but by Order in Council from Westminster, rather than being part of an integrated political and democratic system. He was appalled, and resolved to oppose the measure.

The Commons debated direct rule – in the form of the second reading of the Northern Ireland (Temporary Provisions) Bill – on 28 March, and it meant that Powell, already heavily occupied in the fight against the European Communities Bill, had to open up another front; but it was an offensive, not a defensive, one. Introducing the Bill Whitelaw, who had been made Northern Ireland Secretary, used the language of 1940: 'If the House passes the Bill the British parliament and the House of Commons will have taken on a major responsibility and a daunting task. We can only hope to succeed if we are prepared to see it through together.' He said the Bill would provide a 'fresh start' which must be used 'to promote feelings of tolerance, understanding, fairness and impartiality. If it can do that, then moderate opinion in the minority can be weaned away from the gunman. Then, and in my judgment only then, can the terrorists effectively be defeated and violence ended.'[32] This, in Powell's view, was nonsense. Whitelaw probably thought it was too. When, a year earlier, Cecil King had challenged him over lunch to the effect that the Government's Ulster policy was 'limited to a wish that Ireland and the Irish should go away and get lost', Whitelaw had replied, 'Exactly.'[33]

Powell was one of only eighteen who voted against imposing direct rule. The Government had the support of Labour, and the second reading was carried by a majority of 465. In his speech in the debate he pointed to his own consistent belief that there could be peace only by integration: 'we are all looking for some way to escape from the exclusive concentration of the politics of the Six Counties upon the question of union or non-union'.[34] However, the form of direct rule in the Bill, as he saw it, merely emphasised the difference between the Six Counties and the rest of the Kingdom. He said that the provisional nature of the Bill only made matters worse, renewed as it would have to be every year. 'We create a situation, and set up an organisation, which inherently is and always will be tentative, which every month that it exists carries within itself the seeds not of union but of disunion.'[35] He also made the point, which would become a staple of his criticism of the situation for as long as it lasted, that Ulster was drastically under-represented in Parliament; it had been granted far fewer seats because of the existence of Stormont. For these and other reasons, Powell protested that he found the Bill 'deeply and instinctively offensive'.[36]

He then gave his analysis of why Heath and Whitelaw had taken the steps they had. It was 'the assumption that that support [for the IRA] is tendered to the enemies of law and order and of the Union in Northern Ireland, and is withheld from the forces of law and order, because of things which can be altered or put right or assuaged by constitutional alterations'. Grievances and deprivations had been dealt with increasingly in the preceding two and a half years, and nothing had changed for the better. 'The very course of events', Powell said, 'has been the refutation of that explanation.'[37] He argued that more support had been given to the terrorists because they were seen to be in the ascendant. Fear was the key: 'One cannot, when a man has a gun in his back, expect to gain what is called his co-operation by offering him a position in a cabinet, a constitutional change or some new form of franchise.' The war was being lost, and the people were the prisoners of violence and terror.

The Bill, he went on, was 'founded on a misconception – on a pathetic delusion as to the fundamental reality of the situation in Northern Ireland'. As such, he added, it could only make things worse. The interpretation that the terrorists and their supporters would put on the Bill would be to say: 'You see, violence is succeeding. It is paying off. Another stage has been gained.'[38] He lamented that the pointlessness of this Bill would be aggravated by the refusal to take such essential measures as he had spelled out before: border controls, identity cards and the strengthening of the police. He would, he told the House, resist the 'dangerous temptation' to give the measure a chance by supporting it.[39]

Speaking in Scotland a month later, Powell set out a five-point plan to bring peace to Ulster. He said the main thing that would convince people peace was possible was if the enemy was being beaten; and the Government was manifestly failing in that, because, as always, its leaders had set themselves against any policy that would give the impression the enemy *was* being beaten. The measures he outlined were typical of any country that recognises it is at war. He said communication between the Six Counties and the Republic had to be severed or controlled; no-go areas in Belfast and Londonderry occupied by the IRA had to be reoccupied by the army or the police; police morale, authority and armaments had to be restored; those living in or travelling through Northern Ireland had to be made to carry a means of identification; and the Republic had to be recognised as a foreign country and her citizens as aliens, a course they themselves seemed 'vehemently' to want.

Powell said Whitelaw had told him he had made things more difficult. 'Indeed, I had not,' Powell asserted. 'His task, as he conceived and apparently still conceives it, is inherently not difficult but impossible, and would have been so exactly the same if I had never been born. On the contrary, I had done the one thing that was in my power to help not only him but my fellow citizens.'[40] He added that, in the present circumstances, optimism was the greatest treason, and wondered whether if there had been such violence in Glasgow or Birmingham as there had been in Belfast the Government's first thought would have been to reduce the numbers of the police and demoralise those who were left, the effect of the response to the civil rights movement.

As far as the leadership was concerned, Powell had now gone too far. For the first time since his attack on the policy on Rhodesia nearly four years earlier, Central Office refused to distribute this speech. The decision was taken personally by Lord Carrington, who had just become party chairman and was also Defence Secretary. He told the press, 'I don't think it is right that the Central Office machine should be used to distribute speeches of that sort.' Powell was unfazed, as he had his own distribution network – Jonathan Denby had taken copies to Fleet Street on the evening before delivery – and he knew that the additional notoriety Carrington's refusal would lend to his remarks would only help publicise them. Less than three months after 'Bloody Sunday' – the shooting in January 1972 of thirteen Republican demonstrators by the army in Londonderry – the Government was not prepared to risk confrontations in civilian areas, even if it meant that the rule of law could not be enforced otherwise.

The leadership were further infuriated with Powell because he had, the previous day, chosen a new line of attack against them. As a critic of the Industrial Relations Bill before it had been enacted, he saw no reason to hold off criticising the way the legislation was being operated. He chose to do so as the Government, having dealt with the miners, now faced a challenge from the rail unions. He was especially aggrieved by the Industrial Relations Court, and by the report of a Court of Inquiry into miners' pay presided over by Lord Wilberforce. 'It is time', he said at Inverness on 22 April, 'that a protest was registered against the prostitution of the judicial bench, in particular, by setting it to do work which no judge ought to be called upon to do. To set a judge, or any other person, to adjudicate in a confrontation between unions and Government is merely a device for dressing up and disguising a political decision for which politicians themselves find it inconvenient to take responsibility direct.'[41]

Powell stuck to his line that, in matters where a nationalised industry was negotiating with unions, it was essentially fraudulent to suggest that management had any freedom of manoeuvre. They were merely the 'front men' for the Government, implementing political decisions rather than economic ones; thus industrial disputes in the public sector were political confrontations in which the judiciary should not be involved. 'There are no facts that can be judicially ascertained from which the price of labour or anything else can be deduced,' he said. In order to disguise the political nature of such disputes, the Government had resorted to 'the invocation of a judicial function where no judicial function can subsist'. In any case, as he had often said before, the adjudication of precise percentages of wage claims was fatuous, since they were not the cause of inflation. This would not, however, be the end of it.

II

Powell had slowly formed a friendship since 1970 with Jim Molyneaux, an Ulster Unionist who had entered the House that year and was an instinctive sympathiser. Molyneaux had been one of just two Unionists to vote against the second reading of the European Communities Bill; and shortly after that event Powell asked whether he could spare half an hour to talk about other issues. In the course of their talk, Powell told Molyneaux that, while they had lost one battle, there were two great struggles ahead: the first was to stop the Bill becoming law; the second was to halt the betrayal of Ulster by the Government. Molyneaux agreed that a programme of co-operation between Powell and the Unionists could be fruitful, given the usefulness of Powell's influence when exercised over the Ulster question. Some of his colleagues were suspicious of Powell's integrationist line, but Molyneaux won them over.[42] It was an alliance that would have far-reaching consequences.

After the Easter recess the committee stage of the European Communities Bill resumed. On 18 and 19 April the committee discussed the possibility of a referendum before entry. Powell supported the notion because no indication had been given by the Conservatives at the last election that they would engage in any of the wholesale surrenders of sovereignty this Bill entailed. 'What was meant, and whatever now is meant, by the "full-hearted consent of parliament and people" ', said Powell, 'is that in this matter, though parliament will act and only parliament can act, parliament cannot do so without the consciousness and the evidence of the full-hearted consent of those who sent us here.'[43] That consent had not been obtained at the election, or since.

He stuck by his previous position that he was no friend to the referendum, but argued that when – for he was confident about this – the amendment was passed, a referendum would not necessarily proceed from it. Rather, 'it would begin – it would have to begin – the process of bringing together what sooner or later must be brought together: for this thing cannot go through with a House of Commons and a nation torn apart'.[44] He said the decision to have a referendum would cause something to be done 'to ensure that in due course the forms, the arrangements, the negotiations are so altered that, if possible, full-hearted consent may be forthcoming'.[45] Powell said there was another, more traditional means of gauging support: an election. Heath had, after all, threatened one in his winding-up speech on 17 February.

Powell asked why Heath was going to ask for a dissolution – something he seemed to think would have been electoral suicide – if he had not secured the Bill a second reading. 'What did he suppose the General Election which would follow would be about? What sort of House of Commons was intended to be sent back after the General Election?' He did not dispute Heath's constitutional right to use the threat, comparing it with Lord Grey's being granted a dissolution in 1831 on the matter of the Reform Bill. However, he hinted that, given the temper of the British people, they might well have returned a Labour government if there had been an election, and that Government would have found it impossible – even if it had wanted to – to take Britain in. That, Powell felt, could have been the only result of Heath's 'election'.

The next day, Powell was one of nineteen Conservatives who defied a three-line whip to vote for an advisory referendum. Although Labour's official policy was to vote, on a two-line whip, for the referendum – a Conservative 'rebel' amendment – fifty-two of them did not do so, including the deputy leader, Roy Jenkins, who resigned his post. The Government therefore won relatively comfortably, and the anti-marketeers, who had not expected Labour to break ranks in this way, were beginning to stare at ultimate defeat. Powell had certainly expected the amendment to be won, and wide-ranging consequences destructive of the Bill to flow from it. That the reverse happened was a grievous blow to him. His temper in the committee became shorter, his contempt for some of his opponents, for what he saw as their sharp practice and their ignorance of the real issues, more and more thinly disguised. 'I often think', he said on 19 April, 'that those are least European, have least understanding of what Europe is and what is great and imperishable about Europe, who have appropriated to the European Community, which in many respects is a caricature and even a denial of what is essentially European, the title of "Europe".'

He chose to speak ten days later in Cumberland on the perils of entry, and again Central Office refused to distribute his speech – this time the decision was taken by Jim Prior, a deputy chairman. In that same speech Powell claimed that Jenkins would not be too sorry to have resigned his post, as it was really his ambition 'to exercise his talents on the stage of Europe and to participate in taking decisions not for Britain here at home but for Europe in Brussels, Paris, Luxembourg and wherever else the imperial pavilions may be pitched. He does not, I assure you, foresee his future triumphs and achievements where his predecessors have seen them in the past – at the dispatch box in the House of Commons or in the Cabinet Room at Downing Street.' Jenkins was angered, and sent Powell a note in which he said the construction Powell had put on his motives was 'totally untrue . . . I would be interested to know by what apparent evidence you were mislead [sic].'[46] Powell replied to him, 'I do not think . . . that you should be surprised, or have ground for complaint, if an opponent takes you as the leading figure among Labour Members, supporting the present proposition for British membership of the EEC, and as intending the natural consequences of your policy.'[47] This drew another wounded reply from Jenkins, who did not 'regard it as in any way a satisfactory reply'.[48] Four years later he would leave the front rank of British politics to take up the post of President of the European Commission.

The political transformation Powell was undergoing, blurring for him the rigidities of party that had always dominated his outlook, was profound. Eight years later, recalling the period of the passage of the European Communities Bill, he described how he had come to realise an affinity with the Labour left, and a disgust for the supposedly closer cousins on the right – 'my natural enemy – worse even than Liberals, and more than that I cannot say'.[49] As he trooped, night after night, through the lobbies with the Labour left, he learned they were his truest bedfellows. 'I soon came to know in the weary debates and the 104 divisions against the European Communities Bill who it was with whom I shared feelings of anger, outrage and hatred at what was being perpetrated. I am aware that the "Left" is supposed to be motivated only by the desire to be unimpeded by "Europe" in converting Britain into a socialist state; but I am compelled to depose that the instincts and reasoning of the "Left" opponents of membership . . . were exactly as nationalistic, not to say patriotic, as my own.' Such reasoning also helped explain part of Powell's preternatural distaste for Jenkins, the arch-rightist.

By early May progress on the Bill was becoming so slow that a timetable motion had to be introduced. Powell was incandescent. He had come to the view – indeed, he repeated it in the House on 3 May – that if the European Communities Bill were passed it would become sacrosanct, like the Act of Union with Scotland. Therefore it had to be properly considered. 'Is my right hon Friend', he said to Robert Carr, the Leader of the House, 'seriously contending that one day's debate is proportionate to the importance of the transfer of the power to tax from this House to an authority outside the realm?' Carr had argued that the six days of debate the previous autumn on the White Paper somehow counted towards the time the House had had to consider entry. Powell said, correctly, that there was no link between the two events. The notion of guillotining the debate was repugnant to him: 'This debate is not a debate for or against membership of the Community. It is a debate for or against the continuance of a free House of Commons.'[50] A week later, once the guillotine was through, Powell told a luncheon of the Parliamentary Press Gallery that 'the House of Commons is perishing by its own hand. Week by week, month by month, the House of Commons votes to divest itself of what it had gained through a length of time not much shorter than the history of England itself, the trophies of its past struggles, the prizes of conflicts which will be renowned as long as English history is read.'[51] He denounced the self-interest of colleagues who were merely voting as they were told, thereby bringing this catastrophe about. He was beginning to acknowledge he was defeated.

Powell's high-profile association with Ulster soon sparked rumours that he would abandon his party and sit as a Unionist – two years before his 'shock' move across the Irish Sea.[52] He further endeared himself to the Unionists on 6 May, at a time of growing discontent about direct rule, by denouncing in a speech in County Down the way in which rule by Order in Council was being conducted at Westminster. He said that if 'men, women and children were being killed and mutilated every day and personal and commercial property deliberately destroyed' in the constituencies of Heath, Wilson or Whitelaw, the Commons would 'be loud with it from one end of the week to the other'.[53] However, the removal of the parliamentary voice from Stormont had merely been 'taken as permission to turn over and fall into a deeper sleep'. What Powell described as this 'constitutional twilight' could not, he said, be allowed to last for long: Ulster would have to be fully integrated into the rest of the country, and the laws affecting it debated properly.

He also warned that entry to the Common Market would lead to a united Ireland, a sub-set of the Community's desire to unite Europe. He said the Government was now routinely eschewing any practical or legislative step 'which could be seen as inconsistent with the political aim of the IRA and the Republic'. From this he drew the conclusion that the door was being left open to a policy that might integrate the Six Counties into the Republic. The Unionists formally renounced the Conservative whip, and Powell immediately became one of a seven-strong support group for them within the Conservative party at Westminster. He did not equivocate about his belief in their cause: 'The plantation of Ulster, right or wrong, wise or unwise, beneficent or not, did take place; neither it nor its consequences can be pretended out of existence. The people of this province are a part of the British nation, and the soil of this province is British soil, because the great majority of its inhabitants are so minded.'[54]

Later that month Powell found himself in the news for reasons unconnected with politics. Neighbours of his described how they had seen a man in a brown raincoat and black hat wrench the wing mirrors off a car that was blocking his garage in the mews behind South Eaton Place; having detached them, the man (bearing a distinct resemblance to Powell) then threw them at the windscreen and stormed off. One neighbour, Caroline Rosoman, clearly identified the vandal as Powell. 'I saw Mr Powell come to his garage door, opposite our house, where a Cortina was parked. When he found he could not get his car out he knocked at three of the seven houses in the mews. He asked us if we knew who owned the car, and we said we had no idea.'[55] It was then Powell lost his temper. In fact, the car was owned by a London Transport depot inspector, Thomas Appleton, who had left it there while mending a vacuum cleaner in the house nearby where his wife was a domestic help.

Powell issued a statement saying just that 'the allegations referred to are matters of private dispute'. Mr Appleton said he expected Powell to pay for the damage, and told the press: 'I am going to keep knocking at his door until he agrees to pay.'[56] Powell was not amused. 'Congratulations to the British press,' he said. 'I did not know that even they could make so much out of a non-event.' Nonetheless, so loyal was his personal following now that he received letters from well-wishers commiserating with him, and sharing their own personal experience of difficulties in extricating cars from garages.

His temper was not at its best at that time. He was reviewing Macmillan's latest volume of memoirs for the *Listener*, and gave him the most bilious critique yet: 'The narrative, heavily set with slabs of speech, diary, memorandum and correspondence, flows in a vein midway between a Queen's Speech and a favourable provincial press report.'[57]

He was still receiving 400 to 500 letters a week and, in an interview given to help maintain his public image, told the *Sunday Express*, 'I have been responding to an inner necessity to make statements which I was convinced corresponded with the wishes and opinions of a great body of my fellow countrymen.' He spoke of his 'passionate addiction' to the countryside, his sadness at not being able to ride regularly – he had hunted just before Christmas the previous year, but the strain was beginning to tell on him – and said he could not read the opening of the third book of *Paradise Lost* or the Agincourt speech from *Henry V* without tears coming to his eyes. He concluded the interview on a familiar note: 'I have never been afraid to be alone, either mentally or physically. And I have never been afraid of odds.'[58]

A fortnight later he used the same newspaper to launch a broad assault on Heath's record as Prime Minister, contemplating, ironically as it turned out, what he would say in his next election address. On immigration 'we have done exactly the reverse of what we led the electors to expect'. EEC entry had been pursued in direct contradiction of the last manifesto. Also, 'in contrast with Labour's weak and fumbling policies, we have taken Rolls-Royce aviation into public ownership and put record sums of taxpayers' money into shipbuilding wherever we were sure there was no prospect of profit. New institutions have been set up in Government departments to facilitate public investment in private industry. By our new method of "public equity" we have freed the nationalised industries from the outworn Socialist dogmas of "breaking even" and paying interest on capital.' He could not have made a clearer, nor more public, statement of his almost complete disagreement with virtually every main aspect of Government policy.[59] It was strangely prophetic that, at this time, he should tell a Unionist rally in Belfast on 2 June that 'often, at the end of a parliamentary week, it strikes me as somehow incongruous that I do not return, like my Ulster Unionist colleagues, to a constituency in these six counties'.[60]

Although the guillotine had been imposed, the European Communities Bill was still on the floor of the House at the beginning of June. Powell's disillusion was now endemic. 'When the committee,' he observed on 8 June, 'during the limited time permitted to us, disposed of the previous two subsections of the clause, we abrogated the legislative supremacy of the House of Commons.'[61] It was all being given away too easily, and the giving-away was being masterminded by his own party, utterly divorced by now, as he saw it, from the Tory tradition of Conservatism.

In early June Powell was in Ulster again, telling a Unionist rally at Banbridge what he suspected Heath had said to Whitelaw before sending him over as Northern Ireland Secretary. 'Willie, for God's sake go and put a stop to that squalid nuisance in Northern Ireland at least for the time being. We can't have it interfering with our glorious enterprise in Europe, upsetting the Americans and even annoying my old friend Mr Lynch.' He told his audience to insist on the Union at all costs, and to ignore the 'snares and decoys' sent out from Whitehall.[62] Among the 'dozens of diversions' he believed were being manufactured by the Government were 'provincial autonomy, Ulster nationalism, fancy constitutions, special franchises, artificial links between irreconcilable opponents, community plans, administrative plans, social plans. These are the threads they intend to weave around you, if you will let them, as a spider cocoons its victim. What they fear most – and are determined, if they can, to prevent – is your plain insistence upon loyalty and the Union.' Of Heath and Whitelaw, he said that 'loyalty and the Union are the last things that these men are looking for in Northern Ireland'.[63]

This prompted a hysterical reaction from some sections of the Government. A defence minister, Peter Kirk, accused Powell of making a speech 'bordering on incitement to subversion'. Powell retailed what happened next when he held Kirk up to public derision in a speech the following month, after the situation had taken another turn for the worse. 'I concluded that he could not have seen what I actually said, and sent him the text. To my astonishment he not only persisted in his accusation but cited verbatim in support of it the following sentence: "All the more doggedly, therefore ... must you fortify and entrench yourselves behind the plain uncomplicated things for which you stand." And what were those "plain, uncomplicated things"? I will read on: "The answer is: loyalty to the United Kingdom of Great Britain and Northern Ireland; and union, meaning the union of all its parts, including this one." ' He observed that things had reached an unfortunate pass when such exhortations by a Member of Parliament to his fellow citizens to loyalty could be condemned by a minister – particularly a minister of defence.[64]

Powell's conviction that America was trying to dictate British policy in Ulster would be a theme running through all his future pronouncements on the Province. He kept on his files a copy of a State Department Policy Statement of 15 August 1950, whose principles had not been superseded, in which one of the main United States' aims towards Ireland was stated as 'to ensure in so far as possible the collaboration of Ireland as an ally with the western powers in any future conflict'.[65] The statement went on to say that the 'agitation' caused by partition in Ireland 'lessens the usefulness of Ireland in international organ-isations and complicates strategic planning for Europe', since in 1948 the Free State Government had turned down an invitation to join NATO because of partition and the dispute with the United Kingdom. 'It is desirable', the docu-ment continued, 'that Ireland should be integrated into the defense planning of the North Atlantic area, for its strategic position and present lack of defensive capacity are matters of significance.' The document admitted that pressure was constantly being brought on the Truman administration to 'intrude' into British affairs, and bring partition to an end, but the administration felt it was not proper to do so. Powell felt this self-denying ordinance had weakened in the intervening years, and would continue to do so as American desires to have the British Isles as one strategic entity under NATO increased during the Cold War. The Irish cleverly saw that, as a result, a new lever was in place for them to use to end the partition of the island.

On 16 June Powell was sixty, and at a crossroads in his career. He was still in the Conservative party, but not of it. His attacks on Heath, his colleagues and their policies had now become more virulent than those by the official Opposition. Although a growing number in the parliamentary party were sym-pathetic to his arguments, his tone and approach made it impossible for all but a few who were reconciled to having no ministerial career to support him publicly. His pursuit of principle was closing off the chances of his ever taking power. It was hard to see, even without the benefit of hindsight, how he could fight again under the party banner. It was as much of a problem for the party as for him. They believed if they removed the whip from him he would simply fight Wolverhampton as an independent, beating any 'official' candidate against him; so far, throughout his assaults on Heath he retained the almost total loyalty of his association, because of his stance on immigration.

However, he would soon begin to believe, forcefully, that this last sovereign Parliament of the United Kingdom was the last in which he could serve honour-ably. As inevitable defeat advanced, he turned on Labour for failing to behave like a responsible Opposition. At Sutton Coldfield on 24 June he decided to let the public in on the secret of how the Bill was being put through the Commons, revealing details of Labour co-operation with the Government that would continue to be denied for years to come, but which were eventually admitted. 'The crucial divisions on this great issue', he said,

> are decided not because those who speak and vote one way outnumber, even though it were by the fingers of one hand, those who speak and vote the other way. They are decided by a handful of Members who neither speak nor vote. There is no need to prove that this or that Labour MP pops across to the Government whips to discover how many abstentions are needed to get by on a particular division. The flagrant and undeniable fact is that sufficient, but only just sufficient, Opposition members manage to be missing. The future fate of Britain is not being settled because the serried battalions which speak and vote for entry exceed those that speak and vote against; it is not being settled in the open; it is being settled in the dark, in holes and corners; it is being settled by the methods of the sneak.[66]

Lest he seem a hypocrite, Powell said he did not condemn people who disagreed with their party line; he was one himself. He thought, though, that they should have the courage to advocate their case openly, as he and his few supporters on the Conservative benches had done.

Although he was losing, he sensed the drift of the Heath government towards some sort of national debacle; and it would, he knew, take such a debacle to install him as leader of his party. Heath's friends, when they briefed the press, were always at pains to stress Powell's 'isolation' and 'declining influence': points that trusties like Boyne on the *Daily Telegraph* would make every time Powell's name had to be mentioned. However, Powell then had a great triumph for his influence: the decision on 23 June to float the pound. A run on sterling that started on 16 June, which soon sucked $2,500 million out of the reserves, made the end inevitable. It was a humiliation for Heath and Barber. The Chancellor had said after the dollar crisis, 'I do not believe that completely free floating is practicable ... it would expose any economy to sudden and severe shocks.' As the British economy headed towards the rocks on which, within a year, it would be stranded, it was a chance that had to be taken. Powell called the float 'a fitful gleam of the recovery of sanity'.[67] At a Bow Group cocktail party shortly afterwards, a young member sought to ingratiate himself with Powell by suggesting he must feel glad that everybody had now chosen to follow his policy. Powell told him that to say it had been a matter of choice was rather like believing that a fully clothed man who is pushed into a swimming pool had chosen to dive in.[68]

Barber explained the move to the Commons on 29 June 1972 as a temporary float, which he hoped would end by 1 January the following year – the date of Britain's entry to the EEC. Other economic factors were looking bad. Barber admitted that the increase in the money supply was running at an annual rate of 23 per cent; interest rates had risen another 1 per cent, and had been kept to that level only by a 'special relief', as Barber called it, to the banks by way of subsidy.[69] Despite the obvious problems of so large an increase in liquidity, Barber spoke optimistically about keeping inflation at no more than 6 per cent at sometime in the foreseeable future. This was to prove a terrible hostage to fortune.

Powell said, with heavy irony, that he hoped his friends on the front bench would be 'gratified' to learn that, for once, he would be supporting them. 'But there is just this difficulty. There is that extra word in the Motion. Alas, how often when one thinks that one's hopes have been fulfilled and rushes open-armed to embrace that fulfilment, one finds there is something amiss, something not quite complete, less than perfect; and here, sure enough, it is – the word "temporarily".'[70] He called the word 'the mark of a profound incomprehension', and said that until the Government was free of that incomprehension the economy would not be properly freed up. There was no time that the currency could again be fixed, and no rate at which it could be fixed, at which it would not be vulnerable again to the forces that had compelled the float in the first place. The lesson was, he said, that fixing the price of a commodity that was susceptible to market forces was always wrong.

He reinforced his case by illustrating the fiction that fixed rates brought stability to the business environment. That had not been the case since well before the devaluation of 1967. Fixed rates were also a 'one-way option' for the speculator.[71] In remarks that uncannily prefigured the events of 1987–92, when Britain first rigged too low an exchange rate and then watched the financial markets take their natural course, he also warned that setting a low rate leads to a flood of currency into the country, which leads to inflation. The inflation rampant by 1989–90 led to the endgame of September 1992, as anyone who had read this speech of Powell's could have foretold. Powell said he had for many years advocated a floating rate 'because I am convinced that it would remove at any rate some of the avoidable burdens and evils from the backs of the people'.[72] He concluded with a plea for the word 'temporarily' to be left out so that 'we shall not artificially, for the sake of a shibboleth and a fetish, impose upon this country alternately the evils of deflation and inflation, that we shall not go on repeating the bad film seen so often during the last 25 years'.

Nor was the floating of the currency an isolated example of Powell's moral success. The Industrial Relations Court had proved utterly incapable of stopping the growth of wages, as Powell – who knew the term 'wage inflation' was meaningless – had said it would. His wider economic prescriptions about inflation were manifestly being proved right too, as were his strictures about the pointlessness of pouring money into lame-duck enterprises. He would joke that it was career death for another Conservative to be seen talking to him, but a growing number privately admitted he had a better record of forecasting the economy than either Heath or Barber.

The Industrial Relations Act was proving a particular disaster for Heath, mainly for the reasons Powell had predicted, since it formalised and aggrandised the role of the unions. The Trades Union Congress arranged a meeting with Heath in early July to ask him to shelve the Act, which, without putting nails into his own coffin, he could not do. He still, despite the evidence to the contrary, believed it was a help in the fight against inflation. Powell further aggravated the problems in his party by pointing out, in a speech at Sutton Coldfield on 30 June, that the recent expedient of floating the currency would not be available once the goal of European monetary union was achieved, meaning that Britain would become 'a depressed area in relation to Western Europe'.[73]

On 1 July Powell returned to immigration in a speech at Islington. He linked it with the European question, saying Britain was setting about turning her towns and cities into the ghettos of Europe, which would be regarded by other nations with astonishment and revulsion. They, he told his audience, had been careful to insist on a joint declaration, before the Treaty of Brussels, which settled British entry to the EEC, was signed, in which they had reserved the right to bring before the Community's institutions any 'social situation' that might harm the interests of the group. Powell interpreted this as a determination by our future partners not to have to take a share of what he said they called 'Britain's race problem'.[74] He added, 'I can assure you that it is not the prospect of a sudden inrush of Irish or Norwegians which fills the Europeans with anxiety for their "social situation". The Declaration refers to one thing and one thing only – the present and future coloured population of England – and it gives notice, in terms which are none the less significant for being deliberately veiled, that the European countries are going to be spectators, not participants, in the tragedy of our cities.'

As usual, Powell came under almost universal condemnation from the liberal left. He had spoken of the defeatism of the British people on the question, suggesting that 'either they say: "We have not seen so much about it in the newspaper lately; perhaps after all it has gone away"; or else they say: "It will come; there is no remedy; but we may not be there to witness it." These are the two ways in which all catastrophes that have ever come upon nations have been made inevitable ... it is in this sense that nations deserve their fates.'[75] Referring to the process of the building of ghettos in American cities in the preceding fifteen years, Powell said the same thing was happening in Britain, and would have the same consequences.

Throughout this time, Powell was receiving extensive moral support from a group of friends, led by Ralph Harris, based on the IEA. Frequent private lunches and dinners were arranged for him to meet academics, businessmen and visiting academics and politicians, and to prevent him from experiencing the sense of isolation that Heath's servants in the press were being briefed to write of whenever Powell said anything controversial. Belatedly, on 7 July, Harris and those friends marked Powell's sixtieth birthday with a party in Belgravia and a presentation of the *Encyclopaedia Britannica*. To such people, who were to be instrumental in the development of the philosophy of Thatcherism – Harris so much so that Mrs Thatcher was to acknowledge her debt with a peerage – Powell was the only political hope they had.

Early July saw the denouement of the European Communities Bill. It was a particularly severe defeat for Powell, for not a single amendment had been won. He had been proved wrong: his idealistic belief that the Commons would not sign away so much of its power was unfounded. He fought to the end, watching through the lengthy sittings of the committee of the whole House as the supremacy of Parliament dripped away before him. His line never faltered. In one of his last contributions in the committee, on 5 July, he stated again his belief that 'to pass this Bill lies outside that unwritten contract which all Members of this House have with those who sent them here. We have not been charged by that political will, on which alone rests the independence and sovereignty of parliament and of this country, with the duty or the permission to share it or to abrogate it.'[76] When he professed that this had been 'a business in which on either side of the Committee and on either side of the debate they are sad to have imbrued their hand', he was interrupted with cries of 'Nonsense!' It was a defeat Powell was taking very hard, and personally. 'In their own consciences,' he replied, 'my hon Friends must speak for themselves.'

Yet he also made a clear protestation of his belief that the fight had not ended. He warned that the time would come when the people would see that what Parliament had done was not acceptable to them, and then the people would have to act: 'It is a question of faith whether the people will defend, are determined to defend, have the desire and purpose to defend or, if it is lost, to restore and regain, the supremacy of parliament and the political independence of this country.'[77] Apparently looking forward to the next election, he concluded: 'The question will be decided not in the Lobby when we come to vote, not even by the House of Commons at all. It is a question which will be decided by the people.'[78]

These sentiments were repeated, and amplified, in sombre remarks Powell made in his last parliamentary words on the Bill, at its third reading on 13 July. Earlier on Norman Lamont, who had just entered the House at a by-election in time to vote for the third reading, jested that he had as an undergraduate been converted to the idea of Europe by a speech he had heard Powell make at Cambridge in 1961. Powell, though, was in no good humour. He paid a grand tribute to Foot, 'easily the first, *facile princeps*, among the parliamentarians of this day ... when the history of this episode comes to be written his part in it will be seen to have been at a level with those of the great figures of parliamentary history'.[79] He continued: 'It has often been thought to be a paradox that he and I should have found ourselves not only on the same side but closely allied at every stage. Yet there is no paradox at all.' Both men might have sharp disagreements about most policies, but on the issue of retaining a sovereign parliament, and of allowing the British to determine their own future, they were entirely at one.

Powell warned his colleagues they were deluding themselves if they thought that, after voting to give the Bill a third reading, they could carry on as before; but the Commons would not remain unaltered. He concluded:

> There comes a time … when the House of Commons has to meet its maker; individually and collectively, there comes to us all the time to meet our maker; there comes the time when this House of Commons must be unmade in order to be remade. Although we, this present House of Commons, if we take this step, will have lost the power to reassert our faith in the legislative supremacy of parliament and the sovereignty of the electorate of this country, that power still resides with the people of this country. They have it still; they can use it still; and it is my belief that they will.[80]

He voted against the third reading, the only Conservative not to support his party in any of the 104 divisions on the Bill. Seven others voted against in between sixty-four and seventy-eight divisions. No Labour Member had voted against his or her party; but in 50 of the 104 divisions at least thirty of them failed to vote at all, with one backbencher, Mrs Freda Corbet, missing 102 of those divisions. As Powell had been saying, it had been the Labour abstainers who had helped Heath not merely to get the Bill enacted, but to survive in office.

III

With the Bill on its way to the statute book, Ulster came to dominate Powell's agenda for much of that summer. Whitelaw told the House of Commons on 10 July that he had had a secret meeting with members of the Provisional IRA shortly before the end of the recent ceasefire. Most of his colleagues approved of this, relieved by any attempt to stop the rampant anarchy and bloodshed in the Province. Powell, though, was furious. He issued a statement saying that 'We have now reached the point in the affairs of Northern Ireland where not only those who support the policy of the Secretary of State but those who do not publicly dissociate themselves from them cannot escape responsibility for the consequences.' He repeated his stated view that, far from doing business with the terrorists, only the demonstration by the Government that it was prepared to safeguard Ulster's place in the Union would restore peace in the Province.[81] Later that week a meeting of Conservative backbenchers angrily criticised Whitelaw, as it was detected that the mood in the country was less favourable to him and the Government for its handling of the troubles.

On 19 July Powell was one of eight right-wing MPs who, together with the Ulster Unionists, wrote a letter to *The Times* stating their 'grave alarm at the failure of the Government to prevent widespread murder and anarchy in a part of our country'. It also savaged Whitelaw for negotiating with the IRA and according accredited status to men who employed murder for political ends. 'All areas must be returned to normal civil jurisdiction and those who default on obligations to pay rent, rates and taxes must not be allowed to do so with impunity. The Army must be given a clear mandate to support the civil power in the enforcement of the law.'[82] Heath and Whitelaw were increasingly rattled by the high-octane campaign being run against them by their own side, and the day this letter appeared Heath gave an unequivocal assurance to the Unionists that 'the status of Northern Ireland as part of the United Kingdom will not be altered except by consent'. Whitelaw, for his part, added that the Province would continue to be British 'as long as the majority of the Ulster people want to keep the connection. Nobody is going to be sold down the river.'[83] That evening the Conservative Northern Ireland Committee, which had so angrily dealt with Whitelaw, met again, and renewed its criticism of the Government's activities. There were numerous calls for the ending of no-go areas, and for the pursuit of a policy of enforcing the Union akin to what Powell had been arguing for. He did not speak but, according to one report, 'just sat and glowered'.[84] He had his say in the Commons the next day when Whitelaw answered questions. Powell asked him how many more lives would be 'fruitlessly sacrificed' before he admitted that the policy had been 'proved disastrous'.[85]

A week later he went to County Armagh, and said that Whitelaw inviting people to submit him ideas on how to govern Ulster was as if the policy were 'like a competition in *Tit Bits* or *Home Chat*'.[86] He warned that the feeble policy in Ulster could be the cause of Heath's downfall. His speeches on Ulster were specifically cited by Anthony Speight, the chairman of the Federation of Conservative Students, and David Hunt, the chairman of the Young Conservatives, who jointly called for Powell to resign from the party because of his 'efforts to inflame extremists'.[87] They said Powell had lost credibility with 'men of integrity' and was encouraging those who 'seek to defy the rule of law'.

In fact, at that time Powell believed he had reached a momentous decision. With the European Communities Act now law, he had realised he could no longer hesitate over whether to leave Parliament. His wife was fiercely opposed to his leaving – 'I couldn't believe what I was hearing.'[88] He had looked up some months earlier the formula for use when applying to resign from the Commons, and had kept the form of words in his wallet. By early August 1972 he had drafted the letter to the Chancellor of the Exchequer applying for the Chiltern

Hundreds*; he did not wish to sit in Parliament after the 1971–2 session, 'the last session of the independent parliament of the United Kingdom' as he called it, had ended.[89] He even drafted a statement to his constituency chairman to announce his intended departure:

> With prorogation today the last session of the sovereign Parliament of the United Kingdom has ended. I have no wish to sit in a subordinate legislature. I have therefore requested appointment from tomorrow to the Chiltern Hundreds; and shall be retiring from political life altogether.
>
> My thanks are due to you and to all those who by their help and support over twenty-five years have given me the honour of sitting in this and the previous six parliaments. I only wish that it had been in my power to do anything for the future of the town I have represented.[90]

Knowing none of this, Powell's close-knit circle of friends on the backbenches, led by Nicholas Ridley and John Biffen, were concerned that he was drifting away from the party. They felt the need to try to keep him involved by demonstrating their support, hoping to preserve him for the moment when his hour would come. Ridley founded a group, to include Peter Hordern and Jock Bruce-Gardyne, called the Economic Dining Club, which endorsed Powellite economics, but whose activities had the aim 'of trying to anchor Enoch Powell into the Conservative Party'.[91] Biffen remembered that 'it immediately turned into tutorials': Powell would provide his acolytes with descriptions of the true path. The exercise would not succeed in keeping Powell among them, but it provided Ridley and his colleagues with a priceless spectacle. After the group had stayed so long into the night talking at a private club in Mayfair that they had been locked in, they had to escape unconventionally – with Powell 'climbing down the drainpipe, wearing his black overcoat and black homburg hat'.[92]

What, for the moment, kept him in the House was a new immigration crisis. As he recalled in 1985, 'it had become impossible in the midst of the hue and cry just to put my hat and coat on and walk away'.[93] The decision by the dictator of Uganda, Idi Amin, to expel Asians from his country was the cause of Powell's change of mind. The Government talked of a 'commitment' to allow the expelled Asians with United Kingdom passports to come to Britain, a claim Powell, sojourning in Wolverhampton before leaving for a peripatetic holiday in Guernsey, France and Switzerland, denounced. The immigration restrictions of the 1960s meant that just because some of the Asians had United Kingdom passports they did not have a right to settle here. Powell said, 'Britain should not, and would not, decline her fair share, but it must also be said plainly that

---

* The Stewardship of the Chiltern Hundreds, being an office of profit under the Crown, disqualifies its holder from sitting in the House of Commons.

on any reasonable criteria that due share would be infinitesimal.' A few more Amins, he said, and another 1.5 million people from the Commonwealth might feel they had a right to come to Britain: that was the figure the then Lord Chancellor, Lord Gardiner, had estimated in 1968 for Commonwealth nationals not domiciled in their own countries but in other independent states excluding Britain.[94]

Powell said none of the Asians, in fact, had a right to come to Britain: they were all subject to immigration control. It had been intended to control them ever since the first loopholes were closed in 1962, and no assurances to the contrary had been given. In seeking to find means of letting many of the Asians into Britain, the Government was 'sedulously fostering untruths' about its obligations towards them and was in clear breach of manifesto promises on immigration. Nonetheless, the Government decided to treat the expelled Asians as British nationals, and in a speech at Ramsgate on 12 September Powell made specific attacks on Heath, Sir Peter Rawlinson – the Attorney-General, whom he had already accused of 'prostituting his office' – and Douglas-Home for their behaviour on the question.[95]

To him, the issue was yet another that illustrated the 'yawning gulf' between the nation and its rulers, and he spoke of 'a deliberate intention to deceive the public as to the facts'.[96] He said the Government was guilty of 'errors of fact, errors of tactics, and errors of perception'. He was angry with Rawlinson for being 'put up' by the Government to claim there was an obligation to the Ugandans in international law because they were our own 'nationals'. 'Less than a year before, in order to obtain admission to the European Economic Community, the Government had negotiated with the Community a definition of who our "nationals" are. That definition plainly and indisputably excludes Ugandan Asians.' He also wondered where Rawlinson's definition left all the others who had been deprived of the right to enter Britain under the 1962 Act: 'is Sir Peter Rawlinson telling us we would have to take them, any or all of them, if the occasion arose?' When the leadership had realised there was disquiet over the admission, Douglas-Home had broadcast to the nation about there being no cause for concern over what the Government had done. Powell suggested that the word had gone out: 'Why not try the old trick which invariably works at Conservative party conferences? Bring on Sir Alec Home and let him tell them that everything is all right after all, as otherwise of course he would not have stood for it.' However, as people saw around them the effects of immigration, even that did not convince them, he said.

Powell seemed to be calling for the removal of the Government of which he was still a notional supporter, saying that if it would not recognise public fears 'another must', and 'if these ministers do not do so, others will'. He said Douglas-Home's talk had fallen 'flat on its face' because of 'a still rising wind of public anger' about being misled over immigration. 'To lead is not to lecture or cajole from a safe distance. To lead is to share.' Powell was also concerned that the new intake would gravitate to existing centres of Asian population and aggravate the undue dominance of ethnic minorities in inner cities. He wondered what places like Sidcup, Kinross and Hexham – the constituencies of Heath, Douglas-Home and Rippon respectively – had done 'to be left out in the cold' when it came to accepting their share of the newcomers. As with the Kenyan Asians, he agreed that Britain should take her share, but there was a wider humanitarian obligation to help 'from Russia to Patagonia'.

His new outburst caused an old canard to be resurrected against him. His adversary at the Ministry of Defence, Peter Kirk, wrote to one of his constituents that 'Mr Powell was the first minister to encourage widespread coloured immigration into this country, notably from the West Indies, to staff British hospitals when he was Minister of Health.' Powell wrote immediately to Kirk that there was no sense in which his Ministry, or any other that he knew of, had 'encouraged' immigration. It was the same allegation Rippon had made against him eighteen months before, and he had been unable to find evidence for it then. There was still no evidence now.

Powell had caused offence among a group of supposedly like-minded people the previous week, when he attended the Mont Pelerin Society's annual conference at Montreux in Switzerland. On 6 September, the day after the assassination by Palestinian terrorists of eleven Israeli athletes at the Olympic Games in Munich, Professor Gunter Schmölders, the chairman of the conference, had called for a minute's silence in memory of the victims. To cries of 'Shame!' Powell said the suggestion was wrong; a tribute was irrelevant from a group of economists. Many present were reported to be visibly upset by Powell's protest, though Ralph Harris, the secretary of the Society, said some others 'wholeheartedly agreed with him'.[97] Harris himself privately agreed with Powell, though felt he had caused unnecessary offence; yet, knowing Powell as he did, he understood how Powell's cold intellect and lack of sentiment – not to be confused with a lack of romanticism – would have compelled him to act as he did.[98] Predictably, Powell was unrepentant: 'The question at issue was whether a landslide in Patagonia or a railway accident in Japan or a shooting in Palestine or army deaths in the Bogside were suitable subjects to be discussed or noticed or brought to the hearing in Switzerland at a conference of economists. To my mind they were not.'

His ever loyal wife and daughters were exasperated by this display of their husband's and father's rigid principle. He explained to them that things would have been different if the massacre had happened on Swiss soil, or involved Swiss nationals, as Switzerland was his host country.[99] Three years later, in a press interview, Friedrich von Hayek himself was quoted as having said that the incident caused him to think that Powell might be emotionally unstable. Hayek was alarmed to see these words in print, and wrote to Powell to apologise. Powell replied, 'I am more sorry that you should think I "may be emotionally unstable" than that you should be reported saying so.'[100] In 1980 Powell finally resigned from the Society, explaining to Harris that he felt unease at having to belong to something that had 'a tendency to resolve itself into a Hayek adulation society, with a minor niche for Friedman'.[101] He added that while he admired much of Hayek's work, 'I dislike his teutonic habit of telling the English, whom he does not in the least understand, how to set about governing themselves. After all, Hayek, Friedman and Co. have not put to the practical political test the principles of free market economics. I am content that their academic labours should bring them laurels; but it is perhaps understandable if those who have reaped thorns in the same cause in real life are disinclined to add their contributions to those laurels.'

IV

On his return to England, Powell found the economic problems of the country accelerating towards crisis. Maudling, who had resigned as Home Secretary the previous July because of an association with the corrupt architect John Poulson, had come out in favour of prices and incomes control, saying that 'we cannot go on as we are'. At Leamington Spa on 18 September, Powell said that even a so-called voluntary policy of control could lead to fascism: it was a means of allowing control of the money supply to pass out of the Government's hands and into the hands of those institutions – such as Wilson's Prices and Incomes Board – that had to be set up to administer such a policy.

'By fixing prices and incomes,' he said, 'they would have to replace the entire automatic system of the market and supply and demand – be that good or evil – and put in its place a series of value judgments, economic or social, which they themselves would have to make.'[102] Even if this were a 'voluntary' policy, the institutions would have to exist all the same. 'There is a specific term for this sort of policy. It is, of course, totalitarian, because it must deliberately and consciously determine the totality of the actions and activities of the members of the community. But it is a particular kind of totalitarian regime, namely one in which authority is exercised and decisions are taken by a hierarchy of unions or corporations to which, indeed, on this theory, the effective power has already passed. For this particular kind of totalitarianism the 20th century has a name. That name is "Fascist".'

Referring to Maudling's 'we cannot go on as we are', Powell mentioned the paper he had sent Thorneycroft in December 1957 about the need to control public spending, which had ended: 'we cannot go blundering on'. Both he and Maudling had addressed the need to control inflation, even though the inflation rate about which Powell had been so concerned fifteen years earlier would have been regarded in 1972 as 'a blessed relief and a brilliant achievement'. Yet Powell was advocating the restricting of expenditure, Maudling the control of prices and incomes which, because it would do nothing to control the money supply, would be pointless. Powell said governments were not obliged to 'chase' high wage settlements and create the additional money to finance them, even though unemployment might result if they did not. The power not to do so resided with them; it had nothing to do with the trade unions, which, as always, were a convenient scapegoat for political weakness.

He spoke again on this subject ten days later at Shoreham in Sussex, and was surprised that this was another occasion when Central Office refused to distribute his words. On the list of controversial topics he was wont to broach, incomes policy did seem to rank low down. However, Powell was not to know he had touched an even more raw nerve than usual. He delivered the text to Central Office shortly before Heath announced a prices and incomes policy, the celebrated U-turn that marked the beginning of the end for the Government. When drafting his speech, Powell had suspected from rumours circulating in London and reported from Washington in the press that Heath had this in mind, and Heath was meeting leaders of the CBI and TUC at Chequers, which suggested that something was brewing. Phrases in Powell's speech such as 'the attempt to find an incomes policy is not merely neutral, not merely a waste of time, it is positively harmful' would, in the new context, look intensely wounding.[103] Powell warned that inflation could be stopped only by incurring unemployment; and that those who chose the imaginary world where this did not happen instead of the real one where it did were preferring humbug to candour. Bearing in mind the failed attempts in 1961 and 1966, the new incomes policy was like the British public 'seeing the same film for the third time'.[104]

The economy became the open wound of the Heath Government. Events had helped ensure that the usual 'party sources' could no longer with any conviction brand Powell as mad or intellectually isolated on that key subject. With the party conference approaching, Heath urgently had to mount some sort of defence of his economic record. On the eve of the gathering the Conservative Research Department published a mid-term manifesto entitled *For All the People*. In a foreword, Heath wrote that 'there is just one simple fact we need to remember. The real standard of living of the British people has begun to rise rapidly once again, at nearly double the rate achieved by the Labour government.'[105] This was the ultimate short-term view, as the inflation figure of 17 per cent experienced, as a result of Heath's and Barber's policies, during the first year of the next Labour Government would show. Nonetheless, Heath continued: 'By our policies we have set the scene for prosperity, and the British people are now beginning to achieve it for themselves.' He also advertised his pride at spending more money on the social services, particularly – anathema to Powell – housing subsidies. In a dig at him whose cause went back to 1950, Heath said his generosity with the taxpayer's money was 'in my book ... what belonging to "One Nation" really means' – a direct contradiction of the supremely fiscally responsible original One Nation pamphlet to which Heath had put his name.

He also justified his incomes policy as the only way to tackle inflation, and entered what was interpreted as another shaft at Powell: 'In a free society there will always be a few people who know only how to shout and bully. My aim is to make sure that when such people look round they will find that no-one is following them.' Heath's remarks shared space in the press with some of Powell's made at Ilkley on 7 October, in which he compared the mid-point of Heath's Government with the mid-point of Macmillan's, and in which he suggested that the conclusion of the Heath administration would be the same as that of Macmillan's defeat. He argued that the time when it became necessary to remind a government of its promises and the expectations it had fostered was 'the moment from which its subsequent rejection and defeat dated'. While referring to Northern Ireland, Rhodesia and the admission of the Ugandan Asians, Powell concentrated on the stupidity of Heath's flat-rate incomes policy: 'since when has it been Conservative policy to increase low wages relatively to high wages? To control wages with the object of making low wages higher and high wages lower relatively to one another was as silly as to control prices with the object of making low-priced articles dearer and high-priced articles cheaper.'[106]

Powell could not credit that Heath, having earlier abolished the Prices and Incomes Board, was now planning to set up a new body to help low-pay industries achieve greater productivity and therefore pay higher wages. 'If an advisory body can tell firms how to make profits which they hadn't thought of making or hadn't the intelligence to make, then bang goes the whole Conservative case for competition, capitalism and private enterprise,' he said. 'Do you remember how we used to mock the socialists for their addiction to snoopers? Well, here it is. There is to be "special machinery for monitoring retail prices", and the public are to be invited to report instances of what appear to them to be infringements of the five per cent retail price freeze. Here is a Conservative Prime Minister who claims that new duties for the citizen are created simply by his appearing at a press conference and saying: "the ceilings on prices and incomes are effective from today".' He said Heath had destroyed 'the main portions of the edifice of Conservative policy' with dynamite 'rather than the more laborious methods of demolition', and that the decision to revert to an incomes policy was 'cataclysmic'. Further embarrassment for Heath came from a Labour economic adviser, Professor Nicholas Kaldor, who (while thinking the policy was good for the country) said Heath's ideas were so left-wing he did not think he could carry his party with him. 'The Labour government was not so far to the left,' he said.[107]

Powell had more retaliation to offer before arriving at Blackpool. In Belfast on 9 October he told the Unionists in unequivocal terms that the 'war' against the IRA was being lost. Despite the assurances given by Heath and Whitelaw about the future of the Province, Powell said that 'nobody knows, for sure, neither friend nor foe, citizen nor alien, where the British Government stands'.[108] He discounted the Government's promises about no change without majority consent because every action it took seemed designed to 'discredit and weaken the forces working for the maintenance of the Union'. Provocatively, he added that so many soldiers were now being killed that the shock of such killing was wearing off, adding to the Government's complacency.

Heath's first duty at Blackpool was to address the agents' annual dinner, where he made what was interpreted as another attack on Powell. 'I propose', he told the agents, 'to be consistent to my own views and not those of other people.' He outlined what he claimed were his achievements, but agreed that 'some within our ranks' had taken a different view. He was convinced, however, that he had the support of most of the party for what he did, and said the alternatives had been rejected as 'against the interests of the country'.[109] In fact, on the matter on which Powell was to speak from the floor at the conference – the new immigration from Uganda – Heath had been exactly inconsistent in his views, as Powell had pointed out in a speech at Beaconsfield in September. He read to his audience from a circular letter sent by Heath before the 1970 election to voters who wrote to him expressing their concerns about immigration policy. Heath had assured them that 'future immigrants will only be allowed where they are needed for a specific job in a specific place for a specific time' and that 'a Conservative government will have the power to prevent further immigrants from settling in any area where the pressure on social services is thought to be too great'.[110] As it turned out, neither of these conditions was being applied to the Ugandan Asians.

It was a tactical error for Powell to use the conference to speak on immigration, when he could have done far more damage to Heath by speaking on the economy, and have found a more sympathetic audience. To ensure he had some role in influencing the economic debate, he spoke in Glasgow before going to Blackpool, so his thoughts would appear in the newspapers on the morning the conference discussed the issue. He called the prices and incomes policy 'nonsense from top to bottom and from side to side' and said the notions behind it 'rest upon a simple and self-evident absurdity: the assumption that prices rise in general because people raise prices in particular'. He was infuriated with what he saw as the ignorance and stupidity that had prompted the policy. 'One would have thought that at least in the 20th century a capitalist Government would know better than to ignore or defy the law of supply and demand. But evidently one would have been wrong.' His strictures about the money supply were increasingly hard for the Government to discount. The growth rate in the 'Barber boom' of the preceding year had been 5 per cent; the money supply had risen by 30 per cent in the same period.[111]

The immigration debate was held on 12 October. Since mid-September, nearly 15,000 Ugandan Asians had come into Britain, and the sheer numbers were continuing to alarm many Conservative activists. Powell would normally have had only four minutes to speak, but Harvey Proctor, who had been preparing to propose the motion on behalf of the Hackney South and Shoreditch association, waived his right to do so in favour of the association's president: who happened to be Powell. On 11 October, the day the conference opened, the Powellites immediately showed their anger and their militancy in a gesture more typical of Labour gatherings. Richard Devonald-Lewis, a prominent anti-EEC campaigner, moved an emergency motion at the start of proceedings that the agenda be referred back. He told the conference – and millions watching on television – that the whole event would be an exercise in whitewashing. The resolutions for debate were full of self-congratulation, at a time when the Conservative party had little or nothing to congratulate itself about, and discussion of many controversial issues had been avoided.

Ministers had briefed journalists that this would be the moment when they stood up to the Powellites. Immediately the proceedings started, though, this unprecedented act of defiance challenged their authority, made worse by what one sketch writer described as the 'loud, prolonged rumbles of applause' that interrupted Devonald-Lewis's remarks.[112] He was not, of course, successful, but he had made his point and, more importantly, the leadership were thrown immediately on to the defensive. In his speech the next day Barber, though, showed that he did not intend to be cowed, saying that control of the money supply would lead to economic stagnation and 'that is a price I am not prepared to pay'. As a result he, and the rest of the country, would have to pay a higher one; but the aim was to prevent unemployment at almost any cost. When he announced his hope that the exchange rate could be fixed once more he was greeted with a cry of 'Shame!'

Demonstrating just how far Powell had got under his and Heath's skin Barber said, in phrases that would look deeply embarrassing within three weeks: 'To those who complain that what the Government has proposed involves some interference with the free interplay of market forces, I would reply: "Yes, it does." The purpose of the Government's proposals must be to prevent rip-roaring inflation. It really is time that the latter-day laissez-faire liberal theorists in our party, however great their academic achievements, recognised that the Chequers proposals are in the interest of the whole country and that, at the end of the day, is what matters.'[113] Barber earned a standing ovation, and had taken great comfort from an earlier speech by Angus Maude, one of Powell's friends and supporters. He had come out in favour of 'this extraordinary piece of second generation George Brownery' on the ground that the 'monopoly bargaining powers of trade unions' and the nationalised industries, able to pass uneconomic wage increases on to the consumer, had created a situation 'where economic laws have virtually ceased to operate in this country'.[114]

Powell warmed up for the immigration debate by going on television the evening before it and questioning the probity and motives of several of the most senior members of the Government, saying that they had been 'deceitful' over the rights of admission for the Asians. Pressed to name names, Powell said Hailsham 'knows that my law is right and his is wrong', and said of the Foreign Secretary, 'I'm never quite sure what Sir Alec understands or doesn't understand.' In the same interview, Powell denied he was waging a deliberate campaign against Heath, particularly about his anti-inflationary policy. 'Just because Ted Heath puts himself in the line of fire by proposing to try a futile method again it really isn't my fault.' He also rejected newspaper reports that he and Heath were engaged in 'a struggle for the soul of the Conservative party'. To most spectators, though, that was precisely what they did seem to be doing.[115]

Even before Powell seized on the Asians issue, the leadership had decided to teach him a lesson. This new front provided them with the means to do so. The day before the debate the *Sunday Times*'s political columnist Ronald Butt was told: 'He's been asking for it; now he's going to get it.'[116] The whole machine – ministers and officials briefing the press and television, and the choice of speakers in the debate itself – was to be geared to a humiliation of Powell. As Butt also wrote: 'The Conservative Party, when it has decided on the necessity of political kill, is implacable, pitiless and efficient.' The attack on Douglas-Home further alienated Powell from marginal supporters in the party, making the leadership's task still easier.

Powell argued in his speech in the immigration debate that the Government's 'precipitate acceptance of an unqualified duty' to admit the Asians was, as he had been saying in the country, a departure from the declared policy. The motion he was speaking to declared that the Government's immigration policy – which included provision for voluntary assisted repatriation and strict control on the inflow of immigrants – was 'the only solution likely to be successful and should be implemented by this Government at the earliest opportunity'. The same motion had been passed at the 1969 conference. Now, purely to humiliate Powell, the leadership ensured it was amended to the literally meaningless 'is the only solution likely to be successful and congratulates the Government on its swift action to accept responsibility for the Asian refugees from Uganda'. Although the motion in its original form was unobjectionable, for it to have passed after Powell had proposed it would have been a disaster for the leadership, for he would have used the result to embarrass them for months. Therefore, it was decided to amend it.

Moving the motion, Powell said it was irrefutable that holders of United Kingdom and Colonies passports were subject to the controls introduced in 1962. Also, at the time of the independence of the East African colonies there had been no suggestion that their citizens had a right of entry into Britain, and, indeed, the contrary had been specified in the 1968 Act; and nor was there an overriding obligation in international law. 'This being so,' he said, 'our obligation ... is a moral one which we share no more than equally with all other nations and much less than equally with their true home countries, notably India.'[117] He repeated his warnings about the speed of the growth of the immigrant population, and particularly of its concentration in urban areas. He was loudly applauded when he said that 'the grave consequences which these facts portend can be limited only by the measures which the Conservative party promised before the last election, and which may well have attracted those few additional votes which gave us our narrow majority'. Powell felt the electorate had been misled by the Government, not just about further immigration, but about repatriation; he said the promises made in 1970 'must be renewed this afternoon and they must be carried out', for which he was cheered. There were boos too: and only about 200 Monday Clubbers gave Powell a standing ovation as he returned to his seat, the rest of the applause being less enthusiastic.

The chairman of the Young Conservatives, David Hunt, moved the amendment, and was the first of a group of younger activists with ambitions in the party to show their loyalty to the establishment during the debate, and to create an impression that Powell was being routed. He condemned Powell for his 'slur' on Hailsham and Douglas-Home the previous day. This would have repercussions for Hunt that gave the true measure of feelings about Powell at the grass roots. He had been selected as the prospective candidate for Plymouth Drake, but his local association were so furious at his attack on Powell that they referred his nomination back for further consideration – in other words, deselected him – a fortnight later.[118]

Carr, the new Home Secretary, attacked Powell for his comments on Hailsham and Douglas-Home, and said he spurned Powell's whole approach to the subject. The assisted repatriation policy was not meant to reduce the coloured population, but to help those who desperately wanted to go home because of failure to thrive in Britain; and those coming in, for the most part, were the dependants of those already settled here. He defended the decision to take the refugees as 'part of our imperial heritage and imperial responsibility'; no citizen of a former part of the British Empire would be allowed to become stateless. His speech was sincere and passionate, and was greeted with a huge standing ovation. In a ballot afterwards, Powell's view was rejected by 1,721 to 736, but the Powellites took the consolation from the figures that they spoke for 30 per cent of the party on the issue. The margin was far less than the leadership had hoped for – lobby journalists were briefed in the morning that the Government was looking to win by a ratio of five to one – despite the public relations triumph for them of the debate itself.[119] It contained portents of the internal strife to come. Another figure took a few more days to sink in: there were, by most estimates, more than a thousand abstentions representatives whose natural loyalty to Heath as leader overcame their sympathy with Powell. Analysing the event four years later in his study of Powell's effect on British politics, Douglas Schoen concluded that 'there was no precedent for such a large scale Tory conference rebellion against a united and determined leadership enjoying the advantages of governmental office'.[120] As Schoen pointed out, Powell made the impact he did despite an almost universally hostile press, despite an almost universally hostile party establishment, and despite his own recent record of downright opposition to the party and its leadership.

Powell dominated the conference, though this was the only speech he made at it. Reporters noticed that wherever he went he was attended by groups of admirers, and talking him down was the main preoccupation of the establishment. There was alarm that as many as 736, in an avowedly loyalist gathering, should have supported Powell on immigration. In a show of hands before a ballot was taken, little more than 200 had been prepared to acknowledge their public support for him. The pretence that Powell was a lone figure was over; he seemed, at Blackpool that week, to have an organisation behind him, and a militant one at that. That was the Monday Club, in which both Devonald-Lewis and Proctor were prominent, and it had been unswerving in its support for and promotion of Powell. The immigration motion had been chosen by ballot, and chosen by a higher number of votes than any issue in previous years – thanks to organisation by the Monday Club. Such organisation was necessary: the establishment had orchestrated the immigration debate to unusual lengths, with briefings by the most senior figures in the party before and after it, in an attempt to humiliate Powell once and for all. He, and not Labour, was the principal object of their efforts of political warfare that week. It did not work. A poll taken not long afterwards showed that 38 per cent of Conservative voters thought Powell would make a better Prime Minister than Heath, a massive proportion of a party that prided itself on blind loyalty.[121]

The divisions within the party, which Powell was doing so much to heighten, may or may not have been behind a burglary at the flat of Bee Carthew, Powellight's secretary, shortly after the conference. Although money was taken – mainly in the form of crossed cheques for subscriptions to the group – the motivation behind the burglary appears to have been anything but financial. Most of Powellight's files, listing details of members and their addresses, were stolen too, as well as some Monday Club files – Mrs Carthew was its meetings secretary at the time. She had written to *The Times* about Powellight, a letter that had generated a huge response, but which had also given Powellight's address. The police soon came to the view that the burglary was political; and it set the group back, since among the files stolen was one containing names of would-be applicants for membership.[122] To Powell's closest supporters – with whom he had always had an unofficial relationship only – it was now brought home just what a serious game they were in. Some of the material was published later in the anti-fascist magazine *Searchlight*, and Powellight's organisers drew their own conclusions about who had been responsible. The police arrested a man for the crime, a common housebreaker who seemed unlikely to have done it (none of Mrs Carthew's valuables or jewellery was taken), and who admitted a number of other offences: he told the police that he had taken the files away in one of Mrs Carthew's Union Jack carrier-bags, but Mrs Carthew had no Union Jack carrier-bags.

Soon after the conference, Powell returned to the Ugandan issue. On 27 October he called for an urgent review of the definition of British nationality, since he claimed that those on both sides of the argument over whether to admit the Asians accepted that the confusion about British responsibilities, caused by such terms as 'British passport' and 'United Kingdom passport,' must never be allowed to happen again. All he asked was that Britain legislated about national-ity on the same basis as other countries. He also used Amin's behaviour to draw a moral, in a press article two days later, about the impending renewal of sanctions against Rhodesia. He asked why it was that, with so many vile regimes in Africa – 'I need name no names' – only Rhodesia was singled out for sanctions. 'The hypocrisy of it is sickening.'[123]

He did not let up his campaign against Heath. At Great Yarmouth on 28 October he said he would continue to fight to the end on the Common Market, and accused Heath of breaking his word to the electorate. Directly the European Communities Bill had been enacted, Heath went to Paris and, together with the other heads of government, signed Britain up to the goal of economic and monetary union by 1980. The speed with which Heath acted, and the impli-cations of the policy on a party that had found the lesser step of joining the EEC decisive enough, stunned even some of his close colleagues, not least Douglas-Home. Heath brazenly told them that this implication of joining should have been 'obvious'. Ironically, it was something of which Powell had warned. Now, faced with the reality, he denounced the Government for having acted without any vestige of authority from Parliament or the electorate. 'What we have to ask ourselves', he said at Yarmouth, 'is whether any British party and government, least of all a Conservative government, can do this and survive.'[124] He suspected he knew the answer, and was determined to ensure he was right.

NEMESIS

At a press conference on 3 November 1972 Heath announced further prices and incomes measures, including the extension of welfare support, following the break-up of talks between the Government, the unions and the CBI. Later that day, Powell spoke in Birmingham of his amusement that Common Market finance ministers, meeting in Luxembourg, had called for the growth of the money supply to be cut to the equivalent of the growth in the gross national product plus inflation – a vindication of his views and a humiliation for Barber, just three weeks after his assertion to the contrary at the party conference. The meeting had also pointed the finger 'unequivocally' at growth in public spending as the prime factor in the growth of the money supply: in other words, the finance ministers had condemned two of the most significant actions of the Government that was about to join their number.[1]

Powell found Heath's latest plans intolerable. He came to the Commons on 6 November and, in a moment of high drama, took Heath on in a way a backbencher had not addressed a Prime Minister of his own party since Birch's assault on Macmillan a decade earlier: and Powell was far blunter than Birch. Heath made a statement about the prices and incomes plans. Once Wilson had formally replied, Powell, who had sat brooding throughout, rose and asked, 'Does my right hon Friend not know that it is fatal for any Government or party or person to seek to govern in direct opposition to the principles on which they were entrusted with the right to govern? In introducing a compulsory control of wages and prices, in contravention of the deepest commitments of this party, has my right hon Friend taken leave of his senses?'[2]

There were intakes of breath and whistles of amazement from Powell's colleagues as, his face etched with gloom, he sat down. The Labour benches buzzed with stunned, but pleasant surprise. Heath, predictably, gave the reply of the bureaucrat Powell felt him to be rather than of the politician he notionally was: 'The present Government were returned to power to take action in the national interest when they were required to do so.' Their mutual antagonism, hitherto given voice only in the media, or on party platforms, had now come to the floor of the Commons. Those who knew the intense personal commitment Powell brought to this question understood why he had adopted this tone; but it was counter-productive. However economically sound Powell's solutions were, the use of such language simply convinced most of those with doubts about Heath that Powell was motivated by bitterness and hatred. Nonetheless, this action of

Heath's marked a decisive turning point in his and Powell's fortunes. Heath's would never recover; Powell's were, by this debacle, propelled into a new period of ascendancy that would be ended only by his own hand.

The next day, when the Commons debated the economy, Powell had a greater opportunity to express his feelings. He began with a calculated insult to his own side, congratulating the Labour backbencher who had preceded him on having made 'a thoroughly socialist speech'. The speech had served to remind the House 'that since prices are one of the great levers of the economy it is an essential part of logical and consistent socialism to control them'.[3] Powell went on to say that, if prices and incomes policies worked, then laws restraining prices and incomes would be as normal as laws against burglary and murder; but such policies did not work, and to suppose they did was a 'ludicrous' assumption 'which cannot be matched with reality or with experience'.[4] Only control of the money supply would control inflation, and Powell suspected that Barber had now come to understand this. In case he had not, Powell referred him back to the findings of the finance ministers in Luxembourg the previous week. Powell knew – *The Times*, in a leading article, had reminded him of the fact that very morning – that any attempt to control inflation would lead to unemployment, though he insisted that such a loss of jobs need only be 'transitional': 'it arises from the disappointment of the expectations which are maintained during a period of inflation'.[5] With unemployment at 800,000, a politically unacceptable level at the time, there was already a great obstacle to any anti-inflationary policy that might aggravate matters.

He regarded what Heath was doing as bordering on dishonesty. 'We are engaged in deceiving ourselves if we imagine that a prices and incomes policy or anything else will slow down and eliminate inflation without consequences for unemployment,' he said.[6] 'It is spoof if a freeze, a statutory policy, a counter-inflationary Bill is presented as though it could bridge that gap and resolve that contradiction.' The policy was based on 'a false analysis', making the legislation 'irrelevant' to the problem it was trying to solve. 'It is not on that account merely futile. It will not be merely a waste of time, effort spent for nothing; it will have worse consequences than that, and the worst of consequences will be to create friction and to intensify conflicts where none need be raised or need exist.' Powell's indignation was no artifice; he felt deeply distressed, and destabilised, by what the Government had done. Such was his distraction that, on 8 November, he forgot he was meeting Andrew Freeth at the Commons for one of their regular lunches. He told Freeth that 'I had "taken leave of my senses"', adding that it was the sort of thing that happened 'when life in this place is tense. I am terribly sorry, and do not know what more to say.'[7]

He also explained to the Chief Whip, Francis Pym, why he could not support the Government's counter-inflationary measures in the lobbies: he would be voting in accordance with the manifesto, 'which, so far as I did not explicitly take an individual line, is binding on me personally'.[8] Pym replied to him that 'what I think you find it difficult to comprehend is the fact that the Government still believes fervently in the policy of voluntary arrangements. However, a minority has abused – as it seems to me – the rights and privileges they enjoy. In the national interest, therefore, it is necessary to take action to preserve the ultimate success of what we set out to achieve.'[9] He concluded, 'You say you do not like not always to be able to help as you would wish, and I appreciate that. But if you wanted to help more, you could.' However, Pym could not see Powell's point: that the measures proposed were not just a breach of promise to the electorate, but would also have no beneficial effect.

Most Conservative MPs who sympathised with Powell still kept their feelings to themselves. He had no faction, and did not wish to lead one. However, in other regards party management was becoming increasingly difficult. On 22 November the Government lost, by the massive margin of thirty-five votes, a motion to approve new immigration rules which, it was argued by their opponents, would put Commonwealth citizens at a disadvantage compared with EEC nationals. It was estimated that between thirty-five and fifty-five Conservative MPs deliberately absented themselves; and seven more, including a reportedly 'buoyant' Powell, voted against their party.[10] Partly as a result of this and of the worries caused by the Ugandan Asians episode, the notion of the British passport was redefined by the Government within weeks – which Powell took as a signal victory for him, in the light of the 'pantomime' the leadership had orchestrated at Blackpool to promote the opposite view only the previous month.[11]

Powell spoke in the debate on the immigration policy, having earlier ambushed Douglas-Home with a question about the Government's decision to try to discriminate, for immigration purposes, between Pakistanis who had come to Britain before their country left the Commonwealth, and those who came after. He noted the absurdity of the change that would, as a result of EEC entry, downgrade the immigration status of entrants from the 'white' Commonwealth, even though they were, in law, members of the Queen's realm. In Liverpool two days later he told an audience the defeat had showed that, at last, the Commons was able to respond to the feelings of the people about the Government; and that night, in his constituency, he outlined the broken promises of the Government, on Europe, immigration, involvement by the state in industry and the means of fighting inflation. He reminded his audience that such breaches of faith were what had caused Labour to be thrown out of office.

Such setbacks for Heath did not mitigate the arrogance with which he was seen to conduct his administration. Despite the commitment he had made to take Britain into a European economic and monetary union by 1980, the Commons had never debated the proposition. On 28 November Powell asked Barber, on the floor of the House, whether he would publish a White Paper on the issue that could be debated. Barber refused. It was hardly surprising that, in such a climate, Powell maximised his antagonism. On 19 December, in a debate sanctioning the delegation by the Commons of certain of its Members to be Members of the European Parliament, Powell argued that as MEPs were not liable to censure they would be 'literally irresponsible'.[12] Two days later, in the debate on the second reading of the Coal Bill, he denounced the provisions to increase the subsidy for uneconomic pits. He said the outlay 'represents the deliberate waste of £125m – indeed, much more than £125m – worth of human effort': much more because of the profits the industry would fail to earn.[13] When a fellow backbencher, Patrick Cormack, said later on that 'nobody in this House would suggest that it should be denationalised', Powell interrupted: 'Yes, I would.'[14]

On 1 January 1973 Britain formally entered the EEC, and Heath took a break from superintending the crises around him to say how it was 'for me a very moving occasion'. Powell saw it otherwise: 'How different the circumstances in which it has happened from those he expected two-and-a-half years ago,' he said with no heavy irony, 'when it never occurred to him that such a thing could come about without the enthusiasm of the British people.'[15] Powell warned that the fight was not over, though that seemed a far-fetched statement on the very day of entry. He had just been voted 'Man of the Year' in a BBC radio poll, and opinion polls still showed him to be the most popular politician in Britain. Believing, as he did, that he spoke for voiceless millions spurred him on even at the more obvious moments of defeat.

His main concern remained the economic policy. Before Christmas, he had asked Heath in the Commons by what authority he had 'threatened' negotiators in the gasworkers' wage negotiations, whom Heath had told not to make an offer of increased pay until the guidelines of stage 2 of the incomes policy were known. Heath had replied: 'The authority with which we did it was the authority of the Government, the Head of the Government and the cabinet.' This, said Powell in a speech to the Monday Club on 12 January that echoed his attacks on the Wilson Government's attempts at intervention, made a nonsense of the rule of law, for the Government had only the power accorded to it by law, and 'it is quite certain that neither the Counter-Inflation (Temporary Provisions) Act, nor any other statute, nor any lawful exercise of the prerogative power authorises the government in this country to tell private citizens what offers of remuneration they are to make to one another. How comes it, then, that a Government not merely acts in a breach of the rule of law, but that its action is generally tolerated, and even courted and approved?'[16]

As with the Wilson pay policy, Powell denounced those in the private sector who had agreed to co-operate with the Government when there was no legal obligation, or as he put it, 'to abase themselves at the feet of lawless authority'. He added, 'They have lent themselves, they have become willing co-adjutors, to a gigantic hoax or confidence trick.' The pervading fear of inflation, which he acknowledged, was no excuse to cast the rule of law to one side in trying to fight it, especially when the means used were so simplistic and so wrong. Meanwhile, the rise in prices continued to speed up, and a widespread call for food subsidies rose; things were not getting better. More and more of the Government's supporters were calling for Heath to curb government spending as a means of combating inflation, but still Heath refused. Above all, Powell argued, the Government was now limiting personal freedom in a way it had always been imagined only Labour governments could do.

He developed this argument further on 29 January, when the Commons debated the Counter-Inflation Bill, which implemented stage 2 of the prices and incomes policy – designed to end the absolute freeze on wages. As well as rehearsing his usual objections, Powell mocked his own front bench with more than the usual severity. It was by far the most hostile speech from any part of the House. The policy was, he began, 'one of the hoariest futilities in the recorded history of politics, the attempt to use coercion in some form or other to prevent the laws of supply and demand from expressing themselves in terms of prices'.[17]

The greatest problem the Government would have, he contended, would be the 'hot potato' of how it would be decided when a price should be allowed to rise, and, if so, by how much. This was a task the Government would readily hand to somebody else, and, indeed, a ludicrously complex bureaucracy had been set up to try to match the free-market mechanism that had been outlawed. 'Here,' he said,

> I must congratulate my right hon Friends on having introduced an element of variety into the drama. It is highly desirable; for otherwise the monotony would be almost killing. I had been waiting, I confess, with some anticipation to know whether, when they handed the hot potato over, the recipient would be described as a board or commission. I compliment my right hon Friends; they have done better still: there is a board; there is a commission, and – oh innovation! – agencies. I believe that this is the first time, at any rate in the English versions of the drama, that the term 'agency' has been introduced into the play. It certainly represents a welcome widening and enrichment of our vocabulary, and we should all be grateful.[18]

However, it was not a joke. Powell could not understand why the failures of the incomes policies of 1961–4 and 1966–9 had not been properly understood by the Government; or how no amount of compulsion, 'whether that compulsion be exercised by machine-guns or by firing CBEs, OBEs and MBEs', could stop inflation.[19] He felt the excuse given for ignoring history – that the previous two policies had been conducted in periods of stagnation, whereas this one was being operated during a boom – was 'a little attempt at humour; for it was never before suggested that it is easier to halt inflation in conditions of rising production and growing expectations than under conditions of stagnation and stable output and business'.[20] He proceeded to strip the Government bare intellectually in full public view. The problem was 'a flat self-contradiction'. For eighteen months the Government had had a blatant policy of reflation. Now, it had one of halting inflation. 'They must be promoting inflation and fighting inflation simultaneously in order to fulfil their policies and meet the demands placed upon them,' he said. When a man did such things 'the recourse open to him is the recourse which not only my right hon Friends but politicians through-out the ages – else how should we have survived as a caste or profession – have been able to adopt. That is, to do the one thing and pretend to do the other.'[21]

He knew what was happening: the reflation was continuing, to try to protect what was left of the policy of full employment, and the fight against inflation was entirely bogus. 'The one thing my right hon Friends are most terrified of is that they might actually succeed in slowing down and stopping inflation; for that would annul their policy of reflation.' The Bill was a mere decoy to satisfy public opinion. He concluded in a way that showed no mercy for the reputation of his front bench and which, in hindsight, showed the impossibility of his standing again as a Conservative if Heath still led the party:

> No hon Member out of office may speak for any of his fellows. It is not for any of us to judge what appears to another to be consistency, to be proper political conduct. We can only decide for ourselves. We must judge ourselves, but we may not judge others, even though I find it difficult to understand how those who argued, as we did in the last parliament, against something essentially indis-tinguishable from this Bill, who denounced it in principle and who foreswore anything of the sort when they presented themselves to the electorate, can support it now. Still, we must all answer ourselves. Therefore, I answer the question now, as I shall in the Lobby tonight, by saying that for myself I can not.[22]

Powell's assault had hit its target. Sir Geoffrey Howe, an admirer of his, found himself under orders to hit back during the winding-up speech that it fell to him, as Minister for Consumer Affairs, to make at the end of the debate. He accused Powell of wanting to reduce the money supply. Powell jumped on him immediately: 'I have never advocated reducing the money supply. It is a question of controlling the rate at which the money supply increases.'[23] Howe retorted, 'the tablets of history are being rewritten before our very eyes'. In fact, they were not: Powell had never advocated a reduction in the money supply. Howe tried to justify his remark by quoting from the speech Powell had made in the Commons nearly four years earlier on *In Place of Strife*: 'As I understood his argument there, it was to emphasise that it is by regulation of the money supply and by nothing else that one assails the problem of inflation. On that analysis, therefore, one wonders where the argument takes us.' Howe's interpretation of

Powell's speech was exactly right. But, as Powell had said, regulating the money supply was not the same as reducing it. Ironically, Howe would, after a Damascene conversion barely a year later, go on to become a rigidly monetarist Chancellor of the Exchequer.

The Government won its second reading; Powell's vote against the Bill followed his abstention in a division on the Counter-Inflation White Paper the previous week. He had the consolation, though, of knowing that the pound was still floating, despite Barber's having told the party conference he hoped to have it fixed by 1 January. Such an idea, in the present and worsening climate, looked hopelessly ambitious. When, the following month, Barber told the Commons he remained committed to fixing the pound again, Powell intervened: 'Is the Chancellor aware that I am quite happy to hear him reaffirm his adherence to fixed rates in principle, so long as he allows sterling to float in practice?'[24]

On 6 February Powell went to America for another lecture tour, saying as he left Heathrow that he would be speaking on prices and incomes 'because Americans are as interested in the subject as we are'.[25] On arrival in Washington he gave a press conference, where he was asked to comment on a distinction made by Heath when he was in the American capital the previous week between a 'special' and a 'natural' relationship between Britain and America. Powell replied, 'I am all in favour of natural relations but I didn't know Ted Heath was.'[26] Asked why he was in the United States, he answered, 'Why, to make money of course. I come here once a year. And I get paid in dollars. I can make a substantial part of my income in two weeks.'[27] Powell was disconcerted by this rare encounter with the American sense of humour, finding the local press unamused by his jokes. He rebuked them with 'You are a morose lot.'

In Wichita, Kansas on the last leg of his tour, Powell was candid about the role of the politician. 'I am a politician: that is my profession and I'm not ashamed of it. My race of man is employed by society to carry the blame for what goes wrong. As a very great deal does go wrong in my country there is a lot of blame. In return for taking the blame for what is not our fault, we have learned how not to take the blame for what is our fault.'[28]

Once home, Powell took further steps to maintain his high profile and popularity. He gave another series of interviews to Tony Shrimsley in the *Sun*, and one to the *Daily Express* a week later. Shrimsley tackled head-on a rumour that had been rumbling around for some weeks, in the wake of Powell's mounting popularity, the formation of 'Enoch Powell' societies around the country, and the unbridgeable chasm with Heath: would Powell stay in the party? 'I don't see how I can ever be anything but a Tory,' he replied. 'I was born Tory. I shall die Tory.'[29] This answer was not so obvious as it seemed: it said nothing about the Conservative party. Later in life Powell would say, 'I did not leave the Conservative party. The Conservative party left me.'

Shrimsley pressed him further: did it not seem, from the way he was behaving towards Heath and official party policy, that those ministers were right who said that 'it almost looks as if Enoch wants us to take the whip away'? 'If they really mean that,' Powell replied, 'then they know nothing about politics or about the Conservative party.' So would he set up a Powell party? 'I may be a fool,' Powell replied, 'I am not such a big fool as that.' He was giving nothing away about his thoughts for the future; indeed, given the steep rate of decline in the fortunes of Heath and the Government, there was no point in his doing so. 'I go on living from day to day. I don't try to see my role. That would be a stupid thing to do, like a man who spent his time looking in the mirror.' Having said the pay policy would inevitably end in disaster, Powell was asked whether he would be brought in as leader. 'Oh no, no, no, that would be a false deduction. There is no greater offence than to have been right too soon.'

Later in the series of interviews, Powell was asked why his predictions that entry to Europe would not happen had been wrong.

> I was wrong by eight votes, I agree. I was eight votes out. Why was I eight votes out? Perhaps, at a technical level, because it hadn't, I confess, occurred to me that the Liberal party – even this Liberal party – could march into the Government lobby in favour of guillotining the debate. That I didn't know. I also did not expect that the Conservative Government would dare to outface the absence of the condition which they themselves had stated for accession to Europe – namely the full-hearted consent of the parliament and the people, which nobody can say was present either in the House of Commons or amongst the people. It is not a discreditable expectation on which to be mistaken.[30]

In his *Express* interview – entirely on economics – Powell repeated his call for the money supply to be allowed to increase at no more than the rate of growth in the economy; he said he had never argued for unemployment to be used as a means 'to halt inflation', but said that any serious attempts to deal with inflation would lead to a transitional period of unemployment rising. He repeated his injunctions against regional policy, saying it was 'no service to people to induce or compel industry to be carried on where it is less profitable than elsewhere ... I suppose you would have wished the iron industry to be "induced" to stay in the Sussex Weald because all the charcoal-burners were there? This is a stage-coach mentality.' He boasted, on the matter of floating exchange rates, that 'We are all Powellites now,' but reacted as if stung when his interviewer asked him where he would cut public expenditure. 'When did I ever talk about "cutting expenditure"? Do you misrepresent me deliberately, or out of sheer incomprehension? I wish to reduce the rate at which public expenditure is planned to increase, so as to keep it within the rate of growth of the national income. That used to be Conservative policy until a short time ago!' All that was needed, he claimed, was the 'will' to cut back the rate of increase. He said the Government must, if it was to have any hope of getting the economy back under control, immediately announce it would revise downwards its plans for increasing expenditure; and must increase taxation to eliminate the gap between revenue and spending.[31] Powell was being unusually and unreasonably belligerent with his interviewer who, if he had had to hand a copy of *Income Tax at 4/3 in the £* – Powell's book in which he set out the Morecambe Budget – could easily have repelled Powell's point about never calling for cuts: the cuts listed there, in 1968 prices, totalled £2,874 million, more than funding Powell's projected tax cuts of £2,855 million.

Growing calls in March 1973 to fix the exchange rate caused Powell not just to enlist his usual arguments against such a move, but also to say that doing so would make it easier for the centralisers in Brussels 'to play their complicated games with prices and levies and subsidies, especially in connection with food'.[32] Also, fixing the rate was the necessary prelude to monetary union by 1980. The same weekend, at Southport, he said the Government had developed a deliberate policy of jacking up the price of food to the detriment of the consumer, in collaboration with Brussels: 'We face the proposition that the worker in this country ought to purchase his food not at the best price at which it can be obtained in the world market but at a price fixed by the producers in Western Europe and in their interests. It is as if the Corn Laws were resuscitated, but with the Continental producers in the shoes of the English squirearchy.'[33]

Powell had also become involved in another campaign, and one in keeping with his libertarian beliefs that won him some unusual bedfellows. The Government was legislating to make it compulsory for motorcyclists to wear crash helmets. Unwittingly in league with his old enemies in the National Council for Civil Liberties, Powell was determined to argue against this, on the ground that it was aimed to prevent an individual from harming himself rather than harming society. The Ministry of Transport countered that the wider community stood, in many cases, to be harmed by the death of an individual through his not wearing a crash helmet, to which Powell responded that if that was to be the justification for legally enforceable restraints on an individual's behaviour, there would be no end to the scope for the creation of punishable offences on the ground that they would restrict the likelihood of self-injury.[34]

The furore that accompanied Powell, for years after the Birmingham speech, at public meetings had, for the most part, died down; but it was resurrected by, of all people, the Duke of Devonshire, when he protested about Powell's being invited to address the Chesterfield Conservative Association, of which the Duke was president. He said that unless Powell was told not to come he would resign as president and withdraw the use of Chatsworth for garden parties. In a letter to the association, the Duke said: 'I am totally opposed to Mr Powell's attitude and consider that his recent speeches are both damaging to the country and do a very great disservice to the party.' In the feudal spirit, the Chesterfield association withdrew its invitation to Powell, who merely commented, 'I shall be interested to see what comes of this.'[35]

Needless to say a fine old row blew up, as Powell knew it would, to the great amusement of everyone apart from the Conservative party. The Chesterfield association called a special meeting of its executive to discuss the matter. Richard Devonald-Lewis and another right-winger, Bernard Brook-Partridge, who sat on the political committee of the St Stephen's Club – chaired by the Duke – resigned, accusing him of 'political blackmail'.[36] The Labour MP for Chesterfield, Eric Varley, wondered aloud what right members of the nobility living outside the constituency had to restrict the right of entry by others to it; or perhaps, after all, the landed gentry did still run the party. The association chose to ignore the Duke's wishes and invited Powell after all: another sign of his popularity in the party at the grass roots, even though, as the press commented, he was a far more dangerous opponent of the party leader's than Harold Wilson. The Duke resigned as president; eight years later he joined the SDP.

The Duke's histrionics had a wider effect than he could have imagined. In London, a group of businessmen – who remained anonymous, but were described as 'millionaires' – were so shocked by what they regarded as Devonshire's misunderstanding of Powell's significance to the party that they devised a new campaign to boost Powell and his ideas. David Lazarus, a London businessman and the chairman of Brent Conservative Association, announced that – without Powell's co-operation or knowledge, other than that he gave permission to reproduce speeches he had made – the men would fund a mailshot to all Conservative association chairmen. This would include a letter about their aims, and two recent speeches by Powell on how the Government had gone wrong on both housing and industrial relations. The covering letter argued that Powell was the only Conservative who could win the support of 'the ordinary intelligent man-in-overalls', without whom the next election would be lost. Somewhat disingenuously, it also said that Powell was the only one who could properly present the Government's 'achievements' to the electorate. It rejected the notion that he was disloyal to the party, and claimed that he had made a positive contribution to its thinking.[37] Anthony Fisher, the founder and backer of the Institute of Economic Affairs, was shortly afterwards revealed to be one of the main forces behind the campaign.

Powell would not comment on the initiative which, in its carefully crafted terms, was not so embarrassing as the earlier 'Powell for Prime Minister' campaign had been. News of it broke in the Sunday papers on 25 March, allowing him the excuse of 'keeping the Sabbath' and saying nothing. He told reporters he was observing the Fourth Commandment and had, as usual, not read the Sunday papers. The campaign had, though, brought to the surface once more the belief that Powell, and not Heath, spoke for the Conservative masses. In the Commons Powell's sway was less visible: the smoking room and tea room would empty when he spoke, but none of the 120-strong payroll vote – ministers, Whips and Parliamentary private secretaries – could utter any sound of approval. Nor could anyone with any ambition, whether hearing Powell in the chamber or at the 1922 Committee's weekly meetings. Everyone in the House knew, though, that his parliamentary isolation was the reverse of his public recognition. Intelligent Labour MPs knew they had as much to fear from Powell as Heath did, because of the direct line Powell had to the hearts of their working-class supporters. A Gallup poll at the time seemed to confirm this popular appeal. Asked which of five leading Conservatives – Powell, Heath, Barber, Carr and Douglas-Home – was the greatest asset to the party, Powell won.[38]

The immigration issue had, of course, done more than anything to give Powell that direct line. In early April he returned to the theme, pointing out that the figures for immigrant children in London boroughs' schools covered only those of parents who had entered Britain in the preceding ten years – those who had been in Britain for longer were deemed to have been 'assimilated' – and so were wild understatements of the true numbers. He went on to say that, by the turn of the century, some inner London boroughs would be 'mainly, and in some cases exclusively' coloured. The 'absolute theoretical minimum' proportion would be between a third and a half.[39] Powell had been prompted to speak by a letter he had received from a teacher in Bristol, who had written that 'my school has 127 coloured children and the Department of Education and Science return states 25 immigrants' – the other 102 being deemed 'assimilated'. The figures would, he said, become more inaccurate the more time passed. This was another speech Central Office refused to distribute.

Yet there were also the issues on which Powell's views could not have been more at variance with those of his working-class adherents: his support for the legalisation of homosexuality, for example, and for the abolition of the death penalty. He went into print on the latter subject on 11 April 1973, on the day of a vote in the Commons on a private member's Bill to restore hanging. He opened with an admission of his doubts on the matter: 'Few, if any, Members of Parliament who voted, as I did more than once, for the abolition of the death penalty, can have failed to revolve in their minds many times since then both the reasons for their vote, and what cause there might be to repent of it or to vote otherwise on a future occasion.'[40]

He said he had never had an absolute objection on moral or religious grounds to the taking of life by society; he acknowledged there were circumstances in which to do so would be 'the lesser evil'. It did not worry him that the penalty remained in law for treason: 'I see no parallel or analogy between the punishment of crime within a society and the self-defence of a society against its enemies.' Therefore, he said that if he had been 'reasonably satisfied' that 'substantially fewer' people would be murdered as a result of the existence of the penalty than was the case after abolition, he would support it. Just as he had sought a massive majority in support of entry to the EEC, so he wanted massive evidence of the good the death penalty would do before he would support it. 'It will not do to say, "if the death penalty will save a single life, it is justified".'

There was, he believed, a 'startling and impressive' lack of connection between the prospects of being hanged for a murder and the crime of murder being committed. The evidence, both in Britain and abroad, as noted by the Royal Commission on Capital Punishment in 1953, was ambiguous, or neutral. Because the time of abolition had coincided with a rise in all crimes, both violent and non-violent, Powell argued that it would be 'fallacious' to link the rise in murders since 1965 to the end of the sanction of hanging. This charge was 'not proven' because there was nothing to choose between the incidence of murder and the incidence of other crimes. Pointing to the link between the emergence of terrorism and the fresh calls for restoration, Powell dismissed the notion that this would have any effect: 'the terrorist ... is at least as likely to court what he might regard as a martyr's or a patriot's death as to be deterred by it'.

He accepted that deterrence was not the only form of argument for and against the penalty, but was reluctant to plunge 'into the moral and intellectual deep end of the arguments about retribution'. He did, however, feel crime had risen because people had become more tolerant of it. A sharpening of sentencing policy within the present law would, he said, be no bad thing in order to correct this. He concluded by saying that he might yet change his mind:

> I should be the last to imply that a Member of Parliament ought to subordinate his judgment of what is wise or right to even the most overwhelming majority of opinion. If he believes a thing harmful, he must not support it; if he thinks it unjust, he must denounce it. In those judgments the opinion of those he represents has no claim over him. But capital punishment is not for me in that category; it is not self-evidently harmful, nor self-evidently unjust. I cannot therefore deny that in this context a settled and preponderant public demand ought to be taken into account or that at a certain point it would have to prevail. I do not believe that point has been reached: but it would be disingenuous for me to deny that it could exist.

II

In Northern Ireland that spring the Government was pursuing a policy aimed at setting up a new power-sharing assembly. It would not have the powers of Stormont, but would act like an English local authority. There was no mention, in a White Paper debated in the Commons on 29 March 1973, of increasing the Province's representation in Parliament. In the debate, Powell spoke specifically to attack this failure; he denounced a defence of the position by Whitelaw, that an increase in representation would be an obstacle to enlarging, subsequently, the new assembly, if that were a success. Powell said there would be no obstacle to reducing Ulster's representation if the time came when the assembly could be aggrandised. What most angered him, though, was Heath's claim that representation could not be altered because it would offend what the Prime Minister had called 'a substantial element in the population'.[41] Thus arose a further area of bitter confrontation between the two men.

'I want to ask', Powell said, 'what is this substantial element in the population to which the full parliamentary representation of the people of Northern Ireland would be wholly unacceptable?' He simply could not believe that any element of the population in the Six Counties that wished to remain in the Union could object to being better represented in Parliament; and it was none of Heath's business, as a Conservative, to appease those who wished to break the Union. 'All the politics of Northern Ireland goes back to this fundamental division and clash; to which nation, to which state, is Northern Ireland to belong? The ambiguity ... saturates the White Paper.' The Government was trying to stop the domination of Ulster by Unionist politicians, even though they were all in place as a result of democratic election. 'Here', said Powell, 'is a proposition and a principle totally adverse to any conception of parliamentary or representative government with which we are familiar – the doctrine that in circumstances to be defined by another authority the majority, however large and however clear, shall not exercise the executive power.'[42]

He spelt out what he believed to be Heath's undeclared agenda, of separating Ulster from the rest of the Kingdom; and he could, he said, understand the weariness with the subject that encouraged his colleagues to give initiatives a try, to see whether they could work: 'but we are not sent here to give things a try, to see if they will work. We are sent here to apply our judgment before the event.'[43] He could not vote for the White Paper, and those who did, he said, 'are betraying the trust with which they were sent here and will bear the guilt of what will follow'.[44] In May, when the White Paper was translated into the Northern Ireland Constitution Bill and put to the vote in the Commons, Powell voted against that too. He repeated his reasons for doing so, and in the process he was greatly endearing himself to his future colleagues in the Official Unionist Party. He warned that, because it was illogical, the assembly could not endure, and would merely prolong the agony of Ulster. There were, he emphasised, just two honest alternatives: Union, or separation.

Meanwhile, he kept up his high-pressure assault against the Government's economic unorthodoxies, such as when he asked Rippon, in the Commons on 5 April, about the policy of subsidising building society interest rates. 'Could my right hon and learned Friend say whether there is any longer anything which this Government are not prepared to subsidise?'[45] For a change, Powell turned on Wilson on 14 April, for some observations he had made about inflation. The Leader of the Opposition had said that rent increases for council tenants and the failure to subsidise food prices were to blame. Powell argued that this 'descent into bathos' was not, surely, because Wilson thought that redistributing council housing subsidies could cause an inflation of 10 per cent a year. 'His own argument pointed to the correct explanation. It was, indeed, not the wages of dead bricklayers, but the pressure of live money in 1973, which inflated the price of the old house, as of everything else. It was not the clerks in the building societies that had forced up interest rates, but the Government's necessity to borrow, if possible, an unprecedentedly huge sum of money in the current year.' Wilson had not, he said, 'the slightest intention of denouncing the true causes of inflation, because they are embedded in socialism itself'.[46]

At the end of April Powell kept his date in Chesterfield, and gave a speech that would have confirmed all Devonshire's prejudices about him. He warned that his party risked losing the next election because, like Labour at the last, it looked like choosing to fight it on nothing and to withdraw from debate on all the great issues. 'For anyone who does not sense that this is a nation trying to find itself again and so far baffled by its failure to do so has not much contact with the British people.' His own party was riven with 'deep and severe contradictions', but could still find the means of solving them.[47] The prices and incomes policy – which had now reached its third stage – was, however, at odds with what the party had to do: 'one cannot imagine a more essential repudiation of a free self-directing economy and society'. He concluded: 'we simply cannot inform the people, or allow them to deduce, that since 1970 everything has changed, that we have discovered the nation in practice to be different from what we had supposed and hoped, and that accordingly we propose for them a form of tutelage, where their objects and the means to them will be prescribed on their behalf by others, inside this country and abroad. That course is not seriously open: a party, like a person or a people, has to be true to itself.'[48]

The following month a by-election took place at West Bromwich. The Conservative candidate, David Bell, invited Powell to speak for him; he had been one of Powell's constituents for fourteen years and had 'found him to be a first class MP, very fastidious about the problems of his constituents'. Bell explained to Powell that he did not, however, share his views on either immigration or the EEC; therefore Powell refused to speak in his favour. 'It would put both of us in a false position if I were to ask the people of West Bromwich to vote for you in a by-election which must largely turn upon those very issues,' he said.[49] This refusal, while entirely consistent with Powell's logic and integrity, had a malign side-effect. The National Front candidate, Martin Webster, claimed Powell's refusal to attend as a direct endorsement of him. The Front's policy of compulsory repatriation, not to mention many of their other National Socialist-style policies, was entirely opposed to Powell's own beliefs. At the poll on 24

May the Conservative vote slumped, while Webster recorded 4,789 votes, or 16 per cent of the poll, fewer than 3,000 behind Bell. 'This', said Powell after the result, 'is what I warned Mr Bell would happen'. Other West Midlands Conservatives were quick to spot portents for the next general election.

In the eyes of his colleagues and of the media, Powell's refusal to campaign in West Bromwich proved that he was now so far removed from Heath's orthodoxy that it could only be a matter of time before he left the party altogether, despite his recent protestations to the contrary. They did not take into account, though, that he had been willing to campaign in the Lincoln by-election during March, for Jonathan Guinness, but that Guinness had been told by Central Office to keep Powell away. On 8 June the final breach seemed to be imminent. His advance publicity refined as always, Powell ensured that most of that morning's newspapers carried the flavour of a speech he would make at Stockport that lunchtime, in which it was reported he would say he could no longer advocate his party's right to electoral support. It was the first the leadership heard of the matter: Central Office was now routinely not accepting his speeches for distribution. Powell's friends told the press that, now, it was Heath's carelessness with parliamentary sovereignty that had proved the final straw for him.

When the speech was delivered later that day the expectations did not, in the eyes of most of his colleagues and the press, appear to have been unfounded: it was construed as a clear indication to vote Labour when the opportunity arose. Powell, mischievously, claimed not to understand the disbelief of some Conservatives that he could have implied such a thing; 'many Labour members', he later observed, 'are quite good Tories'.[50] This sentiment would become even more pointed within months. Tony Benn cited it in his diary as 'a great speech'.[51] Powell began by noting the political law that, in a democracy, opposing parties often seem to move closer to each other; the 'physical geography of politics' could be altered only by the earthquakes that occur when that law is suspended, such as when the wing of one party has an object it pursues intently but can be obtained only from its enemies: in this case, the desire to think again on EEC membership, something only Labour was thought likely to offer. The precedent Powell cited was Chamberlain's and his fellow Unionists' decision to break from the Liberal party in 1886 over Home Rule. That rupture had led, with one brief interruption, to the best part of twenty years of Conservative government.

He reminded his audience that the British people, alone of those in the EEC, had been given no say in the decision to join the Community. It had not been an issue at the last election. He suspected it would be at the next, and the voters would have a choice. 'Presented, if they were presented, with two opposing parties which offered them a choice between the option they desired and the option they did not desire, electors would be perverse indeed to choose what they did not want for fear that those who promised what they did want would not perform it.'[52] He reminded them, too, of the real consequences of membership as being much more far-reaching in their implications for loss of sovereignty than Heath would admit. 'The law of the Community overrides the law of parliament; it does so for the most part automatically and silently without so much as the formality of debate or vote; and those who make the law wield the power.'

He was still outraged by Heath's commitment the previous October, without reference to Parliament, to economic and monetary union by 1980. He said this was a commitment to 'unitary government', for when all that concerns economics and money is removed from government, precious little remains ... do not laugh or shrug your shoulders. You have been told: it is your fault if you don't listen.' He listed Heath's abuses of sovereignty: the 'formal cession ... of the supreme right of the Commons to tax, to legislate, and to call the executive to account'. If Heath had his way about monetary union, 'in the next parliament will be completed the absorption of Britain into the new European state as one province along with the others'.

Yet there was one hurdle to be cleared before that parliament: another general election. That would be the moment for the British people to register their 'full-hearted consent'. Powell said he sought to 'assert that a choice, and that of the most fundamental nature, is still to be made'. He concluded:

> I would not conceal, even if I could, where my own counsel lies. Independence, the freedom of a self-governing nation, is in my estimation the highest political good, for which any disadvantage, if need be, and any sacrifice are a cheap price. There is not a state in Africa or Asia, hewn out of some administrative unit of Western colonial rule, which would not scorn to bargain away its independence. It is not for us to judge what others may think it right to do with their own. It is for us, and us alone, to determine if we will continue to be a free, self-governing people. I refuse to imagine that we shall answer no.

In the cacophony that followed, Powell denied he was calling on people to vote Labour: the clear-cut choice he had spoken about did not yet exist; if it did, then 'our opponents offering what so many Conservatives and patriotic people want more than anything else, it would be a horrifying, searing dilemma'. He appeared that evening on *Any Questions* and said, when his speech was mentioned, 'what I was saying to all Conservatives is: "Look out" '. He said his views on Europe were not new, and so should cause no surprise, nor put pressure on him to leave the party. Heath himself, after all, had said that the Common Market was 'a question so profound that every Conservative member – and I am quoting his words – has the right to form his own opinion and to follow it. That's all I've done.' The conclusion was widely drawn that Powell was issuing a personal challenge to Heath, that he would take him on at the hustings if the party's policy on Europe did not alter. He dismissed the notion that he might have any responsibility for splitting the party: 'We would deserve all that is thought about us if we were concerned just with party and then with country.'[53]

The controversy continued for days, and Powell did nothing to quieten it. He appeared on a radio discussion programme with Robin Day, who asked whether he would rather have a Labour government that took Britain out of the Common Market than a Conservative one that did not. Powell answered, 'Well, we shall know as the coming months unroll whether that is the form in which the choice is going to be presented to the electorate and to all of us.'[54] In the same discussion Michael Foot further stirred the pot by musing, 'I don't mind having allies in defending the House of Commons, particularly when there are so many deserters.' Powell said that even if the result of electing an administration that would extract Britain from the Common Market were to mean having Labour in power for the rest of his lifetime, 'I would say: "Well, so be it. But at least we have retained the power to decide under what general principles this nation is going to be governed." ' In the discussion, Powell gave the clearest definition of his philosophy of Parliament: 'The right finds it easy to explain what is and to justify what is, but not to account for change. The left finds it easy to justify change, but not to account for what is, and what is accepted.'[55]

In one respect the Stockport speech backfired: it marked the start in a slow tailing-off of public support for him in the opinion polls. For 'loyal' Conservative Powellites, the apparent call to disown the party was too much to contemplate.[56] Powell was especially wounded by a letter from Nigel Birch, now Lord Rhyl, which (with his customary concision) simply said: 'I am sure you will recapture your enthusiasm for the Market if you think it suits you.'[57] Powell's reply was equally terse: 'I am sorry that you could write a letter such as yours of 13th June.'[58] However, Nicholas Kaldor, the Labour economic adviser who was (as he put it) 'one of your political "enemies",' wrote to say how much he had admired what Powell had said – 'particularly your clear and emphatic declaration that it is the politician's sacred duty to put the national interest first, and party loyalty second'.[59] On the question of party loyalty, Pym, as Chief Whip, let it be known that he had no intention of withdrawing the whip from Powell and making him a 'martyr'.[60]

Powell had sent John Biffen a copy of the speech before it was delivered, which had caused Biffen to give 'troubled thought' to the issues he was trying to raise. He told Powell it would be best if he left the Commons before the end of the Parliament and desisted from 'subsequent political activity'.[61] However, Biffen suspected that Powell would leave early, and use the intervening period to ensure the election of a Labour government. He warned Powell that Labour's own commitment to a renegotiation was not 'sufficiently convincing' to be viable; and that he could not resign the whip and urge a vote for Labour at the next election, whatever Powell might do. 'I want you to know this,' Biffen wrote, 'because I would not wish to mislead you into thinking that at some tactical moment between now and at the next election you could count on me to endorse any appeal to vote other than Conservative.' He said how much he had appreciated Powell's confidence in recent months, but would understand, now, if that confidence had to be withdrawn, for he did not wish to be 'under false colours'. Powell wrote to him sympathetically: their friendship was not affected.

The next episode of Powell's publicity blitz was an appearance on *Panorama* where, once more, he carefully avoided admitting that he was urging people to vote Labour. 'What is important at the next election', he said, 'is the votes that will be cast, in private and in secret, by perhaps small, perhaps large numbers of voters who, by nature and prejudice and pre-disposition, would otherwise vote Conservative.'[62] He said he found it 'difficult to imagine' that Labour would not make Europe an important part of its election programme, for he saw Europe becoming more of an issue in the months ahead. He said he hoped the Conservatives would change their view: 'I still cannot believe, I still cannot get myself to imagine, that I shall live to see an election at which my own party marches under a banner of high food prices for ever and the House of Commons as a provincial council.'

Powell well knew his party would not make the policy changes on Europe that he sought. In his *Panorama* interview he said he hoped they would at least agree to a renegotiation of the terms of entry, but even that was unlikely: so conflict looked inevitable. With hindsight, Stockport was the beginning of the last phase of the process that led to his decision, first, not to fight the election and, second, to endorse Labour eight months later, even though Europe was not the issue that, in the end, caused him not to fight. Powell was beginning to realise the need to make a decision; but, as before, he felt he had until the summer of 1974 to formulate it. Again, in the *Panorama* interview he said he saw no reason why Heath should call an early election. That, of course, would remain his view even after that election was called.

He was still prepared to be personally generous to Heath. He said that 'in many respects I find myself, or used to, in strong sympathy with him. I used to think – I try to think it still – that our views on the working and the importance of a capitalist economy are very similar. I have heard him defend it from the heart in terms very similar to those that have come to my own lips. There is a whole area in which for many years I felt no difference at all.' However, on questions of national identity, institutions and history they were now far apart: and they were the only issues of separation that Powell was prepared, publicly, to admit.

After Powell had spoken about the possible need for a Labour government, Wilson was swift to state that there were no circumstances in which he would work with Powell, but one of his close front-bench colleagues, Peter Shore, a leading anti-marketeer, defended the Stockport speech vehemently, saying it was 'almost inconceivable that he or any other politician should receive so massive a rebuke for advancing the proposition that, in the last resort and on a matter of profound importance, he would put the interests of his own country before that of his party and that of the Common Market'.[63] Even Powell's old adversary, Lord Wigg, said he would support any candidate – including Powell – who stood at the election on an anti-Common Market ticket. He said that 'on the Common Market it seems to me that Mr Powell's position could be compared with General de Gaulle's in 1940'.[64]

Powell's main parliamentary activity in the summer of 1973 was trying, during the committee stage, to mitigate what he regarded as the horrors of the Northern Ireland Constitution Bill. The committee sat through June and into early July, and Powell consistently used its sessions to call for 'the thorough-going total integration and unification of the Six Counties of Northern Ireland with the rest of the United Kingdom'.[65] He said the legislation was designed 'to render the constitution acceptable not to those who accept the union but to those who fundamentally reject the union'.[66] If an assembly were set up it should, he argued, be set up on the same terms that it would be anywhere else in the Kingdom. Above all, the end of the Northern Ireland Government had to be matched by greater representation at Westminster. On 21 June he spoke in favour of a Unionist amendment to try to secure this, but it failed. Powell was not, though, prepared to let the cause fail with it.

Confident of his standing in the party and the country, and equally confident of the growing disrepair of the party establishment, Powell now took his assault against that establishment's deficiencies to ever more abrasive levels. Once the excitement caused by his Stockport speech died down, Powell resumed his criticism of the pay policy, reiterating at Hanley on 7 July that the methods the Government was using against inflation indicated ignorance of the real causes. The policy was 'no more than a sham and a facade, behind which inflation continues unimpeded at whatever speed the increase of money demand dictates'.[67] He denounced the Government for blaming the rise in food prices on 'world shortages', at a time when food mountains were piling up all over Europe. The price of onions had risen by 150 per cent in the previous year, and he put the responsibility for this on Heath directly: 'No doubt all these are imported and I look forward to the MP for Bexley's next shopping expedition and to hearing him explain to the housewives all about the world shortage. Alternatively, pensioners may be driving up the price by putting more onions in their stew to replace the meat. They hardly need to buy more onions to make them cry.'

The ridicule hit its target unimpeded, and caused such outrage that the next most popular man in the party after Powell, Douglas-Home, was charged with making a speech the following weekend to get the establishment's own back. Douglas-Home lacked the killer instinct necessary, and his strictures about how many tomatoes (another foodstuff the rise in whose price Powell had lambasted) were actually imported rather than grown here seemed Pooterish, not to mention beside the point. He reminded his audience that Powell had spoken in his 1964 election address about the importance of 'world market forces'; but Heath had helped put Britain at the mercy of these by his handling of the economy – a point Douglas-Home did not make.[68]

Powell's response to this top-level attack was to go back on BBC radio and say that Heath 'feared' him 'because I represent something in politics which is so foreign to his comprehension and to his scale of things, and his picture of politics and of the world – imagination'. He also claimed that Heath was leading the party to destruction, not out of levity or bad motivation, 'but because I believe he has never seen either politics or the Conservative party in the terms of principles such that his present courses of Government are a reversal, and indeed a destruction, of those principles'.[69]

Ministers were now alert for any means of making Powell look foolish. The Minister for Industrial Development, Christopher Chataway, thought he had found one in a statement on subsidies for the textiles industry on 19 July. In response to an intervention from Powell, he said Powell had supported in a division a similar subsidy to the cotton industry in 1959, apparently daring him to change his attitude now. Powell wrote to him: 'This is not true. No division took place on the second reading of that Bill, during the debate on which I spoke criticising the principle underlying it.'[70] He told Chataway his statement had been 'misleading and damaging', and asked him to seek permission from the Speaker to make a personal statement to correct it. Chataway refused, saying that although there had been no division to vote in on second or third reading, Powell had voted with the government during the committee and report stages.[71] Powell was not placated, and wrote to Pym, as Chief Whip, to say that 'this is the sort of incident which perhaps helps to understand my consistent determination not to go into the Government lobby in any division on the prices and incomes policy, whatever the precise terms of the question before the House may be. One never knows how many years afterwards an unfair misrepresentation may be made.'[72] Pym's reply indicates the loathing in which Powell was now held by the party establishment. 'Frankly, are there any circumstances in which you would be prepared to support the Government in the lobby on prices and incomes policy?' he asked. 'Incidentally, I ought perhaps to tell you, although you may already know, that the restraint shown towards you in the face of some of your own comments is almost more than a number of our colleagues can bear.'[73]

Before Parliament rose for the summer recess Powell had one more opportunity of twisting the knife. The air of crisis, while it had not reached the panic levels of the following autumn, was none the less palpable. On 23 July the Pay Board and the Price Commission – two parts of the market-rigging bureaucracy Powell had denounced in January – were debated in the Commons. He assessed the effect of the policy so far. The previous summer, he said, ministers blamed the unions for the inflation. Since the freeze and the pay policy had come in the previous November, however, the unions had obeyed them to the letter. The policy had been rigidly implemented. 'Yet the result today', he observed, 'is that inflation is running at approximately the same level as it was a year ago, with the additional fact that it is visibly accelerating.'[74] Now the unions could no longer credibly be blamed, the talk was of 'world prices'. Needless to say, he found this explanation 'no more satisfactory'.[75] Some prices were always rising or falling relative to each other, irrespective of whether there was inflation; it had nothing to do with inflation itself.

Barber, he suspected, had at last got the message. He had announced that he was looking for expenditure cuts. The alternative would be to raise taxes, or to print more money, thus further fuelling inflation. Barber could not, of course, admit that he could not print money, because to do so would inculpate himself for the disasters of 1970–2, when printing money was exactly what he had done. As a protective cover, the 'pantomime' of the prices and incomes policy was still being played out.[76] This would necessitate, however, the most difficult part of the pay policy – stage 3 – being executed, the stage in which pay and prices were allowed to move relative to each other. Powell, as a devotee of the markets, simply could not comprehend how this would be done by the 'agencies' charged with doing it.

'The fact is', he said, 'that there is no stage 3. There cannot be a stage 3. No rules can be laid down in advance, or administered by any body of men or Government, so as to decide, prescribe and order, without the most evident and unacceptable injustices, without arbitrary interventions, anomalies and unfairnesses, how all prices and wages are to start to move in relation to one another as well as all moving up together at whatever rate of inflation it is decided to accept for the time being.' To him, it was the ultimate bureaucratic nightmare, the ultimate absurdity for a Government formed by the party of free enterprise to be undertaking. Either, he said, there could be a sham stage 3 – a voluntary agreement no one would honour – or there could be 'ever more stringent compulsion'.[77] That, he said, 'will last for a time; but it will not last for ever; for, with every week it goes on, the contradiction between such a policy and the realities of a live economy will become more screamingly intolerable'. The third option, as always, was the only one worth pursuing, the option now implicit in Barber's policy but which needed to be made explicit. 'Let them do their duty. Let them do what only the Government can do; for only government can cause inflation and only government can stop causing inflation.' It was a devastating speech. Tony Benn, who did not agree with a word of it – not because of the rationale but because of the effect that the rationale, if implemented, would have on unemployment – described it as 'a brilliant academic analysis'.[78] It was generally seen, not least from the Conservative backbenches, that Powell had sent another missile through the superstructure of his own party.

Powell did not allow the normal break in political activity during August to interrupt his crusade. Speaking to women in Wolverhampton on 16 August he said an emergency autumn Budget would be necessary 'in the national interest' to have a 'drastic' downwards revision of the estimates for public spending, and a 'drastic' increase in taxation; the unpleasant side-effects of unemployment and bankruptcies were unavoidable.[79] He attacked Heath, saying it was not leadership 'to tell an inflation-ridden country that it is doing splendidly now and that paradise is round the corner', and that waiting to take the necessary measures after the next election would be too late. What was happening would lead to a national loss of economic confidence, followed by a national loss of confidence in all spheres. The policy Heath was following remained 'futile' because it addressed symptoms not causes: 'like the flowers that bloom in the spring, tra-la, it had nothing to do with the case'. He had not abandoned hope; an administration that had executed as many U-turns as this was always capable of a few more. Maudling, alerted by reporters who had read an advance of the speech (which, as usual, had not gone out through Central Office), dismissed it immediately as 'nonsense' and said, somewhat unfortunately, that Powell did not understand the causes of inflation. With an equal grasp of reality, he said confidently that very few agreed with Powell: the direct opposite of what the opinion polls were showing. Within a coupled of days a cabinet-level assault on Powell was organised, led by Peter Walker, the Trade Secretary, who claimed he was preaching 'human misery'.[80] Powell's response, in a speech in his constituency two days later, was to suggest again that the Conservative party could not seriously intend going into the next election waving a banner marked: 'Dear Food, and Government from Brussels'.[81]

The economic difficulties, not just of the Heath but of the Wilson years, had not helped secure what should have been one of the main features of Powell's political legacy: the ten-year Hospital Plan. Nearly a decade after he had left the Ministry of Health, both the British Medical Association and the new Department of Health and Social Security had to agree that the targets had not been achieved. Many of the slum hospitals and mental hospitals were still standing. Powell had hoped that 230 new district general hospitals each with 600 to 800 beds would be built by 1972; in fact, only forty were. Virtually no investment had taken place in modernising facilities for the mentally ill. although £152 million had been earmarked for hospital building and renovation in 1971–2, compared with £31 million in 1961–2, inflation had eroded the extra money.

Powell soon made another two-day visit to Ulster: he had averaged four trips a year since the troubles began in 1969. He told a gathering in Antrim on 18 September that he now felt closer to the Unionists than to his own party. He said he had been proud to have voted with the Unionists against 'every successive act and policy of the Government over the last three years which has called in doubt Britain's purpose in Ulster'.[82] To Heath's dismay, Powell made this latest high-profile visit just as he was visiting Dublin to hold talks with Liam Cosgrave, the Republic's Prime Minister. When Powell spoke of the 'true guilt' for the problems of Ulster resting at Westminster, and of Heath's and Whitelaw's policy being 'rule of dictatorship by secretary of state', he was applauded lengthily and loudly. He accused Heath of a policy of 'wobble and fumble and drift and blunder' towards the forces of nationalism, or what was becoming known as the 'Irish dimension'.

He soon found a new stick with which to beat the Government: the proposed establishment of the Equal Opportunities Commission. Speaking to the Ilford Chamber of Trade and Commerce, Powell told businessmen to say to the Government, 'It may be the last year before a general election, but do resist the temptation to be daft.'[83] He described the proposals as 'begotten by the monstrous union of the Race Relations Act 1968 and the Equal Pay Act 1970', and asked:

> What sort of society is it, and what state of mind is it, to which it appears desirable or even rational to attempt to impose equality by compulsion where society is most profoundly differentiated? Equalities of economic opportunity for those offering equal prospects and equal reward for equal performance already exist. They are maintained freely and automatically by the force of mutual advantage and the operation of the market. Law and compulsion have to be brought in only where it is desired to prevent equal opportunity and reward for equal prospects and performance. If in any particular employment women give the same overall performance as men, it is impossible for them to long to be remunerated at a lower rate.

The proposed legislation, he concluded, was an injustice to employers, the consumer would suffer, and women too would suffer by being priced out of some jobs.

On 29 September in a speech at Tottenham, Powell explicitly linked, for the first time, the immigration question with the voting intentions of the public at the next election, which he now accepted would be in the next year. He was speaking just three days after a Commons select committee report had said that Government figures on immigrant children in schools were misleading and deficient, and had branded those responsible for collecting the figures as 'misguided' in their determination to keep them low: a vindication of much he had said about the statistics in the preceding five years. He confined himself at that stage to a simple 'I told you so', adding: 'For years I have repeatedly pointed out that the school figures, as collected and published, are grossly and deliberately misleading, and I have demanded genuine statistics instead. The only response has been abuse and ridicule. I congratulate the Select Committee on their belated discovery and wish them better luck.'

At Tottenham, he surmised that many had voted Conservative in 1970 because they felt the party was the only one that would take a properly firm line on immigration. 'They will never do so for that reason again unless a great change comes about – and soon.'[84] Powell said the perceived indifference by the Government to the mounting number of immigrants 'will not be forgotten. It will not be forgiven.' The rate of increase promised to be terrifying: 53 per cent of the immigrant population was under twenty-five, compared with 30 per cent of the rest of the population; and, whereas London was one-tenth coloured, it would be a third in due course. He also rebuked Heath for having taken credit, at the Commonwealth Conference the previous month, for Britain's having 'absorbed' 750,000 people from the New Commonwealth in the previous ten years, in other words after the 1962 Act that had supposedly restricted immigration – another sign that Powell had not been wrong in pointing out the deficiencies of that Act.

Despite the evidence for what he said, this speech brought the usual execration. At the Labour conference, which opened the following day in Black-pool, his prospective opponent in Wolverhampton South-West, Helen Middle-week, accused him of descending to a policy of outright racism. Maudling said Powell had used 'some horrific language', drawing the conclusion that he was hinting at forced repatriation, though the speech contained no mention of such a thing. There were the customary demands by immigrant groups for him to be prosecuted.

For the conference season, Powell chose to publish not one, but two books: *No Easy Answers* described his religious views, and how he had left the church in his youth and then returned to it in early middle age. More provocative in its timing, though, was the publication of *The Common Market: Renegotiate or Come Out*, which contained twenty-four of his speeches on the EEC. For the conference itself, he chose to concentrate on the economy. He wrote his own prologue for the event in *The Times* on 9 October, just before the representatives gathered in Blackpool, looking back to the antics in which the leadership had engaged the previous year in order to try to secure his own humiliation. He addressed his remarks directly to those 'organising the standing ovations'. 'Let those in charge . . . eschew the grosser forms of rigging. Of course, any conference has to be stage-managed, though the Conservative party's constitution does not subject it to the same disagreeable necessities in this respect as the Labour party.'[85]

He claimed the riggers had little idea how 'distasteful' their activities were to the public watching on television, and how the intelligence of those viewers was insulted by the applause given by Conservatives to statements and policies the non-faithful knew to be utterly at odds with the realities of their own lives: particularly the non-faithful 'who know the facts about immigration'. Powell added that his party did not know how it would confront at the polls a nation that it had, against her will, taken into the EEC; and he warned about the foolishness of the party being seen to congratulate itself on economic management, spouting statistics that 'even now ... are being thrust into the hands of ministers and trustworthy speakers. Beware. In the world outside it is not a success story that is visible. What that larger audience knows is not growth but inflation; nor does it need statistics to learn what its daily personal experience tells it all too plainly. If harm is not to be done, these people must be met halfway, and with candour, not euphoria.'

III

Powell's speech in the economic debate on 11 October was, by his standards, restrained. He spoke theoretically, warning once more of the dangers of inflation, and describing it as 'a social evil, an injustice between man and man, and a moral evil – a dishonesty – between Government and people, between class and class'.[86] He made some rare conciliatory remarks about the news that the gap between revenue and expenditure was narrowing, and how the Government needed 'our understanding and support' in the fight against inflation. If it took even sterner action, and imposed rigid control on the money supply, 'we will back you when the measures bite home and the time of testing comes'. There was no direct criticism, and certainly no personal criticism. It was a deliberate ploy. 'One was hoping against hope that the pay policy would be changed,' he said later.[87] He was enough of a psychologist to see that another full-frontal assault would not achieve that aim. The party in the country had had enough of the Government's economic mismanagement, and were well aware that Powell had been proved right: he received a standing ovation as he left the platform. Heath and Barber, who had sat grim-faced throughout, were seen conferring urgently.

The cabinet had long since abandoned any diplomatic niceties with Powell, now seen unequivocally as a great electoral danger. Nonetheless, his speech this time could not remotely be represented as destabilising, but rather as an attempt at burying old differences at what looked like being the last conference before a difficult election – which made Barber's performance at the end of the debate all the more astonishing. He described Powell as a 'frustrated fanatic', saying of him that 'I have no intention of impugning his motives. They are self-evident.' He alleged that he was 'sad' to see an 'old friend' evincing 'all the moral conceit and the intellectual arrogances which are the hallmark of the fanatic'. Barber claimed to have been upset by a recent press release Powell had put out in which he had said that some cabinet ministers were more interested in saving their own skins than doing what was right; and he had taken Powell's talk of 'dishonesty' in his speech personally.

Barber's ploy backfired. The representatives who heard him were shocked by this gratuitous injection of acrimony; his attack was not in the release of his speech given to the press. As they filed out of the hall afterwards, some told journalists they thought Barber had gone too far, especially since Powell had confined himself to a discussion about principle rather than personalities. There was also a recognition that Barber had failed as Chancellor. A comment in the leader columns of the next day's *Daily Telegraph* made the obvious point about the Chancellor's own rectitude: 'Did his [Powell's] economic doctrines, or something like them, seem fanatical to Mr Barber at Selsdon?' In the days that followed, letters of protest arrived at Central Office for Carrington, the party chairman, complaining about Barber's language, and Teddy Taylor, who had resigned from the Government over Europe, said it was 'nonsense' to think of Powell as 'a lone and isolated renegade. His views and consistency have widespread support.' Taylor added that, if the signal was that Powell was to be treated as some sort of parliamentary leper, it would be a grave threat to the whole party.[88] 'I think it was a mistake,' Robert Carr reflected a quarter of a century later.[89] Unfortunately, however right Powell was, the fact that it was he who was right meant that the Government could not be seen to take his medicine. It was no longer the One Nation days, when Powell would give ground, but move his opponents towards him: the battle was of absolutes, on both sides.

Powell had two immediate opportunities to have his own back. Speaking on television shortly afterwards, he described Barber's remarks as 'a grave error of taste', but said he had not been hurt by them. 'I was sorry, because I don't think that personal attacks upon motives and character do a party any good. I don't think they are part of the currency of politics.' He was asked to comment on Barber's assertion that he was conceited and arrogant. He merely said, 'I must leave people to judge for themselves both my character and my motives. At least I give them plenty of material for a judgment.' He also denied he was hoping for Heath's defeat at the next election, and was plotting a coup to replace him in that event. 'I'm not such a fool as to think that.'

That afternoon he went along the coast to make another speech at Lytham St Annes. Barber's friends, soon conscious of the way in which his remarks were backfiring, immediately started to brief the press that he had been getting his retaliation in first for what it was expected Powell would say at Lytham. When he spoke, he made ironic reference to the posters that had featured so prominently in the previous election campaign, featuring Heath's portrait above the motto 'Man of Principle'. 'We came into office', Powell said, 'as a party of principle. It was a word extensively and proudly used – you recall, no doubt, the posters – and we made it plain beyond peradventure what our principle was. In human affairs, and above all in government, principle must ever be tempered to circumstance. But we have not tempered principle; we have reversed it.'[90]

In an uncanny harbinger of events four months later, Powell read out parts of his own election address from 1970, in which he had said: 'If this' – a standard rate of taxation at 40 per cent, inflation, state control of wages and prices, and the possible nationalisation of Rolls-Royce – 'goes on for another few years, Britain will have ceased to be a country where people of initiative, self-respect and independence wish to live and bring up their children.' He and his audience were painfully aware of the Conservatives' record. 'Today, three years later, it would be a bold candidate who would dare to print such a statement. He would be disowned for making a cynical and sarcastic attack upon Mr Heath and the record of his government in office ... The whole course of recent government in Britain, intensified rather than reversed in the last three years, has left us further than ever from pride, as it has from freedom.'

The following week another, apparently remote, portent emerged when it was learned that Powell had received, and refused, an offer to become leader of the Ulster Unionists at Westminster: the stand of the incumbent leader, Brian Faulkner, over power-sharing had caused a split in the Unionist ranks and provoked calls for his removal from office at the Unionists' conference at the end of October. That Powell was now so strongly associated with the Unionist cause should not have been a surprise after his years of campaigning there, but this offer put his links with the party on a new, and far more intense, level.

To the circle of Powell's supporters in the parliamentary party, the assault on him at the conference had triggered terminal despair. Outside, friends like Ralph Harris and Arthur Seldon made no bones to Powell about their belief that he would have to become Prime Minister, and that they and their organisation would do all they could to help. They found Powell remarkably receptive. He was under no illusions about the opportunity the mounting disaster would present him, nor of his ability to stand equal to that challenge. Occasionally that autumn, he met Harris, Seldon and other friends from the IEA to discuss how policy would have to be formulated to achieve the freeing-up of the economy in the event of Powell's forming an administration. In the past Powell had been slightly embarrassed by the well-intentioned enthusiasm of his friends. Now he, and they, were deadly serious. 'The key point', Harris told Powell in a letter of 30 October 1973, 'is that if things go badly wrong under the present administration, then its successor will only succeed if it starts out on the right foot and does not change step when the initial policies run into inevitable headwinds.'[91] It is odd, though, that someone with as strong a grasp of realism as Powell could not foresee the difficulties of such a situation being brought about without an election, or the impossibility of his participating in that election as a Conservative: it was a part of reality to which he seems to have been unable to face up.

In that last, difficult autumn for the Heath Government, leading up to the miners' strike, the three-day week and his ill-fated decision to call a February election, Powell returned to his traditional themes of the economy, immigration and Heath's breach of his promises. On 17 October, soon after Parliament resumed, the Commons debated the price and pay code, and Powell taunted Heath for having made no reference in his own speech to the fact that inflation was at the same level as a year earlier, when the prices and incomes policy had been introduced. As he had said immediately before the recess, all that had changed had been the demonology: the 'whole basis and justification' of the policy when it was implemented in 1972 had been the trade unions and their exorbitant behaviour; now it was world prices that had taken over as the cause of inflation, and as such they necessitated the maintenance of the policy.[92] Wearily, he delivered yet another economics lesson: 'A relative change in prices, even of a group of requirements so important as those which this country habitually imports, is not the same as inflation, and it does not cause inflation.'[93] Powell was right: if the supply of money were kept constant, and if demand for the more expensive goods proved inelastic, the price of other goods in the marketplace would have to fall as fewer resources were available to purchase them, and therefore the demand for them fell.

The policy itself was not even making a pretence of reducing inflation. Powell cited evidence that the chairman of the Pay Board was planning to agree to pay rises at exactly the rate of inflation: 'In other words, the code which is put before us is a code which, so far from imposing controls that will, of themselves, diminish the rate of inflation, accepts the present rate of inflation and proposes to carry it forward.'[94] Now Powell was no longer clear, if that was the case, what was the purpose of 'this grand bureaucracy' set up under the counter-inflation Acts. He noted that Heath was now talking merely of 'containing' inflation: 'when in a battle we say that we have "contained" the enemy's advance, we do not mean that we have driven him back on to his base'.[95] To try and 'contain' an inflation that was already running at 9.5 per cent was, to Powell, verging on the obscene.

Powell was not prepared to reduce the Government's embarrassment. He understood, he said, their dilemma. He said the leadership were 'devoted passionately – Heaven forgive me! I almost said "fanatically" – to growth'.[96] The oblique reference to Barber's attack on him raised hilarity in the chamber. He pointed out that the choice remained between growth and a rise in unemployment; the price of sparing the rise in unemployment was, as always, inflation. There was no other option but these two, and Powell had had enough of the pretence that there was. When some Labour Members barracked him for advocating unemployment, Powell interjected that they should be honest enough to tell their constituents that they wished to insist on inflation continuing to rise at 10 per cent; and when the Labour Members still did not appear to get the point, he offered to conduct a seminar for them.

At a conference in London on 25 October he praised other countries for having followed Britain's lead and floated their currencies, and warned against Britain's being trapped in a European bloc that inflicted huge damage on the prospects of trade with the rest of the world. In his constituency on 2 November his theme was immigration; he accused Carr of 'complete and total ignorance of the facts', judging from what he had said in a speech to the Commons the previous day. The Home Secretary had told the House that to limit immigration 'to the inescapable minimum' would mean that there would be too few people available to work in many blue-collar jobs, especially in transport, and said that the great immigration of the 1950s and early 1960s had partly been used to meet the demand for labour in a period of full employment.[97]

It was an assault on Heath, by far his strongest yet, at the end of November that seemed, at last, to mark the end of Powell's prospects of any future within his party. Not long before, when asked whether Heath might be ousted, Powell had – quoting Housman – said he would be dealt with 'with weapons from the arsenal of divine revenge'. When Robin Day asked him, in an interview, whether Powell thought God was on his side, rather than deny it Powell had mischievously answered, 'Well . . .'[98] This latest attack, though, had somewhat less humour to cushion it. The day before he spoke, Powell sent copies of his speech to newspapers and the Press Association, under embargo, knowing that Central Office would refuse to distribute it. Inevitably, some papers broke the embargo, so that for hours before Powell spoke the country knew the Conservative party's most famous – or infamous – figure was about to savage its leader: which itself generated even more publicity. 'Never before,' the loyal *Daily Express* reported that morning, 'will a leading Tory have spoken in such disparaging terms of his party leader.'[99]

The speech – to a businessmen's luncheon club at the Hilton Hotel in London – lived up to its billing. Powell reminded his audience that, a year earlier, he had asked whether Heath had taken leave of his senses when the prices and incomes policy had been announced: 'a solicitous but not unreasonable inquiry', he quipped. 'The rate of inflation has not been lower during the period of the statutory counter-inflation policy: it has been higher. So official apologists have had to resort to the last refuge of the disconcerted – to claim that things would have been even worse without the policy. This is the version of the old story about the man who threw bits of *The Times* newspaper out of the railway carriage window "to keep the elephants away". It was, he said, self-evidently successful, for where were the elephants?'[100]

He said that the Government's continual reinforcing of its own failure was 'gravely damaging', because it further obscured the only means – means within the Government's control – to rectify the inflation, and perpetuated a policy that set classes and interests within Britain against each other. 'The danger of this was frighteningly illuminated by the Prime Minister's outburst last week against the miners, who, whether or not they are wisely led by their trade unions, have neither done nor threatened to do anything which is against the law.' Heath's threat to the miners, made in a speech in Lancashire, was based purely on the Commons' approval of a White Paper on pay, which had no statutory force and counter to whose precepts the miners were now moving. Heath had asserted, however, that the responsibility of the Government, 'expressed in the price and pay code, is not the responsibility we sought; it is a responsibility which parliament gave us because there is no other way of containing inflation in this country'.

Powell's comment on this remark of Heath's was what took their feud into new territory. 'One cannot but entertain fears for the mental and emotional stability of a head of government to whom such language can appear rational.' Of course, Powell observed, the Government was responsible for the powers Parliament conferred on it; and of course there were other means of fighting inflation, as he had repeatedly told them. 'It is deeply worrying that at a time when past budgetary policies have carried Britain deeper and deeper into inflation, and when the world is waiting to see whether we have the resolution to deal with inflation at its source, more and more symptoms appear that the Government has withdrawn into a world of make-believe of its own, in which disasters are transferred into successes, and responsibility and blame are transferred from where they belong on to synthetic obstacles and enemies.'

Now it was Powell's turn to face accusations that he had gone too far. The *Daily Telegraph*, which had supported him against Barber, wondered whether Powell could hope to advance the just causes in which he believed by using such language – which it defined as 'a premeditated insult, carefully calculated to cause maximum offence'. Powell had enough rational arguments on his side without resorting to that. For others, it seemed the time had come when Powell and Heath's Conservative party would have to go their separate ways. It required too much of a leap of the imagination to see Powell calling for the re-election of a government led by Heath when the time came. As usual, there was no question of Powell's being disciplined for his outburst: not, this time, because of his popularity outside Parliament, but because his remarks had, it was felt, done enough damage to that popularity and to him as it was. For his part, Heath laughed off a question from Joe Ashton, a Labour MP, in the Commons that same afternoon, when Ashton asked the Prime Minister to give an assurance that the Government was not 'barmy'. One of Heath's supporters, John Hunt, said that 'this disgraceful attack on the Prime Minister at a time of grave national crisis must raise doubts about the mental stability of Mr Powell himself'.[101]

Powell even appeared to have gone too far for some of his usually ultra-loyal supporters in Wolverhampton. Ever since his Stockport speech some of them had been increasingly critical in private of his attacks on the leadership. A few, intelligently, had begun to raise the question among themselves of whether Powell could possibly be their candidate when the election came. He was facing particular pressure from a group of activists in the Tettenhall ward, a prosperous area grafted on to the constituency as a result of boundary changes the previous year. Unlike his long-term supporters, the newcomers – who tended not to be from the deferential working-class or lower-middle-class bedrock of Powell's support – were determined he should either stop making an issue of the EEC or get out.

As early as November 1972, at the constituency annual general meeting, protests had been raised against him from Tettenhall; and his constituency chairman, George Wilkes, had warned him that because of some pointed remarks Powell had made at the AGM about the conduct of the Tettenhall members 'you have severely alienated opinion' there.[102] Powell replied offering to conciliate those who had objected to his remarks, though claimed to be innocent of what it was he had said that had caused offence.[103] A rapprochement took place the following January, but Powell's increasingly hostile attitude to the leadership throughout 1973 inflamed feelings again. A meeting was held in the constituency in July, after the Stockport speech, which Powell did not attend. He was mildly rebuked for his absence by Robin Pollard, his loyal agent, for his presence 'would have given those who are "with" you a much needed morale booster' and would have allowed him to explain himself.[104] Pollard said the situation was 'an extremely (and I do not use that word lightly) disturbing one. There are murmurings of a split in the Association.' What worried Pollard was that opposition to Powell was not now confined to the 'new' branches, and that Powell's supporters were increasingly silent. He urged him to take George Wilkes – who had defended Powell in his absence 'magnificently' – fully into his confidence, and to make more effort to explain himself and his actions to the association's management committee. 'I must say that the situation *is* serious – please do not underestimate it.' Wilkes himself wrote to Powell that his attendance at the next management committee meeting was 'absolutely essential as the situation is deteriorating rapidly'.[105] He stressed that all he felt the situation needed was Powell's personal touch: 'There is still an immense fund of goodwill towards you in the Association and this is only awaiting a lead from you.'

In December 1973 these differences finally came into the open. A critical motion about Powell was put down at the annual general meeting, by one of the 'new' branches. Association membership figures were revealed to be down, and Powell was partly blamed for this. Peter Wesson, vice-chairman of the Wolverhampton South-West association and a Tettenhall man, resigned. In an emotive statement, he urged Powell to 'turn aside from the flames of martyrdom. I beg you desist from your obduracy.'[106] Wesson, a well-educated and formidable businessman much respected in the association, specifically attacked the 'bitterness' he said had entered into Powell's language during the last year: 'a great cause has been discredited by its author'. The motion called on Powell to state categorically whether he wished to stand for the constituency at the election if Heath was still leader. Powell advised Wilkes that he was happy for the motion to be debated, and would confront his critics.[107] Pollard warned Powell that 'behind it [the motion] lay the first serious talk of having you replaced as prospective candidate. I think you should know, too, that for the first time many of your most faithful friends have been moaning and feeling that on occasion they cannot defend you.'[108] Pollard told Powell of Wilkes's belief that the association had been unduly loyal to Powell: 'many associations would have "carpeted" you on a number of occasions before now'. To be fair to Powell, the wards from which most of the trouble was coming, Pollard told him, 'didn't much like you from the outset, and have been awaiting an excuse to pounce on you'. They were also wards that did no canvassing, raised little money and undertook no membership drives, which Pollard felt hardly gave them the moral high ground in this battle.

Pollard had also warned Powell to 'bring a plentiful supply of the JEP brand of charisma. I have a feeling you may need it.' At the meeting, Powell made a long speech justifying his actions to his constituents, and analysing the party's breach of promises on the key points of the 1970 manifesto. It was highly dialectical, and its reasoning will have been beyond many of the ordinary members present. He had, he said, been adopted at the previous AGM as the association's candidate for the next election, and this meant it was 'axiomatic' that he 'must stand on the party's manifesto', though he could emphasise such parts of it as he chose and 'may express individual views and aims which lie outside the party's policy but do not conflict with it'.[109] Acceptance of the leader of the party was also 'axiomatic', though not inconsistent with trying to have him replaced – he pointed out that many elected under the leadership of Home in 1964 'did not consider it beneath their dignity to consult together to produce his resignation from that position'. He, though, had never taken part in any such activities.

He went on to say that 'it has never been suggested that to recognise a person as the leader of a party confers upon him a right to the agreement and support of all its members for all his words and actions whatever they may be. A party is not the private property of its leader.' Not being a member of the Government, he added, his was an individual responsibility, not a collective one. He exercised his responsibility to ensure that the pledges of the manifesto on which he had been elected were carried out. He and his colleagues 'were not sent to Westminster with a blank cheque to be filled in by the party's leader ... there is not only no claim of loyalty or duty which constrains a Member to support policies contrary to those on which the Government and he himself were elected, but there is a duty upon him, publicly as well as privately, to expostulate and, if need be, to oppose. Otherwise, all faith and mutual respect between parliament and people is destroyed ... We in Wolverhampton South-West can claim with some pride that we have remained true to the policies on which we fought in 1970.' He quoted the manifesto back at his audience, and compared it with the record; and concluded by saying, 'I am sure, as I am of nothing besides, that for a person or party, government or nation, there is nothing to hope for if we fail to keep faith with ourselves.' He took questions for forty-five minutes and received, finally, a standing ovation.

In one respect, Powell's conduct at the meeting was a disappointment to his senior officers. Both Wilkes and the president of the association, Peter Farmer, had met Powell privately before it and had sought to extract a promise that he would outline what he would do if an election were called in the immediate future. Powell, who had cause to feel discomfort at such a question, dismissed the request, saying that such questions were hypothetical. One of those at the meeting said that Powell 'wasn't himself . . . I got the impression he really wasn't with us.'[110] Wilkes subsequently let it be known that, in the light of Powell's attitude, he had formed the view he would not stand. He warned his fellow officers that a new candidate might be needed at short notice, but was met with disbelief.[111] Certainly, Powell had not answered the fundamental point of how the man who adhered so strongly to the promises of 1970 could possibly expect to be able to support the likely manifesto of 1974 or 1975. 'He hoped against hope against hope that something might happen to enable him to go on,' his wife recalled.[112]

However, a part of Powell was still clinging to the old realities of his political life. With the growing divisions and despair within the Conservative party, the One Nation group had ceased to be a focus for well-organised internal activity, not least because Heath was listening to few outside his circle, and policy-making by anyone else had become otiose. As a result, attendances at its Wednesday dinners were becoming sparser, and these functions were often cancelled. On 12 December Powell wrote to Bill Deedes, the group's chairman, to say:

> I am becoming very anxious about the survival of One Nation, which clearly cannot indefinitely continue if it is simply a residual convenience on Wednesday evenings for those who happen to have nowhere else agreeable to dine on that particular night. Those few Members who still reserve Wednesdays and decline other engagements in order to attend the Nation will not go on doing so for ever, if they are then to suffer one last minute cancellation after another. In any case, the Nation cannot be even mildly effective unless a substantial core of the same Members gather regularly week by week.[113]

The group was important to Powell for two reasons: it was continuous thread running through his parliamentary life from its earliest days; and it was a place where, in his isolation, he could still be included among colleagues. Its decay was a symbol both of his own uncertainty and of his party's.

During December, as the crisis mounted and talk grew of an election to win new authority for a confrontation with the miners, the perception grew that even in this impending disaster Powell's hour had not come. That was despite the fact that Barber, in an emergency Budget, was now seeking to take some of the anti-inflationary measures for which Powell had been branded a "fanatic" by him for advocating. Powell publicly supported him for doing so. Barber was generous in return, telling the Commons, 'I say very genuinely to my right hon Friend, I am grateful.'[114] Powell's support of Barber sent a shock through the Labour party. Benn, recording it in his diary, pointed out that the calculation Labour would have to make would need to be different if Powell was now actively in support of the policy.[115]

However, the talk in the Conservative party at Westminster, faithfully echoed in the press, was that if Heath did forfeit the confidence of his party Whitelaw, and not Powell, would be the man to succeed him and steady the ship. It was not so much that Powell was unpopular for having split the party, or having been proved right, but that he was feared for what was perceived to be his evangelical promotion of the theories of deflation, a creed the Conservative party may have needed, but still was determined not to have. Nor was it felt that Powell had an answer for the militancy of the miners in the face of the Arab oil-price hike, or for train drivers refusing to ship coal from pitheads to power stations. In that crisis, it had gone beyond a question of whether the unions did or did not cause inflation, and was now whether their engagement in political activity could be contained by the Government.

Heath, confronted more immediately with that reality than Powell was, was quickly coming to the view that he would have to make a gesture of militancy that matched the unions'. In theory, the monopoly power exercised by the nationalised industries' rigidly unionised workforce could not be dissipated in the short term, even if the Government was willing. Where Powell was right was in his assertions that the pay policy, roughly constituted in a White Paper, was not the ground on which to confront the unions. Given the circumstances in which both sides found themselves, the conflict was pretty well intractable. The Government, in Powell's eyes, had to refuse to implement a wage increase for the miners on the ground of controlling the money supply, but that would still have left the militancy, the power cuts and the immobilisation of Britain. Not until the miners' strength was broken a decade later, after a battle lasting over a year, could a government view with insouciance their threats to cripple by use of their monopoly.

In the crisis, Powell gave off an air of being almost detached, but then there was no one on the Conservative benches less responsible for what was happening than he, nor who stood to be proved more right by events. Throughout these busy and intense years of politics, Powell never ceased being gregarious, keeping up the round of walking tours, picnics and dinner-parties that had for so long been a feature of his life, or going off regularly to the opera with Richard Ritchie.

Cecil King found Powell in relaxed mood at a dinner party on 13 December given by Nicholas Ridley, the night before his ordeal at Wolverhampton. In quick succession Powell took the conversation through his views on the differences between the sexes – 'men's lives make their faces very different from each other, though they dress alike. Women's faces much more resemble each other (in his view they are almost indistinguishable) but they dress as differently as possible' – to his researches into medieval tombs, and finally to his advice to his wife on what to do on his death: 'Go on a cruise and pick up some nice kind widower, but on her death he expected her to be buried by his side.'[116] His wife remembered that he found it hard to remember all faces, not just women's; and thought the advice he had given her was to marry an old soldier.

Whatever Powell's apparent casualness, Bill Deedes remembers him at this time, however, being deeply affected by the state into which his country had declined. Powell also seemed, to Deedes, angry that the Government, partly because of the history of the last six years, would still not listen to him despite his having been proved right. Deedes saw him as 'the sad spectator of a tragedy that he was powerless to avert'. His failure to compromise had preserved his integrity, but it had also denied him the chance to be brought in to be of service when the crisis came. Even he, though, would have been able to achieve little if he had been brought in. As power supplies began to be widely disrupted, and the union movement prepared for concerted political action against a hated government, it was hard to see how any Conservative – even one as notional as Powell – could have made a difference.

Powell was sufficiently good a politician, however, to realise that in its crisis the Government might, in the national interest, wish to adopt some of his remedies. Barber's latest policy turn seemed to prove this. He may also have been alert to Whitelaw's claim to take over once Heath was finally discredited, and was keen to maintain good personal relations with him. He wrote to the new Employment Secretary – who had direct responsibility for enforcing the counter-inflation policy – on 3 December to say, 'I am sad that, after having had to oppose for nearly two years the policy in pursuance of which you were Secretary of State for Northern Ireland, it is my ill-luck to have to oppose the counter-inflation policy of which you will now be in charge.'[117] He reminded Whitelaw he had done this because the policy was in direct contravention of the promises of 1970, and there was no prospect of his giving assistance until it was 'scrapped'. He concluded, 'Until then, I fear that my consent, though I would wish it to be at your disposal, would be unhelpful.' Whitelaw was too shrewd to rebut this act of comparative goodwill, and replied to Powell, 'I quite understand what you say generously and personally. There might however be occasions even in that context on which I might like to have a word with you and if so, I know that we can do so on a purely private basis. Thank you for writing as you have done.'[118] Events, though, were about to move faster than either expected.

On 18 December, the day after Barber's emergency Budget, the Commons debated the economic and energy crises. Powell was the first speaker called after Heath and Wilson. His intellectual authority was massive. It would never be greater than in what was to turn out to be his twilight as a Conservative MP, and it was generally recognised that he was the Government's most powerful critic. No one left the chamber when he rose. In a moment of what seemed like approaching political apocalypse, the mood could have no finer spokesman.

Powell admitted that the nation had been 'buffeted' by external forces – not that these had caused the inflation – but because of the general increasing scarcity of the goods Britain wished to import, notably oil, the country's terms of trade with the world had deteriorated. Having said that, he had a darker observation: 'The wounds from which this country is bleeding today have not been inflicted by an external enemy. They are self-inflicted wounds; they are what we have done to ourselves.'[119] The 'catastrophic' trade deficits, which had left the country so weak in the face of the recent crisis, were caused by the inflation the Government had been so unwilling to control. Worst of all, the industrial conflict that had set the seal on that crisis was the fruit of the inflation, and of the futile policies used to try to address it – as Powell had predicted.

He defended the miners. They were not, he said, in breach of the law, for stage 3 of the prices and incomes policy lacked the force of law. It was not binding on any citizen; it merely laid down principles with which the Pay Board and the Prices Commission would address cases brought before them. The cause of the disastrous conflict, he said unequivocally, was:

> the determination, incessantly repeated, of Her Majesty's Ministers that their interpretation of what can be extracted by logic from the interstices of the stage 3 price and pay code shall be the *ne plus ultra*, the law of the Medes and the Persians, and that nothing beyond that shall be regarded as in any way reconcilable with the national interest and the national salvation. It is in pursuit of the Ministers' interpretation of statutory control of wages that we have been brought into this conflict, the conflict of which the consequences are not merely before us but are bringing anxiety to every family in the country.[120]

Nor was that all. With Heath sitting a few feet away from him in a silent and tense Commons, Powell reminded the House of the Prime Minister's words of 1970: 'We utterly reject the philosophy of compulsory wage control.' Wilson, in his own speech, had said a Labour government would not repeat the mistakes it had made by having an incomes policy; so why on earth, Powell asked, was Heath so wedded to the idea? He reminded Heath that one of the main motivations the party had had in rejecting a prices and incomes policy in 1970 had been that it did not want to bring 'into the arena of direct conflict between Government and citizen every wage dispute, every bargain, every price and every wage that was fixed'. Powell alluded to Barber's measures of the previous day, and once more endorsed them. When the cry of 'U-turn' went up from some Labour MPs, Powell noted, 'It is not a U-turn for me.'[121] He admitted that, as a result of what Barber had done, there would be a price to pay in unemployment; but he concluded that the people would understand that the correct measures were being taken, and would support a period of stringency. It did not occur to him that there should be any political damage: there did not have to be an election for eighteen months.

IV

On Christmas Eve, more than halfway through his sixty-second year, Powell rode to hounds with the Fernie in Leicestershire, on a horse lent him by Reggie Paget, the Labour MP for Northampton. He had been out a couple of times since 1970, but otherwise had not hunted since 1951. He was twice thrown by his horse, a grey called Zebedee, and returned to Paget's house where the other guests, including the Labour MP Tom Driberg, observed that he was 'white and shaken': as an occasional rider, and at his age, he had found that the intense exertion of hunting was not so easy as it had once been.[122] He had taken his daughter Susan, a good horsewoman, with him, and after his second fall she had said to him, 'Now, Daddy, you go home, and don't come out hunting again.'[123] He took her advice. Once the press got hold of the story the Hunt put out a statement that said, patronisingly, 'It was very courageous of him, but he isn't quite up to Leicestershire standards.' While he was in the field the BBC broadcast a pre-recorded interview with him – to mark his being voted 'Man of the Year' by the *World at One*'s listeners for the second time running – in which he observed that there was, or should be, a limit to the number of U-turns a politician can make. He seemed – though he denied it – to be suggesting that Heath could step down to allow a reversal of the Government's policies, as changing policy by removing ministers was 'one of the beauties of our form of government'.[124]

   Just before New Year Powell left for Australia, to give a series of television interviews about what was happening in Britain. He felt no need to speak equivocally, saying that the Government's policies had led inexorably to the crisis at home, and that if only it had kept its earlier promises it would not be in so much trouble. Asked whether he had been surprised at a recent opinion poll that had shown him well ahead of Heath in public popularity, Powell replied that he seriously doubted whether anyone in Britain had been surprised; but it was of no practical importance to him, since it merely corresponded with what he knew were the realities. If this sounded like vanity, another remark seemed to suggest an unveiling of ambition. He was asked whether he was interested in trying to become leader of his party, to which he answered, 'In active practical politics any politician has to face the possibility that the roulette wheel might stop in front of him.'[125] Just before flying home from Sydney he was more exact, saying, 'Of course I would like to be Prime Minister. It's the nature of all politicians.' He also attacked Gough Whitlam, the Australian Prime Minister, for a comparison he had made between the regime in South Africa and that in Hitler's Germany. It was perhaps unsurprising, in that light, that Whitlam should decline the opportunity to meet Powell, whose lectures he had attended in Sydney thirty-five years earlier.

Once home, Powell found a Britain more deeply in crisis, and with talk rampant of a possible general election. At Derby on 8 January 1974 he said the country lay 'under the shadow of a tragedy. It is a tragedy of the Greek type, where the victim blindly brings disaster upon himself.'[126] He spoke, as he would often do in the weeks ahead, of the 'totally needless conflict' that would flare up over the 'bogus issue' of the prices and incomes policy. He called for the Government to 'have the courage to order the about-turn and extricate all classes from this dangerous cul-de-sac'. At the time, as he must have been aware from speculation in the newspapers, some of Heath's circle were counselling an election on 7 February. There was no hope of reversing the policy.

He went to Wolverhampton for some routine canvassing, unconnected with the prospect of an election, but part of his regular effort to keep in touch with his constituents. He found mischief being made as a result of reports that, contrary to his avowed policy of stopping the immigration of dependants, he had been doing all he could to help the families of three Pakistani constituents of his secure entry to Britain. Robin Pollard, Powell's agent, said this news was ironic 'only in the eyes of the misinformed', as Powell had a long record of helping in this way in cases of particular distress to his constituents. 'This', Pollard continued, 'is what makes us hopping mad when extremist types call him a racist.'[127] Even the local community relations officer was forced to agree that Powell had given 'humanitarian help' on several occasions known to him.

The mounting national crisis now took over Powell's whole political life. On 10 January the House was recalled early from the Christmas recess to debate the three-day working week that Heath, as a result of the energy shortages, had imposed on industry. Powell said the importance of the debate was to give counsel on where policy should lead in the future, and not to dwell on the past; but he added that, inevitably, some consideration of how matters had reached this pitch would be necessary. He said he raked up the past – particularly the Conservative party's abandonment of its promise to the electorate in 1970 to reject a prices and incomes policy – 'in no spirit of criticism or of recrimination', but because there were 'practical and important deductions' to be drawn from what had happened.'[128] The opposition to physical controls had not been purely theoretical, but had been based also on empirical evidence of the two experiments in the 1960s. By remembering this, Powell said, 'we understand that we are not the victims of unforeseen and unforeseeable accidents'.[129] What had happened was what could have been predicted – indeed, had been predicted by Powell – would happen. There could be no escape by blaming external factors, and the country should feel freed from needing to blame the perversity, greed or selfishness of a section of its fellow citizens.

The Conservatives, in 1970, had rejected such a policy as they now followed because it was 'irrelevant'; now, 'we have the grim satisfaction of seeing the realisation and verification of what we ourselves predicted'. However, a new element had been poured into the market-rigging concoction: the talk was all of 'relativities'. This was the notion of rewarding the miners with a relatively higher wage because of the unique nature of the job they did – the gradations which, in a free labour market, the laws of supply and demand took care of. The danger of 'relativities', as Powell pointed out, was that all sorts of trades could advance similar claims, and the relativities were unlikely to remain static. 'One cannot just assess the relative value of a miner and then walk away and leave it, in the hope that that will stay in exactly the same place.'[130] The oil crisis had, overnight, changed the relative values of many trades by changing their relative importance to the economy. In a dynamic economy, where relativities were constantly changing, no mechanism could exist or be contrived that could evaluate the different claims. 'It is', said Powell, 'beyond human imagination.' Only the markets, he maintained, could do it adequately. An early return to free negotiation was essential, and could no longer be prevented on the entirely spurious ground that it would cause inflation.

By the terms of his December financial statement, Barber had, as Powell affirmed, recognised the true cause of inflation. He concluded with a plea for the Government to do as he had advised, but he was not to know that, in the highest counsels of the party, the demonisation of the trade unions had taken the course of the problem far beyond the stage where such a recognition would be possible. Later in the debate, a Conservative backbencher, David Crouch, praised Powell for having 'stuck to his guns' on the prices and incomes policy, a sign that Heath's authority was diminishing in his own party in Parliament. Powell pulled him up: 'In fact, I have stuck to our guns.'[131]

Over the next few days, Powell became more aware of the leadership's real agenda. On 15 January he at last spoke, or rather let out a thunderclap of outrage, about the election rumours. He issued a statement in which he said that to call a poll would be 'an act of total immorality'. He added that 'its sole purpose would be to obtain a larger parliamentary majority and an extended lease of office by false pretences'.[132] He went on to explain himself.

> The Government know perfectly well that, in order to cope with the rising inflation and disastrous trade balance, it is indispensable to budget for a severe increase in taxation and a further reduction in the rate of growth of public

expenditure. They have the majority and the authority to do this now. They do not need an election in order to act in the national interest.

Nor do they need an election to get the country back to full-time work. Neither the miners nor the other trade unions have broken the law or threatened to break it. There is nothing sacrosanct about stage 3 or the Government's interpretations of it. A settlement will have to be found in the mining industry – and in every other industry – which will get the necessary labour into the necessary jobs.

That last point opened up Powell to the old criticisms that he misunderstood what the unions were trying to do. Allowing a market solution in the coal industry, and in many other unionised industries, would first require union reforms of the order of those implemented by the Thatcher Government ten years later, for the unions were not now interested in a market solution, if they ever had been. They were interested, under the emerging influence of regional NUM bosses like Arthur Scargill, in having a political fight with the Government: a fight Heath would shortly be sufficiently foolish to agree to have with them.

Powell's statement continued:

It would be fraudulent – or worse – to fight an election on the cry of 'Who governs the country?' when the Government's first action after the poll would have to be to scrap the irrelevant and impracticable stage 3 and deal with inflation at its source, in the Government's own management of the economy. It is unworthy of British politics, and dangerous to parliament itself, for a Government to try to steal success by telling the public one thing during an election and doing the opposite afterwards.

'Fraudulent' was the adjective that would dominate Powell's thinking and public statements in the weeks ahead. It did not matter whether or not the assumption on which he had built his statement – that Heath would scrap stage 3 if he was returned to office – was accurate. What Powell had done, wittingly or unwittingly, was provide his party with the means of getting rid of him. For the unequivocal language of the statement left no one in any doubt that, if such an election were called, Powell would be unable to fight it as a Conservative. Since he had been aware for some months that by the summer of 1974 he would have to make a judgment on just that point – and his view had increasingly been that it was unlikely he could stand as a Conservative again – for Heath to call an election in such circumstances would provide him with an appropriately dramatic and principled reason for going.

On 16 January he had hinted as much to Pollard during a telephone conversation, and Pollard wrote to him to say that what he had told him had 'perturbed me considerably'.[133] He reminded Powell of a promise earlier not to do anything that would embarrass the association, and added, 'I fear that if you did not stand as a candidate at the last minute this would place the Association in an incredibly difficult position ... I would have thought, and hoped, that you could stand on the basis that *you* were upholding *Conservative* principles, *whatever* the rest of the Party was doing.' Pollard told him that his entreaty was 'sincere and impassioned', and 'from the point of view of the country and your *public* life, you can't and must not give up'. Powell was left in no doubt that, if he did perform what would apparently be the ultimate act of quixotry, he would be letting an awful lot of people down.

His sense of destiny had, however, already taken over. By the time he received Pollard's letter he had prepared a statement, dated 17 January 1974, in the form of a letter to Wilkes explaining why he would not be standing at the coming election, and expecting Wilkes not to be surprised by the news. He said that it was 'impossible to ask the electorate to endorse the opposite policies to those on which, along with all other Conservative candidates, I was elected in 1970'.[134] Had the Parliament run its full course, that objection might have changed. His other one would not, though – that the Government had taken the country into the EEC without the consent of the people. It was no wonder some of his activists would feel there was no excuse for his having left things to the last moment; but this particular letter was not sent, as the election was not called.

Powell had discussed his position with some of his closest political allies, including John Biffen and Nicholas Ridley. He had also, it seems, hinted at his wife's misgivings at the course he was preparing to take. Ridley described their talk in a letter to Pam Powell on 15 January: 'Enoch has discussed with us his decision for the future, if there is a General Election. It was a most moving occasion, but after some thought I am sure he has taken the right decision – at least the only decision which would allow him to be at peace with himself, and perhaps the decision which gives him the best chance to fulfil his life's ambition, too.'[135] Ridley assured her, 'I thought he was right,' and asked her 'not to feel other than that this may be an essential step in his brilliant political career ... we will be able to keep the cause alive, and we will never forget or abandon you.'

On the evening of 15 January, Powell agreed to a television interview in which he was questioned by Robin Day about his motives for issuing his statement about the 'fraudulent' election. 'I felt it was something that had to be said,' he replied.[136] Asked whether he was not deliberately trying to sabotage Heath, he protested that he was merely trying to stop an election being held on a 'fraudulent' basis. He clarified what he meant: that the Government knew the only solution was to regain control of public finance, and wished to 'get off the hook of an absurd and impracticable prices and incomes policy'. He admitted he still wanted to be leader of his party; and he would not commit himself to say that, when the election came, he would campaign for the return of a government led by Heath. When Day asked him, 'Do you want to see Mr Heath defeated?' he replied, 'That will depend upon the policies which Mr Heath and the Conservative Party are standing for at the time.' According to Peter Clarke, Powell's secretary, Powell received at least one emissary from Heath at this time asking what his price was in return for his silence. Clarke believes that Betty Harvie Anderson, a friend of the Powells and a deputy speaker, was asked by Heath to suggest that Powell might like to be ambassador to Washington: a bizarre suggestion, and one, if it was made, Powell had no intention of acting upon, and which he did not relay to his wife.[137]

Two days later Powell had been expected to address the South-East Essex Conservative Association at a meeting in Rayleigh. On a cold evening 450 turned out to hear him at an all-ticket occasion. Instead, they sat in stunned silence while their chairman, Rodney Smith, read out to them a letter the local MP and former under-secretary of Powell's, Bernard Braine, had just received from the expected guest of honour. The letter said:

> In view of the possible imminence of a general election and the fact that I have thought it right publicly and forcibly to condemn such a course were it adopted, I am sure it would be unfair to both you and to your association if, just at this juncture, I were to address the public meeting which your association has done me the honour to arrange for this evening. I hope that this will be understood by those who will have paid me the compliment of being present; and I am glad to think that so many will have the opportunity to hear from you yourself your views and advice on the nation's present predicament.[138]

Powell was immensely fond of Braine, who had been an exemplary colleague a decade earlier, and reassured him that 'nothing can happen to weaken the ties of affection and respect between you and me'. Braine loyally defended Powell to the meeting, noting that 'whatever can be said about him by his critics, he had got Conservatives and the Government going on the issues that he has raised'.

However, it seemed three days later that Powell was beginning to reserve his position. In a speech in Wolverhampton he made a gesture of support for the beleaguered Government. He said he had a duty to give 'loyal encouragement' to the party and would continue to 'speak, vote and act for the Conservatives'.[139] He reminded his constituents how he had cheered Barber's emergency Budget the previous month, and added, 'It was nothing to be surprised at for your Member to say to the Chancellor and the Government, "Carry on, we are with you." ' He did, though, give a warning to those who 'think first of the political consequences and only after of the nation'; and in a letter to *The Times* on 21 January he made the eccentric point that his pledges of support for the Conservatives 'were made in the context of the policies announced by the Chancellor on December 17'. So, once more, it seemed he was keeping open the option not to support his party after all. His position had not changed: he was standing by what his party had stated in its 1970 manifesto, even though his party appeared to have changed its mind without any reference to the electorate.

On 23 January he spoke to the Overseas Women's Club in Bloomsbury of the consequences of the 'non-event' of the 'on–off' election of the previous week. Fleet Street was watching Powell vigilantly: some of the leading political commentators were sent to watch this apparently routine performance, and to dissect it for hidden meanings. They did not have to look too closely. Heath had, the previous day, dismissed talk of an election as something got up by Labour: a manifest untruth. Mentioning the intensive briefing of the press by the Government at that period, Powell derided the scene that had been painted: 'the remarkable picture of a Prime Minister who had never come within miles of wanting to call an election but had manfully and in the end successfully resisted almost intolerable pressure on him to do so'.[140] This picture Powell described as 'bunkum'. Only Heath could have called an election, and 'no Prime Minister would carry preparations for dissolution to the point which was reached last week as a mere feint or tactical manoeuvre in a cabinet tussle or an external confrontation, because the recoil when the bluff was called would be so disastrous'.

He said the nation had, in that week, stood on the edge of a precipice. 'One step further, the one step that was not taken, would have plunged it into a political conflict upon lines which would have created the maximum division and animosity between one class and another in order to approve policies which all concerned knew to be impracticable and about to be abandoned by their own authors.' He said the step back from the precipice would mean the end of one-man government, and the return of cabinet government; but that in itself would not be enough. The Government had to act with the consent of the people – such as it manifestly had not over Europe – and Powell said that as the prospect of economic and monetary union by 1980 was looking daily more and more 'chimerical', it might as well take the opportunity to amend that policy and move back to a position to which the people would consent.

He outlined what would have to be done for Heath to recover his and the party's position: a rise in taxation, an increase in unemployment and a slow-down or stop in economic growth; and even then prices would rise for a while longer. It had to be accepted, as he had said all along, that the anti-inflation policy of the preceding fifteen months had made no difference at all. He ended on a note of hope for the country, and for his party. There was nothing 'fundamentally rotten in the economic state of Britain'. The Government had caused a problem; the Government could cure it. By blaming others, notably the unions, it had created divisions where none need have existed. 'Suddenly, unexpectedly, the fiasco of the last ten days has created the opportunity to start afresh. Not by means of an election but through what is seen to be the impossibility of an election, the Government is being obliged to face the nation again and to win from it the consent which is indispensable.' They would be the last conciliatory words Powell would speak before the breach. As Richard Ritchie put it, his belief that Heath would not be so foolish as to go to the country, and that the Conservatives would have the opportunity of a fifth year in office to start to correct some of the mistakes made since 1970, was an example of Powell's wishful thinking getting the better of his judgment.[141] He felt his statement had stopped the election, but it is more likely to have provoked Heath to think that the right course was to call one.

Now that it was clear – or so he thought – that there would be no election, Powell resumed his routine of speaking to Conservative associations. Expecting that Heath would be vulnerable to pressure to change policies, there was no reason for Powell not to spend the weeks and months ahead exerting it. After all, he had had some conspicuous successes in altering the economic attitudes in the high command in the months beforehand. On 2 February he went to Newham in east London and said that if the miners were given a large wage increase that would mean less, not more, for everybody else, unless the Government chose to expand the money supply still further; if the Government did not do that, there was no certainty of other unions being so fortunate. As soon as Powell had spoken, Heath's supporters briefed the press that, once more, Powell had shown no signs of knowing what he would do if other unions did not follow the example of his logic, but instead engaged in acts of political militancy: one of the few charges they could, at the time, almost make stick on him. He would retort that the political militancy would not have been provoked had not the workers had inflicted upon them the iniquity of a prices and incomes policy in the first place.

On what became the eve of the end of the 1970 Parliament, Barber found himself in the Commons attempting to defend the Government's conduct of its industrial and economic policy. It was a speech which, helped by savage interventions from both sides, was marked by the Chancellor's now customary lack of intellectual command. At a fatal moment, Barber was trapped by the Labour MP Bob Sheldon into confirming that the general increase in prices was inflationary whereas the increase in oil prices had been deflationary. Powell could stand it no more: well aware that Barber, and not the price of oil or the price of food, had caused the inflation, he interrupted to ask: 'Could my right hon Friend explain why the increase in oil prices is deflationary but the increase in all other international prices has apparently been inflationary?'[142]

Tony Benn, in his diary, reported Barber to have been 'completely floored' by Powell.[143] Certainly, Barber's answer, as given by Hansard, is of dramatic economic illiteracy and literally meaningless – 'the consequence of the staggering increase in oil prices at present will be to put up prices in this country' – and it did nothing to appease the growing claque around Powell who felt they had had enough. Nicholas Ridley, who was sitting by Powell, asked the question again a few moments later, and Barber gave the same non-monetarist answer. This time the uproar could hardly be contained. According to another Conservative backbencher of opposite sympathies, Julian Critchley, Powell seemed at the end of his tether. 'Then Enoch again half-rose to his feet and with a sweep of his arms cried loudly "imbecility, imbecility" (his Black Country intonation was very obvious) in the general direction of the Government front bench' – remarks not recorded by Hansard.[144] Critchley adds that Powell was pulled down by Ridley, just before Spencer le Marchant, 'a very large Tory whip' according to Critchley, but in fact then just a backbencher, was about to bear down on him 'presumably to sort him out'.

For Heath, the situation was becoming increasingly desperate. He could not persuade the miners to desist from their strike. He referred their case for a rise to yet another interventionist body, the Relativities Board, which he chose to establish as a means of arbitrating their claim. However, the pressure for him from his closest advisers to call an election became irresistible; and on 6 February he asked the Queen – by telegram as she was in New Zealand – for a dissolution of Parliament. She wired back overnight granting it. After a ninety-minute cabinet meeting on the morning of 7 February the announcement was made: the election would be on 28 February.

V

Heath's theme for the campaign was, he announced, to be 'Firm action for a Fair Britain'. He was not prepared, as Powell would have liked, to take any of the blame for the crisis himself. In a ministerial broadcast justifying his action, he said the election would allow the people to elect a government that would be 'in a far stronger position to reach a settlement with the miners which safeguards your interests as well as theirs'. In a reference to the communist Mick McGahey, vice-president of the NUM, he said: 'There are some people involved in the mining dispute who have made it clear that what they want is to bring down the elected government – not just this Government but any government. They have made it clear they want to change our whole democratic way of life.' Then, in a passage that would look ironic in the light of events, Heath said that the electorate was 'fed up to the teeth' with the miners; and the election 'gives you the chance to make it clear to these people how you feel'.[145]

By the time Heath went on television to make his address that evening, Powell had already put the first of several personal torpedoes through the Conservative battleship. As soon as he had heard the news of Heath's decision earlier that day he had been shocked, but had realised that the decision for which he had prepared was now forced upon him, much to his and particularly his wife's distress – 'It really was awful,' she recalled. 'I was horrified. I felt quite sick.'[146] A new letter was drafted to Wilkes, as chairman of his association, and copied to Pollard. Powell sent his secretary, Peter Clarke, by train to Wolverhampton to deliver them in person; he did so at 5.45 p.m. that day. The letter told Wilkes he would not be standing in the election for the Conservative party and had 'no intention of standing otherwise', because the election Heath had called was 'an act of gross irresponsibility' and 'essentially fraudulent', for the reasons he had outlined in his statement of 15 January. 'The object of those who have called it [the election] is to secure the electorate's approval for a position which the Government itself knows to be untenable, in order to make it easier to abandon that position subsequently. It is unworthy of British politics, and dangerous to parliament itself, for a Government to try to steal success by telling the public one thing during an election and doing the opposite afterwards.'

There was, of course, the wider point, to which Powell had been building up ever since the last election: 'Obviously – and I am sure this will not surprise you – I personally cannot ask electors to vote for policies which are directly opposite to those which we all stood for in 1970, and which I have myself consistently condemned as being inherently impracticable and bound to create the very difficulties in which the nation now finds itself.' He had known for some time he would not be able to stand once the election was called; he had hoped for more time to make and announce his decision, but now his hand had been forced. Wilkes, faced with trying to find a candidate within ten days to fight the seat, took the blow well, though confessed 'it came as a complete shock': which was not the gloss he later put on it, having felt for some weeks that Powell would act in this way. He added: 'We had no inkling Mr Powell was going to make the decision. It has left us in a dilemma. It is going to be a hard slog during the election.' Pollard said it was 'a tragedy'. Nietzsche had given the obvious warning: 'He who thinks much is not suited to be a party member: too soon, he thinks himself through and beyond the party.'[147] Powell knew, and proclaimed, that party was essential to British politics; but it was never going to be suitable for such a free spirit, and such an anti-collectivist, as he.

Back in London, the news having seeped out, the press were after Powell. Before the letter had reached Wolverhampton, Fleet Street had been alerted by a wise House of Commons policeman; he had seen Pam Powell, whom he had known for twenty years, and wished her good luck. She had turned to him and said 'we don't need good luck this time', and left in some distress. 'It was,' she recalled, 'the most terrible thing, politically speaking, that I have ever felt.'[148] Another policeman was reported to have seen Powell, his eyes 'misted over with tears', that morning. The wrench for a man who had identified himself with the institution of parliament was immense. Powell had not gone back into the Commons that afternoon, once he had heard of the election, and where Heath was loudly cheered when he entered the chamber. Nor did he attend the meeting of the 1922 Committee that evening, where strong speeches of support for Heath were made. Powell took care to tell some of his close friends the news before they heard it on the television. Bee Carthew, for example, was summoned for a grim interview, the air heavy with misery. She implored him to form his own party; but Powell told her 'it doesn't work like that'.[149] Andrew Alexander, who also called round that evening, had picked up a hint from Powell of what he intended, and had tried and failed to talk him out of it; but then it was a conversation they had had several times in the preceding two years.[150] Richard Ritchie was entirely unsurprised by Powell's decision; from conversations the two men had had, he knew Powell would simply be unable to stand.[151] Jim Molyneaux had seen Powell, in the distance, leaving the Commons that evening. He had no idea what had happened; had he known, he would have told Powell there and then that a seat could have been found for him in Ulster. It was a cause Molyneaux would address in the next few days.[152]

Eventually the Powells turned up in their car at South Eaton Place, to find reporters waiting. 'There will be no interviews,' Powell told them. 'No further statements. Remember, I am the man who keeps his word.' Mrs Powell, following him in, turned round and said: 'Yes. This is the man who keeps his promises.'[153] Heath, interviewed on television, said he was unconcerned by Powell's decision not to fight. 'That is only a matter for Mr Powell. It doesn't cause any surprise to me. He has been out of sympathy with so much of the Conservative policy and so much of the Conservative party. He is out of sympathy with nearly everyone in the House of Commons.' Later in the year, when he had found his road back to Westminster, Powell said the experience of resignation 'was like descending into hell. ... But I rose again.'[154] It was intensely hard for his wife, a loyal Conservative since long before her days in the Secretariat. It was unclear where the Powells would go from there. Wolverhampton had been everything to him; he had devoted a quarter-century of his life to it, and was grateful to it for allowing him the honour and – as it was in those days – the distinction of being a Conservative MP. The break was anything but casually made. A telegram arrived that evening from Peter Farmer, the President of the Wolverhampton association, 'urgently requesting' Powell's attendance.[155] The reply read: 'Nothing to add to my letter to George, which is final – Powell'.[156] Robin Pollard rang, even before Clarke had arrived in Wolverhampton, and offered to meet Powell at a service station on the M1 to discuss the possibility of his changing his mind; but Pam Powell, who spoke to him, told him it was too late.[157] When Clarke handed over the letter such had been the state of shock in Wolverhampton that Pollard and Wilkes even suggested that he should be the candidate, as he could stand aside when Powell wished to return; but Clarke told them Powell would not be returning.

Other Conservative MPs went around that evening telling journalists: 'Enoch is doing a de Gaulle'. Their instinctive belief was that Powell simply wanted to step aside, to a position where he would be unsullied by party politics, available in the future should the nation send for him: it was not a conception of himself that Powell shared. For him, the decision had been far more visceral, and had nothing to do with long-term strategy. He made a point of rejecting entreaties to stand as an independent, or to form his own party. He also rejected pleas from many of his former colleagues – and not just Conservatives, for Michael Foot was one – to beg him to reconsider. Foot rang him on the evening of 7 February to say 'courageous, magnificent – but reckless.'[158] Some of those, like Jock Bruce-Gardyne, who had supported Powell through thick and thin, felt both amazed and let down. After the election, Bruce-Gardyne quickly forgave Powell, and joined the circle of those who most closely advised him – Biffen, Ronnie Bell and Neil Marten principal among them – who called themselves 'the Privy Council'.[159] Biffen remained loyal throughout, despite disquiet from some of his constituents who knew him as 'a Powell man'. 'But Enoch did not believe in having friends in politics. He believed in causes and ideas,' was how Jonathan Aitken analysed his actions.[160] Alan Clark, who would successfully contest a seat at the election, sent a telegram saying, 'Congratulations Enoch on your courage and honesty. You will have all our loyalty when the call comes.'[161]

For the moment, he did not even accept any speaking engagements. Word went round that there were various candidates who would, if elected, stand aside for him the moment he wished to return. As news of his decision sank in, there was recognition in the press, even from some who had hitherto found reasons to criticise him, that the party was losing (as the *Telegraph* put it) 'one of its finest brains and most gripping speakers'.[162] More than two years later, Powell would tell a Conservative audience of what had motivated him at this time: 'For me the Conservative party ceased to be the Conservative party which I knew and to whose causes my political life had been devoted. It became an incomprehensible stranger to me.'[163] The size of his sacrifice can, in one respect, be judged from the fact that while the respective popularities of Heath and Wilson had risen and fallen over the preceding six years, Powell's approval rating with the public had remained steady at 41 per cent.[164]

He had no intention of pussyfooting around. It seemed to him a matter of national urgency that Heath was removed from office and replaced by someone who could re-open the question of British membership of the EEC; and he intended to do all he could to bring that about. Andrew Alexander, by now a *Daily Mail* political commentator, had a telephone call from Powell, who asked him to come to South Eaton Place. Powell told Alexander he felt it would be useful if contact were made with Wilson's office, to discuss the timing of Powell's intended assault against Heath.[165] Alexander made contact with Joe Haines, Wilson's Press Secretary. Haines was intrigued; but the two men agreed it was important for Wilson and Powell to know what each other intended to say.

Wilson, for his part, was under no illusion about the value Powell could bring to his campaign, provided he was used at arm's length. It was agreed that speeches would be co-ordinated. The co-operation was not so surprising to either party as it might seem. Powell had been talking unofficially to Wilson on and off since June the previous year, and in the most unofficial of places; in the gentlemen's lavatory in the Aye lobby of the House of Commons. Powell told Wilson's biographer, Ben Pimlott, that 'our contacts were incidental rather than by assignment . . . there were half a dozen meetings with Wilson in the loo.'[166] It is further evidence that Powell realised he would have to break with his party long before Heath called his 'fraudulent' election, and his main motivation was Labour's plan to re-negotiate British terms of entry into the EEC.

There was, however, an immediate distraction from the Powell–Wilson plan to finish Heath. On 9 February there were press reports that Powell had been given assurances by Ulster Unionists that, if he wished to have a safe seat in the Province immediately, and leadership of the Unionist coalition after the election, he would be welcomed with open arms. Substantiating the story, several prominent Unionists were quoted in the reports saying Powell was their man. The view was, though, that he would not choose what the *Guardian* called 'the traditional graveyard of Irish politics' when he still had ambitions of leading the Conservatives: the story went away.[167] However, Powell left a contemporary note of a conversation with Molyneaux on the evening of Sunday 10 February, in which he said he had authorised Molyneaux 'confidentially to state on my behalf in response to enquiries from authoritative sources that, only if the "loyal" Ulster Unionists invited me to be their leader and to represent them at Westminster, would I be prepared to consider any approach from Northern Ireland. In the event of that condition being fulfilled, I would think it my duty to give serious consideration to such an invitation, but this did not imply that I would necessarily accept it.'[168] The condition of being leader was not pure vanity on Powell's part: 'Having declined to stand as a Conservative candidate on the grounds stated, I would need to be in personal control of the grounds and policy on which I might otherwise stand for Parliament in present circumstances,' he noted. However, the Unionists had the previous day chosen Harry West as their leader, so there was no vacancy.

Meanwhile, symbolic of the breach her husband had irrevocably made, Pam Powell went quietly to Wolverhampton one day with Ted Curtis, constant in his support of his old friend. The house in Merridale Road had recently suffered three burglaries, they emptied it of its material and sentimental valuables. Powell never set foot in it again. The National Front's chairman, John Tyndall, sent Powell a letter – which appears to be in earnest – inviting Powell to be the party's candidate in Wolverhampton South-West.[169] Powell referred Tyndall to his letter to Wilkes, in which he had said he had no intention of contesting the election for any other party.

For a fortnight Powell said nothing in public, except to preach the sermon on 17 February at his local church, St Peter's Eaton Square, about 'suffering and sacrifice'. He took as his text Matthew, Chapter 14, verse 15, the prelude to the feeding of the five thousand: 'And when it was evening his disciples came to him, saying, this is a desert place, and the time is now past; send the multitude away, and they may go into the villages and buy themselves victuals. But Jesus said unto them, they need not depart; give ye them to eat.' Powell refuted the interpretation put on this passage that it meant the disciples wanted to send the five thousand away, but Christ wanted them fed. What in fact was the case, he said, was that the disciples had proposed an economic way of feeding them – 'they wanted the people to spread out and not force up the price by converging on the nearest village', whereas Christ had decided to perform a miracle. Powell said the passage highlighted the contrast 'between the normal or mundane and the miraculous'.[170]

He went on to argue that if the feeding of the five thousand were to be an example others should imitate, they should know that the miracle Christ performed was to feed them with his own body. 'If we mean seriously what we are saying when we talk about imitating Christ, it is his being crucified and nothing less – for that is the basis of the miracle which we are called to imitate.' Powell outlined how medieval thinkers, in particular, had identified being slain with working miracles. Whenever Christ said 'follow me,' the signpost on the road led to Calvary. 'In order to follow him we are to "take up our cross", which can only mean that we too are to go along the Via Dolorosa. It is our "marked route".' Powell's conclusion was that 'for us also suffering is the supreme form of action. More changes are wrought, and greater miracles performed, by what men allow others to do to them than by anything they do to others.' He received a letter at that time from Milton Friedman, in a remarkably similar vein: 'Congratulations on the stand you have taken,' his fellow monetarist told him.

It is a pleasure for a change to have principle and not expediency triumph. The situation as a whole is a tragedy but you surely have no responsibility for that, and you are surely doing the right and proper thing by refusing to go along with a policy so utterly misguided and so utterly disastrous in its long-run consequences. No one can look very far down the line at the consequences of these developments. That is precisely why principle is sometimes a far better guide than imperfect foresight.[171]

In a less high-minded vein, some of his British supporters were active on what they thought was his behalf, without his knowledge. An Essex farmer, L. H. Lambert, from a body calling itself the Council of Associated Conservative Groups, had had printed 150,000 leaflets quoting Powell's views on the irresponsibility of the election, and was about to distribute them: their message was that Conservatives should abstain from voting in the 'phoney election'. Lambert was a Monday Club activist, but refused to reveal his backers because of the 'witch hunt' he said was being conducted in the party. The leaflet warned that 'a Conservative vote is not a vote for Conservative policies ... NO VOTE IS A VOTE FOR POWELL, FOR DEMOCRACY, FOR BRITAIN.'[172] Lambert added, 'We believe that those who, in the past, have assumed that the Heath Government is the lesser of two evils, will now accept the logic of Mr Powell's action by refusing to support a Government devoted to policies which are Conservative and which have resulted in a divided nation. The time has arrived for all Conservatives and British patriots to demonstrate support for Mr Powell and to register their protest by using the ultimate weapon of democracy – the absent vote.'[173]

The week after he made his decision Powell gave an interview, under a strict embargo, to William Buckley, the American conservative with whom he had held a public dialogue on an earlier visit to America. The interview was not to be broadcast, or its contents revealed, before 24 February. Meanwhile, he was brooding on how to enter the campaign at home. On 20 February he finally motioned that he would break his silence; some of his former colleagues had advanced the theory that by ceasing to be a 'player' Powell would cease to have any influence: an assertion whose manifest wrongness he was determined to prove. To the horror of Heath's circle, who had hoped his self-denying ordinance would last until after the election, he agreed to speak at two rallies organised by the cross-party 'Get Britain Out' campaign. He had been invited on 11 February, and had spent a week weighing up whether or not to do so. His former colleagues were appalled by the posters produced to advertise the rallies, which stated that 'the real enemy of the country is the obsession of one man, Edward Heath. His sole aim is that Britain shall become the province of a European superstate,' and claimed that Labour now spoke for the majority.[174] The first rally would be in Birmingham on the Saturday before the election; the second the following Monday, less than sixty hours before the polls opened, at Saltaire near Shipley in Yorkshire. In public, the Conservatives maintained their insouciance about what Powell might say, the official line being that he was free to speak for whomever he liked. In private they now realised that, although Powell had not wanted the election, Heath had called it, and Powell would use it to reopen the greatest wound of all. He would make the Common Market an issue, and an issue that should prevent people voting Conservative.

To confirm these fears the chairman of the anti-market campaign, Christopher Frere-Smith, said that 'so far this election campaign has been a bore, lacking an element of excitement. Now it will get a new dimension. It would have been an extraordinary election if Mr Powell had not taken part. I think he will have a major influence. It is obvious that Mr Powell thinks the real issue is not the miners but who rules Britain, Brussels or Westminster?' The element of excitement was an understatement: what Powell might or might not say at Birmingham on 23 February started to take on huge significance. There was a growing fear among Conservatives that, if he chose to do so, he could lose the party the election. Had they known that Joe Haines and Wilson had cleared the decks to allow Powell a clear run and to dominate the Sunday and Monday papers with his assault on Heath, that fear would have become a conviction.

Powell had an audience of 1,500 (some of whom had queued for six hours to get in) when he spoke in the incongruous setting of the Mecca Dance Hall in the Bull Ring at Birmingham. Thousands more – some press reports suggested up to 7,000 – had to be turned away.[175] It was a marvellously anachronistic phenomenon: Powell proving by the force of his personality that the received wisdom at the end of the political meeting as a thing of importance in the television age was not, in his case, true. That day there was no high-profile speech by a Labour front-bencher – the fruit of Powell's co-operation with Wilson – so nothing would detract from or interfere with his own attack on Heath. Powell entered the hall to a predictably enthusiastic standing ovation, and the press were glad to note that, among those ovating, were brutish-looking youths wearing National Front insignia. 'Not being a candidate in the present election,' he began,

> I have not thought it proper to put forward once again my views on the immediate circumstances in which the election was called, or the issues on which those who called it hoped that the outcome would exclusively turn. I will only observe that nothing has transpired in the last 15 days to rescue from the charge of fraud an appeal to the public in terms of 'who governs the country', when neither the law has been broken nor the lawful administration defied, and when the Government's embarrassments are the direct consequence of policies adopted in contravention of its own philosophy and promises.[176]

He did not, though, see why this silence should extend to Europe, a matter the Government was as careful to keep from the electorate in 1974 as it had been in 1970. It was, he said, an issue 'on which if there be a conflict between the call of the country and that of party, the call of country must come first'. He then turned Heath's rhetoric back on him:

> Curiously, it so happens that the question 'Who governs Britain?', which at the moment is being frivolously posed, might be taken, in real earnest, as the title of what I have to say. This is the first and last election at which the British people will be given the opportunity to decide whether their country is to remain a democratic nation, governed by the will of its own electorate expressed in its own parliament, or whether it will become one province in a new Europe superstate under institutions which know nothing of political rights and liberties that we have so long taken for granted.

Powell repeated his objection to the commitment Heath had made to economic and monetary union by 1980, as it had not been approved by Parliament; and he noted that there was no mention of it in the brief passage on the EEC in the Conservative manifesto, even though the decision to join would have to be ratified in the next Parliament if the deadline were to be met. 'So here we have the most far-reaching and revolutionary act of policy that can be imagined – and the Conservative party does not think it necessary to tell the electorate, let alone seek the electorate's approval.' He suggested various unlikely reasons for this omission – such as oversight, or a fit of modesty on Heath's part – before telling his audience why Heath had left it out: 'It was suppressed because everybody knew that the electors would detest it if they were allowed to know about it.' This, he said, was consistent with the whole story of Britain's affairs with Europe, 'one long epic of deception' ever since 1970.

He rehearsed his old charges against Heath: the betrayal of the 1970 manifesto, the meaningless promise of 'full-hearted consent' of Parliament and people, the blind acceptance of membership on whatever terms Europe had chosen to offer. He railed against the 'so-called Liberal party' for allowing Heath to get through the House the guillotines that truncated discussion on the Bill. Yet it was Heath, as so often before, who bore the main attack.

> This is the party leader who, on the basis of a few defaulting town councillors at Clay Cross and some foolish utterances by a union official, is heard accusing his political opponents of lacking respect for parliament and the law. It is a savage irony, and not the less so for being unconscious, that these taunts come from the first Prime Minister in 300 years who entertained, let alone executed, the intention of depriving parliament of its sole right to make the laws and impose the taxes of the country and who then, without either electoral or parliamentary authority, took it upon himself to commit this country to economic and monetary unification with eight other nations of Western Europe before the lifetime of the forthcoming parliament is out.

Powell said Heath would never trust the electors with having to decide so important a question, not least because they might reach the opposite decision to his own. The question instead, therefore, was whether the people could be prevented 'from taking back into their own hands the decision about their identity and their form of government which truly was theirs all along'. Powell was in no doubt that they could not be prevented, and it was here he made the final breach with his party:

> They are now, at a general election, provided with a clear, definite and practicable alternative, namely, a fundamental renegotiation directed to regain free access to world food markets and recover or retain the powers of parliament, a renegotiation to be followed in any event by a specific submission of the outcome to the electorate, a renegotiation protected by an immediate moratorium or stop on all further integration of the United Kingdom into the Community. The alternative is offered, as such an alternative must be in our parliamentary democracy, by a political party capable of securing a majority in the House of Commons and sustaining a government.

He spoke of the hundreds of letters he had had since he stood down, imploring him to stand as an independent or to found his own party. As he did so, order at the meeting temporarily broke down, with chanting of 'Enoch, Enoch' from those who had wanted him to lead them. However, he said such people were under a misconception.

> Politics and parliament in this country are about party. Without party neither responsible government nor responsible democracy is possible. If the electors went to the polls to select just 635 good men and true, there would be no correspondence between government and electorate, no means of calling the executive to account, no means of intimating the direction in which public opinion was moving, no means of maintaining intelligent and realistic political debate in the interval between one election and the next. For parliamentary government, as for every other good thing, there is a price to be paid: and that price is party.

He did not use the words 'vote Labour'. There was no need. Reaffirming that Labour offered the chance of reconsidering Britain's membership of the Community, he ended: 'If that for us is the overriding issue – and how it could be less, I do not understand – then we have a clear national duty to help to decide it in the only way of which parliamentary representation admits. We shall be deceiving ourselves, and running away from what we know to be our country's cause, if we try to find some excuse or subterfuge to sacrifice the greater good for the lesser, or the lasting for the transitory.' Taking questions, Powell was asked how the country could be rid of 'that confidence trickster, Heath'. He replied: 'If you want to do it, you can.'

This was strong stuff, even for many of Powell's most devout supporters, for whom the spectre of socialism was worse even than the spectre of Brussels. But that was not how Powell saw it. They had respected his decision not to fight, however much it shocked them, but the clear implication of this speech, that those who felt like Powell did should vote Labour, started to arouse in some of his followers feelings of betrayal. It was widely and immediately seen that his turn against the Conservative party made it impossible for him ever to rejoin it, let alone become its leader. Above all, the consequences of his actions were clear to him. From those in the dance hall, though, he received a thunderous ovation: they needed no persuading he was right.

The Conservative leadership, in private in some cases as well as in public, maintained that Powell's intervention would do nothing to prevent them being returned with an increased majority the following Thursday. As far as they were concerned the villains of the piece were the miners, and Labour – for whom Powell seemed to be urging the public to vote – were the miners' friends. It was as simple as that. The splash headline in the following Monday's *Daily Telegraph* summed up the blinkered complacency of the high command: 'Heath still confident of victory'.[177] There was a further complication for Heath in the form of a surge of support for the Liberals. A Marplan poll completed on the day Powell broke his silence showed the Conservatives ahead with 38.5 per cent, Labour with 31.5 per cent, and the Liberals with 28, a 10.6 point rise for the third party in a week. As for the EEC issue Heath, interviewed while strolling in the grounds at Chequers the day after Powell spoke, said that 'the plain fact is that people have accepted the Community and that's that'.

Powell's interview with Bill Buckley, shown in America on 24 February, was extensively reported in the British press, and (although mainly about economic theory) constituted the first transparent statement he had made explaining his actions of a fortnight earlier. He said, as was obvious, that he could not have endorsed policies to which he had been so opposed, particularly the prices and incomes policy. So it seemed that even if Heath had not called the 'fraudulent' election, but had gone when his mandate had run out, Powell would not have been able to stand unless policies had changed. Asked why he had not declared reservations about aspects of policy, but stood anyway, he replied, 'It would result in my own moral and intellectual self-destruction. A man can't stand up at the election and say: 'I disagree with the very issue on which this election is being fought – I think it is an absurdity – but nevertheless vote for me as an official Conservative candidate." '[178] He said that, in the circumstances that had faced him, 'I found myself confronted with the proposition that I should act in a way in which I found it impossible to act and so I said: "I won't." I hadn't expected it but it happened, so I said "Well, whatever else, I can't do that." ' He rejected Buckley's suggestion that he should have stood but not campaigned: 'That would simply be pathetic, ludicrous cowardice. I would have been running away from the dilemma.'

The leadership had hoped that Powell's second anti-market speech on the Monday evening at Shipley would be less prominently reported, the novelty having worn off. They were disappointed: Powell was now depicted by the press as a one-man nemesis against Heath. His call – so it was inferred – to vote Labour threatened to rock the election. More than 1,000 people packed the hall for the meeting, and another 3,000 were left outside. Powell said clearly he would put his trust in Wilson: 'There are those who desperately try to assure themselves that the Labour party, when it promises fundamental renegotiation and submission of the outcome in any event to the electorate, is not sincere: that, if given a mandate, it will not fulfil it, or – to use the more elegant expression – "Harold Wilson will rat on his undertaking." ' This was an irony too much for Powell.[179]

'Now there are a lot of people about whom it behoves to be very cautious in accusing their political opponents of past or prospective U-turns,' he roared. 'In acrobatics Harold Wilson, for all his nimbleness and skill, is simply no match for the breathtaking, thoroughgoing efficiency of the present Prime Minister.'

At this point, as a spasm of applause laced with jeers died down, the spell was broken. A heckler in the hall cried out, 'Judas!' Electrified, Powell pointed to him. He shouted back: 'Judas was paid! Judas was paid! I am making a sacrifice!'[180]

Neither of the main parties had been particularly good at keeping its promises, he continued, but if the Conservatives were re-elected there would be no prospect of leaving the EEC. Labour had, however, given the firmest commitment to review the issue. He added that he had been surprised by the 'indignation' that had greeted his speech the previous Saturday, when all he had done was restate views expressed again and again during the preceding Parliament, and to bring to the notice of the electorate the fact that they had a choice. On this, he was more direct than at Birmingham. 'It means giving a majority in the next House of Commons to the party which is committed to fundamental renegotiation of the Treaty of Brussels and to submitting to the British people thereafter, for their final yea or nay, the outcome of that renegotiation, succeed or fail.'

Powell reiterated his main objections to the Community – the loss of sovereignty and the institutionalisation of high food prices – and also his view that he could not, after twenty-four years in Parliament, ask electors to support policies opposite to those he had fought for in 1970. He followed that observation with an extension of his now familiar coda:

> I have said before in the same context and I say again now: I was born a Tory, am a Tory and shall die a Tory. It is part of me ... it is something I cannot alter. I am in no wise conscious of having departed from it in anything I have done or said either in the late parliament or now in this election ... For all those in the Conservative party, and indeed elsewhere, who reject the subordination of British interests to others, and the dismantling of our British right to govern and to tax ourselves through parliament, the time has come to understand this. The time has also come to act upon that understanding. If we fail now, the hour will not return.

Meanwhile in Wolverhampton, the Conservatives had selected Nicholas Budgen, a thirty-six-year-old barrister and strong admirer of Powell's, as their candidate; by a coincidence his grandfather, the rector of Newport, had baptised Powell. He was not, however, going to get Powell's vote. Powell had applied for a postal vote, and let it be known in an interview on 26 February, the day after his Shipley speech, that he would be voting for the Labour candidate, Helen Middleweek, who had denounced him publicly earlier for his stand on immigration. He said it was the only decision he could honourably take. What the socialists might do, he said, would be reversible; a Conservative victory, with a renewed commitment to the EEC, would make that central issue impossible to reverse. Miss Middleweek welcomed Powell's support, and said she was 'fighting on the real issues, which include the fact that this election has been dishonestly called and which include the Common Market. Obviously Mr Powell's opinions on both these issues have been helpful.' Budgen found Powell's former supporters in the constituency 'absolutely shattered'. 'A great many of them', he said, 'had not very carefully been following what he had been saying from 1972 to 1974.'[181] Powell believed he had warned his voters of what he might do, but credited them with reading his speeches with the same care with which he had written them. Their shock was intense. His devoted agent, Robin Pollard, eventually had a nervous breakdown.

The damage Powell was doing to the Conservative interest was now apparent right to the highest level. On the evening of 26 February he had been due to give a television interview on the BBC, but it was cancelled at short notice, soon after the Corporation admitted receiving a telephone call from Heath and Carrington about it. ITN considered carrying the interview – which was without question highly newsworthy – instead, but they too refused. Since Powell was not a candidate, there were complications with the Representation of the People Acts.[182] In the end, Powell gave it to Thames Television, the independent London station. In it he confirmed his call to vote Labour and denied he was being disloyal; loyalty, he said, did not mean 'turning when daddy turns' and allowing the party to contradict itself.[183] His first loyalty, as he would maintain repeatedly, was to the people of the country.

When the campaign had started, the Wolverhampton association had had several offers from interested candidates volunteering, if elected, to resign the minute Powell decided to resume his parliamentary career. However, some activists in the association were soon heard expressing relief that Powell had stood down, because his attacks on Heath had embarrassed them. With the 'Vote Labour' exhortation, the mood soured in Wolverhampton and elsewhere. On election eve Powell received a letter from forty Powellites, mainly members of the Monday Club, accusing him of stabbing them in the back over his decision to vote Labour. The organiser of the letter, Charles Paley-Phillips, told the press that 'we have told him that he has taken the Common Market issue completely out of context and that he can never again be representative of the views he originally held'.[184] The letters columns of the Conservative press were not short, either, of complaints from the grass roots about Powell's apparent vindictiveness and disloyalty.

His convictions about the rightness of what he had done were, though, unshakeable. He and his family spent election day in London; and he did not sit up to watch the results. On the morning of Friday 1 March he came downstairs at his usual time of seven o'clock to collect his copy of The Times from the letterbox, and was greeted by the headline 'Mr Heath's general election gamble fails'. He then – as he rejoiced in telling his friends for years afterwards – went upstairs to the bathroom and sang the 'Te Deum'. 'The point being,' he explained, 'as it were, to say "There's justice in the world". You know, I didn't mean it vindictively.'[185] Later on, he was less guarded about his motives: 'I had had my revenge on the man who had destroyed the self-government of the United Kingdom.'[186]

16

ACROSS THE WATER

Powell read on the front of his *Times* that morning that Labour and Liberal gains had wiped out the Conservative majority. It would be some days before it was settled what, exactly, would happen next. Once all the results were in it was clear no party had an overall mandate. In the new 635-seat House of Commons 318 seats gave a majority of one; but Labour had only 301, and the Tories 296. Heath had not done that badly; the main reason for the fall in his party's strength since 1970 was the decision by the Ulster Unionists not to take the Conservative whip. The Conservatives had lost just eleven seats to Labour, and had won two from them, and two from the Liberals. They had, though, lost four seats in Scotland to the Nationalists. In terms of the popular vote, the Conservatives managed 300,000 more than Labour. Nonetheless, the result was a profound shock to Heath and his supporters: they had felt that public feeling against the miners could not but be reflected in a drubbing for Labour. It seemed the public had little confidence in Heath to do better.

Nor was it immediately clear how far Powell had affected the result, even though the press and some of his former colleagues were quick to apportion blame – or credit – to him. In the West Midlands, Powell's heartland, just Dudley West changed hands, though the Conservative vote was down in many seats: Nicholas Budgen saw his majority in Wolverhampton South-West slashed to just over 6,000, but there had been substantial boundary changes. Yet the swing in that region was on average 4 per cent to Labour, against 1 per cent nationally. Budgen himself saw a swing against him of 16 per cent, though he did not have Powell's personal vote. Schoen and Johnson, analysing Powell's effect on the 1970 result, applied themselves to this one too, and found that while there was a national swing of 0.9 per cent to Labour, among Powellites it was 4.8 per cent. For his part, Powell was convinced he was the man responsible for Heath's defeat. Heath appears to have felt it too; his – and Powell's – doctor, Brian Warren, said: 'Ted's got this idea that, were it not for Enoch, he might just have won that election.'[1] It was also, in Warren's view, the final insurmountable obstacle to Heath and Powell ever making up their differences. Powell never bore any grudge against Heath; Heath took his grudge against Powell to great lengths, even refusing, twenty years later, to attend Warren's eightieth birthday party if the Powells were to be invited, and resisting any expression of sympathy to Powell's family when he died.

Heath held a cabinet meeting on 1 March, after which he saw the Queen.

There was no constitutional need for him to resign, for it was far from certain that Wilson could command a majority in the Commons. After seeing the Queen, he began discussions with Jeremy Thorpe, the Liberal leader. Having more than doubled their representation in the House to fourteen seats, the Liberals could help Heath if they chose. Heath wrote to Thorpe on 4 March outlining a basis for a coalition, but the Liberal leadership had received, over the weekend, the strongest representations from their supporters not to do a deal with Heath. Thorpe told Heath there should, instead, be a government of national unity including MPs from all parties. Heath could not accept this, and resigned. Two hours later, Wilson stood on the steps of Downing Street and announced that the Queen had invited him to form a government. He told the Liberals he had no use for them.

While the uncertainty went on, Powell confined himself to a short statement: 'The one clear good to come out of this election has been that the issue of Britain's membership of the Common Market has been decisively kept open. It will now not be possible for much longer to deny the nation the opportunity to decide for itself whether it does wish to belong to the EEC and, if so, on what terms.'[2] He added, in a menacing tone, that 'there has been another gain, though purchased at a heavy cost. The Conservative party is now enabled, and will be obliged, to find its way back to those economic policies – in particular, the rejection of compulsory wage controls – which the whole party was united in supporting in 1970 and which have been abandoned in the last 18 months with such unhappy consequences.'

However, he also had to come to terms with the stern reality that he no longer had a place in Parliament from which to influence the British people. It did not deter him. 'You must remember that it doesn't upset me to be alone,' he told a supporter at this time. 'I have no fear of heights. I am happy on the precipice.'[3] Richard Ritchie, who saw him two or three days after the election, found Powell in higher spirits than for a long time, and convinced there was a way back for him. At this stage, though, he had not formulated what it would be, though Ritchie's memory is that Ulster was an immediately attractive option.[4] If Powell had recovered, his wife, with her lifelong devotion to the Conservative party, was still depressed by events. 'People cut one. All sorts of people no longer asked us to dinner. You can't blame them, I suppose.'[5]

In fact, Powell was already set on a return to Westminster, if necessary as a Conservative: for it was not clear to him that Heath would survive or, if he did, that he could do so without adopting Powellite policies. That was why when senior activists in the Isle of Wight Conservative Association rang Powell and spoke to his private secretary, Peter Clarke, on 2 March, to suggest that he might become their candidate – the seat had just gone to the Liberals by over 7,700 votes – they were not rebuffed. Powell wrote to them on 4 March to say, 'I am grateful to you for communicating with me. I should give my most serious consideration to anything which was put to me.'[6] There was further cor-respondence during March, with Powell signalling that he wished to keep his options open. Friends still in Parliament, like Neil Marten, came and said that a group of MPs wanted to start talk in the tea room about how Heath had to go, and Marten thought immediately after the election that Heath would be out 'in two to three weeks'.[7] Powell was not to know it, but some of the Whips had already come to the same conclusion, and when their leader showed no signs of budging would eventually tell him so, to his horror and disbelief.[8] Such talk encouraged Powell not to rule out a return to the Conservative party, but to keep his options open.

Eight days after the election, once Wilson was in Downing Street and with Heath still reeling, Powell went on *Any Questions* and clashed with Norman St John-Stevas, Arts Minister in Heath's government. He told Powell he would not look so calmly on the present Parliament if he had fought the election. Powell snapped, 'I did, and won it.' Later on in the programme Powell said, 'I have the unfulfilled ambition, but not an ignoble one, of leading the Tory party.'[9] Stevas commented on the bad taste of being seen to boast about or triumph over 'another former colleague to whose defeat one has contributed'. Anthony Howard singled out Powell's performance on this programme as an example of what he, and many others, perceived to be Powell's main flaw – vanity.[10] Like all politicians, Powell had the more than adequate self-regard the job demands. However, his attitude cannot be dismissed so simplistically as 'vanity'. For him, this veneer of arrogance was an essential defence mechanism. Ever since April 1968 he had put himself in the proverbial minority of one, at least among the political classes. Had he not developed what others perceived as this unappealing personal quality, he could not have coped with the highly personal and vicious attacks on him. He had put himself on the margins, but he survived there, with his self-respect intact, even if not fulfilling the conventional aims of a political career.

On the same programme, Powell dismissed the notion that Labour should avoid controversial measures because of its lack of a majority. 'In my view, they ought to attempt to carry out what they think to be right in the interests of the country. If they are defeated in attempting to do so, then they ought to go back to the electorate and allow the electorate once again to have an opportunity of deciding.' The next day he flew to America, to address a conference of 5,000 construction industry executives in San Diego. On 11 March, the day before the state opening of the Parliament of which, for the first time in twenty-four years, he was not a member, he said the Western democracies were routinely denying the principles on which their civilisation was built, and were therefore renounc-ing freedom and fostering communism. He asked, 'what has gone wrong with us?' and, while accepting that in any age there was something 'wrong', felt the problem was a loss of confidence that capitalism was superior to communism.

Speaking of the Western democracies, he said that 'the vast majority support a series of policies and prognostications which imply that regimes that maximise individual liberty and responsibility are wrong and that those that minimise it are right'.[11] He estimated that in Britain 'between 40 and 50 per cent of all the activities of the population are compulsory'; the whole economic framework of the free society was being repudiated, as had been seen by reactions in the West to the energy crisis, its continual pouring out of overseas aid, and, above all, 'the inter-government conspiracy known as the international monetary system, preening itself in the garb of benevolence'. He ridiculed the concepts of 'market failure' and the 'mania of growth', and highlighted the EEC as the exemplar of all he felt was evil, notably in its desire to replace small governments with a big government, and less government by more.

On that day, Powell published, in his absence abroad, an article in *The Times* explaining his actions of the previous month. Though, he said, he had always followed the advice of Horace that it was the mark of a wise man not to be surprised by anything, elements of the campaign had shocked him. He said parliaments and elections were reduced to a charade by 'the assumption so widely, even unquestioningly prevalent now, that any correspondence between the proclaimed intentions and policies of political parties and their actions in office cannot, and perhaps even should not, be expected'.[12] He recalled his chagrin at the reaction to his question to Heath in November 1972, about whether he had taken leave of his senses by failing to govern as he had promised: 'I was immediately told by both low and high ... that this is just what Governments do do, and good luck to them if it works out.'

The policies had not worked. But no one, said Powell, had called into question the reversal of principle, the breach of promise; and when he cited the repudiation of commitments by Heath as a reason why he could not stand in the election, his denunciation of the breach of faith 'was treated as something that could only be accounted for in terms of personal rancour and vindictiveness'. Nonetheless, everyone had expected Powell to stand, despite the breach of principle, and to campaign for 'support and approval for the actual policies he had consistently denounced. To decline to do so was found so paradoxical and quixotic that it had to be supposed a subtle and tortuous machination for self-advancement.' He said if the public expected politicians and their parties to behave so shamelessly, then 'all links in the chain of democratic responsibility are snapped'. He was not merely seeking to justify his own perceived breaches of 'loyalty', he was issuing a warning. 'When the connection of policy with party is assumed to be spurious or reversible, parliamentary politics sink to the level of triviality, and men will begin to look for other ways to influence or control the nation's affairs.'

There was still some unfinished business in Wolverhampton. Powell had never had a reply to his letter to George Wilkes of 7 February, when he announced he was not standing. It arrived on 19 March, Wilkes having been so distressed that he had not trusted himself to write sooner. After twenty-four years of supporting Powell, Wilkes and his wife had felt betrayed, and were uncomprehending – though they said they would forgive him, since they were true friends. However, Wilkes left Powell in no doubt of the chaos and grief he had occasioned in Wolverhampton. 'Your not seeking re-election threw a personal strain and task on me unlike anything I had ever experienced,' Wilkes told him.[13] He added that Powell's decision 'was respected by us all *until* you announced your decision to vote Socialist. By this one act, more than any other word or deed you have lost credibility ... to fling back 24 years friendship and support in one act made a very bitter pill for your many friends to swallow ... your action reduced your friends in some cases to tears and even now, weeks later, I am continually being asked Why?'

Wilkes was offended that Powell had never taken him into his confidence – as Robin Pollard had urged him to do. He was hurt, too, that Powell had not attempted to contact him privately after the letter, to try to explain his actions. He was in no doubt of the import of what Powell had done: 'That you lost the election for the Tory Party is certain – I am sure the defeat will do us all good and we will unite and find a new leader in time who will once more guide us back to true Conservative principles. I with countless others had hoped that leader would have been you.' For all this reproach Wilkes ended, 'We *are* still *your friends.*'

Acknowledging that he had over the years been 'deeply indebted' to 'my old friends in Wolverhampton', Powell replied that he had been 'sorry to read your account of the distress and anxiety' caused by 'events surrounding the election', but he felt there had been no cause for 'surprise or complaint'.[14] He said the party should have been aware of the course he would have to take if an election were called. This was, by his standards, somewhat disingenuous in the light of his performance at the constituency annual general meeting on 14 December, when he had seemed to be avoiding the reality himself – although he had convinced himself, in spite of the rumours in the press of an early election, that he would have until the following summer to make up his mind. He referred to what he had said at Stockport; to his refusal to campaign at West Bromwich; and to his having said in February 1972 that he was prepared to put the Government out of office if that followed from a defeat on the European Communities Bill. Certainly, his association officers should have seen the writing on the wall, but it is hard to excuse Powell, who after all had actually written it, for not having spoken to them in a more straightforward way. He said that 'after the "non-election" of January, I had allowed myself to hope that enough time would elapse to enable the Party to regain a defensible stance on this [the EEC] and other matters before a general election had to be fought; but this was not to be'. Certainly, his supporters had been deluded; but so, it seems, had he. Also, if he had worked out the human consequences of his actions to those devoted to him, he had worked out too a determination to be ruthless about them.

It was as clear to him as to most others that Wilson would need to go to the country sooner rather than later, which meant there would, if he wanted to take it, be an ideal opportunity for Powell's early return to Parliament. In a television interview on 21 March he said he was longing to get back to the Commons. 'It is the great and only place to be in politics in Britain.' Again, he held out the possibility of a return as a Conservative, as he felt sure the party would now move towards the policies he himself had always advocated.[15] Later that week, looking forward to Wilson's first Budget, he said that if he were Chancellor he would increase income tax across the board.

In his absence from Westminster he had renewed one intellectual pursuit and initiated another: he was reading systematically, for the first time since his university days, the Gospels in Greek, and questioning the common interpretation of them; and he was embarking on a monograph about Joe Chamberlain, another Birmingham man who had felt himself drawn to the question of Ireland, and who had had trouble sticking with political parties. He turned down an invitation to write a life of Disraeli. Such things were not to be substitutes for his parliamentary life. However, to return to the Commons he needed a seat where he could be nominated, and which he could win. His raising of his public profile a month after the election coincided with more rumours about Ulster. They were well founded. 'I was approached a fortnight after the general election,' Powell recalled, 'when the Ulster Unionist members said: "When you were a Member of Parliament you voted with us and spoke with us. Now you must join us." I thought that was reasonable.'[16] The offer was put to him by the three leaders of the Ulster Unionist coalition – Harry West, the Official Unionist leader, William Craig of Vanguard, and Ian Paisley of the Democratic Unionists. The triumvirate paid Powell a visit at South Eaton Place – a visit arranged by Molyneaux – to make their entreaty to him. 'Paisley had patent-leather shoes,' Mrs Powell recalled. 'I couldn't believe it.'[17] Certainly, Powell's record of support for the Province did nothing to disqualify him. Also, he was aware that, however much some Conservatives despised him for his disloyalty in making the call to vote Labour, they also realised he had been right about inflation. As a result, a sizeable cross-section of society looked to him for leadership, the more so since the early record of Wilson's Government had been one of surrender to the unions and the imposition of unpopular taxes. The sense was growing that there would shortly be a great national crisis that would necessitate strong measures. Powell, the argument ran, was the only politician with the credibility to implement such measures, given what he had said about the economy throughout the Heath Government. Yet he could not deal with the crisis in any proper sense from outside the Commons. Michael Foot, now a cabinet minister, writing to him on 22 March, seemed to be feeling the loss as much as Powell: 'It has been pitiable to have been in the House of Commons these past few days with you not here. Your absence leaves a hopeless, aching gap.'[18]

On 26 March it was announced that he would address a large Unionist rally in Belfast the following month. John Laird, one of the most prominent Unionists in the Ulster Assembly, said, 'We would welcome Mr Powell to our ranks. I understand that unofficial talks with him have already taken place, the results of which cannot yet be made known.'[19] When asked about this, Powell told the press, 'I know nothing about that.' Talks, though, were under way, both with him and about him. As if to pave the way, Powell announced in early April that he had resigned from the Conservative party and relinquished all honorary offices he had held in it: he was replying to a letter from the Solihull Young Conservatives demanding he resign because of his 'totally irresponsible and misguided behaviour'. This seemed to some at the time the clearest sign that he had finished in politics and could never be a force in it again.

However, while he was on another short lecture tour to America in mid-April, it was made known that before he addressed the Belfast rally he would have talks with Unionist leaders in the Province, though not, it was stressed, on the question of his returning to Westminster as one of their MPs. Harry West made it sound as though Powell was being vetted, saying that 'if Mr Powell was going to stand I would want to make sure we were all on the same wavelength'.[20] This was the purpose of Powell's Belfast talks, in which West and he would be joined by Paisley and Craig. West hinted that Powell's commitment to integration – which the Unionists, wanting Stormont back, did not share – would especially need to be discussed.

Yet even before Powell reached Belfast the Unionists seemed to be falling over themselves to embrace him. Some were quite open about their perception of him as a second Carson, a politician of international weight at home in their six counties. The day after he had talked about the need to discuss where Powell stood on various issues, Harry West announced that he would willingly give up the leadership of the Unionists to Powell if he wanted it and accepted party policy. 'Mr Powell is the only influential friend we have in English politics,' he said.[21] Powell lunched with the Unionist leaders in Belfast on 18 April, and spent much of the afternoon in discussions with them. He dwelt in his speech to the rally that evening on the power the Unionists now had, as a result of the election and their significance as a minor party at a time of minority government, to demand more representation at Westminster: it was an appropriate issue with which to open this new chapter in his relations with the Unionists, as the securing of this representation would be his great cause when he returned to Parliament.

With twelve MPs, Ulster was under-represented by comparison with the rest of the Kingdom, with some constituencies having electorates of over 100,000 compared with an average of under 70,000 in England. Powell said they could demand as many as twenty MPs, and certainly at least eighteen. He argued that to boost the Province's representation at Westminster would also show the world how seriously Britain took her responsibilities for Ulster as part of the United Kingdom. While Stormont had existed the maintenance of under-rep-resentation, while not logical, could be justified. Now it had gone, there was no argument at all against increasing the numbers.

He said Heath had kept Ulster under-represented 'to please a foreign coun-try' – the Irish Republic. It had been 'a plain signal to the Republic and the republicans that the door to what they desire and the majority of Ulster people reject is being unlocked . . . the connection between Westminster representations and death on the streets in Northern Ireland is direct and unequivocal'.[22] He rejoiced that the election had seen the formal end of the alliance between the Unionists and the Conservatives, and said that in three years Heath and his colleagues had done more damage to Ulster than any government of any party had ever done. He denounced Heath for his treatment of Faulkner in 1972, summoning him over to tell him that Stormont was going and that he could 'like it or lump it'; he described the 1973 Constitution as an 'absurdity', an 'outrage' and a 'monstrosity'. He also noted that the voting figures at the election had exploded the myth of a large Roman Catholic minority irreconcilable to Britain; the figures showed clearly that many Catholics had voted for the Union.

No sooner had Powell left the Province – without a hint of his intentions – than it was announced that he would return the following week for a Unionist conference. The rumour also surfaced that Captain Lawrence 'Willy' Orr, the Official Unionist MP for South Down, would create a vacancy for Powell by not standing again. Powell would make no comment on that either, except to say, 'If such a proposition was to be put to me, then I leave it to you to judge by my words and actions in the months and years past what my response would be.'[23] Harry West said that he would offer his seat to Powell, though that might not be such a good idea as it was Fermanagh and South Tyrone, and not safe. Molyneaux offered to surrender South Antrim, the safest seat in the Kingdom, an idea Powell vetoed when put to him.[24] The main purpose of the Unionist conference was to strengthen opposition to Ulster's power-sharing executive, which Powell took every opportunity to attack as 'unrealistic'. On this he was at one with most Unionists, though they were still far apart on integration. He did not shirk from saying that those who wanted a return to Stormont were basing that view on an illusion; but that matter, to his obvious relief, was not pressing.

Powell had received several further approaches from Conservative associ-ations, but was becoming more reserved towards them. Heath showed every sign of staying to fight another election, and no sign of repudiating his old policies. On 17 April Powell told the Isle of Ely association, which had asked him to be their candidate, and towards whom he had initially been sympathetic, that 'I feel that events have to move further in the context of the EEC and the

Conservative Party's position on this subject before it would be possible for me to campaign wholeheartedly as a Conservative candidate.'[25] He said the same to activists at Watford in May, and did not encourage approaches made at around that time by Aldridge Brownhills, Lewisham East, West Bromwich East, Middleton and Prestwich, Ilkeston and Shrewsbury.[26] Most of these were Labour marginals and represented no safe ticket back: the last had a Conservative MP of thirty years' standing, Sir John Langford-Holt, who fully intended to stand again.

Powell kept up his profile with regular speeches, television appearances and newspaper articles. On 5 May in the *Sunday Express* he ridiculed the proposed 'social contract' Wilson was proposing with the unions, on the grounds that it repeated all the old mistakes of the failed Heath incomes policy, and would do nothing to halt inflation. He remained sure the public would not be taken in again, and hoped they realised that Healey's Budget, which had failed to control the money supply, would be as disastrous as Barber's had been.[27] The other threat he perceived from Wilson's Government was its sympathy for devolution in Scotland and Wales, which prompted him, in a speech in Glamorgan on 9 May, to observe that 'there is nothing intermediate between belonging to a particular political unit and not belonging'. In other words, the halfway-house of a devolved assembly with representatives still being sent to Westminster was untenable.

Powell still made no firm arrangement with the Ulster Unionists. One of his Conservative friends in the Commons, Neil Marten, had been consulting with Molyneaux about what could be done. He wrote to Powell on 19 May to confirm that, if a job could be found for Willie Orr, the Unionists would 'fix up his seat' for Powell.[28] He asked Powell whether he had a supporter in business who could come to Orr's aid. Powell, though, spoke to a Conservative group in London on 18 May and his speech seemed to show him holding out an olive branch to his old party. However, it was equally open to the opposite interpretation since it was, in the main, devoted to pouring salt on old wounds and reminding Heath of his failure. It was distributed well in advance, as usual, and heavily trailed. It came at a time when some Conservative backbenchers were beginning in public to express reservations about Heath, largely out of frustration that the uncertainty of Wilson's timing of the next election left them with no opportunity to replace Heath in the short term. Since the recognition that Powell had been right on the main issues was growing, it looked as if there could be a reconciliation between him and his old party.

He said he was sure that in the Conservative party 'in the very widest extension that can be given to the term' – by which it was taken that he meant non-communicants such as himself and other natural Tories who had not supported the party on 28 February – there was a strong yearning to regain the 'unity of purpose' it had once had. In his most conciliatory passage, he said, 'I do not

With Pamela at the count in South Down, 1974

The Brigadier on manoeuvres in Ulster, 1978

With Ted Curtis, c.1976

Susan's wedding, 1977

Holding the baby at the Christening of his first grandchild, Simon Day, 1983, with (left to right) Susan Day, Jennifer Powell, Pamela Powell, Richard Day

With his agent, Jeffrey Donaldson, by the Mountains of Mourne, 1983

On the stump with Jim Molyneaux, 1987

Dressed for wet rain with Andrew Freeth, 1984

The elder statesman and his wife, at Lord Duncan-Sandys's memorial service, 1988

Four old stagers: Sir Hardy Amies, Lord Thorneycroft, Powell, Lord Salisbury at the 80th birthday dinner, 1992

With his family before the 80th birthday dinner: (left to right) Richard Day, Jennifer Lavin, Pamela Powell, Michael Lavin, Susan Day

At the 80th birthday dinner with Greville Howard

Bearing Patch, 1993

With Richard Ritchie, 1989

With his granddaughter Rachel Day, 1990.

With his grandchildren James and
Julia Lavin, 1996

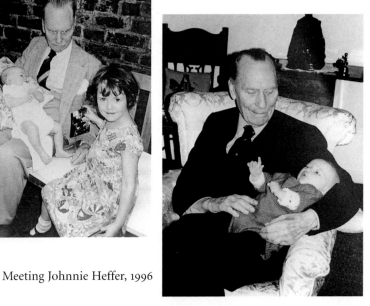

Meeting Johnnie Heffer, 1996

The Last Post: Warwick, 1998

believe ... that the great divisions which destroyed the unity of the party have been dishonourable to those who took one side or the other.'[29] These divisions, like the events that caused them, were history, and Powell was sure that 'neither rancour nor pride ought to keep apart those who are no longer divided by disagreement over real issues'.

Mischievous as ever, he built his thesis on the basis that he had been proved right on so many of those issues on which there had been sharp disagreement, and the old orthodoxies that he had attacked had now disappeared into oblivion. 'It is', he reminded his audience, 'less than three years since advocacy of a floating pound was held to disqualify the advocate not merely from participating in a Conservative administration but from serious attention at all within official Conservative circles.' Nor was it long since allegiance to the concept of 'East of Suez' had been 'the very touchstone of Conservative respectability. To question or discuss the holy mystery was little short of committing the political sin against the Holy Ghost. Equally, economic and monetary union in Europe by 1980 was now manifestly not 'even a bad joke', and even some of the most devoted former adherents of the European dream had realised the concept was in trouble. 'Surely,' Powell said therefore, 'there is no need for the Conservative party to go on tearing itself apart over what we all know is not going to happen – indeed, over what we all know does not exist as a political reality.'

For all the I-told-you-so, which would make the speech impossible for Heath and his friends to interpret as anything other than a renewal of hostilities, Powell did try to make it seem as though he wanted to patch up the quarrel on Europe. 'I recognise', he said, 'that those who were prepared to offer Britain's parliamentary sovereignty as the sacrifice for realising a united Europe were sincere. I for one have never impugned their patriotism nor decried their choice as less honourable than that of their opponents.' He could not help but add that Europe had had nothing on offer that could legitimately command the price of sacrificed sovereignty.

There were two further areas in which he could not help but seem to be rubbing Heath's nose in it. The first was the reversal of principle over a prices and incomes policy, a painful point he brought up to help him argue that no Conservative government would ever be so stupid as to advocate such a move again. 'There is no need to waste time in recrimination and the apportionment of blame. The lesson is learnt; the conclusions drawn; and the Conservative party is once more free to offer the nation the correct diagnosis and prescription for the increasingly feared and devastating scourge of inflation.' The market, and not the arbitrary decisions of politicians and officials, would always be the Conservative way of dealing with wages. The second additional cause of grief was immigration. He said that, in the 1960s, the Conservatives had swallowed 'wildly unreal' assumptions about the eventual size of the immigrant-descended population in Britain. Now, he said, they should have the 'candour and open-mindedness' to present the true picture to the electorate of the prospects for that part of the population, leading to 'a sober and realistic assessment of what those prospects portend and the preventive actions for which they call'.

If Powell had intended his speech to act as the prelude to a rapprochement between himself and his old party – and, if he did, it was with long- rather than short-term intentions, since he would not have fought the next election under Heath even if Heath had let him – it failed. Heath and his friends were angered by Powell's apparent crowing over their discomfort, and had no intention of admitting that he had been proved right and they wrong. One of Heath's press spokesmen, issuing a statement afterwards, simply observed that 'Mr Powell is no longer a member of the party. We have no reaction to make.'[30] Powell's main intention had not been to woo Heath and his colleagues: it had been to rebuild support in constituency associations, where there was still much ill-feeling towards him, even from former close adherents, over his 'Vote Labour' speeches. He had, though, sent a copy of his speech to Whitelaw, who wrote to thank him for it on 20 May. 'I will make no comment on its contents except to say that whatever may be our policy disagreements it is a pity to have no personal relations. I hope you and Pam are well.'[31] At about this time, Powell spoke at a Bow Group dinner, and was closely questioned about why he had deserted the party. Peter Lilley remembers Powell's being interrogated by Peter Lloyd, another future minister. When the interrogation finished Powell said, 'Thank you for examining me so thoroughly.' Lloyd replied, 'You passed.' Powell retorted, 'But I like to pass *cum laude*.'[32]

II

Powell took part in a poetry recital in London on 4 June where, along with Hailsham, Tom Driberg and Lord Gowrie, he read out some of his poems during an evening dedicated to 'the politician as poet'. His participation attracted a hard core of 'anti-racist' hecklers, who attempted to disrupt him. He assured those who had come to hear him, and were distressed by the bad behaviour, that the protesters 'will calm down presently. They always do.'[33] It was a happy diversion for him as he watched, from a respectful distance, the process of Heath's trying not to bring Wilson's Government down, as he felt it was still not the most advantageous time to have to fight an election. Still with no seat to fight, Powell might have been forgiven for thinking the same.

He had now definitely decided that he could not accept any of the overtures from a Conservative association. He wrote, therefore, to Molyneaux on 6 June, after the two men had again discussed the possibility of an Ulster seat, to say that, upon reflection, 'if any opportunity should arise ... I, for my part, would commit myself to it wholeheartedly and undertake whatever was involved in doing so'.[34] Molyneaux replied that he had 'discreetly taken certain steps to safeguard our position and will keep you posted'.[35] This determination not to be reconciled to his old party dismayed John Biffen, who wrote to him sadly on 2 July to say he had the impression 'that you intend to ask people in Oswestry [Biffen's constituency] and elsewhere to vote Labour at an autumn election unless the Conservatives have rid themselves of their leader and become no less explicit "fundamental re-negotiators" than Labour. If my impression is correct I find it very difficult to see what is the point of trying to build bridges between yourself and the Conservative parliamentary party.'[36]

Powell's absorption into the mainstream anti-EEC campaign made him some strange bedfellows. On 19 June he found himself on a platform in Yorkshire with Lord Wigg and Jack Jones, general secretary of the Transport and General Workers Union. Powell said Wilson would not have become Prime Minister without the votes of many who had voted Labour to secure the renegotiation of British membership. He urged Wilson to stick to that promise: no fundamental renegotiation had, thus far, begun. Powell also attacked several newspapers for having written editorials suggesting that Wilson could, with a clear conscience, ditch the promise. He was disturbed by rumours that Wilson intended to do just that, and being out of Parliament he was not easily able to find out how true they were. The following month, when participating in a seminar in London on the practicalities of a referendum on EEC membership, he sought to extract from Labour officials present a promise that Wilson would not try to find a way of avoiding holding a plebiscite. An official of the party's Research Department at the seminar gave Powell that assurance, and Powell made sure the press were informed.

He also used his role in the campaign to settle a few scores with vested interests, such as the CBI and the City, who had been in the forefront of calls for Britain to join the EEC in the first place. He described the fervour for this policy as 'economic illiteracy', and drew a comparison with the CBI's long-standing opposition to a floating exchange rate: once it had been floated against its wishes, the organisation was just as militant in opposing a return to a fixed parity. There was now a new 'delusion' that 'vital interests' were at stake if Britain left the Community, he said.[37] In another anti-market meeting in Norwich on 6 July he mocked the notion of various former Conservative ministers talking of the possibility of a government of 'national unity': 'This is done with no other object than to deny the electorate the one thing which justifies and necessitates the existence of political parties – the power to choose between specifically expressed alternatives for the nation's future.'[38] As Powell saw it, there would have to be an election directly after the summer holidays, and Labour was still the only party promising renegotiation. Until and unless that changed, he would continue to back them.

The Conservative leadership was panicked in June, when word reached

Central Office that Harry d'Avigdor-Goldsmid had told officers in the Aldridge Brownhills seat in the West Midlands that he could 'get' Powell if the local association wanted him; Goldsmid was the president of the constituency party. The local agent had, however, told Goldsmid he had 'no wish' to have Powell in the seat following his activities at the previous election.[39] Yet the notion that Powell might be planning a comeback with the help of some sections of the party would not go away, even though Powell himself had ruled it out. At the end of June Whitelaw drafted a memorandum to Heath about the possibilities. Powell was not, he said, a member of the party, nor was he on the candidates' list. He could not become a party member without Central Office knowing it; 'the probability', Whitelaw mused, 'is that he will seek to be adopted for a Labour held marginal seat in which his personality could well affect the result'. The main fear was that

> he could well be selected – and appear in the press as having been so selected – in a 24–48 hour period. In such an instance we would be faced with (a) a press enquiry as to whether he was an official candidate, (b) a request from the Association for approval, (c) a press call for comment from the Leader and/or the Chairman of the party.
>
> So far as Central Office is concerned we could (a) give him formal endorsement as an ex-MP and Minister or (b) refuse to endorse him on the grounds that he both voted against the party and advised the electorate to do so at the last General Election, in which event the Constituency could proceed regardless with the adoption and we could run an official candidate against him, or (c) not to approve him but not to oppose him.

Whitelaw urged a swift decision by the shadow cabinet as 'we are likely to be confronted with this situation at short notice with very little time to stall'.

Whitelaw developed this into a more detailed memorandum on 2 July, following discussions with colleagues. By this stage, he was concerned that one of Powell's friends in the House might stand down in his favour, and he had asked Central Office agents in the regions to keep an eye out for any Labour marginals in which an attempt might be made to bring Powell in. The seat felt most to be at risk was Dewsbury in Yorkshire, which had a Labour majority of 5,412. Whitelaw felt that if Powell were selected a factual statement should be made to the effect that he, like all other candidates who were not on the approved list, would have to go through the usual procedure of endorsement by Central Office. Unsurprisingly, he advised against providing that endorsement because 'Powell contributed to some degree to the return of a Labour government.' He said that a 'forgive and forget' policy would be 'politically damaging' since 'we would be seeking to dominate the moderate ground in the run-up to the Election'. However, he was also against running an 'official' candidate against Powell as 'the result could well be calamitous. If Powell routed the official candidate, his position would be greatly strengthened especially if we lost the election nationally.' The third option, of neither endorsing nor opposing, seemed to be favoured by Whitelaw, though he admitted it would leave his and Heath's positions exposed and would create accusations of a lack of leadership. A decision was postponed until such times as Powell was selected. In fact, on 4 July, another visit by the 'big three' to South Eaton Place confirmed the prospect of his future as a Unionist.

That summer he made the final breach with Wolverhampton: the five-bed-roomed late-Victorian house in Merridale Road, in which he and his family had spent their time in the constituency for the previous twenty years, was put on the market for £5,650. The press had much fun with the prospect of it being bought, as many around it had been, by an immigrant. Eventually, after a couple of months, it was: by an Irishman who, in an auction, paid £5,700 for it, above the estate agent's asking price. However, the sale fell through, and the house finally sold in early 1975.

Throughout his exile from Parliament, Powell had been closely supported, as usual, by the IEA. That August, they sent him a memorandum advising him of what he would have to do for the country: a little otiose, since he still did not have a seat, but unquestionably well intentioned. To them, Powell was a pro-phetic figure: the first politician correctly to identify the monetary causes of the present inflation, and whose Morecambe Budget six years earlier had defined the tax and spending policies a free economy would need if it were to survive. Now, Powell's friends told him that 'the profound conviction that inspires this memorandum is that many policies hitherto funked as "politically impossible" will become much more readily acceptable to the electorate, the media, and parliament as part of a comprehensive and consistent programme to purge inflation from the British economy by attacking the Budget deficit through large and continuing reductions in total public expenditure'.[40]

However, there was one point on which Powell's 'candid' friends – as they described themselves at the head of the memorandum – took issue with their leader, and that was over Powell's, to them, curious attachment to the welfare state. This was, indeed, the one issue on which Powell the politician seemed to override Powell the ideologue: he knew that to tell the people that their welfare benefits, and especially their health service, were to be scaled down, would be political suicide. Also, he took the view that such a large proportion of the electorate manifestly agreed that the state should provide these services for them with their money that it was not the politician's place to tell them the opposite. 'Your emphasis on the incomparable superiority of the market mechanism over collective decision-making', his friends told him, 'cannot consistently be applied to the economy in general while excluding the welfare sector.'

The signatories hoped that Powell would discuss the matter with them: but events moved urgently on. He had to find a seat and, as he sensed an election would not be delayed long, that need became critical. Standing as a Unionist was his only hope. As well as devoting himself to the anti-EEC crusade, and making occasional speeches on other familiar themes such as inflation – on which he was now regularly corresponding with Milton Friedman – he was reserving much of his spare time to learning Hebrew, an essential requirement for the biblical study he intended to undertake once he eventually retired; but he had no intention of retiring yet since, at sixty-two, he was still fit and physically young for his age. After a short summer break he resumed serious negotiations with the Unionists. Matters were now urgent: Wilson had indicated that the February 1974 parliament would not return after the recess, but that a campaign would start for an October poll.

The Unionists were as keen on Powell as he was on them. As he prepared his endgame, he was helped by the fact that a group of influential Unionists were putting pressure on Orr to stand down and make way for him. Orr was, at fifty-six, six years younger than Powell; at the election his majority had fallen from 13,000 to just over 5,000, which partly explained his association's desire to replace him. He had had personal troubles that had caused him to play less attention to politics than he should have done. Molyneaux was briefed to find him and suggest to him that, perhaps, the time had come for him to stand down.

On 21 August Molyneaux wrote to Powell that 'there has been a dramatic development in the S Down situation'.[41] On 15 August Orr had rung Molyneaux and asked him to meet him for lunch. However, he had not arrived, and subsequent investigations revealed he had 'simply disappeared' without telling his own family. Unionist officials had told the South Down association to deselect Orr as he had become so unreliable, and added, subtly, that it was the unanimous desire of the party's ruling council that Powell should be nominated. Molyneaux warned Powell that both the constituency chairman and secretary were thought to want to succeed Orr, 'but with a bit of pressure these can be overcome'. When it was announced that there would be a selection procedure in South Down, Orr surfaced, ringing Molyneaux and asking what he advised; Molyneaux advised him to stand down, and Orr agreed. Harry West wrote to Powell on 23 August to tell him that Orr 'is definitely out of the running now'.[42] Powell had to be sure he wanted to go through with this, and finally decided to seek the nomination on 25 August, despite his wife's having doubts.

Powell paid a long-arranged visit to Armagh during that week. Harold McCusker, the local MP, drove him from the airport. He found Powell in a state of happy astonishment that the offer was being made, but he made it clear he had no intention of accepting it 'unless he felt he had something to contribute to Northern Ireland'.[43] Before he spoke in public he had a long meeting with West and senior officials of the South Down association. When he arrived he found 300 local people waiting to cheer him. Since his discussion earlier in the year there had been one major development of note: the power-sharing executive under Faulkner had collapsed in May, and Wilson had had plans drawn up for a constitutional convention to replace it. Elections would be held the following spring. For Powell, the collapse of the executive was a further opportunity to push his integrationist line; but the coming of the convention, which he suspected from the start to be a form of introducing power-sharing by other means, would provide him with another target.

Powell used his Armagh speech in a nakedly integrationist way. He renewed his call for more MPs from the Province, strengthening the link between Ulster and the rest of the Kingdom and confirming the Union. Afterwards, he was questioned about his immediate future and replied, 'In view of the close interest that for years in Parliament and outside I have taken in Northern Ireland, and my close association with the Ulster Unionist party, if an appeal were made and a request were made, it is not difficult to know what the answer would be.'[44] Pressed for more detail, he simply said, 'It would be a breach of confidence to say if I had been asked or not asked to stand for this seat.'

A further meeting took place on 30 August. Still no outcome was announced, but once it was made known that day that Orr, who had not been seen in public for some time, was standing down on grounds of ill health, it looked a foregone conclusion that Powell would succeed him. Orr had recommended the association to select Powell; and two other prospective candidates, who were not named, left the race: one withdrew in Powell's favour, the other, as it soon turned out, was Glenn Barr, a member of the hard-line Ulster Defence Association who had helped lead the recent Ulster Workers Council strike. He was unanimously rejected by South Down almost immediately his application was received. Molyneaux wrote to Powell after his conversation with Orr to let him know what had happened. Powell replied that it would be improper of him to solicit the support of South Down's Unionist Association, but that Molyneaux could let them know that, if invited to serve, he would accept.[45]

Now the deed was so close to being done it emerged that not everyone was happy at the idea of Powell becoming an Ulster MP. The Ulster Defence Association, comprised of hard-line Protestants, said it was against him, the group's suspicions – like those of other Unionists – being aroused by Powell's enthusiasm for integration. There was also the assumption, strong at the time, that the Unionists would once more take the Conservative whip and that, once Heath was removed, Powell would stand for the Conservative leadership. The idea that they were being used by a carpetbagger, however strong the evidence was to the contrary given Powell's close interest in Ulster since 1969, was one that stuck with some in Northern Ireland.

Powell faced the prospect of representing a constituency as different from Wolverhampton South-West as could be imagined. Situated south of Belfast and bordering the sea, it contained some of the most stunning countryside in the Province, but also some of the worst 'bandit country'. It had social problems far removed from those of Wolverhampton: no heavy industry, no immigrant community, but pockets of unemployment over 20 per cent in towns such as Newry. It was a predominantly agricultural constituency, and agriculture was something of which Powell had no previous experience. Above all, it was not a safe seat. The electoral roll was divided almost equally, it was estimated, between Protestants and Catholics, and Orr had only been elected with the help of a Catholic Unionist vote. The IRA were reckoned to control Newry and some other stretches of the countryside: the main road and railway between Belfast and Dublin ran through the area, and both forms of transport were regularly attacked by terrorists.

On 3 September Powell's application for the candidature went before the thirty-strong association management committee, and was unanimously approved. All that remained was the formality of his being endorsed by a full meeting of the association. The 'big three' – Paisley, West and Craig – all let it be known that they endorsed him. Back in London, manifestly relieved, he said he was 'proud and honoured' to accept the nomination.[46] Confirming his distance from his former party, Powell said on television that evening that the Conservatives had done more harm to the cause of Ulster than Labour, and spoke supportively of the work of Wilson's Ulster Secretary, Merlyn Rees, who had announced an increase in the strength of the Royal Ulster Constabulary.

The next day Powell flew to Belfast to meet his new colleagues. Shortly before the car bringing him and his wife from the airport arrived at Unionist party headquarters, a van containing a massive bomb was placed outside the building. It was successfully defused, but the IRA had shown the nature of their welcome. Powell would have to live under the terrorist shadow for most of the rest of his life. He announced on arrival that he had no new plans or solutions for the Province's problems, and certainly wanted no return to power-sharing. He added that it would be nonsense to try to redraw the border around Northern Ireland: 'Let peace be restored on the basis that this is part of the Kingdom.'[47] He pledged to serve all his constituents, irrespective of their religion, to the best of his abilities, and paid a warm tribute to Orr's work and courage.

Powell and his wife then went for his first 'meet the people' exercise in his constituency: to Ballynahinch, a small market town. The trip was ill-fated, as the bomb in Belfast had delayed Powell's press conference there, making him arrive in the town after the shops had closed for their half-day; the few people there gave him a polite welcome. He then travelled around his new constituency, acquainting himself with the territory: to Kilmore, Crossgar and Banbridge. The next day he made his first speech in the constituency as candidate, in the Orange Hall at Kilkeel, denouncing the main parties for their handling of the crisis in Ulster. He and his wife had planned to go to Newry, but the plan was changed when the RUC warned that it could not guarantee their safety. Powell said, 'I will go to Newry eventually, as a candidate and as a Member of Parliament.'[48] He did go to Portadown, where he had talks with West, Craig and Paisley. Their coalition, which ranged from moderate Unionists to militants with barely concealed sympathies for loyalist paramilitaries, was already shaky, and the injection of Powell's views would not make it any more stable.

His adoption by South Down was a significant boost for the Unionists. They had been in a political backwater, despite the prominent coverage given in Britain to the troubles; now they had one of the most famous politicians of the day in their ranks. Their cause could not but be better recognised as a result. It was, too, a lifeline for Powell. His influence had waned since February, partly because Heath was no longer in power, but mainly because Powell was not in Parliament. Now that he looked like coming back, his influence would depend largely on what happened in the main political parties. He would, as in the past, rely on them to create the opportunities for him to project himself. One thing, though, would obviously change: as a Conservative, Powell had spoken for a large part of his party at the grass roots, and could claim to have affected the result of the February election. Now he was not a Conservative, there was no guarantee he could continue to influence a constituency within that party, especially since many formerly loyal supporters regarded him as a traitor. The High Tory commentator Peter Utley, who had been a friend of Powell's for years, echoed the feeling of discomfort felt by many at his move to Ulster. 'I subscribe to the view', wrote Utley, 'of Captain Long, Ulster's former Minister of Education: "If the two anonymous candidates who withdrew in South Down were General Amin and Cassius Clay, I think that, on balance, the constituency made the right decision." '[49] Powell was so affronted that he did not speak to Utley for the best part of seven years after reading that, despite attempts by Utley and Bill Deedes, who a few months later became editor of the *Daily Telegraph*, to make Powell see how silly the argument was, and how Utley's remarks were all part of the rough and tumble of political journalism. Eventually Powell, who was not by nature touchy, forgave and forgot, and the two men rebuilt a strong friendship that lasted until Utley's death in 1988.

The translation of Powell to Ulster provoked another interim bout of score-settling from the party he had left behind. Hearing the news, Hailsham commented, 'It is an excellent thing that Mr Powell has joined the Ulster Unionists. They have found a new leader to desert, and he a fresh cause to betray.'[50] It was a remark that he later regarded as 'very cruel' and 'that I rather regret having said at the time'.[51]

Moderate Unionists were concerned about Powell's arrival in Ulster at a time when their notional leader, Faulkner, was politically impotent after the collapse of the power-sharing executive he had done so much to bring about. Nor did it help Powell to become accepted that the general assumption was fostered – though not by him – that he would lead the party at Westminster, and that he was definitely going to challenge Heath for the Conservative party leadership when there was a contest. Some of Powell's relatively sophisticated political pronouncements may have added to the difficulties. In South Down on 14 September, he was asked whether he would, as an Ulster Unionist, feel excluded from any leadership contest that might follow another defeat for Heath. With undue ambiguity, he replied, 'I have felt excluded from the party of which I am a member ever since the Conservative party reversed the policies on which it was elected in 1970. It is that which has excluded me, I hope temporarily, from the party to which I belong.'[52] He went on to say that, in the election campaign, the issue would be far broader than just Northern Ireland, and he would be making speeches on the mainland, particularly about the Common Market and immigration. This talk confirmed the views of some Unionists that Powell was using his new home as a power base for ends unconnected, or largely unconnected, with Ulster.

He made this statement in Raithfriland, where he went about the market square talking to farmers. In learning about their problems, he had merely adapted his basic economic doctrines to the questions affecting them. The farmers were upset about falling prices for their livestock and produce, and wanted them guaranteed by the Government. Powell, of course, wanted no such thing, and made a speech of dazzling economic logic, that, as usual, went far over the heads of most of his audience. They applauded him warmly, but it was only after he had left, and they were questioned by reporters, that they learned he had argued against exactly what they wanted. 'How did you get into this mess?' Powell had asked them. 'You listened to the Government and produced all this meat. What does a politician know about farming? You keep politicians out. They're never right. They should be getting on with their own business, which is keeping law and order, and not fixing prices and saying what's to be needed.'

Powell's rhetoric may have been the same, but in his new constituency his image had changed. The regulation black three-piece suit and homburg had been replaced by a tweed suit and cloth cap. He threw himself into the more easy-going atmosphere of his rural electors, professing particularly to enjoy the distinction the locals made between 'dry' and 'wet' rain. This new image grated with the hard-line Protestants who, despite their Unionism, were more attracted by neo-socialist policies. The magazine of the Ulster Defence Association, the *Ulster Loyalist*, denounced Powell as a member of the 'fur-coated brigade of the landed gentry', and as one embracing policies that would cause 'millions of unemployed'.[53] Its main objection to him, though, was that he was not an Ulsterman, and there was still anger that Glenn Barr had had his attempt to represent South Down, however unlikely given the UDA's distance from the Official Unionists, dismissed so peremptorily.

Powell's campaign developed the themes he had been setting out in his visits to Ulster over the preceding five years. It also contained much of the usual electioneering. Confronting a class of seven-year-olds in a primary school, he asked them what they knew of Enoch in the Bible; very little, as it turned out. 'He comes on the third page or thereabouts of Genesis,' said Powell, 'or perhaps a little further on if it is in big print. He lived rather longer than I shall live. He lived 365 years.' Elsewhere he persuaded a four-year-old boy to lend him a plastic flute he was playing and, to the amusement of a German television crew that was filming him, played the opening bars of the German national anthem.

Addressing more mature audiences, Powell said again that the Government, not the gunmen, were to blame for Ulster's troubles. Even in Ulster, the broader issues appeared. In a small and crowded Orange Hall in South Belfast on 24 September he was asked whether, once more, he would advise a vote for Labour because of the various parties' positions on the EEC. 'I cannot discover that there has been any material change since February last,' he replied.[54] A more direct endorsement would, as he was soon to find out, upset many more moderate Unionists, who in every other respect than Heath's management of Ulster had enjoyed their explicit association with the Conservatives. At Banbridge on 25 September, where Powell made his first big speech of the campaign in his constituency, after a day's solid canvassing of the town and its environs, he concentrated on what united the various parts of the Ulster Unionist coalition rather than what divided it: the abhorrence of power-sharing.

In places, cracks were showing, West had said he would not be happy for Powell to repeat his 'Vote Labour' advice; and, in private, parts of the coalition were becoming increasingly uneasy at the espousal by so prominent a politician of the complete integration of Ulster into the governing structures of the United Kingdom. Powell did not equivocate on this matter at Banbridge: 'Since Ulster is an integral part of the United Kingdom and the majority of its people will have it remain so, it must be treated as such in every respect by the Government and Parliament of the United Kingdom.'[55] He said this was not simply 'the bald statement of a constitutional truism. It is a matter literally of life and death for the men, women and children of this province; for the persistent refusal of successive governments to acknowledge by practical deeds, and not by empty formulae, the status of Northern Ireland as an integral part of the United Kingdom, has been the root cause of the death and destruction that have continued through these last five years and day by day continue still.'

On 29 September he participated in a great act of Unionist solidarity, attending a meeting in Belfast with West, Craig and Paisley to commemorate the signing in 1912 of the Ulster Covenant, which had pledged the resistance of Unionists in the Province to Home Rule. Paisley turned up to profess his delight that Powell was standing, and to express the unity of purpose the various wings of the movement felt; but that did not stop him arriving on the platform halfway through Powell's own speech, prompting the DUP supporters in the hall to interrupt the proceedings with a noisy ovation.

Powell was not personally armed during the campaign, but was surrounded by security men wherever he went. The security presence was heavy during this and subsequent elections, but Powell dispensed with his special RUC crack-shot officer in the late 1970s, feeling he had no need to be protected. On a visit to Newry on 1 October the word went up that the IRA had put a price of £1,000 on his head. His bodyguard was swelled by Royal Marine commandos with blackened faces, toting sub-machine guns. On his visit, which was more symbolic than practical, Powell did not enter the predominantly nationalist heart of the town; 87 per cent of its 13,000 inhabitants were thought to be Catholics. When pressed by reporters as to why he had not done so, he replied, 'What is the point of electioneering where there are no votes?' When a reporter countered with the view that, if he did not go into the centre, people would say he was 'yellow', Powell lost his temper. 'I'm not answering your silly questions. I'm not holding a press conference here,' he said, and walked away.[56] He had been reluctant to have personal security, but the frequency and seriousness of death threats against him put him under intolerable pressure. In 1989 he attended a seminar at the Institute of Historical Research where several former colleagues - Whitelaw, Rippon and Carr among them – greeted him with some embarrassment. Asked by Whitelaw how he was, he replied that 'in a career mainly noted for its failures, I have now received the final humiliation: I have been an MP for an Ulster constituency for many years but nobody has thought it worth trying to assassinate me'.[57]

As the campaign proceeded it became clearer to the Conservatives that Heath would lose again. This further inflamed talk of Powell's future influence on the Conservative party, with 'friends' of his reporting that he would stand back and wait to be called to serve after a great national disaster. One of his admirers in the parliamentary party, Richard Body, said, 'I have always regarded Powell as an Armageddon man, and there is a 50–50 chance that we are going to have Armageddon. I see no-one else who could rise out of the ashes.'[58] More realistic Powellites, like Biffen, felt the nature of Powell's departure still put him beyond the pale; what they were now concerned with was that a means should be found to put Powellite ideas at the forefront of Conservative orthodoxy, if necessary without Powell. Nonetheless, the 'Privy Council' had continued to meet since February, and had tried to persuade Powell to come back. When Ulster had come up, they had not felt this was the ideal solution, but had done nothing to dissuade him.

On 3 October Powell brought his campaign to the mainland, when he addressed an anti-Common Market rally in Bristol. More publicly than hitherto, he made a speech with a clear message that, given the Conservatives' unreconstructed views on Europe, people should vote Labour. Arguing, again, that a Conservative government would not reopen the question of membership, Powell said there was only one course for voters who wanted it reopened. Asked whether he was urging a Labour vote, he replied, 'I should have thought that was the clear implication of what I have said in the last three-quarters of an hour.'[59] The hall cheered him to the echo, though the questioner turned his coat inside out before he sat down. Reflecting sardonically on Britain's membership of the EEC, Powell observed that of all the last Government's achievements it was, already, 'almost the only product of its three and a half years in office which events have not already pulverised and swept away on the rubble heap of history'.

He also took care to link his speech to the official policy of his new party, which was opposed to membership. However, his other remarks were too much for some of his allies across the water. The conviction of some Unionists that Wilson wanted a union between Ulster and the Irish Republic, and the clear statement by Labour of a belief in power-sharing, were policies they found hard to reconcile with Powell's support for Labour. Lieutenant-Colonel Peter Brush, president of the South Down Association and one who had been generous in his endorsement of Powell, merely said that 'we will certainly talk to Mr Powell about this. We are bound to discuss it and we will have to produce an answer. At the moment I would rather not say more.'[60] West said he was sure Powell, as 'a very clever man', would understand the importance of confining his support for Labour to the Common Market issue. For his part, Powell refused to explain, when questioned by reporters, how he reconciled the various parts of his philosophy.

Two days later, on the Saturday before the election, he spoke in England again, this time at Manchester, and made it clear he would not be silenced by the consensus view of the Unionists any more than he had allowed himself to be by the consensus view of his former party. Making no attempt to conciliate, he described himself as one 'exiled from my own party by its flagrant and persistent defiance of the pledge that only full-hearted consent of parliament and people could authorise taking Britain into the Community'. This was still the supreme issue for him. As at the previous election, he warned voters to resist the temptation to put party before country, and widened his attack to embrace other of the Conservatives' sins under Heath, an act that would in retrospect look like the final kicking of a man when he was down: 'The Conservative Government was the chief author of the present wave of inflation which threatens to engulf us. It did so by measures which, it was predicted at the time, would have this result and which reversed the essential policies and promises on which that Government had come to office. No Government in British political history has courted inflation on a comparable scale. There is no reason to suppose that, if restored to office, it would behave differently.'[61]

Powell said that, despite the noises some senior Conservatives had been making about Heath's grasp of economics, there was no sign that the party better understood the real causes of the phenomenon then than it had 'during the years when those who drew attention to them were the constant butt of ridicule and attack'. The Conservatives offered 'no more rational' prospect of attacking the problem than any other party; if they had, then there would have been a dilemma about whom to vote for. Since they compounded this error with their continuing infatuation with Europe, there could be no prospect of supporting them. Twisting the knife, Powell also claimed that 'the Labour Government of 1964 to 1970 did not practise reversal of policies and pledges with the same thoroughness and determination, or on the same comprehensive scale, as characterised the Conservative government of 1970 to 1974'. He repeated that only votes in the Labour interest could secure the renegotiation.

Such sentiments were an extension of those he had voiced in an article, written a few days earlier, in *The Times*. He had seemed to suggest that the party system was breaking down, that 'the old certainties, and with them the old loyalties and moralities, have disappeared'.[62] This, of course, was because of the divisions in both main parties over Europe. 'On both sides there are many who wish desperately for their own army to lose the battle. They wear their familiar, faded uniform still, but only because they possess no other, and because the practical alternative to soldiering on is to quit the service altogether and become spectators.' Deeply unhelpfully to those concerned – most of them former supporters of his who had sacrificed their career prospects under Heath as a result – Powell analysed and named the section in the Conservative party whose hopes depended on Heath's defeat: they were typified by Biffen, Ridley and Bruce-Gardyne, 'who detest and fear the economic policies of the Conservative administration from 1971–74 and whose diagnosis and prescription for the central problem of inflation is, if anything, more opposed to that of Edward Heath than to that of the Labour party'.

Mischievously, though in deadly earnest, Powell quoted remarks by Keith Joseph a few days earlier in which, as he put it, Joseph had 'announced in a thoroughly articulate fashion that the Heath Government to which he belonged had been dead wrong and the Powellite analysis and critique had all the time been correct'. He added the striking claim that Joseph would write to members of the public and tell them, 'Powell was right about inflation.' The problem of explaining his way out of this, Powell went on, typified the 'embarrassment of the many reluctant warriors in the Conservative camp who hope to God King Richard will not leave Bosworth field alive'. With Labour equally divided on Europe – Powell quoted both Roy Jenkins and Shirley Williams as having said they would leave public life if Britain withdrew – it seemed as though the whole party system would have to be redrawn.

These remarks seemed to add arrogance as well as bitterness to Powell's reputation, and did nothing to console traditional Unionists. Most had thought his revenge complete when Heath had lost on 28 February, but the tone of such comments showed the continuing anger Powell felt at his treatment between 1970 and 1974, when, as he believed he could now prove, he had been right all along. In that last week of the campaign, he seemed more interested in the apocalypse he hoped was facing Heath than in anything else. This was not, despite his bitterness, because of a desire for personal revenge against his former colleague: it was because he now felt his old party had to have the stain of Heath and the Heathites expunged from it if it were to face the requisite realities. The role Powell was playing in laying the ground for that expunging could not be understated; and, paradoxically, he would not quickly be forgiven for it.

At Portadown on 7 October he said the question of whether Heath should be replaced as leader was irrelevant to him. 'It's none of my business. I'm not a member of the party.'[63] As to whether he might succeed him, he said that 'no-one can be a Conservative party leader without being a member of it. I don't go around seeking positions. I make observations on current political issues which seem to me important.' Powell derided the Conservative manifesto, in which Heath proposed, if elected, to talk to other politicians, party leaders, industrialists and trade unionists about the best way to govern. 'I am staggered and astonished beyond measure at the sight of a party leader seeking election for his party and himself on the basis that after they are elected they will discover on what policies they would propose to govern. This is the manifesto of the empty box. It is not even the Chinese box within which there are three other boxes.'

At Portadown Powell, who was now registered to vote in the Cities of London and Westminster South seat that included South Eaton Place, indicated that he had voted, by post, 'in accordance with the advice I have consistently given to those electors who share my view that Britain and the European Economic Community is the overriding question'. Asked whether that meant he had voted Labour, Powell said: 'It means exactly what it says.'[64] In order to rebuild some bridges with his own supporters, he said it would be impossible for any Unionist to join the Conservatives, given that party's views on power-sharing.

Thus far the Conservative leadership had ignored Powell, but, almost inevitably, this attack on Heath proved too much for Hailsham. At Preston on 8 October he denounced Powell for saying that the Heath Government had been the main architect of the inflation. 'That is the opposite of the truth,' said Hailsham. 'And Mr Powell either knows it or, in his insane desire to destroy Mr Heath at whatever cost to the country, deliberately shuts his eyes to the truth.' Unfortunately for him, Hailsham then tried to prove that Powell was wrong, but in doing so only proved his own limited understanding of economics. The inflation had, he said, been caused not by the explosion of the money supply, but by 'the quadrupling of oil prices, the doubling of world food and commodity prices, and the trade unions'.[65]

Dealing with the more delicate point, made from closer to home by Keith Joseph, that the Government may have over-reacted to the unemployment left by the last Labour Government, Hailsham showed that Heath's policy had been driven by sentiment rather than reason:

> It is not a point of which I am much ashamed. Having grown up in the 1930s, I have a hatred of unemployment. The reason why we over-reacted, if over-react we did, was because we hoped that, if it could be shown that we were doing our best to deal with avoidable unemployment, the unions would voluntarily restrain their demands and prevent suffering in the community. The truth is that Mr Powell is so intent for personal reasons on ruining Mr Heath that no attack, however violent, however irrational, or however evilly intentioned, is beyond him in his present frame of mind.

The desperation of Hailsham's remarks was properly indicative of the morale of his party on the eve of the election.

The night before the election Powell ended his campaign in Banbridge. In three weeks he had addressed twenty-five public meetings and covered 3,000 miles by car. His eve-of-poll meeting was preceded by a march through the town by pipe and flute bands; he marched at the head of the bands. Election day itself was spent visiting sixty-seven polling stations; there was the strong assumption Powell would win, and he remained confident. He did win, but not resoundingly. The Unionists won ten of the twelve seats, West – who had been elected for the first time in February – losing Fermanagh and South Tyrone. Most of the others won with increased majorities, some of them vastly so, but not Powell. His majority of 3,567 was down even on Orr's low score earlier in the year.

The closeness of his result was a shock for the leaders of the Unionist coalition, who had expected Powell to be given a resounding vote of confidence. He could not be accused of having failed to campaign with sufficient vigour, as he had left hardly a community uncanvassed. His critics within the Unionist movement were quick to blame his 'Vote Labour' message, and reiterated that he had seemed to be using South Down as a power base from which to conduct his battle with Heath, and to settle other scores. Some found his attitude too arrogant: an impression he confirmed in an interview he gave directly his result had been announced. Powell attacked Heath, claimed credit for the Labour victory – Wilson had a bare majority of three, the Conservatives having lost twenty seats – and suggested the Conservatives would need the help of the Unionists to regain power. Given the narrowness of Wilson's victory, the immediate assumption was that there would have to be a third election, probably within a year: few imagined the Parliament just elected would survive well into its fifth year.

Powell said to an interviewer that afternoon, 'I am popularly supposed to have won two, not to say three elections. I wouldn't say single handed. I would say I have had a little help but it is popularly the view that 1970 and 1974 bore the heavy traces of Enoch Powell. People who want to get back don't overlook that kind of evidence.' Such remarks were not designed to endear him to an electorate already suspicious of him.[66] However, in the wider world of Westminster, the reality was plain. Heath's leadership, which had survived so long only because of uncertainty over the timing of the October election, was now in a terminal state. His colleagues made the ritual noises of loyalty, but the fact that they made them at all indicated how perilous things had become for him. Carrington, candidly, advised him to quit at once.

Powell had only one observation to make directly on Heath: 'There is only one person who ruined Mr Heath, and that is Mr Heath.' It was clear there would be no immediate leadership election. It had to be called, in those days, by Heath himself, and his friends were advising him to let the dust settle before making any decision. The pressure on him to move, though, would come almost immediately from those who were not his friends. Some of those thought that, one day, Powell would rejoin the party and become its leader; but this was to ignore the fact that many of the parliamentary party, however much they admired Powell's parliamentary gifts and however much they saw he had been right, still regarded him as a traitor. That perception would, in some quarters, be slow to change, but nonetheless it did. He would not compromise to make any reconciliation easier, which was one main reason why he would miss what some still regarded as his natural destiny.

III

On the Saturday after the election Powell was in Bristol, speaking at an advertising conference. He still saw no reason to lay off Heath. He said the Conservative abandonment of political principles had spread 'a disease which is capable of destroying parliamentary democracy'.[67] He added that 'the devastation of the Conservative party in the last two elections marks a paroxysm of that disease. I hope it will prove to be the crisis at which convalescence sets in. But that will not happen unless we recognise the nature of the disease and how dangerous it is.' He reiterated his call for a fresh establishment of parties. 'Parliamentary government depends, as Disraeli proclaimed 130 years ago in his philippic against Peel, upon the differentiation of party. "Maintain", he said, "the line of demarcation between parties; for it is only by maintaining the independence of parties that you maintain the integrity of public men."' He said the election had seen the final abandonment of principle, the Conservatives relying – fruitlessly – on an appeal to electors to vote for 'moderation'. Labour must, he argued, now restore faith in Parliament – by proceeding with the renegotiation of EEC membership.

Because West had lost his seat speculation began that Powell would become leader of the Unionist coalition. There were, though, many in that coalition determined not to let him. He was still too much of an outsider for them and, in many respects, always would be. Powell himself was not pushing for the post. A list of charges was compiled against him, most of which were simply down to his unfamiliarity with Ulster: during the campaign he had occasionally mispronounced place-names and had refused to accept Irish coinage, which circulated in the Six Counties unofficially. He had condemned state hand-outs to Harland and Wolff, the Belfast shipbuilder, on whom many Protestants depended for their jobs; above all, he had told the British to vote Labour and did not believe in a return of Stormont. One Unionist politician, speaking anonymously, told the *Daily Telegraph*, 'At one time, it was thought he might take over the coalition straight away, but it is now realised he needs time to adjust.'

In other words, the Unionists had thought they were getting a phenomenon when they took Powell into their world, but they had found that his phenomenal aspects were not necessarily those that would make him the right man to come in and lead them. Above all – and this was something those who only knew Powell the public man often could not grasp – he was only human. Instead, the Unionists started to look towards Molyneaux as their new leader. The coalition members met at Westminster on 22 October, convened by Molyneaux as Chief Whip. Powell was proposed and seconded for the leadership. Craig was proposed, but not seconded. Powell said he could take up the duties only if he had complete support; Craig said the same applied to him. To break the deadlock, Harold McCusker proposed Molyneaux, who received unanimous endorsement. Molyneaux accepted the honour reluctantly – he was in favour of Powell.[68] He immediately announced that the Unionists would not be taking the Conservative whip 'at present'.[69] Powell's closest friends believe he was disappointed not to have become leader.

Just because he did not become leader did not mean he had restricted his influence. He was infinitely more experienced and gifted than any of his colleagues, and they had little choice but to defer to that. Three years later McCusker recalled the impact Powell's arrival had had on the group: 'When he joined us ... I thought of us as the new boys rather than him. He used to be a teacher, and at the drop of a hat he becomes one again. He taught us tactics. But he is never overbearing or condescending or holier-than-thou. He has had to deal over the past few years with people who must have strained his patience. To them he has applied just the same vehemence and logic in his arguments as to his peers. Nor is there any question of his dictating what the rest of us do. We are too hard-skinned a bunch for that.'[70] Powell made it his business to support Molyneaux with utter loyalty, even to the extent of addressing him as 'Sir' when a third party was present.[71]

He had a gradual absorption back into Westminster politics, his early weeks as a Unionist MP being devoted to finding his way around his constituency, and establishing a base there. He had been able to walk across his Wolverhampton seat in any direction within half an hour; he now had one that comprised 700 square miles and two ranges of mountains. He had, as a younger man, been 'contemptuous' of those who chose not to live in big, vibrant, dynamic cities; now, he felt his departure to rural Ulster was a 'rejuvenation'.[72] Molyneaux appointed him spokesman on Treasury and economic matters and the EEC; and he found himself speaking in the Commons far more frequently than ever before, representing his party on many of the great issues and in many of the great debates, because of his seniority and expertise.

However, he found himself increasingly distracted by the Conservative party, which was beginning to tear itself apart after its second successive defeat. Keith Joseph and Margaret Thatcher had already signalled a desire to go their own way intellectually with the foundation of the Centre for Policy Studies. Joseph, whom the right had considered their natural leader in the battle they hoped would soon come with Heath, had seemed to rule himself out of the succession following the reaction to a speech he made on 20 October about the need for birth control to be made more available to the lower social classes – caricatured as the 'Pills for Proles' speech. The events of the next few months, which would culminate in Mrs Thatcher's succession, were dispiriting for Powell, despite the fact that many of the policies advocated by the Thatcher–Joseph axis were ones he himself had propounded for the best part of twenty years. He had realised long since that he would not hold office again, and knew that the advice to vote Labour would prevent a reconciliation with his old party. Now, he saw those who had compromised more than he had preparing to prosper with his policies, and to seek the power he had never had to implement them.

As his biographer Roy Lewis commented, Powell observed Joseph setting out the policies with 'no acknowledgements; Powellism without Powell suddenly offered big political rewards'.[73] Lewis aptly described the Centre for Policy Studies as 'an institute to depowellise the alternative Conservatism with which he proposed to transform the party, and perhaps his own position in it'. Though in time the debt to Powell would be acknowledged with good grace, for practical purposes he had become dispensable.

On his return to the Commons, Powell found little had changed. In the debate on 'The State of the Nation' on 5 November he found himself rebuking Foot for misunderstanding the causes of inflation, a lesson he felt even Labour should have learned from the Heath years. In the debate on Healey's Budget the following week, Powell took a far less critical line than he had adopted towards the measures of Healey's predecessor: he praised Healey for using increases in price, either through higher taxation or the removal of subsidies, to ensure economical use of resources. There was, though, still a system of price control, which Powell said he hated and which was 'totally useless'; but Healey's policy was moving in the right direction.[74] He credited the Chancellor with a desire to control public expenditure, and said that that policy would have his full support. As such, if the Opposition chose to vote against the Budget, Powell and the Unionists would not feel justified in joining it. It was an early sign to his erstwhile colleagues of his continuing intransigence, and of the effect it would have on the party to which he now belonged.

Having for the moment exhausted himself where Heath was concerned, Powell now became the moral scourge to flay Heath's collaborators. On 22 November, notwithstanding his recent history, he addressed a Young Conservatives' conference at Eastbourne and, in a speech bilious even by his standards and showing more signs of intolerance of his old party than ever before, said the manoeuvring going on over the leadership was evidence of how politically corrupt the party had become. He talked of the 'spectacle' of Conservative MPs who, in February and October, had urged electors to make Heath Prime Minister, but were now 'declaring to high heaven that "Ted must go" '.[75] Powell asked:

> Why? What has happened since the tenth of October? Edward Heath is the same person now as then. Not one of his faults or imperfections or failings, not one of his virtues or abilities or capabilities, has changed.
>
> Were these Conservative members and candidates mistaken before October 10, so that the scales were only dislodged from their eyes by the shock of defeat? Or did they hold their present opinion of their leader at the very time when they were asking the electors to put him back in Number Ten? The squalid answer is that all they cared for was their seat. As long as those were at stake, it was 'Ted for PM'. The morning after, it was 'Ted must go.' What sort of people must the electorate think these men and women are, and what confidence can it have in any other advice that they tender to it?

This seemed like the final burying, by Powell himself, of any notion that he might lead his old party. He was saying they were morally not sufficiently fit to be led by him, given the sacrifice he had made the previous February. He was pointing at them and telling them they had lied: he alone had told the truth. Margaret Thatcher, who was stung by Powell's attitude, would maintain that it was precisely because she had sat through the compromises and retreats from principle of the Heath years that she was so determined not to emulate them herself.[76]

Powell said that, to keep their jobs, those who had not believed in the EEC or in the incomes policy had exercised 'the excuse of the scoundrel down the ages'. He said that 'in public men it is corruption – the selling of the public interest for private gain ... so deep has become the electorate's cynicism that it no longer expects any correspondence between belief and behaviour, words and actions, on the part of its representatives'. He also referred contemptuously to those MPs who had voted for the European Communities Bill on second reading because they feared they would not be readopted if they rebelled. And he singled out, without naming the men concerned, the 'farce' of Teddy Taylor and Jasper More, who had both resigned from the Government over the Bill and yet had loyally voted for it on second reading – ironically, not unlike his, Birch's and Thorneycroft's vote for the economic policy over which they had just resigned in 1958. Other than them – and they had blotted their copybook – no minister had had 'the common decency to resign' despite the epic U-turn of the Government. Finally, Powell ridiculed Keith Joseph for his recent admission that the Heath economic policy had been wrong.

There could be no possibility of reconciliation. If the Conservatives ditched Heath, the morally unfit would have to choose one of their own to lead them. This tone alarmed some of Powell's friends, notably Ralph Harris, who wanted the Conservative party to embrace Powellite doctrines, and (working within the realities) saw Joseph as the man most likely to bring that about. Harris wrote to Powell on 30 November to beg him to take a more conciliatory attitude, especially in the light of Joseph's public repentance. Powell's reply, dated 2 December, showed there could be no question of this. Speaking of Joseph, Powell wrote:

> his offence does not consist in discovering and confessing past error. If he had been elected in 1970 on a policy of price and wage controls to cure inflation, I would have no complaint if subsequent experience and reflection led him to conclude that the policy was unsound.
>
> That is not what happened. He was elected 'utterly rejecting the philosophy of compulsory wage control'. As an intelligent man, he knew why such a strong assertion could safely be made – namely, the irrelevance of such control to inflation, which therefore had other causes. That policy was suddenly reversed in the third quarter of 1972 by the government to which Joseph belonged; and he was not so immersed in the social services as not to know. He held his peace, however, until he no longer had cabinet office, salary, car and chauffeur to sacrifice and could expect to gain rather than lose personally by re-affirming what he had always been aware of. I did my best, but evidently inadequately, to make this clear at Eastbourne.[77]

Joseph's line, to members of the public who pointed out the discrepancy between his new position and the one he had maintained during the Heath Government, was that 'I accepted the 1970–1974 policies as the least bad options. I was too preoccupied with my departmental work to do the study and brooding that I have done since.'[78] That Powell kept a copy of these remarks in his papers showed how he regarded Joseph's conversion.

Harris, and other of Powell's friends, also had a further concern: that he was deeply unhappy and under immense strain. This was something Powell was determined to contradict:

> I am in fact happier and more at peace with myself now than for two or three years. I can support a cause I had publicly advocated – almost alone among GB politicians – since 1969; I can pursue uninhibited my opposition to membership of the EEC; and I no longer face the dilemma between party allegiance and personal conviction, political or economic. It is only journalism to imagine that I spend time wondering, or, still less, contriving, how I am going to 'lead the country' or all the rest of it. I do not: I am content day by day to say what I deem needs to be said, whether heard or understood or not, and to do the work that lies to my hand with what craftsmanship experience has given me.

Notwithstanding these protestations of contentment, Powell could still be extremely prickly. Not long after he had come back into the House, his successor in Wolverhampton, Nicholas Budgen, went up to him in the lobby to pay his respects. When he had introduced himself, Budgen was looked 'up and down' by Powell who said, 'Thank you very much. I know who you are,' before walking away.[79] A few years later he confided in Jonathan Aitken that, 'when I come to meet St Peter, one of the things I shall find it hardest to answer for is my treatment of Nicholas Budgen in the early days'.[80] Powell soon realised the sincerity of Budgen's regard for him, and the two men became devoted friends.

The Birmingham pub bombings of 21 November 1974 once more concentrated attention on Northern Ireland. The Government introduced the Prevention of Terrorism Bill, on which Powell spoke in the Commons when the second reading took place a week after the outrage. He stressed the difficulty of legislating 'in haste and under the immediate pressure of indignation on matters which touch the fundamental liberties of the subject; for both haste and anger are ill counsellors, especially when one is legislating for the rights of the subject'.[81] He pointed out the unusual – but not unprecedented – step of proscribing membership of certain organisations in Britain, and of ordering the removal of a British subject from one part of the Kingdom to another. However, he agreed with Jenkins, the Home Secretary, that as the Bill was aimed at saving lives in a crisis, the burden of proof rested, for once, on those who said it was uncalled for. He observed, though, that to term the measure 'a Prevention of Terrorism Bill' was 'an almost humorous optimism'.[82] As he had said repeatedly during the Heath years, terrorism was a form of warfare; it would be prevented not by laws and punishments, but by the aggressor's certainty that the war could not be won. Jenkins himself had said in the Commons after the bombings that this was a situation that could not be dealt with by appeasement, and Powell praised him for that.

Powell's main concern about the Bill was that it should treat Northern Ireland and the rest of the Kingdom absolutely identically, so that it could be demonstrated that the Kingdom was at one in its defence against the terrorists. He was concerned that one of its provisions – to keep suspected terrorists off the mainland but not out of Northern Ireland – should be made reciprocal; he moved an amendment to that effect when, later that day, the Bill went into committee. Returning to his constituency the following week, he renewed his earlier call for identity cards in Ulster.

In between the Birmingham atrocity and the Commons debate on the emergency legislation, Powell had a secret meeting with Harold Wilson in the Prime Minister's room in the Commons, with the knowledge only of Molyneaux and Craig among the Unionists. According to Powell's own memorandum of the event, Wilson welcomed him back to the Commons and they agreed that 'the interview had not happened'.[83] Powell told Wilson that for the 'pacification' of Ulster to take place under a Labour government would be a 'more secure result' for the Province than if the Conservatives attempted it. He added that the Unionists 'would do nothing for the sake of embarrassing the Government', and mentioned to Wilson that 'I had in fact told Merlyn Rees that my first duty was to assist government and that I had placed myself at his disposal to that end.' He warned Wilson of the dangers of treating the Six Counties as a separate country from Great Britain, as the Prevention of Terrorism Bill did, because of the encouragement this would give to the IRA, and of being seen to counter terrorism differently in the two parts of the Kingdom. Wilson agreed that in principle the approach to terrorism should be the same throughout the Kingdom, and said that he had instructed Rees and Jenkins to act accordingly. On Powell's other complaint, Wilson foresaw practical difficulties.

Remarkably, Wilson then used the interview to give Powell some political advice. 'The Prime Minister went on to say that from my point of view it was a fortunate accident that a major Northern Ireland subject had come up so early,' Powell recorded, 'since I could satisfy the expectations of my Ulster constituents by operating prominently on it, and then be able to operate at large upon economic and other subjects. He had previously intimated that he studied very carefully everything which I was reported to have said or written, whether on the subject of Northern Ireland or generally, but implied doubt as to whether my views on integration [of Ulster into the political system of Great Britain] were widely shared.' Had Wilson's colleagues in the parliamentary Labour party known of this cosy chat with one of the party's main hate figures, they would have died of horror. Powell wrote to Wilson on 30 November to alert him to 'the great trouble taken by Roy Jenkins and Merlyn Rees to render the Prevention of Terrorism Bill as acceptable as possible', and to say how much the Unionists appreciated it.

Powell and Wilson had generally good relations, based on a great mutual respect that belied the occasional public statements the two men had made about each other. Wilson recognised, sagely, the need his party might have for the Unionists before the end of the parliament, and saw no need not to treat Powell with the respect the former cabinet minister deserved. When that winter the Commons was preparing to take action against the former Postmaster-General John Stonehouse, who had faked his death leaving a string of debts, Powell was prominent among the minority who felt that no precipitate action should be taken against Stonehouse, who was innocent until proved guilty of any crime. When rumours began to circulate that Stonehouse would be removed from the Privy Council, Powell wrote to Wilson of his concerns in this matter, telling him – on Privy Council terms – of his disapproval of Macmillan's striking off Jack Profumo's name from the roll of the Council in 1963. Powell was afraid that, if Stonehouse's name were removed, 'Gresham's Law will speedily set in, and any minister who has been obliged or has decided to resign from office or from membership of the House under a cloud ... will become the subject of unseemly speculation which he will seek to anticipate by volunteering for removal, a request it will seem unreasonable to refuse'.[84] Wilson assured Powell that he would want to be sure of Stonehouse's guilt before sanctioning any such action against him.[85]

The economy, for all the measures Healey had taken in his November Budget, was still in a poor state; and, to help the country out, he had been touring the world trying to raise loans, an activity Powell criticised when he spoke on the Finance Bill shortly before Christmas. He warned that, if disaster were to be avoided, the Government would have to reduce its deficit by one-third. There could be no scope for cutting taxes – a policy in which Powell, the arch tax-cutter, said he would support Healey. Healey, whatever he did, was in a terrible bind: inflation was 18 per cent, not as a result of anything Labour had done. Powell had a score to settle on that front, and chose to settle it with Mrs Thatcher, who had spoken earlier for the Opposition of which she would within two months be leader.

He said of her speech, 'I do not think I have ever heard inflation denounced more convincingly. Satan never rebuked sin with such eloquence as she denounced inflation ... then one waited; for surely something ought to have followed ... namely, the statement of what ought to be done about it.'[86] Powell knew the problem; with Heath in charge, even those, like Thatcher and Joseph, who had worked out the correct analysis could not broadcast it, for to do so would be disloyal, and self-inculpatory. Outside the House, he attacked Wilson too for still refusing to tell the truth about inflation. In his new role as an Ulster Unionist some of the sting had gone out of his criticism. As the press and his colleagues saw it, although he still spoke with massive authority, he was out of the mainstream: the great turbulence now mounting up in his old party would be carried on without him. The power that he had claimed to make and break prime ministers would not so easily be exercised again.

Powell remained, in mind, a Conservative unable to take his eyes off the seismic events in his old party. At the end of 1974 Heath was prevailed upon to call a leadership election, to be held in February 1975. As it was felt by the Powellite right that Joseph was no longer their obvious candidate, Mrs Thatcher was urged to stand against the incumbent. By a happy irony, the right-wing Selsdon Group in the party – named after Heath's ill-fated attempt at Powellism five years earlier – asked Powell to address their annual dinner on the eve of the contest. It gave Powell a legitimate opportunity, in Conservative party circles, to vent his opinions.

Unsurprisingly, he said the leadership crisis had grown out of Heath's decision to reverse the policies of 1970. He took credit for the 1970 election victory, saying that the free-market principles agreed at Selsdon had allowed him to call unequivocally for the Conservatives' election. These principles had then been 'systematically abandoned'. 'Being myself no more concerned in these goings on than any other onlooker, I will permit myself one observation,' he said.

> If the Conservative party is seeking a successor to Mr Heath who will re-establish the principles which were trampled on in office, I will tell them where to look.
>
> It is no use looking among the members of the cabinet which, without a single resignation or public dissent, not merely swallowed but advocated every single reversal of election pledge or party principle. 'Oh,' they say, 'but she – sorry, he – used to grumble a lot in private.' Maybe, but it is not among private murmurers and grumblers, disloyal colleagues, willing to wound but afraid to strike, holding one opinion outside the cabinet room but inside acquiescing in the opposite, that the leadership needed is to be found. All very well to recant now when recantation carries no penalty. It was then that those ladies and gentlemen were found lacking. It was then that they failed the party – far worse than Ted Heath.[87]

Those who find it hard to understand why, when apparently they had so much in common, Powell and Mrs Thatcher (despite willingness on her part) could not get on in the early years of her leadership will find most of the answer in these words. They also reveal the essential difference between Thatcherism and Powellism: the former creed's success was based on a recognition that, first, one must have power. Powell was never convinced, either, that a woman could thrive in high office, let alone in the premiership; he did not believe that Mrs Thatcher had the right instincts to carry the programme through – she was in favour of the EEC. But, above all, he believed that Heath ought not properly be succeeded by someone who had served in the Government he had led.

If Powell was, as many commentators took the opportunity to assert at the time, feeling wretched that this golden chance for him to succeed Heath as leader of the Conservative party could not be taken, he did a remarkably good job of concealing his chagrin. Indeed, when the *Sun* invited him to give his views on the contest, he accepted with an enthusiasm that suggested he felt no personal pain at what was happening. Heath, he said, had not merely acquiesced in the main crimes of his administration; he was the driving force behind them. He had capitalised on a change in the nature of the Conservative party.[88]

'Neither Macmillan nor Churchill nor any Conservative Prime Minister I know of could have made his cabinet and party stand on its head time and again, like a ringmaster with a performing animal, without a single minister resigning or a major outbreak in the ranks,' Powell said. 'The Conservatives in Parliament were no longer that sort of people. Politics for them was no longer that sort of thing. These people were nearer to paid public servants, and their politics to a professional career. The Tory Party had run out of its most characteristic ingredient – gentlemen.' This had, he admitted, followed a trend in the times, the drive towards 'professionals' sustained by staffs of research assistants, perks and large salaries; it was a trend the party should have refused to follow. He never believed that, had he stayed, he would have become leader. 'The Conservative Party', he recalled in 1995, 'was always too wise to be led by me.'[89]

IV

Powell's main concern, while these excitements were being concluded, was to do what he could to get Britain out of the EEC. A renegotiation – the superficiality of which was not yet apparent to him – was now taking place and the referendum had been promised for June. Speaking on 1 February 1975 at a rally in Kent, he insisted that British trade would not be harmed by withdrawal: the other members of the Community needed to trade with Britain far more than she needed to trade with them. He also echoed a sentiment he had uttered in his constituency a week earlier, that Britain did not have so little self-confidence that she needed to belong to the Community. He found himself on the platform with Clive Jenkins, general secretary of the white-collar union ASTMS, whose principal complaints about the EEC were higher food prices and upward pressure on unemployment.

On another occasion one colleague at an anti-Europe meeting was Michael English, a Labour MP, subsequently attacked by colleagues for sharing a platform with Powell; he was one of only three Labour MPs who had said they were prepared to appear in public with him. Defending himself, English pointedly remarked that 'unlike some of my Labour colleagues, I did not want to vote to keep a Conservative government in power when it carried the European Communities Bill with a majority of eight'.[90]

Another constitutional issue was arising, and would run for the rest of the Parliament: the Government's commitments to devolution in Scotland and Wales. The House debated the subject on 4 February. Powell got to the heart of the question in saying that it was not about Scotland, or Wales, but 'the problem of England'.[91] Listening to the Leader of the House, Ted Short, speaking the previous day, Powell said he had 'reflected how gaily the vessel of debate can sail as long as it is traversing the waters of platitude and vagueness'. The main absurdity, as he saw it, was the question of Scottish representation in the Commons; it would only work if the Scots wanted to get out of the Union completely. Powell had always based support for the Union with Northern Ireland on the fact that most in the Six Counties wanted it. When it came to handling Scotland, he said, 'the experience of our forefathers in Ireland is as drastic an object lesson as we could require'.[92] Anything the Scots wanted would have to be instead of, not as well as, the Westminster Parliament. 'The House of Commons', he said, 'brooks no competition and no concurrent authority in any part of the realm.'

When Mrs Thatcher was elected Leader of the Opposition on 11 February, Powell attributed her success to 'luck'. She had been faced by 'supremely unattractive' opponents, and had been 'the number that was up just at that time'.[93] Without a trace of wistfulness, he added that 'of course, if it had been six months earlier it would have been somebody else. If it had been six months later it would have been somebody else. I am not making a complaint, because this is in fact how that particular position nearly always gets filled. It is just who happens to be there at the time.' Mrs Thatcher had said there would be no place for Powell in her shadow cabinet. 'She was right enough,' he said. 'In the first place I am not a member of the Conservative party and secondly, until the Conservative party has worked its passage a very long way it will not be rejoining me. I stand where the Conservative party stood in 1970 on all the major issues. It has got to get back there and when it gets back there, Bless my soul, there will be our old friend Enoch waiting on the shore to welcome them and hand them ashore off the boat.' Powell was not going to miss an opportunity to crack a joke at Heath's expense, even though he was now beyond the grave. 'Perhaps we shouldn't use boat metaphors nowadays, you've got to be careful, you know.'

For the moment, Powell's relevance seemed to have been eclipsed. He regularly spoke in his constituency and elsewhere about the Ulster situation, that month warning the media not to take the IRA so seriously – their credibility being even lower than that of Goebbels – and the Government not to allow any *quid pro quo* to them for any truce or ceasefire. He was working hard in South Down, determined to become acquainted as quickly as possible with its every hamlet, though he had imposed his own way of doing things on a slightly startled populace. There was no surprise that, for example, he always insisted on any questions put to him being written down and sent to the Commons, rather than answered in an oral exchange in the street. In a part of the world where fellow feeling runs high, his apparent lack of warmth – what was really his well-mannered formality towards strangers – did not go unnoticed.

The referendum campaign occupied more and more of his time. At a rally in London on 22 February he said that, even if the vote was to stay in, that would be only an interim measure: it could be reversed, and one day would be. As if distancing himself from a defeat, he said a referendum 'will not decide whether Britain is to be part of the Common Market or not. What it will decide is whether Britain ceases to be part of the Common Market now or somewhat later.'[94] Yet for all his rhetoric Powell could now be little more than a constituency MP, albeit a celebrated one. At the end of February, speaking in Croydon, he returned to immigration, which, as always, secured him plenty of column inches. He renewed his apocalyptic vision of the future, saying that there would be an England 'rent by strife, violence and division on a scale for which we have no parallel'.[95] He also denounced again those who 'covered up' the true immigration figures, and lamented that Parliament no longer felt the need to debate the subject.

Criticism of the speech rumbled on for days, led by Shirley Williams, the Prices Minister. As usual, black community leaders called for Powell to be prosecuted. As usual, he was not. Later that week he attended another anti-EEC rally where, as before, his usual left-wing detractors were on the platform with him. This rally, at Brighton, was attended by more than 1,100 people, with almost as many unable to get in. Powell made his familiar points about national self-determination, and was given a standing ovation. Such sections of opinion were now his constituency within England.

He had an opportunity in late March 1975 to speak outside his now normal areas of concern. He stood up on the second reading of the Sex Discrimination Bill to say he objected to it in principle. He also realised nothing he could say would stop the measure: 'It is an ungrateful task to oppose a piece of legislation which will certainly be wafted on to the statute book by the combined commitment of all political parties. There is a German proverb to the effect that against stupidity the Gods themselves contend in vain; but when the stupidity is fashionable to boot, the frowning battlements are indeed impregnable.'[96]

Powell said he was in favour of removing all legal disabilities from women; what he objected to was the effort the Bill was making 'to detect discrimination and to lay it open to legal proceedings'. Some of the drafting he found simply absurd. The Bill was, he said, 'a denial of the infinite differentiation of jobs and of those best fitted to perform them ... here is a Bill which sets out to eliminate the effects of that differentiation except where it is total or absolute. This is a defiance of reality.'[97] His main argument was that legislation was unnecessary because the market would deal with discrimination against women. Powell admitted there were prejudiced employers, who would pay more than necessary in order to get a man. 'Everyone', he observed, 'is entitled to conduct his own business to his own disadvantage; but those who do so are destined to be in a small and disappearing minority, for the simple processes of society and of the market ensure that those prosper and continue to provide services who pay the going rate for the best available factor of production. It is, therefore, a delusion to suppose in the field of pay that as between men and women there can be unequal pay for identical services.'[98]

The same, he added, applied to other symptoms of discrimination: the market would always ensure that the best person got the job, for if he – or she – did not, the prejudiced employer would be put out of business by someone less restricted in his outlook. He made a prophecy about the Bill that did not turn out wildly inaccurate: he said it would 'introduce suspicion, discord, doubt and anxiety on the part of employer and employee. Wherever it is sought to be enforced there will be the intrusion of the law and of the investigatory powers of the [Equal Opportunities] commission into the affairs not merely of large firms but of all but the smallest. Where before there was a perfectly natural relationship founded upon common sense and on an understanding that the opportunities were adapted to the different propensities and skills which were on offer, in place of that there will be introduced discord and envy.'[99] The one act of over-optimism Powell applied in this attack on what would come to be called 'political correctness' was that the Commission was 'bound to fail'; despite many of the other problems about which he warned coming to pass, it is still with us.

A White Paper was published at the end of March setting out what the Government claimed had been achieved by the EEC renegotiation, and the Commons debated the question over three days in early April. It brought a moment of drama on the last day when Powell and Heath jousted with each other across the chamber, after Heath had interrupted Powell's speech. Heath had spoken earlier, and Powell began his own remarks by referring to what his former leader had said. Heath had recalled that his own maiden speech, twenty-five years earlier, had been about the wisdom of accepting the Schuman Plan; and Powell recalled how, in the division that followed, he had ignored a party line on Europe for the first, but not the last, time. That said, Powell proceeded to devote his speech to the phrase with which he had for years been taunting Heath: 'full-hearted consent'.

Powell asked why it was that membership of the EEC was so unique an act that it, unlike almost anything else that Parliament undertook to do, required 'full-hearted consent'. It was not because of the need to align British policies with those of other Western European states, in order to avoid mis-understandings from which serious consequences could flow; it was not for reasons of defence, or of economics or commerce. Powell was about to explain what the real reason was when Heath rose, and he willingly gave way to him. 'I have never taken the right hon Gentleman up on this point before, but lest he should say that it has gone by default I want to make it absolutely plain that I have never suggested that whole-hearted consent or full-hearted consent in this country would be done other than through Parliament.'[100]

Heath, too, was interrupted, by the former Labour minister Ernest

Fernyhough. 'Parliament and people,' he said, refreshing Heath's memory and expressing an apparent contradiction to what Heath had just said. Heath, in turn, immediately clarified Fernyhough's clarification. 'By people, through Parliament. I still adhere to that.' Powell gave his interpretation. 'I was not concerned with the question whether the consent of Parliament and people was to be one and indivisible. I was concerned with the unique nature of the necessity for full-hearted consent which has been attached to this step. However, since the right hon Gentleman raises the point, I will place on record that the full-hearted consent of Parliament has never been given to this measure.'

This caused cries from pro-marketeers who begged to differ with Powell's analysis. He stated that he did not regard the seven-to-five majority of October 1971 as 'full-hearted'. As for the Bill itself, that had got through 'by reason of a guillotine motion, carried by a majority of 11. So not even Parliament in its legislative capacity, doing its work in its proper way, has yet given its full-hearted consent.'[101] Heath was not prepared to take this, and rose for a second time. He told Powell that the vote of October 1971 was a vote in principle for Britain to go in, and the majority of 112 was 'a substantial majority'. He added, imperiously, 'As the late Sir Winston Churchill said to me on one occasion, "In our system one is enough." That is perfectly true. Nor can the right hon Gentleman object to the procedure of a closure motion being used when it is part of our normal procedure.'

'I can quite understand', Powell replied, 'the right hon Gentleman's sensitivity on this point. It is significant that in the context of a full-hearted consent, which he claimed to be necessary, he refers to the dictum that a majority of one is sufficient.' He said Heath had brought him to his main point, which was that such consent was necessary because of the huge and unprecedented sacrifices of sovereignty that had been entailed. The renegotiation, he said, had changed nothing substantial. The Government, which had earlier been so concerned about many of the provisions of the treaty, was now saying it was really not so bad as it had thought. The decision was still whether to stay in or get out; and Powell saw his old party determined to stay in, despite supposedly being 'devoted to the protection of British institutions', because of its continued search for 'a compensation for the real or believed loss of Empire'.[102] That the EEC had, for many Conservatives, become a 'surrogate for Empire' was 'both a fallacy and a hallucination'. There could not be power and influence for Britain in this context for, by taking part, Britain ceased to be a nation in that sense.

As well as having to deal with Heath, Powell came under attack from other Conservative backbenchers. Sir Anthony Royle – as Tony Royle had become – accused him of having written the One Nation pamphlet on Europe a decade earlier; Powell said he was happy to have the chance to put on the record that he had merely read the pamphlet in draft form, and had commented on it. Patrick Cormack reminded Powell that he had been a member of the cabinet in

1963 when Heath, on Macmillan's behalf, had tried to secure entry to the Common Market; why could Powell not admit he had changed his mind, as others had? This was the one moment of defensiveness in Powell's speech: 'Even if it were true to the fullest extent that I had totally changed my mind on this subject, as totally as the late Conservative administration changed its mind on half a dozen subjects, it would not excuse any hon Member from judging the merits of what I offer to the House and whether or not it is sound.'

If Heath and Macmillan had succeeded in 1963, and Powell had not had other cause to resign, he would have gone along with the decision, despite his 1950 abstention. However, the results of that negotiation were never put to a vote, and so Powell's willingness to resign from the cabinet, as opposed to defying the whip as a senior backbencher, on the question had not been tested. Now, in his peroration, he urged the electorate, when they had their say in June, to vote for Parliament. Thanks to large support from the Conservatives the motion approving the White Paper was carried by a majority of 226, or 396 to 170. Yet Wilson took less than half his party in Parliament with him, and had to sack one minister, Eric Heffer, for opposing the line. The continued strong opposition to Europe in Labour's ranks and the renewed enthusiasm of the Conservatives under Mrs Thatcher helped cement Powell's continuing hostility to his former party. Ironically, Lady Thatcher would later credit Powell with having been 'the first on to Europe'.[103] Powell was intensely dismayed by the shallowness of the renegotiation, and sensed (correctly) that Callaghan, the Foreign Secretary, had been neutered by the Foreign Office. The renegade's enthusiasm for Labour at two elections now looked like a misplaced trust.

Healey's Budget a week later gave Powell a chance to re-enter the debate about economic policy. The realisation that borrowing would have to rise from £7.5 billion to £10.25 billion was, Powell said, akin to walking along a precipice; if Healey could not find the money he would have to print it, which was bound to have a disastrous effect on inflation. As Powell pointed out in an article in the London *Evening News*, there was still 'the awful example of Chancellor Barber who (whether or not he knew what he was doing) budgeted to borrow £4 billion in 1972–73, with the result that in 1973 the money in circulation increased by one-quarter, and last year prices went up by 20 per cent'.[104] In Healey's first year as Chancellor the 'oil profiteers', as Powell termed them had had the money to lend to the Government; now Healey was trying the same trick again, though there was now the added risk that the 'profiteers' would want to draw their money out again, which would leave him having to print money just to stay afloat.

Healey had not quite dared go that far, for that reason and because of the fear of being crippled by interest repayments. Instead of borrowing £10.25 billion he had decided to borrow just £9 billion, and to raise the rest through tax increases. He had not, though, to Powell's distress, said he would cut expenditure – which,

Powell said, in the light of the tax rises, was 'like clapping with one hand'. The Chancellor had promised to look at spending the following year. This, Powell suggested, was because the political unpopularity of putting up taxes was all the Government could take; the unpopularity of cutting services and public sector activities as well would have been too much, particularly given the precariously small majority. Also, Powell knew that Healey was worried about the inevitable concomitant of the tighter policy he was following: the already obvious rises in unemployment.

Speaking later in the debate on the Budget, on 21 April, Powell developed his critique. Most unflatteringly to his former party – for he made it clear that the present inflation was the result of their policies – he said that the situation was akin to Germany in 1923, when hyperinflation had been accompanied by unemployment. He said he found the debate 'weird'.[105] 'In the eerie emptiness of the Chamber during most of the debate one hon Member after another, and especially from each of the front benches, has echoed, literally or by implication, the cry that "we are all monetarists now". Many have tumbled over one another in their eagerness to swear fealty to monetarism.' Powell was not above rubbing it in, and he was not above rubbing in how little the converts understood to what they had been converted. He satirised the beliefs of some of the converts that, at some stages, inflation could be caused by rising prices, at others by rising wages. 'Some of the language used in the debate', he said, 'has been positively antediluvian in its continued belief in such concepts as inflationary price increases, inflationary wage increases and the rest.' In this regard, he said the speech of the Chancellor of the Duchy of Lancaster, Harold Lever, had been 'rather embarrassing, because the House is really fond of the right hon Gentleman'.[106]

He said Healey's failure to reduce the deficit below £9 million, with the hint that he would cut it further next year, was 'total delusion'. The Chancellor had spoken, on taking up his office, of a borrowing requirement of £2.7 billion that had become one of £7.3 billion, and this had borne out a basic fact of Treasury control, 'that for the purposes of Treasury control next year does not exist – it is a non-existent period of time. When a Chancellor of the Exchequer starts talking about what he is going to do to expenditure next year, we may be assured that we are lost.' He saluted Healey's recognition that long-term planning for the purpose of estimates was futile; it could not happen in a period of steeply rising prices. Powell referred again to his objections, as Minister of Health, to the Plowden Committee's report, and said that, at last, he had been vindicated. Healey challenged Powell's assertions about his 'delusion', but Powell told him bluntly that 'unless the net borrowing requirement is halved in the present year, nobody will believe it will be eliminated in the next year'.[107]

His advice on where to find the savings was unequivocal – on roads, and other construction projects. It would mean a severe shock to those industries, but such a shock would have to happen somewhere in the economy. Unemployment would have to happen too; but the longer the delay before imposing the solution, the worse it would be. To do otherwise, he said, would be a dereliction of duty. The Government took no notice. The strictures that would have to be imposed from outside, by the International Monetary Fund eighteen months later, thus became inevitable.

In Northern Ireland, Powell started to concentrate on one of his main goals – expanding the parliamentary representation of Ulster. Speaking in his constituency on 19 April, as the parties were preparing for elections to the constitutional convention, he said under-representation could no longer be justified. This was particularly so because of the debate that had started about Scotland and Wales, and at least the Scottish and Welsh had a full complement of MPs to act for them. Ulster could not be left out of this constitutional review, and its people would need to be properly represented if their interests were to be properly dealt with. Suggestions that Ulster might have its own devolved independence were 'a gift for the opponents of the Union' and 'a trap', and he was filled with 'a burning resentment' that there were not more MPs to mount the correct defence of Ulster's interests.[108]

With the referendum set for 5 June, Powell continued to be unimpressed by the Conservatives under their new leadership, because of the recommendation Mrs Thatcher was making for continued membership. He denounced, in a speech at Bournemouth on 10 May, her line of argument. The original defence of membership had been that 'we shall pool our sovereignty in order to share in a more powerful sovereignty' – a delusion, but an 'honourable' argument. Now it had shifted to the argument that unless Britain stayed in the EEC she would fall prey to communism, or at best hard-line left-wing socialism. It was not an argument that Powell bought for a moment.

He also warned the party against the perception that to be pro-market was a badge of membership of the middle or upper-middle classes, for if Conservatives identified themselves too strongly with such an idea they would risk seeming the party of class division, rather than one of broad support for national institutions. Like Thatcherism after it, Powellism was rooted in the notion that the Conservative party would rest on a solid working-class base, and from that draw its strength, rather than hitherto. He prefaced his remarks as being offered as 'a word of counsel to the party to which I myself until recently belonged and – who knows? – may somehow one day belong again'.[109] However, the gap was still wide, and in the Commons on 21 May, during a debate on a measure to help British Leyland, Powell broadened it further, delivering a scathing lecture to his old party for its failure to understand economics. He urged it to appreciate – as it would before long – that bankruptcies were good for the economy, because they led to the more efficient allocation of scarce resources.

His principal theme in the referendum campaign, which he pushed against overwhelming opposition from the political establishment in all three main parties, was that Britain did have a viable alternative, and not one that involved a retreat into political primitivism. After all, things had been fine before entry, as he said at West Bromwich on 17 May: 'Only two years ago we had a rising export trade widely based throughout the world and not dependent on any particular trading system or alliance, an export trade which owed less and less to the diminishing habits of the Commonwealth, which was exploiting the Continental market successfully through remaining free from the constraints of Community membership but which, above all, was seeking and finding its opportunities in every part of the world.'[110]

As the referendum neared, and opinion polls showed heavy endorsement for the position Wilson had renegotiated, Powell became more and more bilious. The 'No' campaign was at a great disadvantage: its main high-profile speakers were Powell and Benn, who hardly saw eye to eye and strongly divided much opinion against them. The antis were embarrassed when word leaked out that Benn had refused to sit next to Powell on the 'No' side in a debate, staged in a mock-up of the Commons chamber, to be televised shortly before the vote – though Benn's refusal seemed to have more to do with the fact that, in the real House, he would not then be sitting on the same side as Powell, rather than with any personal or political antipathy.

The 'No' campaign could not match the 'Yes' either in funding or in organisation. Powell did not give up, though, until the votes were counted. He went to Arbroath, a centre of the fishing industry, on 30 May to warn that Britain was on 'a hiding to nothing' about control of territorial waters, since in the years ahead there would be common waters in which no country had any more right to fish than any of its neighbours in the Community – or, as Powell put it, 'any other province of the new superstate'. Instead, he complained, 'the Government tell us that they propose to take it up after the referendum. I assume they intend to crawl to Brussels on their knees, or go there barefoot, like the German Emperor begging the Pope's pardon at Canossa. First of all, throw away all your bargaining power and then afterwards see what you get.'[111]

The next day, at Blackpool, he attacked Heath and the other pro-marketeers as 'the men who have been always wrong' and who had devoted themselves to trying 'to frighten and bully the British people into mistrusting their own instincts and common sense'. He added that it looked as though, as the referendum approached, 'the signs accumulate that these irrational fears are starting to weaken'.[112] Such optimism would not bear fruit. By 3 June, two days before the vote, Powell's public pronouncements were taking on a more sombre tone. At the 'No' campaign's main press conference, he said that if the people voted to stay in there would be a 'revulsion' among them at the decision within months; and he said that if they did vote yes, he would not rest from his campaign against the EEC. He was confident that, once membership was confirmed, 'the things that will crawl out from under the carpet and the things which will take place in the months, let alone years, following will be such that the bulk of the British people will say: "We were deceived, taken for a ride, and we will have none of it" '. He condemned the public for not listening to what the EEC was telling them of its intentions, much as Britons had failed to listen to what Hitler told them in the 1930s. The Community 'has been telling us that it intends to become a superstate, and we persist in this country in waving it aside, and the politicians have gone along with the national tendency not to believe what their friends intend to do when they say it'.[113]

Powell was also contemptuous of Mrs Thatcher for not, as he saw it, putting her head above the parapet on the issue, though he conceded it was wise for her to do so because there was no point the new leadership 'spiking itself irrevocably on the policies of the former discredited leadership'. She had made a series of speeches in the north of England on the issue, but none since 6 May – a month before the referendum – as part of a deliberate strategy to keep her distant from Wilson, the better to attack him on other issues once the campaign was over. She also made it clear, on the eve of poll, that a resounding yes was vital. A journalist asked Powell whether he thought Mrs Thatcher was adopting this posture out of tactics or conviction. He replied, 'I find a certain contradiction in the notion of keeping one's head down out of conviction.'[114]

Also on 4 June he wrote an article in *The Times*, largely devoted to an attack on his old party's carelessness about Europe. He said the plebiscite would not be the last chance for the people to assert themselves against the politicians who had duped them; 'if referendum day is not September 1939, at any rate it is September 1938'.[115] The other nations of the EEC had different histories and different cultures that made their sovereignty a less intense issue than it was with the British. That is why the original six of them had felt able to found the Common Market along the politically federalist lines it was now clearly seen to be following; and he warned against the blithe acceptance by the main British parties of the notion of a European parliament, then but a few years away, which would have 'nothing but the name in common with what we mean by parliament or what parliament means to us. It is another instrument for creating a new artificial state.' His final warning would prove starkly accurate: 'The British people have no notion of what the rest of the Community assumes that they are meaning by accepting membership. The mutual misunderstanding would only be heightened and rendered more dangerous if British membership appeared to be confirmed by a method which the rest would mistake for the equivalent of one of their own constitutional procedures.'

The previous evening he had gone on television to reopen the wounds of the 1972 European Communities Bill, which he said 'could not have been passed, even by the majority of eight, but for the fact that individual members were sent for by the Prime Minister and threatened. All the machinery of arm twisting and thumb screws were put on them.' The next evening, the eve of poll, Powell made the same allegation – attested to before and since by some who rebelled with him in 1972 – in Sidcup, in Heath's own constituency. Heath immediately replied that Powell was talking 'absolute nonsense', and said his allegations represented 'the last desperate slander of men who know they have already lost'. Powell used his speech at Sidcup to say that the choice the people were facing was whether or not Britain should remain a nation, for Heath's commitment to economic and monetary union, whose implementation would lead on from a yes vote, would lead to the end of sovereignty.

When the votes were counted, the people – on a low turnout – had voted by two to one to stay in the Community. Powell had expected as much, but the result was a further setback for him as he sought to rebuild his influence in national politics. When the Commons, the following week, debated economic policy in the EEC, Powell described it as the first debate on an EEC topic 'since last week's little local difficulty'.[116] He was not to be deflected. In a newspaper article four days after the poll he explained where he felt things stood now. On the vote of a minority of the electorate – but, of course, of a majority of those who turned out – 'the United Kingdom is no longer a state but has become a province'.[117] He said not one in a hundred of those who had voted yes understood what their vote meant. They had voted in support of the dictum, adduced by Heath in a speech at the Oxford Union during the campaign, that 'the nation state is obsolete', and they did not seem to have grasped the far-reaching implications of that doctrine.

What gave Powell hope was a phrase from the Government's referendum pamphlet – which had advised a yes vote – and which affirmed the perpetuation of the nation state: 'Our continued membership will depend on the continuing assent of Parliament.' He remained in good spirits, despite the result. Tony Benn recalled him coming to a party at the Commons after the poll and telling of how, a few days earlier, he had taken a taxi and the driver had asked him, 'Are you Mr Powell?' 'Yes,' Powell replied. The driver asked: 'Where do you stand on this Common Market business?' Powell said this put him properly in his place; he told the driver that he didn't much like it. The driver said he didn't either – 'because it will mean that we won't be able to rule ourselves'. 'Which shows', Powell said, 'the common sense of the British people.'[118]

LABOUR'S TORY

On 12 June 1975, almost as soon as normal political life had resumed, the Commons came to vote on the principle of having a Register of Members' Interests, a matter proposed while Powell had been out of the House. It agreed to have one by a vote of 181 to 21. Powell, who disapproved, said he would not participate unless an Act of Parliament legally required it; otherwise, the House had no right to impose additional conditions on his membership. He said the decision the previous year had been made in an atmosphere of 'hysteria' about Members' interests; it was as well for the House to reserve the right to change its mind.[1] He explained that he would be opposing the move because he found the proposal 'ineffective and degrading', and because he believed it 'unlawful and unconstitutional'. He wished Members to rely on 'the time-honoured assumption that we behave honourably in this House'. Time would show, though, that however ineffective the register in time turned out to be, Powell's notions of the honour of fellow MPs, based on his own high standards, were well adrift from reality.

The EEC issue disposed of, Powell re-entered other fights, in Northern Ireland and nationally. With inflation now over 20 per cent and climbing – it would peak that autumn at 26.7 per cent, a legacy of Heath's and Barber's management – he saw an obvious target. On 20 June, speaking to Young Conservatives in Littlehampton, he referred to calls from both sides of the Commons to implement an incomes policy. 'The times are dangerous,' he said, 'and at such times there is a morbid fascination for politicians about a policy which has always proved fatal in the past.'[2] The measure was still discussed inside and outside Parliament 'it terms of total illiteracy'. He blamed the continuing inflation on the £9 billion deficit Healey planned to run in the year ahead, and which would lead to Britain's near-bankruptcy in 1976. For the moment, the Government was preparing to blame the people for its own failings, 'while the nation sweeps, like a vessel out of control, towards the economic Niagara'.

If he was angry with his old party for still – in parts – entertaining these fallacies, he was even more outraged at its failure to make a formal response to new immigration figures that showed the rate of inflow running at levels even above those of the mid-1960s. New Home Office figures showed that nearly 90,000 New Commonwealth immigrants had arrived in 1974, way above the average of 35,000 a year in the previous years. 'All the machinery of official misrepresentation was put into operation,' Powell said of the presentation – or otherwise – of this news. 'This startling figure was not even mentioned in the Home Office press statement which accompanied the White Paper. A more violent antithesis to the policy of "no further large-scale immigration" on which the Conservatives won the 1970 election cannot be imagined. Can you imagine an Opposition which sees the policy it promised and which the electorate demanded being reversed so dramatically and not screaming blue murder? Not a bit of it. It is because they know that in 1972 they themselves broke their pledge of "no further large-scale immigration".'[3]

Powell used this speech, at Liverpool, to indict the Conservative party on two other charges. The first was its silence in the case of his old schoolfellow, Denis Hills, condemned to death for treason by Idi Amin in Uganda, but who had been released following the personal intervention of Callaghan, the Foreign Secretary, and the Queen. Powell said Callaghan's behaviour had been improper and should not be repeated; worse, 'The Crown had been humiliated. The nation was outraged. The House of Commons and Her Majesty's Opposition were silent.' Second, he attacked the Conservatives for allowing the 'ludicrous' Sex Discrimination Bill to pass with their 'solemn approval and co-operation.' He followed up his charge against Callaghan in the Commons on 23 June, asking him 'how did the Prime Minister dare to court the humiliation which has been inflicted on the Crown by advising the Queen to write to President Amin?' Callaghan replied that 'the right hon Gentleman is always idiosyncratic in his views'.[4] A decade later, when Hills met Powell at a party – their first meeting for fifty-five years – he told Powell he agreed with his protest. 'The risk of the Queen being humiliated,' Hills told him, 'had I known about it at the time, would have been unacceptable.'[5]

For a time, Powell took a lower profile. He devoted more of his time to the concerns of his constituents and of Northern Ireland in general. On 6 July he made a difficult speech to a rally in Kilkeel, County Down, attempting to define the concept of 'loyalty'. He said that 'to be loyal is, for the Unionist, to accept the will of parliament as expressed in the law of the land, which is made by the Crown in parliament'.[6] Loyalty could not be qualified to a point where it meant accepting some things done in the name of the Crown and not others. 'What, however, no person who calls himself a Unionist can do, without self-contradiction, is to place limits or conditions upon his obedience to the Crown in parliament,' he added. 'He cannot say: "If parliament makes laws I do not like, I will not obey them." He cannot say: "Unless parliament amends the present laws in the way I want, I will go off and declare myself independent." '

He had sensed the controversy this would cause to a group who had long regarded it as their right to pick and choose where Westminster was concerned; he had his speech distributed in London rather than through the Unionist publicity machine in Belfast. What he said provoked some of the more extreme loyalists. Paisley said he inferred from Powell's statements that if Westminster parcelled Ulster off to a united Ireland, the loyalists would have to abide by that decision: something he and his followers would have no intention of doing. West distanced himself from Powell's sentiments, and Craig's Vanguard movement issued a statement condemning it. It read: 'Mr Powell's definition of loyalty is completely unacceptable to us and in our view a total contradiction to Unionist history. Our loyalty is to the Crown because it is a constitutional Protestant monarchy; if we accepted Mr Powell's thinking we could not have carried out things like last year's strike, which brought down the power-sharing executive which had been imposed on us.'

Powell also said the coalition should form its own single leadership, rather than being made up of the Official Unionists, Paisley and Craig, each with separate organisations and agendas. It was immediately assumed that he was making his own bid for that single leadership, but the controversy stirred up by his other remarks settled that, if this was his aim, it was a non-starter. It was also assumed – and this was more likely – that Powell had made these remarks because he wished to distance himself from colleagues who chose to ignore the final report of the constitutional convention. Powell had his own wait-and-see strategy which he hoped – correctly as it turned out – would put paid to the convention by natural causes.

Then, later in July, Powell assaulted some of the other sensibilities of his comrades, this time attacking loyalist dogma about the notions of devolution and direct rule. This annoyed his senior colleagues, who were about to have a conciliatory meeting with Conservatives about Northern Ireland policy. In his speech, in County Antrim on 20 July, Powell directly attacked the notion of the convention, which he saw as a front both for power-sharing – against which almost all the Unionists were set – and for the end of direct rule, which he was almost alone among Unionists in not wanting. He said, 'the fact that it is for the people of Northern Ireland to decide the government of Northern Ireland is the most anti-Unionist proposition that could be devised. It is something that no Unionist can both say and mean. Those who adopt it and repeat it, whether or not they know what they are doing, are repudiating the Union.'[7] He pointed out that no one was suggesting that the people of Kent or East Anglia be asked how they should be governed. 'It is for the United Kingdom and the United Kingdom alone to decide how these and all its parts are to be governed.'

Suspicion of Powell, running at a low level throughout the coalition since his election, was given a serious boost by this inability to conceal his own feelings. Some of his more sophisticated colleagues were aware, though, of logical inconsistencies in the coalition's policies. They recognised that, however embarrassing Powell's outbursts might sometimes be, they were honest. However it was his party's own Chief Whip, Captain Austin Ardill, who was the first to rise in the audience at Ballyhill and question the line Powell had just taken, with its rigid anti-devolutionist stance. 'I felt', he admitted afterwards, 'if I was to sit passively and take all he said I would be betraying my colleagues.' Ardill and his friends simply did not share Powell's faith in the institutions at Westminster. West, further vexed by this, said, 'I don't think Mr Powell has been in Ulster long enough to understand the majority of the people. I will have a discussion with Mr Powell and try to understand his reasoning.'

That month Wilson implied a return to the idea of an incomes policy, with the publication of a White Paper entitled *The Attack on Inflation*. On 22 July, when a full-scale debate was held, Powell made his objections known. Wearily, he condemned the 'staggering lack of novelty' of the proposals, and outlined how measures like them – a freeze, followed by compulsion in wage rises – had repeatedly not worked before.[8] He teased Foot in particular for having participated with him, in the intellectual destruction of the last incomes policy. Referring generally to the Labour front bench, he said that 'there might have been a time, 10 or 15 years ago, when this was a new adventure and some of them actually thought that it might work. But these men, Mr Speaker, are not fools. They have been through it all before, many times, and they are not so stupid as to think that it will turn out as advertised. They know perfectly well by now that such a policy is irrelevant to the causes and therefore to the cure of inflation.'

As when Barber and Heath tried it, Powell attributed this pursuit to the fear of unemployment; but that was going to happen anyway as a result of the fall in inflation from 25 to 10 per cent that Healey had confidently predicted in the year ahead. It would not be obviated by the 'voluntary' nature of the action the Government was proposing. It was the old 'guilt transfer mechanism' of incomes policies from earlier days, the way in which a government tried to avoid blame for something solely within its control.[9] Healey had spoken, in a speech at Tolpuddle the previous weekend, of how 'we have been living above what we are earning'. Powell said he had not made it clear that 'the people living above their means were the Government', just as Heath had not been honest about the causes in 1972–4.[10]

Later that day, the Commons was due to vote on a pay rise for MPs; Powell said he found this juxtaposition ironic, since those who had brought about the present economic mess 'are right hon Members in this Chamber, who sustain Governments, who form Governments and who fail adequately to criticise Governments'. His wrath was not reserved for the Government; it was mainly heaped on 'Her Majesty's Opposition that have had the duty and privilege to speak for England'. What he instead saw on the Opposition front bench was 'a vacuum', in which they sat huddled fearing that someone would ask them the inevitable question: 'The function of an Opposition is to be in the position to replace the Government. No Opposition, when it is challenged to say what in this grave hour needs to be done, dare reply, "You got us into this mess. It is your business to get us out of it." That is non-opposition. That is the renunciation of the constitutional function of Her Majesty's Opposition in the House and in the country.'[11] He felt that both main parties were a disgrace to the country, and urged the Conservatives in particular to advocate a separate, constructive policy. 'The moral issue behind these debates is whether or not we have become the reflection of a nation whose character has changed or whether temporarily we in this House are misrepresenting the nation. For my own part I shall not, as long as I live, believe that the character of this nation has changed. I shall never believe it – never, never, never.'[12]

When the business of the MPs' pay rise was reached, Powell made another quixotic gesture, following on from his stand over the Register of Members' Interests, that set him apart from the rest of the Commons. The House voted itself a £24 a week pay rise, but Powell – as he had first done in 1953, and had last done in 1972 – said he would not accept the rise until his constituents had had the chance to re-elect him, at what they knew would be that level of salary. 'It's a matter of taste, a personal view,' he said. 'Because an MP argues against a tax reduction it would not follow that he has to keep paying the higher rate.' Many of his colleagues thought they should be paid at least £8,000 a year – their pay had just risen from £4,500 to £5,500 – but Powell told them that even before the rise they were better off, in real terms, than MPs had been in 1950. He argued against the notion of linking pay with that of the civil service, a question he asked to have considered in detail by a select committee. He also thought the amounts claimed in parliamentary expenses were becoming excessive, and should be better vouched for: expenses would be paid without proof of the expense being incurred in a way that would not be tolerated anywhere else. His stand was regarded as eccentric, but he said his argument bound only himself; others must make their own judgments about their positions.

By the autumn, the Ulster constitutional convention was putting enormous strains on the coalition. Craig and Paisley were in open disagreement about Craig's belief that the SDLP could be made certain concessions, and offered some form of power-sharing coalition, thereby making it possible for them to remain a partner in the talks. Powell had been horrified by Craig's announcement of his idea at a meeting of coalition leaders on 8 September, and used his experience to squash it. Craig had proposed guaranteed places for nationalists in a Provincial administration, and having the RUC brought under joint control of both communities. He said he had been convinced by protestations from SDLP leaders that they would support Northern Ireland as an entity within the United Kingdom so long as a majority of its inhabitants wanted that – which, to judge from the popular vote at elections, they did. Powell told him that such 'copper fastened guarantees' that stopped short of a formal constitutional settlement would be thrown out of the Commons. It was an assertion Craig simply did not have the weight to dispute. Powell also attacked the convention's chairman, Sir Robert Lowry, for having imagined that the mandate of the body could be changed in this way, and told his colleagues that, if they took part in the convention in the guise of a negotiating body, they would be accepting part of the guilt for the IRA's activities.

Powell, in public maintaining silence on the issue, kept up the pressure in private on his colleagues to repudiate Craig's idea. The Unionist members of the convention, with the exception of the Vanguard leader, duly issued a firm rejection of power-sharing; and on 9 September Craig resigned as leader of the Vanguard Unionists within the convention, saying that his views in favour of power-sharing were simply irreconcilable with those of his former colleagues. In Belfast on 11 September Powell broke his silence, warning the Monday Club of Ulster against the continuation of the convention. He did so in the appropriately apocalyptic surroundings of the bomb-blasted Unionist headquarters in Glengall Street, raising his voice so as to be heard above the beating of rain on the temporary asbestos roof.

His strategy had been to let the convention fray at the edges, giving proof of its own pointlessness, before he moved in to finish off the job with the sledgehammer of his logic and the power of his personality. He had to be careful to garner evidence for his opposition to the convention before striking: otherwise, his intervention might be dismissed as simply consonant with his existing views about integration. Now, he said that 'the field in which the weeds of terrorism and murder spring up has been ploughed and manured, and the dragon's teeth are duly yielding their satanic harvest'.[13] He added that the situation had regressed to the days of the Sunningdale agreement, and that the majority in the Province would be 'bullied into compromising their just and repeated demands and making fateful concessions to their opponents'. He denounced 'that false compromise between incompatible political objectives which has always been the prelude to chaos in Ulster'.[14]

His colleagues – especially Molyneaux, who had almost unqualified admiration for him – got the message. At a four-hour convention meeting at Stormont on 18 September, which only the Unionists attended, Craig – who had been persuaded to come back – renewed his plea for Catholics to be allowed in the cabinet of some future, temporary coalition government in the Province. It was rejected again, by thirty-six to six. The SDLP signalled that there was no point their continuing to take part in talks. Subtly, Powell – at Stormont that day but not a member of the convention – had achieved his aim. An end to direct rule without power-sharing was anathematical to the Government, so direct rule would continue, just as Powell wanted, but with his Unionist colleagues feeling that they had, at least, saved themselves from a greater evil.

He now moved on to stiffer targets. In a speech in his constituency on the same day he attacked the Government and civil servants for continuing to condone the ceasefire between the army and the IRA – something he regarded as akin to collaboration with an enemy – seeming to single out for special criticism the permanent secretary at the Northern Ireland Office, Sir Frank

Cooper. 'It is intolerable', Powell said, 'that civil servants should remain in diligent communication, not denied by the Secretary of State, with thugs and murderers. Indeed, I find it hard to choose words severe enough to reprobate these men who, with their knighthoods and decorations, will submit to be employed in this fashion, let alone misadvise their political chiefs to make themselves responsible for this mischief. They ought, if necessary, to risk their places and their pensions rather than engage in such near-treasonable activities.'[15]

His worst insults, though, were aimed not just at the Government, but at Craig, who had just resigned from his post in the coalition, and was now being kicked even though he was down. 'What fools or knaves must people be', he went on, 'who believe, or pretend to believe, that if two or three members of the Social Democratic and Labour Party were included in an Ulster government, the IRA would flock to surrender their arms at the nearest police stations. The IRA do not care whether there are two or 22 SDLP ministers in a Northern Ireland government. What they care for is an all-Ireland republic and the power which grows out of the barrel of a gun, and which they intend to exercise.'

Four days later, on the eve of the Conservative party conference, Powell spoke to a businessman's lunch in Newcastle-upon-Tyne. He defined inflation as an addictive drug requiring a progressive increase in dosage, but warned, 'there must always be a point somewhere when this acceleration is unsustainable, because even the most imperfect adaptation of prices and relativities becomes impracticable. The wages taken home by wheelbarrow in the German inflation of 1923 are the ideogram for that critical point.'[16] He claimed that, at last, most people had accepted the Powell prescription – 'the disease of inflation in its modern form is caused by an exorbitant increase in money; and, secondly, that increase is caused by governments borrowing from the banking system in order to cover excess public expenditure'. This being so, he added, it should be relatively simple to agree on the main course of treatment: the gap between income and expenditure had to be greatly reduced, to a point where the deficit could be covered by voluntary lending from the private sector. This required convincing the electorate that it had no choice between ending and not ending inflation, but a choice between ending it sooner, or later when 'the life of the patient himself may be endangered by the violence and the side effects of the transition'.

The following week Powell went to South Africa on a four-lecture tour – visiting the country, it was noted, at the same time as his old opponent, George Brown, there to address an investment conference. He predictably found himself questioned on arrival on his views on apartheid. He replied that he was in the country 'merely for the lecture fee' and would not be drawn on issues either at home or in the country he was visiting.[17] 'A great deal of harm is done in the world', he said, 'by politicians commenting on the affairs of a country of which they have no knowledge and putting across judgements which are not sharpened by the necessity of their being held responsible.' Unfortunately for him, interest in his views was itself sharpened by a remark made a few days earlier by the mayoress of one of Johannesburg's smarter suburbs who, in a by-election, had observed that a vote for the Progressive Reform Party was 'a vote for kaffirs in your swimming pool'.

As soon as he was back in England, Powell turned once more to Ulster. Having buried the convention, and with the cabinet thinking anew about what form of devolution it would be best to offer to the Six Counties, he used an article in the *Daily Express* on 27 October to restate his views. 'Uncertainty is the curse of Ulster and the root cause of the bloodshed there, and the responsibility for that uncertainty lies – as I have more than once told them to their face – with successive parliaments and governments of the United Kingdom. They alone can remove the uncertainty and staunch the loss of life.'[18] He repeated his demands for more MPs in the Six Counties, for complete integration, and for the burial of the notion of power-sharing – 'if so-called "power sharing" with political opponents is so necessary, let Harold Wilson make a start by giving Margaret Thatcher and Keith Joseph seats in his cabinet'.

On 12 November, addressing a Conservative Forum in the City of London, he branded plans for devolution – whether in Ulster or elsewhere – as 'constitutional nonsense', and criticised politicians who embraced policies for the most questionable of reasons without understanding their implications. The debate on the issue was, he said, 'based upon a proposition no less objectively false than to assert that two and two make five'. This, he elaborated, was 'the proposition that it is possible to establish one or more local parliaments within the unitary parliamentary state known as the United Kingdom'.[19] Powell defined the distinction between local authorities, which had no power to alter the laws, and assemblies, which manifestly would have that power. From this it followed that 'the establishment of one or more local parliaments must have one of two consequences; either the conversion of the unitary parliamentary state into a federal state, with a written constitution which prescribes the respective spheres and powers of the federal parliament and the local parliaments, or alternatively the dissolution of the unitary state itself into two or more independent states. No third possibility exists.'

A federal state would, he asserted, require a written constitution properly to regulate it and distinguish it from the old, non-federal state it would be replacing. This departure would 'replace the Crown in Parliament by a supreme court as the ultimate sovereign authority; for wherever there is a written constitution, the true sovereign in the state is that piece of paper, and its priesthood – the ultimate human sovereigns – are the judges who authoritatively interpret it'. Powell was sure that, if they were made aware of the choice, the British people would prefer to be ruled by the Crown in Parliament rather than by 'an unelected, unrepresentative judiciary'.

Although he had fenced about the issue during the referendum campaign, Powell had not yet expressed a direct opinion on Mrs Thatcher's performance as Leader of the Opposition. In a BBC interview on 24 November he was finally tempted to do so, noting he had had 'strictures' on those who, when Heath had ruled, 'followed him through thick and thin and now wish it to be generally understood that nevertheless they were not in agreement with what he was doing'. Pressed to name names, he said, 'Well, it could apply to Mrs Thatcher, could it not? It is not necessarily that she herself has gone around saying "I do disagree with it" but she has certainly allowed it to be put about that ... "You know, Margaret Thatcher never went along with a lot of that." '[20]

The Commons debated the economy again on 25 November, on a censure motion put down by the Opposition. As in the past, Powell moved straight to the moral high ground, telling the Government Whips at the start of his speech that the Unionists would not be backing the Conservatives. 'I do not feel called upon', he said, 'to support a motion of economic censure upon the Government moved by an Opposition whose past administration is still a major factor in the inflationary difficulties from which this country suffers – and, moreover, an Opposition who have still not reached the point of being able to answer in an incisive and intelligible manner questions as to the course of action which they are pressing upon the Government.'[21] He added that he felt Healey had, at last, been frank about the problem of the public sector borrowing requirement. He voiced grave reservations about the lengths to which the Chancellor was going, in borrowing large sums from abroad, to stop the exchange rate falling: he repeated his established doctrine that 'it is a profound fallacy to suppose that there is anything to be regretted in a fall in the exchange rate'.[22] It either meant the terms of trade had changed, in which case there was a change in world economic patterns to which Britain should quickly be alerted in the interests of improving her competitiveness, or it merely showed a differential between British rates of inflation and the rates of her competitors. It did not, he emphasised, mean Britain was any worse off. To 'suppress or distort alterations in the exchange rate' was 'denying ourselves the knowledge of what is happening in the real world'; it was 'pure evil'.[23]

On 28 November the Register of Members' Interests was finally published, with Powell the only one of 635 MPs who had not returned his form. The Commons now had the difficulty of deciding how, if at all, to apply any sanction to him for his refusal to co-operate. Despite no one believing that Powell had anything especially worth declaring – his only business interests were believed to be his writing and broadcasting – the Labour left in particular were determined to try to make an example of him. Dennis Skinner, the MP for Bolsover, immediately announced that he would raise Powell's non-compliance with

Selwyn Lloyd, the Speaker. Skinner protested that, if Powell could get away with non-compliance, 'the whole idea would become worthless. Everyone must register or this whole guff is useless.'[24] However, short of passing a law, there was no action that could be taken against Powell.

A by-product of the economic problems had been the need for new arrangements in funding the monarchy, for which the Government introduced a Civil List Bill that winter. When it was debated on 4 December, Powell said that wanting to 'cheesepare' in this area, after the ravages that Government-induced inflation had wrought, was 'a sign that we are still divorced from the pride and self-confidence without which a nation cannot face the world and without which this nation cannot learn to face the world again'.[25] The main change was that money would be taken out of the Consolidated Fund to supplement the Civil List, and without detailed parliamentary scrutiny. This offended Powell's sense of constitutional propriety, and was another issue on which he could rebuke his former party for its inappropriate behaviour. 'I was disappointed', he said later in the debate, 'that the Conservative Party – which used to be the Tory Party – could not find words to interpret the change, and the significance of the change, which is being made by the Bill.'[26]

Throughout December Powell was active on the committee on the Prevention of Terrorism Bill, seeking to secure tightenings of procedures on behalf of his Unionist colleagues. He had, in a speech in the Commons on 26 November on the second reading of the Bill, welcomed some of the revisions to the measure, them being renewed for the first time, and reiterated his opposition to the death penalty being used against terrorists because he said that, to its intended victims, it would be 'an incentive rather than a deterrent'.[27] He had argued for the Six Counties to have the right to operate exclusion orders against people coming from the mainland to commit terrorist acts, and on 11 December led a move for Northern Ireland to have its own power of exclusion under the Bill as the rest of the Kingdom currently enjoyed. This was defeated on the chairman's casting vote, but the junior Home Office minister, Shirley Summerskill, promised that the matter would be given further consideration. The following week the committee wrung a promise out of Jenkins, the Home Secretary, to consult the police further about the use of compulsory identity cards. A Conservative amendment, moved by Ian Gilmour, sought to ensure that no one was admitted to Britain or Northern Ireland without being able to prove who he was. Powell supported the amendment, on the ground that the present level of surveillance on movements between Great Britain, Northern Ireland and the Republic of Ireland was, in his view, unsatisfactory. It was withdrawn in return for Jenkins's promise.

The understated immigration figures about which Powell had been so critical the previous year, provided him with his first big speech of 1976. With advance publicity of the sort hardly seen since his heyday his speech, delivered to Rot-

arians in Surrey, capitalised on an admission made the previous November by
Jenkins – though not widely reported at the time, or noticed even by readers of
Hansard – that 'clerical errors' in the Home Office had led to huge understatements of the figures. Because of a 'double counting of embarkations at
London Airport', the net balance of emigration and immigration should have
been 86,000 in 1973, not 17,000; and the true figure for 1974 should have been
even higher, at 89,000. The Home Office was deeply embarrassed by the disclosure, a fact on which Powell also intended to capitalise.

When he rose to speak in Egham on 5 January, he immediately referred to
the Birmingham speech. He said it had never occurred to him that 'eight years
later we should still be heaping that funeral pyre, not just at the same rate, but
twice as fast'. In the first three-quarters of 1975 the inflow had been 75,000; in
the whole of 1969 it had been 43,000. He said the New Commonwealth population was being recruited 'by an intake approaching the rate of an additional
million per decade'.[28] He poured scorn on academics whose studies had been
used to ridicule him after Birmingham, saying that one of the most widely used
had claimed that in the nine years from 1968 to 1976 the total immigration
would be 360,000; it was already at 450,000 with more than a year's figures to
be taken into account.

This, though, was not all. Despite problems of definition, there was also the
natural increase of this immigrant population to be considered. Powell estimated this at least 50,000 a year, making a total New Commonwealth increase
of at least 140,000 a year. 'However those problems and dangers in themselves
may be assessed, I doubt if there can be many today who would deny that it is
criminal to be still adding to them and in the highest interest of all concerned
to bring the addition to a stop, even if it is not to be replaced by diminution.'
He called for the right of admission of 'so-called dependants' to be ended at
once, and for the end to the apparently automatic right to citizenship for
those who did secure admission to Britain. 'There is neither economic nor
humanitarian justification for it, and control lies wholly in the hands of Government and Parliament.' He was, though, dismayed by the 'connivance' of the
parties, including the Conservatives, in doing nothing about this. In turn, some
Conservatives were cynical about Powell's reasons for bringing the matter up,
however compelling the statistical evidence. It seemed to some he was seeking
to rebuild his own political position with the public, by harking back to his
most popular speech.

For four days in January 1976 the Commons debated the Government's
proposals for devolved assemblies in Scotland and Wales; and Powell, speaking
on the fourth day, made once more his point that it was not possible for the
same electorate to be represented in two legislative assemblies unless the British
unitary state became federal, or its constituent parts separated and had their
separate sovereignties recognised.[29] Disenchanted as he was by the Government's

proposals, Powell said the alternative put forward by the Opposition – a directly elected assembly with legislative powers but one which was, in fact, a 'sub-committee' of the Commons – would, if it had been under discussion, not have survived intact until the fourth day of the debate.[30] The Government's ideas reminded him of Poynings' Laws, the unpopular Act of Tudor times whereby the Irish Parliament could pass any laws it wanted, so long as they were approved of by Westminster.

His view was that the question Joe Chamberlain had put to Gladstone across the cabinet table when Home Rule was discussed in 1886 – 'How is Ireland to be represented in the House of Commons?' – had never been satisfactorily answered, because there was no satisfactory answer.[31] The only answer in a unitary state was federation. It was not possible for Scotland and Wales to be fully represented in the Commons, he argued, influencing legislation and the colour of the party in Government, if they were, elsewhere, legislating for themselves. Even with a reduced representation, it would be difficult for Parliament to determine in some cases which were national and which devolved issues.

Powell also felt the need to make his point as a British nationalist, arguing towards history. Speaking of the period since the Act of Union with Scotland in 1707, he said:

> I do not believe that the loyalty of those many who over those 270 years, and particularly in this century, worked together and died together as part of the union under the Crown, was to the Crown quite simply, even though they wore the Crown on their uniforms and many of them wore it on their hearts. They were not the mercenaries of a Habsburg empire bound together by personal union and dynastic marriages; they were not the servants of a Hohenzollern empire imposed by military force. It was the Crown of the United Kingdom in parliament which was the centre of loyalty, as it is the essential unifying element of this realm, in the name of which and under the inspiration of which men and women these 270 years have worked and lived and died together.[32]

He said that, if devolution took the form of better control and administration, he would support it; if it was to be separation, by 'settled and determined and preponderant wish' of the inhabitants of a specific part of the Kingdom no longer to be part of it, then, with regret, he would accept that. However, if the policy entailed the Commons deceiving itself and setting in train a course of action that would change the Kingdom beyond recognition and destroy the unity of the realm, he could not accept it. 'That, at any rate,' he concluded, 'is the conviction in which I have lived. It is the conviction for the sake of which I tore and destroyed the links of my whole political life. It is a conviction from which I will not depart.'

The speech was received in silent admiration from much of the House, only a few principled Conservative and Labour MPs being brave enough to voice approval in the conventional way. Michael Foot, as Leader of the House responsible for getting the measure through, however sat down and wrote to Powell in terms that glowed: 'What a theme, and what a speech, and what a speaker, and how Oliver Cromwell himself would have been thrilled to hear the parliamentary cause elevated to its rightful pre-eminence ... Writing as an impenitent Leveller who still begs to differ with you (and Oliver Cromwell) in so many matters, I still cannot withhold my wonder and excitement at what I heard there today.'[33] Heath had spoken earlier, and Foot could not forebear to conclude, 'by the way, how, as an added attraction, Bexley was put in the shade'.

In Ulster, Powell's main concern remained the threat of power-sharing. On 6 January, speaking at Brighton, he said that to try and force the concept on the people of the Province without a pledge that they would remain within the United Kingdom would be 'the tocsin of a civil war ... such an attempt is bound to be the signal for resort to force on an unprecedented scale simply because it represents the deliberate discarding of the ballot box as the means of deciding political issues'.[34] He also denounced power-sharing as 'a form of government which applies in no other part of the United Kingdom and which no other part of the United Kingdom would accept', and one which automatically gave undue powers to minorities.

Later that month, in his constituency, he said he feared that the Government had already decided to try to reintroduce power-sharing, claiming to deduce as much from statements made by Merlyn Rees, the Northern Ireland Secretary, who was known to be discussing the possibility of renewing or updating Whitelaw's 1973 Act. Powell said that to do so would simply inflame Catholic expectations that Ireland could be united; and, when that did not happen, old arguments would flare up once more and shatter the executive. Speaking in Newcastle, County Down, on 5 February, he said the convention had never been designed to ascertain what form of government would attract the most widespread support: the continuance of the Province within the Union. He said the people were being threatened that, if they did not agree to power-sharing, there could be no devolution (something Powell, personally, did not want anyway); that power-sharing was the necessary prelude to proper action against terrorism and, without it, there could be nothing but an indefinite continuation of violence; and that without power-sharing there would be no point in giving any economic aid (something else of which Powell, unlike many of his Unionist colleagues, had doubts).

Powell's sustained criticism not just of the Government, but of the Opposition, deepened the unlikelihood of the rift between himself and his old party being patched up. Mrs Thatcher, in answer to a question about Powell's possible return, said, 'No. Not after he refused to fight his own seat in 1974 and, having worked for years with so many devoted Conservative supporters, told the electors to vote Labour.' She said years later that she had been 'deeply shocked' by Powell's advice in February 1974, but admitted unequivocally that her revolution owed its main debt to Powell and to Joseph.[35] Powell retorted, 'Perhaps one day someone will ask Mrs Thatcher whether there is any prospect of her returning to the Tory party.'[36]

On immigration Jenkins, the Home Secretary, had launched a full inquiry into the computation errors, and had reported that there was no evidence of anything other than a mistake, certainly nothing meriting disciplinary action. Powell went on the attack again, at Hackney on 13 February, saying that, on the contrary, a 'considerable ring' of Home Office officials had been engaged in the cover-up. He compounded their embarrassment by reading out a letter he had received in 1973 from immigration officers at Heathrow – a group of whom had, famously, written to him in 1968 to support the Birmingham speech – in which they had detailed the flouting by the Home Office of normal procedures for admission and settlement. Moreover, he said the officers concerned had not reported their suspicions to their superiors because it would have led to a black mark on their records. Powell wanted to know how high up the Home Office hierarchy the information about the cover-up had gone – in other words, who had organised it.

Just as he had argued against anti-discrimination legislation when introduced for Britain, so too did he oppose the Fair Employment Bill, aimed at stopping the favouring of either Protestants or Catholics in Ulster and whose roots were in an inquiry conducted by a Conservative backbencher, William van Straubenzee. Powell agreed with the committee's findings that discrimination in the Province existed 'to some degree', but the only point about the legislation was whether or not it would help. He felt it would not: 'It will heighten the consciousness of divisions within the community.'[37] He especially objected to the Fair Employment Agency, whose role, as he saw it, was 'to go out and find discrimination'. Powell had always operated in a strictly non-sectarian way as a constituency member and told the House, 'I often find myself in some embarrassment as an Anglican wondering whether I am a Catholic or a Protestant.'[38] He made a plea – which went unheard – for the 'forces of fashion' to stop oppressing those who, like him, thought such laws ridiculous.[39] In a similar vein he found himself, a fortnight later, arguing against a fashionable majority on the question of compulsory seat belts. As with his stand on crash helmets for motor-cyclists, he still felt the individual had to have the right to harm himself. To judge from the impact of the helmet law, perhaps not more than forty lives a year would be saved by seat belts. 'I hear someone ask whether 40 lives are not worth saving,' Powell told the Commons on 1 March. 'Of course they are; but I want to know what I am losing at the same time.'[40]

He turned out to have been wrong about the threat of power-sharing. In early March, Rees announced a tightening-up of direct rule. Powell welcomed it for the way it put Ulster on a better footing with the rest of the Kingdom. He made the case, in a speech in Belfast, for this form of government, just the same as those living in Wales, Cornwall or London enjoyed, 'blissfully ignorant of the fact that they are living under "direct rule from Westminster"'. He said direct rule could, or should, be disagreeable only to those who wanted to break up the Kingdom by making Ulster cease to be an integral part of it. 'But for all who uphold the Union there can be nothing distasteful in being governed as a part of the Union, and sharing in the same forms of government, the same rights, duties as the rest of the British people.'[41] Now Powell reinforced his call for better representation of Ulster at Westminster, adding to it the creation of democratic local government, as enjoyed by the rest of the Kingdom.

On 9 and 10 March the Commons debated the latest White Paper on Inflation and Public Spending, whose aim was to 'level off' the rise in spending by the following spring. Labour's left wing were livid at this promise of containment, and Powell, when he spoke in the debate, immediately referred with glee to the 'agony' on the Government benches: 'In its pathos that agony has been reminiscent of a wounded animal in the kind of combination of incomprehension and pain.'[42] Mischievously, he said he wanted to use his speech to try 'to alleviate, as those with natural compassion should, the suffering of fellow Members'.

He gave one of the seminars that now typified his interventions in economics debates, explaining the means by which the state could finance its operations; and admitted that he had, for a time, been wrong when he had thought two years earlier, that the high spending Healey had gone in for would have to be financed by printing money. It had, instead, been financed by unprecedented levels of borrowing. Now Healey had begun to worry about the piling up of debt, and was looking, instead, at increases in taxation; but it looked as though the natural limit of taxation had been reached. The only option was to cut spending, hence the rage of the Labour left. But Powell warned the House, as he had done before, about believing Treasury projections of a continued reduction in spending beyond the following twelve months.

At the end of the debate the Government lost the vote, thanks to abstentions by members of the Tribune group. Wilson had no choice but to call a vote of confidence. The Conservatives had been expecting the Unionists to vote with them against Wilson, which would have run the result close; but they had not been scrutinising Powell's supportive rhetoric on Northern Ireland, and had forgotten his recent spat with Mrs Thatcher. He led seven of his nine coalition colleagues into an abstention – only Paisley and James Kilfedder supported Wilson – and then a statement was put out explaining the action: 'The Opposition have not yet given evidence that their return to office at present would be beneficial to either the United Kingdom economy or to the interests of Northern Ireland.'[43] Powell, although not leader of the group, had talked them into taking this position: it was his first serious blow against Mrs Thatcher, and his former colleagues were aghast. It was a serious earnest of Powell's and the Unionists' intentions towards the Government over the next three years, in which they would continually frustrate the Conservatives.

II

The following month, Powell again inflamed liberal opinion over immigration. At a Police Federation seminar in Cambridge, he sought to prove the truth of his earlier statements that immigration, if left unchecked, would lead to civil unrest. Quoting evidence by the Metropolitan Police to the Select Committee on Race Relations and Immigration – 'Our experience has taught us the fallibility of the assertion that crime rates among those of West Indian origin are no higher than those of the population at large' – Powell suggested that mugging was a racially divisive crime, the very word now being used to describe it having come into currency as a result of the immigration explosion: it was a term used by one part of the divided society to describe its treatment at the hands of the other.[44] His remarks, notwithstanding the police evidence on which they were based, were denounced by race relations workers, notably Mark Bonham Carter, who also attacked the police for inviting him to their seminar. Jenkins, the Home Secretary, immediately said that any assertion that the Asian community was disproportionately involved in crime (which was not what Powell had said at all) was far from the mark – 'indeed my personal opinion, and not without information, is that the reverse is true'.[45]

On 24 May Powell caused more uproar, and embarrassment to the Government, during a Commons debate on immigration and emigration. During his speech he read out part of a confidential Home Office report on immigration from the Indian sub-continent, which showed that the problem was far greater than anyone in officialdom had been prepared to admit. There was the additional difficulty for the Government that Callaghan, on becoming Prime Minister a few weeks earlier after Wilson's surprise retirement, had sacked Alex Lyon, the minister in charge of immigration, for what Lyon claimed were his attempts 'to get justice for the blacks in this country'. Lyon had written his own reply to the report, the author of which was a Foreign Office assistant under-secretary, Donald Hawley, saying it exaggerated the problem in the sub-continent. Lyon claimed that Hawley had been 'misled by the mythology current in the High Commissions of the sub-continent without checking the wider allegations against the facts'.

However, Powell detailed the facts as Hawley, on a visit to India, Pakistan and Bangladesh, had seen them. 'The present position', Hawley had written, 'is unsatisfactory because current procedures and instructions are based on a

Home Office assumption that the immigration problem in the sub-continent is finite, and that we are in the last stage of clearing up a backlog of "entitled" dependants.' Here Powell paused a moment and told the House: 'He always writes entitled in inverted commas, and rightly so – he knows his law.' The report continued: 'All heads of missions and posts are convinced that this assumption is wrong, and I share their view.'[46] Hawley said that in Sylhet – which Powell claimed most MPs would not know how to find on a map – there were 200 travel agents, mostly engaged in arranging for illegal entry of Asians into Britain. He detailed how 'fiancés' bought their way into Britain, being absorbed by the family of their 'bride'; how wives acted as 'couriers' for more than one group of children, but using the same documents; how second and third wives were being admitted into Britain; and how necessary documentation could always be obtained for a price for anyone wishing to emigrate to Britain. Powell was shouted at by Labour MPs when, after reading out details of the report, he said there would one day be armed racial conflict in Britain's cities that would make Belfast seem 'enviable' unless the immigration was halted. Jenkins, replying to the debate, made no mention of the report, but tried to cover his own embarrassment by accusing Powell of 'gross exaggeration'. The damage, though, was done, and Powell compounded it by putting out the complete text of Hawley's report to the Press Association.

The temperature did not cool. A few days later, a Sikh was murdered in Southall, and it was decided that the murder must have a racial motive. Asian leaders immediately blamed Powell for heightening the tension that had led to the murder, and the civil unrest that followed it. Bonham Carter said Powell 'must be pressed to denounce violence', even though it had nothing to do with him; but this was a ploy Powell's opponents had used against him ever since 1968, to try to associate him with extremist elements.[47] His supporters, including some in the Conservative party, took the attacks on him as indicative of the anger the Government felt at having its lassitude towards the illegal immigration industry exposed, and that felt by the immigrant communities here at having been found out.

Meanwhile, Powell returned to two longer-standing concerns. At the time of a new Defence White Paper, he called for the new realities of Britain's strategic position to be better thought about. He still believed there would not be a nuclear confrontation between the Soviet Union and the West, and hoped Britain would establish a conscript army, or people's army, on the model of some European countries. Also in May 1976 he published an updated version of *Medicine and Politics*, in which he sided with the notion that Labour should abolish pay beds in the National Health Service: to do so would allow the private sector the chance to 'stand on its own feet' and flourish like a proper commercial operation, the complete opposite of the results Labour intended from its policy. It would also be good for the NHS in that it would make consultants who currently worked part-time in the NHS, when not attending to their private patients, think about devoting themselves full-time to the NHS. This, too, would encourage a full-time private sector. He also argued for the division of the Department of Health and Social Security to create a separate Ministry of Health again, asserting that the NHS was unsuitable for administration by a political minister. This was a manifestation of his belief that the consensus in favour of the NHS rendered it as something that should be above politics.

The mounting economic crisis was a further opportunity for Powell to reassert his earlier gospels. Speaking in his constituency on 29 May, he said that, were he Chancellor of the Exchequer, he would cut the Bank of England's minimum lending rate – as Bank Rate was now known – from 11.5 per cent to 3 per cent. The current level, he said, was 'a monstrosity. No economy can prosper – it is a miracle if it survives – when money for investment or building is charged at 15 per cent or higher.'[48] His principal complaint was that the rate did not reflect the true level of supply and demand for investible savings, which was its proper function; the level was distorted by massive Government borrowing, and if public spending were brought down to more sensible levels the rate would 'fall like a stone'. 'Nobody would be worse off,' he added, 'because the resources which the Government no longer borrowed and used would be borrowed and used by other people. Everybody would be better off, because the uses to which other people would put these resources would be more profitable in the present and more productive in the future than the uses to which the Government puts them.'

Meanwhile, the controversy Powell had provoked by refusing to submit an entry to the Register of Members' Interests took on new life. The Select Committee on Members' Interests had proposed a standing order that would treat refusal to comply with the requirement to register as a contempt of Parliament. However, the Government now made it known it was unwilling to enforce the rule in this way, not least because of the powerful objections Powell had raised, claiming it was unconstitutional and could not be binding; no useful purpose could be served by penalising Powell, still the only Member to refuse to comply. Also, his fellow backbenchers accepted his point that his objections were based on principle, and not because he had anything to hide.

Another issue from far further back returned to trouble Powell. The *Sunday Times*, was, at this time, campaigning for compensation for victims of the Thalidomide drug, administered to mothers for morning sickness before and during Powell's tenure as Minister of Health. The newspaper's investigation, conducted four years earlier, had only just been published, following a successful plea to lift an injunction covering the details. Powell said that if the Ministry of Health had – as the stories were alleging – accepted the assurances of Distillers, who produced the drug, that the deformed children born to mothers who had taken it were the result of an act of God rather than carelessness in the drug's testing, then that was the considered opinion of the Ministry's professionally qualified advisers. The Minister of Health, not being medically qualified, could not possibly intervene to overrule such a decision. 'I do not know what the state of medicine would be in that case,' said Powell. 'It would be Bedlam if the Ministry, on the responsibility of a lay minister, issued orders to the medical profession.' It had long been accepted that one thing that did not lie within the Minister's province was the exercise of clinical judgment; the medical profession was responsible, though Powell did not blame it for the mistake. 'If we do not want our doctors to make judgments, and therefore make mistakes, let us try to get along without doctors.'[49] The organisers of the campaign for compensation were unconvinced by Powell's denial of responsibility. One of them, Alec Purkis, specifically blamed Powell for not having ordered an inquiry when the first deformities became apparent; the bland acceptance by his Ministry of Distillers' word had, he said, made it harder for the families of the victims to take legal action.

Powell had gradually rebuilt his position since his time in the wilderness in 1974, and was, that summer, coming to be seen as central to the Government's hopes of surviving on so small a majority. He had already been instrumental in helping them survive a vote of confidence, but since then the Unionists had made it clear to the Government they would require further blandishments to keep them co-operative. Powell had persuaded Harold Wilson the previous winter that there was nothing to be gained, and much to be lost, if the Government were to rule out more seats for Ulster.[50] However, the two Oxford academics, Johnson and Schoen, who had undertaken a study into Powell's success in influencing the results of the preceding three elections, reported in it that three senior Conservative MPs had been canvassing the president of Powell's constituency association, Colonel E. H. Brush, to sound him out about having Powell replaced by another prospective candidate more sympathetic to the traditional Unionist tie with the Conservative party. The three named were John Peyton, the shadow Leader of the Commons, Airey Neave and John Biggs-Davison. All that Unionist sources would confirm at the time was that Neave – who had been charged by Mrs Thatcher with the job of bringing the Unionists back to the fold, and who correctly assessed that Powell was the greatest obstacle – had, indeed, been in active contact with Brush, who was known to have strong reservations about Powell's pro-integrationist policies. The study by Johnson and Schoen also claimed to show, from voting data at the 1970 election, that Powell had influenced many Labour voters into abstaining; it was, at that stage, the election with the highest abstention rate in post-war history. Equally, it confirmed the already widespread suspicion that, by whipping up antipathy to Heath, Powell had contributed directly to the Conservative defeats in 1974. However, that Powell had failed to persuade the country to follow him in the 1975 referendum was being taken as a sign his influence had waned.

The government of Northern Ireland was debated on 2 July, when the Order renewing direct rule had to be passed. Powell said the only reason his colleagues and he would not oppose the Order was that, if it failed, the 1973 Constitution Act, which had set up the Assembly, would come into play instead – something they deeply did not want. He made it clear there were still 'four defects' to be remedied: the laws were not made for the Province as for the rest of the Kingdom, the parliamentary representation was inadequate, there was no proper local government, and the Province was being left out of consideration for the devolution being proposed for elsewhere – a point Powell made on behalf more of his colleagues than of himself.[51] There was a fifth grievance, which he had raised before, but which was not appropriate to a discussion of how Ulster should be governed in the same way as the rest of the Kingdom: his call for identity cards. He did, however, have an opportunity to raise that again in an adjournment debate on 4 August, and supported his argument with the claim that pressure in the security forces for such cards, which would greatly assist their surveillance operations, was becoming overwhelming.

Before his summer holiday – this year it was Sicily – Powell took a last swipe at established opinion, saying, in a speech in London, that North Sea oil was a 'curse'. It was inordinately expensive and, what was worse, expensive in sterling. It was not even a foreign-currency asset for the country. He could not believe the idea that Britain 'ought to enjoy paying through the nose for it' and was amused that the Scots, in the midst of the devolution debate, should want to lay claim to it. 'I hope that if the Scots are going to walk out of the United Kingdom,' he said, 'they will take as much North Sea oil with them as possible.'[52] Then, on 8 August, he gave a television interview in which he confirmed – dangerously, in the light of the feeling of some Unionists towards him – that he could not contemplate a return to the Conservative party as it had shown insufficient signs of repentance over the European heresy. Asked what would convince him that repentance was under way, he said that 'time and suffering are needed for the forgiveness which follows upon repentance'.[53] He admitted that his ambition to lead the Conservatives could not be achieved, and said his problem in taking the party seriously was that the front bench, almost without exception, had loyally supported Heath's betrayal of the promises of 1970.

The previous week Powell had been readopted to fight South Down at the next election, whenever it came. The Unionist coalition was breaking up because of disagreement by more militant Unionists with the policy of direct rule. The hard-liners were also irritated that the Official Unionists had been holding conciliatory talks with the nationalist Social Democratic and Labour Party. As a result, Paisley's Democratic Unionists were threatening to run against sitting Unionists such as Powell; a divided vote could put him out of Parliament. Powell was a particular target because of his support for direct rule. Paisley did not want the coalition but wanted the seats split up between the two main Unionist parties, with his men given their fair share.

Paisley represented himself and his supporters as the coalition, and decided to set about 'selecting' candidates. The Official Unionists found this laughable, and put on a show of contempt by having a formal meeting in Banbridge at which, on 16 September, Powell's readoption – which the executive of his party in South Down had already agreed – would be put to a meeting of the full association. The Powells had now lived for more than a year in a modest two-up, two-down cottage in the village of Loughbrickland, and Powell had spent most Saturdays on tours of the constituency with his officials, armed with Ordnance Survey maps and electoral rolls. He would take one square on the map at a time and explore it thoroughly, his usual method when going on his architectural picnics. No one could accuse him of not working hard to defend the seat; and his colleagues knew better than anyone the results of his influence at Westminster, where the question of better representation for Ulster was now actively discussed – a development that would not have happened but for Powell. However, less than a week before the meeting the 'Coalition' – in other words, supporters of Paisley's line though not formal Democratic Unionists – announced their own candidate to fight South Down: Cecil Harvey, a local businessman who had been a convention member for the constituency and was a member of Paisley's church, as well as being prominent in the United Ulster Unionist Movement, in whose name he stood. 'There is a lot of anti-Powell feeling among United Ulster Unionists generally,' Harvey said after his selection.

At Powell's adoption meeting the challenge from Harvey was dismissed, the constituency party proclaiming Powell as the United Ulster Unionist candidate. However, Harvey's supporters reiterated that Powell had forfeited their support by advocating integration rather than devolution, and said they would put Harvey forward again when the coalition – if it still existed – came to make the formal endorsement of candidates at a general election. Powell devoted much of his speech at the meeting to an attack on the Conservatives for their policy towards Ulster, as if to justify better his own line against his former party. He described the Conservatives as 'the architects of Sunningdale' and said they should call for a more robust prosecution of the fight against the terrorists. He mocked the Conservative line of rhetoric about an 'all-out war on terrorism', which, he said, concealed the fact that the party did not have a single constructive proposal to offer on the subject. He blamed the Conservatives, too, for destroying the Northern Ireland parliament by forcing through the power-sharing initiative that had been designed to put the Republicans in power.[54]

Powell did not let these threats to his electoral security impede his style. On 30 September he addressed the South Kensington Young Conservatives, tactfully telling them that Labour was now the patriotic party of Britain. 'In 1940,' he told them, 'the voice which cried "Speak for England" came from a Tory bench. It comes from there no longer.'[55] This, of course, was because of the Conservatives' support for the EEC and, most recently, because of their acceptance of the principle of direct elections to the European Parliament. He forecast that the growing tide of opposition to the EEC would yet lead to Britain leaving it.

These comments, though, were not nearly so controversial as some he would make four days later. In a speech to the Monday Club in Croydon, Powell urged the Government to find £1 billion for a repatriation plan to avert the 'catastrophe of widespread violence' he had been predicting for years.[56] He said it was now only in Parliament and the press that ignorance of the true facts about immigration existed; and stated that the expenditure of £200 million a year for the next five years would (at an estimate of £1,000 per repatriation) allow a million people to return to their countries of origin, and would bring incalculable savings. It was a far better use of the money than investing in projects to stop inner-city 'deprivation', and to devise other schemes to alleviate the lot of the immigrant population. 'Stopping immigration', which some politicians now claimed they were anxious to do, was meaningless. It was too late: the offer of a comprehensive repatriation programme was all that made sense. As Powell had said before, it was the only policy that would make a difference because of the ability of immigrants already settled here to bring in spouses and have children.

He issued as stark a warning about the future as at any time since the Birmingham speech:

> The tag from Virgil's *Aeneid* about the River Tiber has long passed into a byword, but in words devoid of metaphor I have stated my conviction that physical and violent conflict must sooner or later supervene where an indigenous population sees no end to the progressive occupation of its heartland by aliens with whom they do not identify themselves and who do not identify themselves with them. The catastrophe of widespread violence, entrenched in a divided community, can be averted only in the way that other apprehended catastrophes can be averted: namely, by removing its root cause. That root cause is the existing magnitude of the Asian and African population and the certainty of the continuing future increase in that population, proportionately to the rest, which is inherent in its present magnitude and composition. It follows that there is no escape except by way of such a reduction of that existing population as will be sufficient at least to remove the prospect of future growth; in other words to limit to its present dimensions the 'alien wedge' (I use a famous judicial phrase) in the cities and urban areas of England.[57]

He stressed he was still not advocating compulsory repatriation; but if a formal, well-funded voluntary policy existed, there would be no need to offer financial incentives to immigrants to stay, and no need to presume that the only way a family could be reunited was for all its members to come to Britain.

The usual postscript then occurred: leaders of various ethnic communities called on the Government to have Powell prosecuted and, after a respectful interval, the Attorney-General, Sam Silkin, announced that no action could be taken. However, writing to Powell in early December, Silkin warned that if the 1976 Race Relations Act had already been in force, he would have attempted a prosecution. As before, any prosecution would have had to be made under the 1965 Act, which required an intention to incite hatred to be proved. The new Act was looser, saying that a prosecution could be brought if racial hatred was 'likely to be stirred up'.

Powell was irritated that his speech had been interpreted as a demand for a million immigrants to be sent back to their places of origin, so much so that he took the unusual step of going on to the air the following day to clarify what he had said: which was that, if repatriation cost an average £1,000 a head, the expenditure of £1 billion would allow a million to be repatriated. He also explained the origin of the phrase 'alien wedge', which he had been criticised for using: 'It was Lord Radcliffe – Viscount Radcliffe, who was the Lord Justice of Appeal* – who used this expression in addressing a race relations audience some years ago, which is why I do particularly use it; because it shows how the situation can strike an entirely judicial and dispassionate mind.' He added, 'when I use the word alien, this is not an expression of dislike or contempt. It is an expression of fact. Indeed, I am prepared to say it is an expression of respect; because to respect somebody else's difference, and desire and determination to remain different, is, in my view, much more humane than to treat him like just another particle of uniform humanity.'[58] Powell himself had first quoted the phrase at Bradford in July 1969.

The economic crisis reached its peak in early October. The huge additional surge in borrowing – for that was how Healey had chosen to finance spending – had led to a steep rise in interest rates. As Powell had forecast might be the case, the Government could no longer sell enough gilts to support the borrowing. Sterling was in free-fall. Britain was eventually forced to accept a subvention from the International Monetary Fund in order to remain solvent. The Commons debated the situation on 11 October, and Powell dismissed views that it was in Europe's and the world's interests to bail Britain out. 'If we lack determination, if we lack insight, if we lack wisdom and courage,' he said, 'then those qualities will certainly not be supplied by the interested benevolence of other nations. We have to find them for ourselves if we are to use them at all.'[59] He scorned, too, repeated cries for political differences to be put aside and for 'national unity' to be put to the forefront; the only unity Powell felt was needed

---

* Powell errs here, because Radcliffe had actually been a Lord of Appeal in Ordinary (law lord), from 1949 to 1964, and unusually had never been a lord justice of appeal (appeal court judge).

was about the true cause of inflation. He reminded Healey he had warned him in the past about the dangers of not reducing spending, and added a lament that the Government had squandered immense amounts of money it did not have in order to prop up sterling.

Powell's main point was that the 15 per cent minimum lending rate, caused by Healey's borrowing, was a 'grotesque falsification' of the supply of and demand for investible savings; the Government had by this self-inflicted wound distorted the whole market.[60] His view was that savings on the vast scale required – at least £4 billion in the next year – could be obtained only by heavy reductions in the capital programmes of the nationalised industries and other state services. He rebuked Geoffrey Howe, who had led for the Opposition, for ignoring this prospect and instead dealing 'almost in trivialities'.[61] He knew the continuing obsession, on both sides of the House, was that a massive reduction in spending would cause unemployment, the fear of which was all the greater because of the sudden rise in the numbers of unemployed that had accompanied the recent fall in inflation. Therefore, he concluded this particular seminar with the contention that a fall in public spending did not mean money being taken out of the economy, but merely its being reapplied from the private sector.

However obstreperous liberal opinion became about Powell's views on certain issues, the crowning irony was that a left-of-centre government survived now almost entirely thanks to him. In early November 1976 the Government's hold on power was further imperilled by the Conservatives' winning two by-elections. The Government only narrowly secured a guillotine for its highly contentious Bill to nationalise shipbuilding and the aircraft industry – a guillotine Powell voted against. Later that week – speaking for himself rather than for his party – he let it be known he would still prefer to keep Labour in power than allow the Conservatives back; to compound the irony, his view was endorsed by Frank Maguire, the Independent MP for Fermanagh and South Tyrone, a vigorous Republican. This was one occasion on which Powell overstepped the mark. With his customary flair for publicity, he let it be known he would indicate his support for Callaghan in a speech to the City of London Young Conservatives on 10 November. However, reading of his intentions in that morning's newspapers, the chairman of the group, Alan Bradley, immediately withdrew the invitation to Powell to speak, notifying him by hand-delivered letter, telegram and telephone, just to be on the safe side. Powell initially insisted he would deliver the speech, but then decided not to bother.

The Conservative MP for the City of London, Christopher Tugendhat, issued a statement saying that for Powell even to think of using a Conservative platform to declare an intention to keep the party out of power was ill-mannered and an abuse of hospitality. Powell, in turn, released the speech anyway, and blamed newspapers who had broken his embargo for causing the trouble: the newspapers concerned were quick to point out that he had not complained before when his speeches had been heavily trailed in advance, giving him two or sometimes even three days' publicity for a speech that would normally have attracted only one.

The undelivered speech itself was laced with gallows humour, Powell being more than conscious of the ironies of the circumstances in which he was supposed to be making it, but its message was none the less direct. He admitted Labour was now governing 'upon a knife's edge... a perch that can be occupied, with more or less discomfort, for longer periods than is vulgarly expected'.[62] He went quickly to the point. With just one or two more by-elections all that might stand between the Government and its end, 'the question has therefore come upon us, whether the Government ought to be sustained with somewhat greater support than their notional majority or whether every effort should be made to drive, harry or plunge them into a dissolution of parliament and the hazard of a landslide election'.

Powell justified his decision not to support the Conservatives on the ground that he had become an Ulster Unionist in order to sit in Parliament for a party that did not believe in membership of the EEC. He had duties to fulfil towards Ulster in that regard, and in regard of other 'crying injustices' – which he did not enumerate, but which principally meant the under-representation of the Province at Westminster – yet it was in the interests of the whole nation that he felt the need to preserve the existing Government. 'I can find nothing in the essential interest of the United Kingdom, as I understand it, which requires that this administration should, if possible, be replaced by one comprising the present Conservative party. On the contrary, I can see much in the interest of the United Kingdom which might be better served if this Labour Government were able to govern for some time yet and to do so without the hourly hazard of dismissal.'

In case of doubt, Powell went on: 'The great issue of this time is not in my opinion another instalment of the secular debate between socialism and capitalism. It is a struggle for the survival and the soul of this nation, this parliamentary nation, this United Kingdom. When I survey the dangers by which the nation's survival and its soul are threatened, I find not one which the Conservative Opposition, as it exists today, is ready or disposed to confront and overcome.' This was principally because of the continuing enthusiasm in the shadow cabinet for Europe, and enthusiasm Powell believed he saw waning on the Government benches. He may have had some scruple of vindictive intent, and his regard for the moral weakness of the Thatcher front bench was well known. Moreover it pleased him, undeniably, to have a means of exercising power since more conventional means had been denied to him. But Labour, in short, was his only hope of getting Britain out of the Common Market.

Powell's objections went beyond Europe. He said the Opposition had not once, at that stage, made a clear statement of belief in the monetarist means of controlling inflation. He implied that the shadow cabinet, still full of Heath's men, could not credibly renounce the printing of money, as its members had almost all endorsed it less than three years earlier. The matter had an almost religious significance for him. With the International Monetary Fund now taking a close interest, Powell asked, 'Under which administration is Britain more likely to endure successfully the grinding necessity which lies before us of purchasing self-respect by bringing our national accounts into balance, amid the disappointment of short-term hopes and deferment of low percentage rates of unemployment? It was, you may recall, under a Labour Chancellor of the Exchequer that the United Kingdom last balanced its Budget eight years ago.'

Powell also said that he Conservatives showed no sign, still, of coming to terms with immigration, though he admitted that the Government for which he was advocating support was no better. Labour, he pointed out, had been tougher on immigration than it had promised: far from fulfilling a pledge made at the 1964 election to repeal the 1962 Commonwealth Immigrants Act, it had in fact imposed further restrictions by 1968. The Conservatives, for all their tough talk at the 1970 election, had instead failed to capitalise on their rhetoric about repatriation plans and no further large-scale immigration. Given all this, Powell said, the need for Britain to survive as a sovereign nation was paramount, and 'I for one would not at this juncture wish to deny to the present Government the means and the authority to govern.'

Powell's views angered the Conservatives, understandably, and his own colleagues. The mess Healey had been seen to make of the economy, with the IMF now superintending Britain's financial operations, had left even the most hardened Powellites in the Conservative party, who shared his reservation about Mrs Thatcher and her friends, yearning for a change of government. Molyneaux, without naming Powell, said that 'any member' of the coalition who ignored a majority decision to vote against the Government would risk expulsion, a view rapidly and gleefully endorsed by Paisley.[63] However, when the Unionists next had to take part in a crucial vote – on the Dock Work Regulation Bill that same week – Powell, like all his colleagues, voted with the Opposition.

To many of Powell's friends his attitude towards the Thatcher leadership did seem vindictive. The main cause of his disdain, Heath, was history, and the policies the Conservatives were following were coming closer each day to those advocated by Powell himself. He still would not accept, however, that Mrs Thatcher was morally fit to govern Britain, given her collaboration with Heath and her continued, albeit low-profile, support for British membership of the EEC. Some, however, felt they detected another reason: Powell wanted to stave off the election for as long as possible, because he was far from certain of securing final adoption by the coalition to fight his seat, and, if he did, his majority was so small that he might not win it. There was anger that he failed to give any credit to Mrs Thatcher for being so different in her outlook from her predecessor, and for her attempt to transform her party's policies. Powell's critics in the newspaper editorial columns were swift to write him off, saying that this looked like the end of his career in serious politics, and that, in the words of the *Daily Telegraph*, 'the only victim of his revenge will be himself'.[64] He had made an error of taste, but the obsequies were premature.

That same week Powell became the very public target of a left-wing demonstration when, on 12 November, he took part in *Any Questions* broadcast from Basingstoke. The programme had to be taken off the air after demonstrators, others of whom had succeeded in disrupting Powell's last appearance on the programme the previous February, smashed two stained-glass windows in the Unitarian church from which the programme was being broadcast. There were chants of 'Enoch Powell is a murderer'; and his fellow panellist, the Labour MP Judith Hart, was asked by a member of the audience why she had agreed to appear on a platform with a 'racist'. Mrs Hart replied, 'I would rather be here to argue with Mr Powell than have free speech suppressed.'[65] Stewards threw ten demonstrators out of the hall. The BBC launched an inquiry into how so large a group of left-wing extremists had managed to secure tickets to the broadcast.

After these controversies Powell was glad to receive the following weekend a formal statement of support from officials of his constituency party. 'After carefully considering the full text of his proposed speech', a statement ran, referring to the undelivered attack on the Conservatives, 'we have every confidence in Mr Powell as our MP. We feel satisfied that Mr Powell is working in the best interests of the people of Ulster. He has consistently voted with his United Ulster Unionist Council colleagues in the Commons where his attendance and voting record are exemplary.'[66] However, the Conservatives were soon to have further reason to feel angry with him.

When the Commons next debated the economy, on 29 and 30 November, Powell began his speech on the second day by attacking both Maudling, who had been sacked less than a fortnight earlier as shadow Foreign Secretary and had spoken before him, and Jim Prior. Powell claimed to have found Maudling's speech 'both moving and humbling', moving because they had entered politics at the same time over thirty years earlier, and had both made their maiden speeches in the same month in 1950; humbling because 'as I listened to his speech, I realised that it was an anthology, well selected and convincingly expressed, of almost all the propositions which I have been led to combat over the last 20 years. As I listened and said to myself "My right hon Friend seems not to have changed under the impact of events and experience," the humbling thought came to me that perhaps I may be as mistaken as he appeared to be.'[67]

This was verging on the cruel, for Powell was seldom so lacking in self-doubt as in this epoch of his career. He went on to demonstrate this by his assault on Prior, whom he had asked, the previous evening, whether the Opposition were in favour of accepting the IMF loan offered to help keep Britain afloat. He had expected an answer of either yes or no, but 'I was mistaken. I got neither "Yes" nor "No" for an answer. I am not sure whether it was both "Yes" and "No" or neither "Yes" nor "No". But his reply was: "We must accept the loan. We have no alternative but to accept it. But we must also decide for ourselves the terms on which the loan is possible." ' Powell speculated that it would be a wonderful world to live in where one could choose the terms upon which one would borrow, and imagined Prior going to see his bank manager, and dictating the terms of his overdraft.

Powell was, as he told the House, unequivocally opposed to the IMF loan. This was because the problem was of the country's own making, and had to be of its own solution. The loan merely avoided the issue which was, as he had repeatedly said, the nature of the true cause of inflation. This, in turn, brought Powell back to his earlier objections to the continuation of the Plowden system of projecting expenditure for years ahead. However – and this was what really outraged the Conservatives, more than the specific attacks on two of their senior players – he then proceeded to praise Healey's regime at the Treasury, saying that 'never, in my judgment, since the war has the control of public expenditure been exercised with the courage, the determination and the consistency which has been shown in recent months'.[68] What now needed to be addressed was the immense propensity to borrow, now running at the rate of £30 million a day.

Powell told the House that the Unionists would, in recognition of Healey's efforts to restore credibility, continue to support the Government. He said none of the left-wing socialists behind Healey should oppose him, for the alternative was rampant inflation that would further imperil the living standards of their own constituency. Above all, he said the Conservative party should support Healey. It was absurd for them to take a high-minded attitude to his stewardship of the economy. 'Long before the present crunch was reached in the control of expenditure, long before the falling rate of inflation had produced 1.3 million unemployed, an Administration of the party which now forms the official Opposition would have disappeared over the horizon out of sight altogether in a flurry and dustcloud of manufactured money. We know that from the form. We know that, because that was how that Administration behaved in a crunch far less alarming or severe than that wherein we stand at the present time.'[69]

John Biffen had just joined the Conservative front bench, and had the previous day criticised the injection of inflation into the economy. Powell said he was just about the only Conservative MP who, from his actions during the Heath Government, had the moral right to do that. The rest of the party was not purged of its sins. 'I assure them', he said, 'that the sponge will not be passed over the memory and the record of the conflict with the supreme national duty in the years 1970–74, until most of those who were co-operators, connivers or consenters to those events have passed elsewhere.'[70] For the Opposition to say they had no confidence in what the Government was trying to do was 'an impertinence'.

A week later, on 6 December, Powell and his colleagues abstained in a vote in the Commons on the National Insurance Surcharge Bill. As a result, it received a second reading by a majority of just two. Bernard Weatherill, the Opposition Deputy Chief Whip, claimed that Powell had instructed four of his colleagues not to vote; two Labour MPs, who felt that the £950 million additional charge on employers would create more unemployment, voted with the Opposition. Molyneaux, however, specifically refuted the allegation that Powell had led his colleagues into this abstention; the decision to abstain had, he said, been taken a few days earlier by general consent. He added that the decision to abstain had been so as not to obstruct the Government's attempts to reduce borrowing: something of which Powell was, of course, strenuously in favour. The episode was, though, indicative of how demonised Powell had become by his old party, and how they saw him as being the prime mover to keep Callaghan in power.

III

Powell was, however, having problems with his new party, who were internally at odds over devolution. Despite his persistent tutorials about the wrongness of the move, he had failed to persuade his colleagues that a return to self-rule was a bad idea. Molyneaux, anxious to keep all sides together, agreed with the majority view that self-rule should return, but placated Powell by saying nothing should be done in haste. Molyneaux was, though, only the leader in Parliament; the leader of the whole party was still Harry West, and he rejected Molyneaux's strategy out of hand. Powell gave his full support to Molyneaux against West, and hinted to others that the time was coming when Molyneaux ought to replace West as leader. Powell also had acquired another, surprising ally in Roy Mason, who had become Northern Ireland Secretary in succession to Rees the previous September, and who was satisfied with direct rule and committed to making it work as effectively as possible.

The question, however sensitive, was one on which Powell had no intention of keeping quiet, though he did try to address the question at a tangent rather than head-on. The devolution legislation for Scotland and Wales gave him a means of doing this. In the debate on the second reading of the Scotland and Wales Bill on 16 December 1976 he had pointed out that the Commons had made laws separately for Wales and for Scotland, and indeed for Northern Ireland, and could continue to do so without the need for devolved assemblies. But the other member for County Down, James Kilfedder, had interrupted him and argued for the need to restore Stormont, to allow Northern Ireland to be legislated for in a more understanding way than the Commons was capable of.

Powell reminded Kilfedder that he, too, had argued against the destruction of Stormont, but forbore to add that, it having been destroyed, he preferred a different sort of government to replace it.

Then, on 6 January 1977, speaking in his constituency, he set out why the Unionists would oppose the Devolution Bill. 'Like the Home Rule Bills of Gladstone and Asquith,' he said, 'not one of which was ever put into practice, the Scotland and Wales Bill contains at its heart a contradiction not merely insoluble but destructive. It sets up parliaments in parts of the Kingdom, but allows the MPs from those parts to make law for the rest of the country upon the self same subjects over which legislative power is transferred to the new parliaments.'[71] Powell said his party thought the Bill imperilled the very union to which they longed to remain a member; and the conclusion he drew about the results of further agitation by his colleagues for an end to direct rule was clear.

Powell developed the idea of nationalism in two speeches within the next fortnight, moving back from the basic question of national identity to the more incendiary subject of immigration. On 18 January he gave a lunchtime talk at St Lawrence Jewry in the City of London about patriotism, in which he warmed to his theme by referring back to the 'humbug and pretence and self-deception of the British Nationality Act 1948'. Then, three days later, he warned Young Conservatives at Stretford in Manchester of the threat of 'racial civil war'. In his warnings of the violence he believed certain to break out, Powell went far further than in any of his earlier speeches. Journalists who received advance copies of the speech were excited by its tone, so much so that word of it travelled even more efficiently than usual; and Home Office officials even tried to secure copies of it from those journalists, to prepare themselves better for the storm.

The main provocation Powell felt in making his speech was that, within weeks, the new Race Relations Act would come into force and threaten to stop people such as him debating immigration in public; in order to prosecute someone for inciting racial hatred, no intent would need to be proved. He argued that with 'sedulous determination' steps had already been taken to stop the issue being debated in Parliament, and now further attempts would be made to stop debate on it outside Westminster. He cited a precedent with the campaign of isolation waged against those who, in the 1930s, had warned of the risks of war with Germany. This comparison caused an explosion of pompous rage afterwards from Winston Churchill, to whose grandfather Powell was alluding and in whose Stretford constituency he was speaking; Churchill himself would cause controversy fifteen years later when he himself made an intemperate and shallow speech about what he perceived to be the race problem.

Powell adduced the usual reasons for the enforced silence: the belief that if no one mentioned the problem it would go away, but, also, the hidden agenda of the anarchists who wanted the tensions to explode to help them achieve their political ends. He said he no more wanted racial strife than Churchill, in warning about Hitler, had wanted war; but the accusation that he did was just another means of trying to curtail his freedom of speech, and the freedoms of those who agreed with him. He said that, until now, the need for those who accused him of incitement to prove his wicked intent had been a protection to his freedoms. Now, that would be stripped away.

'It is inherently unlikely', he said, stressing the importance of that protection, 'that any subject of public anxiety or apprehension can be discussed or debated without touching upon strong feelings, fears, antagonisms, emotions – indeed, that very probability is proportionate to the importance of the subject. If expression of opinion likely to have that effect is rendered criminal *per se*, irrespective of the intention of the speaker, then all free and open public discussion is rendered impossible, to the manifest endangerment of the public interest, for the public interest depends upon the preservation of free speech.'[72]

Powell had corresponded with Silkin on the intentions of the new Act – and had published the correspondence. He directly accused Silkin, on the basis of what he had learned, of having the political intention of silencing him and others like him. Powell said he was not concerned about the provision in the Act to prosecute for use of 'threatening, abusive or insulting' language, because he had never resorted to such terms and never would. What he was concerned about, though, was that 'the principal law officer of the Crown has asserted that in his view it was insulting to quote, as I did in a speech at Croydon last October, the expression "alien wedge", which Viscount Radcliffe in a public address has applied to New Commonwealth immigrants'. Silkin had further asserted, Powell continued, that 'in his view race hatred against coloured members of our community was likely to be stirred up by what I said. He added that he did not believe a court would find that this was my intention. However, when Section 70 of the new Act comes into force, intention will become irrelevant.'

A decision by Silkin to prosecute in future in such circumstances would, Powell added, be 'radically perverse and one-sided', and contrary to natural justice. It opened up endless debate about what was, or was not, insulting; and it was 'literally inhuman' to indulge in the 'insufferable arrogance' of supposing 'that an Indian or an Iranian or a Bantu want to be, or to be thought of, as an Englishman under the skin'. Powell went on to savage the Archbishop of Canterbury, Donald Coggan, for having said – in a phrase he claimed could just as easily be seen to be as 'insulting' as anything Powell had uttered – that 'the man with a coloured face could be an enrichment to my life and that of my neighbours'. He felt this would hardly go down well in areas where 'whole districts have been transformed into enclaves of foreign lands'. He added, 'It is not so much that it is obvious twaddle. It is that it makes a cruel mockery of the experience and fears of hundreds of thousands, if not millions, of ordinary decent men and women.' Powell was sure that had not been Coggan's 'intention', and he hoped that, if he said such things again, causing such offence to the indigenous population in those parts, Silkin would refrain from having the Archbishop prosecuted.

Powell's other concern about Coggan's remarks was that if so senior a member of the establishment as he could not see the problems and difficulties with which so many were having to contend in their daily life, and did not realise the potential a large concentration of immigrants had for public order, then the people would feel they had to look for a new sort of leadership. He spoke of a 'Gresham's Law' of politics in which the more extreme drove out the less extreme, leading towards outbreaks of physical violence 'in the forms of firearms or high explosive, as being so probable as to be predicted with virtual certainty'. He repeated warnings that the black community would be 'polarised', that those wearing 'the involuntary uniform of colour' would find themselves pressed into a racial conflict on one side or the other, depending on their race. Provocatively, he said that 'colour is a recruiting sergeant, and a recruiting sergeant for officer material'.

The speech provoked calls for Powell to be prosecuted, but – as he had taken pains to point out – until the provisions of the new Act came into force intent had still to be proved. Silkin did not hesitate to play down suggestions that a prosecution might be brought from the moment the subject was first raised with him; and Alex Lyon, the former immigration minister, called for there to be no prosecution, on the grounds that it would only make matters worse.[73] Powell's opponents interpreted what he had said as a dare to the authorities to prosecute him the next time he spoke, once the Act was in force, expecting that his martyrdom would be the undoing of the race relations industry. He did make one convert in Labour's ranks, however: Maureen Colquhoun, the controversial member for Northampton North, said that her colleagues were guilty of 'blind idealism' on race and had lost contact with their constituents on the issue.[74] Predictably, Mrs Colquhoun was attacked by colleagues for her remarks, sufficiently unpleasantly for her to make full retraction within a fortnight.

The following month, Powell's own party felt some embarrassment with him as the untold story of the February 1974 election started to drift out. Joe Haines confirmed his role in the co-ordination between Powell and Wilson at that election; and Powell, unwilling to go into any detail, simply commented that what Haines had said was 'correct'.[75] Wilson, for his part, admitted he had known of Powell's activities, but denied there had been any harmonisation of speeches. The disclosure could not have come at a more sensitive time, as the Government was preparing for a vote of no-confidence, tabled by Mrs Thatcher following the refusal by Labour to vote at the end of a debate on public spending on 17 March. In the debate, Powell had invited the Opposition to table a vote of no-confidence as a means of testing support for the Government. The previous day Callaghan had been warned by his Chief Whip that the Government would lose a vote because of the objections of the left to further cuts, which is why the Prime Minister had opted for what he admitted was 'not a very glorious' procedural device to avoid a defeat.[76] The Liberal party had signalled that it might be prepared to do a deal with Callaghan, not least because the opinion polls – which showed a 16 per cent Conservative lead at the time – suggested a trouncing for the Liberals too. However, it was also suspected that Powell would, as before, corral the Unionists into the lobbies in support of Labour. Labour had, at that stage, just 310 MPs, eight short of an overall majority.

Powell was generally perceived as the brain and motivation of the Unionists, a somewhat exaggerated perception. Nonetheless, as the vote neared, the press started to attribute to him again the power he seemed to have forfeited for ever after 1974: that of making and breaking Prime Ministers. While the Liberals' intentions remained unclear, the Unionist vote was seen to be crucial, and Powell seen to be controlling it. The main card he had to play was, ironically, that the main demand of his colleagues – but not of himself – to have a devolved assembly again in the Province at Stormont was unattractive to Mrs Thatcher, and therefore not something that could be offered to the Unionists to tempt them away from Callaghan. However, with the exception of Molyneaux, Powell's Unionist colleagues were making it known before the vote that they had had enough of Labour; and, seeing which way he thought the wind was blowing, Molyneaux (who had been talking in detail to Foot and Mason) went for formal talks with Mrs Thatcher on 21 March about what she was prepared to offer in return for the party's support. Powell appeared to have been outflanked.

However, on the same day Callaghan held a meeting with David Steel, the Liberal leader, at which he formally solicited that party's support, after several days of informal discussions conducted by some of Callaghan's lieutenants with the Liberal leader. Callaghan also met Powell and Molyneaux the same day. Foot was present at that meeting; and, in Callaghan's account of it, the Prime Minister had opened by offering a formal arrangement with the Unionists, 'but I was not ready to forfeit the Government's self-respect' – something most observers felt had gone some time earlier, not least through the importation of IMF economic policies.[77] Callaghan said that, if too high a price were asked, he would be prepared to go to the country. Powell and Molyneaux replied that, if proper consideration were given to increased representation and a form of local govern-ment for the Province, they might be able to deliver up to six abstentions in the vote of confidence. The matter of more Ulster MPs had been advanced a few weeks earlier by the Conservatives in an attempt to win back the Unionists, but Callaghan had dismissed it. Now, though, times had changes. He said he believed the Government could now, in the absence of Stormont, agree to a Speaker's Conference to consider an increase, and told the two Unionists so, adding that the decision would stand 'even if you are not able to carry your colleagues in the accommodation we are now discussing'.[78] He also promised to have the cabinet consider the question of local government, though he raised concern about the representation of the minority within it. Callaghan led Molyneaux and Powell to believe that, if he had listened to Foot, the Unionists' demands would have been met far sooner, and an accommodation reached earlier.[79] Powell had been putting the case forcefully to Foot for months, and Foot seems to have seen the logic of his position.

It was, however, his meeting with Steel – about which, in advance, Callaghan informed Powell and Molyneaux – that was of greater importance, for it sowed the seeds of the Lib–Lab pact in which Callaghan promised that, in return for support from Steel's thirteen MPs, no legislation be introduced for the rest of the Parliament that was offensive to the Liberals. Powell came under pressure from his constituency to vote against the Government, since feelings were beginning to run high in Northern Ireland about the Government's handling of security questions. He continued, however, to keep his own counsel.

In the vote, Powell and two of his Unionist colleagues – Harold McCusker and John Carson – abstained, Powell doing so shortly after receiving a telegram from his constituency party telling him to vote in line with the whip against Labour. His constituency vice-chairman, William Brown, told the press that the Unionist activists in South Down had been 'very kind' to Powell in the past despite his pro-Labour behaviour, but that they would now be 'very angry' if he did not vote to bring the Government down.[80] Luckily for him, though, his action was immediately defended by Molyneaux, who had voted with the Conservatives. 'I am pleased', the parliamentary leader said, 'that Mr Powell's determination over a period of years with regard to representation has now paid off. He did not think he could vote against a Government which had given what he had been trying so hard to get.' Mainly as result of Molyneaux's strong support, attempts to censure Powell came to nothing. In fact, his abstention was irrelevant to the outcome of the debate. Early in the morning of 23 March, the day the vote took place, Steel and Callaghan agreed their pact. The Government had a majority of twenty-four in the vote, winning by 322 to 298.

That spring saw a further worsening of relations between the Official Union-ists and Paisley's DUP. In April Powell addressed a meeting in an Orange Hall at Lisburn, and afterwards a three-pound bomb was found planted under the stage from which he spoke. It was believed it had been put there after Powell – who was accompanied by his wife and younger daughter – had spoken, but Molyneaux claimed that it had been put there to 'frighten' him.[81] More to the point, he said it seemed to have been an extension of a campaign 'certain members of a Loyalist political party' had been running against Powell – a clear reference to Paisley's supporters. Outraged, Paisley demanded that Molyneaux substantiate the charge or withdraw it. Michael Foot sent Powell a letter express-ing his and his wife's relief at Powell's escape, and added, 'I fear some of the comments immediately uttered when we heard the news were not as considerate as they should have been. Speculation turned to the possible assailants – Mrs Thatcher? Paisley? My candidate is still Ted Heath.'[82]

A week after the bomb was found, Powell made his most unequivocal attack yet on the DUP leader. Paisley was urging, together with Loyalist extremists, support for an economic strike in the Province from the beginning of May. Powell said Paisley's activities were 'irresponsible, unconstitutional and calculated to inflict maximum damage on the interests of Ulster and the Union; and I find it hard to see how, in these circumstances, the Ulster Unionist Parliamentary party could continue to maintain its existing connection with Mr Paisley'.[83] In effect, Powell was calling for the DUP's expulsion from the coalition. Molyneaux, though less outspoken, endorsed Powell's view. Powell's opposition to the strike put a terminal strain on the coalition. Molyneaux tried to explain to Paisley, who had already fallen out badly with West, that it would be counter-productive, particularly as Mason was showing goodwill towards the Unionists.

In early June Powell, in a more relaxed mood, gave an interview in which he talked about his home life and his attitudes to some of his contemporaries. Since giving up hunting he had, he revealed, been even more intent than before on getting out into the countryside on Sundays, walking, picnicking and inspecting architectural sites. He said he never watched television but was undertaking more book reviewing than before, to ensure he forced himself to read books. Of most interest, though, were his views about Heath, not least in the light of his recent admission that he had conspired with Wilson in 1974 to bring his former leader down.

'Edward Heath has every reason to bear me a grudge, since I put him out of office,' he told his interviewer, Ronald Proyer, 'as indeed I promised to do. After he went into the Common Market I promised everybody who cared to listen that I would pull down the Conservative Government and the Conservative party.' That was a rewriting of history: Powell's only explicit warning had been to his senior officers in Wolverhampton in 1972, which was why the rest of his activists, and the country, were so surprised when he left the party two years later. He continued: 'There are some people in one's life from whom one has a physical repulsion. Ted Heath, for me, has never been that sort of person. Although I can't say I've ever quite wanted to cuddle him, I find I have no physical dislike of him at all.'[84]

There were now, indeed, new and more dangerous hate figures. On 1 June Paisley announced that his supporters could not possibly back Powell at the next election, following his criticism of their strike and his instruction to Unionists in recent local elections to withhold their second preference votes from DUP candidates. Being still within the coalition, Paisley's supporters wanted a meeting with officials in South Down to choose someone acceptable at all. The threat was that, if no such candidate were found, the DUP would field their own candidate against him. The officials of his constituency were not prepared to accede to the threat, and they were already promised the intervention at the election of Cecil Harvey. Although Powell's constituency officers issued strong statements defending him and praising his commitment as an MP, one or two of his branches were very much in agreement with the criticisms, not least because of his continued opposition to the end of direct rule.

No activity of Powell's was so innocent that it could not provide ammunition for his opponents in the Province. He and his wife decided to accept a long-standing invitation to make a private visit to Moscow as the guests of René Faessler, the Swiss ambassador and an old friend whose son had been Powell's legal ward for two years in the 1960s and a *de facto* member of the Powell family. Their crime was to make the trip in the week's recess granted to Parliament for the Queen's Silver Jubilee celebrations. Harvey was quick off the mark, ludicrously branding the decision to go at that time a calculated insult to the Queen, and one that would not be speedily forgiven by the loyalists of Ulster.

On his return, Powell wrote an account of his experiences in the Soviet Union for *The Times*. He said it had not been necessary to visit Russia to realise what a 'hair-raising absurdity' the notion was that the outside world could influence the treatment of its nationals. 'There has never been the slightest reason to believe that the Russian state would make, or still less keep, any bargain which it did not consider to be in its own interests on its own view of the world, or to suppose that its view of the world is alterable by anything that the inhabitants of Western Europe, let alone America, think fit to do or say.'[85] The West had been deceived by the facility with which the Russians had learned 'the gobbledegook of the United Nations' into thinking that they were changing, but they were still, Powell wrote with discernible envy, putting their own interests first. Also, he highlighted the danger of trying to influence Russia, since by doing so the West conveyed the right to the Russians to try to influence them.

He discounted the fear that Russia planned an immediate conquest of Western Europe, comparing it with the paranoia felt in the nineteenth century about Russia being poised to invade Britain's Indian Empire, a 'neurosis' that had harmfully dominated British foreign policy right up to the Great War. On his visit, Powell said he had found 'a state at once intensely conservative and intensely nationalist'. That was why, to him, its behaviour was so predictable, both internally and externally, and he feared nothing from it. Disregarding the human rights abuses, and economic rigidities that were anathema to him, Powell gave himself away in his conclusion: 'I have seen a nation which in its past honours itself and its future. I wish I thought I had returned to one.'

On a similar theme, he used a speech to Conservatives in Swansea on 17 June to stigmatise his former colleagues as 'nakedly anti-national', for their support for direct elections to the European Parliament in which Britain would be in a permanent minority.[86] He claimed that the party had written off the nation state, saying its denunciation of political opponents 'for being hesitant or divided over surrendering the right of the British parliament to control British affairs' was 'a national disaster'.[87]

The Commons had discussed the principle of direct elections in a debate on 25 April. While Powell was glad the Government had made it clear, at a recent meeting of EEC heads of government, that the authority of the Commons, and the Government's obedience to that authority, would be maintained, he saw no need for the elections. The Treaty of Rome did not specify a need for them, so there could be no commitment to participate. He noted, too, the irony that under the proposed representation Northern Ireland would have by far the most generous quota of any part of the Kingdom. The sugar was taken off the pill, though, by the realisation that the Province's members would be elected by proportional representation in order to try to ensure that a nationalist representative was elected, which could not have happened under a first-past-the-post system. What really horrified Powell was that the elections seemed to him to lay the foundations for a unitary European state. He repeated these objections on 7 July, when the House came to legislate on the subject.

Earlier in the session, Powell had used an unusually low-key contribution to the Budget debate to call for an abandonment of the 'social contract' or voluntary incomes policy Labour had been operating. On 14 July Callaghan had, to Powell's delight, said that free collective bargaining could be restored. The next day, Healey made a statement on the Government's counter-inflation policy, and Powell asked him what he thought would prevent a 'wage explosion' after the restoration of free collective bargaining.[88] Healey readily admitted that not printing money would help. Five days later the House debated the policy, and Powell hailed such sentiments as Healey and Callaghan were now airing as a 'real turning point' in British economic policy, laden with happy omens for the future. The country had travelled far since Heath's administration had ended 'in a storm of ridicule and disaster' three and a half years earlier.[89] Now, after two years of the 'judiciously vague' social contract, the time for stage 3 had come; and, instead of a pay board, Callaghan had decided to return to free collective bargaining. Powell gave Healey the credit for this: he said he had believed the Chancellor had been a monetarist 'much longer than anyone has ever suspected of him', and had grasped the true causes of inflation at a time when Heath and Barber had not.[90] The culture of thirty years of mistakes had been broken.

A Speaker's Conference on the representation of Ulster was settled, and the Unionists too settled into a posture of general co-operation with the Government. Sensing that this would, together with the Lib–Lab pact, greatly delay their chances of taking power, the Conservatives were livid – such a conference had, after all, originally been their idea – and vented their wrath in particular on Powell. John Biggs-Davison, one of the party's Northern Ireland spokesmen, said that 'suddenly, cynically to postpone the verdict of the electorate, and for reasons that have nothing to do with Northern Ireland, a Socialist Government entered into a pact with a politician whom they abominated as a "racist extremist" '.[91]

Powell had been pleased that Callaghan had adopted Powellism in restoring free collective bargaining. He was, therefore, angry when the Prime Minister, speaking to the TUC in early September, confessed publicly that he would have liked one more year of wage restraint. Powell said that 'to all appearance both he and all those who heard what he said, or reported or commented upon it, were unconscious that by that single statement he repudiated and destroyed the whole basis and theory on which the Government has been purporting to act during the last three years. Nothing could be more obvious.'[92] It was simply not on to blame, even indirectly, the trade unions for what Powell hoped Callaghan had recognised as being a function of the money supply. Powell also wanted the Government to stop falsifying the exchange rate by using the reserves to mount 'rescue' operations for the pound. He remained insistent that the exchange rate did not matter, provided it was honestly set by market conditions.

Powell was once more enjoying himself. Asked by an interviewer that autumn whether he had not committed political suicide, he rejoined, 'If I have, then I'm an uncommonly lively corpse.' His sense of achievement was boosted by the knowledge not just that he had secured the promise of the Speaker's Conference, but also that so much of his wider programme had been accepted by the main parties. Still, two of his main concerns – Europe and immigration – had not been triumphs, which is why, as he put it, 'people still come up to me in the street and thank me for what I am doing. When I tell them I have failed they usually insist that I have not.'[93] That same week Powell's earlier predictions about immigration were reluctantly supported by one of his fiercest critics, Dipak Nandy, the former director of the Runnymede Trust. Speaking on 15 September, Nandy said Powell's 'doom-laden projections' about the concentration of ethnic minorities in certain cities 'were likely to be coming true', thanks to the failure of government and local authorities to operate 'a constructive dispersal policy'. Finding himself extensively reported in the *Daily Telegraph* for saying this, Nandy, now a member of the Equal Opportunities Commission, wrote to the paper claiming he had been misrepresented, an assertion the paper vigorously denied.

Although Powell was still heavily in demand to speak at Conservative functions – even though whenever he turned up he said something highly unhelpful to the party's morale – he was still subject to the occasional protest by those with a different conception of loyalty. On 4 October he had been booked to speak to the Bexleyheath Young Conservatives, but the group cancelled the meeting at short notice because it did not secure the authorisation of the constituency party. This was despite a search being made for a new venue, to stop interference by the constituency party, and even the creation of an *ad hoc* group for Powell to address that was not called the 'Young Conservatives'. As he had done in similar circumstances before, Powell released his speech anyway: it was an attack on what he called 'the community relations industry' whose job was to convince all sides that things were not as bad as they seemed, and then to engage in 'what is fatuously called bringing them together'.[94] The over-reaction was severe; Powell's principal target had been the clergy, not his old party.

He saved that attack for the following week, in an article in the *Spectator* to coincide with the Conservative party conference. He dismissed the leadership as 'the same troupe of ham actors' who had assisted Heath to commit 'wholesale rape ... on a submissive cabinet and a prostrate Conservative party'. He added that 'there are times in the life history of a party, as of a society, when a generation of leaders that has been hopelessly compromised has to disappear and when this necessity is in no way to be avoided'.[95] On 12 October, as the Conservatives in their conference debated Europe and gave their continuing approval to the policy of direct elections to the European Parliament, Powell addressed a meeting at Birmingham on the same subject in which he referred to the fact that, at about the same time, Heath would be speaking in support of direct elections at Blackpool. 'We may reflect, with varying emotions no doubt,' said Powell, 'that he is thereby helping once again to lay the foundations of the next electoral defeat of the Conservative party by identifying it with a decision, happily a reversible decision, that is deeply repugnant to a majority, and an increasingly embittered majority, of the British people.'

For Powell, the legitimation by Westminster Parliament of direct elections to the European one had become the new focus of his antagonism to the EEC. The Bill in the last session had not been found acceptable, and was to be brought back in amended form. Powell said the battle over the legislation would be the most significant since the second reading of the European Communities Bill. He maintained that the usual reason given for supporting direct elections – 'democracy' – was fallacious. Such elections would merely seem to give 'elective authority to the exercise of supra-national powers by institutions and persons who are, in the literal not in the abusive sense of the word, irresponsible'.[96] The decisions currently taken by the delegate assembly could be regarded as of little importance; but once taken by an elected assembly that would change, with Britain finding herself in a minority permanently.

In early November Powell published his biography of Joe Chamberlain. He had been working on it sporadically since 1974, attracted to the subject by the way in which Ireland had served as a turning point in Chamberlain's life, changing him from a Liberal into a Liberal Unionist. He felt a deeper study of Chamberlain would be instructive to him at this point in his own career. Powell had grown up in a household where he had heard his father speak well of Chamberlain, for what he had done for Birmingham. But Powell found that by the time he had finished the book his opinion of his subject was lower than when he had started, because of Chamberlain's unscrupulousness – not least his failure to resign as promptly as he should over the question of tariff reforms in 1903. To some enlightened observers, Powell's similarities with Chamberlain had been apparent for years. Peter Utley, in his book of 1968, had written:

> Chamberlain's mission was to convert the Conservative Party to a vigorous and radical concern for social reform. Powell also conceives himself to have a mission of no less dramatic a kind – the conversion of the Conservative Party from an outmoded imperialism to a realistic patriotism and from a largely dirigist and paternalistic view of economic policy to a radical policy of economic liberalism. Chamberlain sought and Powell is seeking to alter the nature of the Conservative Party – to transform it from a 'safe' party, to be turned to for sound administration in a crisis – into a positive and dynamic party with a defined political and social faith.[97]

The book contains many asides that can be interpreted autobiographically. There is a conscious parallel between Chamberlain, who denied his party – a different party each time – victory first in the election of 1886, then in the election of 1906 – rather as Powell felt himself do in 1974. The way in which Powell describes Radical Joe's gradual comprehension of himself as, above all other things, a Unionist was imitated by his own perception of this trait in himself. One can see, too, an element of *post facto* justification by Powell of his own freelance philosophising when on the Conservative front bench. He says of Chamberlain's activities when he joined the cabinet in 1880 as President of the Board of Trade: 'A minister outside the cabinet can, indeed must, concentrate above all upon his department; but a cabinet minister has only the choice of being a nonentity or else applying his mind and his advice to every successive issue which comes before the government. For Chamberlain there was no question which it had to be. His abilities and personality apart, as representative of the radical element on which the government and its majority depended, his voice had to be heard on every issue.'[98] There is also an echo of part of Powell's justification of the Birmingham speech: referring to Chamberlain's speech on tariff reform, also at Birmingham, in May 1903, Powell wrote, 'as with many speeches that detonate tremendous political explosions, he had said nothing in it that he had not said before, and in public'.[99] By the time Powell comes to Chamberlain's failure to resign from office immediately at this time he is as stern as one who had resigned as often as he had could afford to be: the damage caused by Chamberlain's action was 'never to be repaired'.[100] From this the theme broadens out, to encompass the whole wretchedness of Chamberlain's, and Powell's, existence, until the book reaches its famous conclusion: 'All political lives, unless they are cut off in midstream at a happy juncture, end in failure, because that is the nature of politics and of human affairs.'[101]

IV

The 1977–8 parliamentary year was dominated by constitutional measures, with a new attempt at devolution legislation, separating Welsh and Scottish provisions, as well as the new direct elections Bill. As a result, Powell was heavily engaged in the Commons. A letter at this time from George Thomas, who had become Speaker in succession to Selwyn Lloyd the previous year and had been a friend of Powell's since the 1950s, shows the massive influence Powell had acquired as a parliamentarian. 'Let me thank you for the monumental support which you gave me in the House. Your knowledge of Parliamentary procedure is such that I rely more than you may think on your judgment on Parliamentary affairs,' Thomas wrote to him on 14 November 1977.[102] He told Powell he was aware of the 'very special role' he had to play during the constitutional debates that lay ahead; and he and Powell had regular private meetings during that time, and for the rest of Thomas's Speakership, in which Thomas would solicit and Powell dispense advice on procedure and the handling of difficult issues.

Back in the realm of sheer politics, Powell still would not let the Conservative party forget its wickednesses of 1970–4. When the Commons debated the Scotland Bill on 14 November, he spoke sarcastically of how 'deeply moved' he had been to hear Francis Pym, Heath's Chief Whip, advise that constitutional legislation of this sort should not be passed through a deeply divided House of Commons. Powell said mordantly that he took Pym's observation as 'a sign of grace'.[103]

Yet there were also significant constitutional points to be made: indeed, he had put down an amendment to the Bill denying it a second reading until such time as Northern Ireland was given a form of local government. His point was, as he made clear to Foot when the Lord President intervened, that Northern Ireland did not even have the local powers that already existed in every other part of the Kingdom. He had no objection, he stressed, to better local administration being set up to carry out the provisions of laws framed at Westminster. Yet there were wider issues. Powell noted when he spoke that evening that the Secretary of State for Scotland, Bruce Millan, had, earlier in the debate, utterly failed to answer the question – first raised by the Labour MP Tam Dalyell and named, after his constituency, the West Lothian Question – of what the role would be in a United Kingdom parliament of Scottish members after a devolved assembly had been set up. That Millan could not answer proved to Powell's satisfaction his point that such an assembly could exist only in a federation. The Scottish members, he said again, could hold the balance on great issues of policy. The only way for them not to do so would be for a system to be created – utterly repugnant to him – of first-and second-class members.

Additionally, Powell argued that it would iniquitous if, as proposed, the question of an assembly were decided by a referendum just in Scotland; it should be across the whole of the Kingdom, since the outcome would affect the whole of the Kingdom. He reiterated that his colleagues and he would vote against the measure because their prime concern was the preservation of the Union, though Powell still understood the Union differently from most of his colleagues. Two years later, when Labour, determined this time to get the measure through, imposed a guillotine, Powell raised his usual objections to guillotining constitutional legislation, on the grounds – as he had argued about the European Communities Bill – that it really should have the consent of most of the House, and therefore not be subject to the obstructions that gave rise to the need for a guillotine. He tried to appeal to Foot's sense of the 'good old times', when the two of them had stopped the Parliament (No. 2) Bill, a measure that had received a much larger vote on second reading than the Scotland Bill; but Foot, as Leader of the House, had to obey orders, and deliver something to which his party's manifesto committed him and the Government of which he was a member.[104] Powell took an active part in the committee stage of the Bill, but it reached the statute book in time for the referendum to be held in the spring of 1979.

December 1977 brought a joyous domestic event for the Powells: their elder daughter Susan, now twenty-three, married Richard Day, a Lincolnshire farmer whom she had met while studying at agricultural college. The wedding took place in the Crypt Chapel of the Palace of Westminster; and on each guest's seat in the chapel was placed a short history of the building, written by the bride's father. The marriage was to be a happy and fruitful one; the Days provided the Powells with their first two grandchildren, Simon John Enoch, born in 1983, and Rachel Mary, in 1985. Jennifer, Powell's younger daughter, was completing her studies at Cambridge, where her father, fearing disruption to his daughter's life by student activists, never visited her during her time there.

However much Powell felt the Conservative party morally unfit to govern, he knew the next election would come either later in 1978 or early in 1979. He could tell, even before the Winter of Discontent sealed the issue, that Callaghan's administration would struggle to be re-elected. In January 1978, addressing the South Kensington Young Conservatives, he made a more constructive speech about the Conservatives than for years, but one still steeped in hostility. He told his audience that the party had no long-term future unless it learned to 'speak for England'.[105] He had been heartened by the fact that, in its fight against the devolution Bills, the party seemed to have relearned something about the nature of a United Kingdom and sovereign parliaments. Now, predictably, he saw the true test as the application of this logic to the party's attitudes towards Europe. He felt that during the passage of the Bill to allow direct elections there had been signs of Conservatives at last realising what was going on, and how change affected sovereignty.

There were other signs that Powell was rethinking his priorities. In a speech at Downpatrick two days before South Kensington, he accused Roy Mason of deliberately preventing a framework of democratic local government being established in Ulster in order to break the ties between Great Britain and the Province. He saw Mason's opposition originating in the distrust nationalists had of local government, as it seemed to them to portend integration. With talks continuing at Stormont about the possibilities of some form of devolution, Powell's remarks were seen as a fatal blast against their intentions. He feared that the secret agenda was a return to power-sharing, an aim Mason hoped to achieve by tricks, bribes, cajolery or, if none of these worked, coercion.

In January the Government's latest – and, as it turned out, successful – attempt at a Bill to enable direct elections came to the Commons for its committee stage. After just four days, the Government sought a guillotine, and once more Powell fulminated against what he saw as this abuse of the constitution. He understood that the Government had committed Britain to take part in the elections, scheduled for June the following year, but such a commitment was not binding on Parliament. He could not understand why the Government sought to impose the guillotine, since it had been content for a leisurely progress thus far; it was fear of filibustering in the future, which Powell said was an entirely unaccountable reason, that had prompted the move.

The occasion provided, nonetheless, another assault on the failings of the Opposition, who had not come to a clear view on what, for Powell, could not be a clearer-cut issue. He said the day was fateful for a man of Foot's reputation, for it was he, as Leader of the House, who was once more initiating a manoeuvre which, from the backbenches, he would have condemned; but 'it is also a fateful day for Her Majesty's Opposition, if they are an opposition'.[106] It was their duty, he argued, to protect the rights of backbenchers against the Government, and they were utterly failing to do this, and to give any 'manly' reason for doing so. Thus provoked, Powell embarked on perhaps his most brutal attack on the Thatcher Opposition yet:

> What sort of Opposition are they? They are involved in one of the greatest issues for not merely the House but the country, yet they remain deliberately dumb, deliberately self-contradictory, and give no advice ... to their supporters behind them. Perhaps I am wrong; for it is rumoured that the word has been passed round 'You watch which way who goes'. What a splendid fashion to conduct opposition! ... and so the whisper goes around the corridors and the Benches! 'Let them do the dirty work for us and they will take the blame. In that way the Bill will be on the statute book when we come into office.'[107]

He concluded: 'Those who form an Opposition do so, unless they are a mere faction, so as to have the privilege of governing, the privilege of leading. I say to Her Majesty's Opposition "In God's name, give a lead. For only if you do so will you earn the possibility of being asked by your fellow countrymen to lead them." '

This seemed to set back further any hope of a reconciliation. However, interviewed by Brian Walden, the former Labour MP, on 29 January, Powell said, 'Of course I am very proud of being a Tory. Yes, in my head and in my heart I regard myself as a Tory. As I have said, I was born that way; I believe it is congenital. I am unable to change it. That is how I see the world.'[108] Pressed about whether, one day, the gap between him and his old party might be breached, Powell said the very essence of Toryism was the nation. The EEC 'is the most un-Tory thing that can be conceived'; so, if his old party wanted him back, the nature of its mission was clear. In the Commons, though, relations between Ulster Unionists and the Conservatives had thawed out markedly since the previous summer; and some of Powell's recent speeches and other public statements were taken as signs by the Conservatives that a rapprochement could be achieved.

Certainly, Powell's earlier enthusiasm for the way the Government was conducting the economy had been misplaced. The economic revival had not proceeded as Callaghan had hoped. On 7 February he had announced that the Government would blacklist, by withholding contracts, firms that broke the 10 per cent pay-increase guideline he had set. Unsurprisingly, this brought down a censure motion, which the House debated on 13 February. Powell had to admit to his own disappointment that the Government had not, after all, understood the real causes of inflation, and said at the start of his speech that he and his colleagues regarded the censure as 'largely justified'.[109] This was, he said, irrespective of the correctness of analysis about the causes of inflation; the very methods being threatened by the Government were an outrage. 'We are confronted', he observed, 'with a course of action which the House refused to accept some 300 years ago, that is, a suspensory power in Government – the power of Government as Government to abandon the application of the general law in favour of this or that individual. It is not easy to see what has altered over the last 300 years to make the use of that power more acceptable today.'[110] He also condemned the cowardice of the Government in seeking 'to make up their policy as they go along' rather than embody it 'in a precise justifiable statement'. He concluded, 'This is not good enough. It is not good enough for any Government. It is not good enough for the House of Commons. I hope that the House of Commons will make it clear tonight that it is not.' Nonetheless, the Government, with Liberal support, survived.

If that were to be taken by the Conservatives as a thawing towards them Powell continued to show how far apart he still was by his implacable opposition to the EEC. Even his Unionist colleagues, hard line as they were on the question, were surprised by the tone of a speech made to an unlikely audience of time-and-motion experts at an airport hotel at Heathrow on 10 February. He professed that Britain simply failed to understand 'the depth and durability of the resentment held against us by the Germans and the French. By the Germans for the obvious reason that we defeated them; by the French for the less obvious but still more potent reason that we did not share in their defeat.'[111] The student of *Vom Kriege* took his text direct from Clausewitz, that war was a continuation of politics by other means. He pointed out that few observed that the opposite must also be true, that politics was a continuation of war by other means. The domination Britain's two partners had sought, and failed, to win over her through war had now been secured through diplomacy. Lest he be thought unreasonable, Powell qualified his remarks with the observation, 'nobody is more Francophile than I am'.

Then, as if the wound were not reopened sufficiently, Powell spoke a week later in Coventry about how he had been deceived – and had therefore helped to deceive others – by the Conservative leadership before the 1970 election about the seriousness of their intentions to bring large-scale immigration under control. This was a particularly sensitive time to make such a statement in terms of his party's relations with the Conservatives, as Mrs Thatcher had, at the end of January, made a controversial statement in a television interview about the fears people had of being 'swamped' by immigrants. 'I suppose that I, of all people, ought to have known better,' he reflected. 'I ought to have realised that if the party was likely to fulfil the expectations it encouraged at the 1970 election, they would not have driven out of their counsels two years earlier the one colleague whom ... millions recognised as understanding and voicing their inmost apprehensions.'[112] He said the backtracking and 'noises off' since the 'Thatcher episode' suggested that the deception might be repeated; to talk of stopping or substantially reducing immigration showed that the speaker did not understand the problem that he – or she – was talking about, but was 'deliberately practising upon the gullibility or ignorance of the hearers'.

Powell recalled that controls had already been put in place, in 1962 and 1968, but insufficient had been done to stop the problem of dependants coming to join those allowed to emigrate to Britain. The figures for immigration – 50,000 in 1977 – were the same when he made the Birmingham speech. It was 'the cruellest folly or deception' to suggest that there would be an 'end' to immigration unless steps were taken to ensure that the New Commonwealth population was reduced by actual outflow. For all her talk of being swamped, Mrs Thatcher was not proposing the large-scale programme of voluntary repatriation that he maintained was needed to make any sense of the policy. His remarks were greeted gleefully by Labour MPs – a somewhat unique occurrence – because Powell had highlighted the shortcomings of Mrs Thatcher's rhetoric.

He had not specified by what means the outflow would be achieved, and was attacked by his former Conservative colleague in the Commons, David Lane, now chairman of the Commission for Racial Equality, for appearing to advocate large-scale repatriation. However, in a BBC interview on 9 March, Powell clarified his position. He called, as he had before, for inducements rather than force to be used to 'persuade' a million immigrants to return to their country of origin. In another interview the following month, to mark the tenth anniversary of the Birmingham speech, he went into more detail about the 'inducements': the accrued National Insurance benefits of those returning could be paid to those volunteering for repatriation before retirement; and British firms that depended on immigrant labour could be helped to establish factories in Commonwealth countries to provide work for those returning home.

In April the Speaker's Conference on Ulster concluded with the decision that five more seats would be awarded to the Province, raising its representation by almost half, from twelve to seventeen constituencies. However, in order for Callaghan to keep the Unionists onside, he announced that, while he accepted the decision of the conference, the legislation to create the extra seats would not be introduced until the 1978–9 session. Callaghan had reason to be cautious. The Lib–Lab pact was in danger of fragmenting in forthcoming debates on the Finance Bill, as the Liberals disagreed with some of the provisions of Healey's Budget. The Conservatives were attempting to force a penny cut in the basic rate of income tax, from 34 to 33 per cent, and the Liberals were planning to support them. An additional problem for Callaghan was that his most reliable Ulster supporter, the SDLP MP Gerry Fitt, was furious at the allocation of the extra seats, which he felt would be won by Unionists. Mrs Thatcher, understandably, assured the Unionists that her party would put the legislation through quickly.

The Unionists were the last group to make up their minds on the tax-cut vote, and held the result in the balance. Without them, the House was 311–312 in the Opposition's favour on the issue. The press immediately focused on Powell – his party's Treasury spokesman – as the man they suspected would control the Unionists' support. Powell was keeping quiet. It remained that way until the vote on 8 May when, just a few hours before the division, he made a speech in which, to the astonishment of all who heard it, he announced that he and his six colleagues would support the Opposition amendment to cut a penny off the basic rate.

This seemed to some commentators and MPs a complete reversal of all he had said at second reading, when the Opposition had written off the chance of winning his support: he had focused in the speech on the inadvisability of transferring the burden from direct to indirect taxation, and had sought to demonstrate that the reduction Healey had achieved in the deficit was, in fact, merely temporary, and unable to support a tax cut. In his speech on 8 May,

Powell said Healey had undermined his own position by stating that if he lost the vote, and all the revenue with it, he would merely 'wait and see' what the result was rather than find the cash from elsewhere. Such an attitude, Powell suggested, did not reveal particularly fine judgment. That, though, turned out to be but one reason for the change of heart.

Powell said the debate they were having was not about economics, but about politics, so the Unionists would introduce a nakedly political angle to it. They had promised their electors they would seek redress for the injustices the Ulster people were perceived to suffer by comparison with the rest of the Kingdom. The promise to increase representation had been secured; the next item on the agenda was local government. 'We are not under the delusion', said Powell, 'that the correction of any such injustice can be achieved by a wave of the wand or overnight. In the last resort, it can only be the slow conviction of the House that an injustice has to be removed, by which that result will be achieved; and it will only be firmly achieved if that result is willed and understood by the House of Commons as a whole.'[113] He said there was not even the beginning of a recognition of that injustice; so, in the context of this political debate, it was as good a time as any to start on that process. To this end lay, as he put it, 'the duty of using our position in the House'. He concluded that 'there will be no dereliction of economic or political responsibility when tonight we vote against Her Majesty's Government.'[114] As a result, Labour lost by 312 to 304, the first time ever a government had had the rate of income tax cut against its wishes. Earlier, Callaghan had hinted that such a defeat would mean an election. With the deed done, though, such talk was discounted; Labour would fight on.

Powell took his objections to the direct elections to the European Parliament to their logical conclusion when, in a speech to the Northern Ireland Monday Club on 5 May 1978 – the day the European Assembly Elections Act received the royal assent – he advised a boycott of them. For similar constitutional reasons, he had earlier advised voters in Wales and Scotland that at a general election they should vote only for anti-devolution candidates. He realised that, however much Labour was a party more weighted against continued membership of the EEC than the Conservatives (and the party's opposition to membership was to harden to become a formal party policy by the time of the 1983 election), there was much else the party stood for that Powell simply could not support. He was particularly critical of Callaghan's increasing propensity to blame his former allies in the unions for all that was going wrong. At Eastbourne on 3 June, Powell called this image of union power 'a myth', adding that 'Britain has enough real conflicts to resolve and real evils to encounter without being burdened with spurious fears and unreal divisions.'[115]

It was hardly surprising, therefore, that when speaking to the Safeguard Britain Campaign's rally in London on 3 June Powell should make an important philosophical distinction between his position at the 1974 elections and that at the next one. Rather than issue a blanket endorsement for any party, he instead said that electors should vote for a candidate they believed to be opposed to Britain's membership of the EEC. For a man who had always described the party system as the *sine qua non* of British political life, the admission that that system had 'broken in our hands' was painful. Yet, as he saw it, party lines were no longer relevant. 'Whatever his other services and merits,' he said, 'no Member who before the Referendum voted for the acceptance of the *status quo*, no member who voted for the direct elections Bill, no member who voted to drive that measure through under guillotine, need come before us in the expectation that we will demean ourselves and renounce our deepest convictions by helping to return him.'[116]

The following weekend, addressing a meeting in Billericay on immigration, he was asked whether he could not now return to the Conservative party. He admitted there had been a time the previous winter when he had begun to wonder why he did not, as the differences between his position and the party's seemed to be diminishing; but the party's support for the guillotine that drove through the direct elections Bill had put an end to such imaginings. He also mocked the party for its behaviour in the wake of Mrs Thatcher's 'swamped' interview. 'With the instinctive and impenetrable defensiveness that might be imagined in a convent when the abbess had been delivered of a baby, the entire Conservative establishment swung into action – if I may borrow a phrase from journalism – and plugged the hole again in an instant. Baby? What baby? How dare anyone spread such rumours about Reverend Mother?'[117] Powell had been urging Mrs Thatcher to use an Opposition Day in the Commons for a debate on immigration, as, for different reasons, had Callaghan. But the Conservatives maintained an embarrassed silence, with MPs who sympathised with Powell's views expressing concern that Whitelaw, the deputy leader and home affairs spokesman, was pushing policy back to where it had been under Heath.

On 14 June the House debated another censure motion on the economy. This time it was aimed at Healey for introducing an emergency package the previous week which had included a 2.5 per cent employers' surcharge of a type he had set his face against during the Budget two months earlier. The Opposition, as a result, was demanding a cut of half in his salary. Howe, the Opposition's Treasury spokesman, had delivered a detailed indictment of where Labour had mishandled the economy, though he paid, understandably, little attention to the quality of the legacy the Government of which he had been a member had bequeathed to Labour. Healey had put up, in replying to Howe, a performance magnificent even by his standards of bombast, and an object lesson in how attack is the best form of defence. He had told the House that Howe had 'finally got round' to discussing the package 'a trifle nervously, I thought, after ploughing through a tedious and tendentious farrago of moth-eaten cuttings presented to him by the Conservative Research Department. That part of his speech was rather like being savaged by a dead sheep.'[118]

Continuing the casual approach, Healey did not feel it necessary to stay on the Treasury Bench for all of the rest of the debate, a discourtesy Powell regretted. He said it had been negligent of Healey to have needed to introduce a new package so soon after his Budget. The trouble was, as Powell pointed out, that the Government had once more found it could no longer sell all the gilts it needed to fund its public sector borrowing requirement; and the sum Healey had been forced to raise the previous week was the sum by which taxation had been cut in the vote on 8 May. It fell to Powell to deflate, in his absence, some of Healey's exuberance: 'Year after year the Chancellor has come to this House with the air of a boy riding a bicycle with his hands off the handlebar saying "See, no hands. Whatever the PSBR is, I get away with it." This time he has not got away with it.'[119] It was not, Powell said, the £500 million shortfall; it was that the £8 billion deficit was 'unsustainable' in the way in which it was being financed. The Government had exhausted its credit in the markets. Again, Powell had had his expectations of what Labour might be able to do disappointed. His confidence that they could win re-election, despite everything, was diminishing. He concluded his speech by expressing the hope that both front benches now realised the need for the country to stop being at the mercy of inflationary forces, but gave no clue how he would vote. In fact, he abstained, and the Government won.

Before the House rose for the summer recess, he had another opportunity to reprimand his fellow politicians for their lack of control over the economy, when the House debated Members' salaries. Powell had still never taken a rise during a parliament and did not intend to break that rule now. He reminded his colleagues that the inflation that had ravaged their salaries had been caused by politicians. 'It is an addition of shamelessness to use our power of the purse', he said, 'to vote ourselves an offset to see that we are all right, Jack. That is . . . why I consider this to be a shameful thing that we are doing.'[120] When Powell presented figures that showed how, in real terms, MPs' disposable income was the same in 1978 as when he had entered the House in 1950, he was pulled up by a Labour MP, James Lamond, who told him that living standards and expectations had risen in that time. Powell snapped back, 'The desire to be in this House has neither increased nor diminished, so far as I observe.'[121]

Throughout that summer, Powell continued to make demands in the Commons for a debate on immigration, for the reason, as he put it on 6 July, that the electorate needed to be forewarned against 'misleading and fraudulent statements' on the question that would most likely be made at the forthcoming election – statements made by (though Powell did not say so) the Conservative party more than anyone. Heath, at this time, gave his party an assurance that he would work with it at the next election – though his friends suspected that his promise was not unconnected with an ambition to return to high office. Powell's friends on the Conservative benches hoped he would do the same; but there was no prospect of that. For him, the evils of the past perpetrated against him had still not been exorcised or atoned for.

The publication in July of his latest collection of speeches, *A Nation or No Nation?*, reinforced the division between Powell and the Conservatives: it comprised speeches in which he set out, from 1972 onwards, why and how he had been betrayed by his old party, and why the dishonesty of Heath and his ministers had forced him to leave it – speeches whose import was highlighted by the succinct but pointed commentary by his archivist and friend Richard Ritchie. The book further highlighted what Peter Utley, reviewing it in the *Sunday Telegraph*, described as the 'paradox' of Powell despising the role of the independent in politics, yet now being one himself.[122] Powell often remarked that his intellectual arrogance made him impervious to a sense of isolation, but the truth was – and it was one that the camouflage of his membership of the Unionist party had perhaps prevented even him seeing clearly – that he was completely alone in Parliament, however much support he had in the country; and, because of the intensely individualistic nature of his views and his unpolitician-like integrity, he was unlikely to find anyone with whom he could band together. He had admirers in the Commons, and not just in the Conservative party, but his distance, reserve and intellect meant he could more easily have disciples than friends in the House.

Once Mrs Thatcher had discussed the consequences of mass immigration, Powell would not let the subject go. Speaking to the Wiltshire Monday Club on 21 July, he suggested that the backtracking since her original remarks was a clear bid by the Conservatives to win the minority vote at the election. He regretted her retreat from her original view, which had been 'an echo of the overwhelming public response which greeted a speech I made in Birmingham ten years before. However prissily expressed, people knew what she meant, and they knew it was the truth. The fear was a real fear. The swamping was a real swamping.'[123] Once she had spoken a 'chloroformed gag was immediately clapped over her mouth'. Now the kidnappers had, he said, let her out again – to address a meeting of the Anglo-Asian Conservative Society in her constituency, at which the talk was no longer of an end to immigration. Now, said Powell, it was about 'revised regulations to control the rate of immigration'. She was, he added, no longer concerned about the fears of the indigenous population, but of the immigrant one. It all came down to the party's calculations about votes – 'an activity to which their ruthless dedication is incomparable'. After all, he added, no one who feared being 'swamped' would vote Labour or Liberal, so the Conservatives could have it both ways.

Once Powell had raised the temperature again, Whitelaw, as home affairs spokesman, found himself under particular attack. He went too far, however, when he wrote angrily to one of Powell's supporters – who sent the letter on to him – that it was 'of course' Powell 'as Minister of Health in the early 1950s who was responsible for a large number of Asians coming here'.[124] Powell wrote to Whitelaw:

> I know you better than to be surprised by the enclosed; but if you are inclined to send this type of letter out in future, you may care to bear in mind that
>
> 1. I was not Minister of Health in the early 1950s;
> 2. The Ministers of Health did not recruit or employ NHS staff;
> 3. Until July 1962 there was no control or identification of persons entering the UK from the Commonwealth for residence or employment;
> 4. Staff employed from overseas (not only the Commonwealth) in the NHS normally returned after serving one to three years to get experience and qualifications.
> 5. Total New Commonwealth personnel employed in the NHS was at all times a tiny fraction of New Commonwealth residents in the UK.[125]

His next big speech, on 28 July, was an assault on the continuing ignorance of the Government – and the survivors of Heath's administration – about the economy. 'My considered conclusion', he said, 'is that a considerable and increasing proportion [of MPs], including most of the occupants of both front benches, do know they are talking nonsense, but they go on doing so because they are ashamed to stop after so long, because it gives them something to say, and because as everybody is talking the same nonsense, they feel quite safe.' Particular contempt was reserved for the Government, which had just published a White Paper with the 'stupid' title of *Winning the Battle against Inflation* and which did not include a single reference to the importance of the money supply.

Yet it was just as predictable that, when in early September the Conservatives, now effectively fighting an election campaign, claimed they would handle the economy better than Labour, Powell derided them. He simply did not believe that Mrs Thatcher and her colleagues were prepared to be sufficiently radical, and to offer a 'rupture' with the past. But then he was not to know the opportunity for radical action that the climate of public opinion created by the Winter of Discontent was about to give to the Opposition.

V

The approach of the election created other matters of urgency for the Unionists. What had, in 1974, been a coalition was now in open disarray; and when, at the Trades Union Congress in early September Callaghan announced that he would not be calling an election that autumn, the Unionists took the opportunity to have talks to try to put together a united front for the following spring, when the contest was expected. At local level, Official Unionist and DUP councillors were having meetings, but the fear remained that Paisley would put up a candidate in every constituency against the Official Unionist; and Powell was still threatened by a rogue candidacy from Cecil Harvey.

Powell was so convinced an autumn election would be called that he had started drafting valedictory letters to colleagues with whom he was friendly and who he knew would not be standing again. He was equally convinced he would hold his seat. Nor did he intend to alter his integrationist policy, and, indeed, in electoral terms, there was no need. Having first converted Molyneaux to the argument, he had now converted all but the DUP hard-liners. Opinion polls in the Province showed that, as Stormont became a distant memory and the importance of asserting Ulster's place as a part of the Kingdom became more pressing, so support for integration had grown. Now 80 per cent of Unionists were shown by polls to favour it. Powell had worked the constituency so assiduously in the preceding four years that he felt he had nothing to fear. Whereas at first it had been hard to go into Newry he had, by now, visited almost every house in every street in the town. If there were any houses where he was told he was not welcome, he would simply raise his hat and leave. Roy Lewis, his schoolfellow and now biographer, accompanied him on one such visit and found Powell 'absolutely fearless'.[126] Ironically, not being an Orangeman had helped him to bridge the sectarian divide. He had won the respect of the minority population, and, as the forthcoming election would show, some of their votes. He had built up a formidable organisation, including, for the first time in South Down, a full-time agent. He also predicted that, having succeeded in securing more MPs for the Six Counties, there would soon be a proper system of democratic local government there: a promise Callaghan was beginning to hold out in the event of his being returned to office, and continuing to receive Unionist support.

Callaghan having met Parliament again with a Queen's Speech, attention was once more focused on the Unionists, and how long they would support him. Powell had given few clues in his speeches during the recess, heaping obloquy on both parties in more or less equal measure. When the Conservatives put down a censure amendment against the Government on the Queen's Speech, however, Powell said his party would not be supporting it. He said the Unionists had a 'compelling duty' to see that the legislation in increasing the number of Ulster MPs was on the statute book before the end of the session. But he also took the opportunity of dismissing the assertion by the Conservatives that if they formed a government they could 'create lasting prosperity'. 'When I read those words,' said Powell, for they were set out in the motion on the Order Paper, 'it occurred to me that the Greeks had a word for it. To assert that an administration can create lasting prosperity is an assertion that no self-respecting politician ought to allow himself to make. Least of all should such an assertion come from a party which once had some affiliation with Toryism."[127]

He continued, 'It is indeed possible for Administrations to assist to some extent the endeavours of a people. It is certainly possible for Administrations more seriously to hamper them. But to suggest to the House and to the people that an Administration is capable of "creating a lasting prosperity" falls under the definition of *hubris*.'[128] He went on to warn against the obsession with incomes policy, and with the damage that could be done by trade unions – a doctrine that would sound less well composed a couple of months later, once the Winter of Discontent was under way. He hoped it was now realised that no increases in wages could be paid unless the money supply were expanded to allow it. He allowed himself, in this context, a poke at Heath: 'Sometimes I think that even the right hon Member for Sidcup has received some intimations of this truth.'[129] He surmised that, from the confusion they were still in about the incomes policy – Mrs Thatcher had been talking about a 'norm' in pay settlements – the Conservatives just did not know how to run the economy. The decision of his party to back the Government in order to secure Ulster its additional representation was not, therefore, difficult: 'there has been no painful dilemma which we have had to resolve between the national interest as a whole and our own peculiar duty'.[130]

Before the realities of the impending industrial crisis engulfed political life, Parliament had an opportunity – one repeatedly refused by Heath's administration, though he had committed Britain to monetary union – to debate the first stage of that union, a European Monetary System. Talks had been going on between officials, and now a meeting was scheduled between ministers of the EEC, to try to establish a foundation for this system. In the debate Powell followed a Labour backbencher, John Prescott, a future deputy leader of his party, who had spoken categorically of his objections to a federal Europe and to economic and monetary union. Powell warmly endorsed his view. He regretted that Howe, who had spoken for the Conservatives, had welcomed a system of fixed exchange rates, though one which – and Powell did not refrain from highlighting this paradox, which was to dog the Conservative Government until its entry into the Exchange Rate Mechanism in 1990 – could have its rates adjusted before, and not after, intervention was necessary. 'One would have thought', Powell observed, 'that a system of exchange rates that are free to change later whenever necessary without an intervention is remarkably difficult to distinguish from a system of freely floating exchange rates.'[131]

He said categorically that a system of controlled rates 'is unworkable and always will be unworkable, both inside and outside the European Economic Community'. His evidence was not least the Bretton Woods system, the pursuit of which had 'had a devastating effect upon the life of this country and upon its morale in the past 30 years'.[132] He said that differential rates of inflation, or differentials of expected rates of future inflation, would cause differences in exchange rates, and the supply of and demand for different currencies would be affected by any other number of factors, and lead to an impossibility of fixing them. Powell said that even if a way could be found of managing the internal value of a currency so that it was completely stable, that would still not guarantee a stable exchange rate. It would still be at the mercy of what was happening elsewhere. He issued another warning, which would be of great relevance after ERM entry in 1990: the lesson of the return to the gold standard in 1925 had been one of 'grinding deflation'; now there would be a gold standard without gold, but the effect would be the same.

There was also the constitutional worry, that there would need to be a single European monetary authority to control this fixity of the currencies, or, if it came to this extreme, the eventual single European currency. He said that, within the nation, some areas were economically disadvantaged compared with others, which is why some politicians advocated a regional policy. A single currency throughout the EEC simply magnified that problem, and prevented it from being contained within national bounds. The consequences would be fearsome: 'the result of a common market and a common monetary system is to intensify and throw into relief all those economic trends which the component nations would endeavour to digest separately in accordance with their own judgments and their own national characters and intentions'.[133] Healey had said that Britain had no independence to surrender with regard to the exchange rate, because it was not set by Britain. Powell knew this to be self-evidently true, but said it was illogical to surrender a floating currency and to surrender, therefore, a means of controlling the money supply and with it inflation.

'All economic decisions lead back, feed back, to the exchange rate,' he said.[134] 'Surrender the right to control the exchange rate – surrender control over it to another body – and one has, directly or indirectly, surrendered the control of all the economic levers of government.' Powell realised some political manoeuvring might be necessary to save the diplomatic sensibilities of Britain's European partners – such as 'The EMS [European Monetary System] is a splendid thing so long as we are not in it' – and urged the Government to maintain the substance of political independence.[135] It was notable, though, that in the debate those who presented the most enthusiastic arguments for British membership were on the Conservative benches. Most of the opposition came from the Government and their supporters. Neil Marten, a Conservative anti-marketeer, told Tony Benn in the autumn of 1978 that, when Parliament was sitting, he, Powell, Douglas Jay and the Labour MP Brian Gould would meet on Mondays to discuss the most effective way of countering European integration – a meeting Marten termed 'the unusual channels'.[136]

On 8 December Powell ventured into a new, and highly potent, field of controversy. Occasionally, in the now exhaustive newspaper speculation about whom the Prince of Wales might marry, it was mooted that his bride might be a Roman Catholic. That this might displease many of his Protestant supporters was scarcely the point; such a marriage would also be illegal. Saying 'I dislike and deplore unnecessary and impertinent intrusions into the personal and private aspects of the life of the Sovereign and the Royal Family,' he felt this particular aspect was one upon which comment 'if respectfully expressed' was in order. Indeed, because of the legal standing of such a marriage, it was not purely a private matter.[137]

He proceeded to give a historical exposition to help him make the point. He detailed the exclusion from the succession of any who would 'marry a papist'. He said that even though the laws laying this down were drafted by 'men living under the immediate impression of the events of 1688 and the impression, less immediate but still profound, of the events of 1553–58' one should not conclude that, as the present day was far more remote, 'provision of law may be treated as obsolete and thus as readily repealable if convenience should require'. No doubt with his constituents in mind, he said that 'immense emotional forces' still came to bear on a question that, he hoped, would remain academic. He also stressed that it was not a religious issue, and that did not impinge on questions of religious toleration; his objection to the heir to the throne marrying a Roman Catholic was not rooted in religious bigotry.

'The question is political,' he said. 'The question is national ... what does make the issue political is the nature – what is today the unique nature – of the British state.' That state was, he added, a prescriptive monarchy, whose authority was derived from 'immemorial' acceptance by the British people of the power of the Crown. With Britain's unwritten constitution, the 'central, essential fact about the British state' was the monarchy. The English – the preponderant constituents of that state – had made the specific choice that that source of authority in it, and its church, should be one and the same thing – the Crown. 'Acceptance of what the Bill of Rights called "reconciliation to the Church of Rome" involves acceptance of a source of authority external to the realm and, in the literal sense, foreign to the Crown in Parliament,' he pointed out. 'Between Roman Catholicism and the royal supremacy there is, as St Thomas More concluded, no reconciliation.'

His conclusion was unequivocal. 'A Roman Catholic Crown would signify by definition the destruction of the Church of England because it would contradict the essential character of that church,' he said. That was not all.

When Thomas Hobbes wrote that 'the Papacy is no other than the ghost of the deceased Roman Empire sitting crowned upon the grave thereof', he was promulgating an enormously important truth. Authority in the Roman Church is the exertion of that *imperium* from which England in the 16th century finally and decisively declared its national independence as the *alter imperium*, the 'other empire', of which Henry VIII declared 'This realm of England is an empire'.

It was an event which neither the toleration of other churches and religions nor the decline (if such there be) in the Christian religion itself can reverse, so long as the nation continues to be a nation – to be itself.

Powell had a more profound political point. External authority had been admitted by the nature of British participation in the EEC. That was bad enough, and a struggle was continuing to change it. Yet for the Church of England, too, to surrender to such authority 'would be the capitulation of a key position, both morally and practically,' he added. 'It would signal the beginning of the end of the British monarchy. It would portend the eventual surrender of everything that has made us, and keeps us still, a nation.'

Irrespective of the political point Powell wished to make about Europe, the constitutional point he made was absolutely clear. The effective separation of the authority of the Crown in Parliament and the Crown in the established church would have profound effects on the perception of the British monarchy, and of Rome's role in British life. Yet he was immediately attacked for making these statements of fact. An unnamed official of the Vatican Secretariat for Christian Unity, founded a decade earlier to try to establish closer relationships between the Anglican and Roman Catholic churches, accused him of being 'hopelessly outdated' and talking 'utter nonsense'.[138] Hailsham, who for some time had not bothered to attack Powell in public, surfaced with the view that his old rival 'was simply trying to out-flank Paisley in his constituency and win popular support there. He was speaking out of turn and should have kept his mouth shut.' He believed the constitution would simply have to be changed if the Prince chose to marry a papist. Buckingham Palace said that the Prince of Wales had no intention of marrying a Roman Catholic 'or anyone else'.[139]

Lest he be accused of whipping up anti-Catholic feeling, Powell used a speech the very next evening, to an Orange lodge, to remind Orangemen that their order had a rule not to admit anyone who was seen to be intolerant of others because of their religious beliefs: Powell endorsed this rule. However, even one of his own colleagues, James Kilfedder, was appalled by his remarks on the Prince of Wales, saying it was 'outrageous' that Powell, as a Privy Councillor, should raise the issue.[140] 'By taking this stand now, Mr Powell may think he will gain greater support in the next election. However, he should know that Ulster people are not morons, they are not stupid or susceptible.' Few of Powell's colleagues thought he had made the speech when he did for any other reason than to try to pre-empt a Paisleyite threat.

In the months until the election – 1979 had to be an election year, as Callaghan's mandate could not extend beyond October – Powell continued to make prominently reported speeches on a wide range of issues. Molyneaux, who saw him just before he returned to London at the end of the Christmas recess, spoke to him about the chance of securing more concessions from the Government in return for the Unionists' co-operation. It was agreed that Powell would tell Callaghan that the end of the process of co-operation had not necessarily been reached. Powell conveyed the message but, as the winter went on, the Unionists received the impression that Callaghan was too distressed by the conduct of some of his own notional supporters to have any heart to do more deals with the Unionists to prolong the Parliament.[141]

Powell continued to goad his old party. In comments with a mischievous tinge – in that they seemed to separate his old friend Thorneycroft, who was now the Conservative party chairman, from some of his Heathite colleagues in the Conservative leadership – Powell commented on 2 January 1979 that his former chief had been right about inflation in 1957, when he had discharged policy on the basis that it was caused by failure to control the money supply. In sharp contrast to those who disagreed with that policy now, Thorneycroft 'took the old-fashioned course dating from the days when politicians were gentlemen and not players'.[142] Rather than remind everyone that he had been expounding the policy for the last twenty years – while Thorneycroft himself had kept quiet about it – Powell now argued that what had been heresy was now orthodoxy. 'The old superstitions and errors about inflation being caused by greed or by trade union monopoly or by the failure of anchovies off the South American coast have been routed and driven from the intellectual battlefield.'

This was a somewhat provocative statement: the Government (which Powell was not addressing) still harboured such beliefs, and the shadow cabinet (the real target of his remarks) had its share of Heathmen who believed in a prices and incomes policy. He claimed that recent speeches by Mrs Thatcher on inflation had convinced him that 'if the Conservatives get in again they would be off once more on a policy of price and income control before you could say Jack Robinson'. Hence the embarrassment for Thorneycroft, who found a neat way of sidestepping it. 'I have known Mr Powell for many years,' the chairman said. 'We resigned together in disagreement over Government policy. Mr Powell's comments are welcome. He himself played a very important part at the time.'

Then came the sting. 'In addition to the monetarist lines he was talking about, he did join with me in the establishment of the "three wise men", an early attempt at incomes policy. It was an attempt at public discussion of the monetary and economic situation of the country so that individuals, Government and unions were able to inform each other of the kind of outlook that lay ahead. It was a system not dissimilar to that used in Germany today and that set out in "The Right Approach to the Economy", published recently by the Conservatives.' These unifying words further fuelled Powell's suspicions that Mrs Thatcher would, in economics, be no better than Heath.

The breakdown during January of the Government's attempts to deal with the public sector unions over pay – the Winter of Discontent – further reinforced

Powell's views. The Commons debated the crisis on 16 January, and he cheerfully told the Government that the way in which this Parliament was ending bore a stark resemblance to the way in which the one over which Heath had presided had finished. This was, he said, hardly surprising, since they both came at the end of a period when the Government had been trying to control prices and wages. 'The 'industrial chaos' that was breaking out 'is a consequence of the framework into which the unions and the employers have both been pinned by the policies of the past three or four years'.[143] As in 1974, the main grievance was over relativities, the system of which had been broken down by flat percentage pay increases.

He attacked Mrs Thatcher for dealing, once more as he saw it, with a symptom rather than the cause of the unrest. He agreed with her that laws against secondary picketing would be important, but they were not the heart of this particular issue. He picked up on a despairing remark by Callaghan that strike action had always used to be 'the last resort'. 'I will tell him', said Powell, 'why strike action is now the first resort. It is that men know that the restrictions which it is attempted to place upon their remuneration in the next 12 months are unreasonably drawn and unsustainable, and they see instances where, by strike action, that unsustainability has been demonstrated. So they say to themselves "Very well, we know what to do. We will strike first and negotiate afterwards." '[144] It might well be that the law allowed the unions too much leeway, but it was the Government, by distorting the market rate of wages, that had provoked them to exploit that leeway. It was, as ever, the consequence of the Government not financing its expenditure honestly, and of not properly controlling the money supply. These assertions brought an immediate accusation from a Labour backbencher, Ron Thomas, that Powell was a 'militant monetarist' and could not see what problems the rise in food prices, for example, caused by the Common Agricultural Policy, was causing. Wearily, Powell told him that, of course, the CAP had raised food prices relative to other prices in the economy; but that was not inflation, which was the rising of all prices, and which was enabled by a larger supply of money.

Speaking in his constituency on 26 January, he claimed that Callaghan's policy had brought the country to 'the nearest approximation to a general strike'. The Prime Minister had made the Government the principal party in every industrial dispute, thereby forcing the unions to form a common front against it. It was, he said, 'impossible' for Callaghan to tell the workers there could be 8 per cent inflation, but not more than 5 per cent increases in pay to meet it; and, as a cure for inflation, the whole policy was 'futile' anyway.

Yet, in the middle of the social and industrial chaos seizing the country, Powell still had time for more philosophical ruminations. He used a speech at Doncaster on 20 January to claim that Russia – in the view of most politicians, even in the Labour party, a potential enemy in a full-scale nuclear confrontation – was in fact Britain's natural ally. He admitted that some might find his remarks 'strange', but said that necessity would bring the two countries closer together over the rest of the century. He observed that in the two world wars, and in the Napoleonic conflicts, Russia had been 'the ultimate guarantee of the survival of Britain as an independent nation'. He interpreted the recent refusal of Britain to join the European Monetary System as a sign that she did not really want to be part of a European power bloc, and would soon return to her earlier distrust of continental hegemony. That was when Russia as an ally and a counterweight would become more significant, resuming her former role as 'the great power out beyond Britain's continental enemy'.[145]

After his visit there in 1977, Powell had said how struck he was by the sense of nation in Russia. Nor was he concerned about the vastly different political systems and philosophies of the two countries: political affinity and friendship were irrelevant to this argument. 'The word "friendship", as used in the inter-course of peoples, is hollow and delusory,' he said. 'Necessity, not sympathy, is the only sure bond in the world of nations ... the *entente* will not be *cordiale*; but *entente* it will still be.'

Such matters of high international diplomatic theory were far from the growing difficulties in the Unionist party as it neared the election. In early February one of its MPs, James Kilfedder, resigned from the party, saying he would fight the election as an independent. In a statement, he cited as his reason for going the fact that Harry West 'was allowing Enoch Powell to lead the party by the nose'.[146] Kilfedder's objections to Powell were contradictory: he resented the Official Unionists' estrangement from the Conservative party, but resented even more Powell's continued arguments in favour of direct rule – which the Conservatives had, of course, introduced – as a prelude to full integration. Powell was untroubled by Kilfedder's assertions, telling constituents that the Unionists would, after the grant of the additional seats, probably be the third largest party in the Commons. This would bring 'a new-found respect' towards the Province and the 'non-aligned force' of the Unionist party from the rest of the political establishment that would only cement Ulster's importance in the Kingdom.

It seemed the election could not long be delayed. Fitt, on whom Callaghan depended for his majority, was making it clear that he was less and less impressed with Labour's conduct, and the Government's already battered reputation had been further assaulted by the Winter of Discontent. Yet Powell the strategist felt this was not the time to remove the props from the Government; it was a time to make more demands for the benefit of the Province. Even though agreement would buy Callaghan only a few more months at most, Powell told him on 16 March that the Unionists would continue to support Labour in return for a gas pipeline linking the Six Counties with the mainland. The project would cost £100 million, but it would bring the costs of gas in Ulster – which could use only the more expensive manufactured town gas – down to British levels. Similarly, Ulster should be linked to the electricity grid. Powell told the government it was not the case that these aims were neither politically nor economically possible, because they were.

The demand was provoked by the leak of a private report, undertaken by a senior Northern Ireland Office civil servant, to Roy Mason telling him that the demand for the pipeline was economic nonsense. Not only could the Government not afford it, but the Province could produce more electricity than it could use, so it was pointless subsidising gas. Mason was set against the concession. The Government did, though, hint to Unionists that there would soon be more shipbuilding contracts to benefit the workers in Belfast's shipyards. Powell shifted his ground: while not retreating from his integrationist position, he renewed calls in a speech in his constituency on 17 March for more local government functions – principally health, schools and social services – to be returned to Ulster. He promised that in the weeks ahead the Unionist MPs would be 'vigilant to miss no opportunity for genuine advance' on these questions.[147]

The Government, in desperate trouble, quickly announced that it would welcome agreement on widening local democracy in the Province. Callaghan invited Powell to put forward specific proposals. At the same time, Mrs Thatcher made remarks in the Commons about Europe that further proved Powell's thesis that she was little better than Heath, and which offended some of the more right-wing members of her front-bench team. She criticised Callaghan for having been 'abrasive' at the most recent EEC summit when he had warned the other eight countries that Britain was no longer prepared to support and heavily finance the Common Agricultural Policy. Her trade spokesman, John Nott, praised what Callaghan had said as a 'necessary protest', and others resented the opportunity she had given to Callaghan to put himself forward as the better defender of Britain's interests in Europe. With speculation that another vote of confidence would soon be tabled, Powell saw no reason why he and his colleagues should do anything to help Mrs Thatcher gain power.

Powell had assumed the role of chief negotiator with the Government on behalf of the Unionists, and he found that most of his demands were quite acceptable to Callaghan. He wanted Healey to introduce a fiscally and monetarily tight Budget the following month, and expected Callaghan to maintain his pressure on Brussels to reform the CAP. The matter became critical on 22 March, when Mrs Thatcher, sensing her chance as all the other opposition parties were united behind her, tabled another motion of no-confidence. The spur was Callaghan's predicament over Scottish devolution. The Scots had voted in their referendum insufficiently to allow the establishment of assemblies – the Welsh had comprehensively rejected the chance to have theirs – and the Welsh and Scottish secretaries were now bound to advise the Queen not to give the royal assent to the Acts of Parliament that were passed by Parliament and would have set the assemblies up. The Government's dilemma was that a majority had voted for devolution in both referendums, but in neither had the proposals won the support of the required 40 per cent of the electorate. So Callaghan, anxious about losing votes in both regions at the election, was determined that this should be the end of the matter.

Before sanctioning withdrawal of the Acts, Callaghan wanted talks with all the other parties on the subject, and issued invitations. Mrs Thatcher ignored hers, and tabled her motion instead. Speculation immediately centred upon what the Ulster parties would do. Both Fitt and the nationalist independent Frank Maguire let it be known that the deliberate creation of more seats for Unionists by the Government was not an act for which Callaghan could expect gratitude. However, for the moment, there seemed to be enough to allow Powell to persuade his group to support Callaghan. However, on 25 March, the Sunday papers carried a well-informed leak that the Government would soon publish a Green Paper explaining its decision not to finance the gas pipeline. This was a blow to Powell, who had said that this remained a key factor in maintaining the support of his colleagues for the Government. He and other Unionists were under renewed pressure from the grass roots to revert to type and support the Conservatives; if there was to be no pipeline, such pressure would be harder to resist. One consolation for Powell was that West had been to see Mrs Thatcher earlier in the week, but had managed to wring no additional concessions out of her either.

Up until the vote on 28 March the likely result was too close to call. Powell could not convince all his colleagues to support the Government; there was manifestly nothing in it for them now. The pipeline issue still grated. When David Steel, the Liberal leader, mentioned it, Powell snapped that, far from being merely the latest concession sought by the Unionists, his party had been in negotiations about it for three years. Fitt had spoken in the debate and signalled that, because of what he perceived as Mason's failure to root out police brutality, he could not support the Government. He had also speculated about another element of Powell's motivation, saying that 'the last thing that the right hon Member for Down, South wants is a Government of any description with a big enough majority to legislate. He loves his present position, where he can hold the balance. He can go to little villages and towns in Down, South and tell everyone how important he is, and he does that every weekend. I have not met another hon Member who suffers from such delusions of grandeur.'[148] Stripping away from those remarks the bitterness of an opponent, one is still left with a painful truth that would soon impact upon Powell: that his days as an important political mover in the Commons were almost at an end.

He did not speak in the debate. Molyneaux, who did, said Ulster had a right to local democracy and was still being denied it; the implication was clear. Powell told his wife later that evening, when he stole home for a quick supper (the Commons' catering staff were, like much of the rest of the country, on strike), that Callaghan had been making more positive noises about the return of local government in Ulster, but it was too late. Yet, as she went through the lobbies with her supporters, Mrs Thatcher herself was seen apologising to them for not having pulled off her attempt to remove the Government. Two Unionists did in fact vote with Callaghan; five others, including Powell, voted with the Conservatives. When the votes were counted, Mrs Thatcher had a surprise; the Opposition had won by 311 votes to 310. The election was set for 3 May.

There were a few odd Bills to be tidied up before the dissolution, and Powell was speaking on one of them – the Credit Unions Bill – on the afternoon of 30 March when the sound of an explosion was heard in the Commons. A few minutes later, the Speaker interrupted Powell and suspended the sitting for fifteen minutes; a car had been blown up on its way out of the car park into New Palace Yard. The bomb killed Airey Neave, the Conservatives' Northern Ireland spokesman. Powell was asked by a television station to comment later on, and seemed to many to allow his feelings about Conservative policy in Northern Ireland to override normal sensitivity. 'I am sure', he said, 'that Airey Neave would have wished nothing better than to share the same end as so many of his innocent fellow citizens for whom the House of Commons is responsible.' Asked to clarify the remarks by journalists reporting on how appalled other MPs had been by them, Powell refused to add or subtract anything from what he had said.[149] As with Macleod's death, Powell was not prepared, in a public forum, to take his emotions out of the freezer.

Gerry Fitt made sure the press were immediately told how he had been especially upset by Powell's attitude, as it had been he who, during the suspension of the sitting, had told Powell it had been Neave who had been killed. Powell's response horrified him. 'He sat down with an expressionless face,' Fitt recalled. 'He showed no emotion and made no comment. He was as cold as ice. Then he got up and carried on as if nothing had happened. He even said something like "Following this interruption" and then carried on. I was shocked.'[150] What Hansard in fact records Powell as having said upon the resumption was 'I take it, Mr Deputy Speaker, that it is your wish that we should proceed with the debate?' While not betraying any normal human emotions – which it was not in Powell's character to do in public – that is hardly the same as Fitt's recollection.[151]

A man who had longed to die in the war knew what he meant by what he said about Neave, yet could not see how others incapable of understanding that complex emotion would put a different interpretation upon it. It was soon brought home to Powell, privately, that his bare words had been taken offensively, not least in Fleet Street. One who told him pointedly was his long-standing friend and admirer Andrew Alexander, who for his pains was met with 'waves of hostility' and had the telephone put down on him.[152] Powell soon apologised, telling Alexander, 'I am sure that journalists, like the politicians whom they observe, are from time to time under severe emotional pressure – perhaps most when they show it least – and react accordingly. I hope this enables us, when necessary, to make allowance for one another's uncharacteristic moments.'[153] In the meantime, Powell had sought to repair the most obvious damage, writing to Neave's widow the day after the assassination to say that 'whatever others thought, Airey himself would have known what my few words about him meant, and would have understood them as one soldier's salute to another, far better and more gallant than himself'.[154] Mrs Neave thanked him, adding that 'Airey knew you were a soldier of renown – and would understand and appreciate what you meant.'[155]

Neave's murder thrust the Ulster question into the forefront of a campaign that the Conservatives had hoped would be mainly about two conflicting ideologies. For the Unionists, the most important thing still to resolve was the threat by Paisley's supporters to oppose Official Unionist candidates. Talks in Londonderry on 8 April to try and resolve the issue were not even attended by the DUP, and ended in stalemate. Cecil Harvey was still threatening to stand; but, at the very last moment, he announced that, in the interests of Unionist unity, he would give Powell a clear run. His SDLP opponent, Eddie McGrady, a local chartered accountant, immediately confided in the press that his high hopes of winning the seat had been hampered by Harvey's decision. Elsewhere, some of Powell's colleagues were not so lucky. In seven seats both a DUP candidate and an Official Unionist stood.

Powell opened his campaign at Banbridge on 19 April, claiming that the last Parliament had seen a 'fantastic change for the better' in Ulster. Statistically, this was true, as the incidence of terrorist activity had been falling since 1977: Powell had not foreseen the bloody few months ahead, which would include the murder of Lord Mountbatten and a slaughter of soldiers at Warrenpoint. The Unionist manifesto, launched the same day, presented Powell with a doctrinal problem, in that it put the return of devolved government for Ulster at the top of the agenda. But he knew the unlikelihood of this taking place, and was prepared to work assiduously for the devolution of powers to a democratic local government, as in the rest of the Kingdom.

Unlike his first campaign in Ulster, this was relatively low-profile. The prospect of a woman prime minister, and the slick and compelling nature of the Conservative campaign on the mainland, prevented Powell from securing as much publicity as in the past. In his campaign he acted with typical English intellectual reserve. Early on four RUC men were killed by the IRA at Bessbrook, ten miles from Loughbrickland, where Powell lived when in the constituency. Asked to comment on the murders, he refused, saying it was not his practice to make public comments on such matters. 'I write privately to the bereaved and make it known that I am available to them ... I don't seek to make publicity for myself out of their troubles.'[156] Harvey, on the other hand – and he had not at that stage decided not to stand – used the incident to demand the restoration of hanging and the drafting in of the SAS, and roundly condemned the atrocity. Powell was bemused by concern that he had failed to condemn the murders; to him, such condemnation was both implicit and obvious, and therefore pointless and self-serving. His supporters, though, were dismayed by his tight-lipped reluctance to go through the usual motions. As the commentator and former Irish minister Conor Cruise O'Brien noted, 'Ulster is a place where Mr Powell represents a force for moderation.'

On the Saturday before the poll he came to the mainland and spoke in Birmingham, where he repeated advice he had given the previous year: votes should be cast only for those against the EEC, and, if there was no such candidate, an abstention was the correct course. He stated his dissatisfaction with Labour's renegotiation of 1975, claiming that its present manifesto was nearly as bad as the Conservatives'. He said the task for the British people was whether they could prove 'they still deserve to be numbered among the nations of the earth'.[157]

How many still listened cannot be computed: to judge from the result, relatively few. Powell had made an important difference to the outcome of the previous three elections; he would not do so at a fourth. In the preceding years he had, in effect, enjoyed more power than ever at Westminster, thanks to the bargaining strength his strategic guile had brought to the Unionists. Yet at the same time his removal to Ulster, and the length of his alienation from his traditional Conservative supporters, had reduced his influence. His last reported remarks in the campaign were about the malign influence of America on the politics of the Six Counties – an issue which, admittedly, would loom large in the years ahead, and about which Powell was utterly, if over-dramatically, accurate. But at that stage of the campaign it was, even in Ulster, less than centrally relevant. On the mainland he still had a widespread, in some parts fanatical, following. However, it was no longer big enough to make a difference. The old issues had moved on: 'we are all monetarists now'.

Ironically, though Powell seemed not to see it, the election was at last about the great question he had posed nearly twenty years earlier: about socialism versus the free society. The free society won, though Powell did not believe it. He held his seat by a greatly increased majority of 8,000. When asked how he regarded Mrs Thatcher's historic victory, he simply replied: 'Grim.'[158]

18

THE OLD STATESMAN

The Unionists, and even someone of Powell's position, were diminished by the Conservative victory. Mrs Thatcher's majority of forty-three meant she did not need them in the way Callaghan had. Powell's political hostility to her was unequivocal. In the preceding months he had attacked her grasp of economics – he never believed she had a proper understanding of monetarism and its implications – her attitude to Europe, and her sincerity about immigration. To this he now added her infatuation with America, a country which, in a speech just before polling day, Powell had claimed was now engaged in a high-level campaign of 'ignorant and impertinent meddling' to get Britain out of Ulster.[1] The omens for reconciliation, despite the avowedly Powellite intent of the Thatcher programme, were not plentiful.

One of Powell's first acts after Labour's defeat was to write in sincere sorrow to 'My dear Jim' Callaghan, to thank him for his 'staunch and repeated defence of Ulster during the election campaign' and to 'look forward, on Ulster's account and the country's, to our continued co-operation and understanding in the new parliament'.[2] He wrote similarly to Roy Mason, speaking of the 'unfortunate results' of both the no-confidence motion and the election.[3] However, one of Powell's most fervent admirers on the Conservative benches, Ian Gow, was appointed as the new Prime Minister's parliamentary private secretary; and over the next four years would largely succeed in bringing her and Powell closer together, and establishing an understanding between two people who had, if only Powell could realise it, much in common.

There was, however, little time for Powell to brood. The direct elections to the European Parliament were less than a month away. He rethought his position on the elections. Though he disagreed with the notion in principle still, he suggested that the electorate should now go out and vote for candidates determined to allow Britain to remain British – something not interpreted as a call to support the Conservative party, which he said was keen to ensure that the 1972 European Communities Act remained irreversible. Labour, already moving left since its defeat, was far more hostile. Powell saw the European Parliament as a forum in which Britain's rights could be recovered, and said that 'we ought to recover them, whether the rest of the EEC agrees or not'.[4] While he said he understood the views of those who wanted a boycott – he had, after all, wanted one himself – he felt that, as the Parliament was an accomplished fact, the elections to it should be participated in, and the chance should be taken to vote for Britain as a nation rather than as a European province.

On the eve of that election, he took his pessimism about the national psyche a stage further. He posed the question, in an article for the *Guardian*, why 'class affiliation across national borders' had led to a desire for 'external rule in preference to native misrule'.[5] It could possibly be, he mused, that 'the British have actually ceased to be a nation. Being a nation is, in the last resort, subjective; those who feel they are a nation and behave accordingly are one. On this hypothesis, the British by their indifference (to put it at its mildest) towards the surrender of all the essential marks of a nation have proved *ipso facto* that, whatever they were in 1940 or more recently, the are now a nation no longer.' The other possibility was that the nation, as St Mark might have put it, was 'not dead but sleepeth'. The people were merely displaying their willingness to be walked over, because the establishment had told them that was what was best for them. If this was so, Britain would come to her senses and 'take back, and take back brutally, the sovereign rights which have been sequestered. If Britain is, after all, still a nation, there can sooner or later be no other outcome.'

Powell noted that Labour had promised 'to amend the 1972 European Communities Act so as to restore to the House of Commons the power to decide whether or not any EEC regulation, directive or decision should be applicable to the UK', regardless of whether the rest of the Community approved or not. With intentional self-reference, he mused that this 'proves that whether Britain is "a nation or no nation" is a question not decided yet'. It was another clear sign that he believed Labour should be supported. The big victory the Conservatives won was therefore the second great disappointment to him in barely a month.

A striking vignette took place two days before the election: Powell and Heath speaking on opposite sides of a European motion at the Cambridge Union. Powell warned his fellow Cantabrigians that they might one day have to fight for the right to remain a sovereign state; Oxford had famously rejected a motion, before the last war, to fight for King and Country, but many who voted against did fight when the time came. 'They responded to the reality of the nation,' Powell said. 'The question of nation or no nation is the most important and fundamental question that people can ask themselves and answer themselves.' Heath, showing an appreciation of reality consistent with that of 1971–2, stated that sovereignty was 'not an issue'. A convincing majority of the Union's members backed him.[6]

The issue of nationhood, always significant in Powell's political outlook, had now risen to dominate it. It was a part of his approach to politics becoming less tactical and more philosophical, now that his day-to-day influence in the affairs of government had been negated. Ironically, the coming of Thatcherism, for which he felt such disdain, had led to the assessment of Powell the political philosopher superseding that of Powell the philosophical politician. In June 1979, reviewing Roy Lewis's impressive book on Powell's thought, the commentator Peregrine Worsthorne summed up the impact Powell had made: 'Powellism is now part of the English intellectual and moral tradition; part of the nation's mythology. The man, too, is a legend in his lifetime.' Beyond that, though, Worsthorne identified a crueller truth. 'So in a sense his work is done. For whatever eventually happens to him his ideas have now entered the bloodstream of the British body politic, guaranteeing them a kind of immorality. Of no other living British statesman could the same be said.'[7] A few weeks later John Biffen, elevated to the cabinet as Chief Secretary to the Treasury, asked Powell whether he would have any objection to his donating Lewis's book to the Cabinet Room library. Powell replied, 'Certainly. Lewis on Powell will be a most salutary work for perusal by the inmates.'[8]

The idea that Powell's work had finished was commonplace, even among his supporters; and coming back to the Commons after the election, almost thirty years after he had first entered it, he found that the composition of the place had changed greatly. He was even more remote from the mass of his fellow parliamentarians than before, because of the peculiarity of his intellect, his status as a folk hero or villain, but above all because of his undoubted supremacy as a House of Commons performer. One new Labour MP who would, in time, become a friend of Powell's, Frank Field, recalled the forbidding impression Powell made on junior colleagues: 'There's an atmosphere around Enoch that makes immediate or casual contact difficult ... he would always assume that you might not want to talk to him. There was that huge element of reserve. Enoch always held himself at a distance from one.'[9] Field felt that the reserve was based upon courtesy, a wish not to intrude, rather than on aloofness. The ice was broken between the two men later on in the 1979 Parliament, when Field ventured to tell Powell that he regretted having missed a series of theological lectures Powell had given. Within an hour, Field found copies of the lectures had been sent to him; and when he next saw Powell the conversation moved to Powell's suggestion that both he and Field should be worshipping John the Baptist. When Field responded that this might have the makings of a good heresy trial in South Down, Powell said he would welcome such a thing, as it might improve his vote.

Mrs Thatcher herself would join Powell in the ranks of the political immortals, not many years hence, and the radicalism with which she took on the vested interests in society allowed her quickly to eclipse the attention given to all other politicians, including Powell. The 1979 election was, for him, the clear watershed between his being an active player and being an elder statesman. The years that remained to him in the Commons were those in which he remained unchallenged, except perhaps by Foot, as the supreme parliamentarian, almost always present in the chamber. The House would inevitably fill when the annunciators showed he was speaking. However, the battles now being fought in Britain were ones on which all he could do, from however influential a position, was spectate.

For the moment, Powell did not hurry to intervene or participate in debates in the new House of Commons. There was an air that, just as after Heath's victory in 1970, he was waiting for mistakes to be made before he would strike; he had no reason, as he saw it, to believe that the protestations of neo-Powellite rectitude in economic policy would turn out any differently from those in the era of Selsdon man. Yet in his first intervention in the Commons, during a debate on the economy, he found himself forced to the defence of the new Prime Minister. Eric Heffer, a left-wing Labour backbencher but, for all that, a long-time admirer of Powell's, sought to attack Mrs Thatcher's earlier statement that 'there is no such thing as collective compassion'. Powell, sitting near him, interjected, 'There is not.'[10]

Heffer told him that, while he and Powell would agree on many things, on this Powell was, like Mrs Thatcher, 'totally wrong'. He cited the welfare state and the National Health Service as examples of the phenomenon. Powell intervened again. 'Might I', he asked, 'indicate the difficulty which some of us feel over collective compassion? The good Samaritan had compassion. If two good Samaritans had compassion, that would still be individual compassion, not collective compassion. If the good Samaritan had been obliged by decree of the Roman Emperor to assist the traveller, that would not be compassion at all, because it would be done under obligation.' Heffer, a deeply committed Christian, contented himself with saying, 'I remind the right hon Gentleman that Jesus Christ was nailed to the cross for preaching collective compassion ... that is why I believe that the basic doctrines of the Bible and Socialism are not very far removed.'[11] It was rare for Powell to be taken head-on in the Commons like this, and would become rarer still. Frank Field observed that 'because Enoch came with a reputation and because linguistically he was clever, people were frightened of him ... you had to go to the very foundations of the argument. There would be no fault in the construction; if there was any fault it would be in where it started from. He commanded a position here much based on fear of what he could do to you.'[12]

When not in the chamber, Powell was in the library, writing away slowly and carefully with a dip-pen, further emphasising – wilfully – his distance, separateness and isolation. He had a regular seat at the head of a table, well positioned in terms of light and access to materials. After the 1983 election a new member, Gerry Malone, sat in this place and sensed, when he saw Powell standing 'rigidly' near him, that he must be in Powell's place, and offered to move. 'No, no,' said Powell, pushing Malone back into his seat. 'In this church we are all equal. No one has the right to reserve a pew.' Malone recalled that 'he moved off to an alternative seat, but did nothing other than look longingly towards the place I had usurped. After a respectable five minutes I made a show of completing my correspondence, gathering it up and moving towards the tea room. We exchanged courteous nods as I passed his chair. I couldn't resist returning after two minutes or so and found him installed in what I subsequently gathered was a place he had occupied for years.'[13]

Howe, who had become Chancellor, introduced his first Budget six weeks after the election, and Powell spoke on it on 18 June. The Government was advertising its policies as monetarist, but they were not sufficient for the most militant monetarist of all. Powell said all Budgets were so packed with illusion that they were 'to some extent mythical', and Howe's effort had been 'a rather more mythical Budget than most'.[14] He singled out for particular opprobrium the 'myth' that the process had started of 'rolling back the boundaries of the public sector'. He said the savings, of approximately £1.7 billion, which Howe had advertised were illusory. They were mostly to be secured by the imposition of cost limits below the going rate of inflation, and by an adjustment of the contingency reserve – which was not a saving at all. 'It would not be true', he said, 'to say that the Government have tried to have their cake and eat it. They are trying to have their cake before they have baked it.'[15]

Nor, he said, did the £2.5 billion cut in borrowing signify a shift from public to private sectors, as the level of borrowing was merely lower than Labour had forecast the previous year, and much of that proposed reduction would accrue from the sale of assets that had not yet been put on the market. He did, though, praise Howe for raising minimum lending rate to 14 per cent out of regard for the enormous size of the PSBR. He renewed his earlier criticism – made before the Conservatives had regained office – of a shift from direct to indirect taxes. Powell had always believed in income tax because of its progressive nature. A shift that added £2.5 billion on to the indirect tax bill was, however, not progressive at all. 'There may be exceptions here and there,' he said, 'but, taken generally, the pockets from which that £2.5 billion will now be extracted are the pockets of those on lower incomes than those from which it would have been drawn if that transfer had not happened.'[16]

This was not his most fundamental criticism of what Thatcherism had, at this early stage, showed itself to mean. He dismissed the idea that a tax cut motivated people to work harder, saying that the notion 'betrays a crass misunderstanding of human nature, individual and social'. People worked hard, or in certain ways, he said, for reasons other than of taxation; the reasons for cutting taxation were ideological, and concerned with the size and role of the state, not personal motivation. It is not a speech that reads well in retrospect. While Powell's economic reasoning is sound, his disbelief in the incentive effects of tax cuts was not borne out by events, which throughout the 1980s justified the supply-side theory of economics – that the more taxes were cut, the more revenues were raised. It also had a tone of grudge and nit-picking which would, for a few years yet, characterise his dealings with the policies of his old party.

Some of Powell's non-economic philosophical excursions left others feeling extremely curious too. With the memory of his remarks on Airey Neave still fresh in the mind, he courted further opprobrium in July by asserting that Britain, not being bound by ties of race or history, had no special obligation to come to the aid of the Vietnamese boat people, scenes of whose torment were being replayed nightly on British news bulletins. The Government had promised to admit a further 10,000 refugees from where they had landed in Hong Kong, and put the plight of the boat people on the same level as that of the Jews under Hitler. Powell, in a question to the deputy Foreign Secretary, Sir Ian Gilmour, on 18 July, rejected this notion unequivocally.

The following month, addressing Banstead Young Conservatives, he demanded an end to dual nationality for Commonwealth immigrants, so that those who retained the citizenship of their country of origin would become 'non-British'. This was another angle on his current favourite theme: while the Conservatives talked about amending the law of nationality, there was 'an almost total absence of preparatory thought or debate on the most vital of all subjects for a nation – the definition of who belongs in it'.[17] For Britain to allow – as many other nations did not – the notion of a citizen having two loyalties merely recreated 'the disastrous hallucination implicit in the 1948 [British Nationality] Act', which the Government now purported to want to end. Powell's argument was that it would be wrong to alter nationality law to render anyone stateless, but those with another state to go would not be in that category.

The assassination of Lord Mountbatten at the end of August, and the visit of the Pope to the Republic of Ireland soon afterwards, provoked Powell towards further controversy. At the funeral of two other victims of the explosion on Mountbatten's boat, the Archbishop of Canterbury, Donald Coggan, had told the congregation, 'Let us not, today, hark back to the tragedy which led to their deaths, except in so far as to register our determination not to let hate reign, but rather to give ourselves, in so far as we can, to the extermination of the conditions which led to these dreadful acts perpetrated by wicked men.'[18] Speaking in his constituency three days before the Pope's visit, Powell said he interpreted the Archbishop's words as a calling into question of the Union between Great Britain and Northern Ireland; or, as he paraphrased it, it had been a 'mealy-mouthed circumlocution' that had said, 'We shall now have to think more seriously about quitting; so carry on, boys, you can't lose.'

Coggan's office immediately denied the Primate had meant such a thing. His press secretary said the word 'conditions' had referred not to the Union, but to the climate of hatred in Ulster. Powell also attacked Cathal Daly, the Roman Catholic Bishop of Ardagh and Clonmacnois, for saying there was an 'unpardonable political vacuum' in Ulster that had led to the killings. According to Powell, this amounted to the Bishop's saying, 'If you want to stop terrorism your only course is to start giving the IRA what they want.' He had been 'denouncing the Union of Great Britain and Northern Ireland, neither more nor less'. Powell said that those, such as the two churchmen, who 'treat it as self-evident that the Union is foredoomed and that its maintenance being the cause of the warfare being waged against it, [it] must obviously be abandoned if that warfare is to end' were the real accomplices of the murderers.

Lord Brabourne – at whose son's and mother's funeral the Archbishop had been speaking – wrote angrily to Powell to complain of the 'distress and anguish you have caused my wife and myself by the misinterpretation of what the Archbishop has said, for your own political ends'.[19] Brabourne told Powell that 'it is surely obvious to any unbiased person' that Coggan had been calling for an end to hatred and violence, not to the Union. He said he did not wish to enter into an argument with Powell, but wanted 'to ask you to be more careful in future before you cause people who have suffered enough to be again upset as we are at your outburst'. Powell told Brabourne in reply that 'you have a right to sympathy, which I readily offer; but that does not excuse the offensive nature of your letter'.[20] He continued: 'I can understand why you preferred abuse to argument, into which you say you "do not wish to enter"; for it is a defiance of the natural meaning of words to suppose that hatred and the use of violence would be described as "conditions" which "lead" to terrorist murder and ought to be "exterminated".'

Once the Pope arrived in Ireland, he too came under Powell's lash. An appeal by him to politicians not to 'cause or condone or tolerate' conditions which gave excuses or pretexts to terrorists for their actions effectively put the practitioners of violence in the seat of power, he said; it put the onus on politicians to find a way of satisfying their claims. 'In fact,' Powell said, 'you could not more accurately express the technique of modern violence, which is to latch on to the pretext of grievance and thereby put lawful and constituted authority into the dock as the real instigator of violence.'[21]

He wrote a curtain-raiser in the *Sun* for the Conservative party conference, which he accepted would be something of a victory rally. He also, with remarkably little grace, gave the Conservatives credit for moving to avoid a second consecutive Winter of Discontent by refusing to confront the unions. He castigated Howe for having arranged to take a larger share of the nation's income for use in the public sector than Healey had the previous year; and, while obviously surprised that the Government had put the EEC on notice that it wanted the elimination of Britain's £1 billion net contribution to the Community, he said the Europeans had no intention of doing any such thing, because it would mean the end of the CAP. Although Mrs Thatcher did not succeed in eliminating the net contribution, the massive reduction she did win was one way in which Powell underestimated her. He claimed that 'one day it will be the Conservative party's failure to "speak for England" that is its undoing', and as he surveyed policy in Europe and Ulster, and the impending review of national-ity, he thought he saw that day coming quite clearly.[22]

In the longer term, Powell was right. The defeat of the Major Government in 1997 – the end of a period of eighteen years of continuous Conservative rule that had begun in May 1979 – could be directly attributed to the Conservative party's divisions over Europe, and especially to its failure to 'speak for England' in putting the supposed interests of Europe first in maintaining British mem-bership of the Exchange Rate Mechanism from 1990 to 1992. In the short term, though, his harsh criticism of the Thatcher Government – one that, for all its shortcomings, was more Powellite than any since Lord Salisbury's – made him seem churlish, even cantankerous. However, he was still more capable than most in the new Government of highlighting the correct path for it to take, and his value in the 1980s was to consist largely of that.

With the Government still to put flesh on the bones of its policy for reform of the unions, Powell wrote in the *Guardian* on 22 October of the need to end the closed shop. He said it could be justified only if unions were of economic benefit to their members, as it was logically right that all members should contribute to a benefit that they all received. If it could not be shown that all unions were so beneficial – and Powell was convinced it could not – then the case for the closed shop fell. It was now up to the Government, he argued, to do as he did, and 'support legislation which effectively guarantees the right, self-evidently equitable upon my premises, of free choice to join or not to join a union'.[23] What greatly concerned him, though, was that the rhetoric still emerging from the Conservative party was that the unions were a good idea, and should be preserved. Powell realised that 'it is much to ask of a political party to explode a popular economic myth', so he was not expecting miracles, but the logic of reform of the closed shop, at least, should be obvious. 'It is time', he concluded, 'that someone set about providing the Conservative party with a workable philosophy of trade unionism.' This philosophy was needed not just to strip away economic myths, but also to make the Conservatives see they could not justify their own toleration of private coercion: 'a tax collector is one thing; but a highwayman is another'.

That week the Government executed an economic policy that Powell could at last warmly endorse: the lifting of exchange controls. This time, there was no element of grudge. 'Is the Chancellor aware', he asked in the Commons on 23 October, when the announcement was made, 'that I envy him the opportunity and the privilege of announcing a step that will strengthen the economy of this country and will help restore our national pride and confidence in our currency?'[24] Howe told him he was grateful for the sentiment. The usual, cyclical rumours about Powell and the Conservatives making up were given a new boost.

What was happening in Powell's own backyard was, though, sufficient to make a mockery of such thoughts. In Ulster the Northern Ireland Secretary, Humphrey Atkins, was planning a new initiative to restore to local administration some of the functions discharged from Westminster, to be preceded by all-party talks to which four invitations were issued: to the Official Unionists, now reduced to five MPs following the split with Paisley; to the DUP, which had secured three seats; to the SDLP and the Alliance party. However, when the invitations were issued on 19 October the Unionists, still the biggest party and the one with the highest share of the popular vote, refused to accept. Molyneaux, who remained strongly under Powell's influence, had private talks with Atkins, in which he had made it clear in advance that his MPs could not take part in what he termed 'just a window-dressing exercise' by the Government. The party wanted Ulster's future settled in Parliament at Westminster, not in some form of new assembly.

Because of the strong performance by the DUP in both the general and the European elections – Paisley himself had been elected a Euro-MP in addition to his Westminster seat – it was also assumed that the Official Unionists would be keen to avoid any process that might lead to local elections, and a further opportunity for Paisley and his followers to prove their strength. However, the Unionists had also picked up the hint from Atkins that the Government might be considering a new assembly that, with built-in safeguards for the minority population, would smack horribly of power-sharing. Within a week, Paisley too had rejected the invitation to talks, saying he would change his mind only if the Government implemented sterner anti-IRA measures.

Indeed, the praise Powell had lavished on the exchange-control policy was but one swallow and did not make a summer. When the Prime Minister signalled her determination to wring financial concessions from the EEC, Powell dismissed it as 'empty bluster'.[25] On 8 November, the Government introduced its Southern Rhodesia Bill, designed to take the colony to legal independence, Powell – who had always opposed the Smith regime, and had always opposed sanctions too – lambasted it in the House. He said the powers the Bill would confer on the Government in Rhodesia were objectionable in being so sweeping. He repeated his long-held view that the Government could have no responsibility in Rhodesia because it had no power to enforce its will there. Powell's main objection, though, was that the Government, in planning to send a governor and a train to rule Rhodesia, was planning to act out the fantasy it and its predecessors had harboured for the previous fourteen years about having 'power' in that land. He concluded by warning that the Government was about to embark upon 'a dangerous charade which may well leave us exposed, in the face of the world, impotent to ridicule and without conferring one atom of safety, security or well-being upon those for whom we purport to be responsible and for whom Labour Members like to think themselves responsible'.[26] His fears were, though, soon proved groundless; the transition to independence was, from that point, accomplished quickly and smoothly.

In a debate on economic policy on 28 November, Powell seemed to be becoming reconciled to the Thatcher administration. Howe, a few days earlier, had said categorically that Britain had to master inflation, and it could be done only by controlling and reducing the growth in the money supply. 'The supposed alternatives to these policies', he had said, 'are a delusion.'[27] This was a moment of utter triumph for Powell: Howe, from the Treasury Bench, had enunciated pure Powellism, and Powell quoted his words with relish. 'I have waited a long time, a matter of 20 years or so, to hear those principles declared so clearly and firmly by a Government and made, at any rate initially, the basis of that Government's actions.' He gave the Government his support and encouragement; he reminded it of the practical and political difficulties of the task it had set itself. He specifically reminded the Government of what the cost would be in unemployment, as expectations adjusted. His speech turned into a detailed seminar, a distillation of all he had said on the economy from the backbenches in the late 1960s and throughout the 1970s. But, at last, he had been heard.

When the Unionists, on 23 November, made clear their refusal to take part in Atkins' proposed talks – which they thought meant that any plans Atkins had would have to be presented direct to Parliament rather than, first, to the Ulster parties – Powell published a minatory open letter to Mrs Thatcher, in which he told her that 'any deal or agreement with the Government of the Irish Republic, whereby that Government would somehow assist Britain in return for political concessions in Ulster, would be the road to disaster'. He went on: 'I have to warn you solemnly that, if Her Majesty's Government were now to throw the affairs of Ulster back into the melting pot of the dark era of 1972 to 1975, it would incur a needless and fearful responsibility.'[28]

Nonetheless, Atkins prepared for talks to start after Christmas, and the Conservatives roundly blamed Powell for the Official Unionists' boycott. It was a decision that threatened to backfire: Paisley's DUP did not hesitate to take part, which left him appearing to be the sole spokesman for the Unionist community; and there were fears that Paisley might pull off some sort of deal, negating the power of the Official Unionists. That did not happen, as Powell had believed it would not. The Official Unionists maintained that, since the Government had ruled out any form of elected assembly, the implementation of regional councils in the Province could take place without further talks.

In his letter to the Prime Minister, Powell added that it was a delusion to suppose constitutional change would placate the terrorists. It would merely convince them their goal was achievable, and further damage the morale of the Unionist population. In a speech that same day at Banbridge, he referred directly to the pressure he knew was being put on Britain to make 'progress' in her relations with Ireland, both by the EEC and by America. In the years ahead

Powell would make much of American interference, and of the readiness of the Foreign Office to accede to influence from Washington – a theory proved by the conclusion of the Anglo-Irish Agreement in 1985. After he left the Commons, shortly after the Iran–Contra arms scandal had rocked the Reagan administration, Powell asserted that, in the light of what had happened in Central America and the Middle East, the CIA could well have 'used' the IRA – which would have included funding them.[29]

He reflected this view on 3 January 1980, speaking to an Orange Lodge in his constituency. 'To the Foreign Office the fact that five-sixths of the inhabitants of this Province are, and intend to remain, integrally citizens of the United Kingdom is less than nothing. Its thoughts are not of us. Its eyes and its affections are fixed outside the realm – on Dublin, on Brussels, on the Vatican, above all on Washington DC, for whose favour and delectation this Province is to be offered up a sacrifice, if the arts of skullduggery will avail us to do the trick.'[30] He was sure that the Foreign Office was acting in Ulster as the CIA did in countries it wished to destabilise, but that the 'granite rock of Ulster's Unionist determination' would help see off the danger. Nonetheless, he felt the Union was in more peril than at any time since the Heath Government, and not because of the Provisional IRA. He was angry that the Government, in proposing any initiative or any change to the way Ulster was governed, was concerned principally to have the backing of the SDLP; the other parties did not matter. His only remotely conciliatory comments were that he did not blame either Atkins or Mrs Thatcher for the new crisis. 'I refer to that nest of vipers, that nursery of traitors, which is known as the British Foreign Office.'

Within a fortnight he overturned another pillar of Foreign Office orthodoxy, this time the conventional view of the cold war. He took further his heretical idea of the Soviet Union in a speech in Lisburn on 14 January. He said it was a mistake for Britain to base her defence policy on the assumption that the Soviet Union was the only enemy. He reflected that Soviet forces could have swept across Europe to the Channel ports at any time in the preceding thirty years; the real question was whether it had ever been their intention to do so. His observations had been prompted by a slight rise in real defence spending by the new Government, the reversal of a trend that had lasted over thirty years; and he warned that the nuclear deterrent, in which he had never really believed, was 'not a substitute for, or an alternative to, the means of rational attack and defence'.[31]

The other backdrop to the speech was the recent invasion by the Soviet Union of Afghanistan, a move that had thrown Britain closer to America and increased Government hostility towards Russia. There was not, Powell said, the faintest resemblance in Russian behaviour in 1980 with the aggression that preceded the Second World War. Therefore, 'British defence cannot be based on, or deduced from, the size and composition of the armed forces of the Soviet Union.' It had to be based on the relative priority of different forms of defence for protecting these islands against an enemy operating from the adjacent continent', whoever that enemy might be. He was not against expanding the armed forces, but trusted they would be expanded to meet the needs they were likely to have to face.

He developed this view in a speech in a Commons debate on East–West relations on 28 January. He described as 'almost . . . hysteria' the reaction to the Afghan crisis. 'I have been irresistibly reminded', he said, 'of the character in Noel Coward's play "Cavalcade" who, on setting off for the Boer War as a volunteer, declared his conviction that unless we beat the Boers they would speedily be found in London, spreading fire, rapine and murder on all sides.'[32] As usual – and not necessarily because of his admiration for the Soviet Union – Powell was preaching a strict policy of non-intervention. 'To me,' he told the House, 'it seems utter delusion to suppose that Afghanistan is perceptibly related to the defence or the interests of the United Kingdom.'[33] He said he suspected it was because of the recent 'preoccupation' with nuclear matters that the importance of geography had been forgotten. If properly understood, it would soon follow that Afghanistan became, to Britain, an 'irrelevance'. Britain did not have the power to fulfil any defence obligations in that region; therefore, she should not talk of doing so. There had been an over-reaction, he concluded, although if Britain had meant what she said about protecting the 'security and independence' of the region it was an under-reaction too. 'We should not have reacted at all.'[34]

II

With constitutional talks now under way in Ulster, Atkins was having little success. Powell, speaking in his constituency on 25 January, rubbed this in uncompromisingly. He accused the Northern Ireland Secretary of behaving towards the Province 'as if he were the man in the moon paying us a visit', though he blamed this attitude on the 'sheer bad advice' Atkins was receiving from his civil servants.[35] He said this problem would be eased if the civil servants – most of them Ulstermen – who had served the old Stormont parliament were allowed to serve the Northern Ireland Office, which was mainly staffed by recruits from other Whitehall departments. Instead, Atkins had been severely let down: 'In small things and in great, in matters of timing and manner as in matters of policy, he has from his earliest days in office made a series of gaffes and blunders from which any ordinarily competent department would have saved him.' Such fire distracted the Official Unionists from their worries about non-participation in the talks: the party was split on the question, with anti-integrationists convinced that Powell was manipulating them.

For all his continued guerrilla warfare against the Conservatives, Powell began to be gratified that many of his most important economic prescriptions were now being adopted. Soon after the lifting of exchange controls, he made a speech to some Hertfordshire businessmen acknowledging that the Government now understood the true causes of inflation – and adding that this proved how right the 'mavericks' who had for years argued for the control of the money supply had been.[36] When the economic situation was the subject of a Commons confidence motion on 28 February, he defended the Government. Inflation had reached 19 per cent, but Powell said this was the fault of policies pursued by Healey two years earlier, just as Healey himself had, rightly, blamed the difficulties of 1975 and 1976 on Heath and Barber. He said that he, and the other Unionists, regarded an attempt to censure the Government's economic management after just ten months as 'premature', and would not support it.[37]

His support was not, however, unconditional. He said – and the Government knew he was right – that the PSBR, at £9 billion, was still 'dangerously high', and had urgently to be cut. 'We should', he said, 'be aiming at a nil net borrowing requirement.'[38] Challenged by a left-wing Conservative, Hugh Dykes, as to whether he would accept cuts in the heavy subsidies paid to Ulster as a means of reducing the deficit, Powell said clearly that the Province was prepared to pay its part in the sacrifices that were generally needed: integration cut both ways. As for the reduction, his experience as a former Treasury minister told him it could be 'done by mirrors'; but he preferred more definite measures, starting with a reduction in the British contribution to the EEC's funds. Perhaps, he added, £1 billion or £2 billion could be raised in taxes; but, above all, there would need to be the deferment of substantial capital projects. Above all, boldness was required. The savings needed could not be achieved 'by a gradual gnawing, eroding process, which is constantly undone again, like footprints covered up as we walk across the sand. It has to be done by large, massive acts which will free the Government boldly from their present borrowing incubus.'[39] Powell did not attempt to deny this would reduce jobs in the construction industry.

He suggested that one way for Howe to find more money was to realise part of the asset of the Government's $24 billion reserves, the only purpose of which was, he suggested, to gamble on the foreign exchanges or to try to rig the exchange rate. Using it to bring down the deficit was just like selling off parts of the nationalised industries, or issuing gilts, and no more inflationary. He concluded his speech with a passage helpful to the Government. He pointed out with complete clarity the contradictions of the stance of the Opposition, which was still committed to high borrowing and to other inflationary policies, but which had complained about high interest rates that would only get worse as borrowing increased. He asked the Opposition whether it did not, at last, understand that many of the divisions and tensions in society were caused by inflation of the sort it was recommending.

In other areas, though, he remained dissatisfied. With the constitutional conference in Ulster going nowhere Powell asked Atkins, on 6 March, whether during his 'long periods of boredom and frustration as he presides over the time-wasting conference will he find time to reflect that for the protection of minorities and for the securing of power-sharing no instrument has been devised which compares with the House of Commons?' Unsurprisingly, Atkins denied that the conference, destined to end in stalemate, was a waste of time.

Then, on 10 March, Powell used a Commons debate on new immigration rules to complain about the still inadequate policing of entry from abroad. The question was not, he said, about immigration, but about what the Government now defined as 'persons of New Commonwealth and Pakistan ethnic origin'. In other words, as that section of the population, which was predominantly young, grew, the question was about that whole section of society, not to be defined by whether it had immigrated to Britain.[40] Indeed, Powell said the figures of the ethnic population were becoming harder to calculate as, officially, they no longer included births in which both parents had been born in this country. The fact was that the problem of immigration, which he had tried to address twelve years earlier, would not now go away: 'That is a delusion which we merely feed by pretending that by controlling immigration, by tinkering with, by rendering rational . . . the immigration rules we can appreciably alter that which, on these facts as they are, lies before this country.'[41]

At this point Powell was interrupted by Alex Lyon, the former immigration minister with whom he had jousted in 1976. Lyon told him that the population would stabilise at 3.3 million and, when it did, society would be 'settled and harmonious' because the ethnic minorities would be 'British in their outlook'. Powell immediately disputed the notion that the population would stabilise; the fact of such large immigrant communities would, he said, make further immigration inevitable, whatever the rules. He hinted at, but did not this time specifically call for, repatriation to avert the crisis he was still convinced would one day occur. The proposed tightening of the rules was, he said, merely 'fiddling' and would make no long-term difference.[42]

He was even sterner against the Government for its policy of advocating a boycott of the forthcoming Moscow Olympics in response to the Soviet invasion of Afghanistan. This view was provoked not so much by Powell's sympathy for the Russians – he never defended Soviet aggression – as by his regard for proprieties, and for the fact the Government was seeking to follow a line initiated by the Americans. Writing in the *Sunday Express* on 14 March he said he 'thought the Conservative party had learnt – at least since the days of Mr Heath – what the rule of law means. One part of the rule of law is that the citizen is perfectly free to do what the law does not forbid.'[43] If Mrs Thatcher did not like Britons going to participate in the games, she should change the law to prevent them; otherwise she should keep quiet.

Rather than introduce an 'Olympic Games (Boycott) Bill', the Government had instead 'proceeded to try to get its way in the manner which its members had so often reprobated in others – by threats, by bullying, by cajolery, by all the arts of a chief whip disciplining recalcitrant party members'. If the Government were allowed to get away with this, there was no telling what precedent it would set. He mocked the notion that a boycott would achieve anything. 'That the Russian people, discovering the stadia half empty and being told, upon enquiry, that their capitalist enemies had boycotted – or tried to boycott – the Games, would say to themselves: "Deary me, if that is how the Americans and the British feel about us, we must be a very, very naughty people and ought to mend our ways" is pathetic to the point of farce.'

Even in the Budget debate on 1 April Powell was unable to maintain his support for the economic policy, except for Howe's having taken what he had always advanced as the logical step of presenting proposals for taxation and spending together in the financial statement. He said Howe appeared already to have lost the battle, in announcing a proposed deficit of £8.5 billion against an out-turn of £9 billion the previous year. Not sparing the Chancellor's feelings, he observed that 'that is not the Budget that the right hon and learned Gentleman wanted. That is not what he perfectly well knew was required by the firm belief that not only this Government profess and hold as to the nature and causation of inflation, but the belief that has been held, when in office, by Chancellors of the Exchequer from the Labour party.'[44] Powell's mischievous conclusion was that the Government would, instead, pursue a course of 20 per cent inflation per annum that would make a deficit of £8–10 billion hardly worth worrying about.

Later that month, when there was still no sign of the Government moving to implement regional councils in Northern Ireland, Powell urged it to recognise that the concept of devolution was dead, and that direct rule should be ended and replaced by a structure similar to that operating in Wales and Scotland. Speaking in Londonderry, he said he still believed that the Government was holding out for some form of power-sharing, which he knew the people of Ulster would not accept. He could not, he said, understand the reluctance to give Ulster normal local government; if it were to happen, he predicted, 'not a mouse would squeak'.[45] As spring became summer, stalemate persisted.

As the Government persisted with its radical overhaul of Britain, so Powell's profile continued to wane. In Parliament, while he still contributed on the big issues, he also selflessly devoted much of his time to making highly detailed contributions to debates on matters purely of parochial interest to his constituents – particularly agriculture and fisheries. These, understandably, attracted him little attention. On certain of the big issues, too, he devoted himself to the Ulster angle, such as in a debate on defence in the Commons on 29 April 1980. Powell used part of his speech to propound his non-sectarian standards, praising the bravery of the dwindling number of Roman Catholics in the Ulster Defence Regiment. 'I am proud to have some of those men in my constituency and to know them personally,' he said, adding that fear for their lives, not prejudice, was why so few of them remained in the regiment.[46]

The crisis concerning the taking of American hostages in Iran enlisted the support of the strongly pro-American Thatcher administration, and resulted in a sanctions Bill being brought before the Commons on 12 May. Douglas Hurd, a junior Foreign Office minister, told the House that the question of the hostages was 'not just a quarrel between the US and Iran' and that the programme of sanctions and visa restrictions being proposed were 'necessary for the good health of the alliance'.[47] This was hardly Powell's view. He said Hurd had made a speech devoid of any content as to the effect the sanctions were supposed to have, and reminded the House that sanctions had had no effect in Rhodesia, but that it had been the events leading on from the collapse of the Portuguese Empire that had resolved the matter there. That they might do anything to the fanatical regime in Iran was beyond comprehension. He was sure the result would be 'to promote greater determination and greater pertinacity' among the Iranians.[48]

He particularly seized upon the notion 'that as we are allies and friends of the United States we should do whatever the United States wishes and asks us to do, even if we believe it to be unwise, futile and counter-productive'.[49] The alliance, as far as Powell was prepared to admit to it, was founded in NATO, and the question of Iran, as far as he was concerned, lay well outside NATO's sphere of interest. There was, therefore, only one argument, and 'it seems to me a poor and unacceptable argument to say that it can be the implication of alliance and friendship – even in the broadest sense – that one should do an unwise thing at the behest of one's friend and ally'. He then noted that the Americans did not interpret the meaning of alliance and friendship in quite the same way, and cited their behaviour in the Ulster problem as an example. The only other reason that remained for doing what the Americans wanted was if it gave Britain some sort of influence over them; but the fact that they had recently tried a disastrous 'rescue mission' without any word of consultation with the British proved that Britain would have no consultative role at all. He urged the Bill be not passed, but it was.

The following month, on another matter of foreign affairs, he once more went against the consensus, when the Commons debated the Brandt Report on the development of third world countries. Powell said he felt some difficulty in taking part since he was 'unable to share or even in a degree to understand the vocabulary and the assumptions with which the subject of aid, development and the under-developed countries is discussed'.[50] Heath, who had served on the Commission that compiled the report, had spoken before him, and Powell – who had long been willing, unlike Heath, to let bygones be bygones – praised the 'breath-taking comprehensiveness and competence' of the speech Heath had made, but did not agree with the content. Heath had outlined a proposed structure of international finance, much of it to do with the treatment of debt, that he claimed would help afflicted countries. Powell submitted that, in practice, this would be impossible.

He said there could be no answer to the question of why large parts of the world remained under-developed; and, reflecting on how the organisation of Mogul India had been superior to that of Tudor England, he said – perhaps with an eye on his less informed critics – that under-development 'is not due to any difference in intellectual capacity, human ability or insight. It is an absurd notion that the European is intellectually superior to vast millions of the human race in Asia and elsewhere.'[51] Nor, he argued, was the solution to be found in the handing-out by the West of huge sums of money. He cited the story of how the bishop in Hugo's *Les Misérables* transforms the morality of a convict by the gift of two candlesticks, but argued that if every convict had been given such silver by the state it would not have been recognised as 'a transmuting act of generosity'.

Powell continued:

> The mistake we make is to believe that compulsion can do the work of freedom and that the engine of compulsion, the state, can perform what can only be performed by human beings acting, whether in the sphere of commerce, intellect or any other, upon one another. By our narrow concept, our mechanical concept, our materialistic concept of development and of the world, we are giving a stone where what we mean to give is bread.[52]

The biblical allusion was significant. He concluded with the observation that Europe had once sought to export Christianity to the world, as the means of improving it; now it exported cash, or thought merely in material terms, because of the loss of faith. Money had, he lamented, become 'the screen for the ever-present desire to impose one's standards upon others, to exalt one's achievements over those of others, and to find a reason for exercising power over one's fellow men'. It was not a speech against aid *per se*, but a speech against the compulsion to exercise imperialism by whatever means.

Much of what Powell now had to say was optimistic in tone, which is perhaps why it attracted so little attention. Speaking to the Yorkshire Monday Club in May, he claimed that Britain was seriously underestimating herself. 'We are, in fact, masters of our situation, politically, militarily and economically. By failing to understand this and to behave accordingly, we are in danger of losing it all in real earnest and of reducing ourselves in fact to the level of our own false estimate.'[53] Later in the summer, as the Government made pleas to the public to economise with energy, Powell attacked this despairing notion. 'The real price of oil-based energy will decline during the years ahead,' he told a meeting in London on 9 July. 'So plentiful and so fiercely competitive will be the sources of energy in general that many of those who are now investing heavily on the contrary assumption will be ruined.'[54] He added that the nervous Governmental urgings for restraint were 'futile and pathetic'.

On his sixty-eighth birthday that June he was guest of honour at a Bow Group dinner. Asked whether he had any regrets, he said, as usual, that he was not conscious of any. One of those present, Peter Lilley, recalled another member asking Powell whether, since politics was about the pursuit and exercise of power, his own career had not been something of a waste of time. Lilley recalled Powell's answer thus: 'Power is a very elusive concept. Do you mean by power the holding of office, only obtained by mortgaging your freedom to choose which lever to pull; or do you mean something more akin to influence, such that when you stand up in the House of Commons, the chamber fills, and when you sit down, it empties again?'[55]

He could still be shaken out of these sunlit views. When riots broke out in the predominantly black St Paul's area of Bristol in the summer of 1980 – precursor of far worse disturbances in London and Liverpool the following year – Powell accused the media of habitually suppressing news of such incidents, which had been happening in cities for years. That, he claimed in a speech in Dorking on 11 July, was why the widely reported events in Bristol had caused such panic among politicians and the public. The 'race relations industry' was now warning of the likelihood of further disturbances. There was no reason to suspect that the problems would become any less marked as the numbers of Commonwealth-descended people in Britain grew.

As usual, he did not stint in his prophecies. 'Far less than the foreseeable New Commonwealth and Pakistan ethnic proportion would be sufficient to constitute a dominant political force in the United Kingdom able to extract from government and the main parties terms calculated to render its influence still more impregnable,' he warned. 'Far less than this proportion would provide the bases and citadels for urban terrorism, which would in turn reinforce the overt political leverage of simple numbers.'[56] He believed the Government was still hampered by 'silence and blindness', and still not speaking for the people.

Yet Powell had, since his disdain for Howe in the Budget debate, come to be more impressed by the way in which the administration was handling the economy. On 22 July, at Prime Minister's Questions, he asked Mrs Thatcher to 'take the opportunity today and every day to make clear to the country, as only she can, that the courses that are being commended to her by the official Opposition and by many other voices mean nothing but a deliberate return to hyper-inflation'.[57] This encomium brought gasps of 'Oh!' from the House, so much so that the Speaker, George Thomas, called for order and asked, 'Now that hon Members have got over their surprise, they should listen quietly.' Mrs Thatcher was unequivocal. 'I agree with the right hon Gentleman. One cannot create genuine jobs on printed money.'

Then, a week later, just before the House rose for the summer recess, Powell was one of four Official Unionists who voted with the Government after a motion of confidence tabled by Labour, which the Government comfortably won: the notion of colluding with the remnants of Heathism by such action seemed to be wearing off. Powell felt that the motion, prompted by a rise in unemployment to over two million, was dishonest. The Opposition, so recently in government, would have had no choice – to judge from the actions actually taken – but to conduct the economy in the way the Government had, as he saw it. Callaghan had called for a cut in interest rates and an increase in spending, but Powell said he knew as well as anybody what the result of that would be: 'It would not only increase the amount that the Government require to borrow in order to meet their outlays, but would also ensure that they failed to do so on a massive scale.'[58] He said the message of the Opposition was that 'inflation reduces unemployment and we should have more inflation'.[59]

Powell was assailed during his speech by several Labour backbenchers angry at his support for the Government and at the meticulous way he was dissecting Callaghan's arguments. One, Norman Atkinson, repeatedly complained that, if Powell was against public spending, why did he not agree to it being stopped in Northern Ireland and the Six Counties being given to the Republic? Powell insisted that Atkinson had not understood that just because one was in favour of limiting spending it did not follow that one was in favour of ending it altogether. For this, Atkinson called Powell 'a charlatan'. Powell, conscious of the donnish way in which he operated during these debates, replied that 'willing as I am to conduct seminars, this is a debate in which many hon Members wish to take part, and all of us are under the constraints of time'.[60]

Cheered to an extent by its approach to economic issues, Powell not only felt that he could support what the Government was doing, but also felt more able to offer it constructive advice. Though, in a speech on 5 August, he had condemned the Government for assisting in 'an exhibition of the inordinate and unsatisfied craving of the EEC to behave as a state' by agreeing to a common foreign policy communiqué on the Middle East from the Venice summit a few weeks earlier, Powell used his first main speech after his summer holiday to urge specific policies on Mrs Thatcher.[61] He told a conference in Nottingham that the Government would have to increase taxes 'heavily, ruthlessly and comprehensively' in order to restore the proper financing of public expenditure. Its three aims – aims that Powell shared – of reducing taxation, reducing public spending and reducing the funding of that spending by inflation could not, he said, all be achieved at once. The Government had not, he believed, thought this matter out sufficiently before being elected. Now the best route out of its troubles was to fund public spending more adequately, with less resort to borrowing: the totals had risen as a result of the steep rise in unemployment since May 1979.

Controversially, Powell said unemployment was actually 'the best form of national investment, for it is the indispensable key to the redeployment of effort and resources into the pattern that will be needed in the 1980s and 1990s. It is only fair that the rest of the community should pay, and pay generously, to maintain those who have to carry the burden of this transaction directly.'[62] No minister could possibly have used such language. But, as the next Budget would show, Powell's prescription was one the Government would follow to the letter, and he was careful to specify in his Nottingham speech that the Government's aims were entirely practicable, and right.

Nonetheless, on some issues he still found himself in sympathy with Labour, and wrote a piece in the *Daily Telegraph* explaining why. He outlined the struggle he had been through, intellectually, in the winter of 1972, when he had been with the Labour left against the European Communities Bill; how he had always been in sympathy with them against incomes policies; how he was revolted by the Conservatives' leanings towards America and their 'periodic fits of hysterical Russophobia'. He said he parted company with Labour only 'because of my blind, high Tory ultimate faith in the people. If they are the people that I thought and still want to think that they are, those who represent them will assuredly be pulled back in time from the betrayal of their birthright of parliamentary freedom either to a European state or to a Marxist bureaucracy'. Little, it seemed, could shake his mood of optimism.[63]

In October 1980, shortly after Mrs Thatcher had told her party's conference that she was 'not for turning', he renewed his endorsement of the Government's economic policies in an article in the *Guardian*. He defended the Thatcherites against the growing clamour from the 'wets' in the Government – the term Mrs Thatcher and her closest supporters used to describe those who still clung to the Heathite heresies they had almost all once supported – that the pursuit of the economic objectives the Government had settled upon would militate against other desirable aims. Extra verve was given to his attack by the fact that the two prominent wets outside the Government, Heath himself and Macmillan, had also been making these assertions. It gave Powell a magnificent opportunity to settle old scores. He mocked the idea that there was 'a kind of choice ... between dealing with inflation and promoting economic well-being ... the reason people talk and think in this way is that they simply have not grasped what inflation is.'[64]

Powell defined inflation as, 'quite simply, a means of financing public expenditure'. It was 'dishonest taxation, inasmuch as it enables governments to get what they want without asking parliament and then to put the blame on everybody else for what they themselves have brought about'. He claimed that

Macmillan and Heath were telling the people that only by taxing dishonestly –
as they had both done when in office, especially Heath in 1972 – could other
desirable ends be achieved, such as the reduction of unemployment. Powell
described this attitude as 'Carry on cheating!' He, for one, had always been
honest about the inevitability of unemployment following on from the control
of inflation, and said he wished Mrs Thatcher 'would get out of the habit of
saying that inflation causes unemployment. This is true only in the sense that
sunrise brings on darkness, because day is inexorably succeeded by night'.

He reminded his readers that the result of Heath's binge in 1972 had been
inflation at nearly 30 per cent three years later; Mrs Thatcher's case was, he said,
stronger even than she realised. Heath and Macmillan were 'victims of their
own past propaganda' who 'inhabit a never-never land where it would be
possible – given "moderation" on all sides – to enjoy the sweetness of inflating
the currency without suffering the punishment which follows. It is too bad that
so many are found who will still believe them.' Powell's influence was still such
that this strong endorsement of Mrs Thatcher was deeply welcome to her in the
battle she was fighting, and which would within weeks move on a stage further
with a purge of some of the 'wets' from the Government. This did not happen,
though, before she had distressed Powell by imposing a 6 per cent limit on
public sector pay, something he felt that she, as a monetarist, should have known
better than to do.

III

In Ulster that autumn IRA prisoners took a new turn in their campaign to be
granted political status, and went on a hunger strike. To Powell's fury, the
Government, while refusing to grant political status, made other concessions in
the regime at the Maze prison, including the end of the requirement for prisoners
to wear uniform. He was particularly angry that Atkins chose to leave it to a
junior minister to answer questions on this matter in the Commons, while he
remained in Belfast. When the next day, 28 October, the Commons debated a
Temporary Provision Bill for British prisons – caused by an industrial dispute
by prison officers – Powell used the fact that its measures could be imposed on
Ulster by Order in Council to launch another assault on policy in the Six
Counties. He called Atkins's actions 'ambiguous, contradictory and self-defeating', and said they had called into question the 'competence and sincerity' of
the whole government of the Province.[65]

As the old Heathites increased their attacks on the Government's economic
policy during the autumn, so Powell stuck to his defence of them. In a debate
on the economic situation on 27 November he followed both Callaghan (who
had just been succeeded as party leader by Michael Foot) and Heath – who had

been taunted in his speech by fellow Conservative MPs for his criticism of the high unemployment that had occurred under the Thatcher Government, with Jock Bruce-Gardyne calling out, 'How many elections did you lose?'[66] Powell referred to the speeches of the two former prime ministers, saying both men 'set out, with conviction and sincerity, to put the economy to rights. For both of them, it ended in open and humiliating failure.'[67] He repeated his warning that the PSBR, which Howe had just announced would be £3 billion greater than expected, still had to be brought under control, and praised Howe for trying to raise taxes to deal with it. However, the severe economic situation that would culminate in the watershed deflationary Budget of the following spring – when £5 billion in extra taxes were raised – was already unavoidable.

Powell started a new religious controversy – the first since his speech about the possible bride of the Prince of Wales – when speaking to East Grinstead Young Conservatives in early December about the possibilities of a papal visit to Britain. He argued there had been no discussion of the 'implications' of such a visit, and there should be; and, once that happened, if in the light of it a substantial body of opinion felt it would be better for the Pope not to come, those views should be respected. He stressed that religion had nothing to do with his objection; it was a political issue. The Pope was a head of state and if he came to Britain it would be as a result of a political decision taken by the Government.

There would be, he said, an 'English nerve' touched by the visit, because only in England was the Crown supreme judicial authority in the national church. From this, he concluded that 'it is constitutionally and logically unthinkable for England to contain both the Queen and the Pope. Before that could happen the essential character of the one or the other would have to be surrendered.' It was, for Powell, a question of the surrender of yet another national symbol, 'the last possessions of a nation, without which it cannot renew itself'.[68]

Within a few days, though, he would have a more immediate provocation. Without even telling most of her cabinet, Mrs Thatcher went to Dublin for secret talks with Charles Haughey, the Irish Prime Minister. Powell was outraged by what he suspected to be the collusion behind this meeting. While pointing out that he did not know what had happened there – neither side was making other than a terse public statement – Powell said he would have thought the public were in a position to 'form a judgement by seeing the Prime Minister and three senior members of the British Government go across to hobnob with the Prime Minister of a country which actually claims sovereignty over a part of the United Kingdom and come away with an agreed communiqué almost dictated in his own language. I think they'll form their own opinion about that, and maybe they'll form it more quickly about this mini-Munich than they did about the major one in 1938.' He added the event had been a 'visible humiliation' for the Government, since Haughey, soon to face a general election, was sure to gain from it.[69]

For years Powell had been calling for a measure to define British citizenship properly, and when the British Nationality Bill had its second reading on 28 January 1981 he spoke on it. He reminded the House that the earlier Nationality Act, thirty-three years beforehand, had been rushed through before legislators had had a chance adequately to consider the implications of changing the basis of the status of a British subject from the allegiance to the Crown to 'an aggregation of separate citizenships'.[70] It had been one thing to equate the citizenships of the Dominions with British subjectship, quite another to give citizenship of 'the United Kingdom and Colonies', resulting in the 'crass offence' of inventing a citizenship 'to which no state, no reality, no actuality corresponded'.[71]

He knew that the intention of the new Bill was to reunite 'status and reality, status and statehood, status and rights and duties', but he felt it failed. The different categories of citizenship it sought to create still did not always correspond to a state, or carry with them duties as well as rights. He was not clear about the rights of entry to the realm, or to the franchise; or about 'the right – it is as well a duty and a privilege – of serving the nation in peace and particularly – the ultimate test of nationality – in war'.[72] What especially confused him was the proposed basis for citizenship: 'it is not to be all who are born in the United Kingdom; it is those who are born in the United Kingdom of a particular descent'. He argued against the notion of 'descent by residence', by which those who had acquired the right of residence should be allowed to pass on British nationality to their descendants by virtue of remaining resident. To him, this once more compromised his notion of what a Tory Conservative government should understand by nationhood, a concept that required much stronger underpinning: 'Allegiance is the very essence of nationhood, there is no meaning in nationhood without allegiance. Nationhood means that a man stands to one nation, to one loyalty, against all others – that is what it is about.'[73]

Powell was becoming increasingly concerned by the closeness of the relations between the British and American governments, a new acceleration of which had taken place following the election the previous November of Ronald Reagan, an ideological soul-mate of Mrs Thatcher's, as President. When, on 3 March 1981, the Commons debated the nuclear deterrent, Powell reiterated his long-standing theories about nuclear blackmail, but added that the debate was now more political than military, and that Britain did not in fact have an 'independent' deterrent, however much that might be claimed. Through NATO, Britain was bound in to the nuclear deterrence policy of the United States, and bound thereby to America's 'strategy, to its view of the world and to its concept of the politics of the world as a whole'.[74]

To approbation from the Labour benches, he described Mrs Thatcher as having used in her own statements on the subject 'the authentic terminology of the American view of the world'. He defined this as follows: 'It is, in the strictest terms, Manichean. It divides the world into two monoliths – the goodies and the baddies, the East and the West, even the free and the enslaved. It is a nightmarish distortion of reality. Indeed, to call it a distortion is too complimentary to it. It is a view of the world which this country cannot possibly share, or can share only at its own greatest peril.' As with the desire to be part of the emerging superstate in Europe, he added, the impetus to ally with America had been part of the desperate urge for a post-imperial role. Powell said Britain could still be strong on her own: 'We have that which is true of few other nations: we have proved invincible. That power can exist, however, and be realised only at the price that it is accompanied by independence. Once we attach ourselves to the philosophy, to the outlook and to the purposes of other nations differently situated and differently constituted, we forfeit that importance, that greatness which is not boastful but rightly ours and which we still have.'

In Ulster throughout the spring of 1981 Powell had taken an active part in the campaign for the much delayed local elections, at last set for 20 May. One inevitable by-product of the elections was to confirm the acrimony between the various wings of the Unionist movement, a process in which Powell assiduously participated in a speech in Belfast on 8 May. He described Paisley as being 'afraid for his own skin and afraid of the fringe-men of violence on whose backs he would fain ride'.[75] He claimed that because Paisley was a 'bully and a coward' he had not joined other Unionists in protesting about special-category status for more than 300 inmates of what Powell termed 'the Maze Academy of Terrorism'. He added that 'enemies of the Union' such as the Northern Ireland and Foreign Offices were longing for the DUP to do well in the elections, because of what he believed to be Paisley's wish to be leader of an independent Protestant Ulster outside the Union. When the Commons debated the renewal of the Emergency Provisions for Ulster on 22 July, Powell renewed his attack on Paisley – who was not present – complaining of 'his contempt for the House ... his readiness to abuse the House both inside it and outside, and ... his repudiation of any allegiance to the House'.[76] He reopened the wound about Paisley having tried to use the strike of 1977 to wreck the economy of the Province and to coerce the House, saying that most of his actions over the years had amounted to 'a repudiation of the authority of the House'.

In that same speech, Powell also attacked the latest flowering of Atkins's initiative, an advisory council – advising the Secretary of State – drawn from people in the Province already elected to public office, whether as district councillors of MEPs. This he described as a 'monstrosity'. The body was also to act as a constitutional convention, but his main outrage was prompted by the fact that, contrary to any constitutional practice elsewhere in the Kingdom, they would be advising Atkins on legislation rather than just policy, something

Powell called 'a sinister absurdity'.[77] He concluded, 'We would not dream in any other circumstances of setting up a political advisory body in a part of the Kingdom represented in this House. We would not dream of saying "You should have an Executive which is recruited from people who have been elected to do opposite things." All the proposals, small and great, for the government of Northern Ireland fly in the face of the constitutional principles upon which this House exists. That is the reason why they all fail and why they all founder.'[78] He told Atkins his proposals would help 'the enemies of this country'; and the Conservative MP who followed Powell, Michael McNair-Wilson, immediately conceded he had done 'an incredible demolition job' on Atkins.[79]

The spring and summer of 1981 saw rioting on the streets of London and Liverpool, in predominantly black areas, that seemed to fulfil some of Powell's darkest prophecies. He had spoken to Ashton-under-Lyne Young Conservatives on 28 March in tones more apocalyptic than he had used for some years. He warned of 'the uncertainty of violence on a scale which can only adequately be described as civil war' if the immigrant areas were not diluted, and he discounted what he regarded as the prevailing, defeatist mentality that it was 'too late to do anything'.[80] He warned that if the situation were reversed there would have to be 'a reduction in prospective numbers as would represent re-emigration hardly less massive than the immigration which occurred in the first place', though he did not use the word repatriation. However, such a policy, which had looked unlikely enough in 1968 when most heads of immigrant families were first-generation settlers, seemed highly improbable almost a generation later. Also, Powell's critics were not slow to point out that the apocalypse he had so often predicted had not manifested itself.

Roy Hattersley, the shadow Home Secretary, denounced Powell for using 'Munich beer-hall language'. He said that 'any Pakistani mugged by skinheads tonight will believe that Mr Powell was in part responsible for the attack'.[81] When, within days, some of the most violent and destructive rioting seen on British streets in modern times occurred in Brixton, the controversy about how far Powell had had a role in stoking up anger broke out again. Even Mrs Thatcher began to sound worried about his rhetoric. An interviewer quoted to her a remark by Powell made after Brixton that, given the prospective increase of the immigrant population, the people of Britain 'have seen nothing yet'. She replied, 'I heard him say that and it was a very, very alarming remark, and I hope with all my heart that it is not true.'[82]

However, when, in July, riots flared in the Liverpool suburb of Toxteth, Powell repeated his observation that there was still worse to come. He used a speech during the later stages of the British Nationality Bill to call for a tightening of the new definition of citizenship beyond what the Government was proposing, and to say again that many of New Commonwealth descent, even including some born in Britain, would be happier to settle in the Commonwealth. When

Whitelaw made a statement in the Commons on Toxteth on 6 July, Powell, to his horror, asked him, 'in which town or city does the right hon Gentleman expect the next pitched battle against the police to be fought?'[83]

He spoke at greater length, and caused even more outrage, in a Commons debate on the civil disturbances on 16 July. Under constant interruption from Labour backbenchers, Powell questioned Whitelaw's use of the phrases 'working to prevent tensions' and to 'promote mutual tolerance and understanding', saying that the House 'should ask itself seriously how far those phrases and those intentions correspond with practical reality'.[84] What was happening could not, he said, be divorced from the 'over-arching fact' that in many large cities a young generation, up to the age of twenty-five, was between a quarter and a half New Commonwealth. Because of the youth of the population, the proportion was set to double over the next generation and treble beyond that. Unless the population was decentralised or its fertility declined – neither of which he thought likely – the catastrophe he had always predicted still, he said, lay ahead.

In the manner of 1968, he then read to the Commons a letter from a member of the public complaining about the effects of immigration. The extract he read out ended: 'As they continue to multiply and as we can't retreat further there must be conflict.'[85] Martin Flannery, a Labour backbencher, shouted out that Powell was delivering 'a National Front speech'. Powell pressed on, predicting 'inner London becoming ungovernable or violence which could only effectually be described as civil war'. Flannery shouted at him again, asking what Powell knew about inner cities. Powell rose to the provocation. 'The hon Member asked me what I know about inner cities. I was a Member for Wolverhampton for a quarter of a century. What I saw in those early years of the development of this problem in Wolverhampton has made it impossible for me ever to dissociate myself from this gigantic and tragic problem.'

He emphasised that it was the concentration of the ethnic minority population in cities that was the problem, and took issue with an assertion by Hattersley that the causes of the trouble were largely economic. 'Are we seriously saying', asked Powell, 'that so long as there is poverty, unemployment and deprivation our cities will be torn to pieces, that the police in them will be the objects of attack and that we shall destroy our own environment? Of course not.'[86] He said there was a 'lesser evil' that might prevent the doubling or trebling of the population, for which he was assailed by Labour Members for having a 'cattle truck mentality'. Dame Judith Hart, one of them, said his words were 'an evil incitement to riot'. Powell told her, 'I am within the judgment of the House, as I am within the judgment of the people of this country, and I am content to stand before either tribunal.'

He added that more and more members of the New Commonwealth population wanted to know whether there was a means of avoiding the conflict that, he felt, they like he knew was inevitable. The recently elected socialist government in France had proposed that an agreement be reached with immigrant workers about 'their eventual return home'. Powell could not see why such a solution should be so unthinkable on the British side of the Channel. He did not want the Government necessarily to go that far; he just wanted them to be honest with people who lived in London and other cities about the prospects '10, 20 or 30 years ahead'. He said he received many letters from elderly people who told him how glad they were to be old, for they would not live to see what the country was coming to. Once more he was assailed by Labour Members demanding to intervene upon him; once more he refused, and order threatened to break down. He concluded that he was confident the British would see sense before the crisis finally erupted, but only if the Government was honest with them.

His criticisms of the Government's probity were, though, highly specific. His support for the stringent economic measures – he had confined his observations in the Budget debate to an assault on Labour's desire for an even more massive deficit, and an incomes policy, to try to bring down unemployment – had, despite his profound disagreements over Ulster and reservations about immigration policy, helped thaw his relations with the Conservative leadership. Mrs Thatcher, who had always admired him, was heard to refer to him privately as 'that golden-hearted Enoch'.[87] In early July 1981 it emerged he would attend the party conference in October – his first time since 1973, when Barber had denounced him – to speak to an anti-Common Market meeting on the fringe. Powell made it clear he would not attend the main conference. Asked whether he would linger in Blackpool, he told a reporter, 'Certainly not. I should not think anyone would want to stay in Blackpool a moment longer than he has to.'[88]

When he addressed the meeting, on 14 October, he was given a hero's welcome by more than 400 representatives. He called for withdrawal from the EEC and, when asked whether he would be advocating a Labour vote at the next election, he said that he hoped the Conservatives would have changed their mind on the subject by then. With a diplomacy he had been reluctant for some time to show in this context, he added, 'I'm not going to foreclose on that hope by anything I do or say.'[89] Eight Conservative MPs shared the platform with Powell, who was met with cries of 'You should never have left us.' Sir Nicholas Bonsor, one of the MPs present and a future Foreign Office minister, said he hoped Powell would rejoin the party, bringing 'his talent and immense national loyalty which we cannot do without'.

The following week, Powell further impressed his old party in an economic censure debate in the Commons. Mrs Thatcher had, earlier, made an uncompromising defence of monetarism, telling her critics – more those on her own benches than opposite – that she would not feed the public on 'a diet of illusion'.[90]

By common consent, Powell – the first speaker called after Mrs Thatcher – made the best speech in the debate. He fundamentally disputed the proposition that underpinned the censure motion, that the total of unemployed – now three million – was the fault of the Government; and that the policies being suggested by the Opposition to ameliorate the problem would be of any help. Foot, who had led the attack, had advocated a massive increase in public expenditure, but Powell argued that increases in spending for most of the preceding seven years had not prevented a continued rise in unemployment. Also, the increase in spending was, Foot had specified, to be met not by more taxation, but by more borrowing, so the inflationary effect would be additionally severe, since much of the additional borrowing of the previous years had been from the banks, and had greatly increased the money supply. Labour was relying on the increased money supply not being translated into higher prices or higher wages; and, as he pointed out, this had been tried many times before, and had failed every time.

He addressed, directly, the most emotional part of this issue: 'The three million people who are unemployed in this country', he said, 'have a right to expect they will not be deceived by those who pretend to them that resort to policies which have been disproved and exploded in the past, to measures which can be refuted both theoretically and practically, will be the means of rescuing them now.'[91] These were the chickens not of the past two years, but of the past eleven years, coming home to roost, and Powell would not have the issue deflected from stern reality. Foot intervened, and Powell gave way to him. The Leader of the Opposition admitted that Powell had put the Government's case far better than the Government, but would he say how much extra unemployment, particularly in Northern Ireland, would be caused by what he was advocating?

Powell retorted that Foot had not been able to make good the causal connection between the Government's policies and the high unemployment. The unemployment was mainly, he said, caused by the radical changes in the economy, and not least by the reliance on oil that had led to Britain having both a huge surplus on the current account of the balance of payments and three million unemployed at the same time. No short-term palliative policies could address that problem: 'It is a large scale readjustment to change which this country is called upon to face by the events of the last few years. We deceive those who are affected if we pretend otherwise to them. The motion on the Order Paper is not merely an insult to the intelligence of the House. It is an insult to three million unemployed people.'

This display prompted twenty-seven Conservative MPs to put down an early day motion urging Powell to sit again as one of their number. He would not be drawn on their invitation. The motion was soon amended to call for him to be given a place in the Government, a notion taken up enthusiastically in the leader columns of the *Daily Telegraph*. The Government was deeply unpopular, and bringing Powell into it, the paper said, would be looked on by Mrs Thatcher's opponents as 'recourse to a strategic nuclear deterrent; but, after all, the Prime Minister believes in such deterrents'.[92]

Having avoided specific mention of repatriation in his comments about immigration earlier that year, Powell addressed the subject in a speech on 7 November. He said repatriation was necessary, on a large scale, but should be voluntary and heavily financially assisted. He also claimed that the mass export of such human resources would do more for the developing countries to which the immigrants would return than the money Britain was pouring into them in overseas aid. He said he was well aware that many of the immigrant-descended population would want to stay, but that 1.5 million could return over the next ten years at a cost of £300 million a year – well under the £750 million aid budget. He said such a voluntary scheme was 'the only rational step' and would probably be welcomed by the countries of origin to which the immigrants still, for the most part, had an unconditional right of re-entry.[93] Powell also attacked Michael Heseltine, the Environment Secretary, for having refused to confirm or deny Powell's own projections for the content of the population of the inner cities in the future; and he took as an admission of guilt Heseltine's remarks that 'Mr Powell wants everyone to have the figures so that they know the scale of the problem. The only consequence of the projection of the figures Mr Powell produces, plus the language of voluntary repatriation, is to foment the very anxieties and tensions that he is forecasting.'[94] This was, for Powell, evidence that 'the Government's conclusion is really the same as mine', but, if they were to 'come clean' with the public, the cry for repatriation would be deafening.

Such episodes showed the difficulties that would have followed from Powell's taking the Conservative whip. Ulster, however, would always be a worse provocation to him. A meeting later that month between Mrs Thatcher and the Irish Prime Minister, Garret FitzGerald, provoked Powell to draw unhappy conclusions about what was going on behind the scenes in discussions about the future of Northern Ireland. When the meeting was announced, Powell asked Mrs Thatcher in the Commons, 'Does the Prime Minister not recognise that a nation cannot secure its own peace and security by entering into arrangements which its own people rightly regard as a conspiracy against them with their enemies?'[95] Mrs Thatcher replied that she doubted all people would take that view. Powell felt that she said such things with a heavy heart, never agreeing privately with what her officials in the Northern Ireland and Foreign Offices had persuaded her it was in Britain's interests for her to say.

Within a few days, an incident occurred that raised the temperature on the issue still higher: the murder on 14 November by the IRA of one of Powell's Unionist colleagues, the Rev. Robert Bradford. Powell led the tributes to him in the Commons on the afternoon of 16 November, and Mrs Thatcher followed him, endorsing his every word. Paisley, shortly afterwards, in a speech of sincere regret, added his belief that Bradford would not be the last MP to die in this way before Christmas came; and Fitt, after him, said the murderers 'are trying to drive the Northern Ireland community into total conflict and civil war'.[96] It was the House, though, that was the immediate scene of conflict: Jim Prior, who had succeeded Atkins as Northern Ireland Secretary, then sought to make a statement about the security situation in the Province – Bradford's murder was but one of several horrific incidents in the preceding days – but was soon interrupted by Paisley and his two fellow DUP MPs, who shouted him down. The sitting had twice to be suspended for ten minutes before order could be restored, and the three MPs were suspended. The Speaker, on resuming the sitting, said he believed the three men had come with the explicit intention of disrupting the proceedings, a view Powell had long held about Paisley.

When Prior eventually finished his statement, Powell questioned him. He asked whether Prior was aware that what he had described as a 'black week' for Northern Ireland 'was the sequel and, to a large extent, the consequence, of what was done at the Downing Street meeting on 6 November?' – the summit with FitzGerald.[97] Powell said the Government had been warned of the consequences of this meeting, and were 'therefore guilty of the consequences of which they were warned'. He asked Prior to refrain from making matters worse 'by referring to things like political progress and agreements, which indicate to people in Northern Ireland that Her Majesty's Government share, if not the methods, then at any rate the aims of the IRA'. This immediately brought cries of 'disgraceful,' and an assertion by Prior that Powell's remarks would do 'a great deal of damage' to the search for peace.

Powell would not, though, be deflected from his belief that the Government's attitude was a principal sponsor of terrorism. Speaking at Coleraine on 5 December he alleged that British, American and Irish officials were working to bring about a united Ireland within NATO, filling what Powell felt the Americans regarded as the greatest strategic gap in that organisation; and that the British role in this scheme was not necessarily known of by Mrs Thatcher. He predicted – accurately, in the light of the events of 1985 – that a key part of this change would be the creation of 'an Anglo-Irish institution in which Ulster is to be represented as a third and distinct element and thus drawn progressively into economic and political relations with the Irish republic. Of all this, the essential prerequisite is to have in existence an Ulster representative institution.'[98]

Wrongly, he said that to appease the Republic the Government would renege on its earlier promise to add five extra seats to Ulster's parliamentary representation. The Boundaries Commission had been told to delay its final report, a move from which Powell concluded that the Commission was not to pre-empt the plans to establish some sort of Ulster assembly. His suspicions had been further fuelled by talks between Prior and William Clark, the American deputy Secretary of State, in which Powell was convinced that further pressure was being put on Britain to help with the development of NATO to include an all-Ireland state. He asked a question of the Prime Minister and the cabinet – which he admitted he could not answer – 'Do they understand the part that they themselves, as principals, or puppets, are playing in the plot of selling into bondage a portion of their own country and people in order to purchase the goodwill of doubtful allies and buy off the hostility of enemies?'[99]

The immigration issue then returned. After the summer's riots the Government had commissioned a law lord, Lord Scarman, to conduct an inquiry into their nature and into the policing of the affected areas. When the Commons considered his report on 10 December, Powell drew out in his speech the evidence Scarman had found of the racial element in the disturbances. Much of this bore out Powell's long-standing theses: he quoted the opinion that the police had 'stood between our society and a total collapse of law and order in the streets of an important part of the capital', and that this near-collapse had been characterised by 'a strong racial element'.[100] However, he felt he had found a 'gap in reasoning' in a section where Scarman had concluded that 'if alienation among the black community is not to develop, there should be a more ready recognition of the special problems and needs of the ethnic minorities than hitherto'. The 'gap', as Powell saw it, was Scarman's assumption 'that the black community is alienated because it is disadvantaged ... it is by no means self-evident, and by no means necessary, that the two facts should be connected as cause and effect'.

Applying his logic to the problem, Powell said the community was alienated because it was alien; and, being so large and so concentrated, it was manifestly alien. He applied Scarman's evidence of the composition of the population to show that tensions would worsen. Whereas in Lambeth the non-white population stood at 25 per cent, it was 40 per cent of those of secondary-school age. Both the community itself, and those looking on at it, would feel more alienated in the years ahead as a result of the inevitable explosion in the population because of the relatively high fertility of the ethnic group. Powell said the Government should be honest with the people and tell them that, thirty years hence, the black population of an already tense and volatile Lambeth would have doubled in size. He defied a Government spokesman to gainsay his projections, based on Scarman's evidence: none came forward to do so.

Early in the new year, speaking in his constituency, Powell renewed his dire warnings for Ulster's future. On 6 January 1982 he said Northern Ireland was as much a part of the United Kingdom as Finchley – Mrs Thatcher's constituency – but most of the Ulster people were nearing the precipice of breaking away from the rest of the country, and might be tempted by the Paisley solution of an independent Protestant state. Powell warned that Paisley would get such a mandate if the people of Ulster were 'rattled and frightened, hysterical, bewildered and deceived', a condition that British policy seemed determined to bring about.[101]

He placed the main responsibility for the shifts in Ulster policy on the Americans. Since the assumption of office by President Reagan, there had been many examples of closer ties between the two governments, which Powell found alarming and distasteful. On 28 January Powell asked Prior what reason he had 'for assuming that he is made aware of all the communications that pass between officials of his Department, officials of the Irish Government and officials of the American embassy in Dublin.'[102] Prior answered that he had that confidence 'because I am Secretary of State for Northern Ireland in Her Majesty's Government and because I have more confidence in my officials' integrity than has the right hon Gentleman'. A few minutes later Powell intervened again, saying that the 'principal threat' from the United States to peace in Ulster came not from the Irish-American community, whose fund-raising activities on behalf of the IRA ministers had condemned, but from the State Department and the Pentagon.[103] He would make a habit, in the next two years before Prior was replaced, of mocking him at Question Time. Perhaps the most painful episode occurred later that spring when, on 25 March, Powell recounted words used by Prior to Unionist MPs the day after Robert Bradford's funeral to the effect that 'we were not expecting Robert Bradford to be murdered'. 'Who', asked Powell, 'were they expecting to be murdered, and will the Secretary of State invite his officials to explain to him what he meant?'[104]

He continued to worry that the Thatcher administration was acquiring some of the imperialist tendencies he attributed to the Americans. Earlier in January he had courted further controversy when he interrupted remarks made in the Commons by the Prime Minister about the clampdown by the military regime in Poland. When she said, 'We all deeply and bitterly regret that action is being taken to extinguish the flame of freedom,' Powell called out, 'Why?' He explained later on that he had interrupted because of the impossibility of Britain taking responsibility for Poland, having neither the power nor the knowledge to influence Polish affairs any more than the Polish Government could become involved in British affairs.

The Lord Privy Seal, Humphrey Atkins – who spoke on Foreign Office matters in the Commons as Carrington, the Foreign Secretary, was in the Lords – had said the Government would maintain a stance of non-intervention in the matter. That had now manifestly changed, and Powell felt sure it had done so because of American pressure. The Reagan administration had put sanctions on the Soviet Union as a mark of its displeasure at how the Polish military dictatorship was fulfilling the wishes of the Soviet leadership. Powell felt that this had placed the ball in Mrs Thatcher's court, and the Americans were waiting for Britain to match their action. 'We were dragged into folly by the Americans over Iran,' he said. 'We were dragged into folly by the Americans over Afghanistan. Neither national interest nor moral obligation requires us to be dragged by them into folly over Poland.'[105]

In a newspaper article the following month Powell continued his theme, saying Britain was, if she only realised it, almost impregnable militarily, politically and economically. 'Yet we slink about like whipped curs ... our self-abasement principally takes the form of subservience to the United States.'[106] He added that 'we are under no necessity to participate in the American nightmare of a Soviet monster barely held at bay in all quarters of the globe by an inconceivable nuclear armament and by political intervention everywhere from Poland to Cambodia. It is the Americans who need us in order to act out their crazy scenario.' Powell outlined Britain's strengths: principally self-sufficiency in oil, and massive lending to foreign countries to finance the world's trading deficit with Britain. 'We simply do not need to go chasing up and down after the vagaries of the next ignoramus to become President of the United States.'

In the same article, Powell extended his theory of British subservience to include obeisance to Europe as well as America, a point he developed the next month in an attack on the European Court of Human Rights. Speaking in Ilford on 13 March, he referred to two recent adjudications by the courts – demanding the legalisation of homosexual relations between consenting adults in Northern Ireland, and allowing parents to object to the use of corporal punishment in British schools. Powell had supported the legalisation of homosexuality, and was a consistent opponent of corporal punishment, but he said, 'I would sooner receive injustice in the Queen's courts than justice in a foreign court. I hold that man or woman to be a scoundrel who goes abroad to a foreign court to have the judgments of the Queen's courts overturned, the actions of her Government countermanded or the legislation of parliament struck down.'[107]

IV

By the time of the Budget in March 1982 the economic situation seemed so dire, with unemployment showing no sign of falling and taxes still high, that the Government's chances of another election victory had been all but written off: no one had foreseen the effects of the international crisis about to grip Britain, and how it would deliver the Conservatives their greatest election triumph since the war. Speaking in the Budget debate on 15 March, Powell found himself again coming to the Government's defence, but in what was, for him, a more enjoyable fashion than usual. He spoke directly after Heath, who had preceded his own speech by telling the press – and Powell quoted these words eagerly – that 'the intellectual battle against monetarism has been won'.[108] He did not feel this was typical Heath: 'the right hon Gentleman's former colleagues know that there was one certain way of sending him into a paroxysm of irritation and impatience;

that is, to suggest that the major issues of politics are subject to and capable even of resolution by intellectual debate. The wilderness is a wonderful place.'

Powell teased Heath for his comment – strictly true – that reflation was not the same as inflation. Reflation was the stimulation of additional demand, and the challenge was to achieve this without causing inflation. 'If the right hon Member for Sidcup will forgive me for saying so,' Powell continued, 'on this matter he was disappointing.' Heath had been vague about the size of the new demand he wanted to create, and about how it was to be created, unlike Labour, which had specified £9 billion extra spending, to be financed by massive borrowing and tempered by an incomes policy. Powell then dissected a speech by Peter Shore, the shadow Chancellor, in which Shore had tried to explain how he would improve the economy by these methods. Powell, though, came to the conclusion that Labour still did not see how the whole economy, largely under pressure from technological change, had undergone a revolution, and that in its financial notions it still did not understand realities either of economics or of capitalism.

He argued that because of this change employment patterns would have to undergo a similar revolution. Shore was compelled to intervene in this withering assault and admit that 'once again, the right hon Gentleman has played his part as the intellectual Lone Ranger coming to the aid of the devastated Government Benches'.[109] Shore tried to make Powell admit that the problem with the economy was that the exchange rate had been allowed to remain so high at a time of rapidly rising costs, but Powell returned to his earlier contention that the problem was Britain's self-sufficiency in oil, which had led to a large balance of payments surplus and prevented the need to buy too much foreign currency, thus depressing the exchange rate. It was important, Powell concluded, for the Government to relay to the people the nature of the causes of the economic crisis, and that much of what the policy would have to respond to was outside the control of any government. He praised Howe for having removed Labour's employment surcharge, thereby creating more incentives for employers to take labour on in difficult times. Once more, it was felt that Powell had done the Government a massive favour for – as Shore had obliquely said – no one on the Conservative benches had been able to outline the sense of the Government's policies, and the nonsense of the Opposition's, as well as he had.

Paisley also spoke in the House that day, despite having not attended the rest of the debate. Powell was so angry that he used his friendship with the Speaker, George Thomas, to write to him in what were for Powell unprecedented terms. Writing to 'Dear George' – all Powell's other letters to Thomas are, despite the closeness of their acquaintance, addressed to 'Dear Mr Speaker' – Powell had clearly had enough. 'I have never presumed before to refer to the exercise by the Chair of its prerogative of calling hon Members to speak; but the calling of Ian Paisley in the Budget debate yesterday was a humiliation of the House,' he wrote.[110] 'The Member concerned comes here, insults the House, and repudiates its authority; but he can count on turning up after the opening speeches on the last day of a debate he has not attended and being called within two hours in prime time before many other members. He can then dispense with attending the wind-up, before reappearing to "chat up" the occupant of the Chair during the division. The House has only itself to blame if a bully and a braggart treats it in this way.' Thomas replied that he had a 'dread of bearing malice, or of appearing unfair in my dealings with Members with whom I have clashed in public. This dread certainly influences me in my dealings with Ian Paisley, but your letter puts a very different perspective on the matter. I can only say that in noting your unusually severe comments, I shall be mindful of them in the future.'[111]

In the run-up to Powell's seventieth birthday in June 1982 he increasingly attracted the attentions of the profile writers and interviewers. He reflected to the *Daily Mail* on the continuing nature of his fame and popularity: 'It is not unknown for people coming to my house to be told by the taxi-driver that there is no charge. It is an unintended and unsought testimonial, but I would be surprised if what I feel is not what the mass of my fellow countrymen feel. I don't feel separate just because I was a professor of Greek. My countrymen say: "This man sees what we see, he feels as we feel, he's one of us, thank God." '[112] The reaching of his biblical span seemed to confirm Powell in his role as revered, unique elder statesman, but other events that spring demonstrated his continuing importance and relevance to contemporary politics.

In the first week of April Argentina invaded the Falkland Islands. For Powell, it was a defining moment in his regard for the Government, and he was not disappointed, except that he drew from the resolute response towards the aggression conclusions about the attitude of the Thatcher administration towards Ulster that were over-optimistic. Once the crisis broke out, Powell, as a Privy Councillor and on behalf of his party, was given secret briefings about the progress of the conflict. The House was recalled on a Saturday, 3 April, to debate the matter, and Powell – in a speech that lasted only a little over six minutes – made a telling intervention.

He began with a direct appeal to Mrs Thatcher, arguing that it would be 'grotesque' to proceed with the Northern Ireland policy at a time when the country had, rightly, been alerted to the importance of maintaining British sovereignty over a more remote piece of territory; and he asked for the publication of the Northern Ireland White Paper to be deferred.[113] As for the Falklands, Powell suggested that the time for inquests would come later. He agreed it was right, in accordance with Britain's international duty, that the matter had been put before the United Nations, but reminded the House that nothing compelled the Government to wait upon the UN's deliberations before doing what was necessary to re-establish British sovereignty in the islands. The use of force was, he said, essential, and he praised the Government for setting in train the necessary measures; 'but there must be nothing which casts doubt upon their will and their intention to do it'.[114]

For all the speed and purpose of the remedial action being set in train, Powell was unimpressed by the Government's handling of the issue. Before the invasion, when the news came of the aggressive activities of the Argentinians on South Georgia, he had asked Richard Luce, a Foreign Office minister, whether the Government believed that the public would support the use of force in maintaining British sovereignty over the Falklands and their dependencies. Luce had said it would be the Government's duty to take such steps. Now Powell delivered his judgment: 'The Government have failed to do that duty. They have manifestly failed. They have failed in the face of the world.' In concluding, he turned his gaze upon Mrs Thatcher. 'The Prime Minister, shortly after she came into office, received a sobriquet as the "Iron Lady". It arose in the context of remarks which she made about defence against the Soviet Union and its allies; but there was no reason to suppose that the right hon Lady did not welcome and, indeed, take pride in that description. In the next week or two in this House, the nation and the right hon Lady herself will learn of what metal she is made.' Powell had made the remark because he feared that he saw, as he had so often seen before, a Conservative party shrinking from a necessary confrontation. According to Mrs Thatcher's circle, his statement had a 'devastating impact' upon her, and helped form her resolve to fight.[115] A task force was being assembled to go to the islands. When it arrived, it would be used ruthlessly to achieve objectives that would not disappoint Powell.

A further debate was held on 14 April, when the Commons had had more time to consider what was happening. When he spoke Powell did not dwell on the initial failure to have pre-empted the invasion – the reasons for which were still not fully understood – but contended that 'it is difficult to fault the military and especially the naval measures which the Government have taken'. Soon significant naval power would be in the area; but then, he warned, there would need to be a fight. For the moment, he wished to refer to 'dangers of a political character'.[116] Powell asked that the campaign be not justified purely because of the desire of the Falkland Islanders to remain British; 'I do not think that we need be too nice about saying that we defend our territory as well as our people. There is nothing irrational, nothing to be ashamed of, in doing that. Indeed, it is impossible in the last resort to distinguish between the defence of territory and the defence of people.'[117] The echoes of his views on Ulster were obvious.

His second point was a product of his feelings about the United Nations. He was concerned about the ambiguity in part of the Security Council's resolution calling for a 'peaceful solution'. Powell would have liked the invasion to be overturned without bloodshed, but another form of peaceful solution – 'a negotiated settlement or compromise between two incompatible positions' –

was utterly unacceptable. 'That cannot be the meaning of the resolution of the Security Council. It cannot be meant that one country has only to seize the territory of another country for the nations of the world to say that some middle position must be found between the two parties, that some compromise must be the object of diplomacy, some formula that takes account of the objects and interests of the aggressor as well as of those of the aggressed.' If this interpretation could be put on the resolution 'it would be a pirates' charter. It would mean that any claim anywhere in the world had only to be pursued by force, and points would immediately be gained and a bargaining position established by the aggressor.' His conclusion was literally uncompromising, and reflected entirely the Prime Minister's view: 'We are under no obligation to try to find a middle position between what the Falkland Islanders and we have the right to and what might be found tolerable by an aggressor.'

Asked by the *Daily Telegraph* to contribute an article on the matter, he gave the paper instead – and they published – the speech he had made to Conservatives in York in January 1969, mocking a statement in the House of Commons by Denis Healey, then Defence Secretary, about the absence of any strategic significance of the Falklands to Britain for the future. Those were the days, Powell had said, when the prospect of nuclear war dominated strategic thinking. But, even in 1969, the United States had begun to consider at greater length the prospect of a conventional war involving extensive naval engagements. In any war, Powell had argued, Britain would still have to command the Atlantic, and he asked what was, to him, the obvious question: 'If the Falkland Islands belonged to the Soviet Union, would their Minister of Defence be saying: "These islands do not have any contribution to make to our future strategy?" '[118] He rather suspected not.

There were, for Powell, obvious similarities between the defence Britain was being called upon to make of the Falklands and the defence he believed needed better to be made of Ulster's place within the United Kingdom. It was both ironic and appropriate that, at the same time as the conflict was proceeding, Prior should bring before the House proposals for devolution – proposals Powell felt had been hurried along by the IRA's intense aggression the previous autumn. He told Prior candidly how 'disappointing' it must be for him to have spent so many months on these proposals only to find them rejected by almost every side to whom they would apply. 'He was attempting the impossible,' Powell said, 'and it was no discredit to him if he failed.' He sought to explain the impossibility to him, saying it was a result of the 'in-built contradiction in the behaviour of successive Governments of this country towards Ulster.'[119]

There was a parallel contradiction. 'We assured', Powell said, 'the people of the Falkland Islands that there should be no change in their status without their agreement. Yet at the very same time that those assurances were being repeated, the actions of the Government and their representatives elsewhere were belying or contradicting those assurances and showing that part at any rate of the Government was looking to a very different outcome that could not be approved by the people of the islands.' The same, he continued, had happened to Northern Ireland. The problem was that when similar assurances had been given in 1920 to the people of Ulster, the Government had set up in the Six Counties a microcosm of the government for all Ireland designed by Asquith's Home Rule legislation of 1912, when all Ulster had really wanted was to be governed in the same way as the rest of the Kingdom.

This decision, Powell added, had meant that conventional political parties had disappeared in the Six Counties, the divide being simply whether one was for or against the Union. This had contradicted the democratic principle by ensuring one-party rule until the end of Stormont in 1972 when, as Powell saw it, pressure from the Irish Republic and from America, with her strategic interest in Ireland, put an end to the parliament there. Power-sharing, which had been the way around this problem, had not survived either, because it too contradicted the democratic principle. Powell said Prior was simply trying to revive the 1973 Act that had brought about that unworkable situation, but with changes that would make matters even worse. 'The notion that one will begin with an Assembly with no responsibilities,' he argued, 'and work up gradually to an Executive, some of whose members are responsible in one direction and some in another, only adds a new nightmare on top of the old. It is absolutely asking for what has been predicted repeatedly in this debate, that such an institution will become a focus not of co-operation or mutual understanding but of a sharpening of differences, a focus of alienation between the people of the Province and the Government of the United Kingdom, which, after all, carries the ultimate sovereign responsibility.'[120] He concluded by reminding the Government of the dangers inherent in the 1973 Act, of which he had warned at the time, and about which he had been proved right. He begged them not to try to repeat the error, above all at a time when the country was in a state of war.

When the Commons next discussed that war the task force still had not reached the islands, and Powell remained anxious to rebut the opinion that Britain could act only under the United Nations charter. 'The right of self-defence', he argued, '– to repel aggression and to expel an invader from one's territory and one's people whom he has occupied and taken captive – is, as the Government have said, an inherent right. It is one which existed before the United Nations was dreamt of.'[121] The Parliament and people had, he said, resolved to take such just action, but they should bear in mind the implications. 'One is that having willed and approved that action we must, as a nation, be prepared to take the consequences ... it ought to be understood that we were accepting and expressing the will, if necessary, to maintain a long and difficult course of action in which there may be reverses and severe losses. We must not allow that to be misunderstood or played down outside the House.'

He also attacked the notion that, once the islands were recovered, their continued existence as British territory was unsustainable. 'We owe it to those whom we have involved by our decision,' he said, '– our governmental decision, our parliamentary decision, our national decision – to be clear with ourselves that the possession of the Falkland Islands is integral to our national defence and interests and that it is, if necessary, indefinitely sustainable.'[122] This meant, fundamentally, that sovereignty could not be negotiated away. 'I hope that the Government will make it clear that they remain resolved to retain the power to exercise that right,' he concluded. 'If they make that clear, I believe the nation will support them.'[123]

On 10 May the Northern Ireland Bill, embodying the proposals in Prior's White Paper for 'rolling devolution' with power-sharing, had its second reading. Powell was unequivocal in his opposition. It was still his view that the assembly would exacerbate differences in Ulster. He also outlined what he believed to be the sequence of events since the Government's election three years earlier, when the Americans had started to put pressure on for a resolution of the conflict; and they had found, Powell said, a willing helper in Carrington, who had just resigned as Foreign Secretary over the Falklands debacle, and who was felt to have had no attachment to Unionism.

Powell recalled the meetings Mrs Thatcher had had with her Irish counterparts during those years – Lynch, Haughey and FitzGerald – and especially how at the meeting with FitzGerald the previous November it had been agreed that there should be 'an Anglo-Irish Council with a parliamentary tier in which the Republic, the United Kingdom and Northern Ireland as a separate entity would each be represented'.[124] As Powell told the story, FitzGerald found himself criticised by Haughey for not having gone far enough or fast enough; but FitzGerald, speaking in the Dail, had replied that he believed it wise 'not to press ahead at this stage with an Anglo-Irish parliamentary council because of the difficulties involved in securing fair representation from Northern Ireland where there was no elected representative body'. So Powell now understood what Prior's proposals were all about: his plans would, with power-sharing, create such a body, and provide a next step in what he claimed Northern Ireland Office officials 'colloquially referred to' as 'the reunification exercise'. That was the only purpose of this otherwise pointless assembly.

Prior intervened to say that neither he, nor his predecessor, had ever heard of the phrase 'reunification exercise'. Powell accepted his word, but said that made it all the more worrying, since in that case Prior was unaware of 'the ride for which he is being taken', the ride designed to achieve 'that reunification which is desired not only by the nation which claims Northern Ireland as part of its territory, but also by the most powerful nation on earth – the United States'.[125] He concluded with another affirmation that it would be as wrong to support this legislation as it had been to support its predecessor in 1973.

Three days later the House once more debated the Falklands, in the light of a statement by the new Foreign Secretary, Francis Pym, about what he called an 'interim agreement' – which as it turned out was not accepted by the Argentinians – in which there would have been a 'withdrawal of Argentine forces ... matched by corresponding withdrawal of British forces'.[126] This would have been entirely unacceptable to Powell. 'There is', he said,

> no withdrawal of British force that 'corresponds' to the withdrawal from the territory of the islands of those who have unlawfully occupied them. We have a right to be there; those are our waters, the territory is ours and we have the right to sail the oceans with our fleets whenever we think fit. So the whole notion of a 'corresponding withdrawal', a withdrawal of the only force which can possibly restore the position, which can possibly ensure any of the objectives which have been talked about on either side of the House, is in contradiction of the determination to repossess the Falklands.[127]

Equally offensive to him was another facet of the failed interim agreement, which would have created an interim administration under a small group of countries acceptable to both sides. Powell saw this as Foreign Office capitulation of the worst sort: 'we had been told that our object was to restore British administration ... such an interim administration prejudices, and is intended to prejudice, the eventual outcome against this country'. He was outraged that Pym had even contemplated so needless a gesture, and one so at odds with what Parliament had already agreed: 'It may well be that the Foreign Secretary is not in agreement with his colleagues in the Cabinet. It may be that the divergence to which I have drawn attention and which I believe is indisputable represents an internal difference of opinion in the Government. If so, the right hon Gentleman can resolve it. If he is not agreed with his colleagues on the purposes for which this operation is being conducted, there is an honourable course that he can take.' No more was heard of the plan: the task force proceeded with the objectives agreed for it by Parliament.

As soon as British forces had retaken the Falklands, Powell called for the islanders to be granted full citizenship, which would have meant the reversal of a decision made immediately before the invasion took place, when Parliament had considered the British Nationality Bill. He also paid tribute to Mrs Thatcher, making it clear that, by her resolution against the attempts at compromise offered her by the United Nations and the Foreign Office, she had passed the test he had set her on 3 April. 'Is the right hon Lady aware', he asked her at Questions on 17 June, two days after the victory, 'that the report has now been received from the public analyst on a certain substance recently subject to analysis and that I have obtained a copy of the report? It shows that the substance under test consisted of ferrous matter of the highest quality, that is of exceptional tensile strength, is highly resistant to wear and tear and to stress, and may be used with advantage for all national purposes?'[128] 'I think that I am very grateful indeed to the right hon Gentleman,' replied the Prime Minister. 'I agree with every word that he says.' Those lines, and the original question Powell had put to Mrs Thatcher, were printed and framed, and presented to her by their mutual friend Ian Gow; she hung them in her office.

For Powell, the most significant result of the conflict had been the way in which he felt it should alter perceptions of Britain's relations with America. He wrote, in *The Times* a fortnight after the ceasefire, of his belief that the Americans had secretly wanted the Falklands to pass out of British control and into the hands of a power who might have been even more amenable to them than Britain was. He believed this because he felt that the Falklands, situated in close relation to 'the most critical of all routes for American naval strategy' around Cape Horn, were highly desired as a naval base by the Americans.[129] This was, he hinted, also because of what he called the 'Hispanic factor' in American race relations, about which predominantly white Anglo-Saxon America had 'phobias' – as if, though he did not say it directly, America wanted a base off the sub-continent of South America from which to police it. He asserted that 'the American struggle to wrest the islands from Britain has only commenced in earnest now that the fighting is over'.

Three months later, in the *Guardian*, Powell repeated his assertion that the Falklands War had thrown into doubt the importance of the alliance with America in NATO. He lauded the fact that, thanks to the success of the operation, 'Britain now no longer looked upon itself and the world through American spectacles.' The view it had obtained was 'more rational; and it was more congenial; for, after all, it was our own view'.[130] He mocked claims made by both Britons and Americans that the United States was the leader of the free world. Quoting an observation that Americans believed theirs was 'a unique society ... where God has put together all nationalities, races and interests of the globe for one purpose – to show the rest of the world how to live', Powell attacked the 'manic exaltation of the American illusion' and contrasted it with the 'American nightmare'. Again, quoting the observation of an American, he defined this as 'the idea that we may one day find ourselves all alone in a sea of grim and envious and unfree people', rather than continuing to preside over the end of the Soviet Union.

This introduced one of Powell's most explicit statements of his reasons for his anti-Americanism: the belief Americans had that 'they are authorised, possibly by the deity, to intervene, openly or covertly, in the internal affairs of other countries anywhere in the world'. His provocation, more immediate than the Falklands, was the involvement of American troops in the war in the Lebanon. He was aggrieved by British complicity in this. 'It is not', he said, 'in Britain's self-interest alone that Britain should once again assert her own position. A world in which the American myth and the American nightmare go unchallenged by question or by contradiction is not a world as safe or as peaceable as human reason, prudence and realism can make it.'

The surrender at Port Stanley coincided, happily, exactly with Powell's seventieth birthday. In an interview given the week beforehand he touched upon themes that were, naturally enough for him, to dominate the rest of his life: the contemplation of, and preparation for, mortality, or what he called 'the one great certainty'. He said that 'one hopes for it to be sudden, to be merciful, like the death which Odysseus hoped for and was promised, like the gentleness of a mother to a child'. He added, with in retrospect great poignance, that 'unless I succeed in dying of a wasting disease they will have to put a little extra cloth into my brigadier's uniform if I am to be buried in it'.[131]

The excitement of the Falklands over, Powell spent much of that summer in committee trying to dilute the provisions of the Northern Ireland Bill; but it was a measure only the Official Unionists, the SDLP and a few Conservatives were minded to oppose. Other than delaying, there was little Powell could do to stop Prior's proposals becoming law. On 22 June it was decided to guillotine the debate, and Powell made a speech of barely controlled fury on the motion in the Commons. He said it was unlike any other guillotine because 'it involves in its fortunes the life and death of men, women and children; the predictable and certain death of more persons than would otherwise have suffered the fate in the coming months and years'.[132] He said that the House had a duty to think again about what it was doing by forcing through the measure. He was especially outraged that the Liberal party should have been supporting it. 'If one scratches a Liberal,' he observed, 'one will commonly find a dictator.'

He noted that the Opposition – then firmly committed to a policy of reunification – was not opposing the Bill or the guillotine, for it would, if enacted, forward its own policy in the Province. He cited evidence, not long made known to him, of the Conservative party's own agenda: that, in notes circulated to candidates a week before the general election of 1979, it had been said explicitly that 'the next Government will come under considerable pressure to launch a new high-powered political initiative on Northern Ireland with the object of establishing another "power-sharing" government in the Province which could pave the way for a federal constitution linking Ulster to the Irish Republic'.[133] It had specified that the pressure was coming, as Powell had long claimed it was, not just from the Republic but from the United States. It had all proved accurate.

He condemned recent remarks by Prior that integration of the Province into the United Kingdom would be incompatible with 'meaningful relations' with the Irish Republic. Devolution was what the Republic wanted, because of the progress it signalled towards a federal system. 'Everyone in Northern Ireland who is opposed to the Union', he added, 'must draw comfort, satisfaction and assurance for the future from this legislation and the Government's determination to force it through.'[134] Prior was stung by this and asked how Powell could reconcile two separate points he had made: one that the level of violence would increase as a result of the Bill, and the other that the Bill handed the IRA all it wanted. 'Surely the logical conclusion of his argument', Prior contended, 'is that, if the IRA believes that it has what it wants, there is no need for it to resort to violence?' Powell replied that 'the legislation is a standing encouragement to the IRA. It is a standing encouragement to those who believe that by violence they can anticipate or ensure that the foreseen fate of Northern Ireland is in their hands. It is a standing encouragement to those who are sufficiently light-headed or unwise to believe that terror and the escalation of terror can be met with the escalation of terror. The right hon Gentleman has taken my point and understood my argument.'[135]

Paisley, who followed Powell, attacked him and his thesis. He said that, in fact, the Republicans were opposed to the Bill – he cited statements to that effect made by the Sinn Fein MP Owen Carron, who had never taken his seat – and this was precisely why he and the DUP wanted the assembly. Paisley was also outraged that since Powell had, rightly, pointed out the mission of both main British parties to be rid of Ulster, he should still want the electors of Ulster to put their faith in Westminster: Paisley said he would prefer faith to be put in the assembly. He alleged that, before Mrs Thatcher's meeting with Haughey, the Official Unionists had sent her a list of items they wished to be discussed with him, so they had been collaborating in the talks that they had, ever since, been so ostentatiously condemning. Powell intervened, and said that if Paisley would read out the items suggested, 'the House will see that they were inconsistent with any political arrangement between the United Kingdom and the Irish Republic and consistent with the union of Northern Ireland with the rest of the United Kingdom'.[136] Four times Powell asked Paisley to read out the list; four times Paisley refused.

A week later, during the last session on the Bill, Powell caused the greatest discomfort to the Government. He began a long speech with an attack on Labour, whose policy in favour of reunification had now, he said, become one of reunification without consent. He added that such compulsion was, in any case, the hidden agenda of the Bill, as dictated during the series of meetings Mrs Thatcher had had with her Irish counterparts in the preceding years, and would be effected through the federal constitution about which he had already warned. However, what he went on to say relied on more than just informed assertion.

'The Conservative party', he told the House, 'has learnt that in the Bill it is witnessing . . . prophesied subversion or inversion of its policy towards Northern Ireland.'[137] This was, he said, 'corroborated by information of which it is right the House should be put in possession. In doing so, I have no alternative but to implicate officials.' Powell reminded his colleagues of the conventions concerning the actions of officials under the British constitution; responsibility lay with ministers, since it was they, and not officials, who made the decision on whether to act upon the advice they were given. There was one exception to this rule, however: 'it arises where there is reason to suppose that the advice tendered to Ministers has not been *bona fide* and that the information supplied to them has been misleading or incomplete'.

Powell singled out an official in Prior's office, Clive Abbott, who he said had been more or less the 'onlie begetter' of the Bill. Powell wondered whether it had been Abbott's briefing that had led Prior to assure the House that the Bill would strengthen the Union. He then quoted from replies Abbott had given sixteen months earlier, in February 1981, to questions from an academic researcher with connections to the Unionists, Geoffrey Sloan. In response to the question 'is it true to say that between May and October 1979 there was consultation between the two governments' – the Republic's and the British – 'on Northern Ireland and that after coming to power the Tory Party changed its policies on Northern Ireland?' the official had apparently answered: 'Before the Conservative Party came to power in 1979 it had promised that local government functions would be returned to local councils. We had to tell them that it was just not on. In terms of the future government of Northern Ireland integration is a non-starter for two main reasons. First, we would automatically lose the co-operation we are getting from Haughey over border security. Secondly, we couldn't break certain undertakings we have given to the Irish government over the constitutional future of Northern Ireland.'[138]

Prior, stultified on the Treasury Bench, asked Powell to repeat the second reason he had given 'as I did not quite get it'. Powell obliged, and added that he had never doubted the Secretary of State's sincerity in the reasons he had given for not restoring proper local government – in that, being inevitably Unionist-controlled, such authorities would exacerbate conflict. He was sure, he went on, that if Prior had been told that to restore such a system would affect security policy 'he would manfully and plainly have told the House and his party "This is what we had intended to do; but we cannot do it because we are being blackmailed by the Irish Government." '[139] To make matters worse for Prior one of his own backbenchers, Lord Cranborne, jumped up and demanded an explanation.

Powell said Prior had been put in a 'false position' by his officials, as, possibly, had his predecessor Roy Mason, since the 'unbreakable undertakings' had apparently existed before the change of government. He called for a full investigation, and said Molyneaux, as leader of the party, would be placing all the evidence before the Prime Minister, given her direct responsibility for the civil service; and he argued that, since the Bill now appeared to have been founded on a false premise, it could not possibly receive the royal assent until the matter was cleared up. Julian Amery, one of the Conservatives' most senior backbenchers, called, unsuccessfully, for an immediate adjournment to give

Prior the chance to explain himself. However, Prior made his inquiries while the debate continued, and just over an hour later intervened to answer Powell's points.

Somewhat nervously, he put on record immediately the provisions of the 1973 Constitution Act, which had specified that 'without the consent of the majority of the people of Northern Ireland' there would be no change in the Six Counties' position as part of the United Kingdom. He had not yet seen the document from which Powell had quoted, but noted his implication that it was official in nature. 'So far as I am aware,' Prior stated, 'it was nothing of the sort.' It was, in fact, notes made by Sloan who 'took down his record of what he thought the junior official at the Northern Ireland Office had said'.[140] Sometimes, Prior continued, such researchers would check back that their remarks were accurate. That had not happened in this case. Therefore, there was no justification for what Powell had said.

Prior then stated categorically that 'there are no such undertakings as the right hon Gentleman accuses the Civil Service or a junior civil servant or the Government of having given'. He reiterated the doctrine that ministers make policy, and said, 'I do not even believe that it is correct to say that the gentleman concerned said those things, but even if he had said them it would have been quite wrong to believe that they were undertakings given by the Government, because they were not.'[141] He added that Haughey's objections to local govern-ment reform were well known, and that 'where a state has a land border with another state, and where we have had so much trouble with security, it is not necessarily wrong to take the views of that other state into consideration when considering the importance of security aspects. We would be extremely neg-ligent if we did not do so. On that point there is no problem.'

He then specifically attacked Powell for naming Abbott, whom Prior said he had not met until the previous February. Adding that he deplored Powell's behaviour, he continued: 'the right hon Gentleman has been pursuing his theory of a conspiracy for a long time against members of my Department. He has been wrong to do so.' He said he would take Powell's accusations seriously only if the text from which he had quoted was signed by Abbott, but Powell interrupted him and said he had told the House he was quoting from notes of replies, and that was what he would be showing to Prior. Prior, becoming angry, asked Powell what the status of the notes was. Powell told him, 'that is a matter that the right hon Gentleman must investigate'. At that, Prior exclaimed, 'That is disgraceful.' He demanded that Powell apologise to Abbott, but Powell made it clear that he was satisfied with Prior's admission 'that the Government have been influenced in their constitutional proposals for Northern Ireland by what they regarded would be the effect on cross-border security'.[142]

The Unionists were not, however, remotely satisfied by Prior's denial, and, after a stern protest from Molyneaux, Mrs Thatcher agreed to have the matter fully investigated. She asked the cabinet secretary, Sir Robert Armstrong, to do this. Armstrong met Powell on 25 October 1982, and Powell informed him of the nature of his information and of its source. A week later, on 1 November, Armstrong and Powell met again at Powell's request, this time in the presence of Ian Gow, and Powell questioned Armstrong about the results of his inquiry into the accuracy of the Sloan–Abbott conversations. He also made some startling further allegations about the behaviour of officials of the Northern Ireland Office, saying that officials had approached members of the Unionist party 'and had fostered discontent in order to forward the policies of the NIO'.[143] When Armstrong reflected that this was a 'very serious charge', Powell informed him that Merlyn Rees, when Northern Ireland Secretary, had confirmed that Foreign Office officials had acted as *agents provocateurs* in a similar way in the Province in 1975. Abbott, Powell suggested, was simply another NIO official playing deliberately in politics, but shaping policy accordingly, and his remarks to Sloan proved this.

Powell went on to assert that NIO officials had been in touch with the Government in Dublin without the knowledge of ministers; Armstrong denied this. In any case, the cabinet secretary added, it had not been any part of his brief from Mrs Thatcher to inquire into such a thing. As to what he had inquired into, he told Powell that Abbott had admitted that the conversations had happened and that the questions were as stated. 'However,' the official note records, 'there the agreement ended.' Abbott had told Armstrong that Sloan's account was 'inaccurate, incomplete, misleading and distorted'. Powell and Armstrong then argued about the accuracy of Sloan's notes, which Powell was forced to agree were 'fragmentary'. After much cavilling, Powell asked Armstrong whether Abbott denied the important point, 'such as that there had been an understanding with the Irish Government'. The cabinet secretary replied that Abbott did, indeed, deny this. He concluded that he could take no action against Abbott on the 'very limited evidence' of his wrongdoing, and added, for good measure, that the vice-chancellor of Sloan's university had suggested that Sloan was 'a man with strongly held political views, whose mind tended to filter what it received so that it accorded with his views'.

Armstrong – who would later achieve wider fame when admitting, in another context, that he had occasionally to be 'economical with the truth' – said that there was no evidence that Government policy had been changed on the initiative of officials in collusion with Dublin. In a later letter to Powell, Armstrong set great store by Sloan's failure to check his record of the conversations with Abbott at the time.[144] What shocked Powell most about Armstrong's remarks at their meeting was when he had said, in response to Powell's question about whether there might have been improper contacts with the Republic, 'I am agnostic.' Powell later noted that this was 'a reply which in all the circumstances must be regarded as highly remarkable'.[145] He formed his own conclusions, which was that the Government had altered its policy towards Ireland because of initiatives by officials such as Abbott, and in contradiction of its stated political intentions before the 1979 election. He spoke outside the Commons on what Abbott was reputed to have said, and in January 1983 revealed that he had, the previous August, invited Armstrong to sue him for defamation over what Powell had said about Armstrong; no proceedings were issued.[146]

Prior proceeded to set up the assembly, but Powell claimed that as part of the 'certain undertakings' there had been an understanding with the Irish that this would be linked with the Anglo-Irish Council, thus involving the Republic directly. He claimed that Prior knew he would not get the necessary legislation through Parliament if he admitted there had been such an agreement, so he denied its existence, which had led to protests from the Irish Government, and to Prior having to explain himself on a visit to Washington the previous week. Writing a few days after the IRA had let off two bombs in London, one in a bandstand in Regent's Park killing six members of the Royal Green Jackets, and another in Hyde Park killing two soldiers of the Blues and Royals and seven of their horses, Powell said, 'If you seek the true causes of Tuesday's carnage and of the deeds of blood which went before it, you will find them in the duplicity, the deception and the disaffection of persons in high places who have been responsible for the affairs of Northern Ireland.'

V

His profile having risen again after the Falklands episode, Powell was more in demand than ever as both speaker and writer. With the news editors, however, according less space on their pages to reports of his speeches, he made his voice heard more and more by writing on the features pages instead. The month after the Falklands conflict was resolved, Powell reviewed the history of the Government's conduct of Northern Ireland policy since 1979, noting how Neave's assassination had allowed a policy of initiatives aimed at creating power-sharing to be created, with the help of 'pressure' in the form of the murder of Lord Mountbatten and the Warrenpoint killings in August 1979. The Anglo-Irish summit of December 1980 had, he said, been the price of calling off the hunger strikes before Christmas, strikes renewed when Mrs Thatcher failed to put the same construction on the import of the talks as Charles Haughey had done. The strikes had ended again only when Mrs Thatcher had met FitzGerald the previous autumn, 'at which further and more definite terms of capitulation could be dictated'.[147] The Anglo-Irish Council had been the result, and Mrs Thatcher's attempts to play this down had led to the murder, earlier that year, of Robert Bradford.

That autumn speculation arose again about a reconciliation between Powell and his old party. For all his ferocious attacks on Northern Ireland policy, Powell's unqualified admiration for the conduct of the Falklands campaign had brought him back closely into line with the mainstream of the party. His approval of the economic course did not stint either. In a speech at Stevenage in early September 1982 he drew parallels between the Suez campaign, when the operation had been called off because of threats by the Americans to cut off loans to Britain, and the Falklands, when despite American opposition the war had been prosecuted to a successful conclusion – all because the Government had stopped worrying about the value of sterling. 'The fact that Britain, after two decades of deliberate debauchery, opted for honesty in its money and its public finance and stuck by its decision is a phenomenon no more lost on the outside world than the Union Jack at the top of the flagpole in Port Stanley.'[148]

However, in a speech to a meeting of the Conservative Political Centre in Cornwall on 16 October, Powell seemed finally to end all hopes that he might go back. He said it would be 'moral suicide' for him to do so, because for all the party's pursuit of Powellism in certain respects it was still as committed to Europe as it had been on the day he had left; and there were his obvious reservations about the Northern Ireland policy, which he defined as one designed to 'get Ulster out of the United Kingdom'.[149] The imminence of the elections to the ill-fated assembly was concentrating his mind on the policy. Speaking in Belfast on 12 October he advised a vote for the Official Unionists in the elections, and not for the 'Protestant Sinn Fein' of Paisley. Those, he claimed, were doing the bidding of the 'quislings', 'stoolpigeons' and 'running dogs' of the Northern Ireland Office, who, in collaboration with the Foreign Office, wanted a final solution to the Ulster question. Powell said the Paisleyites were anti-British and anti-Unionist, and were determined to use the assembly 'as a launching pad for unlawful action and rebellion'.[150] Paisley countered with a repudiation of 'the venomous hatred and the mad rantings of the arch anti-Unionist Enoch Powell'. Once the Commons returned in late October, Powell taunted Mrs Thatcher about her personal opposition to the assembly, saying the policy had been forced upon her against her will.

Shortly before the assembly was due to meet for the first time, in the second week of November, Powell used the debate on the Queen's Speech to reiterate his opposition to it. He referred to violence that had taken place since the passage of the Bill, adding that 'there can be few mistakes made by a Government, few disastrous pieces of legislation, that have been punished so swiftly as the Northern Ireland Act. Unfortunately, the punishment in this case falls not upon the guilty, but upon the innocent.'[151] He saw no future for the body: Paisley and his supporters were almost the only attenders at the assembly, the Official Unionists having boycotted it, and either they were to be allowed to run it on a straight majority, or they would have to submit to power-sharing. It was no basis for 'rolling' devolution, by which the assembly would eventually be given both power and responsibility. He made another plea for integration; he was not heard.

That autumn Powell disquisited elsewhere on less weighty matters, and in doing so gave the public a rare view of the man, stripped of his forbidding public persona, that only his friends and family usually saw. The death of the French actor, writer and director Jacques Tati, he wrote in *The Times*, caused him 'a pang of deprivation'.[152] He revealed that when, thirty years earlier, he had first seen one of the Hulot films, 'I started to laugh during the credits and never stopped until the end, wave after wave of delight like sparkling seawater foaming up a beach.' Tati's attraction to Powell was that he was 'a profound and generous, even an indulgent, observer of humanity and the human condition ... the ridiculous was never cruel or bitter, always kindly and comprehending.' Powell knew France and the French well, and Tati had captured and reproduced his own perception of them. Powell liked the way Tati's work showed 'the affection for children which is the mark of other great humorists', and how 'the interplay of the individual with the mass' was so absorbing to Tati. He called the five films 'as far as any work of art is complete, a complete commentary in terms of visualised humour upon French humanity and upon humanity in general. That is why they will not grow stale or become mere period curiosities.'

The Commons debated immigration on 11 November 1982, and once more Powell had an opportunity to put his own personal record straight. He was told by the Labour MP Sydney Bidwell that 'he must accept the responsibility, which he appears to deny, for recruiting medical staff during 1960 to 1963 when he was the successful Minister of Health. He recruited doctors from the subcontinent and nurses from the West Indies.' Now that twenty years had passed, Powell felt no need for restraint in answering an allegation that had become as boring as it was wrong. He told Bidwell that 'until July 1962 no distinction whatsoever could be made, and no limitation could be placed, on the entry of British subjects to this country. When the books are opened it will be found that, as a member of the Government, I strongly supported the measure taken to introduce such a possibility of control by the Commonwealth Immigrants Act 1962, and that I argued persistently for the narrowest possible use of the available scope for immigration under the 1962 Act.'[153]

Noting the steep rise in the Conservative party's popularity since the Falklands War, Powell deduced – correctly – that 1983 was sure to be an election year. He was at threat not from the nationalists or Republicans, but from the likelihood of one of Paisley's supporters splitting the Unionist vote and preventing him from winning. To help his campaign he wrote a series of high-profile articles in the press on the betrayal of Ulster by the Government, with particular reference to Prior's continued attempts to establish an assembly. He also kept up the pressure in the Commons, frequently reminding Mrs Thatcher of the casualties being sustained in the Province in the aftermath of the Northern Ireland Act. After an atrocity in early December at the Droppin Well discotheque in Ballykelly, which resulted in the deaths of sixteen people – including eleven soldiers – Powell, accompanied by cries of 'Disgraceful!', told the junior Northern Ireland minister John Patten that the carnage had been the direct fault of the legislation. He told Patten the Government was striving for a united Ireland, and when Patten denied he had any such policies, Powell said to him, 'May you be forgiven.'[154]

When, later that month, Powell saw rumours in the press that there was to be another Anglo-Irish summit at which Mrs Thatcher could meet Garret FitzGerald, who had just become Prime Minister, Powell wrote to her that 'I would consider myself at fault if I did not put on record that, so long as the present assembly exists, even the prospect, let alone the occurrence, of any such meeting with the Irish premier would have dire consequences in the province, where it would be seen by all as proof of intentions on the Government's part inconsistent with its commitments regarding the constitutional status of Northern Ireland.'[155] Mrs Thatcher replied that there were no plans for such a meeting 'at present', but if one took place there would be 'no foundation' for a supposition that it would affect the constitutional status of the Six Counties. 'The position will not be compromised in any meetings I may have with Dr FitzGerald.'[156]

Speaking in Downpatrick in early January, Powell outlined why a vote for an Official Unionist was essential, and why, in the new, enlarged representation of seventeen seats that would be in force at the election, the twelve or thirteen seats likely to be won by the Unionists would best be won by Official ones. He said that 'we can afford no longer the damage which has been inflicted upon the cause of Ulster and the Union by persons who, masquerading as Unionists, oppose us and lose no opportunity to attack and denigrate us . . . whose purpose is not, as ours is, the maintenance and entrenchment of the Union'. His main fear was that the assembly Prior wanted was the necessary autonomous institution that would allow Ulster to participate in a tripartite arrangement with the Republic and Britain, as a prelude to coercion into an all-Ireland state.

He still, though, had some sympathy with the Government. In an attempt to rebuild its own position, Labour put down a censure motion on the economy, debated on 19 January 1983. Powell once more came to the aid of his old party. He was still bemused as to why the Government made no mention of the huge current account surplus it was still running. There were now well over three million unemployed, industrial output was 20 per cent down on 1979, and yet the trading surplus was between £6 billion and £7 billion annually. The exchange rate had plummeted, and Powell said the only means of reducing it further – what Labour wanted – was to print money and sell it on the foreign exchanges.

He had spoken in earlier debates about the problems of technological change that reduced labour-intensiveness. Now, he argued that attention should be paid to how 'one of the greatest forms of wealth – leisure – can be introduced into our society without the damaging effect of its being concentrated in the form of involuntary leisure'.[157] He wanted to look at reform of the social security system that would prevent the 'fossilising of an obsolete pattern of work'. Above all, Britain had to reconcile herself to becoming a service rather than a manu-facturing economy; additional demands for such an economy would be made by the ageing population. He ended on what he meant to be an optimistic note: 'In this House and in this country, we are invited to contemplate what may be as large an impending revolution for the people of the United Kingdom as the industrial revolution was 150 years ago.'[158]

Before the election campaign, Powell continued to tour Conservative associ-ations -- where he was still welcome, despite denouncing aspects of party policy. At Aldershot on 4 February he said it was 'disgraceful' for the Government to keep Britain in the United Nations, when the UN had been a main cause of the Falklands War, by encouraging Argentina in her aspirations.[159] At Marlow on 18 February he attacked the Government's decision to lend its defeated Argentinian adversaries large amounts of money to save them from 'bankruptcy' – a concept he denounced.[160] At Southend on 26 February he questioned the moral and legal basis of British soldiers being included in a so-called peacekeeping force in the Lebanon; observing Mrs Thatcher's regard for President Reagan and his management of affairs, Powell was increasingly alert to British attempts to try to join in with America's self-appointed role as world policeman. His activities were stepped up because he could not understand why Mrs Thatcher was delaying the election: he freely admitted that, if he had been in her shoes, he would have had it immediately after the Falklands victory, the effect of which became a greater wasting asset with each day that passed.

As Labour started to enunciate its own new policies – which would culminate in a manifesto derided by the party's right wing as 'the longest suicide note in history' – one in particular provoked Powell: the promise to make foxhunting illegal. It had been nearly ten years since he had last ridden to hounds, but his passion for the sport had not abated. Ridiculing the idea, he observed in an article that angling was infinitely more cruel, and that it might be just as logical to ban the boiling alive of lobsters, or the eating of live oysters. Above all, he felt the ceremonial side to the sport reflected 'a side of our national character which is deeply antipathetic to the Labour party'.[161]

As the election neared, Powell's main preoccupation became, inevitably, his constituency. Boundary changes had removed substantial areas of Unionist support, with Powell's supporters believing that 55 per cent of the population was now Catholic. The fight would be arduous. Under Powell's influence, Moly-neaux was still keen to reject overtures from the DUP for a joint Unionist campaign, because of the deep differences over devolution and integration; and, once the poll was called for 9 June, Powell discovered that his old would-be adversary, Cecil Harvey, was planning to stand for the DUP against him. Justifying the decision to split the vote, Paisley himself repudiated Powell as 'a foreigner and an Anglo-Catholic'.[162] The assumption grew that Powell, defending a majority of 8,221, would lose. If it was any consolation, Paisley and his followers were given an almost universally bad press for their intransigence in having Harvey stand against Powell. It was to be an almighty struggle nonetheless.

Powell had made the most of what would – had he lost – have been his last opportunity to speak in the Commons, in a debate on 12 May on the extension of the 1974 Northern Ireland Act, by which direct rule was enforced. He was annoyed the debate was taking place so early – the annual renewal was not needed until 16 July, leaving plenty of time for the measure to be put through after the election. It hardly, he felt, came in the category of 'essential business' to be put through the House before the dissolution the following day. One possibility was that the Government wanted the measure through while Members' minds were on other things and thus unable to give it the requisite scrutiny; the other that it was worried there would be difficulty forming an administration after the election and before the 16 July deadline. Powell said this gave the lie to the 'brassy, hubristic self-confidence' with which ministers spoke of the forthcoming triumph.

He also used the speech to advertise a new militancy. He had, like his colleagues, had enough of the Province being ruled by Order in Council, and told the Government that 'we shall not go on indefinitely putting up with this order being renewed year after year'.[163] He rebuked Paisley for 'sniggering', which prompted his victim to ask Powell why during the Labour Government he had voted for the renewal of the Act he was now condemning, and Powell veered to a rare example of what was, by his elevated standards, vulgar abuse, saying that 'the hon Gentleman would do better to stay away and abuse this House and parliament from long range instead of coming here to make a mockery of it by his presence'.[164] It was a sign of the pressure Powell was feeling at the threat of the challenge from the DUP. He said, in conclusion, that the desire to renew the Order was a further sign that the Government was not serious about governing Ulster in a way that removed hope from the terrorists that their aims would be achieved; he asked, unsuccessfully, for it to be thrown out. Then, not content with his assault on Paisley, he made a series of bad-tempered interruptions in the speech of the Independent Unionist, James Kilfedder, who attempted to defend the assembly – a body which, as Powell shouted at him repeatedly, had nothing to do with the Order they were debating, and of which Kilfedder happened to be chairman.

He then made a series of interventions in a speech by Fitt, mild compared with the argument he had with Paisley, who spoke next. Paisley claimed apostolic succession from Carson and Craigavon, who, he said with limited historical accuracy, had 'rejected' the Westminster Parliament when it passed the Home Rule Act. He thanked God Powell had not been leading the Ulster people then, 'because if he had been they would have been sadly betrayed and sold to the enemy'.[165] He said Powell knew nothing about the people of Ulster, which prompted Powell to shout out, 'They elect me!'[166] Paisley then accused Powell of no longer being deputy leader of the Official Unionists – a post Powell had never formally held. Powell asked Paisley who, in that case, was deputy leader. A schoolboy argument flared across the chamber, which Powell attempted to resolve by proclaiming there was no deputy leader. Paisley then proclaimed, in his turn, that 'the right hon Gentleman has been sacked and the post declared obsolete'. The turmoil between the various wings of the Unionist movement could not have been more clearly illustrated on the very eve of one of its sternest tests.

In the campaign, Powell toured his constituency energetically and extensively, leaving few communities uncanvassed in his quest to maximise support. The belief in the media that he would lose simply drove him on all the harder, and he made more speeches and met more electors than in either of his previous campaigns. A strong constituency association, who had taken him to their hearts not just because of his sincerity but also because of his obvious fondness for the landscape and people of South Down, worked tirelessly for him. He also found time to concentrate on the wider issues of the national debate, notably the question of nuclear disarmament – which would play a significant part in the unilateralist Labour party's massive defeat. Speaking in Killyleagh on 2 June Powell asserted that no set of circumstances could be 'constructed or imagined' in which it would make sense for the United States to use a nuclear weapon. Two days earlier, at Downpatrick, he had repeated his 'suicide' theory, and restated his belief that no one was prepared to engage in such an act. This had won him unusual applause from the left, both politicians and the press. When some of his local supporters accused him of diverting from the main issues, Powell reminded them that the CIA's involvement in Northern Ireland brought the question of nuclear defence very much home to the people of South Down.

As he toured the area, Mrs Powell driving him in one car and another full of bodyguards trailing behind, Powell never believed he would lose. When he found, in village after village and housing estate after housing estate, indifference among the electors to what was happening, he was not deterred. He told journalists who came to see him that, like Queen Victoria, he was not interested in the possibilities of defeat. At a 300-strong rally in Rathfriland on the day before the poll he was still apparently tireless, microphone in hand, addressing the people to an accompaniment by seven local pipe bands. The fact that the bands had been brought to the rally was a sign to Powell's opponents of how concerned the Unionists were he might lose, and how every effort to mobilise had to be made. At the rally, other Unionist speakers used the fact that a vote for Harvey would, effectively, be a vote for a republican to try to squeeze out the extra votes: Powell and his supporters had had a rule during the campaign of ignoring Harvey, the message being disseminated that a vote for the DUP was a wasted vote.

In the end, Powell scraped home by just 548 votes out of a poll of more than 51,000. Eddie McGrady, his SDLP opponent, was second: his defeat was attributed to a lethargy born of a complacency that Powell was sure to lose, reflected in the fact that the SDLP had already booked the band and the venue for a victory celebration. Jeffrey Donaldson, Powell's agent, believed that a substantial number of the Catholic majority in the seat had not voted, because Powell's record as a constituency MP in helping them made it impossible for them to vote against him.[167] Harvey had taken 3,743 votes, which had just proved insufficient to remove Powell and give the DUP the satisfaction of seeing a nationalist elected. Donaldson felt Powell owed his victory to the non-sectarian way in which he had run not just his campaign, but all his affairs there since 1974. It was an asset for Powell to have remained a national figure not merely for the recognition it gave him, but because he did not seem to have an obsession just with the local, narrow issues of Northern Ireland that might otherwise have marginalised him. His agent noted that well over half the requests Powell received from constituents for help came from Catholics, some of whom registered Unionist sympathies.[168] It was also a help to Powell now, as it had not earlier been, that he was a Tory who objected to the way in which the Conservative party had continually betrayed Unionism.

The lustre was taken off Powell's victory by a grave personal blow just before the end of the campaign: Ted Curtis, his oldest friend, died. Their friendship had not declined with the years: Curtis and, after he was widowed, his sister Hester had been frequent holiday companions of the Powells. Living near the Powells in Belgravia, he was a frequent and welcome visitor. He had been one of the few people who would take Powell on in an argument, the length of their friendship meaning that Curtis was not intimidated, as most others were, by Powell. He would venture criticism, but always affectionately. Curtis's sister remembers them only once having anything resembling an acrimonious exchange. Curtis was one of the few people outside his family with whom Powell would relax, and with whom he would lower his guard, and admit to mistakes. He spoke to him of the Birmingham speech once in those terms, apparently hinting that the strategy might not have paid off.[169] He was the nearest Powell had had to a brother, and his loss was shattering. 'Gloom descended upon us,' his wife remembered. 'He was terribly cut up, and so was I.'[170] As well as losing so close a friend, Powell had lost a contemporary, which pointed up his own mortality. But his life had, paradoxically, just been given a new lease, and he would not be surrendering it yet.

19

EVENING

At least the huge Conservative majority – 144 over all other parties – seemed to suggest it would be some time before Powell had to defend his precarious hold on Down South. Safely returned to Westminster, he quickly found a source of mischief in Mrs Thatcher's decision to revive, after almost twenty years, the practice of granting hereditary peerages. She had recommended a viscounty for William Whitelaw, the Deputy Prime Minister, and for Powell's friend George Thomas, the retiring Speaker. Powell was amused by this reversion to tradition – 'does Mrs Thatcher cherish close to her heart, year after long year, just as if she were a Tory like myself, the determination that sooner or later she will resume hereditary creations, and then pounce when the irresistible merits of a Whitelaw open a back door to the achievement of her purpose?'[1] He suspected she had only made the award in order to keep Whitelaw sweet, and observed that the new viscount had no son to inherit his title.

However, he had a serious point. A precedent had been set. There was now nothing to stop further creations. 'Rejoice, rejoice, as somebody once said. Suddenly a second chamber, in the only possible form in which providence could have endowed us with one, has become defensible again in rational terms.' Powell looked back to 1969, recalling that he and Foot had found 'there is no alternative method of constituting a second chamber for the parliament of the United Kingdom that is not manifestly worse than the semi-hereditary composition which history has bequeathed to us'. He believed that Mrs Thatcher's action, whatever its motivation, had shored up an otherwise tottering part of the constitution. For the moment, his relations with the Prime Minister continued amicably. Although his main link with her, Ian Gow, had been promoted from his job as her parliamentary private secretary, he had been replaced by another of Powell's long-term admirers, Michael Alison. Gow, in a letter to his successor, told him that 'whenever he [Powell] wished to see the Prime Minister, she saw him. JEP never abused the direct access which the Prime Minister was always willing to accord to him. More frequently, he used to communicate to the Prime Minister through me.'[2] So, for the moment, it would continue.

Ted Curtis's funeral took place immediately after the election; Powell gave the address, reflecting on the fifty-two years of their close association. He touched upon the importance of Curtis to him. A reticent man – so reticent that Powell had not known until after his death that his friend had been mentioned in dispatches in 1940 – he was able to absorb himself in his interest in his friends' lives and careers, particularly Powell's. Like Powell, he had had an 'inexhaustible and voracious inquisitiveness about every aspect of human activity and thought'. Powell recalled Curtis's being there to meet him on his arrival in Cairo, and concluded, 'I know that I ought not; yet I half believe that when I get my posting to a more distant station than Egypt, I shall find waiting for me when I land, as kind as ever, as young as ever, as handsome as ever, my friend Ted.'[3] As he came down from the pulpit Powell stopped and placed his hand on his friend's coffin.

Life went on. Speaking in the debate on the address*, Powell found himself looking at a sea of unfamiliar faces, the product of the Conservative landslide: 'we raddled harridans of parliamentary life are apt to feel rather lost in an ocean of virginity'.[4] There was a new Speaker, Jack Weatherill, with whom Powell was on good terms, and to whom – as with his predecessor – he showed many kindnesses in never using his extensive knowledge of procedure to embarrass him.[5] Powell's speech on the address was on the nuclear deterrent. He had hoped it would have been debated before the end of the old Parliament; but it had not. Then, he had hoped it would be an issue in the campaign; it was not, except that unilateralism was prominent on the long list of issues on which Labour had lost. So he was determined to raise it now, and took as his text an answer Mrs Thatcher had given to his question of whether she would use the deterrent even as a last resort. She had said yes, but Powell said he did not believe that, when the crunch came, she would. Speaking admiringly of how she had carried the responsibility for the operation to retake the Falklands, he said, 'I do not believe that that Prime Minister would take a decision that would consign a whole generation to destruction in any conceivable circumstances whatsoever.'[6]

He sought to argue the point from history – that, had Britain possessed the deterrent in 1940, as she awaited the apparently inevitable German invasion, she would not have used it even then. Leaping forward, he said he believed that were the Warsaw Pact countries in the position the Germans had held, and were they to demand immediate surrender or the use of nuclear weapons against Britain, Britain would still pause. Powell suggested that, in those circumstances, the Russians would bomb – 'I am not attempting to be jocular' – Rockall. The enemy would then invite Britain to see what the weapon could do, and say the next strike would be on somewhere more strategically important and heavily populated.

'What would the United Kingdom do?' he asked. 'Would it discharge Polaris, Trident or whatever against the main centres of population of the Continent of Europe or in European Russia? If so, what would be the consequence? The consequence would not be that we should survive, that we should repel our

---

* The debate, usually lasting at least a week, on matters raised in the Queen's Speech at the start of a session of Parliament.

antagonist – nor would it be that we should escape defeat. The consequence would be that we would make certain, as far as is humanly possible, the virtual destruction and elimination of the hope of the future in these islands.' He did not believe, given that assessment, that anyone would use it. 'I would much sooner that the power to use it was not in the hands of any individual in this country at all.'[7]

He claimed that even if an invasion had already been launched against Britain – and no position could, he thought, be more like the last resort than that – it would entail similar consequences to launch a retaliatory nuclear strike. 'We should', he contended, 'be condemning, not merely to death, but as near as may be the non-existence of our population.' Therefore, with or without the nuclear deterrent, an invasion would take place. Therefore, there was no point in keeping it. He stated baldly that, after years of consideration, he had decided there were no 'rational grounds on which the deformation of our defence preparations in the United Kingdom by our determination to maintain a current independent nuclear deterrent can be justified'.[8] Michael Heseltine, the new Defence Secretary, intervened briefly towards the end of Powell's speech to seek clarification. Coming from a Tory, the policy Powell was enunciating left the modern Conservative party numb with incomprehension.

With so large a Government majority, the Unionists had even less scope for influence than the little they had enjoyed during the previous Parliament. Powell, though, had no view to retiring. At seventy-one he was as active in Parliament as ever, and as attentive to the demands of his constituents. His non-political side now began to assert itself more than for some years. On 17 July he wrote a long, reflective piece in the *Sunday Times* in which he unveiled his intellectual hinterland, and described what had always made him tick: his insatiable curiosity, his desire to find out how one thing in life came to fit with another: 'felix qui potuit rerum cognoscere causas,' as Lucretius had put it – 'Happiness is in the knack of getting to understand how one thing causes another.'[9] He described how this line of thought had diverted him more as he became older: 'Ordinary observations, events, experiences, which one had taken for granted as uninteresting and unproblematic, become absorbing puzzles.'

He explained how it fascinated him to travel in an Underground train – which he still did every day on the District Line between Sloane Square and Westminster – and simply try to imagine what had led to his fellow travellers being there, dressed as they were, looking like they did. At another level, he wrote of the Mountains of Mourne in his constituency, a favourite site for the weekend picnics. 'I enjoyed them passively, visually, uncritically,' he said.

> Then suddenly – I think it was when contemplating one day the complex geo-metric patterns of the stone boundary walls on a mountain side – I said to myself: 'There must be some comprehensible, discoverable explanation for all that.'

> From that moment the nature of my pleasure was altered and enhanced: the
> landscape was peopled with problems, doubts, questions, puzzlements. I became
> an enthusiastic amateur of field-patterns, settlement history, a dabbler in geology,
> a traveller in search of ever more answers to ever more questions.

This attitude would become typical of Powell's mind and outlook in the later
part of his life, and one reason why those who did not know him found him,
on almost any subject they cared to discuss with him, intellectually intimidating.
Most notably, he applied it on his many architectural excursions, always detecting an original Saxon church where Pevsner, or some other authority, told him
the building was, at the earliest, Norman. 'Even if, quite exceptionally, both the
concept and the execution turn out to be unitary – one period, one style, one
stone quarry – the unsatisfied curiosity still demands the reasons for the very
exception. Whose thought? Whose wealth? What purpose? And why, and by
what enchantment, the untouched survival?' It was not that Powell had, in his
old age, become a new sort of philosopher; it was that the constraints imposed
hitherto on his time for such interests and such curiosity had been lifted, and
he could not stop himself.

The new awakening of old interests had positive consequences. Two subjects
in particular obsessed him: the authorship of the plays of Shakespeare, which,
since he had read the corpus again in 1963–4, in preparing some talks for the
BBC World Service, he had believed could not have been the work of one man;
and the Greek New Testament, the first three Gospels of which he had re-read
in 1972, and which he was determined to subject to thorough and detailed
textual criticism. The second of these was already assuming its place as the
leading intellectual preoccupation of his declining years. It would be there,
ready and waiting for him to devote himself to it full-time, the moment he had
recovered from the blow of leaving Parliament four years later.

The crushing defeat of Labour in 1983 also effected a change in Powell's
outlook. The early signals were that, after that defeat, Labour would be reviewing
many of its policies, and it was soon made known that the hard-line decision
to leave the EEC was up for review. Addressing an anti-market meeting in
Eastbourne on 2 September, Powell said that the party was undergoing a 'moral
collapse'; his sympathies for it, sustained over nine years because of its view on
Europe, were now being reviewed too.[10] Without a mainstream political party
that followed his line, though, his own isolation would become more intense.
However, in one respect his views became ever closer to Labour, as he showed
in a speech in Somerset on 16 September, in which he attacked the new Foreign
Secretary, Sir Geoffrey Howe, for 'slavishly' following American policies, notably
in the Middle East, and thereby putting British lives in danger. He said Britain
had 'no moral right' to send troops to Beirut, and called for precisely the sort
of radical review of foreign policy Labour had been demanding, to avoid the

further 'Finlandisation' of Britain in respect of America – where sovereignty was only notional.[11]

Powell paid a guerrilla-warfare-style visit to the Conservative party conference in early October, to denounce the Northern Ireland policy. He warmed up for this with two attacks on Mrs Thatcher. First, at Torquay on 7 October, he criticised remarks she had made about the Soviet Union being an aggressive power, remarks Powell thought could be better applied to America. Russia's disastrous intervention in Afghanistan was the exception that proved the rule, he said, for otherwise 'no Russian soldier stands today an inch beyond where Russian soldiers stood in 1948'.[12] He added that 'if Russia is bent on world conquest, she has been remarkably slothful and remarkably unsuccessful'. Two days later, on television, he said Mrs Thatcher was 'too strident' and behaving as though she were still fighting the election. Powell advised her, in light of her massive victory, to indulge in 'more relaxation and greater magnanimity'.[13] However when, the following month, Mrs Thatcher followed a bilateral meeting with FitzGerald with a statement to the Commons in which she unequivocally ruled out joint sovereignty with the Republic over the Six Counties, Powell wrote to her that 'Perhaps more than anyone else, I am in a position to recognise the skill and the magnitude of the achievement represented by your statement and answers in the House today. ... I am deeply grateful to you.'[14] He might have been less grateful had he known, as Mrs Thatcher admitted in her memoirs, that once FitzGerald left she and her officials sat down and began to design proposals for the governance of Ulster that would result, two years later, in the Anglo-Irish Agreement.[15]

One particular action that autumn – the invasion by American marines of the former British colony of Grenada in the Caribbean – seemed to confirm most of his foreign policy views. To him, it showed the Commonwealth as a sham, and America's loyalty to her British ally a sham too. When the Commons debated the issue on 26 October Powell speculated upon the discomfort of Howe, having come to the House one day saying he was in the 'closest touch' with the Americans over Grenada, and believing they would not invade, but having to return the next and announce that the Americans had, after all, gone in.[16] The events had proved, Powell said, that the only yardstick by which the United States operated was that of her own interests. It was but the latest example – he cited others, such as the Yom Kippur War of 1973 and the action against Iran more recently, in which the Americans had acted entirely without consultation of their European allies.

Powell was worried by more than events in the Caribbean. 'At the invitation of Her Majesty's Government,' he reminded the House, 'the United States is about to station on the soil of the United Kingdom nuclear weapons which, we are told, will be used only after consultation and by joint decision with Her Majesty's Government. Anyone who, after the experience of the last few days and of recent years, imagines that the United States will defer to the views of the Government of this country is living in a dangerous fool's paradise. Anyone in office who entertains that illusion is in no position to serve the security of this country.'[17] He denounced the 'two mutually supporting delusions' that dominated America's thinking: the first was that, by the use of military force, it could 'create what it calls freedom and democracy by external military force'; the second, as he had said before, the 'Manichean struggle between the powers of light and the powers of darkness', the mantle of the leader of the power of light having fallen upon the United States.

These were, he said, 'nationwide' delusions 'held and expressed by Americans of every class and creed'. These were not beliefs that could involve much consultation with allies; and they were the reason why, if American weapons were stationed on British soil, the power of decision over their use should rest with Britain. If the Americans could not shake off their delusions, which prevented them from understanding the true condition of the world, then Britain should shake off her 'fondness' for America 'which has turned this country into something horribly resembling a satellite of the United States'.[18] He addressed a similar theme in the House a week later, when he called for the removal of British troops from the Lebanon, where their only function appeared to be to service what, again, the Americans – in what he termed a 'hallucination' – regarded as a vital part of their international interests.[19]

Writing in the *Daily Telegraph* on 22 November, he exposed the contradiction of how a British task force had not been summoned up to retake Grenada; and noted that the conferral of statehood on colonies at independence was entirely bogus. As he had said in his speech on the 1953 Royal Titles Bill, once the Queen's realm was divided there could be no pretence of sovereignty over territories within that division, as what had happened in Grenada now showed. He said, again, it was time to stop the charade of the Commonwealth, whose biennial conference was about to open in Delhi. 'Some time,' he wrote, 'there will have to be an end to this make-believe. Some day the Queen's ministers will have to stop advising her to undertake another and yet another journey through the phantasmagoria of cheering crowds and empty ceremonies which mock the memory of a power that was but is no longer.'[20]

Similar thoughts compelled him, the following month, to urge Britain to stop trying to reunify Cyprus, but to let the Turks there form their own country if that was what they wanted. He suspected the need to retain bases on the island was what motivated Britain, but Powell argued that these could be ditched as they were no longer necessary to British interests; it was now just a dream that Britain could be a military power in the Middle East. For this, as before, he blamed the American influence over the Foreign Office. However, there was one American activity that December that he very prominently cheered: the decision to withdraw from UNESCO, on the ground that America had been financing international propaganda campaigns contrary to her own interests. Powell hoped this would be another occasion where Britain would follow America's lead, and would take the principle further, applying it to the United Nations itself.

December 1983 saw the marriage of the Powells' younger daughter, Jennifer. Of the two girls she was the more like her father, having been to Cambridge to read not classics, but history, and having then worked in Australia. The father–daughter relationship was, as with that with Susan, exceptionally close. The professor who had shunned women found himself in a house with three of them, all exceptionally strong characters, as if as a form of divine retribution. Susan had always managed to conduct herself in a way that avoided attracting her father's disapproval, but Jennifer had been less co-operative. During her teens Powell had teased her remorselessly about her various acts of rebellion, pointing out that by rebelling she was simply being drearily conventional; but he had also sought to coach her in her 'A' level Latin and Greek. Her marriage was a proud moment for him, and it caused him great pain when, within a few years, it ended in divorce. However, he would be cheered by her second marriage to Michael Lavin in 1991, and particularly by the two grandchildren, Julia Margaret and James John Enoch, born in 1992 and 1996.[21]

After Christmas Powell devoted himself mainly to Ulster. In Downpatrick on 5 January 1984 he said that FitzGerald shared the IRA's aims for a united Ireland, and was 'not so unobservant that he will have failed to notice how it was terrorism and violence that first got him co-operation from the British in making political progress towards achievement of this object'.[22] This, though, was mild compared with other comments he made that weekend: he said in an interview that the CIA had been responsible for the assassination of Mountbatten, and that the two murdered MPs, Airey Neave and Robert Bradford, had both been victims of an American conspiracy.

Powell claimed that his evidence came from members of the Royal Ulster Constabulary to whom he had spoken. He said the police were convinced 'of the effective existence of a policy and motivation outside and above the IRA and INLA', which had led to 'a series of assassinations which can be distinguished from run-of-the-mill murders of persons connected with the security forces'.[23] This developed a point he had made in the Commons on 8 December 1983, during the debate on the Emergency Powers Act, when he had claimed that the former permanent secretary at the Northern Ireland Office, Sir Kenneth Stowe, had told him that the series of ministerial meetings between the British and Irish governments had arisen out of a decision taken to improve communications directly after Mountbatten's murder. All the initiatives, and all the bloodshed since, stemmed, Powell had argued, from that important concession, and the impression it had created that Britain had been ready to do business about the future of the Six Counties.

He added that such murders were designed to create the maximum 'high level political impact'. They had urged on the Prime Minister in her series of meetings with three successive Irish leaders, and in the search for a compromise that would lead to a 'federal' Ireland; and Powell reiterated his earlier claim that American strategic fears, bred of uncertainty about the future of their bases in Britain and on the continent and their desire to have bases in a united Ireland, had been behind the events. Merlyn Rees, the former Northern Ireland Secretary, was but one prominent politician who did not immediately dismiss Powell's claims, but said the Government should make a statement about the operations, if any, of American intelligence in Northern Ireland.

Powell found a further opportunity to attack the Americans a few days later, in a speech at West Bromwich, in which he referred to the plans for the Group of Seven economic summit, to be held in London in June. He claimed that event was 'dangerous nonsense', on the ground there was no such thing as a world economy. But, above all, it was a vehicle designed to promote 'personal publicity of leading political figures', notably President Reagan, who faced re-election in the autumn. 'This nation is an island,' he said, 'and islands, especially islands of sanity, have no business to be attending, let alone hosting, international economic conferences.'[24]

It was a return to one of his most reliable causes of outrage that really put Powell back in the spotlight. At Leicester on 20 January he criticised the Queen's Christmas Broadcast of the previous month, in which she had appeared to praise the regime of Mrs Gandhi in India. He said the broadcast and other recent pronouncements 'suggest that she has the affairs and interests of other countries in other continents as much, or more, at heart than those of her own people'.[25] He added that 'even here, in the United Kingdom, she is more concerned for the susceptibilities and prejudices of a vociferous minority of newcomers than for the great mass of her subjects whose stake and title in this kingdom is coeval with her own'. The Queen could act only on the advice of her ministers, but Powell said that those ministers 'have seemed afraid for her to speak as a Christian monarch to a Christian people or as a British monarch to the British people'. Such advice, he said, was 'pregnant with peril for the future'.

His was not the first criticism of the speech. Some right-wing Conservative MPs had got there before him, but, lacking his clout, had not caused the stir he now did. Much of the surprise among his colleagues stemmed from the fact that Powell, as a Privy Councillor, was in an unusually delicate position from which to make such an observation. He himself, however, referred to this in his speech, saying it was his 'duty' to point out that 'the place of the Crown in the affections of the people would be threatened if they began to sense that the Crown was not in that unique and exclusive sympathy with the people of the United Kingdom as their mutual dependence ought to imply'. By apportioning blame where, he felt, it constitutionally belonged, Powell had avoided any insult to the Queen, but her press secretary immediately countered with the observation that, as the message was to all the peoples of the Commonwealth, it had not been formulated on the advice of one government, and was a 'personal' message. One unnamed source, apparently from the Foreign Office, told the *Observer* that from what he knew of what traffic the Government had had with the Palace on these matters Powell's remarks were 'wicked, mischievous and frankly loony'.[26] Even one of his admirers, John Biggs-Davison, said it would have been preferable had Powell tendered his views to the Queen on Privy Council terms, rather than in public.

Powell was more concerned by what he felt to be the constitutional aspects of the claim that the Queen had not acted on ministerial advice in delivering her message. He even said he was considering making a second speech on the implications of some of the comments made about his original remarks. In fact, later that week, he expressed his further reservations in an article in *The Times*. He said the consequences of the assertion that the Queen did not speak on the advice of her ministers when addressing the Commonwealth were 'peculiar and alarming'.[27] He could discuss this matter without impugning the Sovereign because 'ministerial advice that ministerial advice is not requisite is also ministerial advice, for which ministers must take responsibility and stand question'. He conceded that there were difficulties in operating the convention that the Queen only spoke anywhere on the advice of the ministers in that place, if she would have to speak on the advice of two or more lots of ministers at once, as in the Christmas broadcast. However, when the Queen addressed citizens of a republic, such as India, she could be expected to act constitutionally not on the advice of that republic's ministers, but on the advice of her own in the United Kingdom. However, if she spoke as head of the Commonwealth, and the Commonwealth had no government and therefore no ministers, she would have to speak without responsible advice.

This problem, he reminded his readers, was just the sort he had warned of in 1953: the 'make-believe' of the Commonwealth was exposed when the Queen tried to speak to countries over which she did not reign. As a result of Powell's warnings not being heeded, he said the monarch had been placed in a position that was 'constitutionally inexplicable and indefensible'. The blame had to lie with ministers who had, in order to make Britain feel better about losing her Empire, invented the 'chimera' of the Commonwealth. The fact that it continued – and that the Queen continued to be put in this embarrassing predicament – was also the fault of her ministers. The following weekend, Powell announced that of the letters he had received on the subject, a proportion of eleven to one was in favour of his view.

In February the Commons debated the report of the inquiry into a mass escape from the Maze prison on 25 September the previous year; and, during his speech, Powell read out evidence from a secret document, from prison records, comprising a log of how a Northern Ireland Office official and a Catholic clergyman, acting as an intermediary, had tried to end the hunger strikes of 1980 and 1981. He said the meetings had been designed to come up with a list of concessions which the clergyman could put to the strikers to buy them off; and Powell, in leaking the document to *The Times*, said it had manifestly been successful. He attacked Prior for his admission that he had no idea how low morale was among staff in the Maze. It was, Powell said, his job to know such things. He added that Prior had had a duty to provide leadership to such people, and had conspicuously failed.

It was, he said, the 'buying off' of the hunger strikes that had had so bad an effect on morale. They had, he continued, been bought off at two meetings Mrs Thatcher had had with Irish prime ministers in 1980 and 1981, each hunger strike ending a matter of days beforehand. Powell said he accepted that the second hunger strike – in which ten Republican prisoners had died – had been brought to an end in a fashion far less discreditable than the first. But, nonetheless, both had been bought off, and morale in the prison service had collapsed under this political interference in operational activities. Prior would not take this, and intervened to tell Powell that he 'must desist from building up conspiratorial theories that have no grounds of truth whatsoever'.[28] Powell snapped back, 'It is not I who am in the dock for being unaware of what was going on.' Without specifically calling for his resignation, he told Prior – who had, he later revealed in his memoirs, offered to resign immediately after the debacle – that he should accept responsibility for what he had done, or failed to do.

On 9 March he referred once more to the 'obtuse and irresponsible' policy of the United States, this time in the Middle East. Speaking at Warwick, Powell was concerned that the Royal Navy, patrolling in the Gulf, might be engaged there with American forces, so concerned that he had asked the Prime Minister to specify the Government's intentions. Mrs Thatcher had told him that no guarantee could be given, as the Government would always act to protect Britain's interests. These interests, as she defined them, extended to co-operating with the Americans to protect that part of the world and the oil supplies for the West. Powell could not understand from whom this part of the world was being protected, or, indeed, what that 'part of the world' meant. Iran and Iraq, fighting a war among themselves, did not seem a problem; and Russia was certainly not interested. He dismissed, too, the notion that the oil supplies were vital to Britain. 'In fact,' he said, if those supplies were cut off, 'Britain would be "quids in" on the rise in price that would still further increase our already disgustingly large surplus on current trading accounts.'[29] Powell said that if Mrs Thatcher had been straight about which part of the world would actually be dis-advantaged – Japan – she would have had 'half the House of Commons chort-ling'. He said that, as usual, Britain was taking the view she did because of the 'obsessive belief that Britain is necessitated to "join with American forces" upon demand whatever they are doing and wherever they are doing it'.

As he neared his seventy-second birthday, Powell was still in robust health, but that April was put in bed by an attack of vertigo that affected his balance, due to an inner-ear infection. It kept him out of action for more than a week. As soon as he was fit again he joined the battle over the miners' strike, which had just started, condemning the Archbishop of York for 'moral and – I must risk saying it – religious bankruptcy' for telling the Government that pits should be exhausted before they were closed. Powell argued that it was immoral to urge miners to produce coal that cost more to mine than it could be sold for. 'The immorality is to attempt, by ecclesiastical authority on his grace's part, by physical coercion on the miners' part, to compel our fellow men to waste their brains and labour so that we may continue to waste our own.'[30]

In May he stepped up his campaign to enforce a better security policy in Ulster. Speaking in his constituency on 26 May he made remarks interpreted as urging Britain to take direct military action within the Irish Republic in order to counter terrorism. 'The killing continues,' he said with reference to the murder of a UDR sergeant, 'because the Irish Republic enables and aids it to continue. It continues because Britain, along with the United States and Europe, enables and aids the Irish Republic to enable and aid it to continue.' Saying that the Republic was allowing a terrorist campaign in the Province to be conducted from her territory, Powell demanded that Britain 'treat the Republic exactly as any other nation would treat a neighbouring state that behaved in that way'. He admitted that such an attitude would not appeal to the Americans or to 'our ex-enemies (how "ex" are they really?)' in the EEC', but he had a blunt message for them: 'get lost'.[31]

Before the Commons rose for its summer recess it debated a censure motion against the Government for its handling of the miners' strike, then in its twenty-second week. Powell said he felt the public were 'appalled' by what they saw, 'not so much by the duration of the strike, the severe losses, both private and public, that it is inflicting or even the scenes of violence so frequently presented to the viewing public as by the absurdity and the futility of the dispute'.[32] He said the miners were not fools, and should be capable of understanding the economic realities. They should all, he claimed, be aware that their future livelihoods were bound up with the modernisation of the industry. There had been, he said, 'a colossal failure of leadership' on the part of the management that had brought about the dispute.[33] While he condemned this – Powell believed that the modernisation could have been handled successfully, which suggests a misunderstanding on his part of the political agenda of Arthur Scargill, the miners' leader – he stuck to his view that uneconomic pits had to be closed.

Even one as adept at securing publicity as Powell found, as the 1983 Parliament wore on, that it was not so easy as before. The main issue on which he now campaigned – the end of direct rule and its replacement by the full integration of Ulster into the United Kingdom – was of almost no interest to the public. For the second half of 1984 his profile was lowered, though he worked assiduously to keep up Unionist pressure on the Government to make no concessions to nationalist feeling. In July Powell had been unsettled by Prior's assertion that a parliamentary tier would be established in the Anglo-Irish Council, his latest initiative. He did not doubt that representatives from Ulster would be found who would serve on such a body, and 'thus will come about what the majority in Ulster have always feared and always rejected – Ulster representation in a Dublin Parliament. That reality will not be altered by the pretext that the body represents the British Isles, nor concealed by the pretence that Ulster's participation is voluntary.'[34] He warned that, if this happened, Unionists 'will see themselves back again in 1912 [at the time of the passage of Asquith's Home Rule Bill]; and they will not be mistaken. Their anger and their sense of betrayal will be made manifest in unforeseeable but violent ways.' Powell wrote to Mrs Thatcher on 18 July spelling this out. He requested a meeting with her, and she saw him just over a week later.

They met alone, without officials or even Michael Alison being present, but Powell made a note of the meeting directly afterwards. Mrs Thatcher told him she had been 'shocked' by his letter, having not realised how differently the process was perceived by Unionists.[35] Powell told her he had heard facilities were being provided for NATO to conduct surveillance in Irish waters, but Mrs Thatcher said she knew nothing of this. She added that she had never understood why the Americans were so interested in Ireland as a strategic base, given the country's historic neutrality. She also reaffirmed that the Anglo-Irish Council was not intended to threaten the Union. But Powell argued that obtaining such a body had been part of the Republican strategy since the Free State was formed, and later sent her a historical memorandum in which he sought to outline the precedents. The Prime Minister asked Powell whether anything could be done in Ulster, or whether the issue was 'one of the impossibles'. He told her that the situation was improving, that the two communities could and did get on, as he saw for himself in his constituency; and he implored her to have the Government abandon talk of 'political progress', which made his supporters feel the Union was threatened. When Mrs Thatcher countered that many Unionists wanted Stormont, Powell said this was out-of-date intelligence, and blamed it on the 'generation gap'. Writing to her afterwards, he told the Prime Minister that he had 'valued the privilege' of their talk, and that he intended to take up her invitation to renew it.[36]

The next great 'event' in Anglo-Irish relations was the attempt by the IRA to kill Mrs Thatcher and the cabinet when bombing the Grand Hotel at Brighton during the 1984 Conservative party conference. Powell would subsequently regard this incident as the crucial application of pressure that tipped the Government over into the concessions of the following year's Anglo-Irish Agreement;

but at the time Mrs Thatcher's response to it impressed him. He had been about to send her another letter warning of the possibly violent reaction by Unionists if a parliamentary tier were included in the Anglo-Irish Council, and told her, 'I find that my draft ended with the words: "A million and a half British citizens are in your hands." After what has happened, they will know that they have more reason than ever to rely on your courage and insight.'[37]

A categorical announcement by Mrs Thatcher at the end of November 1984 that Ulster would remain in the Union was taken by him to mean the final end to the point of direct rule – which, he continued to maintain, was to create the transitory state in Ulster that would lead to Ulster's participating in an all-Ireland state. Powell wrote to her again on 21 November to say, 'I would be very remiss if I did not express to you my personal gratitude and admiration for the stand you took at the Anglo-Irish summit. I realise something of what it must have involved; but you can rest assured that you have opened the way to a better future for Ulster and an end to the recurrent disasters of the last fifteen years. If that happens, it will be you whom Ulster has to thank.'[38] He did, however, warn her about a phrase in the communiqué issued after the summit, concerning 'two communities' in Ulster: he pointed out that there would be no problem recognising two identities in Ulster, but both those identities had to be allowed their full expression under British sovereignty. It was not possible, he warned, to have one identity that recognised that authority, while another was allowed not to do so. Speaking at Warrenpoint on 30 November, he wrote off the chances of Labour's acting in Ulster's interests, but, encouraged by Mrs Thatcher's statement, said that 'it is through the Conservative party that those Ulster electors who would be supporters and members of the Conservative Party in Great Britain must find a way to participate in the politics of their country'.[39]

These were the most supportive remarks Powell had made in public about the Thatcher administration since the Falklands, nearly three years earlier. They were interpreted as a sign that the Official Unionists might reapply for the Conservative whip. However, as so often, Powell acted quickly to stress his independence. Speaking on 5 December, barely a week later, he said Mrs Thatcher's insistence that funds for education be diverted towards the sciences in the interests of increasing national prosperity was the way to an 'inhuman and barbarous state'. He added that learning was 'to the glory of God' and not intended to be useful.[40]

The year ahead would be one in which Powell's political activities were to resume something like their former place in the spotlight, for two reasons. The second, chronologically, was the startling development in Anglo-Irish relations that autumn, the preparations for which Powell and Molyneaux were alerted to just after Christmas 1984; the first Powell's decision, when drawn favourably high in the ballot for Private Members' Bills, to announce that he would introduce a measure to outlaw embryo experimentation, a scientific technique then being developed. A committee under Dame Mary Warnock, the Mistress of Girton, had been convened during 1984 by the Government to look into questions of human fertilisation and embryology; and, after Powell had announced his intentions, health ministers said the Government would introduce a comprehensive Bill in the next session of Parliament, in the light of the committee's recommendations.

Powell's Bill was published on 1 February 1985, and was immediately criticised by specialists not merely for its proclaimed intent of ending experimentation, but also because, they claimed, the obstacles it would create to test-tube baby treatment would mean the technique would virtually cease to be possible. It was also said that experimentation would enable the avoidance of congenital abnormalities in children. A second reading was set for 15 February, and before that MPs were bombarded with vast petitions from anti-abortion and pro-life groups all over the country. At the beginning of the week of the debate, two million signatures had been collected. On the day before the debate Cardinal Hume, the Archbishop of Westminster, wrote to every MP putting the weight of the Roman Catholic Church behind Powell. The Government itself decided to adopt a position of neutrality, though the two ministers most responsible, Norman Fowler, the Secretary of State for Social Services, and Kenneth Clarke, the Minister of Health, both stated that they would oppose it.

Moving the second reading, Powell said the Bill had 'a single purpose ... to render it unlawful for a human embryo created by *in vitro* fertilisation to be used as the subject of experiment or, indeed, in any other way or for any other purpose except to enable a woman to bear a child'.[41] He assured the House that the Bill was drawn up in such a way as not to affect the rights to fertility treatment of women having difficulty conceiving. What he wanted to stop was experimentation, and he explained why: 'When I first read the Warnock report I had a sense of revulsion and repugnance, deep and instinctive, towards the proposition that a thing, however it may be defined, of which the sole purpose or object is that it may be a human life, should be subjected to experiment to its destruction for the purpose of the acquisition of knowledge.'[42] The predicament had been made worse for him by Warnock's suggestion that responsibility for allowing these acts should be passed from the normal legislative body – Parliament – to a committee of 'experts'.

Powell said he was not going to attempt to settle a definition of an embryo that would seek to answer the question about when a human being became a human being. 'That question', he observed, 'is unanswerable, because it goes to the heart of the great unanswerable question: what is man?' He accepted that those with the most intensely motivated objections were the deeply religious, but he said he would make his plea in the same way 'if I were addressing an assembly of atheists in an atheist country'.[43] The objections were more fundamental even than religion: 'this is the recognition by a human society of its obligations to itself, to future generations and to human nature'. He did not doubt that much valuable information could be gleaned if experiments were permitted, but said he hoped the House would decide that 'the moral, human and social cost of that information being obtained in a way that outrages the instincts of so many is too great a price to pay'. He concluded with a plea to his colleagues that they should 'uphold and assert the dignity of man by giving the Bill a Second Reading'.

As Powell had risen in the Commons that Friday morning to move the second reading, women from the Revolutionary Communist Party in the public gallery hurled contraceptives down on to the benches below. Four were arrested and locked up for the day in the Commons' cells. At the end of the debate Powell and his supporters won by 238 votes to 66, a majority of 172; and a leading Catholic on the Conservative benches, Norman St John-Stevas, suggested that the Government should try to reach some sort of compromise with Powell by seeking to draft some of its own proposals on to the Bill. Since Powell's intentions went further than the Government had been planning, and since Powell had pre-empted that legislation with apparently massive support, the Conservative leadership was faced with a dilemma. The scientific community, however, was quite clear and apparently united in its attacks on the measure, the ferocity of which were stepped up immediately the size of Powell's victory was clear.

II

That same week was also the tenth anniversary of Mrs Thatcher's election as leader of the Conservative party, and the occasion provoked a tribute from Powell of, by his standards, exceptional warmth. Referring to the miners' strike, then in its eleventh month and crumbling, he said it provided a 'very good illustration of the skill and determination, the sheer courage and willpower of the Prime Minister. She has sustained through difficulties a quite definite purpose, an intelligible purpose, and a self-evidently right purpose from the point of view of the economy and of the coal industry itself.'[44] His only reservation was that Mrs Thatcher, as a woman, could not speak to the miners about the irrationality of their leadership and its actions in the way a man would have done, 'as one man talks to other men, as one soldier talks to other soldiers'. The antagonism between Arthur Scargill, the leader of one of the miners' unions, and Mrs Thatcher was, he thought, accentuated by the gender difference, and the two opponents were harder to reconcile as a result.

Powell also described Mrs Thatcher as 'somebody who is in her own style a consummate politician. Political action, that is her business. And she is an artiste in the way she goes about it.' In her first five years, he added, she had laid down her principles 'clearly, decisively, dramatically', and he said, 'I marvel at the patience, as well as the skill, with which she lived more or less unscathed through those years.' However, these were generous sentiments that the shock of the Anglo-Irish Agreement would cause him more than to retract later in the year.

Until the middle of March Powell sat on the committee that examined his Bill, whose proceedings concluded with a twenty-hour all-night sitting that ended at 1 p.m. on 14 March. He and his supporters won all twenty-seven votes on the Bill, and expressed their confidence that the measure would become law by the summer. The Bill's opponents, however, immediately stated their determination to fight it to the bitter end, if necessary trying to ensure it ran out of parliamentary time. Powell's thirty-five years in the House left him equal to such a challenge. 'Something will give way,' he said after the completion of the committee stage, 'but it will not be me.'[45]

By the time the Commons reassembled after Easter, his opponents were formulating their tactics. Their plan was to slow up proceedings on other Private Members' Bills so that there would not be time to conclude business on Powell's. No guarantee of parliamentary time had been made by the Government, despite the great preponderance of Conservative MPs being in favour of it. In the weeks before the report stage, scheduled for 3 May, Powell took the opportunity to speak in the country on other matters, making a call for withdrawal from the Common Agricultural Policy. He was in good spirits. On 20 April, addressing the Monday Club, he said, 'If you think the Conservative Party would kill its own grandmother for votes you are wrong. In fact, the Conservatives would kill the old girl and eat her afterwards.'[46]

When the report stage of the Unborn Children (Protection) Bill took place its opponents lighted upon a preceding measure, whose aim was to allow seven days for drivers stopped by the police to produce their documents rather than five, and sought to spin it out for much of the morning. By the time Powell's Bill was reached there was little time left to debate it, and as his opponents were outlining their case for an amendment he leaped up and demanded a division. His opponents objected but the Deputy Speaker, Harold Walker, agreed with Powell. Tempers were lost and a group of Powell's opponents surrounded the Speaker's chair and argued with Walker; one of them banged his fist and broke the chair. What little time remained for parliamentary discussion was mostly spent on points of order of varying degrees of legitimacy. The Bill seemed to have been talked out; it was not clear that any more parliamentary time could be found for it.

Powell said afterwards that he trusted the Government would, in the light of the evidence of the Bill's strong support in the House, find time for it to pass through all its stages. However, at the next Prime Minister's Questions after the scenes at the report stage, Mrs Thatcher said she would not alter the Government's practice of not making time specially available to Private Members' Bills.

This was not, though, to be the end. A Conservative MP, Andrew Bowden, who had won the right to have a Bill debated on 7 June, announced that he would use the time to help the Powell Bill through its remaining stages. This was immediately criticised by Government business managers, who hoped they had buried the problem. Bowden had tabled a motion saying the Commons should not adjourn at its usual time of 2.30 p.m. on the Friday but should continue until all amendments on Powell's Bill had been discussed – which, as there were twenty of them, could have taken some time. The Leader of the House was Powell's close friend John Biffen, who was not prepared to do anything to prevent the motion being debated if the Speaker adjudged it in order. However, because of the precedent such a motion would set – it could have led to Bills being debated well into the weekend – Biffen announced that he would argue for the motion to be voted down.

On 7 June a procedural device even more fiendish than Bowden's was used to thwart Powell and his supporters. Dennis Skinner, the left-wing Labour MP and an opponent of the Bill, rose at the start of business and moved the writ for a pending by-election at Brecon and Radnor. Speeches on this writ lasted throughout the morning; then a filibuster was instituted on further petitions that had been presented, leaving barely half an hour for Powell's Bill. The proceedings ended without a vote at 2.30 p.m.; the chances of the Bill passing into law were now extinguished, and Powell's supporters announced they would be pressing the Government to incorporate the Bill's provisions into its own legislation. It was a vain hope.

Powell accepted the inevitable and resumed a political life beyond the issue that had dominated his life for six months. The night the Bill's proceedings ground to a halt he went to Bristol and, referring to the call by black activists for black sections within the Labour party, said it was but a matter of time before blacks called for a quota system of representation in Parliament. He drew a distinction between the call from an ethnic minority for representation within the party and that historically demanded by, for example, trade unions: 'A black section is different in kind from any other element in a party; its members cannot alter their identification though all who share that identification are under a moral and social pressure to adhere to it. It thus becomes a peculiarly effective force in any body that operates by majority decision; for it is an element which does not wax or wane with the ebb and flow of opinion or the influence of circumstance or opinion.'[47]

He also turned back to economic matters, rebuking the Chancellor, Nigel Lawson, for allowing growth in the money supply to push inflation up to 7 per cent. The Government had borrowed more than it had needed and had lent the surplus to the banks, who in turn had used it to expand credit. 'Insistence on sound money or its synonym, honest money, is not an optional item on an *à la carte* menu of desirables,' he said. 'It is not an objective which can wisely or safely be diluted with others, for the simple reason that no other objectives are acceptable which require inflation to be artificially maintained, let alone created.'[48] In the debates on the Finance Bill earlier in the session, Powell had been annoyed by what he thought the arrogant statement that the Government had brought inflation down, and planned to bring it down further. As a monetarist, he agreed with the presumption that these things were within the Government's power; but he had asked why, if the Government was now admitting it had this power, it did not strive to bring inflation down more quickly than it planned.

Throughout the summer, Powell's agitation at the diplomatic toing and froing between the British and Irish governments led him to suspect that a deal was being cooked up. Early in July 1985 he said Mrs Thatcher and President Reagan had failed to live up to their promises to beat terrorism in condoning the status of the Irish Republic as a 'safe haven' for terrorism.[49] A month later, at Kilkeel in his constituency, he said that the Government acted in this way because 'a power which it regards as mightier than itself – a power whose shoes it is continually bending down to lick – demands that it shall be seen to be purchasing the Republic's goodwill not to Britain but to the Western Alliance by the old, old device of betraying Ulster'. He emphasised that no deal could be done for any purpose, let alone to appease the Americans. He and Molyneaux wondered whether to seek a briefing on what was going on, on Privy Council terms, but agreed it would compromise them in terms of the action they could then take.

Before that question could move to its denouement, the worst consequences of immigration manifested themselves again, in riots that autumn in Birmingham and London. Those in the Birmingham suburb of Handsworth in the second week of September came, Powell admitted, as 'no surprise' to him: after all, he pointed out, they had happened 'not a mile and a half away from the very spot' where he had spoken of a nation 'busily engaged in heaping up its own funeral pyre. Sooner or later the torch would be put to that pyre.'[50] He reasserted his belief that civil war in England was the obvious likely result of what had been allowed to happen, and that only a massive repatriation could have avoided it; and it was still not too late to implement that policy.

A week later he made the case even more clearly, in a speech at Birkenhead to Conservative women, prompting the Labour deputy leader, Roy Hattersley, to describe him as 'the Alf Garnett of British politics'.[51] Liberal Conservatives were upset that Powell had used a party occasion to make his speech, bringing, as they saw it, embarrassment on the party he had left eleven years earlier. Powell had gone back, as often before, to the statistics, and found that 30 per cent of births in Birmingham, Bradford and inner London between 1981 and 1983 had been to mothers of New Commonwealth or Pakistani descent. In Leicester and Blackburn the figure had been even higher, at 33 per cent. He challenged Mrs Thatcher to repudiate his views, or to act on them, adding, 'The time of truth is coming at last for those who sit in the seats of authority. If they can dissent neither from my projections nor from my judgment of that future Britain they cannot now, with a shrug of the shoulders and a roll of the eyes declare: "Well it's just too bad." [52] Despite the execration from Hattersley and others, Powell told a Monday Club meeting in Southampton that he had felt an inner compulsion to make his repatriation call: 'Enoch, I said to myself, you just have to get up and tell everyone: "I told you so." '[53] When it was put to him that he was like Alf Garnett, Powell replied, 'Garnett? Alf Garnett? Who's he? One of the new ministers?'

He remained utterly unrepentant about his warnings on immigration. The previous autumn he had received an entirely gratuitous letter from Jim Thompson, the Bishop of Stepney. He told Powell that after eighteen years of working in London's East End he had decided that 'your contributions on the race issue in this country have been the most damaging and harmful statements to [sic] everything that the Christian Church in East London has tried to achieve'.[54] The Bishop ended with the intensely Christian observation, 'I can only think that when you meet your Maker you will weep.' Powell replied that 'it is depressing to have to learn that a person in your responsible position can so delude himself as to think that people would not have noticed and resented the change in the population of their cities, towns and country if I had not spoken about it'.[55] He concluded, 'At the Last Judgment I shall have no different plea from yourself or any other man living.'

Powell's main theme at Southampton had been not immigration, but Ireland. Referring to the talks between FitzGerald and Mrs Thatcher, he said their very continuance seemed rooted in the idea that the Republic had a legitimate interest in the internal affairs of the Six Counties; and he wondered how the people of Yorkshire or Cornwall would feel if they, too, had been the subject of such talks. He said that if any deal were done – and the leaks from their talks led Powell to expect some joint council of the two countries' ministers would be established – it would provoke the 'passionate resentment' of the people of Ulster.[56] A fortnight later, speaking in his constituency after another outbreak of rioting at Broadwater Farm in north London, Powell linked the racial tensions in England with what was happening in Ulster. Forecasting that troops would soon be on the streets of the capital trying to keep order, he said, 'what is astonishing is that a Government face to face with insurrection in the capital city and elsewhere on the mainland should be engaged at the very same time in a negotiation with the Irish republic which is calculated to recreate those selfsame conditions in Ulster'.[57]

Ironically, in the month before the signing of the Anglo-Irish Agreement, Powell made a speech predicting the end of the United States' domination of the West. He concentrated at this time on more philosophical speeches, telling the Cambridge University Conservative Association on 20 October that the

Government had made a mistake in pushing through so much legislation: 'There has been more law reform than could be properly digested, with the result that a large proportion of Members just opted out of concern with Bills too extensive, too complicated and too technical for the ordinary MP to keep track of.'[58] He said it was impossible, under such a weight of legislation, for the MP to exercise his proper duty of vigilance.

Powell also worried about radical departures in the exercise of law, some of which he regarded as a breach of ancient principles. A suggestion from the Home Office that victims of crime could enter into some sort of negotiation with the criminals to discuss reparation was condemned by him, since it impinged upon the state's duty to maintain the law and regulate the punishment of crime. 'The essence of crime', he said, 'is a wrong done not to an individual but to the community as represented and personified by the sovereign authority.' Similarly, at Oxford a fortnight later, Powell told that University's Conservatives of his reservations about the policy of confiscating the assets of drug traffickers. He warned that 'anger and fear are the natural parents of bad law: and we are in a period when too much law is being enacted under emotional impulse of indignation and alarm. The principle, once it finds a place in our law, that a person on conviction is put in peril of being mulcted of all his property does not remain inert. It is presently found to have hands and feet; it walks and it grasps.'[59]

On 23 October, in the wake of the recent riots, the House debated the urban disturbances. Powell dismissed the notion that another judicial inquiry, in the fashion of Scarman, was needed. 'What we need', he argued, 'is for those who are in office, who are in positions of authority and responsibility, to acknowledge the truths – some of them appalling, some of them embarrassing – which are known and understood by the people who live in those cities.'[60] After the Handsworth riot he had point-blank asked Mrs Thatcher whether she accepted his projections for the future composition of the population and, if she did, 'what sort of a Britain, and what sort of a London, did she believe there would be?' He had had no answer, and demanded one again. He drew the conclusion that the Prime Minister had been told by her officials that his projections were accurate, for otherwise she would have wasted no time in putting the contrary view. 'The answer she more probably got', he added provocatively, 'was that the true projection was higher than the one which I had put to her and that, therefore, she would be wise to leave it alone.'[61] Ministers were prepared to admit that much of the trouble in areas with a high concentration of ethnic minorities was drug related, and sought to take measures to limit the drugs traffic; but here, too, Powell warned again of the dangers of infringing normal civil liberties by reviving the medieval penalty of confiscation of assets.

However, the Anglo-Irish Agreement now took over Powell's political activity completely. As the signing was reported to be imminent, Powell said on 12

November that Mrs Thatcher should be treating the Ulster question in the same way as she had the Falklands. The attempt, as he saw it, by Dublin to persuade Britain to cede some of her sovereignty over the Six Counties was presenting 'a more testing struggle than 1982'.[62] Putting the Prime Minister on notice, he reminded her that 'she has at her personal command the means of ending the long agony of Ulster. A single syllable can stop the futile but bloodstained campaign to sell the province out and can give to all the people the reconciling assurance that their place in the Union is no longer to be negotiable.'

When, on 14 November, it was made known that the agreement would be signed the next day, Powell, other Unionists and right-wing Conservatives attacked Mrs Thatcher, at Question Time, with bitter comments. Powell's own assault was the most withering: 'Does the right hon Lady understand – if she does not yet understand she soon will – that the penalty for treachery is to fall into public contempt?' Mrs Thatcher, reported by lobby correspondents to have had her eyes blazing with anger, told the House, 'I find his remarks deeply offensive.'[63] She stuck to her position, arguing that no agreement of any sort could be implemented unless approved by Parliament first. She bore Powell no grudge for his attack, despite it being couched in such personal terms: she believed he had to represent his constituents as he saw fit, and to the best of his abilities.[64]

Whatever the agreement meant for the people of Ulster, it threw the Unionists into confusion. The breach between Official and Democratic Unionists was put to one side, and there was a consensus that, if the Commons approved the accord, all the Unionists would resign and fight by-elections to demonstrate the support they had in the Province. Powell, though, signalled his reluctance to resign. His seat was highly marginal, and even though the vote would not be split (as it had been in 1983) by a Democratic Unionist against him, he could not be sure to hold it. He kept up what pressure he could in the House, telling Biffen, who stood in for Mrs Thatcher at Prime Minister's Questions on 21 November while she was abroad, that he had received an 'increasing flood of communication' about the agreement and her personal part in it'.[65] Hardly ever, in his political career, had Powell turned an issue, even one as sensitive as this, into something so personal.

However, suspicion about a breach between him and his colleagues was heightened when, alone of the fifteen Unionist MPs, Powell did not attend a rally in Belfast on 23 November, at which all the others signed a declaration of intent to surrender their seats if the Commons approved the accord. Tens of thousands of people attended the rally, bringing Belfast to a standstill for hours. It was the sort of dramatic, collective gesture Powell would have felt intensely uncomfortable making, even if he had been as willing as the others to resign. Molyneaux, loyal as always, explained away his absence by referring to engagements on the mainland from which Powell had found it impossible to extricate himself. However, other colleagues and supporters were less impressed by Powell's excuses, and some signalled that they would be pressing him to declare he would resign, thereby preserving the unity of the parliamentary Unionists. Some activists made little secret of their belief that Powell's absence had undermined and overshadowed the impact of the rally. Molyneaux was pressed, the next day, to say what he understood Powell's position to be. He answered that 'when a party leader issues an invitation we would always hope that invitation would be accepted. I would have been disappointed if any of my other colleagues had refused to resign their seat.'[66]

Once all the MPs were back at Westminster on 26 November, Molyneaux had no choice but to put Powell on the spot. However much Powell might have carried the party in the Commons in the previous eleven years – and no Official Unionist had had so forceful or so active a presence in the chamber as he – Molyneaux realised he could not allow Powell to go his own way on so vital an issue. Part of Powell's value to the party was that he had enjoyed, at times, privileged access to Mrs Thatcher, who had treated him with increasing affection and respect until his 'treachery' outburst; but that direct line had clearly ended, a personal failure for Powell. He pre-empted an approach from Molyneaux by sending him, on the morning before the House was due to begin a two-day debate on the agreement, a letter construed as a qualified offer to resign his seat. Saying the decision to apply for the Chiltern Hundreds was a matter of personal responsibility no one else could share, he added, 'Nevertheless I would like you to know against the background of our long friendship and collaboration that, if you were to intimate that I could be of help to you in particular circumstances by resigning my seat with a view to re-contesting it, I would be disposed to do so. I am sure you would only envisage this action if you were assured that it could be given the intended effect.'[67] Powell explained that his hesitation had not been caused by fear of losing his seat, but by fear that the Commons might not move the writ for a by-election, delaying the contest indefinitely. Powell added that it was Molyneaux's responsibility, as leader, to ensure that all the by-elections could be fought at the same time.

Powell spoke near the end of the second day of the debate, in a state of profound depression. The debate had not, he said, been about Ulster, but 'about the United Kingdom; or, to put the same point in another way, it has been about this House, for what we have been debating these two days is the proposition that the Government should be approved for having made with another country an agreement whereby a conference will be set up to exercise surveillance over the administration of the United Kingdom'.[68] To him this was 'unacceptable and deeply offensive', and the House was on the verge of a unique and 'unprecedented breach in the Governance of the United Kingdom, an unprecedented arrangement whereby a formal position is allocated to another country in respect of the conduct of affairs in the United Kingdom'.[69] What further affronted him was that this arrangement applied to just one part of the Kingdom. 'We cannot all' – he spoke for himself and the other Unionists – 'come here accepting law made by a majority in this House, because we are all part of the United Kingdom, and then see that law imposed differently – different laws made for different parts of the Kingdom.' Where such different laws had been made – as, for example, with the distinctiveness of the Scottish legal system – it had been with the express consent of those affected.

He added that if the vote, on a resolution, was passed, the law of the United Kingdom would not be altered: the House had no power to do that by resolution. Pending an Act of Parliament that enshrined a treaty, the people of Ulster would be under no obligation to accept the agreement. He questioned the two claims made for the agreement: that it would bring reconciliation and help fight terrorism. He did not see how reconciliation between two bodies of opinion could be achieved 'by installing an external authority to have a special responsibility for being the protector and representative of one of those bodies'.[70] This would merely inflame the quarrel; and he knew the Prime Minister was sufficiently rational to see this. He also doubted that the Irish Government would want to be seen to do anything that hindered the IRA, as such a perception would be too politically damaging for it at home.

Powell asked why it was that officials had succeeded, in the preceding year, in turning Mrs Thatcher around to their view, and how had other ministers who, like her, had not wanted the agreement, been brought in to support it? He maintained that in her heart she had not wanted it. One 'had only to watch the Prime Minister at the signing at Hillsborough to understand that here was someone doing what she knew was wrong and what she knew was contrary to her instincts and knowledge of the position'.[71] This was met by cries of 'Rubbish.' He went on to explain his 'treachery' outburst: if, he said, he had used an expression 'which the Prime Minister found offensive, it was because I was indignant at a result being produced for purposes and reasons which were not the real ones'.

He immediately outlined the real one: 'This has been done because the United States insisted that it should be done.' This prompted ridicule, which provoked Powell. 'The Ministers on the Front Bench, though they may grin and waggle their heads, know perfectly well, as does the Prime Minister, that that is the case.' Ireland had been told by the Americans that, if it would enter NATO, thereby assisting the United States strategically, the Americans would help supply 'a visible prospect which it can interpret as progress towards an all-Ireland state'.[72] He ended on a note of gloom and menace deeper even than that on which he had begun: 'When in the coming months the consequences of this understanding work themselves out and the Prime Minister watches with uncomprehending compassion the continued sequence of terrorism, murder and death in Northern Ireland which this agreement will not prevent but will maintain and foment, let her not send to ask for whom the bell tolls. It tolls for her.' His plea was, as he knew it would be, in vain. The resolution was carried massively, by 473 votes to 47.

As soon as the result was known, Paisley and his DUP colleague, Peter Robinson, announced their resignations. The Official Unionists indicated that they would follow soon; all that was required was an assurance that no obstruction would be put up by the Government to a resignation *en masse*, with simultaneous by-elections. On 28 November Mrs Thatcher gave the assurance that the Chancellor of the Exchequer, who was responsible for the administration of the resignations, would not divert from custom and practice. Powell's decision to resign could now be made; and he wrote in a newspaper the following Sunday of how, in doing so, he was reminded of Britain's shame in appeasing Hitler and how what had just been done to Ulster was, in his view, even more of a betrayal than the entry into Europe that had so nearly prompted his resignation from Parliament in the summer of 1972.

In his article, he explained that the Hillsborough accord had had three features that were 'peculiarly repulsive': that oversight of the administration of part of the United Kingdom had been granted to foreign ministers, a grant sanctioned by the House of Commons ('did Pierre Laval and Marshal Pétain do worse than that?'); that the Commons had sanctioned this without any suggestion of agreement from the inhabitants of the Six Counties; and that all this had been done because of a form of duress to which the Government would not publicly admit. The terms of the 'capitulation' were not, he said, 'dictated to Britain by the Irish Republic. They were dictated from the White House and the Pentagon, cynically holding up to ransom an ally supposedly dependent on their military strength.'[73]

In the midst of this struggle over the agreement, the almost surreal diversion took place of the House debating whether or not it should agree to having its proceedings televised, following the precedent of the House of Lords. Powell was fervently against the proposals – which were agreed, but only implemented when he was no longer a Member. He said that he and all other Members were holders of a trust, and it was their duty to pass on that trust 'as little as possible diminished' to those who succeeded them – for, if this particular trust was destroyed, it could not be recreated. Parliamentary debate was at the heart of the way in which the Commons did things; there was nothing else like it anywhere.

'We do not', he observed,

> stride to a rostrum to make orations to our fellow Members; we rise where we sit, from among our fellows; we belong, and are aware of belonging, to a collective corporate entity ... we address the House with the purpose of being heard by, and winning a hearing from, our fellows and equals. Those who occupy offices

of state are, for the purposes of debate, no more than the equals of the rest. We address a gathering which knows us, and by all of whom we are known. It is part of the nature of our debate that everyone, as he seeks his own way of bringing his point of view home to the rest, judges the House, and is judged by the House from moment to moment as he does so. Debate in this House is a seamless garment; the whole collectivity of what happens in the chamber is a single thing.[74]

All this being so, he said, to televise the House would lead to a complete misrepresentation: 'the one certain way to falsify it is to abstract from it one element. Partial representation is essentially falsification.' This early prophecy about the damaging culture of the sound-bite went, however, unheeded.

On 17 December the remaining Unionist MPs resigned – Powell applying for the Stewardship of the Manor of Northstead, the Chiltern Hundreds having already been allocated to another – and the writ for all fifteen by-elections was moved. The Unionists expressed the wish that the poll could be held on 23 January, the earliest possible date. This was acceded to, and, directly after Christmas, the Unionists began a campaign in the depths of an unremitting, cold, wet winter. Much of the press attention in the campaign focused on Powell, not merely because he was by far the best known of the candidates, but also because he was defending a majority of only 548. He fought the campaign with as much energy as he had any of its predecessors, despite being in his seventy-fourth year; and the feeling from the start was that, because of the staunchly non-partisan way in which he had striven in the preceding eleven years to serve Protestants and Catholics alike without any favours, he would manage to get home – helped by the fact that there was no other Unionist candidate.

In an interview on the Sunday before the election, Powell said his main achievement in Ulster had been to secure the Province its full representation at Westminster, and he had no regrets about his years there. Pressed about his future if he lost his seat, he was asked whether he had set his face against a peerage. He replied, with what anyone who knew him would recognise as a rare public outing for his highly satirical sense of humour: 'I would regard the prospect of the offer of a hereditary earldom being made as a remote one, or the offer of the Garter, but a man would not wish, from cold as it were, to announce in advance that an earldom or the Garter would be refused.' Earnestly, his interviewer asked whether he would refuse a life peerage. 'Yes,' he answered, because 'it does not correspond to what I regard as my place in British politics.'[75]

The campaign for the by-elections coincided with the Government's own crisis over the split in the cabinet on whether to order new helicopters for the army from a European or American supplier – the Westland affair. Powell alleged that Mrs Thatcher had been blackmailed by the Americans into backing the Sikorsky option, just as she had been blackmailed by them into offering concessions in Ulster. Powell's opponent in South Down was once more Eddie

McGrady, one of the SDLP's four advisers to the Dublin Government during the negotiations that had led to the agreement. McGrady was, as in 1983, handicapped by having a Sinn Fein opponent to split the nationalist vote. Those observing the election felt that Powell would not lose, and that his campaign had won over many Unionists in his constituency who had never overcome the scepticism they felt towards him when he first represented them in 1974. The predictions were sound. Powell got home by 1,842, three times his 1983 majority, but still precarious.

III

Once back at Westminster, the Unionists – all but one of whom held his seat – were divided over what tactics to adopt now they had won their real, and moral, victories. The policy they abhorred was still in place, and the Government had no intention of reversing it, however unpopular it might have been with those it directly affected. Two of the three DUP MPs, and some of the Official Unionists, announced that they intended to take the oath and then boycott the Commons. Paisley said he would issue an ultimatum to Mrs Thatcher to start to reverse the policy within a month, or face a boycott. Powell and Molyneaux were the only MPs from the group who argued that they should attend the Commons, in order to continue to highlight the injustices of the Agreement and to use their places to persuade the Government to think again. In the face of this divide, the boycott never properly came about; and nor did any compromise by the Government.

This last phase of Powell's parliamentary career – though he did not know at the time how short, or how final, it was to be – saw no diminution in what were now regarded as his licensed maverick activities. Long a national institution, he was increasingly seen, as he advanced in years, to have lost some of his bite, but none of his powers of perception or entertainment. The refusal of the Government to back down on the Hillsborough Agreement was another, inevitable mark of his impotence; but this new failure did not affect his morale. He continued to give economic lectures, reflecting in the spring of 1986 – almost the height of the boom years of Thatcherism – that British industry was far more of a success than it was given credit for, and that the flood of Japanese imports about which so many commentators were so worried was really a boon; they were 'bargains' without which 'the massive blessings of the international division of labour could never be reaped'.[76] Less concerned than ever what others thought of him, his humour became increasingly mordant. Interviewed by some Conservative students, he was asked whether he was 'anti-American'. He replied 'Most people are. The only change is that it has become a term of abuse.' Asked why he was anti-American, he said, 'Well, I just don't like America, or

Americans. It is like saying you like sugar in your tea. *De gustibus non est disputandum.*[77]

He gave a wireless interview in April 1986 that further marked out his singlemindedness – and in which he gave full vent to his normally suppressed romanticism. It also caused a rare difference of opinion between Powell and his family. He talked of his return to the church and of his commitment to institutions; he talked about his poetic impulse, which led on to his discussing the war, and reading his poem on El Alamein. In doing so, he broke down. Composing himself, he went on to talk about the unsuitability of women in the Commons, and then immigration ('yes, but we've agreed on the dominant importance in human affairs of gut reaction, haven't we?').[78] However, what caused his wife and daughters to be upset, and what astounded other listeners, was his reply to the last question from his interviewer, Anne Brown. 'How would you like to be remembered?' 'I should like to have been killed in the war.' As he became older, he thought more and more about the war, the defining experience in his life. After broadcasting that remark, he 'received dozens of letters from people saying I'm glad you said that because I felt the same and I've never known it before. There's a secret guilt about those who served and were not killed that they too – that they too were not killed.'[79]

If he was prepared to be so ruthless with himself, it was hardly surprising that in other contexts he acted with such unconcern for the views of others. Ulster issues gave him plenty of scope to shake the usual assumptions. Appearing on television on 8 April, he said the Prime Minister had been guilty of 'criminal' activity in signing the agreement, and that a recent upsurge of violence by loyalists protesting against it had left the Government with 'blood on their hands'. Most controversially, Powell refused to condemn attacks by loyalists on the homes of RUC officers, saying these were the responsibility of the Government for having given such encouragement to the IRA. He persisted in the view that the overwhelming vote given in the Commons for Hillsborough was meaningless: 'they voted wrong'.[80]

Early that month Powell had had another personal blow that affected him deeply: the death of another of his few long-standing friends, Andrew Freeth, whom he had first met almost fifty years before. Freeth's son remembers Powell being deeply upset by his father's death, and Powell wrote warmly to Freeth's widow, Roseen: 'I feel that, as time goes on, Andrew's place and his achievement will be more and more secure and a source of pride and consolation to you.'[81] With Curtis gone, it left Powell with only Michael Strachan as the survivor of those close friends who had known him since before his political life took over, and who, therefore, knew the real Powell.

The main challenge he set himself during the spring and summer of 1986 was in his opposition to the Single European Act, the means by which a single market and new common institutions were created in the European Community. When

the House debated the principle on 5 March, he complained that since the Act –
an amendment of the 1972 European Communities Act – would greatly change
a piece of legislation the House had spent nearly six months discussing, it should
not be dealt with too quickly. As in 1972, he felt the Government was not being
'candid'.[82] 'Every alteration proposed in the new treaty', he said, 'is an alteration
which diminishes the powers of the House ... which means a further erosion
of the opportunity for the British people to influence the policy and the laws
under which they live.' He was especially concerned about allowing some
matters, in future, to be decided in the Council of Ministers by a qualified
majority, rather than, as hitherto, unanimity. Many of the decisions the Council
had to take, Powell added, were fed into it by the European Parliament, another
institution against which he had argued. All around, the Commons' power was
waning. He urged that, when the time came to legislate, the House should bear
in mind the further erosions of its standing that were being threatened.

Although it would be another year before Lawson, as Chancellor, embarked
upon his policy of 'shadowing the Deutschmark' as a precursor to entry into a
European fixed exchange rate system, the advocates of entry were already making
their case. Leon Brittan, who had resigned as Trade Secretary after the Westland
crisis two months earlier and would, in time, serve as a European Commissioner,
made the case in the Budget debate on 24 March. Powell spoke after him, and
rebutted his case forcefully. One of Brittan's arguments had been that a fixed
rate would help with balance of payments problems, though Powell pointed out
that the balance of payments would operate 'inexorably, whether or not one
messes around with the exchange rate'.[83]

He then gave a lesson that would reflect the exact, and predictable, problems
the Treasury would have in first shadowing, and then joining, a fixed exchange
rate system over the next six years. 'If', he postulated, 'one decides to fix the
exchange rate, one does so at one's own expense, in two ways: to keep the rate
down one manufactures one's own currency and sells it; to push the rate up one
borrows other people's currencies and sells that. It is a simple and rather hair-
raising game, is rigging the exchange rate. In the end the cost always recoils on
the country which does it – either by the consequences of providing currency
of its own in order to depress the rate, or by the consequences of the international
debt incurred in operations to force the exchange rate up.' Powell had already
detected Mrs Thatcher's opposition to such a move, having questioned her
about it in the Commons on 6 March, three weeks earlier. She agreed that such
a system would have caused great problems for Britain, and Powell reminded
the House of her views.

By contrast, he said that in his support of the principle, Brittan

evidently believes that we have walked out of history. He believes that we have
left behind us the period when factors which none of us foresaw, not years before,

but only a few weeks before, could alter the balance of supply and demand for sterling. For myself, I cannot believe that the change in economic variables throughout the world which comes home to roost in terms of a movement of the sterling exchange rate lies behind us once and for all and that therefore it would now be painless to attach ourselves to an external norm. I believe that we would still find ourselves paying dearly to maintain that norm, and ultimately at our own cost.

Throughout the spring of 1986 the Northern Ireland assembly had limped on, but was now moribund. The SDLP had never taken their seats, which meant the assembly's task of preparing proposals for devolution was made impossible; and the Unionists in the assembly had refused to undertake the other function, the monitoring of the activities of government in the Province. On 13 March the assembly had formally resolved to do nothing except meet once a week to debate aspects of the Anglo-Irish Agreement. Tom King, the Northern Ireland Secretary, had warned the assembly's members that, if it did not carry out the functions that had been designed for it, it might have to be closed down. They ignored the warning, and would not even talk to King about it. He therefore announced, on 12 June, that he was having the assembly dissolved.

He stressed he was not abolishing the body, new elections to which were due in the autumn, but simply leaving open the date for those elections. For the sake of form, King told the House that the dissolution in no way conflicted with the Government's desire for devolved government, and he urged those Unionists still boycotting the Commons to return so that the future could be discussed. To Powell, this represented a victory, and a justification of his warnings in 1982 about the body. He asked King whether the views of the two main Unionist parties, who had opposed the assembly, and the Conservative Members who had supported them, had now been validated by what King was having to do. The Secretary of State, understandably, refused to agree.

The Single European Act – or the European Communities (Amendment) Bill, as it was formally known at that stage – was a tougher proposition. As the House debated it throughout the summer, Powell revisited the arguments and the tactics of fourteen years earlier. He was unconcerned by the predicament the Government would find itself in if the Bill were not carried, when all other parties to it would amend it. All that concerned him was the need to preserve what was left of the powers of the House of Commons. The main argument he had to counter was that the Bill would lead to greater freedom of trade. He told the Commons on 26 June, 'I have a deep-rooted prejudice in favour of freedom of trade. I am sorry about that, and apologise for it, but it is so deep as to be ineluctable.'[84] However, he added that 'the EEC – despite its earlier legends – has nothing to do with freedom of trade.' It had, he said, 'disastrously' interfered with trade relations between its member states and the outside world. And the very legislation they were considering was a self-contradiction. 'The internal free trade of the EEC is procured by compulsion and by an attempt to enforce similar regulations, practices and laws on all the participant countries. One of the beautiful advantages of free trade is that one does not have to interfere with anyone else to enjoy it.'

He argued that free trade did not need the sort of compulsion contained in this legislation, and was not achievable by compulsion. What, in fact, the Bill was really about was not economics, but politics. It was like the *Zollverein* in nineteenth-century *Mitteleuropa*, which he reminded the House had been an instrument not of liberation, but of pressurising smaller states in central Europe to join a political union under the lead of Prussia. The free market the new legislation was trying to create was overtly political in intent, and was based upon common political institutions. 'It is', he said, 'about compulsion and not about freedom.' He lambasted the wording of the Bill as 'vague and almost meaningless', and on that principle alone called for it not to be incorporated into United Kingdom law.[85]

As in 1972, a small group of opponents, including Powell, held up progress; and on 1 July the Government sought to impose – and, with the help of an increasingly pro-European Labour party, succeeded in imposing – the guillotine. It was, to Powell, just like the old days. He told the House, in the debate on the guillotine, that this time it was a decision on political union that was being rushed through; and Powell had one other reason to feel disappointed. 'It is a cruel irony', he said,

> that this act is committed to the hands of the right hon Member for Shropshire, North [Biffen, the Leader of the House]. The House knows, and the country knows, the right hon Gentleman's view of British membership of the European Economic Community. Through all his years in office he has preserved his honour on this subject in the sense that by no word or gesture has he conveyed to anyone approval of the decision that was taken in 1972 ... yet it falls to him, by cruel chance, to propose that the House of Commons should be guillotined in order to pass this further instalment of abnegation.[86]

Powell suspected that Biffen was under pressure in the same way Mrs Thatcher was, from a Foreign Office already, as Powell saw it, issuing threats about what would happen if a policy of opposition to the development of the EEC were to hold sway. He quoted a prominent former diplomat, Sir Anthony Parsons, who was on record as saying that, in those circumstances, Foreign Office mandarins 'would find it impossible conscientiously to implement the new policies'.[87] Powell could not foresee the causes of the Prime Minister's removal from office four years later, but he uncannily came close. What Parsons had said was 'a description of the prison which has been constructed and in which the Prime Minister finds that her instincts and her will are "cribb'd, cabin'd and confin'd".

It is under those pressures and under that kind of blackmail and dictation that the House finds itself being compelled, at the gunpoint of a guillotine, to pass the legislation. ... It is blackmail, and it is blackmail from a quarter from which the House ought not to accept blackmail. It is a blackmail imposed by those who are not, as we are, the elected representatives of the people of this country. ... As for myself, I will have none of it.' Yet, as in 1972, the measures passed.

Powell's most prophetic remarks about the Bill were made on 10 July, when he elaborated on his earlier contention that it was about political union, not about better economic arrangements within the EEC. He began his speech by stating that 'in this debate we are arguing and eventually voting for or against the principle of monetary union'; and he read from Article 20 of the Treaty, which specified co-operation in European economic and monetary policy 'in order to ensure the convergence of economic and monetary policies which is necessary'.[88] Foreshadowing arguments that were to tear the Conservative party apart during the 1990s, he pronounced that 'there is nothing which comes nearer to sovereignty, self-government or what politics is about than control of money'. The 'principal issue' at elections, he said, was how the respective parties would use 'the money-making power'. He stressed that 'if there is to be monetary union, that decision is to be taken away from the British people. It is no longer to be a subject of politics in this country. It is a subject which will be decided by the general and common authorities of a monetary union. Consequently, there is nothing more directly and clearly inimical to the political process in this country than the professed intention to enter into a monetary union.'[89] If the legislation, as set out, were passed, he continued, that intention would be exactly what the Commons would be expressing.

This was something the Government was playing down. Referring to Lynda Chalker, the Foreign Office minister, who was seeing the Bill through, he said:

it is all very well, and it will no doubt happen, for the Minister to tell us from the Dispatch Box to take no notice. She will say that it is not binding, that it is the preamble and that it is just words and has no effect. However, that is not what we will be told when it becomes an Act. That is not what we shall be told when steps are taken and enforced upon us, possibly by a guillotine in due course, towards economic and monetary union. We shall be told 'In 1986 the House of Commons said so. The House of Commons embodied those words in an Act of Parliament.' ... are we to be told that those words will never be quoted against us in future and that we shall never be told that we approved those objectives solemnly and put them on the statute book of this country by writing the words of a preamble into an Act of Parliament?

Indeed, when John Major's opponents, a decade later, accused him of comparative weakness in handling the European issue, his supporters would respond that it had been Mrs Thatcher, and not he, who by driving through the Single

Act had established the authority of the European political institutions that so trammelled sovereignty.

Ironically, Powell was beginning to repair his relations with the Prime Minister, badly damaged in the rain of hard words after the Hillsborough accord. When Mrs Thatcher went into hospital in August 1986 for an operation on her hand, Powell wrote with good wishes; and, referring to her opposition to sanctions on South Africa, added that her conduct of the policy had been 'skilful as well as determined. I believe that, not for the first time, you have the mass of the British people on your side.'[90] After such an overture he was dismayed to receive no reply, but that was, as it turned out, because the Prime Minister had never seen the letter. When finally she did she told Michael Alison, her PPS, that she was 'doubly delighted' at Powell's 'wonderful comments'.[91] The great rapprochement had begun.

Powell kept up his remorseless round of weekly, or often twice-weekly, speaking engagements throughout that summer, and his journalistic practice thrived. He wrote regularly for the editorial pages of *The Times* and reviewed books widely. He also noticed, that summer, that his hearing was becoming less acute; one of the few signs of physical decline apparent to him at the age of seventy-four. He was not prepared to settle for decline; unless he was rattling cages he was unhappy. On 17 October there was a smell of the old days when a mob prevented him from delivering a speech at Bristol University, jumping up on to the platform from which he was speaking and smashing the sound equipment. Powell had to be escorted away by ten members of the University rugby club, one of whom said, 'It was terrifying. People went absolutely berserk.'[92]

This, though, was nothing compared with the stir Powell caused the following day, when he went to address Conservative students in Birmingham. He told them that the murder of Airey Neave in 1979 had not been carried out by the Irish National Liberation Army, but by 'high contracting parties' made up of 'MI6 and their friends'. Neave had been set to become Northern Ireland Secretary and was committed to a programme of integration – as was Powell. His murder had, he said, been designed to shake the Government into taking a course more favourable to the United States in her aim of uniting Ireland and taking it into NATO. Many of Powell's fellow politicians execrated him for his remarks. Even one of his closest supporters in the Commons, Ian Gow, who had resigned over the Anglo-Irish Agreement and who would himself be murdered by terrorists four years later, said Powell's notions were 'absurd'.[93]

For the rest of the parliamentary session Powell was as active as at any time in his career. On 27 November 1986 he sought to atone for what he felt had been a fault of his during the passage of the Drug Trafficking Offences Act the previous session. He did so during the second reading debate of the Criminal Justice Bill, when he complained about the extension to other sorts of crime of the principle of confiscation of assets, which the Drug Act had established. Powell said that, when that first measure had gone through Parliament, there were some like him who, though they disapproved of confiscation of the assets of criminals, disapproved of the crime far more. He, and others like him, had 'let it go by on the basis that it would not be drawn into precedent or extended beyond the context which was originally thought to justify it'.[94]

The new Bill proposed that confiscation should apply to any crime 'that can be associated with pecuniary gain'. Powell had argued outside the House against this precept when the Drug Bill was before Parliament, but had not done so in the House. Lamenting his failure, he said that 'one of the irrecoverables of life is the dissent that one did not express, the vote that one failed to cast. At any rate, by this brief speech this evening, I am endeavouring to expiate what I left undone last Session.' Powell was interrupted by David Mellor, the Home Office minister, and asked what his possible objection could be to criminals being prevented from benefiting from their crimes. He replied that he felt it violated the principles of criminal justice by superimposing 'what is in effect an additional penalty – and a severe one – upon the penalties which have been prescribed by statute for the offences in question'. The punishments for those crimes had been set to take into account the fact that profit might have been made from them. Now, he said, 'we pile on top of these indiscriminately the engine of confiscation'.[95]

The ultra-hard line that the Unionists were taking against the Government, and had taken since Hillsborough, was largely driven by Powell, with the complete agreement of his Ulster-born colleagues. In February 1987, a few months short of his seventy-fifth birthday and still in robust health, he announced that he would be happy to contest the South Down seat at the next election. His wish was unanimously endorsed by his supporters in the constituency. He had not let up a jot in his energies in representing his constituents; he would still spend at least one weekend in two there, and much of the parliamentary recesses, and still had not exhausted his interest in walking the land with his Ordnance Survey maps and picnicking out of the wind behind stone walls. However, boundary changes had brought more nationalist communities into his seat. It was not going to be easy, and the SDLP seemed to have learned the lessons of 1983, and of the 1986 by-election.

That February Powell came to the *Daily Telegraph*, then still in Fleet Street, for lunch with its editor, Max Hastings, the leader writers, senior executives and political correspondents. On such occasions Powell could be wilfully uncooperative, particularly if he sensed he might be bored by the company; and this was one such occasion. I engaged him in a conversation about the authorship of Shakespeare, which seemed to liven him up; but Hastings, wanting to draw Powell out on political matters of the moment, interrupted and asked a junior political reporter whether he had a question. The journalist, who had hoped to remain silent, was flustered, but asked Powell what he thought would be the result of the election.

'I wasn't aware one had been called,' Powell replied tersely.

Taken aback, Hastings sought to put a more precise question to his guest. He asked Powell what he thought about the newly unleashed Aids epidemic. 'Well,' replied Powell, barely able to conceal his ennui, 'as a man of seventy-five who has been happily married for thirty-five years, I hardly think it affects me.'[96]

By early April Powell accepted the consensus that the Conservatives, energised after a successful party conference the previous October and still well placed in the opinion polls, would choose the coming summer to go to the country. Writing in the *Guardian* on 6 April, he noted that, unlike many other governments that had served two terms, the Conservatives' ideological mandate is unexhausted, if not inexhaustible'.[97] There were more denation-alisations (as Powell still insisted on calling them) to accomplish; however, he also observed that the novelty of this programme had worn off, and the public were no longer excited by it. Even income tax at 25 per cent – 'not yet quite "income tax at 4/3 in the pound" which a Conservative politician once displayed to a disbelieving fringe-meeting almost 20 years ago' – was not exciting. 'Mental and moral palates', he asserted, 'have become jaded.' His own recipe for livening up the palate was to engage in radical acts of foreign policy, which he did not specify but which could, without much effort, be imagined.

The Prime Minister's visit to the Soviet Union, where she conducted what was tantamount to a pre-election rally under the stewardship of President Gorbachev, prompted Powell, in a Commons speech on 7 April, to return to his earlier musings on the nuclear question. This was precisely the sort of foreign policy departure he had hoped for, a British Conservative Prime Minister in the heart of Mother Russia, signifying once and for all an end to the belief that the Russians were planning to unleash nuclear war over the British Isles, or to unleash a third world war of any description. A friendship formed with Russia would, he maintained, allow Britain to stop having her foreign policy dictated from outside, namely by the Americans.

As expected, the election was called in May for 11 June; and the final debate of the 1983 parliament in which Powell took part was on security policy in Northern Ireland. In a concise, closely argued and uninterrupted exposition of just twenty minutes he outlined how the security situation in the Six Counties had been worsened by the Anglo-Irish Agreement of eighteen months earlier. The Republic, he reminded his colleagues, still had in its constitution the aim to include the Six Counties within its own state; the IRA operated largely from the Republic; therefore, for Britain to have entered into such an agreement with the Republic was an open inducement to the IRA to believe its main aims were near achievement, and it sought to make the last lunge for superiority by further violence.

He argued, too, that the many inhabitants of the Six Counties who were Catholic or anti-Union, but who did not support the IRA, no longer felt it worthwhile to take the risks incumbent on not toeing the Republican line 'in order to sustain a state that is despaired of even by the Government of the country to which it belongs'.[98] Thus the Agreement had further reduced active opposition to the terrorists. The Agreement had been the culmination of a policy of appeasement of the terrorists that had lasted since 1969; and, until it was reversed, 'until the United Kingdom is seen decisively to have abandoned a course designed to lead to the separation of Ulster from the United Kingdom and its embodiment in some kind of all-Ireland state', the terror and the bloodshed would continue. He ended his speech with an appeal to the Government to use the power it still had to abrogate the agreement and reverse the policy of which it had been the crowning glory. Later that night, when the House considered a Police Order for the Province, to set up new procedures to deal with complaints against the RUC, Powell intervened in a speech being made by Sir Eldon Griffiths, a Conservative MP, to ask, 'Is the hon Gentleman sure that we shall have an opportunity to debate the regulations?'[99] They were the last words he would utter in the House of Commons.

With Parliament dissolved, Powell immediately went into battle with his customary energy and apparent inexhaustibility. He would not believe he could lose; a sincere belief that drove him on. His tent on the battlefield was his home at Ballynahinch, to which the Powells had moved after a boundary change at the 1983 election. There his strategy was plotted after each day's canvassing, and they were long days, the twilight not starting in early June in Ulster until ten o'clock. He did, though, misread the campaign from the start. 'I have the feeling of 1945,' he said at the start of a campaign that was to see the Conservatives home with a majority of 100 – a decline since their 144-seat triumph in 1983, but a handsome victory nonetheless. 'Mrs Thatcher has never known losing office as Gladstone did and the need to face changing circumstances and clear new obstacles before returning to power.'[100]

He was as confident of his own success as he was about Mrs Thatcher's impending difficulties. 'I see no rational grounds for contemplating defeat. No chances are being taken here. I never do and South Down Unionists don't either.' The Catholic votes that had helped him at all his previous elections were still being counted on; and so studiously non-sectarian had Powell been in his approach over the preceding years, and so assiduous in working for his constituents, that there was no 'rational' ground for thinking things would be different this time. The SDLP, however, believed most of the 4,000 new voters on the roll since 1983 were their voters, and would swing the result for them, despite the intervention of Sinn Fein, a Workers' Party and an Alliance candidate, all of whom were after Catholic votes.

Notwithstanding the pressure from the SDLP (who were once again fielding Eddie McGrady) – or perhaps because of it – Powell maintained a maudlin good humour. Stephen Robinson, who covered the events for the *Daily Telegraph*, noted that Powell 'seemed to find the pomp and grind of Ulster politics boring and embarrassing, and would deal with this by establishing an ironic detachment from the political fray. Hence, after making a point about the Anglo-Irish agreement or attacking a member of the Government, he would say: "Mr Powell adds acidly", or, "a typical classical reference from Mr Powell"'.[101] Robinson also felt that much of Powell's agenda was not relevant to the concerns of his electors – an interview he conducted with him was used by Powell to discuss his distaste for American foreign policy. 'He smiled,' Robinson recalled, 'gently mocking me when I asked him what the "issues" might be in the election.' His interviewer felt that Powell had nothing in common with his fellow Ulster Unionists, taking instead an entirely Anglocentric view of Unionism: 'He was always uncomfortable in the extreme when required to join a marching band or at events where the faithful would savage popery.' Robinson incurred the wrath of Pam Powell for writing a piece, based on interviews with a cross-section of Powell's constituents, in which he suggested that Powell might have trouble holding the seat because of a perception that he did not spend enough time in the constituency. As Mrs Powell truthfully pointed out to Robinson, they were there at least every other weekend. However, given the typical military thoroughness with which Powell conducted his canvass, it became clear that it was not his assiduity that was in question. Although the vote did not divide strictly along sectarian lines, the growth in the nationalist population was a greater obstacle.

Powell moved around the constituency in his loudspeaker-car, addressing housing estates and villages for votes, uttering polite 'thank yous', and driving relentlessly on. There were 72,000 electors to reach, spread over 700 square miles; and since January, Powell had been systematically visiting the homes of all those who had come on the electoral roll since the last general election. No chances, indeed, were being taken. He reminded his voters of the treachery of the Prime Minister, and how he had, to her face, accused her of that crime across the floor of the House of Commons. 'I am here defending you,' he said through his loudspeaker as he drove round.

Yet it was not enough. On polling day, 11 June, he and his wife toured all fifty-eight polling stations in the constituency in a bullet-proof RUC car. He had been disturbed to see the turnout in nationalist areas at seven o'clock in the morning, as the polls opened, and had the first intimations that he was not going to win. The votes were not counted in South Down until the Friday, once the ballot boxes had been brought in from the outlying villages and hamlets.

On the Thursday evening Powell had returned with his wife, their police guards and his agent to their bungalow at Ballynahinch, and at the end of the evening had announced, as he went to bed, 'Goodnight, ladies and gentlemen, and I am afraid I think that, unfortunately, we are going to lose this seat tomorrow.'[102] This came as a great shock to those present. As was his custom, Powell did not arrive at the count at Dromore High School until it was well under way, at about two in the afternoon. When he arrived, his agent took him to one side and told him it was not looking good. However his last agent had said the same thing to him at the same juncture four years earlier, and he had got home then.

Reporters watching the scene noticed a look of deep concern becoming rooted on Powell's face. He had been told by his agent that the relatively small number of Sinn Fein votes was the problem: the more moderate nationalist appeared to have squeezed the extremist vote. Powell knew, this time, after the first count that he had lost. The result was so close that a recount was called, though that was mainly for the sake of the Unionist party workers. The recount confirmed the earlier finding; and at 5.15 p.m. it was announced that, even though Powell's share of the vote had increased by 5.4 per cent since 1983, McGrady had won by 731 votes. Having recalled the lesson of 1983, McGrady and his supporters had worked furiously to get their vote out, and the Sinn Fein vote had collapsed. Powell, looking pale, was seen to tremble as the result was read out. Jeffrey Donaldson, no longer the constituency agent but nonetheless a helper in the campaign, recalled that Powell was shocked by what had happened, given his strong showing in the by-election.[103]

Both men made speeches of dignity – McGrady, first, paying tribute to his predecessor, recognising the respect in which he had been held by both traditions in the constituency; and Powell made a brief farewell, his face etched with crushing disappointment, but throughout he maintained the bearing of a soldier. 'For the rest of my life,' he said, 'when I look back on the 13 years I shall be filled with affection for the Province and its people, and their fortunes will never be out of my heart.'[104] The predominantly nationalist audience gave him a warm ovation: their verdict had not been personal. As he came down from the stage, he was heard by Stephen Robinson to utter the words Burke used in his speech declining the poll at Bristol in 1780, referring to the death of another candidate at the moment of the election: 'What shadows we are, what shadows we pursue.'[105] Powell's shock was palpable, and he seemed to Robinson to be near breaking down. Yet, when a BBC reporter, somewhat fatuously, asked him to explain his defeat, he replied: 'My opponent polled more votes than me.'

His wife, his agent and a handful of other close helpers returned to Powell's constituency home for a sombre evening. An inquest took place. 'He was very philosophical about it,' recalled Donaldson, who was among those present. His career in the Commons had had its reverses, many of them self-inflicted, before. Now it was over for ever. There was an echo of words he had uttered there five years earlier, on the death of Rab Butler: 'When we go hence, our room is soon filled, and we are soon forgotten.'[106] It was not true of Butler, and would not be true of Powell either.

LIFE AFTER DEATH

There had been periods of depression in Powell's career before – notably after Heath's victory in 1970, and after his failure to stop the European Communities Bill two years later – but his grief at losing his seat was unprecedented. In public, he came to terms with it quickly, his passionate temperament no more on display after his defeat than it had been before it. In private, it created a period of disorientation, from which – unlike in February 1974 – there was no apparent road back. He had once said, 'Take Parliament out of the history of England and that history itself becomes meaningless. The British nation could not imagine itself except with and through its parliament.'[1] The same, quite clearly, applied to Powell himself.

Those who knew him little or not at all suspected he would move effortlessly to the House of Lords. John Biffen, however, who came to see him on the Saturday after the election – just as he had been sacked from the cabinet by Mrs Thatcher – on entering the house told Powell he hoped he would remain 'the great commoner'.[2] Ian Gow had rung already to say that Mrs Thatcher was minded to give Powell a peerage, and Lord Thorneycroft told Powell not to turn one down without consulting him first. Innumerable other friends, among them Michael Foot, implored Powell not to reject the offer when it was made. On 22 June Gow called at South Eaton Place with Archie Hamilton, the Prime Minister's new PPS: for the first, but not the last, time the offer was tentatively made.

However, there would be no reversal of his earlier decision to reject a life peerage, and no prospect of his being offered a hereditary one. This was despite Mrs Thatcher's decision, after the 1983 election, to revive hereditary honours; despite the baronies and viscounties showered, a generation earlier, on Powell's ministerial contemporaries from the Macmillan era whose contributions to British political life had been far less than his; and despite his having no son to inherit a peerage. Mrs Thatcher, notwithstanding some of their past dis-agreements, had been prepared to consider his claim on an hereditary honour, but senior colleagues of hers said it would set a precedent, and necessitate such peerages being given to other retiring MPs. Whitelaw, the last-but-one Conservative recipient of a hereditary honour, was particularly hostile, and Mrs Thatcher could not win Heath's former lieutenant over. She felt the Lords was the right place for Powell, and saw nothing inappropriate in his sitting there as a hereditary peer.[3]

Among some of the more literal-minded occupants of the Government benches there was also a sense of disbelief that Powell could receive such an accolade after twice telling the people to vote Labour. When the honours list was published without his name, some of Mrs Thatcher's so-called 'friends' briefed the press that it was because of the 'treachery' remark. This was completely untrue, and an indication of how much that came, allegedly, out of Downing Street in those years – and since – had but a precarious association with the facts. Powell's own view on retirement honours had been outlined in a letter he sent to Harold Wilson in 1976, when the ex-Prime Minister received the Garter: 'I used to think that a dignified and honourable withdrawal into the House of Lords was the fitting crown of an English statesman's career. I have long ago learnt better, and come to believe that the Garter is now the only really nice thing left.'[4]

His political career was, it seemed, destined to continue on the Friday night political dinner circuit, in the columns of newspapers, anywhere except in the Palace of Westminster. There was no diminution in the number of speeches he gave around the country; there was more time for journalism. However, there was more time for all the other recreations and interests that Powell had hitherto had to push to the margins of his crowded life. He could now apply himself more devotedly to what he had set out as the task of his final years, the examination of the texts of the Gospels, starting with St Matthew. There was also more opportunity for him to indulge his literary and antiquarian interests. He would become, in 1990, president of the Johnson Society, and became active in the Church Monuments Society.

His first journalistic outing after his defeat was in *The Times* in early July, where he argued that, if the Scots wanted to leave the United Kingdom – one of the conclusions that might be drawn from the poor performance of the Conservative party north of the border at the recent election – they should be allowed to do so. 'The attempt to deny that wish to the people of what is now the Irish Republic, after they had plainly and unmistakably expressed it at the "khaki election" of 1918, was the cause of immense tragedy and wrath.'[5]

The first general public sighting of Powell after his defeat was at the *Spectator*'s summer garden party early in July 1987. He was not in the best of spirits, answering inquiries about his well-being with the dismal refrain, 'I'm dead.' He would later write, 'I have got a sympathy now for the dead that I never had before, when I go through a cemetery, I say to myself, "I know just how they are feeling! They are not there"'[6] Yet the work he had set himself to do, and the fact that, more than most in his position, he had many interests to pursue, soon, it seemed, helped restore his spirits. He allowed his sense of humour to emerge more than before, which lulled those who met him into believing he had recovered from the blow. However, the humour was often dark, both with memories of defeat, and with resignation not to death – of which he was unafraid – but to old age.

Although he had a legendary reputation as a parliamentarian, few even among his friends had understood just what being an MP meant to him. His working life had revolved around the Commons. Once he had gone through his morning routine – consuming a flask of tea prepared by his wife the night before, reading *The Times* from cover to cover, eating a traditional English breakfast ('a voracious appetite and good digestion ... I consider the indispensable basis of mental activity') and going through the correspondence with Monica Wilson, his devoted secretary, when she arrived at South Eaton Place at nine o'clock – he would set off for Westminster.[7] He had assiduously attended, and spoken in, the Commons. When not in the chamber he shunned the normal apparatus of an office – as a Privy Councillor and former cabinet minister he could have had a grand one – but had preferred to do his work in the library. His reading and gathering of information he would do before lunch – which he would often take at home – as well as any constituency business that had required a personal reply. In the afternoons he would write, whether journalism or speeches. These collegiate surroundings, in which he had been able to regulate his life and activities perfectly according to his mental predispositions, were now cut off from him. It was that loss, coupled with his having no constituents to represent and help, that he took the hardest. He had had a genuine fondness for South Down and maintained his links there, attending the opening of new Unionist constituency offices shortly after his defeat and becoming patron of the Unionist association.

That summer he went through the therapeutic exercise of collaborating with a television company in a documentary about his life and career, shown on Channel Four in October 1987. In it, Powell seemed to be defining to himself what had been the point of the previous thirty-seven years: 'My self-imposed business in my political life has been telling the English about themselves – who they are and what they are, how they govern themselves in that way, and why they do it.'[8] If that raised a doubt about the nature of the exercise he had been conducting in Ulster since 1974, Powell further aggravated it by admitting to his interviewer, Nick Ross, that he had no regrets about his career, but that he did feel remorse: for choosing, against his earlier decision, to continue to sit in Parliament after it had ceased to be sovereign. In a career famous for its absolutism, this did indeed look to have been the great compromise. What Powell was saying, and what had become obvious to his friends since his defeat, was that he had been addicted to the Commons like a drug, and had lacked the willpower, in 1974, to give it up permanently. Now, he had no choice.

In October 1987, speaking to the Salisbury Group – an association of High Tory intellectuals whose spiritual leader he was – he reflected on his leaving the Commons. He began by saying he had asked himself what had happened in the preceding thirty-seven years that, if he had been told in 1950 that he would live to see, he would not have believed. He said he could have believed the retreat from Empire; could have believed that the British, 'or at least those whom the British permitted to speak for them, were compulsively, besottedly, gripped by the delusion that something called the Commonwealth was making them "mightier yet" '. He would even have been able to comprehend the 'horrific' prophecy about the ethnic composition of many of Britain's inner cities.[9] What he could not have brought himself to believe was that Britain would abandon any desire to remain a nation, to subjugate herself to America and to allow herself to be subsumed into Europe. He would never have believed that the Commons could have passed the European Communities Act; he had been mistaken.

Later that month, I had arranged to give Powell lunch at Simpson's in the Strand. Walking through the gardens on the Embankment I saw him, dressed in black jacket and striped trousers and crowned by a bowler hat, escorting Pam. They had just been to the memorial service for Peter Goldman, the defeated Conservative candidate in the Orpington by-election of 1962. 'I'm just taking Pam to the tube,' he said funereally, 'and then I'll be back for lunch.'[10]

'Why don't you bring her too?' I suggested, detecting that Powell was not in one of his more relaxed moods, and his wife's traditional role as icebreaker and restorer of equilibrium might be a blessing.

'But won't she get in the way?' he asked.

We agreed she would not, and proceeded to Simpson's. While heartily consuming smoked eel followed by tripe and apple pie, he spoke like a man who felt he had no future. It soon became too much for his wife, who urged me to tell him that he ought to take a peerage, and therefore continue to have a place in Parliament. Powell was not grateful the subject had been brought up, but his wife persisted. Though she had worked tirelessly for his re-election, she had privately felt that 'it would not be the most disastrous thing in the world' had he lost, because 'I did not see, otherwise, how we were ever going to stop him being an MP.'[11] She thought the Lords would give him somewhere to work, and somewhere to be actively involved in politics: she could not, she recalled, get used to his being at home in the evening to watch the six o'clock news with her. However, she knew he could not be pushed into it.

Mrs Thatcher had made another attempt, through an intermediary, to see whether Powell would reconsider his refusal to take a life peerage. He had again refused, on the ground that ever since he had made his position clear in the debates on the 1958 Life Peerages Bill he had maintained that such creations were 'a constitutional abomination'. To change his tune now, he felt, would prompt others to say, 'I had no integrity.' When it was suggested that thirty years had passed, and no one would blame him for observing the new realities – and, indeed, few would remember – he observed, 'I would remember.'

Molyneaux, who as his party leader would have made the formal recommendation, also urged him to think again, and Powell did: but after two days
said he could not do it.[12] He later said, not in jest, that a 'life peerage is a sort of
insult, isn't it? Look at the people that are given them.'[13]

That autumn the *Spectator*, making its annual Parliamentarian of the Year
awards, gave a special prize to Powell. It was collected by his wife, Powell being
in Germany lecturing to British soldiers, and the huge ovation she received
from the assembled politicians and political correspondents was as much for
her as for him, in his absence. Powell was now able to travel more; he had more
time for broadcasting, and enjoyed doing it more than he ever had; but, above
all, he had more time for reading and writing, and particularly for the reading
and writing of history. The tercentenary of the Glorious Revolution – an event
that had done more than anything to shape the place he had just finished
representing in Parliament – fell in 1988, and in the first week of the year he
wrote a celebration of it in the *Daily Telegraph*, calling it 'the English miracle
... England had entered as a decisive player into the grand game of maintaining
the European balance of power.' Moreover, it had preserved 'the three most
precious of our national possessions, the three things without which we would
not be the people that we are: our monarchy, our Parliament, and our church'.[14]
That week also brought evidence of his other, more important studies: an article
in *The Times*, about the narrative of the Three Kings of the Nativity that occurs
in St Matthew's Gospel, and some contradictions apparent within it.

Powell had long ago made the resolution not to write an autobiography. It
was a mark of self-professed intellectual arrogance, his status as a 'loner' entirely
committed to his own judgments, that he felt no need to enter into the self-
justificatory exercise that, in the hands of a politician, such works usually
become. His writings in the press increasingly threw up fragments of autobiography, such as an article that spring in the *Spectator* on the National Health
Service, twenty-five years after he had ceased to run it. His comments on
contemporary politics could still gain him column inches, such as when in
March 1988 in a speech in Staffordshire he launched a formidable assault on
Neil Kinnock, saying that under his five-year leadership Labour had failed to be
an effective Opposition. 'You would not exaggerate very greatly', Powell said, 'if
you said that for five years British parliamentary democracy has been in eclipse
because it lacked the ingredient of a principled opposition without which it
cannot work.'[15]

Opposition was, Powell went on, about principle 'in a way that government,
with its constant practical involvement in management and subterfuge, cannot
ever be'. Instead, Labour had 'exchanged the true parliamentary function of
opposition for the practice and morality of a firm of public relations consultants'.
He cited the party's retreat from outright opposition to the EEC since its
hammering at the 1983 election as one main item of evidence; as a result, the

party was in no position to criticise the Government over its difficult relations with Europe. It could not credibly say, 'We told you what would happen if you did not recover your national rights.' Nor could Labour any more enter into the debate on the value of the nuclear deterrent, having ditched its opposition to that too. Powell seethed with contempt that the party was now preparing to ask the people what policies they would like it to adopt, dismissing Kinnock and his colleagues as 'an exceptional coincidence of voluble but empty-headed nonentities'.

Within a fortnight, this time in a press article, Powell was back on the rampage against Labour, for the way in which the weakness of its activities as an Opposition was allowing the Government to get away with its damaging Northern Ireland policy. He also turned on the press for failing, in the absence of a decent Opposition, to do the job for them. The particular incident that provoked Powell's fury was the 'massive self-congratulation' of politicians and press after the shootings in Gibraltar, by members of the SAS, of three IRA terrorists who were believed to be about to let off a bomb. The lawfulness of what had been done, Powell said, could only be determined judicially; but why was no one calling for such a tribunal to do this?[16]

On one issue in April 1988 the press was not silent: it was the twentieth anniversary of the Birmingham speech, and much space was devoted to examining whether or not Powell had been justified in his predictions. He himself wrote in *The Times* on the day before the anniversary that he did not take back one word of what he had said. 'Re-read after 20 years,' he wrote, somewhat mischievously, 'I am struck by its sobriety.'[17] He quoted official figures published only three weeks earlier that had shown the ethnic minority population to be around 5 per cent of the total, or nearly three million; and set to rise to 7 per cent, or 4 million, by the year 2000 if the then rate of increase was maintained. However, because of the numbers of immigrants reaching child-bearing age, the statistics came with the warning that the rate of increase was likely to be far higher during the 1990s. 'It was therefore hardly a wild conjecture in 1968', he added, 'that at the end of the century the figure on the trends then current "must be in the region of approximately one-tenth of the population".' Powell also claimed that Hailsham had, in 1968, said to a colleague, 'Enoch's figures are right: we know that.'

Two days later, at the St George's Day meeting of the Birmingham branch of the Royal Society of St George, Powell continued his unrepentance. 'England is the country of the English,' he said. 'England is a stage on which the drama of English history was played and the setting within which the English became conscious of themselves as a people ... when politicians and preachers attempt to frighten and cajole the English into pretending away the distinction between themselves and people of other nations and other origins, they are engaged in undermining the foundation upon which democratic government by consent and peaceable civilised society in this country are supported.' He concluded that 'those who at the end of the twentieth century wish to keep alive that consciousness of being English, which seemed so effortless and uncontroversial to our forefathers, will discover that they are called upon, if they take their purpose seriously, to confront the most arrogant and imposing prejudices of their time'.[18]

As well as continuing his work on the Gospels, Powell pursued other studies, publishing a defence that summer of his view of the authorship of Shakespeare. He said that his re-reading of the history plays in 1963–4 had convinced him that the writer had an insider's knowledge of the exercise of political power; and he felt it was unlikely that the man called Shakespeare had acquired all this knowledge when writing the plays in his twenties and thirties. Powell had verified the existence of a man called Shakespeare, born in 1564 at Stratford and dying there in 1616; but it was not until six years after his death, when the folio edition of his plays was published, that anyone had associated the Shakespeare who wrote the plays with the man who had lived and died at Stratford. Indeed, there was no mention Powell could find of any connection with Stratford before that time.

He then noted that, in that age of 'diarists and compulsive scribblers', nobody ever seemed to have met the playwright. Was this mere invisibility, he wondered, or non-existence?[19] Also, the folio was claimed to have been edited by two of Shakespeare's fellow actors, who said the plays had been public property before but incorrectly printed. Powell called this 'an absolute lie', as sixteen of the thirty-six plays in the edition had never been printed before; indeed, of some of them there was no trace even of any public performance. The two actors had been made bequests in Shakespeare's will, as if to confirm their link with him. Powell had been to look at the will, and found that the two men's names had been entered later, by a different hand. Nor did the will contain any reference to books, or to the manuscripts of the plays. 'So here was one of the world's greatest poets, a man so widely read that allusions to ancient and modern literature flowed onto his pen unbidden as he wrote; yet when he died he left not a book, not a word of provision for his still unpublished masterpieces. The folio edition, I could no longer doubt, had been launched with a tissue of deliberate deceit.'

The final part of his case was that the plays appeared to have dried up in 1609, after a period in which they had appeared for nearly twenty years at the rate of almost two a year, but seven years before the death of Shakespeare of Stratford-upon-Avon.

The plays, I believe, were court productions, written in the first place at the court and for the court by courtiers – the modern word is 'politicians' – not necessarily all by the same one, though there was a towering figure among them. They remained private and personal property, their existence and the identity of the authors a closely guarded and official secret, until most of those concerned were dead and its seemed a shame (especially if the enterprise might be profitable) not to release them. When that was done, the pseudonym 'William Shakespeare' was carefully preserved and even given, if not flesh and blood, at any rate dead bones and a local identity in a small provincial town. It was an outrageous imposture. But it worked.

However, no Shakespeare scholar of note felt that Powell had added anything of substance to the debate.

II

Because of his popularity with grass-roots Conservatives and the general public, Powell was able to enjoy as high-profile a life as if he were still an elected politician. Being no longer required to attend the Commons allowed him to speak more in the country, but also to travel more extensively than at any time since the war. In June 1988 he went to Moscow for the celebrations of the millennium of the Christian church in Russia. The new tolerance afforded to the church, and the greater evidence of other liberalisations under the Gorbachev regime, reinforced him in his view that Russia was no threat to Europe. He wrote that she had 're-entered what in old-fashioned parlance used to be the Concert of Europe; and she re-enters it as a nation among nations, sharing with the rest of Europe – and not least with the United Kingdom – responsibility for a European equilibrium upon which the peace of Europe and thus of the world will depend'.[20]

Then, later that summer, marking the half-centenary of his arrival there as Professor of Greek, he returned to Sydney to give a lecture, appropriately on the fictitious nature of the Commonwealth. He found an Australia that was 'in real, human terms ... as far away by Qantas capsule in 23 hours from London as it was by the lumbering flying-boats of Imperial Airways'.[21] He found the Australians still a unique nation, unique in their remoteness, because 'they live with no consciousness that anybody is looming over them'. He was struck also by the natural courtesy of the Australians towards him, the more so since his name and face meant nothing to almost all of them, so he knew he was not the recipient of special treatment because of his standing in Britain. He was bewildered not to recognise the centre of Sydney, completely rebuilt in the preceding half-century; but, when visiting the rooms of his successor as Professor of Greek, he was startled to see, on the wall, a photograph of himself as an officer cadet in 1940.

Shortly after his return from Australia Powell witnessed a historic, and seismic, shift in the attitudes of some of the Conservative leadership towards

Europe, to the point where it seemed almost to be prepared to adopt Powellite policies. In September 1988 Mrs Thatcher, inflamed by an address the President of the European Commission, Jacques Delors, had made to the annual conference of the Trades Union Congress in Bournemouth, delivered a rebuke in Bruges in which she warned Europe – and the avidly pro-European left of her party – that the frontiers of the state had not been rolled back in Britain over the preceding decade in order for them to be reimposed by the Commission. Powell was pleasantly surprised. A few days after her speech he was in Halifax, stepping up his own unending campaign against Brussels, and seeking to counter the received wisdom about the move towards the Single European Market due to reach fruition in 1992. 'What the EEC is bent upon has nothing to do with free trade or free anything,' he said. 'It is a naked assertion of the will to power, the will to create a unified state to which instead of our own national organs of representation and government we are all to be subordinated.'[23]

However, Mrs Thatcher continued to offend him over Ulster. Powell had written some articles since losing his seat about the reluctance with which, he knew, the Prime Minister had signed the Hillsborough Agreement, and about the burden she had to bear as a result. He had been to the Province several times since he lost his seat to speak, with his usual lack of equivocation, about the Government's betrayal of the Ulster people. Now he took his campaign a stage further, and used a fringe meeting at the Conservative party conference on 12 October to say that Mrs Thatcher was 'personally responsible' for the 'nightmare' of Northern Ireland.[24]

More often than not, when Powell made his regular excursions into print it was to castigate the Government for abandoning what he had marked out for them as the true path. Speaking in Wimbledon on 22 November he warned of the unacceptability of the prevailing inflation rate of 6 per cent, caused by 'government flooding the place with new money in order to meet public expenditure'.[25] The Government blamed the banks for the credit boom; but it was the Government which had supplied the banks with the funds in the first place. Powell perceived that Lawson, the Chancellor, was intervening to affect the value of sterling on the foreign exchanges – the so-called 'shadowing of the Deutschmark' – which required him to 'sell sterling like mad' to keep its value down. To sell this sterling, he had to create it, and much of the surplus was being spent, with inflationary consequences, at home.

Then, in the *Sunday Telegraph* on 4 December 1988, he pointed out that the pursuit of monetarism had not merely strengthened the economy but had also enabled the Government's trade union reforms to be executed: 'The unions were powerless to cause or to prevent inflation: so why toady to them?'[26] The policy had provided the resolve to control public expenditure, and had displayed the pointlessness of exchange controls, which had ended. He continued his attack upon Lawson, and his attempt to pre-empt Britain's entry into the

European Exchange Rate mechanism, a policy to which the Prime Minister (who was becoming more Powellite by the day) was viscerally opposed. The Government was trying to staunch the credit boom by putting up interest rates, which had the counter-productive side-effect of pushing up sterling; whereas Powell said it should have 'cut back the banks' reserves' – which were supplying all the credit – 'by using its own surplus to cancel its own paper', in other words, to stop the central bank, as lender of last resort, pumping out so much money to the banks and instead calling their reserves in. 'So the Government has got into a nice old vicious circle, rigging interest rates, rigging the rate of sterling, and now threatening to rig everything else ... it should cut the credit base of the banks and steady the growth in money.' None of this advice, which was deeply prophetic, was heeded. The policy Lawson was following, and which his two successors would follow, would culminate in the humiliation of Black Wednesday in September 1992, and the adoption, once more, of something like the policies Powell had been advocating.

As the Soviet Union, under Gorbachev, became more sympathetic to the West, Powell thought he saw the vindication of another of his policies, and was already, in 1988, anticipating the coming down of the Berlin Wall the following year. It was, as he rejoiced in writing in the *Guardian* on 7 December, a moment that brought about 'the death and burial of the American empire'.[27] The British, like the rest of Europe, now no longer saw the Americans as indispensable to their safety and security. And Chancellor Kohl of West Germany, choosing a visit to Moscow to talk of reunifying his country with the Eastern part (under Soviet control since 1945), had signalled the final gasp of America's power in Europe; and it would, as he had often predicted, be succeeded by a new balance of power in the continent dependent not on military force, but on the 'recognition of the restraints which the ultimate certainty of failure places upon the ambitions of the respective national states'.

In an end-of-year interview in December 1988 with the *Sunday People* Powell quite brazenly blew his own trumpet. As well as signifying his belief that his old party was 'rejoining Enoch' over the EEC, he referred to the adoption of his anti-inflationary policies by the Government after 1979; but he also referred to the main point on which he had been paid insufficient attention, immigration, and once more predicted civil war.[28] 'I still cannot foresee', he said, 'how a country can be peaceably governed in which the composition of the population is progressively going to change, in the way the population of great parts of England is certainly going to change. I am talking about violence on a scale which can only be described as civil war. I cannot see there can be any other outcome.' He specified he was not talking about a race war, but 'about people who revolt against being trapped in a situation where they feel at the mercy of a built-in racial majority, whatever its colour'. To give the pot an extra stir, Powell added that the highest levels of Government knew of the potential for civil war, and were making plans for it. There was no alternative, he said, but to have large-scale repatriation, even though many second- and third-generation blacks had been born in Britain; the cost of this in welfare payments and pension entitlements was, he said, well worth paying.

The beginning of 1989 saw another fillip for Powell's 'posthumous' reputation as an active politician. Under the thirty-year rule the cabinet papers for 1958 were made public, and the circumstances of his resignation in January of that year were almost universally interpreted to the discredit of Macmillan, not least because it had taken another twenty years for anyone to pay heed to the necessary action for the establishment of a sound money economy. Leaving aside the detail, contrasts were drawn with an earlier age where resignation on principle was, if not common, certainly unexceptional, and modern times, when the art of such resignations had almost entirely decayed. In an echo of old acrimonies, another of Powell's contemporaries was provoked to put his side of the case. Heath said that the argument over the spending cut was, in fact, a plot to remove Macmillan from the premiership: an assertion that lacked only hard evidence to substantiate it. 'The only way in which it was historic', Heath said, mocking the idea that the resignations had been on a point of principle, 'was that it showed that some people who wanted to get rid of Harold Macmillan as Prime Minister failed to do so. I have no doubt that they wanted to get rid of Mr Macmillan. They disliked him and his approach as Prime Minister, particularly towards the social services.'

Unlike Powell's assertions about, for example, CIA involvement in terrorism in Ulster, which although somewhat wild have never been categorically disproved, Heath's claims were easier to refute. Powell certainly came to loathe Macmillan, Birch even more so, and more quickly; but there is no suggestion that Powell's distaste was the cause of the events of 1958, as it was not, at that stage, fully formed. Also, Macmillan was in so strong a position in his party at that time – he would, the following year, lead it to re-election with an overall majority of 100 – that it defies belief that three so sensible and shrewd operators as Birch, Powell and Thorneycroft would have thought there was a chance of removing him. At best, Heath's analysis was based on anachronistic considerations. Powell explained, again, why he and his colleagues had done what they had, arguing that had they been listened to the 'disaster of the Heath years' might have been avoided.[29]

That winter, Powell was the guest on *Desert Island Discs*, for which, as usual, he made no compromises. His eight records comprised each of the four operas from Wagner's *Ring* cycle, two Beethoven symphonies ('his music was better than his politics'), his opera *Fidelio* and, finally, Haydn's *The Creation* ('a good, moral religious character. I do enjoy being with Josef Haydn'). As is not usual on that programme, most were accompanied by short but detailed analysis by the chooser. It was an interesting selection by a man who also confessed that he had been a little 'afraid' of music since the war, because of the emotional effect it might have on him. In the interview, Powell admitted that his wife had 'taken personally' his remark of three years before, about his wish that he had been killed in the war, but claimed that his wish did not invalidate all that he had done since. Repudiating his logical image, he said he was driven by emotion, something plainly true to any who knew him. He wanted no book other than the Bible (the Old Testament in Hebrew, the New in Greek, 'in order that I can continue to apply my mind to it') and Shakespeare, which were sent with him anyway. His luxury was a fish smoker, a revelation that led to his being sent smoked fish by admirers for some time afterwards.[30]

Following the success of his Australian trip, Powell planned further excursions during 1989. His health was still good, and there was no shortage of sponsors prepared to take him. The BBC was keen for him to make a television pro-gramme about India, where Powell had not set foot since February 1946. He was as keen to make the documentary as they were, and the formalities were set in train. A plan was made for him to revisit old haunts in Delhi, areas of North-West India and some former army outposts. However, the Indian high commission in London refused him a visa. No reason was given, but the wide-spread assumption was that it had much to do with Powell's speeches on immigration. Publicly the high commission was apologetic; it had received an order direct from Delhi and was powerless to do anything about it. Instead, Powell accepted an approach from another film-maker to go to Russia for the second time in a year, and to make a programme about his impressions of that country. There was no chance of his being refused entry there.

His profile at home rose greatly again that spring, with the publication, and widespread notice of Patrick Cosgrave's biography of him. The timing of the publication was fortuitous for Powell, coming as it did when enough evidence was now available to credit him with having been right about the economy, and with the climate of Conservative opinion moving in his direction on the European issue after the Bruges speech. Appearing as the book did on the eve of Mrs Thatcher's tenth anniversary in Downing Street, the elevation of Powell as one of her philosophical inventors was inevitable, but also justified. The arrival of the first biography since Powell left Parliament also allowed prominent commentators and politicians to take a view on him in an obituary sense as if, as he had gone around himself saying, he was already 'dead'. The consensus that he had had more influence than was usually credited was general, but so too was the view that the last thirteen years of his parliamentary career had been a time of sad anti-climax, and that Powell was, in fact, a man who had never been cut out for politics. Douglas Hurd, the Home Secretary, reviewing the book in *The Times*, said that Powell, though the greatest parliamentarian, had done nothing constructive in his political life apart from the Hospital Plan: all else had been negative, an epic of denunciation and opposition, and few of the apparent achievements of the Conservatives since 1979 owed anything to him. Hurd was especially dismissive of Powell's work in Northern Ireland and in opposing the EEC. The old enmities harboured by the Heathmen – Hurd had spent the Heath years as the Prime Minister's private secretary – were still there, and indeed survived Powell himself.

That spring Powell went to Russia to make his television documentary, which was shown the following July. The programme was a plea for a better understanding of the country, which had to be seen in the context of its history. In one scene, he went to the huge cemetery containing the remains of 600,000 people who perished in the siege of Leningrad and voiced his incredulity that a people who had suffered so much, and so recently, would willingly start another war. Powell attended a veterans' parade, at which he wore his own medals, and, through an interpreter, conversed with Russian soldiers. He went on to Moscow, where his romantic view of Russia was tempered by memories of the mass murders under Stalin. He visited the place where relatives of those killed under that regime were still coming to look at relics in the hope of identifying members of their families. He met a group of people devoted to compiling a record and archive of what Stalin had done. He was shocked by the scale of what he saw, but found himself asking what law, if any, Stalin had broken in his purges, for in all the limited reparations made since 1953 there had been no admission of fault on the part of the authorities. It was another example of his excess of logic exceeding his normally abundant humanity. The conclusion he now came to about Russia was that it was a country engaged in the search for legitimate authority.

Powell's programme attracted some hostile reaction when it was shown, some critics arguing, with justification, that so entranced had he been by Russia's sense of national identity that he had glossed over the threat presented by the Soviet Union to the West since the war. But it was a threat which Powell would not admit had existed, and which the events of 1989 seemed, one by one, to prove more and more absurd. However, his pleas – made in several places that summer – for an alliance to be forged between Russia and Britain as a matter of urgency in the light of the likely reunification of Germany – were treated with greater seriousness than some of the rest of his analysis.

Fired up by his visit to Russia and by the events taking place there, Powell devoted a large proportion of his public speeches to the theme of foreign policy during the rest of 1989. He was impressed, too, by the resilience with which Mrs Thatcher was taking the fight to Brussels, and defended her more than once against the attacks from her own left wing. When, in May 1989, Heath launched one such assault on his successor, Powell, in a speech at the Oxford Union, dismissed him as 'the old virtuoso of the U-turn'.[31] Back in Oxford three weeks later he returned to this theme of the end of American power in Europe, and how Russia and Britain between them still retained the ability, by force of arms, to hold the balance of power in Europe in check as they had done in the Second World War. It was in phrases such as 'Britain and Russia wore down and destroyed the greatest military machine on earth', without making any mention of America's role in the campaign from 1942 onwards, that helped continue to alienate Powell from many on the Thatcherite right of the Conservative party.[32]

The effects of Lawson's economic policy, about which Powell had been so scathing the previous year, were now becoming more apparent, with inflation reaching double figures and interest rates at 15 per cent. For all his new absorption in what the Americans were starting to call the 'new world order', Powell was able to divert his attention to this latest, predictable consequence of apostasy from his own creed. As in the 1960s, he found himself haranguing ministers who offered excuses for the new burst of inflation; and, twisting the knife in Lawson, he offered what he called 'a brief preliminary catechism':

Q: Who caused the inflation?
A: The Chancellor of the Exchequer.
Q: How did he cause it?
A: By putting a flood of new money into circulation.
Q: Why did he do *that*?
A: To prevent the exchange rate of the pound rising last year.
Q: Why did he want to stop it rising?
A: To keep level with the Deutschmark.
Q: What for?
A: To make it easier to join the EMS.[33]

He also, though, pointed to the problem that would undermine Mrs Thatcher terminally: that every other party leader, most of her senior colleagues, the self-appointed leaders of business and industry and almost the whole of European opinion were in favour of the European Monetary System too. Against that larger problem, the difficulty of Lawson's not owning up to having caused a quite unnecessary bout of inflation by his economic mismanagement would become quite insignificant.

In early September Powell published his first collection of speeches for more than a decade. *Enoch Powell on 1992*, edited by his friend Richard Ritchie, was a testament to the fact that he had not simply packed up his campaign against the EEC when the referendum had gone against him in 1975, and it contained extracts from speeches made on the question throughout the late 1970s and 1980s. Brian Walden, interviewing Powell on the publication of book, taxed him with the observation that he had, for years, said that the British people would not tolerate the EEC, yet they had tolerated it. Powell explained this away by using Bagehot's phrase, that the English are a 'deferential' people. Moreover, 'it is also a characteristic of the English that they dislike theory. You might even say, harshly, that they dislike logic. They dislike seeing a deduction drawn from something and then being confronted with that deduction and told: "But this is a logical deduction." They don't like that. It's not their way of proceeding.'[34] At the launch of the book at Chatham House on 6 September, Powell urged Mrs Thatcher to fight the next election on a nationalist platform, outflanking Labour but in sympathy with the newly emergent nationalist feelings right across Europe as the Iron Curtain came down. For Powell, this was a period of massive hope. He could not see that, in adopting what were essentially Powellite attitudes in this question every bit as zealously as he could have hoped, Mrs Thatcher would present the dagger to her internal opponents.

Throughout the following months, as pressures mounted on the Prime Minister, Powell spoke more and more enthusiastically in her support. Speaking in Surrey on 19 September he rejected the notion that the new Brugesist policy on Europe was Mrs Thatcher's alone: her colleagues, by not resigning, had signed up to it as well under the doctrine of collective responsibility, and the sniping some of them were conducting against her should be seen in that context. Amused, too, by Labour's disarray, and with a nod at his own position in Heath's shadow cabinet, he told Neil Kinnock, the Labour leader, that there was 'no collective responsibility in opposition'. Addressing a fringe meeting at the Conservative party conference at Blackpool in early October, he confessed 'I find myself today less on the fringe of that party than I have done for 20 years.'[35]

While the European policy conducted by the Prime Minister met with his approval, the economic dimension of this policy, led by Lawson, continued to distress him. Speaking on 19 October, Powell savaged Lawson for having shown 'how easy it is for a clever man to fool the ignorant' and for restoring the country to 'the tyranny of internationally fixed exchange rates'.[36] Goading Mrs Thatcher for her tolerance of this policy, Powell asked 'whether the grasp of the Conservative party upon the underlying theory of its economic policy was ever sufficiently sound or sure'. He thought it had been, but now the Conservatives had 'immolated their economic policy and the country's economic achievements upon the altar of the European Monetary Union'. Lawson was in daily conflict with Mrs Thatcher's own economic guru, Sir Alan Walters, whose views were identical to Powell's. When Mrs Thatcher refused to sack Walters ten days later, Lawson resigned.

Powell continued to support Mrs Thatcher against her internal enemies. When she once more defied the centralising and federalising tendencies of her European counterparts at a summit at Strasbourg in November, Powell wrote to her parliamentary private secretary, Mark Lennox-Boyd, to ask him to pass on to Mrs Thatcher 'my respectful congratulations on her stand'.[37] He added that 'she both spoke for Britain and gave a lead to Europe – in the line of succession of Winston Churchill and William Pitt. Those who lead are always out in front, alone.' Mrs Thatcher replied to him, 'I am deeply touched by your words. They give me the greatest possible encouragement.'[38]

His most emphatic public assertion of support for her yet came when addressing the Merseyside Conservative Ladies' Luncheon Club in Liverpool on 5
January 1990, saying the Conservatives could win the next election if they played
the 'British card'. Referring to the contrast between Mrs Thatcher and her
predecessor, Heath, who was energetically criticising her from the sidelines,
Powell said that 'a struggle is in progress between yesterday's people and tomorrow's people'.[39] He added that the new mood in Britain for 'self-determination'
had provided a 'beacon' for the newly liberated nations of Eastern Europe; if
necessary, and not for the first time, Britain should stand alone for European
freedom. In language calculated to send the Prime Minister into raptures, he
said, 'We are taunted – by the French, by the Italians, by the Spaniards – for
refusing to worship at the shrine of a common government superimposed upon
them all … where were the European unity merchants in 1940? I will tell you.
They were either writhing under a hideous oppression or they were aiding and
abetting that oppression. Lucky for Europe that Britain was alone in 1940.' The
question the Conservatives would have to ask, sooner or later – best of all at the
next election – was: 'Do you intend still to control the laws which you obey, the
taxes you pay and the policies of your government?'

A few days later, Mrs Thatcher revealed her continuing admiration for Powell,
despite everything. 'I have always read Enoch Powell's speeches and articles very
carefully,' she said in an interview with the *Daily Telegraph*. 'He was not helpful
over things like the Anglo-Irish Agreement. I think he has been absolutely right
about the economy – inflation is a monetary phenomenon. I always think it was
a tragedy that he left. He is a very, very able politician. I say that even though
he has sometimes said vitriolic things against me.'[40] Speculation surged that
Powell and the Conservatives were about to reunite; but, as on so many similar
occasions, Powell immediately found some other issue on which to attack the
Prime Minister.

Returning to South Down on 26 January, to address the annual general
meeting of his Unionist association, he observed that 'the British Government
is still in the business of obeying the demand of the United States that Ulster be
handed over to an all-Ireland state as the price at which (allegedly) Irish neutrality can be bought out and the whole of Ireland drawn into NATO'.[41] He was
angry that the Government had offered full support to the United States for a
recent invasion of Panama and arrest of that country's President, General
Noriega, ostensibly on drug-trafficking charges. Provocatively, he noted that
this support came from the same Government that, 'when a similar act of
aggression was committed by the Argentine against the Falkland Islands, despat-
ched a military expedition to the South Atlantic and took them back'.[42]

Nonetheless, the last year of the Thatcher leadership saw Powell once more
openly – rather than covertly – spoken of as a leading influence on the party's
policy: or, more accurately, the policy of that section of the party that followed

Mrs Thatcher. The Conservatives faced a difficult by-election – which they lost heavily, increasing the pressure on Mrs Thatcher – in Mid-Staffordshire. The poll tax and not, for the moment, Europe was the issue causing most pain to the Government. Powell, who had long believed there was no substitute for rates, wrote on the day of the by-election that there was no point not admitting that the tax was 'a disaster'.[43] What mattered most to the people of Mid-Stafford-shire in his view was the question of who runs Britain, and only the Con-servatives were, at last, showing a readiness to stand up to the principle that the British should run themselves. Mrs Thatcher was, he observed, accused of being 'dictatorial' for wanting to 'go it alone' in Europe. 'Well, I do not mind somebody being dictatorial in defending my own rights and those of my fellow countrymen ... lose self-government, and I have lost everything, and for good.' So, for the first time since 1970, Powell was commenting on a parliamentary contest in which he was urging the voters to vote Conservative.

III

That spring a collected edition of Powell's poetry was published – the first time some of it had been in print since 1937. Since he had become famous in another sphere, those who learned that he was a poet were often keen to read his work – and he had kept a stash of *Dancer's End* and *The Wedding Gift* that he would sell, at cost price, to anyone who bothered to ask him. When, in 1983, a bookseller had written to offer him a copy of this double volume of poems for £12, Powell had replied, 'I was interested to learn from your letter of 24 March that you can get £12, postage free, for my book. I have evidently been undercharging those members of the public to whom I have been selling my remaindered copies direct.'[44]

With this full reprint of the poems the enigmas within them were not unwrap-ped, not even by Powell's own introduction and epilogue. 'I am glad', he admit-ted, 'in a vaguely melancholy way that they are to be in print again.'[45] In an afterword to the poems, Powell asked the obvious question about his poetic impulse: 'Well, what became of it? What happened to that irresistible imperative? Where has it gone to? One cannot be content just to answer: "It stopped." '[46] He concluded that the river of inspiration had gone underground, where it still flowed; he felt that the impulse had been channelled into his speeches as a politician. 'It was an ex-poet whom my fellow countrymen still today, more fitfully, hear admonishing them still. The words, and the compulsion to utter them, are drawn, I suspect, from the same source, though long since hidden underground, as the poetry which has now been reprinted in this volume.' The *Times Literary Supplement*'s review of the collection distinguished between the pre-war poems (stigmatised as 'Housman without the street credibility') and the post-war ones, and said that Powell wrote with 'real force' when he cast off the shackles of his mentor.[47]

Only the barest factual information about the poems was given to orientate the reader. Powell agreed to some newspaper interviews to mark the publication – he was as alert as any other author to the benefits of promotion and marketing – but only on condition that he was not asked about the poems themselves. He preferred to talk about his continuing, and increasingly time-consuming, work on St Matthew's Gospel: 'The crucial event was my perception or rather conviction that it was demonstrable that Matthew was the source of the other Gospels,' he told an interviewer. He was seeking to overturn the established view of the last century or so that the reverse was true, and instead to shore up the previously established theory that Matthew had been the first of the Gospels. For Powell, such apparent cussedness about established theological beliefs had long been merely an extension of his political nature.

Later that spring Powell went to South Africa, to give some lectures and to see the country at a time of great change, on the eve of the end of apartheid. He was impressed by the optimism he found there, faced as South Africa was by a period of deep uncertainty. He felt as strongly she should be left alone by the West to sort out her own problems after the end of institutionalised discrimination as he had felt that she should be left alone before. Soon after his return he renewed his defence of Mrs Thatcher in a speech at Sutton, proclaiming that she deserved the support of her party, and that the party deserved the support of the electorate. He condemned Labour for having shifted its policy on Europe since Delors' propitiation of them in 1988, and said that, come the election, 'I shall tell you to vote to keep the right to govern your own country. That will mean voting for the party and the person who proclaim unambiguously in the face of Europe and the world that they intend Britain to be a proud, independent sovereign nation.'[48] It was a cry he repeated in several speeches over the succeeding weeks, though it had a maudlin undercurrent to it. As he said at Sutton about his own campaign against the EEC, 'I stand before you as one who has to confess that his personal resistance and protests against it have been thrust aside with ridicule and indifference.'[49]

At the end of May 1990 Powell had an accident that would, in retrospect, mark the end of his long middle age. Staying with some friends, he rose in the middle of the night to go to the bathroom. Not wishing to wake his wife he did not put the light on, and tripped over, hitting his head on a cabinet. Though dazed and in some pain, he did not believe any damage had been done. However, a couple of days later he began to realise his co-ordination was going, he was plagued by headaches and he could not think straight. A doctor was called, and soon determined Powell had a blood clot on his brain. To remove the threat to his life an emergency operation was necessary. It entailed boring two holes in his skull to drain the blood. The operation was a success; but once he appeared again in public after a convalescence of several weeks, a sign of his ordeal – a slight indentation on one of his temples – was plainly visible. A sudden frailty, unsurprisingly, seemed to have come over him. For the first time, his friends began to see him as physically vulnerable.

That summer the Ulster question took on a new urgency. The IRA mounted a renewed terror campaign on the mainland, the nadir of which was the murder of Ian Gow at his home in Sussex on 30 July 1990, by a car bomb. Gow had particularly gained Powell's admiration for his resignation on principle after the signing of the Anglo-Irish Agreement in 1985. Powell felt that the indirect killers of his friend had been the Government, and this was not a view Powell kept to himself or to his circle. A few days after Gow's assassination he wrote in the *Daily Express* that the 'horrendous' murders of Gow and others had been 'made more horrendous by the downpour of sanctimonious humbug about "not giving in to terrorism" which is their invariable accompaniment'.[50] He accused the Government of cowardice and appeasement towards the IRA over many years: 'One would have to be a fool indeed to believe that, if the Provisional IRA had never existed, Her Majesty's Government would have pursued the same policy towards Northern Ireland as it has been doing since the early 1970s.' Powell was milder on Mrs Thatcher than he had been previously, the impetus to attack her having lessened greatly since the speech at Bruges. He wrote that 'the grief inflicted upon her by every terrorist response is too genuine to be doubted'; she had been obviously distraught at Gow's death, as she had at Neave's eleven years earlier and after the casualties of the Brighton bombing in 1984. She was, however, still in thrall to the Americans, Powell suggested, and since the coming down of the Iron Curtain there had been no need for this. He urged her to try to make Gow's death the final motivation to stop giving in to terrorism.

Soon after Gow's funeral the Powells went on a motoring holiday to Tuscany, to return, late in August, to find the police waiting for them. Powell had been a terrorist target from the start of his association with Ulster. New information came into the hands of the police suggesting that the threat to Powell had moved from being more or less latent to being active. A 'death list' had been discovered, linked to a heavily armed IRA cell, and they had reason to believe that Powell was highly likely to be attacked. The Powells had always been reluctant to have any security – he himself had refused, almost uniquely among Ulster MPs, to carry a firearm when still in Parliament – but the terms used by Scotland Yard to spell out to him the gravity of the threat as they now understood it left him and his wife with no sensible option but to comply.

The house at 33 South Eaton Place was well known: Powell had insisted on publishing not only his address, but also his private telephone number, in several reference books. It was now heavily fortified with locks, alarms, sensors, reinforced windows and bomb-proof curtains. The Powells were told to keep away from the windows in case of a sniper's having found his way into one of the overlooking buildings. Also, Powell's habit of travelling on the tube had to end. For the duration of the threat – which lasted until the following year – he had to go everywhere in an armour-plated Jaguar with two policemen; and another two rode in a similar car in front. It was saturation security of a sort usually only applied to the Prime Minister and one or two senior cabinet ministers, but Scotland Yard was taking no chances.

The security, inevitably, interfered with everything the Powells wanted to do; and, having always been an intensely independent and self-reliant couple, the prospect of a round-the-clock chauffeur-driven service, and of having one's shopping done – little perks that often appealed to others with Special Branch protection – held no attraction for them. The policemen attached to them quickly, however, became like members of the family, and in some cases friends for life, so the situation was one to which the Powells found it relatively easy to adapt. It even managed to have its funny side, without which it might have been difficult to bear.

I had arranged to take the Powells to Sussex at the start of September 1990, to write a feature for the *Daily Telegraph* about his belief that so-called 'Norman' churches were, in fact, Saxon structures – usually detectable from the height of their chancel arches and their towers – that the Normans had 'vandalised' by imposing their forms of decoration upon them. After some discussion we had chosen Sussex because Powell's researches had told him that this part of the country was rich in such buildings.

Instead of my picking him and Pam up one Monday morning and driving them there, we were driven down in the second of the two armour-plated Jaguars (which, the driver proudly told us, did eight miles to the gallon on a clear run) while the first, filled with policemen, cruised in front. No one knew the details of our itinerary, the police the previous week having ordered complete confidentiality. All that day and the next the two big cars – conspicuous even on a busy road, and all the more so on virtually deserted country lanes – would pull up outside isolated churches, with the policemen jumping out before they came properly to a halt and running back to guard Powell's exit from his car, their hands on their chests. The landscape was scoured for lingering terrorists as we made our way inside to look at the buildings. The only violence occasioned was when one of the burlier policemen forced open a door, somewhat to our embarrassment, of a church we could not otherwise enter. We talked mainly of the crisis in the Gulf following Iraq's invasion of Kuwait, which Powell was, as ever, deeply opposed to the British intervening in. However absorbed we were in other matters, and however much we tried to forget about the high security under which we were travelling, the knowledge that Ian Gow had been murdered a few miles along the coast just over a month earlier was never far away.[51]

Powell had outlined his concerns over Britain's attitude to the Gulf only days after Saddam Hussein's invasion of Kuwait. In a letter to the *Daily Telegraph* on 11 August he berated Labour for its failure to demand a recall of Parliament to discuss the crisis. 'We seem no longer to possess the asset of a parliamentary opposition,' he complained. 'It is not that the Opposition Front Bench have gone on holiday. The trouble is they are too busy collecting from the Americans brownie points which they fondly imagine can be converted into votes at a general election.'[52] He said that although the Americans had declared Saudi Arabia an ally, and had pledged to defend her territorial integrity, the country was not an ally of Britain's in the formal sense. No alliance Britain had with America, he asserted, required the British to become engaged in the defence of Saudi Arabia; however, naval and air forces had already been committed to that end. There was no need for Britain to become involved: 'Saddam Hussein has a long way to go yet before his troops come storming up the beaches of Kent or Sussex.'

He suggested that talk of 'appeasing' Saddam, in the way Britain had appeased Hitler in the late 1930s, was 'nonsense'. Then, that had been a question of the balance of power in Europe. This was a question of the balance of power in the Middle East, which had ceased to matter to Britain at the end of Empire. 'Saddam Hussein may not be nice and his form of Government not to our taste. That is no business of ours nor of the United States,' he wrote. If troops were to be committed, Parliament should be consulted. That was the message Labour should have been putting out. But, Powell concluded, 'can they be trusted to govern if they cannot even be trusted to oppose?'

Parliament was recalled, at the end of September, and no impediments were put in the way of a commitment of British troops to assist in the defence of Saudi Arabia – or, as it was to become, the expulsion of the Iraqis from Kuwait. Powell continued to maintain that the conflict was none of Britain's business. The internment, as hostages, of British nationals in Kuwait and Iraq was, he said, no reason to start a war. He drew a parallel with the internment of enemy aliens by both sides in 1939, which was somewhat inexact, since such aliens had not explicitly been hostages in the way these Britons were. 'The world is full of evil men engaged in doing evil things,' he wrote on 21 October. 'That does not make us policemen to round them up nor judges to find them guilty and to sentence them. What is so special about the ruler of Iraq that we suddenly discover that we are to be his jailers and his judges?'[53] He dismissed the notion that, because of other sources of supply, the events in Kuwait would have any long-term effect on the price of oil, and said, categorically, that 'we as a nation have no interest in the existence or non-existence of Kuwait or, for that matter, Saudi Arabia as an independent state'. He concluded, 'I sometimes wonder if, when we shed our power, we omitted to shed our arrogance.'

For the moment, though, the Conservative party was concerned with fights closer to home. Returning from a summit of European heads of government at Rome at the end of October, where she had been ambushed into making further commitments to a single currency, Mrs Thatcher had uttered a series of uncompromising remarks about her determination to defend British monetary independence. These, in turn, had been construed as sufficient provocation by Michael Heseltine, her former Defence Secretary, to break earlier declarations of intent not to stand against her for the leadership. The more uncompromising Mrs Thatcher had become, the more resolutely Powell had spoken in her defence, culminating, once the contest was called, in a promise by him to apply to rejoin the party and urge people to support it (and therefore to support the continuation of national independence) if Mrs Thatcher survived in office. Such was Powell's conviction, at last, that Mrs Thatcher was a fit leader for his old party and his country that he wrote to one of her closest supporters, Norman Tebbit, on 16 November – the night after he had pledged his support to her in a speech at Ewell – telling him that she was welcome to use his name and the fact of his intentions in any way she saw fit.[54]

On 20 November she came top of the poll against Heseltine, but by an insufficient margin to be re-elected leader. Her intention was to fight again, but it was quickly made clear to her by several self-interested ministers who had higher hopes of advancement under a successor that they would not give her their support. So, on 22 November, she resigned. Powell, writing in the press the following Sunday, was philosophical. 'Good news is seldom so good, nor bad news so bad, as at first sight appears,' he said, referring to the abject gloom into which the Powellite–Thatcherite wing of the Conservative party, with its deep antipathy to European integration, had been plunged since her demise.[55] Coldly, he analysed that she had fallen from power because few of her most important colleagues were as Powellite on the European policy as she was. He did not doubt she had taken a line that had improved the popularity of her party with the electorate, and for that reason it had been foolish of her internal enemies to be rid of her.

He was not, though, entirely despondent. 'The battle has been lost, but not the war. The fact abides that, outside the "magic circle" at the top, a deep and rooted opposition has been disclosed in Britain to surrendering to others the right to make our laws, fix our taxes, or decide our policies. Running deep beneath the overlay of years of indifference is still the attachment of the British public to their tradition of democracy. Their resentment on learning that their own decisions can be overruled from outside remains as obstinate as ever.' He agreed that matters, for the moment, looked bad, but warned that it was a perilous business to try to govern in the face of the wishes of the people. She had rekindled the flame of independence after more than a decade of its being doused; and 'what has happened once can happen again ... sooner or later those who aspire to govern ... will have to listen'. These were prophetic words:

the internecine struggle in the Conservative party had only just started, and would bedevil Mrs Thatcher's successors as much as, if not more than, it had bedevilled her.

When British troops finally went into action against the Iraqis in January 1991, Powell did not relent from his earlier opposition to the conflict. Writing in the *Daily Telegraph*, he protested as he had before that 'no national interest of Britain is at stake' in the occupation of Kuwait.[56] The whole exercise had been aimed at upholding something he could not believe existed – the 'authority of the United Nations'. This, in turn, was merely a vehicle for 'the aspiration of the United States to project its new-found power in the defence of something called "the world" against a moral antibody known as "communism"' '. The sanctioning by Parliament of the use of British forces was, he contended, 'immoral'.

That spring, as he neared his seventy-ninth birthday, his mental and physical activity remained undimmed. It soon became clear to Powell – and he reflected the perception in the speeches he was still making, relatively frequently, up and down Britain – that Mrs Thatcher's successor, John Major, had none of her understanding of the political imperatives of the European question. The Budget of March 1991 also offended him. Child benefit, which the previous admin-istration was allowing to fade away by not uprating it, had been restored in value; and Powell said this was a 'reversion to the Socialist hosepipe methods for allocating welfare payments'.[57] He found it odd, too, that an interview with the Chancellor of the Exchequer, Norman Lamont, should have cited Iain Macleod as a great influence on many contemporary Conservative ministers, for Powell knew that the Macleod of *Needs and Means*, forty years earlier, would never have dreamed of using the 'hosepipe'. Powell, writing on this subject in the *Independent* after the Budget, reminded his readers that Macleod had left no written philosophical legacy, which 'perhaps accounts for his name having been so inappropriately inscribed on the banners of a Conservative party fleeing from beneath the fall-out from the Thatcher detonation. Alas, poor Iain; how surprised he would be to find himself the darling of the refugees from That-cherism.'

In early July Powell attended a party at 11 Downing Street, a house he had hardly visited since his resignation from the Treasury in 1958. As he left the house at the end he looked behind him and, with a nod towards Hailsham's first volume of memoirs, said to John Patten, a Home Office minister, 'Ah, the door whereout I came.'[58] His mood of reflectiveness was further heightened by the preparatory work for the publication later in the year of a substantial compendium of his writings, broadcasts and speeches, *Reflections of a Statesman*. Writing the foreword to it that summer, Powell mused on what might have been, and on what he would have liked to have been. He recognised that his particular approach to politics was not conducive to achieving office:

If an act of choice was involved, it was a choice implicit already in my own personality. I do not deny that I would like to have been Secretary of State for Defence or Chancellor of the Exchequer; but that would have been at the price of renouncing the freedom to speak my mind on matters which seemed to me to be of transcendent interest and importance and on which my own conclusions were out of line with the commonly accepted views, conclusions and conventions. To decline to pay that price was a renunciation which proved to be congenial; but to avow this casts no aspersion on colleagues whose choice was different.[59]

He devoted himself more and more to literary, rather than political, endeavours. There was always a book to review, and his work on Matthew was now sufficiently advanced for him to be looking around for a publisher. Through the autumn, after a holiday abroad, he worked hard at this theological studies. At the end of the year he was diverted by two continental events: the Maastricht summit, and the break-up of Yugoslavia, events he contrasted with each other: the so-called new Europe, and the old, at which Britain could not be at the heart, but which – as Germany, in her recognition of Slovenia and Croatia as independent states, was showing – was about the balance of power and spheres of interest. 'Whether Yugoslavia dissolves into two states or half a dozen states or does not dissolve at all makes no difference to the safety and well being of the United Kingdom,' he wrote in December.[60] The lesson of Maastricht was a continuation of the lesson he had been trying to teach, in several contexts, for years: that where Britain's genuine interests were concerned, the country had to have 'a foreign policy which befits the sole insular and oceanic state in Europe'. He correctly detected the accelerant nature of the treaty on the smouldering resentment against Europe in the Conservative party.

The following year was one of great landmarks, but also of ominous portents for the future, for Powell and his family. On 2 January he and Pam had been married for forty years, and held a Ruby Wedding dinner on 18 January to which they asked their closest friends and family. The Strachans, who had not been able to come to the original ceremony, came this time. Powell had the sensation of being increasingly bereaved, his life more and more becoming a round of memorial services. Still working as hard as he was, and feeling restored after his accident of the previous year, he had plenty to occupy him, and his family and friends were planning an even greater celebration, or series of celebrations, for the summer: his eightieth birthday.

Before that, however, another general election intervened, and Powell chose to make a remarkable intervention to the campaign. He went back to Wolverhampton South-West – only the third time since 1974 – to speak for his successor, Nicholas Budgen, who was now, because of demographic changes, fighting what had become a marginal seat. It was just like the old days: the people packed out the room in a local hotel where the meeting was held. The doorman saluted him. An anti-racist demonstration welcomed him outside. He endorsed Budgen for his opposition to Maastricht, but condemned the rest of the Conservative party for supporting it and, with it, yet further surrenders of sovereignty. One questioner, afterwards, asked Powell, 'Is this your last campaign?' He replied, 'I do not know when the Lord will take me.'[61]

There were not, though, to be that many more such outings. Slowly, gradually, Powell was winding down, still spurred relatively often to protest on his old themes in the newspapers, or on public platforms, but more, now, content to be at home in his small study overlooking the garden, with his books and his wife. He was spending more time reading than for years, mainly because of the weight of book reviewing he was doing, but also because he found that the speed at which he read had declined. Meanwhile, that spring, preparations for his eightieth birthday continued.

There were three notable occasions making up the celebrations. First, he and his wife gave a party for their close friends at the Athenaeum – which Powell had joined after losing his parliamentary seat, and where he would lunch about once a fortnight. This happily coincided with the news that Yale University Press had accepted his book on St Matthew's Gospel for publication. Then, his friends still in Parliament, led by Patrick Cormack and Jonathan Aitken, gave a small private dinner for him in Aitken's house, to which former parliamentary colleagues, chosen by Powell, were asked. John Biffen, Richard Body and Peter Shore were veterans of the fight against Europe; Michael Foot, who came with his wife, of Powell's and his great triumph against the Parliament (No. 2) Bill; Jim Molyneaux and Robert Cranborne reflected Powell's Ulster interests, and Jane Gow was there in place of her murdered husband. Julian Amery, Peter Tapsell, Peter Hordern and Jack Weatherill, who had just retired as Speaker, were old friends; Richard Shepherd, Nick Budgen, William Waldegrave and Neil Hamilton were from a younger generation of admirers. His former colleagues presented him with a silver salver on which were inscribed the words 'Scholar, poet, soldier, statesman'. Finally, there was a great dinner to which friends, colleagues and many prominent in national life, including Lady Thatcher, came, which Andrew Alexander and Greville Howard had organised. It was presided over by the 6th Marquess of Salisbury, who presented Powell with a fine bronze of his great-grandfather, Victoria's Prime Minister. Powell made a moving speech of thanks as the climax of the evening. He had aged, it seemed to many of us, more than we would have liked since his accident. His voice was becoming thinner, less resonant, less powerful. Suddenly, he seemed an old man. The celebrations also provided an opportunity for Powell to demonstrate that he was not now a man to harbour grudges; among those invited was Clement Jones, to whom he had barely spoken since 1968.

In early June I had interviewed Powell for the *Spectator*, and we had turned, as seemed natural, almost immediately to the subject of death. 'How', he asked me rhetorically, 'can a man of 80 say he is happier than he was at 35? I have aged! If a man of 25 were to wake up feeling as I do as a man of 80, he would cry out: "What's wrong with me? I'm ill!" '[62] He continued that death, now, 'appears under a more friendly guise. After all, for most of one's life, one is keeping him at bay. But now he is a potential friend. This is something, one grows old by jerks. And I remember, when I grew old by a jerk in my forties, having a sensation like a hand laid on my shoulder, as I worked in the garden. It said to me, You know, you're in your forties now. Similarly, death is like the hand laid on the shoulder. It says, It's all right, old chap, you don't have to worry, I'll come and take you away.'

For all his absorption in literary pursuits, and for all the demand he was still in as a speaker and broadcaster, Powell revealed in the interview that he still deeply missed being a Member of Parliament. He did not, to his surprise, especially miss the Commons, but 'I still miss the constituency. I still miss places and people who expect something from me. Places and people to whom I can go and say, "You have a problem here, I'm your Member of Parliament, will you show me?" ' He repeated his belief that, looking back on his career, he had not failed: 'We are in danger of identifying political activity with the exercise of office.' He mocked the assumption 'that what matters is to grab the levers. It matters equally to be in a position to advise and consent.'

He felt confident he would be proved right on Europe, and claimed that he had no regrets or grudges. His sacking in 1968 had been 'a liberation for me. I became, dare I say it, my own man. I've always wanted to be friends with Ted, though I'm not at all sure it's reciprocated. He has a very nice sense of humour. And I have no repulsion from Ted at all.' Of Hailsham he said, 'when you're dealing with Quintin you must remember that you're dealing with the man who never grew up. He receives the tolerance which adults give to the young. He's a very able young man, and we put up with the inconvenience of having him about the house because he is so bright, you know.' Powell never bore a grudge against the man who had, perhaps, been most responsible for ensuring he was sacked in 1968. Reviewing a philosophical tract by his old adversary two years later, Powell wrote, 'if I had to point, among the public men of our time, to the possessor of the highest talent, I would unhesitatingly nominate Lord Hailsham, however much I might be inclined to qualify that encomium by declining to extend to it maturity of judgment'.[63]

Before our interview closed, I asked him, for the record, whether he would change his mind and settle down, in his remaining years, to write his auto-biography. His answer was unequivocal. 'No autobiography. No vomit.' It held no attraction to him to 'regurgitate' what he thought he had thought in the past; it was something he wished to leave to another. He outlined a more pervasive truth about himself, and his record, in one of his other birthday interviews: 'Perhaps I've been too interested in politics to be a good politician.'[64]

IV

The preoccupation of the Conservative party in the winter of 1992–3 with getting through Parliament the Bill that would ratify the Treaty of Maastricht was a great fillip to Powell. In the new, firm resistance to the treaty among some Conservative MPs he saw that the message he, with only a handful of others, had sought to convey at the time of the passage of the European Communities Bill twenty years earlier had not been lost. The ignominious retreat by Britain from the Exchange Rate Mechanism in September 1992 was another vindication of Powellism, from which the opposition to Maastricht flowed effortlessly on. Writing in the *European* on 5 November 1992 Powell said he was not expecting the European Communities Act to be repealed, or even amended, in the near future. 'Still, something has happened. There has been an explosion. Politicians, political parties, the public itself have looked into the abyss.' He stuck to his view that 'the British people, somehow or other, will not be parted from their right to govern themselves in parliament'.[65]

During the autumn of 1992 his health began to give him and his family concern. His increasing frailty, and the tremor in his usually strong voice and in his movements, seemed to suggest something was wrong. A doctor diagnosed Parkinson's disease in its early stages. The disease would not kill him, but it threatened to restrict him severely. Powell was determined not to take the threat passively; as with everything else in his life, he resolved to fight. For some time, hardly anyone outside the family was told of his illness, and he did all he could to carry on life as normal.

The spring of 1993 saw the twenty-fifth anniversary of the Birmingham speech, and found Powell still unrepentant. The 1991 Census had shown the immigrant-descended population to be 5.9 per cent of the total, compared with the 'little over 6 per cent' that the Eastbourne speech of November 1968 had predicted for the year 2000, but still some way below Powell's upper-end estimate of perhaps 10 per cent in the Birmingham speech. His predictions about the concentration of ethnic minorities in certain inner cities were correct, indeed had somewhat understated the reality; his predictions of civil war had yet to come true, but he was still maintaining that the last years of the century would, because of the predominant age group in which the immigrant-descended population was placed, see the greatest increase in numbers, and therefore risk of violence, yet.

He wrote an article in *The Times* on the anniversary itself in which he proclaimed his lack of regret at his remarks of twenty-five years earlier. The 1991 Census had also shown what he called 'a great disparity in the age structure of the two populations' – being the indigenous and the immigrant-descended – 'which will continue to cause the relative size of the ethnic minority to increase as far ahead as it is worthwhile to look'.[66] He stressed, as before, that the problem was made worse by the concentration of immigrants in certain areas. This, he said with the lack of understatement he habitually used in addressing these matters, would lead to 'communalism', which would have a profound effect on the electoral system in Britain: 'communalism and democracy, as the experience of India demonstrates, are incompatible'.

As a significant part of the Conservative party had hardened in its opposition to the Government's official policy on Europe, so Powell's status as a figurehead for their views had been resurrected. I interviewed him in front of a packed house at the Bow and Poplar Conservative Association in March 1993, where he was cheered to the echo by fully paid-up Conservative supporters for denouncing their party's policy on Europe. In early May he went to Newbury, where the Government was defending the seat in a by-election, and spoke on behalf of Alan Sked, standing for the United Kingdom Independence Party on a platform of opposition to Maastricht. Powell's name brought more than 400 people to a rally for Sked on the evening of 4 May, where Powell urged them not to support any party 'who will take away from you that which you value'.[67] The vital question, in the by-election and beyond, was, he said again, 'by whom are you going to be governed?' In a nostalgic touch, Powell was heckled by communists who kicked the car in which he arrived.

At the end of May 1993 the Powells attended the fortieth birthday party of Michael Portillo at the Spanish Club. Margaret Thatcher, seeing Powell, came up to him and greeted him effusively, and with genuine affection. Ever since her endorsement of her successor in the general election of the previous year Powell had cooled again towards her, feeling that the endorsement was also a repudiation of what she had been fighting for between the Bruges speech and her removal from office. 'Enoch, I haven't seen you since your eightieth-birthday dinner. How are you?' she asked. 'I'm eighty-one,' he replied.[68] Some of Powell's most entertaining – intentionally or otherwise – remarks were made at such gatherings: he adored parties more as he became older, not least because of the chance that he would meet someone genuinely interesting. When he did not, he could be wilfully mordant.

At one such event he was elsewhere in the room when his wife met the actor Sir Donald Sinden. She told Sinden what a great admirer she had always been of his, and how she had enjoyed many of his films; and, when Sinden discovered she was Powell's wife, he asked to be introduced. The formalities over, Sinden told Powell at some length, and with thespian eloquence, how much he had always admired him. The eulogy over, Powell fixed Sinden with a stare and said, 'Thank you. And, might I ask, what line of business might you be in?'[69]

In the summer of 1993 an old policy of Powell's came back to haunt him: his zeal, as Health Minister thirty years earlier, to have the mentally ill removed from their Victorian institutions and cared for 'in the community'. In the space of five weeks that summer three people were murdered by former mental patients, adding to a tally of approximately forty such killings in the previous two years. The Health Secretary, Virginia Bottomley, promised a review of the policy. Powell went into print on 13 July to outline why his policy could have worked, but had not.

He stressed that those known to be criminally insane should never have been included in such a programme; Broadmoor and Rampton were still there for them. The problem he claimed to have identified from the moment in 1962 when he first envisaged the policy, but which none of his successors had managed successfully to tackle, was that of funding. 'The new forms of care were going to require more and not less money than the old, inasmuch as they were decentralised and more intimate as well as more human.'[70] The Health and Welfare Plan of 1963, which had followed the Hospital Plan of 1962, had had the sub-title 'The Development of Community Care'. It had assumed, drawing on the local authority plans which then existed, capital expenditure on community care of £200 million in the following ten years and an increase of 45 per cent in staff. These things had not happened.

As the local authorities, whose responsibility it now was to care for the former inmates, received their finances from local rates and central government grants, whereas the NHS was funded directly out of taxation, a huge transfer of money from one area of government to another was needed if the community care policy was to be operated properly; but it had not happened. Instead, he observed, there had throughout the preceding fifteen years been 'open warfare' between central and local government, so the assumptions upon which the policy had earlier been based had now proved groundless. As a result, institutional care had been run down without the resources for community care being expanded. Nothing short of 'the reinstatement of responsible democratic local government' would turn the policy round, for, as he had always seen it, the care of the mentally ill and handicapped in the community 'is a proper responsibility for elective local government'.

Though it was now six years since he had lost his seat, Powell was still a regular visitor to Ulster and retained his membership of the Official Unionist party, whose annual conference each autumn he would usually address. He delivered the Ian Gow Memorial Lecture to the Friends of the Union in June 1993, in which he claimed that it was still the undeclared aim of the Government to have Northern Ireland removed from the United Kingdom. This was apposite, since in the last months of 1993 the rumour mill was active, as it had been during 1985, of accommodations being reached between the governments in London and Dublin; and, as he had eight years earlier, Powell went into print to denounce the participation by the Conservative Government in any initiative that might give the IRA cause to believe that, by turning up the pressure of its violence just a little more, it could soon achieve its long-standing aims. Powell, writing in *The Times* in November 1993, urged a 'clean break' with the past. But instead, the following month, the two governments concluded a new accord in London.[71]

Powell treated the Downing Street Declaration with predictable contempt. He detected that the policy had been driven, as usual, by a determination in Whitehall to get shot of Ulster once and for all. If only, he wrote the day after the declaration had been made, the 'proconsular, undemocratic legislation by Order in Council' were abandoned in favour of proper integration, and Ulster was governed like the rest of the Kingdom, there would be no need for concessions. However, he was not heard any more than at any other time in the preceding quarter-century when he had made this call.

In early 1994 Powell's health took a noticeable downturn. At no time in his illness, even towards the end, was he prepared to admit defeat. He became progressively less steady on his feet, which inevitably placed some restriction on his activities. He began to lose weight – not that he had ever been anything other than trim – and his voice became less and less powerful. He accepted fewer speaking engagements, and by the following year had to give up public platforms altogether. He was still able to write, and was determined not to be silent completely.

The first part of the year was devoted to correcting the proofs of his work on Matthew, *The Evolution of the Gospel*, publication of which was set for that autumn. He still found the opportunity, occasionally, to take part in the debate about Britain's future in Europe, sensing that the prophecies he had made about the nature of the beast were, at last, being accepted as true. On 16 May he spoke to the anti-federalist Bruges Group in London, where he observed that the European issue had 'destroyed one Prime Minister and will destroy another Prime Minister yet'.[72] His main message was for the Government to repatriate the powers surrendered to the European Court of Justice, which he said was 'committed to upholding the unifying purposes of the Community'.

The following month he wrote in the *Daily Mail* that 'Britain is waking from the nightmare of being part of the continental bloc, to rediscover that these offshore islands belong to the outside world and lie open to its oceans.'[73] He felt that many of the aberrations currently present in society – whether the European experiment, or the rejection of the two-parent family, or an apparent breakdown in law and order – would be seen to be only temporary. As he himself became frailer, he was suffused with optimism about the country: 'When exploration has run its course, we shall revert to the normal type of living to which nature and instinct predispose us. The decline will not have been permanent. The deterioration will not have been irreversible.' History, he said, had showed fluctuations 'between periods of rupture and periods of conformity'.

One constant, it seemed, was the strife in Ulster. In August 1994, on the twenty-fifth anniversary of the troops being sent in to restore order, Powell wrote that the determination of the people of the Six Counties – Protestant and Catholic – to remain in the United Kingdom had been clearly expressed at every general election since 1918; seventeen out of seventeen seats in the Province had, at the 1992 election, returned candidates who took their seats at Westminster. Yet, ever since 1918, the 'English State' had 'cold-bloodedly' persisted in its desire to be rid of Ulster.[74] The determination was, he believed, still there to force home rule upon the Six Counties, and then to make them see the sense of linking up with the Republic. 'It is', he concluded, 'the tragedy of a Government committed to objectives which it dare not avow.'

The publication of *The Evolution of the Gospel* caused a stir weeks before any copies reached the shops. Powell had lost none of his old talent for publicity. His supposition that there was an original Gospel in which Christ was not crucified, but was stoned to death, was the most shocking thing for his critics, but Powell relied on his well-used tools of textual criticism to justify the point. He was even accused of trying to fan anti-Semitism, for his case was that Jesus had been stoned by the Jews as a blasphemer, though the oldest teachings on this question also point to stoning. The Dean of Lichfield, Dr Tom Wright, opined that while Powell's was obviously a work of 'great erudition', it 'seems to have lost touch with the distinction between that which is possible and that which is plausible'.[75]

The *Daily Telegraph*'s reviewer, Peter Jones, was savage: 'This, then, is good old 19th-century source analysis, of the sort German scholars deployed to show there were eight (or three, or six, or 14) authors of Homer's *Iliad*. The method depends on the *a priori* assumption that inconsistency demonstrates multiple authorship, and encourages a nit-picking, literalistic myopia.'[76] Powell had not, this critic asserted, understood the metaphorical quality of the literature, and had therefore chosen to discard the translations of many words that, unless interpreted metaphorically, did not make sense. Nor had Powell paid heed to the historical sources that mentioned the crucifixion, preferring to rely on his textual interpretations for asserting that there had not been one. He rebuked Powell for paying heed to no one's studies but his own, and called the work 'a dereliction of scholarly and intellectual responsibility'.

The outrage of theologians that Powell could suggest that Matthew had been the first Gospel to be written, and that it badly distorted the story, was reminiscent of the opprobrium and derision heaped on him twenty-five years earlier for suggesting that control of the money supply could constrain inflation. His theological work was taken by his critics to symbolise all that was wrong with Powell the politician – his disdain for the view of others in the same field, his bloody-mindedness in the face of an established consensus, his pedantry, the absurdity of his remorseless logic, his refusal to compromise, and what one who studied him closely, D. L. W. Ashton, has called 'the preference for being an odd-man-out rather than top-man-in'.[77] Nonetheless, recognising by this stage what an influence he had had by operating in this way in the political sphere, Powell was not minded to moderate his tone in matters of religion.

He made what turned out to be his last visit to a Conservative party conference in October 1994, arriving in Bournemouth on a day of extraordinary heat and beauty for so late in the year and addressing a Monday Club meeting on Northern Ireland. The room, in a small hotel, was packed and overflowing; many had to stand outside in a courtyard to hear him. The size of the attendance was taken as a clear sign by conference managers that the party did not approve of the Government's more conciliatory policy towards nationalism, in the wake of a ceasefire offered by the IRA a month earlier.

In his speech – made without a note, as the tremor in his hand made it difficult for him to read from a text if he held it – Powell said the ceasefire was a sign the IRA believed it was close to achieving its objectives. To counter this, he continued, a proper structure of local government had to be restored in Ulster; and the flavour of the meeting, from questions asked afterwards, was that there should be no concessions to Sinn Fein until the IRA had disbanded and its arms had been handed over – a position the Government would not adopt. That Powell could still act as a rallying point for the dissenters within the Conservative party, twenty years after he had left it, was remarkable. As he spoke, the signs of his growing infirmity were now becoming harder to conceal. He was still dynamic, however, and spoke for perhaps twenty minutes. He received a lengthy and emotional ovation, many of those in attendance rightly supposing that it might be their last opportunity to display their affection for him so directly. He went out into the courtyard afterwards to be surrounded by the press, and gave some short television interviews, before joining a small group of the Club's officials and other friends for a simple lunch of fish and chips, and a discussion of the apparently inevitable failure of the Government to grasp the European question any better than its predecessors.

For all the physical constraints on what he could now do, he still had his reading and writing. The pile of books for review did not shrink, and he was still in demand for journalism, though he found writing more and more of an effort. He could still write in an increasingly shaky hand and produce a manuscript that his secretary, Monica Wilson, would type out, but it was more time-consuming, and harder, than it had been. He nurtured the plan of studying and writing about St John's Gospel in the way he had about St Matthew's. It was an ambition that, from the start, looked mountainous, though a manuscript lay uncompleted at his death.

He was determined not to be made either a physical or mental prisoner by his illness; that was one of the attractions journalism held for him. When a committee was set up under Lord Nolan in the autumn of 1994 to examine and rule upon standards in public life, Powell was ready with his views based on nearly half a century in politics. He said that such a committee was 'the most futile and self-defeating operation that can be imagined. There is a word which people have become afraid to use in this connection, but there is no substitute for it. That word is "gentleman". A Member of Parliament should be expected to behave as a gentleman would.'[78]

Outlining a view painfully anachronistic – on the Conservative benches at least – in the 1990s, he added that the status of an MP 'is not the reward for any inconveniences or duties to which a Member of Parliament is subject, and it is a reward which, therefore, cannot be paid in cash. The man or woman who receives that status may have other income, earned or unearned, but must not go around looking out to be paid.' MPs had privileges – notably parliamentary privilege – that enabled them to do their jobs properly without fear of outside encroachment. 'If all this sounds old fashioned,' Powell concluded, 'that is only a symptom of our malady. The "classless society", to which John Major aspires, is a society in which there are no "privileges" and in which there are no "gentlemen" ... alas, in these days of registers of Members' interests and definitions by committee of acceptable behaviour in public life, we have moved a long way from, and below, the class society which created our free institutions.'

Throughout 1995 Powell's health slowly deteriorated, but there were still good days when he seemed almost like his old self. He was still able to get out, and enjoyed doing so, though the experience could be exhausting. Although he had to cut down drastically what he could do, especially in public, there were important exceptions. In May 1995 he made the last of countless memorial addresses, and for him one of the most poignant, at the funeral of the former Garter King of Arms Sir Anthony Wagner. The Powells and the Wagners had been friends since 1956, the friendship fuelled by the two men's love of the past, and conducted over many picnics and church-crawls. Wagner had helped Powell extensively with his work on the House of Lords, and his death was a grievous loss to Powell. The tribute the now frail statesman paid to his friend was, according to those present, one of the most moving of his life.

On his eighty-third birthday he seemed more alert and genial than for months. A BBC film crew were making a documentary about him, and although this was tiring him he, and Pam, were both enjoying the experience. It allowed a precious insight into his view, in reflective old age, of his achievement, and into his life as a combative invalid, still busily at work on the Gospels: 'I spend more time thinking than reading, which is how it should be,' was the note on which the documentary ended.

Nothing could impair his enthusiasm for politics. As the Conservative party continued to tear itself in two over Europe, Powell returned to the doctrine of 1974. He told a journalist that, for the Conservatives, 'a defeat [at the next election] would help. It helps one to change one's tune.' He felt the party was just 'slithering around'.[79] What he saw was a comfort to him; he said he saw 'a cyclical movement in human affairs and, if you're right, you're proved right in the end'. He summoned up the energy that same month for his last outing to the Cambridge Union, where he was on the winning side in a debate about

Europe. It was a stunning and uplifting performance, despite his infirmity and the growing weakness of his voice. The president, Nicholas Boys-Smith, said afterwards: 'A lot of people used to think Powell was dead. It came as a shock to find that he wasn't . . . he is credited with the revival of the right. Everyone looks at modern politicians and thinks they are all so grey, but he is far from boring. He is a political character in an age that is bereft of them.' By surviving, and by his rareness, he had become a cult figure. But there would be no more public speeches.

From the distant sidelines, Powell was absorbed by the contest for the Conservative leadership in early July 1995, prompted by the resignation of John Major and his standing for re-election. Immediately the contest was called, Powell went into print to vent his constitutional fury at the way Major had conducted himself. 'He says to the Sovereign: "I no longer am leader of the majority party in the House of Commons; but I am carrying on as your Prime Minister." Now I don't think anybody can say that – at least without inflicting damage on the constitution.'[80] He said that for someone who felt he could no longer command a majority in the Commons to seek to offer the Queen advice was 'tantamount to treating the monarch herself with disrespect and denying the very principle on which our parliamentary democracy is founded'. John Redwood, who took up Major's challenge, did so on a broadly Powellite platform of cutting public spending and governing Britain from Westminster rather than Brussels. Powell sent a message of consolation to Redwood after his defeat: 'Dear Redwood,' he wrote, 'You will never regret the events of the last week or two. Patience will evidently have to be exercised – and patience is the greatest of the political virtues – by those of us who want to keep Britain independent and self-governed.'[81]

Although Powell had been exhausted by the demands of the documentary makers, his condition did appear to have stabilised by July. Then, however, things took another turn for the worse. His family drove him to southern France for a holiday in the middle of what turned out to be the third hottest summer since 1659. The heat debilitated him, and the farmhouse where they were staying was not designed for elderly invalids. There were many stone steps, and Powell was by now most unsteady on his feet. To make matters worse the Powells' three-year-old granddaughter, Julia, was taken seriously ill with what was feared to be – but fortunately was not – meningitis. By the end of the holiday Powell was in a state of near complete collapse. He had lost further weight off his already spare frame, and his friends began to fear for his life. A short spell in hospital allowed more tests to be carried out and a brief period of rest and recuperation; but things would now have to change.

He had recovered sufficiently by the end of August to be brought out by his wife for a weekend with us in the country. The trip was ostensibly work: I had begun to undertake detailed research for this book, and no research was more

serious than talking to my subject. We managed several hours of taped conversations over the weekend, though Powell still tired easily. In other respects
he seemed well: his appetite had returned, and, charmed as ever by children, he
was keen to amuse our two-year-old son with twitches of his moustache. On
the Sunday morning we took him for a drive around the countryside, and he
talked learnedly of Anglo-Saxon field systems. His mind was as sharp as ever; it
was his body that was giving up, though not without a fight. He still wanted to
write: he was persuaded to compose for the *Daily Telegraph* that autumn some
memories and an appreciation of Housman for the centenary of *A Shropshire
Lad*, due the following year. 'I can still in my mind's eye see', he wrote, 'his tall,
taut figure striding firmly along King's Parade to the lecture room through
milling crowds of undergraduates as if they were not there at all.'[82] He would
often say that he never wrote anything without hearing Housman's voice saying
to him, 'Now, you haven't thought about that properly, have you?'

Another spell in hospital followed that autumn, preventing him from attending the seventieth birthday reception given by the Prime Minister for Lady
Thatcher at Downing Street. Another former leader, Lord Home, died in early
October, and Powell put out a statement saying that 'though I refused a seat in
his cabinet in 1963 I always regarded Alec as the rarest thing in politics – a
politician whose word one could trust'.[83] Once discharged from hospital, Powell
spent much of his time quietly at home, though he did make a point of venturing
out, for nostalgic reasons, to see the revival of *Cavalcade* at Sadler's Wells. Such
excursions were, though, rare. Hand-rails were fitted in the Powells' house to
help prevent him from falling over, and the first of a series of devoted nurses
was brought in. Friends would still call on him frequently, and on good days
signs of the old Enoch were still there; on bad ones he found that even talking
required the most enormous effort. The broadcasting of the BBC documentary
about him on 11 November renewed interest in him, though his gaunt and
strained appearance caused concern among many who had not seen him for
some time. The main excitement of the programme was Powell's speaking for
the first time about Barbara, and her public identification: she was now a widow
living in retirement in Yorkshire, and one of the best woman shots in the
country. Yet the documentary showed the human face of Powell beyond this:
his daughters admitting that he used to yell out like a baby when having his hair
washed, to their great amusement; and scenes of him trying to teach his small
granddaughter the alphabet.

Shortly after the programme was broadcast Barbara Hawkins wrote to Powell,
their first contact for forty-four years after his earlier refusal to contemplate
friendship with her. She said she had had to summon the 'nerve' to write, and
how 'horror struck' she had been about the media attention, but how pleased
she had been to see what a 'happy life' the Powells had had together.[84] She
concluded that she was 'very proud to have counted you as a friend' and added

a sad footnote to Pamela Powell: 'I wish that I had met you.' It was a few weeks before Powell replied, but he did reply. 'It was good of you to write to us as you did.' he added, 'I am becoming reconciled to the pains and disappointment of increasing age.'[85]

The Powells had a happy Christmas in Lincolnshire with Susan and her family, and in the first weeks of 1996 he was strong enough – having put on a little weight by now – to venture out occasionally other than for short walks. In the last week of January he attended Alec Home's memorial service at Westminster Abbey, his presence captured in a ghostly photograph in *The Times*. Three days later he went to the annual party given at Scotland Yard by Special Branch, who had guarded him five years earlier. The effort of that was exhausting, leaving him drained for two days afterwards: but his morale depended on his being able to do such things. He also managed to keep up his role as a church warden at St Margaret's, Westminster, the parliamentary church, despite his illness, and he never lost his keen interest in how that particular church was conducting itself within the Church of England. Nor did he cease to be a regular attender on almost every Sunday, so long as he was able to go out.

In those two days he summoned up all his powers of recuperation to be fit for a surprise party, organised by their daughters, for Pam's seventieth birthday on 28 January. Powell had played along with the story that it was to be a dinner, and he had spent ages with Pam agonising over the placement. In a speech he made at the party he described this as 'just about the only act of deceit and dishonesty I have ever practised during our marriage', and complimented his wife on being just the same as she had been when they were first married. None of their friends required any evidence of their complete devotion to each other; and, weakened by age and illness though he was, Powell was still able to show himself as the constant romantic.

Perhaps the greatest blow in his intellectual life was the difficulty he now had in communicating his thoughts to the outside world. He had not lost his keen interest in politics, not least because the growth of opposition to the European Union during the spring of 1996, with senior politicians now openly talking about the option of withdrawal, seemed to him a vindication of what had always stood for. Whatever the predations of old age, he had the consolation, as he saw it, of living long enough to be seen to be proved right. In one of his last journalistic exercises, he made a point in saying so, when the *Daily Express* asked him to contribute to a series in which leading figures expressed their impatience with decisions being imposed on Britain from Brussels – most particularly, at this time, a world-wide ban that had been imposed by the EU on British beef for fear it was contaminated. 'Those who consented to the surrender made in 1972 will have to think again,' Powell wrote. 'Thinking again means that activity most unthinkable for politicians – unsaying what has been said.'[86] He remained completely defiant. 'The surrender ... we have made is not irrevocable. Parliament still has the power (thank God) to reclaim what has been surrendered by treaty. It is time we told the other European nations what we mean by being self-governed.'

Writing was now an immense effort; his voice was sometimes so weak that dictation too was difficult. Book reviewing became almost impossible as a result, though he still spent much of time reading, his mind as active as ever. Once it was known among his friends that his mobility was limited, but that he was glad to receive visitors, the flow of friends to South Eaton Place increased. Powell would soon become animated and show glimpses of his old self. His memory was good – a great help to his biographer – and he enjoyed talking about the past. In the second half of 1996 his condition seemed to stabilise, helped, ironically, by a decision not to try to be as ambitious as the previous year, and not to take a holiday. There were still occasional excursions, mainly to memorial services and, in September 1996, to Westminster Abbey, where he unveiled the Housman memorial in Poets' Corner.

The following month he gave his last interview, to Matthew d'Ancona of the *Sunday Telegraph*. He received d'Ancona at South Eaton Place, looking frail but – as he would always receive his visitors, even in the depths of his own illness – still dressed in a three-piece suit: his carpet slippers were his only concession to his age and infirmity. His feelings as expressed in this on-the-record meeting were just as he would have put them in private: 'I have lived into an age in which my ideas are now part of common intuition, part of a common fashion. It has been a great experience, having given up so much, to find that there is now this range of opinion in all classes, that an agreement with the EEC is totally incompatible with normal parliamentary government.' Asked why this had happened, Powell replied, 'The nation has returned to haunt us.'[87] Still smarting from the campaign of 1975, Powell revealed that he would not be putting the weight of his reputation behind the Referendum Party of Sir James Goldsmith, then mobilising to fight the forthcoming general election on the single issue of Europe.

The greatest peril for Powell – and a cause of terrible strain for his ever-solicitous wife – was his propensity to fall over. His injuries, fortunately, were usually not serious – just cuts and bruises, though he did once have severe concussion. As when learning to ride he remained undaunted, but would simply be helped up again and would keep carrying on. At Christmas 1996 the Powells went to Lincolnshire again, and he had his most serious fall yet, down a flight of stairs on Christmas Eve. Nothing was broken, but he had to be driven back to London by ambulance, and was forced to take to his bed for a month. A new weakness appeared to have descended upon an already frail frame, though even in this adversity he continued to display a determination not to give up. Though he had difficulty holding a book, he willed himself to continue to read. He drove himself to try to work at his commentary on St John; and for relaxation returned, at last, to Wagner, watching videos of the *Ring*. However, his life became, inevitably, more solitary, despite the regular parade of friends. Walking even short distances became nearly impossible, and at last Powell consented to a wheelchair, which at least allowed him to be taken out.

He followed the 1997 election keenly, though inevitably at a remove. He was not prepared to allow his incapacity to prevent him from playing a part in the election, though what he could do was mostly symbolic. He wrote for public circulation a letter to his successor, Nick Budgen, once more defending Wolverhampton South-West, and urged his electors to vote for him because of his record in opposing the federal project of the European Union. Since that same week there had been an avalanche of Conservative candidates using their election addresses to signal their distance from the official party line on Europe, Powell's words made the front pages. It was a mark of the place he still held, ten years after leaving Parliament, in the public's estimation. However, Budgen lost, ending forty-seven years of Conservative possession since Powell's first campaign. He went down as part of a landslide that saw Labour win a majority of 179 seats, the largest since 1906, and the Conservatives reduced to an English rump – none of their candidates was returned in either Wales or Scotland – of 165 members. Asked by his wife what he felt the election meant, Powell mournfully replied, 'They have voted to break up the United Kingdom.'[88] He was still not sufficiently convinced by the Conservative party, when it acquired a new leader, to seek to resume his membership of it; but his wife, in the wake of the apocalypse of 1 May, rejoined the party the next day after twenty-three years.

V

The last summer and autumn of Powell's life were predominantly peaceful. Able to walk only with the greatest difficulty, he scarcely left South Eaton Place. The constant attentions of his wife and nurses eased his suffering and frustration; a steady succession of visitors illuminated his twilight. His eighty-fifth birthday was celebrated with a few close friends at home, and his health was drunk in champagne. He was never bedridden: right to the end he would get up each day and, dressed smartly, would receive his visitors on the ground floor of his house. The falls became less frequent, as he tried to be less ambitious about what he could do; and, though weak, his condition, once more, appeared to have stabilised. There seemed no immediate threat of death, nor threat of further, sharp, distressing decline.

The family had a quiet, but happy, Christmas. A great source of pleasure to Powell was his eighteen-month-old grandson, James, by now walking and uttering his first words. It was not a harsh winter, and he settled down into his now daily routine of sitting and reading, and thinking. To visitors he seemed cheerful, and was easily stirred to laughter; there was a strong spark in him to the end, and an undiminished interest in the life of his nation. He pushed on with his work on St John: the last book he ever read was *The Fourth Gospel*, by the Cambridge scholar Edwyn Clement Hoskyns. He also maintained his religious devotion. No longer able to attend St Margaret's, where the congregation prayed for him every Sunday, the Rector, Donald Gray, would regularly take him Communion from the Reserved Sacrament.

On the evening of Friday 6 February 1998 the Powells entertained some old friends for drinks, and went to bed at their usual time. In the night, without any warning, Powell suffered an aneurysm, just as his father had done. His doctor had him admitted to the King Edward VII Hospital for Officers in Marylebone the next morning, the place already besieged by photographers and reporters awaiting news of the condition of Queen Elizabeth the Queen Mother, who had suffered a broken hip. Powell almost died in the ambulance, but his fighting spirit rallied him again. His doctors relieved his pain, but, after conducting extensive tests, admitted that there was no hope. Later in the day, his wife excused herself for a moment to get some lunch, which prompted Powell to ask where his was. His wife indicated the means by which he was being fed intravenously. 'I don't call that much of a lunch,' he replied. In the manner of Pitt the Younger asking for one of Bellamy's veal pies, they were his last words. He soon slipped out of consciousness for the last time. Canon Gray came that evening to administer the full rites of the church to him. Surrounded by his family, he died peacefully at 4.30 a.m. on 8 February, in the eighth month of his eighty-sixth year.[89]

As the first word went around his circle that Sunday morning the shock was profound: although he had been so ill there had been no inkling the end would come so quickly or so suddenly. A press release early that afternoon alerted the world, and it soon became apparent that the years that had passed since Powell was last active in politics had done nothing to dim the regard and affection in which he was held by the British people. News bulletins led with the story of his death for the rest of the day; newspapers praised him the next morning. Tony Blair, the Prime Minister, said that 'however much we disagreed with many of his views, there was no doubting the strength of his convictions or their sincerity, or his tenacity in pursuing them, regardless of his own political self-interest'.[90] Lady Thatcher, who owed him more than most, was effusive: 'There will never be anybody else as compelling as Enoch. He had a rare combination of qualities all founded on an unfaltering belief in God, an unshakeable loyalty to family and friends and an unswerving devotion to our country which in war and peace he served so well.' Her successor-but-one as party leader, William Hague, said Powell's contribution to the Conservative party 'helped to shape the history of our party and our times. He will not be forgotten.' Tony Benn and Denis Healey had words of admiration too, despite earlier conflicts; Powell had believed that his friendship with Benn was as genuine and as pleasant as it was possible to achieve in politics.[91] Heath, bearing his hatred of Powell to the grave, was admirably consistent: 'I am not making any statement.' The chairman of the Association of Black Clergy did put out a statement, saying that 'Powell was not a single-subject person and served his country well. Each person stands before God as an equal and deserves the same level of love.'[92]

Of all the press comment – most of it favourable but some raking up Powell's supposed role as a racial agitator – perhaps the most insightful was the *Daily Telegraph*'s leading article:

> For those who saw and heard Enoch Powell, the memory is indelible – the black moustache, the burning eyes, the hypnotic, metallic voice, the precision of language, the agility in debate. These will be largely lost to future generations. But, in a more important respect, Powell will survive more surely than any other British politician of the 20th century except Winston Churchill. His speeches and writings will be read so long as there exists a political and parliamentary culture in which speaking and writing matter. And if there comes a time when such a culture is all but destroyed, those brave few who wish to restore it will find in the thoughts of Enoch Powell something approaching their Bible.

VI

The funeral, which Powell had planned fifteen years earlier, took place on 18 February. Rejecting any notion that it had been morbid of him to organise the event so meticulously, he had said simply that 'a man should tidy up after himself ... we live our life in contemplation of the end of it'.[93] The obsequies began in St Faith's Chapel in Westminster Abbey at eight in the morning, with a requiem attended just by Powell's close family. During the service there was a reading from his own translation of St Matthew. There had been complaints by bishops in the Church of England that Powell should not rest in this 'national shrine' overnight before the funeral, because of his part, as they saw it, in exciting racial tension. It was a privilege to which Powell, as a church warden of St Margaret's and as one who with his wife had worshipped there for more than twenty years, was properly entitled, as Canon Gray forcefully pointed out, publicly condemning the 'chief pastors who were adding quite thoughtlessly and insensitively to [the family's] grief and pain in their time of bereavement'.[94] In the true spirit of modern Christianity, the church he loved ensured that controversy surrounded Powell literally to the grave.

Then, at eleven o'clock on a bright, still morning, the first of two public funeral services was held – this the political one, in Parliament's parish church, St

Margaret's Westminster. The church overflowed, with many of the congregation standing at the back, and many more outside who could not get in. Statesmen, politicians and friends joined Powell's family for a service in the high Anglican rite. The Queen was represented; the last Conservative administration was there in force too, led by the ex-Prime Minister, John Major. Sir Denis Thatcher represented his wife, who was abroad. Tony Benn, whose sincere devotion to Powell as a man overcame their deep political differences, was there too. As is not the fashion, the coffin was covered with the Union Flag: it made for an arresting entrance, richly symbolic of one of the few men whose convictions could justify such a gesture, and symbolic, too, of the fundamental thing in which Powell had believed. Lord Biffen, the oldest surviving Powellite, gave the address, in which he quoted Disraeli: 'I had to prepare the mind of the country, and to educate our party.' Powell's elder daughter Susan gave a reading. So too did two others who had been at Powell's side in the darkest, but most exhilarating days, and with whom he had close and special bonds of friendship: Greville Howard and Richard Ritchie. Outside, a few members of the public had left wreaths. 'You were right, Enoch,' read the card on one of them. 'The country is now going to the dogs. Ninety per cent of the people I know say that you should have been Prime Minister.'

With the military precision of which Powell would have been proud, the mourners then embarked on coaches for Warwick, for the second part of the proceedings. It was Powell's wish to be buried, in the uniform of a brigadier of his regiment, in the Warwickshire Regiment plot after a service in Warwick parish Church, which houses the regimental chapel. 'If I was asked "what place were you happiest in", it would be Warwick', he had said.[95] He had, without any fuss or ceremony, always attended the regiment's annual commemoration service at the church, until infirmity finally prevented him. Many of his old comrades, with whom he had marched past the flag after each service, now filled the church for him. The streets approaching it were lined with people, some of them weeping. Six senior NCOs of the Warwicks' successor regiment, the Royal Regiment of Fusiliers, bore the coffin into the grand perpendicular church just after two-thirty in the afternoon. The mourners from London were greatly outnumbered by hundreds of ordinary people from Powell's own West Midlands, who had come to bid him farewell. Powell's younger daughter, Jennifer, gave the reading; another former parliamentary colleague, Sir Patrick Cormack, gave an address. With the church sunlit through high windows, the moment of most intense emotion came when two buglers beneath the chancel arch sounded the 'Last Post' and 'Reveille'; and, finally, the congregation sang 'God Save the Queen'. His coffin was carried out by the soldiers.

After the service, the mourners stood outside the church as Brigadier Powell was taken to rest among his brother soldiers, a few paces from his old batman Arthur 'Dixie' Lee. The ten days since the Brigadier's death had seen unseasonably warm weather: the first flowers were pushing through the grass, and the first buds were preparing to burst, a little early, on the trees. The poet appeared to have arranged it that he might, this time, cheat the sadness of spring.

EPILOGUE

THE CLOVEN HOOF

Most politicians, as they become older, become more skilled in compromise. The sacrifice of what were once deeply held, and prominently advertised, convictions troubles their consciences less and less; it certainly leaves no moral imprint. In an age when many politicians have ceased to have a life outside politics, survival and the retention of power become paramount. What in normal society would constitute shameful duplicity is, by a modern politician, executed shamelessly: nobody expects better of them, least of all themselves, and they do not therefore disappoint. Retreating from principle, bending, concealing or sometimes even abandoning the truth are normal, everyday activities. Anyone who points out the depravity of such behaviour is seen as painfully unsophisticated.

In perhaps the most insightful piece of journalism ever written about Powell – the *Observer* profile of February 1961, before he became widely known – it was recorded: 'For a long time Powell's critics have been saying how extraordinary it is that a man who could have risen to somewhere near the top as proconsul, staff officer, civil servant or academic should have chosen politics, the one career which seemed certain to defeat him. For the outstanding thing about Powell has been that he is not a politician, which means, quite honourably, a compromiser.'[1] Thus it was identified less than a third of the way through his parliamentary career that he lacked the mechanism needed to survive at the highest level, and to exercise the power most politicians believe is the sole point of their existence. Even in those far-off days, to be so little motivated by self-regard was considered a charming eccentricity. Today it is felt to be just plain daft.

It is a matter of historical record that once Powell renounced office in 1963 he did not hold it again. It is a matter of perception that he had decided never again to follow a path in government with which he could not reconcile the relentless engine of his conscience, or which offended against the truth as his logic defined it. If such attitudes made him a maverick, they are of a piece with his romantic self-belief. It is the word 'honourably' in that *Observer* profile with which he would have had the greatest difficulty; and he would not accept that to refuse to compromise meant to pass up any chance of governing the country remotely effectively. He would never believe, as most politicians do, that the secret was to lead public opinion by only a little way if at all. Powell cared for public opinion, but in a way that made him determined to lead it as radically as possible, for the sake of its own enlightenment. This was the talent of the brilliant polemicist, or evangelist, rather than of the statesman. He could, in later life, become a little rueful about his lack of evasiveness as a politician: 'I've probably explained too much in politics, more than I ought to have done.'[2]

However unsuited he was to the calling, he loved being a politician. None was more respected as a House of Commons man than he when, against his will, he left Westminster. 'He was', the Prime Minister of the time, Lady Thatcher, said, 'the best parliamentarian I ever knew.'[3] He knew why he had sought the job: 'It is not for career, nor for remuneration or perquisites. It is, quite simply, for the sake of being a Member of Parliament, for that is held to be an honourable thing to be. It is a matter, if one dare breathe the word in this "classless" society, of status; the esteem of oneself and of one's fellow citizens.'[4] The job was its own reward, and the only reward needed by a patriot. Powell was unlike many of his fellows in this respect above all.

Early on he had a facility for compromise, for pragmatism, for grinning and bearing it while, under collective responsibility, all sorts of perversions and ignorances were perpetrated partly in his name. He endured the humiliation of Suez without resigning; he tolerated the 'dangerous nonsense' of an incomes policy while sitting in the cabinet; he voted with his party line for the principle of negotiating to enter the Common Market. However, such accommodations deeply affected him, and caused him shame. The experience of seeing at first hand Macmillan's conduct of high office had revolted him. Being complicit in such behaviour was something he was determined not to repeat after October 1963: it explains the intensity and hostility of his opposition to Heath, and its consequences. He would not then, and would not in future, come to a point where he had to 'turn all the mirrors round'. He felt – though scarcely anybody else did – that he had compromised himself enough by staying in parliament after Britain joined the EEC, even though he used his place there to fight wholeheartedly against rule from Brussels and for all his other causes.

Once he lost his limited facility to comply, to conform and to prevaricate, he lost the opportunity to remain as a front-rank politician in the conventional sense. Less than halfway through his thirty-seven years in Parliament he sat on the front bench for the last time. In sheer legislative terms, as measured by the statute book, he thereafter achieved very little. By refusing to compromise, he had thrown away his chance to serve, and he could not play his part in the executive of the nation. The unequivocal stand he took on several questions – notably immigration, but also his titanic assault on Heath from 1971 – made it impossible for the lesser men who might have rallied to him to do so. Moreover, Powell did not really seem to care whether they did or not. In terms of support, it mattered to him most that the public were behind him, for each arrival of the postman seemed to confirm his own special mandate from them. He was sustained, too, for much of this time by his simple religious faith. In moments of frustration or disappointment he would intone to his family and friends, simply: 'The Lord will provide.'

Many of his colleagues, who had learned and tolerated the arts of compromise, regretted what they saw as Powell's wasted opportunities. To them, he could have reached almost any height had he simply restrained his independence and his intellectual arrogance. Lord Carr, who knew him from 1950, and who would be pitched against him as a senior member of the Heath Government, said that 'however much I may have disagreed with him, particularly in later years, he was a special man, and one of the very few substantial people of my generation'.[5] Powell knew he was unsuited, as other politicians would see it, to take part in their profession: 'I never played the game, the game of snakes and ladders; I was never interested in playing that game,' he said late on in his life. 'So I was the odd man out, like the man on a playing field who isn't playing the game.'[6] For all his strictures about the importance of party, he was proof that parties cannot easily contain men with such a capacity for independence as his. Although after his death some who could not think outside these traditional parameters rebuked him for not having submitted himself to the collective will of the Conservative party, the fact that he did not made little difference to the party, or to him. His lesson, especially in economics, was irresistible and compelling. As John Biffen said in the address at his funeral, 'He did not achieve power but, more important, he achieved influence and respect on a scale which perhaps only history will come to recognise.'[7] The difficulty Heath had with him was that he could not understand him. Powell recalled, late in his life, that whenever he had confronted Heath with an idea, his leader had turned red in the face and started to bluster.[8]

Even after Powell's death, Heath was still proclaiming that the Birmingham speech was 'a racist speech, quite obviously so ... no respectable politician would use that language'.[9] To Heath, Powell was 'a super-egotist', and that was that. Powell's own defence against accusations of racism was perhaps best made in a sermon at St Lawrence Jewry in the City of London in January 1977:

> Though legend relates otherwise, I would not have chosen, if I could have avoided it, to become the eponymous exponent of the conviction that by no contrivance can the prospective size and distribution of our population of 'New Commonwealth ethnic origin' ... prove otherwise than destructive of this nation. The basis of my conviction is neither genetic nor eugenic; it is not racial, because I can never understand what 'race' means and I have never arranged my fellow men on a scale of merit according to their origins. The basis is political. It is the belief that self-identification of each part with the whole is the one essential precondition of being a parliamentary nation, and that the massive shift in the composition of the population of the inner metropolis and of major towns and cities of England will produce, not fortuitously or avoidably, but by the sheer inevitabilities of human nature in society, ever increasing and more dangerous alienation.[10]

II

Powell's contribution to British national life was greater and longer-lasting than most executive action could ever be. His effect on the thinking of others, from the highest ministerial level down to the British elector, was perhaps more profound than that of any other practising politician of the twentieth century. The very direction of British political economy after 1979, as, eventually, pursued by both main parties, was greatly according to the Powell blueprint. That marks Powell out among the most significant people in British public life of his century. It was clear that by conducting his political career solely on his terms after 1963 he might have ruled out the conventional baubles some politicians seek, but had retained an intact integrity. It became more subtly apparent, and will become more so, that the truths about the interdependence of the free society and the free market that he fought to establish are to become cornerstones of our polity in the early twenty-first century. The recognition that, as a safeguard of democratic freedoms, the English at least still cling to the idea of nation, and therefore must order their politics accordingly, may follow not far behind. In his restless, evangelical crusade to tell the English about themselves he was unique among politicians, but it was that crusade which more than anything took him to the people's hearts. The painter Bernard Cohen, who met Powell at Harry d'Avigdor-Goldsmid's in the 1960s, had always been opposed to Powell's ideas. On leaving, Cohen observed: 'Thank God I don't live in that man's constituency, or I'd have to vote for him.' His was also an influence that spread abroad more than many might have credited. Visiting Britain in 1969, for example, the Singaporean leader Lee Kwan Yew sought a meeting with Powell, not remotely concerned that Powell no longer held even shadow office, but wanting to meet and learn from this phenomenon.

Commenting in 1989 on the success of Margaret Thatcher, Powell said that one of her 'remarkable characteristics, which stamps her as a superb politician, is her ability to put up with things and go along with them, even though she doesn't agree with them, until the time comes when they can be dealt with. Now not possessing that quality myself – having the loquacity which always impels me to say: "I don't agree" – I admire this.'[11] She claimed, in return, that the two greatest influences on her as Conservative leader had been Powell and Keith Joseph, 'both of them very great men'.[12] This, like her comments at the time of his death, was a great compliment to Powell, but no less than his due. It accords him his rightful place in the Conservative movement, and in history. It is the place of a philosopher, though, not of a practitioner, a role for which baser skills are required.

Powell took nothing for granted. For him, there was no such thing as received wisdom. Every thought, every action had to be questioned and analysed. In economic policy, the battle was eventually won: others were still being fought when he died. His main, unresolved conflict with his opponents was the question of whether the British people wished to remain a nation. It was a question he put not just to their political representatives, who to the greater extent controlled the people's destinies, but directly to the people themselves. On immigration they listened immediately, and in some regards with destructive effects he had not foreseen. On British subsumption into a European Union, it was only in his declining years that the people seemed to hear him, and began to take up his call, using arguments with which he had provided them. It was in economics that he had his greatest victory. He lived to see a Labour Chancellor of the Exchequer subscribe to the monetary theory of inflation, the theory he had been the first senior British politician to propound in the age of Keynes.

The galvanising of Britain as a nation against an external enemy in 1939–40 was the key moment in Powell's life. His failing in relation to it, though, was that he expected his fellow Britons to treat the survival of their nation with no less seriousness once the war was over. He would not admit that they failed to share his urgency about it, or that, one day, they might fail to assert themselves against political threats that were the continuation of the war by other means. Nor was Powell content to have them on his side unless they understood why it was right they should be there. The Oxford don R. W. Johnson remembered him demolishing the case for devolution at a meeting in the University in 1978; and then, as he was set for 'a standing ovation' from an audience that had come to attack him, he proved the point that an undergraduate had put to him about it being possible for Oxford to vote for independence from the Kingdom. However, he then asked, 'with real venom, eyes flashing', why not talk about places that were really different, such as Bradford, Brixton or Southall? It was 'a collective slap in the face . . . everyone filed out in silence, as if physically beaten'. Johnson asked Powell why he had done that. Powell replied, 'Oh yes, I could see I had won them over, so I thought, if you want to accept me, it's got to be the whole package, not just my views on devolution. So I showed them the cloven hoof. I don't want any easy victories.'[13]

Such intellectual aggression borne of deep integrity helps show why Powell was unsuited to be a politician. Yet it was from his politician's platform that he ended up having more influence on Britain in the last quarter of the twentieth century than most of his peers. Michael Foot was categorical about what he thought Powell would have achieved but for the Birmingham speech, but for that one moment when any conventional politician would have resisted the urge to unveil his feelings: 'The Tory Kingdom would sooner or later have been his to command, for he had all the shining qualities which the others lacked. Heath would never have outmanoeuvred him; Thatcher would never have stepped into the vacant shoes. It was a tragedy for Enoch, and a tragedy for the rest of us too.'[14] What Foot always saw in Powell was a deep and total humanity, one that too often could not be picked out amid the intellectual bombardment, one Powell himself obscured by showing, instead, 'the cloven hoof'. It made many hate him, not least because they perceived him as a crude racialist; and to that others, notably vehement critics like Roy Hattersley, have added accusations of conceit and fundamental failure – though rare is the politician who, with his hand on what passes for his heart, can claim to have been unvisited by those two demons.

We know how Powell would have liked to be remembered: he wished he had been killed in the war, to have made the only sacrifice he felt was worth making, to have made the ultimate act of self-identification with his nation. That was not to be. He might, perhaps, have been happier had he become Field Marshal Lord Powell, but his effect on the country and its governance would have been incalculably less. He left the army to strive to become viceroy, but that opportunity was removed. He wanted to be prime minister or at least leader of his party, but the Conservatives could never have accepted him with his vice of absolutes, or with his Olympian mind, however much he tried to hide them when in his guise of The People's Enoch. For all his outward display of rigid conformity he was a Tory anarchist, the object of his anarchy being an unthinking, compromising, morally cowardly establishment. He devoted himself to beating that establishment – which, in February 1974, he as much as anyone did – and those he could not beat he at least strove to educate.

He never gave way to regret or disappointment. His achievements as a man outside politics were more than enough to sustain him, for only he knew how hard and how properly he had worked for them, and how, unlike political advancement, they were not dependent upon the caprice or fancies of others. I took him out to lunch on his seventy-seventh birthday in 1989 and, by chance, three other former cabinet ministers were in the same restaurant. I noted the surfeit of Privy Councillors, but he said, 'Yes, but I think I am the only professor and the only brigadier present.'

His detractors assailed him for hyperbole, for vanity and for sins moral and ideological, for his temerity in thinking that, at times, he knew better than the Conservative party, and had a right to condemn its moral and intellectual failings. As a counter to the eulogies produced on his death, there were still, thirty years after Birmingham, the constant accusations that he had made racialism respectable, and had helped engineer a climate in which some people in Britain, purely on account of the colour of their skin, felt they had to live in fear. In many respects, the gamble he took with that one speech did not pay off; yet he did not regret it, for he knew the cost to his integrity, and to his ideal of how a Member of Parliament should act, of his having otherwise remained silent. The troubles of which he warned have not occurred, but he died convinced there was no certainty they would never occur. If they do, it will not simply be a case that Powell had foreseen them; some will argue that he was principally responsible for creating a climate in which they could happen.

Immigration and its consequences, though, comprised but one area of his thought. It was the best example of his belief in the power of free speech, and of the importance of challenging orthodoxies and conspiracies of silence such as existed in the main political parties on immigration control in the 1960s. In other respects, a formidable case can be made for him as prophet and sage. When one considers the magnitude of his achievement as scholar and soldier, and as a politician without self-interest, his takes on many of the aspects of a heroic life.

Powell once said of all political careers – not just his own – that 'at the end of a lifetime in politics ... when a man looks back, he discovers that the things he most opposed have come to pass and that nearly all the objects he set out with are not merely not accomplished, but seem to belong to a different world from the one he lives in'.[15] Not just because of his intellectual arrogance, but because of his moral certainty rooted in his version of Christianity, he was unworried by criticism, or by the frustration of his aims: 'If you're right, well, then you will be found right in the end.'[16] He was not always right, and not least in the line of his that will be remembered even if one day all else is forgotten: 'All political lives ... end in failure, because that is the nature of politics and of human affairs.' He did not fail.

BIBLIOGRAPHY

A note on sources

My principal source, the Powell Papers, has yet to be formally catalogued. At the time of writing the final destination of the papers remains to be decided by Powell's literary trustees. It would be pointless to give the exact provenance from specific files in Powell's archive as such references are almost certain to be changed when formal cataloguing takes place, given the eclectic system Powell used. Almost all letters quoted are from Powell's 'Personal' files, arranged chronologically. The notable exception is the correspondence between Powell and his parents, which is to be found in his file marked 'Letters to Parents'; and letters from Italy to them in 1935, and from various walking holidays of the period, are to be found in his file entitled 'Juvenilia'.

For ease of reference to general readers, I have wherever possible sourced Powell's speeches either to his published works or to newspaper reports. I have only used a Powell Papers reference for a speech where the speech concerned was neither anthologised nor reported in the national press: a rare event between 1968 and 1979 especially. Powell himself was a good judge of significance, and ensured that his most important speeches were published in his various anthologies. With the exception of the papers from the Conservative Party Archive and the Public Record Office, all other papers quoted remain in private hands.

All interviews listed below were recorded with the permission of the interviewees, and the tapes remain in my possession.

1. Works by J. Enoch Powell

LH: *A Lexicon to Herodotus* (Cambridge University Press, 1938).

GU: *Greek in the University: An Inaugural Lecture* (Oxford University Press, 1938).

HH: *The History of Herodotus* (Cambridge University Press, 1939).

H: *Herodotus: A Translation* (Clarendon Press, 1949).

ON: *One Nation*, with others (CPC, 1950).

SFS: *Saving in a Free Society* (Hutchinson/IEA, 1960).

RN: *Rebirth of a Nation*, contributor (Pan, 1964).

ANNA: *A Nation Not Afraid*, ed. John Wood (Batsford, 1965).

FR: *Freedom and Reality*, ed. John Wood (Batsford, 1969).

IT: *Income Tax at 4/3 in the £*, ed. Anthony Lejeune (Stacey, 1970).

PE: *Powell and the 1970 Election*, ed. John Wood (Elliott, 1970).

CMCA: *The Common Market: The Case Against* (Elliott, 1971).

STD: *Still to Decide*, ed. John Wood (Batsford, 1972).

NEA: *No Easy Answers* (Sheldon, 1973).

WWTA: *Wrestling with the Angel* (Sheldon, 1977).

JC: *Joseph Chamberlain* (Thames & Hudson, 1977).

ANONN: *A Nation or No Nation?*, ed. Richard Ritchie (Batsford, 1978).

1992: *Enoch Powell on 1992* ed. Richard Ritchie (Anaya, 1989).

RS: *Reflections of a Statesman* (Bellew, 1990).

CPEP: *Collected Poems* (Bellew, 1990).

2. Unpublished sources

PP: Papers of the late J. Enoch Powell.

CP: Papers of Miss Hester Curtis.

DP: Papers of Lord Deedes of Aldington.

FP: Papers of the late H. Andrew Freeth.

HP: Papers of Lord Harris of High Cross.

MCP: Papers of Mr Michael Cockerell. These are principally the transcripts of interviews by Mr Cockerell for his 1995 BBC documentary on Powell.

RP: Papers of Mr Bryan Rayner.

SP: Papers of Mr Michael Strachan.

WP: Papers of Mr Hywel Williams.

CPA: Conservative Party Archive, Bodleian Library, Oxford.

PRO: Government papers in the Public Record Office, Kew.

3. Published sources

AF: *Australia's First: A History of the University of Sydney*, vol. I: *1850–1939*, by Clifford Turney, Ursula Bygott and Peter Chippendale (The University of Sydney, 1992).

Alexander-Watkins: *The Making of the Prime Minister 1970*, by Andrew Alexander and Alan Watkins (Macdonald, 1970).

Amery: *The Empire at Bay: The Leo Amery Diaries 1929–45* (Hutchinson, 1988).

Attallah: *Asking Questions*, by Naim Attallah (Quartet, 1996).

Baker: *The Turbulent Years*, by Kenneth Baker (Faber & Faber, 1993).

Benn I: *Diaries, Papers and Letters 1940–62*, by Tony Benn (Hutchinson, 1984).

Benn II: *Out of the Wilderness (Diaries 1963–67)*, by Tony Benn (Hutchinson, 1987).

Benn III: *Office without Power (Diaries 1968–72)*, by Tony Benn (Hutchinson, 1988).

Benn IV: *Against the Tide (Diaries 1973–6)*, by Tony Benn (Hutchinson, 1989).

Benn V: *Conflicts of Interest (Diaries 1977–80)*, by Tony Benn (Hutchinson, 1990).

Benn VI: *The End of an Era (Diaries 1980–90)*, by Tony Benn (Hutchinson, 1992).

Berkeley: *The Odyssey of Enoch*, by Humphry Berkeley (Hamish Hamilton, 1977).

Brittan: *The Treasury under the Tories 1951–64*, by Samuel Brittan (Pelican, 1964).

Butler: *The Art of the Possible*, by Lord Butler (Hamish Hamilton, 1971).

Butler–Pinto: *The British General Election of 1970*, by David Butler and Michael Pinto-Duschinsky (Macmillan, 1971).

Callaghan: *Time and Chance*, by James Callaghan (Collins, 1987).

Campbell: *Edward Heath*, by John Campbell (Jonathan Cape, 1993).

Charmley: *A History of Conservative Politics 1900–96*, by John Charmley (Macmillan, 1996).

Cockett: *Thinking the Unthinkable*, by Richard Cockett (HarperCollins, 1994).

Colville: *Footprints in Time*, by John Colville (Collins, 1976).

Comfort: *Brewer's Politics*, ed. Nicholas Comfort (Cassell, 1993).

Cosgrave I: *Carrington: A Life and a Policy*, by Patrick Cosgrave (Dent, 1985).

Cosgrave II: *The Strange Death of Socialist Britain*, by Patrick Cosgrave (Constable, 1992).

Cowling: *Religion and Public Doctrine in Modern England*, by Maurice Cowling (Cambridge University Press, 1980).

Crawford: *The Profumo Affair*, by Iain Crawford (White Lodge, 1963).

Crick: *Michael Heseltine*, by Michael Crick (Hamish Hamilton, 1997).

Critchley: *A Bag of Boiled Sweets*, by Julian Critchley (Faber & Faber, 1994).

Crossman I: *The Diaries of a Cabinet Minister*, vol. I: *Minister of Housing 1964–6*, by Richard Crossman (Hamish Hamilton and Jonathan Cape, 1975).

Crossman II: *The Diaries of a Cabinet Minister*, vol. II: *Lord President of the Council and Leader of the House of Commons 1966–8*, by Richard Crossman (Hamish Hamilton and Jonathan Cape, 1976).

Crossman III: *The Diaries of a Cabinet Minister*, vol. III: *Secretary of State for Social Services 1968–70*, by Richard Crossman (Hamish Hamilton and Jonathan Cape, 1977).

Daniel: *Some Small Harvest*, by Glyn Daniel (Thames & Hudson, 1986).

Day: ... *But with Respect*, by Sir Robin Day (Weidenfeld, 1993).

Dell: *The Chancellors*, by Edmund Dell (HarperCollins, 1996).

Driberg: *Ruling Passions*, by Tom Driberg (Jonathan Cape, 1977).

Evans: *Downing Street Diary*, by Harold Evans (Hodder & Stoughton, 1981).

Fforde: *The Bank of England and Public Policy 1941–58*, by John Fforde (Cambridge University Press, 1992).

Fisher: *Iain Macleod*, by Nigel Fisher (André Deutsch, 1973).

Foot M: *Loyalists and Loners*, by Michael Foot (Collins, 1986).

Foot P: *The Rise of Enoch Powell*, by Paul Foot (Penguin, 1969).

Fowler: *Ministers Decide,* by Norman Fowler (Chapmans, 1991).

Gilbert: *Never Despair: Winston Churchill 1945–65,* by Martin Gilbert (William Heinemann, 1988).

Gilmour: *Whatever Happened to the Tories?* by Ian Gilmour, with Mark Garnett (Fourth Estate, 1997).

Goodhart: *The 1922,* by Philip Goodhart (Macmillan, 1973).

Greenleaf: *The Ideological Heritage,* by W. H. Greenleaf (Methuen, 1983).

Hailsham I: *The Door Wherein I Went,* by Lord Hailsham (Collins, 1975).

Hailsham II: *A Sparrow's Flight,* by Lord Hailsham (Collins, 1990).

Hall: *The Robert Hall Diaries 1954–61,* ed. Alec Cairncross (Unwin Hyman, 1991).

Healey: *The Time of my Life,* by Denis Healey (Michael Joseph, 1989).

Heffer: *Moral Desperado: A Life of Thomas Carlyle,* by Simon Heffer (Weidenfeld & Nicolson, 1995).

Hennessy I: *Whitehall,* by Peter Hennessy (Secker & Warburg, 1989).

Hennessy II: *Never Again: Britain 1945–51,* by Peter Hennessy (Jonathan Cape, 1992).

Hills: *Tyrants and Mountains,* by Denis Hills (John Murray, 1992).

Horne II: *Macmillan 1957–86,* by Alistair Horne (Volume II of the Official Biography), (Macmillan, 1989).

Howard: *RAB: The Life of R. A. Butler,* by Anthony Howard (Jonathan Cape, 1987).

Howarth: *Cambridge Between the Wars,* by T. E. B. Howarth (Collins, 1978).

Howe: *Conflict of Loyalty,* by Geoffrey Howe (Macmillan, 1994).

Hunt: *A Don at War,* by Sir David Hunt (revised edn, Cass, 1990).

Hurd: *An End to Promises,* by Douglas Hurd (Collins, 1979).

Hutchinson: *Edward Heath,* by George Hutchinson (Longman, 1970).

James: *A Last Eccentric: A Symposium Concerning the Reverend Canon F. A. Simpson,* ed. Eric James (Christian Action, 1991).

Kilmuir: *Political Adventure,* by the Earl of Kilmuir (Weidenfeld & Nicolson, 1964).

King I: *The Cecil King Diary 1965–70,* by Cecil King (Jonathan Cape, 1972).

King II: *The Cecil King Diary 1970–4,* by Cecil King (Jonathan Cape, 1975).

Laing: *Edward Heath, Prime Minister,* by Margaret Laing (Sidgwick & Jackson, 1972).

Lewis: *Enoch Powell: Principle in Politics,* by Roy Lewis (Cassell, 1979).

Macmillan IV: *Riding the Storm,* by Harold Macmillan (Macmillan, 1971).

Macmillan V: *Pointing the Way,* by Harold Macmillan (Macmillan, 1972).

Macmillan VI: *At the End of the Day,* by Harold Macmillan (Macmillan, 1973).

Maudling: *Memoirs,* by Reginald Maudling (Sidgwick & Jackson, 1978).

Middlemas: *Britain in Search of Balance 1940–61,* by Keith Middlemas (Macmillan, 1986).

Morley: *Robert Morley's Book of Bricks*, by Robert Morley (Pan, 1979).

Mortimer: *In Character*, by John Mortimer (Penguin, 1983).

Nietzsche I: *Daybreak: Thoughts on the Prejudices of Morality*, by Friedrich Nietzsche (Cambridge University Press, 1982).

Nietzsche II: *Human, All Too Human*, by Friedrich Nietzsche (Penguin Classics, 1994).

Norton: *Conservative Dissidents: Dissent within the Conservative Party 1970–4*, by Philip Norton (Temple Smith, 1978).

Pimlott: *Harold Wilson*, by Ben Pimlott (HarperCollins, 1992).

Powys: *Wolf Solent*, by John Cowper Powys (Penguin, 1964 edn).

Prior: *A Balance of Power*, by Jim Prior (Hamish Hamilton, 1986).

Rhodes James: *Ambitions and Realities: British Politics 1964–70*, by Robert Rhodes James (Weidenfeld & Nicolson, 1972).

Ridley: *My Style of Government*, by Nicholas Ridley (Hutchinson, 1991).

Roth I: *Enoch Powell: Tory Tribune*, by Andrew Roth (Macdonald, 1970).

Roth II: *Heath and the Heathmen*, by Andrew Roth (Routledge & Kegan Paul, 1972).

Schoen: *Enoch Powell and the Powellites*, by Douglas E. Schoen (Macmillan, 1977).

Seldon-Ball: *Conservative Century*, ed. by Anthony Seldon and Stuart Ball (Oxford University Press, 1994).

Shepherd I: *Iain Macleod*, by Robert Shepherd (Hutchinson, 1994).

Shepherd II: *Enoch Powell*, by Robert Shepherd (Hutchinson, 1996).

Thatcher I: *The Path to Power*, by Margaret Thatcher (HarperCollins, 1995).

Thatcher II: *The Downing Street Years*, by Margaret Thatcher (HarperCollins, 1993).

Thorpe I: *Selwyn Lloyd*, by D. R. Thorpe (Jonathan Cape, 1989).

Thorpe II: *Alec Douglas-Home*, by D. R. Thorpe (Sinclair-Stevenson, 1996).

Timmins: *The Five Giants*, by Nicholas Timmins (HarperCollins, 1995).

Trott: *No Place for Fop or Idler: The Story of King Edward's School, Birmingham*, by Anthony Trott (James & James, 1992).

Utley: *Enoch Powell: The Man and his Thinking*, by T. E. Utley (Kimber, 1968).

Whitelaw: *The Whitelaw Memoirs*, by William Whitelaw (Aurum, 1989).

Wilson I: *The Labour Government 1964–70*, by Harold Wilson (Weidenfeld & Nicolson, 1971).

Wilson II: *Final Term*, by Harold Wilson (Weidenfeld & Nicolson, 1979).

4. Taped interviews

Powell I: J. Enoch Powell, 26 August 1995.

Powell II: J. Enoch Powell, 27 August 1995.

Powell III: J. Enoch Powell, 19 March 1996.

Powell IV: J. Enoch Powell, 31 July 1996.

Howard: Greville Howard, 17 August 1995.

Carthew: Mrs Bee Carthew, 28 September 1995.

Lewis: Roy Lewis, 28 September 1995.

C Jones: Clement Jones, 8 October 1995.

G Jones: George Jones, 14 October 1995.

Amies: Sir Hardy Amies, 13 December 1995.

Hunt: Sir David Hunt, 8 January 1996.

Warren: Sir Brian Warren, 9 January 1996.

Hills: Denis Hills, 6 February 1996.

Godber: Sir George Godber, 19 February 1996.

Aitken: Jonathan Aitken, 27 February 1996.

Harris: Lord Harris of High Cross, 20 March 1996.

Biffen: John Biffen, 26 March 1996.

Donaldson: Jeffrey Donaldson, 12 April 1996.

Deedes: Lord Deedes of Aldington, 15 April 1996.

Alport: Lord Alport, 20 April 1996.

Benn: Tony Benn, 15 May 1996.

Lilley: Peter Lilley, 19 May 1996.

Molyneaux: Sir James Molyneaux, 22 May 1996.

Alexander: Andrew Alexander, 3 June 1996.

Budgen: Nick Budgen, 9 June 1996.

Curtis: Miss Hester Curtis, 10 June 1996.

Post: Colonel Kenneth Post, 7 September 1996.

Freeth: Martin Freeth, 16 October 1996.

Ritchie: Richard Ritchie, 8 November 1996.

Thatcher: Baroness Thatcher of Kesteven, 5 December 1996.

Field: Frank Field, 19 December 1996.

Waldegrave: William Waldegrave, 9 January 1997.

James: Canon Eric James, 18 February 1998.

Harrison: Bernard Harrison, 24 March 1998.

Carr: Lord Carr of Hadley, 2 April 1998.

Beddows: Ian Beddows, 18 April 1998.

MPP I: Pamela Powell, 29 April 1998.

Gray: Canon Donald Gray, 30 April 1998.

MPP II: Pamela Powell, 11 May 1998.

Weatherill: Lord Weatherill, 11 May 1998.

IWM: Interview conducted by staff of the Imperial War Museum with J. Enoch Powell, 1987, and in the Powell archive.

NOTES

Chapter 1: 'My earliest dwelling'

1 PP: Memorandum of 1988 by J Enoch Powell on his ancestors.
2 Ibid.
3 Ibid.
4 *Panorama*, 2 December 1968.
5 NEA, p2.
6 *Panorama*, 2 December 1968.
7 *Sunday Express*, 17 April 1966.
8 *Listener*, 28 May 1981.
9 Roth I, p10.
10 *Listener*, 26 April 1970.
11 Mrs Marjorie Dyson, letter to the author, 26 December 1995.
12 RS, p69.
13 Attallah, p342.
14 *Sunday Express*, 26 April 1966.
15 *Sunday Times*, 18 November 1979.
16 MCP: Powell interview.
17 *Sunday Express*, 26 April 1966.
18 PP: Memorandum of 1988 by J Enoch Powell on his ancestors.
19 Powell interview I.
20 Lewis interview.
21 MCP: Powell interview.
22 *Panorama*, 2 December 1968.
23 BBC Radio 4 interview, 13 April 1986.
24 Hills interview.
25 Hills, p9.
26 MCP: Interview with CF Evans.
27 Lewis interview.
28 Hills interview.
29 Trott, p93.
30 *Panorama*, 2 December 1968.
31 Ibid.
32 PP: Undated note in Powell's papers, c 1985.
33 Private information.
34 *Sunday Express*, 26 April 1966.
35 MCP: Powell interview.
36 Cowling, p432.
37 RS, p104.
38 *The Times*, 8 July 1960.
39 Ibid, 27 September 1962.
40 NEA, p49.
41 PP: Letter from Powell to Ted Curtis, 19 April 1934.
42 *Daily Mail*, 9 September 1974.
43 *Sunday Telegraph Magazine*, 28 August 1977.
44 Hills, p15.
45 MCP: Powell interview.
46 *The Times*, 17 February 1998.
47 Ibid, 27 September 1962.

Chapter 2: The sadness of spring

1 *Sunday Times*, 5 February 1956.
2 *Odd Man Out*, BBC Television, 11 November 1995.
3 *Panorama*, 2 December 1968.
4 *Sunday Express*, 26 April 1970.
5 MCP: Powell interview.
6 *Sunday Express*, 26 April 1970.
7 *Desert Island Discs*, 19 February 1989.
8 PP: Letter from Powell to his parents, 22 April 1951.
9 MCP: Powell interview.
10 MPP interview II.
11 *Panorama*, 2 December 1968.
12 Nietzsche I, p188.
13 *Panorama*, 2 December 1968.
14 For a full bibliography of Powell's classical work, see *Quaderni di storia 42* (edizioni Dedalo, 1995), for an exhaustive article by Professor Robert B. Todd. I am greatly indebted to Professor Todd's work, and for his drawing it to my attention.
15 Powell interview IV.
16 *Daily Telegraph*, 13 February 1991.
17 Roth I, p19.
18 MCP: Powell interview.
19 *Odd Man Out*, BBC Television, 11 November 1995.
20 MCP: Powell interview.
21 GU, p5.
22 *The Times*, 27 September 1962.
23 CP: Undated card from Ted Curtis to his mother.
24 PP: Memoir by Powell of Ted Curtis, undated, c 1985.

25 *Housman Society Journal*, vol 1, 1974.
26 *Listener*, 28 May 1981.
27 *Sunday Times*, 17 July 1983.
28 *Charismatics*, BBC Radio 4, 1 May 1995.
29 *Daily Telegraph*, 21 October 1995.
30 Powell interview II.
31 Hunt interview.
32 *Housman Society Journal*, vol 1 1974.
33 *Desert Island Discs*, 19 February 1989.
34 *Sunday Telegraph*, 5 January 1975.
35 *Old Lady*, December 1988.
36 *Daily Telegraph*, 30 May 1992.
37 Powell interview I.
38 James, p73.
39 *Old Lady*, December 1988.
40 PP: Letter from Powell to his parents, 6 April 1935.
41 *Sunday Times*, 6 November 1977.
42 PP: Letter from Powell to his parents, 18 April 1935.
43 IWM interview.
44 *Spectator*, 6 June 1992.
45 *The Times*, 27 September 1962.
46 Nietzsche II, p33.
47 Ibid, p85.
48 Roth I, p24.
49 IWM interview.
50 PP Undated note by Powell in collection of letters to parents, c 1935.
51 Howarth, p183.
52 Ibid, p184.
53 *Sunday Express*, 26 April 1970.
54 *Panorama*, 2 December 1968.
55 *Sunday Express*, 26 April 1970.
56 *Daily Telegraph*, 13 February 1991.
57 PP: Juvenilia: 'On Cambridge, by a Cambridge Undergraduate'.
58 Ibid: Letter from Powell to his parents, 8 July 1935.
59 Powell interview III.
60 *Housman Society Journal*, vol I, 1974.
61 James, p73.
62 Ibid, p74.
63 *The Times*, 21 August 1986.
64 PP: Letter from Powell to his parents, 30 April 1935.
65 Ibid.
66 Howarth, p184.
67 LH, preface.
68 *Classical Review*, 1938.
69 In a private interview with Miss Fiona McPhillips.
70 *The Times*, 6 January 1936.
71 *Observer*, 24 April 1966.
72 Powell interview II.
73 IWM interview.
74 Powell interview II.
75 *Sunday Telegraph*, 8 October 1972.
76 PP: Letter from Powell to FA Simpson, 24 January 1940.
77 Cowling, p433.
78 CPEP, p vii.
79 Attallah, p345.
80 FR, p256.
81 CPEP, p vii.
82 WWTA, p71.
83 Attallah, p345.
84 CPEP, p3.
85 Ibid, p4.
86 Ibid, p30.
87 Ibid, p31.
88 Ibid, p37.
89 Ibid, p43.
90 Ibid, p41.
91 Ibid, p19.
92 Ibid, p5.
93 Ibid, p47.
94 Ibid, p46.
95 Ibid, p52.
96 *Times Literary Supplement*, 15 January 1938.
97 PP: Letter to Powell from John Masefield, undated, c November 1937.
98 Ibid: Letter to Powell from Hilaire Belloc, 19 November 1937.
99 *The Times*, 10 February 1998.
100 PP: Letter from Powell to AWJ Thomas, 10 November 1937.
101 MCP: Powell interview.
102 *Daily Telegraph*, 4 October 1971.
103 *Spectator*, 16 April 1983.
104 Ibid.
105 PP: Letter from Powell to his parents, 26 June 1938.
106 *Times Higher Education Supplement*, 1 September 1995.
107 *Times Educational Supplement*, 28 February 1964.
108 PP: Testimonial for Powell by Ernest Harrison, August 1937.
109 Ibid: Testimonial for Powell by Paul Maas, July 1937.
110 Ibid: Testimonial for Powell by FH Sandbach, August 1937.
111 PP: Card from Powell to Ted Curtis, undated, c 1937.
112 Attallah, p343.

[113] *Daily Telegraph*, 15 October 1988.

[114] PP: Letter from Powell to his parents, 18 February 1938.

[115] Ibid: Letter from Powell to his parents, 25 February 1938.

[116] *Daily Telegraph*, 15 October 1988.

[117] *Times Educational Supplement*, 28 February 1964; Powell interview I.

[118] PP: Letter from Powell to his parents, 27 February 1938.

[119] *Sunday Telegraph*, 17 March 1968.

[120] *Daily Telegraph*, 15 October 1988.

[121] IWM interview.

[122] *Times Educational Supplement*, 28 February 1964.

[123] PP: Letter from Powell to his parents, 28 February 1938.

[124] Ibid: Letter from Powell to his parents, 17 April 1938.

[125] Ibid: Letter from Powell to his parents, 6 March 1938.

[126] Ibid: Letter from Powell to his parents, 27 March 1938.

[127] Ibid: Letter from Powell to his parents, 10 April 1938.

[128] *Times Educational Supplement*, 28 February 1964.

[129] PP: Letter from Powell to his parents, 12 March 1938.

[130] AF, p506.

[131] PP: Letter from Powell to his parents, 19 March 1938.

[132] *Times Educational Supplement*, 28 February 1964.

[133] *Sunday Express*, 1 December 1985.

[134] CPEP, p64.

[135] PP: Letter from Powell to his parents 19 March 1938.

[136] *Sunday Express*, 26 April 1970.

[137] MCP: Powell interview.

[138] PP: Letter from Powell to his parents, 22 May 1938.

[139] *Sunday Telegraph Magazine*, 28 August 1977.

[140] *Sunday Express*, 26 April 1970.

[141] *Times Educational Supplement*, 28 February 1964.

[142] PP: Letter from Powell to his parents, 19 March 1938.

[143] Ibid: Letter from Powell to his parents, 17 April 1938.

[144] AF, p507.

[145] GU, p3.

[146] Ibid, p4.

[147] Ibid, p5.

[148] Ibid, pp5–6.

[149] Ibid, pp8–9.

[150] Ibid, p9.

[151] *Classical Quarterly*, 1938, p108.

[152] H, p iii.

[153] PP: Letter from Powell to his parents, 22 May 1938.

[154] Ibid.

[155] Ibid: Letter from Powell to his parents, 21 August 1938.

[156] Ibid: Letter from Powell to his parents, 7 August 1938.

[157] Ibid: Letter from Powell to his parents, 15 August 1938.

[158] Ibid: Letter from Powell to his parents, 11 September 1938.

[159] Ibid: Letter from Powell to his parents, 18 September 1938.

[160] Ibid: Letter from Powell to his parents, 2 October 1938.

[161] Ibid: Letter from Powell to his parents, 9 October 1938.

[162] Ibid: Letter from Powell to his parents, 27 October 1938.

[163] Ibid: Letter from Powell to his parents, 18 May 1939.

[164] *Journal of Hellenic Studies*, 1939, p238.

[165] *Classical Review*, 1939, p123.

[166] HH, preface.

[167] PP: Letter from Powell to his parents, 19 March 1939.

[168] Ibid: Letter from Powell to Ted Curtis, 10 April 1939.

[169] Ibid: Letter from Powell to Basil Blackwell, 21 December 1938.

[170] Powys, p11.

[171] CPEP, p55.

[172] Ibid, p72.

[173] Ibid, p74.

[174] Ibid, p63.

[175] Ibid, p65.

[176] Ibid, p85.

[177] Ibid, p86.

[178] Ibid, p87.

[179] Ibid, p88.

[180] Ibid, p95.

[181] *Odd Man Out*, BBC Television, 11 November 1995.

[182] CPEP, p95.

[183] *Times Literary Supplement*, 24 June 1939.

[184] *Cambridge Review*, 14 October 1939.

[185] PP: Letter from Powell to his parents, 9 April 1939.
[186] Ibid: Letter from Powell to his parents, 27 June 1939.
[187] Ibid: Letter from Powell to his parents, 9 July 1939.
[188] IWM interview.
[189] PP: Letter from Powell to his parents, 15 August 1939.
[190] Morley, p69.
[191] Daily Telegraph, 15 October 1988.
[192] IWM interview.
[193] Times Educational Supplement, 28 February 1964.

Chapter 3: The separating flame

[1] Sunday Telegraph, 6 February 1966.
[2] Spectator, 6 June 1992.
[3] Private information.
[4] PP: Letter to Powell from AWJ Thomas, 4 October 1939.
[5] Sunday Express, 26 April 1970.
[6] Enoch: A Life in Politics, Channel 4, 16 October 1987.
[7] IWM interview.
[8] Sunday Express, 26 April 1970.
[9] Panorama, 2 December 1968.
[10] Sunday Telegraph, 8 October 1972.
[11] Listener, 28 May 1981.
[12] IWM interview.
[13] Ibid.
[14] Old Lady, December 1988.
[15] Sunday Express, 15 May 1966.
[16] Attallah, p350.
[17] Powell interview III.
[18] Hunt interview.
[19] Hunt, p15.
[20] Hunt interview.
[21] Amies interview.
[22] Battledress, May/June 1940.
[23] PP: Letter from Powell to Ted Curtis, 10 June 1939.
[24] Ibid: Memoir of Ted Curtis by Powell, undated, c 1985.
[25] Ibid: Letter from Powell to Ted Curtis, 12 May 1940.
[26] Ibid: Letter from Powell to his parents, 26 May 1940.
[27] AJ Marsden, letter to the author, 13 November 1995.
[28] The Times, 30 April 1969.
[29] PP: 'Appreciation of the Battle in France',

15 June 1940; 'Armies', 16 June 1940; and 'The Defence of Britain', 18 June 1940.
[30] Ibid: 'The Chances of Victory'.
[31] IWM interview.
[32] Sunday Express, 26 April 1970.
[33] IWM interview.
[34] Michael Strachan, letter to the author, 31 January 1996.
[35] PP: Letter to Powell from Maj-Gen MB Brocas Burrows, 27 June 1941.
[36] SP: Letter from Powell to Michael Strachan, 22 July 1941. The places mentioned are on the Norwegian–Finnish border.
[37] SP: Letter from Powell to Michael Strachan, 17 August 1941. The German means 'puzzling and incomprehensible'.
[38] PP: Letter to Powell from Maj-Gen MB Brocas Burrows, 20 August 1941.
[39] Ibid: Letter to Powell from Maj-Gen MB Brocas Burrows, 7 September 1941.
[40] Ibid: Letter to Powell from Maj-Gen MB Brocas Burrows, 24 September 1941.
[41] Ibid: Letter from Powell to Colonel T Robbins, 24 Setember 1941.
[42] Ibid: Letter to Powell from Colonel T Robbins, 26 September 1941.
[43] Ibid: Letter to Powell from his parents, 9 October 1943.
[44] Ibid: Letter from Powell to his parents, 19 October 1941.
[45] Ibid: Letter from Powell to his parents, 25 October 1941.
[46] Ibid: Letter from Powell to his parents, 20 January 1942.
[47] Powell interview III.
[48] PP: Letter from Powell to his parents, 2 November 1941.
[49] Ibid: Letter from Powell to his parents, 9 November 1941.
[50] Ibid: Letter from Powell to his parents, 23 May 1942.
[51] Powell interview III.
[52] IWM interview.
[53] PP: Letter from Powell to his parents, 29 June 1942.
[54] Ibid: Letter from Powell to his parents, 13 July 1942.
[55] Roth I, p36.
[56] IWM interview.
[57] PP: Letter from Powell to his parents, 22 July 1942.
[58] SP: Letter from Powell to Michael Strachan, 29 July 1942.

[59] PP: Letter from Powell to his parents, 31 August 1942.

[60] Ibid: Letter from Powell to his parents, 18 September 1942.

[61] Ibid: Letter from Powell to his parents, 11 November 1942.

[62] Ibid: Letter from Powell to his parents, 25 November 1942.

[63] Ibid: Letter from Powell to his parents, 14 December 1942.

[64] Ibid: Letter from Powell to his parents, 24 January 1943.

[65] Ibid: Letter from Powell to his parents, 14 January 1943.

[66] Ibid: Letter from Powell to his parents, 5 January 1943 (misdated 1942).

[67] RS, p33.

[68] Attallah, p357.

[69] PP: '1943'.

[70] Ibid: Letter from Powell to his parents, 24 January 1943.

[71] Ibid: Letter from Powell to his parents, 7 February 1943.

[72] Ibid: Letter from Powell to his parents, 25 July 1943.

[73] Sunday Express, 26 April 1970.

[74] Ibid, 17 March 1967.

[75] IWM interview.

[76] PP: Letter from Powell to his parents, 16 February 1943.

[77] Ibid: Letter from Powell to his parents, 28 February 1943.

[78] Ibid: Letter from Powell to his parents, 9 March 1943.

[79] Old Lady, December 1988.

[80] Professor JM Thoday, letter to the author, 10 March 1998.

[81] London Gazette, 18 February 1943.

[82] PP: Letter from Powell to his parents, 28 February 1943.

[83] Michael Strachan, op cit.

[84] The Times, 17 February 1998.

[85] Blackwood's Magazine, May 1949, pp379–92.

[86] PP: Letter from Powell to his parents, 16 June 1943.

[87] Michael Strachan, op cit.

[88] Ibid.

[89] Sunday Express, 17 April 1966.

[90] The Times, 7 May 1983.

[91] PP: Letter from Powell to his parents, 21 May 1943.

[92] Ibid: Letter from Powell to his parents, 25 July 1943.

[93] Ibid: Letter from Powell to his parents, 7 August 1943.

[94] Ibid: Letter from Powell to his parents, 17 August 1943.

[95] SP: Letter from Powell to Michael Strachan, 5 February 1943.

[96] The Times, 7 May 1983.

[97] Oldie, 2 October 1992.

[98] Powell interview I.

[99] PP: Letter from Powell to his parents, 28 August 1943.

[100] Ibid: Letter from Powell to his parents, 2 September 1943.

[101] SP: Letter from Powell to Michael Strachan, 23 September 1943.

[102] PP: Letter from Powell to his parents, 16 September 1943.

[103] SP: Letter from Ellen Mary Powell to Michael Strachan, 10 October 1943.

[104] Roth I, p34.

[105] SP: Letter from Powell to Michael Strachan, 23 September 1943.

[106] Daniel, p154.

[107] PP: Letter from Powell to his parents, 23 September 1943.

[108] Ibid: Letter from Powell to his parents, 15 October 1943.

[109] Ibid: Letter to Powell from his parents, 27 October 1943.

[110] Ibid: Letter from Powell to his parents, 24 November 1943.

[111] SP: Letter from Powell to Michael Strachan, 23 September 1943.

[112] MCP: Powell interview.

[113] SP: Letter from Powell to Michael Strachan, 23 September 1943.

[114] Sunday Times, 28 April 1968.

[115] SP: Letter from Powell to Michael Strachan, 13 November 1943.

[116] PP: Letter from Powell to his parents, 19 December 1943.

[117] Ibid: 'British War Aims in the Far East', 16 October 1943.

[118] Ibid: Memo to Powell from RP Fleming, 16 October 1943.

[119] SP: Letter from Powell to Michael Strachan, 13 January 1944.

[120] PP: Letter from Powell to his parents, 27 January 1944.

[121] Powell interview II.

[122] SP: Letter from Powell to Michael Strachan, 20 May 1944.

[123] PP: Letter from Powell to his parents, 16 April 1944.

[124] SP: Letter from Powell to Michael Strachan, 17 June 1944.

[125] *Panorama*, 2 December 1968.

[126] PP: Letter from Powell to his parents, 5 July 1944.

[127] Ibid: Letter from Powell to his parents, 8 July 1944.

[128] Ibid: Letter from Powell to his parents, 10 July 1944.

[129] Ibid: Letter from Powell to his parents, 18 June 1944.

[130] Ibid: Letter from Powell to his parents, 30 July 1944.

[131] Ibid: Letters from Powell to his parents, 21 May 1944 and 5 July 1944.

[132] Ibid: Letter to Powell to his parents, 1 September 1944.

[133] Ibid: Letter from Powell to his parents, 1 September 1944.

[134] SP: Letter from Powell to Michael Strachan, 17 October 1944.

[135] PP: Letter from Powell to his parents, 24 September 1944.

[136] Ibid: Letter from Powell to his parents, 19 November 1944.

[137] SP: Letter from Powell to Michael Strachan, 3 September 1944.

[138] Ibid: Letter from Powell to Michael Strachan, 17 October 1944.

[139] Ibid: Letter from Powell to Michael Strachan, 17 July 1945.

[140] Ibid: Letter from Ellen Mary Powell to Michael Strachan, 18 August 1945.

[141] Ibid: Letter from Powell to Michael Strachan, 14 December 1944.

[142] PP: Letter from Powell to his parents, 4 November 1944.

[143] *Daily Telegraph*, 27 February 1988.

[144] SP: Letter from Powell to Michael Strachan, 14 December 1944.

[145] PP: Letter from Powell to his parents, 10 December 1944.

[146] SP: Letter from Powell to Michael Strachan, 15 February 1945.

[147] PP: Letter from Powell to his parents, 22 January 1945 (misdated 1944).

[148] Powell interview III.

[149] SP: Letter from Powell Michael Strachan, 15 April 1945.

[150] Ibid: Letter from Powell to Michael Strachan, 17 July 1945.

[151] PP: Letter from Powell to his parents, 3 June 1945.

[152] Ibid: Letter from Powell to his parents, 30 June 1945.

[153] Ibid: Letter from Powell to his parents, 14 July 1945.

[154] Ibid: Letter from Powell to his parents, 29 July 1945.

[155] Ibid: Letter from Powell to his parents, 9 August 1945.

[156] Ibid: Letter from Powell to his parents, 12 August 1945.

[157] Ibid: Letter from Powell to his parents, 13 May 1945.

[158] Ibid: Letter from Powell to his parents, 21 April 1945.

[159] *Spectator*, 26 July 1968.

[160] PP: Letter from Powell to his parents, 14 July 1945.

[161] SP: Letter from Powell to Michael Strachan, 11 November 1945.

[162] Daniel, p154.

[163] PP: Letter from Powell to his parents, 6 January 1946.

[164] *Daily Telegraph*, 8 July 1989.

[165] *Spectator*, 6 April 1974.

Chapter 4: The third life

[1] *Sunday Times*, 27 October 1963.

[2] Nietzsche II, p222.

[3] PP: Letter from Powell to his parents, 10 December 1944.

[4] Powell interview I.

[5] RS, p54.

[6] Charmley, p132.

[7] Greenleaf, p195.

[8] RS, p53.

[9] Ibid, p54.

[10] *Sunday Telegraph Magazine*, 28 August 1977.

[11] Alport interview.

[12] Butler, pp140–1.

[13] Maudling, p28.

[14] Ibid, p42.

[15] CPA: CRD 2/25/1.

[16] SP: Memorandum on Indian Policy, 16 May 1946, para 2.

[17] Ibid, para 4.

[18] Ibid, para 5.

[19] Ibid, para 7.

[20] Ibid, para 9.

[21] Ibid, para 10.

[22] Ibid, para 11.

[23] Ibid, para 12.

[24] Ibid, para 19.

[25] Ibid, para 25.
[26] Ibid, para 32.
[27] Ibid, para 34.
[28] Ibid, para 35.
[29] *Sunday Times*, 15 September 1946.
[30] *Sunday Telegraph*, 12 February 1967.
[31] Beddows interview.
[32] SP: Memorandum on Indian Policy, 3 December 1946, para 1.
[33] Ibid, para 2.
[34] Ibid, para 4.
[35] Ibid, para 9.
[36] Butler, p141.
[37] Powell interview I.
[38] *Evening Standard*, 14 January 1947.
[39] Powell interview I.
[40] *Sunday Express*, 3 May 1970.
[41] PP: Address to the Electors of the Normanton Division, 24 January 1947.
[42] *Pontefract and Castleford Express*, 31 January 1947.
[43] *Yorkshire Post*, 30 January 1947.
[44] Ibid, 8 February 1947.
[45] Ibid.
[46] CPA: RAB 4/2/245.
[47] Gilbert, p312, *Daily Telegraph*, 7 February 1947.
[48] *Daily Telegraph*, 13 February 1947.
[49] SP: Letter from Powell to Michael Strachan, 12 March 1947.
[50] *Yorkshire Post*, 13 February 1947.
[51] PP: Memorandum from Powell to JPL Thomas, 17 February 1947.
[52] Ibid: Letter to Powell from HL Hartley, 17 March 1947.
[53] RS, p55.
[54] Hennessy II, p235.
[55] Berkeley, p52.
[56] PP: Letter from Powell to Henry Hopkinson, 6 June 1947.
[57] SP: Letter from Powell to Michael Strachan, 9 August 1947.
[58] PP: Letter from Harold Macmillan to Powell, 17 June 1947.
[59] Powell interview I.
[60] RS, p55.
[61] *Odd Man Out*, BBC Television, 11 November 1995.
[62] CPA: CRD 2/37/2/235.
[63] H, piii.
[64] SP: Letter from Powell to Michael Strachan, 25 January 1948.
[65] CPA: CRD 2/37/2/252.

[66] Ibid, CCO 4/2/183.
[67] Ibid.
[68] PP: Speech at the Royal Commonwealth Society, 22 January 1969.
[69] *Sunday Telegraph*, 7 June 1992.
[70] Foot P, p16.
[71] Ibid, p17.
[72] Hansard (Fifth series), 453:388.
[73] Ibid, 453:394.
[74] Ibid, 453:411.
[75] Ibid, 453:412.
[76] CPA: CRD 2/37/2/253.
[77] Ibid: CRD 2/37/2/285.
[78] Powell interview III.
[79] Ibid.
[80] CPA: CRD 2/23/6.
[81] CPA: CRD 2/37/2/297a.
[82] SP: Letter from Powell to Michael Strachan, 24 December 1948.
[83] David Clarke, letter to the author, 23 March 1998.
[84] MCP: Powell interview.
[85] PP: Letter from Iain Macleod to Powell, undated (c October 1947).
[86] Ibid: Draft speech by Macleod for Powell, c October 1948.
[87] *Sunday Express*, 3 May 1970.
[88] C Jones interview.
[89] CPA: CCO 1/7/279.
[90] SP: Letter from Powell to Michael Strachan, 24 December 1948.
[91] CPA: CRD 2/44/4.
[92] SP: Letter from Powell to Michael Strachan, 28 January 1949.
[93] Rhodes James, p168.
[94] CPA: CRD 2/53/5.
[95] PP: Letter from RA Butler to Powell, 29 May 1949.
[96] CPA: CCO 1/7/279.
[97] *Newcastle Journal*, 30 July 1949.
[98] *Sunday Express*, 3 May 1970.
[99] SP: Letter from Powell to Michael Strachan, 5 December 1949.
[100] BBC radio interview, 13 April 1986.
[101] Nietzsche II: pp84–5.
[102] BBC radio interview, 13 April 1986.
[103] Mortimer, p48.
[104] NEA, p3.
[105] *Sunday Express*, 3 May 1970.
[106] PP: Letter to Powell from JPL Thomas, 27 July 1949.
[107] SP: 'A Letter from your Conservative Candidate, Enoch Powell', general election 1950.

[108] Powell interview I.

Interlude: Powell and God

[1] *Oldie*, 2 October 1992.
[2] Mortimer, p48.
[3] NEA, p4.
[4] WWTA, p79.
[5] PP: 'The Church' (undated, c 1951).
[6] Ritchie interview.
[7] WWTA, p71.
[8] *The Times*, 18 August 1994.
[9] *Sunday Times*, 21 August 1994.
[10] NEA, p2.
[11] Ibid, p10.
[12] Field interview.
[13] See WWTA, pp54–7.
[14] Ibid, p57.
[15] Ibid, p70.
[16] For a detailed description of Carlyle's theology, see Heffer, pp14–18.
[17] WWTA, p86.
[18] Gray interview.
[19] Cowling, p432.
[20] Ibid, p437.
[21] NEA, p11.
[22] *The Times*, 4 March 1973.
[23] Ibid, 20 July 1973.
[24] NEA, p12.
[25] Ibid, p29.

Chapter 5: A public life

[1] C Jones interview.
[2] SP: Letter from Powell to Michael Strachan, 19 February 1950.
[3] Mortimer, p50.
[4] Hansard, 472:1315.
[5] Ibid, 472:1316.
[6] Ibid, 472:1318.
[7] Ibid, 472:1319.
[8] Ibid, 472:2368.
[9] *Listener*, 28 May 1981.
[10] SP: Letter from Powell to Michael Strachan, 3 April 1950.
[11] Roth I, p64.
[12] Transcript of interview with Rebecca Hardy, 6 November 1995. I am indebted to Miss Hardy for the use of this material.
[13] Roth I, p60.
[14] PP: Letter to Powell from Michael Strachan, 8 March 1950.
[15] Ibid: Letter to Powell from Barbara Kennedy, 21 July 1950.
[16] Transcript of interview with Rebecca Hardy.
[17] PP: Draft of letter from Powell to Barbara Kennedy, 1 August 1950.
[18] Ibid: Letter to Powell from Barbara Kennedy, 3 August 1950.
[19] Ibid: Draft of letter from Powell to Barbara Kennedy, 27 August 1950.
[20] Ibid: Letter to Powell from Barbara Kennedy, 3 September 1950.
[21] Ibid: Draft of letter from Powell to Barbara Kennedy, 5 September 1950.
[22] Transcript of interview with Rebecca Hardy.
[23] *Odd Man Out*, BBC Television, 11 November 1995.
[24] SP: Letter from Powell to Michael Strachan, 30 May 1950.
[25] Ibid: Letter from Powell to Michael Strachan, 13 June 1950.
[26] PP: Letter from Jonathan Cape to Powell, 16 January 1947.
[27] Ibid: Letter from Powell to Jonathan Cape, 23 April 1947.
[28] CPEP, p viii.
[29] Ibid, p ix.
[30] Ibid, p108.
[31] PP: Letter from Powell to Ted Curtis, 10 June 1939.
[32] CPEP, p114.
[33] Ibid, p115.
[34] Ibid, p113.
[35] Ibid, p128.
[36] Ibid, p147.
[37] Ibid, p149.
[38] Ibid, p135.
[39] Ibid, p vii.
[40] Ibid, p ix.
[41] Ibid, pp ix–x.
[42] Ibid, p x.
[43] Ibid, p157.
[44] Ibid, p158.
[45] Ibid, p160.
[46] Ibid, p165.
[47] Ibid, p167.
[48] Ibid, p170.
[49] Ibid, p169.
[50] Ibid, p173.
[51] Ibid, p172.
[52] *Sunday Telegraph*, 12 November 1967.
[53] Miscalled because England is the Mother of Parliaments, not the English Parliament itself.
[54] *Listener*, 28 May 1981.

[55] Powell interview I.
[56] Ibid.
[57] Alport interview.
[58] Carr interview.
[59] ON, p92.
[60] Ibid, p9.
[61] Ibid, p18.
[62] Ibid, p20.
[63] PP: Letter to Powell from Iain Macleod, undated (c August 1950).
[64] ON, pp27–8.
[65] Ibid, pp30–1.
[66] Ibid, p33.
[67] PP: Letter to Powell from Macleod, undated (c August 1950).
[68] Freeth interview.
[69] I am indebted to Mrs Michael Strachan for this information.
[70] Alport interview.
[71] SP: Letter from Powell to Michael Strachan, 14 October 1950.
[72] CPA: CCO 1/8/279.
[73] Powell interview I.
[74] *The Times*, 13 November 1950.
[75] *Daily Telegraph*, 17 November 1950.
[76] Ibid, 18 November 1950.
[77] CPA: CCO 1/8/279.
[78] Ibid.
[79] Ibid.
[80] *Daily Telegraph*, 20 November 1950.
[81] *Manchester Guardian*, 21 November 1950.
[82] SP: Letter from Powell to Michael Strachan, 21 November 1950.
[83] PP: Letter from Powell to his parents, 2 December 1950.
[84] CPA: CCO 1/8/279.
[85] Ibid.
[86] Ibid.
[87] *Daily Telegraph*, 24 January 1951.
[88] CPA: CCO 1/8/279.
[89] PP: Letter from Powell to his parents, 19 February 1951.
[90] CPA: CCO 1/8/279.
[91] Hansard, 481:884.
[92] Ibid, 482:295.
[93] Ibid, 482:296.
[94] Ibid, 482:301.
[95] Roth I, p73.
[96] *Spectator*, 15 December 1950.
[97] Hansard, 485:1438.
[98] Ibid, 485:1439.
[99] Ibid, 485:1441.
[100] Ibid, 486:1788.

[101] Ibid, 487:312.
[102] Ibid, 487:314.
[103] Ibid, 487:1201.
[104] Ibid, 488:1190.
[105] Ibid, 490:364.
[106] PP: 'A Letter from your Conservative Candidate, Enoch Powell', general election 1951.
[107] Goodhart, p159.
[108] CPA:CRD 2/23/10.
[109] *The Times*, 3 June 1970.
[110] *Listener*, 28 May 1981.
[111] *Odd Man Out*, BBC Television, 11 November 1995.
[112] MPP interview I.
[113] *Sunday Express*, 17 April 1966.
[114] C Jones interview.
[115] Alport interview.
[116] MCP: Pamela Powell interview.
[117] Carr interview.
[118] PP: Letter to Powell from Barbara Hawkins, 12 December 1951.
[119] Confirmed by Barbara Hawkins, letter to the author, 14 April 1998.
[120] Hennessy II, ppxiv–xv.
[121] Hansard, 494:2454.
[122] Ibid, 494:2455.
[123] Ibid, 496:1532.
[124] SP: Letter from Powell to Michael Strachan, 2 January 1952.
[125] Ibid: Letter from Powell to Michael Strachan, 19 February 1952.
[126] Ibid: Letter from Powell to Michael Strachan, 25 February 1952.
[127] *The Social Services: Needs and Means*, by Iain Macleod and J Enoch Powell; Preface.
[128] Fisher, p331.
[129] *Needs and Means*, p5.
[130] Ibid, p32.
[131] PP: Letter from Powell to Winston Churchill, 27 February 1952.
[132] Ibid: Letter to Powell from Winston Churchill, 2 March 1952.
[133] Hansard, 498:886.
[134] Ibid, 498:1951–2.
[135] Deedes interview.
[136] PP: Letter to Powell from Iain Macleod, 27 May 1952.
[137] MPP interview I.
[138] Carr interview.
[139] MPP interview I.
[140] *Spectator*, 16 July 1965.
[141] Gilmour, p136.
[142] *The Times*, 19 August 1952.

143 *Daily Mail*, 27 August 1952.
144 Colville, pp250–1.
145 MPP interview I.
146 RS, p57.
147 Powell interview I.
148 Deedes interview.
149 PP: Letter from Powell to the Director of Personnel Administration, War Office, 30 October 1952.
150 Hansard, 507:1443.
151 Ibid, 509:1432–3.
152 Roth I, p95.
153 *Evening Standard*, 27 April 1953.
154 Seldon-Ball, p421.
155 Hansard, 512:193–4.
156 Ibid, 512:194.
157 Ibid, 512:197.
158 Ibid, 512:242.
159 Ibid, 512:243.
160 Ibid, 512:244.
161 Ibid, 512:245.
162 Ibid, 512:246.
163 Ibid, 512:247.
164 Ibid, 512:253.
165 PP: Letter to Powell from Iain Macleod, undated (c March 1953).
166 Hansard, 515:260.
167 MPP interview I.
168 SP: Letter from Powell to Michael Strachan, 25 May 1953.
169 MCP: Powell interview.
170 Hansard, 517:970.
171 Ibid, 520:343.
172 Ibid, 520:347–8.
173 *Daily Telegraph*, 21 November 1953.
174 Benn I, p268.
175 Amery, p1064.
176 CPA:CRD 2/34/1.
177 Hansard, 521:892.
178 CPA:CRD 2/23/11.
179 *The Times*, 6 August 1993.
180 Aitken interview.
181 FP: Letter from Pamela Powell to Roseen Freeth, 29 January 1954.
182 Freeth interview.
183 *Change Is our Ally*, edited by Enoch Powell and Angus Maude, p9.
184 Ibid, p98.
185 *The Social Services: Needs and Means*, by Iain Macleod and J Enoch Powell (2nd edn, 1954), p27.
186 *Daily Herald*, 19 November 1954.
187 *Needs and Means* (2nd edn) p37.

188 *The Times*, 25 June 1954.
189 *Spectator*, 26 July 1986.
190 *Sunday Telegraph*, 19 January 1986.
191 Foot P, p25.
192 Ibid; *Express and Star*, 23 October 1954.
193 *Tradition and Change* (CPC, 1954) p41.
194 Ibid, p49.
195 Ibid, p52.
196 Hansard, 529:2544.
197 PP: Letter to Powell from Duncan Sandys, 29 October 1954.
198 Hansard, 531:1676–7.
199 *Daily Telegraph*, 8 January 1955.
200 *Observer*, 6 February 1955.
201 Hansard, 536:1325.
202 Ibid, 536:1479.
203 Ibid, 536:1466.
204 PP: Letter from Powell to the Bishop of Lichfield, 26 February 1955.
205 Ibid: Letter to Powell from the Bishop of Lichfield, 2 March 1955.

Chapter 6: Minister of the Crown

1 PP: Transcript of interview between Powell and Anthony Seldon, 28 May 1980.
2 Hansard, 543: 1661.
3 CPA: CRD 2/23/12.
4 Ibid: Transcript of 'Live from the conference', 6 October 1955.
5 Benn interview.
6 CPA: Speech (No. 5244) at Shrewsbury, 23 October 1955.
7 Ibid: Speech (No. 5245) at Halesowen, 24 October 1955.
8 *The Times*, 5 March 1955.
9 *Manchester Guardian*, 21 January 1956.
10 Hansard, 546:1081.
11 Ibid, 546:1083.
12 Roth I, p127.
13 Private information: Memorandum in the author's possession from Edward Heath to Sir Anthony Eden, 4 November 1955.
14 Powell interview III.
15 Post interview.
16 Hansard, 548:2374.
17 Ibid, 550:2162.
18 Ibid, 550:2173.
19 PP: Details taken from Powell's own note of the meetings, 27 February 1956 and 25 April 1956.
20 Ibid: Letter from Powell to the 5th Marquess of Salisbury, 4 March 1971.

21 Ibid: Note by Powell, dated 21 June 1971, on a letter to Salisbury of 7 June 1971.

22 Foot P, pp32–3.

23 Benn I, p268.

24 *Evening Standard*, 28 September 1956.

25 *Daily Sketch*, 29 September 1956.

26 *Manchester Guardian*, 25 October 1956.

27 *Daily Telegraph*, 3 November 1956.

28 *The Times*, 13 October 1987.

29 Benn I, p268.

30 *The Spectator*, 26 July 1986.

31 *Enoch: A Life in Politics*, Channel 4, 16 October 1987.

32 Hansard, 560:162.

33 Ibid, 560:1777.

34 Howard, p241.

35 *Spectator*, 10 January 1987.

36 Roth I, p159.

37 *Daily Herald*, 18 February 1957.

38 PP: Letter to Powell from Sir Anthony Eden, 17 January 1957.

39 Ibid: Letter to Powell from Harold Macmillan, 16 January 1957.

40 Cockett, p164.

41 *Spectator*, 23 July 1954.

42 Fforde, p669.

43 Hall, p94.

44 CPA: CRD 2/53/24.

45 Hansard, 568:1308.

46 Ibid, 568:1316.

47 Ibid, 568:1317–18.

48 Ibid, 568:1320.

49 *Daily Telegraph*, 8 May 1957.

50 Fforde, p674.

51 Hansard, 573:1012.

52 Ibid, 573:1014–15.

53 Ibid, 573:1528.

54 *Sunday Telegraph*, 16 August 1987.

55 CPA: Speech (No. 6061) at Sheringham Hall, 3 August 1957.

56 Brittan, pp190–1.

57 PRO: CAB 129/90 C(57)168.

58 Brittan, pp190–1.

59 PRO: T 233/1369.

60 Ibid.

61 Fforde, p676.

62 Hall, p119.

63 *Manchester Guardian*, 16 September 1957.

64 Hall, p125.

65 Ibid, p126.

66 PRO: CAB 128/31/2 CC(57)66.

67 Fforde, p677.

68 PRO: CAB 128/31/2 CC(57)68.

69 Hall, p126.

70 PRO: CAB 128/31/2/71(57).

71 Ibid: PREM 11/1823.

72 Ibid: PREM 11/1824.

73 Hall, p126.

74 Ibid.

75 Fforde, p686.

76 PRO: PREM 11/1823.

77 Ibid.

78 Ibid: CAB 129/88 c(57)225.

79 Ibid: T 233/1429/1.

80 *Daily Telegraph*, 27 September 1957.

81 Ibid, 5 October 1957.

82 PRO: T 233/1429/59.

83 *Daily Telegraph*, 5 October 1957.

84 CPA: Speech (No. 6106) at Wednesfield, 4 October 1957.

85 *Daily Telegraph*, 11 October 1957.

86 *The Times*, 21 October 1957.

87 *Financial Times*, 14 December 1957.

88 Hansard, 577:1090.

89 Ibid, 577:1271.

90 CPA: Speech (No. 6211) at Newcastle, 29 November 1957.

91 PRO: T 233/1459.

92 MPP interview I.

93 PRO: T 233/1459.

94 Ibid.

95 Horne II, p75.

96 Dell, p216.

97 PRO: T 233/1459.

98 Ibid.

99 Ibid.

100 Hall, p140.

101 Horne II, p71.

102 PP: Letter from Powell to Nigel Birch, 24 December 1957.

103 PRO: CAB 128/31/2/86(57).

104 PRO: T 233/1459.

105 Ibid.

106 PRO: CAB 128/32/1/(58).

107 Horne II, pp71–2.

108 PRO: CAB 128/32/2/(58).

109 PRO: CAB 128/32/3/(58).

110 Horne II, p72.

111 Middlemas, p294; Powell interview IV.

112 Hall, p143.

113 Private information.

114 Macmillan IV, p368.

115 Shepherd I, p132.

116 Macmillan IV, p369.

117 Powell interview I.

118 Butler, p232.

[119] *Daily Telegraph*, 7 January 1958.
[120] *The Times*, 7 January 1958.
[121] Macmillan IV, p370.
[122] *The Times*, 7 January 1958.
[123] Ibid; Powell interview IV.
[124] PP: Letter from Powell to Harold Macmillan, 6 January 1958.
[125] Campbell, p239.
[126] Hailsham II, p318.
[127] *The Times*, 7 November 1970.
[128] Macmillan IV, p372.
[129] Ibid, p373.
[130] Ibid.
[131] *Daily Telegraph*, 8 January 1958.
[132] Ibid.
[133] Hall, pp143–4.
[134] PP: Letter to Powell from William Whitelaw, 7 January 1958.
[135] *Daily Telegraph*, 9 January 1958.
[136] Ibid, 10 January 1958.
[137] *The Times*, 10 January 1958.
[138] Shepherd II, p183.
[139] Mark Jarvis, 'The 1958 Treasury Dispute', *Contemporary British History* (forthcoming). I am indebted to Mr Jarvis for allowing me early sight of his work.
[140] Hall, p144.
[141] PP: Memorandum on the Treasury resignations, 22 January 1958.
[142] Ibid: Letter to Powell from Sir Bruce Fraser, 12 January 1989.
[143] *Listener*, 28 May 1981.
[144] Powell interview I.
[145] Nietzsche II, p17.

Chapter 7: The way back

[1] *Daily Telegraph*, 11 January 1958.
[2] Benn I, p262.
[3] *Daily Telegraph*, 15 January 1958.
[4] *Manchester Guardian*, 3 February 1958.
[5] Hansard, 582:436.
[6] Ibid, 582:437.
[7] Ibid, 582:438.
[8] Ibid, 582:439.
[9] Ibid, 582:440.
[10] Ibid, 582:441.
[11] Ibid, 582:442.
[12] Ibid, 586:217.
[13] Ibid, 586:218.
[14] Ibid, 586:219.
[15] PP: Letter from Powell to Peter Thorneycroft, 19 April 1958.
[16] Ibid: Letter from Powell to Peter Thorneycroft, 26 April 1958.
[17] *Daily Telegraph*, 9 June 1958.
[18] *Manchester Guardian*, 1 January 1959.
[19] Benn I, p297.
[20] Powell interview IV; MPP interview I.
[21] PP: Letter from Powell to Nigel Birch, 22 January 1959.
[22] Ibid: Letter from Powell to Peter Thorneycroft, 21 February 1959.
[23] CPA: CRD 2/53/24.
[24] Ibid: CRD 2/53/26.
[25] Ibid: CRD 2/53/28.
[26] Hansard, 602:694.
[27] Ibid, 602:695.
[28] Ibid, 602:698.
[29] Ibid, 602:699.
[30] Harris interview.
[31] *Spectator*, 6 March 1959.
[32] *Lloyd's Bank Review*, April 1959, p19.
[33] Hansard, 603:251.
[34] Ibid, 603:253.
[35] Ibid, 603:255.
[36] Healey, p146.
[37] PP: Letter from Powell to Alan Lennox-Boyd, 18 June 1959.
[38] Hansard, 610:232.
[39] Ibid, 610:235.
[40] Ibid, 610:236.
[41] Ibid, 610:237.
[42] *Daily Telegraph*, 28 July 1959.
[43] Hansard, 610:249–50.
[44] PP: Letter to Powell from Mark Bonham Carter, 28 July 1959.
[45] Ibid: 'A Letter from your Conservative Candidate, Enoch Powell', general election 1959.
[46] Roth I, p219.
[47] Ibid, p221.
[48] *Daily Telegraph*, 26 October 1959.
[49] Powell interview I.
[50] Hansard, 612:327.
[51] Ibid, 612:330.
[52] Ibid, 612:331–2.
[53] Ibid, 612:332.
[54] Ibid, 614:650.
[55] Ibid, 614:652.
[56] Ibid, 614:653 (quoting para 498 of Radcliffe report).
[57] Ibid, 614:654.
[58] Ibid, 614:655.
[59] Ibid, 614:656.
[60] *Financial Times*, 7 January 1960.
[61] Benn I, p323.

[62] *The Times*, 25 February 1960.
[63] *Financial Times*, 19 May 1960.
[64] Hansard, 621:613.
[65] Ibid, 621:615.
[66] Ibid, 621:617.
[67] Ibid, 624:478.
[68] Ibid, 624:93.
[69] *Observer*, 5 February 1961.
[70] Alport interview.
[71] *Daily Telegraph*, 25 July 1960.
[72] Macmillan V, p231.
[73] Powell interview IV.
[74] Macmillan V, p231.
[75] *Panorama*, 2 December 1968.
[76] Pamela Powell, note to the author, March 1998.
[77] Powell interview I.
[78] Kilmuir, pp313–14.

Chapter 8: Power

[1] *Spectator*, 20 February 1988.
[2] HP: Letter from Ralph Harris to Powell, 29 July 1960.
[3] Ibid: Letter from Powell to Ralph Harris, 20 August 1960.
[4] *Spectator*, 20 February 1988.
[5] RP: Memorandum on Enoch Powell – Minister of Health 1960–63.
[6] Harrison interview.
[7] Powell interview III.
[8] *Spectator*, 20 February 1988.
[9] Godber interview.
[10] PRO: PREM 11/3438.
[11] *Daily Telegraph*, 29 August 1960.
[12] *Daily Express*, 2 February 1961.
[13] *Daily Mail*, 6 October 1960.
[14] Ibid, 21 May 1962.
[15] SFS, p8.
[16] Ibid, p22.
[17] Ibid, p26.
[18] Ibid, p36.
[19] *Daily Telegraph*, 26 September 1960.
[20] SFS, p93.
[21] Ibid, p96.
[22] Ibid, p130.
[23] CPA: Speech (No. 7217) at Barry, 10 September 1960.
[24] *The Times*, 12 September 1960.
[25] CPA: Speech (No. 7282) at Manchester, 18 November 1960.
[26] PRO: CAB 129/102/2/C(60)135.
[27] *Daily Telegraph*, 17 October 1960.
[28] Ibid.
[29] PRO: PREM 11/3438.
[30] Ibid.
[31] Ibid.
[32] CPA: CRD 2/30/14.
[33] PRO: CAB 128/34/CC/54(60).
[34] ANNA, p43.
[35] Ibid, p44.
[36] *The Times*, 22 November 1960.
[37] CPA: CRD 2/30/12.
[38] Godber interview.
[39] PRO: MH 90/83.
[40] Ibid.
[41] Hansard, 632:1258.
[42] PRO: CAB 128/34/CC/65(60).
[43] Macmillan V, p366.
[44] PRO: PREM 11/3438.
[45] Timmins, p210.
[46] *Daily Telegraph*, 18 January 1961.
[47] *Observer*, 5 February 1961.
[48] Hansard, 634:406.
[49] *Daily Telegraph*, 9 February 1961.
[50] Hansard, 634:408.
[51] Ibid, 634:414.
[52] Ibid, 634:426.
[53] Ibid, 634:435.
[54] Ibid, 634:1902.
[55] Ibid, 634:1911.
[56] *Daily Telegraph*, 2 March 1961.
[57] Hansard, 636:167–8.
[58] Ibid, 635:197.
[59] *The Times*, 10 March 1961.
[60] ANNA, p46.
[61] Timmins, p210.
[62] Godber interview.
[63] Timmins, p211.
[64] ANNA, p46.
[65] Timmins, p212.
[66] G Jones interview.
[67] *The Times*, 27 April 1961.
[68] *Daily Express*, 14 March 1961.
[69] *Daily Telegraph*, 18 May 1961.
[70] *Sunday Telegraph*, 11 June 1961.
[71] Hansard, 644:219–20.
[72] Ibid, 644:235–6.
[73] Ibid, 644:238.
[74] PRO: PREM 11/3238.
[75] Ibid: CAB 134/1469 CCM (60) 1.
[76] Ibid: CAB 134/1469 CCM (61) 1.
[77] Ibid.
[78] Ibid: CAB 134/1469 CCM (61) 7.
[79] Ibid: CAB 134/1469 CCM (61) 2.

[80] Ibid: CAB 134/1469 CCM (61) 12.
[81] Ibid: CAB 128/35/2/CC/47(61).
[82] Ibid: CAB 128/35/2/CC/48(61).
[83] PRO: T 298/115.
[84] Ibid.
[85] *Sunday Telegraph*, 1 October 1961.
[86] *The Times*, 2 October 1961.
[87] RS, p526.
[88] Ibid, p527.
[89] Ibid, p535.
[90] Timmins, p209.
[91] *Daily Mail*, 26 January 1962.
[92] PRO: CAB 128/35/2/CC/72(61).
[93] Ibid: CAB 128/36/1/CC/3(62).
[94] Ibid: CAB 128/36/1 CC(62)14.
[95] *Daily Telegraph*, 27 February 1962.
[96] *The Times*, 24 March 1962.
[97] PRO: CAB 128/36/1/CC/19(62).
[98] Godber interview.
[99] PRO: CAB 128/36/1/CC/20(62).
[100] *The Times*, 10 March 1962.
[101] *Sunday Telegraph*, 11 March 1962.
[102] Hansard, 656:1081.
[103] Ibid, 656:1095.
[104] Ibid, 656:1098.
[105] Ibid, 656:1101.
[106] *The Times*, 24 March 1962.
[107] CPA: CRD 2/52/7.
[108] Ibid: CRD 2/52/8.
[109] Ibid: CRD 2/52/9.
[110] Ibid.
[111] PRO: CAB 128/36/2/CC/46(62).
[112] Ibid: CAB 128/36/1/CC/32(62).
[113] Ibid: CAB 134/2568 WN (62)1.
[114] Ibid: PREM 11/5203.
[115] Hansard, 659:945.
[116] *Sunday Telegraph*, 20 May 1962.
[117] *Daily Telegraph*, 15 May 1962.
[118] Harrison interview.
[119] PRO: CAB 128/36/1/CC/37(62).
[120] *Daily Mail*, 21 May 1962.
[121] Hansard, 661: 157.
[122] *The Times*, 22 June 1962.
[123] PRO: CAB 128/36/1/CC/41(62).
[124] *Spectator*, 1 March 1980.
[125] *Flashback: Night of the Long Knives*, BBC Radio 4, 9 July 1995.
[126] PP: Letter to Powell from Sir Bruce Fraser, 13 July 1962.
[127] Ibid: Letter to Powell from Edward Heath, 16 July 1962.
[128] Harrison interview; PP: Letter from Herbert Peplow to Powell, 15 July 1962.
[129] PP: Letter from Powell to Herbert Peplow, 17 July 1962.
[130] Pamela Powell, note to author, March 1998.
[131] *Daily Telegraph*, 17 July 1962.
[132] PRO: CAB 128/36/2/CC/47(62).
[133] Thorpe I, p355.
[134] PP: Letter to Powell from Edith Pitt, 17 July 1962.
[135] Hansard, 663:888.
[136] Ibid, 663:894.
[137] Horne II, p72.
[138] *Spectator*, 3 April 1982.
[139] Hansard, 663:945.
[140] Ibid, 663:946.
[141] Bernard Harrison; letter to the author, 26 March 1998.
[142] PRO: CAB 128/36/2/CC/51(62); CAB 128/36/2/CC/55(62).
[143] Powell interview IV.
[144] *Evening Standard*, 7 August 1962.
[145] *Daily Telegraph*, 14 September 1962.
[146] Ibid, 12 December 1962.
[147] Hansard, 665:330.
[148] Ibid, 665:338.
[149] Roth I, p274.
[150] PRO: CAB 128/37/CC/5(63).
[151] Ibid: CAB 128/37/CC/6(63).
[152] *The Times*, 28 March 1963.
[153] *Daily Telegraph*, 9 March 1963.
[154] Ibid, 18 May 1963.
[155] PR: CAB 128/36/2/73(62).
[156] DP: Meeting at Chequers, Sunday April 28, 1963, Section 1, para 1.
[157] Ibid, Section I, para 3.
[158] Ibid, Section I, para 5.
[159] Ibid, Section II, para 5.
[160] Ibid, Section II, para 19.
[161] *Sunday Times*, 5 May 1963.
[162] Evans, pp38, 264.
[163] PRO: CAB 128/36/2/32(62).
[164] *Daily Telegraph*, 27 May 1963.
[165] Hansard, 677:439.
[166] Ibid, 677:453.
[167] Ibid, 677:455.
[168] PP: Letter from Powell to Harold Wilson, 15 January 1975.
[169] *Daily Telegraph*, 13 June 1963.
[170] Deedes interview.
[171] PRO: CAB 128/37/38(63).
[172] *Daily Telegraph*, 14 June 1963.
[173] MPP interview I.
[174] PP: Telegram to Powell from the editor of the *Daily Sketch*, 13 June 1963.

[175] Ibid: Letter to Powell from Dr P Pattison, Dr AS MacAskill and Dr AR Barber, 13 June 1963.
[176] Ibid: Letter to Powell from Donald McLachlan, 14 June 1963.
[177] Ibid: Letter from Powell to Donald McLachlan, 17 June 1963.
[178] *Daily Telegraph*, 15 June 1963.
[179] *Sunday Telegraph*, 16 June 1963.
[180] Ibid.
[181] Ibid, 7 July 1963.
[182] PP: 'Narrative of the events of 8–19 October 1963 so far as known to me directly'.
[183] Powell interview I.
[184] Hansard, 696:95–6.
[185] Ibid, 696:96–7.
[186] Ibid, 696:98.
[187] Amery, p568.
[188] Hansard, 696:99.
[189] Crawford, pp85–6.
[190] ANNA, p25.
[191] *Daily Express*, 9 July 1963.
[192] *Daily Telegraph*, 2 October 1963.
[193] Ibid, 21 September 1963.
[194] ANNA, p xi.
[195] *Sunday Telegraph*, 6 October 1963.
[196] Godber interview.
[197] PP: Letter to Powell from Kenneth Robinson, 20 October 1963.
[198] Horne II, p541.
[199] PP: 'Narrative of the events ...'
[200] Horne II, p541.
[201] Seldon-Ball, p93.
[202] PP: 'Narrative of the events ...'
[203] Ibid.
[204] Thorpe II, p293.
[205] PP: 'Narrative of the events ...'
[206] Ibid.
[207] *Sunday Telegraph*, 13 October 1963.
[208] Ibid.
[209] Horne II, p544.
[210] PP: 'Narrative of the events ...'
[211] Thorpe II, p289.
[212] PP: 'Narrative of the events ...'
[213] Macmillan VI, p513.
[214] Thorpe II, p301.
[215] *Spectator*, 17 January 1964.
[216] Macmillan VI, p514.
[217] Deedes interview.
[218] PP: 'Narrative of the events ...'
[219] Ibid.
[220] *Spectator*, 17 January 1964.
[221] PP: 'Narrative of the events ...'
[222] Ibid.
[223] Howard, p320.
[224] Macmillan VI, p515.
[225] *Spectator*, 13 October 1973.
[226] PP: 'Narrative of the events ...'
[227] Ibid.
[228] Ibid.
[229] Ibid.
[230] *Panorama*, 2 December 1968.
[231] Powell interview I.
[232] *Sunday Telegraph*, 19 January 1986.
[233] *Daily Telegraph*, 21 October 1963.
[234] Ibid, 26 October 1963.
[235] PP: Letter to Powell from Kenneth Robinson, 20 October 1963.
[236] Thorpe I, p383.
[237] Macmillan VI, p516.
[238] *Spectator*, 13 October 1973.

Interlude: 'Backward travels our gaze'

[1] In the two collections of Powell's speeches in which the St George's speech has been reprinted, *A Nation Not Afraid* and *Freedom and Reality*, the date of delivery is wrongly given as 22 April 1964. The original copy of the speech in the Powell Papers is dated 1961, and a notice of the dinner appeared on the Court page of the *Daily Telegraph* on Monday 24 April 1961.
[2] FR, pp254–7.

Chapter 9: Powellism

[1] *Daily Telegraph*, 22 October 1963.
[2] Ibid, 25 October 1963.
[3] Lewis, p67.
[4] *The Times*, 25 October 1963.
[5] *Sunday Times*, 27 October 1963.
[6] RS, pp57–8.
[7] *Political Quarterly*, vol XXIV, Nos 1–4, 1953, p157.
[8] PP: Telegram to Powell from Richard Ingrams, 1 November 1963.
[9] *Daily Telegraph*, 7 November 1963.
[10] PP: Letter to Powell from WH Smith, 6 December 1963; letter from Powell to WH Smith, 7 December 1963.
[11] *Sunday Times*, 15 December 1963.
[12] Private information.
[13] Thorpe II, p322.
[14] Ibid, p343.
[15] *Daily Telegraph*, 17 January 1964.

16 Thorpe II, p344.
17 Hansard, 688:82.
18 Ibid, 688:86.
19 *The Times*, 29 January 1964.
20 *Observer*, 22 December 1963.
21 *The Times*, 29 January 1964.
22 *Sunday Telegraph*, 2 February 1964.
23 *Daily Mail*, 13 February 1964.
24 *Daily Telegraph*, 13 February 1964.
25 *Sunday Telegraph*, 22 March 1964.
26 *The Times*, 4 April 1964.
27 *Daily Telegraph*, 4 April 1964.
28 *Sunday Telegraph*, 5 April 1964.
29 *The Times*, 1 April 1964.
30 Ibid, 2 April 1964.
31 *Guardian*, 7 April 1964.
32 *Sunday Telegraph*, 5 April 1964.
33 *Daily Telegraph*, 7 April 1964.
34 *Observer*, 10 April 1964.
35 Seldon-Ball, p371.
36 PP: Draft of Education section for 1964 manifesto.
37 Ibid: Draft of Health section for 1964 manifesto.
38 Hennessy I, p174.
39 Hansard, 693:477.
40 Ibid, 693:479.
41 Ibid, 693:481.
42 Ibid, 693:482.
43 *Daily Telegraph*, 23 April 1964.
44 *The Times*, 22 April 1964.
45 *Daily Telegraph*, 23 April 1964.
46 *Sunday Telegraph*, 3 May 1964.
47 RN, p256.
48 Ibid, pp262–3.
49 Ibid, p265.
50 Ibid, p266.
51 *Daily Telegraph*, 26 May 1964.
52 Ibid, 17 June 1964.
53 *The Times*, 30 July 1964.
54 Hansard, 699:1894.
55 Ibid, 699:1895.
56 *Sunday Times*, 6 September 1964.
57 *Daily Telegraph*, 29 September 1964.
58 PP: A Letter from your Conservative Candidate, Enoch Powell, General Election 1964.
59 Fowler, p58.
60 Powell interview I.
61 Ibid.
62 Foot P, p35.
63 Roth I, p310.
64 *Express and Star*, 10 October 1964.
65 ANNA, p11.
66 *Daily Telegraph*, 2 October 1964.
67 Ibid, 3 October 1964.
68 ANNA, p64.
69 Ibid, p65.
70 Ibid, p13.
71 *Sunday Telegraph*, 18 October 1964.
72 Ibid, 12 February 1967.
73 Utley, pp34–5.
74 Pamela Powell, note to the author, March 1998.
75 Hansard, 701:1347.
76 CPA: LCC minutes, 18 November 1964.
77 Utley, p56.
78 ANNA, p100.
79 Ibid, p102.
80 *Daily Telegraph*, 30 November 1964.
81 CPA: LCC minutes, 2 December 1964.
82 HP: Letter to Powell from Ralph Harris, 8 January 1965.
83 Harris interview.
84 ANNA, p80.
85 *Daily Telegraph*, 19 December 1964.
86 *The Times*, 18 December 1964.
87 *Daily Telegraph*, 16 January 1965.
88 *The Times*, 5 February 1965.
89 FR, p48.
90 *Guardian*, 6 February 1965.
91 Hansard, 705:920.
92 ANNA, p84.
93 Ibid, p86.
94 *Sunday Telegraph*, 14 February 1965.
95 *Daily Telegraph*, 18 February 1965.
96 Ibid, 26 February 1965.
97 CPA: LCC minutes, 22 February 1965.
98 Ibid: LCC minutes, 23 February 1965.
99 Ibid: LCC minutes, 23 March 1965.
100 Ibid: LCC minutes, paper LCC (65) 23.
101 Ibid: LCC minutes, 29 March 1965.
102 PP: Letter from Powell to Sir Alec Douglas-Home, 26 January 1965.
103 Ibid: Letter to Powell from Sir Alec Douglas-Home, 28 January 1965.
104 Ibid: Note by Powell of remarks in a speech by Sir Alec Douglas-Home, 3 February 1965.
105 CPA: LCC minutes, 31 March 1965.
106 *Sunday Express*, 4 April 1965.
107 *Guardian*, 5 April 1965.
108 *The Times*, 8 April 1965.
109 CPA; LCC minutes, 13 April 1965.
110 *Sunday Telegraph*, 2 May 1965.
111 Ibid, 25 April 1965.
112 *The Times*, 22 May 1965.
113 CPA:CRD 3/16/1.

[114] PP: Letter from Powell to Sir Alec Douglas-Home, 27 May 1965.
[115] See, for example, Nietzsche I, pp120–2.
[116] *Spectator*, 16 July 1965.
[117] *Sunday Times*, 18 July 1965.
[118] *Sunday Telegraph*, 25 July 1965.
[119] *Observer*, 18 July 1965.
[120] *Spectator*, 9 October 1976.
[121] *Daily Telegraph*, 23 July 1965.
[122] Ibid, 27 July 1965.
[123] Biffen interview.
[124] Baker, p157.
[125] Howe, p39.
[126] *Birmingham Post*, 4 May 1968; Richard Ritchie, letter to the author, 16 July 1998.
[127] *Sunday Telegraph*, 18 February 1979.

Chapter 10: The silent member

[1] Powell interview I.
[2] Ibid.
[3] FP: Letter from Powell to H Andrew Freeth, 6 August 1965.
[4] MPP interview I.
[5] Roth II, p188.
[6] Hansard, 717:1882.
[7] *Daily Telegraph*, 6 September 1965.
[8] *The Times Guide to the House of Commons*, 1966, p286.
[9] Carr interview.
[10] Thatcher interview.
[11] Thatcher II, p141.
[12] Thatcher interview.
[13] Carr interview.
[14] Ibid.
[15] *Sunday Telegraph*, 19 September 1965.
[16] *Daily Telegraph*, 20 September 1965.
[17] FR, p170.
[18] Alexander interview.
[19] Crossman I, p354.
[20] *Sunday Telegraph*, 17 October 1965.
[21] Ibid.
[22] *Daily Telegraph*, 20 October 1965.
[23] *Sunday Telegraph*, 31 October 1965.
[24] Carr-interview.
[25] *Sunday Telegraph*, 7 November 1965.
[26] *Daily Mail*, 22 November 1965.
[27] Hansard, 722:1579.
[28] Ibid, 722:1583.
[29] Ibid, 722:1585.
[30] *Daily Mail*, 21 December 1965.
[31] *Daily Telegraph*, 3 January 1966.
[32] Ibid, 5 January 1966.
[33] Ibid, 13 January 1966.
[34] Ibid, 15 January 1966.
[35] Ibid, 18 January 1966.
[36] Ibid, 19 January 1966.
[37] Ibid, 20 January 1966.
[38] CPA: LCC minutes, 31 January 1966.
[39] Ibid, 16 February 1966.
[40] Hansard, 725:239.
[41] Utley, p111.
[42] Hansard, 725:240.
[43] Ibid, 725:242.
[44] Ibid, 725:243.
[45] *Daily Telegraph*, 26 February 1966.
[46] Ibid, 16 March 1966.
[47] *Guardian*, 20 May 1970.
[48] Alexander interview.
[49] Hansard, 725:1748.
[50] Ibid, 725:1750.
[51] Ibid, 725:1760.
[52] Ibid, 725:1767.
[53] Ibid, 725:1768.
[54] Ibid, 725:1771.
[55] Ibid, 725:1774.
[56] Ibid, 725:1775.
[57] *The Times*, 17 March 1966.
[58] FR, p222.
[59] *Daily Telegraph*, 26 March 1966.
[60] Powell interview I.
[61] *Sunday Telegraph*, 27 March 1966.
[62] Ibid.
[63] Alexander-Watkins, p82.
[64] Powell interview III.
[65] *Daily Telegraph*, 28 March 1966.
[66] Roth II, p199.
[67] *Sunday Telegraph*, 3 April 1966.
[68] *The Times*, 14 April 1966.
[69] *Sunday Express*, 17 April 1966.
[70] Prior, p43.
[71] Carr interview.
[72] *Daily Telegraph*, 20 April 1966.
[73] Hansard, 727:648.
[74] Ibid, 728:414.
[75] Ibid, 728:418.
[76] *Spectator*, 19 August 1966.
[77] *The Times*, 23 July 1966.
[78] Hansard, 732:1850.
[79] CPA: LCC minutes, 25 July 1966.
[80] Ibid: LCC minutes, 1 August 1966.
[81] FR, p39.
[82] Ibid, p97.
[83] *Glasgow Herald*, 17 September 1966.
[84] *Spectator*, 3 April 1982.
[85] *Daily Telegraph*, 14 September 1966.

86 Ibid, 16 September 1966.
87 PP: Speech at Blackpool, 24 September 1966.
88 *Daily Telegraph,* 30 September 1966.
89 Ibid, 1 October 1966.
90 FR, p173.
91 *Daily Telegraph,* 27 October 1966.
92 Ibid, 5 November 1966.
93 Crossman II, p107.
94 *Sunday Telegraph,* 6 November 1966.
95 *Daily Telegraph,* 12 November 1966.
96 Ibid, 19 November 1966.
97 FR, p43.
98 *Daily Telegraph,* 2 December 1966.
99 Ibid, 24 November 1966.
100 Ibid, 25 November 1966.
101 Ibid, 12 January 1967.
102 FR, p75.
103 *The Times,* 16 January 1967.
104 Prior, p45.
105 *Daily Telegraph,* 13 January 1967.
106 *The Times,* 16 January 1967.
107 *Daily Telegraph,* 14 January 1967.
108 Ibid, 17 January 1967.
109 Powell interview III.
110 CPA: LCC minutes, 23 January 1967.
111 Ibid: LCC minutes, 6 February 1967.
112 *Spectator,* 3 February 1967.
113 *Sunday Telegraph,* 12 February 1967.
114 DP: Submission on denationalisation policy by J Enoch Powell (undated).
115 Powell interview IV.
116 PP: Letter to Powell from Sir Michael Fraser, 21 July 1967.
117 Ibid: Letter from Powell to Edward Heath, 29 August 1967.
118 Ibid: Letter from Powell to Michael Alison, 20 June 1975.
119 *Daily Telegraph,* 16 February 1967. As for Powell's distinction between immigration and race, he said, for example, in a letter to Matthew d'Ancona of 24 October 1996, 'I have never made a speech on race.'
120 Hansard, 740:864.
121 Ibid, 742:120.
122 Ibid, 742:135.
123 *The Times,* 6 March 1967.
124 Hansard, 742:1194.
125 Ibid, 742:1196.
126 Ibid, 742:1198.
127 *Daily Telegraph,* 13 March 1967.
128 Ibid, 1 April 1967.
129 *Daily Telegraph Magazine,* 22 March 1967.
130 FR, p17.
131 *The Times,* 4 April 1967.
132 CPA: LCC minutes, 24 April 1967.
133 *Daily Telegraph,* 29 April 1967.
134 Ibid, 10 May 1967.
135 *Sunday Times,* 14 May 1967.
136 *Guardian,* 26 May 1967.
137 *Daily Telegraph,* 26 May 1967.
138 *Observer,* 25 June 1967.
139 CPA: LCC minutes, 19 July 1967.
140 Hansard, 751:985.
141 Ibid, 751:1008.
142 Ibid, 751:1010.
143 Ibid, 751:1011.
144 Ibid, 751:1013.
145 PP: 'Conservative Policy on Immigration and Race Relations', August 1967.
146 Ibid: Letter from Powell to Edward Heath, 7 August 1967.
147 Ibid: Letter to Powell from Edward Heath, 28 July 1967.
148 Ibid: Letter from Powell to Edward Heath, 7 August 1967.
149 *Evening Standard,* 3 August 1967.
150 *Glasgow Herald,* 6 September 1967.
151 *Daily Express,* 7 October 1967.
152 FR, p70.
153 Ibid, p71.
154 *Daily Telegraph,* 19 October 1967.
155 Roth I, p341.
156 MPP interview I.
157 *Sunday Telegraph,* 15 October 1967.
158 Ibid, 17 March 1968.
159 Hansard, 754:1146.
160 Ibid, 754:1311.
161 FR, pp238–42.
162 Alexander-Watkins, p83.
163 Hansard, 755:46.
164 Ibid, 755:47.
165 Ibid, 755:50.
166 FR, p76.
167 Ibid, p80.
168 *Daily Telegraph,* 8 December 1967.
169 *Spectator,* 10 February 1973.
170 Powell interview III.
171 *Daily Telegraph,* 8 December 1967.
172 Ibid, 23 December 1967.
173 Ibid, 11 January 1968.
174 PP: Letter to Powell from Maurice Cowling, 16 January 1968.
175 Ibid: Letter from Powell to Stanley Bell, 19 January 1968.
176 Hansard, 756:1890.

177 Ibid, 756:1894.
178 Ibid, 756:1897.
179 Ibid, 756:1901.
180 Utley, p114.
181 *Sun*, 2 March 1973.
182 CPA: LCC minutes, 7 February 1968.
183 *Daily Telegraph*, 12 February 1968.
184 *Guardian*, 12 February 1968.
185 *Daily Telegraph*, 19 February 1968.
186 Laing, p196.
187 *Sunday Times*, 5 May 1968.
188 C Jones interview.
189 HP: Letter from Powell to Ralph Harris, 8 March 1968.
190 FR, p176.
191 PP: LCC (68) 231st Meeting.
192 Carr interview.
193 PP: LCC (68) 231st Meeting.
194 Thatcher I, p144.
195 See Ian Aitken, Whitelaw's biographer, in the *Guardian*, 12 February 1998.
196 Hailsham I, p234.
197 Prior, p51.
198 PP: Letter to Powell from Edward Heath, 16 April 1968.

Chapter 11: 'The great betrayal'

1 C Jones interview.
2 *Sunday Express*, 14 July 1968.
3 *Enoch: A Life in Politics*, Channel 4, 16 October 1987.
4 WWTA, p5.
5 FR, pp213–19.
6 *The Times*, 6 August 1993.
7 *Sunday Telegraph*, 5 May 1968.
8 Aitken interview; Pamela Powell, diary, 7 July 1968.
9 *The Times*, 12 February 1998.
10 Rhodes James, p164.
11 Hailsham I, p234.
12 Ibid, p235.
13 Whitelaw, p64.
14 Carr interview.
15 Utley, p17.
16 Ibid, p39.
17 C Jones interview.
18 *Daily Telegraph*, 22 April 1968.
19 *Sunday Times*, 2 April 1968.
20 Benn III, p59.
21 Shepherd I, p501.
22 *Daily Telegraph*, 22 April 1968.
23 Hutchinson, p175.
24 Whitelaw, p64.
25 *Odd Man Out*, BBC Television, 11 November 1995.
26 Thatcher I, p146.
27 Carr interview.
28 Thatcher I, p147; Thatcher interview; Pamela Powell, diary, 8 July 1968.
29 *The Times*, 22 April 1968.
30 Ibid.
31 Ibid, 23 April 1968.
32 Ibid, 22 April 1968.
33 MCP: Jennifer Lavin interview.
34 *Guardian*, 22 April 1968.
35 *The Times*, 22 April 1968.
36 *Daily Telegraph*, 22 April 1968.
37 *The Times*, 23 April 1968.
38 CPA: LCC minutes, 22 April 1968.
39 *Daily Telegraph*, 23 April 1968.
40 *The Times*, 23 April 1968.
41 Utley, p43.
42 *Daily Telegraph*, 24 April 1968.
43 Ibid.
44 Ibid.
45 Crossman III, p21.
46 Deedes interview.
47 PP: Letter to Powell from 'JMD', 23 April 1968.
48 *Daily Telegraph*, 24 April 1968.
49 *The Times*, 29 April 1968.
50 *Daily Telegraph*, 27 April 1968.
51 Ibid, 23 April 1968.
52 *Financial Times*, 27 April 1968.
53 *Daily Telegraph*, 27 April 1968.
54 Ibid, 30 April 1968.
55 Crossman III, p29.
56 Race Relations Act 1965.
57 *Birmingham Post*, 4 May 1968.
58 *Sunday Telegraph*, 5 May 1968.
59 *Daily Telegraph*, 8 May 1968.
60 Ibid, 6 May 1968.
61 *The Times*, 8 May 1968.
62 *Daily Telegraph*, 10 May 1968.
63 *Sunday Telegraph*, 12 May 1968.
64 *Sunday Times*, 12 May 1968.
65 Comfort, p475.
66 SP: Letter from Powell to Michael Strachan, 13 May 1968.
67 Biffen interview.
68 MPP interview I.
69 Howard interview.
70 *Daily Telegraph*, 15 June 1968.
71 *Sunday Telegraph*, 16 June 1968.
72 *The Times*, 20 June 1968.

73 *Daily Telegraph*, 11 July 1968.
74 *Daily Mail*, 11 July 1968.
75 *Daily Telegraph*, 19 July 1968.
76 Ibid, 18 July 1968.
77 *Sunday Telegraph*, 1 September 1968.
78 *Daily Telegraph*, 28 September 1968.
79 *Sunday Times*, 1 September 1968.
80 *Daily Telegraph*, 2 September 1968.
81 *Daily Express*, 5 September 1968.
82 *Daily Telegraph*, 9 September 1968.
83 *Sunday Times*, 8 September 1968.
84 *The Times*, 13 September 1968.
85 *Daily Telegraph*, 20 September 1968.
86 *The Times*, 18 September 1968.
87 *Sunday Express*, 28 September 1968.
88 *Daily Telegraph*, 23 September 1968.
89 Ibid, 2 October 1968.
90 Ibid, 8 October 1968.
91 Ritchie interview.
92 *Daily Telegraph*, 11 October 1968.
93 Ritchie interview.
94 IT, p25.
95 Ibid, p26.
96 Ibid, p29.
97 Ibid, p37.
98 *Observer*, 13 October 1968.
99 *Daily Telegraph*, 14 October 1968.
100 *Sunday Express*, 17 November 1968.
101 *Sunday Telegraph*, 13 October 1968.
102 *Daily Telegraph*, 19 October 1968.
103 Ibid, 26 October 1968.
104 Ibid, 8 October 1968.
105 Ibid, 9 November 1968.
106 *The Times*, 5 November 1968.
107 Ibid.
108 *Sunday Telegraph*, 8 November 1968.
109 *Daily Mail*, 11 July 1968.
110 FR, pp226–37.
111 *Daily Telegraph*, 18 November 1968.
112 PP: Letter from Powell to the Earl of Warwick, 17 October 1968.
113 Private information.
114 Ibid: Letter to Powell from Anthony Barber, 20 November 1968.
115 *Daily Telegraph*, 22 November 1968.
116 *The Times*, 18 November 1968.
117 The Runnymede Trust's estimate in between the 1991 and 2001 Censuses.
118 Hansard, 773:1131.
119 Ibid, 773:1133.
120 Ibid, 773:1150.
121 Ibid, 773:1163–4.
122 Ibid, 773:1165.
123 Ibid, 773:1166.
124 Ibid, 773:1167.
125 Ibid, 773:1168.
126 Ibid, 773:1169.
127 *Daily Telegraph*, 20 November 1968.
128 Hansard, 773:1300.
129 *Daily Telegraph*, 21 November 1968.
130 Ibid.
131 *The Times*, 25 November 1968.
132 *Daily Telegraph*, 27 November 1968.
133 Private source: Note of One Nation meeting, 27 November 1968.
134 James Ramsden, letter to the author, 29 April 1998.
135 James Ramsden, letter to the author, 25 April 1998.
136 James Ramsden, letter to the author, 29 April 1998.
137 *The Times*, 30 November 1968.
138 *Daily Telegraph*, 2 December 1968.
139 *The Times*, 3 December 1968.
140 PP: Letter to Powell from Barrie Sales, BBC *Panorama*, 12 December 1968.
141 *Daily Telegraph*, 7 December 1968.
142 Powell interview IV.
143 PP: Speech at Thetford, 13 December 1968.
144 *Listener*, 26 December 1968.
145 Crossman III, p299.
146 *Daily Telegraph*, 4 January 1969.
147 PP: Letter to Powell from Anthony Kershaw, 3 January 1969.
148 *The Times*, 18 January 1969.
149 *Daily Telegraph*, 16 January 1969.
150 Foot P, p121.
151 *Guardian*, 21 January 1969.
152 *Daily Telegraph*, 9 January 1969.
153 *Daily Express*, 18 January 1969.
154 *Daily Telegraph*, 25 January 1969.
155 *Sunday Telegraph*, 26 January 1969.
156 *Daily Telegraph*, 27 January 1969.
157 Ibid, 28 January 1969.
158 Ibid.

Chapter 12: An enemy within

1 Hansard, 777:1351.
2 Ibid, 777:1352.
3 Ibid, 777:1411.
4 Ibid, 777:1412.
5 Ibid, 778:306.
6 Ibid, 778:341.
7 Ibid, 778:383.
8 Ibid, 778:384.

9 Ibid, 778:427–8.
10 Ibid, 778:433.
11 Ibid, 778:505.
12 Ibid, 778:506.
13 Ibid, 778:1380.
14 Ibid, 778:1488.
15 Ibid, 778:1592.
16 Ibid, 779:41.
17 Ibid, 779:86.
18 Ibid, 779:92–3.
19 *Daily Telegraph*, 8 March 1969.
20 *The Times*, 7 March 1969.
21 Ibid, 10 March 1969.
22 PP: Letter from Powell to Anthony Barber, 14 March 1969.
23 Ibid: Letter to Powell from Anthony Barber, 17 March 1969.
24 Hansard, 780:350.
25 *The Times*, 22 March 1969.
26 CMCA, p9.
27 PP: Transcript of *Any Questions*, 18 March 1966.
28 *The Times*, 22 March 1969.
29 MCP: Powell interview.
30 Benn III, p192.
31 *Daily Telegraph*, 10 April 1969.
32 Ibid, 11 April 1969.
33 Benn III, p161.
34 PP: Speech at the Hyde Park Hotel, 17 April 1969.
35 Hansard, 781:1279.
36 *Daily Telegraph*, 24 April 1969.
37 Ibid, 30 April 1969.
38 Ibid, 7 June 1969.
39 Ibid, 10 June 1969.
40 *The Times*, 10 June 1969.
41 Ibid, 13 June 1969.
42 DP: Memorandum to Heath and Hogg from Patrick Cosgrave regarding Powell's Speech of 9 July 1969 at Wolverhampton.
43 *Daily Telegraph*, 14 June 1969.
44 *Guardian*, 17 June 1969.
45 PP: Speech at Bradford, 18 July 1969.
46 King I, p268.
47 *The Times*, 21 August 1969.
48 Ibid, 28 August 1969.
49 *Daily Telegraph*, 1 September 1969.
50 *The Times*, 6 September 1969.
51 King I, p274.
52 Ibid, p275.
53 *Daily Telegraph*, 26 September 1969.
54 Ibid, 30 September 1969.
55 Ibid, 3 October 1969.
56 *The Times*, 4 October 1969.
57 *Sunday Telegraph*, 5 October 1969.
58 *Brighton Evening Argus*, 10 October 1969.
59 *Sunday Express*, 25 January 1970.
60 Hansard, 788:639.
61 Ibid, 788:641.
62 Ibid, 788:642.
63 Ibid, 788:643.
64 Ibid, 791:242.
65 Ibid, 791:257.
66 SP: Notes on a meeting with Powell, 6 November 1969.
67 PP: Speech at Wolverhampton, 7 November 1969.
68 Hansard, 791:1256.
69 Ibid: 793:1385–6.
70 Ibid: 793:1390–1.
71 Ibid: 793:1410.
72 Ibid, 793:1413–14.
73 PP: Speech at Wolverhampton, 6 January 1970.
74 *The Times*, 13 January 1970.
75 FP: Letter from Pamela Powell to Roseen Freeth, 13 January 1970.
76 *Sunday Telegraph*, 18 January 1970.
77 *Daily Telegraph*, 19 January 1970.
78 PP: Letter to Powell from Quintin Hogg, 19 January 1970.
79 Ibid: Speech to St Andrews Conservative Association, 23 January 1970.
80 *Sunday Express*, 25 January 1970.
81 Wilson I, p524.
82 PP: Letter from Powell to Edward Heath, 2 February 1970.
83 Alexander-Watkins, p113.
84 PP: Letter to Powell from Edward Heath, 3 February 1970.
85 Ibid: Letter from Powell to Edward Heath, 4 February 1970.
86 *Guardian*, 6 February 1970.
87 *Daily Telegraph*, 9 February 1970.
88 *Daily Mirror*, 9 February 1970.
89 Ibid.
90 PP: Letter to Powell from Iain Macleod, 14 February 1970.
91 *Daily Telegraph*, 7 February 1970.
92 Ibid, 9 February 1970.
93 Hansard, 796:1263.
94 Ibid, 796:1264.
95 Ibid, 796:1265.
96 Ibid, 796:1266–7.
97 Ibid, 796:1270.
98 Ibid, 797:467.

99 Ibid, 797:468.
100 Ibid, 797:472.
101 Ibid, 797:479.
102 *Daily Telegraph*, 13 March 1970.
103 Crossman III, p828.
104 *The Times*, 17 March 1970.
105 Butler, p141.
106 PP: Letter to Powell from Lord Butler, 4 June 1971.
107 *Daily Telegraph*, 23 March 1970.
108 Hansard, 799:290.
109 Ibid, 799:291.
110 Ibid, 800:111.
111 Ibid, 801:103–4.
112 PP: Letter from Sir Edward Boyle to Horace King, 7 May 1970.
113 Ibid: Letter from Powell to Fred Peart, 7 May 1970.
114 Ibid: Letter to Powell from Fred Peart, 15 May 1970.
115 Ibid: Letter from Powell to Fred Peart, 21 May 1970.
116 Ibid: Letter from Powell to Horace King, 6 May 1970; Pamela Powell, note to the author, July 1998.
117 Ibid: Letter from Horace King to Powell, 7 May 1970.
118 Ibid: Letter from Powell to Horace King, 21 May 1970.
119 Ibid: Letter to Powell from Horace King, 22 May 1970.
120 Hansard, 801:235.
121 Ibid, 801:236.
122 Ibid, 801:237.
123 Ibid, 801:238.
124 *The Times*, 19 May 1970.
125 *Sunday Telegraph*, 31 May 1970.
126 Butler–Pinto, p310.
127 Ritchie interview.
128 PP: Vote Powell on Thursday 18th June (1970 election address).
129 *Daily Telegraph*, 29 May 1970.
130 Butler–Pinto, p233.
131 *Guardian*, 20 May 1970.
132 *Daily Telegraph*, 4 June 1970.
133 Ibid.
134 Ritchie interview.
135 *The Times*, 9 June 1970.
136 Benn III, p288.
137 Benn interview.
138 Crossman III, p939.
139 Benn IV, p92.
140 *Daily Telegraph*, 5 June 1970.

141 Ibid, 2 June 1970.
142 Ibid, 5 June 1970.
143 Alexander-Watkins, p180.
144 *The Times*, 3 June 1970.
145 *Daily Telegraph*, 9 June 1970.
146 Ibid, 15 June 1970.
147 *The Times*, 15 June 1970.
148 Alexander-Watkins, p189.
149 Ibid.
150 *Sunday Times*, 14 June 1970.
151 Ibid.
152 *Daily Telegraph*, 15 June 1970.
153 *The Times*, 15 June 1970.
154 Alexander-Watkins, p191.
155 Ibid.
156 *The Times*, 16 June 1970.
157 Fisher, p304.
158 PP: Letter to Powell from Iain Macleod, 16 June 1970.
159 *Daily Mail*, 16 June 1970.
160 *The Times*, 16 June 1970.
161 *Daily Telegraph*, 17 June 1970.
162 *The Times*, 17 June 1970.
163 Ibid.
164 *Guardian*, 17 June 1970.
165 *The Times*, 18 June 1970.
166 *Sunday Times*, 14 June 1970.
167 Hurd, p22.
168 *Daily Telegraph*, 18 June 1970.
169 *The Times*, 19 June 1970.
170 *Daily Telegraph*, 19 June 1970.

Chapter 13: Unfinished victory

1 Crick, p135.
2 Ritchie interview.
3 MPP interview I.
4 PP: Letter to Powell from Lord Alport, 23 June 1970.
5 Ibid: Letter to Powell from Lord Thorneycroft, 24 June 1970.
6 Ibid: Letter from Powell to his wife, 30 June 1970.
7 *Observer*, 21 June 1970.
8 *Sunday Times*, 28 June 1970.
9 *London Review of Books*, 23 January 1997.
10 PE, p19.
11 Ibid, p27.
12 Ibid, p29.
13 *Daily Telegraph*, 22 July 1970.
14 Fisher, p66.
15 Powell interview I.
16 *Observer*, 1 December 1985.

[17] PP: Letter from Powell to Ian Harvey, 10 July 1973.
[18] Lilley interview.
[19] *Daily Telegraph*, 1 October 1970.
[20] Ibid, 17 October 1970.
[21] Ibid, 19 October 1970.
[22] *Spectator*, 24 October 1970.
[23] *Financial Times*, 23 October 1970.
[24] *The Times*, 9 November 1970.
[25] *Daily Telegraph*, 11 November 1970.
[26] *Sunday Express*, 8 November 1970.
[27] Cowling, p432.
[28] Hansard, 806:265.
[29] PP: Speech at Southport, 12 November 1970.
[30] Hansard, 807:499.
[31] Ibid, 807:554.
[32] *Sunday Telegraph*, 29 November 1970.
[33] *Sunday Express*, 3 January 1971.
[34] *Guardian*, 16 January 1971.
[35] *The Times*, 18 January 1971.
[36] *Daily Telegraph*, 7 January 1971.
[37] Ibid, 18 January 1971.
[38] Ibid, 21 January 1971.
[39] PP: Speech at Birmingham, 22 January 1971.
[40] Hansard, 809:1369.
[41] Ibid, 809:1371.
[42] Ibid, 809:1372–3.
[43] Ibid, 809:1374.
[44] Ibid, 809:1376.
[45] Ibid, 809:1377.
[46] *Daily Telegraph*, 8 February 1971.
[47] *The Times*, 11 February 1971.
[48] *Guardian*, 2 May 1970.
[49] *Daily Telegraph*, 15 December 1970.
[50] *Spectator*, 9 October 1976.
[51] *Daily Express*, 10 February 1971.
[52] PP: Speech at Lyon, 12 February 1971.
[53] *The Times*, 16 February 1971.
[54] *Guardian*, 22 February 1971.
[55] *Sun*, 3 March 1971.
[56] Ibid, 4 March 1971.
[57] Ibid, 5 March 1971.
[58] Hansard, 813:76.
[59] Ibid, 813:78.
[60] Ibid, 813:80.
[61] Ibid, 813:83.
[62] *The Times*, 24 March 1971.
[63] *Sunday Express*, 28 March 1971.
[64] *The Times*, 30 March 1971.
[65] *Daily Telegraph*, 7 April 1971.
[66] Hansard, 815:72.
[67] Ibid, 815:72–3.
[68] Ibid, 815:74.
[69] Ibid, 815:75.
[70] Carr interview.
[71] *Daily Telegraph*, 17 April 1971.
[72] Ibid, 19 April 1971.
[73] *The Times*, 19 April 1971.
[74] *Daily Telegraph*, 8 May 1971.
[75] DP: Letter from Powell to Bill Deedes, 11 May 1971.
[76] *The Times*, 12 May 1971.
[77] *Daily Telegraph*, 18 May 1971.
[78] *Sunday Express*, 30 May 1971.
[79] *The Times*, 28 May 1971.
[80] Ibid, 31 May 1971.
[81] Hansard, 819:563.
[82] Ibid, 819:564.
[83] Godber interview.
[84] Hansard, 820:42.
[85] Ibid, 820:72.
[86] Ibid, 802:79.
[87] *Sunday Telegraph*, 1 August 1971.
[88] PP: Letter from Powell to Sir Gilbert Longden, 18 April 1974.
[89] *Sunday Times*, 1 August 1971.
[90] *Daily Telegraph*, 12 September 1971.
[91] *The Times*, 4 September 1974.
[92] *Sunday Express*, 5 September 1971.
[93] *The Times*, 9 September 1971.
[94] Ibid, 14 September 1971.
[95] *Daily Telegraph*, 17 September 1971.
[96] *Sunday Telegraph*, 19 September 1971.
[97] *The Times*, 13 September 1971.
[98] Hansard, 823:39.
[99] Ibid, 823:40.
[100] Ibid, 823:45.
[101] Ibid, 823:46.
[102] *Daily Telegraph*, 30 September 1971.
[103] Ibid, 14 October 1971.
[104] Ibid, 20 October 1971.
[105] *The Times*, 16 October 1971.
[106] PP: Speech at Cardiff, 18 October 1971.
[107] Ibid: Speech at Newport, 22 October 1971.
[108] Hansard, 823:2185.
[109] Ibid, 823:2186.
[110] Ibid, 823:2189.
[111] *The Poisoned Chalice*, BBC Television, 16 May 1996.
[112] Alexander-Watkins interview.
[113] *Sunday Telegraph*, 7 November 1971.
[114] *The Times*, 1 November 1971.
[115] Hansard, 826:1110.
[116] *Powellight*, November/December 1971.
[117] Hansard, 826:1205.

[118] Ibid, 826:1206.
[119] *Powellight*, November/December 1971.
[120] Hansard, 827:1554.
[121] Ibid, 827:1556.
[122] Ibid, 827:1559.
[123] Ibid, 828:1150.
[124] Ibid, 828:1151.
[125] Ibid, 828:1152.
[126] Ibid, 828:1157.
[127] Ibid, 828:59.
[128] *Daily Telegraph*, 13 January 1972.
[129] Beddows interview.
[130] *Sunday Telegraph*, 16 January 1972.
[131] *The Times*, 25 January 1972.
[132] Hansard, 829:701.
[133] *Sunday Express*, 30 January 1972.

Chapter 14: A battle for Britain

[1] *The Times*, 14 February 1972.
[2] Private information.
[3] Hansard, 831:266.
[4] Ibid, 831:267.
[5] Ibid, 831:268.
[6] Ibid, 831:700.
[7] Ibid, 831:701.
[8] Ibid, 831:702.
[9] Ibid, 831:703.
[10] Ibid, 831:704.
[11] Ibid, 831:705.
[12] Ibid, 831:706.
[13] Ibid, 831:707.
[14] Ibid, 831:758.
[15] Pamela Powell, note to the author, July 1998.
[16] Hansard, 831:1181.
[17] Ibid, 831:1187.
[18] *Observer*, 27 February 1972.
[19] *Daily Telegraph*, 1 March 1972.
[20] Hansard, 832:465.
[21] Ibid, 832:466.
[22] Ibid, 832:467.
[23] Ibid, 832:471.
[24] *Observer*, 5 March 1972.
[25] Hansard, 832:1041.
[26] *Guardian*, 11 March 1972.
[27] Hansard, 832:1300–1.
[28] Ibid, 832:1519–20.
[29] *Sunday Telegraph*, 9 April 1972.
[30] *The Times*, 10 April 1972.
[31] *Sunday Telegraph*, 19 March 1972.
[32] Hansard, 834:240.
[33] King II, p80.
[34] Hansard, 834:270.

[35] Ibid, 834:271.
[36] Ibid, 834:272.
[37] Ibid, 834:273.
[38] Ibid, 834:274.
[39] Ibid, 834:276.
[40] *Sunday Telegraph*, 23 April 1972.
[41] *Guardian*, 22 April 1972.
[42] Molyneaux interview.
[43] Hansard, 835:343.
[44] Ibid, 835:347.
[45] Ibid, 835:348.
[46] PP: Letter to Powell from Roy Jenkins, 1 May 1972.
[47] Ibid: Letter from Powell to Roy Jenkins, 3 May 1972.
[48] Ibid: Letter to Powell from Roy Jenkins, 12 May 1972.
[49] *Daily Telegraph*, 14 September 1980.
[50] Hansard, 836:282.
[51] ANONN, p41.
[52] *Daily Telegraph*, 6 May 1972.
[53] *Sunday Times*, 7 May 1972.
[54] *Economist*, 8 July 1972.
[55] *Daily Express*, 18 May 1972.
[56] *Daily Telegraph*, 19 May 1972.
[57] *Listener*, 10 June 1972.
[58] *Sunday Express*, 21 May 1972.
[59] Ibid, 4 June 1972.
[60] ANONN, p65.
[61] Hansard, 838:728.
[62] *Sunday Telegraph*, 11 June 1972.
[63] *Daily Telegraph*, 12 June 1972.
[64] *The Times*, 29 July 1972.
[65] PP: Policy Statement Prepared in the Department of State, Washington, August 15 1950.
[66] *Powellight*, June 1972.
[67] *The Times*, 24 June 1972.
[68] Lilley interview.
[69] Hansard, 839:1710.
[70] Ibid, 839:1751.
[71] Ibid, 839:1753.
[72] Ibid, 839:1755.
[73] *Daily Telegraph*, 1 July 1972.
[74] *Powellight*, July 1972.
[75] *The Times*, 3 July 1972.
[76] Hansard, 840:566.
[77] Ibid, 840:568.
[78] Ibid, 840:569.
[79] Ibid, 840:1925.
[80] Ibid, 840:1930.
[81] *Daily Telegraph*, 11 July 1972.
[82] *The Times*, 19 July 1972.

[83] *Daily Telegraph*, 20 July 1972.
[84] Ibid.
[85] Hansard, 841:926.
[86] *The Times*, 29 July 1972.
[87] *Guardian*, 29 July 1972.
[88] MPP interview I.
[89] *Sunday Express*, 1 December 1985.
[90] PP: 'Draft prepared in July 1972.
[91] Ridley, p20.
[92] Biffen interview.
[93] *Sunday Express*, 1 December 1985.
[94] *Daily Telegraph*, 17 August 1972.
[95] *Guardian*, 28 August 1972.
[96] *The Times*, 13 September 1972.
[97] *Sunday Telegraph*, 17 September 1972.
[98] Harris interview.
[99] Pamela Powell, note to the author, July 1998.
[100] PP: Letter from Powell to Friedrich von Hayek, 10 October 1975.
[101] Ibid: Letter from Powell to Ralph Harris, 17 May 1980.
[102] *Daily Telegraph*, 19 September 1972.
[103] *The Times*, 28 September 1972.
[104] *Daily Telegraph*, 28 September 1972.
[105] Ibid, 9 October 1972.
[106] *Sunday Telegraph*, 8 October 1972.
[107] *Daily Telegraph*, 9 October 1972.
[108] *Guardian*, 10 October 1972.
[109] *Daily Telegraph*, 11 October 1972.
[110] *Powellight*, October 1972.
[111] *Daily Telegraph*, 12 October 1972.
[112] Ibid.
[113] Ibid, 13 October 1972.
[114] Ibid.
[115] *The Times*, 12 October 1972.
[116] *Sunday Times*, 15 October 1972.
[117] Ibid, 13 October 1972.
[118] *Daily Telegraph*, 26 October 1972.
[119] *The Times*, 13 October 1972.
[120] Schoen, pp94–5.
[121] *Sun*, 28 February 1973.
[122] Carthew interview.
[123] *Sunday Express*, 29 October 1972.
[124] Ibid.

Chapter 15: Nemesis

[1] *Daily Telegraph*, 4 November 1972.
[2] *The Times*, 7 November 1972; Hansard, 845:63–2.
[3] Hansard, 845:884.
[4] Ibid, 845:885.
[5] Ibid, 845:888.
[6] Ibid, 845:890.
[7] FP: Letter from Powell to H Andrew Freeth, 8 November 1972.
[8] PP: Letter from Powell to Francis Pym, 8 November 1972.
[9] Ibid: Letter to Powell from Francis Pym, 8 November 1972.
[10] Norton, p129.
[11] *Sun*, 2 March 1973.
[12] Hansard, 848:1275.
[13] Ibid, 848:1657.
[14] Ibid, 848:1666.
[15] *Daily Telegraph*, 2 January 1973.
[16] Ibid, 13 January 1973.
[17] Hansard, 849:977.
[18] Ibid, 848:979.
[19] Ibid, 849:980.
[20] Ibid, 849:981–2.
[21] Ibid, 849:983.
[22] Ibid, 849:984.
[23] Ibid, 849:1069.
[24] Ibid, 851:659.
[25] *Daily Telegraph*, 6 February 1973.
[26] *Guardian*, 8 February 1973.
[27] *Daily Mail*, 14 February 1973.
[28] Ibid.
[29] *Sun*, 28 February 1973.
[30] Ibid, 2 March 1973.
[31] *Daily Express*, 5 March 1973.
[32] *Sunday Express*, 11 March 1973.
[33] *Sunday Telegraph*, 11 March 1973.
[34] *Daily Telegraph*, 7 March 1973.
[35] Ibid, 14 March 1973.
[36] Ibid, 15 March 1973.
[37] *Daily Telegraph*, 26 March 1973.
[38] Schoen, p97.
[39] *Sunday Telegraph*, 8 April 1973.
[40] *Daily Telegraph*, 11 April 1973.
[41] Hansard, 853:1591.
[42] Ibid, 853:1592.
[43] Ibid, 853:1594.
[44] Ibid, 853:1595.
[45] Ibid, 854:624.
[46] *The Times*, 16 April 1973.
[47] *Daily Telegraph*, 30 April 1973.
[48] ANONN, p85.
[49] *Daily Telegraph*, 16 May 1973.
[50] *Enoch: A Life in Politics*, Channel 4, 16 October 1987.
[51] Benn IV, p44.
[52] *Daily Telegraph*, 9 June 1973.
[53] Ibid.

[54] Ibid, 11 June 1973.

[55] *The Times*, 11 June 1973.

[56] Schoen, p118.

[57] PP: Letter to Powell from Lord Rhyl, 13 June 1973.

[58] Ibid: Letter from Powell to Lord Rhyl, 15 June 1973.

[59] Ibid: Letter to Powell from Nicholas Kaldor, 10 June 1973.

[60] *The Times*, 11 June 1973.

[61] PP: Letter to Powell from John Biffen, 7 June 1973.

[62] *Daily Telegraph*, 12 June 1973.

[63] Ibid, 15 June 1973.

[64] Ibid, 16 June 1973.

[65] Hansard, 857:1828.

[66] Ibid, 857:1830.

[67] *Sunday Telegraph*, 8 July 1973.

[68] Ibid, 15 July 1973.

[69] *Daily Telegraph*, 16 July 1973.

[70] PP: Letter from Powell to Christopher Chataway, 20 July 1973.

[71] Ibid: Letter to Powell from Christopher Chataway, 23 July 1973.

[72] Ibid, Letter from Powell to Francis Pym, 24 July 1973.

[73] Ibid: Letter to Powell from Francis Pym, 26 July 1973.

[74] Hansard, 860:1214.

[75] Ibid, 860:1215.

[76] Ibid, 860:1217.

[77] Ibid, 860:1219.

[78] Benn IV, p55.

[79] *Daily Telegraph*, 16 August 1973.

[80] Ibid, 20 August 1973.

[81] ANONN, p49.

[82] *Daily Telegraph*, 19 September 1973.

[83] Ibid, 26 September 1973.

[84] *Sunday Telegraph*, 30 September 1973.

[85] *The Times*, 9 October 1973.

[86] *Daily Telegraph*, 12 October 1973.

[87] Powell interview III.

[88] *Daily Telegraph*, 16 October 1973.

[89] Carr interview.

[90] *Daily Telegraph*, 12 October 1973.

[91] HP: Letter to Powell from Ralph Harris, 30 October 1973.

[92] Hansard, 861:239.

[93] Ibid, 861:240.

[94] Ibid, 861:242.

[95] Ibid, 861:243.

[96] Ibid, 861:244.

[97] *Daily Telegraph*, 3 November 1973.

[98] I am indebted to Sir Robin Day for this information.

[99] *Daily Express*, 29 November 1973.

[100] *Daily Telegraph*, 30 November 1973.

[101] Ibid.

[102] PP: Letter to Powell from George Wilkes, 27 November 1972.

[103] Ibid: Letter from Powell to George Wilkes, 28 November 1972.

[104] Ibid: Letter to Powell from Robin Pollard, 11 July 1973.

[105] Ibid: Letter to Powell from George Wilkes, 13 July 1973.

[106] *Daily Telegraph*, 15 December 1973.

[107] PP: Letter from Powell to George Wilkes, 7 December 1973.

[108] Ibid: Letter to Powell from Robin Pollard, 10 December 1973.

[109] Ibid: Speech at the AGM of the Wolverhampton SW Conservative Association, 14 December 1973.

[110] Schoen, p124.

[111] Ibid, p125.

[112] MPP interview I.

[113] DP: Letter from Powell to Bill Deedes, 6 December 1973.

[114] Hansard, 866:973.

[115] Benn IV, p79.

[116] King II, p330.

[117] PP: Letter from Powell to William Whitelaw, 3 December 1973.

[118] Ibid: Letter to Powell from William Whitelaw, 6 December 1973.

[119] Hansard, 866:1198.

[120] Ibid, 866:1199–1200.

[121] Ibid, 866:1203.

[122] Driberg, p189.

[123] Powell interview II.

[124] *Daily Telegraph*, 27 December 1973.

[125] *The Times*, 2 January 1974.

[126] ANONN, p82.

[127] *Daily Telegraph*, 12 January 1974.

[128] Hansard, 867:214.

[129] Ibid, 867:215.

[130] Ibid, 867:217.

[131] Ibid, 867:241–2.

[132] *Daily Telegraph*, 16 January 1974.

[133] PP: Letter to Powell from Robin Pollard, 16 January 1974.

[134] Ibid: Letter (unsent) from Powell to George Wilkes, 17 January 1974.

[135] Ibid: Letter to Pamela Powell from Nicholas Ridley, 15 January 1974.

[136] *Powellight*, January 1974.
[137] Pamela Powell, note to the author, July 1998.
[138] *Daily Telegraph*, 18 January 1974.
[139] Ibid, 19 January 1974.
[140] Ibid, 24 January 1974.
[141] Ritchie interview.
[142] Hansard, 885:1232.
[143] Benn IV, p104.
[144] Critchley, p136.
[145] *Daily Telegraph*, 8 February 1974.
[146] MPP interview I.
[147] Nietzsche II, p246.
[148] Powell interview II.
[149] Carthew interview.
[150] Alexander interview.
[151] Ritchie interview.
[152] Molyneaux interview.
[153] *Daily Telegraph*, 8 February 1974.
[154] *Daily Mail*, 9 September 1974.
[155] PP: Telegram to Powell from Peter Farmer, 7 February 1974.
[156] Ibid: Draft of telegram from Powell to Peter Farmer, 7 February 1974.
[157] MPP interview I.
[158] MPP interview II.
[159] Ibid.
[160] Aitken interview.
[161] PP: Telegram to Powell from Alan Clark, 8 February 1974.
[162] *Daily Telegraph*, 9 February 1974.
[163] Ibid, 1 October 1976.
[164] Cosgrave II, p125.
[165] Alexander interview.
[166] Pimlott, p611.
[167] *Guardian*, 9 February 1974.
[168] PP: 'Note of a telephone conversation with James Molyneaux, Esq, 22.45hrs, Sunday 10 February' (1974).
[169] Ibid: Letter to Powell from John Tyndall, 12 February 1974.
[170] *The Times*, 18 February 1974.
[171] HP: Letter from Milton Friedman to J Enoch Powell, 11 February 1974.
[172] PP: Leaflet 'DON'T VOTE IN THE PHONEY ELECTION', February 1974.
[173] *The Times*, 18 February 1974.
[174] Ibid, 21 February 1974.
[175] See, for example, ibid, 12 May 1975.
[176] *Sunday Telegraph*, 24 February 1974.
[177] *Daily Telegraph*, 25 February 1974.
[178] Ibid.
[179] Ibid, 26 February 1974.

[180] *Enoch: A Life in Politics*, Channel 4, 16 October 1987.
[181] Budgen interview.
[182] I am indebted to Professor John Ramsden for pointing this out to me.
[183] *The Times*, 27 February 1974.
[184] Ibid, 28 February 1974.
[185] *Daily Mail*, 9 September 1974.
[186] *Odd Man Out*, BBC Television, 11 November 1995.

Chapter 16: Across the water

[1] Warren interview.
[2] ANONN, p102.
[3] *The Times*, 12 May 1975.
[4] Ritchie interview.
[5] MPP interview.
[6] PP: Letter from Powell to Ivor Davies, 4 March 1974.
[7] MPP interview II.
[8] Weatherill interview.
[9] *Daily Telegraph*, 9 March 1974.
[10] *Sunday Times*, 6 October 1996.
[11] Ibid, 12 March 1974.
[12] *The Times*, 11 March 1974.
[13] PP: Letter to Powell from George Wilkes, 18 March 1974.
[14] Ibid: Letter from Powell to George Wilkes, 21 March 1974.
[15] *The Times*, 22 March 1974.
[16] Powell interview III.
[17] Ibid.
[18] PP: Letter to Powell from Michael Foot, 22 March 1974.
[19] *Daily Telegraph*, 27 March 1974.
[20] Ibid, 15 April 1974.
[21] *Guardian*, 16 April 1974.
[22] *Daily Telegraph*, 19 April 1974.
[23] *The Times*, 20 April 1974.
[24] Molyneaux interview.
[25] PP: Letter to EG Morton, 17 April 1974.
[26] Ibid: Note by Pamela Powell, May 1974.
[27] *Sunday Express*, 5 May 1974.
[28] PP: Letter to Powell from Neil Marten, 19 May 1974.
[29] *Daily Telegraph*, 20 May 1974.
[30] Ibid.
[31] PP: Letter to Powell from William Whitelaw, 20 May 1974.
[32] Lilley interview.
[33] *Daily Telegraph*, 5 June 1974.

34 PP: Draft of letter from Powell to James Molyneaux, 6 June 1974.

35 Ibid: Letter to Powell from James Molyneaux, 11 June 1974.

36 Ibid: Letter to Powell from John Biffen, 2 July 1974.

37 *The Times*, 26 June 1974.

38 *Sunday Telegraph*, 7 July 1974.

39 CPA: CCO 20/66/16.

40 HP: Draft Memorial to JEP from some (candid) friends, August 1974.

41 PP: Letter to Powell from James Molyneaux, 21 August 1974.

42 Ibid: Letter to Powell from Harry West, 23 August 1974.

43 *Sunday Telegraph Magazine*, 28 August 1977.

44 *Daily Telegraph*, 30 August 1974.

45 Molyneaux interview.

46 *Daily Telegraph*, 4 September 1974.

47 Ibid, 5 September 1974.

48 Ibid, 6 September 1974.

49 Ibid, 7 September 1974.

50 *Observer*, 1 December 1985.

51 MCP: Lord Hailsham interview.

52 *Daily Telegraph*, 15 September 1974.

53 Ibid, 16 September 1974.

54 *Guardian*, 25 September 1974.

55 *Powellight*, October 1974.

56 *Daily Telegraph*, 2 October 1974.

57 I am indebted to Professor John Ramsden for this information.

58 *Daily Telegraph*, 3 October 1974.

59 *The Times*, 4 October 1974.

60 *Daily Telegraph*, 4 October 1974.

61 *Sunday Telegraph*, 6 October 1974.

62 *The Times*, 4 October 1974.

63 *Daily Telegraph*, 7 October 1974.

64 Ibid, 8 October 1974.

65 Ibid, 9 October 1974.

66 Ibid, 12 October 1974.

67 *Sunday Telegraph*, 13 October 1974.

68 Molyneaux interview.

69 *Daily Telegraph*, 23 October 1974.

70 *Sunday Telegraph Magazine*, 28 August 1977.

71 Molyneaux interview.

72 Powell interview II.

73 Lewis, p223.

74 Hansard, 881:673.

75 *Daily Telegraph*, 23 November 1974.

76 Thatcher I, p196.

77 HP: Letter from Powell to Ralph Harris, 2 December 1974.

78 PP: Letter from Sir Keith Joseph to Mrs S Leach, 4 February 1975.

79 Budgen interview.

80 Aitken interview.

81 Hansard, 882:667.

82 Ibid, 882:669.

83 PP: Memorandum on meeting between Powell and Harold Wilson, 26 November 1974.

84 Ibid: Letter from Powell to Harold Wilson, 15 January 1975.

85 Ibid: Letter to Powell from Harold Wilson, 21 January 1975.

86 Hansard, 883:1413.

87 *Daily Telegraph*, 1 February 1975.

88 *Sun*, 3 February 1975.

89 Powell interview II.

90 *Guardian*, 7 March 1975.

91 Hansard, 885:1199.

92 Ibid, 885:1203.

93 *The Times*, 13 February 1975.

94 1992, p1.

95 *Daily Telegraph*, 28 February 1975.

96 Hansard, 889:539–40.

97 Ibid, 889:541.

98 Ibid, 889:542.

99 Ibid, 889:543.

100 Ibid, 889:1295.

101 Ibid, 889:1296.

102 Ibid, 889:1300.

103 Thatcher interview.

104 *Evening News*, 16 April 1975.

105 Hansard, 890:1036.

106 Ibid, 890:1037.

107 Ibid, 890:1039.

108 *Sunday Telegraph*, 20 April 1975.

109 *Daily Telegraph*, 12 May 1975.

110 *Sunday Telegraph*, 18 May 1975.

111 *The Times*, 31 May 1975.

112 *Sunday Telegraph*, 1 June 1975.

113 *Daily Telegraph*, 4 June 1975.

114 Ibid.

115 *The Times*, 4 June 1975.

116 Hansard, 893:604.

117 *Daily Telegraph*, 9 June 1975.

118 Benn interview.

Chapter 17: Labour's Tory

1 Hansard, 893:741.

2 *The Times*, 21 June 1975.

3 *Daily Telegraph*, 28 June 1975.

4 Hansard, 894:166.

5 Hills, p221.
6 *The Times*, 7 July 1975.
7 Ibid, 22 July 1975.
8 Hansard, 896:379.
9 Ibid, 896:382.
10 Ibid, 896:383.
11 Ibid, 896:385.
12 Ibid, 896:386.
13 *The Times*, 12 September 1975.
14 *Sunday Telegraph*, 14 September 1975.
15 *The Times*, 1 October 1975.
16 Ibid, 7 October 1975.
17 Ibid, 13 October 1975.
18 *Daily Express*, 27 October 1975.
19 *The Times*, 13 November 1975.
20 Ibid, 25 November 1975.
21 Hansard, 901:749.
22 Ibid, 901:753.
23 Ibid, 901:754.
24 *Daily Mail*, 29 November 1975.
25 Hansard, 901:1990.
26 Ibid, 901:1992.
27 Ibid, 901:926.
28 *Daily Telegraph*, 6 January 1976.
29 Hansard, 903:998.
30 Ibid, 903:999.
31 Ibid, 903:1001.
32 Ibid, 903:1006.
33 PP: Letter to Powell from Michael Foot, 19 January 1976.
34 *The Times*, 7 January 1976.
35 Thatcher interview.
36 *Sun*, 9 February 1976.
37 Hansard, 905:1050.
38 Ibid, 905:1051.
39 Ibid, 905:1055.
40 Ibid, 906:953.
41 *Daily Telegraph*, 7 March 1976.
42 Hansard, 907:491.
43 *Daily Telegraph*, 13 March 1976.
44 *The Times*, 12 April 1976.
45 Ibid, 13 April 1976.
46 Hansard, 912:49; *Daily Telegraph*, 25 May 1976.
47 *The Times*, 10 June 1976.
48 *Sunday Telegraph*, 30 May 1976.
49 *Daily Telegraph*, 28 June 1976.
50 PP: Letter from Powell to Harold Wilson, 6 January 1976; letter to Powell from Harold Wilson, 12 January, 1976.
51 Hansard, 914:867.
52 *The Times*, 5 August 1976.
53 *Daily Telegraph*, 9 August 1976.

54 *The Times*, 17 September 1976.
55 *Daily Telegraph*, 1 October 1976.
56 Ibid, 5 October 1976.
57 *The Times*, 5 October 1976.
58 *Daily Telegraph*, 6 October 1976.
59 Hansard, 917:87.
60 Ibid, 917:91.
61 Ibid, 917:92.
62 Ibid.
63 *Daily Telegraph*, 11 November 1976.
64 Ibid.
65 Ibid, 13 November 1976.
66 Ibid, 15 November 1976.
67 Hansard, 921:758–9.
68 Ibid, 921:762.
69 Ibid, 921:764.
70 Ibid, 921:765.
71 *The Times*, 7 January 1977.
72 *Daily Telegraph*, 22 January 1977.
73 Ibid, 25 January 1977.
74 Ibid, 24 January 1977.
75 Ibid, 18 March 1977.
76 Callaghan, p451.
77 Ibid, p453.
78 Ibid, p454.
79 Molyneaux interview.
80 *Daily Telegraph*, 24 March 1977.
81 Ibid, 19 April 1977.
82 PP: Letter to Powell from Michael Foot, 19 April 1977.
83 *Daily Telegraph*, 28 April 1977.
84 *Sunday Express*, 5 June 1977.
85 *The Times*, 21 June 1977.
86 *Daily Telegraph*, 18 June 1977.
87 *The Times*, 18 June 1977.
88 Hansard, 935:996.
89 Ibid, 935:1658.
90 Ibid, 935:1659.
91 *Daily Telegraph*, 25 July 1977.
92 Ibid, 10 September 1977.
93 *Daily Express*, 12 September 1977.
94 *The Times*, 5 October 1977.
95 *Daily Telegraph*, 13 October 1977.
96 *Financial Times*, 25 October 1977.
97 Utley, p171.
98 JC, pp46–7.
99 Ibid, p136.
100 Ibid.
101 Ibid, p151.
102 PP: Letter to Powell from George Thomas, 14 November 1977.
103 Hansard, 939:86.
104 Ibid, 939:609.

105 *The Times*, 17 January 1978.
106 Hansard, 942:1648.
107 Ibid, 942:1649.
108 *Daily Telegraph*, 30 January 1978.
109 Hansard, 944:75.
110 Ibid, 944:79.
111 *Daily Telegraph*, 11 February 1978.
112 *Sunday Telegraph*, 19 February 1978.
113 Hansard, 949:828.
114 Ibid, 949:829.
115 *Daily Telegraph*, 3 June 1978.
116 Ibid, 5 June 1978.
117 *Sunday Telegraph*, 11 June 1978.
118 Hansard, 951:1027.
119 Ibid, 951:1064.
120 Ibid, 954:2041.
121 Ibid, 954:2043.
122 *Sunday Telegraph*, 16 July 1978.
123 *Daily Telegraph*, 22 July 1978.
124 PP: Letter from William Whitelaw to Mrs Stather, 25 July 1978.
125 Ibid: Letter from Powell to William Whitelaw, 2 August 1978.
126 Lewis interview.
127 Hansard, 957:1247.
128 Ibid, 957:1248.
129 Ibid, 957:1250.
130 Ibid, 957:1256.
131 Ibid, 959:506.
132 Ibid, 959:507.
133 Ibid, 959:511.
134 Ibid, 959:512.
135 Ibid, 959:513.
136 Benn V, p363.
137 *Daily Telegraph*, 9 December 1978.
138 *Sunday Telegraph*, 10 December 1978.
139 Ibid.
140 *Daily Telegraph*, 11 December 1978.
141 Molyneaux interview.
142 *Daily Telegraph*, 3 January 1979.
143 Hansard, 960:1562.
144 Ibid, 960:1564.
145 *Observer*, 21 January 1979.
146 *Daily Telegraph*, 12 February 1979.
147 *Sunday Telegraph*, 18 March 1979.
148 Hansard, 965:518.
149 *Daily Telegraph*, 31 March 1979.
150 *Sunday Telegraph*, 1 April 1979.
151 Hansard, 965:877.
152 PP: Letter to Powell from Andrew Alexander, 1 April 1979.
153 Ibid: Letter from Powell to Andrew Alexander, 4 April 1979.
154 Ibid: Letter from Powell to Diana Neave, 31 March 1979.
155 Ibid: Letter to Powell from Diana Neave, 25 April 1979.
156 *Observer*, 22 April 1979.
157 *Sunday Telegraph*, 29 April 1979.
158 *Daily Telegraph*, 5 May 1979.

Chapter 18: The old statesman

1 *Daily Telegraph*, 1 May 1979.
2 PP: Letter from Powell to James Callaghan, 6 May 1979.
3 Ibid: Letter from Powell to Roy Mason, 6 May 1979.
4 *Daily Telegraph*, 2 June 1979.
5 *Guardian*, 4 June 1979.
6 *Daily Telegraph*, 6 June 1979.
7 *Sunday Telegraph*, 10 June 1979.
8 PP: Note in Powell's hand on letter to him from John Biffen, 10 September 1979.
9 Field interview.
10 Hansard, 967:963.
11 Ibid, 967:964.
12 Field interview.
13 Gerry Malone, letter to the author, 15 April 1998.
14 Hansard, 968:948–9.
15 Ibid, 968:950.
16 Ibid, 968:954.
17 *Daily Telegraph*, 16 August 1979.
18 Ibid, 27 September 1979.
19 PP: Letter to Powell from Lord Brabourne, 27 September 1979.
20 Ibid: Letter from Powell to Lord Brabourne, 2 October 1979.
21 *Daily Telegraph*, 1 October 1979.
22 *Sun*, 7 October 1979.
23 *Guardian*, 22 October 1979.
24 Hansard, 972:205.
25 *Guardian*, 10 November 1979.
26 Hansard, 973:693.
27 Ibid, 974:1339.
28 *The Times*, 24 November 1979.
29 *Enoch: A Life in Politics*, Channel 4, 16 October 1987.
30 *Daily Telegraph*, 4 January 1980.
31 *Guardian*, 21 January 1980.
32 Hansard, 977:972.
33 Ibid, 977:973.
34 Ibid, 977:977.
35 *Daily Telegraph*, 26 January 1980.
36 Ibid, 7 February 1980.

37 Hansard, 979:1619.
38 Ibid, 979:1621.
39 Ibid, 979:1624.
40 Ibid, 980:1041.
41 Ibid, 980:1044.
42 Ibid, 980:1047.
43 *Sunday Express*, 14 March 1980.
44 Hansard, 982:261.
45 *Daily Telegraph*, 26 April 1980.
46 Hansard, 983:1225.
47 Ibid, 984:913.
48 Ibid, 984:941.
49 Ibid, 984:942.
50 Ibid, 986:1190.
51 Ibid, 986:1191.
52 Ibid, 986:1194.
53 *Daily Telegraph*, 19 May 1980.
54 *Financial Times*, 10 July 1980.
55 Lilley interview.
56 *The Times*, 12 July 1980.
57 Hansard, 989:267.
58 Ibid, 989:1326.
59 Ibid, 989:1328.
60 Ibid, 989:1329.
61 *The Times*, 6 August 1980.
62 *Daily Telegraph*, 6 September 1980.
63 Ibid, 14 September 1980.
64 *Guardian*, 20 October 1980.
65 Hansard, 991:233.
66 Ibid, 994:603.
67 Ibid, 994:606.
68 *Daily Telegraph*, 6 December 1980.
69 Ibid, 11 December 1980.
70 Hansard, 997:963.
71 Ibid, 997:965.
72 Ibid, 997:966.
73 Ibid, 997:967.
74 Ibid, 1000:157.
75 *Daily Telegraph*, 9 May 1981.
76 Hansard (Sixth Series), 7:1108.
77 Ibid, 7:1111.
78 Ibid, 7:1113.
79 Ibid, 7:1114.
80 *Sunday Telegraph*, 29 March 1981.
81 *Daily Telegraph*, 30 March 1981.
82 Ibid, 14 April 1981.
83 Hansard, 8:26.
84 Ibid, 8:1411.
85 Ibid, 8:1412.
86 Ibid, 8:1414.
87 Private information.
88 *Sun*, 25 August 1981.
89 *Daily Telegraph*, 15 October 1981.

90 Hansard, 10:887.
91 Ibid, 10:889–90.
92 *Daily Telegraph*, 30 October 1981.
93 *Sunday Telegraph*, 8 November 1981.
94 *Sunday Express*, 8 November 1981.
95 Hansard, 12:425.
96 Ibid, 13:21.
97 Ibid, 13:26.
98 *Daily Telegraph*, 7 December 1981.
99 *Sunday Telegraph*, 6 December 1981.
100 Hansard, 14:1018.
101 *Daily Telegraph*, 7 January 1982.
102 Hansard, 16:995.
103 Ibid, 16:986.
104 Ibid, 20:1080–1.
105 *The Times*, 8 January 1982.
106 *Sunday Express*, 4 February 1982.
107 *Sunday Telegraph*, 14 March 1982.
108 Hansard, 20:43.
109 Ibid, 20:46.
110 PP: Letter from Powell to George Thomas, 16 March 1982.
111 Ibid: Letter to Powell from George Thomas, 16 March 1982.
112 *Daily Mail*, 13 April 1982.
113 Hansard, 21:643.
114 Ibid, 21:644.
115 Cosgrave I, p35.
116 Hansard, 21:1158.
117 Ibid, 21:1159.
118 *Daily Telegraph*, 20 April 1982.
119 Hansard, 22:922.
120 Ibid, 22:925.
121 Ibid, 22:1003.
122 Ibid, 22:1004.
123 Ibid, 22:1005.
124 Ibid, 23:540.
125 Ibid, 23:541.
126 Ibid, 23:976.
127 Ibid, 23:977.
128 Ibid, 25:1082.
129 *The Times*, 29 June 1982.
130 *Guardian*, 18 October 1982.
131 *Sunday Express*, 13 June 1982.
132 Hansard, 26:176.
133 Ibid, 26:177.
134 Ibid, 26:179.
135 Ibid, 26:180.
136 Ibid, 26:182.
137 Ibid, 26:769.
138 Ibid, 26:770.
139 Ibid, 26:771.
140 Ibid, 26:788.

141 Ibid, 26:789.
142 Ibid, 26:790.
143 PP: Official Note of meeting between Powell, Sir Robert Armstrong and Ian Gow, 1 November 1982.
144 Ibid: Letter to Powell from Sir Robert Armstrong, 6 December 1982.
145 Third Ian Gow Memorial Lecture, delivered by Powell, 10 June 1993.
146 *The Times*, 20 January 1983.
147 *Sunday Express*, 25 July 1982.
148 *The Times*, 11 September 1982.
149 *Daily Telegraph*, 18 October 1982.
150 Ibid, 13 October 1982.
151 Hansard, 31:348.
152 *The Times*, 13 November 1982.
153 Hansard, 31:711.
154 Ibid, 33:726.
155 PP: Letter from Powell to Margaret Thatcher, 16 December 1982.
156 Ibid: Letter to Powell from Margaret Thatcher, 23 December 1982.
157 Hansard, 35:366.
158 Ibid, 35:367.
159 *The Times*, 5 February 1983.
160 Ibid, 19 February 1983.
161 *Sunday Telegraph*, 3 April 1983.
162 *Daily Telegraph*, 1 June 1983.
163 Hansard, 42:940.
164 Ibid, 42:941.
165 Ibid, 42:948.
166 Ibid, 42:949.
167 Donaldson interview.
168 Ibid.
169 Curtis interview.
170 MPP interview II.

Chapter 19: Evening

1 *The Times*, 22 June 1983.
2 PP: Letter from Ian Gow to Michael Alison, 12 July 1983.
3 Ibid: Address by Powell at Edward Curtis's Funeral, June 1983.
4 Hansard, 44:494.
5 Weatherill interview.
6 Hansard, 44:495.
7 Ibid, 44:496.
8 Ibid, 44:497.
9 *Sunday Times*, 17 July 1983.
10 *Daily Telegraph*, 3 September 1983.
11 Ibid, 17 September 1983.
12 Ibid, 8 October 1983.
13 Ibid, 10 October 1983.
14 PP: Letter from Powell to Margaret Thatcher, 8 November 1983.
15 Thatcher II, p396.
16 Hansard, 47:307.
17 Ibid, 47:308.
18 Ibid, 47:309.
19 Ibid, 47:1054.
20 *Daily Telegraph*, 22 November 1983.
21 MCP: Jennifer Lavin interview.
22 *Sunday Telegraph*, 6 January 1984.
23 *Guardian*, 9 January 1984.
24 *Daily Telegraph*, 14 January 1984.
25 Ibid, 21 January 1984.
26 *Observer*, 22 January 1984.
27 *The Times*, 26 January 1984.
28 Hansard, 53:1063.
29 *Guardian*, 12 March 1984.
30 *Daily Telegraph*, 28 April 1984.
31 *Sunday Express*, 27 May 1984.
32 Hansard, 65:287.
33 Ibid, 65:288.
34 PP: Letter from Powell to Margaret Thatcher, 18 July 1984.
35 Ibid: Note of a meeting between Powell and Margaret Thatcher, 27 July 1984.
36 Ibid: Letter from Powell to Margaret Thatcher, 31 July 1984.
37 Ibid: Letter from Powell to Margaret Thatcher, 18 October 1984.
38 Ibid: Letter from Powell to Margaret Thatcher, 21 November 1984.
39 *The Times*, 1 December 1984.
40 *Daily Telegraph*, 6 December 1984.
41 Hansard, 73:637.
42 Ibid, 73:640.
43 Ibid, 73:641.
44 *Daily Mail*, 11 February 1985.
45 *Daily Telegraph*, 15 March 1985.
46 Ibid, 20 April 1985.
47 Ibid, 8 June 1985.
48 Ibid, 29 June 1985.
49 *The Times*, 8 July 1985.
50 *Sunday Express*, 15 September 1985.
51 *Daily Telegraph*, 22 September 1985.
52 *Daily Mail*, 21 September 1985.
53 *Sunday Mirror*, 22 September 1985.
54 PP: Letter to Powell from the Bishop of Stepney, 13 November 1984.
55 Ibid: Letter from Powell to the Bishop of Stepney, 20 November 1984.
56 *Sunday Telegraph*, 22 September 1985.
57 *Daily Telegraph*, 12 October 1985.

[58] Ibid, 21 October 1985.

[59] *Sunday Telegraph*, 3 November 1985.

[60] Hansard, 84:375.

[61] Ibid, 84:376.

[62] *Daily Telegraph*, 13 November 1985.

[63] *Daily Mail*, 15 November 1985; Hansard, 86:682.

[64] Thatcher interview.

[65] Hansard, 87:414.

[66] *The Times*, 26 November 1985.

[67] *Daily Telegraph*, 27 November 1985.

[68] Hansard, 87:950.

[69] Ibid, 87:951.

[70] Ibid, 87:953.

[71] Ibid, 87:954.

[72] Ibid, 87:955.

[73] *Sunday Express*, 1 December 1985.

[74] Hansard, 87:309.

[75] *Sunday Telegraph*, 19 January 1986.

[76] *The Times*, 3 May 1986.

[77] Ibid, 9 April 1986.

[78] RS, p51.

[79] MCP: Powell interview.

[80] *Daily Telegraph*, 9 April 1986.

[81] FP: Letter from Powell to Roseen Freeth, 14 April 1986.

[82] Hansard, 93:351.

[83] Ibid, 94:655.

[84] Ibid, 100:554.

[85] Ibid, 100:558.

[86] Ibid, 100:944.

[87] Ibid, 100:946.

[88] Ibid, 101:526.

[89] Ibid, 101:527.

[90] PP: Letter from Powell to Margaret Thatcher, 5 August 1986.

[91] Ibid: Copy of note from Margaret Thatcher to Michael Alison, 23 October 1986.

[92] *Daily Telegraph*, 18 October 1986.

[93] *Sunday Telegraph*, 19 October 1986.

[94] Hansard, 106:490.

[95] Ibid, 106:491.

[96] Author's private diary.

[97] *Guardian*, 6 April 1987.

[98] Hansard, 115:796.

[99] Ibid, 115:823.

[100] *The Times*, 28 May 1987.

[101] Stephen Robinson, letter to the author, 9 December 1996.

[102] MPP interview II.

[103] Donaldson interview.

[104] *Daily Telegraph*, 13 June 1987.

[105] Stephen Robinson, letter to the author, 9 December 1996.

[106] Hansard, 19:848.

Chapter 20: Life after death

[1] Day, p177.

[2] PP: Note of events after polling day, 1987, by Pam Powell.

[3] Thatcher interview.

[4] PP: Letter from Powell to Sir Harold Wilson, 24 April 1976.

[5] *The Times*, 8 July 1987.

[6] RS, p61.

[7] *Sunday Times Magazine*, 11 May 1986.

[8] *Enoch: A Life in Politics*, Channel 4, 16 October 1987.

[9] *The Times*, 13 October 1987.

[10] Author's private diary.

[11] MPP interview II.

[12] Molyneaux interview.

[13] MCP: Powell interview.

[14] *Daily Telegraph*, 4 January 1988.

[15] *Guardian*, 19 March 1988.

[16] *Independent*, 1 April 1988.

[17] *The Times*, 19 April 1988.

[18] *Independent*, 23 April 1988.

[19] *Evening Standard*, 22 April 1988.

[20] *Spectator*, 25 June 1988.

[21] *Daily Telegraph*, 15 October 1988.

[22] Author's private diary.

[23] 1992, p33.

[24] *Daily Telegraph*, 13 October 1988.

[25] PP: Speech at Wimbledon, 22 November 1988.

[26] *Sunday Telegraph*, 4 December 1988.

[27] *Guardian*, 7 December 1988.

[28] *Sunday People*, 11 December 1988.

[29] *Daily Telegraph*, 2 January 1989.

[30] *Desert Island Discs*, 19 February 1989.

[31] *Sunday Express*, 21 May 1989.

[32] *Guardian*, 13 June 1989.

[33] Ibid, 24 July 1989.

[34] *Sunday Times*, 3 September 1989.

[35] *Spectator*, 14 October 1989.

[36] PP: Speech at Ewell, 19 October 1989.

[37] Ibid: Letter from Powell to Mark Lennox-Boyd, 9 November 1989.

[38] Ibid: Letter to Powell from Margaret Thatcher, 13 December 1989.

[39] *Independent*, 6 January 1990.

[40] *Daily Telegraph*, 12 January 1990.

[41] RS, p441.

[42] Ibid, p440.

[43] *Daily Telegraph*, 22 March 1990.

44 PP: Letter from Powell to TE Meaker, 25 March 1983.
45 CPEP, p vii.
46 Ibid, p191.
47 *Times Literary Supplement*, 17–23 August 1990.
48 *Daily Telegraph*, 14 May 1990.
49 PP: Speech at Sutton-in-Ashfield, 12 May 1990.
50 *Daily Express*, 3 August 1990.
51 Author's private diary.
52 *Daily Telegraph*, 11 August 1990.
53 *Sunday Correspondent*, 21 October 1990.
54 PP: Letter from Powell to Norman Tebbit, 16 November 1990.
55 *Sunday Correspondent*, 25 November 1990.
56 *Daily Telegraph*, 19 January 1991.
57 *Independent*, 27 March 1991.
58 I am indebted to the Rt Hon Lord Patten for this information.
59 RS, p xi.
60 *Sunday Telegraph*, 22 December 1991.
61 *Daily Telegraph*, 4 April 1992.
62 *Spectator*, 6 June 1992.
63 *Daily Telegraph*, 30 July 1994.
64 *Sunday Telegraph*, 7 June 1992.
65 *European*, 5 November 1992.
66 *The Times*, 20 April 1993.
67 *Daily Telegraph*, 5 May 1993.
68 I am indebted to the Hon Bernard Jenkin MP for this information.
69 I am indebted to Sir Donald Sinden for confirming this information.
70 *Evening Standard*, 13 July 1993.
71 *The Times*, 1 November 1993.
72 *Daily Telegraph*, 17 May 1994.
73 *Daily Mail*, 29 June 1994.
74 *The Times*, 10 August 1994.
75 *Independent*, 16 August 1994.
76 *Daily Telegraph*, 18 September 1994.
77 DLW Ashton, letter to the author, 20 July 1996: I am much indebted to Mr Ashton for his thoughtful observations on Powell's theology.
78 *Daily Mail*, 27 October 1994.
79 From an unpublished interview with Sarah Baxter, April 1995: I am greatly indebted to Miss Baxter for providing me with this material.
80 *Daily Mail*, 27 June 1995.

81 WP: Letter from Powell to John Redwood, 6 July 1995.
82 *Daily Telegraph*, 21 October 1995.
83 PP: Press statement on the death of Lord Home, 9 October 1995.
84 Ibid: Letter to Powell from Barbara Hawkins, 18 December 1995.
85 Ibid: Letter from Powell to Barbara Hawkins, 3 February 1996.
86 *Daily Express*, 24 April 1996.
87 *Sunday Telegraph*, 27 October 1996.
88 I am indebted to Pamela Powell for this information.
89 MPP interview II.
90 *Daily Telegraph*, 9 February 1998.
91 I am indebted to Mr Richard Ritchie for this information.
92 *Daily Telegraph*, 9 February 1998.
93 MCP: Powell interview.
94 Rector's Annual Report, St Margaret's Westminster, 1998.
95 MCP: Powell interview.

Epilogue: The cloven hoof

1 *Observer*, 5 February 1961.
2 Attallah, p351.
3 *Odd Man Out*, BBC Television, 11 November 1995.
4 *The Times*, 19 May 1995.
5 Carr interview.
6 *Odd Man Out*, BBC Television, 11 November 1995.
7 *Daily Telegraph*, 19 February 1998.
8 I am indebted to Professor John Ramsden for this information, which appears in *Contemporary Record*, Vol 3, No 3, February 1990.
9 MCP: Transcript of untransmitted interview with Sir Edward Heath conducted for BBC documentary by Michael Cockerell, June 1998.
10 WWTA, p5.
11 *Sunday Times*, 3 September 1989.
12 Thatcher interview.
13 *London Review of Books*, 23 January 1997.
14 Foot M, p192.
15 Richard Ritchie, letter to the author, 16 July 1998.
16 MCP: Powell interview.

INDEX

Issues with which Powell was most concerned appear under their own headings. All speeches are Powell's unless otherwise stated. All characters are titled as they appear within the text.

Garland

" AND FOR MY NEXT TRICK I SHALL